WALT DISNEY'S

BY FLOYD GOTTFREDSON

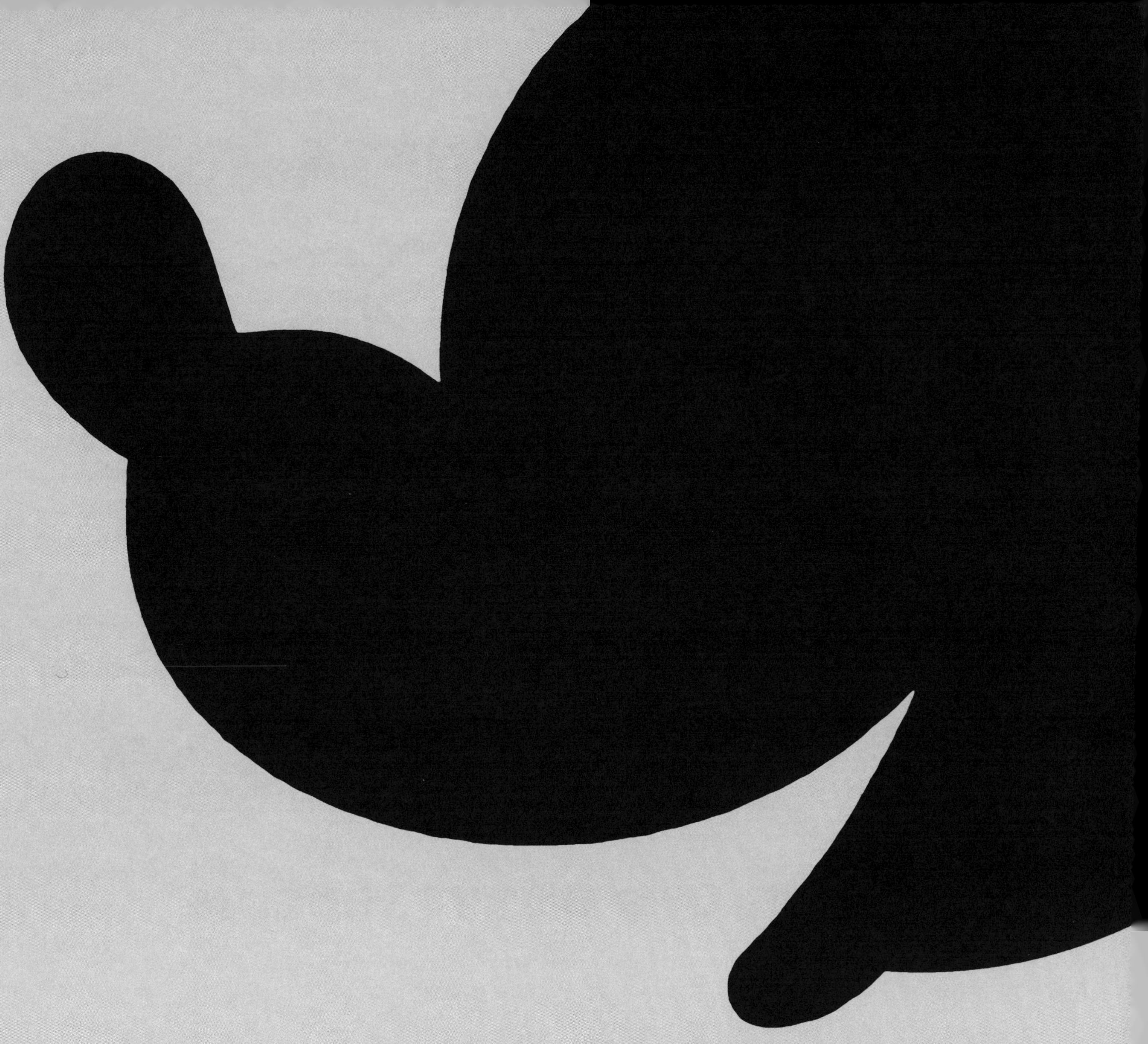

WALT DISNEY'S

MICKEY MOUSE

BY FLOYD GOTTFREDSON

VOLUME TWO

Color Sundays

"ROBIN HOOD RIDES AGAIN"

Series Editors: David Gerstein and Gary Groth

LEFT: Pauncho Malarky, the villain in this volume's "Sheriff of Nugget Gulch," roughly resembles a dog version of Pegleg Pete. It was not the first time Gottfredson had drawn a Pete-like canine villain. An earlier instance came in about 1931, when Gottfredson experimented with his own non-Disney tiger cartoon character— and a strikingly proto-Pauncho bad guy. Image © and courtesy Floyd Gottfredson Estate; used with permission of Colleen Gottfredson Toomay.

The Floyd Gottfredson Library

Series Editors: DAVID GERSTEIN with GARY GROTH
Series Designers: JACOB COVEY and TONY ONG
Colorists: DIGIKORE STUDIOS
Production: PAUL BARESH
Associate Publisher: ERIC REYNOLDS
Publishers: GARY GROTH and KIM THOMPSON

To receive a free catalogue of graphic novels, newspaper strip reprints, prose novels, art books, cultural criticism and essays, and more, call 1-800-657-1100 or visit our website at www.fantagraphics.com.

Distributed in the U.S. by W.W. Norton and Company, Inc. (800-233-4830)
Distributed in Canada by Canadian Manda Group (800-452-6642 x862)
Distributed in the U.K. by Turnaround Distribution (44 (0)20 8829-3002)
Distributed to comic stores by Diamond Comics Distributors (800-452-6642 x215)

ISBN 978-1-60699-686-7

Printed in Singapore.

IT'S A STATEMENT I once never thought I'd make: as of this volume, for the first time ever, all of Floyd Gottfredson's Sunday color work is easily available. Every last *Mickey Mouse*—even stragglers from years after Gottfredson's regular run. And for completeness' sake, a few "guest star" stories with Donald and other Disney heroes.

We'd never have gotten here without help. Ken Shue, Disney Publishing Worldwide's Vice President of Global Art and Design Development, his Secretary Iliana Lopez, and Consultant Floyd Norman were invaluable in securing surviving Gottfredson line art stats for us. Strip collectors Thomas Andrae, Thomas Jensen, and Fredrik Strömberg provided color tearsheets and substitutes for damaged masters. Danny Saeva and Jason McNaughton, our DPW category managers, were there to aid us with cross-Disney communications.

Numerous other scholars contributed artwork, essays, knowledge, and archival items. We're grateful to Director Rebecca Cline, Archivist Michael Buckhoff, Contractor Kevin Kern, and Senior Secretary Alesha Reyes at the Walt Disney Archives; also to Creative Director Lella Smith, Research Manager Fox Carney, and Researchers Ann Hansen and Jackie Vasquez at the Walt Disney Animation Research Library. I'd also like to thank Thomas Andrae, Arlene Balkansky, Alberto Becattini, Franco Bellazzi, Geoffrey Blum, John Clark, Arthur Faria Jr., Ferdi Felderhof, Gilles Garrigues, Dan Gonzales, Leonardo Gori, Colleen Gottfredson Toomay, Jan Gottfredson, Joakim Gunnarsson, the Hake's Americana staff (including Alex Winter, Terence Kean, and Deak Stagemeyer), Elizabeth Helms, Andy Hershberger/Geppi's Entertainment Museum, Linda Hope, Lars Jensen, J. B. Kaufman, Thad Komorowski, Mauro Lepore, Larry Lowery, Philippe Marcilly, Mike Mashon, Mike Matei, Jan Morrill, Tom Neely, Christoph Overberg, Jesse Post, Stefano Priarone, Thom Roep, Timo Ronkainen, Ulrich Schroeder, Zoran Sinobad, Frank Stajano, Julie Svendsen, Ted Toomay, Joe Torcivia, Fernando Ventura, Malcolm Willits, and Dejan Zivkovic.

Others, too, have provided crucial support and encouragement. First and foremost come my parents, Susan and Larry Gerstein, and my brother Ben. Then come friends including Céline and Stefan Allirol-Molin, Garry Apgar, Christopher and Nicky Barat, Jerry Beck, Leonid Breydo, Diane Disney Miller, Byron Erickson, César Ferioli, Fabio Gadducci, Lana German, Didier Ghez, Jonathan Gray, Nelson Hughes, Mark and Cole Johnson, Vincent Joseph, Mark Kausler, Jim Korkis, Raquel Lopez, Jean Marie Metauten, Geoffrey Moses, Martin Olsen, KaJuan Osborne, Tarkan Rosenberg, Travis Seitler, Warren Spector, Tom Stathes, Kwongmei To, Esther Torcivia, Germund Von Wowern, and Wilbert Watts.

In mid-1935, the *Mickey Mouse* Sunday strip changed aspect ratio: from two-thirds of a newspaper page to a half-page—thus the deep margins, in this volume, above and below each strip. On the upside, this gives us more breathing room for the strips' episode titles: created, in most cases, for 1940s comic book reprints. The few that weren't named then have been named now, their monikers carefully chosen in the spirit of the originals.

—David Gerstein
May 2013

TABLE of CONTENTS

Setting the Stage

The Sundays: Floyd Gottfredson's Mickey Mouse Stories With Introductory Notes

TABLE of CONTENTS

MICKEY'S SUNDAY BEST

FLOYD GOTTFREDSON AND THE DISNEY COLOR COMICS

1936-1938: *Moving On*

» *FOREWORD BY J. B. KAUFMAN*

THE MINUTE a popular phenomenon stands still, it begins to lose something. By the mid-1930s Mickey Mouse was, by any standard, a popular phenomenon. He had achieved a level of world fame that no other cartoon character had ever enjoyed before, or, arguably, ever has since. His early years had been marked by a series of breakthroughs as, day by day, delighted new admirers discovered him. The surprise success of his first films had quickly grown, spread to exponential levels, and burst the bounds of the screen: now he could be seen not only in the movies but in other showcases—notably the comics. The first experimental steps of his daily newspaper comic strip, and then of a parallel series in full color on the Sunday pages, had added greatly to his legend (and, happily, have now been collected by Fantagraphics in earlier volumes of this series). Through it all, Mickey had remained his smiling, ingenious, resourceful, and thoroughly engaging self, meeting each new challenge with good cheer and a courageous spirit. By the end of 1935 he had scaled every imaginable height in the cartoon universe. What would happen next? Would he relax, rest on his laurels, grow complacent—and lose his edge?

Thankfully, *nothing* stood still for very long at the Disney studio—least of all in the mid-1930s, when Walt and his artists were elevating the art of animation itself to spectacular and unprecedented heights. The exciting creative energy that reigned at the studio permeated every level of Disney activity, including the comics. By this time Floyd Gottfredson and his colleagues had assumed semi-autonomous control over the daily and Sunday comic strips, but their work was still subject to Walt's supervision and their art was still a direct outgrowth of the studio's art. Charged with representing the face of Disney on newspaper comic

ABOVE: Floyd Gottfredson at his drawing board in 1951, just over a decade after he moved on from the *Mickey* Sunday strip. Image courtesy Disney Publishing Worldwide.

pages during this richly creative time, they continued to rise to the challenge with varied, surprising, and masterfully drawn comic adventures. The results will be seen in the pages of this volume.

Readers of Mickey's earlier Sunday pages may recall that the Mouse had displayed varying facets of his personality during the first four years of the Sunday feature. By turns playful, purposeful, a can-do hero and a comic fall guy, Mickey proved a versatile protagonist but was still recognizably Mickey at all times. Now, as he proceeds through the second half of the decade, he demonstrates that he's still full of surprises. Tackling a series of domestic chores in March 1936, he's every bit the responsible home handyman. When Donald or Goofy  bring on some disaster with their inept efforts to help, it's up to Mickey to play the grownup. But only a few months later he finds a book on ventriloquism and gleefully plunges into a series of pranks, scaring the daylights out of Pluto and others, his playful side clearly on display.

This mischievous streak had been a part of Mickey's makeup from the beginning, perhaps more prominent in the comics than on the screen. In the late 1930s, it's sometimes dormant but alive and well. Mickey hitches a ride on the back of a sled full of groceries as the nephews struggle to pull it along the sidewalk; skylarking as he helps Minnie pack her kitchen goods, he manages to drop and break every one of her dishes. Sometimes he goes to extremes for the sake of a practical joke: in February 1937 he ties the entire contents of a fruit basket to the branches of a tree, trying to convince Goofy that this array of produce has all sprouted from the same plant. Mickey's pranks backfire on him more often than not, but he invariably bounces back before long with another gag.

Elsewhere Mickey displays varying aspects of his personality according to the needs of the story. Consider his moral scruples during "The Robin Hood Adventure" in 1936: ordered by Robin to rob a wealthy traveler passing through Sherwood Forest, Mickey loves the idea of a hearty adventure but balks at stealing. Yet only a few months earlier he cheerfully circumvents the *letter* of the law for the sake of a greater good: preventing the dogcatcher from dragging Pluto off to the pound.

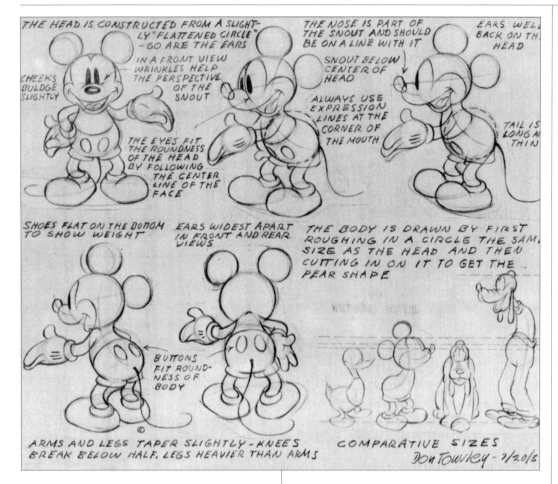

THE HEAD IS CONSTRUCTED FROM A SLIGHT- LY "FLATTENED CIRCLE" - SO ARE THE EARS

CHEEKS BULDGE SLIGHTLY

IN A FRONT VIEW WRINKLES HELP THE PERSPECTIVE OF THE SNOUT

THE EYES FIT THE ROUNDNESS OF THE HEAD BY FOLLOWING THE CENTER LINE OF THE FACE

THE NOSE IS PART OF THE SNOUT AND SHOULD BE ON A LINE WITH IT

SNOUT BELOW CENTER OF HEAD

ALWAYS USE EXPRESSION LINES AT THE CORNER OF THE MOUTH

EARS WELL BACK ON TH. HEAD

TAIL IS LONG AN THIN

SHOES FLAT ON THE BOTTOM TO SHOW WEIGHT

EARS WIDEST APART IN FRONT AND REAR VIEWS

THE BODY IS DRAWN BY FIRST ROUGHING IN A CIRCLE THE SAM. SIZE AS THE HEAD AND THEN CUTTING IN ON IT TO GET THE PEAR SHAPE

BUTTONS FIT ROUND- NESS OF BODY

ARMS AND LEGS TAPER SLIGHTLY - KNEES BREAK BELOW HALF, LEGS HEAVIER THAN ARMS

COMPARATIVE SIZES

Don Towsley - 2/20/3

ABOVE: Mickey model sheet by animator Don Towsley, 1937. Mickey's design in later Gottfredson Sunday strips approximates this look. Image courtesy Disney Publishing Worldwide.

In January 1937 Clarabelle asks Mickey to shoot the rabbits that have been raiding her garden, but his tender-hearted side asserts itself and he just can't bring himself to harm them. This episode contrasts vividly with a later installment that today's reader may find more than a little disturbing: the nephews, about to be caught stealing bread and jam, frame Pluto for their crime. When Mickey finds Pluto with the faked evidence, he *pretends* he's about to beat

the poor dog with a baseball bat! The ruse works— the terrified nephews confess in order to save Pluto—but only in the last panel does Gottfredson reveal Mickey's benign intentions, a paltry gesture of reassurance at the very last moment.

Mickey's *visual* design having been established before the debut of the comic strip, his appearance remains stable throughout the contents of this book, subject only to the inevitable evolution of details in Gottfredson's style. Some of the other major characters, however, were still in flux during the late 1930s, and the changes in their designs are

fascinating to the Disney devotee. Donald Duck offers a prime, if elusive, example. By 1936 Donald's appearances in the *Mickey* strip—both daily and Sunday editions—were dwindling in frequency as the Duck moved toward a solo strip of his own.[1] But 1936 was a pivotal year for Donald on the screen. His appearance underwent a major and deliberate design change in the theatrical films of that year, and when he does appear in the Mickey comics, his design reflects those changes. Step by step, we can track the stages in his transformation.

Goofy provides us with an even more extended case study. Disney enthusiasts will remember that this character had already undergone a series of alterations, both on and off the screen: introduced in the movies in 1932 as an unnamed bit player, then developed as an eccentric supporting character called Dippy Dawg. By mid-1934 he had been taken in hand by animator Art Babbitt, who saw greater possibilities in him. Babbitt argued that "the Goof" was not merely a generic halfwit but a character with a colorful, distinctive psychology all his own, and made his point with a series of memorable animation set-pieces in cartoons like *On Ice* (1935) and *Moving Day* (1936). Exit Dippy Dawg, enter Goofy—a far more versatile and durable character.

At the same time, Goofy's makeover was also taking place in the parallel universe of the comics. Gottfredson and writer Ted Osborne had already featured Dippy Dawg prominently in the Mickey comics; now they coordinated their efforts with those of the filmmakers. Dippy made his last appearance in the Mickey Sunday page in December 1935; in this volume we see the first appearance of Goofy in March 1936—both his name and his appearance consistent with those of his screen counterpart. More importantly, the character's *personality* is changed in keeping with the fanciful flights of reasoning that Babbitt had suggested for him. This Goof is not merely a simpleton, but an individual with a delicately precise illogic. This is the character who knocks a gaping hole in a roof during a rainstorm, hoping it will help him locate a leak; who labors furiously at building a fence, trying to finish it before he runs out of lumber. When Mickey finds that book on ventriloquism and goes around trying it out on his friends, Goofy is the one who remains unimpressed. Confronted with the illusion that Pluto is talking to him, Goofy doesn't find the spectacle of a talking dog particularly remarkable (happily, no one complicates the issue by pointing out that Goofy *himself* is a talking dog). But when he learns that it *is* an illusion—that Mickey has learned to throw his voice—now *that's* something!

As this suggests, and as David Gerstein writes elsewhere in this volume, Goofy's reinvented persona sometimes has the effect of reducing Mickey to the role of straight man. Several of Mickey's practical jokes during this period are directed at Goofy—in one May 1937 page, low on funds, he rather unkindly suggests mocking Goofy as a cheap form of amusement—and they invariably fall flat because Goofy *never* reacts to anything in the way Mickey expects. Finding that tree that seems to have sprouted an assortment of fruit, Goofy is merely annoyed because there are no plums. In one December 1936 page, Mickey hides a brick underneath a top hat on the sidewalk, hoping Goofy will kick it. Instead, Goofy notices that the silk hat is much nicer than his own and decides to make a swap. Lifting the silk topper from its place, he substitutes his ratty old hat, carefully fits it over the brick—and *then* kicks it.

Of course the late 1930s didn't mark the end of Goofy's character development; and, in fact, in later years he continued to evolve in far more varied and unpredictable ways than some of the other characters. In the movies, the Art Babbitt Goofy was succeeded by the Goof of director Jack Kinney, who featured him in a series of wildly inventive sports parodies. But the late 1930s, the period covered by this volume, did mark a turning point for Goofy in the comics. The persona that Gottfredson and his writers developed at this time proved so useful that they continued to develop it and use it further. Right up to the present day, this version of Goofy continues to appear in new comics as a sidekick to Mickey, independent of the course followed by his screen counterpart.

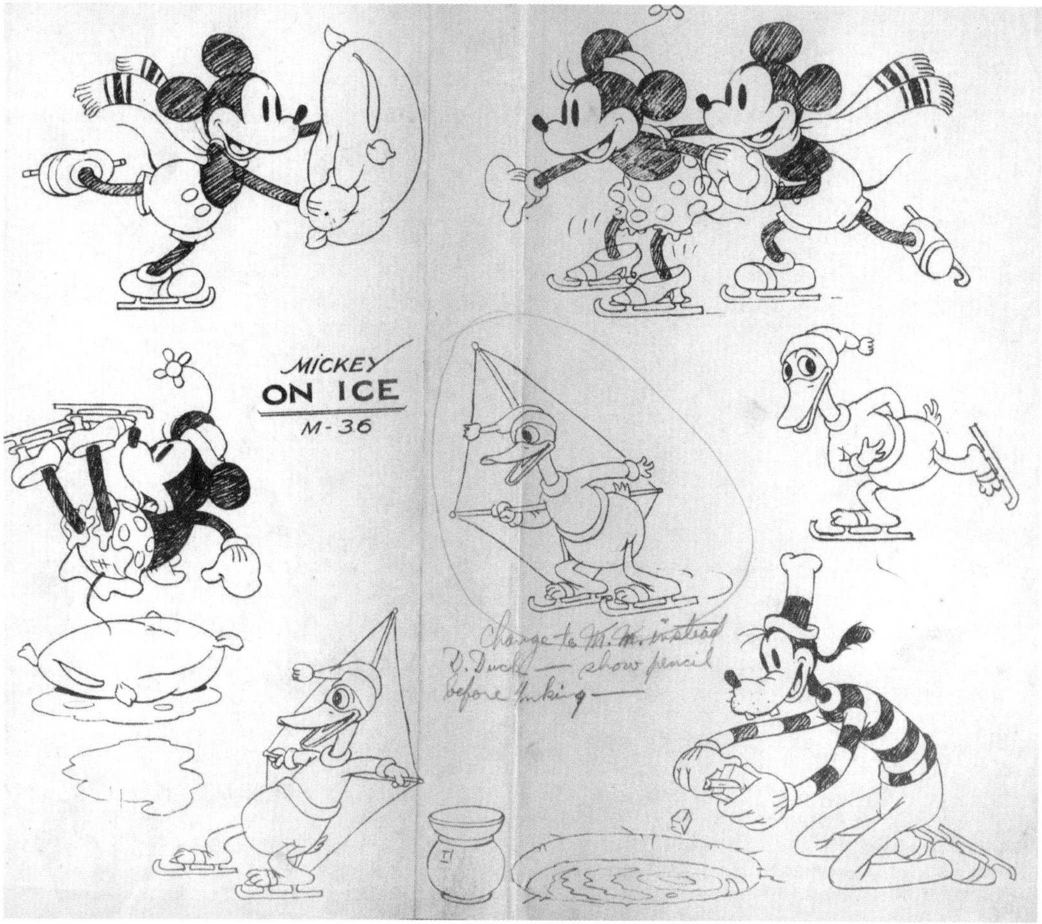
MICKEY
ON ICE
M-36
Change to M.M. instead
D. Duck — show pencil
before inking —

RIGHT: A model sheet for *On Ice* (1935) captures Goofy midway through his evolution. Image courtesy Walt Disney Archives.

In the meantime, what of the story content in the 1936-38 *Mickey Mouse* Sunday pages? Readers of the previous volume in this series may remember that, from the beginning, the Sunday page had developed a story style all its own. The daily strip had largely been adapted to a series of exciting continuities, featuring Mickey as a scrappy little adventurer, but the Sunday page—with its extended length and intermittent appearances—seemed suited to other kinds of stories: comedies or elaborate fantasies. Sometimes these stories were drawn out in extended continuities that ran for months; at other times they might be self-contained within a single page.

In this volume we can see that the same patterns continued through the late 1930s. Here we find slapstick and situation comedy as Mickey essays simple (?) home repairs or tests his ventriloquist skills; imaginative fantasy in "The Robin Hood Adventure" and "Brave Little Tailor"; and any number of isolated gags. The extended "Sheriff of Nugget Gulch" continuity in 1937, like the earlier "Lair of Wolf Barker" (1933), is the exception that proves the rule: a Western adventure story, but one very unlike those in the daily strip. Here the adventures are triggered by comedy situations, and Mickey becomes a hero almost by accident. And here again, Goofy's new persona is a key ingredient in the story. As he and Mickey prepare for a train journey to the gold fields out west, Goofy can't resist firing his sixguns recklessly from the observation platform—not realizing that such behavior is frowned upon. Word of his escapade quickly spreads, and by the time the two harmless tourists arrive out West, they've been preceded by reputations as notorious desperadoes. Before they know it they've been drawn into the center of a local conflict with a *real* desperado. Of course, once heroism is thrust upon him, Mickey rises to the occasion, defeating the bad guy with his characteristic blend of ingenuity and steely nerve.

Much of the fascination of Disney comic strips lies in their parallels with contemporary Disney films. These parallels are many and varied in the *Mickey* Sundays, and they range from subtle—almost hidden—visual references to open duplications of characters, story situations, and sometimes entire films.

For the Disney enthusiast, the most subtly hidden connections in these strips are the most enjoyable. In the 25 April 1937 page, as Mickey and Goofy exit the vaudeville theater in the first panel, they pass a poster advertising the well-known artiste, Madame Clara Cluck. In fact Madame Cluck was currently appearing in a theatrical Mickey Mouse short, *Mickey's Amateurs*, which had been in the works for well over a year, and which was released a scant week before this page was published. In January 1938 Clarabelle Cow enlists Mickey's help to catch her pet parrot, which has escaped from its cage. As Clarabelle anxiously frets over the safety of "the poor creature," Mickey climbs a tree in pursuit of the parrot (which looks easily big enough and strong enough to take care of itself) and is soundly thrashed for his pains. The appearance of this parrot reflects the bird's intended screen debut—also as Clarabelle's pet—in the shelved cartoon "Interior Decorators." It also reflects his eventual use in *Mickey's Parrot*, which was currently in production and was released to theaters later the same year. The bird in *Mickey's Parrot* is nobody's pet, but the resemblance and tough mannerisms are unmistakable.

Sometimes the movie references are more artfully mixed. Disney fans reading the opening installments of 1936's "Robin Hood Adventure" will be instantly reminded of *two* Mickey pictures: *Mickey's Garden*, which had been released the previous year and had featured hallucinatory images of supersized plants and insects, and *The Worm Turns*, then in production, in which Mickey's further experiments produced behavioral oddities like the belligerent fly seen here. As if for good measure, Gottfredson and Ted Osborne also include a page of flypaper gags—inevitably recalling the famed "flypaper sequence" in *Playful Pluto* (1934)—and the end of the "Robin Hood" continuity, with Mickey escaping from the storybook, bears comparison with the ending of yet another film, *Thru the Mirror*, released a few months earlier in 1936.

Conversely, sometimes Gottfredson and Osborne begin with a *situation* from one of the films but develop the story along very different lines. The "Service with a Smile" continuity appeared in newspapers in the spring of 1938, a full three years after the film *Mickey's Service Station* had played in theaters. On screen, the service-station setting had been the springboard for a series of slapstick gags as Mickey,

HEH
HEH
HEH
HEH
HEH
HE

BELOW: Donald is tailed by Clarabelle's parrot in storyboards for the unfinished "Interior Decorators" (c. 1936; see page 262 for an additional sequence). Art by Otto Englander; image courtesy Disney Animation Research Library.

PUBLICITY ON WALT DISNEY'S MICKEY MOUSE in "Mickey's Service Station"

Released thru UNITED ARTISTS

NEW MOVEMENTS FOR OLD MOTORS

MECHANIC

DONALD

When Mickey cleans an automobile motor, you may be sure that that motor will be in a perfect state of prophylactic cleanliness. Only the best grade of toothpaste is used to clean the teeth of the gears, and when valves are to be ground, the studio meatgrinder is brought into service!

Mickey, the mechanic supreme, with Donald Duck and the Goof as his capable assistants, make their appearance in the latest Walt Disney production, "MICKEY'S SERVICE STATION," coming to the .... Theatre. When this crew of mechanical men get finished with a car, the motor has a movement all its own.

Donald Duck seems to be a victim of deflation. At any rate, it's evident that he does not believe in "MICKEY'S SERVICE STATION" slogan—"Service with a smile." Plant this mat in your newspapers for cooperative tie-ups. Write to the United Artists office for your mat. It's gratis.

Service With A Smile!

"Where Donald goes disaster follows!" seems to be a motto around the Walt Disney Studio, for Donald Duck simply oozes trouble wherever he travels.

It was a unique inspiration on the part of Uncle Walt Disney when he cast the delightful Duck in the role of a trouble hunter in Mickey Mouse's latest picture, "MICKEY'S SERVICE STATION," coming to the .... Theatre .... next.

A HOBBY DUCK

Donald Duck has acquired the reputation of being the Walt Disney Studio's "Hobbyist." His mania for collecting and experimenting is well-known to his fellow workers. While working in "MICKEY'S SERVICE STATION," Walt Disney's latest Mickey Mouse production, coming to the .... Theatre, Donald unfolded his plan to build a combination airship, house-boat and automobile all rolled into one!

MICKEY OPENS SERVICE STATION FIXES AUTOS OF THE NATION

Amidst a scene of much gaiety and laughter, Mickey Mouse opened his automobile service station yesterday at the .... Theatre. Many of his friends attended the opening and gave Mickey a hilarious send-off on his new venture.

EXPERT AUTO FIXER-UPPERS!

Donald Duck and the Goof are Mickey's capable assistants in this new Walt Disney release, while Peg-leg Pete supplies whatever menace is lacking. Mickey has always maintained that Donald Duck is menace enough in every picture he plays in. "MICKEY'S SERVICE STATION," Walt Disney's latest Mickey Mouse production is now showing at the .... Theatre.

TIRE TECHNIQUE

The Goof visited Clarabelle Cow's sewing circle in preparation for his role in Walt Disney's latest Mickey Mouse production, "MICKEY'S SERVICE STATION," now showing at the .... Theatre. Goofy uses his stitching technique to good effect by patching blown out inner tubes with a semi-hem-stitching movement all his own.

MICKEY'S MIRTH

When you hear that Mickey is running an automobile service station, you may be sure that his customers will be given service with Mickey's infallible smile, and not even pugnacious Peg-leg Pete can shake it loose. Donald Duck and the Goof support Mickey in his latest Walt Disney production, "MICKEY'S SERVICE STATION," coming to the .... Theatre .... next.

A GOOFY GAG

Goofy inadvertently introduced a new method of testing batteries, using himself as both tester and method, in Walt Disney's latest Mickey Mouse production, "MICKEY'S SERVICE STATION," coming to the .... Theatre. Mechanic Goof picked up an electric bulb in one hand and accidently touched the terminals of a battery with his other. The bulb glowed, and went out as Goofy, with a yell, discarded his new testing system for something less shocking.

Donald, and Goofy scrambled to repair Pete's car. In the newspaper continuity, Donald Duck is no longer available—having departed to star in his own strip by this time—and the gags center on the dynamic between Mickey and Goofy. Endeavoring to assist Mickey in running the station, Goofy works earnestly to make good in the oil business, with a predictable rate of success.

As it happens, the most obvious of these movie references in the 1936-38 comics—references so explicit that they amount to "advertisements" for their respective films—occur, like bookends, at the beginning and the end of the selections reproduced in this volume. "Mickey's Rival," which opens 1936, features Mortimer, Minnie's obnoxious former suitor, who would appear on movie screens later the same year in the cartoon of the same title. David Gerstein introduces us to Mortimer later in these pages. For now we'll simply observe that, during Mortimer's four visits to the comics, Mickey gets the best of the offensive prankster on two occasions—giving him a score of fifty percent, a far better average than he ever manages to achieve in the film!

Far more remarkable is "The Brave Little Tailor," in late 1938. The theatrical *Brave Little Tailor*, released in September, was a highlight among the studio's 1938 releases. Produced on a lavish scale for a short subject, even by Disney standards, the film was earmarked as something special upon its release to theaters. The studio promoted it with more than the usual publicity, including this Sunday-comic continuity, which was more or less the equivalent of the special *Snow White* comic continuity that had appeared in newspapers in 1937-38. Thad Komorowski comments on the unusual circumstances surrounding the "Tailor" continuity in 1938, and the unusual "movie-within-a-comic-strip" result that appeared in the finished pages.

LEFT: Original press kit cover for *Mickey's Service Station* (1935). Image courtesy Walt Disney Archives.

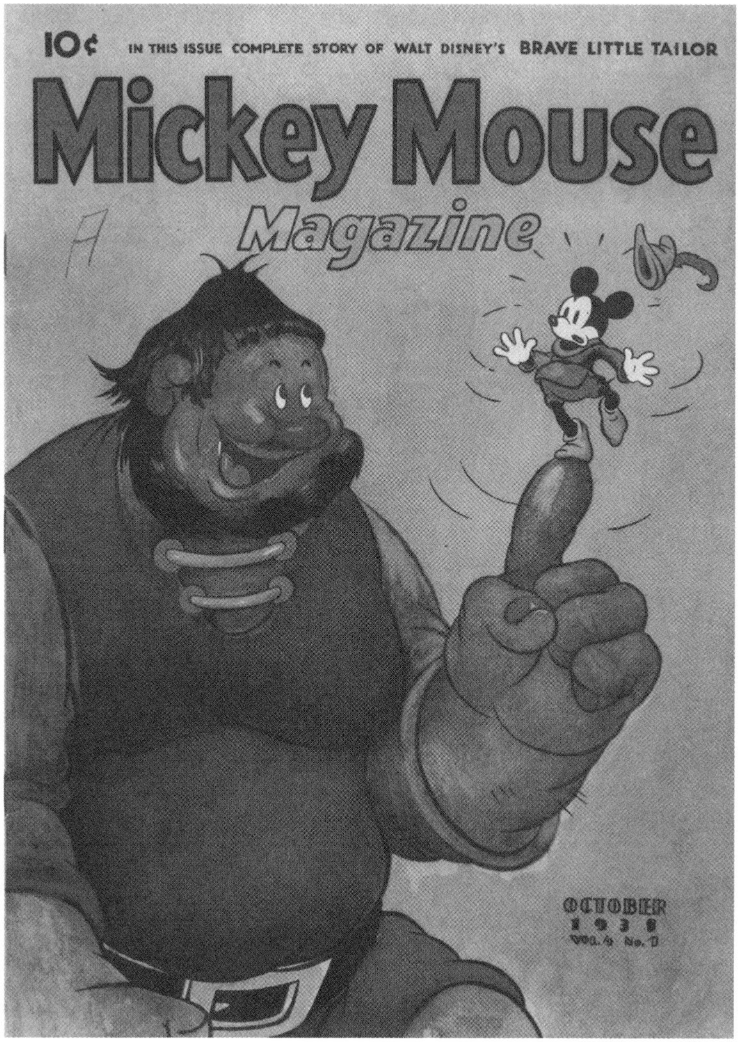
10¢
IN THIS ISSUE COMPLETE STORY OF WALT DISNEY'S BRAVE LITTLE TAILOR
Mickey Mouse
Magazine
OCTOBER
1938

As it turned out, this device served more than its original purpose. Behind the scenes, it also provided a transitional means for Gottfredson to bow out of the Mickey Sunday comics. By this time Gottfredson had been carrying the artistic responsibilities of both the daily *and* Sunday *Mickey Mouse* strips, an enormous workload, for nearly seven years. At various times in 1937 and 1938, Sunday inker Al Taliaferro assisted with the pencils as well, but this was only a temporary fix.[2] Gottfredson could not sustain this pressure indefinitely, and when he became ill in late 1938, it was clearly time to pass the Sunday page to another artist. Taliaferro, having recently launched the *Donald Duck* daily strip, was carrying a workload of his own and was no longer available. The candidate nominated for the job was Manuel Gonzales, late of the studio's publicity department, whom we'll meet later in these pages. Because of the unusual nature of the "Brave Little Tailor" continuity, it became an ideal vehicle for Gonzales' "audition," and as we can see in this volume, he passed the test with flying colors. Within a few months he had officially inherited the assignment.

LEFT: Brave Little Tailor was the cover feature in *Mickey Mouse Magazine* 37 (1938). This splendid drawing by Hank Porter was also used for the cartoon's original theatrical poster. Image courtesy Geppi's Entertainment Museum.

And so—aside from a few isolated occasions later on—Floyd Gottfredson's work on the *Mickey Mouse* Sunday comic page came to an end. It wasn't the end of an era; Gottfredson's work on the daily strip was still going strong and would continue for another four decades. But his formative seven years of the Sunday page would remain an important and impressive part of his body of work, a treasure that we're privileged to have preserved in these two volumes. As for Mickey himself, he took scant notice of the changes behind the scenes. From his beginnings in 1928 he had refused to stand still, and this was no time to start. Eager to find the next adventure, he moved on and never looked back. •

1 David Gerstein and Thad Komorowski, "The Cast: Donald," in *Walt Disney's Mickey Mouse: House of the Seven Haunts!* (Vol. 4 of Fantagraphics' companion daily strip series), p. 256.

2 David Gerstein, "Sharing the Spotlight: Al Taliaferro," in *Walt Disney's Mickey Mouse: Race to Death Valley* (Vol. 1 of Fantagraphics' companion daily strip series), p. 275. In addition, comics scholar and artist Joakim Gunnarsson has cited Mickey's posture, the shape of Goofy's muzzle, and the design of incidental players as the easiest means of detecting Taliaferro's pencil work.

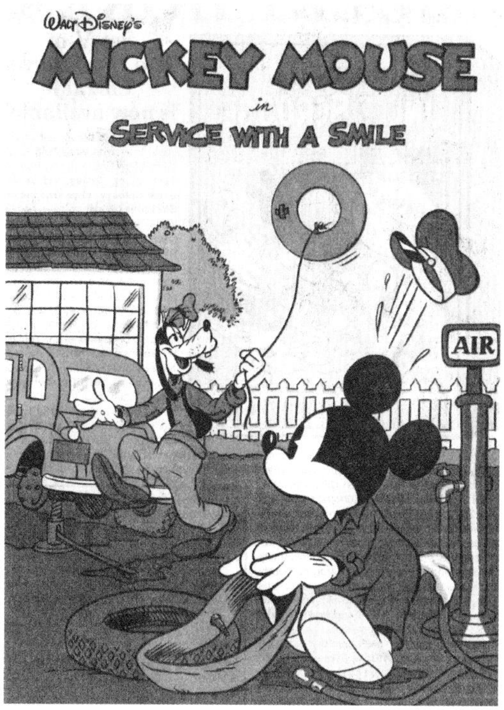
Walt Disney's
MICKEY MOUSE
in
SERVICE WITH A SMILE
AIR

RIGHT: This full-page illustration for Gottfredson's "Service With a Smile" appeared in the comic book *Mickey and Donald* 18 (1990). Art by Murad Gumen.

Of Blots and Stressed-Out Bodies

» *Appreciation by Tom Neely*

Where do I begin to write about Floyd Gottfredson? I'm a fan and an artist who has been enormously influenced by Gottfredson in many ways throughout the years. His Mickey Mouse comics were the first comics I even remember reading. My earliest recollection of really getting interested in comics was when I discovered Bill Blackbeard's *Smithsonian Collection of Newspaper Comics* (1977)—my grandmother gave that landmark anthology to me one Christmas, and that's where I first saw Floyd Gottfredson's Mickey Mouse.[1]

In some ways, Floyd Gottfredson was my first art teacher. I was drawn to the *Smithsonian* Mickey reprint because I was already a fan of Disney cartoons and had an interest in the moving image. But now that I had the comics, I could finally see the characters when they *weren't* moving—and this made it easier for me to copy the drawings and learn from them. Imitating their style taught me to draw. And reading about the artists in the *Smithsonian Collection* made me realize that I could maybe be a cartoonist when I grew up. By the time I had reached middle school I was very serious about wanting to be an animator and comic book artist.

My desire receded for awhile; as my interest in funny animals and superheroes gave way to more "serious" aspirations, I moved away from comics. For some years, I became more interested in fine arts and pursued painting. But when I was in art school in San Francisco—feeling completely, and unexpectedly,

UH... MICKEY!
QUIET GOOF!
I THINK I FOUND A CLUE.

lost—rediscovering my love of old comics as well as discovering the independent comics scene changed my entire perspective and made me want to create comics again.

When I began to seriously pursue my first graphic novel, I once again returned to the comics of my youth for inspiration. I wanted to do a very personal story and it made sense to go back to my earliest influences: Mickey comics and surrealism. The result was a book drawn in a style very much informed by Gottfredson—and E. C. Segar's Popeye, another childhood favorite. I told a surrealistic story about a nameless man plagued by a mysterious cloud

WALT DISNEY'S Brave Little Tailor
PAINT AND CRAYON BOOK
PICTURES BY THE WALT DISNEY STUDIOS

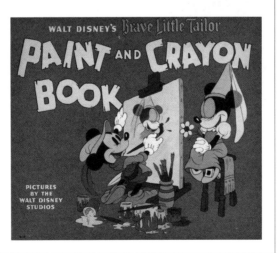

Above and opposite right: Gawrsh! Stylized Mickey, Goofy, and Phantom Blot as drawn by Neely for an unrealized licensed project. Art courtesy of the artist.

Left: *Brave Little Tailor* was actually marketed to young fans as a seminal role for Mickey-the-actor. Pencil art by Hank Porter courtesy Walt Disney Photo Library; published version courtesy David Gerstein.

of ink that eventually takes over his life, tears it apart, but then gives him a new hope. I named that book *The Blot* (2007) as a slight nod to one of Gottfredson's best creations, the villainous Phantom Blot.

I feel like Floyd Gottfredson's comics are all burned into the back of my brain somewhere; all his random distilled moments, full of pathos and drama. The energy that Gottfredson infused into his compositions compels you through every strip and

ABOVE: Tom Neely tips his hat to Gottfredson with a very non-Disney *Blot* (2007). Art © and courtesy Tom Neely.

every page—always moving forward! Each character pose creates a frenetic feeling that is mesmerizing. And the drama of their acting—like the vaudevillian and silent screen stars of the time, these characters act with every bit of their bodies! When Mickey is surprised, his entire body shoots up in the air, back arched, with sweat and tears flying in every direction. When Goofy is confused, you see it from the top of his lumpy head right down to the sagginess of his shoes. Even when Mickey is standing still in a "relaxed" position, his body looks as if it is coiled and taut and ready to spring into action. Gottfredson's characters' bodies are always under so much stress that, I like to imagine, they must have been exhausted at the end of the day when Floyd was through drawing them!

Acting is one of the strongest qualities of Floyd's comics. It's easy to imagine that Gottfredson was influenced by attitudes at the Disney Studio, where Walt often represented Mickey and the gang as actors: like Harold Lloyd, Charlie Chaplin and Buster Keaton, Mickey was a star and he worked many roles. In the stories reprinted in this volume, Gottfredson took the concept to its logical conclusion—establishing the comic strip as a behind-the-scenes look at the "real life" of the actor seen on screen! We get to watch Mickey talking to his director, reading his scripts, and driving onto the Disney lot before settling into his role as "The Brave Little Tailor."

I still look to Floyd for guidance when I need to make my characters come to life. Last year I got to design a new character, a mysterious boxer called the Phantom Crusher, for IDW's recent line of Popeye comics. Writer Roger Langridge and I both agreed that I had to pay homage again and model the Crusher after the Phantom Blot.

Like Floyd, I've even been working for Disney, drawing comics for *Phineas and Ferb Magazine*—actually one of the funnest jobs I've had in a dozen years of freelancing for the Studio. Even in my current independent comic *Henry & Glenn Forever*—the fictionalized adventures of musicians Glenn Danzig

and Henry Rollins—I see Gottfredson's hand guiding mine in the way that I make my characters act: they have exaggerated, coiled-up and stressed-out little bodies like Mickey and the gang.

Until *this* series of Mickey Mouse books was announced by Fantagraphics, the comics I most sought out to collect were Gottfredson's! As I look through my life, Floyd Gottfredson has been an influence all along. ●

1 The *Smithsonian Collection* reprinted the daily serial "Race for Riches" (1935) in its entirety. "Race" also appears in Vol. 3 of Fantagraphics' companion daily strip series.

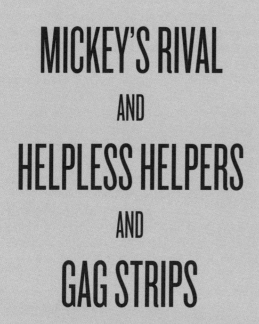

MICKEY'S RIVAL
AND
HELPLESS HELPERS
AND
GAG STRIPS

JANUARY 5, 1936
–
APRIL 19, 1936

MICKEY MOUSE
REGISTERED U.S. PATENT OFFICE

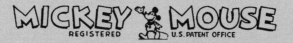

BALANCING ACTS—AND WHEN HELPFULNESS LACKS

Floyd Gottfredson's *Mickey Mouse* daily strip frequently built on the subject matter of Walt Disney's animated shorts, often expanding on the basic premises in wonderful ways. Simple gag cartoons turned into complex adventure comics: *The Steeplechase* (1933) became "Mickey Mouse and His Horse Tanglefoot" (1933), *Lonesome Ghosts* (1937) was adapted during production into "The Seven Ghosts" (1936), and we continue to enjoy both versions today.

The seven-day intervals and shorter duration of the Sunday continuities, however, would necessitate that Gottfredson and his writers adjust their cartoon adaptation process to suit the larger and more colorful weekly showcase. While some gag cartoons still became adventure comics on Sunday—the 1934 short *Camping Out* evolved into the epic "Dr. Oofgay's Secret Serum" (1934)—a more practical method of adapting short to strip was for the Sunday page to run "gag-for-gag" with its animated antecedent. Certain gag-based cartoons, by their nature, were best translated into gag-based comics.

Two such examples are presented here: "Mickey's Rival," based on the cartoon of the same name, and "Helpless Helpers," salvaged from the remnants of an unproduced Mickey, Donald, and Goofy cartoon.[1]

As on the screen, Mickey would be set against an obstinate opponent or other source of problems, typically winning some battles and comically losing others. First up would be the lanky, obnoxious irritant who would become the titular "Mickey's Rival" for the hand of fair Minnie—Mortimer Mouse.

After establishing Mortimer as a "Bluto" to Mickey's "Popeye"—or later "Reggie" to the Mouse's "Archie"—Gottfredson and writer Ted Osborne proceed with a narrative "balancing act" of comic rivalry between the two antagonists. Neither Mouse maintains the upper hand for longer than the duration of a single strip! The back-and-forth battle culminates in a *literal* balancing act, into which Mick maneuvers Mort as the deciding factor in their conflict.

Similar to "Mickey's Rival," "Helpless Helpers" is a four-installment continuity, pitting Mickey not against rivals, but pests. Though firmly in "do-it-yourself-mode" to fix up Minnie's house, Mickey faces unwanted assistance from Donald Duck in three installments and Goofy in the remaining one, nicely converting various bits of animation-style business to the comic pages.

As four separate, only tangentially related gags, "Helpless Helpers" is a rapid romp with which it's hard to find fault. Unless you're *Mickey*, who might wish for the balancing act of comic contention seen in "Mickey's Rival." There, Mickey had a fifty-fifty success rate at outwitting Mortimer; in "Helpers," Mickey succeeds in his tasks only *once*. Donald dooms Mickey's efforts in weeks one and four, while Goofy applies his own unique problem-solving logic to week two's task.

Taken as a continuity, "Helpers" might seem stronger overall if Donald were the singular, consistent thorn in Mickey's midsection, omitting Goofy's segment entirely. But don't despair, Duck fans. Donald makes up for this with some legitimate hand-lending in the strips of April 12 and 19, also seen in the coming pages.

—JOE TORCIVIA

1 "Interior Decorators" drifted in and out of development several times between 1935 and 1938. See page 262 for more details.

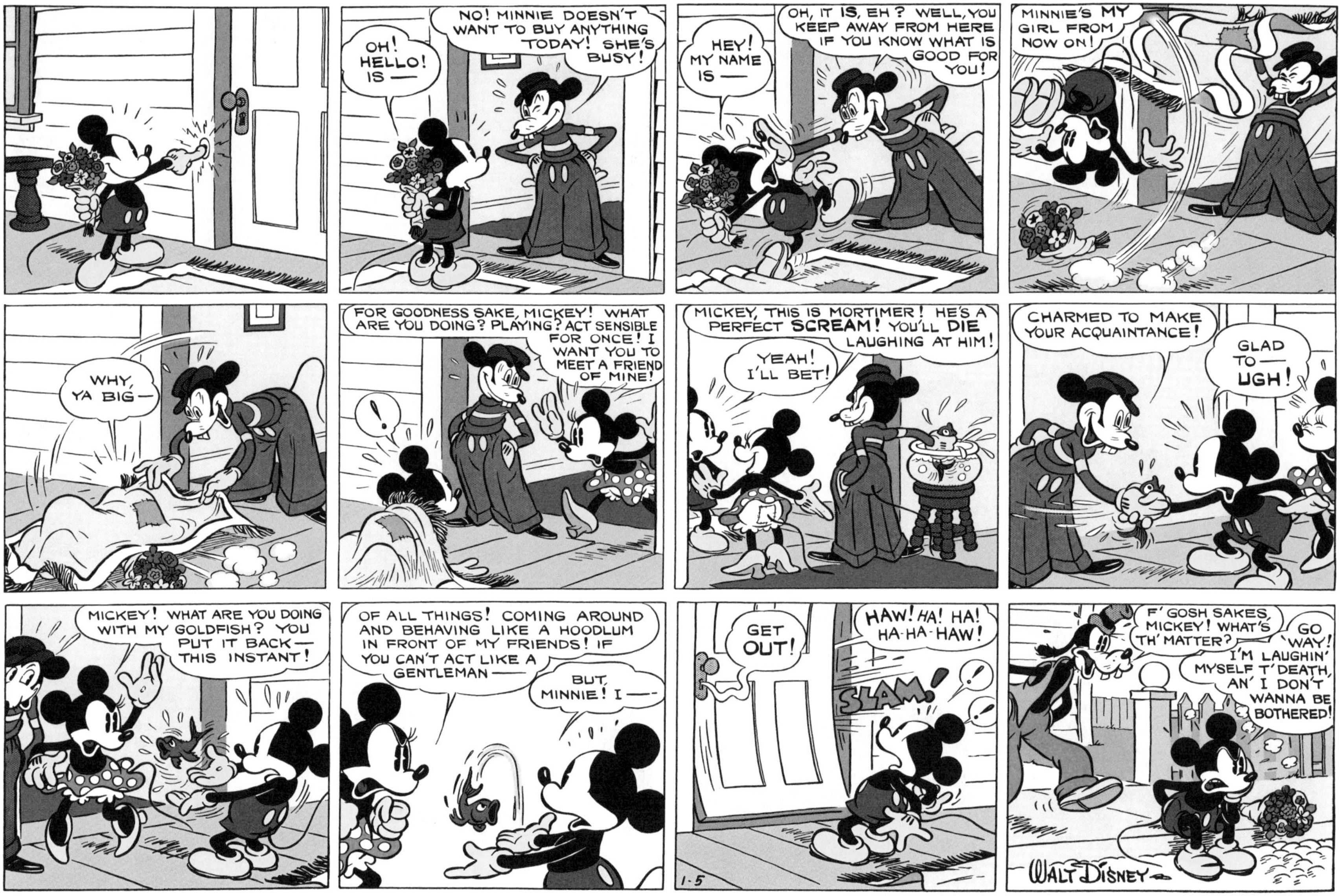

OH! HELLO! IS —
NO! MINNIE DOESN'T WANT TO BUY ANYTHING TODAY! SHE'S BUSY!
HEY! MY NAME IS —
OH, IT IS, EH? WELL, YOU KEEP AWAY FROM HERE IF YOU KNOW WHAT IS GOOD FOR YOU!
MINNIE'S MY GIRL FROM NOW ON!
WHY, YA BIG —
!
FOR GOODNESS SAKE, MICKEY! WHAT ARE YOU DOING? PLAYING? ACT SENSIBLE FOR ONCE! I WANT YOU TO MEET A FRIEND OF MINE!
MICKEY, THIS IS MORTIMER! HE'S A PERFECT SCREAM! YOU'LL DIE LAUGHING AT HIM!
YEAH! I'LL BET!
CHARMED TO MAKE YOUR ACQUAINTANCE!
GLAD TO — UGH!
MICKEY! WHAT ARE YOU DOING WITH MY GOLDFISH? YOU PUT IT BACK — THIS INSTANT!
OF ALL THINGS! COMING AROUND AND BEHAVING LIKE A HOODLUM IN FRONT OF MY FRIENDS! IF YOU CAN'T ACT LIKE A GENTLEMAN —
BUT, MINNIE! I —
1-5
GET OUT!
HAW! HA! HA! HA-HA-HAW!
SLAM!
F' GOSH SAKES, MICKEY! WHAT'S TH' MATTER?
GO 'WAY! I'M LAUGHIN' MYSELF T' DEATH, AN' I DON'T WANNA BE BOTHERED!
WALT DISNEY

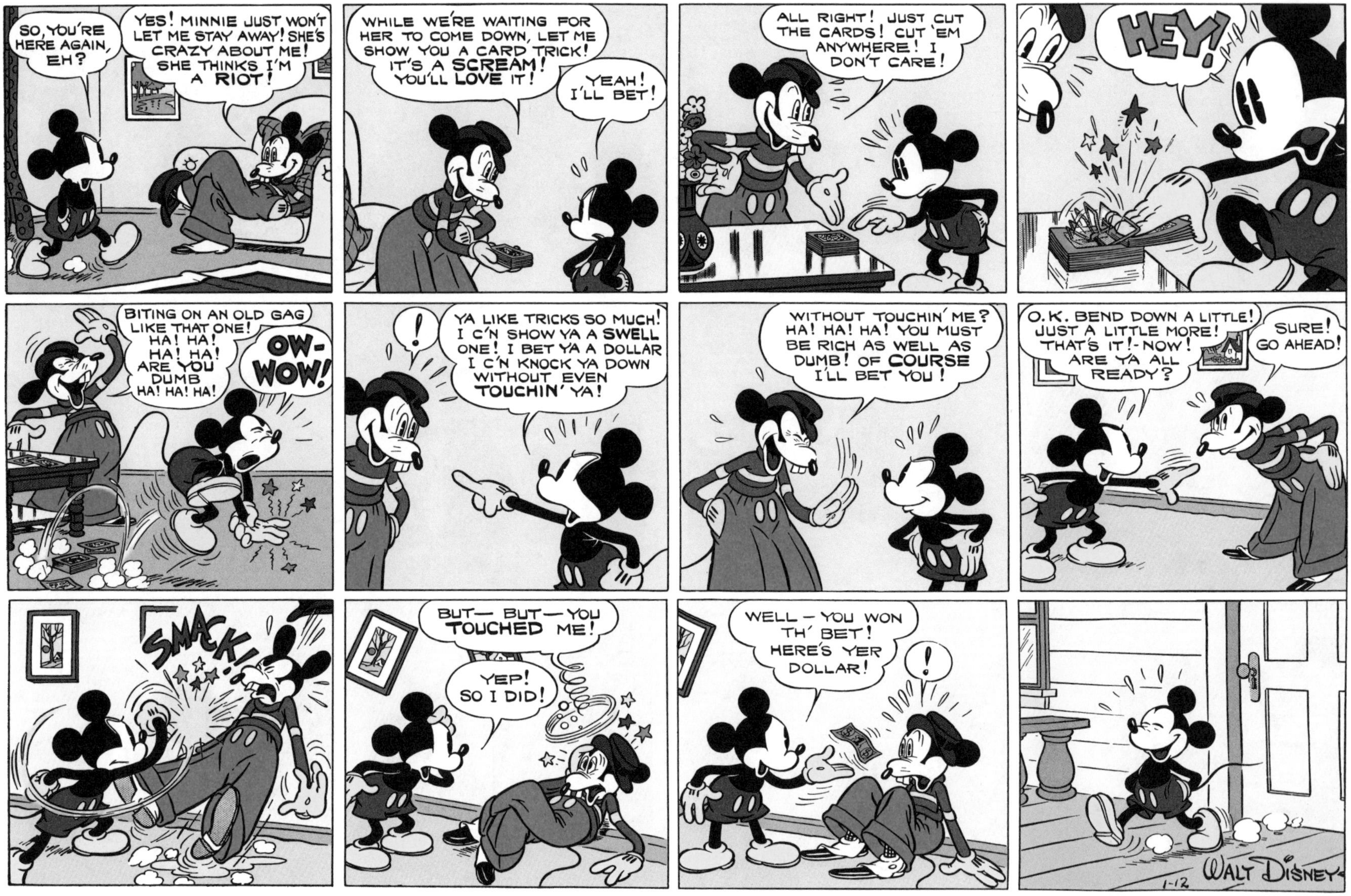

SO, YOU'RE HERE AGAIN, EH?
YES! MINNIE JUST WON'T LET ME STAY AWAY! SHE'S CRAZY ABOUT ME! SHE THINKS I'M A RIOT!
WHILE WE'RE WAITING FOR HER TO COME DOWN, LET ME SHOW YOU A CARD TRICK! IT'S A SCREAM! YOU'LL LOVE IT!
YEAH! I'LL BET!
ALL RIGHT! JUST CUT THE CARDS! CUT 'EM ANYWHERE! I DON'T CARE!
HEY!
BITING ON AN OLD GAG LIKE THAT ONE! HA! HA! HA! HA! ARE YOU DUMB HA! HA! HA!
OW-WOW!
!
YA LIKE TRICKS SO MUCH! I C'N SHOW YA A SWELL ONE! I BET YA A DOLLAR I C'N KNOCK YA DOWN WITHOUT EVEN TOUCHIN' YA!
WITHOUT TOUCHIN' ME? HA! HA! HA! YOU MUST BE RICH AS WELL AS DUMB! OF COURSE I'LL BET YOU!
O.K. BEND DOWN A LITTLE! JUST A LITTLE MORE! THAT'S IT!- NOW! ARE YA ALL READY?
SURE! GO AHEAD!
SMACK!
BUT— BUT— YOU TOUCHED ME!
YEP! SO I DID!
WELL - YOU WON TH' BET! HERE'S YER DOLLAR!
!
1-12
WALT DISNEY

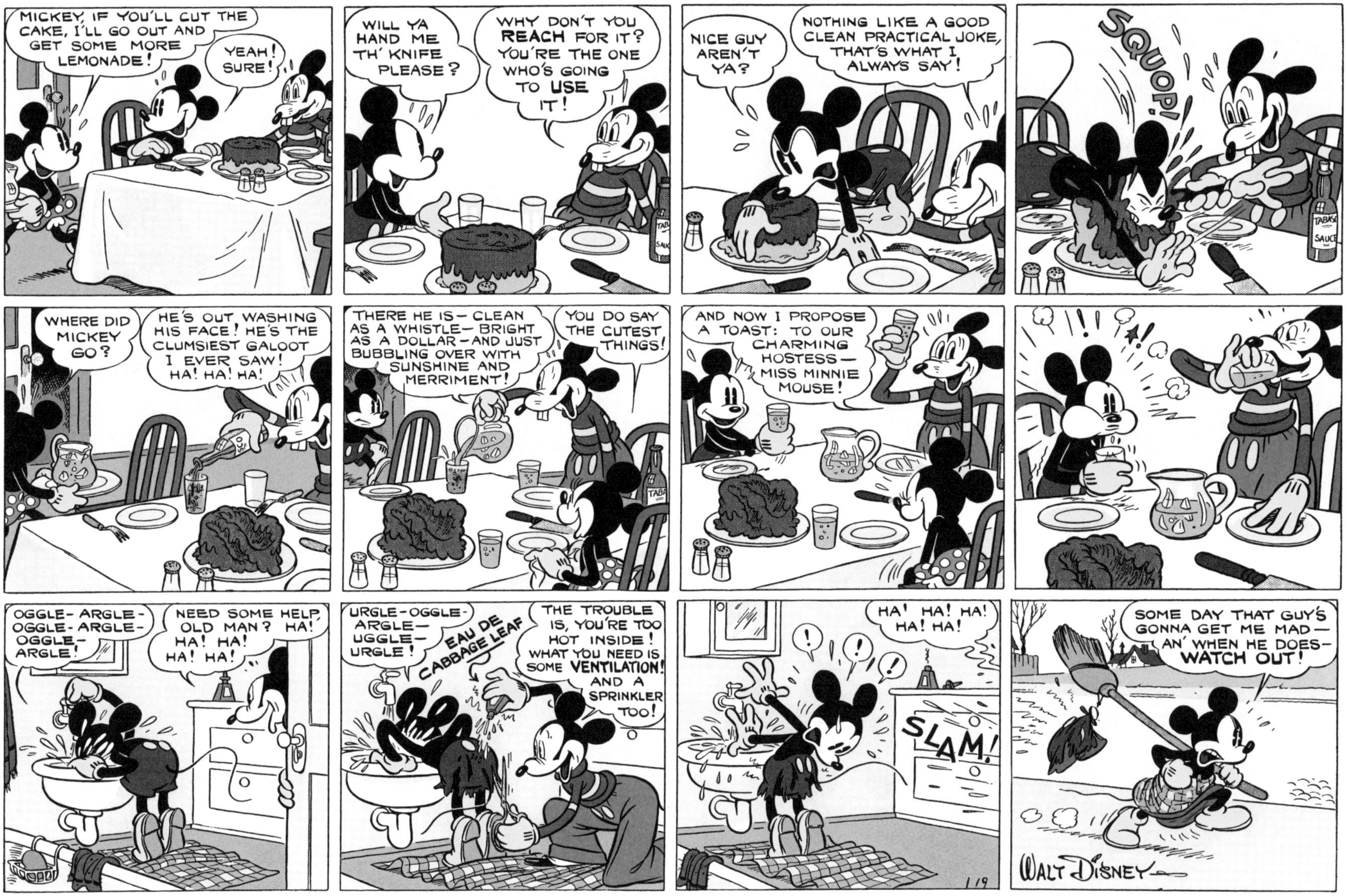
MICKEY, IF YOU'LL CUT THE CAKE, I'LL GO OUT AND GET SOME MORE LEMONADE!
YEAH! SURE!
WILL YA HAND ME TH' KNIFE PLEASE?
WHY DON'T YOU REACH FOR IT? YOU'RE THE ONE WHO'S GOING TO USE IT!
NICE GUY AREN'T YA?
NOTHING LIKE A GOOD CLEAN PRACTICAL JOKE, THAT'S WHAT I ALWAYS SAY!
SQUOP!
WHERE DID MICKEY GO?
HE'S OUT WASHING HIS FACE! HE'S THE CLUMSIEST GALOOT I EVER SAW! HA! HA! HA!
THERE HE IS— CLEAN AS A WHISTLE— BRIGHT AS A DOLLAR— AND JUST BUBBLING OVER WITH SUNSHINE AND MERRIMENT!
YOU DO SAY THE CUTEST THINGS!
AND NOW I PROPOSE A TOAST: TO OUR CHARMING HOSTESS— MISS MINNIE MOUSE!
OGGLE- ARGLE- OGGLE- ARGLE- OGGLE- ARGLE!
NEED SOME HELP OLD MAN? HA! HA! HA! HA! HA!
URGLE- OGGLE- ARGLE- UGGLE- URGLE!
EAU DE CABBAGE LEAF
THE TROUBLE IS, YOU'RE TOO HOT INSIDE! WHAT YOU NEED IS SOME VENTILATION! AND A SPRINKLER TOO!
HA! HA! HA! HA! HA!
SLAM!
SOME DAY THAT GUY'S GONNA GET ME MAD— AN' WHEN HE DOES— WATCH OUT!
WALT DISNEY

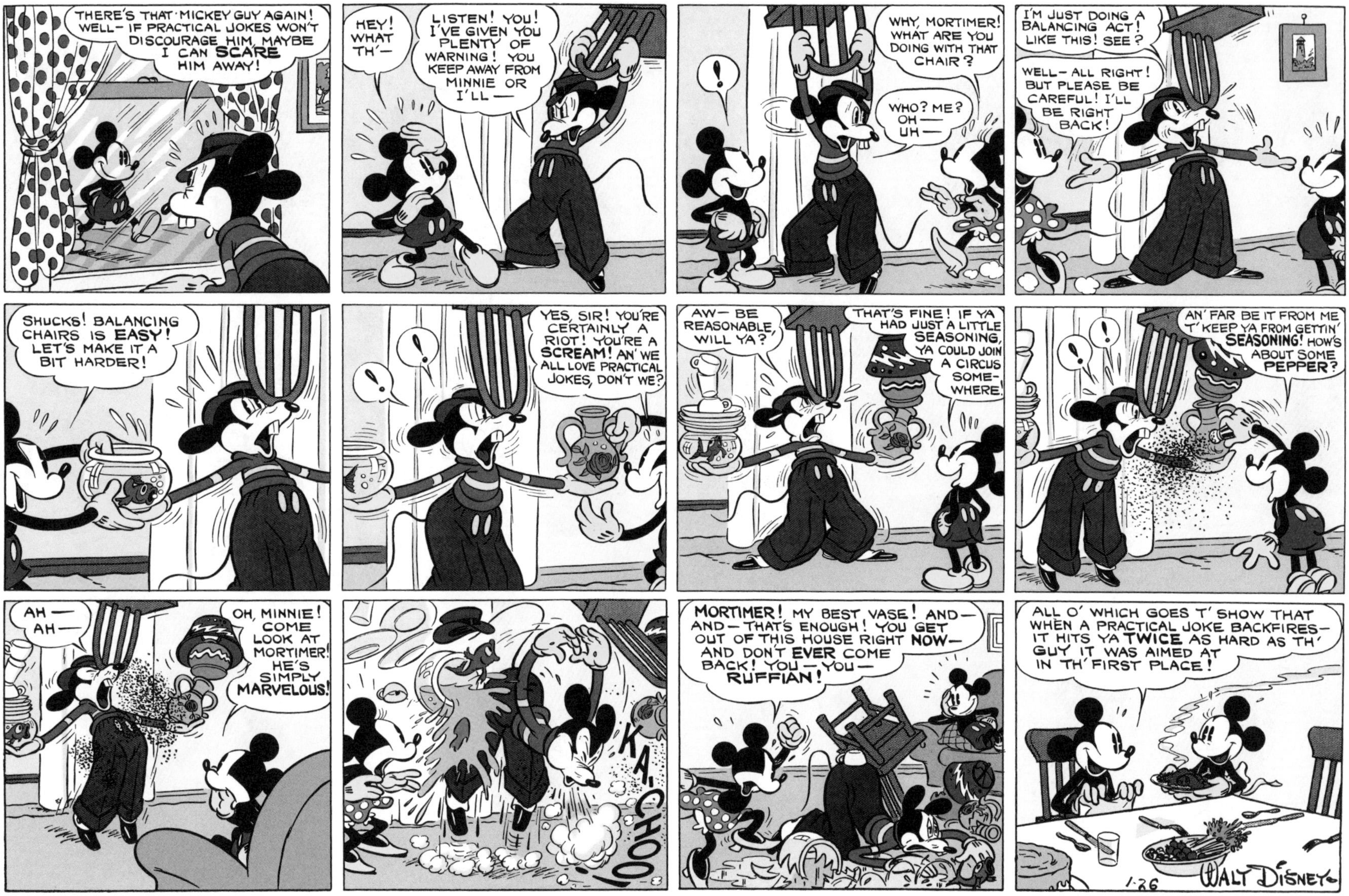
THERE'S THAT MICKEY GUY AGAIN! WELL– IF PRACTICAL JOKES WON'T DISCOURAGE HIM, MAYBE I CAN SCARE HIM AWAY!
HEY! WHAT TH'–
LISTEN! YOU! I'VE GIVEN YOU PLENTY OF WARNING! YOU KEEP AWAY FROM MINNIE OR I'LL —
!
WHY, MORTIMER! WHAT ARE YOU DOING WITH THAT CHAIR?
WHO? ME? OH — UH —
I'M JUST DOING A BALANCING ACT! LIKE THIS! SEE?
WELL– ALL RIGHT! BUT PLEASE BE CAREFUL! I'LL BE RIGHT BACK!
SHUCKS! BALANCING CHAIRS IS EASY! LET'S MAKE IT A BIT HARDER!
!
YES, SIR! YOU'RE CERTAINLY A RIOT! YOU'RE A SCREAM! AN' WE ALL LOVE PRACTICAL JOKES, DON'T WE?
AW– BE REASONABLE, WILL YA?
THAT'S FINE! IF YA HAD JUST A LITTLE SEASONING, YA COULD JOIN A CIRCUS SOME-WHERE!
! !
AN' FAR BE IT FROM ME T' KEEP YA FROM GETTIN' SEASONING! HOW'S ABOUT SOME PEPPER?
AH — AH —
OH, MINNIE! COME LOOK AT MORTIMER! HE'S SIMPLY MARVELOUS!
KA-CHOO!
MORTIMER! MY BEST VASE! AND– AND– THAT'S ENOUGH! YOU GET OUT OF THIS HOUSE RIGHT NOW– AND DON'T EVER COME BACK! YOU — YOU — RUFFIAN!
ALL O' WHICH GOES T' SHOW THAT WHEN A PRACTICAL JOKE BACKFIRES– IT HITS YA TWICE AS HARD AS TH' GUY IT WAS AIMED AT IN TH' FIRST PLACE!
1-26
WALT DISNEY

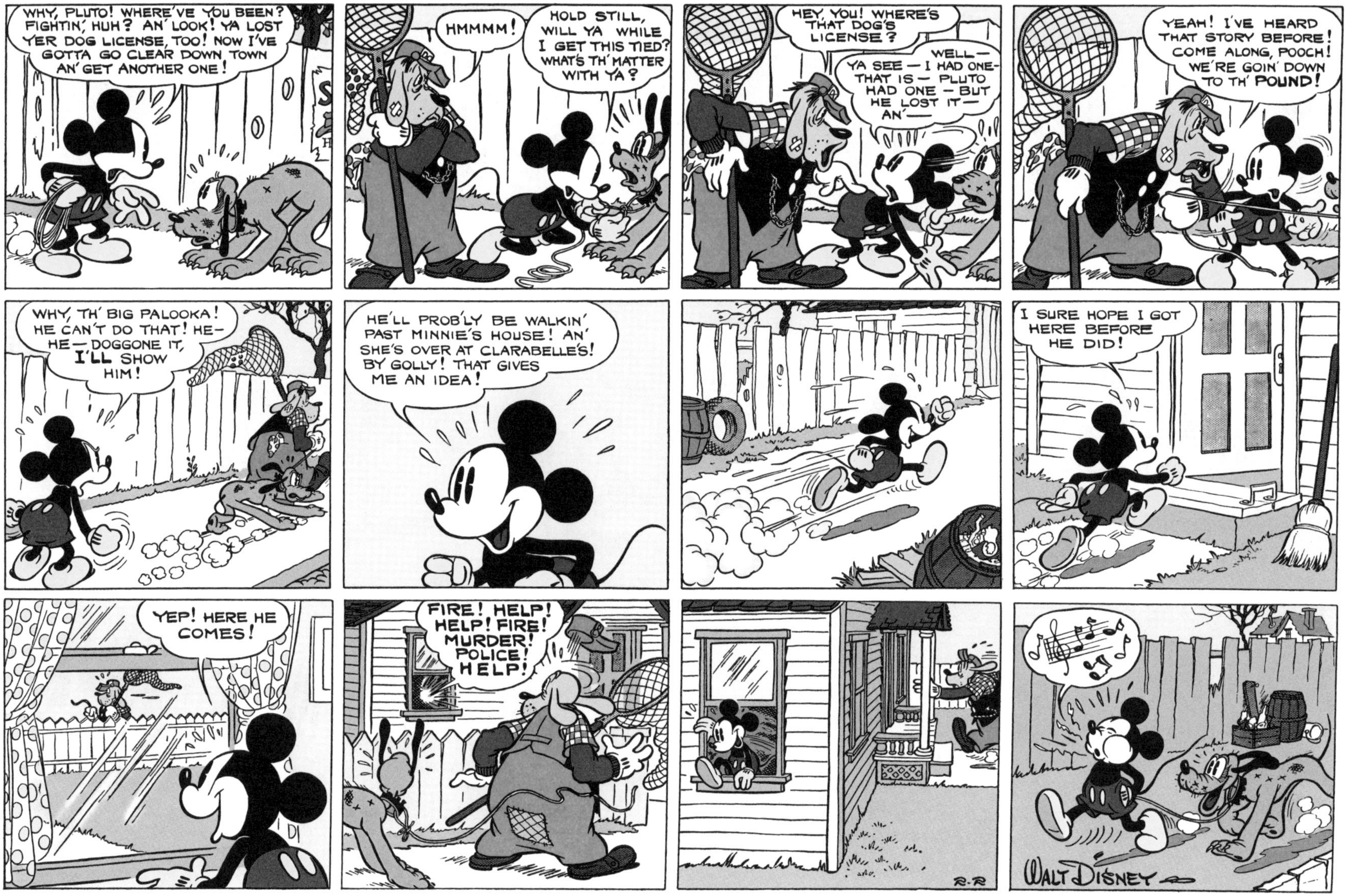
WHY, PLUTO! WHERE'VE YOU BEEN? FIGHTIN', HUH? AN' LOOK! YA LOST YER DOG LICENSE, TOO! NOW I'VE GOTTA GO CLEAR DOWN TOWN AN' GET ANOTHER ONE!
HMMMM!
HOLD STILL, WILL YA WHILE I GET THIS TIED? WHAT'S TH' MATTER WITH YA?
HEY, YOU! WHERE'S THAT DOG'S LICENSE?
WELL— YA SEE — I HAD ONE— THAT IS — PLUTO HAD ONE — BUT HE LOST IT— AN'—
YEAH! I'VE HEARD THAT STORY BEFORE! COME ALONG, POOCH! WE'RE GOIN' DOWN TO TH' POUND!
WHY, TH' BIG PALOOKA! HE CAN'T DO THAT! HE— HE— DOGGONE IT, I'LL SHOW HIM!
HE'LL PROB'LY BE WALKIN' PAST MINNIE'S HOUSE! AN' SHE'S OVER AT CLARABELLE'S! BY GOLLY! THAT GIVES ME AN IDEA!
I SURE HOPE I GOT HERE BEFORE HE DID!
YEP! HERE HE COMES!
FIRE! HELP! HELP! FIRE! MURDER! POLICE! HELP!
R-R
WALT DISNEY

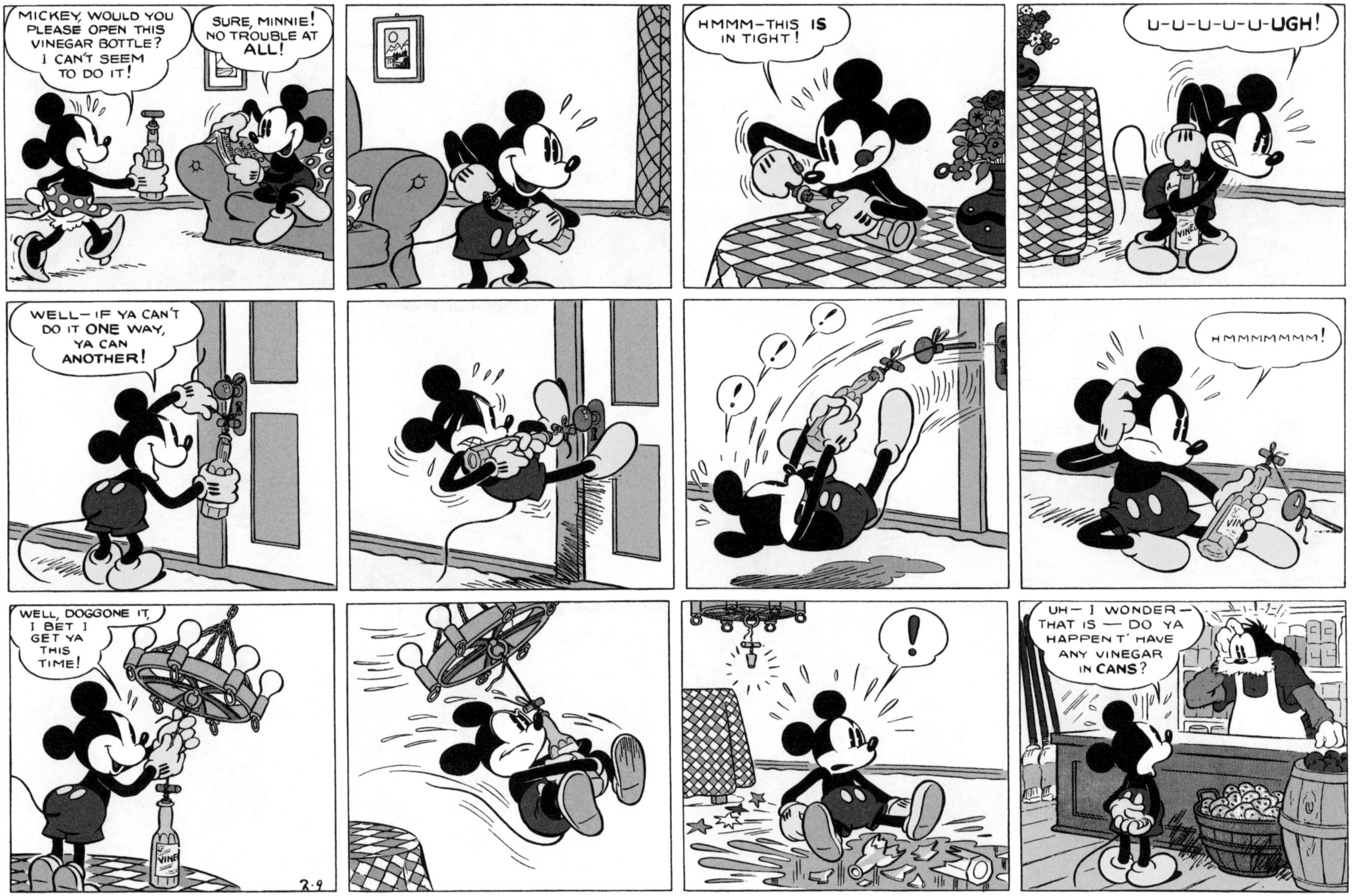
MICKEY, WOULD YOU PLEASE OPEN THIS VINEGAR BOTTLE? I CAN'T SEEM TO DO IT!
SURE, MINNIE! NO TROUBLE AT ALL!
HMMM—THIS IS IN TIGHT!
U-U-U-U-U-UGH!
WELL—IF YA CAN'T DO IT ONE WAY, YA CAN ANOTHER!
!
!
!
HMMMMMMM!
WELL, DOGGONE IT, I BET I GET YA THIS TIME!
!
UH—I WONDER—THAT IS—DO YA HAPPEN T' HAVE ANY VINEGAR IN CANS?

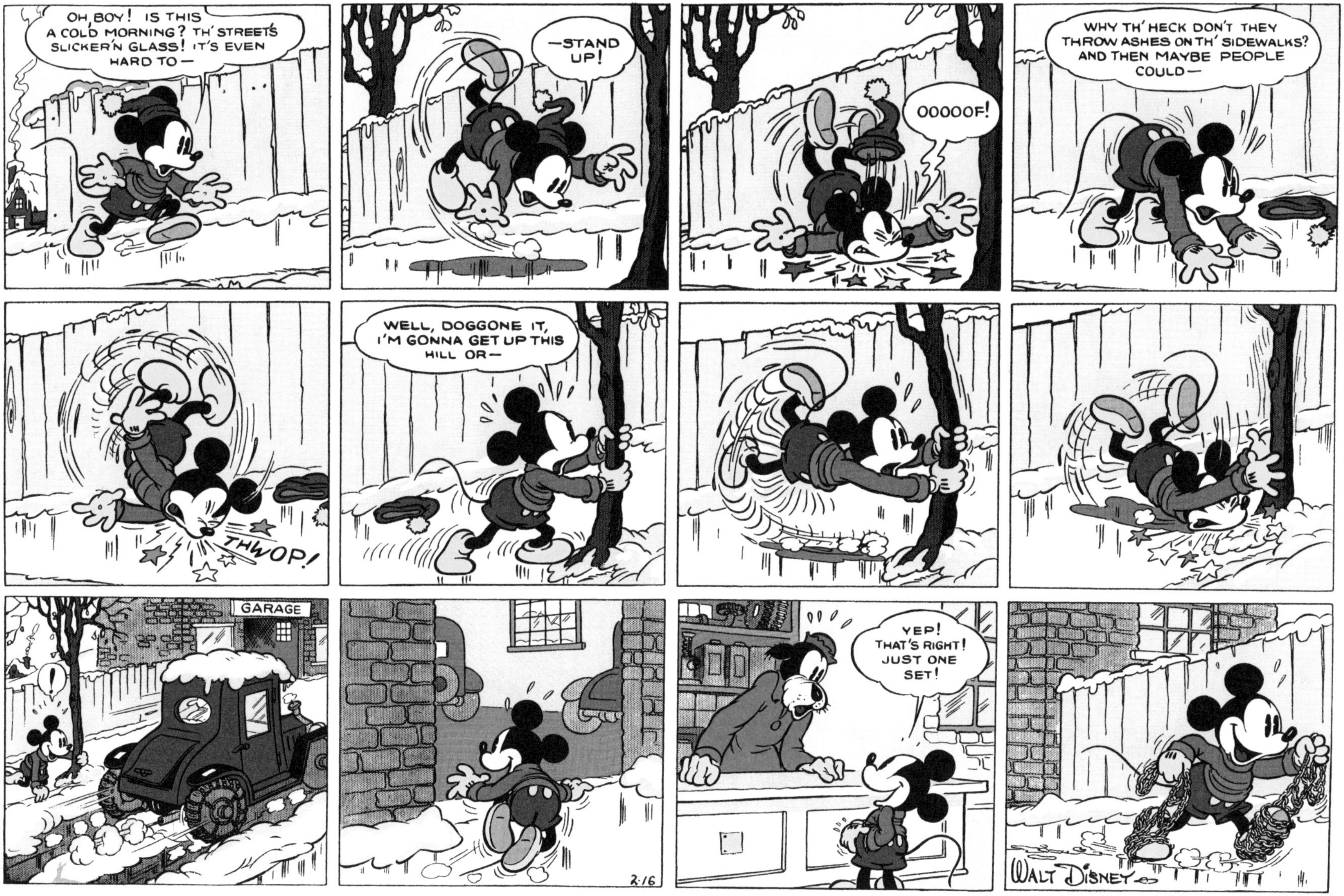
OH, BOY! IS THIS A COLD MORNING? TH' STREETS SLICKER'N GLASS! IT'S EVEN HARD TO —
—STAND UP!
OOOOOF!
WHY TH' HECK DON'T THEY THROW ASHES ON TH' SIDEWALKS? AND THEN MAYBE PEOPLE COULD —
THWOP!
WELL, DOGGONE IT, I'M GONNA GET UP THIS HILL OR —
GARAGE
!
2·16
YEP! THAT'S RIGHT! JUST ONE SET!
WALT DISNEY

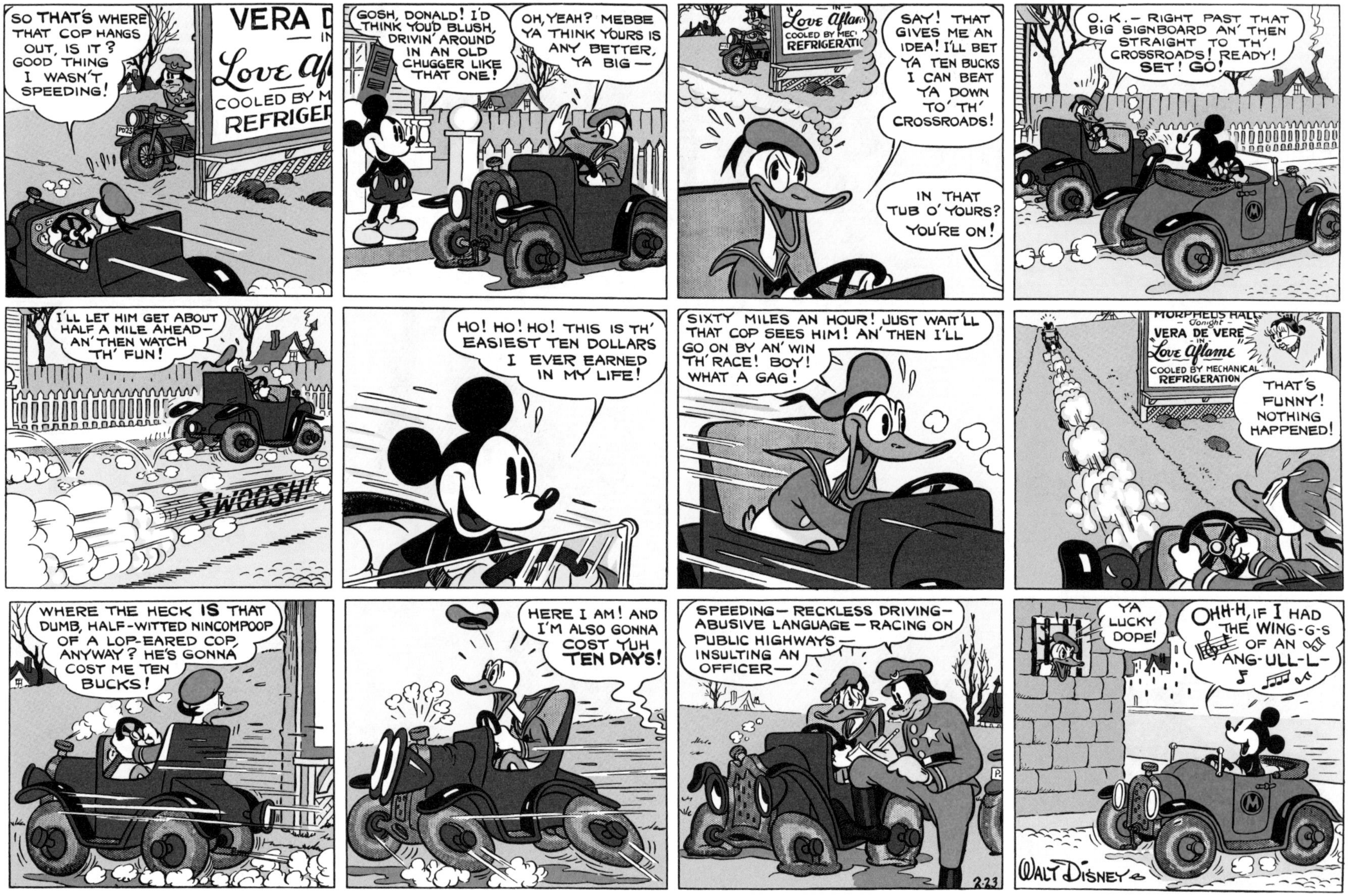
SO THAT'S WHERE THAT COP HANGS OUT, IS IT? GOOD THING I WASN'T SPEEDING!
VERA D
IN
Love af
COOLED BY M
REFRIGER
GOSH, DONALD! I'D THINK YOU'D BLUSH, DRIVIN' AROUND IN AN OLD CHUGGER LIKE THAT ONE!
OH, YEAH? MEBBE YA THINK YOURS IS ANY BETTER, YA BIG —
Love Aflam
COOLED BY MEC
REFRIGERATIO
SAY! THAT GIVES ME AN IDEA! I'LL BET YA TEN BUCKS I CAN BEAT YA DOWN TO' TH' CROSSROADS!
IN THAT TUB O' YOURS? YOU'RE ON!
O. K. — RIGHT PAST THAT BIG SIGNBOARD AN' THEN STRAIGHT TO TH' CROSSROADS! READY! SET! GO!
I'LL LET HIM GET ABOUT HALF A MILE AHEAD— AN' THEN WATCH TH' FUN!
SWOOSH!
HO! HO! HO! THIS IS TH' EASIEST TEN DOLLARS I EVER EARNED IN MY LIFE!
SIXTY MILES AN HOUR! JUST WAIT'LL THAT COP SEES HIM! AN' THEN I'LL GO ON BY AN' WIN TH' RACE! BOY! WHAT A GAG!
MORPHEUS HALL
Tonight
VERA DE VERE
IN
Love Aflame
COOLED BY MECHANICAL
REFRIGERATION
THAT'S FUNNY! NOTHING HAPPENED!
WHERE THE HECK IS THAT DUMB, HALF-WITTED NINCOMPOOP OF A LOP-EARED COP, ANYWAY? HE'S GONNA COST ME TEN BUCKS!
HERE I AM! AND I'M ALSO GONNA COST YUH TEN DAYS!
SPEEDING— RECKLESS DRIVING— ABUSIVE LANGUAGE — RACING ON PUBLIC HIGHWAYS — INSULTING AN OFFICER—
2-23
YA LUCKY DOPE!
OHH-H, IF I HAD THE WING-G-S OF AN ANG-ULL-L-
WALT DISNEY

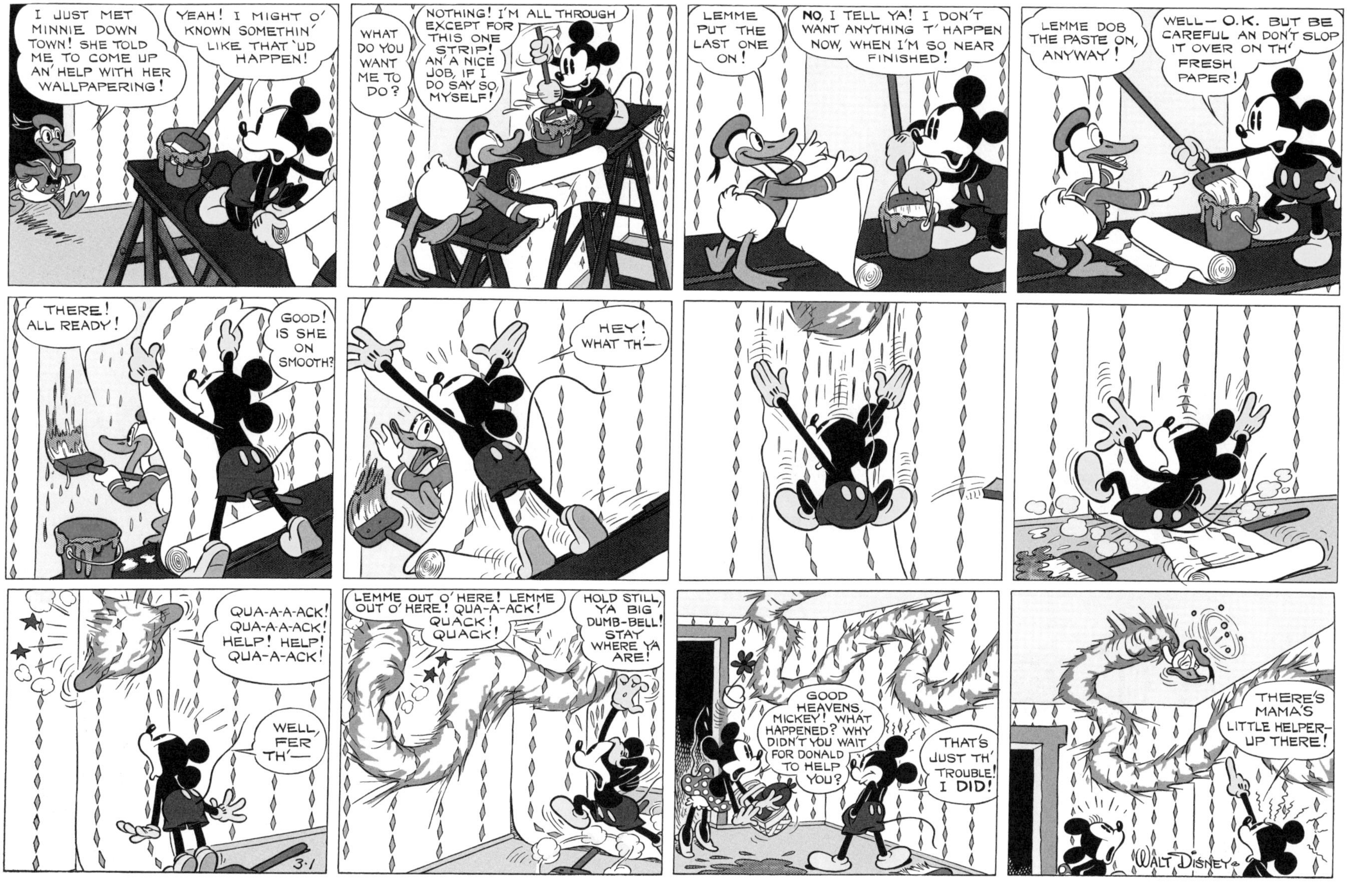
I JUST MET MINNIE DOWN TOWN! SHE TOLD ME TO COME UP AN' HELP WITH HER WALLPAPERING!
YEAH! I MIGHT O' KNOWN SOMETHIN' LIKE THAT 'UD HAPPEN!
WHAT DO YOU WANT ME TO DO?
NOTHING! I'M ALL THROUGH EXCEPT FOR THIS ONE STRIP! AN' A NICE JOB, IF I DO SAY SO, MYSELF!
LEMME PUT THE LAST ONE ON!
NO, I TELL YA! I DON'T WANT ANYTHING T' HAPPEN NOW, WHEN I'M SO NEAR FINISHED!
LEMME DOB THE PASTE ON, ANYWAY!
WELL— O.K. BUT BE CAREFUL AN DON'T SLOP IT OVER ON TH' FRESH PAPER!
THERE! ALL READY!
GOOD! IS SHE ON SMOOTH?
HEY! WHAT TH'—
QUA-A-A-ACK! QUA-A-A-ACK! HELP! HELP! QUA-A-ACK!
WELL, FER TH'—
3·1
LEMME OUT O' HERE! LEMME OUT O' HERE! QUA-A-ACK! QUACK! QUACK!
HOLD STILL, YA BIG DUMB-BELL! STAY WHERE YA ARE!
GOOD HEAVENS, MICKEY! WHAT HAPPENED? WHY DIDN'T YOU WAIT FOR DONALD TO HELP YOU?
THAT'S JUST TH' TROUBLE! I DID!
THERE'S MAMA'S LITTLE HELPER— UP THERE!
WALT DISNEY

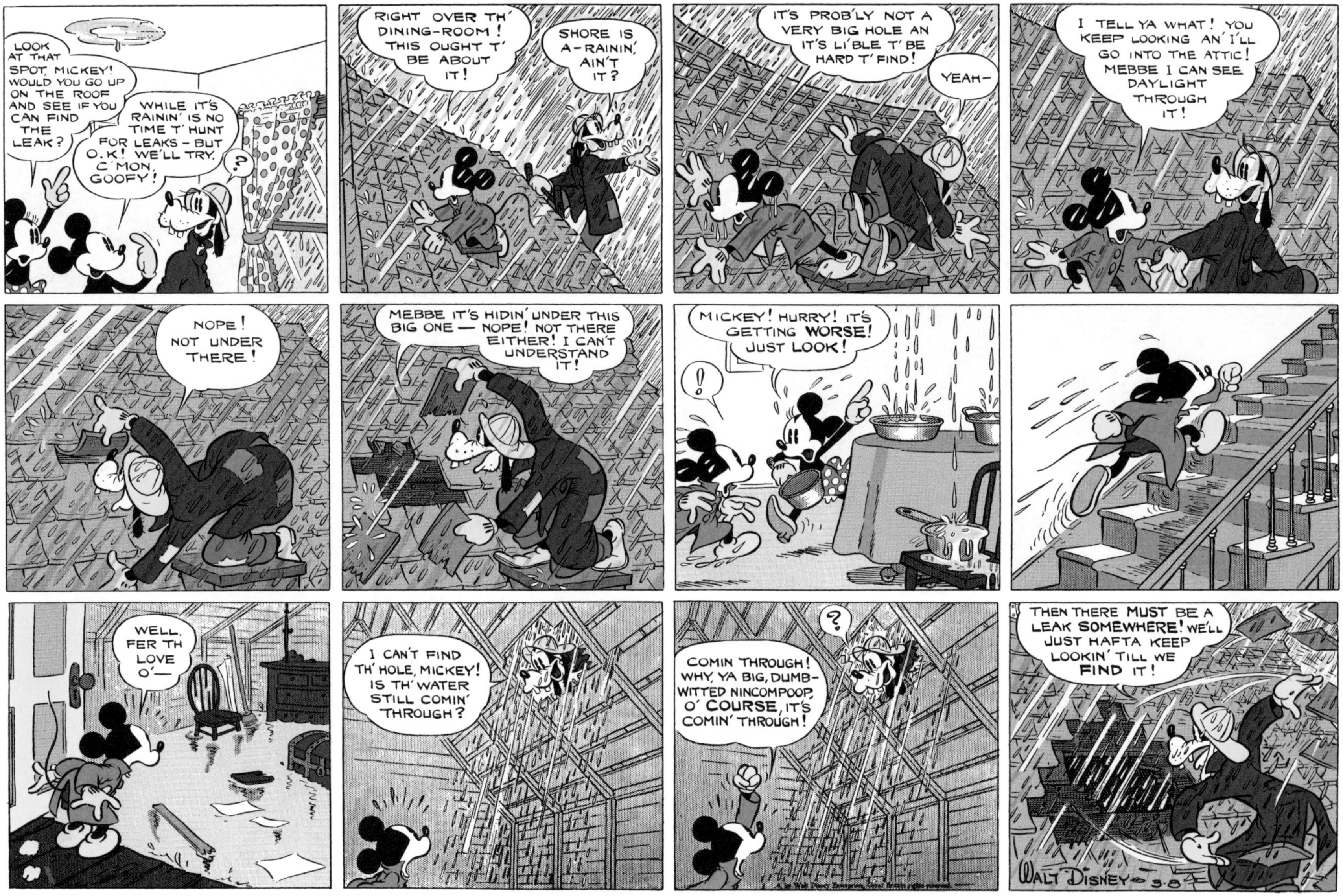
LOOK AT THAT SPOT, MICKEY! WOULD YOU GO UP ON THE ROOF AND SEE IF YOU CAN FIND THE LEAK?
WHILE IT'S RAININ' IS NO TIME T' HUNT FOR LEAKS - BUT O.K.! WE'LL TRY. C'MON, GOOFY!
?
RIGHT OVER TH' DINING-ROOM! THIS OUGHT T' BE ABOUT IT!
SHORE IS A-RAININ', AIN'T IT?
IT'S PROB'LY NOT A VERY BIG HOLE AN IT'S LI'BLE T' BE HARD T' FIND!
YEAH-
I TELL YA WHAT! YOU KEEP LOOKING AN' I'LL GO INTO THE ATTIC! MEBBE I CAN SEE DAYLIGHT THROUGH IT!
NOPE! NOT UNDER THERE!
MEBBE IT'S HIDIN' UNDER THIS BIG ONE — NOPE! NOT THERE EITHER! I CAN'T UNDERSTAND IT!
MICKEY! HURRY! IT'S GETTING WORSE! JUST LOOK!
!
WELL, FER TH LOVE O'—
I CAN'T FIND TH' HOLE, MICKEY! IS TH' WATER STILL COMIN' THROUGH?
?
COMIN THROUGH! WHY, YA BIG, DUMB-WITTED NINCOMPOOP, O' COURSE, IT'S COMIN' THROUGH!
THEN THERE MUST BE A LEAK SOMEWHERE! WE'LL JUST HAFTA KEEP LOOKIN' TILL WE FIND IT!
WALT DISNEY 3-8

28. HELPLESS HELPERS

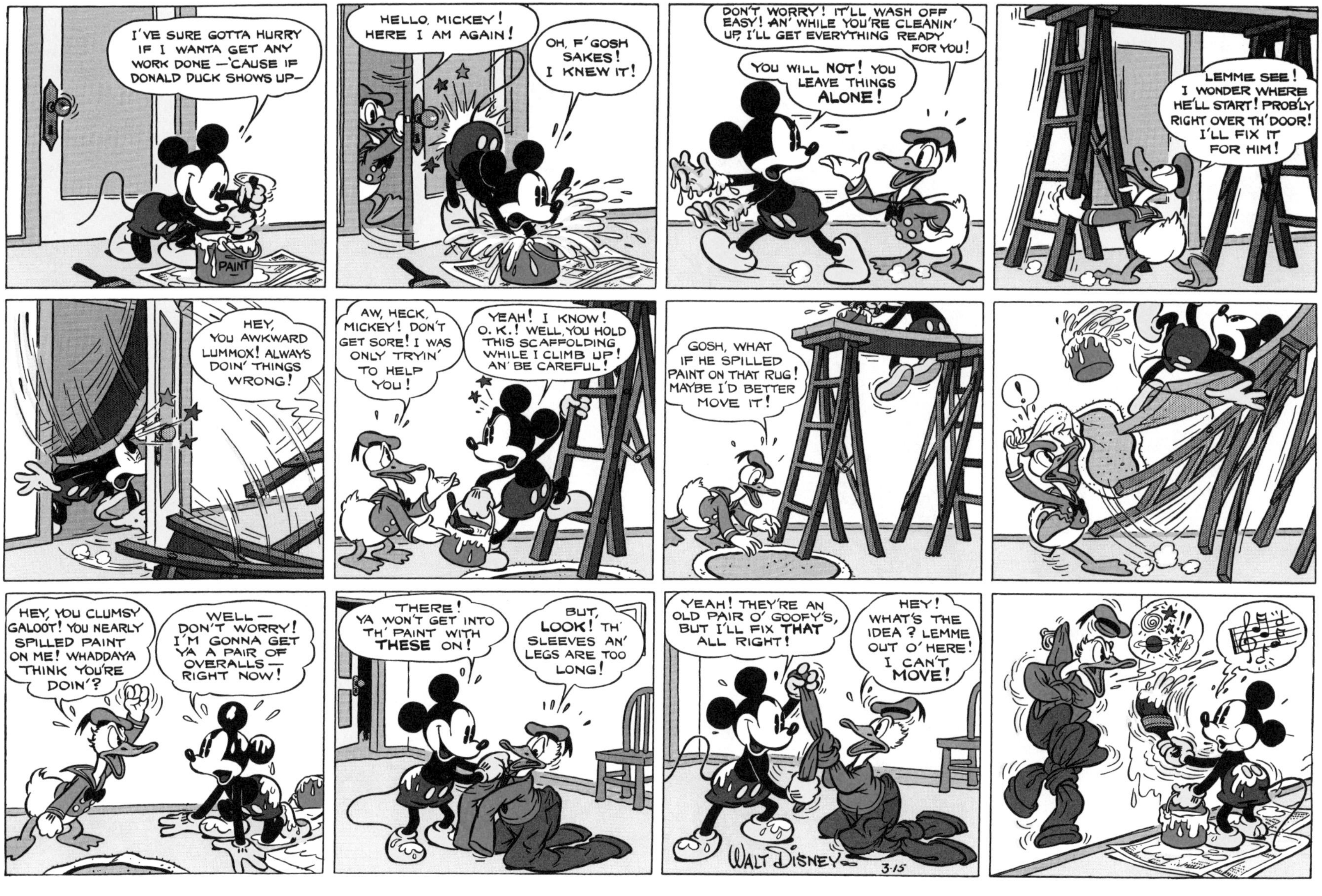

I'VE SURE GOTTA HURRY IF I WANTA GET ANY WORK DONE —'CAUSE IF DONALD DUCK SHOWS UP—
PAINT
HELLO, MICKEY! HERE I AM AGAIN!
OH, F'GOSH SAKES! I KNEW IT!
DON'T WORRY! IT'LL WASH OFF EASY! AN' WHILE YOU'RE CLEANIN' UP, I'LL GET EVERYTHING READY FOR YOU!
YOU WILL NOT! YOU LEAVE THINGS ALONE!
LEMME SEE! I WONDER WHERE HE'LL START! PROB'LY RIGHT OVER TH' DOOR! I'LL FIX IT FOR HIM!
HEY, YOU AWKWARD LUMMOX! ALWAYS DOIN' THINGS WRONG!
AW, HECK, MICKEY! DON'T GET SORE! I WAS ONLY TRYIN' TO HELP YOU!
YEAH! I KNOW! O.K.! WELL, YOU HOLD THIS SCAFFOLDING WHILE I CLIMB UP! AN' BE CAREFUL!
GOSH, WHAT IF HE SPILLED PAINT ON THAT RUG! MAYBE I'D BETTER MOVE IT!
HEY, YOU CLUMSY GALOOT! YOU NEARLY SPILLED PAINT ON ME! WHADDAYA THINK YOU'RE DOIN'?
WELL — DON'T WORRY! I'M GONNA GET YA A PAIR OF OVERALLS — RIGHT NOW!
THERE! YA WON'T GET INTO TH' PAINT WITH THESE ON!
BUT, LOOK! TH' SLEEVES AN' LEGS ARE TOO LONG!
YEAH! THEY'RE AN OLD PAIR O' GOOFY'S, BUT I'LL FIX THAT ALL RIGHT!
HEY! WHAT'S THE IDEA? LEMME OUT O' HERE! I CAN'T MOVE!
WALT DISNEY
3-15

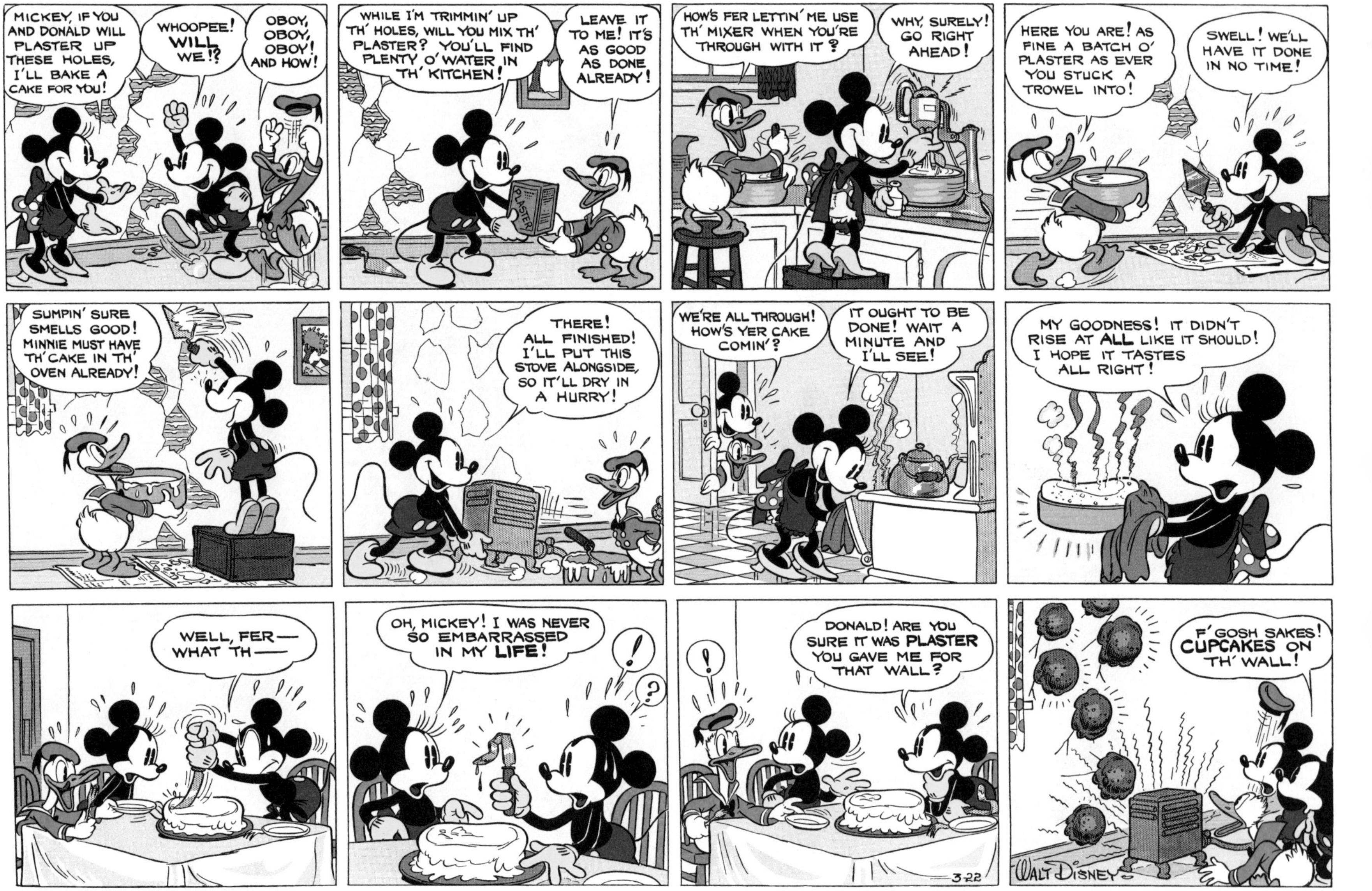
MICKEY, IF YOU AND DONALD WILL PLASTER UP THESE HOLES, I'LL BAKE A CAKE FOR YOU!
WHOOPEE! WILL WE!?
OBOY, OBOY, OBOY! AND HOW!
WHILE I'M TRIMMIN' UP TH' HOLES, WILL YOU MIX TH' PLASTER? YOU'LL FIND PLENTY O' WATER IN TH' KITCHEN!
LEAVE IT TO ME! IT'S AS GOOD AS DONE ALREADY!
PLASTER
HOW'S FER LETTIN' ME USE TH' MIXER WHEN YOU'RE THROUGH WITH IT?
WHY, SURELY! GO RIGHT AHEAD!
HERE YOU ARE! AS FINE A BATCH O' PLASTER AS EVER YOU STUCK A TROWEL INTO!
SWELL! WE'LL HAVE IT DONE IN NO TIME!
SUMPIN' SURE SMELLS GOOD! MINNIE MUST HAVE TH' CAKE IN TH' OVEN ALREADY!
THERE! ALL FINISHED! I'LL PUT THIS STOVE ALONGSIDE, SO IT'LL DRY IN A HURRY!
WE'RE ALL THROUGH! HOW'S YER CAKE COMIN'?
IT OUGHT TO BE DONE! WAIT A MINUTE AND I'LL SEE!
MY GOODNESS! IT DIDN'T RISE AT ALL LIKE IT SHOULD! I HOPE IT TASTES ALL RIGHT!
WELL, FER— WHAT TH—
OH, MICKEY! I WAS NEVER SO EMBARRASSED IN MY LIFE!
!
?
!
DONALD! ARE YOU SURE IT WAS PLASTER YOU GAVE ME FOR THAT WALL?
3-22
F' GOSH SAKES! CUPCAKES ON TH' WALL!
WALT DISNEY

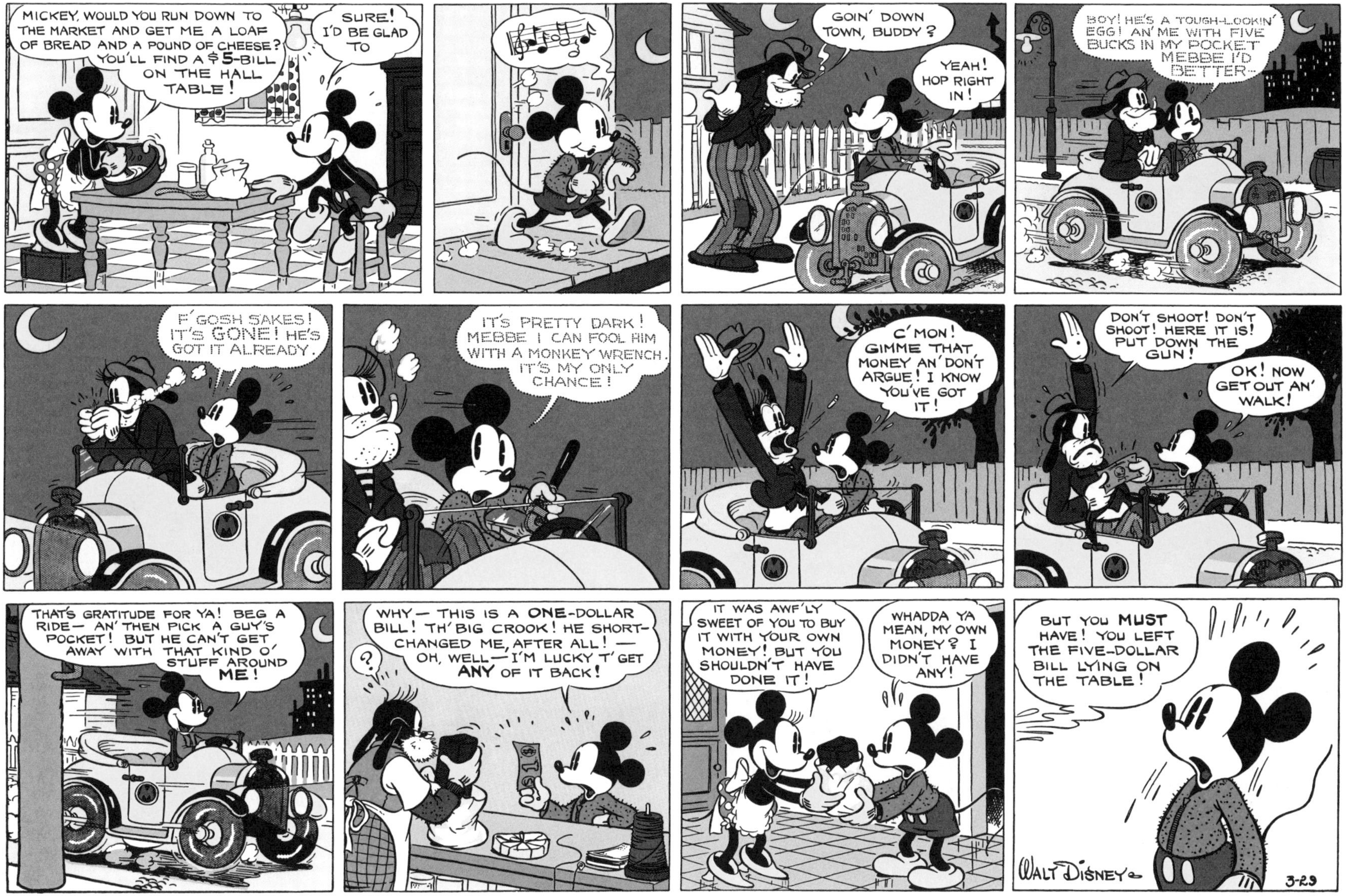
MICKEY, WOULD YOU RUN DOWN TO THE MARKET AND GET ME A LOAF OF BREAD AND A POUND OF CHEESE? YOU'LL FIND A $5-BILL ON THE HALL TABLE!
SURE! I'D BE GLAD TO
GOIN' DOWN TOWN, BUDDY?
YEAH! HOP RIGHT IN!
BOY! HE'S A TOUGH-LOOKIN' EGG! AN' ME WITH FIVE BUCKS IN MY POCKET. MEBBE I'D BETTER--
F'GOSH SAKES! IT'S GONE! HE'S GOT IT ALREADY.
IT'S PRETTY DARK! MEBBE I CAN FOOL HIM WITH A MONKEY WRENCH. IT'S MY ONLY CHANCE!
C'MON! GIMME THAT MONEY AN' DON'T ARGUE! I KNOW YOU'VE GOT IT!
DON'T SHOOT! DON'T SHOOT! HERE IT IS! PUT DOWN THE GUN!
OK! NOW GET OUT AN' WALK!
THAT'S GRATITUDE FOR YA! BEG A RIDE— AN' THEN PICK A GUY'S POCKET! BUT HE CAN'T GET AWAY WITH THAT KIND O' STUFF AROUND ME!
WHY— THIS IS A ONE-DOLLAR BILL! TH' BIG CROOK! HE SHORT-CHANGED ME, AFTER ALL! — OH, WELL—I'M LUCKY T' GET ANY OF IT BACK!
?
IT WAS AWF'LY SWEET OF YOU TO BUY IT WITH YOUR OWN MONEY! BUT YOU SHOULDN'T HAVE DONE IT!
WHADDA YA MEAN, MY OWN MONEY? I DIDN'T HAVE ANY!
BUT YOU MUST HAVE! YOU LEFT THE FIVE-DOLLAR BILL LYING ON THE TABLE!
WALT DISNEY
3-29

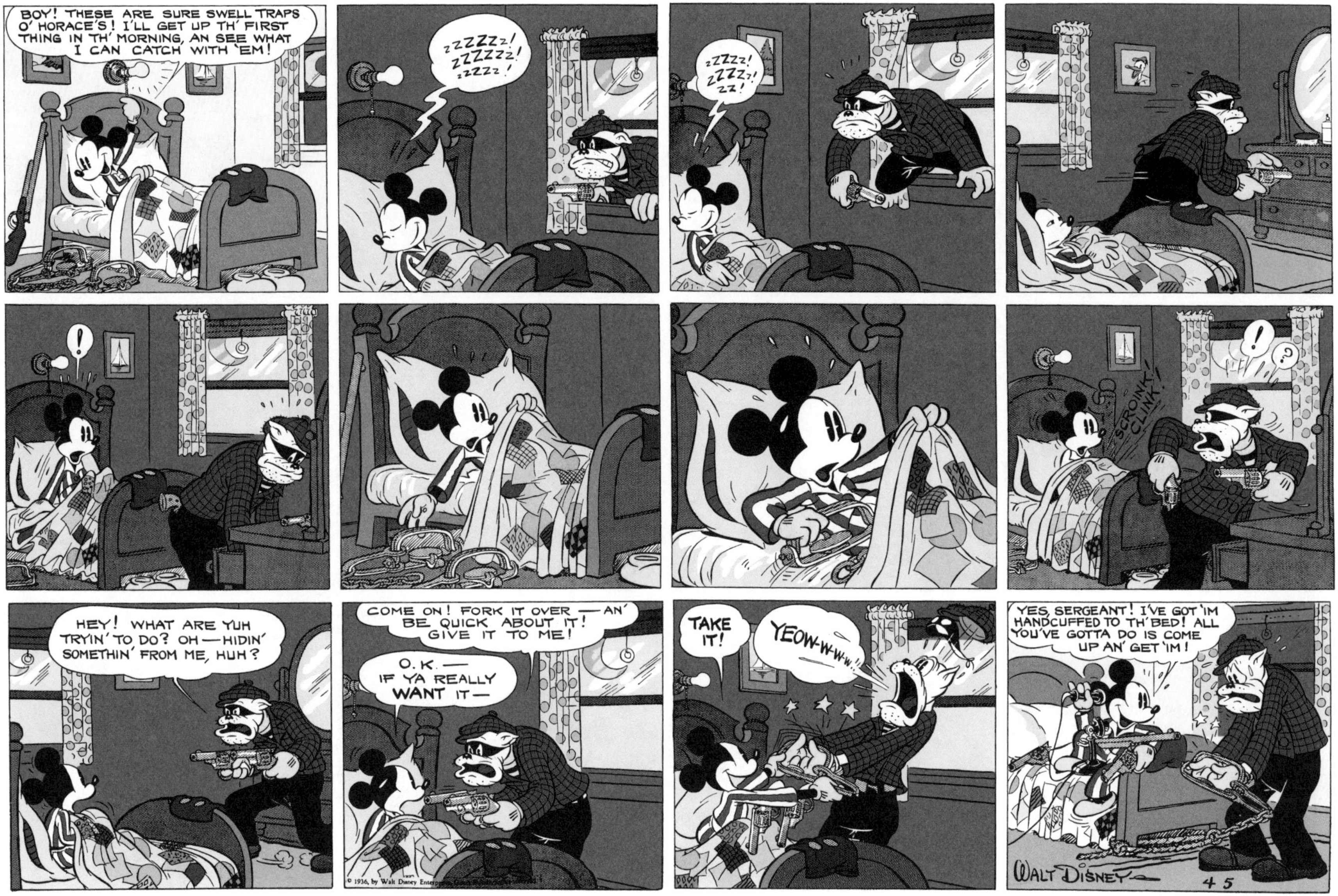
BOY! THESE ARE SURE SWELL TRAPS O' HORACE'S! I'LL GET UP TH' FIRST THING IN TH' MORNING, AN SEE WHAT I CAN CATCH WITH 'EM!
zZZZZz! ZZZZZZ! zZZZz!
zZZZz! ZZZZz! zz!
!
!
?
SCROINK! CLINK!
HEY! WHAT ARE YUH TRYIN' TO DO? OH — HIDIN' SOMETHIN' FROM ME, HUH?
COME ON! FORK IT OVER — AN' BE QUICK ABOUT IT! GIVE IT TO ME!
O.K. — IF YA REALLY WANT IT —
TAKE IT!
YEOW-W-W-W!
YES, SERGEANT! I'VE GOT 'IM HANDCUFFED TO TH' BED! ALL YOU'VE GOTTA DO IS COME UP AN' GET 'IM!
WALT DISNEY
4 5

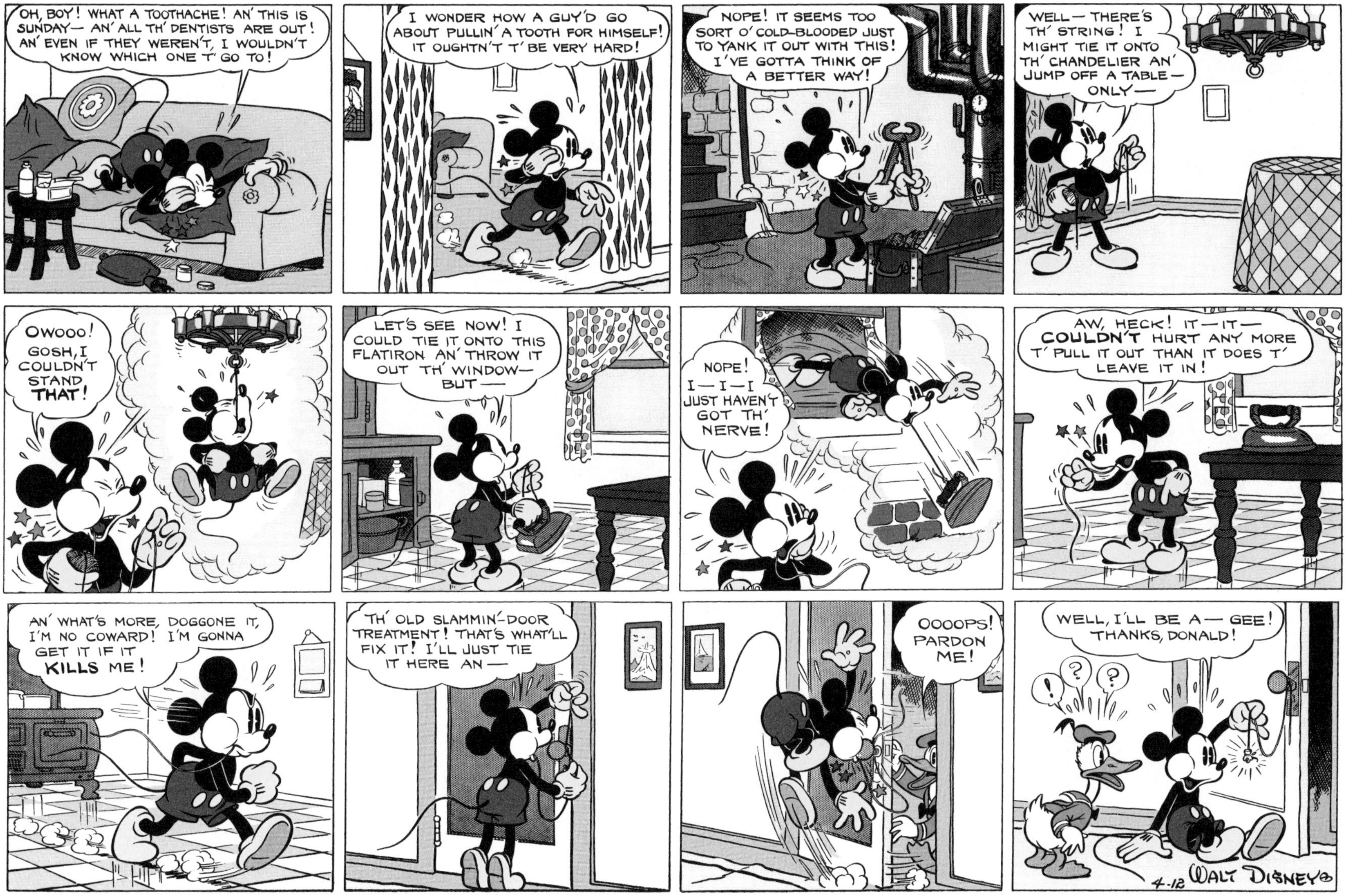
OH, BOY! WHAT A TOOTHACHE! AN' THIS IS SUNDAY— AN' ALL TH' DENTISTS ARE OUT! AN' EVEN IF THEY WEREN'T, I WOULDN'T KNOW WHICH ONE T' GO TO!
I WONDER HOW A GUY'D GO ABOUT PULLIN' A TOOTH FOR HIMSELF! IT OUGHTN'T T' BE VERY HARD!
NOPE! IT SEEMS TOO SORT O' COLD-BLOODED JUST TO YANK IT OUT WITH THIS! I'VE GOTTA THINK OF A BETTER WAY!
WELL— THERE'S TH' STRING! I MIGHT TIE IT ONTO TH' CHANDELIER AN' JUMP OFF A TABLE— ONLY—
OWOOO! GOSH, I COULDN'T STAND **THAT**!
LET'S SEE NOW! I COULD TIE IT ONTO THIS FLATIRON AN' THROW IT OUT TH' WINDOW— BUT—
NOPE! I—I—I JUST HAVEN'T GOT TH' NERVE!
AW, HECK! IT—IT— **COULDN'T** HURT ANY MORE T' PULL IT OUT THAN IT DOES T' LEAVE IT IN!
AN' WHAT'S MORE, DOGGONE IT, I'M NO COWARD! I'M GONNA GET IT IF IT **KILLS** ME!
TH' OLD SLAMMIN'-DOOR TREATMENT! THAT'S WHAT'LL FIX IT! I'LL JUST TIE IT HERE AN—
OOOOPS! PARDON ME!
!
?
?
WELL, I'LL BE A— GEE! THANKS, DONALD!
4-12
WALT DISNEY©

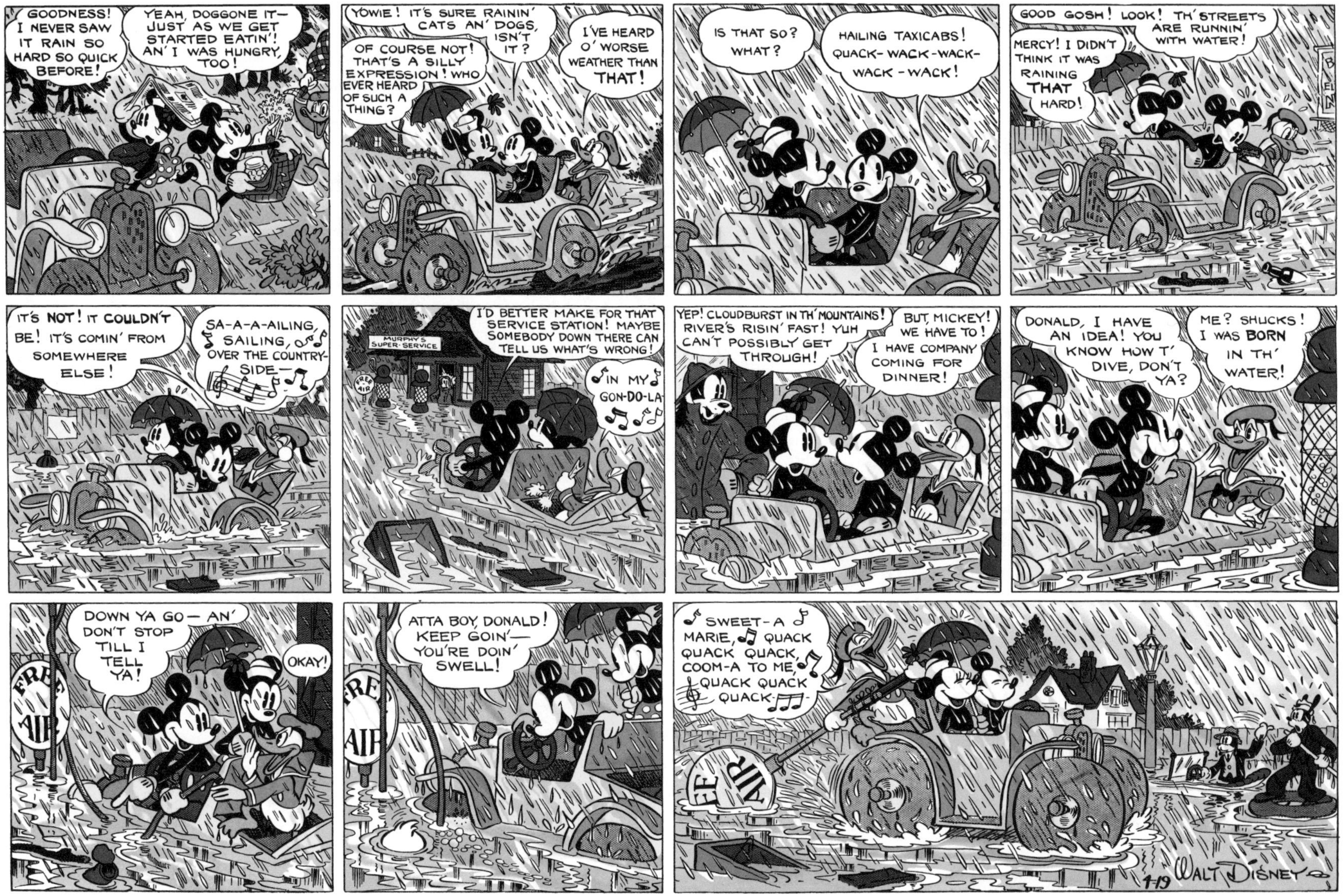
GOODNESS! I NEVER SAW IT RAIN SO HARD SO QUICK BEFORE!
YEAH, DOGGONE IT— JUST AS WE GET STARTED EATIN'! AN' I WAS HUNGRY, TOO!
YOWIE! IT'S SURE RAININ' CATS AN' DOGS, ISN'T IT?
OF COURSE NOT! THAT'S A SILLY EXPRESSION! WHO EVER HEARD OF SUCH A THING?
I'VE HEARD O' WORSE WEATHER THAN THAT!
IS THAT SO? WHAT?
HAILING TAXICABS! QUACK-WACK-WACK-WACK-WACK!
GOOD GOSH! LOOK! TH' STREETS ARE RUNNIN' WITH WATER!
MERCY! I DIDN'T THINK IT WAS RAINING THAT HARD!
IT'S NOT! IT COULDN'T BE! IT'S COMIN' FROM SOMEWHERE ELSE!
SA-A-A-AILING, SAILING, OVER THE COUNTRY-SIDE—
MURPHY'S SUPER-SERVICE
FREE AIR
I'D BETTER MAKE FOR THAT SERVICE STATION! MAYBE SOMEBODY DOWN THERE CAN TELL US WHAT'S WRONG!
IN MY GON-DO-LA
YEP! CLOUDBURST IN TH' MOUNTAINS! RIVER'S RISIN' FAST! YUH CAN'T POSSIBLY GET THROUGH!
BUT, MICKEY! WE HAVE TO! I HAVE COMPANY COMING FOR DINNER!
DONALD, I HAVE AN IDEA! YOU KNOW HOW T' DIVE, DON'T YA?
ME? SHUCKS! I WAS BORN IN TH' WATER!
DOWN YA GO— AN' DON'T STOP TILL I TELL YA!
OKAY!
FREE AIR
ATTA BOY, DONALD! KEEP GOIN'— YOU'RE DOIN' SWELL!
SWEET-A MARIE, QUACK QUACK QUACK, COOM-A TO ME, QUACK QUACK QUACK
FREE AIR
1-19 WALT DISNEY

THE ROBIN HOOD ADVENTURE

APRIL 26, 1936
–
OCTOBER 4, 1936

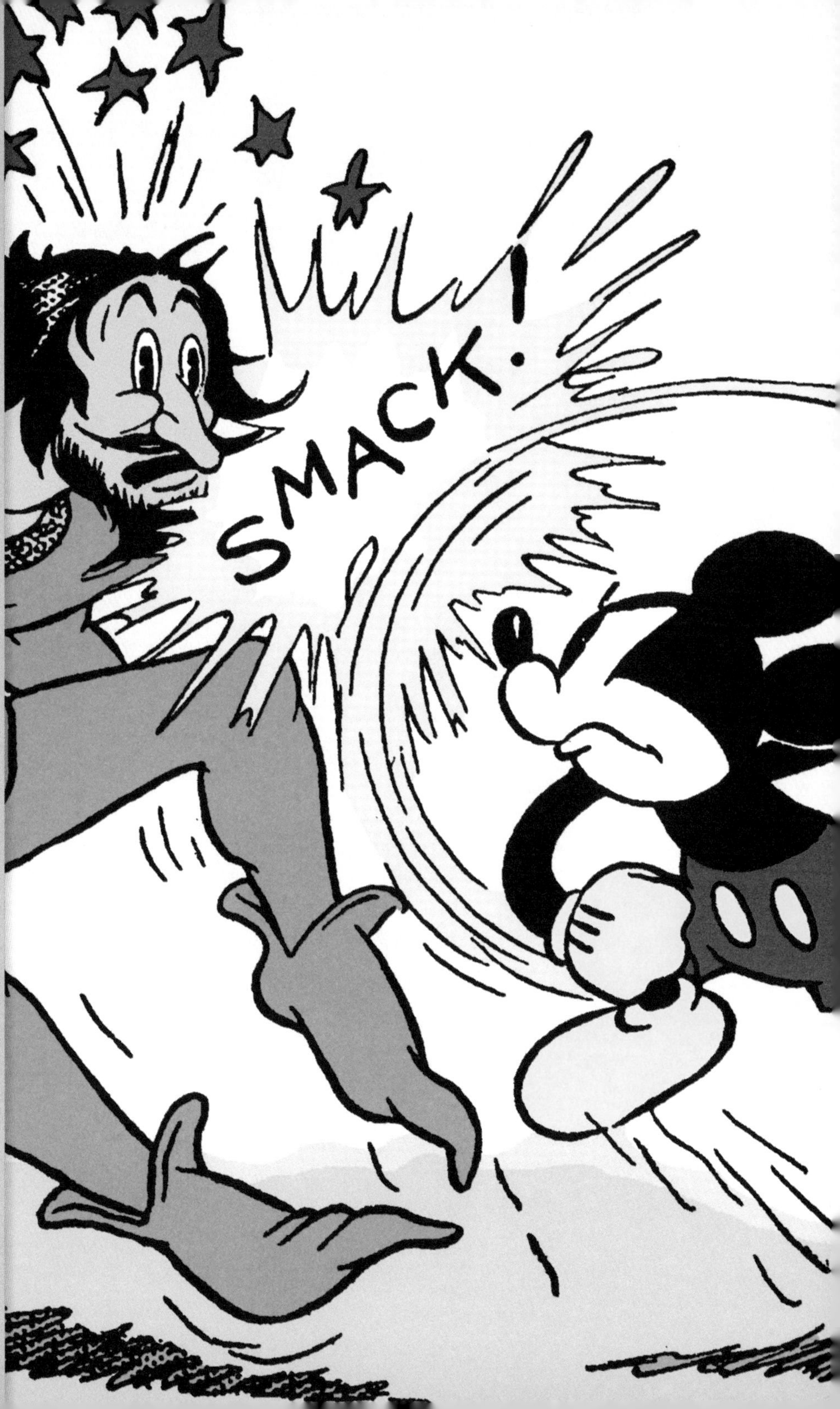
SMACK!

MICKEY MOUSE
REGISTERED U.S. PATENT OFFICE

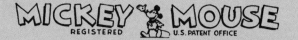

POSTMODERN TIMES

What makes a work of literature "classic"? Italian novelist Italo Calvino famously stated that "a classic is a book that has never finished saying what it has to say." This definition easily applies to "The Robin Hood Adventure," the only late 1930s Sunday serial that Floyd Gottfredson plotted as well as drew.

Determined to improve his garden, Mickey creates a fertilizer that makes plants grow bigger and bigger, along with a serum to shrink them in case of emergencies. Soon, fighting with an enlarged plant, Mickey accidentally sprinkles the shrink-serum on himself. Reduced to the size of—er, a *normal* mouse—Mickey ends up, Gumby-style, in the pages of a book, all ready to fight medieval evil.

"The Robin Hood Adventure" anticipates modern TV's *The Simpsons* in its storytelling style: it uses a small-scale "a-story" as the teaser for an epic, almost entirely unrelated "b-story." The first six strips—with Mickey enlarging and reducing plants and insects—have little in common with the seventeen-page Old English thriller that follows. Only the final page brings us back to 1930s America.

The disparate plots reflect the way Gottfredson and Ted Osborne mixed up inspiration from different sources. The cartoons *Mickey's Garden* (1935) and *The Worm Turns* (1937, then in production) both featured Mickey as chemist, mixing formulas not too far removed from his fertilizer and shrinker. Meanwhile, the comic strip *Dickie Dare* by Milton Caniff—a comics contemporary much admired by Gottfredson[1]—had already shown its hero sharing adventures with Robin Hood. Gottfredson was evidently driven to send Mickey down the same path.

Yet Mickey doesn't share adventures with the *real* Robin Hood... or does he? In a strikingly postmodern take on the material, Mickey is fully aware that he has journeyed into a *book*, not into the actual Sherwood Forest—and he clarifies his awareness by openly calling Robin and his band "poor illustrations"! Indeed, the Merry Men differ strongly from their portrayal in classic canon: they are more like common thieves than heroes. Of course, the same was likely true of the real-life Merry Men, if they ever existed. Fairy tales and legends, Gottfredson seems to say, are never as glamorous as we think. Traditional heroes like Robin Hood are asking to be deconstructed—along with our expectations of fiction.

Perhaps 1930s readers considered "The Robin Hood Adventure" merely a humorous, exciting flight of fancy, but now we can read it in a different way. Like all true classics, this story always has more to tell us.

— Stefano Priarone

1 Floyd Gottfredson to Bruce Hamilton, *Mickey Mouse in Color* deluxe edition (Prescott: Another Rainbow, 1988), p. 102.

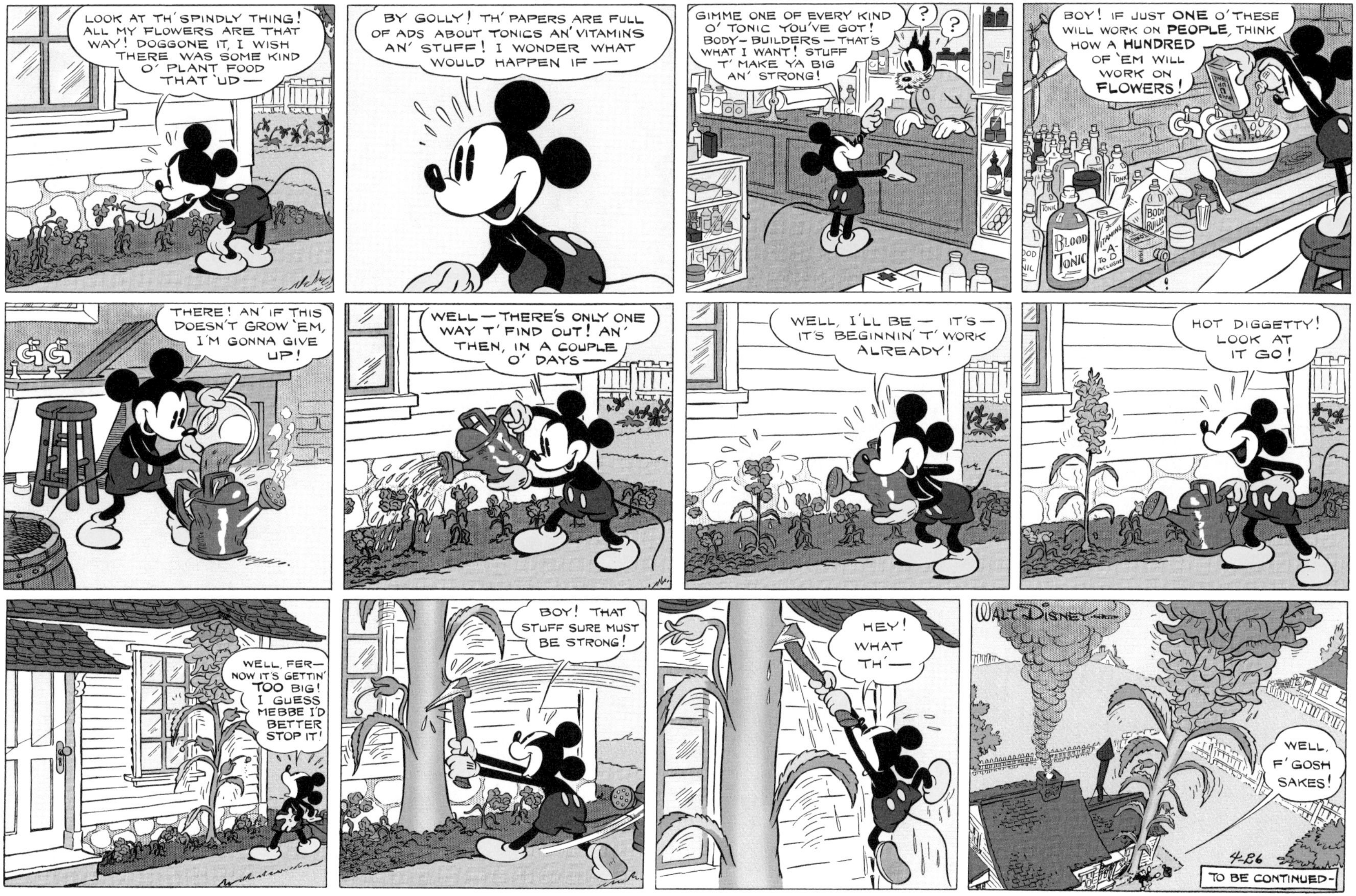
LOOK AT TH' SPINDLY THING! ALL MY FLOWERS ARE THAT WAY! DOGGONE IT, I WISH THERE WAS SOME KIND O' PLANT FOOD THAT 'UD —
BY GOLLY! TH' PAPERS ARE FULL OF ADS ABOUT TONICS AN' VITAMINS AN' STUFF! I WONDER WHAT WOULD HAPPEN IF —
GIMME ONE OF EVERY KIND O' TONIC YOU'VE GOT! BODY-BUILDERS — THAT'S WHAT I WANT! STUFF T' MAKE YA BIG AN' STRONG!
? ?
BOY! IF JUST ONE O' THESE WILL WORK ON PEOPLE, THINK HOW A HUNDRED OF 'EM WILL WORK ON FLOWERS!
BLOOD TONIC
VITAMINS -A- TO D INCLUSIVE
BODY BUILDER
THERE! AN' IF THIS DOESN'T GROW 'EM, I'M GONNA GIVE UP!
WELL — THERE'S ONLY ONE WAY T' FIND OUT! AN' THEN, IN A COUPLE O' DAYS —
WELL, I'LL BE — IT'S — IT'S BEGINNIN' T' WORK ALREADY!
HOT DIGGETTY! LOOK AT IT GO!
WELL, FER — NOW IT'S GETTIN' TOO BIG! I GUESS MEBBE I'D BETTER STOP IT!
BOY! THAT STUFF SURE MUST BE STRONG!
HEY! WHAT TH' —
WALT DISNEY
WELL, F' GOSH SAKES!
4-26
TO BE CONTINUED -

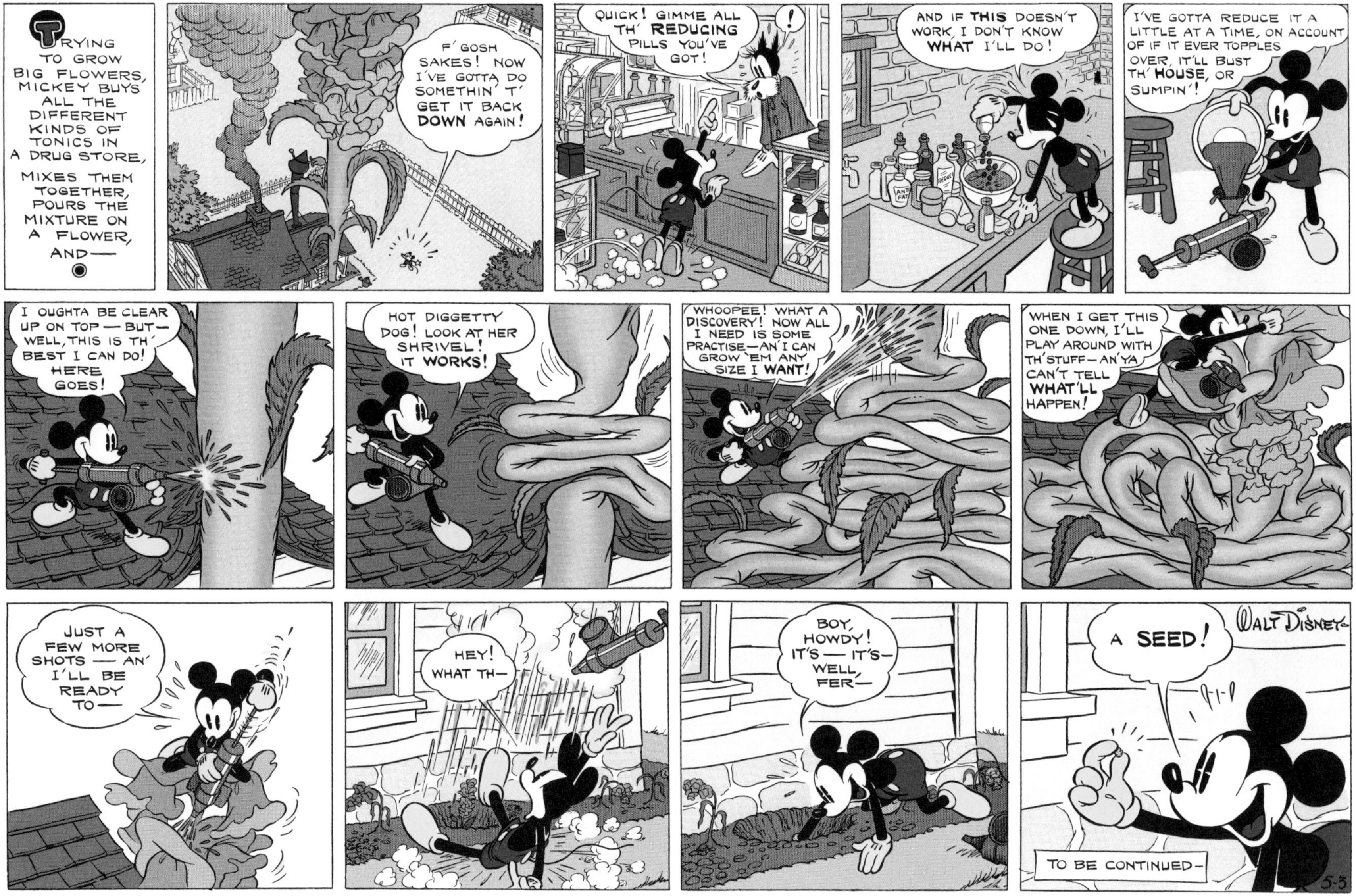
TRYING TO GROW BIG FLOWERS, MICKEY BUYS ALL THE DIFFERENT KINDS OF TONICS IN A DRUG STORE,
MIXES THEM TOGETHER, POURS THE MIXTURE ON A FLOWER, AND—
F'GOSH SAKES! NOW I'VE GOTTA DO SOMETHIN' T' GET IT BACK DOWN AGAIN!
QUICK! GIMME ALL TH' REDUCING PILLS YOU'VE GOT!
!
AND IF THIS DOESN'T WORK, I DON'T KNOW WHAT I'LL DO!
I'VE GOTTA REDUCE IT A LITTLE AT A TIME, ON ACCOUNT OF IF IT EVER TOPPLES OVER, IT'LL BUST TH' HOUSE, OR SUMPIN'!
I OUGHTA BE CLEAR UP ON TOP — BUT — WELL, THIS IS TH' BEST I CAN DO! HERE GOES!
HOT DIGGETTY DOG! LOOK AT HER SHRIVEL! IT WORKS!
WHOOPEE! WHAT A DISCOVERY! NOW ALL I NEED IS SOME PRACTISE—AN' I CAN GROW 'EM ANY SIZE I WANT!
WHEN I GET THIS ONE DOWN, I'LL PLAY AROUND WITH TH' STUFF—AN' YA CAN'T TELL WHAT'LL HAPPEN!
JUST A FEW MORE SHOTS — AN' I'LL BE READY TO—
HEY! WHAT TH—
BOY, HOWDY! IT'S — IT'S — WELL, FER—
A SEED!
WALT DISNEY
TO BE CONTINUED—
5-3

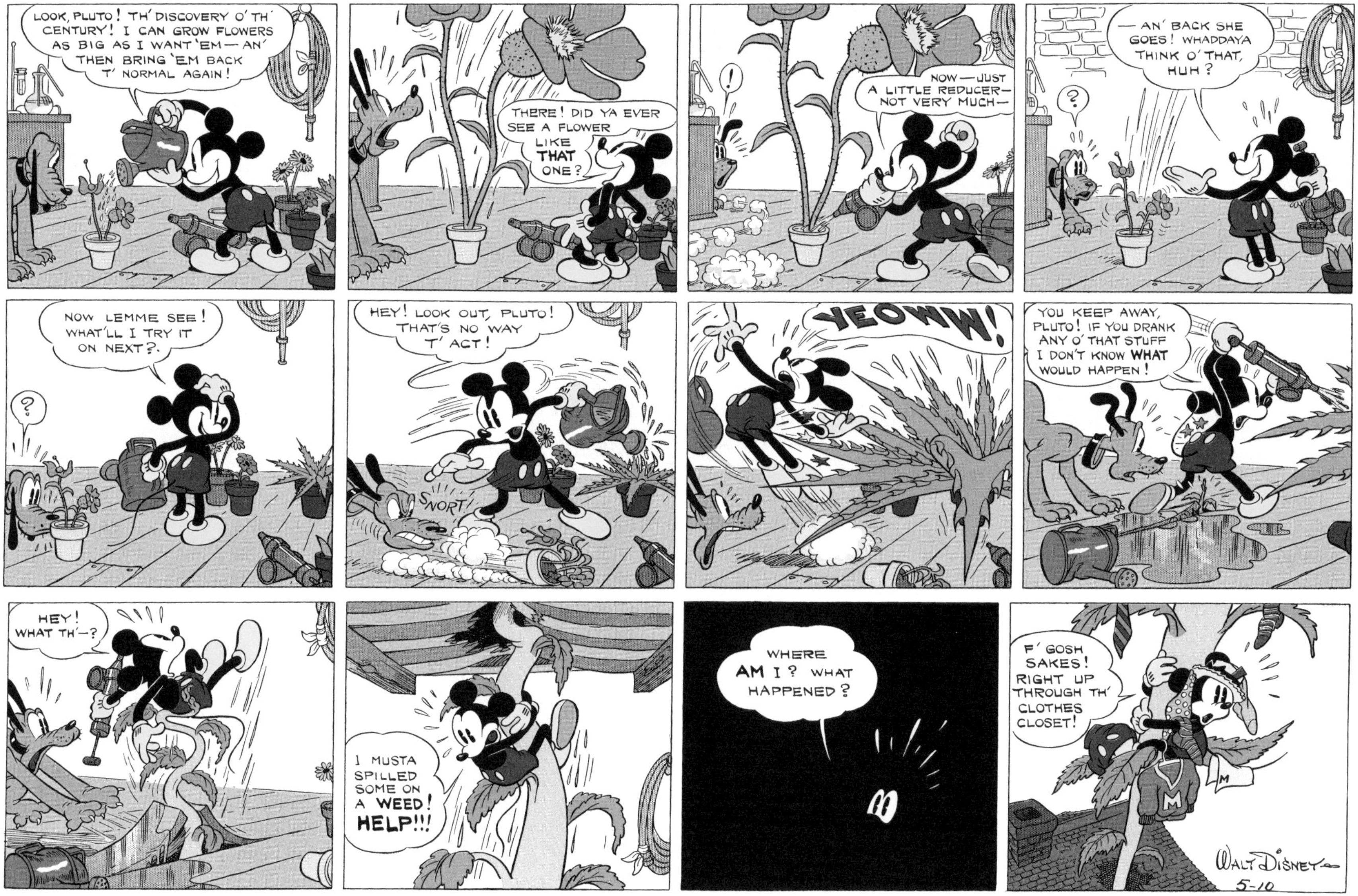
LOOK, PLUTO! TH' DISCOVERY O' TH' CENTURY! I CAN GROW FLOWERS AS BIG AS I WANT 'EM — AN' THEN BRING 'EM BACK T' NORMAL AGAIN!
THERE! DID YA EVER SEE A FLOWER LIKE **THAT** ONE?
!
NOW — JUST A LITTLE REDUCER — NOT VERY MUCH —
?
— AN' BACK SHE GOES! WHADDAYA THINK O' THAT, HUH?
NOW LEMME SEE! WHAT'LL I TRY IT ON NEXT?.
?
HEY! LOOK OUT, PLUTO! THAT'S NO WAY T' ACT!
SNORT!
YEOWW!
YOU KEEP AWAY, PLUTO! IF YOU DRANK ANY O' THAT STUFF I DON'T KNOW **WHAT** WOULD HAPPEN!
HEY! WHAT TH' —?
I MUSTA SPILLED SOME ON A **WEED**! **HELP!!!**
WHERE **AM** I? WHAT HAPPENED?
F' GOSH SAKES! RIGHT UP THROUGH TH' CLOTHES CLOSET!
WALT DISNEY
5-10

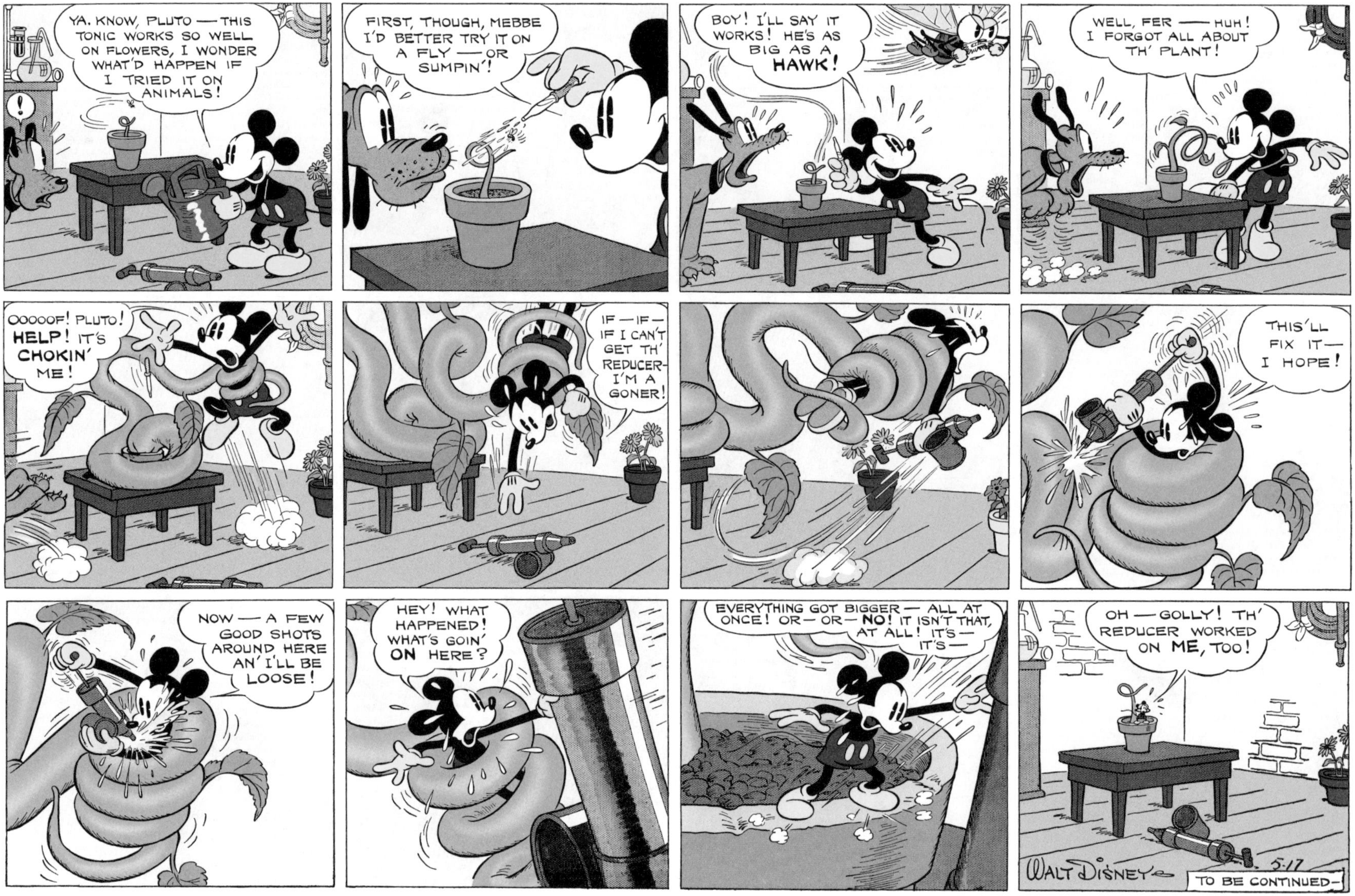

YA. KNOW, PLUTO — THIS TONIC WORKS SO WELL ON FLOWERS, I WONDER WHAT'D HAPPEN IF I TRIED IT ON ANIMALS!
!
FIRST, THOUGH, MEBBE I'D BETTER TRY IT ON A FLY — OR SUMPIN'!
BOY! I'LL SAY IT WORKS! HE'S AS BIG AS A HAWK!
WELL, FER — HUH! I FORGOT ALL ABOUT TH' PLANT!
OOOOOF! PLUTO! HELP! IT'S CHOKIN' ME!
IF — IF — IF I CAN'T GET TH' REDUCER — I'M A GONER!
THIS'LL FIX IT — I HOPE!
NOW — A FEW GOOD SHOTS AROUND HERE AN' I'LL BE LOOSE!
HEY! WHAT HAPPENED! WHAT'S GOIN' ON HERE?
EVERYTHING GOT BIGGER — ALL AT ONCE! OR — OR — NO! IT ISN'T THAT, AT ALL! IT'S — IT'S —
OH — GOLLY! TH' REDUCER WORKED ON ME, TOO!
WALT DISNEY
5-17
TO BE CONTINUED —

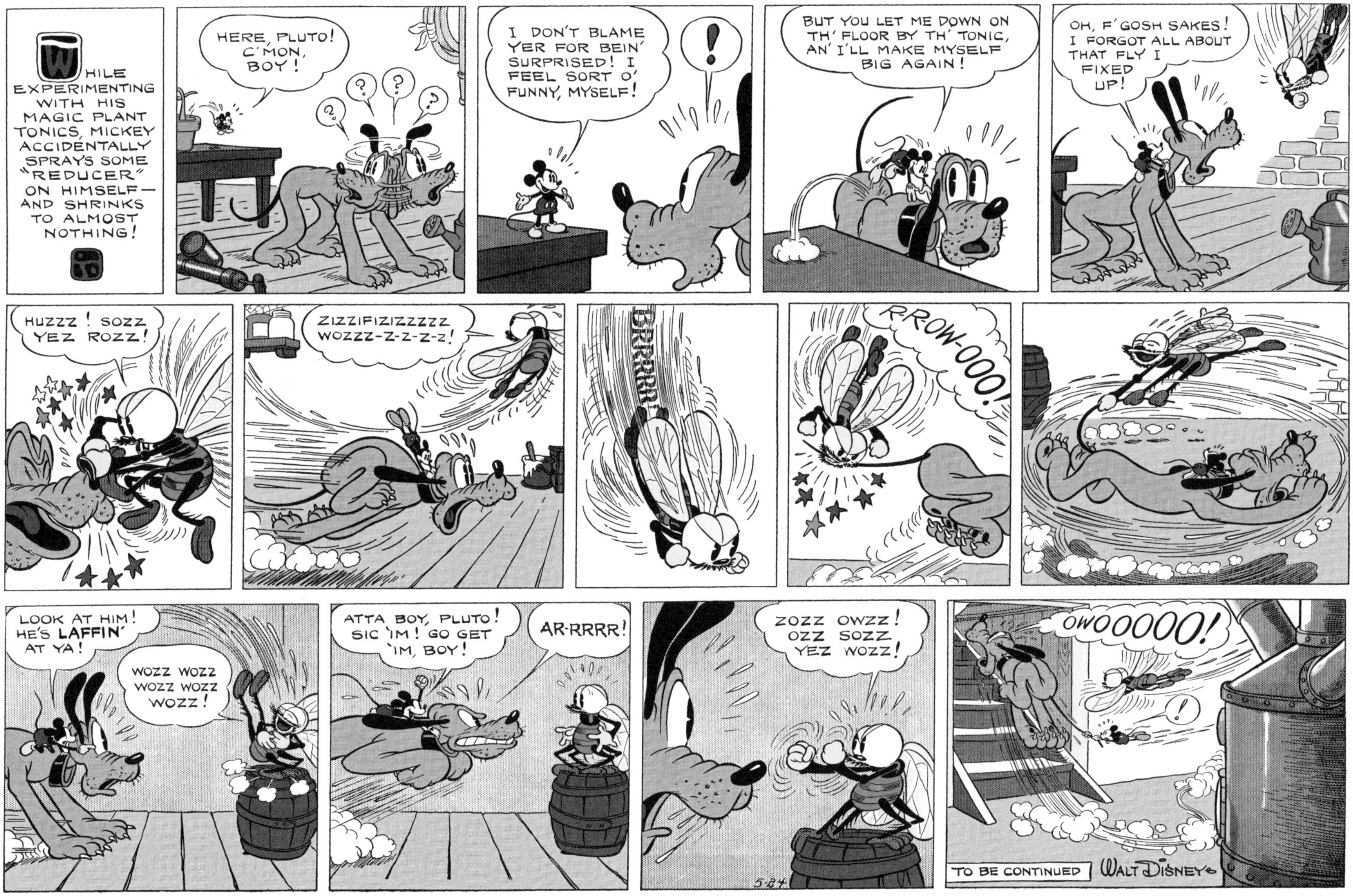
WHILE EXPERIMENTING WITH HIS MAGIC PLANT TONICS, MICKEY ACCIDENTALLY SPRAYS SOME "REDUCER" ON HIMSELF— AND SHRINKS TO ALMOST NOTHING!
HERE, PLUTO! C'MON, BOY!
I DON'T BLAME YER FOR BEIN' SURPRISED! I FEEL SORT O' FUNNY, MYSELF!
!
BUT YOU LET ME DOWN ON TH' FLOOR BY TH' TONIC, AN' I'LL MAKE MYSELF BIG AGAIN!
OH, F'GOSH SAKES! I FORGOT ALL ABOUT THAT FLY I FIXED UP!
HUZZZ! SOZZ YEZ ROZZ!
ZIZZIFIZIZZZZZ WOZZZ-Z-Z-Z-Z!
BRRRRR!
R-ROW-OOO!
LOOK AT HIM! HE'S LAFFIN' AT YA!
WOZZ WOZZ WOZZ WOZZ WOZZ!
ATTA BOY, PLUTO! SIC 'IM! GO GET 'IM, BOY!
AR-RRRR!
ZOZZ OWZZ! OZZ SOZZ YEZ WOZZ!
OWOOOOO!
!
TO BE CONTINUED
WALT DISNEY

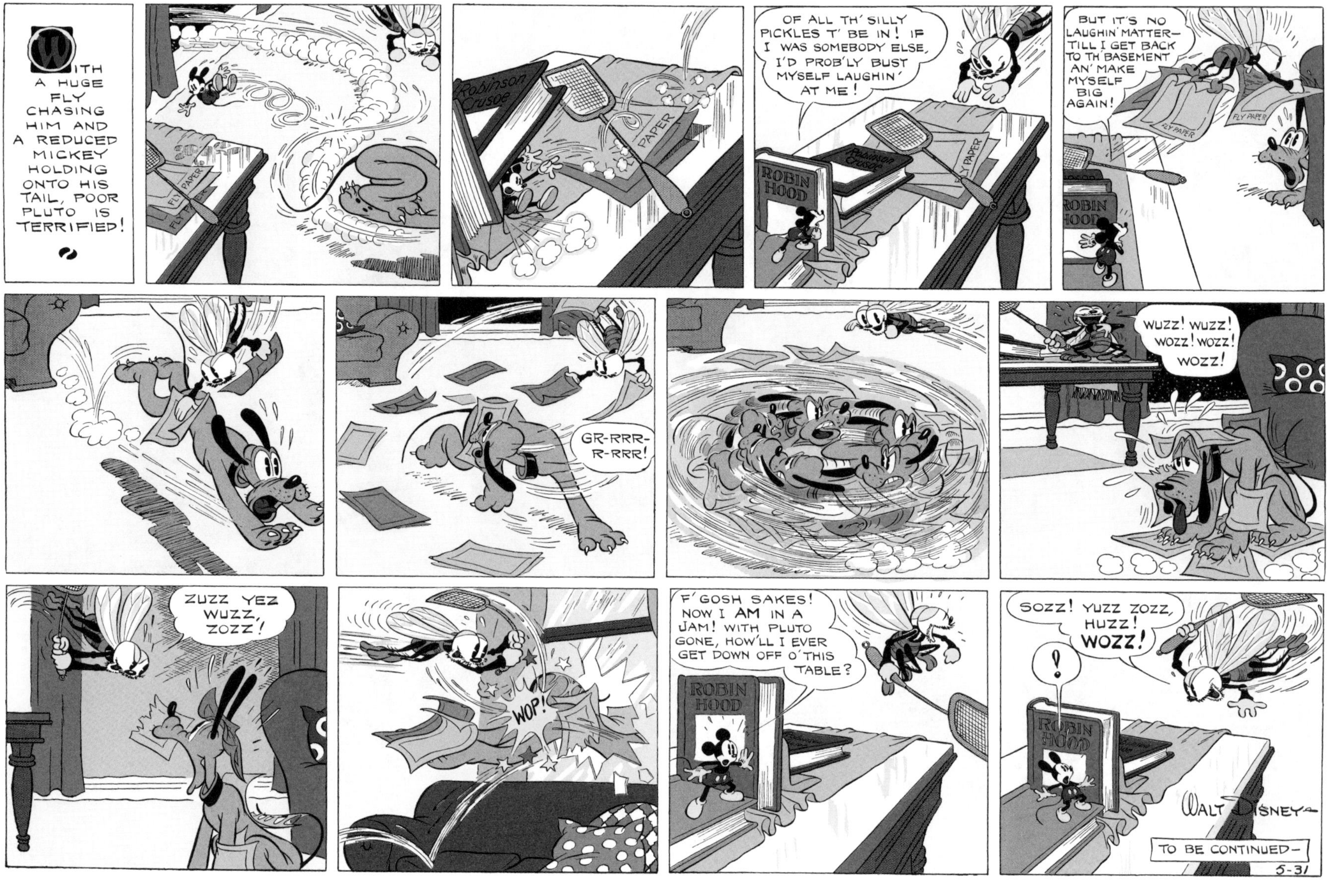
WITH A HUGE FLY CHASING HIM AND A REDUCED MICKEY HOLDING ONTO HIS TAIL, POOR PLUTO IS TERRIFIED!
Robinson Crusoe
FLY PAPER
PAPER
OF ALL TH' SILLY PICKLES T' BE IN! IF I WAS SOMEBODY ELSE, I'D PROB'LY BUST MYSELF LAUGHIN' AT ME!
ROBIN HOOD
BUT IT'S NO LAUGHIN' MATTER-TILL I GET BACK TO TH' BASEMENT AN' MAKE MYSELF BIG AGAIN!
FLY PAPER
GR-RRRR-R-RRR!
WUZZ! WUZZ! WOZZ! WOZZ! WOZZ!
ZUZZ YEZ WUZZ, ZOZZ!
WOP!
F'GOSH SAKES! NOW I AM IN A JAM! WITH PLUTO GONE, HOW'LL I EVER GET DOWN OFF O'THIS TABLE?
ROBIN HOOD
SOZZ! YUZZ ZOZZ, HUZZ! WOZZ!
!
ROBIN HOOD
WALT DISNEY
TO BE CONTINUED-
5-31

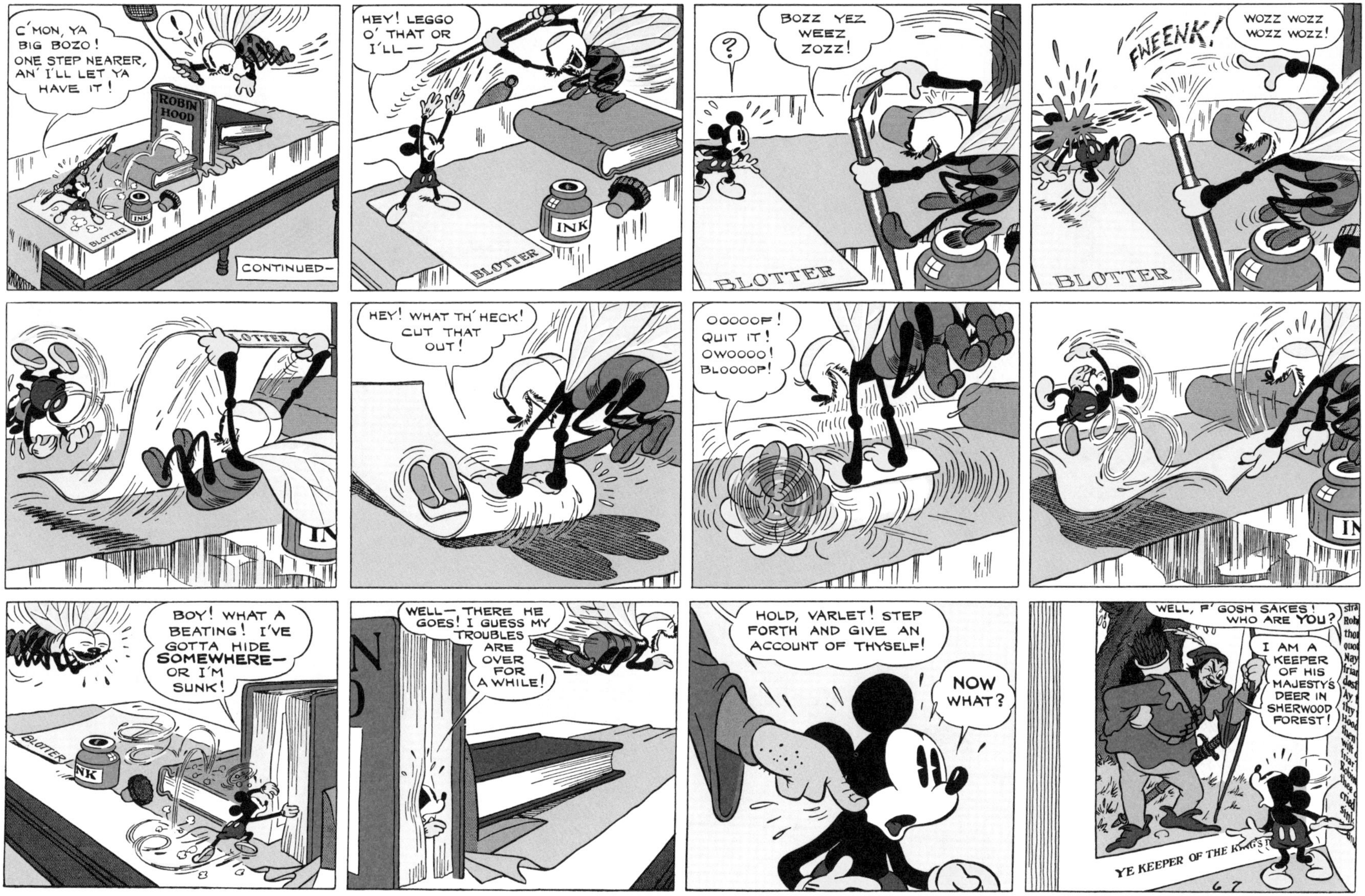

C'MON, YA BIG BOZO! ONE STEP NEARER, AN' I'LL LET YA HAVE IT!
!
ROBIN HOOD
BLOTTER
INK
CONTINUED-
HEY! LEGGO O' THAT OR I'LL—
INK
BLOTTER
?
BOZZ YEZ WEEZ ZOZZ!
BLOTTER
FWEENK!
WOZZ WOZZ WOZZ WOZZ!
BLOTTER
HEY! WHAT TH' HECK! CUT THAT OUT!
OOOOOF! QUIT IT! OWOOOO! BLOOOOP!
BOY! WHAT A BEATING! I'VE GOTTA HIDE **SOMEWHERE**— OR I'M SUNK!
BLOTTER
INK
WELL— THERE HE GOES! I GUESS MY TROUBLES ARE OVER FOR A WHILE!
HOLD, VARLET! STEP FORTH AND GIVE AN ACCOUNT OF THYSELF!
NOW WHAT?
WELL, F' GOSH SAKES! WHO ARE **YOU**?
I AM A KEEPER OF HIS MAJESTY'S DEER IN SHERWOOD FOREST!

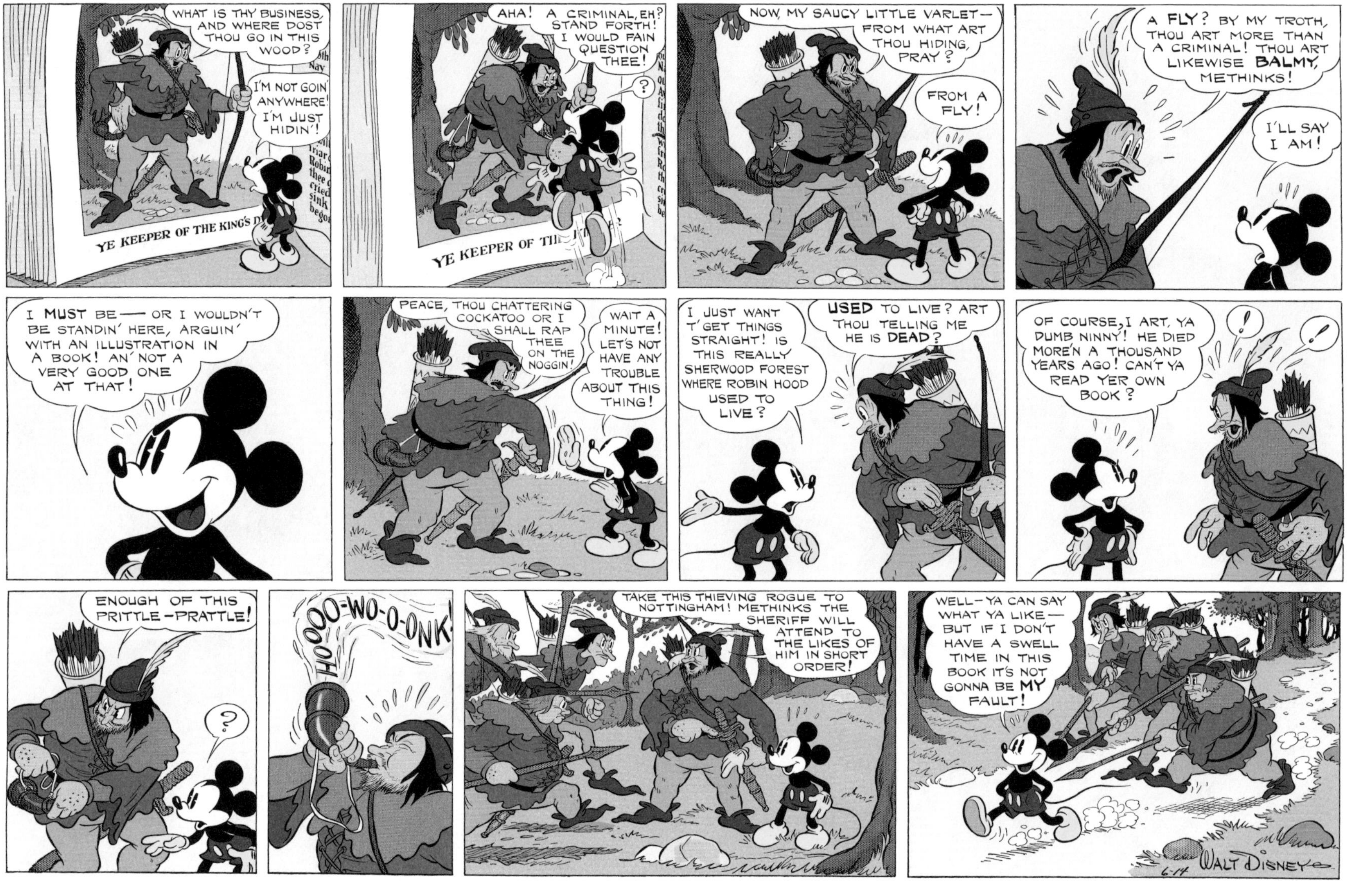

WHAT IS THY BUSINESS, AND WHERE DOST THOU GO IN THIS WOOD?
I'M NOT GOIN' ANYWHERE! I'M JUST HIDIN'!
YE KEEPER OF THE KING'S
AHA! A CRIMINAL, EH? STAND FORTH! I WOULD FAIN QUESTION THEE!
?
YE KEEPER OF
NOW, MY SAUCY LITTLE VARLET— FROM WHAT ART THOU HIDING, PRAY?
FROM A FLY!
A FLY? BY MY TROTH, THOU ART MORE THAN A CRIMINAL! THOU ART LIKEWISE BALMY, METHINKS!
I'LL SAY I AM!
I MUST BE— OR I WOULDN'T BE STANDIN' HERE, ARGUIN' WITH AN ILLUSTRATION IN A BOOK! AN' NOT A VERY GOOD ONE AT THAT!
PEACE, THOU CHATTERING COCKATOO OR I SHALL RAP THEE ON THE NOGGIN!
WAIT A MINUTE! LET'S NOT HAVE ANY TROUBLE ABOUT THIS THING!
I JUST WANT T' GET THINGS STRAIGHT! IS THIS REALLY SHERWOOD FOREST WHERE ROBIN HOOD USED TO LIVE?
USED TO LIVE? ART THOU TELLING ME HE IS DEAD?
OF COURSE, I ART, YA DUMB NINNY! HE DIED MORE'N A THOUSAND YEARS AGO! CAN'T YA READ YER OWN BOOK?
!
!
ENOUGH OF THIS PRITTLE-PRATTLE!
?
HOOOO-WO-O-ONK!
TAKE THIS THIEVING ROGUE TO NOTTINGHAM! METHINKS THE SHERIFF WILL ATTEND TO THE LIKES OF HIM IN SHORT ORDER!
WELL—YA CAN SAY WHAT YA LIKE— BUT IF I DON'T HAVE A SWELL TIME IN THIS BOOK IT'S NOT GONNA BE MY FAULT!
WALT DISNEY
6-14

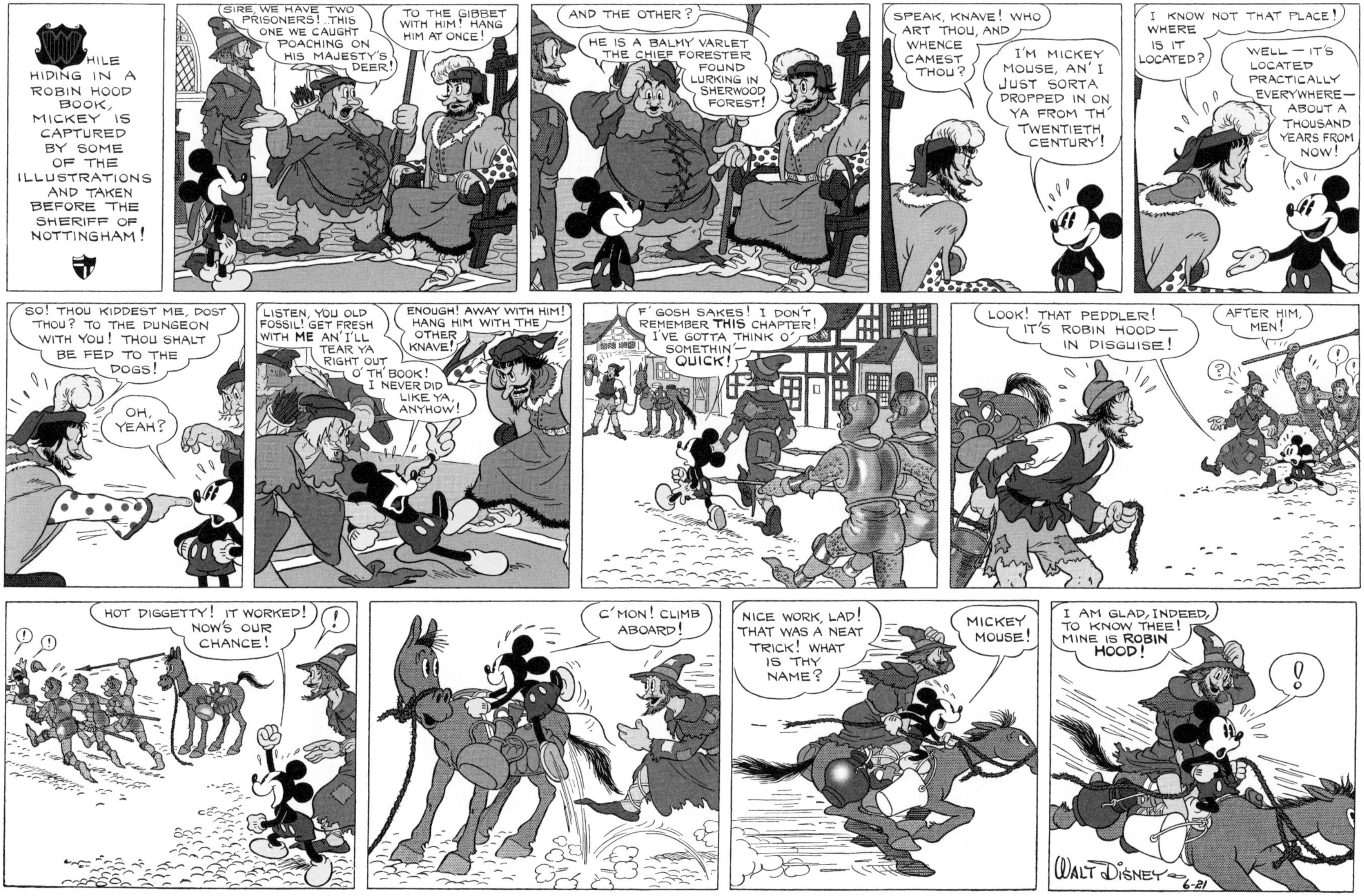
WHILE HIDING IN A ROBIN HOOD BOOK, MICKEY IS CAPTURED BY SOME OF THE ILLUSTRATIONS AND TAKEN BEFORE THE SHERIFF OF NOTTINGHAM!
SIRE, WE HAVE TWO PRISONERS! ..THIS ONE WE CAUGHT POACHING ON HIS MAJESTY'S DEER!
TO THE GIBBET WITH HIM! HANG HIM AT ONCE!
AND THE OTHER?
HE IS A BALMY VARLET THE CHIEF FORESTER FOUND LURKING IN SHERWOOD FOREST!
SPEAK, KNAVE! WHO ART THOU, AND WHENCE CAMEST THOU?
I'M MICKEY MOUSE, AN' I JUST SORTA DROPPED IN ON YA FROM TH' TWENTIETH CENTURY!
I KNOW NOT THAT PLACE! WHERE IS IT LOCATED?
WELL — IT'S LOCATED PRACTICALLY EVERYWHERE— ABOUT A THOUSAND YEARS FROM NOW!
SO! THOU KIDDEST ME, DOST THOU? TO THE DUNGEON WITH YOU! THOU SHALT BE FED TO THE DOGS!
OH, YEAH?
LISTEN, YOU OLD FOSSIL! GET FRESH WITH ME AN' I'LL TEAR YA RIGHT OUT O' TH' BOOK! I NEVER DID LIKE YA, ANYHOW!
ENOUGH! AWAY WITH HIM! HANG HIM WITH THE OTHER KNAVE!
F' GOSH SAKES! I DON'T REMEMBER THIS CHAPTER! I'VE GOTTA THINK O' SOMETHIN'— QUICK!
LOOK! THAT PEDDLER! IT'S ROBIN HOOD — IN DISGUISE!
AFTER HIM, MEN!
HOT DIGGETTY! IT WORKED! NOW'S OUR CHANCE!
C'MON! CLIMB ABOARD!
NICE WORK, LAD! THAT WAS A NEAT TRICK! WHAT IS THY NAME?
MICKEY MOUSE!
I AM GLAD, INDEED, TO KNOW THEE! MINE IS ROBIN HOOD!
!
WALT DISNEY
6-21

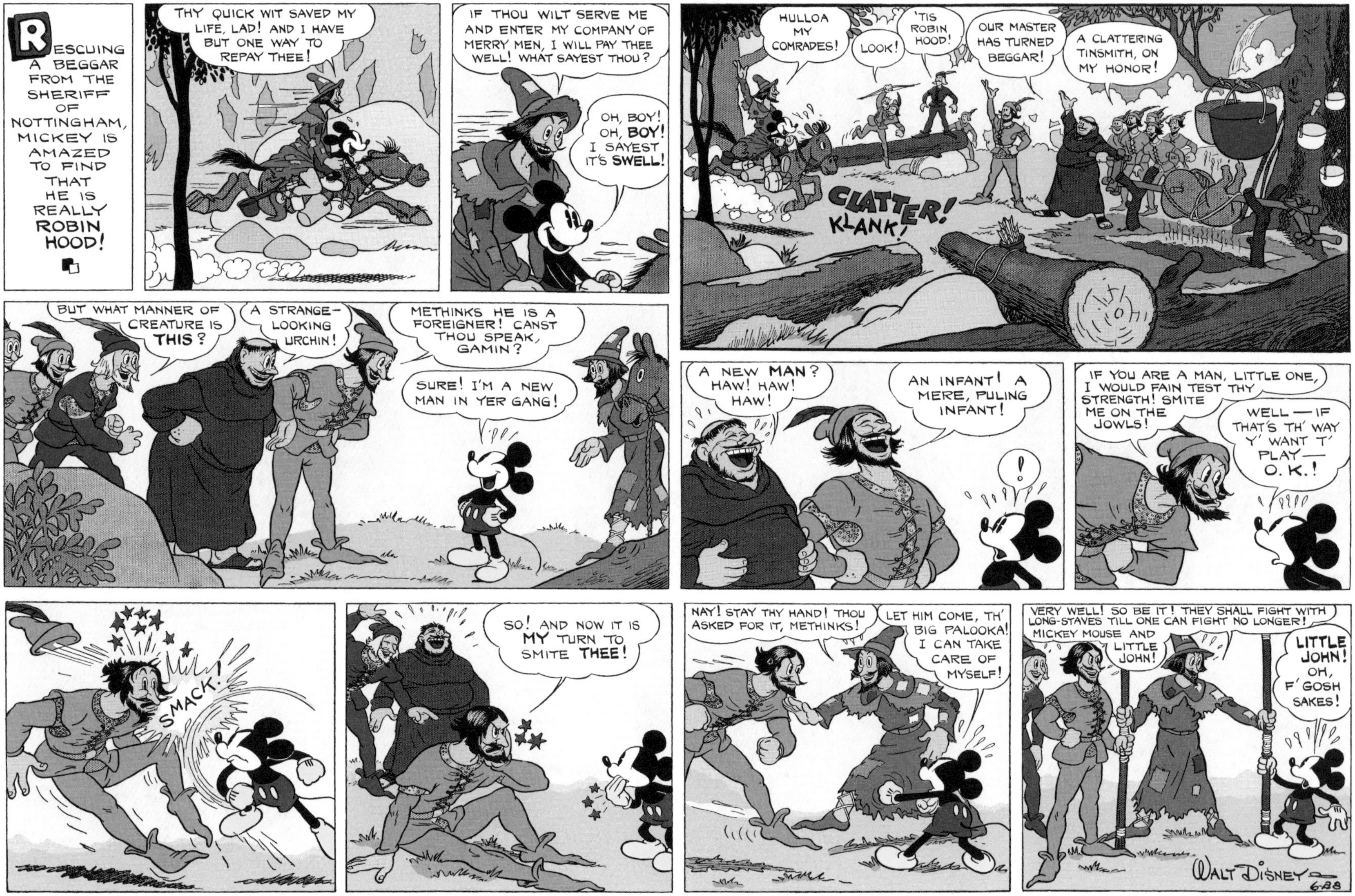
RESCUING A BEGGAR FROM THE SHERIFF OF NOTTINGHAM, MICKEY IS AMAZED TO FIND THAT HE IS REALLY ROBIN HOOD!
THY QUICK WIT SAVED MY LIFE, LAD! AND I HAVE BUT ONE WAY TO REPAY THEE!
IF THOU WILT SERVE ME AND ENTER MY COMPANY OF MERRY MEN, I WILL PAY THEE WELL! WHAT SAYEST THOU?
OH, BOY! OH, BOY! I SAYEST IT'S SWELL!
HULLOA MY COMRADES!
LOOK!
'TIS ROBIN HOOD!
OUR MASTER HAS TURNED BEGGAR!
A CLATTERING TINSMITH, ON MY HONOR!
CLATTER!
KLANK!
BUT WHAT MANNER OF CREATURE IS THIS?
A STRANGE-LOOKING URCHIN!
METHINKS HE IS A FOREIGNER! CANST THOU SPEAK, GAMIN?
SURE! I'M A NEW MAN IN YER GANG!
A NEW MAN? HAW! HAW! HAW!
AN INFANT! A MERE, PULING INFANT!
!
IF YOU ARE A MAN, LITTLE ONE, I WOULD FAIN TEST THY STRENGTH! SMITE ME ON THE JOWLS!
WELL — IF THAT'S TH' WAY Y' WANT T' PLAY — O.K.!
SMACK!
SO! AND NOW IT IS MY TURN TO SMITE THEE!
NAY! STAY THY HAND! THOU ASKED FOR IT, METHINKS!
LET HIM COME, TH' BIG PALOOKA! I CAN TAKE CARE OF MYSELF!
VERY WELL! SO BE IT! THEY SHALL FIGHT WITH LONG-STAVES TILL ONE CAN FIGHT NO LONGER! MICKEY MOUSE AND LITTLE JOHN!
LITTLE JOHN! OH, F'GOSH SAKES!
WALT DISNEY
6-28

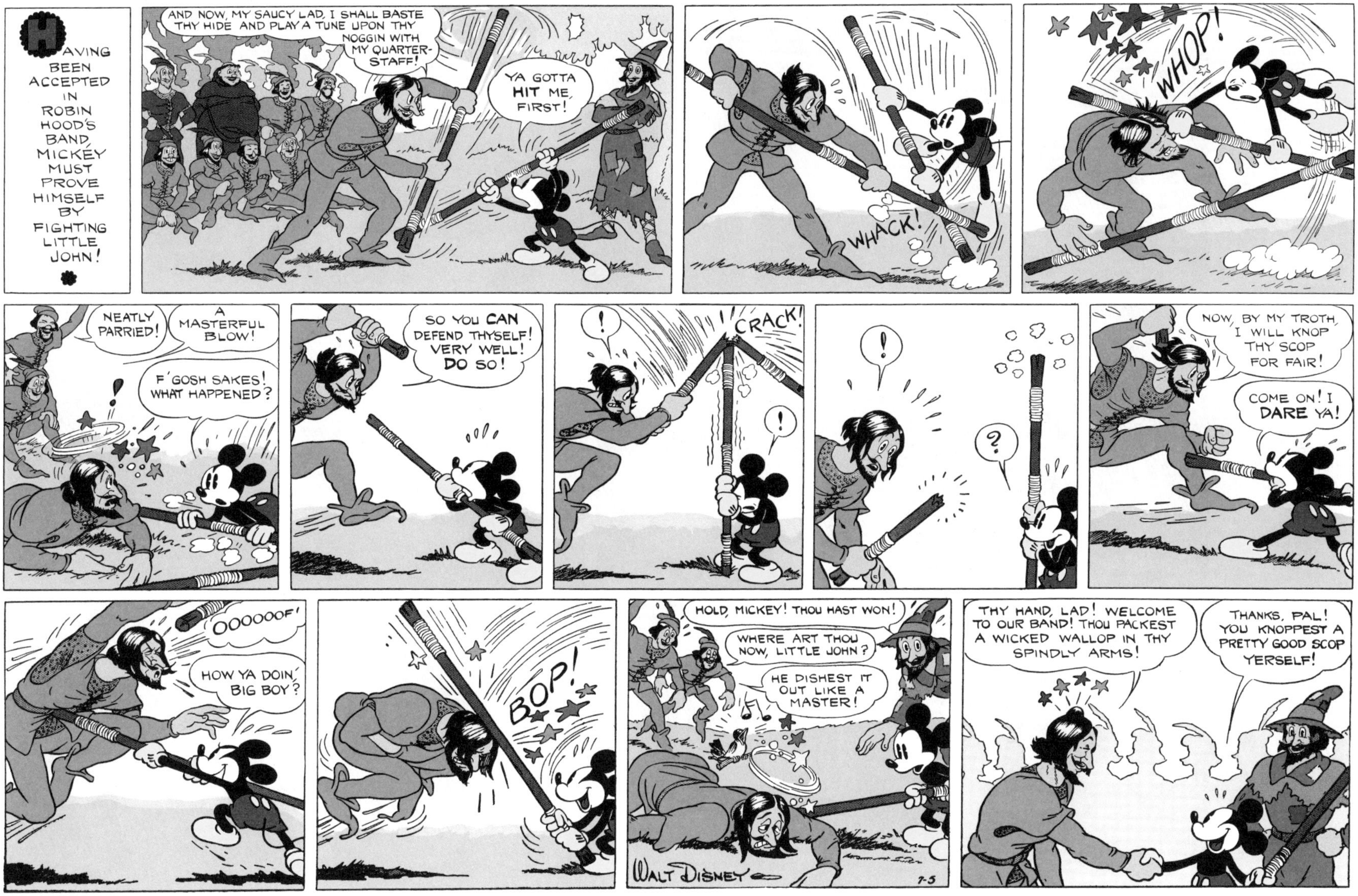
HAVING BEEN ACCEPTED IN ROBIN HOOD'S BAND, MICKEY MUST PROVE HIMSELF BY FIGHTING LITTLE JOHN!
AND NOW, MY SAUCY LAD, I SHALL BASTE THY HIDE AND PLAY A TUNE UPON THY NOGGIN WITH MY QUARTER-STAFF!
YA GOTTA HIT ME, FIRST!
WHACK!
WHOP!
NEATLY PARRIED!
A MASTERFUL BLOW!
F'GOSH SAKES! WHAT HAPPENED?
SO YOU CAN DEFEND THYSELF! VERY WELL! DO SO!
CRACK!
NOW, BY MY TROTH, I WILL KNOP THY SCOP FOR FAIR!
COME ON! I DARE YA!
OOOOOOF!
HOW YA DOIN', BIG BOY?
BOP!
HOLD, MICKEY! THOU HAST WON!
WHERE ART THOU NOW, LITTLE JOHN?
HE DISHEST IT OUT LIKE A MASTER!
WALT DISNEY
7-5
THY HAND, LAD! WELCOME TO OUR BAND! THOU PACKEST A WICKED WALLOP IN THY SPINDLY ARMS!
THANKS, PAL! YOU KNOPPEST A PRETTY GOOD SCOP YERSELF!

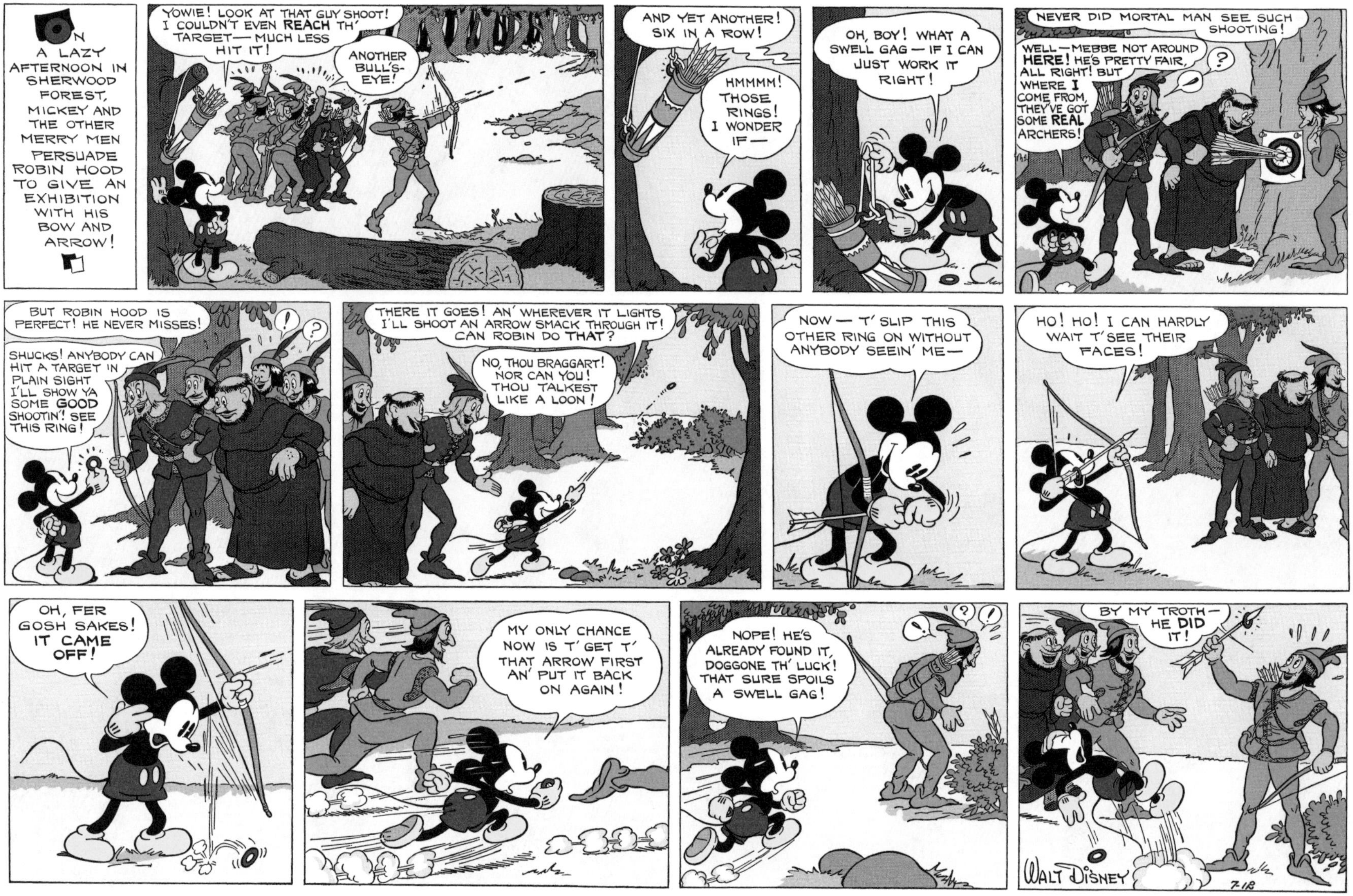
ON A LAZY AFTERNOON IN SHERWOOD FOREST, MICKEY AND THE OTHER MERRY MEN PERSUADE ROBIN HOOD TO GIVE AN EXHIBITION WITH HIS BOW AND ARROW!
YOWIE! LOOK AT THAT GUY SHOOT! I COULDN'T EVEN REACH TH' TARGET— MUCH LESS HIT IT!
ANOTHER BULL'S-EYE!
AND YET ANOTHER! SIX IN A ROW!
HMMMM! THOSE RINGS! I WONDER IF—
OH, BOY! WHAT A SWELL GAG — IF I CAN JUST WORK IT RIGHT!
NEVER DID MORTAL MAN SEE SUCH SHOOTING!
WELL — MEBBE NOT AROUND HERE! HE'S PRETTY FAIR, ALL RIGHT! BUT WHERE I COME FROM, THEY'VE GOT SOME REAL ARCHERS!
?
BUT ROBIN HOOD IS PERFECT! HE NEVER MISSES!
SHUCKS! ANYBODY CAN HIT A TARGET IN PLAIN SIGHT I'LL SHOW YA SOME GOOD SHOOTIN'! SEE THIS RING!
!
?
THERE IT GOES! AN' WHEREVER IT LIGHTS I'LL SHOOT AN ARROW SMACK THROUGH IT! CAN ROBIN DO THAT?
NO, THOU BRAGGART! NOR CAN YOU! THOU TALKEST LIKE A LOON!
NOW — T' SLIP THIS OTHER RING ON WITHOUT ANYBODY SEEIN' ME—
HO! HO! I CAN HARDLY WAIT T' SEE THEIR FACES!
OH, FER GOSH SAKES! IT CAME OFF!
MY ONLY CHANCE NOW IS T' GET T' THAT ARROW FIRST AN' PUT IT BACK ON AGAIN!
NOPE! HE'S ALREADY FOUND IT, DOGGONE TH' LUCK! THAT SURE SPOILS A SWELL GAG!
?
!
BY MY TROTH — HE DID IT!
WALT DISNEY
7-18

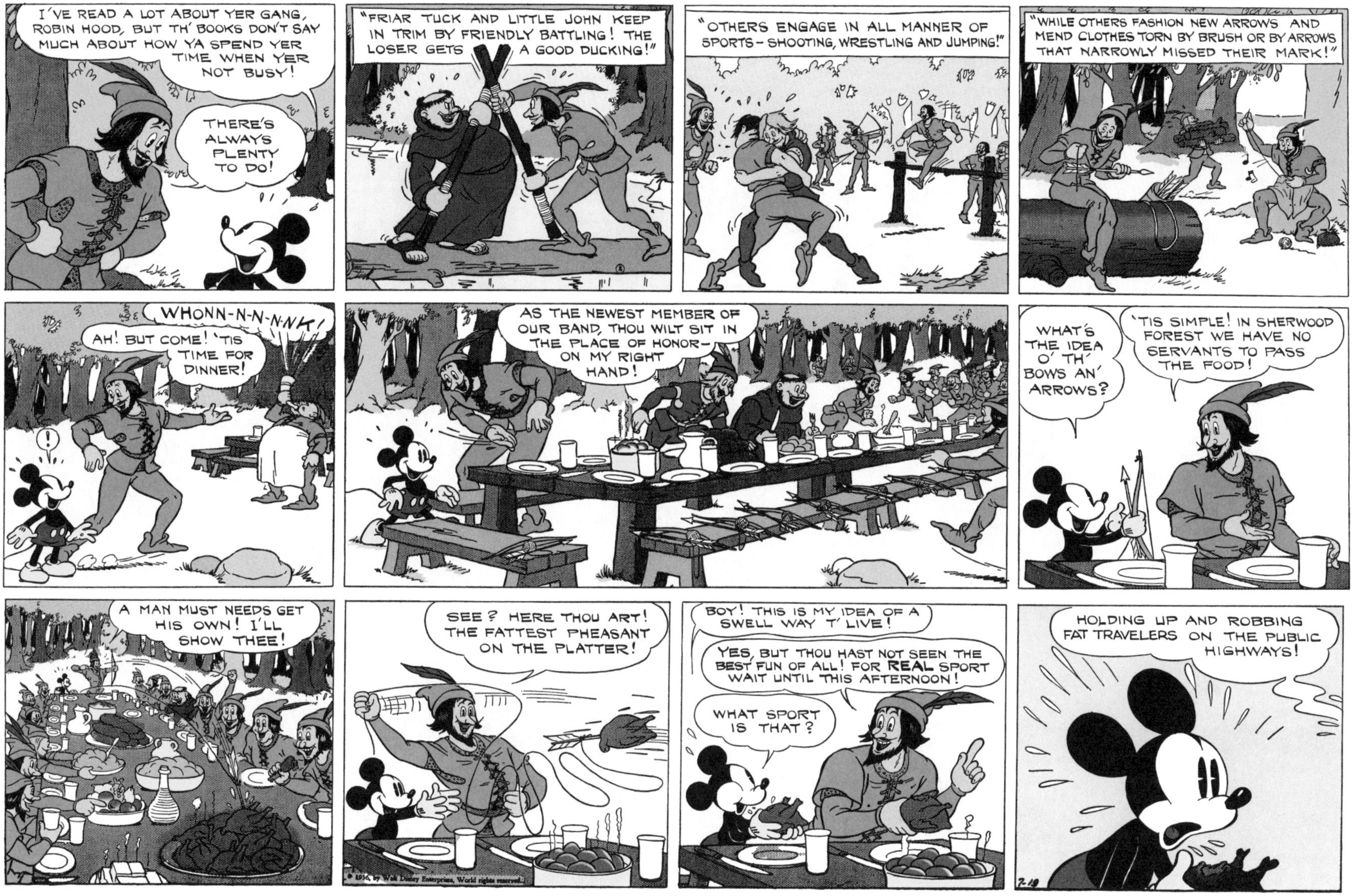

I'VE READ A LOT ABOUT YER GANG, ROBIN HOOD, BUT TH' BOOKS DON'T SAY MUCH ABOUT HOW YA SPEND YER TIME WHEN YER NOT BUSY!
THERE'S ALWAYS PLENTY TO DO!
"FRIAR TUCK AND LITTLE JOHN KEEP IN TRIM BY FRIENDLY BATTLING! THE LOSER GETS A GOOD DUCKING!"
"OTHERS ENGAGE IN ALL MANNER OF SPORTS – SHOOTING, WRESTLING AND JUMPING!"
"WHILE OTHERS FASHION NEW ARROWS AND MEND CLOTHES TORN BY BRUSH OR BY ARROWS THAT NARROWLY MISSED THEIR MARK!"
WHONN-N-N-N-NK!
AH! BUT COME! 'TIS TIME FOR DINNER!
!
AS THE NEWEST MEMBER OF OUR BAND, THOU WILT SIT IN THE PLACE OF HONOR– ON MY RIGHT HAND!
WHAT'S THE IDEA O' TH' BOWS AN' ARROWS?
'TIS SIMPLE! IN SHERWOOD FOREST WE HAVE NO SERVANTS TO PASS THE FOOD!
A MAN MUST NEEDS GET HIS OWN! I'LL SHOW THEE!
SEE? HERE THOU ART! THE FATTEST PHEASANT ON THE PLATTER!
© 1936, by Walt Disney Enterprises, World rights reserved.
BOY! THIS IS MY IDEA OF A SWELL WAY T' LIVE!
YES, BUT THOU HAST NOT SEEN THE BEST FUN OF ALL! FOR **REAL** SPORT WAIT UNTIL THIS AFTERNOON!
WHAT SPORT IS THAT?
7-19
HOLDING UP AND ROBBING FAT TRAVELERS ON THE PUBLIC HIGHWAYS!

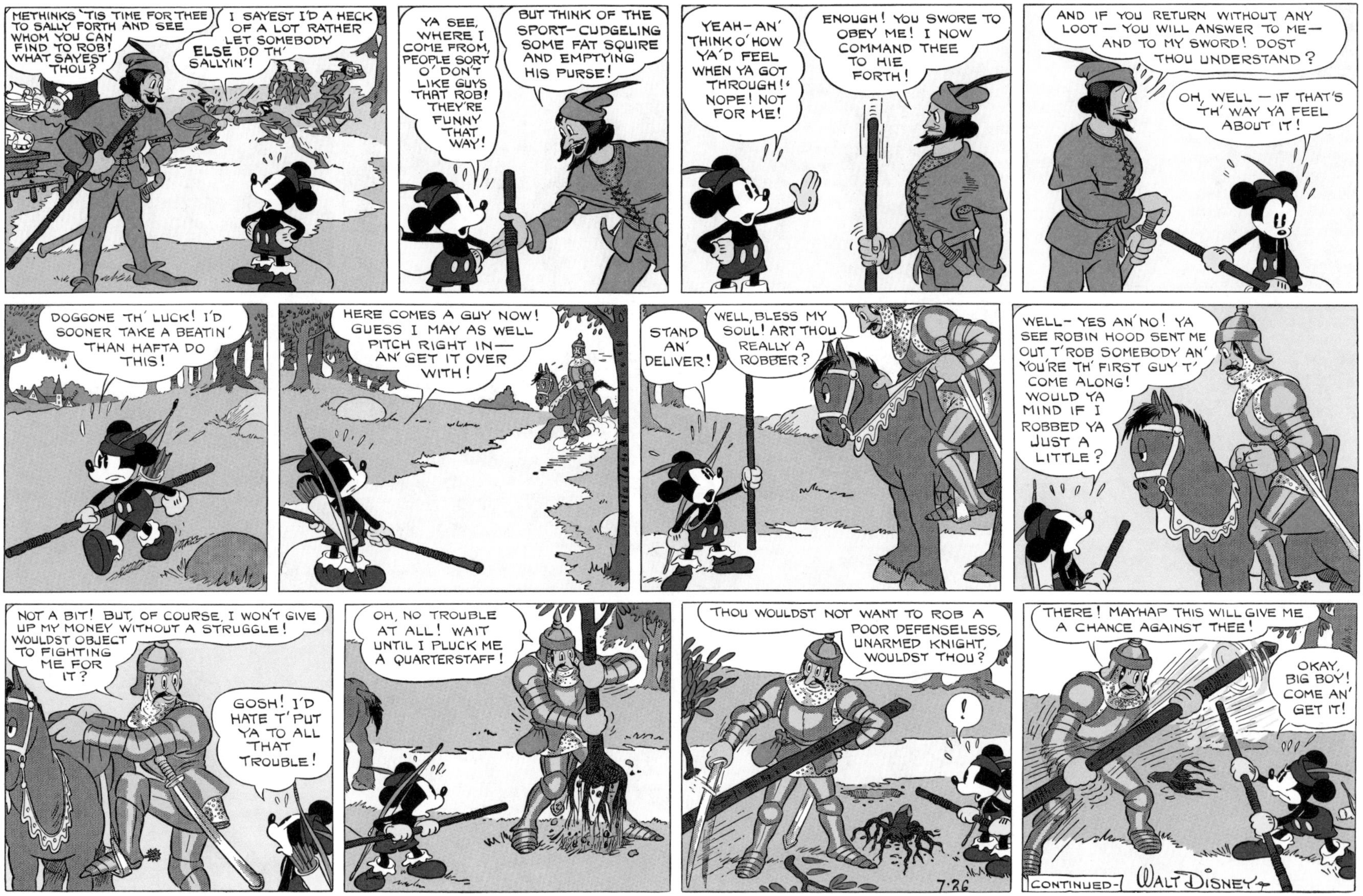
METHINKS 'TIS TIME FOR THEE TO SALLY FORTH AND SEE WHOM YOU CAN FIND TO ROB! WHAT SAYEST THOU?
I SAYEST I'D A HECK OF A LOT RATHER LET SOMEBODY ELSE DO TH' SALLYIN'!
YA SEE, WHERE I COME FROM, PEOPLE SORT O' DON'T LIKE GUYS THAT ROB! THEY'RE FUNNY THAT WAY!
BUT THINK OF THE SPORT—CUDGELING SOME FAT SQUIRE AND EMPTYING HIS PURSE!
YEAH—AN' THINK O' HOW YA'D FEEL WHEN YA GOT THROUGH! NOPE! NOT FOR ME!
ENOUGH! YOU SWORE TO OBEY ME! I NOW COMMAND THEE TO HIE FORTH!
AND IF YOU RETURN WITHOUT ANY LOOT — YOU WILL ANSWER TO ME—AND TO MY SWORD! DOST THOU UNDERSTAND?
OH, WELL — IF THAT'S TH' WAY YA FEEL ABOUT IT!
DOGGONE TH' LUCK! I'D SOONER TAKE A BEATIN' THAN HAFTA DO THIS!
HERE COMES A GUY NOW! GUESS I MAY AS WELL PITCH RIGHT IN— AN' GET IT OVER WITH!
STAND AN' DELIVER!
WELL, BLESS MY SOUL! ART THOU REALLY A ROBBER?
WELL—YES AN' NO! YA SEE ROBIN HOOD SENT ME OUT T' ROB SOMEBODY AN' YOU'RE TH' FIRST GUY T' COME ALONG! WOULD YA MIND IF I ROBBED YA JUST A LITTLE?
NOT A BIT! BUT, OF COURSE, I WON'T GIVE UP MY MONEY WITHOUT A STRUGGLE! WOULDST OBJECT TO FIGHTING ME FOR IT?
GOSH! I'D HATE T' PUT YA TO ALL THAT TROUBLE!
OH, NO TROUBLE AT ALL! WAIT UNTIL I PLUCK ME A QUARTERSTAFF!
THOU WOULDST NOT WANT TO ROB A POOR DEFENSELESS, UNARMED KNIGHT, WOULDST THOU?
!
7-26
THERE! MAYHAP THIS WILL GIVE ME A CHANCE AGAINST THEE!
OKAY, BIG BOY! COME AN' GET IT!
CONTINUED—
WALT DISNEY

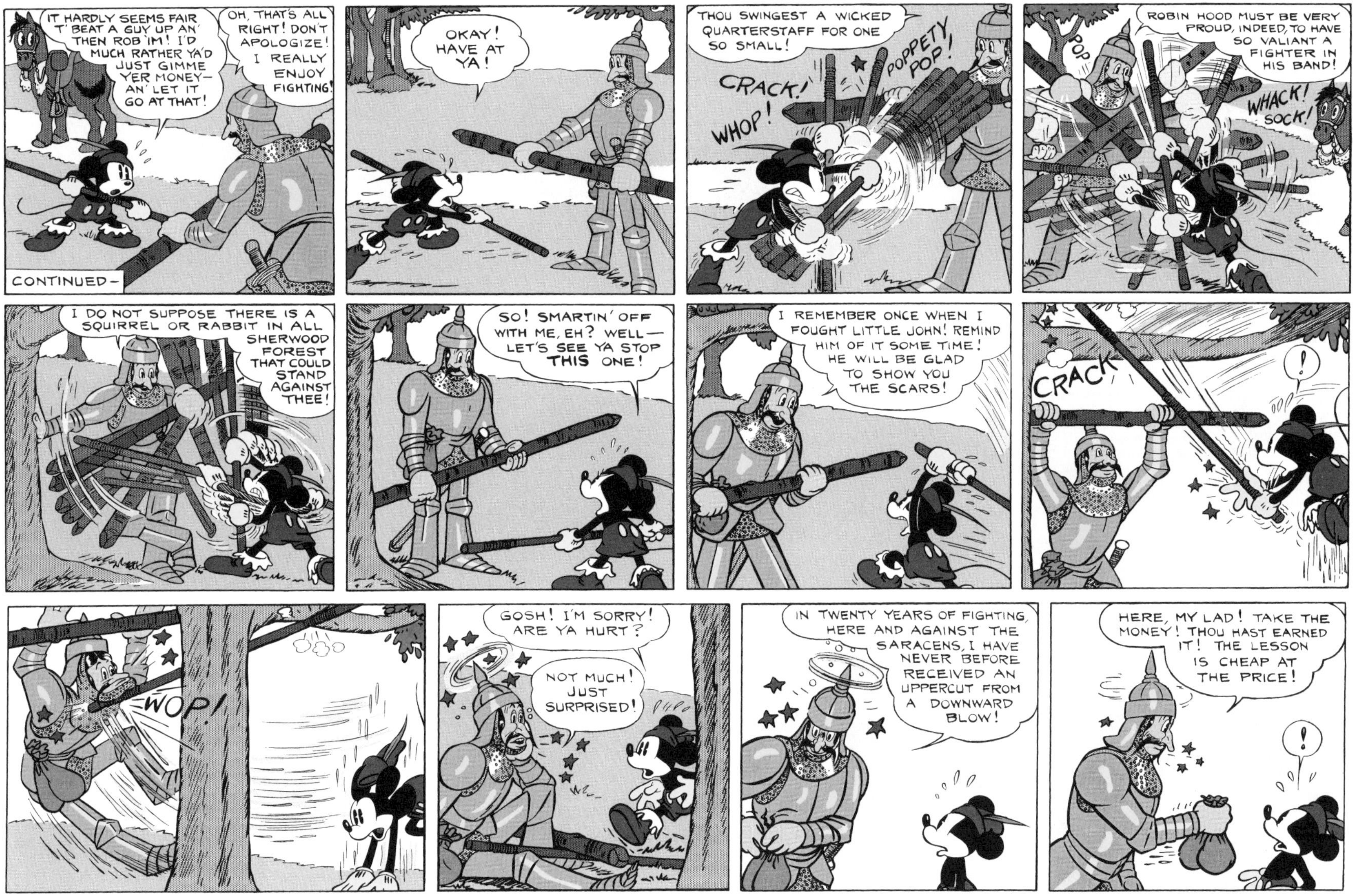
IT HARDLY SEEMS FAIR T' BEAT A GUY UP AN' THEN ROB 'IM! I'D MUCH RATHER YA'D JUST GIMME YER MONEY— AN' LET IT GO AT THAT!
OH, THAT'S ALL RIGHT! DON'T APOLOGIZE! I REALLY ENJOY FIGHTING!
CONTINUED—
OKAY! HAVE AT YA!
THOU SWINGEST A WICKED QUARTERSTAFF FOR ONE SO SMALL!
CRACK!
WHOP!
POPPETY POP!
ROBIN HOOD MUST BE VERY PROUD, INDEED, TO HAVE SO VALIANT A FIGHTER IN HIS BAND!
POP
WHACK!
SOCK!
I DO NOT SUPPOSE THERE IS A SQUIRREL OR RABBIT IN ALL SHERWOOD FOREST THAT COULD STAND AGAINST THEE!
SO! SMARTIN' OFF WITH ME, EH? WELL— LET'S SEE YA STOP THIS ONE!
I REMEMBER ONCE WHEN I FOUGHT LITTLE JOHN! REMIND HIM OF IT SOME TIME! HE WILL BE GLAD TO SHOW YOU THE SCARS!
CRACK
!
WOP!
GOSH! I'M SORRY! ARE YA HURT?
NOT MUCH! JUST SURPRISED!
IN TWENTY YEARS OF FIGHTING, HERE AND AGAINST THE SARACENS, I HAVE NEVER BEFORE RECEIVED AN UPPERCUT FROM A DOWNWARD BLOW!
HERE, MY LAD! TAKE THE MONEY! THOU HAST EARNED IT! THE LESSON IS CHEAP AT THE PRICE!
!

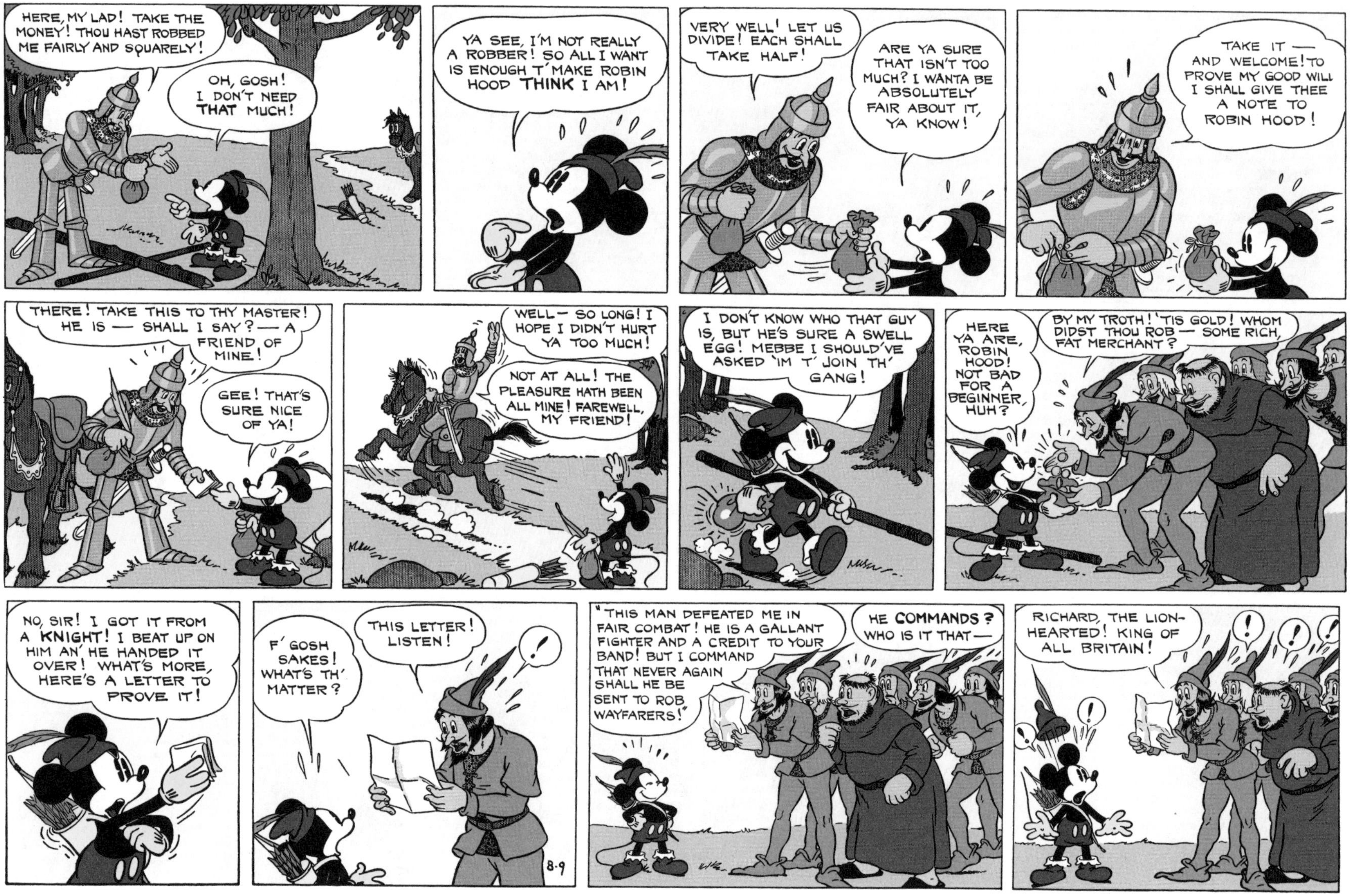
HERE, MY LAD! TAKE THE MONEY! THOU HAST ROBBED ME FAIRLY AND SQUARELY!
OH, GOSH! I DON'T NEED THAT MUCH!
YA SEE, I'M NOT REALLY A ROBBER! SO ALL I WANT IS ENOUGH T' MAKE ROBIN HOOD THINK I AM!
VERY WELL! LET US DIVIDE! EACH SHALL TAKE HALF!
ARE YA SURE THAT ISN'T TOO MUCH? I WANTA BE ABSOLUTELY FAIR ABOUT IT, YA KNOW!
TAKE IT — AND WELCOME! TO PROVE MY GOOD WILL I SHALL GIVE THEE A NOTE TO ROBIN HOOD!
THERE! TAKE THIS TO THY MASTER! HE IS — SHALL I SAY? — A FRIEND OF MINE!
GEE! THAT'S SURE NICE OF YA!
WELL — SO LONG! I HOPE I DIDN'T HURT YA TOO MUCH!
NOT AT ALL! THE PLEASURE HATH BEEN ALL MINE! FAREWELL, MY FRIEND!
I DON'T KNOW WHO THAT GUY IS, BUT HE'S SURE A SWELL EGG! MEBBE I SHOULD'VE ASKED 'IM T' JOIN TH' GANG!
HERE YA ARE, ROBIN HOOD! NOT BAD FOR A BEGINNER, HUH?
BY MY TROTH! 'TIS GOLD! WHOM DIDST THOU ROB — SOME RICH, FAT MERCHANT?
NO, SIR! I GOT IT FROM A KNIGHT! I BEAT UP ON HIM AN' HE HANDED IT OVER! WHAT'S MORE, HERE'S A LETTER TO PROVE IT!
F' GOSH SAKES! WHAT'S TH' MATTER?
THIS LETTER! LISTEN!
!
8-9
"THIS MAN DEFEATED ME IN FAIR COMBAT! HE IS A GALLANT FIGHTER AND A CREDIT TO YOUR BAND! BUT I COMMAND THAT NEVER AGAIN SHALL HE BE SENT TO ROB WAYFARERS!"
HE COMMANDS? WHO IS IT THAT —
RICHARD, THE LION-HEARTED! KING OF ALL BRITAIN!
!
!
!
!
!
!

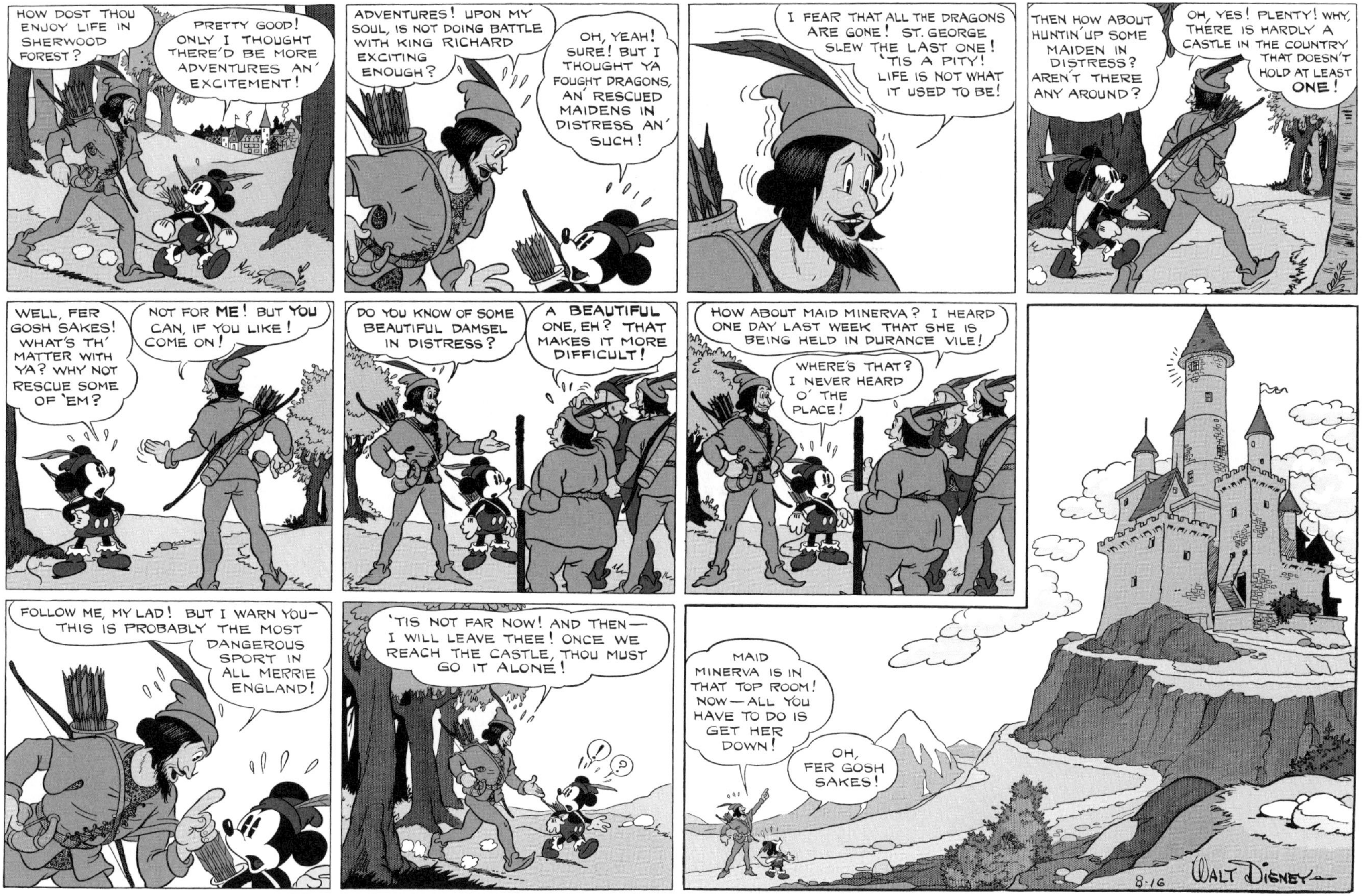

HOW DOST THOU ENJOY LIFE IN SHERWOOD FOREST?
PRETTY GOOD! ONLY I THOUGHT THERE'D BE MORE ADVENTURES AN' EXCITEMENT!
ADVENTURES! UPON MY SOUL, IS NOT DOING BATTLE WITH KING RICHARD EXCITING ENOUGH?
OH, YEAH! SURE! BUT I THOUGHT YA FOUGHT DRAGONS, AN' RESCUED MAIDENS IN DISTRESS AN' SUCH!
I FEAR THAT ALL THE DRAGONS ARE GONE! ST. GEORGE SLEW THE LAST ONE! 'TIS A PITY! LIFE IS NOT WHAT IT USED TO BE!
THEN HOW ABOUT HUNTIN' UP SOME MAIDEN IN DISTRESS? AREN'T THERE ANY AROUND?
OH, YES! PLENTY! WHY, THERE IS HARDLY A CASTLE IN THE COUNTRY THAT DOESN'T HOLD AT LEAST ONE!
WELL, FER GOSH SAKES! WHAT'S TH' MATTER WITH YA? WHY NOT RESCUE SOME OF 'EM?
NOT FOR ME! BUT YOU CAN, IF YOU LIKE! COME ON!
DO YOU KNOW OF SOME BEAUTIFUL DAMSEL IN DISTRESS?
A BEAUTIFUL ONE, EH? THAT MAKES IT MORE DIFFICULT!
HOW ABOUT MAID MINERVA? I HEARD ONE DAY LAST WEEK THAT SHE IS BEING HELD IN DURANCE VILE!
WHERE'S THAT? I NEVER HEARD O' THE PLACE!
FOLLOW ME, MY LAD! BUT I WARN YOU— THIS IS PROBABLY THE MOST DANGEROUS SPORT IN ALL MERRIE ENGLAND!
'TIS NOT FAR NOW! AND THEN— I WILL LEAVE THEE! ONCE WE REACH THE CASTLE, THOU MUST GO IT ALONE!
!
?
MAID MINERVA IS IN THAT TOP ROOM! NOW—ALL YOU HAVE TO DO IS GET HER DOWN!
OH, FER GOSH SAKES!
8-16
WALT DISNEY

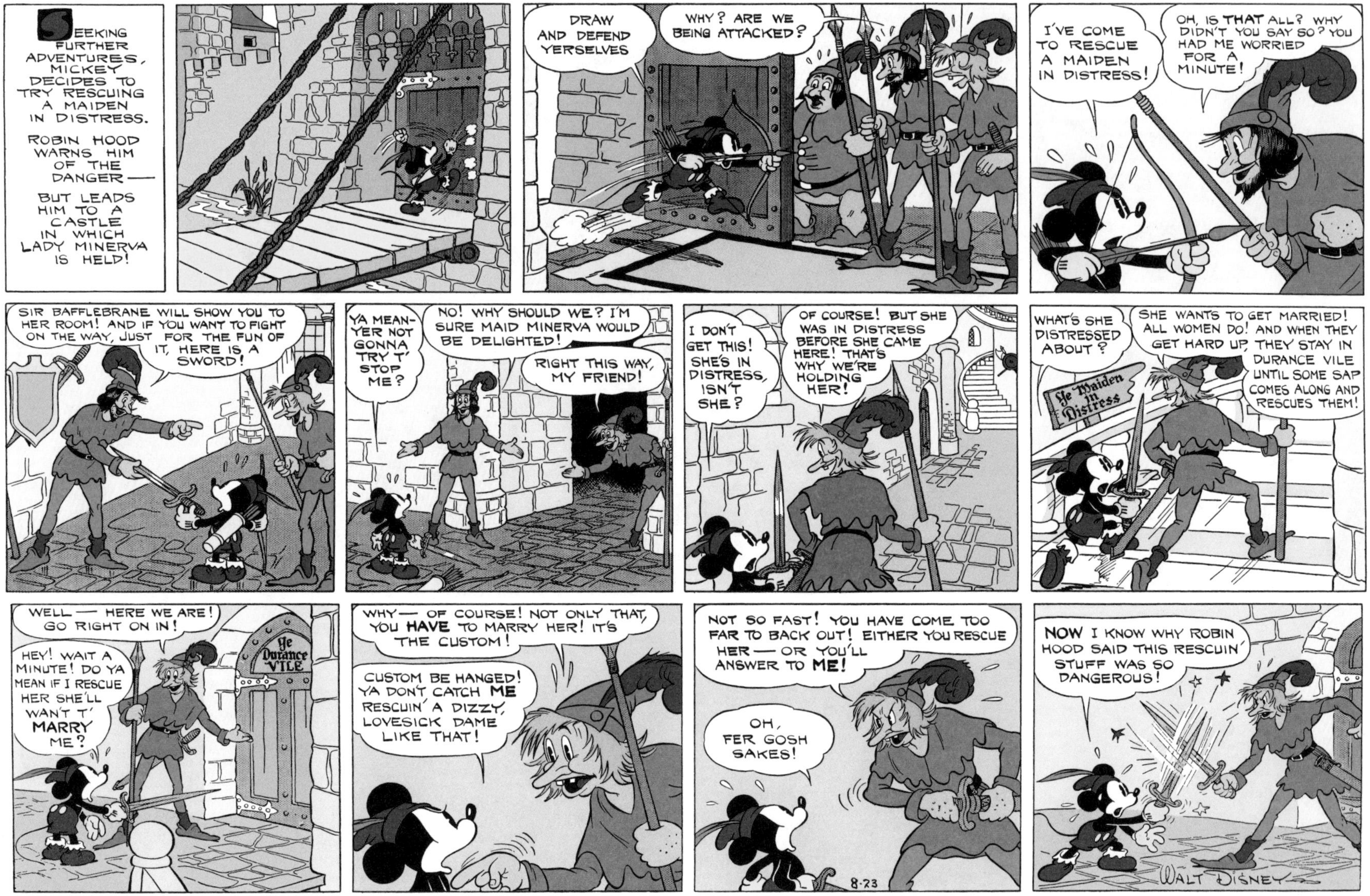
SEEKING FURTHER ADVENTURES, MICKEY DECIDES TO TRY RESCUING A MAIDEN IN DISTRESS.
ROBIN HOOD WARNS HIM OF THE DANGER—
BUT LEADS HIM TO A CASTLE IN WHICH LADY MINERVA IS HELD!
DRAW AND DEFEND YERSELVES
WHY? ARE WE BEING ATTACKED?
I'VE COME TO RESCUE A MAIDEN IN DISTRESS!
OH, IS THAT ALL? WHY DIDN'T YOU SAY SO? YOU HAD ME WORRIED FOR A MINUTE!
SIR BAFFLEBRANE WILL SHOW YOU TO HER ROOM! AND IF YOU WANT TO FIGHT ON THE WAY, JUST FOR THE FUN OF IT, HERE IS A SWORD!
YA MEAN-YER NOT GONNA TRY T' STOP ME?
NO! WHY SHOULD WE? I'M SURE MAID MINERVA WOULD BE DELIGHTED!
RIGHT THIS WAY, MY FRIEND!
I DON'T GET THIS! SHE'S IN DISTRESS, ISN'T SHE?
OF COURSE! BUT SHE WAS IN DISTRESS BEFORE SHE CAME HERE! THAT'S WHY WE'RE HOLDING HER!
WHAT'S SHE DISTRESSED ABOUT?
SHE WANTS TO GET MARRIED! ALL WOMEN DO! AND WHEN THEY GET HARD UP, THEY STAY IN DURANCE VILE UNTIL SOME SAP COMES ALONG AND RESCUES THEM!
Ye Maiden in Distress
WELL — HERE WE ARE! GO RIGHT ON IN!
HEY! WAIT A MINUTE! DO YA MEAN IF I RESCUE HER SHE'LL WAN'T T' MARRY ME?
Ye Durance VILE
WHY— OF COURSE! NOT ONLY THAT, YOU HAVE TO MARRY HER! IT'S THE CUSTOM!
CUSTOM BE HANGED! YA DON'T CATCH ME RESCUIN' A DIZZY, LOVESICK DAME LIKE THAT!
NOT SO FAST! YOU HAVE COME TOO FAR TO BACK OUT! EITHER YOU RESCUE HER — OR YOU'LL ANSWER TO ME!
OH, FER GOSH SAKES!
8·23
NOW I KNOW WHY ROBIN HOOD SAID THIS RESCUIN' STUFF WAS SO DANGEROUS!
WALT DISNEY

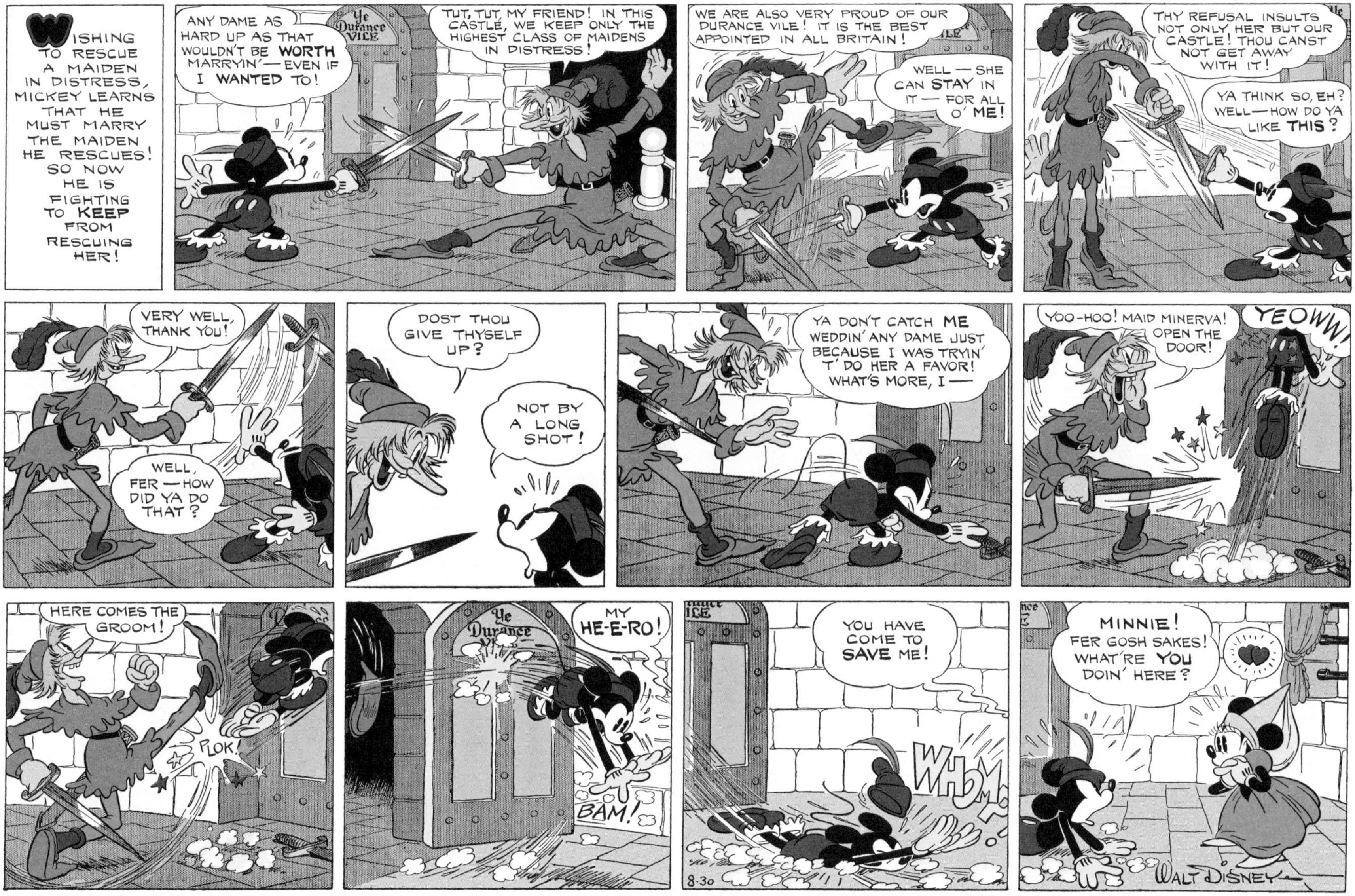
WISHING TO RESCUE A MAIDEN IN DISTRESS, MICKEY LEARNS THAT HE MUST MARRY THE MAIDEN HE RESCUES! SO NOW HE IS FIGHTING TO KEEP FROM RESCUING HER!
ANY DAME AS HARD UP AS THAT WOULDN'T BE WORTH MARRYIN'— EVEN IF I WANTED TO!
Ye Durance VILE
TUT, TUT, MY FRIEND! IN THIS CASTLE, WE KEEP ONLY THE HIGHEST CLASS OF MAIDENS IN DISTRESS!
WE ARE ALSO VERY PROUD OF OUR DURANCE VILE! IT IS THE BEST APPOINTED IN ALL BRITAIN!
WELL — SHE CAN STAY IN IT — FOR ALL O' ME!
THY REFUSAL INSULTS NOT ONLY HER BUT OUR CASTLE! THOU CANST NOT GET AWAY WITH IT!
YA THINK SO, EH? WELL— HOW DO YA LIKE THIS?
VERY WELL, THANK YOU!
WELL, FER — HOW DID YA DO THAT?
DOST THOU GIVE THYSELF UP?
NOT BY A LONG SHOT!
YA DON'T CATCH ME WEDDIN' ANY DAME JUST BECAUSE I WAS TRYIN' T' DO HER A FAVOR! WHAT'S MORE, I —
YOO-HOO! MAID MINERVA! OPEN THE DOOR!
YEOWW!
HERE COMES THE GROOM!
PLOK!
Ye Durance
MY HE-E-RO!
BAM!
YOU HAVE COME TO SAVE ME!
WHOMP
8·30
MINNIE! FER GOSH SAKES! WHAT'RE YOU DOIN' HERE?
WALT DISNEY

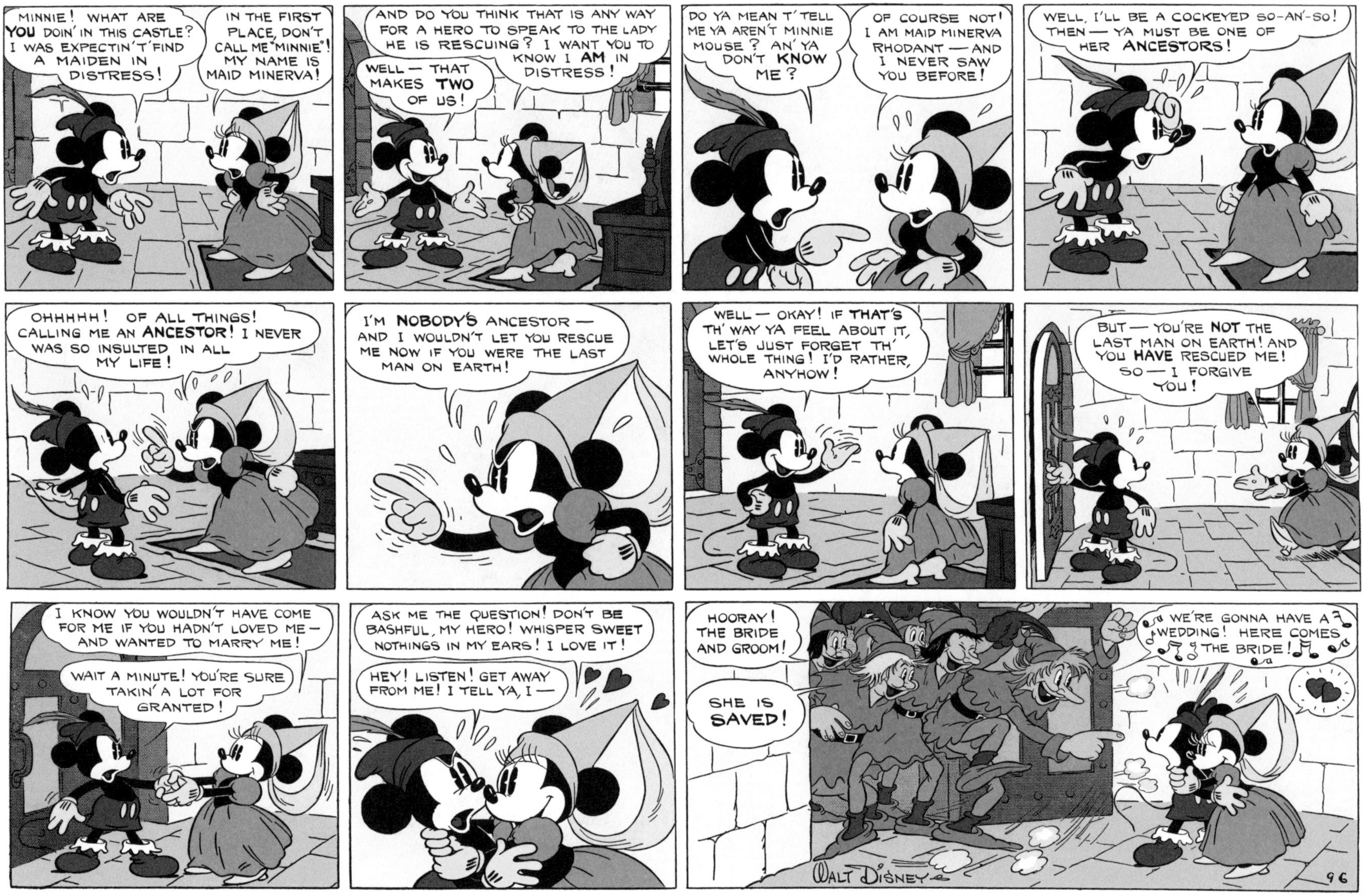
MINNIE! WHAT ARE YOU DOIN' IN THIS CASTLE? I WAS EXPECTIN' T' FIND A MAIDEN IN DISTRESS!
IN THE FIRST PLACE, DON'T CALL ME "MINNIE"! MY NAME IS MAID MINERVA!
AND DO YOU THINK THAT IS ANY WAY FOR A HERO TO SPEAK TO THE LADY HE IS RESCUING? I WANT YOU TO KNOW I AM IN DISTRESS!
WELL — THAT MAKES TWO OF US!
DO YA MEAN T' TELL ME YA AREN'T MINNIE MOUSE? AN' YA DON'T KNOW ME?
OF COURSE NOT! I AM MAID MINERVA RHODANT — AND I NEVER SAW YOU BEFORE!
WELL, I'LL BE A COCKEYED SO-AN'-SO! THEN — YA MUST BE ONE OF HER ANCESTORS!
OHHHHH! OF ALL THINGS! CALLING ME AN ANCESTOR! I NEVER WAS SO INSULTED IN ALL MY LIFE!
I'M NOBODY'S ANCESTOR — AND I WOULDN'T LET YOU RESCUE ME NOW IF YOU WERE THE LAST MAN ON EARTH!
WELL — OKAY! IF THAT'S TH' WAY YA FEEL ABOUT IT, LET'S JUST FORGET TH' WHOLE THING! I'D RATHER, ANYHOW!
BUT — YOU'RE NOT THE LAST MAN ON EARTH! AND YOU HAVE RESCUED ME! SO — I FORGIVE YOU!
I KNOW YOU WOULDN'T HAVE COME FOR ME IF YOU HADN'T LOVED ME — AND WANTED TO MARRY ME!
WAIT A MINUTE! YOU'RE SURE TAKIN' A LOT FOR GRANTED!
ASK ME THE QUESTION! DON'T BE BASHFUL, MY HERO! WHISPER SWEET NOTHINGS IN MY EARS! I LOVE IT!
HEY! LISTEN! GET AWAY FROM ME! I TELL YA, I —
HOORAY! THE BRIDE AND GROOM!
SHE IS SAVED!
WE'RE GONNA HAVE A WEDDING! HERE COMES THE BRIDE!
WALT DISNEY
96

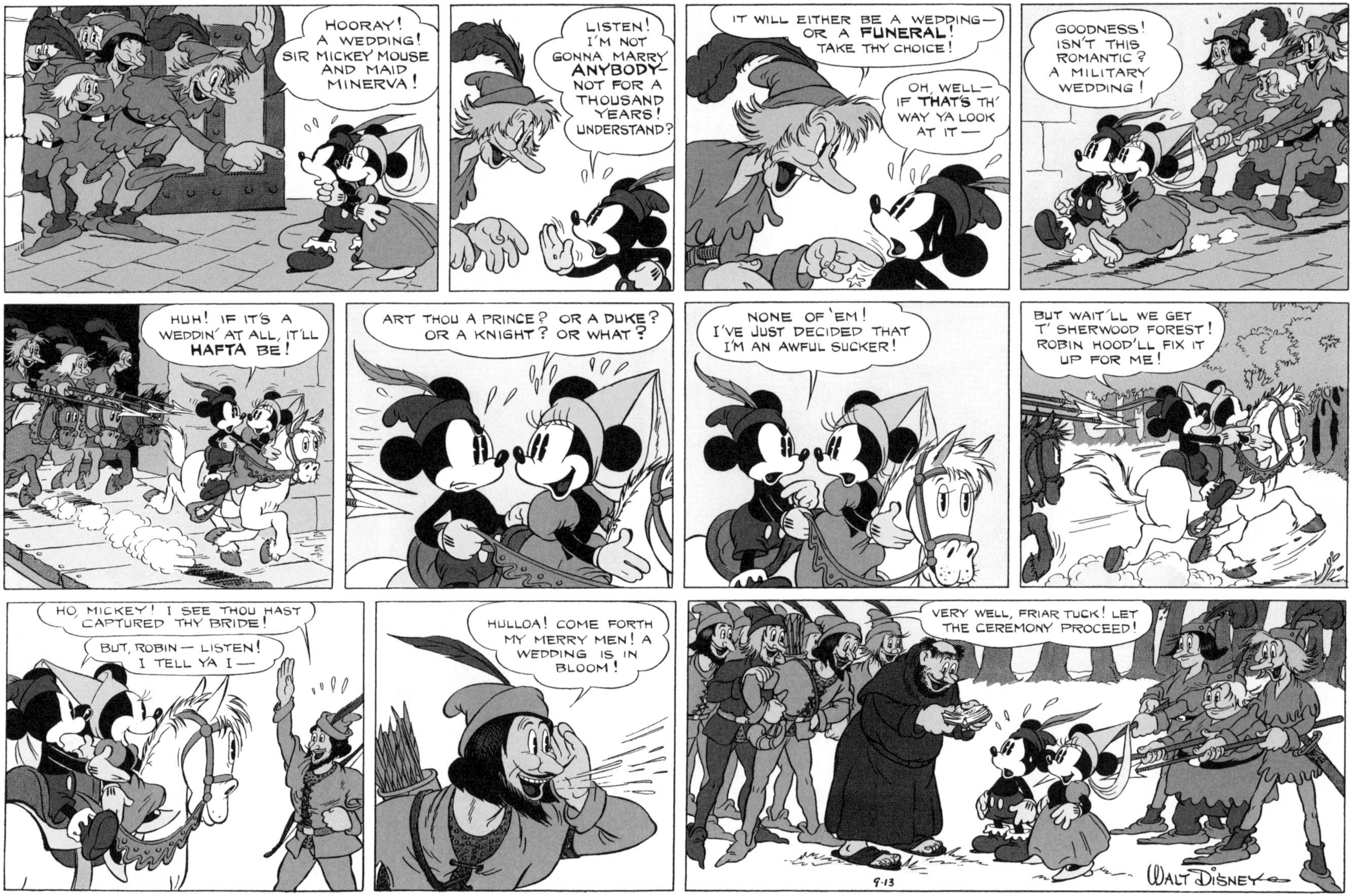
HOORAY! A WEDDING! SIR MICKEY MOUSE AND MAID MINERVA!
LISTEN! I'M NOT GONNA MARRY ANYBODY- NOT FOR A THOUSAND YEARS! UNDERSTAND?
IT WILL EITHER BE A WEDDING— OR A FUNERAL! TAKE THY CHOICE!
OH, WELL— IF THAT'S TH' WAY YA LOOK AT IT —
GOODNESS! ISN'T THIS ROMANTIC? A MILITARY WEDDING!
HUH! IF IT'S A WEDDIN' AT ALL, IT'LL HAFTA BE!
ART THOU A PRINCE? OR A DUKE? OR A KNIGHT? OR WHAT?
NONE OF 'EM! I'VE JUST DECIDED THAT I'M AN AWFUL SUCKER!
BUT WAIT'LL WE GET T' SHERWOOD FOREST! ROBIN HOOD'LL FIX IT UP FOR ME!
HO, MICKEY! I SEE THOU HAST CAPTURED THY BRIDE!
BUT, ROBIN — LISTEN! I TELL YA I —
HULLOA! COME FORTH MY MERRY MEN! A WEDDING IS IN BLOOM!
VERY WELL, FRIAR TUCK! LET THE CEREMONY PROCEED!
9-13
WALT DISNEY

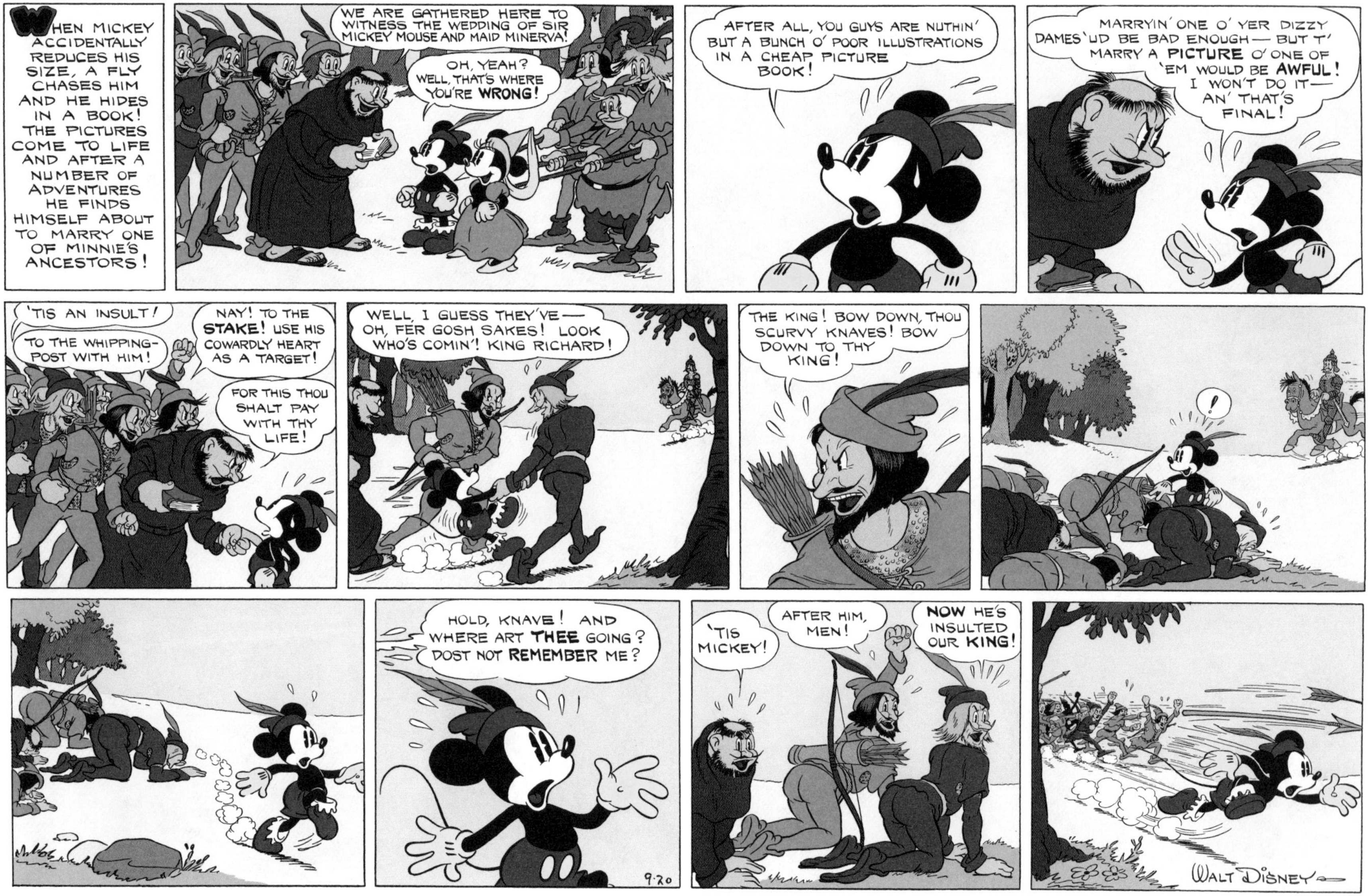
WHEN MICKEY ACCIDENTALLY REDUCES HIS SIZE, A FLY CHASES HIM AND HE HIDES IN A BOOK! THE PICTURES COME TO LIFE AND AFTER A NUMBER OF ADVENTURES HE FINDS HIMSELF ABOUT TO MARRY ONE OF MINNIE'S ANCESTORS!
WE ARE GATHERED HERE TO WITNESS THE WEDDING OF SIR MICKEY MOUSE AND MAID MINERVA!
OH, YEAH? WELL, THAT'S WHERE YOU'RE WRONG!
AFTER ALL, YOU GUYS ARE NUTHIN' BUT A BUNCH O' POOR ILLUSTRATIONS IN A CHEAP PICTURE BOOK!
MARRYIN' ONE O' YER DIZZY DAMES 'UD BE BAD ENOUGH — BUT T' MARRY A PICTURE O' ONE OF 'EM WOULD BE AWFUL! I WON'T DO IT — AN' THAT'S FINAL!
'TIS AN INSULT!
TO THE WHIPPING-POST WITH HIM!
NAY! TO THE STAKE! USE HIS COWARDLY HEART AS A TARGET!
FOR THIS THOU SHALT PAY WITH THY LIFE!
WELL, I GUESS THEY'VE — OH, FER GOSH SAKES! LOOK WHO'S COMIN'! KING RICHARD!
THE KING! BOW DOWN, THOU SCURVY KNAVES! BOW DOWN TO THY KING!
!
HOLD, KNAVE! AND WHERE ART THEE GOING? DOST NOT REMEMBER ME?
9-20
'TIS MICKEY!
AFTER HIM, MEN!
NOW HE'S INSULTED OUR KING!
WALT DISNEY

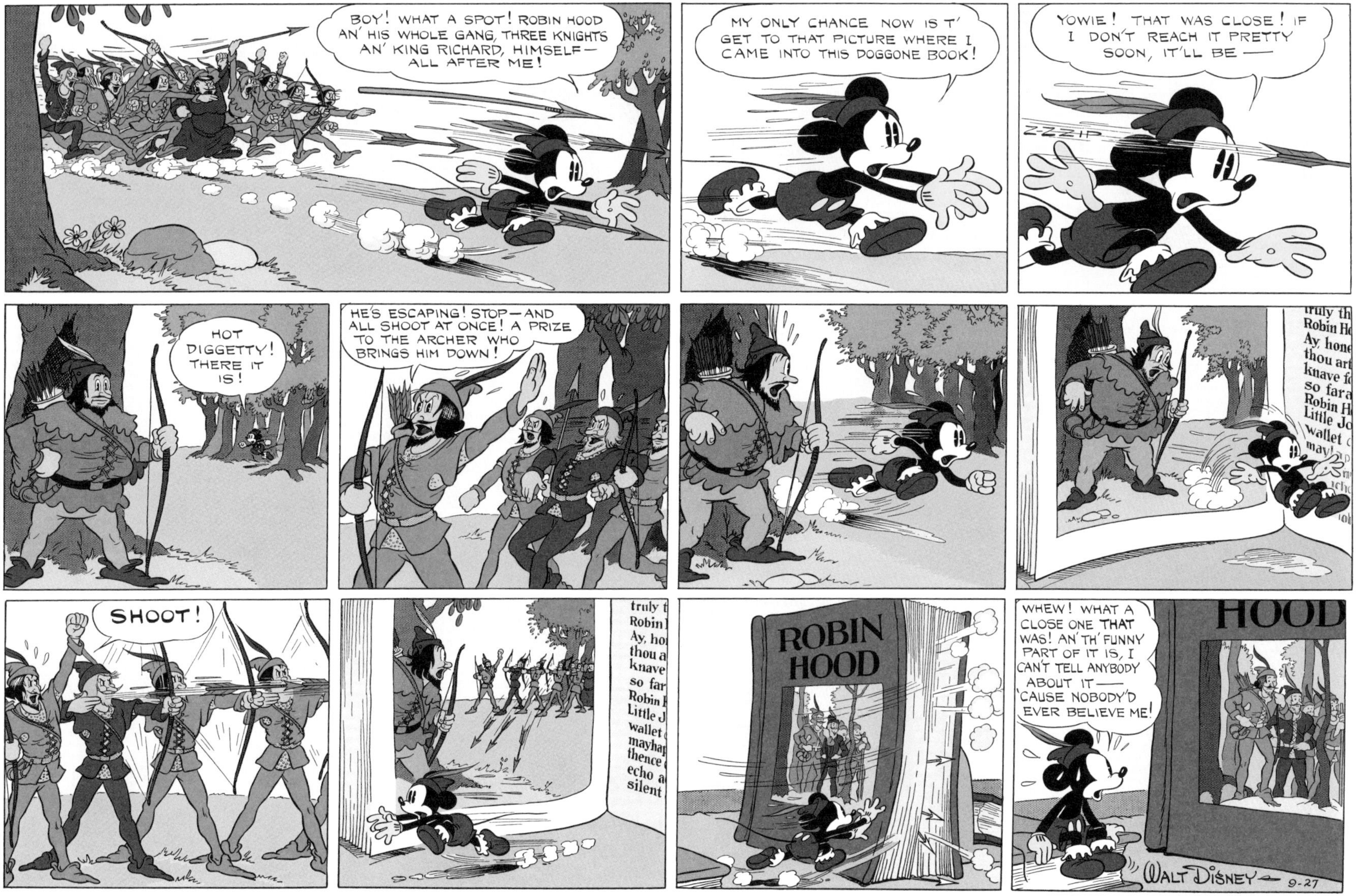
BOY! WHAT A SPOT! ROBIN HOOD AN' HIS WHOLE GANG, THREE KNIGHTS AN' KING RICHARD, HIMSELF— ALL AFTER ME!
MY ONLY CHANCE NOW IS T' GET TO THAT PICTURE WHERE I CAME INTO THIS DOGGONE BOOK!
YOWIE! THAT WAS CLOSE! IF I DON'T REACH IT PRETTY SOON, IT'LL BE —
Z-Z-ZIP
HOT DIGGETTY! THERE IT IS!
HE'S ESCAPING! STOP—AND ALL SHOOT AT ONCE! A PRIZE TO THE ARCHER WHO BRINGS HIM DOWN!
SHOOT!
ROBIN HOOD
WHEW! WHAT A CLOSE ONE THAT WAS! AN' TH' FUNNY PART OF IT IS, I CAN'T TELL ANYBODY ABOUT IT— 'CAUSE NOBODY'D EVER BELIEVE ME!
HOOD
WALT DISNEY
9-27

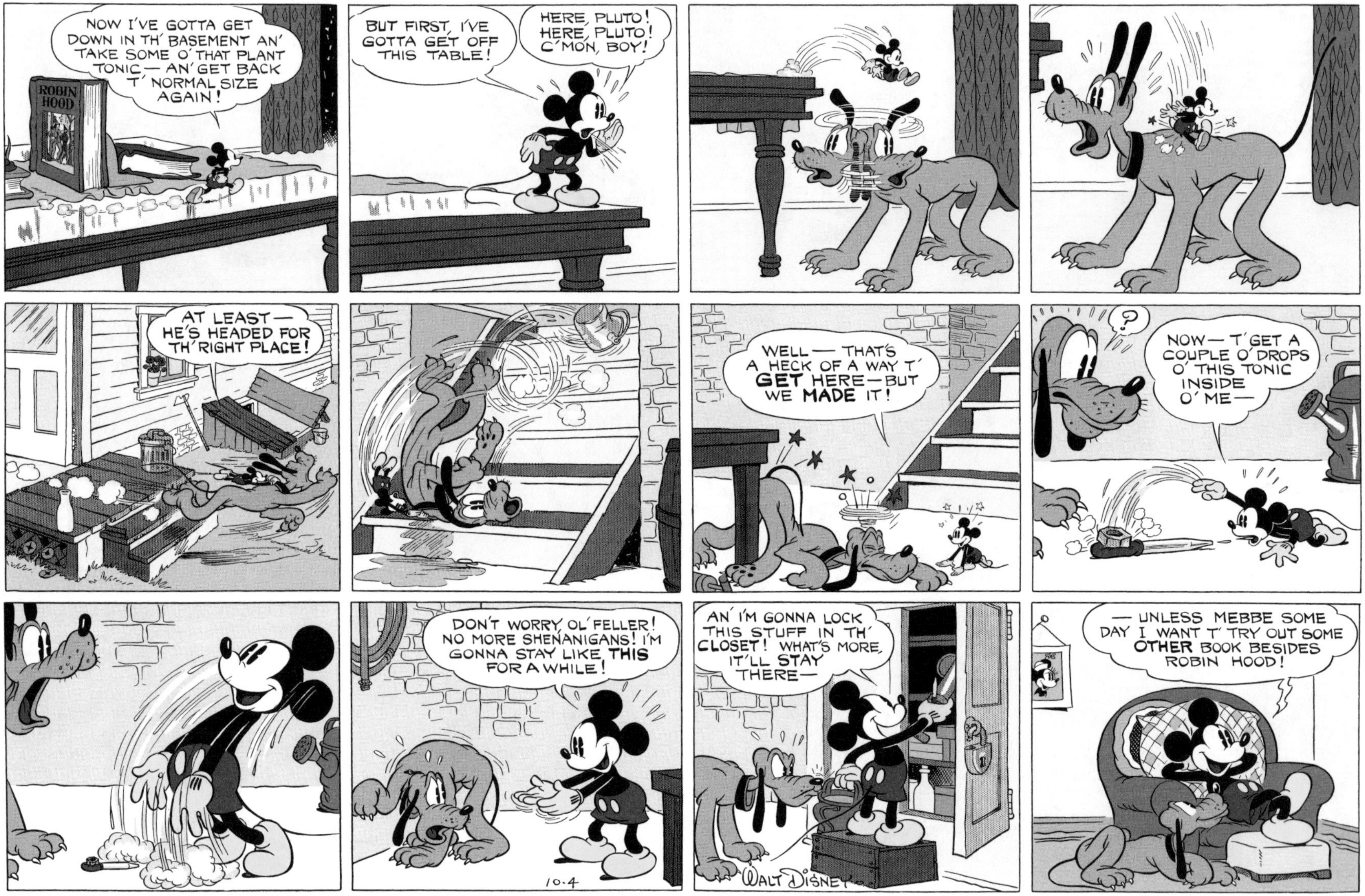
NOW I'VE GOTTA GET DOWN IN TH' BASEMENT AN' TAKE SOME O' THAT PLANT TONIC— AN' GET BACK T' NORMAL SIZE AGAIN!
ROBIN HOOD
BUT FIRST, I'VE GOTTA GET OFF THIS TABLE!
HERE, PLUTO! HERE, PLUTO! C'MON, BOY!
AT LEAST— HE'S HEADED FOR TH' RIGHT PLACE!
WELL— THAT'S A HECK OF A WAY T' GET HERE—BUT WE MADE IT!
?
NOW— T' GET A COUPLE O' DROPS O' THIS TONIC INSIDE O' ME—
DON'T WORRY, OL' FELLER! NO MORE SHENANIGANS! I'M GONNA STAY LIKE THIS FOR A WHILE!
10-4
AN' I'M GONNA LOCK THIS STUFF IN TH' CLOSET! WHAT'S MORE, IT'LL STAY THERE—
WALT DISNEY
— UNLESS MEBBE SOME DAY I WANT T' TRY OUT SOME OTHER BOOK BESIDES ROBIN HOOD!

THE VENTRILOQUIST

AND

GAG STRIPS

OCTOBER 11, 1936
–
MAY 9, 1937

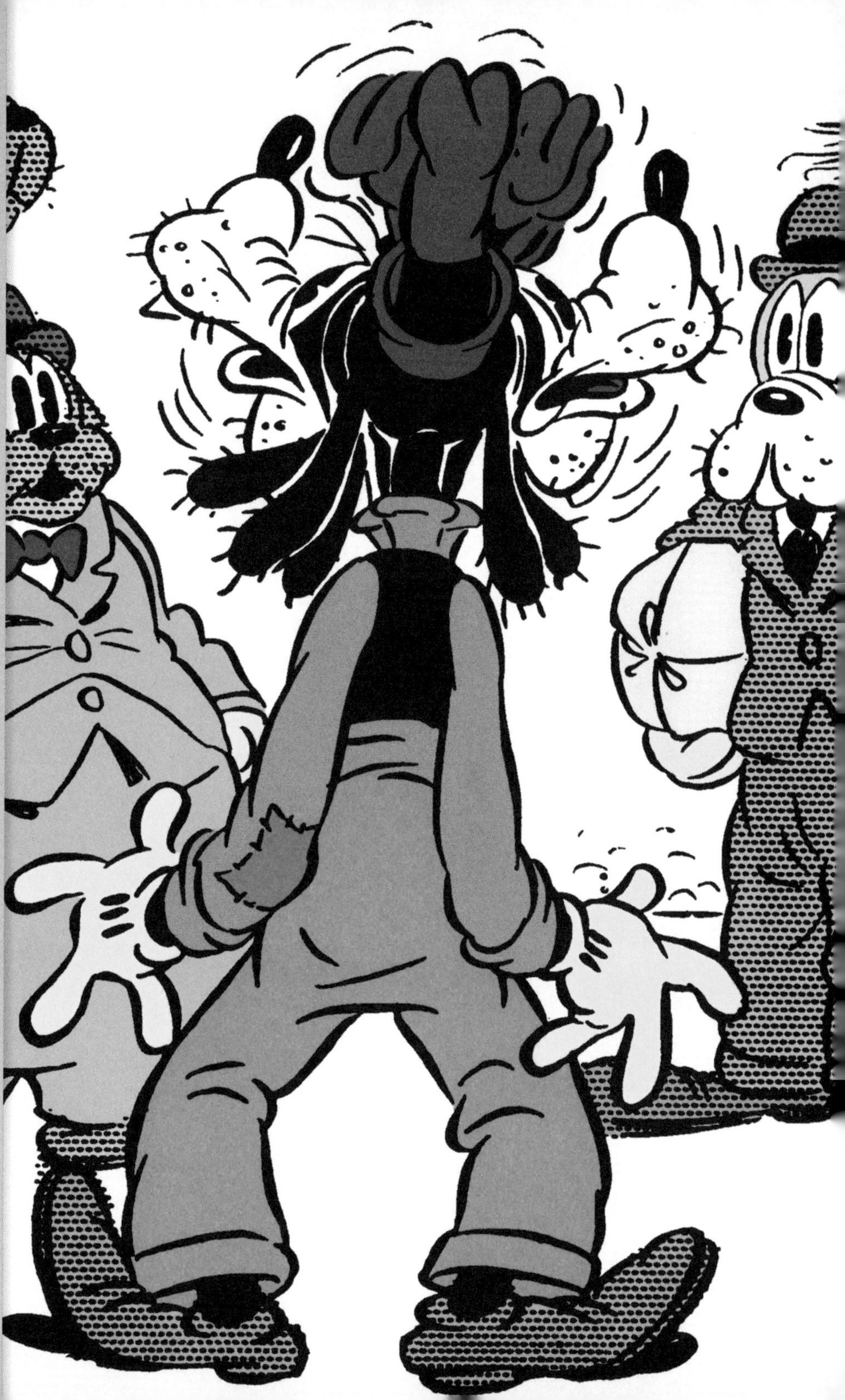

MICKEY MOUSE

REGISTERED U.S. PATENT OFFICE

GROWING UP, GROWING DOWN

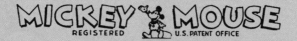

Readers of our companion daily strip series will already be familiar with Mickey's mid-1930s evolution. While the adventurous tone of the daily remained unchanged, the character of Mickey slowly grew from an impulsive boy hero into a strategizing young adult. It was a transformation much like Mickey was then experiencing on screen: the trickster who had once played music on a cow's teeth was now—increasingly often—a proper master of ceremonies. Some cartoons arguably took the trend too far, casting the Mouse as a gentrified figure: a "sissy do-gooder," as famed animator Ward Kimball remembered him.[1] Luckily, Gottfredson's adventurous dailies were free of such missteps.

What, then, of the Sundays, with their frequently more gag-oriented approach? The Sunday Mickey of 1935 had already become a bit more mature than the Sunday Mickey of 1932. His relationship with his nephews and Pluto had evolved from near-rowdiness to well-meaning big-brotherhood. In this new role, Mickey could not be quite as foolhardy or aggressive as before. But he was still an overenthusiastic, comically unlucky figure; and sometimes, still, a trickster. In "The Ventriloquist," the last Sunday serial of 1936, we find Mickey the prank-puller—Mickey the *kid*—in a series of set-pieces that might as well have emerged from the earliest days of his career.

Yet just a month after "The Ventriloquist," things begin to change. As if to back away from the focus on trickster Mickey, we find Osborne and Gottfredson moving into an unprecedented exploration of Goofy: his goofy logic, his clumsiness, and his growing ability to carry gags like never before. This is not to say Mickey is pushed offstage; early on, as we see, he even tries to prank the Goof. But in a gag format, Goofy's sheer eccentricity unavoidably moves Mickey into the straight man role: the eternal domain of the slightly-less-funny. Mickey makes a *humorous* straight man, capable of deadly snark and a hilarious flip-take—but a straight man he remains. He has slipped a notch on the comedic scale.

In the daily strip, Mickey's maturity enabled stories to take a more serious, more gripping, and more complex tone; leading, inarguably, to Gottfredson's finest string of adventures. In the Sunday strip, Mickey's maturity made an unprecedented star out of Goofy. We're sure Mickey didn't mind doing his friend the favor. [DG]

---

1 Ward Kimball, letter to Justin Knowles, March 1986.

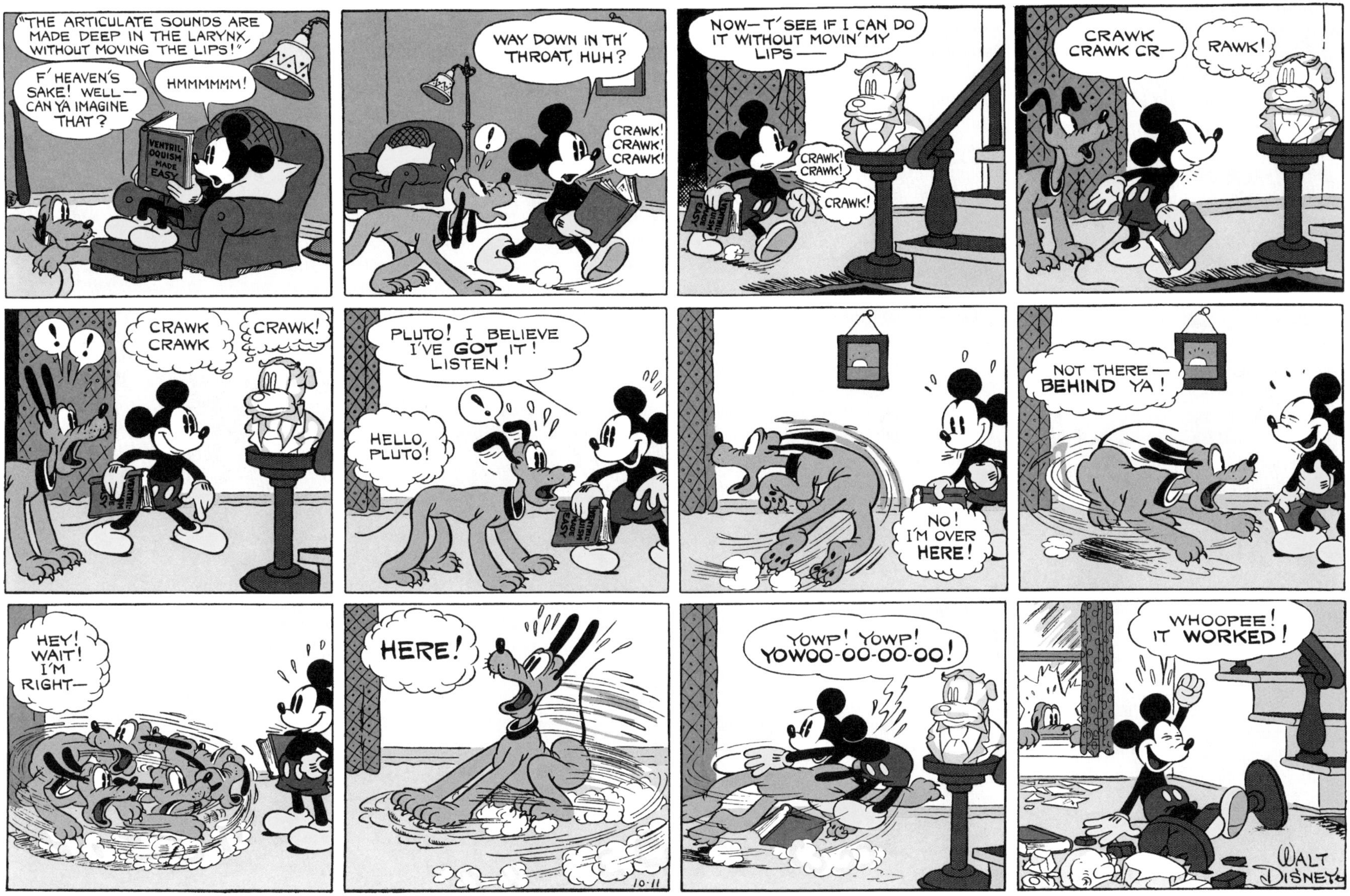
"THE ARTICULATE SOUNDS ARE MADE DEEP IN THE LARYNX, WITHOUT MOVING THE LIPS!"
F' HEAVEN'S SAKE! WELL— CAN YA IMAGINE THAT?
HMMMMMM!
VENTRILOQUISM MADE EASY
WAY DOWN IN TH' THROAT, HUH?
!
CRAWK! CRAWK! CRAWK!
NOW— T' SEE IF I CAN DO IT WITHOUT MOVIN' MY LIPS —
CRAWK! CRAWK!
CRAWK!
CRAWK CRAWK CR—
RAWK!
CRAWK CRAWK
CRAWK!
PLUTO! I BELIEVE I'VE **GOT** IT! LISTEN!
!
HELLO, PLUTO!
NO! I'M OVER **HERE**!
NOT THERE— **BEHIND** YA!
HEY! WAIT! I'M RIGHT—
HERE!
10-11
YOWP! YOWP! YOWOO-OO-OO-OO!
WHOOPEE! IT **WORKED**!
WALT DISNEY

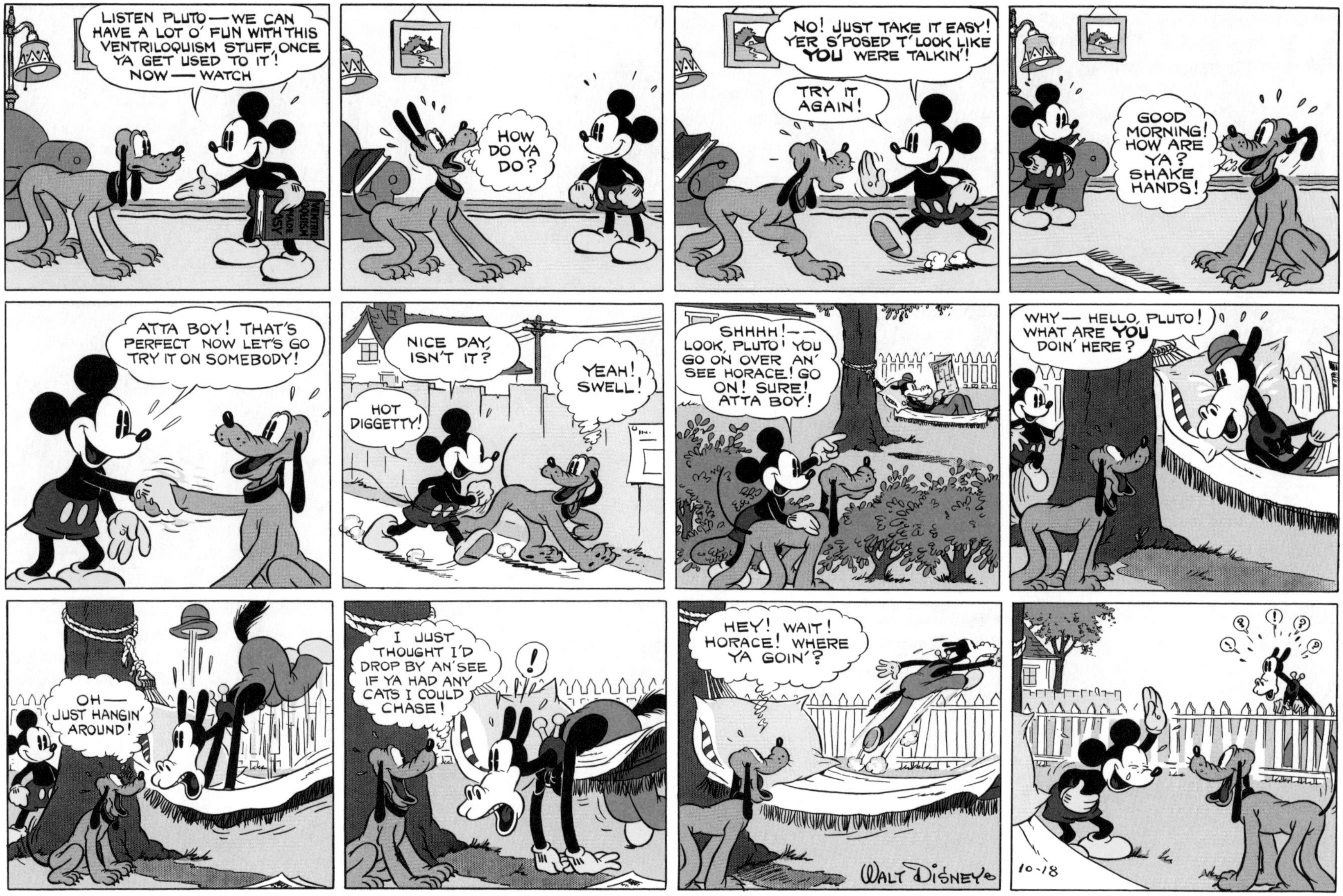

LISTEN PLUTO — WE CAN HAVE A LOT O' FUN WITH THIS VENTRILOQUISM STUFF, ONCE YA GET USED TO IT! NOW — WATCH
HOW DO YA DO?
NO! JUST TAKE IT EASY! YER S'POSED T' LOOK LIKE YOU WERE TALKIN'!
TRY IT AGAIN!
GOOD MORNING! HOW ARE YA? SHAKE HANDS!
ATTA BOY! THAT'S PERFECT NOW LET'S GO TRY IT ON SOMEBODY!
NICE DAY, ISN'T IT?
HOT DIGGETTY!
YEAH! SWELL!
SHHHH!-- LOOK, PLUTO! YOU GO ON OVER AN' SEE HORACE! GO ON! SURE! ATTA BOY!
WHY — HELLO, PLUTO! WHAT ARE YOU DOIN' HERE?
OH — JUST HANGIN' AROUND!
I JUST THOUGHT I'D DROP BY AN' SEE IF YA HAD ANY CATS I COULD CHASE!
HEY! WAIT! HORACE! WHERE YA GOIN'?
WALT DISNEY
10-18

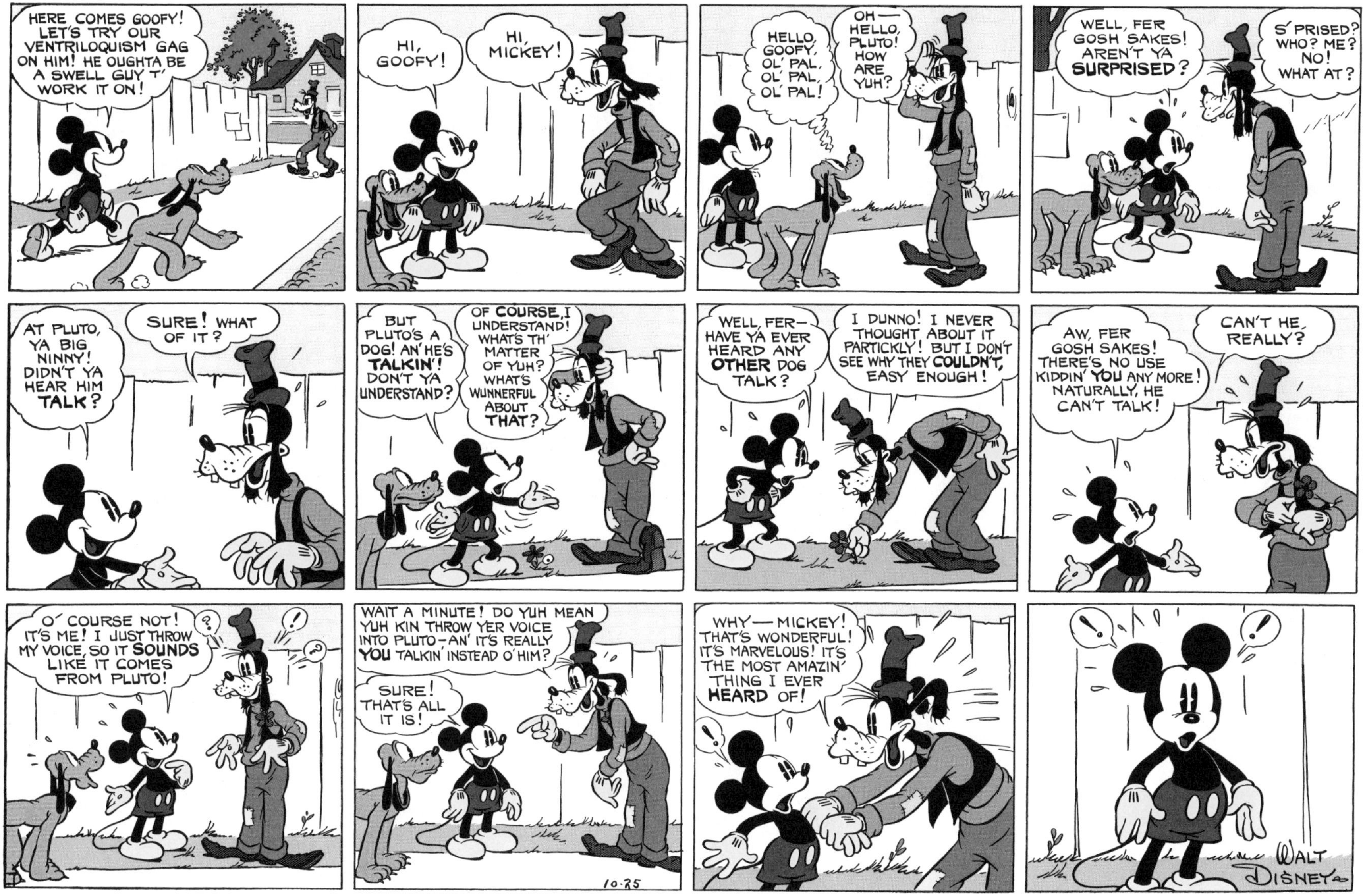
HERE COMES GOOFY! LET'S TRY OUR VENTRILOQUISM GAG ON HIM! HE OUGHTA BE A SWELL GUY T' WORK IT ON!
HI, GOOFY!
HI, MICKEY!
HELLO, GOOFY, OL' PAL, OL' PAL, OL' PAL!
OH— HELLO, PLUTO! HOW ARE YUH?
WELL, FER GOSH SAKES! AREN'T YA SURPRISED?
S'PRISED? WHO? ME? NO! WHAT AT?
AT PLUTO, YA BIG NINNY! DIDN'T YA HEAR HIM TALK?
SURE! WHAT OF IT?
BUT PLUTO'S A DOG! AN' HE'S TALKIN'! DON'T YA UNDERSTAND?
OF COURSE, I UNDERSTAND! WHAT'S TH' MATTER OF YUH? WHAT'S WUNNERFUL ABOUT THAT?
WELL, FER— HAVE YA EVER HEARD ANY OTHER DOG TALK?
I DUNNO! I NEVER THOUGHT ABOUT IT PARTICKLY! BUT I DON'T SEE WHY THEY COULDN'T, EASY ENOUGH!
AW, FER GOSH SAKES! THERE'S NO USE KIDDIN' YOU ANY MORE! NATURALLY, HE CAN'T TALK!
CAN'T HE, REALLY?
O' COURSE NOT! IT'S ME! I JUST THROW MY VOICE, SO IT SOUNDS LIKE IT COMES FROM PLUTO!
WAIT A MINUTE! DO YUH MEAN YUH KIN THROW YER VOICE INTO PLUTO—AN' IT'S REALLY YOU TALKIN' INSTEAD O' HIM?
SURE! THAT'S ALL IT IS!
10-25
WHY—MICKEY! THAT'S WONDERFUL! IT'S MARVELOUS! IT'S THE MOST AMAZIN' THING I EVER HEARD OF!
WALT DISNEY

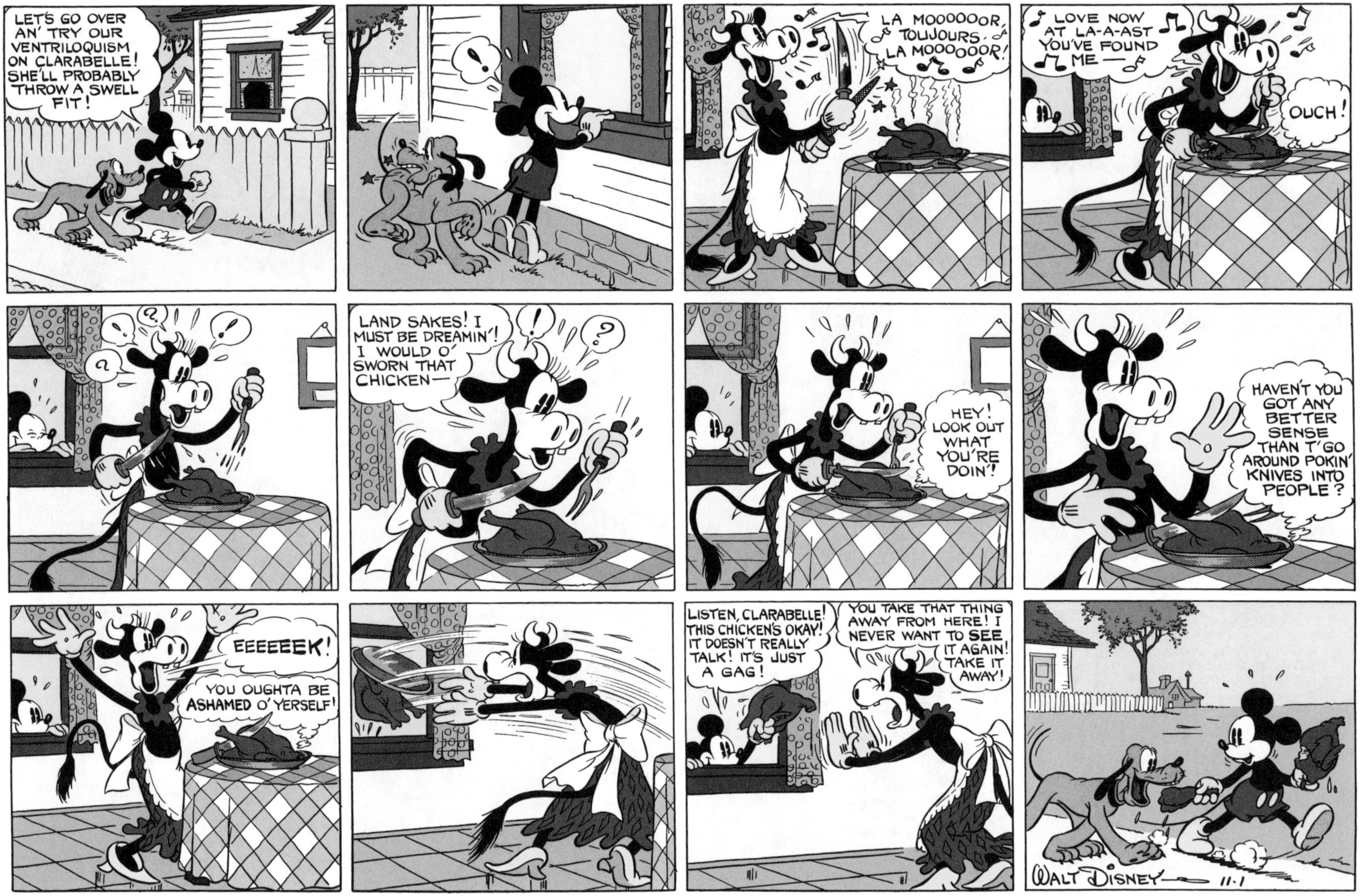

LET'S GO OVER AN' TRY OUR VENTRILOQUISM ON CLARABELLE! SHE'LL PROBABLY THROW A SWELL FIT!
!
LA MOOOOOOR, TOUJOURS, LA MOOOOOOR!
LOVE NOW AT LA-A-AST YOU'VE FOUND ME —
OUCH!
?
!
?
!
LAND SAKES! I MUST BE DREAMIN'! I WOULD O' SWORN THAT CHICKEN—
!
?
HEY! LOOK OUT WHAT YOU'RE DOIN'!
HAVEN'T YOU GOT ANY BETTER SENSE THAN T' GO AROUND POKIN' KNIVES INTO PEOPLE?
EEEEEEK!
YOU OUGHTA BE ASHAMED O' YERSELF!
LISTEN, CLARABELLE! THIS CHICKEN'S OKAY! IT DOESN'T REALLY TALK! IT'S JUST A GAG!
YOU TAKE THAT THING AWAY FROM HERE! I NEVER WANT TO SEE IT AGAIN! TAKE IT AWAY!
WALT DISNEY 11·1

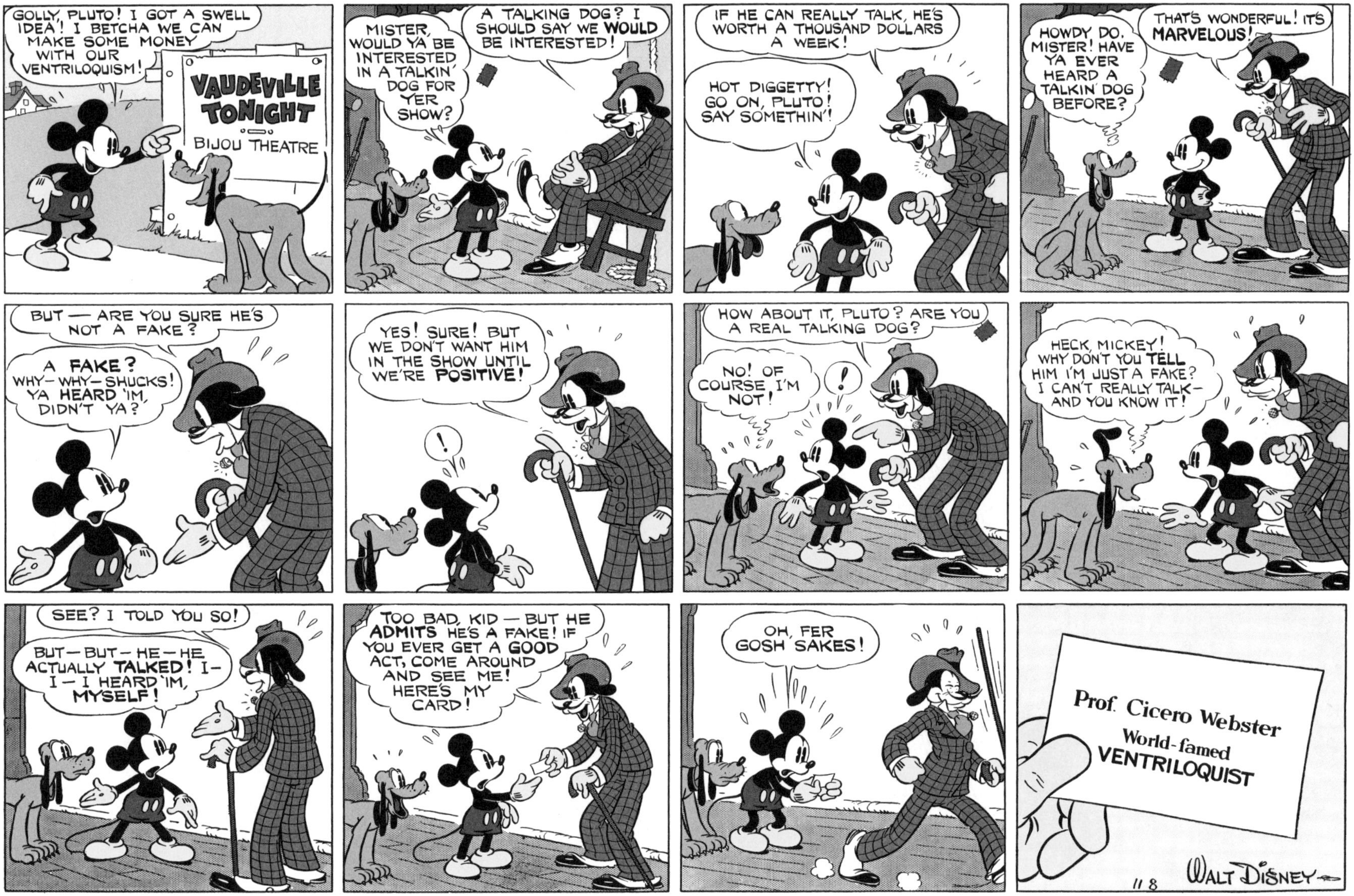
GOLLY, PLUTO! I GOT A SWELL IDEA! I BETCHA WE CAN MAKE SOME MONEY WITH OUR VENTRILOQUISM!
VAUDEVILLE TONIGHT
BIJOU THEATRE
MISTER, WOULD YA BE INTERESTED IN A TALKIN' DOG FOR YER SHOW?
A TALKING DOG? I SHOULD SAY WE WOULD BE INTERESTED!
IF HE CAN REALLY TALK, HE'S WORTH A THOUSAND DOLLARS A WEEK!
HOT DIGGETTY! GO ON, PLUTO! SAY SOMETHIN'!
HOWDY DO, MISTER! HAVE YA EVER HEARD A TALKIN' DOG BEFORE?
THAT'S WONDERFUL! IT'S MARVELOUS!
BUT — ARE YOU SURE HE'S NOT A FAKE?
A FAKE? WHY— WHY— SHUCKS! YA HEARD 'IM, DIDN'T YA?
YES! SURE! BUT WE DON'T WANT HIM IN THE SHOW UNTIL WE'RE POSITIVE!
!
HOW ABOUT IT, PLUTO? ARE YOU A REAL TALKING DOG?
NO! OF COURSE, I'M NOT!
!
HECK, MICKEY! WHY DON'T YOU TELL HIM I'M JUST A FAKE? I CAN'T REALLY TALK— AND YOU KNOW IT!
SEE? I TOLD YOU SO!
BUT— BUT— HE— HE ACTUALLY TALKED! I— I— I HEARD 'IM, MYSELF!
TOO BAD, KID — BUT HE ADMITS HE'S A FAKE! IF YOU EVER GET A GOOD ACT, COME AROUND AND SEE ME! HERE'S MY CARD!
OH, FER GOSH SAKES!
Prof. Cicero Webster
World-famed
VENTRILOQUIST
11 8
WALT DISNEY

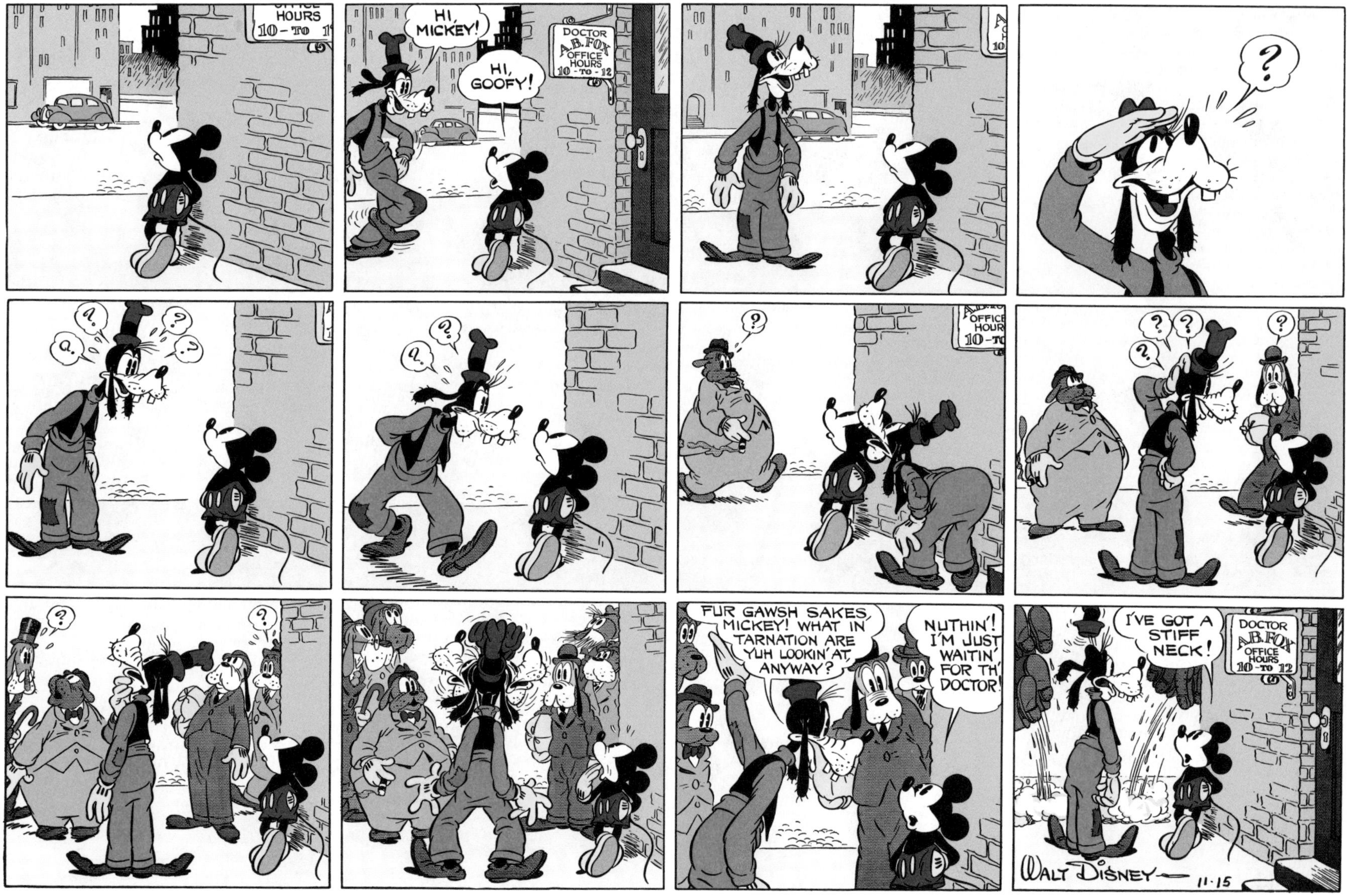
OFFICE
HOURS
10 - TO 1
HI,
MICKEY!
HI,
GOOFY!
DOCTOR
A.B. FOX
OFFICE
HOURS
10 - TO - 12
?
?
?
?
?
?
?
?
?
?
?
?
OFFICE
HOURS
10 - TO
?
?
FUR GAWSH SAKES,
MICKEY! WHAT IN
TARNATION ARE
YUH LOOKIN' AT,
ANYWAY?
NUTHIN'!
I'M JUST
WAITIN'
FOR TH'
DOCTOR!
I'VE GOT A
STIFF
NECK!
DOCTOR
A.B. FOX
OFFICE
HOURS
10 - TO 12
WALT DISNEY
11.15

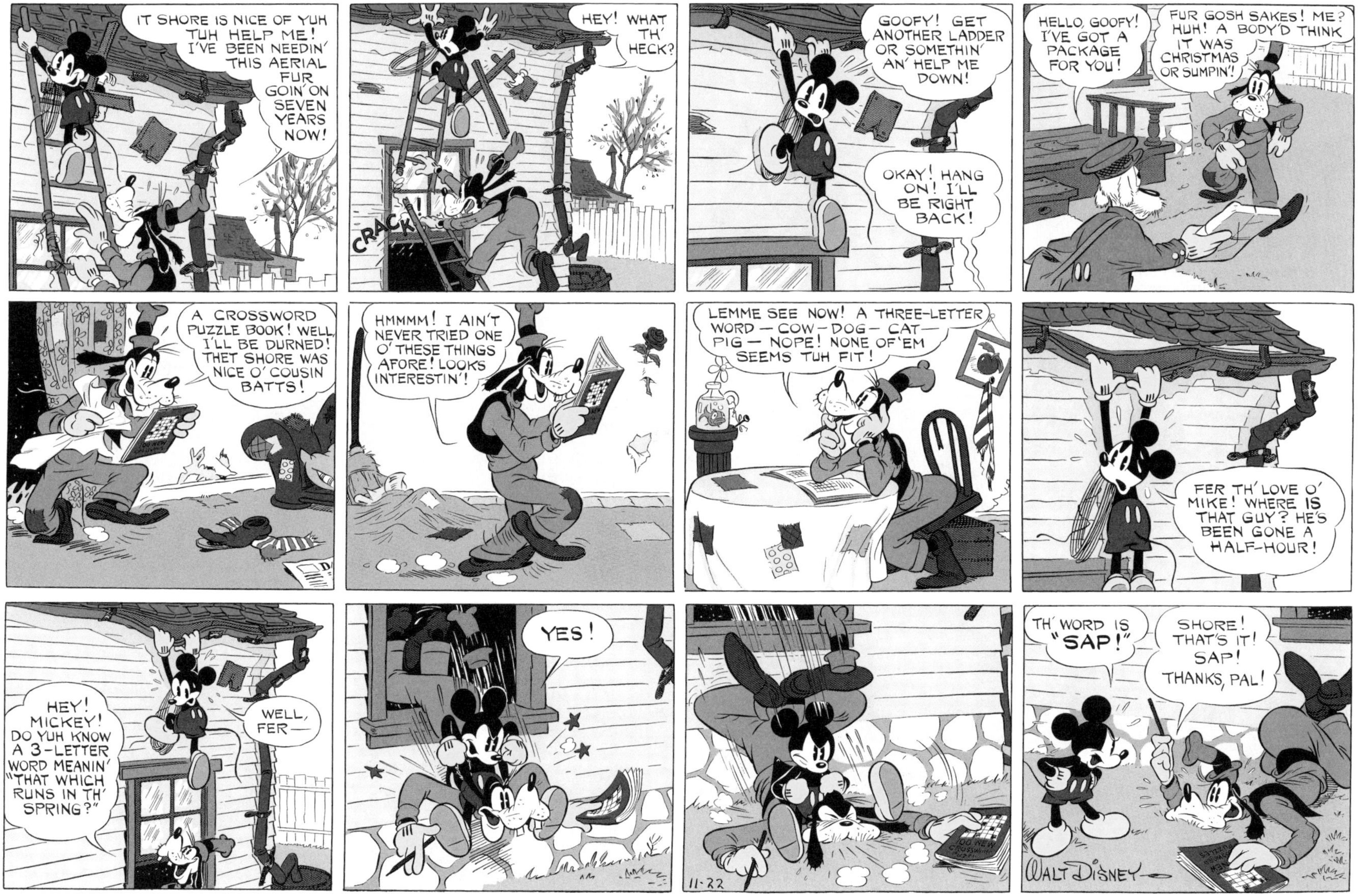
IT SHORE IS NICE OF YUH TUH HELP ME! I'VE BEEN NEEDIN' THIS AERIAL FUR GOIN' ON SEVEN YEARS NOW!
HEY! WHAT TH' HECK?
CRACK!
GOOFY! GET ANOTHER LADDER OR SOMETHIN' AN' HELP ME DOWN!
OKAY! HANG ON! I'LL BE RIGHT BACK!
HELLO, GOOFY! I'VE GOT A PACKAGE FOR YOU!
FUR GOSH SAKES! ME? HUH! A BODY'D THINK IT WAS CHRISTMAS OR SUMPIN'!
A CROSSWORD PUZZLE BOOK! WELL, I'LL BE DURNED! THET SHORE WAS NICE O' COUSIN BATTS!
HMMMM! I AIN'T NEVER TRIED ONE O' THESE THINGS AFORE! LOOKS INTERESTIN'!
LEMME SEE NOW! A THREE-LETTER WORD — COW — DOG — CAT — PIG — NOPE! NONE OF 'EM SEEMS TUH FIT!
FER TH' LOVE O' MIKE! WHERE IS THAT GUY? HE'S BEEN GONE A HALF-HOUR!
HEY! MICKEY! DO YUH KNOW A 3-LETTER WORD MEANIN' "THAT WHICH RUNS IN TH' SPRING?"
WELL, FER—
YES!
11-22
TH' WORD IS "SAP!"
SHORE! THAT'S IT! SAP! THANKS, PAL!
WALT DISNEY

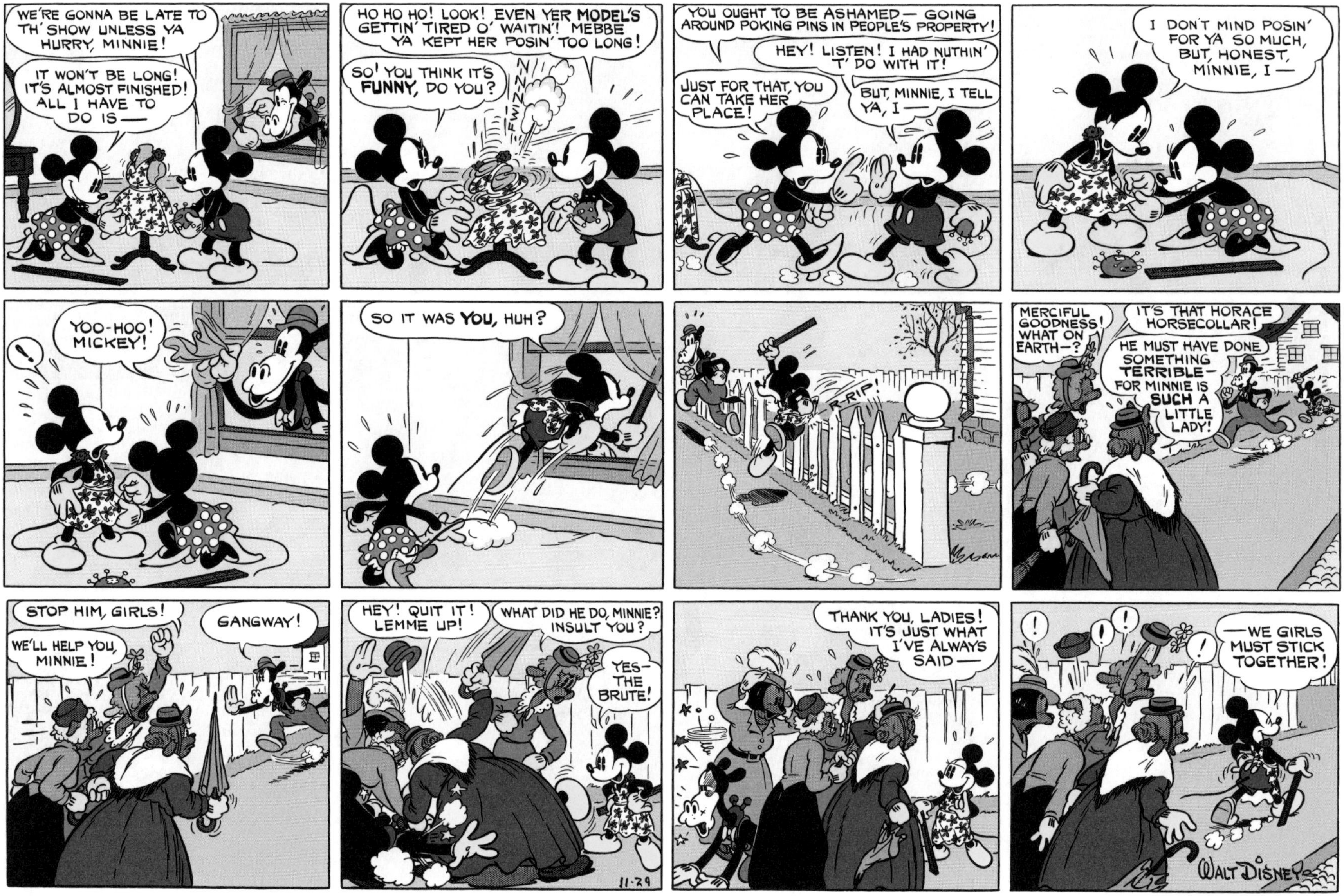

WE'RE GONNA BE LATE TO TH' SHOW UNLESS YA HURRY, MINNIE!
IT WON'T BE LONG! IT'S ALMOST FINISHED! ALL I HAVE TO DO IS—
HO HO HO! LOOK! EVEN YER MODEL'S GETTIN' TIRED O' WAITIN'! MEBBE YA KEPT HER POSIN' TOO LONG!
SO! YOU THINK IT'S FUNNY, DO YOU?
YOU OUGHT TO BE ASHAMED— GOING AROUND POKING PINS IN PEOPLE'S PROPERTY!
HEY! LISTEN! I HAD NUTHIN' T' DO WITH IT!
JUST FOR THAT, YOU CAN TAKE HER PLACE!
BUT, MINNIE, I TELL YA, I—
I DON'T MIND POSIN' FOR YA SO MUCH, BUT, HONEST, MINNIE, I—
!
YOO-HOO! MICKEY!
SO IT WAS YOU, HUH?
R-RIP!
MERCIFUL GOODNESS! WHAT ON EARTH—?
IT'S THAT HORACE HORSECOLLAR!
HE MUST HAVE DONE SOMETHING TERRIBLE— FOR MINNIE IS SUCH A LITTLE LADY!
STOP HIM, GIRLS!
WE'LL HELP YOU, MINNIE!
GANGWAY!
HEY! QUIT IT! LEMME UP!
WHAT DID HE DO, MINNIE? INSULT YOU?
YES—THE BRUTE!
11-29
THANK YOU, LADIES! IT'S JUST WHAT I'VE ALWAYS SAID—
!
!
!
!
—WE GIRLS MUST STICK TOGETHER!
WALT DISNEY

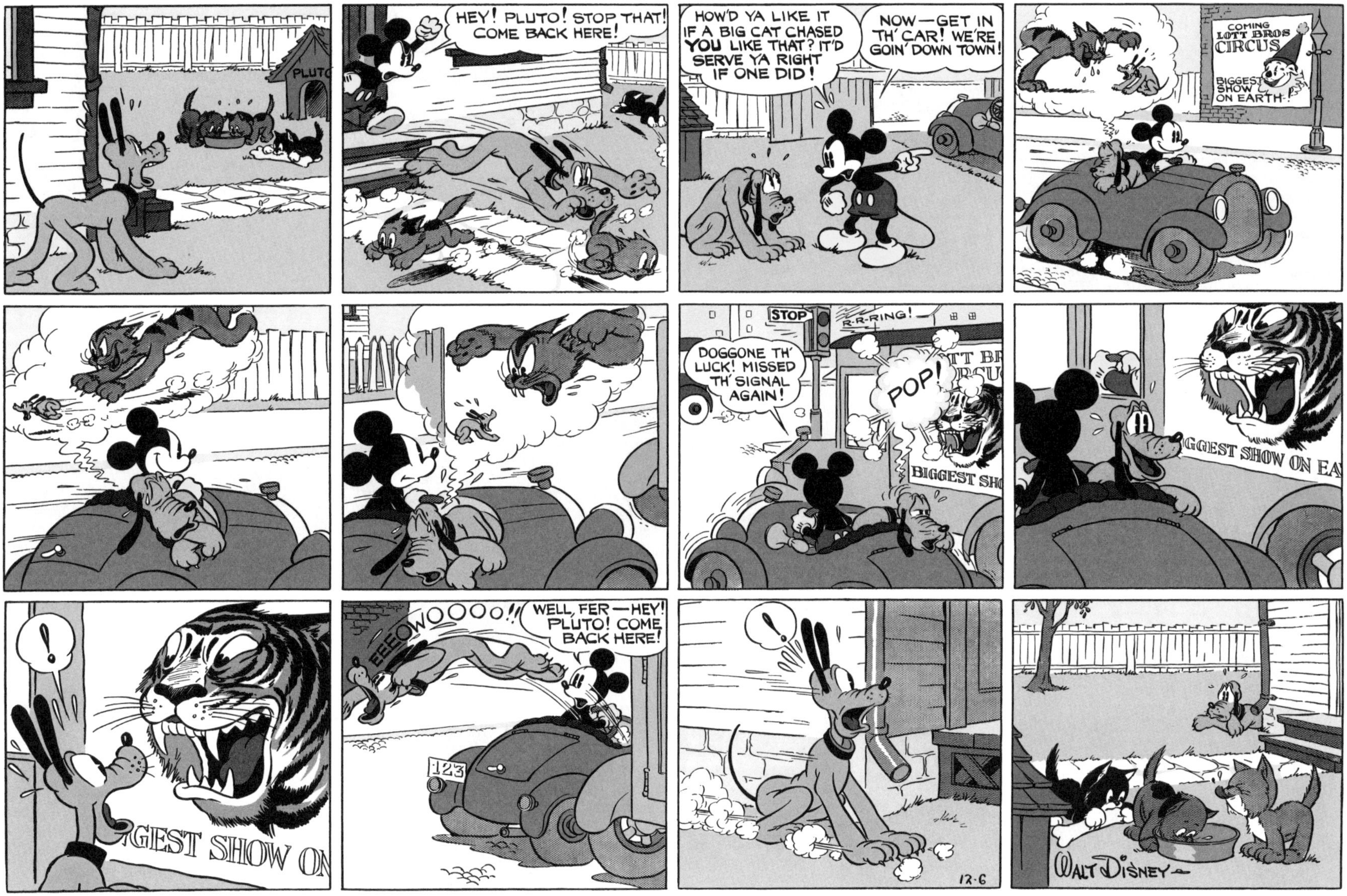
PLUTO
HEY! PLUTO! STOP THAT! COME BACK HERE!
HOW'D YA LIKE IT IF A BIG CAT CHASED YOU LIKE THAT? IT'D SERVE YA RIGHT IF ONE DID!
NOW—GET IN TH' CAR! WE'RE GOIN' DOWN TOWN!
COMING LOTT BROS CIRCUS
BIGGEST SHOW ON EARTH
STOP
R-R-RING!
DOGGONE TH' LUCK! MISSED TH' SIGNAL AGAIN!
POP!
BIGGEST SHO
GGEST SHOW ON EA
!
GEST SHOW ON
EEEOWOOOOo!!
WELL, FER—HEY! PLUTO! COME BACK HERE!
123
!
12-6
WALT DISNEY

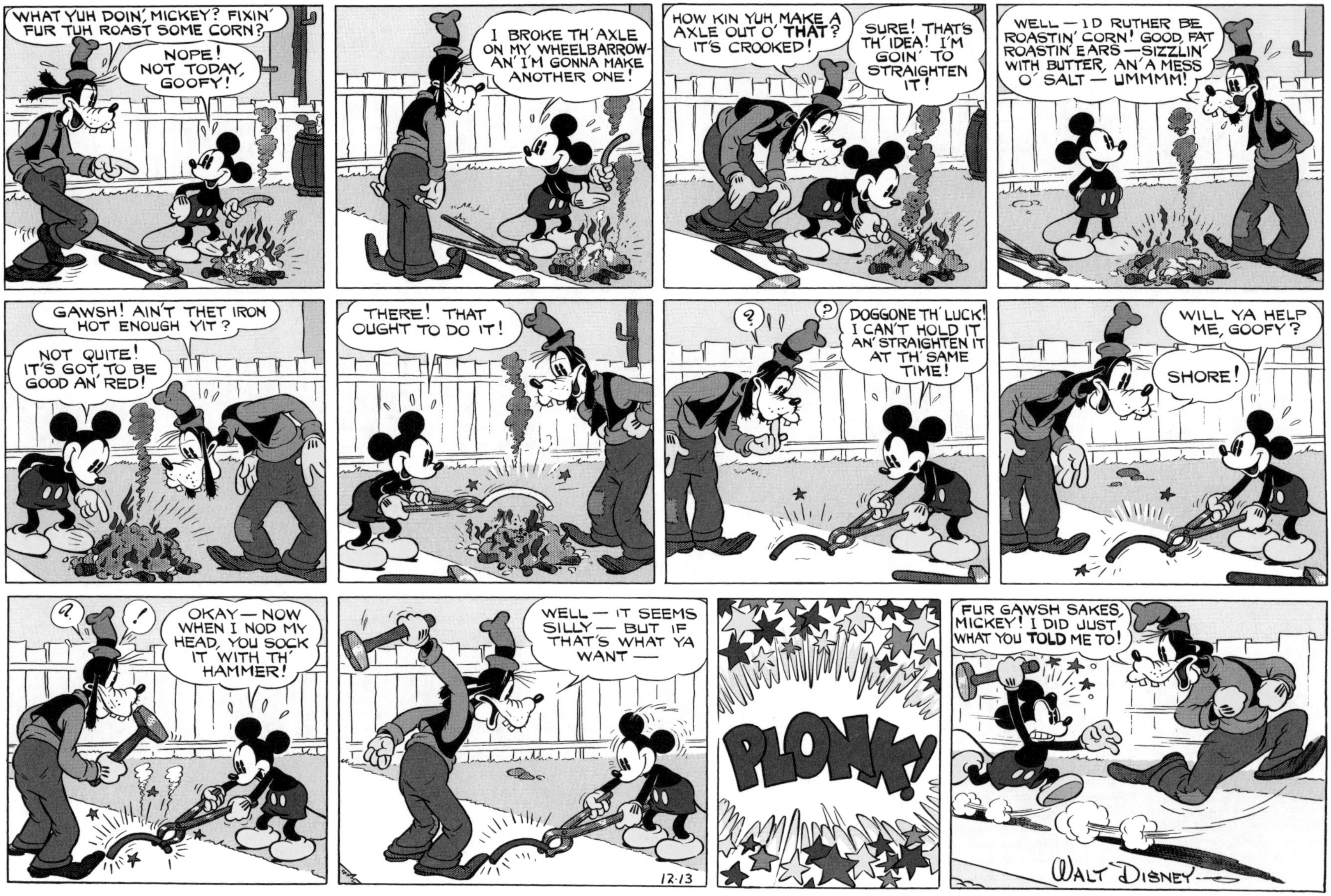

WHAT YUH DOIN', MICKEY? FIXIN' FUR TUH ROAST SOME CORN?
NOPE! NOT TODAY, GOOFY!
I BROKE TH' AXLE ON MY WHEELBARROW-AN' I'M GONNA MAKE ANOTHER ONE!
HOW KIN YUH MAKE A AXLE OUT O' **THAT**? IT'S CROOKED!
SURE! THAT'S TH' IDEA! I'M GOIN' TO STRAIGHTEN IT!
WELL — I'D RUTHER BE ROASTIN' CORN! GOOD, FAT ROASTIN' EARS — SIZZLIN' WITH BUTTER, AN' A MESS O' SALT — UMMMM!
GAWSH! AIN'T THET IRON HOT ENOUGH YIT?
NOT QUITE! IT'S GOT TO BE GOOD AN' RED!
THERE! THAT OUGHT TO DO IT!
?
?
DOGGONE TH' LUCK! I CAN'T HOLD IT AN' STRAIGHTEN IT AT TH' SAME TIME!
WILL YA HELP ME, GOOFY?
SHORE!
?
!
OKAY — NOW WHEN I NOD MY HEAD, YOU SOCK IT WITH TH' HAMMER!
WELL — IT SEEMS SILLY — BUT IF THAT'S WHAT YA WANT —
12-13
PLONK!
FUR GAWSH SAKES, MICKEY! I DID JUST WHAT YOU **TOLD** ME TO!
WALT DISNEY

72. GOOFY DID A BANG-UP JOB

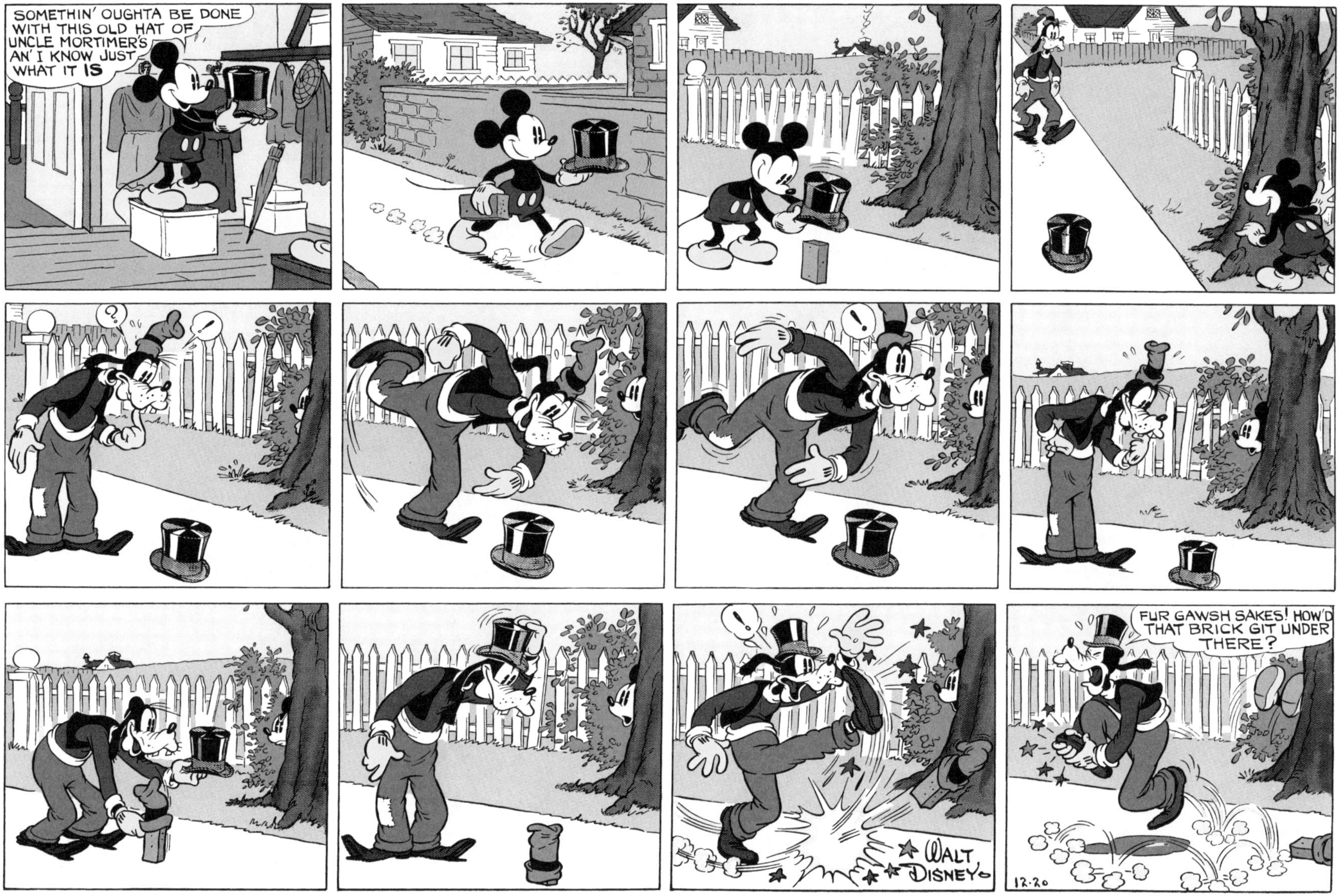
SOMETHIN' OUGHTA BE DONE WITH THIS OLD HAT OF UNCLE MORTIMER'S AN' I KNOW JUST WHAT IT IS
?
!
!
!
FUR GAWSH SAKES! HOW'D THAT BRICK GIT UNDER THERE?
WALT DISNEY
12-20

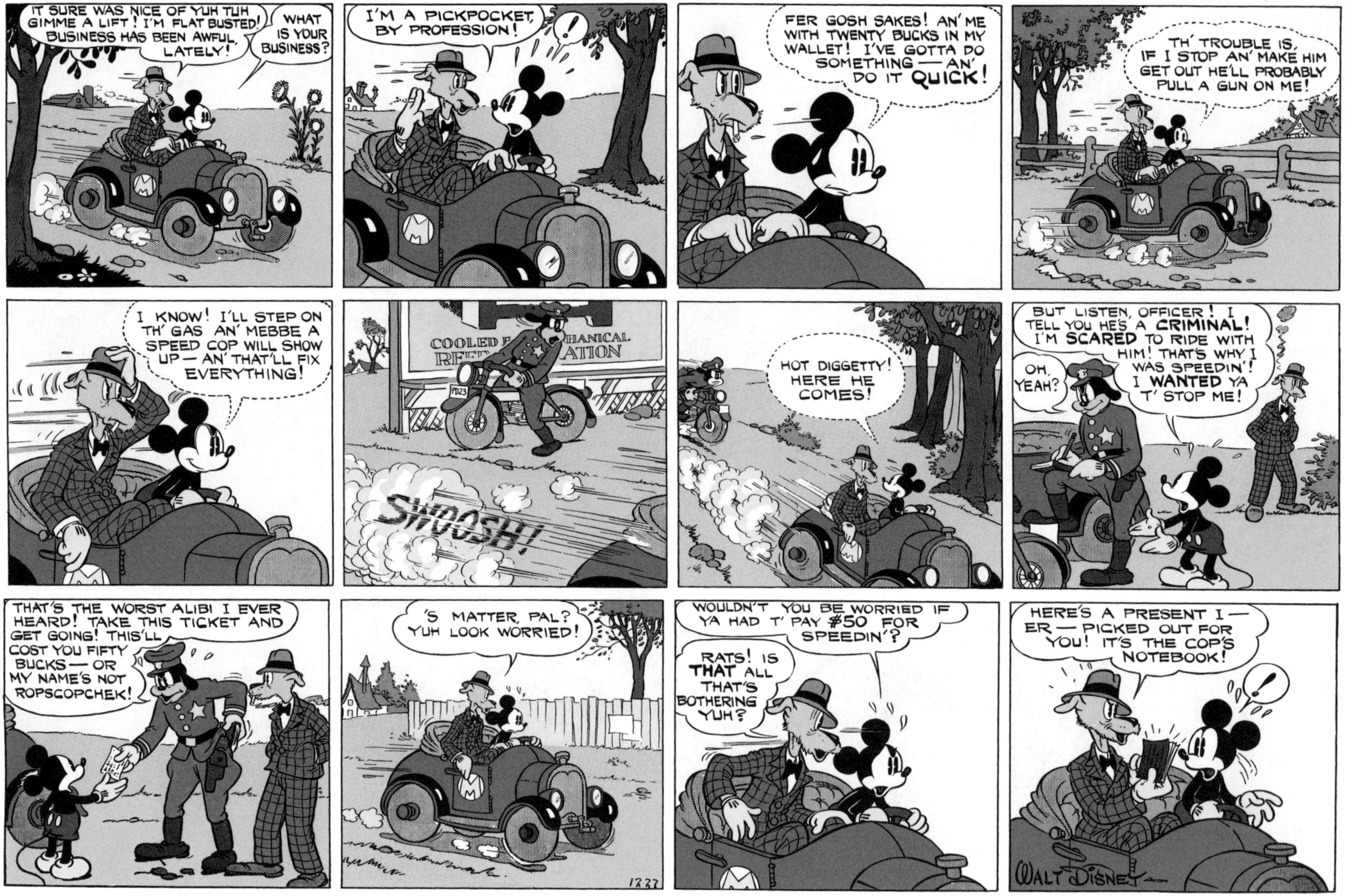

IT SURE WAS NICE OF YUH TUH GIMME A LIFT! I'M FLAT BUSTED! BUSINESS HAS BEEN AWFUL, LATELY!
WHAT IS YOUR BUSINESS?
I'M A PICKPOCKET, BY PROFESSION!
!
FER GOSH SAKES! AN' ME WITH TWENTY BUCKS IN MY WALLET! I'VE GOTTA DO SOMETHING — AN' DO IT QUICK!
TH' TROUBLE IS, IF I STOP AN' MAKE HIM GET OUT HE'LL PROBABLY PULL A GUN ON ME!
I KNOW! I'LL STEP ON TH' GAS AN' MEBBE A SPEED COP WILL SHOW UP — AN' THAT'LL FIX EVERYTHING!
PD23
SWOOSH!
HOT DIGGETTY! HERE HE COMES!
BUT LISTEN, OFFICER! I TELL YOU HE'S A CRIMINAL! I'M SCARED TO RIDE WITH HIM! THAT'S WHY I WAS SPEEDIN'! I WANTED YA T' STOP ME!
OH, YEAH?
THAT'S THE WORST ALIBI I EVER HEARD! TAKE THIS TICKET AND GET GOING! THIS'LL COST YOU FIFTY BUCKS — OR MY NAME'S NOT ROPSCOPCHEK!
'S MATTER, PAL? YUH LOOK WORRIED!
WOULDN'T YOU BE WORRIED IF YA HAD T' PAY $50 FOR SPEEDIN'?
RATS! IS THAT ALL THAT'S BOTHERING YUH?
HERE'S A PRESENT I — ER — PICKED OUT FOR YOU! IT'S THE COP'S NOTEBOOK!
!
WALT DISNEY

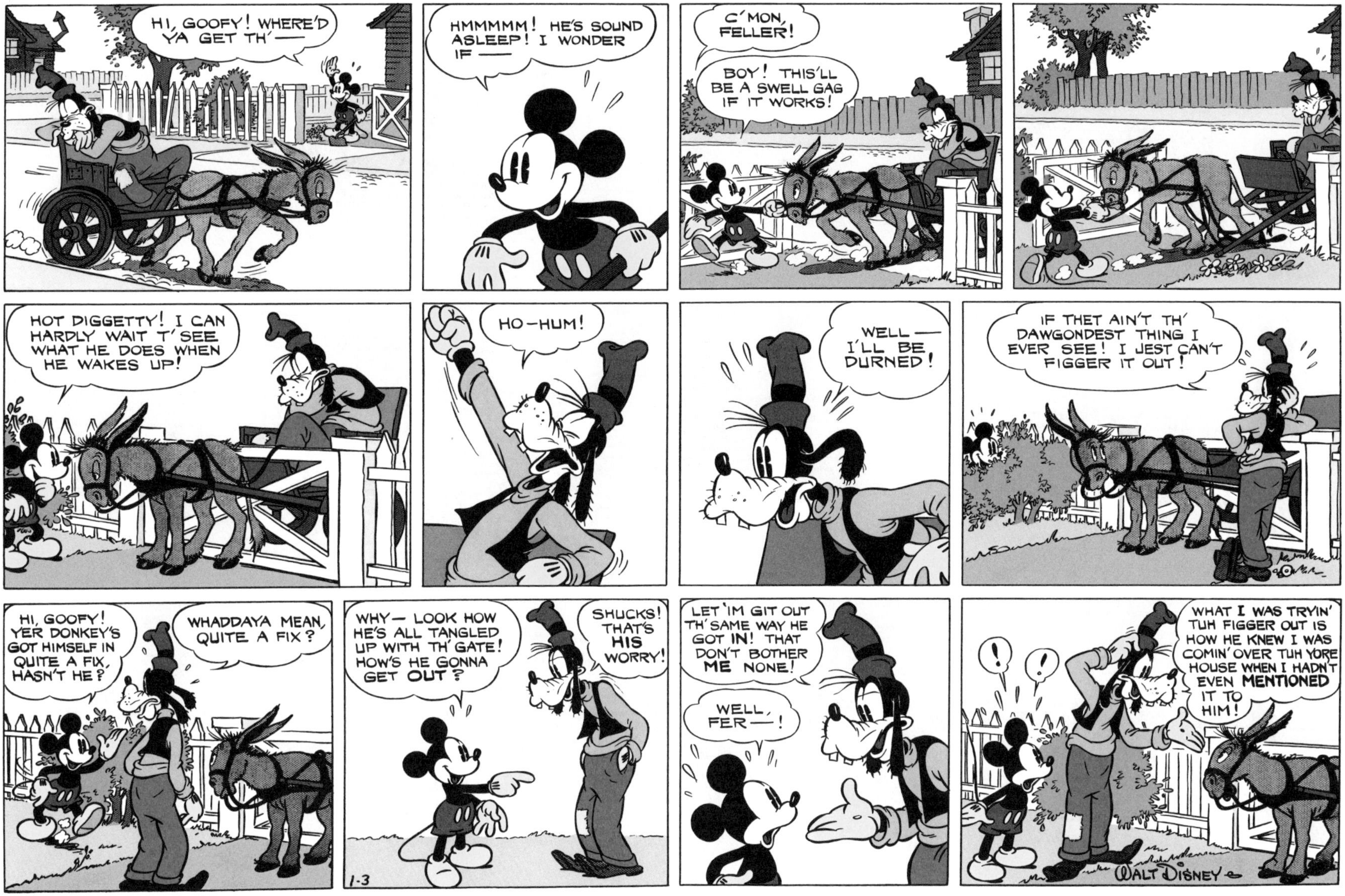
HI, GOOFY! WHERE'D YA GET TH'—
HMMMMM! HE'S SOUND ASLEEP! I WONDER IF—
C'MON, FELLER!
BOY! THIS'LL BE A SWELL GAG IF IT WORKS!
HOT DIGGETTY! I CAN HARDLY WAIT T' SEE WHAT HE DOES WHEN HE WAKES UP!
HO-HUM!
WELL— I'LL BE DURNED!
IF THET AIN'T TH' DAWGONDEST THING I EVER SEE! I JEST CAN'T FIGGER IT OUT!
HI, GOOFY! YER DONKEY'S GOT HIMSELF IN QUITE A FIX, HASN'T HE?
WHADDAYA MEAN, QUITE A FIX?
WHY— LOOK HOW HE'S ALL TANGLED UP WITH TH' GATE! HOW'S HE GONNA GET OUT?
SHUCKS! THAT'S HIS WORRY!
1-3
LET 'IM GIT OUT TH' SAME WAY HE GOT IN! THAT DON'T BOTHER ME NONE!
WELL, FER—!
WHAT I WAS TRYIN' TUH FIGGER OUT IS HOW HE KNEW I WAS COMIN' OVER TUH YORE HOUSE WHEN I HADN'T EVEN MENTIONED IT TO HIM!
WALT DISNEY

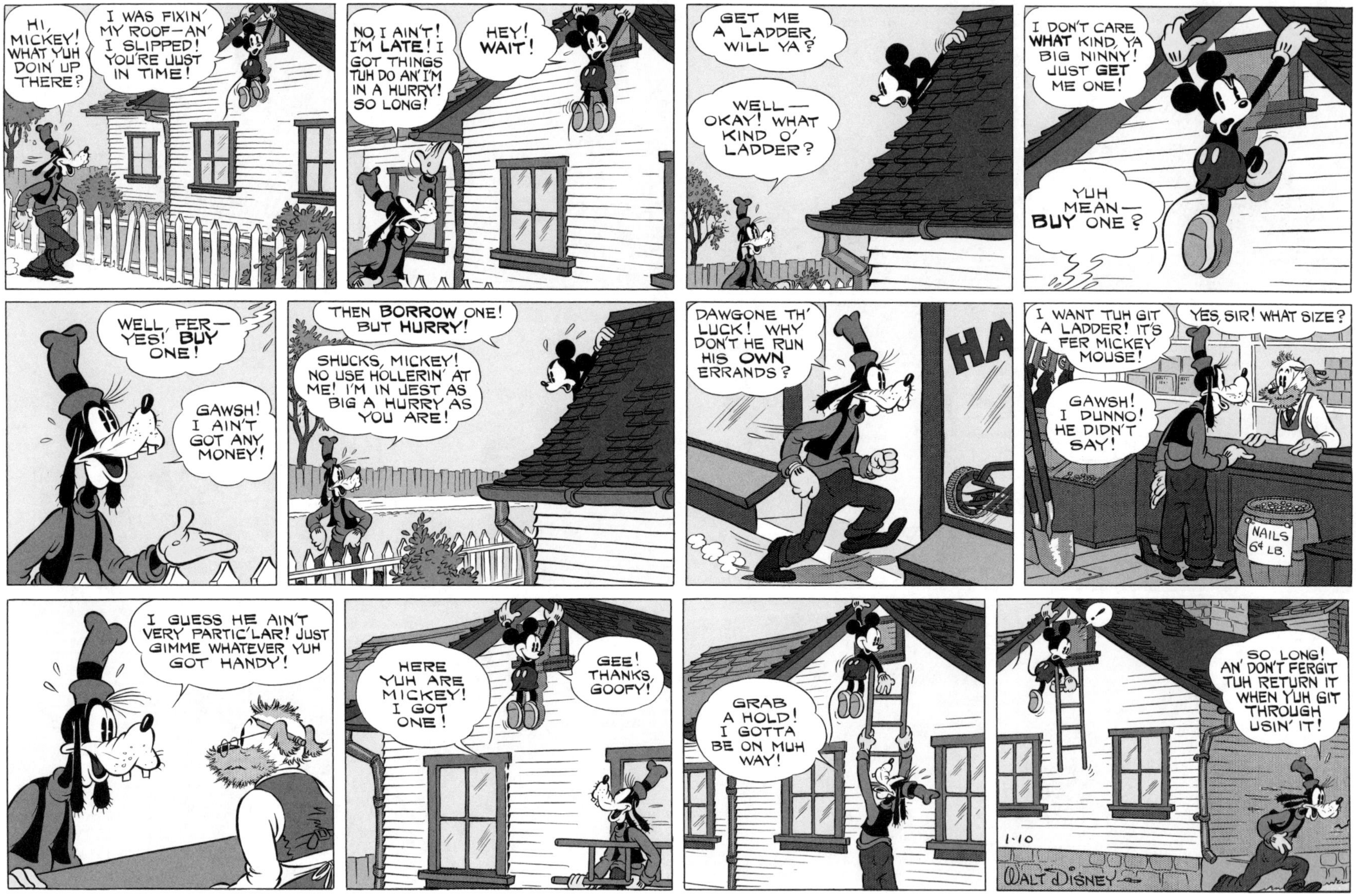
HI, MICKEY! WHAT YUH DOIN' UP THERE?
I WAS FIXIN' MY ROOF—AN' I SLIPPED! YOU'RE JUST IN TIME!
NO, I AIN'T! I'M LATE! I GOT THINGS TUH DO AN' I'M IN A HURRY! SO LONG!
HEY! WAIT!
GET ME A LADDER, WILL YA?
WELL— OKAY! WHAT KIND O' LADDER?
I DON'T CARE WHAT KIND, YA BIG NINNY! JUST GET ME ONE!
YUH MEAN— BUY ONE?
WELL, FER— YES! BUY ONE!
GAWSH! I AIN'T GOT ANY MONEY!
THEN BORROW ONE! BUT HURRY!
SHUCKS, MICKEY! NO USE HOLLERIN' AT ME! I'M IN JEST AS BIG A HURRY AS YOU ARE!
DAWGONE TH' LUCK! WHY DON'T HE RUN HIS OWN ERRANDS?
HA
I WANT TUH GIT A LADDER! IT'S FER MICKEY MOUSE!
YES, SIR! WHAT SIZE?
GAWSH! I DUNNO! HE DIDN'T SAY!
NAILS 6¢ LB.
I GUESS HE AIN'T VERY PARTIC'LAR! JUST GIMME WHATEVER YUH GOT HANDY!
HERE YUH ARE MICKEY! I GOT ONE!
GEE! THANKS, GOOFY!
GRAB A HOLD! I GOTTA BE ON MUH WAY!
!
SO LONG! AN' DON'T FERGIT TUH RETURN IT WHEN YUH GIT THROUGH USIN' IT!
1·10
WALT DISNEY

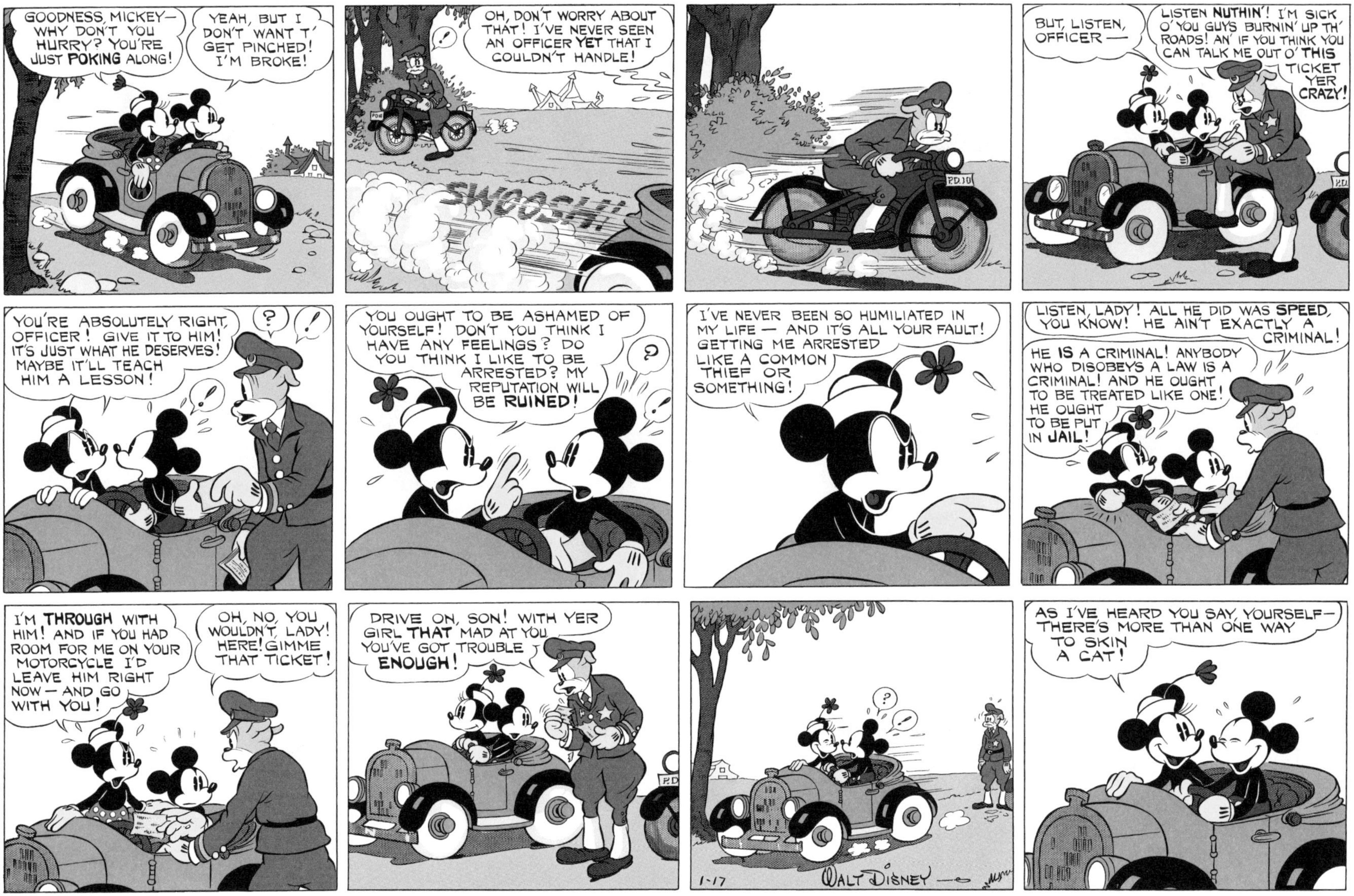
GOODNESS, MICKEY— WHY DON'T YOU HURRY? YOU'RE JUST POKING ALONG!
YEAH, BUT I DON'T WANT T' GET PINCHED! I'M BROKE!
OH, DON'T WORRY ABOUT THAT! I'VE NEVER SEEN AN OFFICER YET THAT I COULDN'T HANDLE!
SWOOSH!!
BUT, LISTEN, OFFICER —
LISTEN NUTHIN'! I'M SICK O' YOU GUYS BURNIN' UP TH' ROADS! AN' IF YOU THINK YOU CAN TALK ME OUT O' THIS TICKET YER CRAZY!
YOU'RE ABSOLUTELY RIGHT, OFFICER! GIVE IT TO HIM! IT'S JUST WHAT HE DESERVES! MAYBE IT'LL TEACH HIM A LESSON!
YOU OUGHT TO BE ASHAMED OF YOURSELF! DON'T YOU THINK I HAVE ANY FEELINGS? DO YOU THINK I LIKE TO BE ARRESTED? MY REPUTATION WILL BE RUINED!
I'VE NEVER BEEN SO HUMILIATED IN MY LIFE — AND IT'S ALL YOUR FAULT! GETTING ME ARRESTED LIKE A COMMON THIEF OR SOMETHING!
LISTEN, LADY! ALL HE DID WAS SPEED, YOU KNOW! HE AIN'T EXACTLY A CRIMINAL!
HE IS A CRIMINAL! ANYBODY WHO DISOBEYS A LAW IS A CRIMINAL! AND HE OUGHT TO BE TREATED LIKE ONE! HE OUGHT TO BE PUT IN JAIL!
I'M THROUGH WITH HIM! AND IF YOU HAD ROOM FOR ME ON YOUR MOTORCYCLE I'D LEAVE HIM RIGHT NOW — AND GO WITH YOU!
OH, NO, YOU WOULDN'T, LADY! HERE! GIMME THAT TICKET!
DRIVE ON, SON! WITH YER GIRL THAT MAD AT YOU YOU'VE GOT TROUBLE ENOUGH!
1-17
WALT DISNEY
AS I'VE HEARD YOU SAY, YOURSELF— THERE'S MORE THAN ONE WAY TO SKIN A CAT!

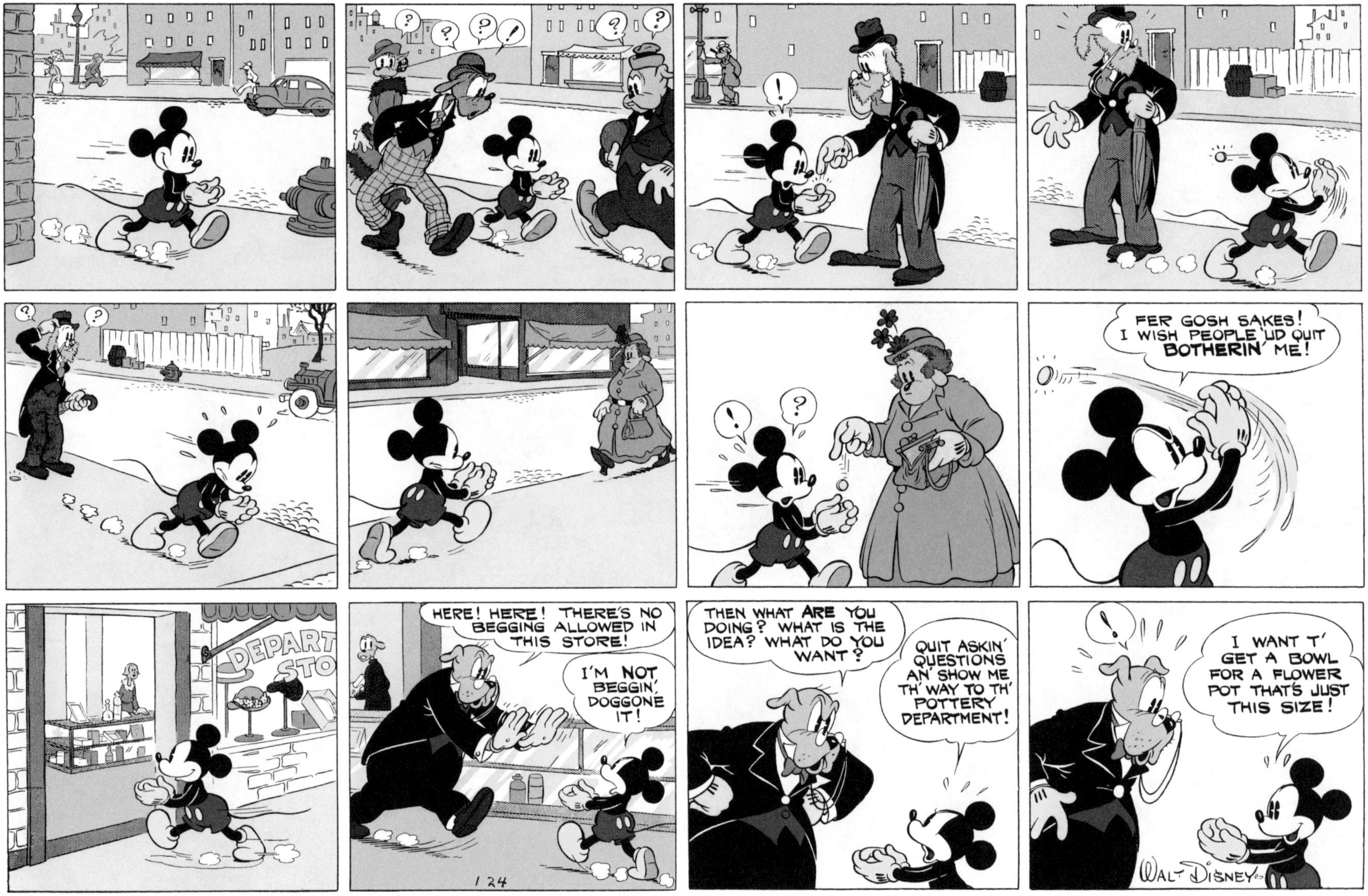
?
?
?
!
?
?
!
?
?
!
?
FER GOSH SAKES! I WISH PEOPLE 'UD QUIT BOTHERIN' ME!
DEPART
STO
HERE! HERE! THERE'S NO BEGGING ALLOWED IN THIS STORE!
I'M NOT BEGGIN', DOGGONE IT!
1 24
THEN WHAT ARE YOU DOING? WHAT IS THE IDEA? WHAT DO YOU WANT?
QUIT ASKIN' QUESTIONS AN' SHOW ME TH' WAY TO TH' POTTERY DEPARTMENT!
!
I WANT T' GET A BOWL FOR A FLOWER POT THAT'S JUST THIS SIZE!
WALT DISNEY

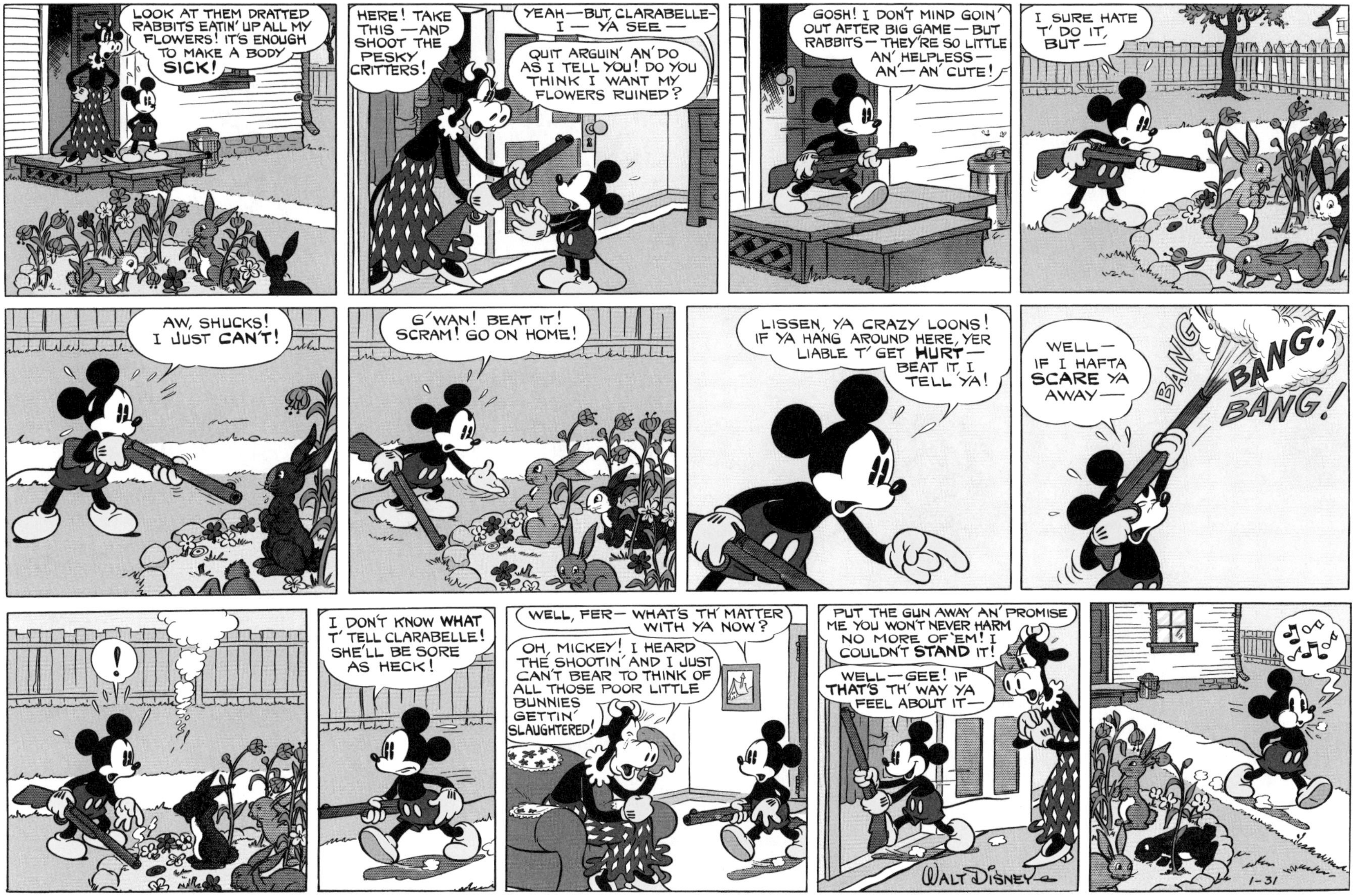
LOOK AT THEM DRATTED RABBITS EATIN' UP ALL MY FLOWERS! IT'S ENOUGH TO MAKE A BODY SICK!
HERE! TAKE THIS —AND SHOOT THE PESKY CRITTERS!
YEAH—BUT, CLARABELLE—I — YA SEE —
QUIT ARGUIN' AN' DO AS I TELL YOU! DO YOU THINK I WANT MY FLOWERS RUINED?
GOSH! I DON'T MIND GOIN' OUT AFTER BIG GAME—BUT RABBITS—THEY'RE SO LITTLE AN' HELPLESS— AN'— AN' CUTE!
I SURE HATE T' DO IT, BUT —
AW, SHUCKS! I JUST CAN'T!
G'WAN! BEAT IT! SCRAM! GO ON HOME!
LISSEN, YA CRAZY LOONS! IF YA HANG AROUND HERE, YER LIABLE T' GET HURT— BEAT IT, I TELL YA!
WELL— IF I HAFTA SCARE YA AWAY—
BANG! BANG! BANG!
!
I DON'T KNOW WHAT T' TELL CLARABELLE! SHE'LL BE SORE AS HECK!
WELL, FER— WHAT'S TH' MATTER WITH YA NOW?
OH, MICKEY! I HEARD THE SHOOTIN' AND I JUST CAN'T BEAR TO THINK OF ALL THOSE POOR LITTLE BUNNIES GETTIN' SLAUGHTERED!
PUT THE GUN AWAY AN' PROMISE ME YOU WON'T NEVER HARM NO MORE OF 'EM! I COULDN'T STAND IT!
WELL—GEE! IF THAT'S TH' WAY YA FEEL ABOUT IT—
WALT DISNEY
1-31

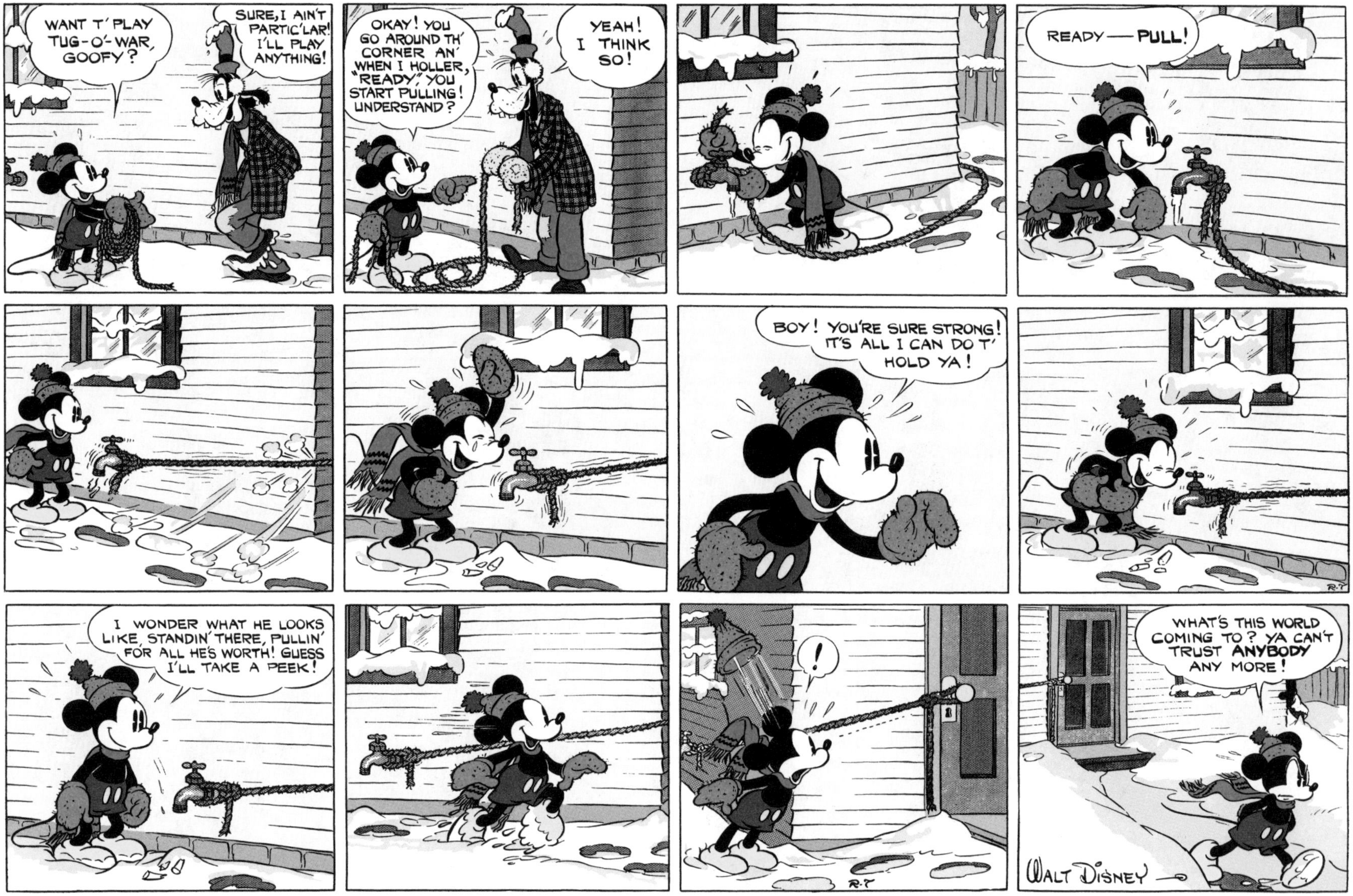
WANT T' PLAY TUG-O'-WAR, GOOFY?
SURE, I AIN'T PARTIC'LAR! I'LL PLAY ANYTHING!
OKAY! YOU GO AROUND TH' CORNER AN' WHEN I HOLLER, "READY," YOU START PULLING! UNDERSTAND?
YEAH! I THINK SO!
READY — PULL!
BOY! YOU'RE SURE STRONG! IT'S ALL I CAN DO T' HOLD YA!
I WONDER WHAT HE LOOKS LIKE, STANDIN' THERE, PULLIN' FOR ALL HE'S WORTH! GUESS I'LL TAKE A PEEK!
!
WHAT'S THIS WORLD COMING TO? YA CAN'T TRUST ANYBODY ANY MORE!
WALT DISNEY

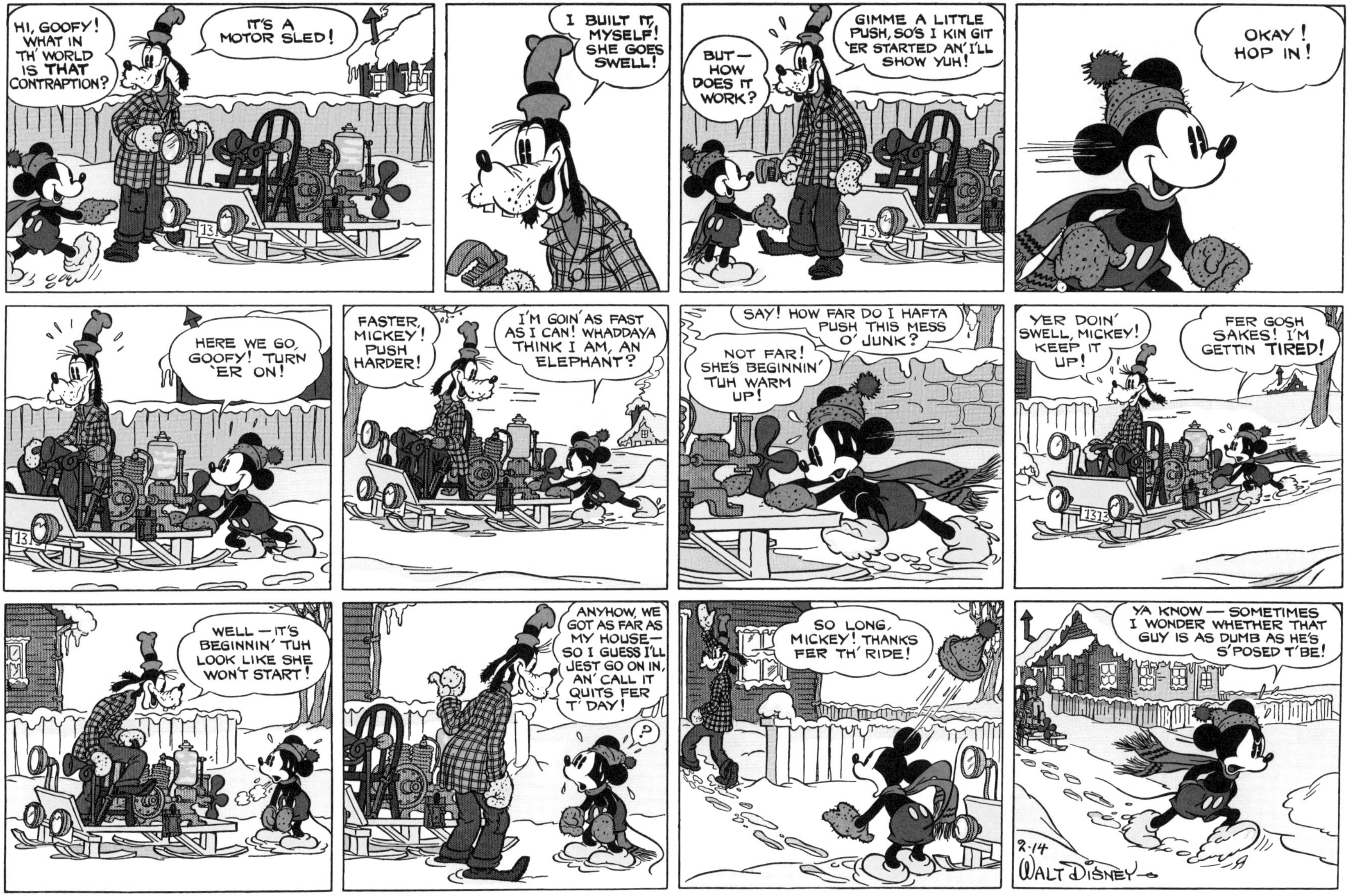
HI, GOOFY! WHAT IN TH' WORLD IS THAT CONTRAPTION?
IT'S A MOTOR SLED!
I BUILT IT, MYSELF! SHE GOES SWELL!
BUT— HOW DOES IT WORK?
GIMME A LITTLE PUSH, SO'S I KIN GIT 'ER STARTED AN' I'LL SHOW YUH!
OKAY! HOP IN!
HERE WE GO, GOOFY! TURN 'ER ON!
FASTER, MICKEY! PUSH HARDER!
I'M GOIN' AS FAST AS I CAN! WHADDAYA THINK I AM, AN ELEPHANT?
SAY! HOW FAR DO I HAFTA PUSH THIS MESS O' JUNK?
NOT FAR! SHE'S BEGINNIN' TUH WARM UP!
YER DOIN' SWELL, MICKEY! KEEP IT UP!
FER GOSH SAKES! I'M GETTIN TIRED!
WELL — IT'S BEGINNIN' TUH LOOK LIKE SHE WON'T START!
ANYHOW, WE GOT AS FAR AS MY HOUSE— SO I GUESS I'LL JEST GO ON IN, AN' CALL IT QUITS FER T' DAY!
SO LONG, MICKEY! THANKS FER TH' RIDE!
YA KNOW — SOMETIMES I WONDER WHETHER THAT GUY IS AS DUMB AS HE'S S'POSED T'BE!
2-14
WALT DISNEY

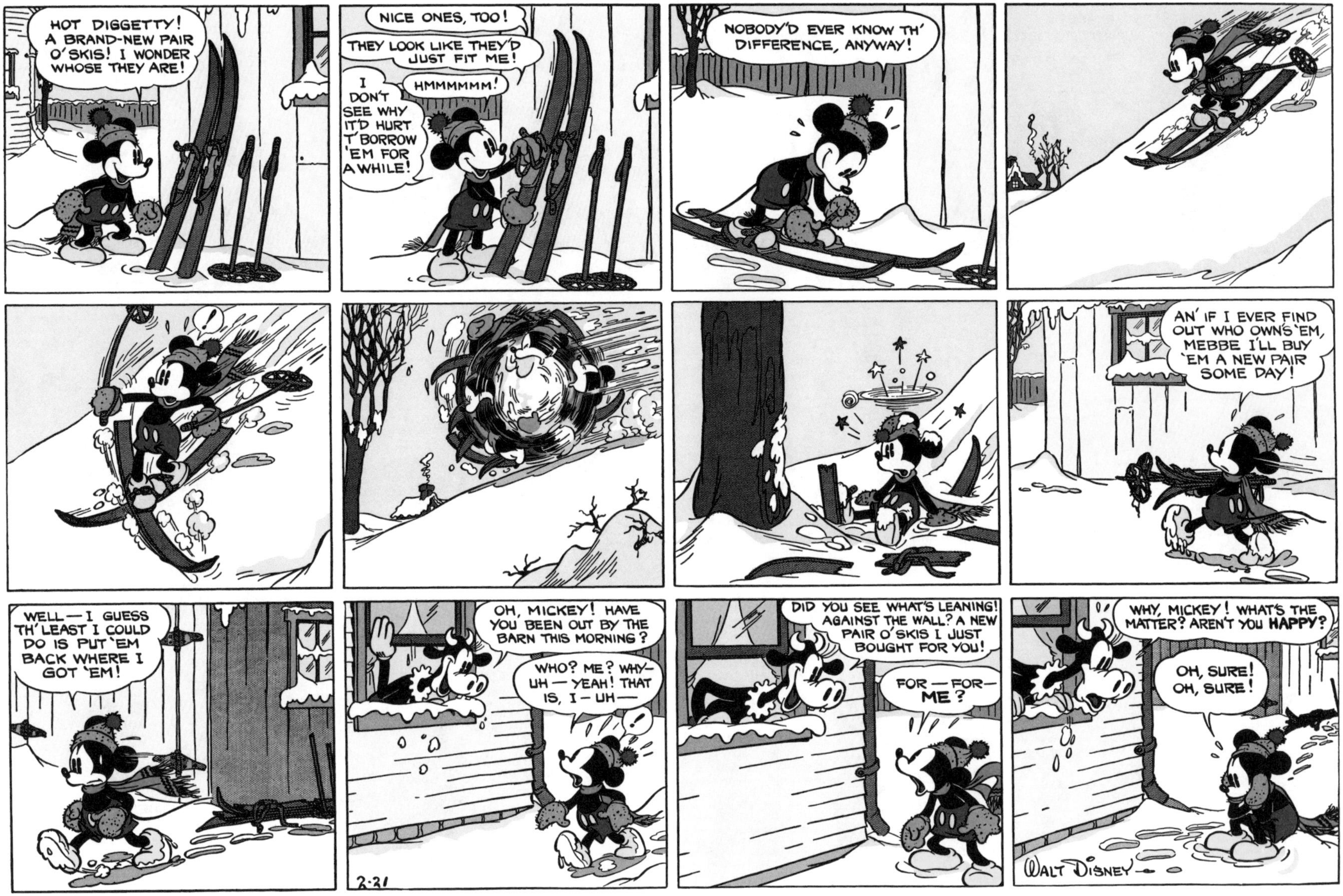
HOT DIGGETTY! A BRAND-NEW PAIR O' SKIS! I WONDER WHOSE THEY ARE!
NICE ONES, TOO!
THEY LOOK LIKE THEY'D JUST FIT ME!
HMMMMMM!
I DON'T SEE WHY IT'D HURT T'BORROW 'EM FOR A WHILE!
NOBODY'D EVER KNOW TH' DIFFERENCE, ANYWAY!
!
AN' IF I EVER FIND OUT WHO OWN'S 'EM, MEBBE I'LL BUY 'EM A NEW PAIR SOME DAY!
WELL — I GUESS TH' LEAST I COULD DO IS PUT 'EM BACK WHERE I GOT 'EM!
OH, MICKEY! HAVE YOU BEEN OUT BY THE BARN THIS MORNING?
WHO? ME? WHY-UH — YEAH! THAT IS, I — UH —
!
2-31
DID YOU SEE WHAT'S LEANING! AGAINST THE WALL? A NEW PAIR O' SKIS I JUST BOUGHT FOR YOU!
FOR — FOR — ME?
WHY, MICKEY! WHAT'S THE MATTER? AREN'T YOU HAPPY?
OH, SURE! OH, SURE!
WALT DISNEY

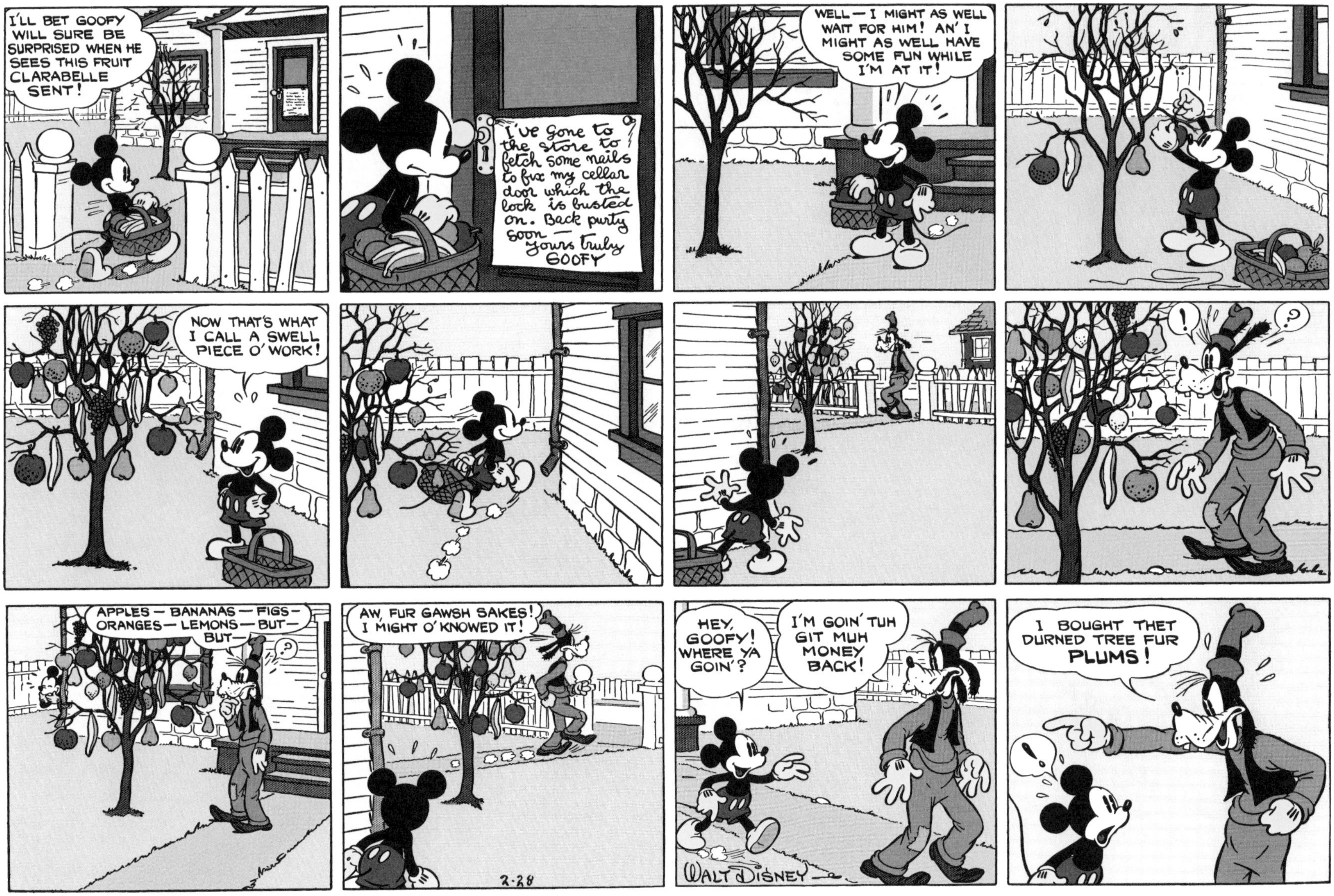
I'LL BET GOOFY WILL SURE BE SURPRISED WHEN HE SEES THIS FRUIT CLARABELLE SENT!
I've gone to the store to fetch some nails to fix my cellar door which the lock is busted on. Back purty soon — Yours truly GOOFY
WELL — I MIGHT AS WELL WAIT FOR HIM! AN' I MIGHT AS WELL HAVE SOME FUN WHILE I'M AT IT!
NOW THAT'S WHAT I CALL A SWELL PIECE O' WORK!
!
?
APPLES — BANANAS — FIGS — ORANGES — LEMONS — BUT — BUT —
?
AW, FUR GAWSH SAKES! I MIGHT O' KNOWED IT!
2-28
HEY, GOOFY! WHERE YA GOIN'?
I'M GOIN' TUH GIT MUH MONEY BACK!
WALT DISNEY
I BOUGHT THET DURNED TREE FUR PLUMS!
!

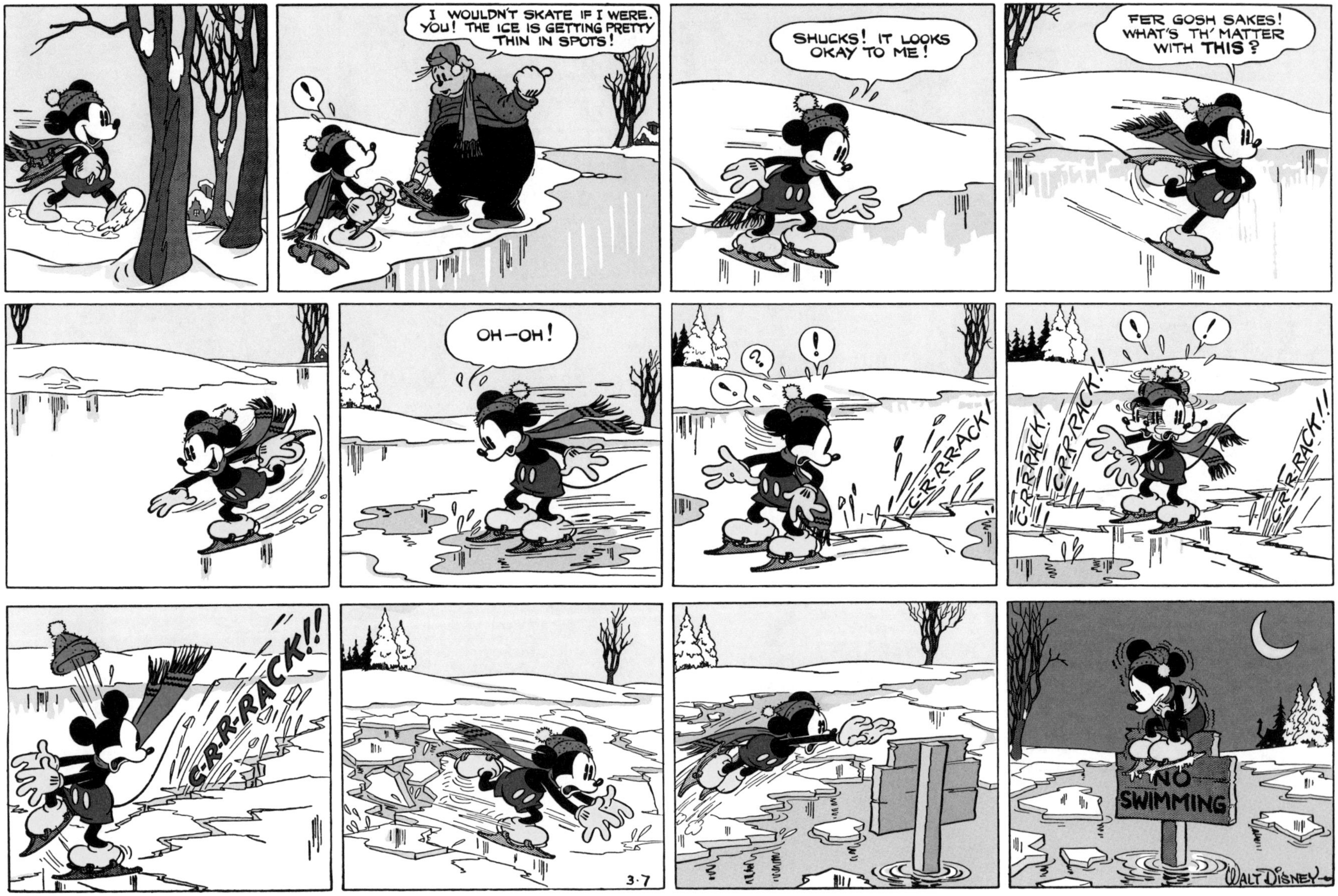
I WOULDN'T SKATE IF I WERE. YOU! THE ICE IS GETTING PRETTY THIN IN SPOTS!
!
SHUCKS! IT LOOKS OKAY TO ME!
FER GOSH SAKES! WHAT'S TH' MATTER WITH THIS?
OH—OH!
!
?
!
C-R-R-RACK!
!
!
C-R-RACK!
C-R-R-RACK!!
C-R-RACK!!
C-R-R-RACK!!
3·7
NO SWIMMING
WALT DISNEY

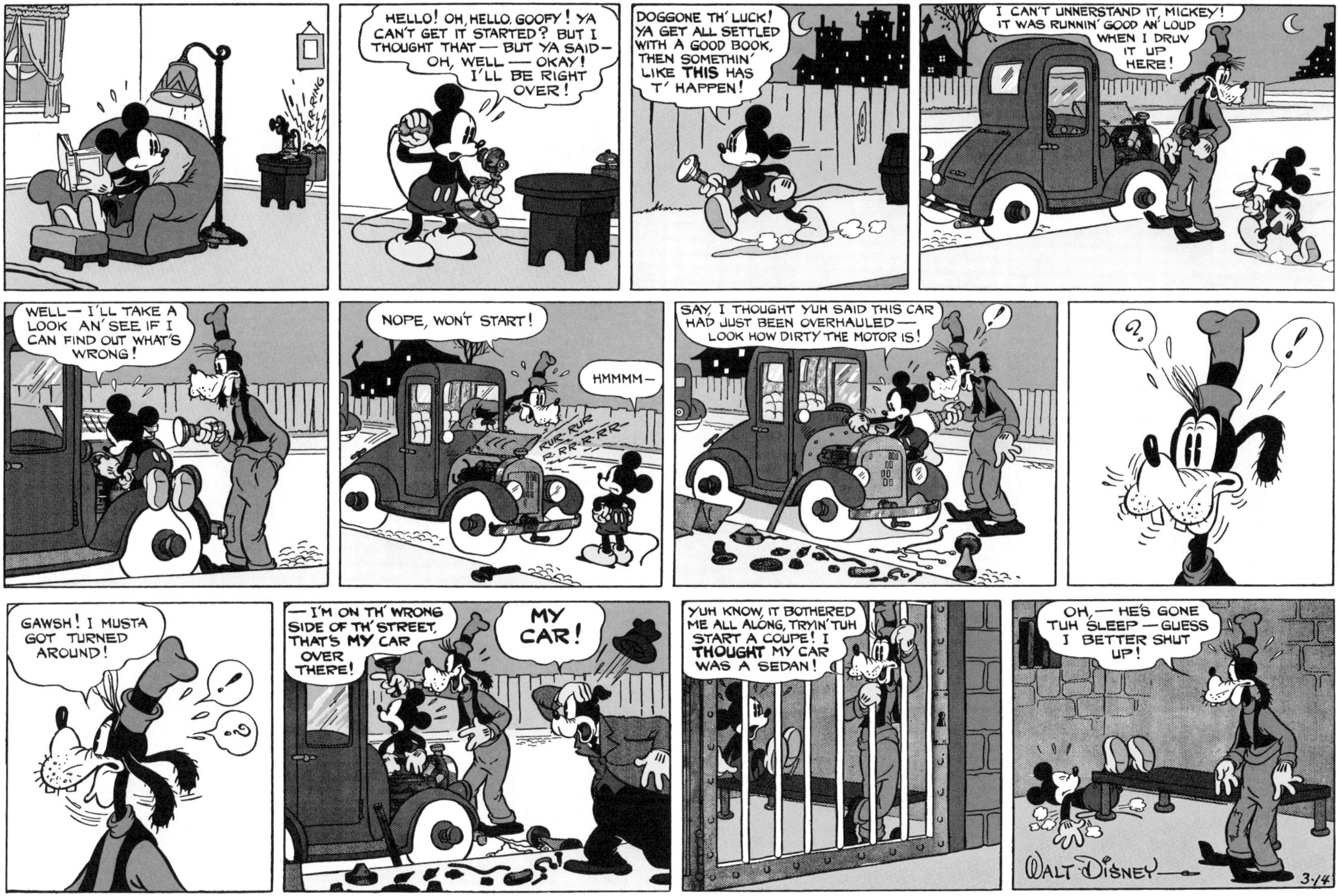
R-R-RING
HELLO! OH, HELLO, GOOFY! YA CAN'T GET IT STARTED? BUT I THOUGHT THAT — BUT YA SAID — OH, WELL — OKAY! I'LL BE RIGHT OVER!
DOGGONE TH' LUCK! YA GET ALL SETTLED WITH A GOOD BOOK, THEN SOMETHIN' LIKE **THIS** HAS T' HAPPEN!
I CAN'T UNNERSTAND IT, MICKEY! IT WAS RUNNIN' GOOD AN' LOUD WHEN I DRUV IT UP HERE!
WELL — I'LL TAKE A LOOK AN' SEE IF I CAN FIND OUT WHAT'S WRONG!
NOPE, WON'T START!
HMMMM —
RUR-RUR R-RR-R-RR —
SAY, I THOUGHT YUH SAID THIS CAR HAD JUST BEEN OVERHAULED — LOOK HOW DIRTY THE MOTOR IS!
GAWSH! I MUSTA GOT TURNED AROUND!
— I'M ON TH' WRONG SIDE OF TH' STREET, THAT'S **MY** CAR OVER THERE!
MY CAR!
YUH KNOW, IT BOTHERED ME ALL ALONG, TRYIN' TUH START A COUPE! I **THOUGHT** MY CAR WAS A SEDAN!
OH, — HE'S GONE TUH SLEEP — GUESS I BETTER SHUT UP!
WALT DISNEY
3-14

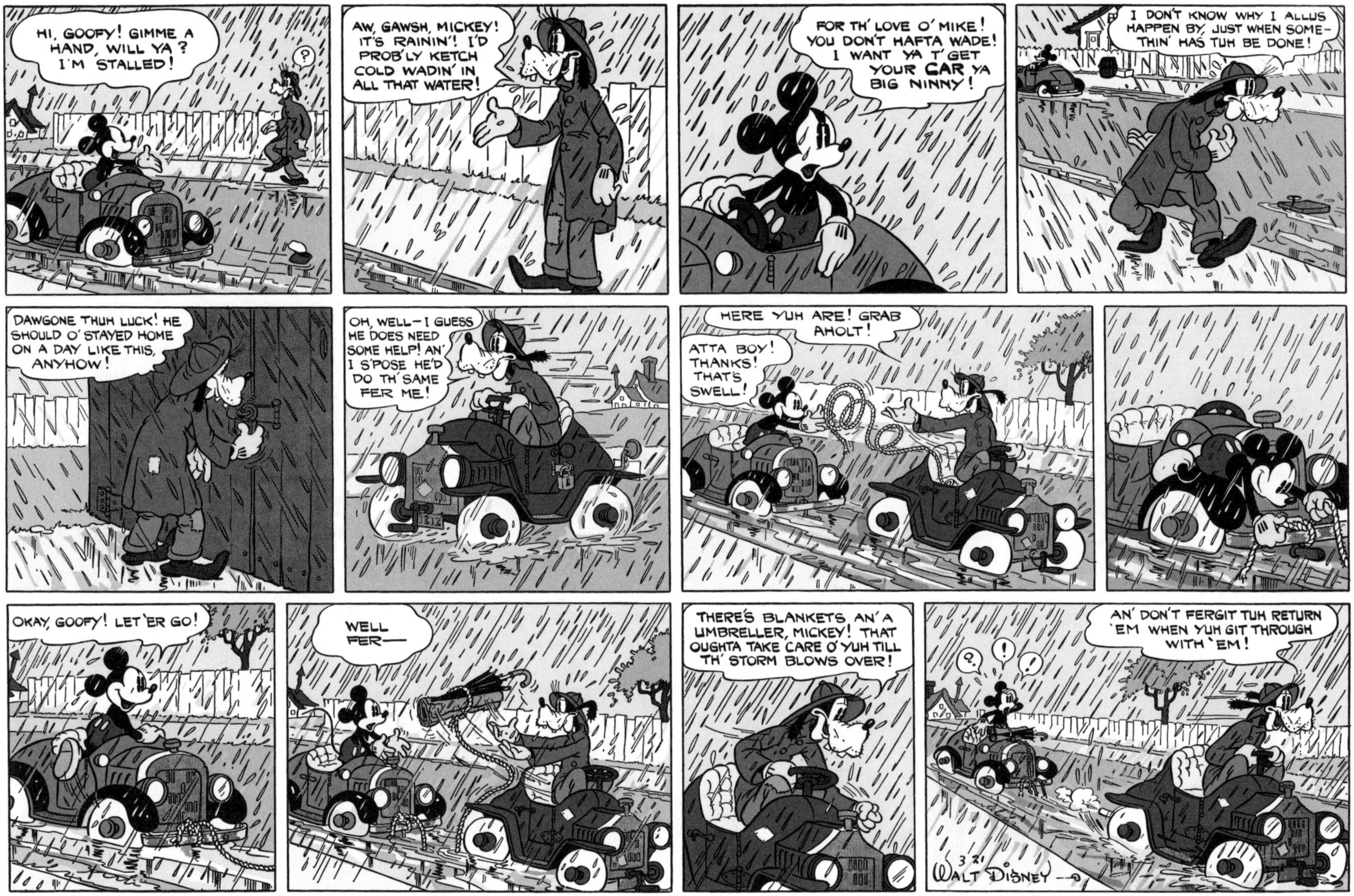
HI, GOOFY! GIMME A HAND, WILL YA? I'M STALLED!
?
AW, GAWSH, MICKEY! IT'S RAININ'! I'D PROB'LY KETCH COLD WADIN' IN ALL THAT WATER!
FOR TH' LOVE O' MIKE! YOU DON'T HAFTA WADE! I WANT YA T' GET YOUR CAR YA BIG NINNY!
I DON'T KNOW WHY I ALLUS HAPPEN BY, JUST WHEN SOME-THIN' HAS TUH BE DONE!
DAWGONE THUH LUCK! HE SHOULD O' STAYED HOME ON A DAY LIKE THIS, ANYHOW!
OH, WELL—I GUESS HE DOES NEED SOME HELP! AN' I S'POSE HE'D DO TH' SAME FER ME!
HERE YUH ARE! GRAB AHOLT!
ATTA BOY! THANKS! THAT'S SWELL!
OKAY, GOOFY! LET 'ER GO!
WELL FER—
THERE'S BLANKETS AN' A UMBRELLER, MICKEY! THAT OUGHTA TAKE CARE O' YUH TILL TH' STORM BLOWS OVER!
AN' DON'T FERGIT TUH RETURN 'EM WHEN YUH GIT THROUGH WITH 'EM!
?
!
!
3 21
WALT DISNEY

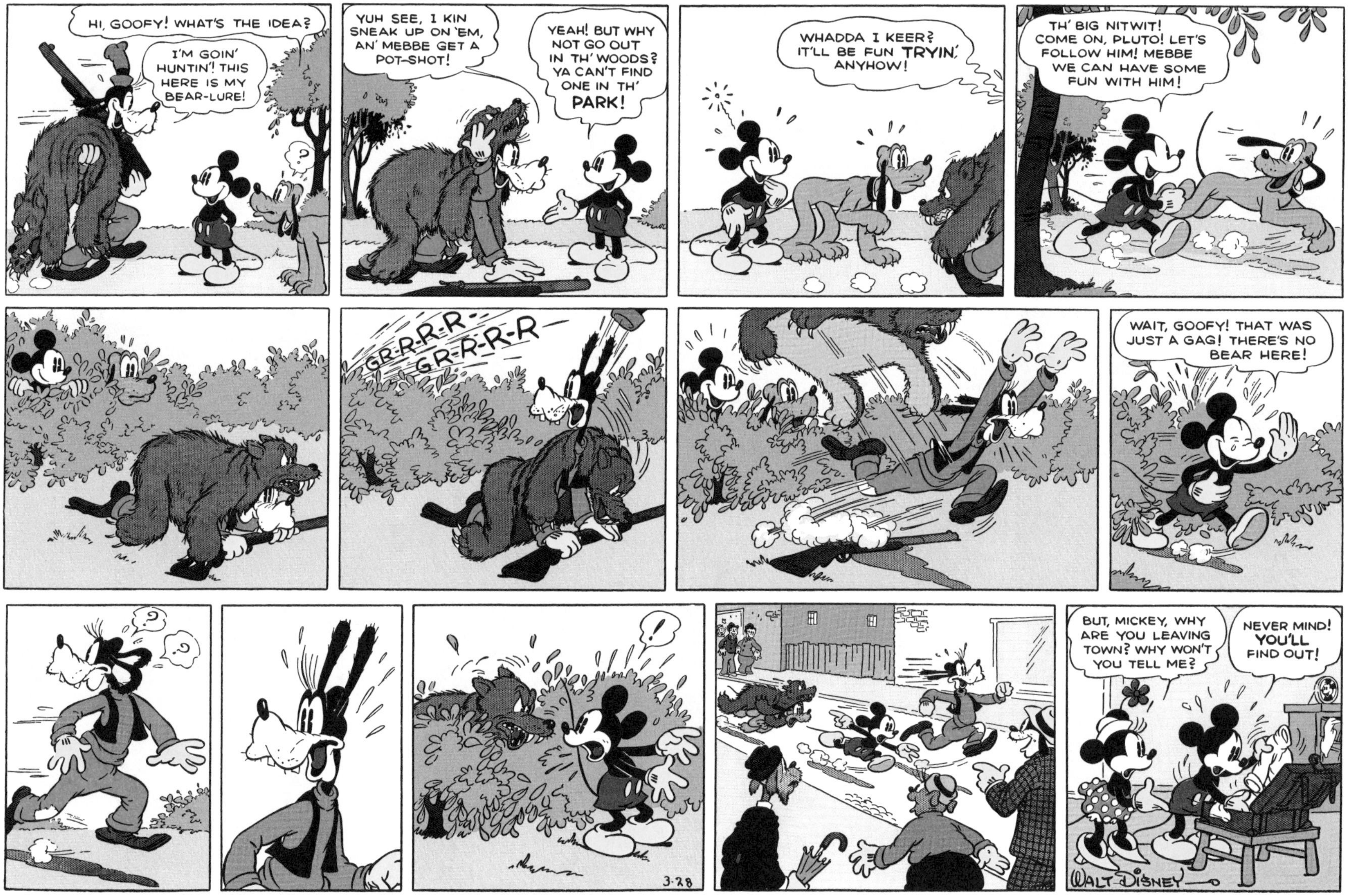
HI, GOOFY! WHAT'S THE IDEA?
I'M GOIN' HUNTIN'! THIS HERE IS MY BEAR-LURE!
?
YUH SEE, I KIN SNEAK UP ON 'EM, AN' MEBBE GET A POT-SHOT!
YEAH! BUT WHY NOT GO OUT IN TH' WOODS? YA CAN'T FIND ONE IN TH' PARK!
WHADDA I KEER? IT'LL BE FUN TRYIN' ANYHOW!
TH' BIG NITWIT! COME ON, PLUTO! LET'S FOLLOW HIM! MEBBE WE CAN HAVE SOME FUN WITH HIM!
GR-R-R-R-
GR-R-R-R
WAIT, GOOFY! THAT WAS JUST A GAG! THERE'S NO BEAR HERE!
?
?
!
3-28
BUT, MICKEY, WHY ARE YOU LEAVING TOWN? WHY WON'T YOU TELL ME?
NEVER MIND! YOU'LL FIND OUT!
WALT DISNEY

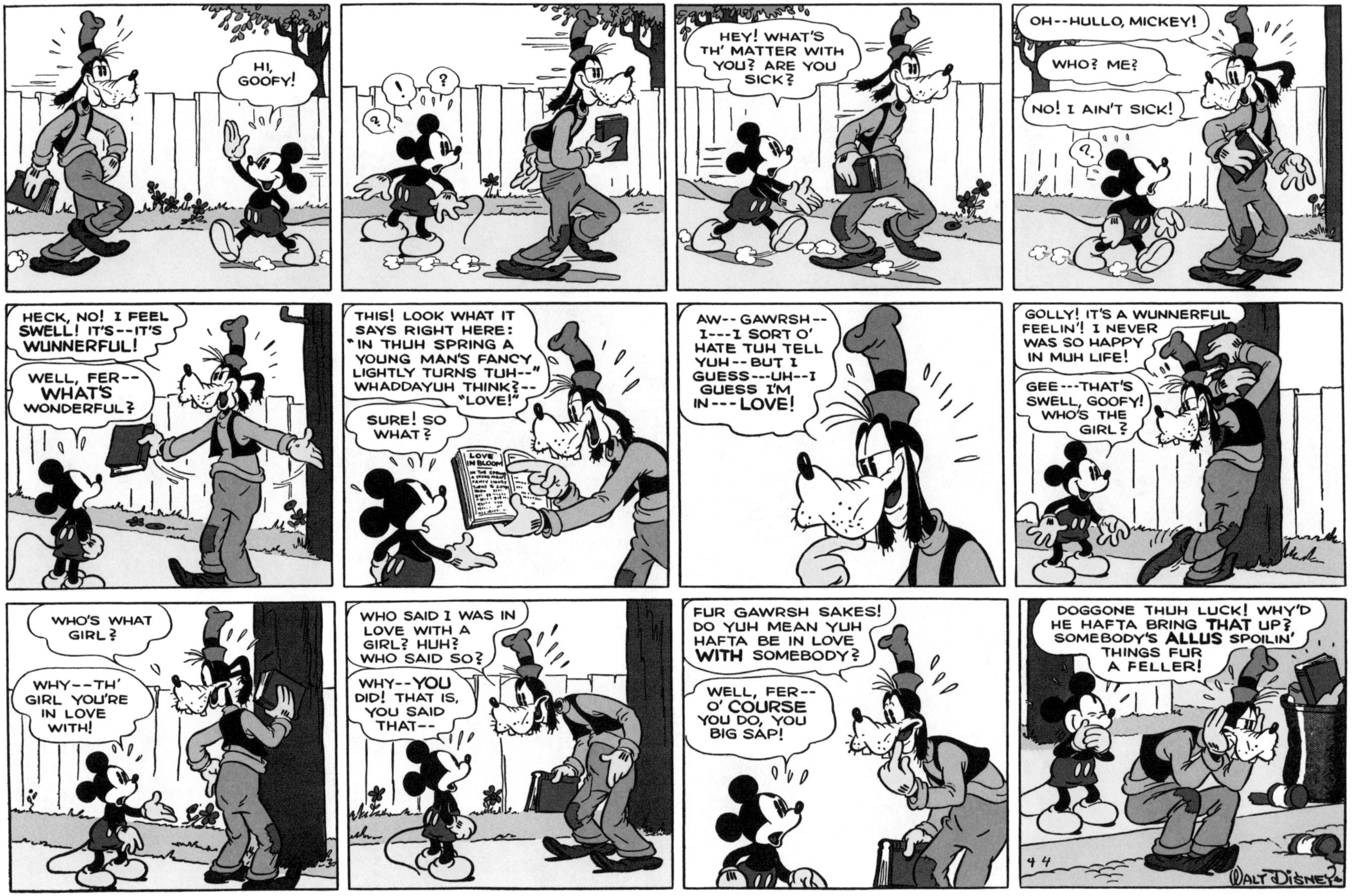
HI, GOOFY!
?
!
?
HEY! WHAT'S TH' MATTER WITH YOU? ARE YOU SICK?
OH--HULLO, MICKEY!
WHO? ME?
NO! I AIN'T SICK!
?
HECK, NO! I FEEL SWELL! IT'S--IT'S WUNNERFUL!
WELL, FER-- WHAT'S WONDERFUL?
THIS! LOOK WHAT IT SAYS RIGHT HERE: "IN THUH SPRING A YOUNG MAN'S FANCY LIGHTLY TURNS TUH--" WHADDAYUH THINK?-- "LOVE!"
SURE! SO WHAT?
LOVE IN BLOOM
AW--GAWRSH-- I---I SORT O' HATE TUH TELL YUH--BUT I GUESS---UH--I GUESS I'M IN---LOVE!
GOLLY! IT'S A WUNNERFUL FEELIN'! I NEVER WAS SO HAPPY IN MUH LIFE!
GEE---THAT'S SWELL, GOOFY! WHO'S THE GIRL?
WHO'S WHAT GIRL?
WHY--TH' GIRL YOU'RE IN LOVE WITH!
WHO SAID I WAS IN LOVE WITH A GIRL? HUH? WHO SAID SO?
WHY--YOU DID! THAT IS, YOU SAID THAT--
FUR GAWRSH SAKES! DO YUH MEAN YUH HAFTA BE IN LOVE WITH SOMEBODY?
WELL, FER-- O' COURSE YOU DO, YOU BIG SAP!
DOGGONE THUH LUCK! WHY'D HE HAFTA BRING THAT UP? SOMEBODY'S ALLUS SPOILIN' THINGS FUR A FELLER!
WALT DISNEY

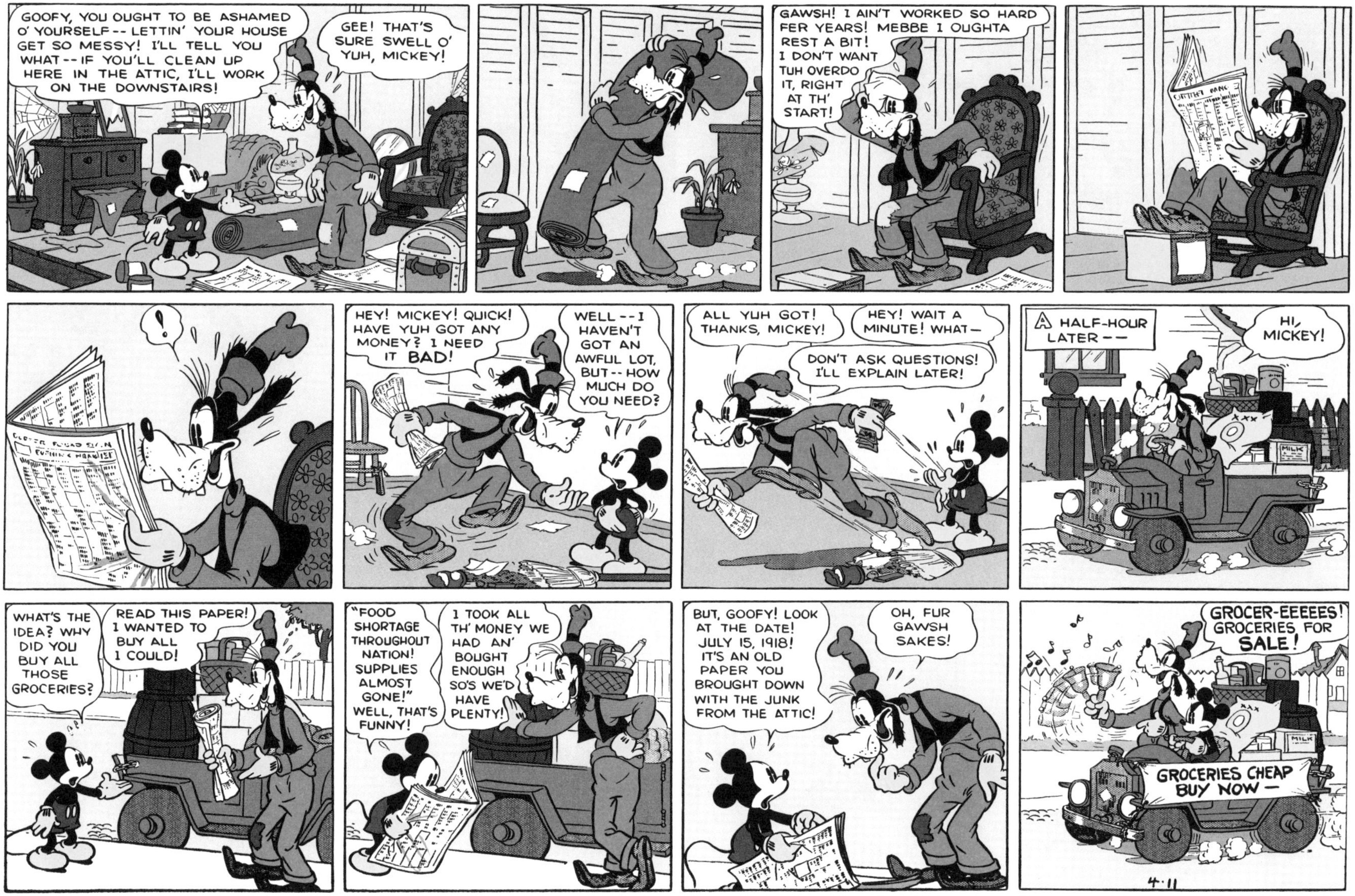
GOOFY, YOU OUGHT TO BE ASHAMED O' YOURSELF-- LETTIN' YOUR HOUSE GET SO MESSY! I'LL TELL YOU WHAT-- IF YOU'LL CLEAN UP HERE IN THE ATTIC, I'LL WORK ON THE DOWNSTAIRS!
GEE! THAT'S SURE SWELL O' YUH, MICKEY!
GAWSH! I AIN'T WORKED SO HARD FER YEARS! MEBBE I OUGHTA REST A BIT! I DON'T WANT TUH OVERDO IT, RIGHT AT TH' START!
!
HEY! MICKEY! QUICK! HAVE YUH GOT ANY MONEY? I NEED IT BAD!
WELL--I HAVEN'T GOT AN AWFUL LOT, BUT--HOW MUCH DO YOU NEED?
ALL YUH GOT! THANKS, MICKEY!
HEY! WAIT A MINUTE! WHAT—
DON'T ASK QUESTIONS! I'LL EXPLAIN LATER!
A HALF-HOUR LATER--
HI, MICKEY!
MILK
WHAT'S THE IDEA? WHY DID YOU BUY ALL THOSE GROCERIES?
READ THIS PAPER! I WANTED TO BUY ALL I COULD!
"FOOD SHORTAGE THROUGHOUT NATION! SUPPLIES ALMOST GONE!" WELL, THAT'S FUNNY!
I TOOK ALL TH' MONEY WE HAD AN' BOUGHT ENOUGH SO'S WE'D HAVE PLENTY!
BUT, GOOFY! LOOK AT THE DATE! JULY 15, 1918! IT'S AN OLD PAPER YOU BROUGHT DOWN WITH THE JUNK FROM THE ATTIC!
OH, FUR GAWSH SAKES!
GROCER-EEEEES! GROCERIES FOR SALE!
MILK
GROCERIES CHEAP BUY NOW—
4-11

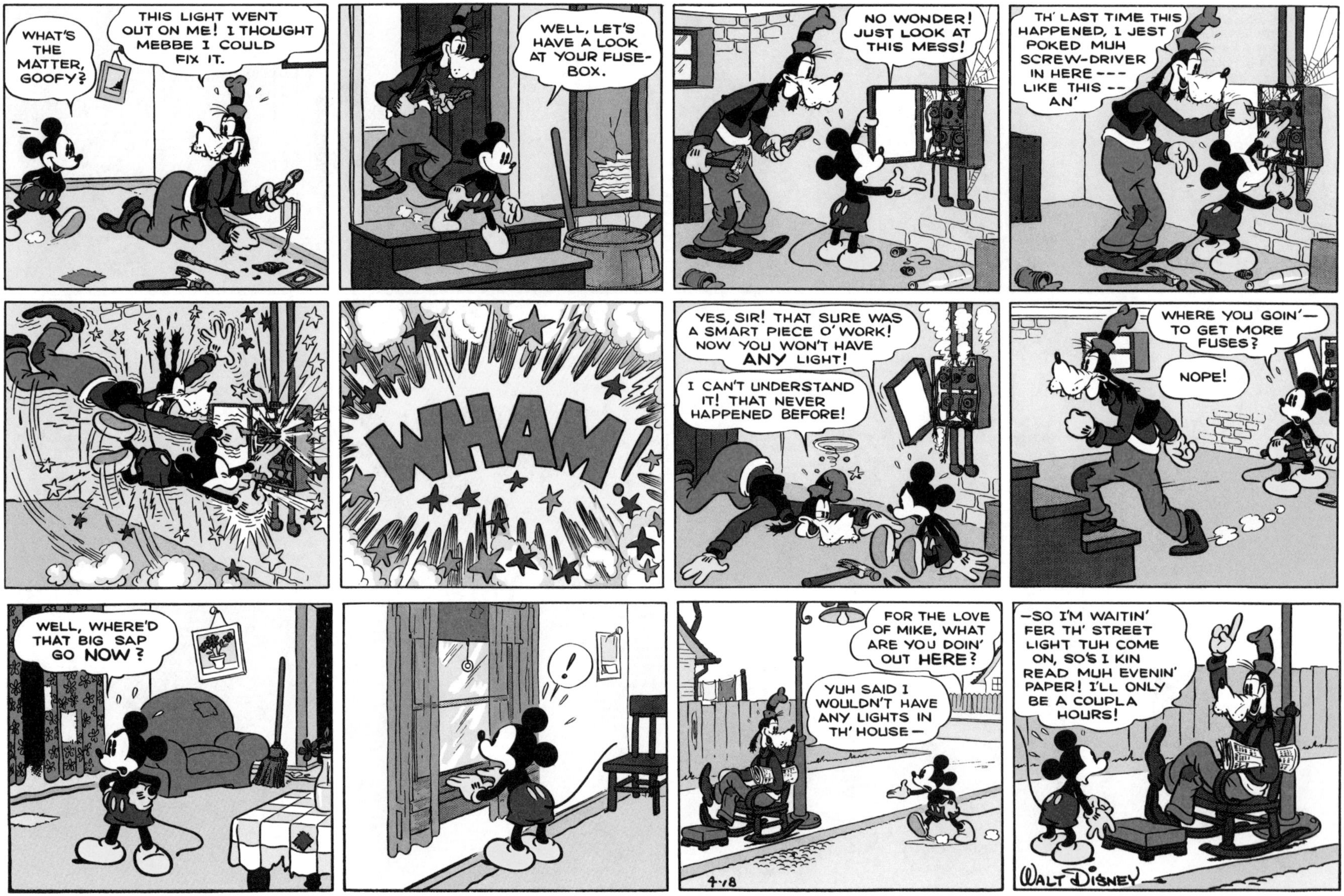

WHAT'S THE MATTER, GOOFY?
THIS LIGHT WENT OUT ON ME! I THOUGHT MEBBE I COULD FIX IT.
WELL, LET'S HAVE A LOOK AT YOUR FUSE-BOX.
NO WONDER! JUST LOOK AT THIS MESS!
TH' LAST TIME THIS HAPPENED, I JEST POKED MUH SCREW-DRIVER IN HERE--- LIKE THIS -- AN'
WHAM!
YES, SIR! THAT SURE WAS A SMART PIECE O' WORK! NOW YOU WON'T HAVE ANY LIGHT!
I CAN'T UNDERSTAND IT! THAT NEVER HAPPENED BEFORE!
WHERE YOU GOIN'— TO GET MORE FUSES?
NOPE!
WELL, WHERE'D THAT BIG SAP GO NOW?
!
FOR THE LOVE OF MIKE, WHAT ARE YOU DOIN' OUT HERE?
YUH SAID I WOULDN'T HAVE ANY LIGHTS IN TH' HOUSE—
—SO I'M WAITIN' FER TH' STREET LIGHT TUH COME ON, SO'S I KIN READ MUH EVENIN' PAPER! I'LL ONLY BE A COUPLA HOURS!
4-18
WALT DISNEY

90. IT WAS ALL VERY CON-FUSE-ING

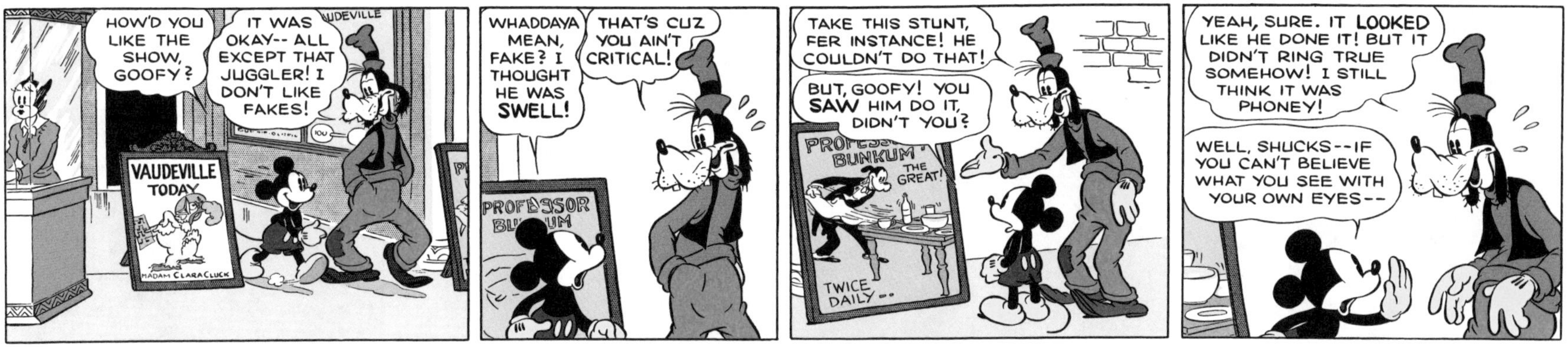
HOW'D YOU LIKE THE SHOW, GOOFY?
IT WAS OKAY-- ALL EXCEPT THAT JUGGLER! I DON'T LIKE FAKES!
VAUDEVILLE TODAY
MADAM CLARA CLUCK
WHADDAYA MEAN, FAKE? I THOUGHT HE WAS **SWELL**!
THAT'S CUZ YOU AIN'T CRITICAL!
PROFESSOR
TAKE THIS STUNT, FER INSTANCE! HE COULDN'T DO THAT!
BUT, GOOFY! YOU **SAW** HIM DO IT, DIDN'T YOU?
BUNKUM THE GREAT!
TWICE DAILY..
YEAH, SURE. IT **LOOKED** LIKE HE DONE IT! BUT IT DIDN'T RING TRUE SOMEHOW! I STILL THINK IT WAS PHONEY!
WELL, SHUCKS--IF YOU CAN'T BELIEVE WHAT YOU SEE WITH YOUR OWN EYES--

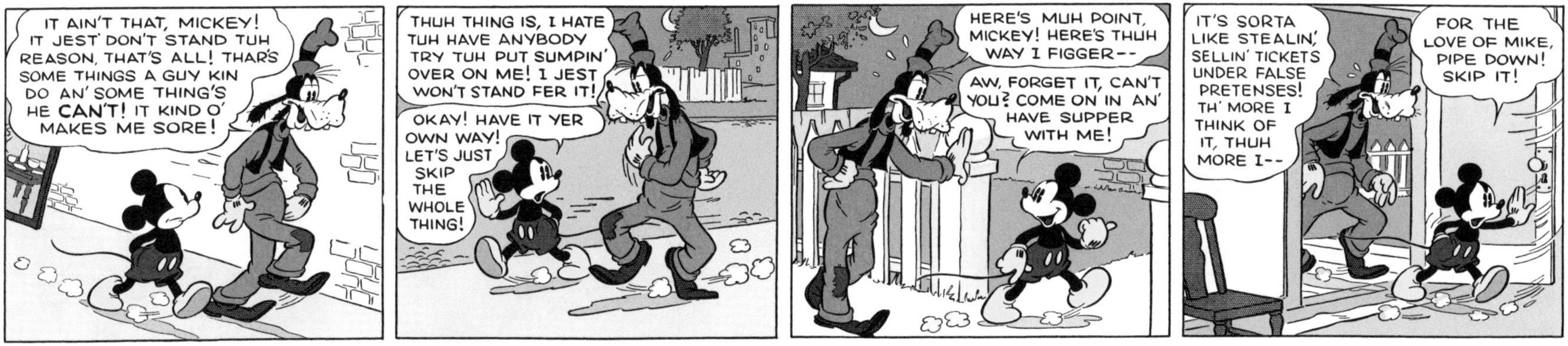
IT AIN'T THAT, MICKEY! IT JEST DON'T STAND TUH REASON, THAT'S ALL! THAR'S SOME THINGS A GUY KIN DO AN' SOME THING'S HE **CAN'T**! IT KIND O' MAKES ME SORE!
THUH THING IS, I HATE TUH HAVE ANYBODY TRY TUH PUT SUMPIN' OVER ON ME! I JEST WON'T STAND FER IT!
OKAY! HAVE IT YER OWN WAY! LET'S JUST SKIP THE WHOLE THING!
HERE'S MUH POINT, MICKEY! HERE'S THUH WAY I FIGGER--
AW, FORGET IT, CAN'T YOU? COME ON IN AN' HAVE SUPPER WITH ME!
IT'S SORTA LIKE STEALIN', SELLIN' TICKETS UNDER FALSE PRETENSES! TH' MORE I THINK OF IT, THUH MORE I--
FOR THE LOVE OF MIKE, PIPE DOWN! SKIP IT!

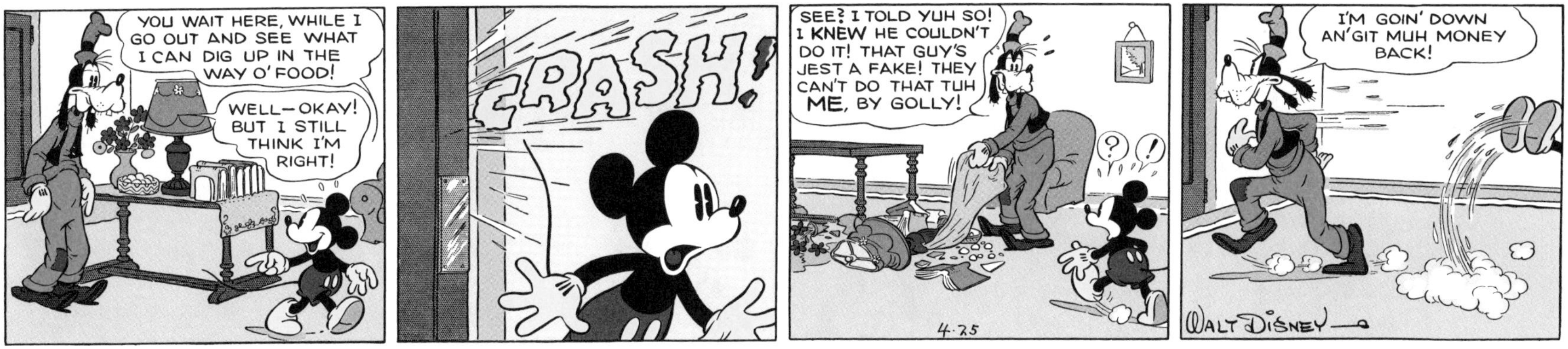
YOU WAIT HERE, WHILE I GO OUT AND SEE WHAT I CAN DIG UP IN THE WAY O' FOOD!
WELL—OKAY! BUT I STILL THINK I'M RIGHT!
CRASH!
SEE? I TOLD YUH SO! I **KNEW** HE COULDN'T DO IT! THAT GUY'S JEST A FAKE! THEY CAN'T DO THAT TUH **ME**, BY GOLLY!
?
!
4-25
I'M GOIN' DOWN AN' GIT MUH MONEY BACK!
WALT DISNEY

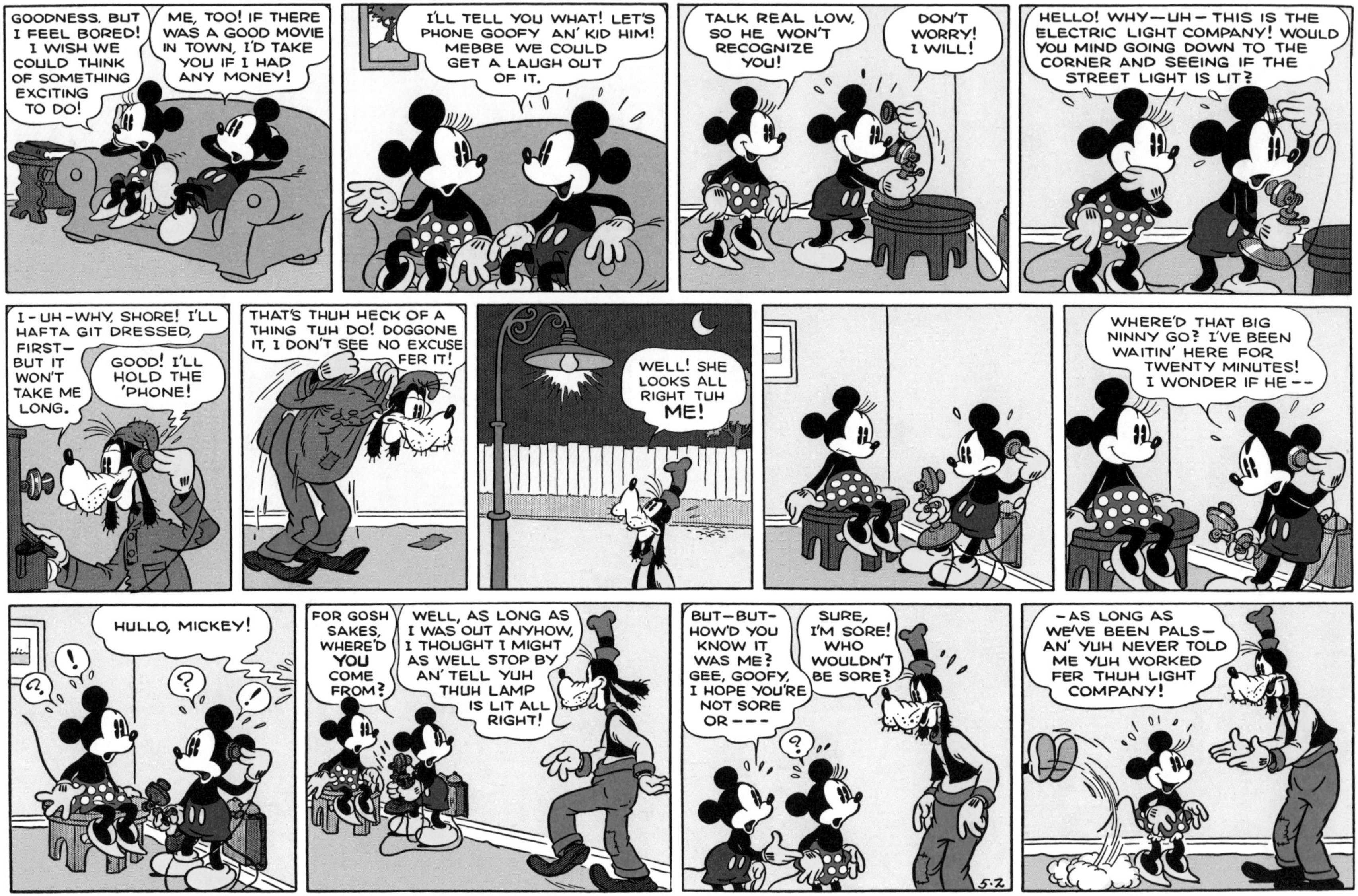
GOODNESS, BUT I FEEL BORED! I WISH WE COULD THINK OF SOMETHING EXCITING TO DO!
ME, TOO! IF THERE WAS A GOOD MOVIE IN TOWN, I'D TAKE YOU IF I HAD ANY MONEY!
I'LL TELL YOU WHAT! LET'S PHONE GOOFY AN' KID HIM! MEBBE WE COULD GET A LAUGH OUT OF IT.
TALK REAL LOW, SO HE WON'T RECOGNIZE YOU!
DON'T WORRY! I WILL!
HELLO! WHY—UH—THIS IS THE ELECTRIC LIGHT COMPANY! WOULD YOU MIND GOING DOWN TO THE CORNER AND SEEING IF THE STREET LIGHT IS LIT?
I-UH-WHY, SHORE! I'LL HAFTA GIT DRESSED, FIRST—BUT IT WON'T TAKE ME LONG.
GOOD! I'LL HOLD THE 'PHONE!
THAT'S THUH HECK OF A THING TUH DO! DOGGONE IT, I DON'T SEE NO EXCUSE FER IT!
WELL! SHE LOOKS ALL RIGHT TUH ME!
WHERE'D THAT BIG NINNY GO? I'VE BEEN WAITIN' HERE FOR TWENTY MINUTES! I WONDER IF HE --
HULLO, MICKEY!
FOR GOSH SAKES, WHERE'D YOU COME FROM?
WELL, AS LONG AS I WAS OUT ANYHOW, I THOUGHT I MIGHT AS WELL STOP BY AN' TELL YUH THUH LAMP IS LIT ALL RIGHT!
BUT—BUT—HOW'D YOU KNOW IT WAS ME? GEE, GOOFY, I HOPE YOU'RE NOT SORE OR ---
SURE, I'M SORE! WHO WOULDN'T BE SORE?
—AS LONG AS WE'VE BEEN PALS—AN' YUH NEVER TOLD ME YUH WORKED FER THUH LIGHT COMPANY!
5-2

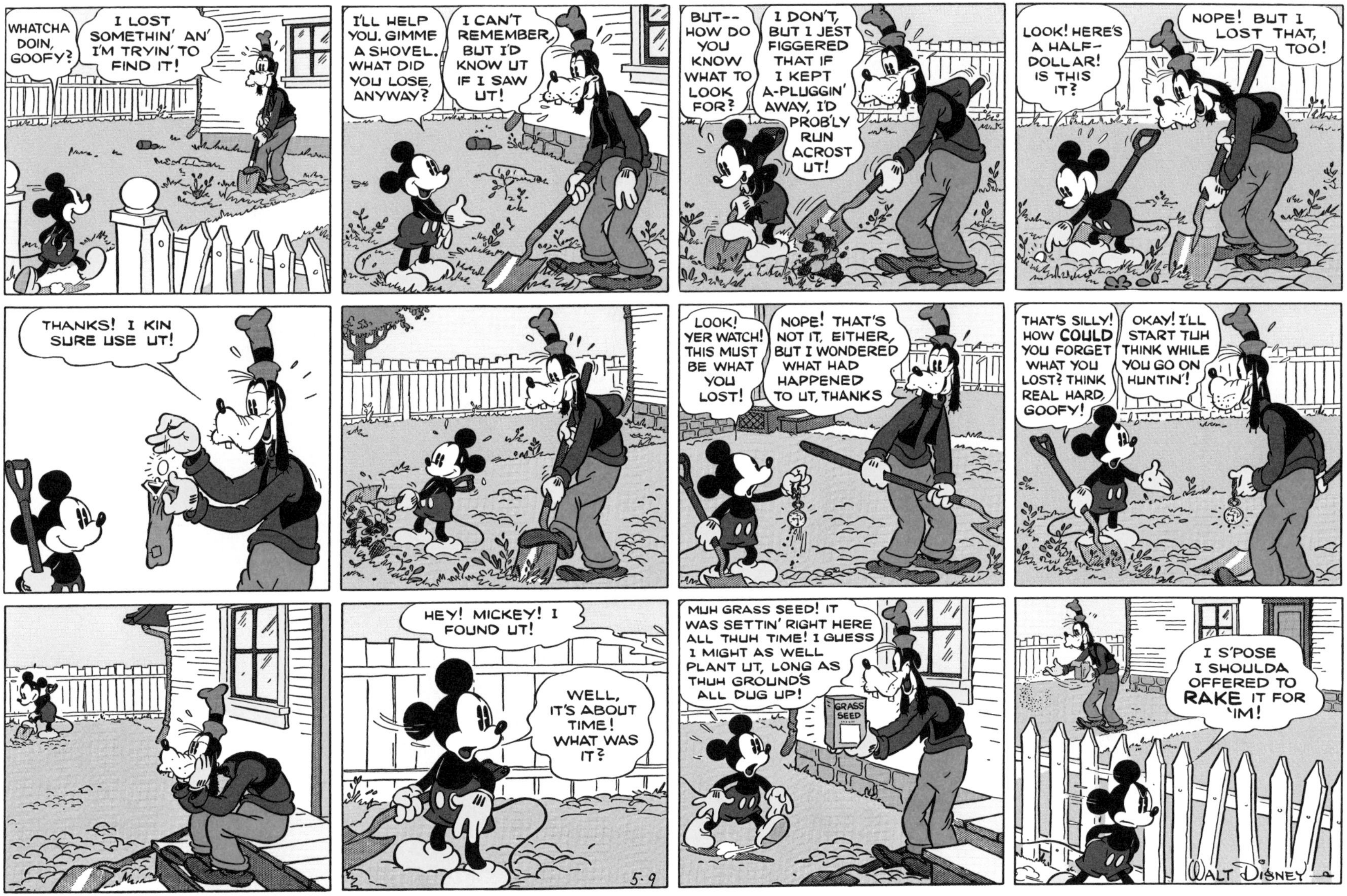
WHATCHA DOIN, GOOFY?
I LOST SOMETHIN' AN' I'M TRYIN' TO FIND IT!
I'LL HELP YOU. GIMME A SHOVEL. WHAT DID YOU LOSE, ANYWAY?
I CAN'T REMEMBER, BUT I'D KNOW UT IF I SAW UT!
BUT-- HOW DO YOU KNOW WHAT TO LOOK FOR?
I DON'T, BUT I JEST FIGGERED THAT IF I KEPT A-PLUGGIN' AWAY, I'D PROB'LY RUN ACROST UT!
LOOK! HERE'S A HALF-DOLLAR! IS THIS IT?
NOPE! BUT I LOST THAT, TOO!
THANKS! I KIN SURE USE UT!
LOOK! YER WATCH! THIS MUST BE WHAT YOU LOST!
NOPE! THAT'S NOT IT, EITHER, BUT I WONDERED WHAT HAD HAPPENED TO UT, THANKS
THAT'S SILLY! HOW COULD YOU FORGET WHAT YOU LOST? THINK REAL HARD, GOOFY!
OKAY! I'LL START TUH THINK WHILE YOU GO ON HUNTIN'!
HEY! MICKEY! I FOUND UT!
WELL, IT'S ABOUT TIME! WHAT WAS IT?
5-9
MUH GRASS SEED! IT WAS SETTIN' RIGHT HERE ALL THUH TIME! I GUESS I MIGHT AS WELL PLANT UT, LONG AS THUH GROUND'S ALL DUG UP!
GRASS SEED
I S'POSE I SHOULDA OFFERED TO RAKE IT FOR 'IM!
WALT DISNEY

Very best wishes to ULRICH SCRÖDER

Floyd Gottfredson

© W.D.P.

Floyd Gottfredson loved his Wild West stories—including this volume's "Sheriff of Nugget Gulch," but also some half-dozen more Mickey horse operas over the years. Gottfredson drew this 1980s image of cowboy Mickey for Disney scholar/artist Ulrich Schröder (misspelled "Scröder" in his dedication). Image courtesy Ulrich Schröder.

SHERIFF OF NUGGET GULCH AND GAG STRIPS

MAY 16, 1937
–
FEBRUARY 27, 1938

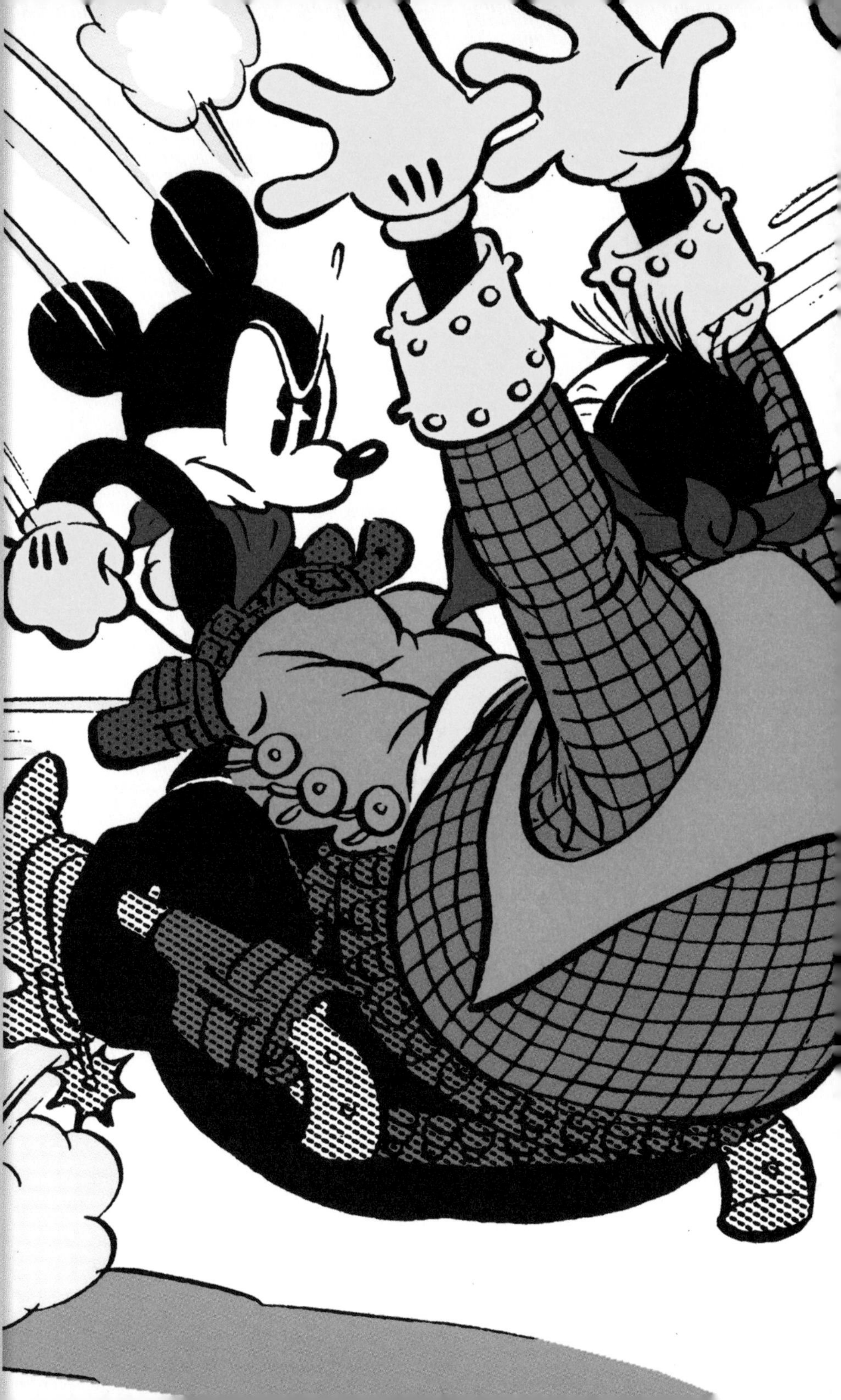

MICKEY MOUSE

REGISTERED U.S. PATENT OFFICE

THE GOOD, THE BAD, AND THE SUNDAY

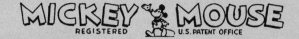

Mickey and Goofy are off to the Wild West yet again; a setting of which Gottfredson was obviously fond, even if it isn't quite as wild as Goofy imagines. Emptying his guns in the air in a juvenile display of enthusiasm, he lands both himself and an innocent Mickey behind bars—twice!—while earning them a reputation as desperados. Of course, they're really just city boys dressed up as cowboys; and the misunderstanding provides the source of many gags throughout the story, the most memorable being their shooting lessons from Minnie's assertive old aunt.

As exemplified by "Sheriff of Nugget Gulch," Sunday page serials have a different rhythm from daily strip serials. Within both formats, each individual strip needs to close with some kind of "bang": a gag, an element of surprise, a cliffhanger. But in the daily strip this happens every four panels; so if a meaningful plot is to be developed, each strip must be strongly connected to the neighboring days' strips. The Sunday page, on the other hand, has enough panels that each installment can almost function as its own microstory. And that's just as well: first, because installments appear a full week apart, so the writer must assume readers will have forgotten ongoing details; second, because the readers themselves may represent a different audience. As a rough generalization, it is typically grownups who follow the weekday newspaper, while kids get the comics in the Sunday edition. This, in turn, influences the writing—as we can see by comparing the relatively unsophisticated plot of "Nugget Gulch" with the elaborate daily serials of the same year, such as "In Search of Jungle Treasure" and "Monarch of Medioka."

"Nugget Gulch"'s unsophisticated nature even allows for some glaring plot holes and logic inconsistencies. For example, Goofy and Mickey—owing to their notorious reputation as outlaws—are accused by miners of holding up a stagecoach, shooting the sheriff, and escaping with a whole shipment of gold. A vigilante captures them and brings them into town, where in an unexpected twist, the miners make Mickey the new sheriff: as the toughest guy in town, he will now be responsible for any future hold-ups. The miners' decision arguably makes sense; but if they really think Mickey and Goofy robbed them, why not get their gold back from the pair before installing them in power?

Another glitch comes at the end of the story, when Mickey proves his worth as the sharpest shot in town—but some of us still remember that until recently, he was so hopeless with a revolver that he needed emergency remedial lessons.

Sunday comic sections brought hours of mindless relaxation to tired Depression-era kids. We like to imagine that Gottfredson and his collaborators, too, treated these Sundays as a bit of mindless relaxation.

— Francesco Stajano and Leonardo Gori

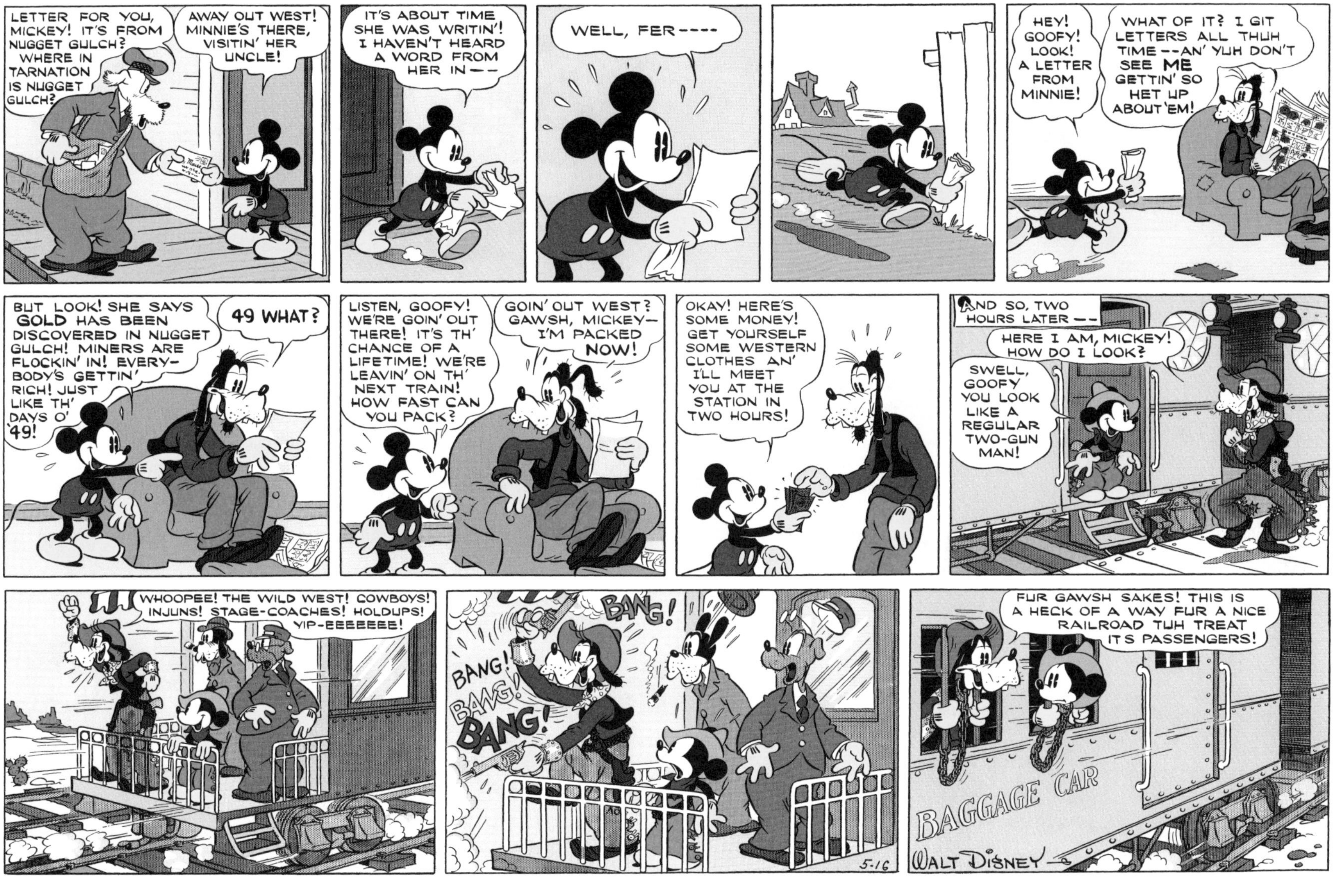

LETTER FOR YOU, MICKEY! IT'S FROM NUGGET GULCH? WHERE IN TARNATION IS NUGGET GULCH?
AWAY OUT WEST! MINNIE'S THERE, VISITIN' HER UNCLE!
IT'S ABOUT TIME SHE WAS WRITIN'! I HAVEN'T HEARD A WORD FROM HER IN--
WELL, FER----
HEY! GOOFY! LOOK! A LETTER FROM MINNIE!
WHAT OF IT? I GIT LETTERS ALL THUH TIME--AN' YUH DON'T SEE ME GETTIN' SO HET UP ABOUT 'EM!
BUT LOOK! SHE SAYS GOLD HAS BEEN DISCOVERED IN NUGGET GULCH! MINERS ARE FLOCKIN' IN! EVERY-BODY'S GETTIN' RICH! JUST LIKE TH' DAYS O' '49!
49 WHAT?
LISTEN, GOOFY! WE'RE GOIN' OUT THERE! IT'S TH' CHANCE OF A LIFETIME! WE'RE LEAVIN' ON TH' NEXT TRAIN! HOW FAST CAN YOU PACK?
GOIN' OUT WEST? GAWSH, MICKEY--I'M PACKED NOW!
OKAY! HERE'S SOME MONEY! GET YOURSELF SOME WESTERN CLOTHES AN' I'LL MEET YOU AT THE STATION IN TWO HOURS!
AND SO, TWO HOURS LATER--
HERE I AM, MICKEY! HOW DO I LOOK?
SWELL, GOOFY YOU LOOK LIKE A REGULAR TWO-GUN MAN!
WHOOPEE! THE WILD WEST! COWBOYS! INJUNS! STAGE-COACHES! HOLDUPS! YIP-EEEEEEE!
BANG!
BANG!
BANG!
BANG!
5-16
FUR GAWSH SAKES! THIS IS A HECK OF A WAY FUR A NICE RAILROAD TUH TREAT ITS PASSENGERS!
BAGGAGE CAR
WALT DISNEY

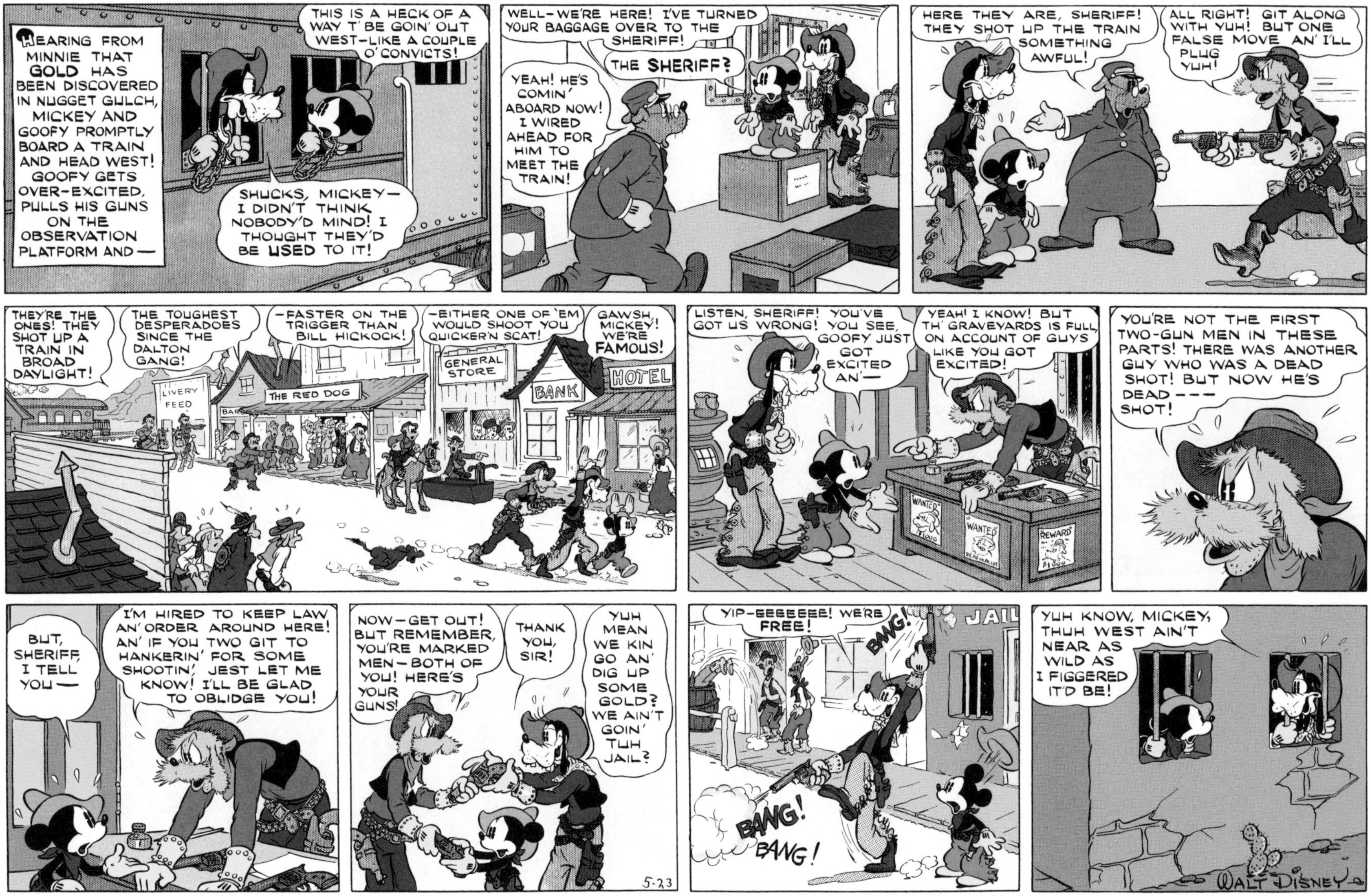
HEARING FROM MINNIE THAT GOLD HAS BEEN DISCOVERED IN NUGGET GULCH, MICKEY AND GOOFY PROMPTLY BOARD A TRAIN AND HEAD WEST! GOOFY GETS OVER-EXCITED, PULLS HIS GUNS ON THE OBSERVATION PLATFORM AND—
THIS IS A HECK OF A WAY T' BE GOIN' OUT WEST—LIKE A COUPLE O' CONVICTS!
SHUCKS, MICKEY— I DIDN'T THINK NOBODY'D MIND! I THOUGHT THEY'D BE USED TO IT!
WELL—WE'RE HERE! I'VE TURNED YOUR BAGGAGE OVER TO THE SHERIFF!
THE SHERIFF?
YEAH! HE'S COMIN' ABOARD NOW! I WIRED AHEAD FOR HIM TO MEET THE TRAIN!
HERE THEY ARE, SHERIFF! THEY SHOT UP THE TRAIN SOMETHING AWFUL!
ALL RIGHT! GIT ALONG WITH YUH! BUT ONE FALSE MOVE AN' I'LL PLUG YUH!
THEY'RE THE ONES! THEY SHOT UP A TRAIN IN BROAD DAYLIGHT!
THE TOUGHEST DESPERADOES SINCE THE DALTON GANG!
—FASTER ON THE TRIGGER THAN BILL HICKOCK!
—EITHER ONE OF 'EM WOULD SHOOT YOU QUICKER'N SCAT!
GAWSH, MICKEY! WE'RE FAMOUS!
LIVERY FEED
BAR
THE RED DOG
GENERAL STORE
BANK
HOTEL
LISTEN, SHERIFF! YOU'VE GOT US WRONG! YOU SEE, GOOFY JUST GOT EXCITED AN'—
YEAH! I KNOW! BUT TH' GRAVEYARDS IS FULL ON ACCOUNT OF GUYS LIKE YOU GOT EXCITED!
WANTED
WANTED
REWARD
YOU'RE NOT THE FIRST TWO-GUN MEN IN THESE PARTS! THERE WAS ANOTHER GUY WHO WAS A DEAD SHOT! BUT NOW HE'S DEAD - - - SHOT!
BUT, SHERIFF, I TELL YOU—
I'M HIRED TO KEEP LAW AN' ORDER AROUND HERE! AN' IF YOU TWO GIT TO HANKERIN' FOR SOME SHOOTIN', JEST LET ME KNOW! I'LL BE GLAD TO OBLIDGE YOU!
NOW—GET OUT! BUT REMEMBER, YOU'RE MARKED MEN—BOTH OF YOU! HERE'S YOUR GUNS!
THANK YOU, SIR!
YUH MEAN WE KIN GO AN' DIG UP SOME GOLD? WE AIN'T GOIN' TUH JAIL?
5-23
YIP-EEEEEEE! WE'RE FREE!
JAIL
BANG!
BANG!
BANG!
YUH KNOW, MICKEY, THUH WEST AIN'T NEAR AS WILD AS I FIGGERED IT'D BE!
WALT DISNEY

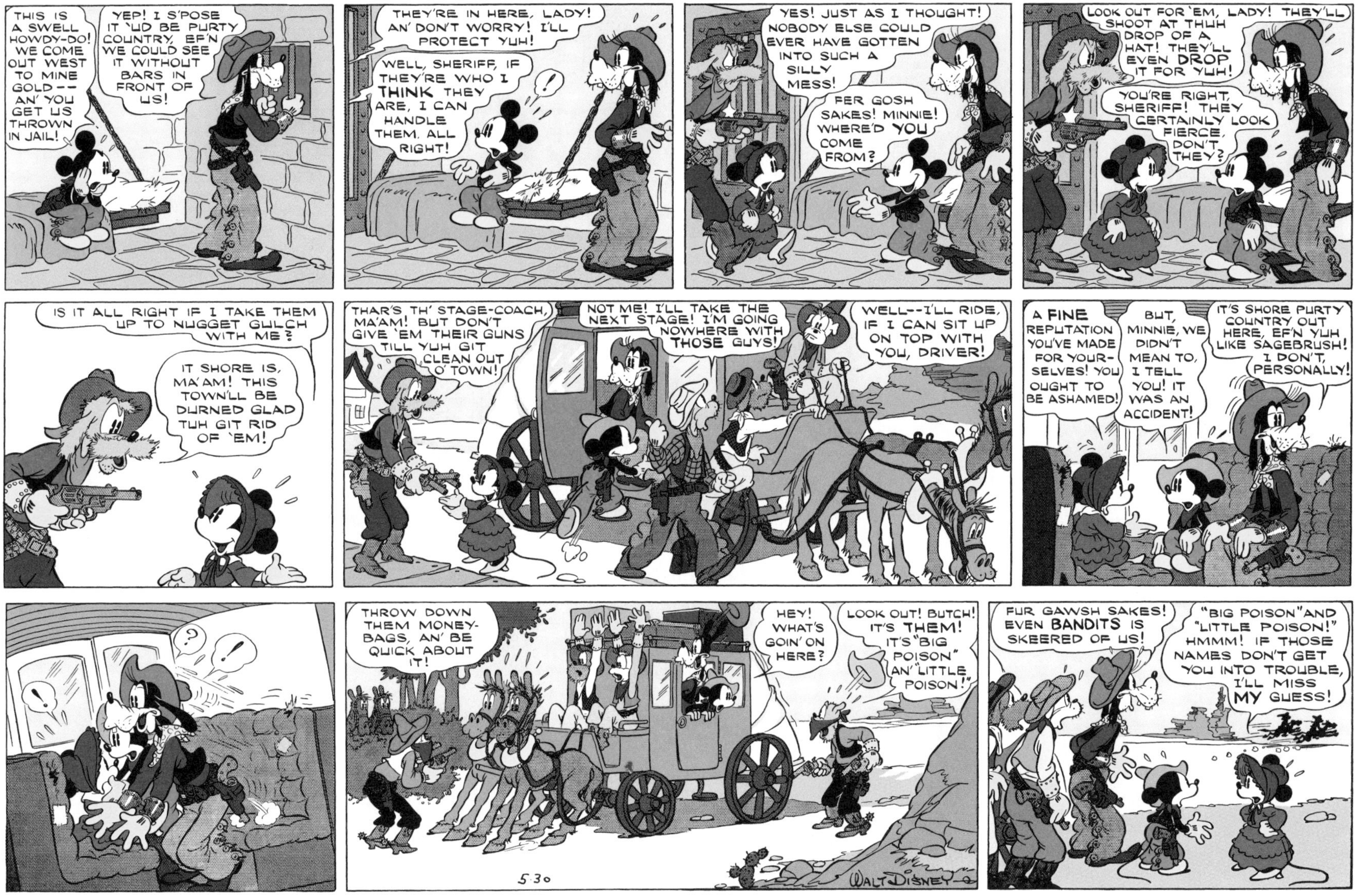
THIS IS A SWELL HOWDY-DO! WE COME OUT WEST TO MINE GOLD-- AN' YOU GET US THROWN IN JAIL!
YEP! I S'POSE IT 'UD BE PURTY COUNTRY, EF'N WE COULD SEE IT WITHOUT BARS IN FRONT OF US!
THEY'RE IN HERE, LADY! AN' DON'T WORRY! I'LL PROTECT YUH!
WELL, SHERIFF, IF THEY'RE WHO I **THINK** THEY ARE, I CAN HANDLE THEM. ALL RIGHT!
!
YES! JUST AS I THOUGHT! NOBODY ELSE COULD EVER HAVE GOTTEN INTO SUCH A SILLY MESS!
FER GOSH SAKES! MINNIE! WHERE'D **YOU** COME FROM?
LOOK OUT FOR 'EM, LADY! THEY'LL SHOOT AT THUH DROP OF A HAT! THEY'LL EVEN **DROP** IT FOR YUH!
YOU'RE RIGHT, SHERIFF! THEY CERTAINLY LOOK FIERCE, DON'T THEY?
IS IT ALL RIGHT IF I TAKE THEM UP TO NUGGET GULCH WITH ME?
IT SHORE IS, MA'AM! THIS TOWN'LL BE DURNED GLAD TUH GIT RID OF 'EM!
THAR'S TH' STAGE-COACH, MA'AM! BUT DON'T GIVE 'EM THEIR GUNS TILL YUH GIT CLEAN OUT O' TOWN!
NOT ME! I'LL TAKE THE NEXT STAGE! I'M GOING NOWHERE WITH **THOSE** GUYS!
WELL--I'LL RIDE, IF I CAN SIT UP ON TOP WITH YOU, DRIVER!
A **FINE** REPUTATION YOU'VE MADE FOR YOURSELVES! YOU OUGHT TO BE ASHAMED!
BUT, MINNIE, WE DIDN'T MEAN TO, I TELL YOU! IT WAS AN ACCIDENT!
IT'S SHORE PURTY COUNTRY OUT HERE, EF'N YUH LIKE SAGEBRUSH! I DON'T, PERSONALLY!
?
!
!
THROW DOWN THEM MONEY-BAGS, AN' BE QUICK ABOUT IT!
HEY! WHAT'S GOIN' ON HERE?
LOOK OUT! BUTCH! IT'S **THEM**! IT'S "BIG POISON" AN' "LITTLE POISON!"
5.30
WALT DISNEY
FUR GAWSH SAKES! EVEN **BANDITS** IS SKEERED OF US!
"BIG POISON" AND "LITTLE POISON!" HMMM! IF THOSE NAMES DON'T GET YOU INTO TROUBLE, I'LL MISS **MY** GUESS!

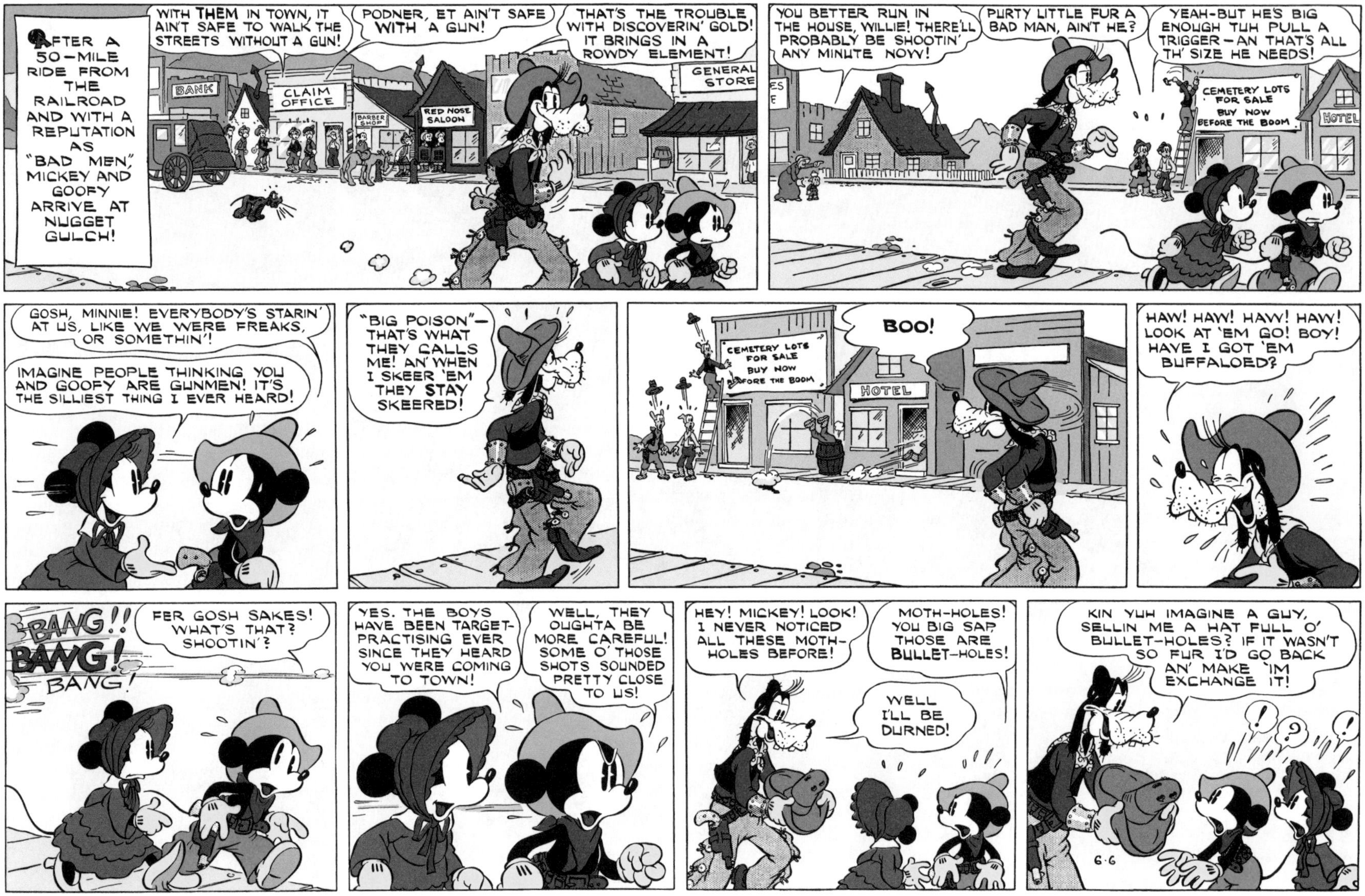

AFTER A 50-MILE RIDE FROM THE RAILROAD AND WITH A REPUTATION AS "BAD MEN," MICKEY AND GOOFY ARRIVE AT NUGGET GULCH!
WITH THEM IN TOWN, IT AIN'T SAFE TO WALK THE STREETS WITHOUT A GUN!
PODNER, ET AIN'T SAFE WITH A GUN!
THAT'S THE TROUBLE WITH DISCOVERIN' GOLD! IT BRINGS IN A ROWDY ELEMENT!
BANK
CLAIM OFFICE
BARBER SHOP
RED NOSE SALOON
GENERAL STORE
YOU BETTER RUN IN THE HOUSE, WILLIE! THERE'LL PROBABLY BE SHOOTIN' ANY MINUTE NOW!
PURTY LITTLE FUR A BAD MAN, AIN'T HE?
YEAH-BUT HE'S BIG ENOUGH TUH PULL A TRIGGER—AN THAT'S ALL TH' SIZE HE NEEDS!
CEMETERY LOTS FOR SALE BUY NOW BEFORE THE BOOM
HOTEL
GOSH, MINNIE! EVERYBODY'S STARIN' AT US, LIKE WE WERE FREAKS, OR SOMETHIN'!
IMAGINE PEOPLE THINKING YOU AND GOOFY ARE GUNMEN! IT'S THE SILLIEST THING I EVER HEARD!
"BIG POISON"—THAT'S WHAT THEY CALLS ME! AN' WHEN I SKEER 'EM THEY STAY SKEERED!
BOO!
CEMETERY LOTS FOR SALE BUY NOW FORE THE BOOM
HOTEL
HAW! HAW! HAW! HAW! LOOK AT 'EM GO! BOY! HAVE I GOT 'EM BUFFALOED?
BANG!! BANG! BANG!
FER GOSH SAKES! WHAT'S THAT? SHOOTIN'?
YES. THE BOYS HAVE BEEN TARGET-PRACTISING EVER SINCE THEY HEARD YOU WERE COMING TO TOWN!
WELL, THEY OUGHTA BE MORE CAREFUL! SOME O' THOSE SHOTS SOUNDED PRETTY CLOSE TO US!
HEY! MICKEY! LOOK! I NEVER NOTICED ALL THESE MOTH-HOLES BEFORE!
MOTH-HOLES! YOU BIG SAP! THOSE ARE BULLET-HOLES!
WELL I'LL BE DURNED!
KIN YUH IMAGINE A GUY, SELLIN ME A HAT FULL O' BULLET-HOLES? IF IT WASN'T SO FUR I'D GO BACK AN' MAKE 'IM EXCHANGE IT!
! ? !
6-6

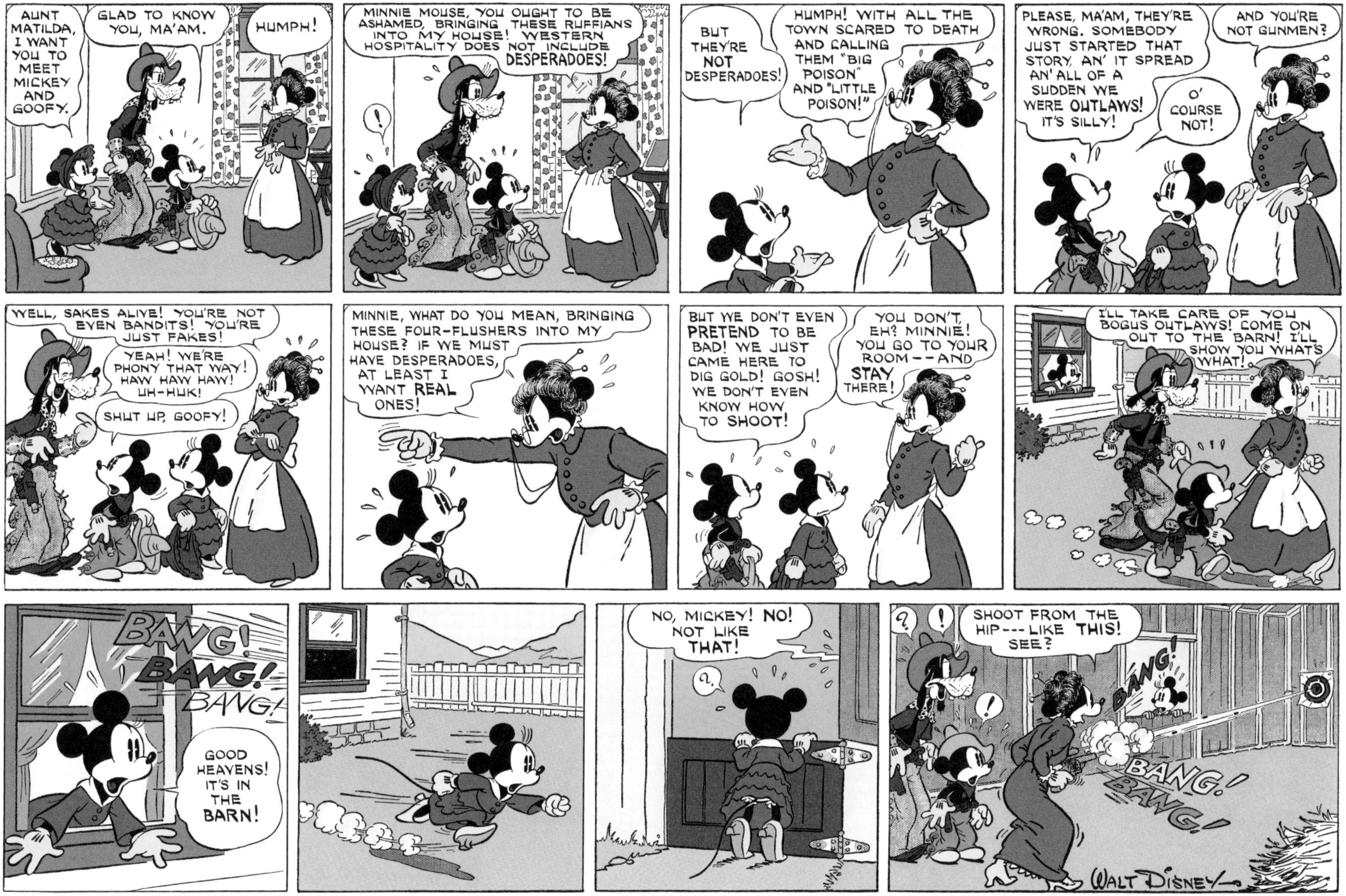
AUNT MATILDA, I WANT YOU TO MEET MICKEY AND GOOFY.
GLAD TO KNOW YOU, MA'AM.
HUMPH!
MINNIE MOUSE, YOU OUGHT TO BE ASHAMED, BRINGING THESE RUFFIANS INTO MY HOUSE! WESTERN HOSPITALITY DOES NOT INCLUDE DESPERADOES!
!
BUT THEY'RE NOT DESPERADOES!
HUMPH! WITH ALL THE TOWN SCARED TO DEATH AND CALLING THEM "BIG POISON" AND "LITTLE POISON!"
PLEASE, MA'AM, THEY'RE WRONG. SOMEBODY JUST STARTED THAT STORY, AN' IT SPREAD AN' ALL OF A SUDDEN WE WERE OUTLAWS! IT'S SILLY!
O' COURSE NOT!
AND YOU'RE NOT GUNMEN?
WELL, SAKES ALIVE! YOU'RE NOT EVEN BANDITS! YOU'RE JUST FAKES!
YEAH! WE'RE PHONY THAT WAY! HAW HAW HAW! UH-HUK!
SHUT UP, GOOFY!
MINNIE, WHAT DO YOU MEAN, BRINGING THESE FOUR-FLUSHERS INTO MY HOUSE? IF WE MUST HAVE DESPERADOES, AT LEAST I WANT REAL ONES!
BUT WE DON'T EVEN PRETEND TO BE BAD! WE JUST CAME HERE TO DIG GOLD! GOSH! WE DON'T EVEN KNOW HOW TO SHOOT!
YOU DON'T, EH? MINNIE! YOU GO TO YOUR ROOM--AND STAY THERE!
I'LL TAKE CARE OF YOU BOGUS OUTLAWS! COME ON OUT TO THE BARN! I'LL SHOW YOU WHAT'S WHAT!
BANG! BANG! BANG!
GOOD HEAVENS! IT'S IN THE BARN!
NO, MICKEY! NO! NOT LIKE THAT!
?
? !
SHOOT FROM THE HIP---LIKE THIS! SEE?
!
BANG! BANG! BANG!
WALT DISNEY

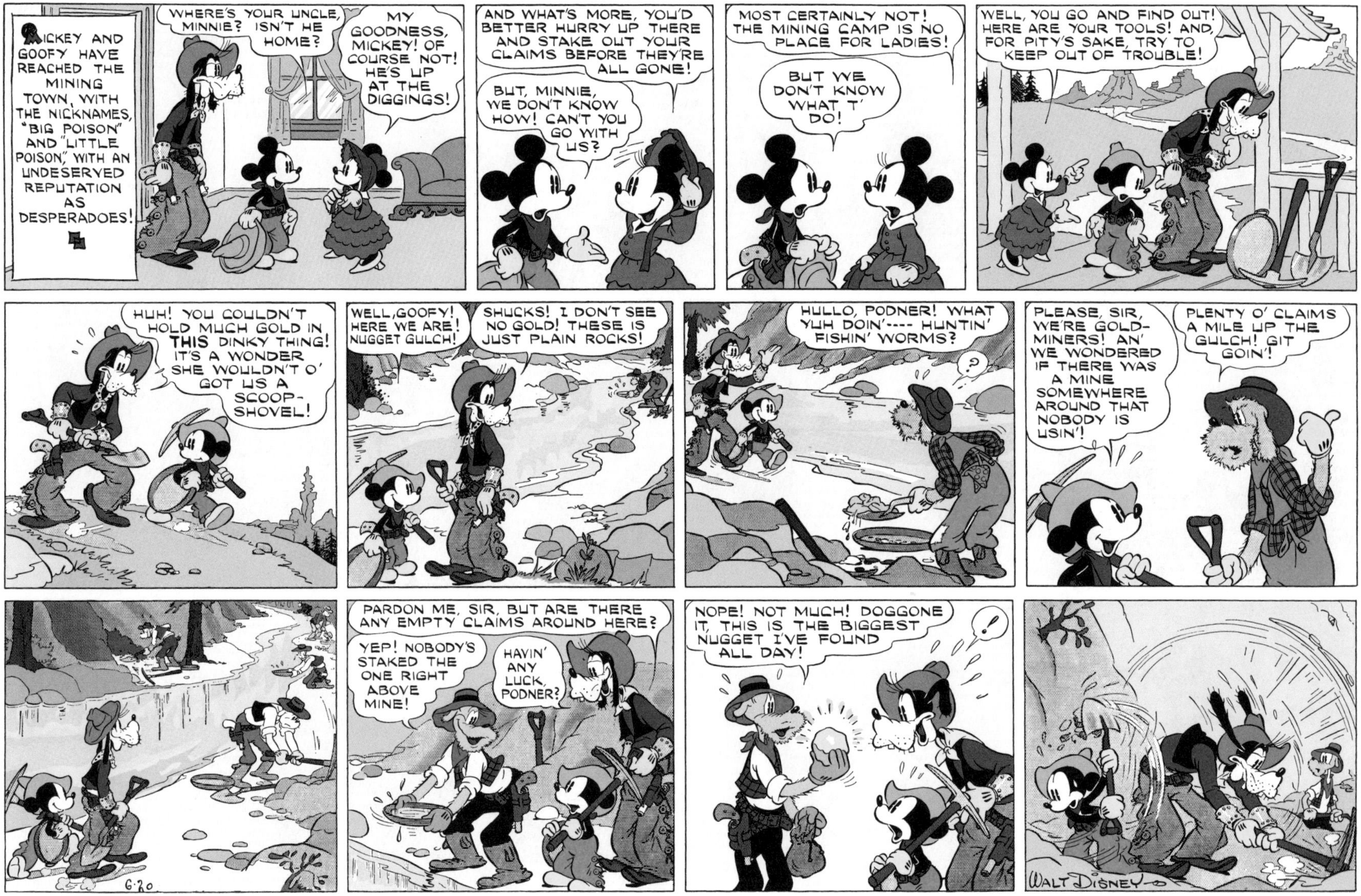
MICKEY AND GOOFY HAVE REACHED THE MINING TOWN, WITH THE NICKNAMES, "BIG POISON" AND "LITTLE POISON," WITH AN UNDESERVED REPUTATION AS DESPERADOES!
WHERE'S YOUR UNCLE, MINNIE? ISN'T HE HOME?
MY GOODNESS, MICKEY! OF COURSE NOT! HE'S UP AT THE DIGGINGS!
AND WHAT'S MORE, YOU'D BETTER HURRY UP THERE AND STAKE OUT YOUR CLAIMS BEFORE THEY'RE ALL GONE!
BUT, MINNIE, WE DON'T KNOW HOW! CAN'T YOU GO WITH US?
MOST CERTAINLY NOT! THE MINING CAMP IS NO PLACE FOR LADIES!
BUT WE DON'T KNOW WHAT T' DO!
WELL, YOU GO AND FIND OUT! HERE ARE YOUR TOOLS! AND, FOR PITY'S SAKE, TRY TO KEEP OUT OF TROUBLE!
HUH! YOU COULDN'T HOLD MUCH GOLD IN **THIS** DINKY THING! IT'S A WONDER SHE WOULDN'T O' GOT US A SCOOP-SHOVEL!
WELL, GOOFY! HERE WE ARE! NUGGET GULCH!
SHUCKS! I DON'T SEE NO GOLD! THESE IS JUST PLAIN ROCKS!
HULLO, PODNER! WHAT YUH DOIN'---- HUNTIN' FISHIN' WORMS?
?
PLEASE, SIR, WE'RE GOLD-MINERS! AN' WE WONDERED IF THERE WAS A MINE SOMEWHERE AROUND THAT NOBODY IS USIN'!
PLENTY O' CLAIMS A MILE UP THE GULCH! GIT GOIN'!
6-20
PARDON ME, SIR, BUT ARE THERE ANY EMPTY CLAIMS AROUND HERE?
YEP! NOBODY'S STAKED THE ONE RIGHT ABOVE MINE!
HAVIN' ANY LUCK, PODNER?
NOPE! NOT MUCH! DOGGONE IT, THIS IS THE BIGGEST NUGGET I'VE FOUND ALL DAY!
!
WALT DISNEY

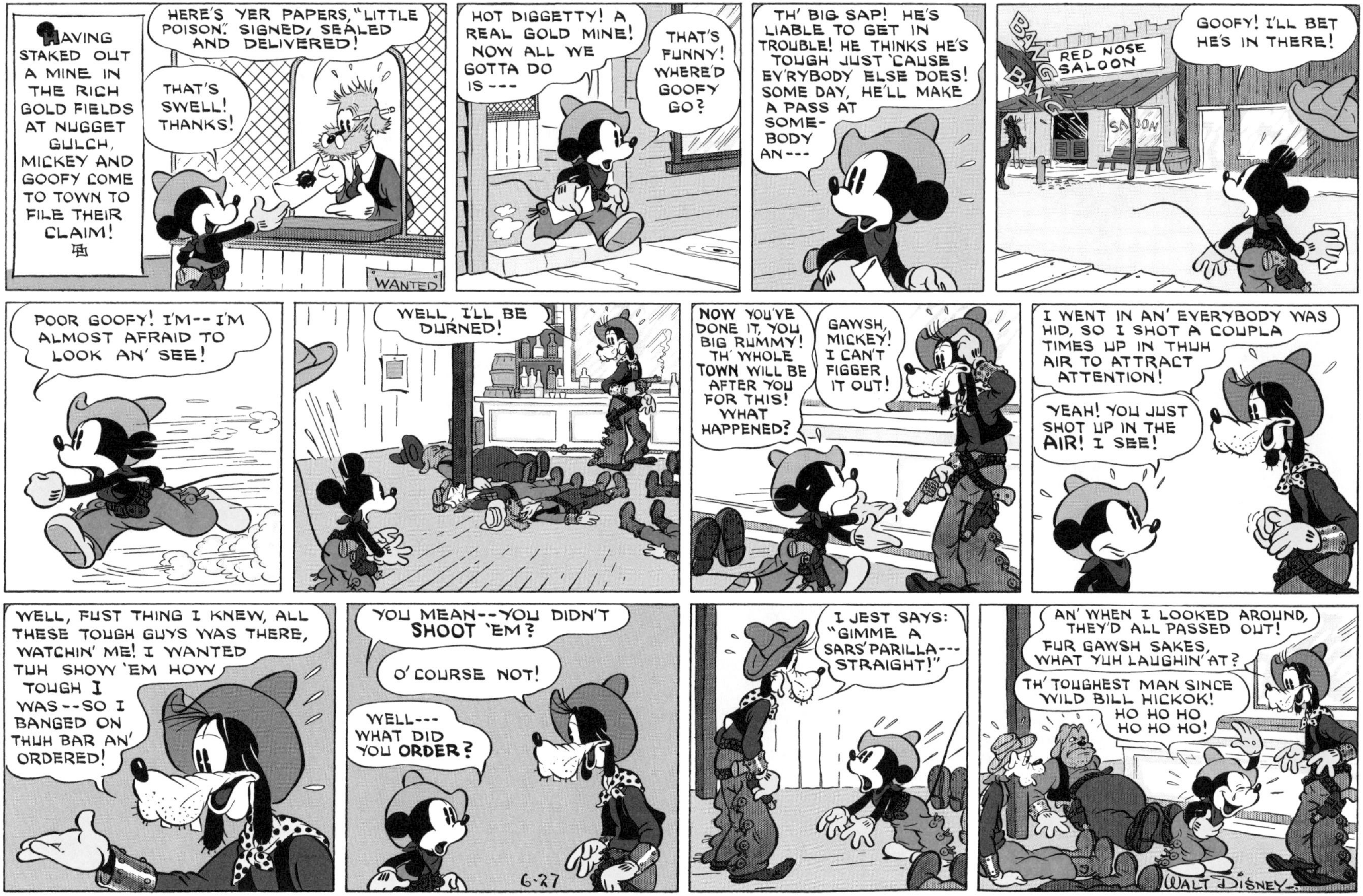

HAVING STAKED OUT A MINE IN THE RICH GOLD FIELDS AT NUGGET GULCH, MICKEY AND GOOFY COME TO TOWN TO FILE THEIR CLAIM!
HERE'S YER PAPERS, "LITTLE POISON". SIGNED, SEALED AND DELIVERED!
THAT'S SWELL! THANKS!
WANTED
HOT DIGGETTY! A REAL GOLD MINE! NOW ALL WE GOTTA DO IS ---
THAT'S FUNNY! WHERE'D GOOFY GO?
TH' BIG SAP! HE'S LIABLE TO GET IN TROUBLE! HE THINKS HE'S TOUGH JUST 'CAUSE EV'RYBODY ELSE DOES! SOME DAY, HE'LL MAKE A PASS AT SOME-BODY AN---
BANG
BANG
RED NOSE SALOON
SALOON
GOOFY! I'LL BET HE'S IN THERE!
POOR GOOFY! I'M--I'M ALMOST AFRAID TO LOOK AN' SEE!
WELL, I'LL BE DURNED!
NOW YOU'VE DONE IT, YOU BIG RUMMY! TH' WHOLE TOWN WILL BE AFTER YOU FOR THIS! WHAT HAPPENED?
GAWSH, MICKEY! I CAN'T FIGGER IT OUT!
I WENT IN AN' EVERYBODY WAS HID, SO I SHOT A COUPLA TIMES UP IN THUH AIR TO ATTRACT ATTENTION!
YEAH! YOU JUST SHOT UP IN THE AIR! I SEE!
WELL, FUST THING I KNEW, ALL THESE TOUGH GUYS WAS THERE, WATCHIN' ME! I WANTED TUH SHOW 'EM HOW TOUGH I WAS--SO I BANGED ON THUH BAR AN' ORDERED!
YOU MEAN--YOU DIDN'T SHOOT 'EM?
O'COURSE NOT!
WELL--- WHAT DID YOU ORDER?
6-27
I JEST SAYS: "GIMME A SARS'PARILLA--- STRAIGHT!"
AN' WHEN I LOOKED AROUND, THEY'D ALL PASSED OUT!
FUR GAWSH SAKES, WHAT YUH LAUGHIN' AT?
TH' TOUGHEST MAN SINCE WILD BILL HICKOK! HO HO HO HO HO HO!
WALT DISNEY

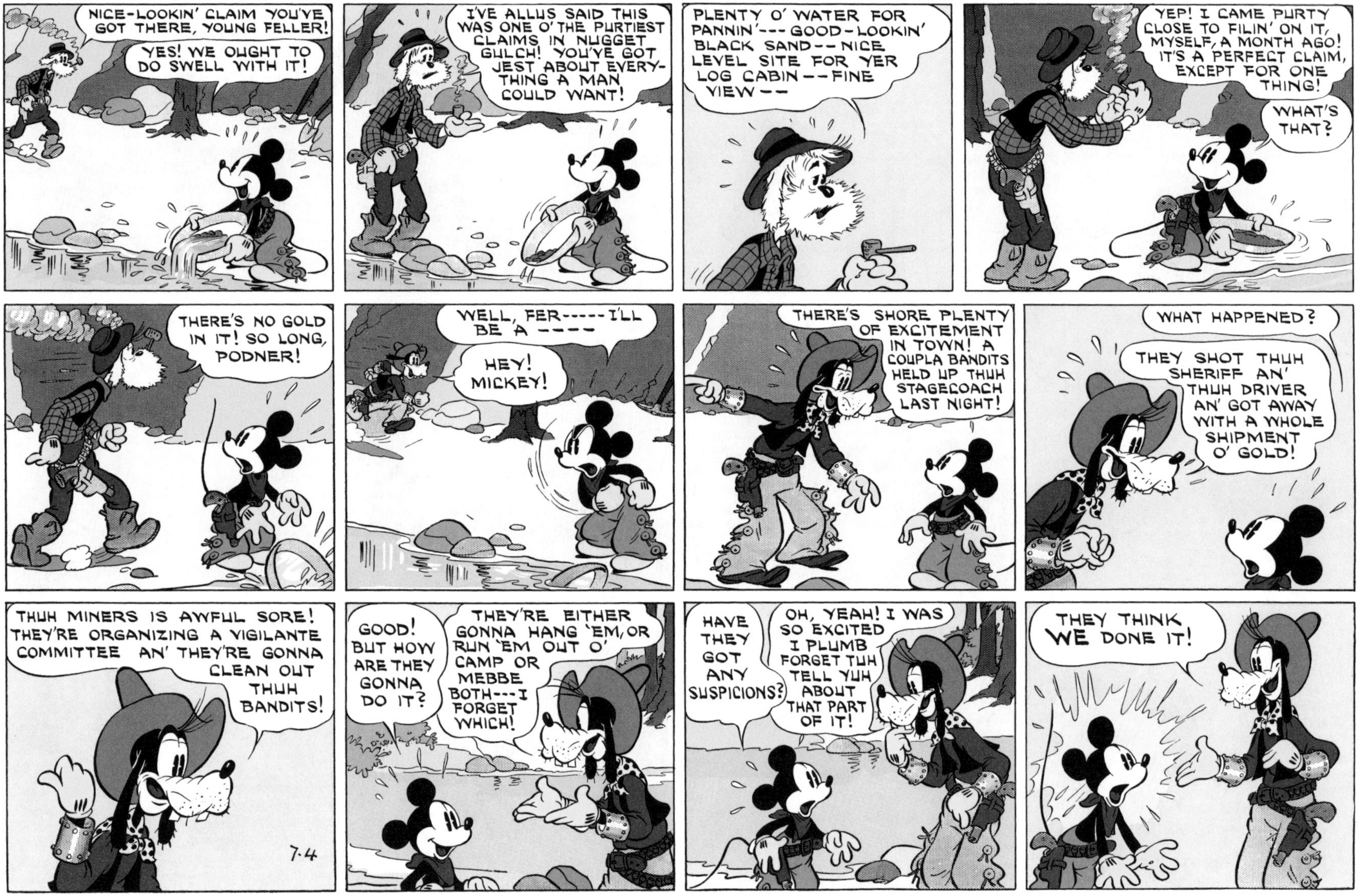

NICE-LOOKIN' CLAIM YOU'VE GOT THERE, YOUNG FELLER!
YES! WE OUGHT TO DO SWELL WITH IT!
I'VE ALLUS SAID THIS WAS ONE O' THE PURTIEST CLAIMS IN NUGGET GULCH! YOU'VE GOT JEST ABOUT EVERY-THING A MAN COULD WANT!
PLENTY O' WATER FOR PANNIN'--- GOOD-LOOKIN' BLACK SAND-- NICE LEVEL SITE FOR YER LOG CABIN -- FINE VIEW --
YEP! I CAME PURTY CLOSE TO FILIN' ON IT, MYSELF, A MONTH AGO! IT'S A PERFECT CLAIM, EXCEPT FOR ONE THING!
WHAT'S THAT?
THERE'S NO GOLD IN IT! SO LONG, PODNER!
WELL, FER----- I'LL BE A ----
HEY! MICKEY!
THERE'S SHORE PLENTY OF EXCITEMENT IN TOWN! A COUPLA BANDITS HELD UP THUH STAGECOACH LAST NIGHT!
WHAT HAPPENED?
THEY SHOT THUH SHERIFF AN' THUH DRIVER AN' GOT AWAY WITH A WHOLE SHIPMENT O' GOLD!
THUH MINERS IS AWFUL SORE! THEY'RE ORGANIZING A VIGILANTE COMMITTEE AN' THEY'RE GONNA CLEAN OUT THUH BANDITS!
7-4
GOOD! BUT HOW ARE THEY GONNA DO IT?
THEY'RE EITHER GONNA HANG 'EM, OR RUN 'EM OUT O' CAMP OR MEBBE BOTH--- I FORGET WHICH!
HAVE THEY GOT ANY SUSPICIONS?
OH, YEAH! I WAS SO EXCITED I PLUMB FORGET TUH TELL YUH ABOUT THAT PART OF IT!
THEY THINK WE DONE IT!

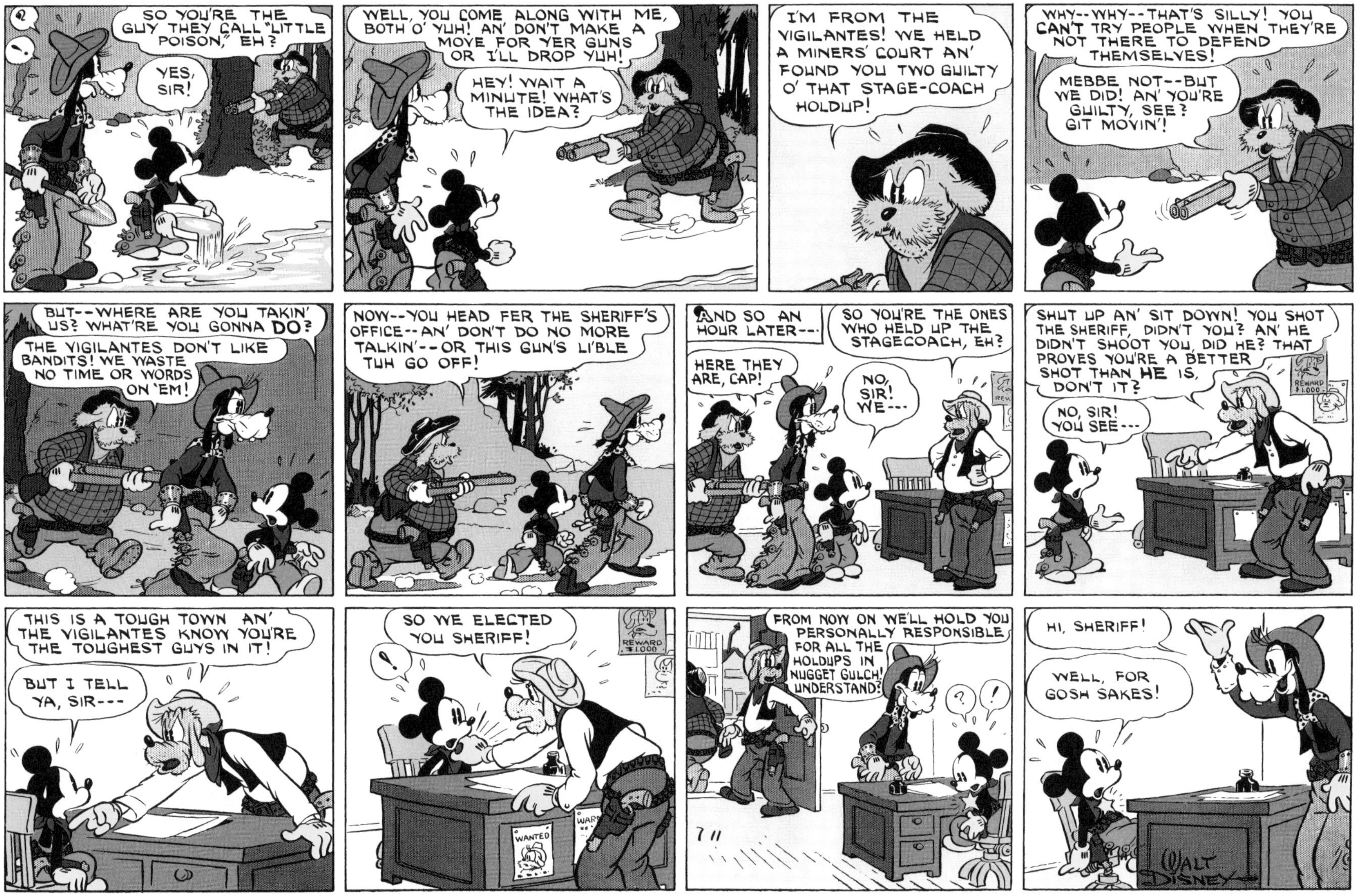

SO YOU'RE THE GUY THEY CALL "LITTLE POISON," EH?
!
YES, SIR!
WELL, YOU COME ALONG WITH ME, BOTH O' YUH! AN' DON'T MAKE A MOVE FOR YER GUNS OR I'LL DROP YUH!
HEY! WAIT A MINUTE! WHAT'S THE IDEA?
I'M FROM THE VIGILANTES! WE HELD A MINERS' COURT AN' FOUND YOU TWO GUILTY O' THAT STAGE-COACH HOLDUP!
WHY--WHY--THAT'S SILLY! YOU CAN'T TRY PEOPLE WHEN THEY'RE NOT THERE TO DEFEND THEMSELVES!
MEBBE NOT--BUT WE DID! AN' YOU'RE GUILTY, SEE? GIT MOVIN'!
BUT--WHERE ARE YOU TAKIN' US? WHAT'RE YOU GONNA DO?
THE VIGILANTES DON'T LIKE BANDITS! WE WASTE NO TIME OR WORDS ON 'EM!
NOW--YOU HEAD FER THE SHERIFF'S OFFICE--AN' DON'T DO NO MORE TALKIN'--OR THIS GUN'S LI'BLE TUH GO OFF!
AND SO AN HOUR LATER--
SO YOU'RE THE ONES WHO HELD UP THE STAGECOACH, EH?
HERE THEY ARE, CAP!
NO, SIR! WE---
SHUT UP AN' SIT DOWN! YOU SHOT THE SHERIFF, DIDN'T YOU? AN' HE DIDN'T SHOOT YOU, DID HE? THAT PROVES YOU'RE A BETTER SHOT THAN HE IS, DON'T IT?
REWARD $1,000
NO, SIR! YOU SEE---
THIS IS A TOUGH TOWN AN' THE VIGILANTES KNOW YOU'RE THE TOUGHEST GUYS IN IT!
BUT I TELL YA, SIR---
SO WE ELECTED YOU SHERIFF!
!
REWARD $1,000
WANTED
FROM NOW ON WE'LL HOLD YOU PERSONALLY RESPONSIBLE FOR ALL THE HOLDUPS IN NUGGET GULCH! UNDERSTAND?
? !
HI, SHERIFF!
WELL, FOR GOSH SAKES!
WALT DISNEY

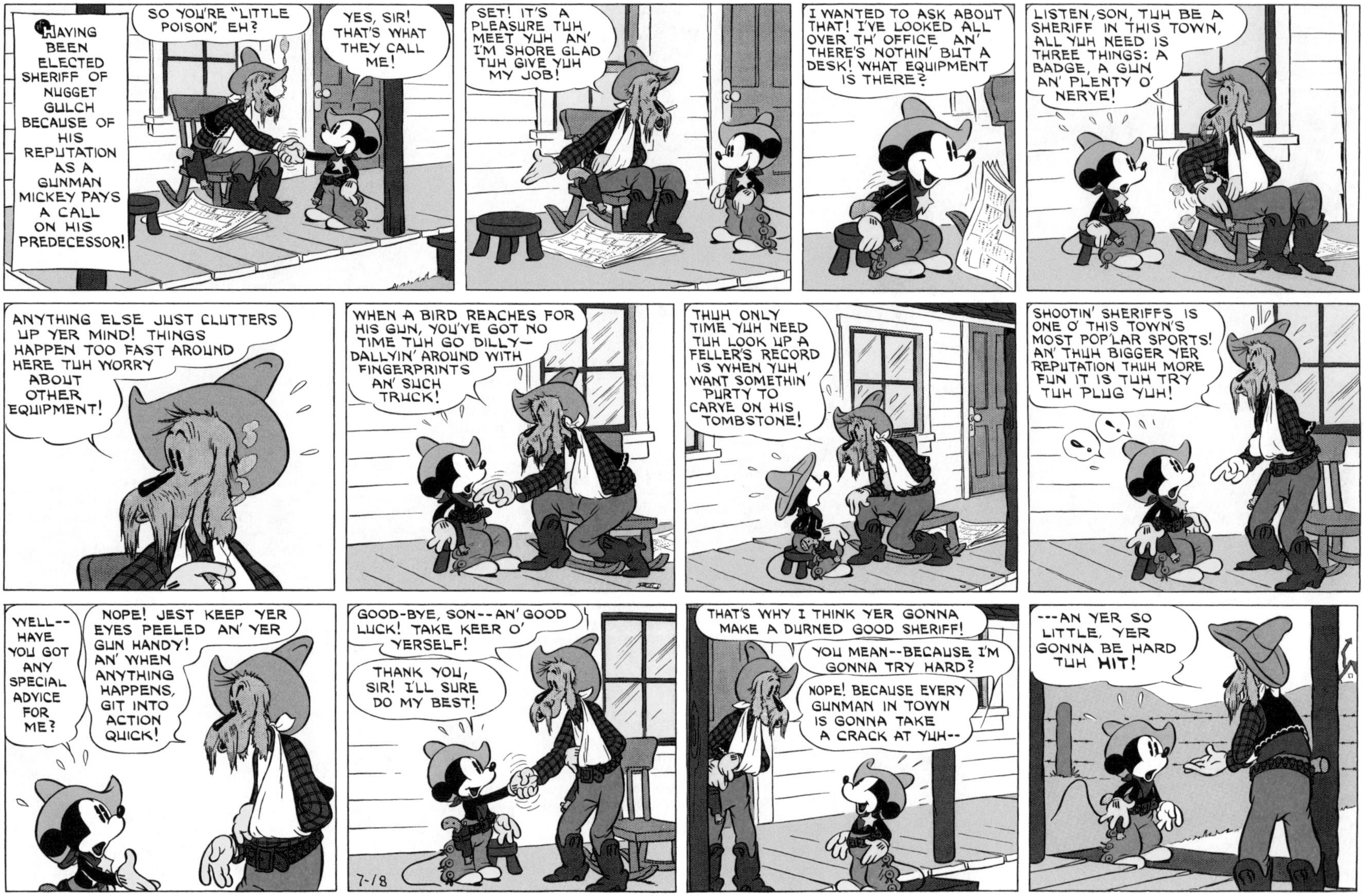
HAVING BEEN ELECTED SHERIFF OF NUGGET GULCH BECAUSE OF HIS REPUTATION AS A GUNMAN MICKEY PAYS A CALL ON HIS PREDECESSOR!
SO YOU'RE "LITTLE POISON", EH?
YES, SIR! THAT'S WHAT THEY CALL ME!
SET! IT'S A PLEASURE TUH MEET YUH AN' I'M SHORE GLAD TUH GIVE YUH MY JOB!
I WANTED TO ASK ABOUT THAT! I'VE LOOKED ALL OVER TH' OFFICE AN' THERE'S NOTHIN' BUT A DESK! WHAT EQUIPMENT IS THERE?
LISTEN, SON, TUH BE A SHERIFF IN THIS TOWN, ALL YUH NEED IS THREE THINGS: A BADGE, A GUN AN' PLENTY O' NERVE!
ANYTHING ELSE JUST CLUTTERS UP YER MIND! THINGS HAPPEN TOO FAST AROUND HERE TUH WORRY ABOUT OTHER EQUIPMENT!
WHEN A BIRD REACHES FOR HIS GUN, YOU'VE GOT NO TIME TUH GO DILLY-DALLYIN' AROUND WITH FINGERPRINTS AN' SUCH TRUCK!
THUH ONLY TIME YUH NEED TUH LOOK UP A FELLER'S RECORD IS WHEN YUH WANT SOMETHIN' PURTY TO CARVE ON HIS TOMBSTONE!
SHOOTIN' SHERIFFS IS ONE O' THIS TOWN'S MOST POP'LAR SPORTS! AN' THUH BIGGER YER REPUTATION THUH MORE FUN IT IS TUH TRY TUH PLUG YUH!
WELL--HAVE YOU GOT ANY SPECIAL ADVICE FOR ME?
NOPE! JEST KEEP YER EYES PEELED AN' YER GUN HANDY! AN' WHEN ANYTHING HAPPENS, GIT INTO ACTION QUICK!
GOOD-BYE, SON--AN' GOOD LUCK! TAKE KEER O' YERSELF!
THANK YOU, SIR! I'LL SURE DO MY BEST!
7-18
THAT'S WHY I THINK YER GONNA MAKE A DURNED GOOD SHERIFF!
YOU MEAN--BECAUSE I'M GONNA TRY HARD?
NOPE! BECAUSE EVERY GUNMAN IN TOWN IS GONNA TAKE A CRACK AT YUH--
---AN YER SO LITTLE, YER GONNA BE HARD TUH HIT!

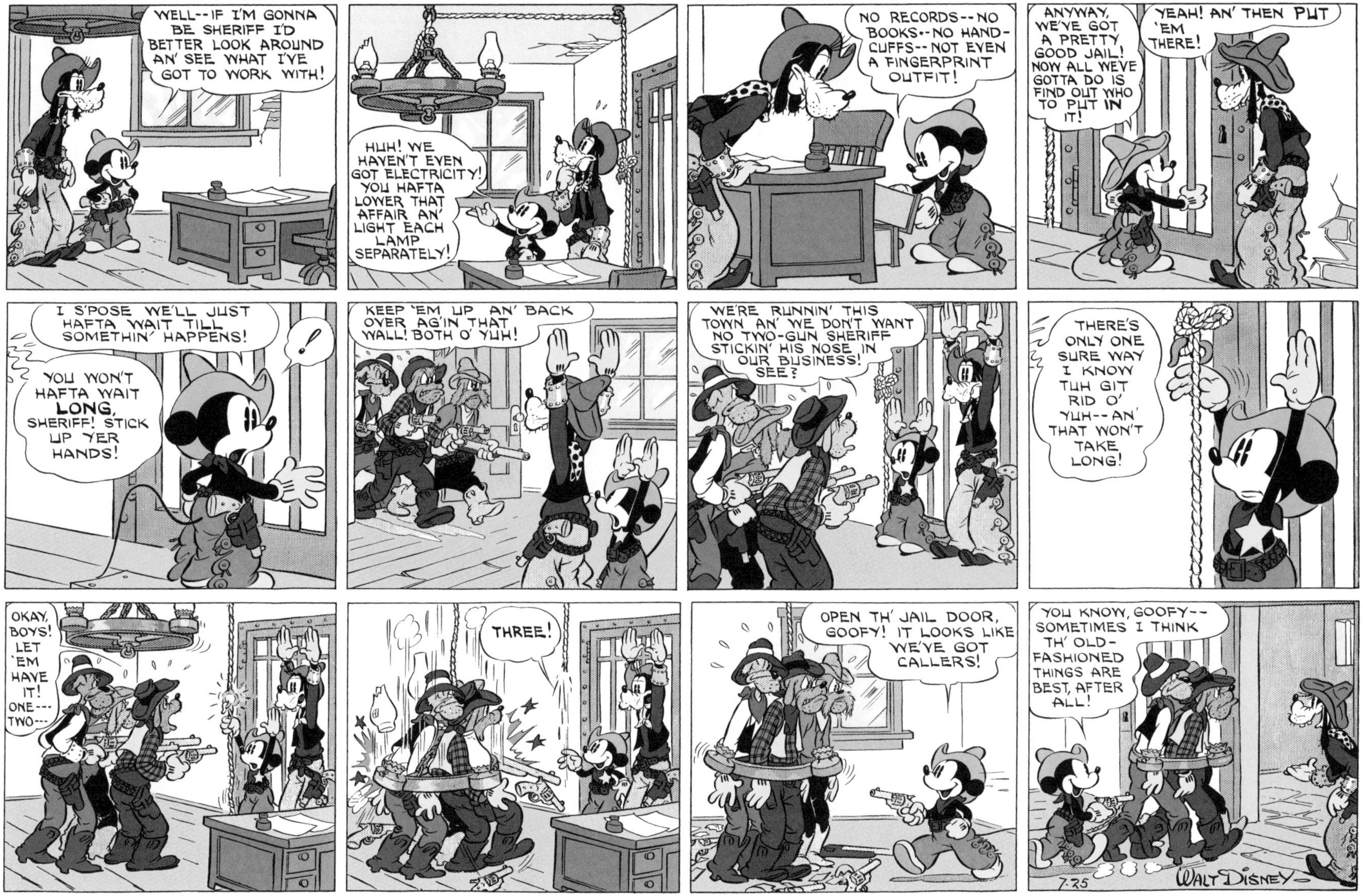

WELL--IF I'M GONNA BE SHERIFF I'D BETTER LOOK AROUND AN' SEE WHAT I'VE GOT TO WORK WITH!
HUH! WE HAVEN'T EVEN GOT ELECTRICITY! YOU HAFTA LOWER THAT AFFAIR AN' LIGHT EACH LAMP SEPARATELY!
NO RECORDS--NO BOOKS--NO HAND-CUFFS--NOT EVEN A FINGERPRINT OUTFIT!
ANYWAY, WE'VE GOT A PRETTY GOOD JAIL! NOW ALL WE'VE GOTTA DO IS FIND OUT WHO TO PUT IN IT!
YEAH! AN' THEN PUT 'EM THERE!
I S'POSE WE'LL JUST HAFTA WAIT TILL SOMETHIN' HAPPENS!
!
YOU WON'T HAFTA WAIT LONG, SHERIFF! STICK UP YER HANDS!
KEEP 'EM UP AN' BACK OVER AG'IN THAT WALL! BOTH O' YUH!
WE'RE RUNNIN' THIS TOWN AN' WE DON'T WANT NO TWO-GUN SHERIFF STICKIN' HIS NOSE IN OUR BUSINESS! SEE?
THERE'S ONLY ONE SURE WAY I KNOW TUH GIT RID O' YUH--AN' THAT WON'T TAKE LONG!
OKAY, BOYS! LET 'EM HAVE IT! ONE--- TWO---
THREE!
OPEN TH' JAIL DOOR, GOOFY! IT LOOKS LIKE WE'VE GOT CALLERS!
YOU KNOW, GOOFY--SOMETIMES I THINK TH' OLD-FASHIONED THINGS ARE BEST, AFTER ALL!
7-25
WALT DISNEY

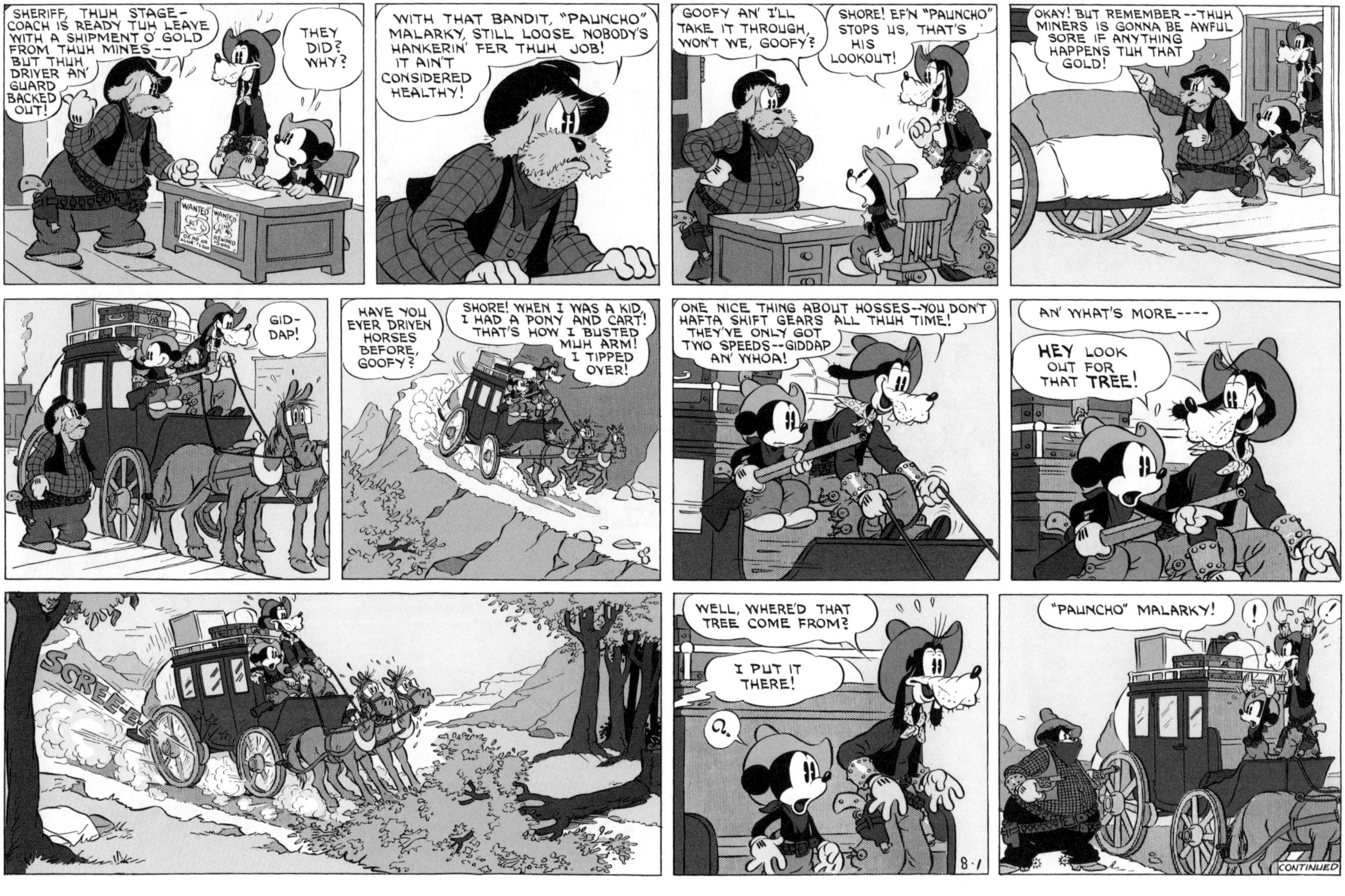
SHERIFF, THUH STAGE-COACH IS READY TUH LEAVE WITH A SHIPMENT O' GOLD FROM THUH MINES -- BUT THUH DRIVER AN' GUARD BACKED OUT!
THEY DID? WHY?
WANTED
WANTED
WITH THAT BANDIT, "PAUNCHO" MALARKY, STILL LOOSE NOBODY'S HANKERIN' FER THUH JOB! IT AIN'T CONSIDERED HEALTHY!
GOOFY AN' I'LL TAKE IT THROUGH, WON'T WE, GOOFY?
SHORE! EF'N "PAUNCHO" STOPS US, THAT'S HIS LOOKOUT!
OKAY! BUT REMEMBER -- THUH MINERS IS GONNA BE AWFUL SORE IF ANYTHING HAPPENS TUH THAT GOLD!
GID-DAP!
HAVE YOU EVER DRIVEN HORSES BEFORE, GOOFY?
SHORE! WHEN I WAS A KID, I HAD A PONY AND CART! THAT'S HOW I BUSTED MUH ARM! I TIPPED OVER!
ONE NICE THING ABOUT HOSSES -- YOU DON'T HAFTA SHIFT GEARS ALL THUH TIME! THEY'VE ONLY GOT TWO SPEEDS -- GIDDAP AN' WHOA!
AN' WHAT'S MORE ----
HEY LOOK OUT FOR THAT TREE!
SCREEEE
WELL, WHERE'D THAT TREE COME FROM?
I PUT IT THERE!
?
8-1
"PAUNCHO" MALARKY!
!
!
CONTINUED

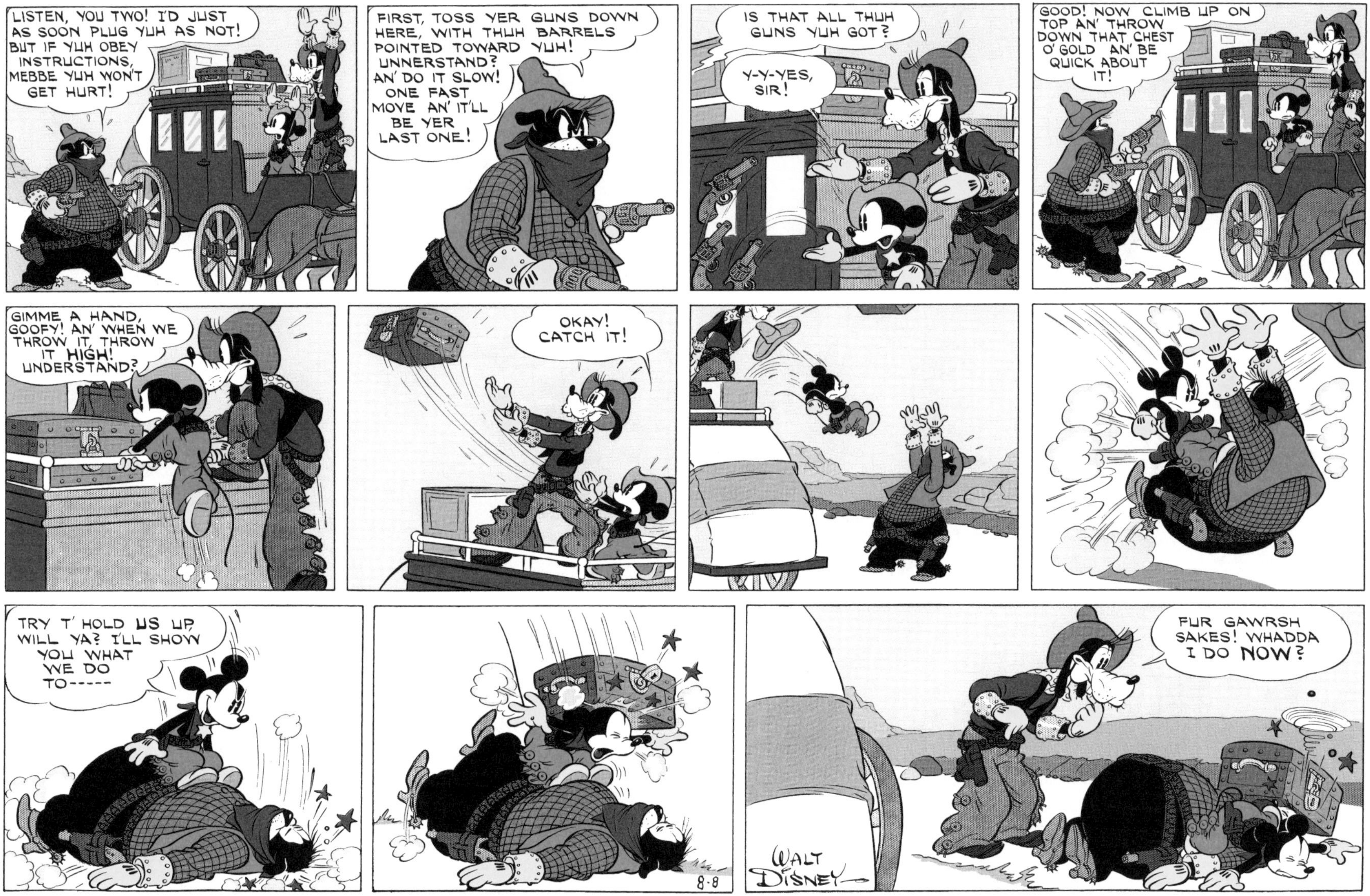
LISTEN, YOU TWO! I'D JUST AS SOON PLUG YUH AS NOT! BUT IF YUH OBEY INSTRUCTIONS, MEBBE YUH WON'T GET HURT!
FIRST, TOSS YER GUNS DOWN HERE, WITH THUH BARRELS POINTED TOWARD YUH! UNNERSTAND? AN' DO IT SLOW! ONE FAST MOVE AN' IT'LL BE YER LAST ONE!
IS THAT ALL THUH GUNS YUH GOT?
Y-Y-YES, SIR!
GOOD! NOW CLIMB UP ON TOP AN' THROW DOWN THAT CHEST O' GOLD AN' BE QUICK ABOUT IT!
GIMME A HAND, GOOFY! AN' WHEN WE THROW IT, THROW IT HIGH! UNDERSTAND?
OKAY! CATCH IT!
TRY T' HOLD US UP, WILL YA? I'LL SHOW YOU WHAT WE DO TO-----
8-8
WALT DISNEY
FUR GAWRSH SAKES! WHADDA I DO NOW?

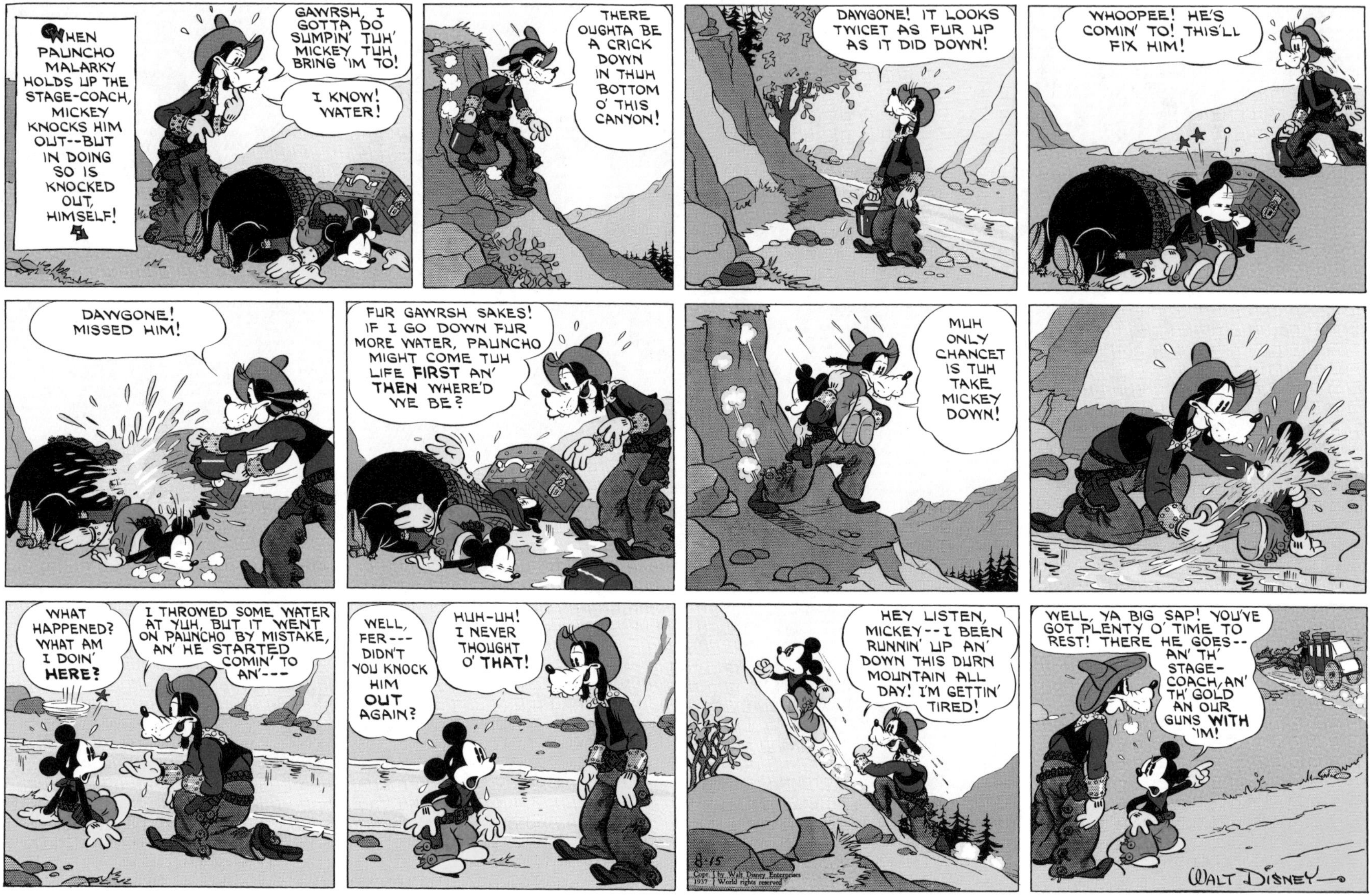
WHEN PAUNCHO MALARKY HOLDS UP THE STAGE-COACH, MICKEY KNOCKS HIM OUT--BUT IN DOING SO IS KNOCKED OUT, HIMSELF!
GAWRSH, I GOTTA DO SUMPIN' TUH' MICKEY TUH BRING 'IM TO!
I KNOW! WATER!
THERE OUGHTA BE A CRICK DOWN IN THUH BOTTOM O' THIS CANYON!
DAWGONE! IT LOOKS TWICET AS FUR UP AS IT DID DOWN!
WHOOPEE! HE'S COMIN' TO! THIS'LL FIX HIM!
DAWGONE! MISSED HIM!
FUR GAWRSH SAKES! IF I GO DOWN FUR MORE WATER, PAUNCHO MIGHT COME TUH LIFE FIRST AN' THEN WHERE'D WE BE?
MUH ONLY CHANCET IS TUH TAKE MICKEY DOWN!
WHAT HAPPENED? WHAT AM I DOIN' HERE?
I THROWED SOME WATER AT YUH, BUT IT WENT ON PAUNCHO BY MISTAKE, AN' HE STARTED COMIN' TO AN'---
WELL, FER--- DIDN'T YOU KNOCK HIM OUT AGAIN?
HUH-UH! I NEVER THOUGHT O' THAT!
HEY LISTEN, MICKEY--I BEEN RUNNIN' UP AN' DOWN THIS DURN MOUNTAIN ALL DAY! I'M GETTIN' TIRED!
8-15
Copr. 1937 by Walt Disney Enterprises World rights reserved
WELL, YA BIG SAP! YOU'VE GOT PLENTY O' TIME TO REST! THERE HE GOES-- AN' TH' STAGE-COACH, AN' TH' GOLD AN OUR GUNS WITH 'IM!
WALT DISNEY

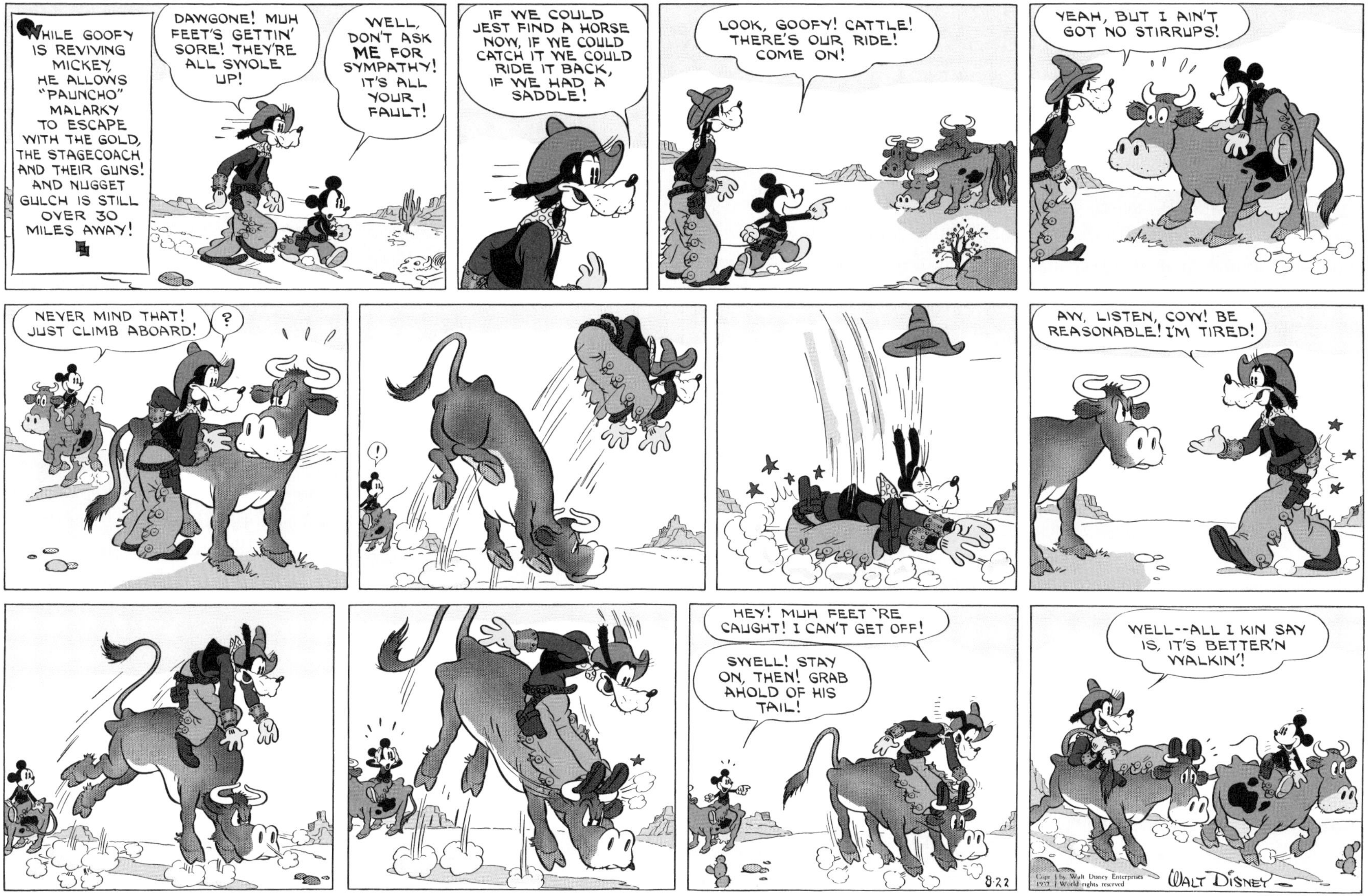
WHILE GOOFY IS REVIVING MICKEY, HE ALLOWS "PAUNCHO" MALARKY TO ESCAPE WITH THE GOLD, THE STAGECOACH AND THEIR GUNS! AND NUGGET GULCH IS STILL OVER 30 MILES AWAY!
DAWGONE! MUH FEET'S GETTIN' SORE! THEY'RE ALL SWOLE UP!
WELL, DON'T ASK ME FOR SYMPATHY! IT'S ALL YOUR FAULT!
IF WE COULD JEST FIND A HORSE NOW, IF WE COULD CATCH IT WE COULD RIDE IT BACK, IF WE HAD A SADDLE!
LOOK, GOOFY! CATTLE! THERE'S OUR RIDE! COME ON!
YEAH, BUT I AIN'T GOT NO STIRRUPS!
NEVER MIND THAT! JUST CLIMB ABOARD!
?
!
AW, LISTEN, COW! BE REASONABLE! I'M TIRED!
HEY! MUH FEET 'RE CAUGHT! I CAN'T GET OFF!
SWELL! STAY ON, THEN! GRAB AHOLD OF HIS TAIL!
8-22
WELL--ALL I KIN SAY IS, IT'S BETTER'N WALKIN'!
Copr 1937 by Walt Disney Enterprises World rights reserved
WALT DISNEY

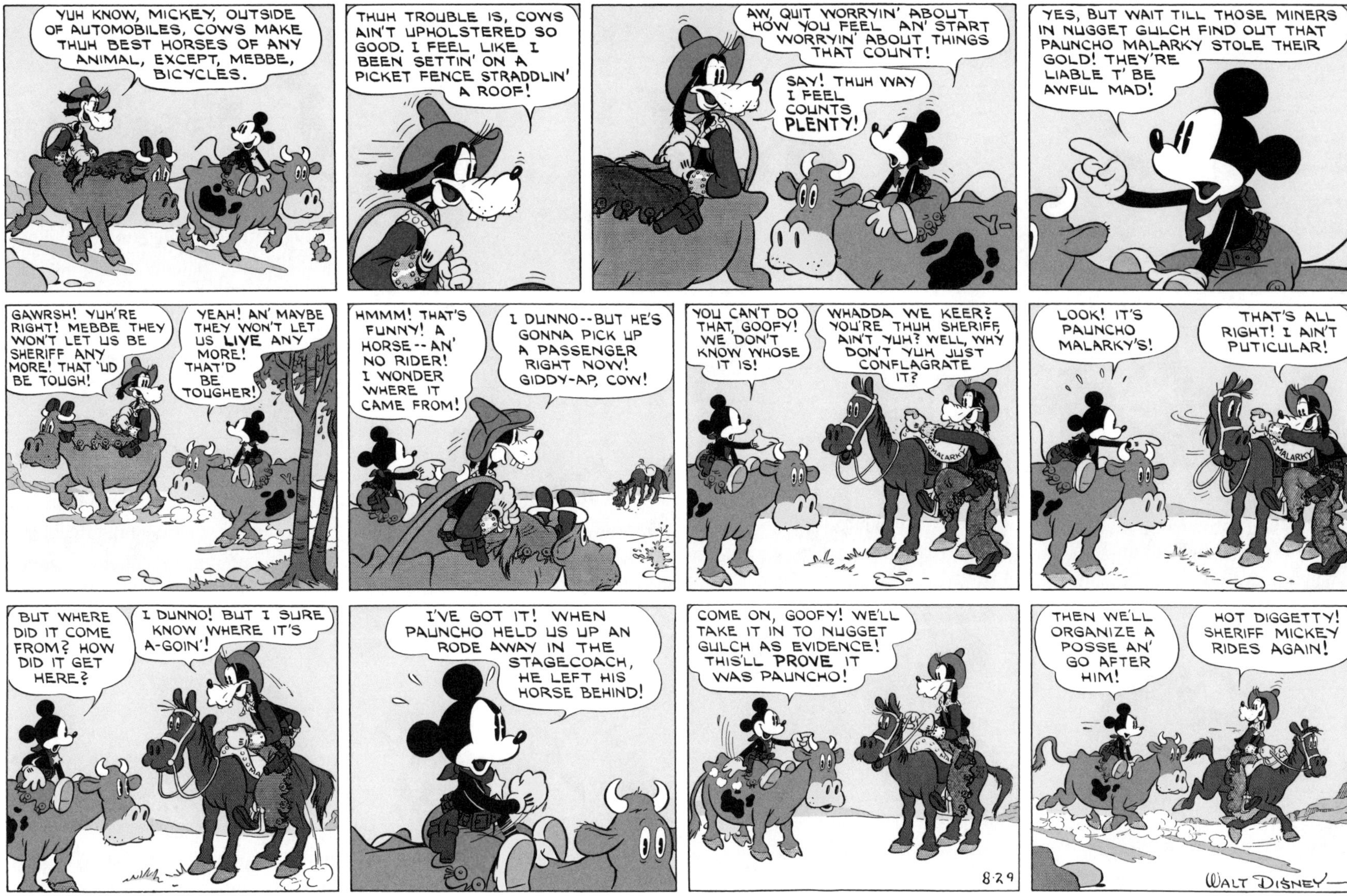
YUH KNOW, MICKEY, OUTSIDE OF AUTOMOBILES, COWS MAKE THUH BEST HORSES OF ANY ANIMAL, EXCEPT, MEBBE, BICYCLES.
THUH TROUBLE IS, COWS AIN'T UPHOLSTERED SO GOOD. I FEEL LIKE I BEEN SETTIN' ON A PICKET FENCE STRADDLIN' A ROOF!
AW, QUIT WORRYIN' ABOUT HOW YOU FEEL AN' START WORRYIN' ABOUT THINGS THAT COUNT!
SAY! THUH WAY I FEEL COUNTS **PLENTY**!
Y-
YES, BUT WAIT TILL THOSE MINERS IN NUGGET GULCH FIND OUT THAT PAUNCHO MALARKY STOLE THEIR GOLD! THEY'RE LIABLE T' BE AWFUL MAD!
GAWRSH! YUH'RE RIGHT! MEBBE THEY WON'T LET US BE SHERIFF ANY MORE! THAT 'UD BE TOUGH!
YEAH! AN' MAYBE THEY WON'T LET US **LIVE** ANY MORE! THAT'D BE TOUGHER!
HMMM! THAT'S FUNNY! A HORSE--AN' NO RIDER! I WONDER WHERE IT CAME FROM!
I DUNNO--BUT HE'S GONNA PICK UP A PASSENGER RIGHT NOW! GIDDY-AP, COW!
YOU CAN'T DO THAT, GOOFY! WE DON'T KNOW WHOSE IT IS!
WHADDA WE KEER? YOU'RE THUH SHERIFF, AIN'T YUH? WELL, WHY DON'T YUH JUST CONFLAGRATE IT?
MALARKY
LOOK! IT'S PAUNCHO MALARKY'S!
THAT'S ALL RIGHT! I AIN'T PUTICULAR!
MALARKY
BUT WHERE DID IT COME FROM? HOW DID IT GET HERE?
I DUNNO! BUT I SURE KNOW WHERE IT'S A-GOIN'!
I'VE GOT IT! WHEN PAUNCHO HELD US UP AN RODE AWAY IN THE STAGECOACH, HE LEFT HIS HORSE BEHIND!
COME ON, GOOFY! WE'LL TAKE IT IN TO NUGGET GULCH AS EVIDENCE! THIS'LL **PROVE** IT WAS PAUNCHO!
8·29
THEN WE'LL ORGANIZE A POSSE AN' GO AFTER HIM!
HOT DIGGETTY! SHERIFF MICKEY RIDES AGAIN!
WALT DISNEY

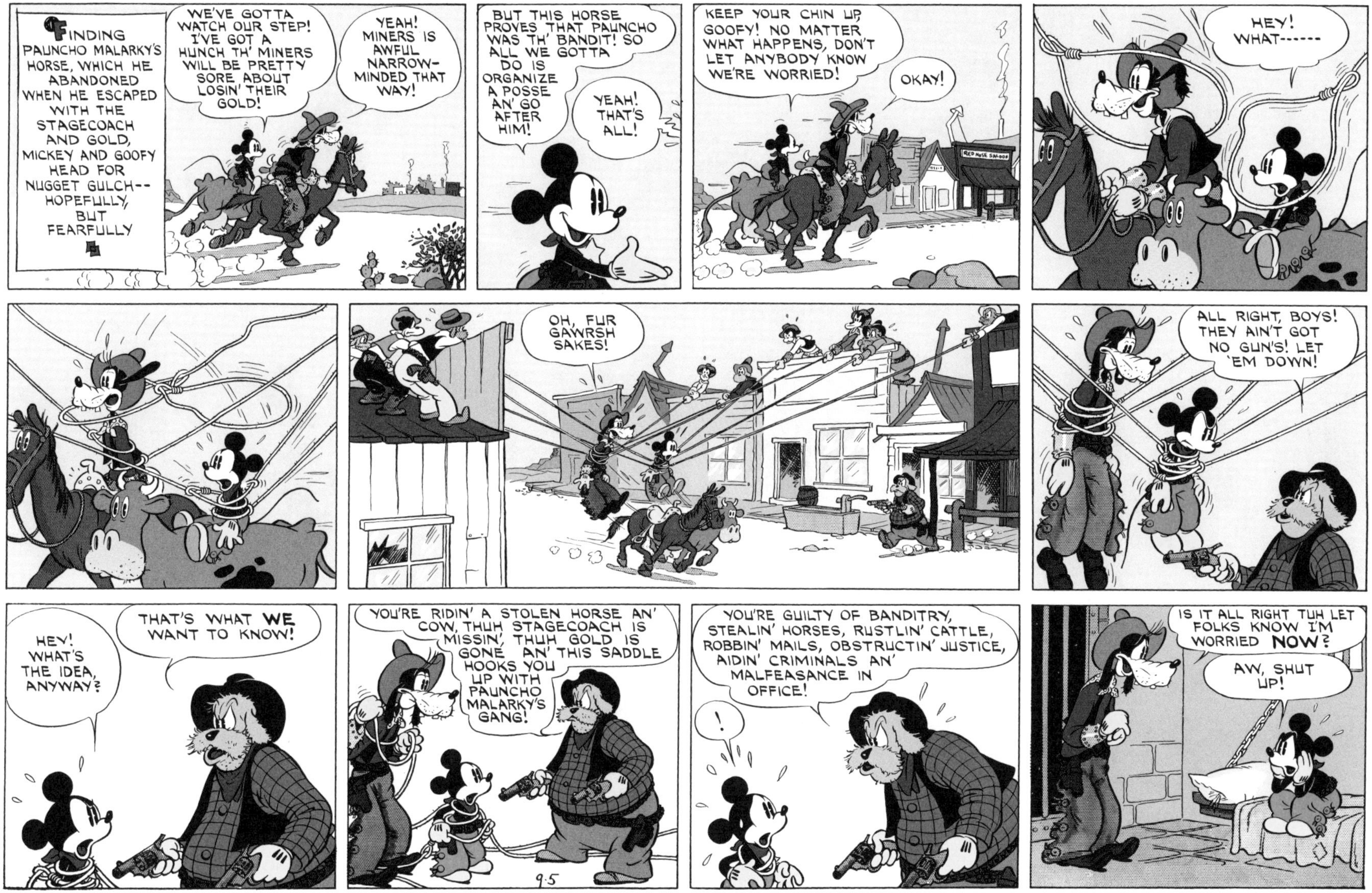
FINDING PAUNCHO MALARKY'S HORSE, WHICH HE ABANDONED WHEN HE ESCAPED WITH THE STAGECOACH AND GOLD, MICKEY AND GOOFY HEAD FOR NUGGET GULCH-- HOPEFULLY, BUT FEARFULLY
WE'VE GOTTA WATCH OUR STEP! I'VE GOT A HUNCH TH' MINERS WILL BE PRETTY SORE ABOUT LOSIN' THEIR GOLD!
YEAH! MINERS IS AWFUL NARROW-MINDED THAT WAY!
BUT THIS HORSE PROVES THAT PAUNCHO WAS TH' BANDIT! SO ALL WE GOTTA DO IS ORGANIZE A POSSE AN' GO AFTER HIM!
YEAH! THAT'S ALL!
KEEP YOUR CHIN UP, GOOFY! NO MATTER WHAT HAPPENS, DON'T LET ANYBODY KNOW WE'RE WORRIED!
OKAY!
RED NOSE SALOON
HEY! WHAT------
OH, FUR GAWRSH SAKES!
ALL RIGHT, BOYS! THEY AIN'T GOT NO GUNS! LET 'EM DOWN!
HEY! WHAT'S THE IDEA, ANYWAY?
THAT'S WHAT WE WANT TO KNOW!
YOU'RE RIDIN' A STOLEN HORSE AN' COW, THUH STAGECOACH IS MISSIN', THUH GOLD IS GONE AN' THIS SADDLE HOOKS YOU UP WITH PAUNCHO MALARKY'S GANG!
9-5
YOU'RE GUILTY OF BANDITRY, STEALIN' HORSES, RUSTLIN' CATTLE, ROBBIN' MAILS, OBSTRUCTIN' JUSTICE, AIDIN' CRIMINALS AN' MALFEASANCE IN OFFICE!
!
IS IT ALL RIGHT TUH LET FOLKS KNOW I'M WORRIED NOW?
AW, SHUT UP!

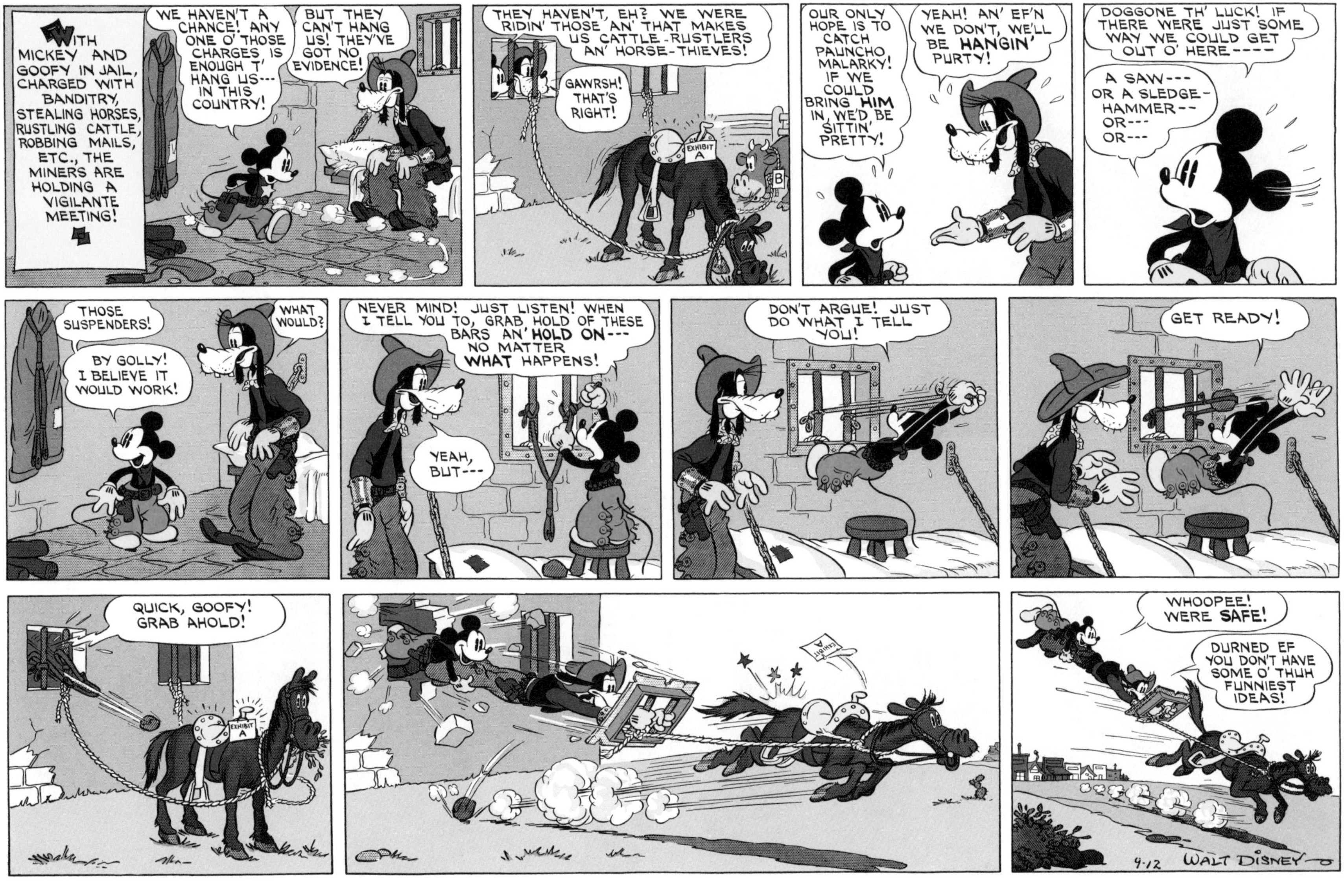
WITH MICKEY AND GOOFY IN JAIL, CHARGED WITH BANDITRY, STEALING HORSES, RUSTLING CATTLE, ROBBING MAILS, ETC., THE MINERS ARE HOLDING A VIGILANTE MEETING!
WE HAVEN'T A CHANCE! ANY ONE O' THOSE CHARGES IS ENOUGH T' HANG US--- IN THIS COUNTRY!
BUT THEY CAN'T HANG US! THEY'VE GOT NO EVIDENCE!
THEY HAVEN'T, EH? WE WERE RIDIN' THOSE AN' THAT MAKES US CATTLE-RUSTLERS AN' HORSE-THIEVES!
GAWRSH! THAT'S RIGHT!
EXHIBIT A
B
OUR ONLY HOPE IS TO CATCH PAUNCHO MALARKY! IF WE COULD BRING **HIM** IN, WE'D BE SITTIN' PRETTY!
YEAH! AN' EF'N WE DON'T, WE'LL BE **HANGIN'** PURTY!
DOGGONE TH' LUCK! IF THERE WERE JUST SOME WAY WE COULD GET OUT O' HERE----
A SAW--- OR A SLEDGE-HAMMER-- OR--- OR---
THOSE SUSPENDERS!
WHAT WOULD?
BY GOLLY! I BELIEVE IT WOULD WORK!
NEVER MIND! JUST LISTEN! WHEN I TELL YOU TO, GRAB HOLD OF THESE BARS AN' **HOLD ON**--- NO MATTER **WHAT** HAPPENS!
YEAH, BUT---
DON'T ARGUE! JUST DO WHAT I TELL YOU!
GET READY!
QUICK, GOOFY! GRAB AHOLD!
EXHIBIT A
WHOOPEE! WERE **SAFE**!
DURNED EF YOU DON'T HAVE SOME O' THUH FUNNIEST IDEAS!
9-12
WALT DISNEY

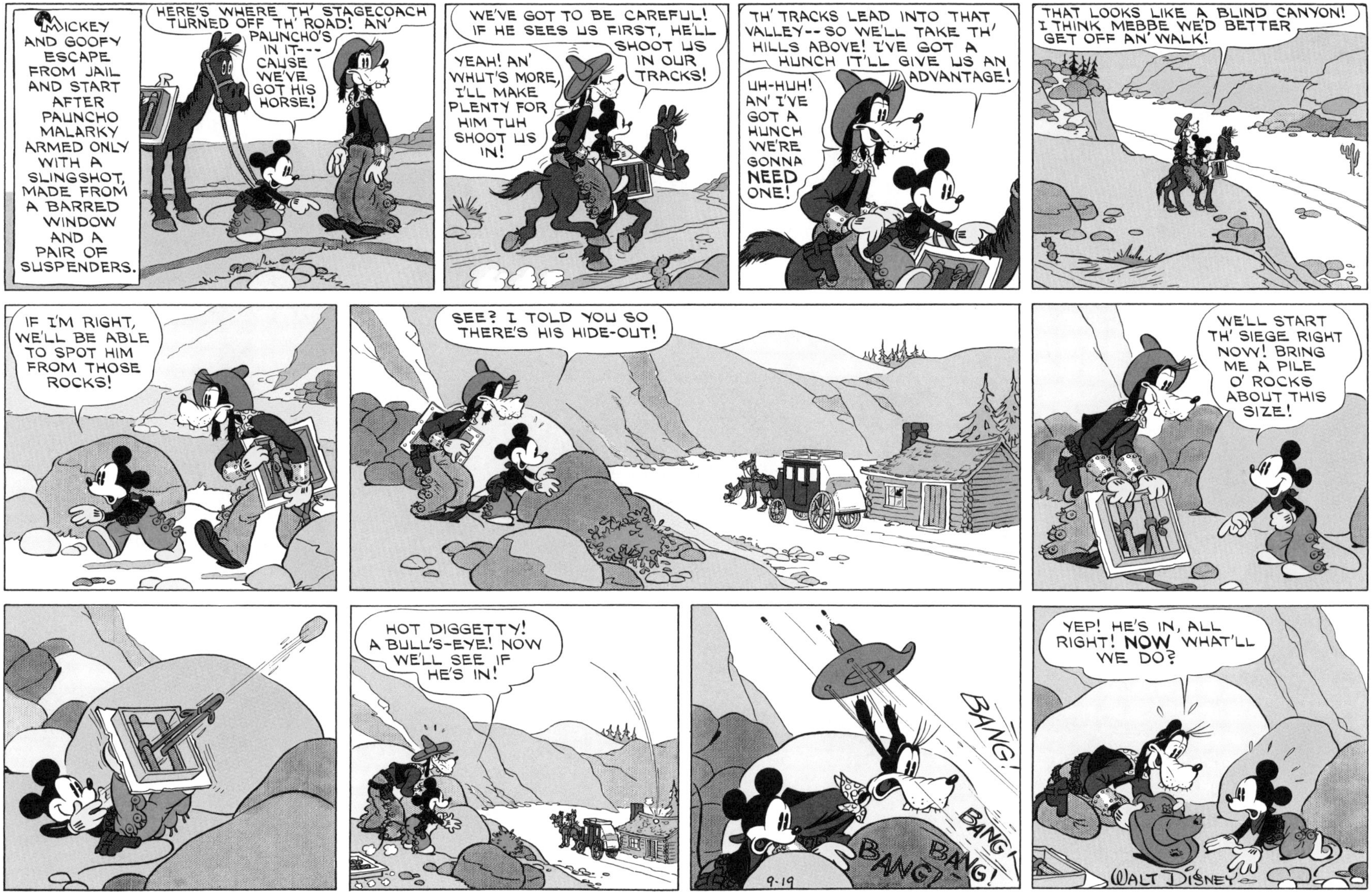
MICKEY AND GOOFY ESCAPE FROM JAIL AND START AFTER PAUNCHO MALARKY ARMED ONLY WITH A SLINGSHOT, MADE FROM A BARRED WINDOW AND A PAIR OF SUSPENDERS.
HERE'S WHERE TH' STAGECOACH TURNED OFF TH' ROAD! AN' PAUNCHO'S IN IT--- CAUSE WE'VE GOT HIS HORSE!
WE'VE GOT TO BE CAREFUL! IF HE SEES US FIRST, HE'LL SHOOT US IN OUR TRACKS!
YEAH! AN' WHUT'S MORE, I'LL MAKE PLENTY FOR HIM TUH SHOOT US IN!
TH' TRACKS LEAD INTO THAT VALLEY--SO WE'LL TAKE TH' HILLS ABOVE! I'VE GOT A HUNCH IT'LL GIVE US AN ADVANTAGE!
UH-HUH! AN' I'VE GOT A HUNCH WE'RE GONNA NEED ONE!
THAT LOOKS LIKE A BLIND CANYON! I THINK MEBBE WE'D BETTER GET OFF AN' WALK!
IF I'M RIGHT, WE'LL BE ABLE TO SPOT HIM FROM THOSE ROCKS!
SEE? I TOLD YOU SO THERE'S HIS HIDE-OUT!
WE'LL START TH' SIEGE RIGHT NOW! BRING ME A PILE O' ROCKS ABOUT THIS SIZE!
HOT DIGGETTY! A BULL'S-EYE! NOW WE'LL SEE IF HE'S IN!
BANG!
BANG!
BANG!
BANG!
9-19
YEP! HE'S IN, ALL RIGHT! NOW WHAT'LL WE DO?
WALT DISNEY

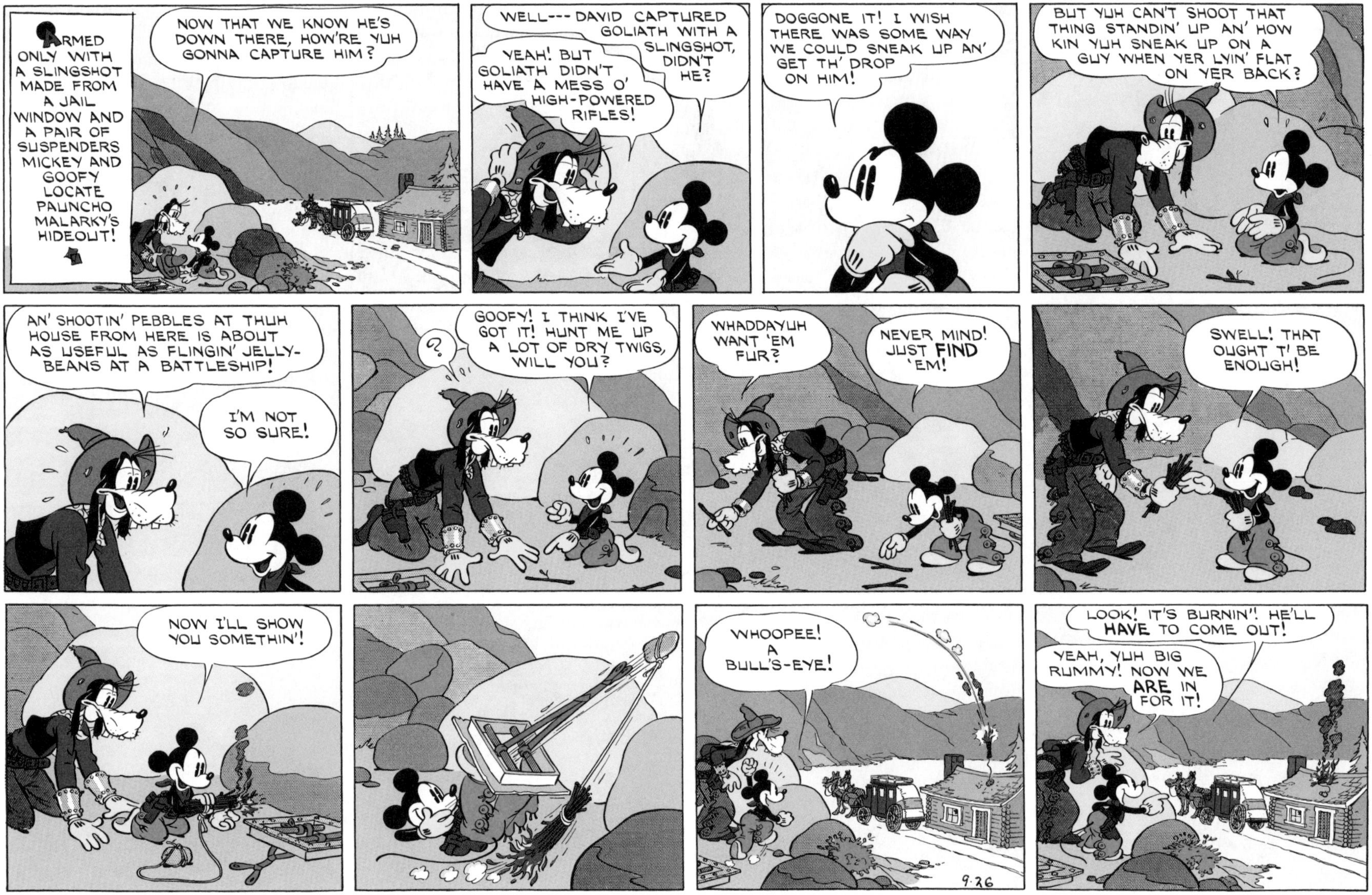
ARMED ONLY WITH A SLINGSHOT MADE FROM A JAIL WINDOW AND A PAIR OF SUSPENDERS MICKEY AND GOOFY LOCATE PAUNCHO MALARKY'S HIDEOUT!
NOW THAT WE KNOW HE'S DOWN THERE, HOW'RE YUH GONNA CAPTURE HIM?
WELL--- DAVID CAPTURED GOLIATH WITH A SLINGSHOT, DIDN'T HE?
YEAH! BUT GOLIATH DIDN'T HAVE A MESS O' HIGH-POWERED RIFLES!
DOGGONE IT! I WISH THERE WAS SOME WAY WE COULD SNEAK UP AN' GET TH' DROP ON HIM!
BUT YUH CAN'T SHOOT THAT THING STANDIN' UP AN' HOW KIN YUH SNEAK UP ON A GUY WHEN YER LYIN' FLAT ON YER BACK?
AN' SHOOTIN' PEBBLES AT THUH HOUSE FROM HERE IS ABOUT AS USEFUL AS FLINGIN' JELLY-BEANS AT A BATTLESHIP!
I'M NOT SO SURE!
?
GOOFY! I THINK I'VE GOT IT! HUNT ME UP A LOT OF DRY TWIGS, WILL YOU?
WHADDAYUH WANT 'EM FUR?
NEVER MIND! JUST **FIND** 'EM!
SWELL! THAT OUGHT T' BE ENOUGH!
NOW I'LL SHOW YOU SOMETHIN'!
WHOOPEE! A BULL'S-EYE!
9-26
LOOK! IT'S BURNIN'! HE'LL **HAVE** TO COME OUT!
YEAH, YUH BIG RUMMY! NOW WE **ARE** IN FOR IT!

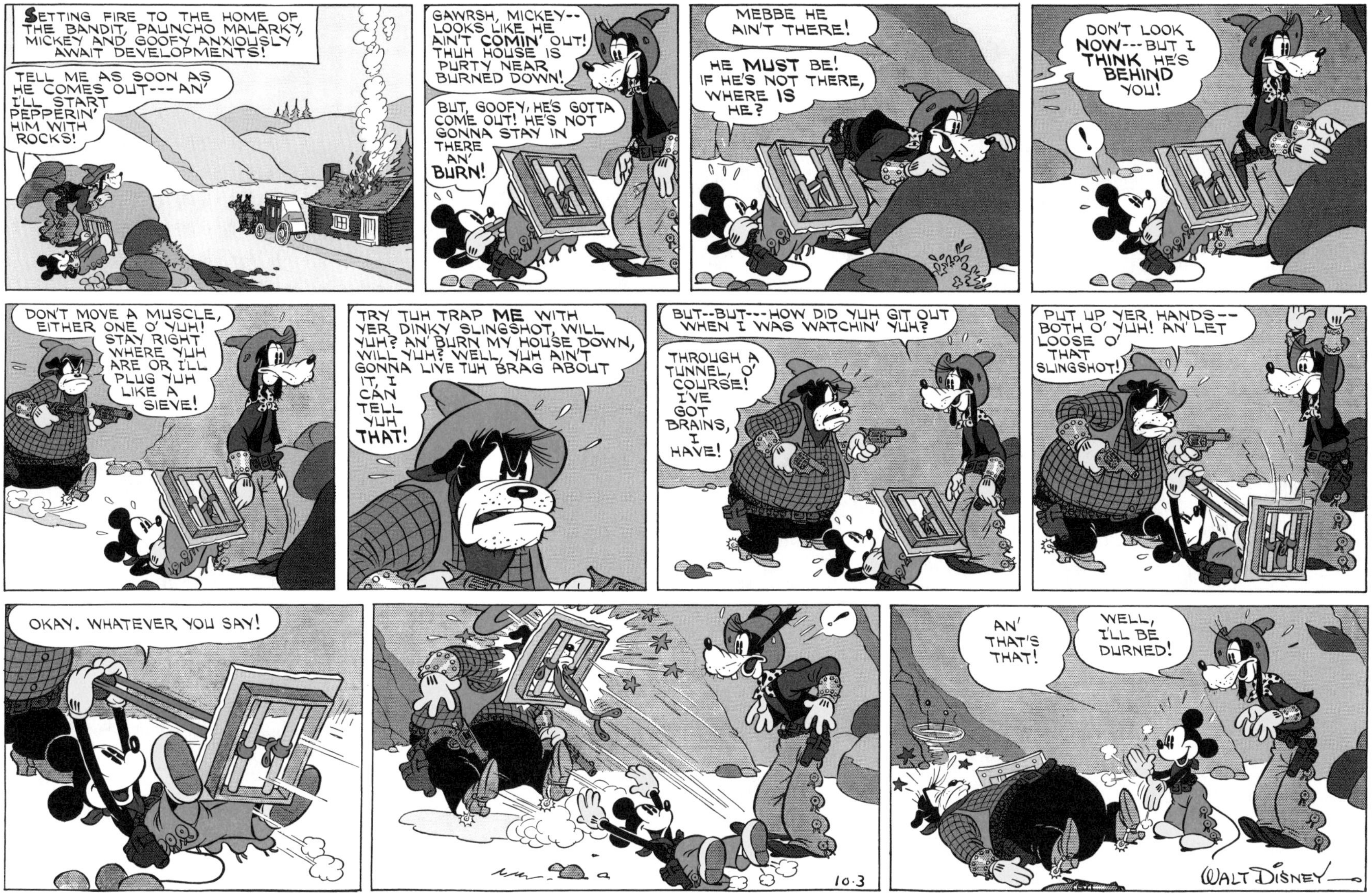
SETTING FIRE TO THE HOME OF THE BANDIT, PAUNCHO MALARKY, MICKEY AND GOOFY ANXIOUSLY AWAIT DEVELOPMENTS!
TELL ME AS SOON AS HE COMES OUT--- AN' I'LL START PEPPERIN' HIM WITH ROCKS!
GAWRSH, MICKEY-- LOOKS LIKE HE AIN'T COMIN' OUT! THUH HOUSE IS PURTY NEAR BURNED DOWN!
BUT, GOOFY, HE'S GOTTA COME OUT! HE'S NOT GONNA STAY IN THERE AN' BURN!
MEBBE HE AIN'T THERE!
HE MUST BE! IF HE'S NOT THERE, WHERE IS HE?
DON'T LOOK NOW--- BUT I THINK HE'S BEHIND YOU!
!
DON'T MOVE A MUSCLE, EITHER ONE O' YUH! STAY RIGHT WHERE YUH ARE OR I'LL PLUG YUH LIKE A SIEVE!
TRY TUH TRAP ME WITH YER DINKY SLINGSHOT, WILL YUH? AN' BURN MY HOUSE DOWN, WILL YUH? WELL, YUH AIN'T GONNA LIVE TUH BRAG ABOUT IT, I CAN TELL YUH THAT!
BUT--BUT--- HOW DID YUH GIT OUT WHEN I WAS WATCHIN' YUH?
THROUGH A TUNNEL, O' COURSE! I'VE GOT BRAINS, I HAVE!
PUT UP YER HANDS-- BOTH O' YUH! AN' LET LOOSE O' THAT SLINGSHOT!
OKAY. WHATEVER YOU SAY!
!
10-3
AN' THAT'S THAT!
WELL, I'LL BE DURNED!
WALT DISNEY

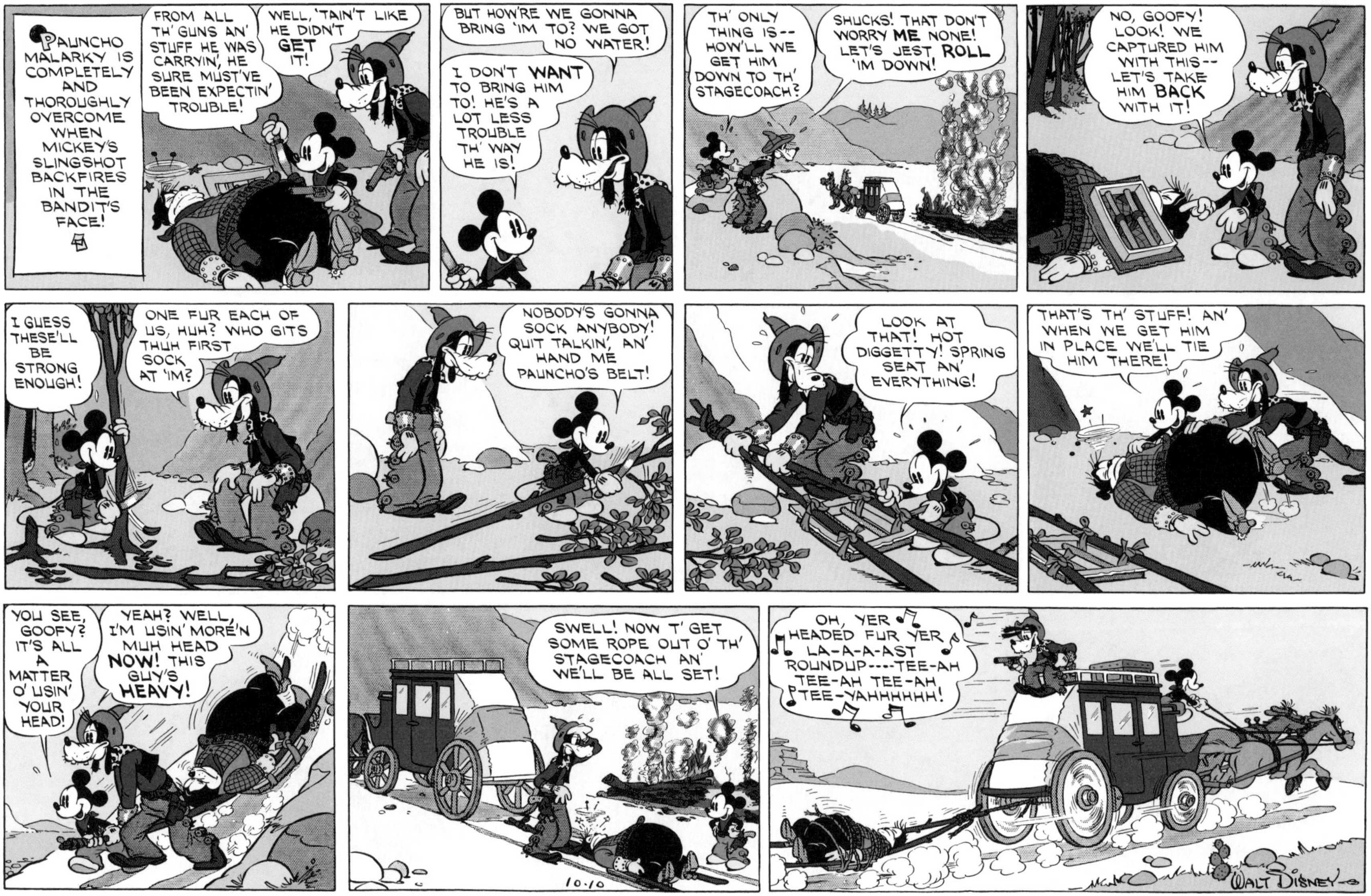
PAUNCHO MALARKY IS COMPLETELY AND THOROUGHLY OVERCOME WHEN MICKEY'S SLINGSHOT BACKFIRES IN THE BANDIT'S FACE!
FROM ALL TH' GUNS AN' STUFF HE WAS CARRYIN', HE SURE MUST'VE BEEN EXPECTIN' TROUBLE!
WELL, 'TAIN'T LIKE HE DIDN'T GET IT!
BUT HOW'RE WE GONNA BRING 'IM TO? WE GOT NO WATER!
I DON'T WANT TO BRING HIM TO! HE'S A LOT LESS TROUBLE TH' WAY HE IS!
TH' ONLY THING IS-- HOW'LL WE GET HIM DOWN TO TH' STAGECOACH?
SHUCKS! THAT DON'T WORRY ME NONE! LET'S JEST ROLL 'IM DOWN!
NO, GOOFY! LOOK! WE CAPTURED HIM WITH THIS-- LET'S TAKE HIM BACK WITH IT!
I GUESS THESE'LL BE STRONG ENOUGH!
ONE FUR EACH OF US, HUH? WHO GITS THUH FIRST SOCK AT 'IM?
NOBODY'S GONNA SOCK ANYBODY! QUIT TALKIN', AN' HAND ME PAUNCHO'S BELT!
LOOK AT THAT! HOT DIGGETTY! SPRING SEAT AN' EVERYTHING!
THAT'S TH' STUFF! AN' WHEN WE GET HIM IN PLACE WE'LL TIE HIM THERE!
YOU SEE, GOOFY? IT'S ALL A MATTER O' USIN' YOUR HEAD!
YEAH? WELL, I'M USIN' MORE'N MUH HEAD NOW! THIS GUY'S HEAVY!
SWELL! NOW T' GET SOME ROPE OUT O' TH' STAGECOACH AN' WE'LL BE ALL SET!
10-10
OH, YER HEADED FUR YER LA-A-A-AST ROUNDUP----TEE-AH TEE-AH TEE-AH TEE-YAHHHHHH!
WALT DISNEY

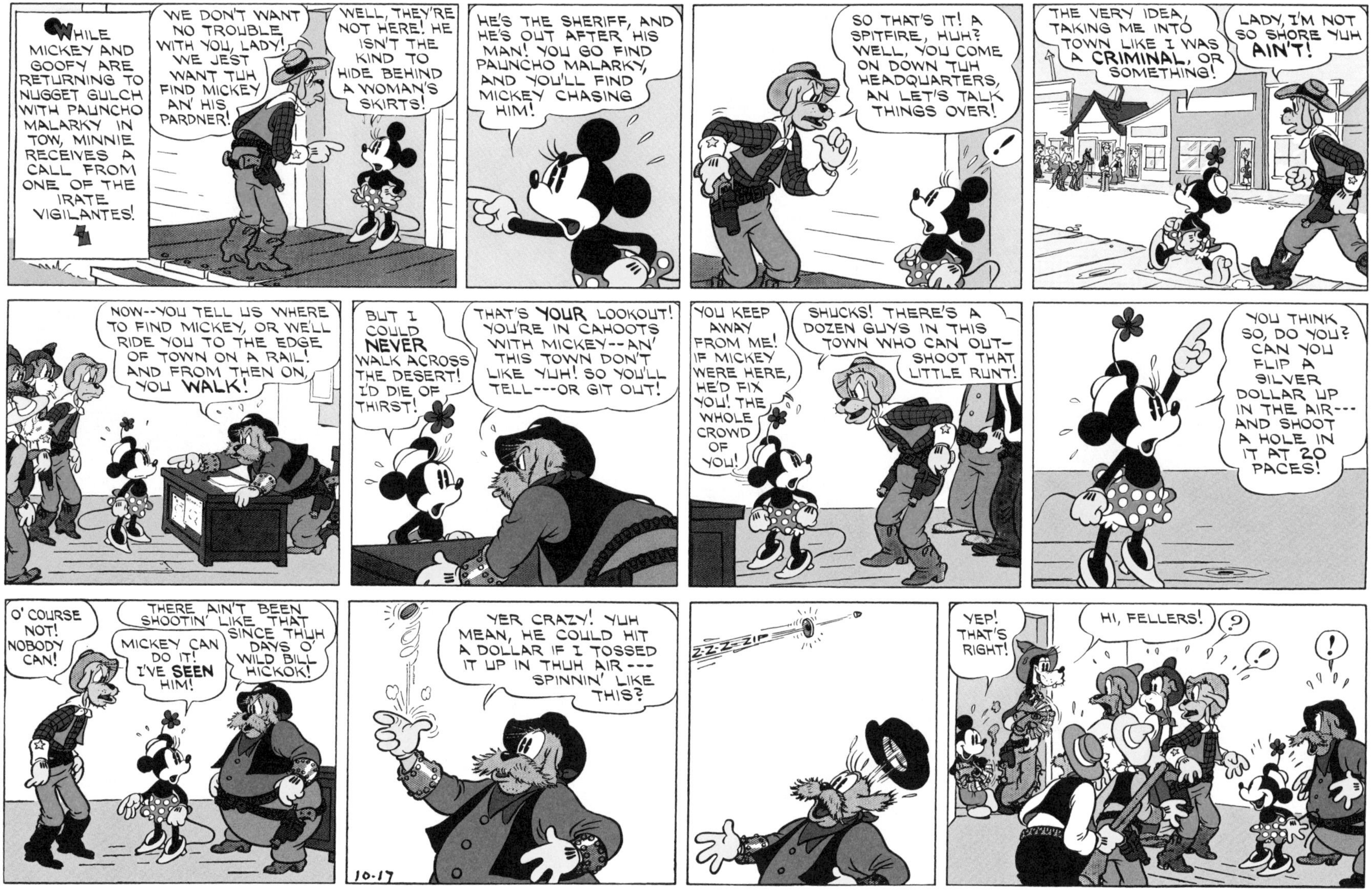
WHILE MICKEY AND GOOFY ARE RETURNING TO NUGGET GULCH WITH PAUNCHO MALARKY IN TOW, MINNIE RECEIVES A CALL FROM ONE OF THE IRATE VIGILANTES!
WE DON'T WANT NO TROUBLE WITH YOU, LADY! WE JEST WANT TUH FIND MICKEY AN' HIS PARDNER!
WELL, THEY'RE NOT HERE! HE ISN'T THE KIND TO HIDE BEHIND A WOMAN'S SKIRTS!
HE'S THE SHERIFF, AND HE'S OUT AFTER HIS MAN! YOU GO FIND PAUNCHO MALARKY, AND YOU'LL FIND MICKEY CHASING HIM!
SO THAT'S IT! A SPITFIRE, HUH? WELL, YOU COME ON DOWN TUH HEADQUARTERS, AN LET'S TALK THINGS OVER!
!
THE VERY IDEA, TAKING ME INTO TOWN LIKE I WAS A **CRIMINAL**, OR SOMETHING!
LADY, I'M NOT SO SHORE YUH **AIN'T**!
NOW--YOU TELL US WHERE TO FIND MICKEY, OR WE'LL RIDE YOU TO THE EDGE OF TOWN ON A RAIL! AND FROM THEN ON, YOU **WALK**!
BUT I COULD **NEVER** WALK ACROSS THE DESERT! I'D DIE OF THIRST!
THAT'S **YOUR** LOOKOUT! YOU'RE IN CAHOOTS WITH MICKEY--AN' THIS TOWN DON'T LIKE YUH! SO YOU'LL TELL---OR GIT OUT!
YOU KEEP AWAY FROM ME! IF MICKEY WERE HERE, HE'D FIX YOU! THE WHOLE CROWD OF YOU!
SHUCKS! THERE'S A DOZEN GUYS IN THIS TOWN WHO CAN OUT-SHOOT THAT LITTLE RUNT!
YOU THINK SO, DO YOU? CAN YOU FLIP A SILVER DOLLAR UP IN THE AIR---AND SHOOT A HOLE IN IT AT 20 PACES!
O' COURSE NOT! NOBODY CAN!
THERE AIN'T BEEN SHOOTIN' LIKE THAT SINCE THUH DAYS O' WILD BILL HICKOK!
MICKEY CAN DO IT! I'VE **SEEN** HIM!
YER CRAZY! YUH MEAN, HE COULD HIT A DOLLAR IF I TOSSED IT UP IN THUH AIR---SPINNIN' LIKE THIS?
10-17
Z-Z-Z-ZIP
YEP! THAT'S RIGHT!
HI, FELLERS!
?
!
!

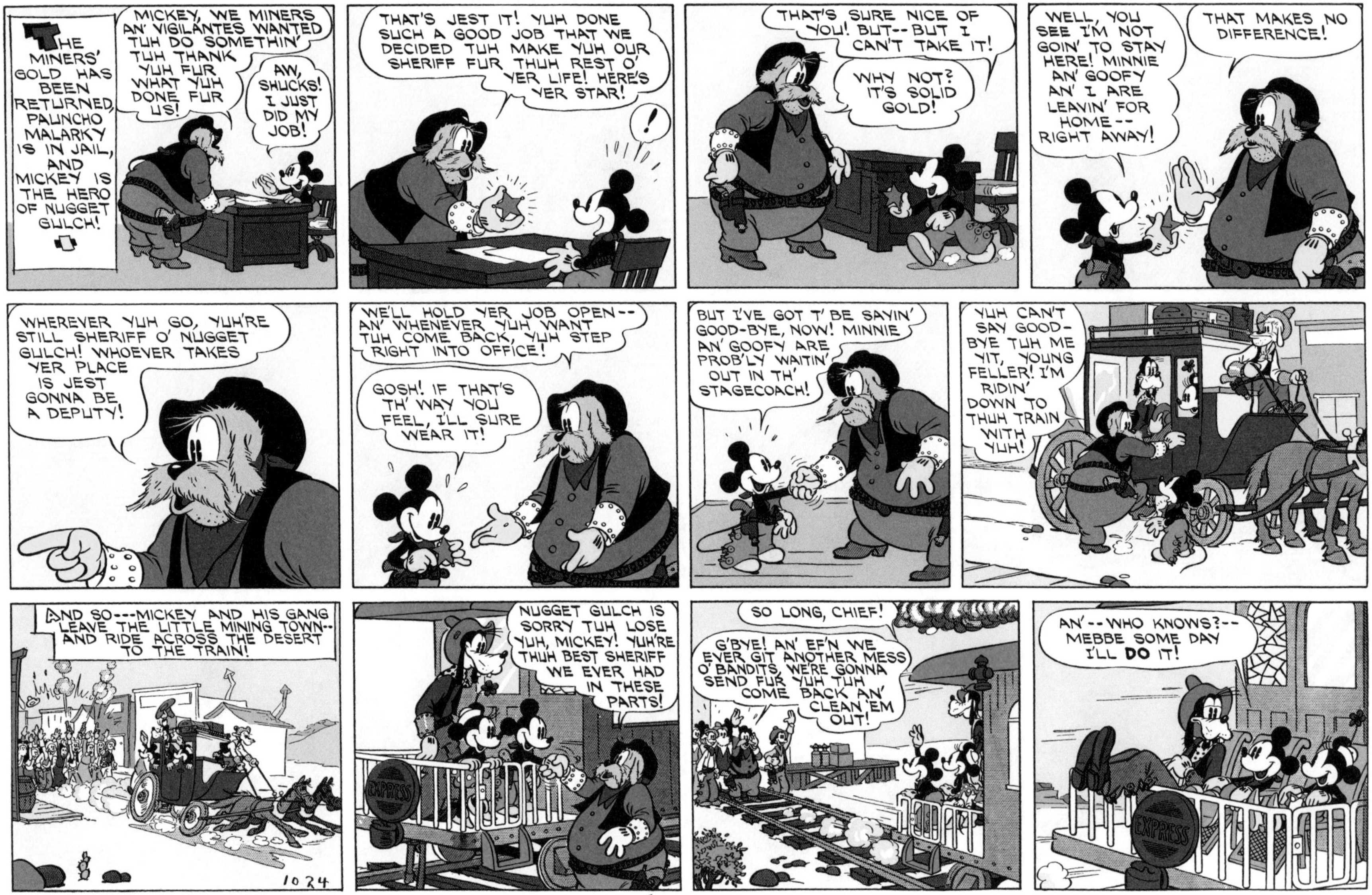
THE MINERS' GOLD HAS BEEN RETURNED, PAUNCHO MALARKY IS IN JAIL, AND MICKEY IS THE HERO OF NUGGET GULCH!
MICKEY, WE MINERS AN' VIGILANTES WANTED TUH DO SOMETHIN' TUH THANK YUH FUR WHAT YUH DONE FUR US!
AW, SHUCKS! I JUST DID MY JOB!
THAT'S JEST IT! YUH DONE SUCH A GOOD JOB THAT WE DECIDED TUH MAKE YUH OUR SHERIFF FUR THUH REST O' YER LIFE! HERE'S YER STAR!
!
THAT'S SURE NICE OF YOU! BUT--BUT I CAN'T TAKE IT!
WHY NOT? IT'S SOLID GOLD!
WELL, YOU SEE I'M NOT GOIN' TO STAY HERE! MINNIE AN' GOOFY AN' I ARE LEAVIN' FOR HOME-- RIGHT AWAY!
THAT MAKES NO DIFFERENCE!
WHEREVER YUH GO, YUH'RE STILL SHERIFF O' NUGGET GULCH! WHOEVER TAKES YER PLACE IS JEST GONNA BE A DEPUTY!
WE'LL HOLD YER JOB OPEN-- AN' WHENEVER YUH WANT TUH COME BACK, YUH STEP RIGHT INTO OFFICE!
GOSH! IF THAT'S TH' WAY YOU FEEL, I'LL SURE WEAR IT!
BUT I'VE GOT T' BE SAYIN' GOOD-BYE, NOW! MINNIE AN' GOOFY ARE PROB'LY WAITIN' OUT IN TH' STAGECOACH!
YUH CAN'T SAY GOOD-BYE TUH ME YIT, YOUNG FELLER! I'M RIDIN' DOWN TO THUH TRAIN WITH YUH!
AND SO---MICKEY AND HIS GANG LEAVE THE LITTLE MINING TOWN-- AND RIDE ACROSS THE DESERT TO THE TRAIN!
10 24
NUGGET GULCH IS SORRY TUH LOSE YUH, MICKEY! YUH'RE THUH BEST SHERIFF WE EVER HAD IN THESE PARTS!
EXPRESS
SO LONG, CHIEF!
G'BYE! AN' EF'N WE EVER GIT ANOTHER MESS O' BANDITS, WE'RE GONNA SEND FUR YUH TUH COME BACK AN' CLEAN 'EM OUT!
AN'--WHO KNOWS?-- MEBBE SOME DAY I'LL **DO** IT!
EXPRESS

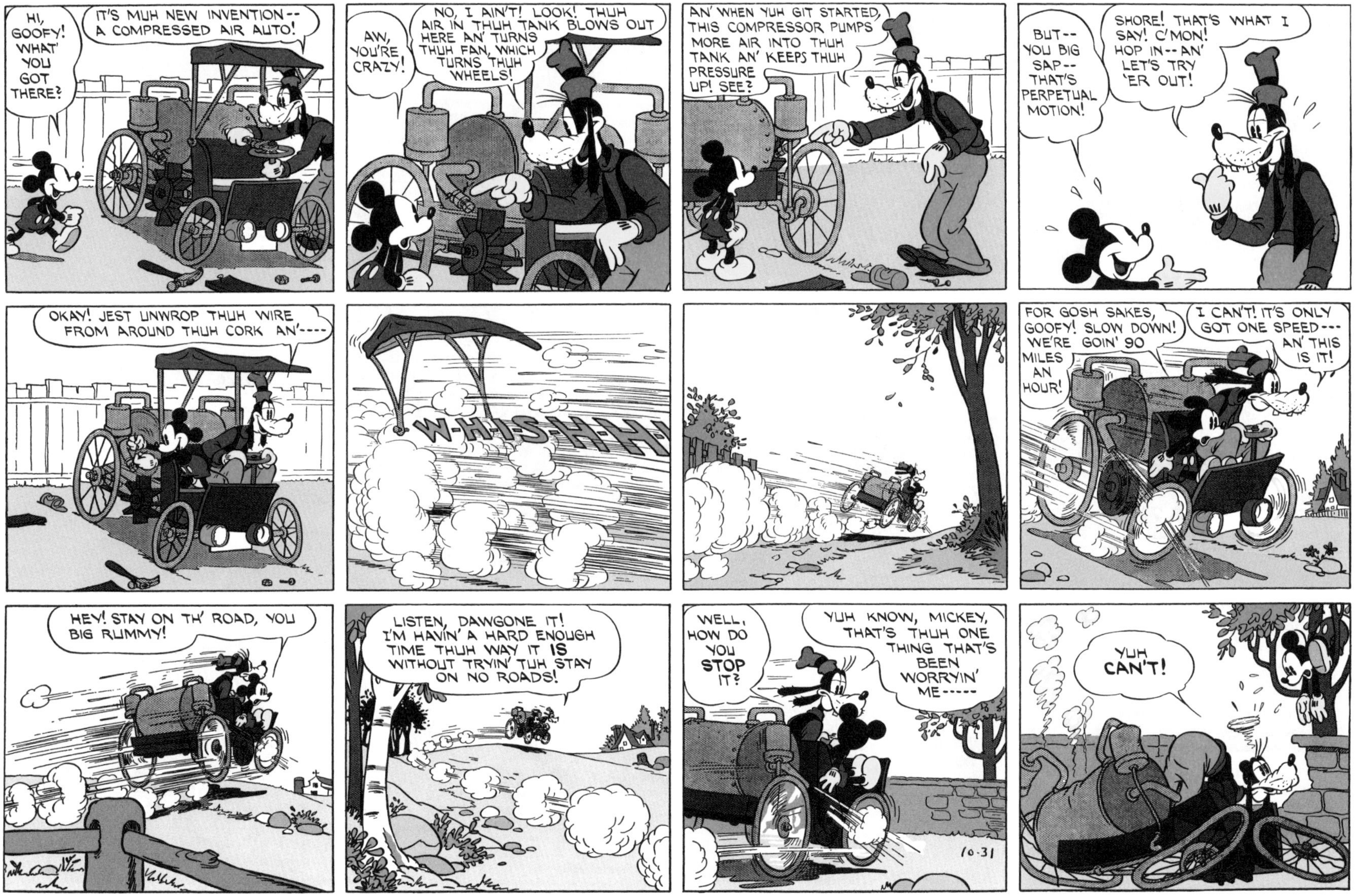

HI, GOOFY! WHAT' YOU GOT THERE?
IT'S MUH NEW INVENTION-- A COMPRESSED AIR AUTO!
AW, YOU'RE CRAZY!
NO, I AIN'T! LOOK! THUH AIR IN THUH TANK BLOWS OUT HERE AN' TURNS THUH FAN, WHICH TURNS THUH WHEELS!
AN' WHEN YUH GIT STARTED, THIS COMPRESSOR PUMPS MORE AIR INTO THUH TANK AN' KEEPS THUH PRESSURE UP! SEE?
BUT-- YOU BIG SAP-- THAT'S PERPETUAL MOTION!
SHORE! THAT'S WHAT I SAY! C'MON! HOP IN--AN' LET'S TRY 'ER OUT!
OKAY! JEST UNWROP THUH WIRE FROM AROUND THUH CORK AN'----
W-H-I-S-H-H-H
FOR GOSH SAKES, GOOFY! SLOW DOWN! WE'RE GOIN' 90 MILES AN HOUR!
I CAN'T! IT'S ONLY GOT ONE SPEED--- AN' THIS IS IT!
HEY! STAY ON TH' ROAD, YOU BIG RUMMY!
LISTEN, DAWGONE IT! I'M HAVIN' A HARD ENOUGH TIME THUH WAY IT IS WITHOUT TRYIN' TUH STAY ON NO ROADS!
WELL, HOW DO YOU STOP IT?
YUH KNOW, MICKEY, THAT'S THUH ONE THING THAT'S BEEN WORRYIN' ME-----
10-31
YUH CAN'T!

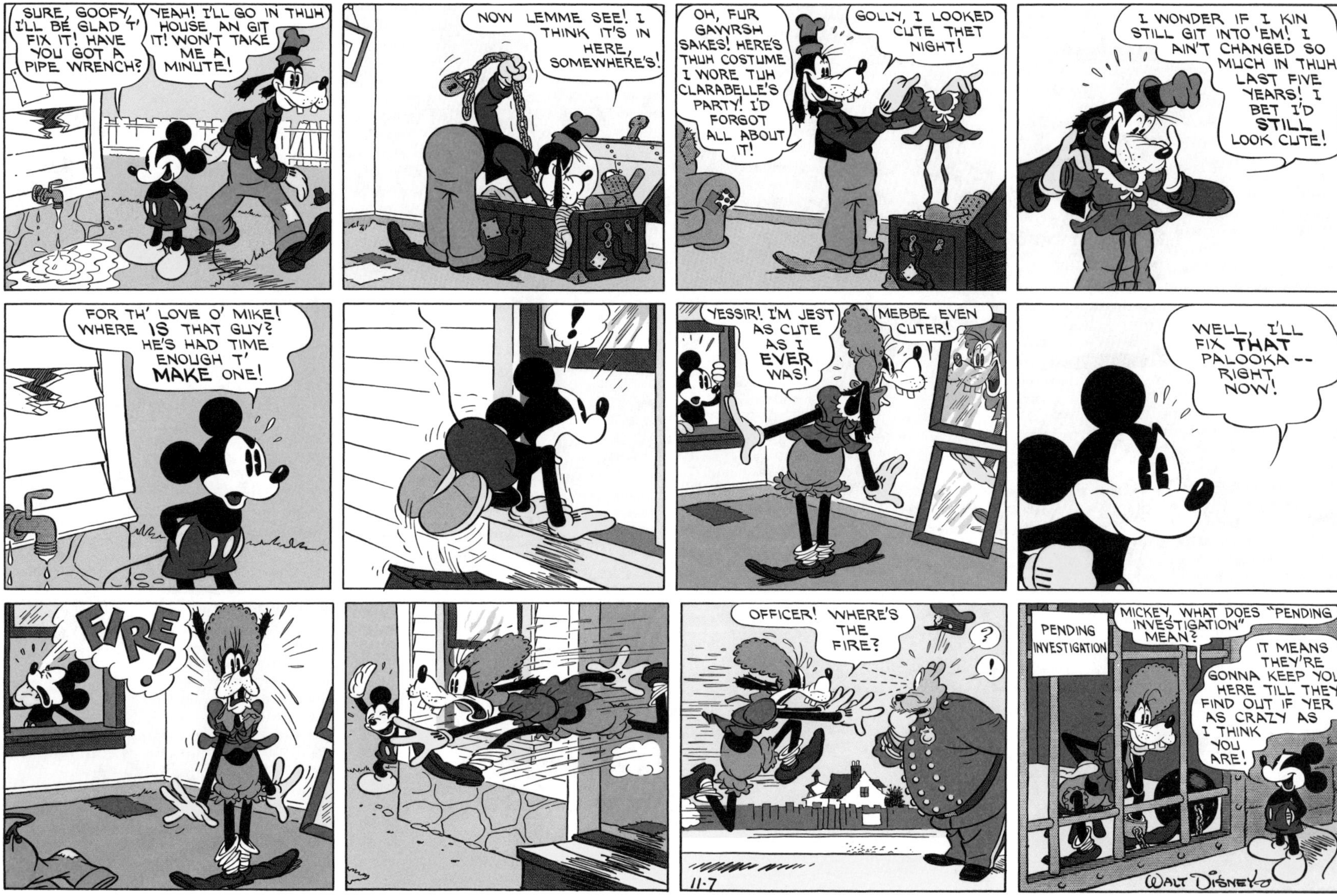
SURE, GOOFY, I'LL BE GLAD T' FIX IT! HAVE YOU GOT A PIPE WRENCH?
YEAH! I'LL GO IN THUH HOUSE AN GIT IT! WON'T TAKE ME A MINUTE!
NOW LEMME SEE! I THINK IT'S IN HERE, SOMEWHERE'S!
OH, FUR GAWRSH SAKES! HERE'S THUH COSTUME I WORE TUH CLARABELLE'S PARTY! I'D FORGOT ALL ABOUT IT!
GOLLY, I LOOKED CUTE THET NIGHT!
I WONDER IF I KIN STILL GIT INTO 'EM! I AIN'T CHANGED SO MUCH IN THUH LAST FIVE YEARS! I BET I'D STILL LOOK CUTE!
FOR TH' LOVE O' MIKE! WHERE IS THAT GUY? HE'S HAD TIME ENOUGH T' MAKE ONE!
!
YESSIR! I'M JEST AS CUTE AS I EVER WAS!
MEBBE EVEN CUTER!
WELL, I'LL FIX THAT PALOOKA -- RIGHT NOW!
FIRE!
OFFICER! WHERE'S THE FIRE?
?
!
11-7
PENDING INVESTIGATION
MICKEY, WHAT DOES "PENDING INVESTIGATION" MEAN?
IT MEANS THEY'RE GONNA KEEP YOU HERE TILL THEY FIND OUT IF YER AS CRAZY AS I THINK YOU ARE!
WALT DISNEY

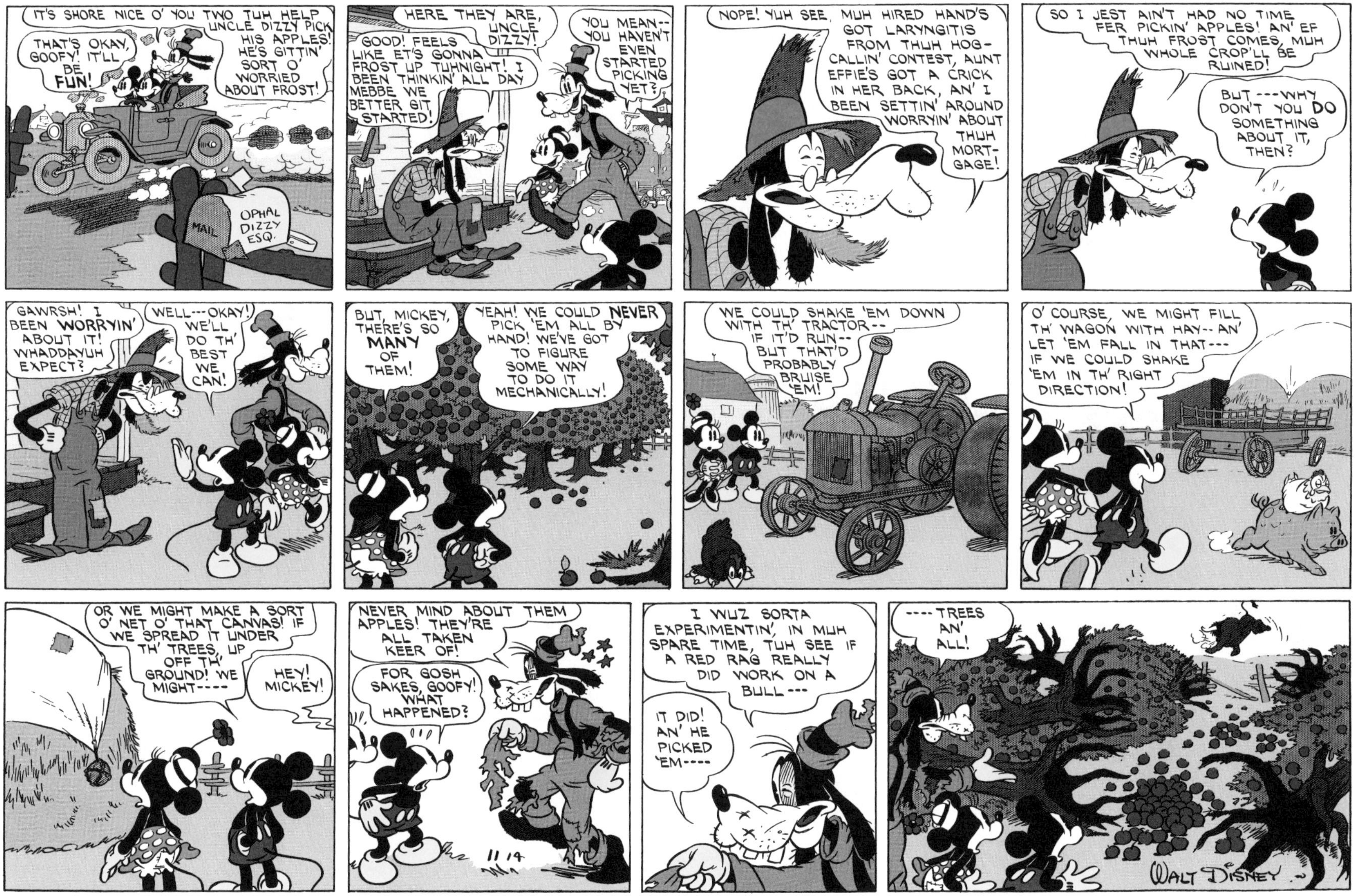
IT'S SHORE NICE O' YOU TWO TUH HELP UNCLE DIZZY PICK HIS APPLES! HE'S GITTIN' SORT O' WORRIED ABOUT FROST!
THAT'S OKAY, GOOFY! IT'LL BE FUN!
MAIL
OPHAL DIZZY ESQ.
HERE THEY ARE, UNCLE DIZZY!
GOOD! FEELS LIKE ET'S GONNA FROST UP TUHNIGHT! I BEEN THINKIN' ALL DAY MEBBE WE BETTER GIT STARTED!
YOU MEAN-- YOU HAVEN'T EVEN STARTED PICKING YET?
NOPE! YUH SEE, MUH HIRED HAND'S GOT LARYNGITIS FROM THUH HOG-CALLIN' CONTEST, AUNT EFFIE'S GOT A CRICK IN HER BACK, AN' I BEEN SETTIN' AROUND WORRYIN' ABOUT THUH MORT-GAGE!
SO I JEST AIN'T HAD NO TIME FER PICKIN' APPLES! AN' EF THUH FROST COMES, MUH WHOLE CROP'LL BE RUINED!
BUT ---WHY DON'T YOU DO SOMETHING ABOUT IT, THEN?
GAWRSH! I BEEN WORRYIN' ABOUT IT! WHADDAYUH EXPECT?
WELL---OKAY! WE'LL DO TH' BEST WE CAN!
BUT, MICKEY, THERE'S SO MANY OF THEM!
YEAH! WE COULD NEVER PICK 'EM ALL BY HAND! WE'VE GOT TO FIGURE SOME WAY TO DO IT MECHANICALLY!
WE COULD SHAKE 'EM DOWN WITH TH' TRACTOR-- IF IT'D RUN-- BUT THAT'D PROBABLY BRUISE 'EM!
O' COURSE, WE MIGHT FILL TH' WAGON WITH HAY-- AN' LET 'EM FALL IN THAT--- IF WE COULD SHAKE 'EM IN TH' RIGHT DIRECTION!
OR WE MIGHT MAKE A SORT O' NET O' THAT CANVAS! IF WE SPREAD IT UNDER TH' TREES, UP OFF TH' GROUND! WE MIGHT----
HEY! MICKEY!
NEVER MIND ABOUT THEM APPLES! THEY'RE ALL TAKEN KEER OF!
FOR GOSH SAKES, GOOFY! WHAT HAPPENED?
11 14
I WUZ SORTA EXPERIMENTIN', IN MUH SPARE TIME, TUH SEE IF A RED RAG REALLY DID WORK ON A BULL---
IT DID! AN' HE PICKED 'EM----
----TREES AN' ALL!
WALT DISNEY

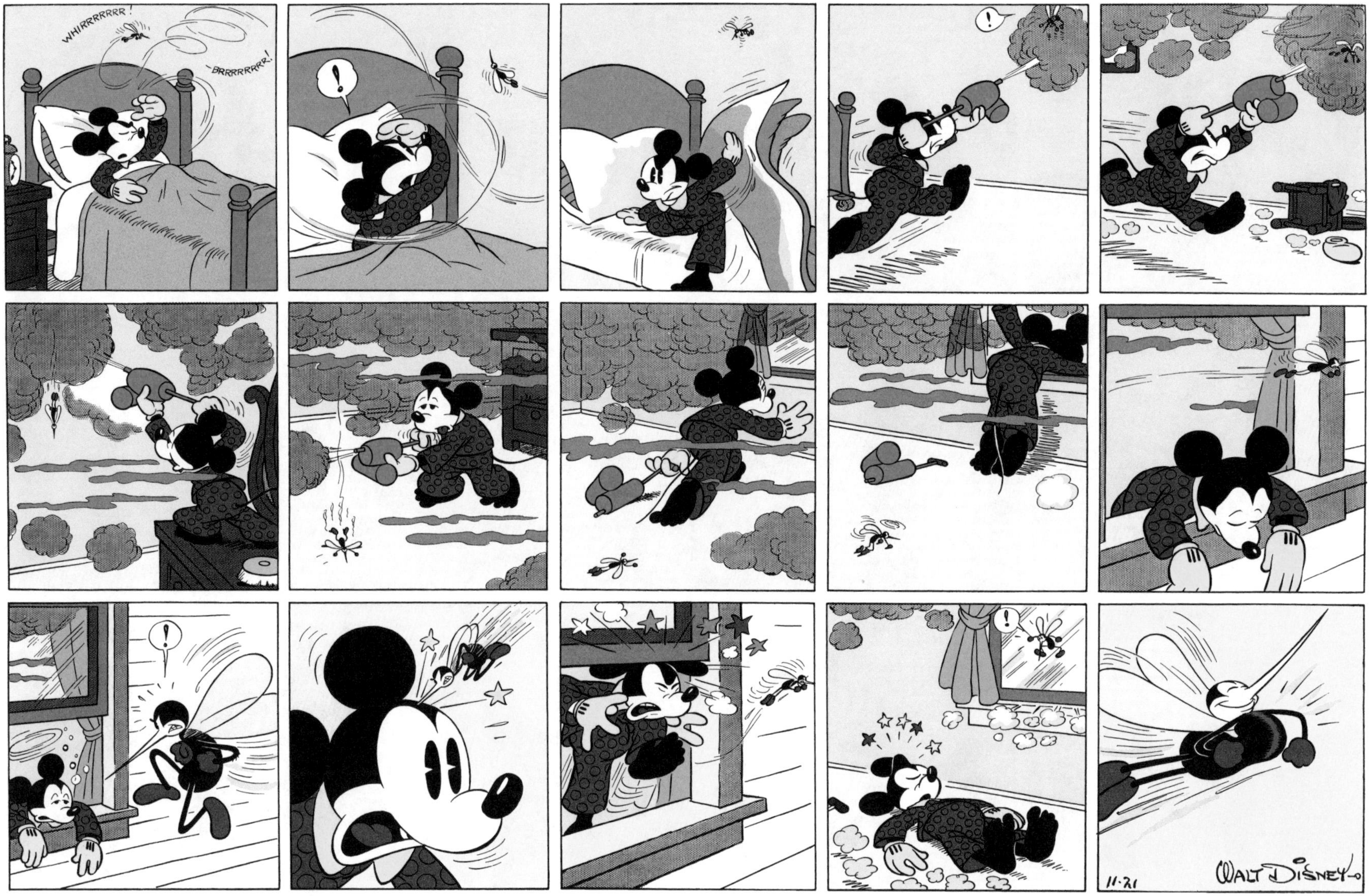
WHIRRRRRRR!
-BRRRRRRRR!
!
!
!
!
!
11·21
WALT DISNEY

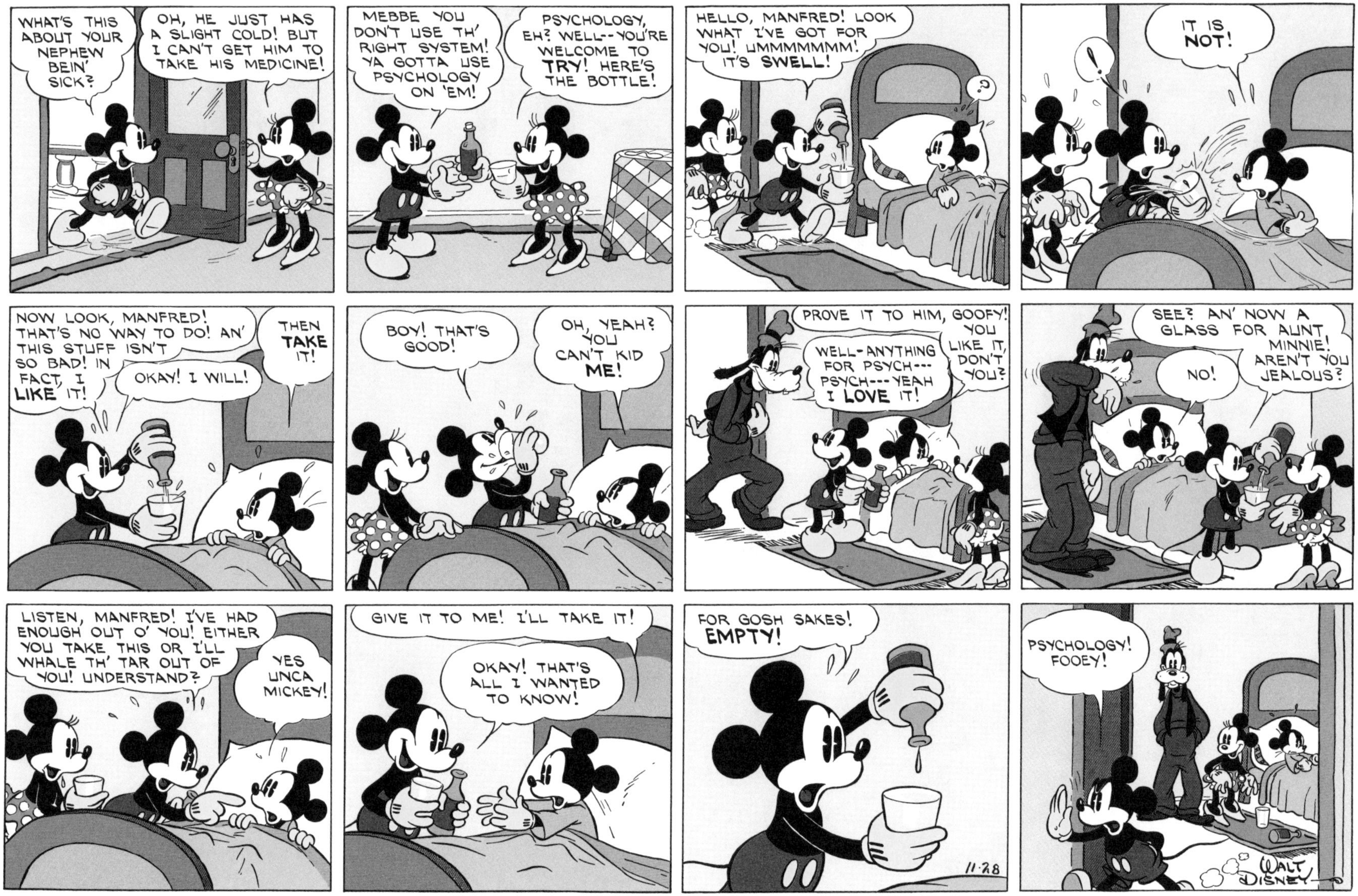
WHAT'S THIS ABOUT YOUR NEPHEW BEIN' SICK?
OH, HE JUST HAS A SLIGHT COLD! BUT I CAN'T GET HIM TO TAKE HIS MEDICINE!
MEBBE YOU DON'T USE TH' RIGHT SYSTEM! YA GOTTA USE PSYCHOLOGY ON 'EM!
PSYCHOLOGY, EH? WELL--YOU'RE WELCOME TO TRY! HERE'S THE BOTTLE!
HELLO, MANFRED! LOOK WHAT I'VE GOT FOR YOU! UMMMMMMMM! IT'S SWELL!
IT IS NOT!
NOW LOOK, MANFRED! THAT'S NO WAY TO DO! AN' THIS STUFF ISN'T SO BAD! IN FACT, I LIKE IT!
THEN TAKE IT!
OKAY! I WILL!
BOY! THAT'S GOOD!
OH, YEAH? YOU CAN'T KID ME!
PROVE IT TO HIM, GOOFY! YOU LIKE IT, DON'T YOU?
WELL-ANYTHING FOR PSYCH--- PSYCH---YEAH I LOVE IT!
SEE? AN' NOW A GLASS FOR AUNT MINNIE! AREN'T YOU JEALOUS?
NO!
LISTEN, MANFRED! I'VE HAD ENOUGH OUT O' YOU! EITHER YOU TAKE THIS OR I'LL WHALE TH' TAR OUT OF YOU! UNDERSTAND?
YES UNCA MICKEY!
GIVE IT TO ME! I'LL TAKE IT!
OKAY! THAT'S ALL I WANTED TO KNOW!
FOR GOSH SAKES! EMPTY!
11·28
PSYCHOLOGY! FOOEY!
WALT DISNEY

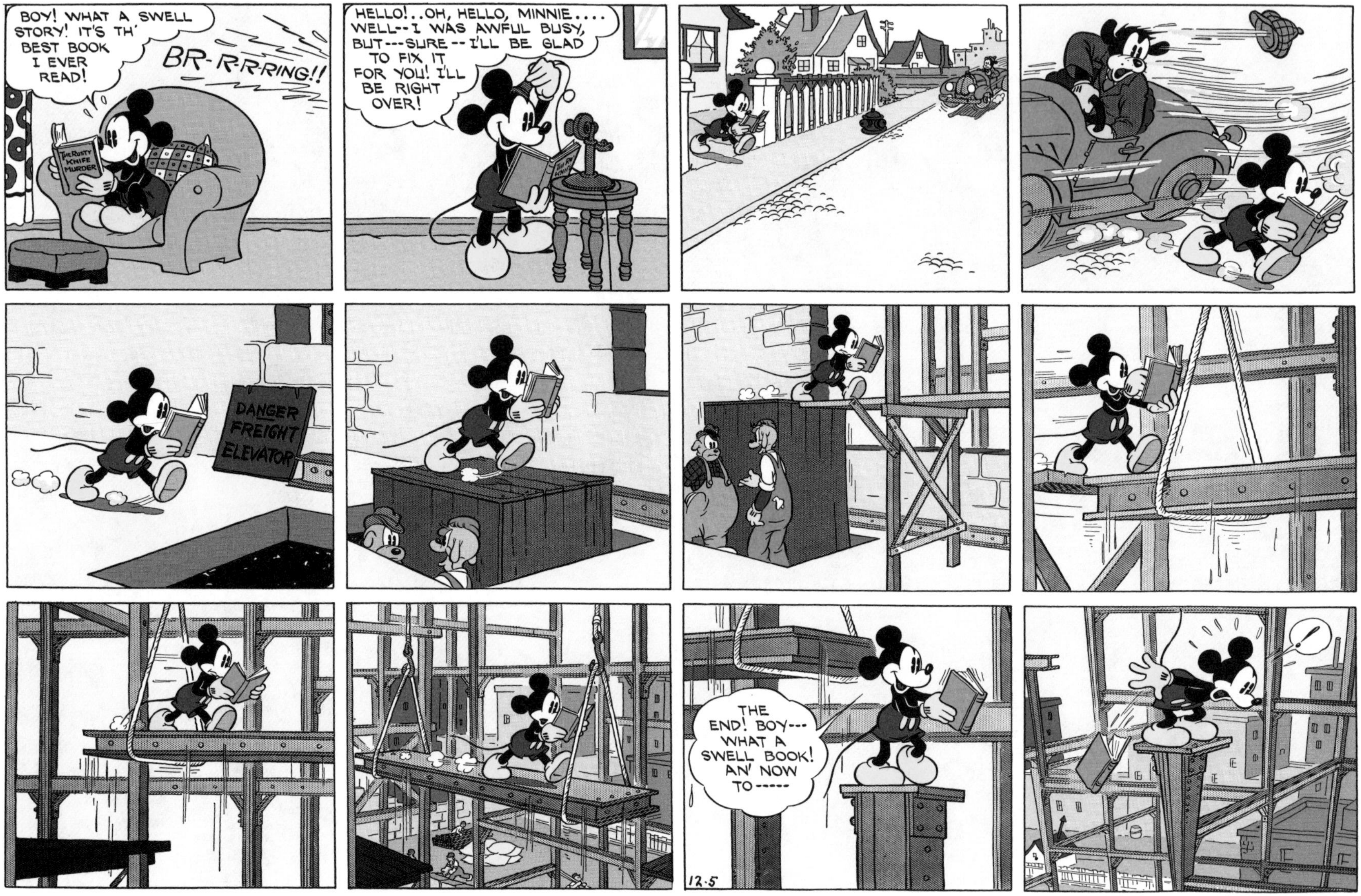

BOY! WHAT A SWELL STORY! IT'S TH' BEST BOOK I EVER READ!
BR-R-R-RING!!
THE RUSTY KNIFE MURDER
HELLO!..OH, HELLO, MINNIE.... WELL--I WAS AWFUL BUSY, BUT---SURE--I'LL BE GLAD TO FIX IT FOR YOU! I'LL BE RIGHT OVER!
DANGER FREIGHT ELEVATOR
THE END! BOY--- WHAT A SWELL BOOK! AN' NOW TO-----
12.5

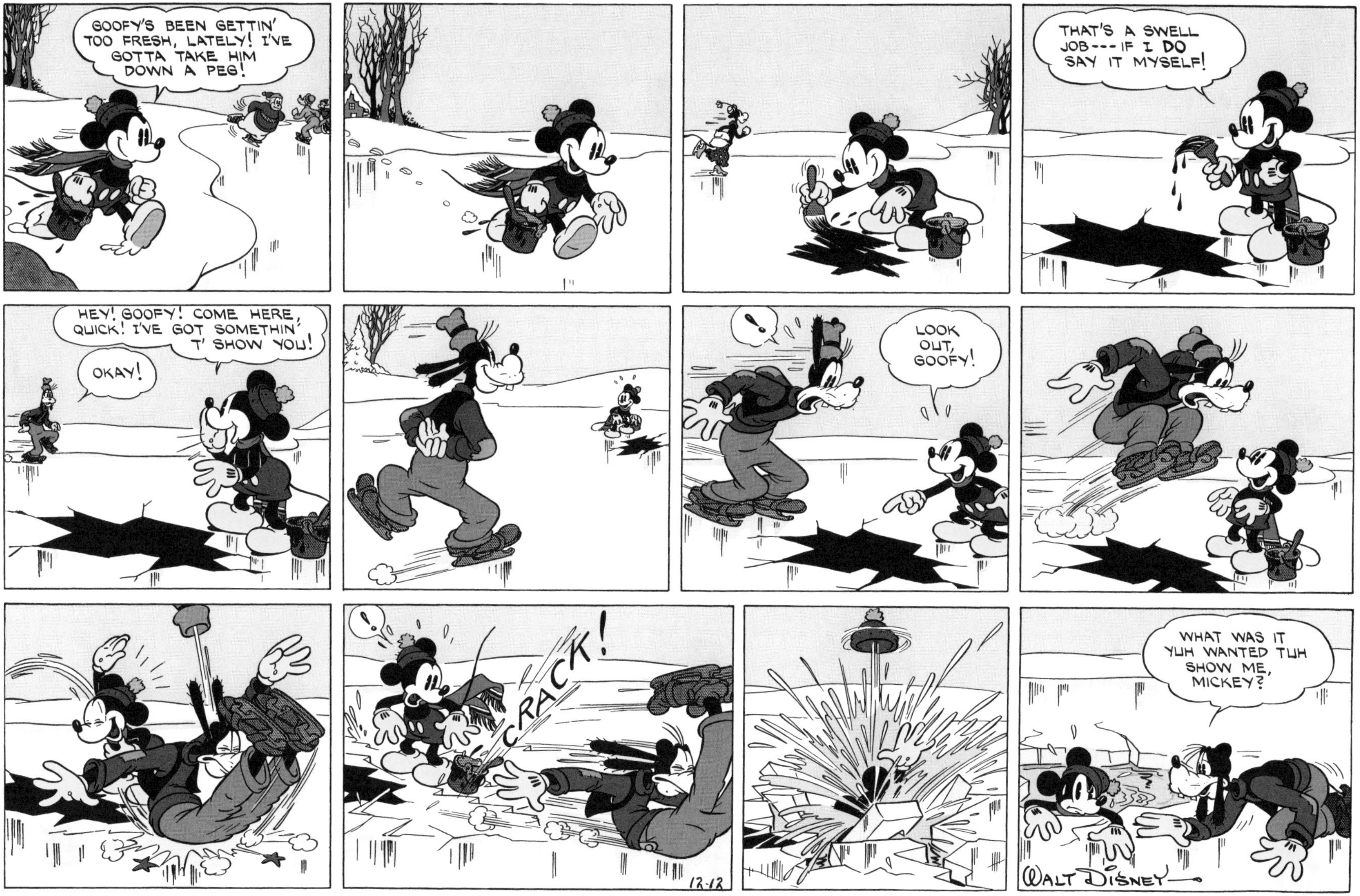
GOOFY'S BEEN GETTIN' TOO FRESH, LATELY! I'VE GOTTA TAKE HIM DOWN A PEG!
THAT'S A SWELL JOB--- IF I DO SAY IT MYSELF!
HEY! GOOFY! COME HERE, QUICK! I'VE GOT SOMETHIN' T' SHOW YOU!
OKAY!
!
LOOK OUT, GOOFY!
!
CRACK!
12-12
WHAT WAS IT YUH WANTED TUH SHOW ME, MICKEY?
WALT DISNEY

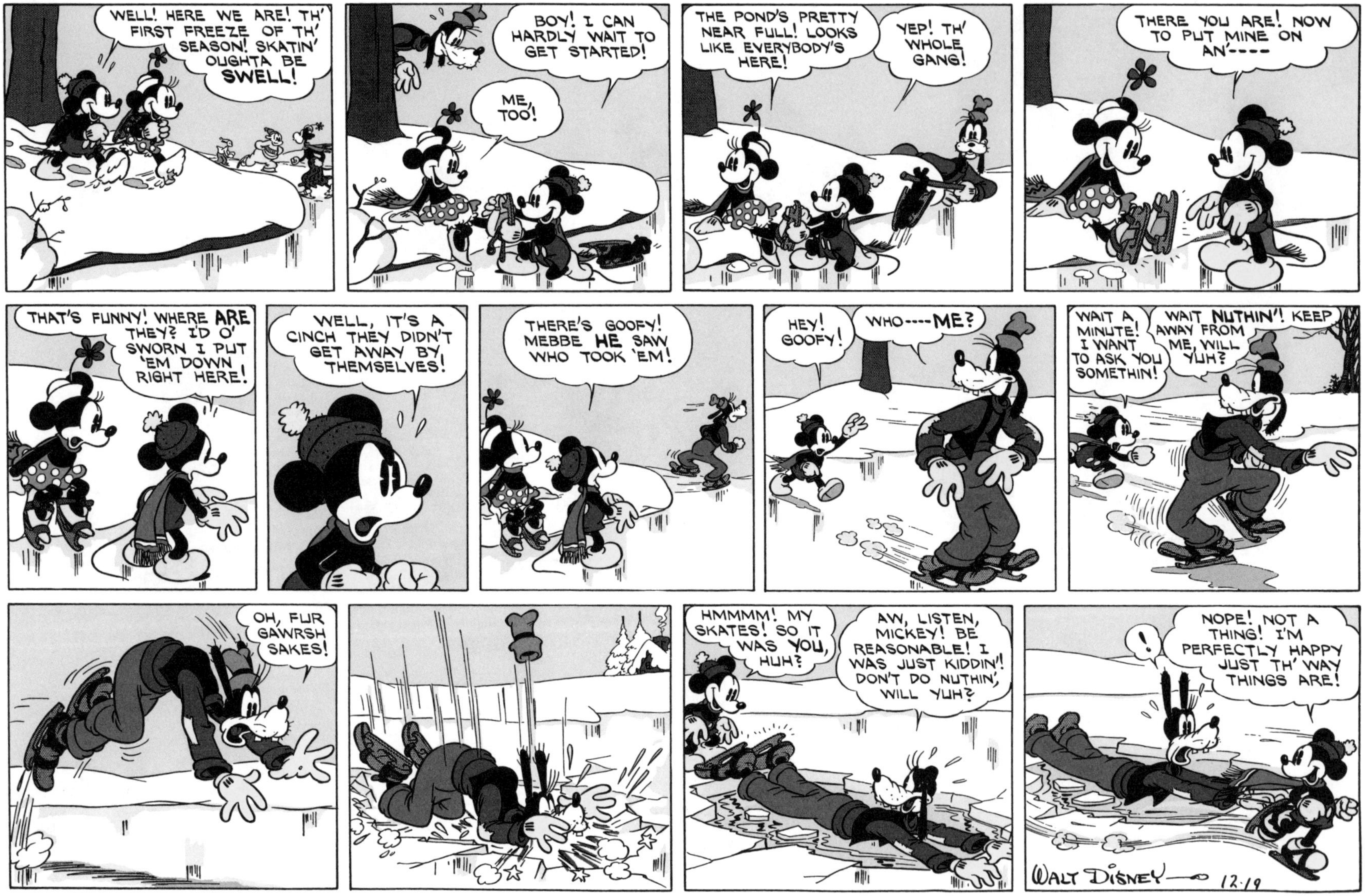
WELL! HERE WE ARE! TH' FIRST FREEZE OF TH' SEASON! SKATIN' OUGHTA BE **SWELL**!
BOY! I CAN HARDLY WAIT TO GET STARTED!
ME, TOO!
THE POND'S PRETTY NEAR FULL! LOOKS LIKE EVERYBODY'S HERE!
YEP! TH' WHOLE GANG!
THERE YOU ARE! NOW TO PUT MINE ON AN'----
THAT'S FUNNY! WHERE **ARE** THEY? I'D O' SWORN I PUT 'EM DOWN RIGHT HERE!
WELL, IT'S A CINCH THEY DIDN'T GET AWAY BY THEMSELVES!
THERE'S GOOFY! MEBBE **HE** SAW WHO TOOK 'EM!
HEY! GOOFY!
WHO----**ME**?
WAIT A MINUTE! I WANT TO ASK YOU SOMETHIN!
WAIT **NUTHIN'**! KEEP AWAY FROM ME, WILL YUH?
OH, FUR GAWRSH SAKES!
HMMMM! MY SKATES! SO IT WAS **YOU**, HUH?
AW, LISTEN, MICKEY! BE REASONABLE! I WAS JUST KIDDIN'! DON'T DO NUTHIN', WILL YUH?
!
NOPE! NOT A THING! I'M PERFECTLY HAPPY JUST TH' WAY THINGS ARE!
WALT DISNEY 12.19

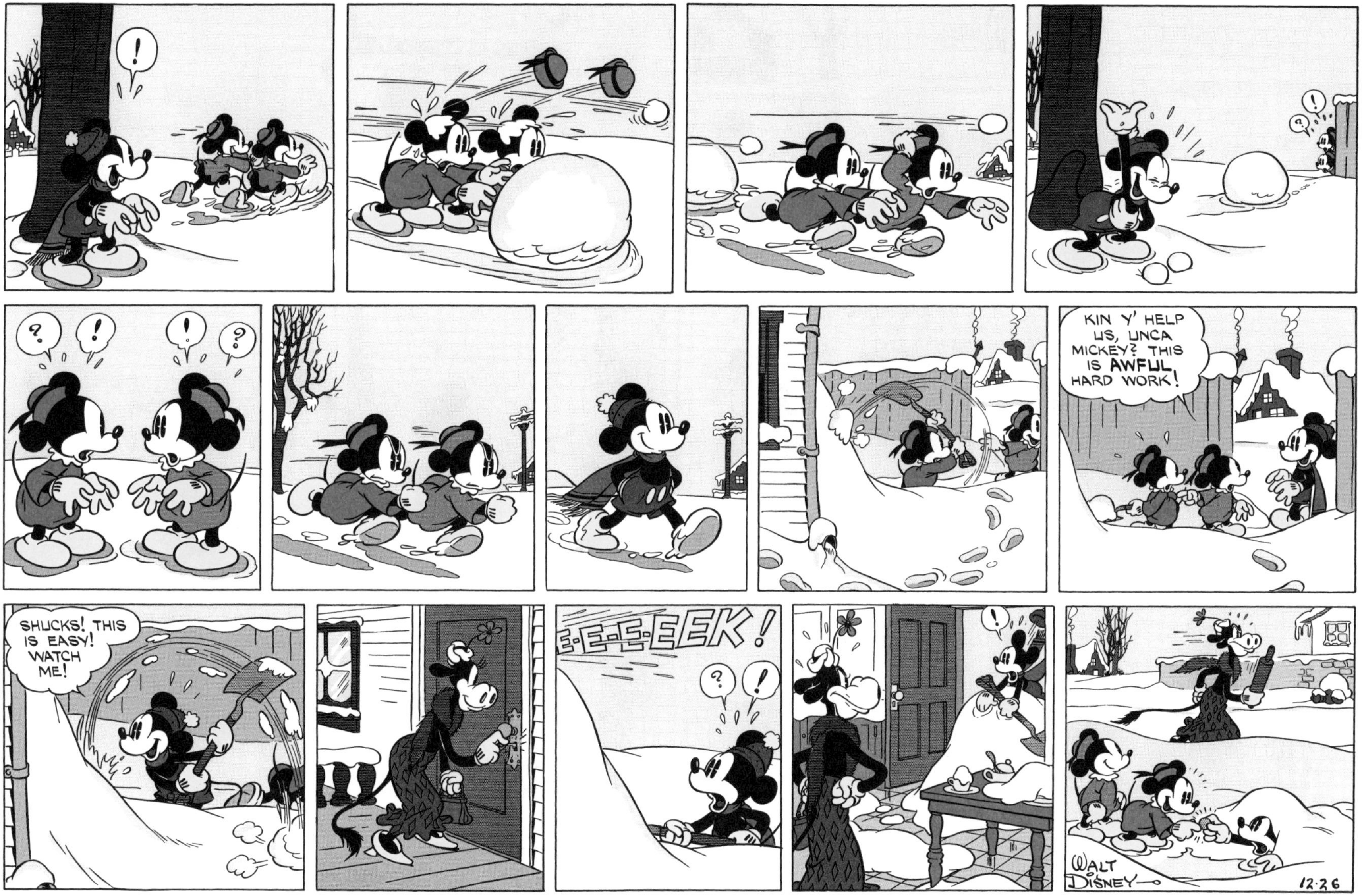
!
!
?
!
?
!
!
?
KIN Y' HELP US, UNCA MICKEY? THIS IS AWFUL HARD WORK!
SHUCKS! THIS IS EASY! WATCH ME!
E-E-E-E-EEK!
?
!
!
WALT DISNEY
12-26

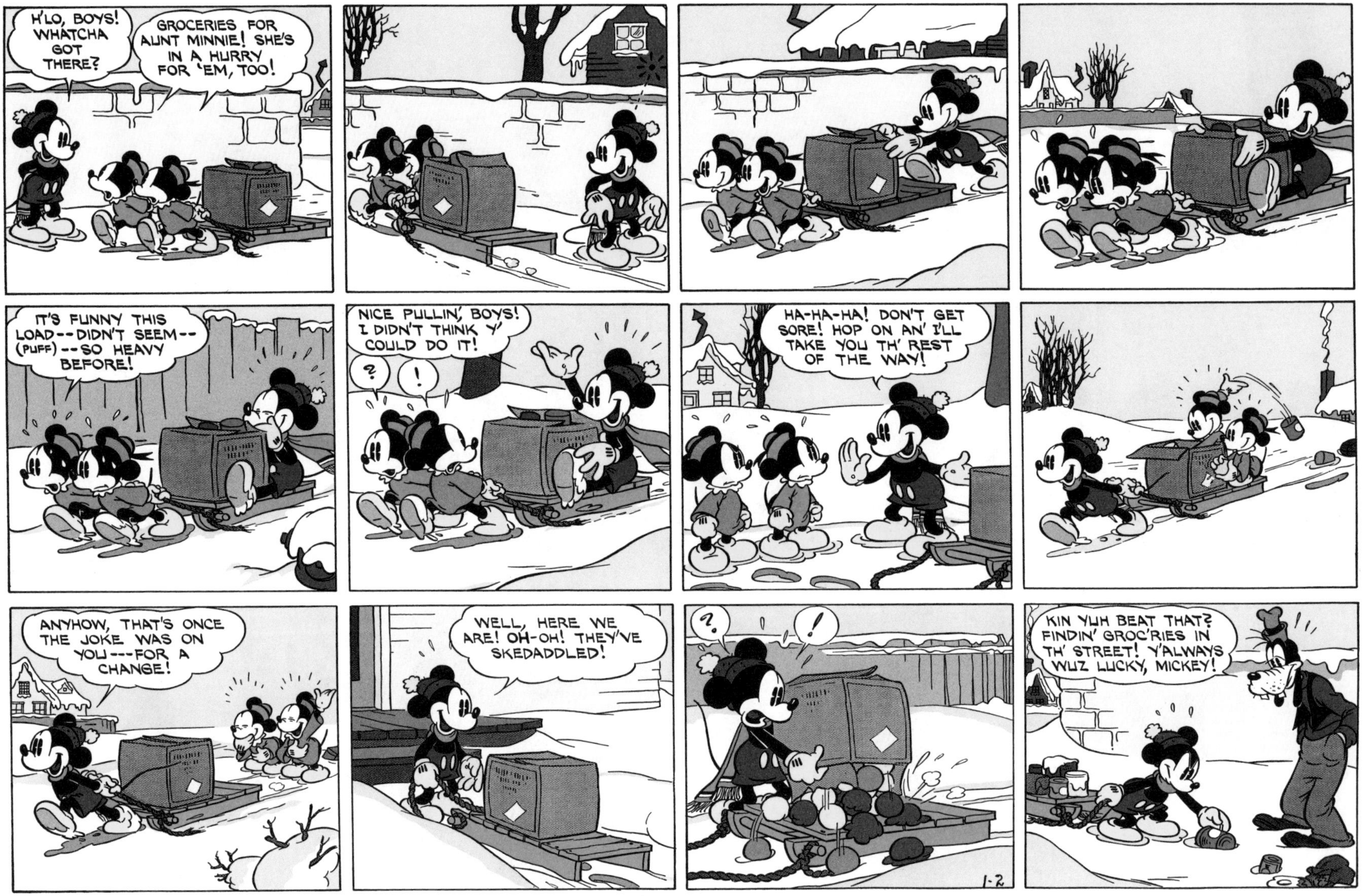
H'LO, BOYS! WHATCHA GOT THERE?
GROCERIES FOR AUNT MINNIE! SHE'S IN A HURRY FOR 'EM, TOO!
IT'S FUNNY THIS LOAD--DIDN'T SEEM--(PUFF)--SO HEAVY BEFORE!
NICE PULLIN', BOYS! I DIDN'T THINK Y' COULD DO IT!
?
!
HA-HA-HA! DON'T GET SORE! HOP ON AN' I'LL TAKE YOU TH' REST OF THE WAY!
ANYHOW, THAT'S ONCE THE JOKE WAS ON YOU---FOR A CHANGE!
WELL, HERE WE ARE! OH-OH! THEY'VE SKEDADDLED!
?
!
1-2
KIN YUH BEAT THAT? FINDIN' GROC'RIES IN TH' STREET! Y'ALWAYS WUZ LUCKY, MICKEY!

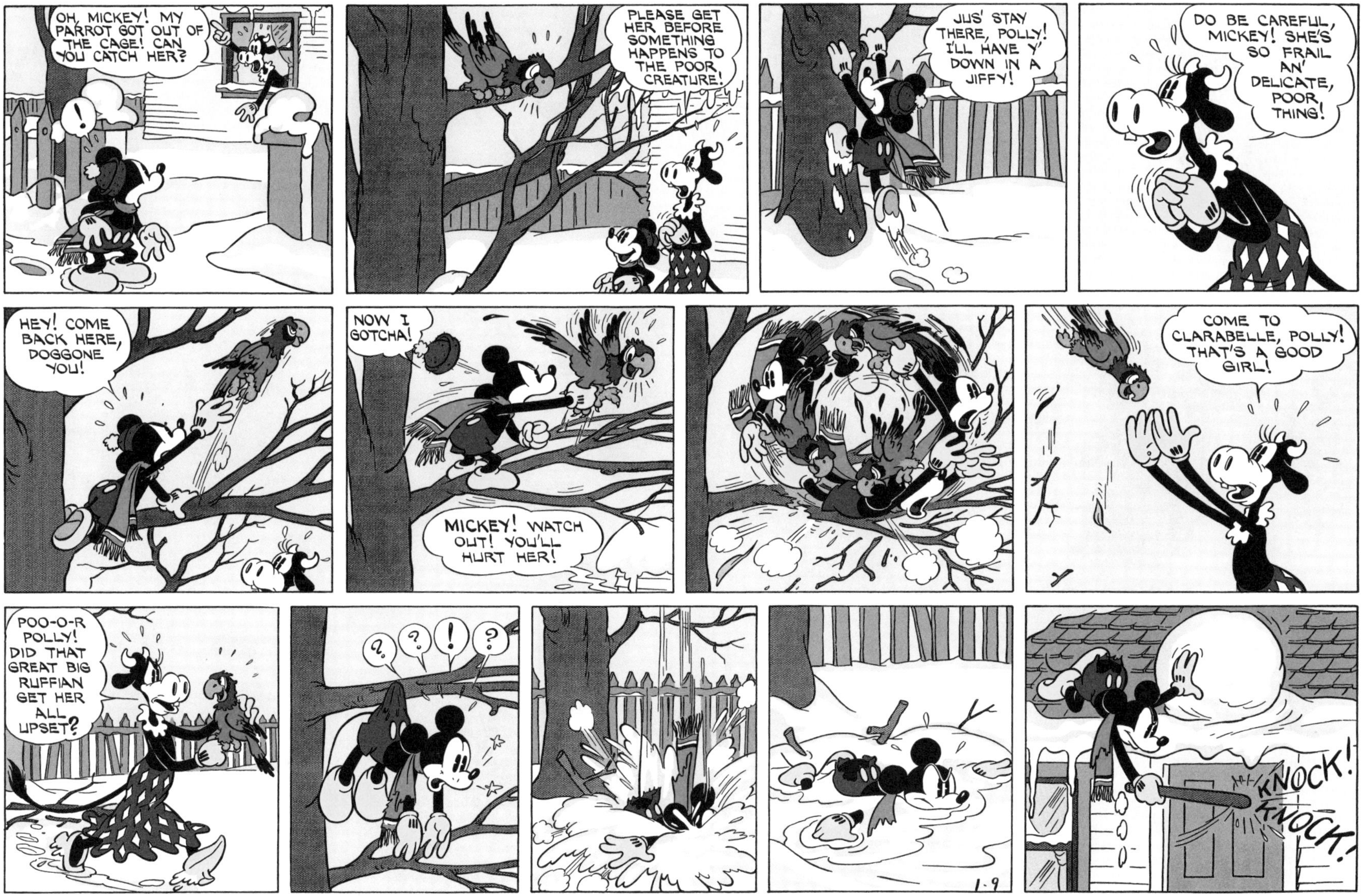
OH, MICKEY! MY PARROT GOT OUT OF THE CAGE! CAN YOU CATCH HER?
!
PLEASE GET HER BEFORE SOMETHING HAPPENS TO THE POOR CREATURE!
JUS' STAY THERE, POLLY! I'LL HAVE Y' DOWN IN A JIFFY!
DO BE CAREFUL, MICKEY! SHE'S SO FRAIL AN' DELICATE, POOR THING!
HEY! COME BACK HERE, DOGGONE YOU!
NOW I GOTCHA!
MICKEY! WATCH OUT! YOU'LL HURT HER!
COME TO CLARABELLE, POLLY! THAT'S A GOOD GIRL!
POO-O-R POLLY! DID THAT GREAT BIG RUFFIAN GET HER ALL UPSET?
? ? ! ?
1-9
KNOCK! KNOCK!

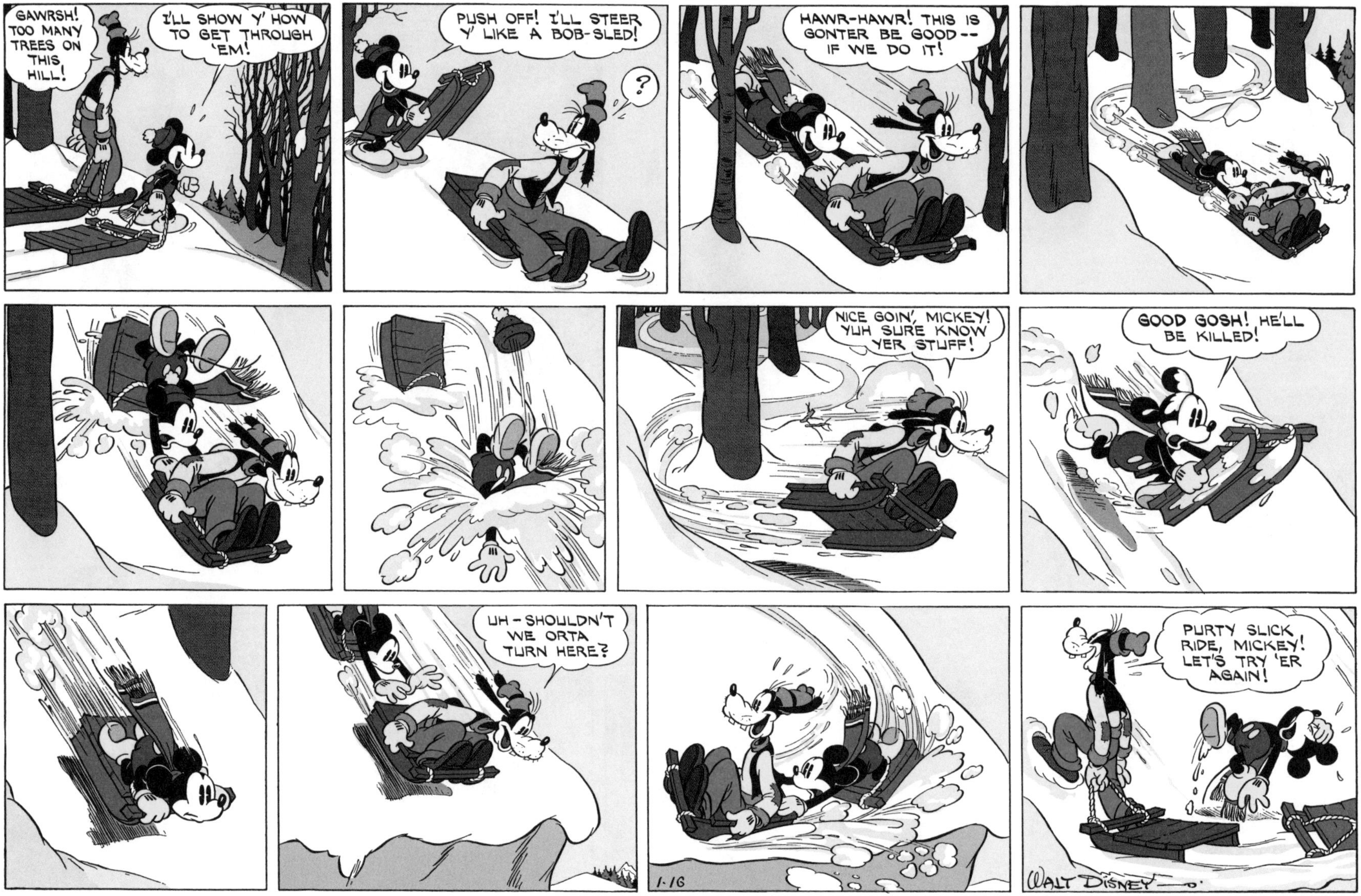
GAWRSH! TOO MANY TREES ON THIS HILL!
I'LL SHOW Y' HOW TO GET THROUGH 'EM!
PUSH OFF! I'LL STEER Y' LIKE A BOB-SLED!
?
HAWR-HAWR! THIS IS GONTER BE GOOD -- IF WE DO IT!
NICE GOIN', MICKEY! YUH SURE KNOW YER STUFF!
GOOD GOSH! HE'LL BE KILLED!
UH - SHOULDN'T WE ORTA TURN HERE?
1·16
PURTY SLICK RIDE, MICKEY! LET'S TRY 'ER AGAIN!
WALT DISNEY

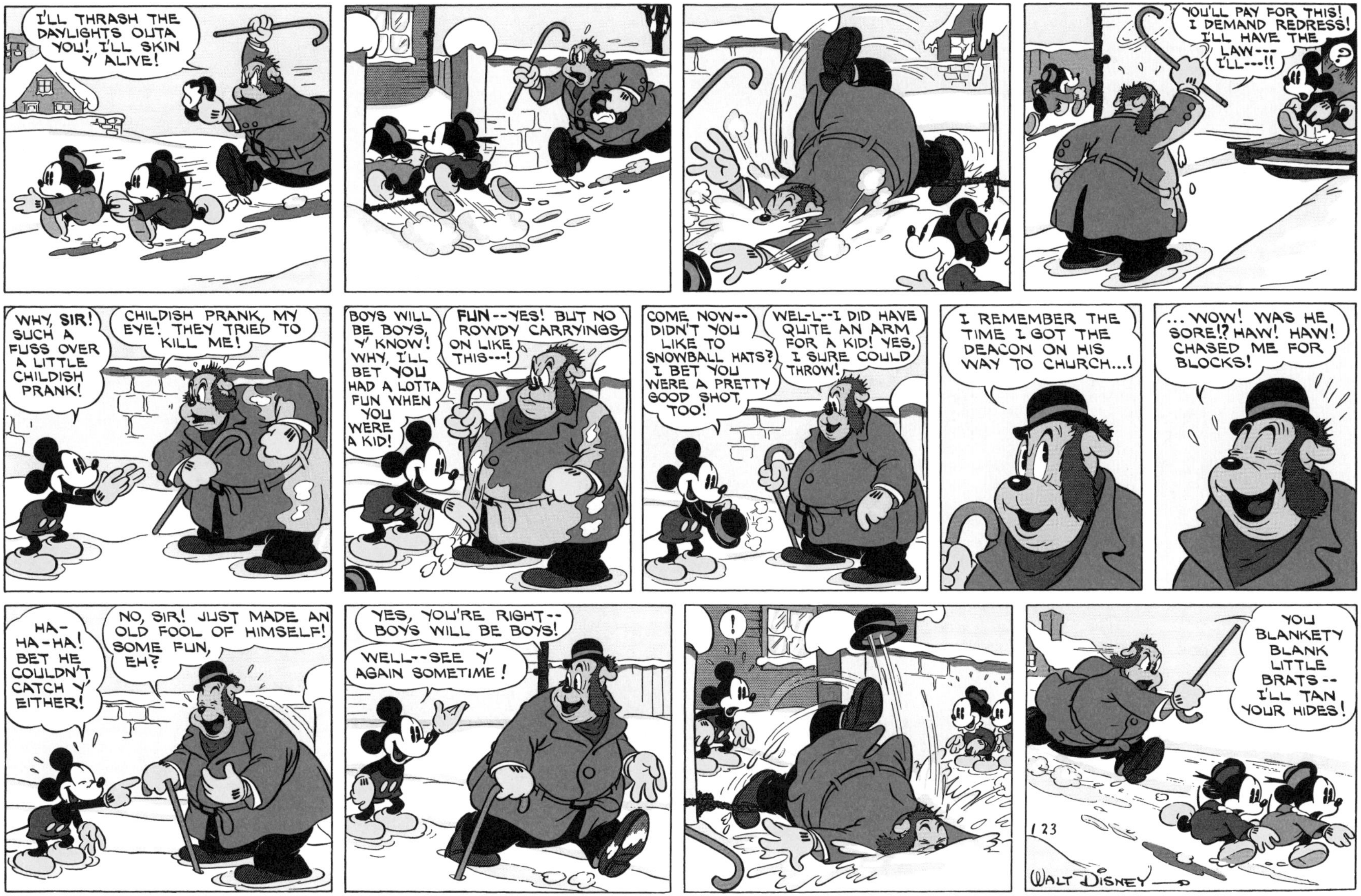
I'LL THRASH THE DAYLIGHTS OUTA YOU! I'LL SKIN Y' ALIVE!
YOU'LL PAY FOR THIS! I DEMAND REDRESS! I'LL HAVE THE LAW--- I'LL---!!
?
WHY, SIR! SUCH A FUSS OVER A LITTLE CHILDISH PRANK!
CHILDISH PRANK, MY EYE! THEY TRIED TO KILL ME!
BOYS WILL BE BOYS, Y' KNOW! WHY, I'LL BET YOU HAD A LOTTA FUN WHEN YOU WERE A KID!
FUN--YES! BUT NO ROWDY CARRYINGS-ON LIKE THIS---!
COME NOW--DIDN'T YOU LIKE TO SNOWBALL HATS? I BET YOU WERE A PRETTY GOOD SHOT, TOO!
WEL-L--I DID HAVE QUITE AN ARM FOR A KID! YES, I SURE COULD THROW!
I REMEMBER THE TIME I GOT THE DEACON ON HIS WAY TO CHURCH...!
...WOW! WAS HE SORE!? HAW! HAW! CHASED ME FOR BLOCKS!
HA-HA-HA! BET HE COULDN'T CATCH Y' EITHER!
NO, SIR! JUST MADE AN OLD FOOL OF HIMSELF! SOME FUN, EH?
YES, YOU'RE RIGHT--BOYS WILL BE BOYS!
WELL--SEE Y' AGAIN SOMETIME!
!
YOU BLANKETY BLANK LITTLE BRATS--I'LL TAN YOUR HIDES!
1 23
WALT DISNEY

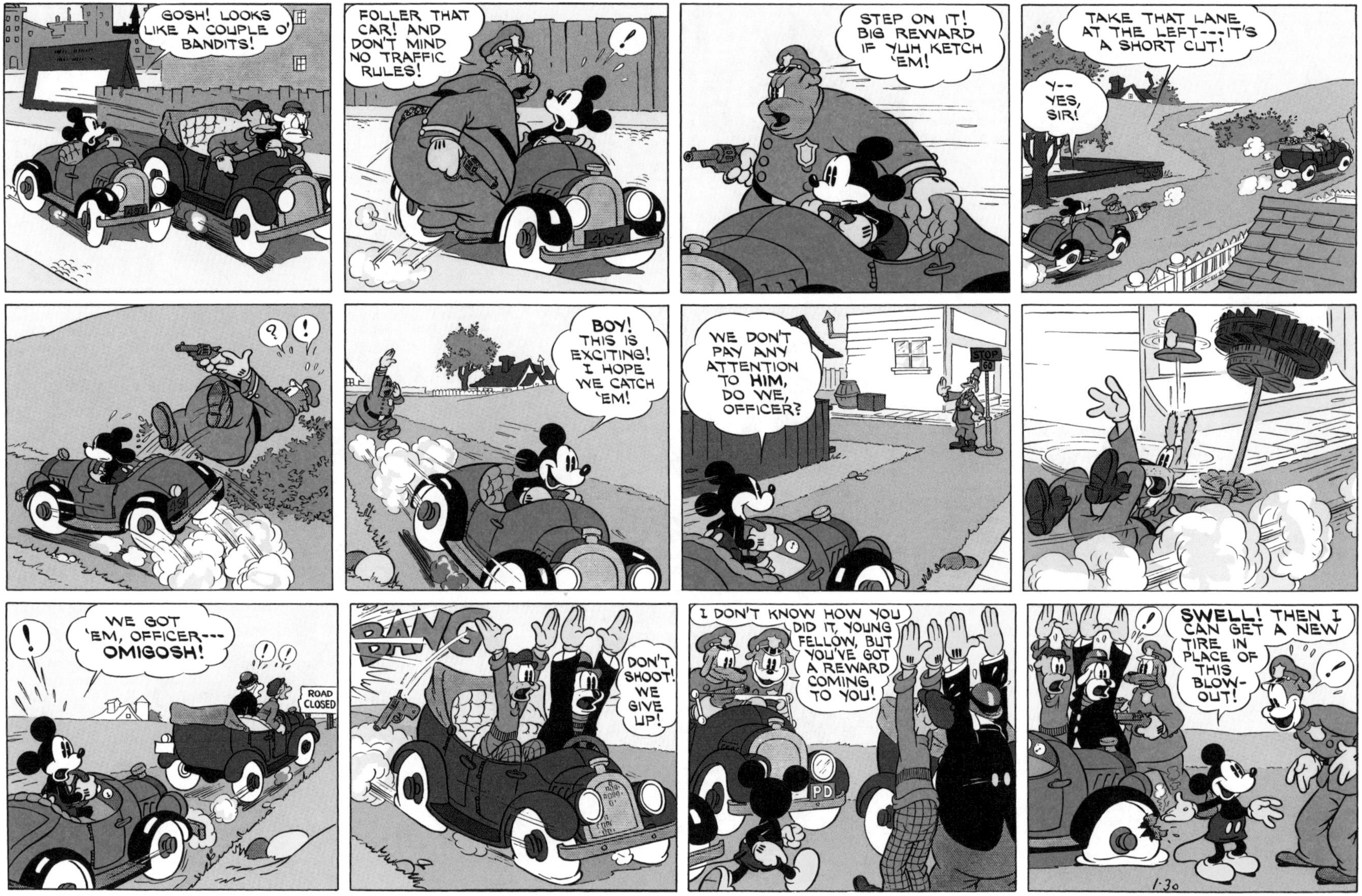
GOSH! LOOKS LIKE A COUPLE O' BANDITS!
FOLLER THAT CAR! AND DON'T MIND NO TRAFFIC RULES!
!
STEP ON IT! BIG REWARD IF YUH KETCH 'EM!
TAKE THAT LANE AT THE LEFT---IT'S A SHORT CUT!
Y-- YES, SIR!
? !
BOY! THIS IS EXCITING! I HOPE WE CATCH 'EM!
WE DON'T PAY ANY ATTENTION TO HIM, DO WE, OFFICER?
STOP
60
!
WE GOT 'EM, OFFICER--- OMIGOSH!
! !
ROAD CLOSED
BANG
DON'T SHOOT! WE GIVE UP!
I DON'T KNOW HOW YOU DID IT, YOUNG FELLOW, BUT YOU'VE GOT A REWARD COMING TO YOU!
PD
1-30
!
SWELL! THEN I CAN GET A NEW TIRE IN PLACE OF THIS BLOW-OUT!
!

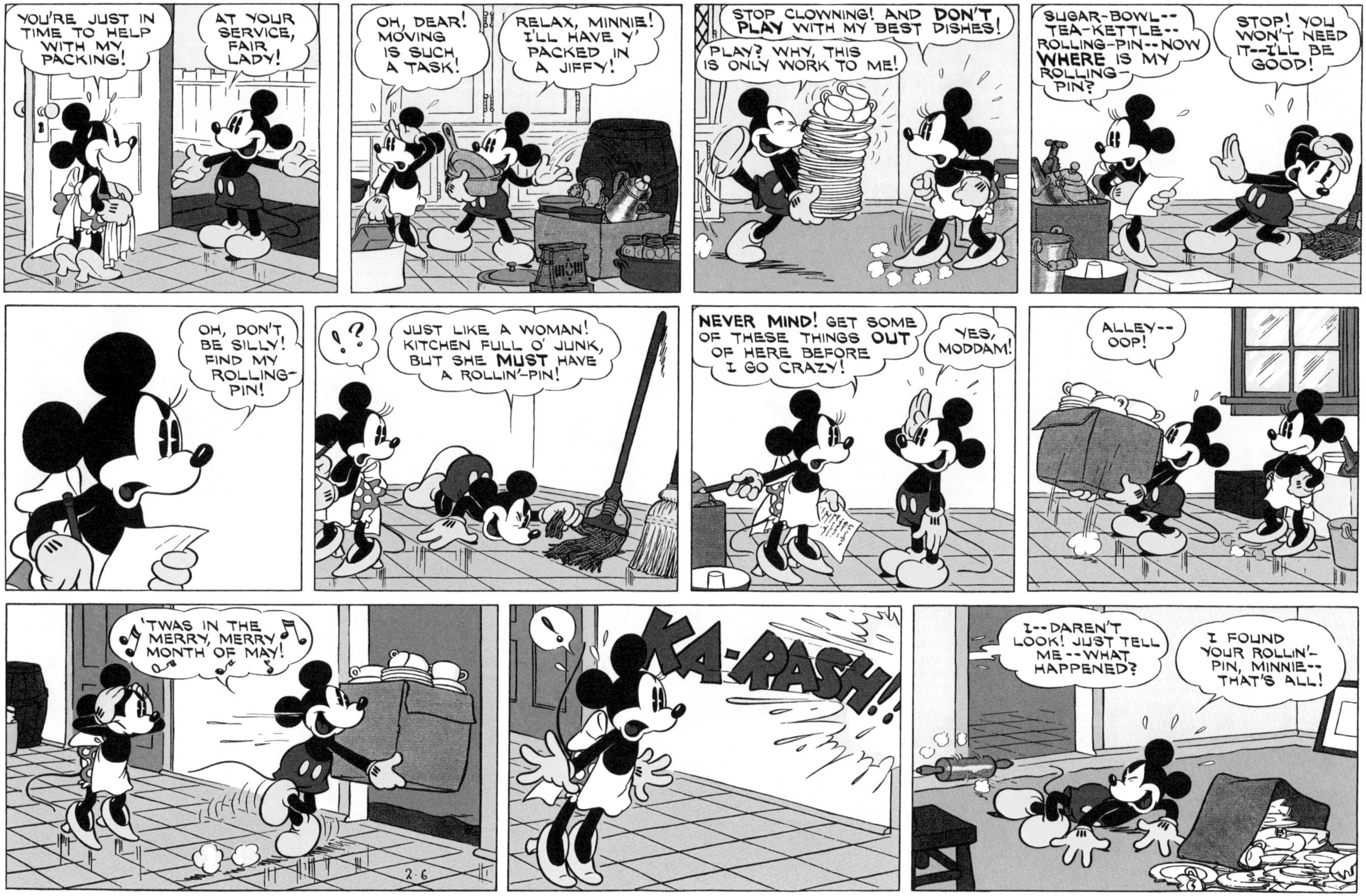

YOU'RE JUST IN TIME TO HELP WITH MY PACKING!
AT YOUR SERVICE, FAIR LADY!
OH, DEAR! MOVING IS SUCH A TASK!
RELAX, MINNIE! I'LL HAVE Y' PACKED IN A JIFFY!
STOP CLOWNING! AND DON'T PLAY WITH MY BEST DISHES!
PLAY? WHY, THIS IS ONLY WORK TO ME!
SUGAR-BOWL-- TEA-KETTLE-- ROLLING-PIN--NOW WHERE IS MY ROLLING-PIN?
STOP! YOU WON'T NEED IT--I'LL BE GOOD!
OH, DON'T BE SILLY! FIND MY ROLLING-PIN!
!?
JUST LIKE A WOMAN! KITCHEN FULL O' JUNK, BUT SHE MUST HAVE A ROLLIN'-PIN!
NEVER MIND! GET SOME OF THESE THINGS OUT OF HERE BEFORE I GO CRAZY!
YES, MODDAM!
ALLEY-- OOP!
'TWAS IN THE MERRY, MERRY MONTH OF MAY!
!
KA-RASH!!
2-6
I--DAREN'T LOOK! JUST TELL ME--WHAT HAPPENED?
I FOUND YOUR ROLLIN'-PIN, MINNIE-- THAT'S ALL!

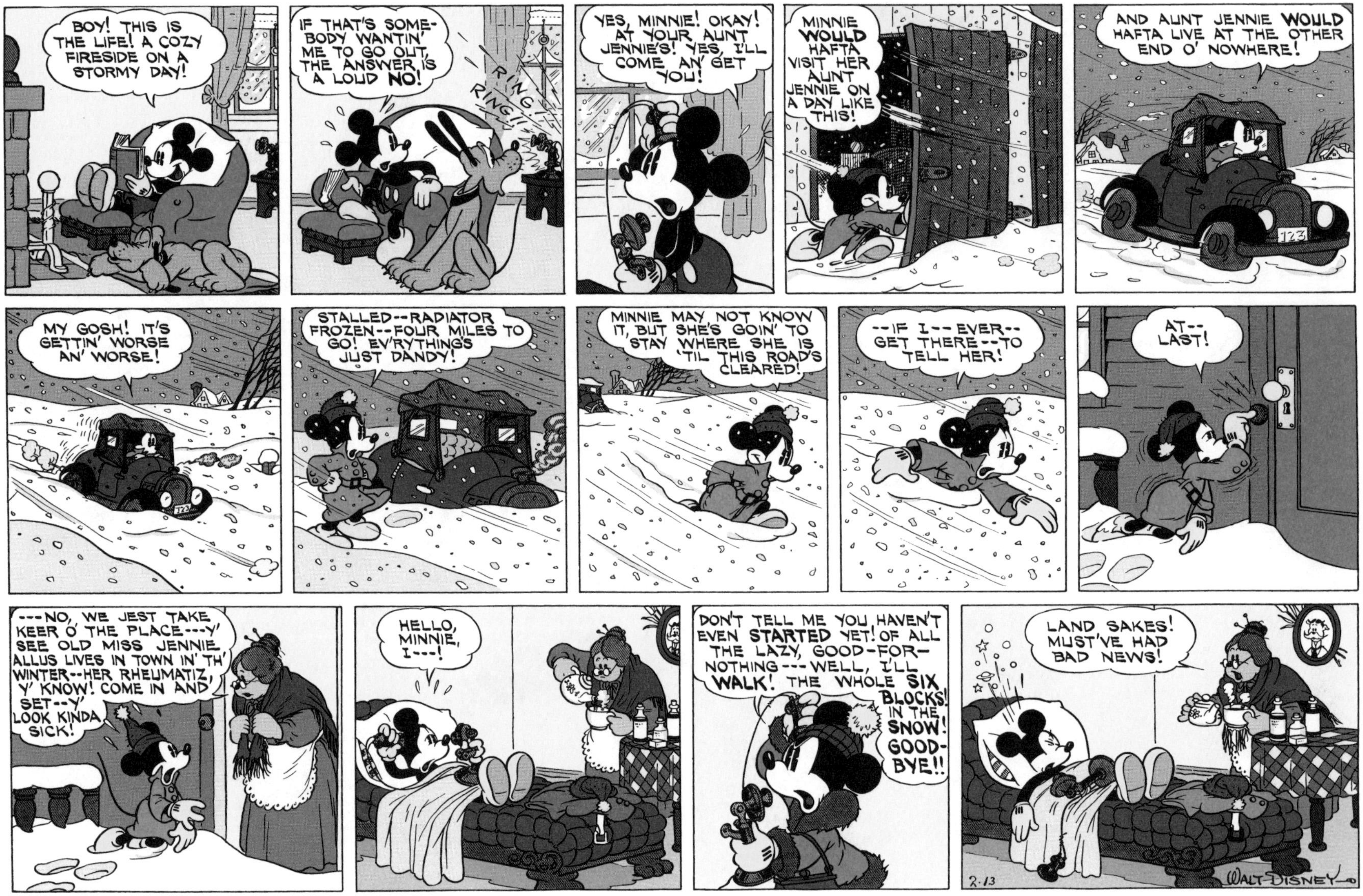
BOY! THIS IS THE LIFE! A COZY FIRESIDE ON A STORMY DAY!
IF THAT'S SOMEBODY WANTIN' ME TO GO OUT, THE ANSWER IS A LOUD NO!
RING RING!!
YES, MINNIE! OKAY! AT YOUR AUNT JENNIE'S! YES, I'LL COME AN' GET YOU!
MINNIE WOULD HAFTA VISIT HER AUNT JENNIE ON A DAY LIKE THIS!
AND AUNT JENNIE WOULD HAFTA LIVE AT THE OTHER END O' NOWHERE!
MY GOSH! IT'S GETTIN' WORSE AN' WORSE!
STALLED--RADIATOR FROZEN--FOUR MILES TO GO! EV'RYTHING'S JUST DANDY!
MINNIE MAY NOT KNOW IT, BUT SHE'S GOIN' TO STAY WHERE SHE IS 'TIL THIS ROAD'S CLEARED!
--IF I--EVER--GET THERE--TO TELL HER!
AT--LAST!
---NO, WE JEST TAKE KEER O' THE PLACE---Y' SEE OLD MISS JENNIE ALLUS LIVES IN TOWN IN' TH' WINTER--HER RHEUMATIZ, Y' KNOW! COME IN AND SET--Y' LOOK KINDA SICK!
HELLO, MINNIE, I---!
DON'T TELL ME YOU HAVEN'T EVEN STARTED YET! OF ALL THE LAZY, GOOD-FOR-NOTHING---WELL, I'LL WALK! THE WHOLE SIX BLOCKS! IN THE SNOW! GOOD-BYE!!
LAND SAKES! MUST'VE HAD BAD NEWS!
2-13
WALT DISNEY

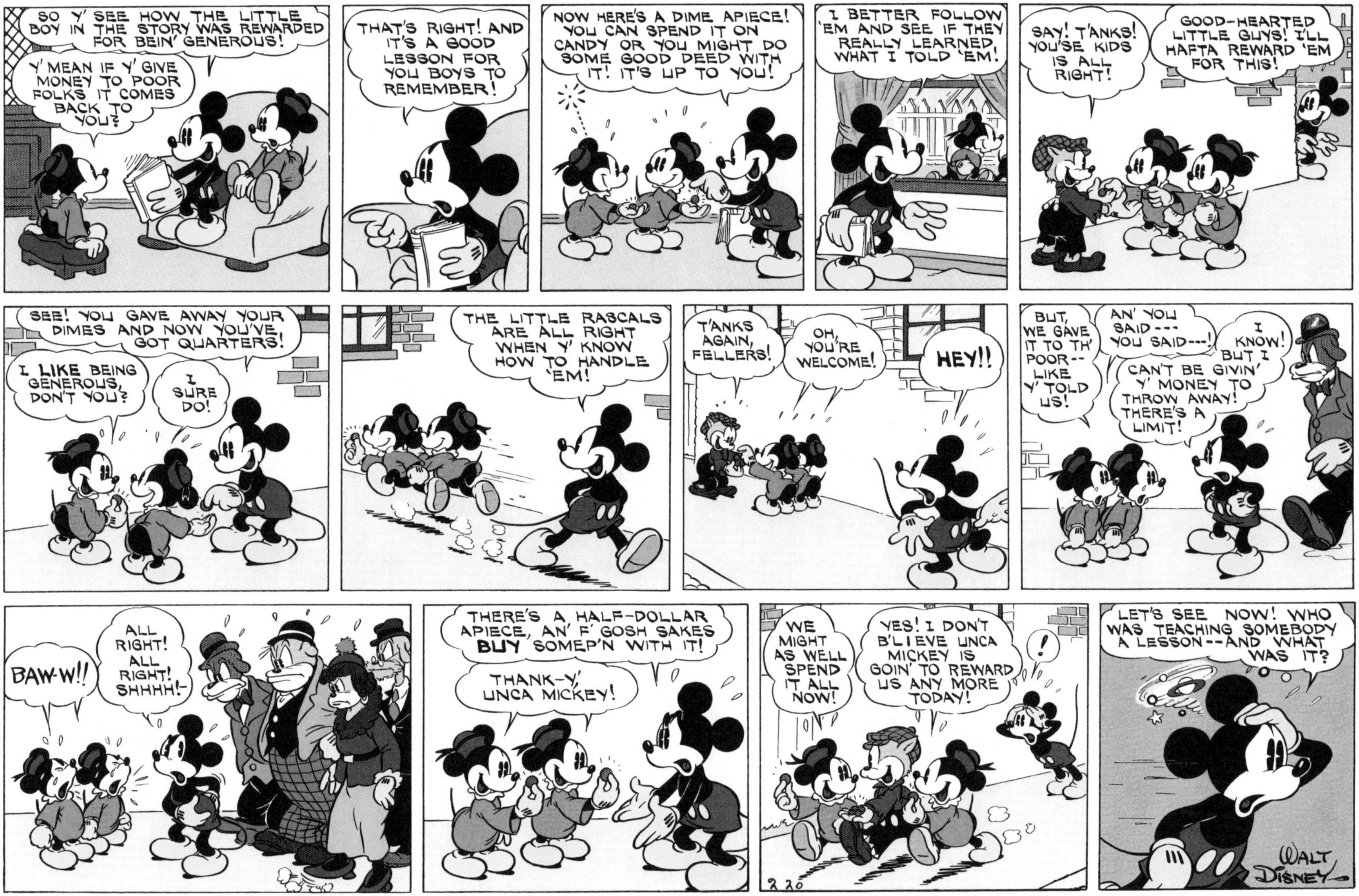
SO Y' SEE HOW THE LITTLE BOY IN THE STORY WAS REWARDED FOR BEIN' GENEROUS!
Y' MEAN IF Y' GIVE MONEY TO POOR FOLKS IT COMES BACK TO YOU?
THAT'S RIGHT! AND IT'S A GOOD LESSON FOR YOU BOYS TO REMEMBER!
NOW HERE'S A DIME APIECE! YOU CAN SPEND IT ON CANDY OR YOU MIGHT DO SOME GOOD DEED WITH IT! IT'S UP TO YOU!
I BETTER FOLLOW 'EM AND SEE IF THEY REALLY LEARNED WHAT I TOLD 'EM!
SAY! T'ANKS! YOU'SE KIDS IS ALL RIGHT!
GOOD-HEARTED LITTLE GUYS! I'LL HAFTA REWARD 'EM FOR THIS!
SEE! YOU GAVE AWAY YOUR DIMES AND NOW YOU'VE GOT QUARTERS!
I LIKE BEING GENEROUS, DON'T YOU?
I SURE DO!
THE LITTLE RASCALS ARE ALL RIGHT WHEN Y' KNOW HOW TO HANDLE 'EM!
T'ANKS AGAIN, FELLERS!
OH, YOU'RE WELCOME!
HEY!!
BUT, WE GAVE IT TO TH' POOR-- LIKE Y' TOLD US!
AN' YOU SAID--- YOU SAID---!
I KNOW! BUT I CAN'T BE GIVIN' Y' MONEY TO THROW AWAY! THERE'S A LIMIT!
BAW-W!!
ALL RIGHT! ALL RIGHT! SHHHH!-
THERE'S A HALF-DOLLAR APIECE, AN' F' GOSH SAKES BUY SOMEP'N WITH IT!
THANK-Y', UNCA MICKEY!
WE MIGHT AS WELL SPEND IT ALL NOW!
YES! I DON'T B'LIEVE UNCA MICKEY IS GOIN' TO REWARD US ANY MORE TODAY!
!
LET'S SEE NOW! WHO WAS TEACHING SOMEBODY A LESSON--AND WHAT WAS IT?
WALT DISNEY

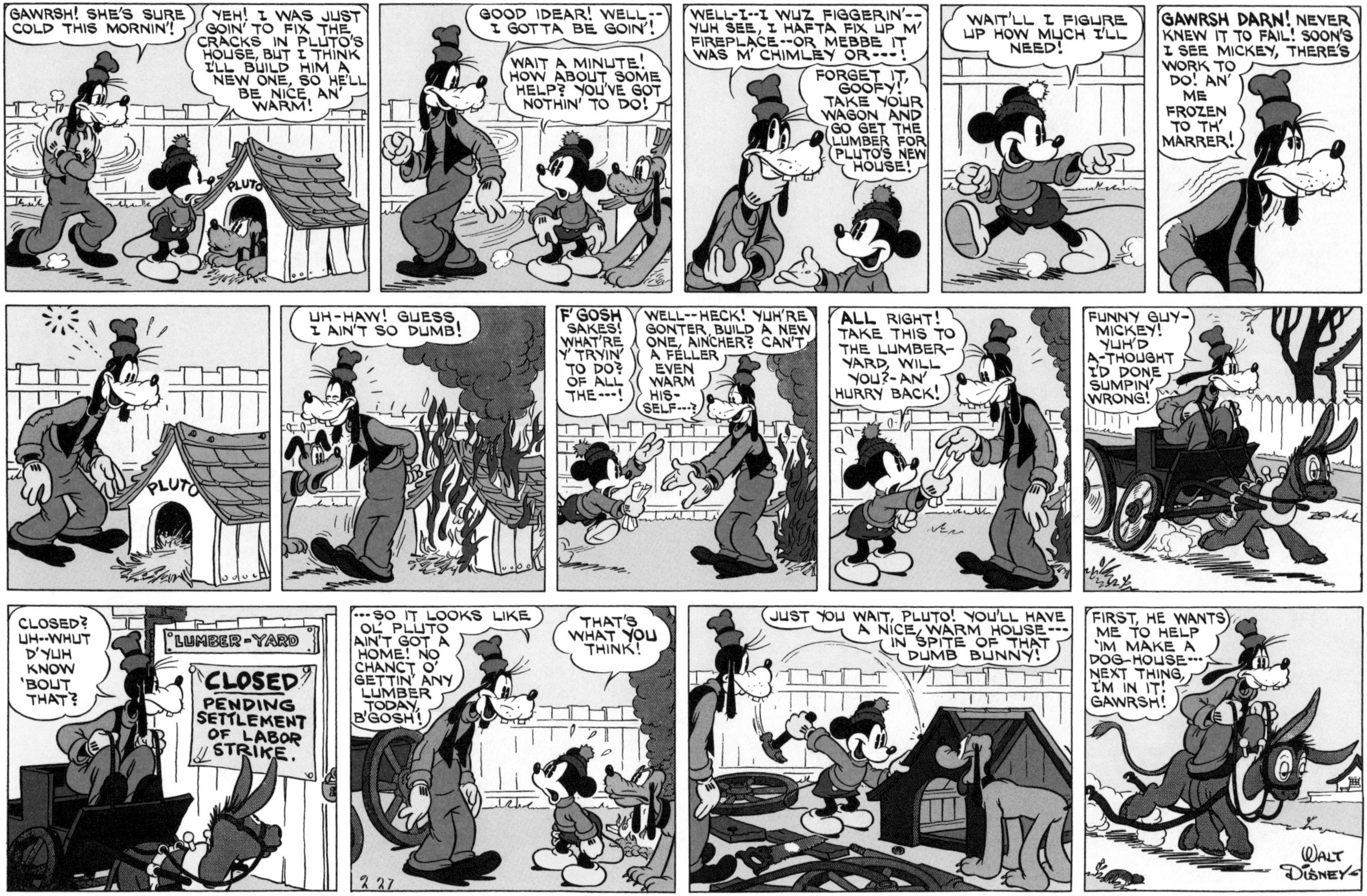
GAWRSH! SHE'S SURE COLD THIS MORNIN'!
YEH! I WAS JUST GOIN' TO FIX THE CRACKS IN PLUTO'S HOUSE, BUT I THINK I'LL BUILD HIM A NEW ONE, SO HE'LL BE NICE AN' WARM!
PLUTO
GOOD IDEAR! WELL-- I GOTTA BE GOIN'!
WAIT A MINUTE! HOW ABOUT SOME HELP? YOU'VE GOT NOTHIN' TO DO!
WELL-I--I WUZ FIGGERIN'-- YUH SEE, I HAFTA FIX UP M' FIREPLACE--OR MEBBE IT WAS M' CHIMLEY OR---!
FORGET IT, GOOFY! TAKE YOUR WAGON AND GO GET THE LUMBER FOR PLUTO'S NEW HOUSE!
WAIT'LL I FIGURE UP HOW MUCH I'LL NEED!
GAWRSH DARN! NEVER KNEW IT TO FAIL! SOON'S I SEE MICKEY, THERE'S WORK TO DO! AN' ME FROZEN TO TH' MARRER!
PLUTO
UH-HAW! GUESS I AIN'T SO DUMB!
F'GOSH SAKES! WHAT'RE Y' TRYIN' TO DO? OF ALL THE---!
WELL--HECK! YUH'RE GONTER BUILD A NEW ONE, AINCHER? CAN'T A FELLER EVEN WARM HIS-SELF---?
ALL RIGHT! TAKE THIS TO THE LUMBER-YARD, WILL YOU?- AN' HURRY BACK!
FUNNY GUY- MICKEY! YUH'D A-THOUGHT I'D DONE SUMPIN' WRONG!
CLOSED? UH--WHUT D'YUH KNOW 'BOUT THAT?
LUMBER-YARD
CLOSED PENDING SETTLEMENT OF LABOR STRIKE.
---SO IT LOOKS LIKE OL' PLUTO AIN'T GOT A HOME! NO CHANCT O' GETTIN' ANY LUMBER TODAY, B'GOSH!
THAT'S WHAT YOU THINK!
2 27
JUST YOU WAIT, PLUTO! YOU'LL HAVE A NICE, WARM HOUSE--- IN SPITE OF THAT DUMB BUNNY!
FIRST, HE WANTS ME TO HELP 'IM MAKE A DOG-HOUSE--- NEXT THING, I'M IN IT! GAWRSH!
WALT DISNEY

SERVICE WITH A SMILE AND GAG STRIPS

MARCH 6, 1938
–
AUGUST 21, 1938

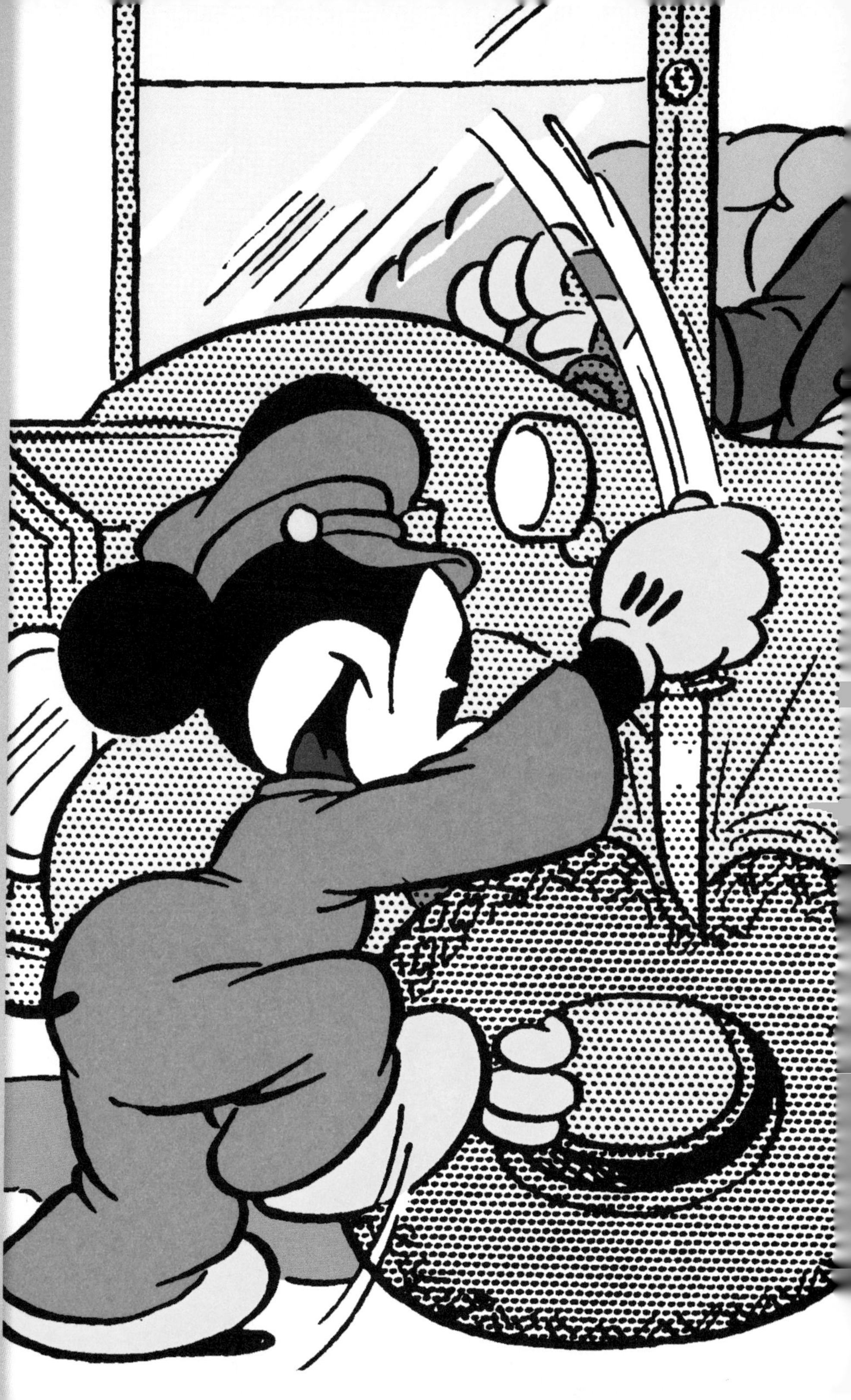

MICKEY MOUSE
REGISTERED U.S. PATENT OFFICE

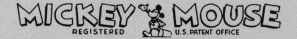

WITH FRIENDS LIKE THESE...

What does Mickey do when he's not traveling the world looking for adventure, lost treasure or criminals? The early 1938 Sunday pages show us Mickey's more mundane day-to-day routine—with his co-stars, and their relationships, now closely anticipating the modern Disney comics milieu. Mickey is the common element from strip to strip; but somehow, the other characters often feel like the real heroes of the gags.

While each page stands alone as its own story, the strips comprising "Service With a Smile" are loosely connected by the common theme of Mickey and Goofy running a gas station. It's Goofy who is showcased here, with his own absurd but backwardly logical way of thinking. We split the proceeds fifty-fifty? Okay; then if I get a punch in the eye, so do you. This customer wants extra proof that our puncture-proof tires are better? Okay; then let's puncture her regular tires. I've been slapped in jail? Okay; then the joke's on the authorities, 'cause I'm the wrong guy. Goofy is like a chess player who only considers the current move—blissfully and totally unaware of its potentially disastrous long-term consequences. His personality will of course evolve a little more over the years. But what makes this 1938 Goofy both so irritating and so funny is that we recognize in him an exaggerated version of our own stubbornness and naïveté—and that of our acquaintances.

Minnie, on the other hand, is a much more sensible character, though of course not without her quirks. Some Mickey-Minnie gags based on "gender wars" may feel dated, as society has evolved towards a more balanced outlook in the intervening seventy years. But even if we view the clichés for what they are, we can still laugh at how Gottfredson and his writers made fun of them.

Even more troublesome than Goofy and Minnie are Morty and Ferdie—unstoppable, hyperactive kids who always manage to get themselves into trouble. Half the fun is witnessing what new mess they will land in this time; the other half is figuring out how Mickey can possibly cope with it and restore some semblance of order. Sometimes we are left guessing! We have to imagine him fixing things in the blank space between one Sunday and the next.

We feel a bit sorry for Mickey—forced to put up with all of these troublesome companions. But in the end, his means of coping with the challenges they provide are also opportunities for the authors to define his positive personality. If Mickey can beat Pegleg Pete in a daily strip epic, can he beat his friends' eccentricities on Sunday? Maybe not... but he's game to try.

—Leonardo Gori and Francesco Stajano

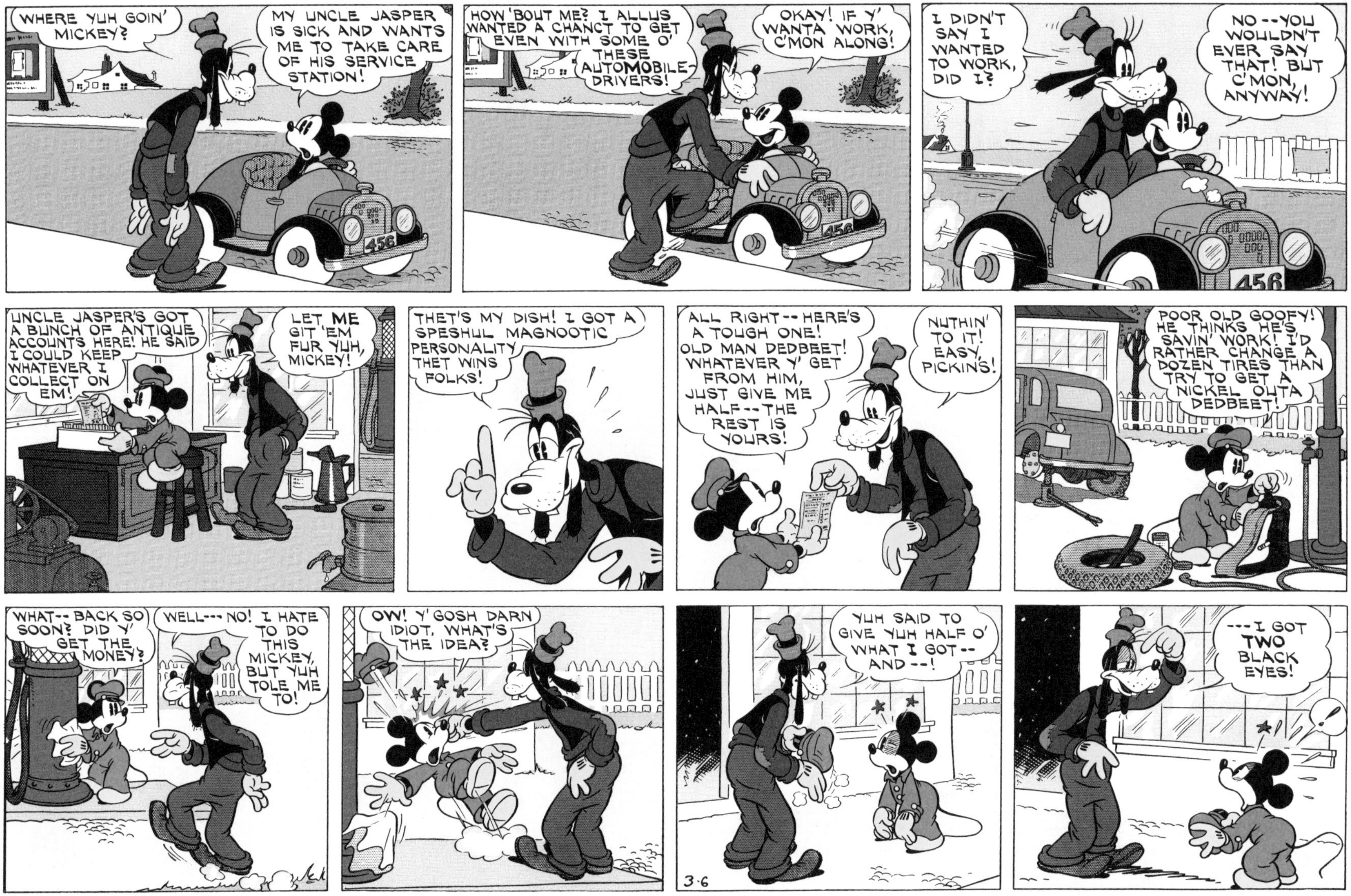
WHERE YUH GOIN' MICKEY?
MY UNCLE JASPER IS SICK AND WANTS ME TO TAKE CARE OF HIS SERVICE STATION!
456
HOW 'BOUT ME? I ALLUS WANTED A CHANCT TO GET EVEN WITH SOME O' THESE AUTOMOBILE-DRIVERS!
OKAY! IF Y' WANTA WORK, C'MON ALONG!
456
I DIDN'T SAY I WANTED TO WORK, DID I?
NO -- YOU WOULDN'T EVER SAY THAT! BUT C'MON, ANYWAY!
456
UNCLE JASPER'S GOT A BUNCH OF ANTIQUE ACCOUNTS HERE! HE SAID I COULD KEEP WHATEVER I COLLECT ON 'EM!
LET ME GIT 'EM FUR YUH, MICKEY!
THET'S MY DISH! I GOT A SPESHUL MAGNOOTIC PERSONALITY THET WINS FOLKS!
ALL RIGHT -- HERE'S A TOUGH ONE! OLD MAN DEDBEET! WHATEVER Y' GET FROM HIM, JUST GIVE ME HALF -- THE REST IS YOURS!
NUTHIN' TO IT! EASY PICKINS!
POOR OLD GOOFY! HE THINKS HE'S SAVIN' WORK! I'D RATHER CHANGE A DOZEN TIRES THAN TRY TO GET A NICKEL OUTA DEDBEET!
WHAT -- BACK SO SOON? DID Y' GET THE MONEY?
WELL --- NO! I HATE TO DO THIS MICKEY, BUT YUH TOLE ME TO!
OW! Y' GOSH DARN IDIOT, WHAT'S THE IDEA?
YUH SAID TO GIVE YUH HALF O' WHAT I GOT -- AND --!
3·6
--- I GOT TWO BLACK EYES!
!

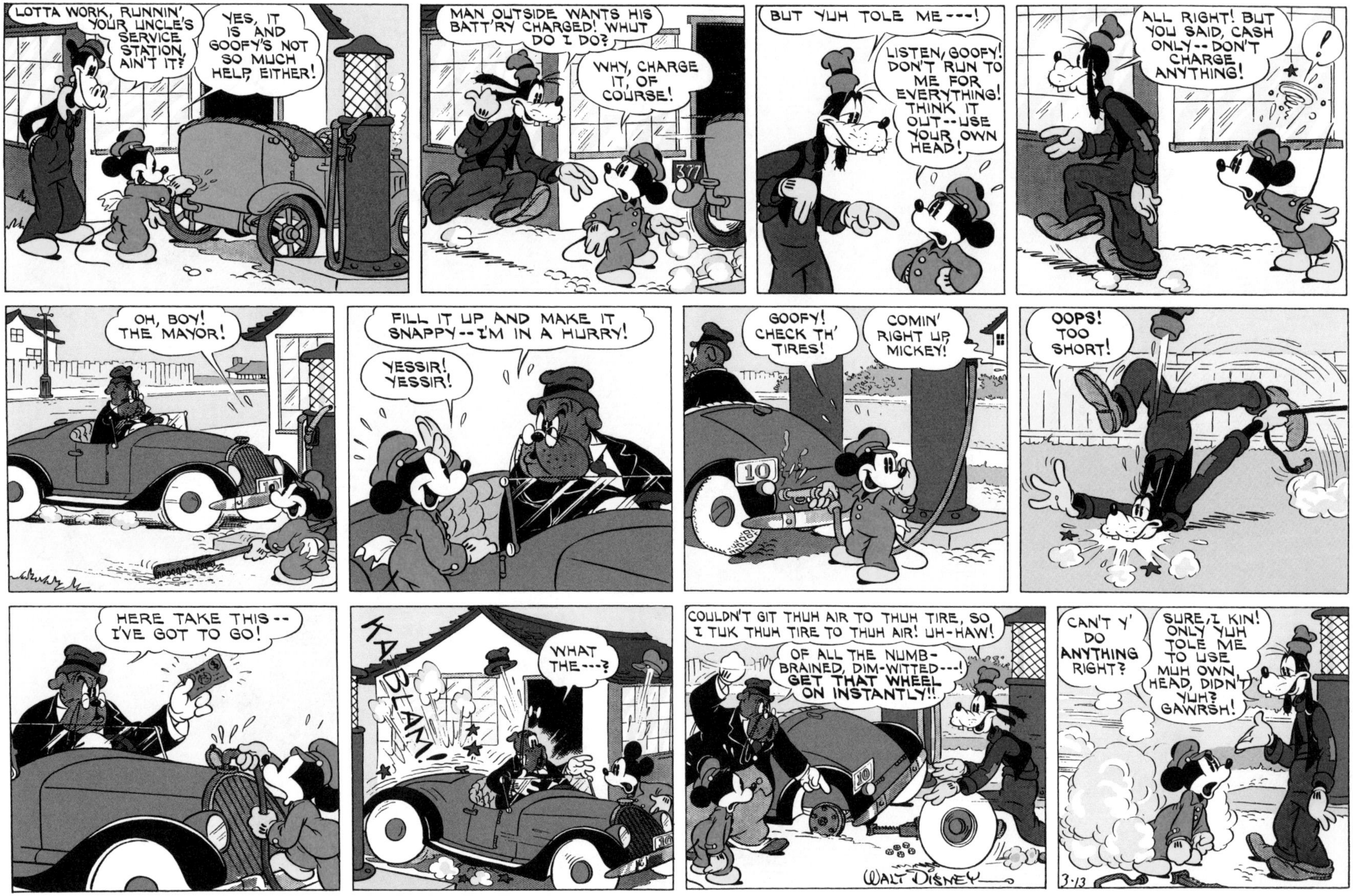
LOTTA WORK, RUNNIN' YOUR UNCLE'S SERVICE STATION, AIN'T IT?
YES, IT IS AND GOOFY'S NOT SO MUCH HELP, EITHER!
MAN OUTSIDE WANTS HIS BATT'RY CHARGED! WHUT DO I DO?
WHY, CHARGE IT, OF COURSE!
377
BUT YUH TOLE ME---!
LISTEN, GOOFY! DON'T RUN TO ME FOR EVERYTHING! THINK IT OUT--USE YOUR OWN HEAD!
ALL RIGHT! BUT YOU SAID, CASH ONLY--DON'T CHARGE ANYTHING!
!
OH, BOY! THE MAYOR!
FILL IT UP AND MAKE IT SNAPPY--I'M IN A HURRY!
YESSIR! YESSIR!
GOOFY! CHECK TH' TIRES!
COMIN' RIGHT UP, MICKEY!
10
OOPS! TOO SHORT!
HERE TAKE THIS--I'VE GOT TO GO!
KA BLAM!
WHAT THE---?
COULDN'T GIT THUH AIR TO THUH TIRE, SO I TUK THUH TIRE TO THUH AIR! UH-HAW!
OF ALL THE NUMB-BRAINED, DIM-WITTED---! GET THAT WHEEL ON INSTANTLY!!
WALT DISNEY
CAN'T Y' DO ANYTHING RIGHT?
SURE, I KIN! ONLY YUH TOLE ME TO USE MUH OWN HEAD, DIDN'T YUH? GAWRSH!
3-13

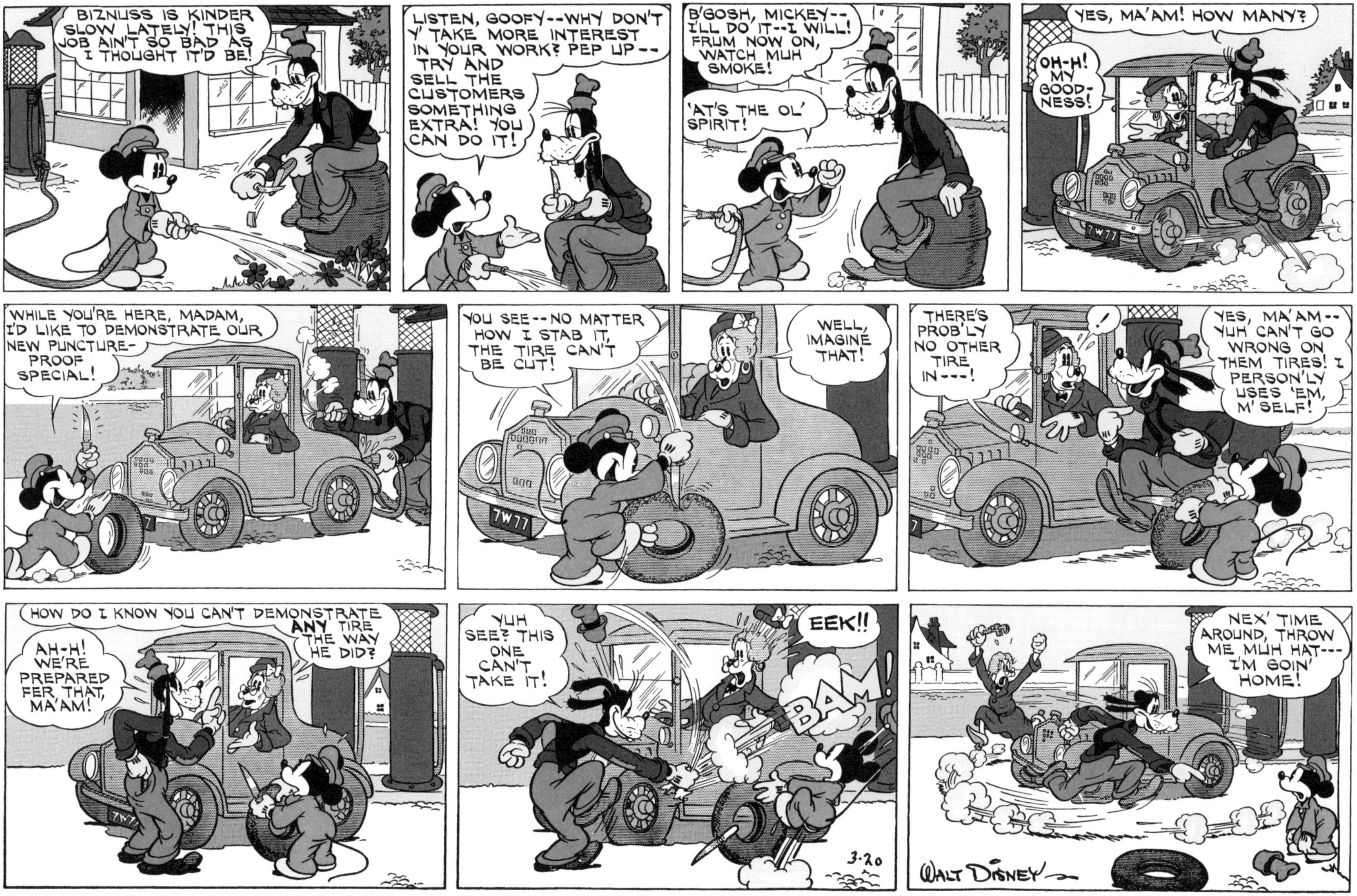
BIZNUSS IS KINDER SLOW LATELY! THIS JOB AIN'T SO BAD AS I THOUGHT IT'D BE!
LISTEN, GOOFY--WHY DON'T Y' TAKE MORE INTEREST IN YOUR WORK? PEP UP--TRY AND SELL THE CUSTOMERS SOMETHING EXTRA! YOU CAN DO IT!
B'GOSH, MICKEY--I'LL DO IT--I WILL! FRUM NOW ON, WATCH MUH SMOKE!
'AT'S THE OL' SPIRIT!
YES, MA'AM! HOW MANY?
OH-H! MY GOODNESS!
7W77
WHILE YOU'RE HERE, MADAM, I'D LIKE TO DEMONSTRATE OUR NEW PUNCTURE-PROOF SPECIAL!
YOU SEE--NO MATTER HOW I STAB IT, THE TIRE CAN'T BE CUT!
WELL, IMAGINE THAT!
7W77
THERE'S PROB'LY NO OTHER TIRE IN---!
!
YES, MA'AM--YUH CAN'T GO WRONG ON THEM TIRES! I PERSON'LY USES 'EM, M'SELF!
HOW DO I KNOW YOU CAN'T DEMONSTRATE ANY TIRE THE WAY HE DID?
AH-H! WE'RE PREPARED FER THAT, MA'AM!
YUH SEE? THIS ONE CAN'T TAKE IT!
EEK!!
BAM!
3-20
NEX' TIME AROUND, THROW ME MUH HAT---I'M GOIN' HOME!
WALT DISNEY

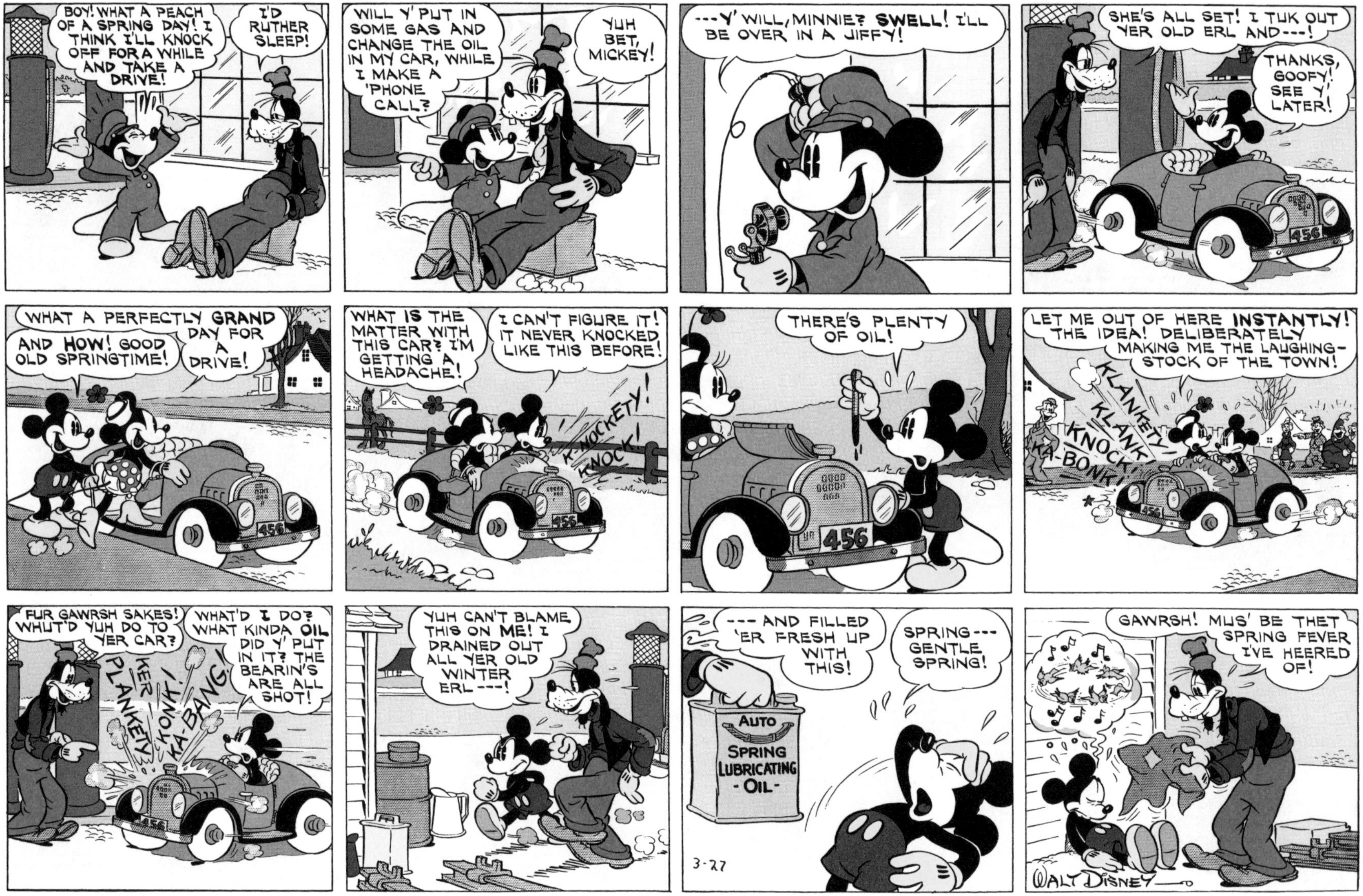
BOY! WHAT A PEACH OF A SPRING DAY! I THINK I'LL KNOCK OFF FOR A WHILE AND TAKE A DRIVE!
I'D RUTHER SLEEP!
WILL Y' PUT IN SOME GAS AND CHANGE THE OIL IN MY CAR, WHILE I MAKE A 'PHONE CALL?
YUH BET, MICKEY!
---Y' WILL, MINNIE? SWELL! I'LL BE OVER IN A JIFFY!
SHE'S ALL SET! I TUK OUT YER OLD ERL AND---!
THANKS, GOOFY! SEE Y' LATER!
456
WHAT A PERFECTLY GRAND DAY FOR A DRIVE!
AND HOW! GOOD OLD SPRINGTIME!
456
WHAT IS THE MATTER WITH THIS CAR? I'M GETTING A HEADACHE!
I CAN'T FIGURE IT! IT NEVER KNOCKED LIKE THIS BEFORE!
K-NOCKETY!
KNOCK!
456
THERE'S PLENTY OF OIL!
456
LET ME OUT OF HERE INSTANTLY! THE IDEA! DELIBERATELY MAKING ME THE LAUGHING-STOCK OF THE TOWN!
KLANKETY
KLANK
KNOCK
KA-BONK!
456
FUR GAWRSH SAKES! WHUT'D YUH DO TO YER CAR?
WHAT'D I DO? WHAT KINDA OIL DID Y' PUT IN IT? THE BEARIN'S ARE ALL SHOT!
KER-PLANKETY
KONK!
KA-BANG!
456
YUH CAN'T BLAME THIS ON ME! I DRAINED OUT ALL YER OLD WINTER ERL---!
---AND FILLED 'ER FRESH UP WITH THIS!
SPRING--- GENTLE SPRING!
AUTO SPRING LUBRICATING -OIL-
3-27
GAWRSH! MUS' BE THET SPRING FEVER I'VE HEERED OF!
WALT DISNEY

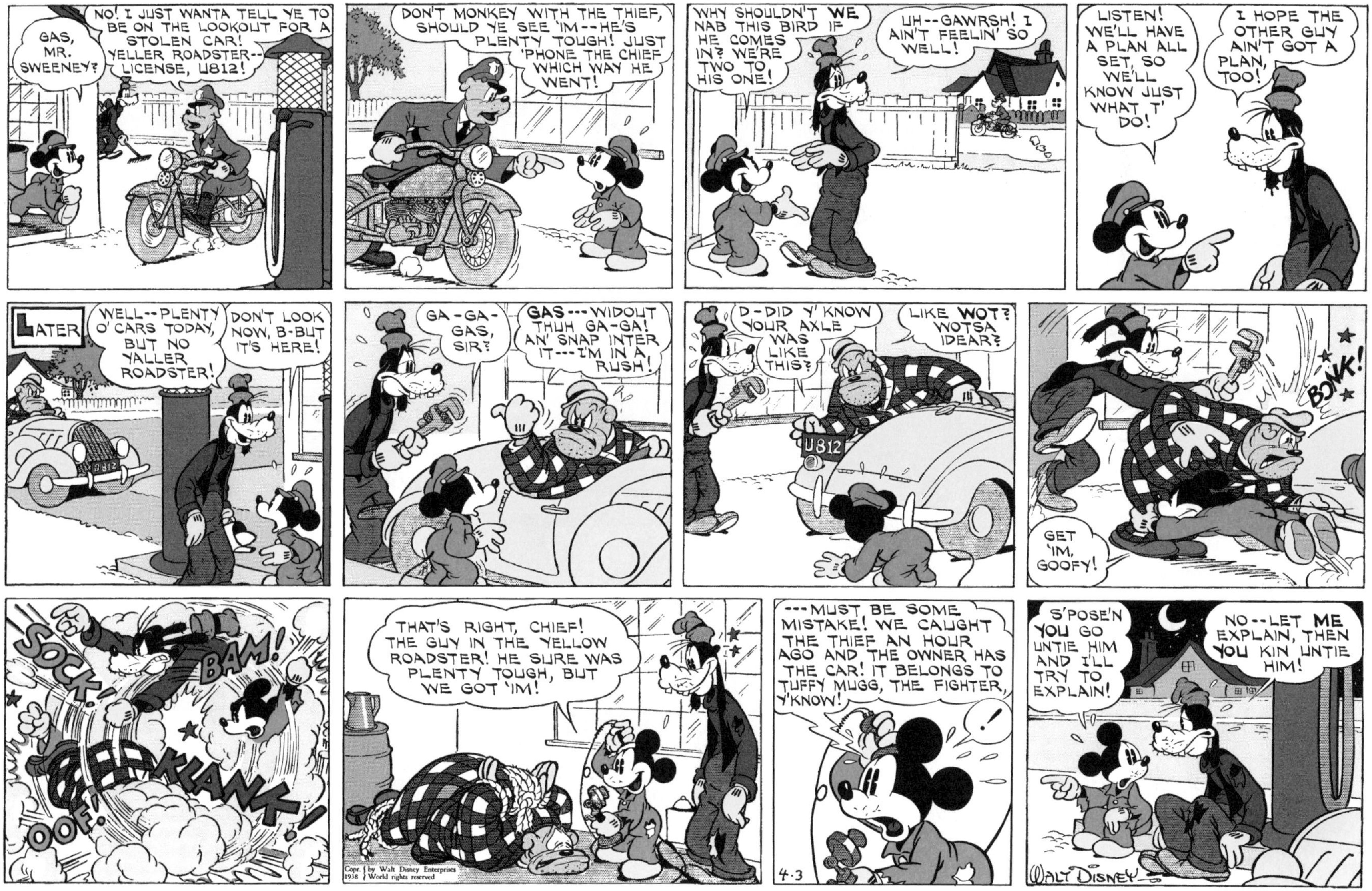
GAS, MR. SWEENEY?
NO! I JUST WANTA TELL YE TO BE ON THE LOOKOUT FOR A STOLEN CAR! YELLER ROADSTER-- LICENSE, U812!
U812
DON'T MONKEY WITH THE THIEF, SHOULD YE SEE 'IM--HE'S PLENTY TOUGH! JUST 'PHONE THE CHIEF WHICH WAY HE WENT!
WHY SHOULDN'T WE NAB THIS BIRD IF HE COMES IN? WE'RE TWO TO HIS ONE!
UH--GAWRSH! I AIN'T FEELIN' SO WELL!
LISTEN! WE'LL HAVE A PLAN ALL SET, SO WE'LL KNOW JUST WHAT T' DO!
I HOPE THE OTHER GUY AIN'T GOT A PLAN, TOO!
LATER
WELL--PLENTY O' CARS TODAY, BUT NO YALLER ROADSTER!
DON'T LOOK NOW, B-BUT IT'S HERE!
U812
GA-GA-GAS, SIR?
GAS---WIDOUT THUH GA-GA! AN' SNAP INTER IT---I'M IN A RUSH!
D-DID Y' KNOW YOUR AXLE WAS LIKE THIS?
LIKE WOT? WOTSA IDEAR?
U812
BONK!
GET 'IM, GOOFY!
SOCK!
BAM!
KLANK!
OOF!
THAT'S RIGHT, CHIEF! THE GUY IN THE YELLOW ROADSTER! HE SURE WAS PLENTY TOUGH, BUT WE GOT 'IM!
Copr. 1938 by Walt Disney Enterprises World rights reserved
---MUST BE SOME MISTAKE! WE CAUGHT THE THIEF AN HOUR AGO AND THE OWNER HAS THE CAR! IT BELONGS TO TUFFY MUGG, THE FIGHTER, Y'KNOW!
!
4-3
S'POSE'N YOU GO UNTIE HIM AND I'LL TRY TO EXPLAIN!
NO--LET ME EXPLAIN, THEN YOU KIN UNTIE HIM!
WALT DISNEY

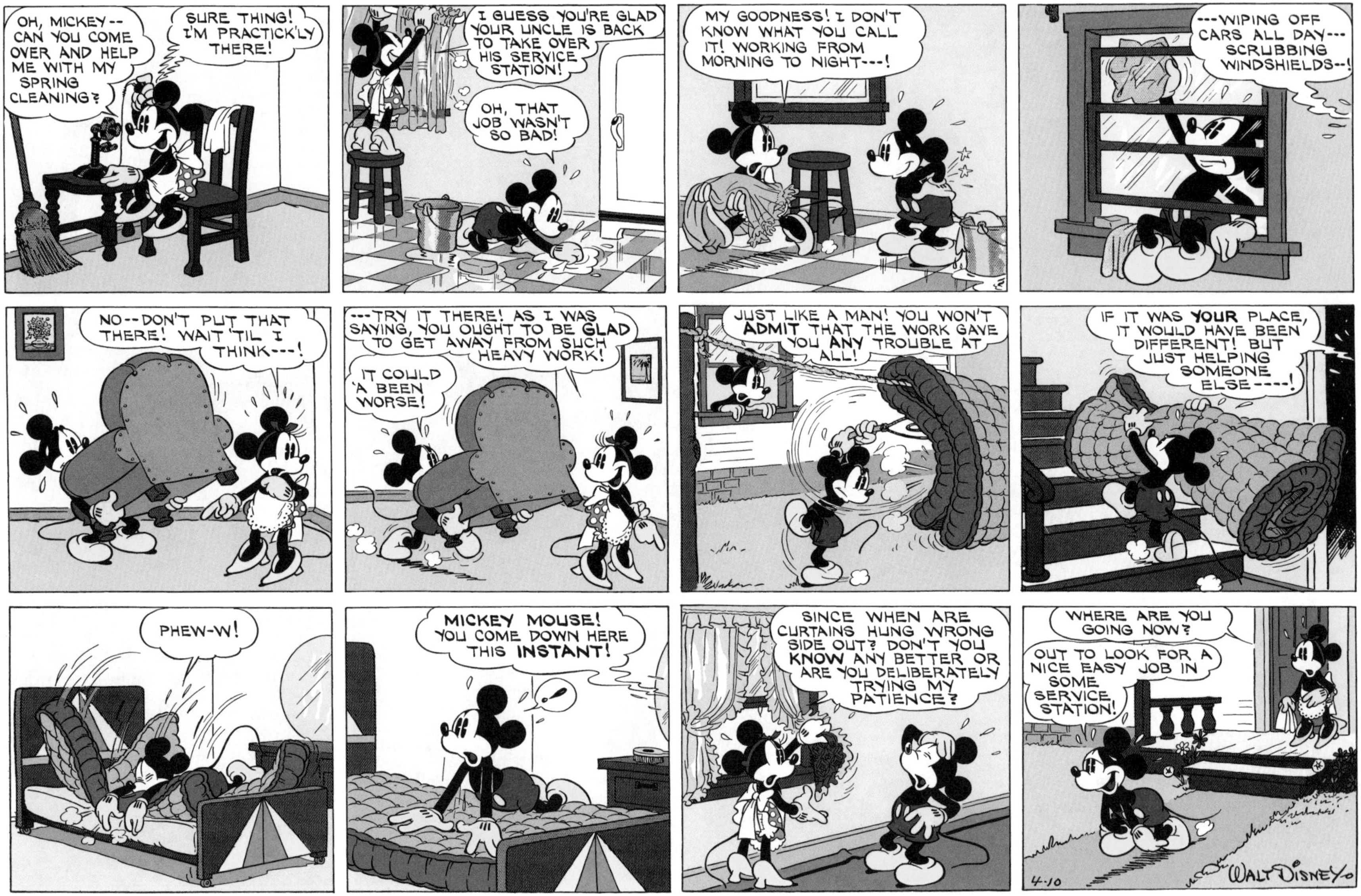
OH, MICKEY-- CAN YOU COME OVER AND HELP ME WITH MY SPRING CLEANING?
SURE THING! I'M PRACTICK'LY THERE!
I GUESS YOU'RE GLAD YOUR UNCLE IS BACK TO TAKE OVER HIS SERVICE STATION!
OH, THAT JOB WASN'T SO BAD!
MY GOODNESS! I DON'T KNOW WHAT YOU CALL IT! WORKING FROM MORNING TO NIGHT---!
---WIPING OFF CARS ALL DAY--- SCRUBBING WINDSHIELDS--!
NO--DON'T PUT THAT THERE! WAIT 'TIL I THINK---!
---TRY IT THERE! AS I WAS SAYING, YOU OUGHT TO BE GLAD TO GET AWAY FROM SUCH HEAVY WORK!
IT COULD 'A BEEN WORSE!
JUST LIKE A MAN! YOU WON'T ADMIT THAT THE WORK GAVE YOU ANY TROUBLE AT ALL!
IF IT WAS YOUR PLACE, IT WOULD HAVE BEEN DIFFERENT! BUT JUST HELPING SOMEONE ELSE----!
PHEW-W!
MICKEY MOUSE! YOU COME DOWN HERE THIS INSTANT!
!
SINCE WHEN ARE CURTAINS HUNG WRONG SIDE OUT? DON'T YOU KNOW ANY BETTER OR ARE YOU DELIBERATELY TRYING MY PATIENCE?
WHERE ARE YOU GOING NOW?
OUT TO LOOK FOR A NICE EASY JOB IN SOME SERVICE STATION!
4-10
WALT DISNEY

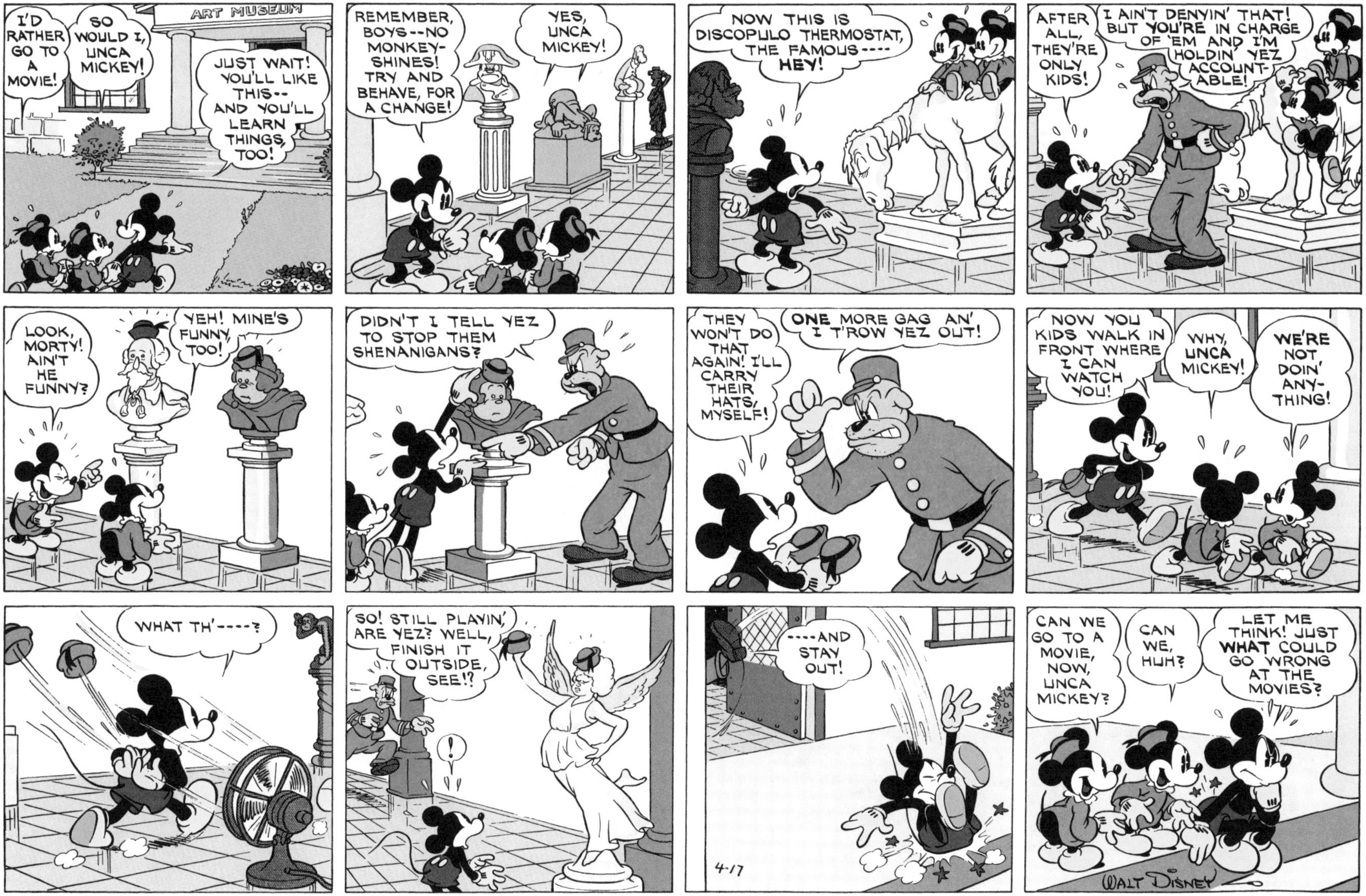
ART MUSEUM
I'D RATHER GO TO A MOVIE!
SO WOULD I, UNCA MICKEY!
JUST WAIT! YOU'LL LIKE THIS-- AND YOU'LL LEARN THINGS, TOO!
REMEMBER, BOYS--NO MONKEY-SHINES! TRY AND BEHAVE, FOR A CHANGE!
YES, UNCA MICKEY!
NOW THIS IS DISCOPULO THERMOSTAT, THE FAMOUS---- HEY!
AFTER ALL, THEY'RE ONLY KIDS!
I AIN'T DENYIN' THAT! BUT YOU'RE IN CHARGE OF 'EM AND I'M HOLDIN' YEZ ACCOUNT-ABLE!
LOOK, MORTY! AIN'T HE FUNNY?
YEH! MINE'S FUNNY, TOO!
DIDN'T I TELL YEZ TO STOP THEM SHENANIGANS?
THEY WON'T DO THAT AGAIN! I'LL CARRY THEIR HATS, MYSELF!
ONE MORE GAG AN' I T'ROW YEZ OUT!
NOW YOU KIDS WALK IN FRONT WHERE I CAN WATCH YOU!
WHY, UNCA MICKEY!
WE'RE NOT DOIN' ANY-THING!
WHAT TH'----?
SO! STILL PLAYIN', ARE YEZ? WELL, FINISH IT OUTSIDE, SEE!?
!
----AND STAY OUT!
4-17
CAN WE GO TO A MOVIE, NOW, UNCA MICKEY?
CAN WE, HUH?
LET ME THINK! JUST WHAT COULD GO WRONG AT THE MOVIES?
WALT DISNEY

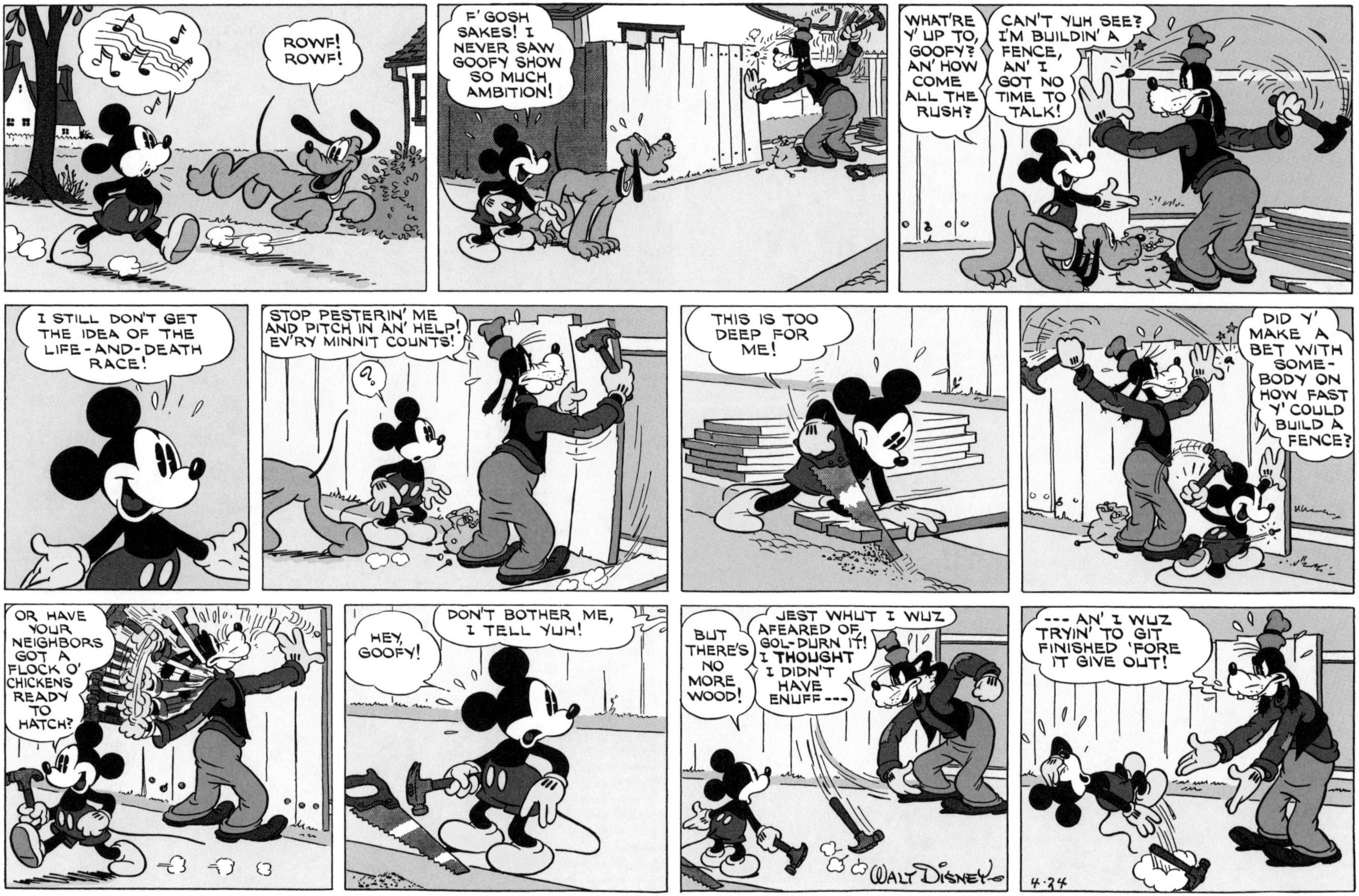
ROWF! ROWF!
F' GOSH SAKES! I NEVER SAW GOOFY SHOW SO MUCH AMBITION!
WHAT'RE Y' UP TO, GOOFY? AN' HOW COME ALL THE RUSH?
CAN'T YUH SEE? I'M BUILDIN' A FENCE, AN' I GOT NO TIME TO TALK!
I STILL DON'T GET THE IDEA OF THE LIFE-AND-DEATH RACE!
STOP PESTERIN' ME AND PITCH IN AN' HELP! EV'RY MINNIT COUNTS!
?
THIS IS TOO DEEP FOR ME!
DID Y' MAKE A BET WITH SOME-BODY ON HOW FAST Y' COULD BUILD A FENCE?
OR HAVE YOUR NEIGHBORS GOT A FLOCK O' CHICKENS READY TO HATCH?
HEY, GOOFY!
DON'T BOTHER ME, I TELL YUH!
BUT THERE'S NO MORE WOOD!
JEST WHUT I WUZ AFEARED OF, GOL-DURN IT! I **THOUGHT** I DIDN'T HAVE ENUFF ---
WALT DISNEY
--- AN' I WUZ TRYIN' TO GIT FINISHED 'FORE IT GIVE OUT!
4-24

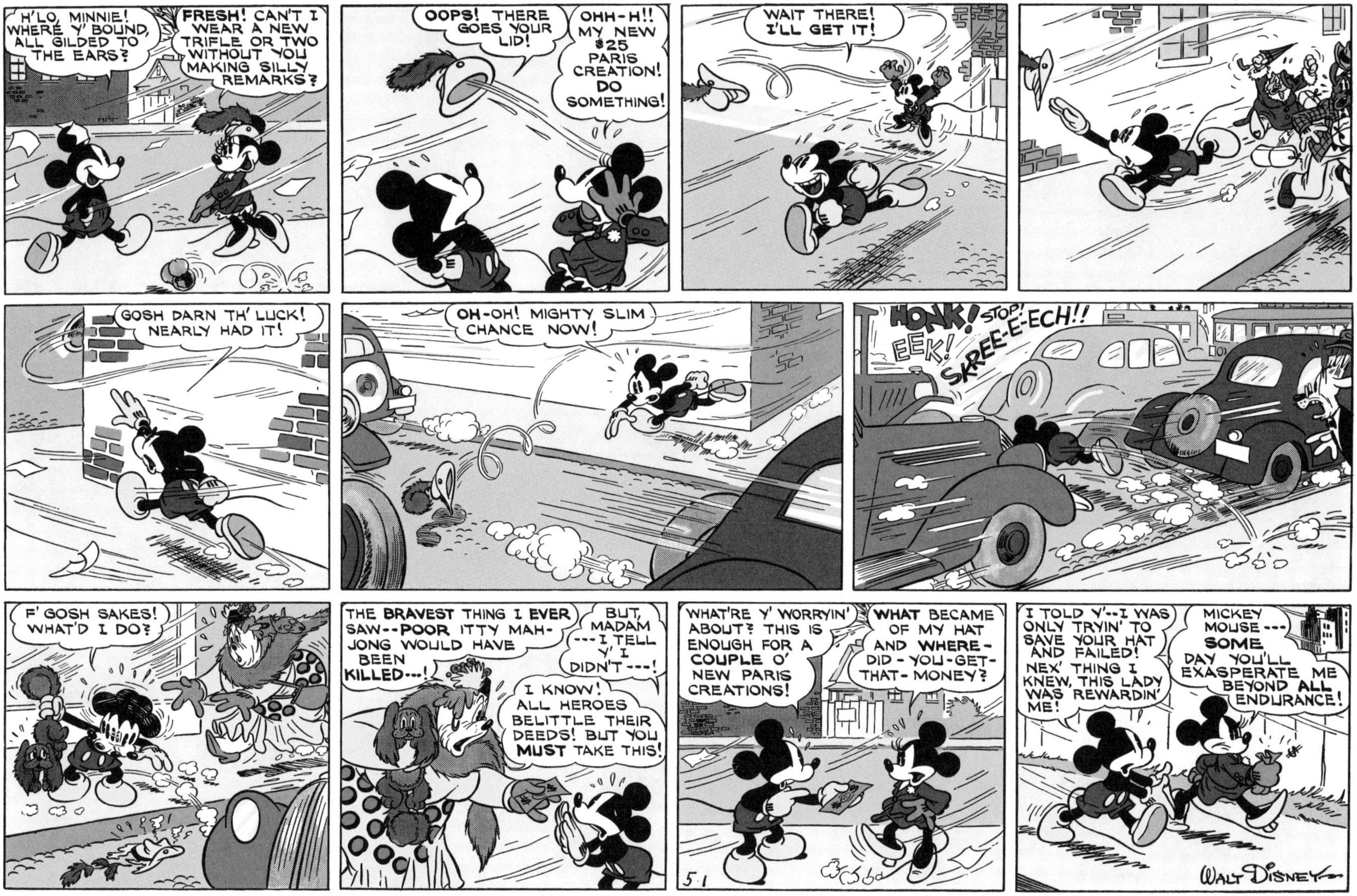

H'LO, MINNIE! WHERE Y' BOUND, ALL GILDED TO THE EARS?
FRESH! CAN'T I WEAR A NEW TRIFLE OR TWO WITHOUT YOU MAKING SILLY REMARKS?
OOPS! THERE GOES YOUR LID!
OHH-H!! MY NEW $25 PARIS CREATION! DO SOMETHING!
WAIT THERE! I'LL GET IT!
GOSH DARN TH' LUCK! NEARLY HAD IT!
OH-OH! MIGHTY SLIM CHANCE NOW!
HONK!
STOP!
EEK!
SKREE-E-ECH!!
F' GOSH SAKES! WHAT'D I DO?
THE BRAVEST THING I EVER SAW--POOR ITTY MAH-JONG WOULD HAVE BEEN KILLED---!
BUT, MADAM ---I TELL Y' I DIDN'T---!
I KNOW! ALL HEROES BELITTLE THEIR DEEDS! BUT YOU MUST TAKE THIS!
WHAT'RE Y' WORRYIN' ABOUT? THIS IS ENOUGH FOR A COUPLE O' NEW PARIS CREATIONS!
WHAT BECAME OF MY HAT AND WHERE-DID-YOU-GET-THAT-MONEY?
I TOLD Y'--I WAS ONLY TRYIN' TO SAVE YOUR HAT AND FAILED! NEX' THING I KNEW, THIS LADY WAS REWARDIN' ME!
MICKEY MOUSE--- SOME DAY YOU'LL EXASPERATE ME BEYOND ALL ENDURANCE!
5-1
WALT DISNEY

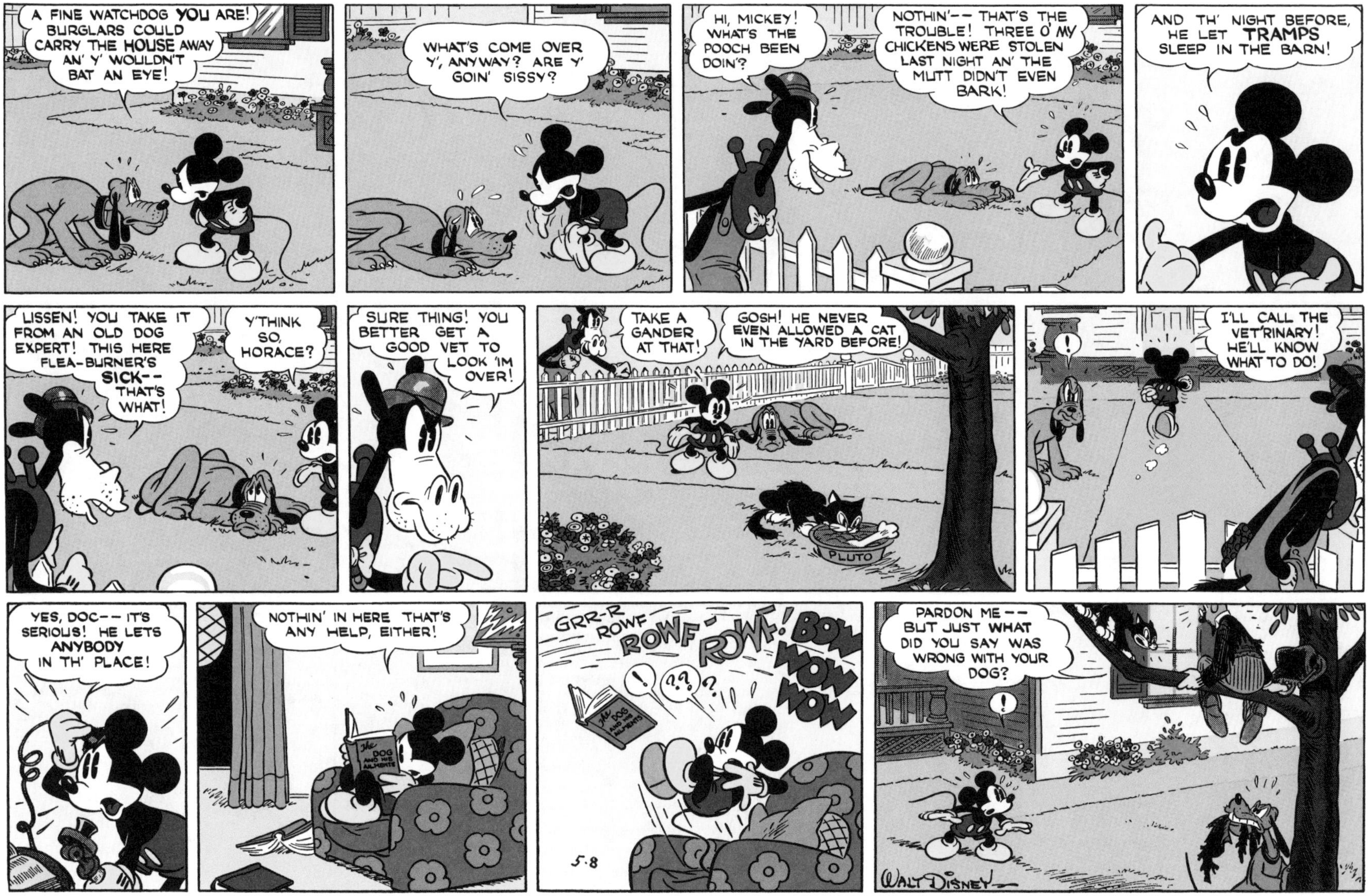

A FINE WATCHDOG YOU ARE! BURGLARS COULD CARRY THE HOUSE AWAY AN' Y' WOULDN'T BAT AN EYE!
WHAT'S COME OVER Y', ANYWAY? ARE Y' GOIN' SISSY?
HI, MICKEY! WHAT'S THE POOCH BEEN DOIN'?
NOTHIN'-- THAT'S THE TROUBLE! THREE O' MY CHICKENS WERE STOLEN LAST NIGHT AN' THE MUTT DIDN'T EVEN BARK!
AND TH' NIGHT BEFORE, HE LET TRAMPS SLEEP IN THE BARN!
LISSEN! YOU TAKE IT FROM AN OLD DOG EXPERT! THIS HERE FLEA-BURNER'S SICK-- THAT'S WHAT!
Y'THINK SO, HORACE?
SURE THING! YOU BETTER GET A GOOD VET TO LOOK 'IM OVER!
TAKE A GANDER AT THAT!
GOSH! HE NEVER EVEN ALLOWED A CAT IN THE YARD BEFORE!
PLUTO
!
I'LL CALL THE VET'RINARY! HE'LL KNOW WHAT TO DO!
YES, DOC-- IT'S SERIOUS! HE LETS ANYBODY IN TH' PLACE!
NOTHIN' IN HERE THAT'S ANY HELP, EITHER!
The DOG AND HIS AILMENTS
GRR-R ROWF ROWF-ROWF! BOW WOW WOW
! ??? ?
5-8
PARDON ME-- BUT JUST WHAT DID YOU SAY WAS WRONG WITH YOUR DOG?
!
WALT DISNEY

150. PLUTO SHOWED MICKEY HE WAS ALL VET

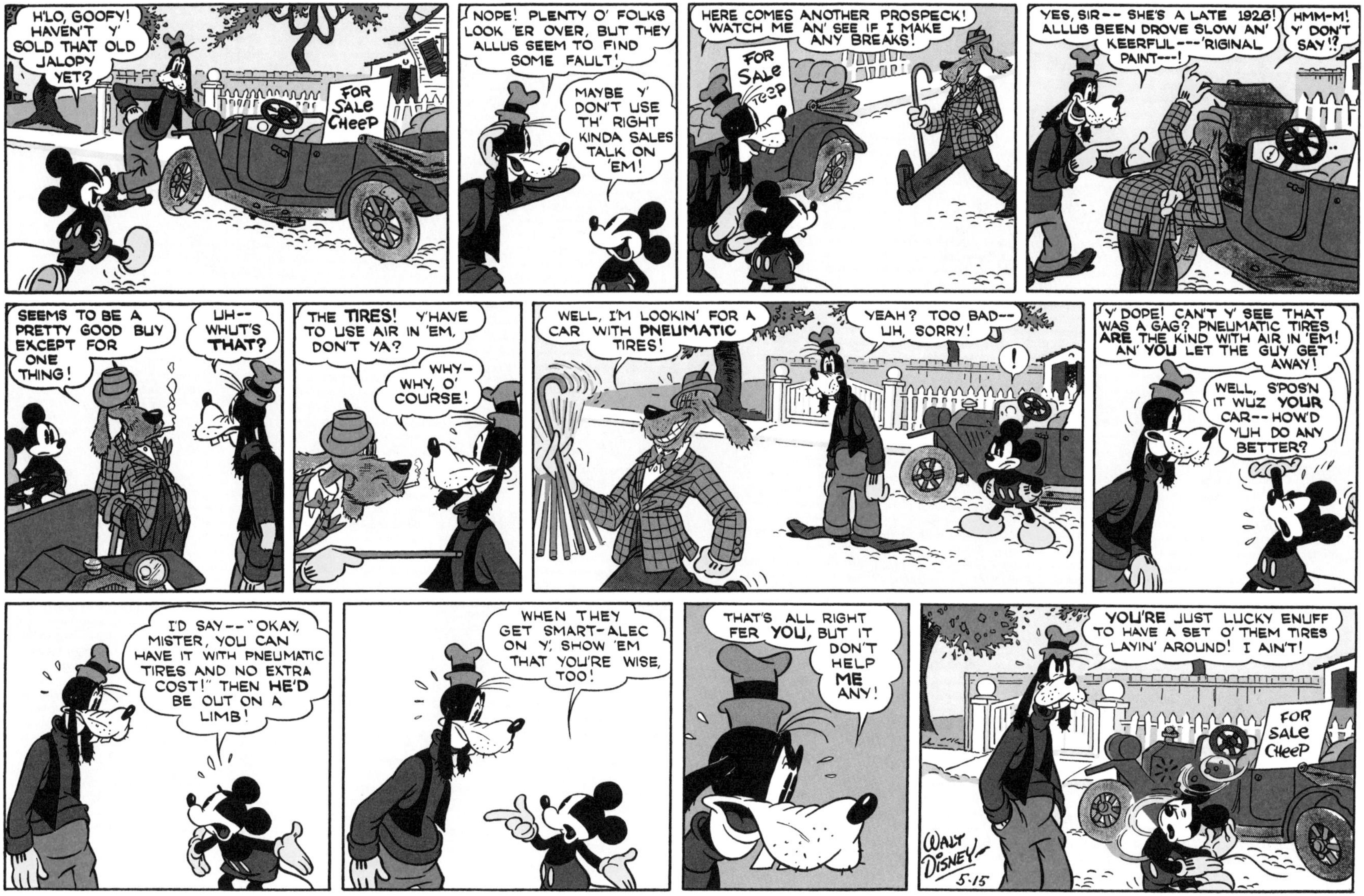
H'LO, GOOFY! HAVEN'T Y' SOLD THAT OLD JALOPY YET?
FOR SALE CHEEP
NOPE! PLENTY O' FOLKS LOOK 'ER OVER, BUT THEY ALLUS SEEM TO FIND SOME FAULT!
MAYBE Y' DON'T USE TH' RIGHT KINDA SALES TALK ON 'EM!
HERE COMES ANOTHER PROSPECK! WATCH ME AN' SEE IF I MAKE ANY BREAKS!
FOR SALE
YES, SIR-- SHE'S A LATE 1926! ALLUS BEEN DROVE SLOW AN' KEERFUL---'RIGINAL PAINT---!
HMM-M! Y' DON'T SAY!?
SEEMS TO BE A PRETTY GOOD BUY EXCEPT FOR ONE THING!
UH-- WHUT'S THAT?
THE TIRES! Y'HAVE TO USE AIR IN 'EM, DON'T YA?
WHY- WHY, O' COURSE!
WELL, I'M LOOKIN' FOR A CAR WITH PNEUMATIC TIRES!
YEAH? TOO BAD-- UH, SORRY!
!
Y' DOPE! CAN'T Y' SEE THAT WAS A GAG? PNEUMATIC TIRES ARE THE KIND WITH AIR IN 'EM! AN' YOU LET THE GUY GET AWAY!
WELL, S'POS'N IT WUZ YOUR CAR-- HOW'D YUH DO ANY BETTER?
I'D SAY--"OKAY, MISTER, YOU CAN HAVE IT WITH PNEUMATIC TIRES AND NO EXTRA COST!" THEN HE'D BE OUT ON A LIMB!
WHEN THEY GET SMART-ALEC ON Y', SHOW 'EM THAT YOU'RE WISE, TOO!
THAT'S ALL RIGHT FER YOU, BUT IT DON'T HELP ME ANY!
YOU'RE JUST LUCKY ENUFF TO HAVE A SET O' THEM TIRES LAYIN' AROUND! I AIN'T!
FOR SALE CHEEP
WALT DISNEY
5-15

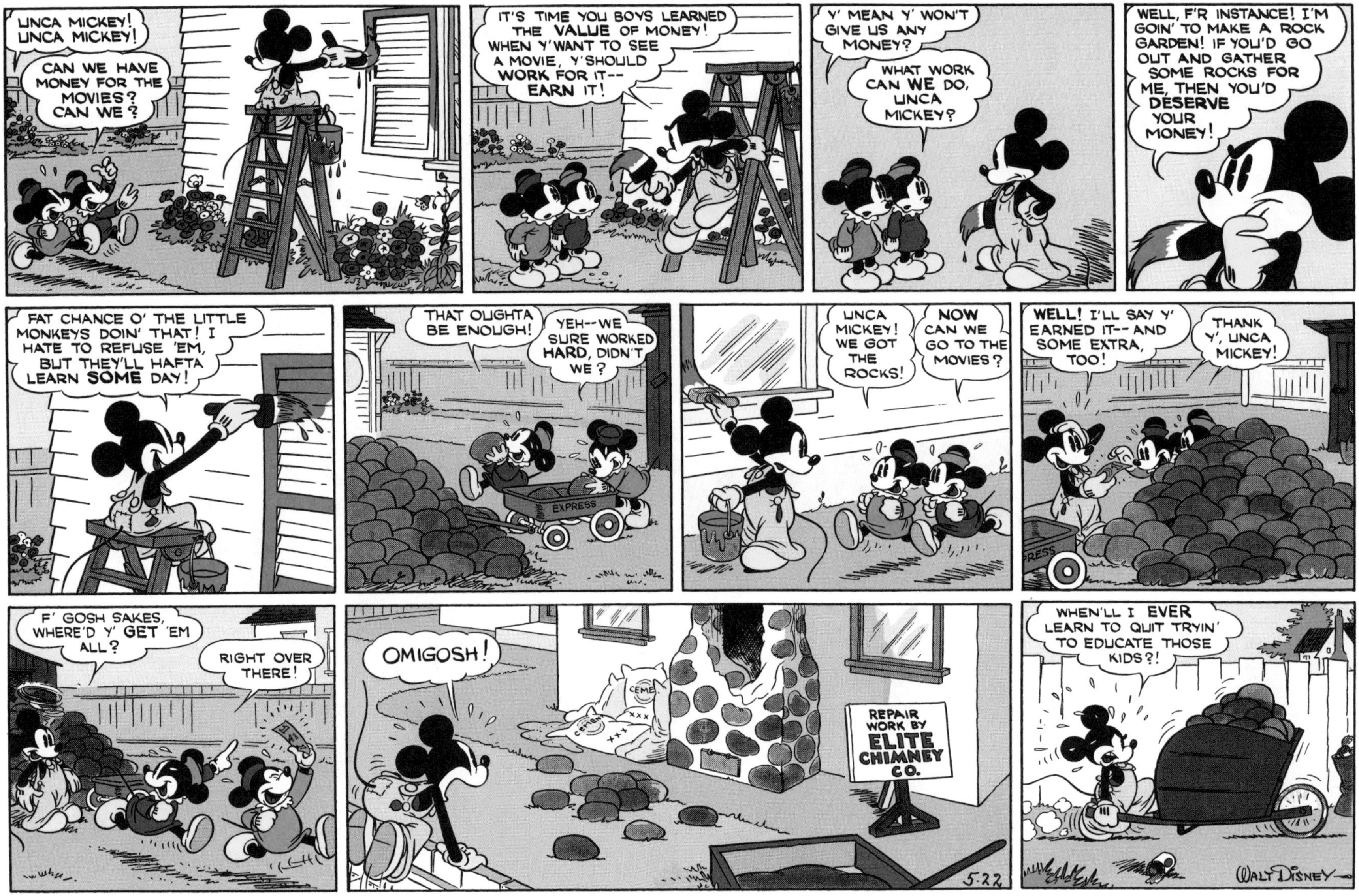

UNCA MICKEY! UNCA MICKEY!
CAN WE HAVE MONEY FOR THE MOVIES? CAN WE?
IT'S TIME YOU BOYS LEARNED THE VALUE OF MONEY! WHEN Y'WANT TO SEE A MOVIE, Y'SHOULD WORK FOR IT-- EARN IT!
Y' MEAN Y' WON'T GIVE US ANY MONEY?
WHAT WORK CAN WE DO, UNCA MICKEY?
WELL, F'R INSTANCE! I'M GOIN' TO MAKE A ROCK GARDEN! IF YOU'D GO OUT AND GATHER SOME ROCKS FOR ME, THEN YOU'D DESERVE YOUR MONEY!
FAT CHANCE O' THE LITTLE MONKEYS DOIN' THAT! I HATE TO REFUSE 'EM, BUT THEY'LL HAFTA LEARN SOME DAY!
THAT OUGHTA BE ENOUGH!
YEH--WE SURE WORKED HARD, DIDN'T WE?
EXPRESS
UNCA MICKEY! WE GOT THE ROCKS!
NOW CAN WE GO TO THE MOVIES?
WELL! I'LL SAY Y' EARNED IT-- AND SOME EXTRA, TOO!
THANK Y', UNCA MICKEY!
F' GOSH SAKES, WHERE'D Y' GET 'EM ALL?
RIGHT OVER THERE!
OMIGOSH!
REPAIR WORK BY ELITE CHIMNEY CO.
5-22
WHEN'LL I EVER LEARN TO QUIT TRYIN' TO EDUCATE THOSE KIDS?!
WALT DISNEY

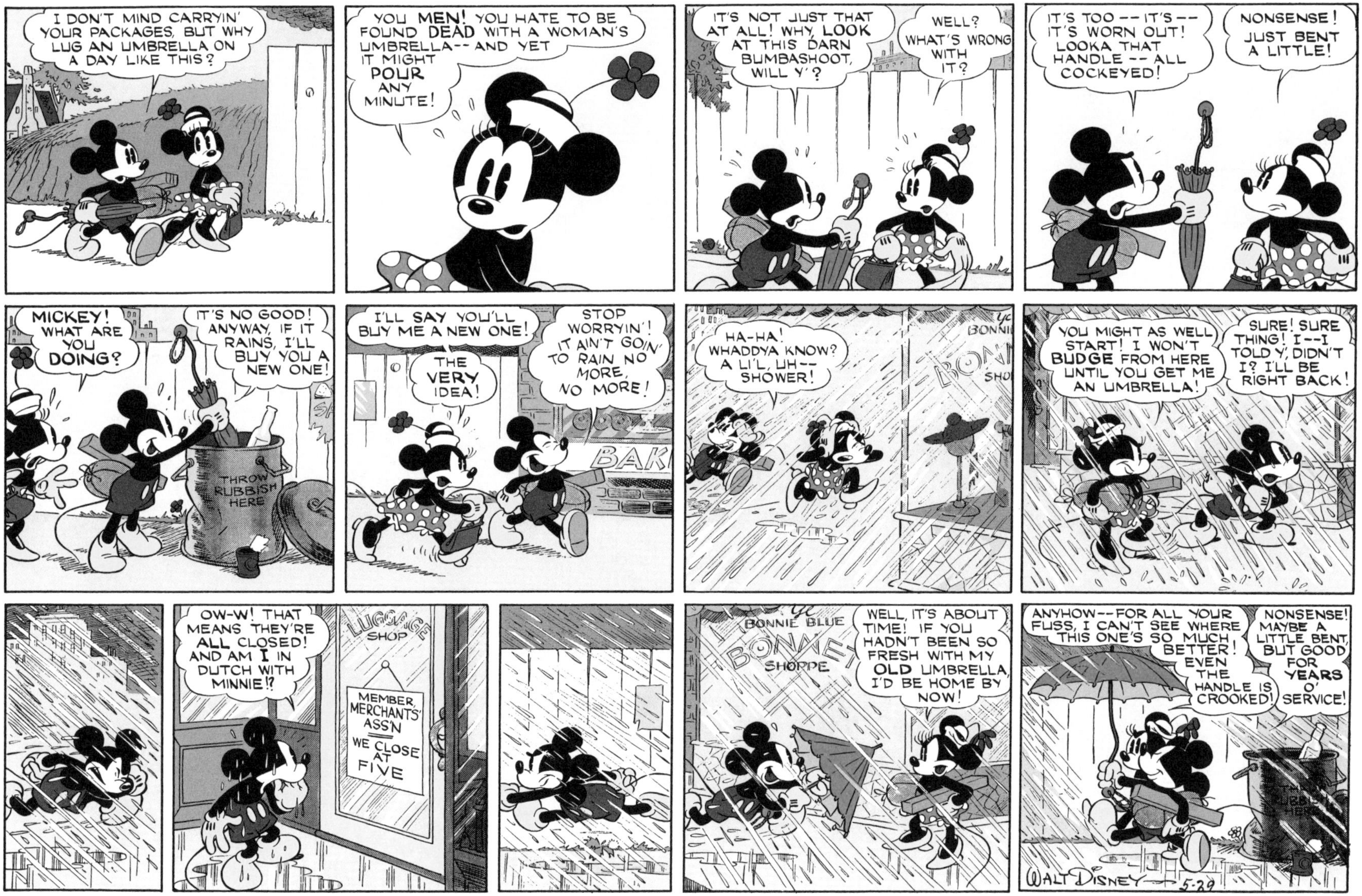
I DON'T MIND CARRYIN' YOUR PACKAGES, BUT WHY LUG AN UMBRELLA ON A DAY LIKE THIS?
YOU MEN! YOU HATE TO BE FOUND DEAD WITH A WOMAN'S UMBRELLA-- AND YET IT MIGHT POUR ANY MINUTE!
IT'S NOT JUST THAT AT ALL! WHY, LOOK AT THIS DARN BUMBASHOOT, WILL Y'?
WELL? WHAT'S WRONG WITH IT?
IT'S TOO -- IT'S -- IT'S WORN OUT! LOOKA THAT HANDLE -- ALL COCKEYED!
NONSENSE! JUST BENT A LITTLE!
MICKEY! WHAT ARE YOU DOING?
IT'S NO GOOD! ANYWAY, IF IT RAINS, I'LL BUY YOU A NEW ONE!
THROW RUBBISH HERE
I'LL SAY YOU'LL BUY ME A NEW ONE!
THE VERY IDEA!
STOP WORRYIN'! IT AIN'T GOIN' TO RAIN NO MORE, NO MORE!
BAK
HA-HA! WHADDYA KNOW? A LI'L, UH-- SHOWER!
BONNI
SHO
YOU MIGHT AS WELL START! I WON'T BUDGE FROM HERE UNTIL YOU GET ME AN UMBRELLA!
SURE! SURE THING! I--I TOLD Y', DIDN'T I? I'LL BE RIGHT BACK!
OW-W! THAT MEANS THEY'RE ALL CLOSED! AND AM I IN DUTCH WITH MINNIE!?
LUGGAGE SHOP
MEMBER MERCHANTS' ASS'N
WE CLOSE AT FIVE
BONNIE BLUE BONNET SHOPPE
WELL, IT'S ABOUT TIME! IF YOU HADN'T BEEN SO FRESH WITH MY OLD UMBRELLA, I'D BE HOME BY NOW!
ANYHOW--FOR ALL YOUR FUSS, I CAN'T SEE WHERE THIS ONE'S SO MUCH BETTER! EVEN THE HANDLE IS CROOKED!
NONSENSE! MAYBE A LITTLE BENT, BUT GOOD FOR YEARS O' SERVICE!
WALT DISNEY 5-29

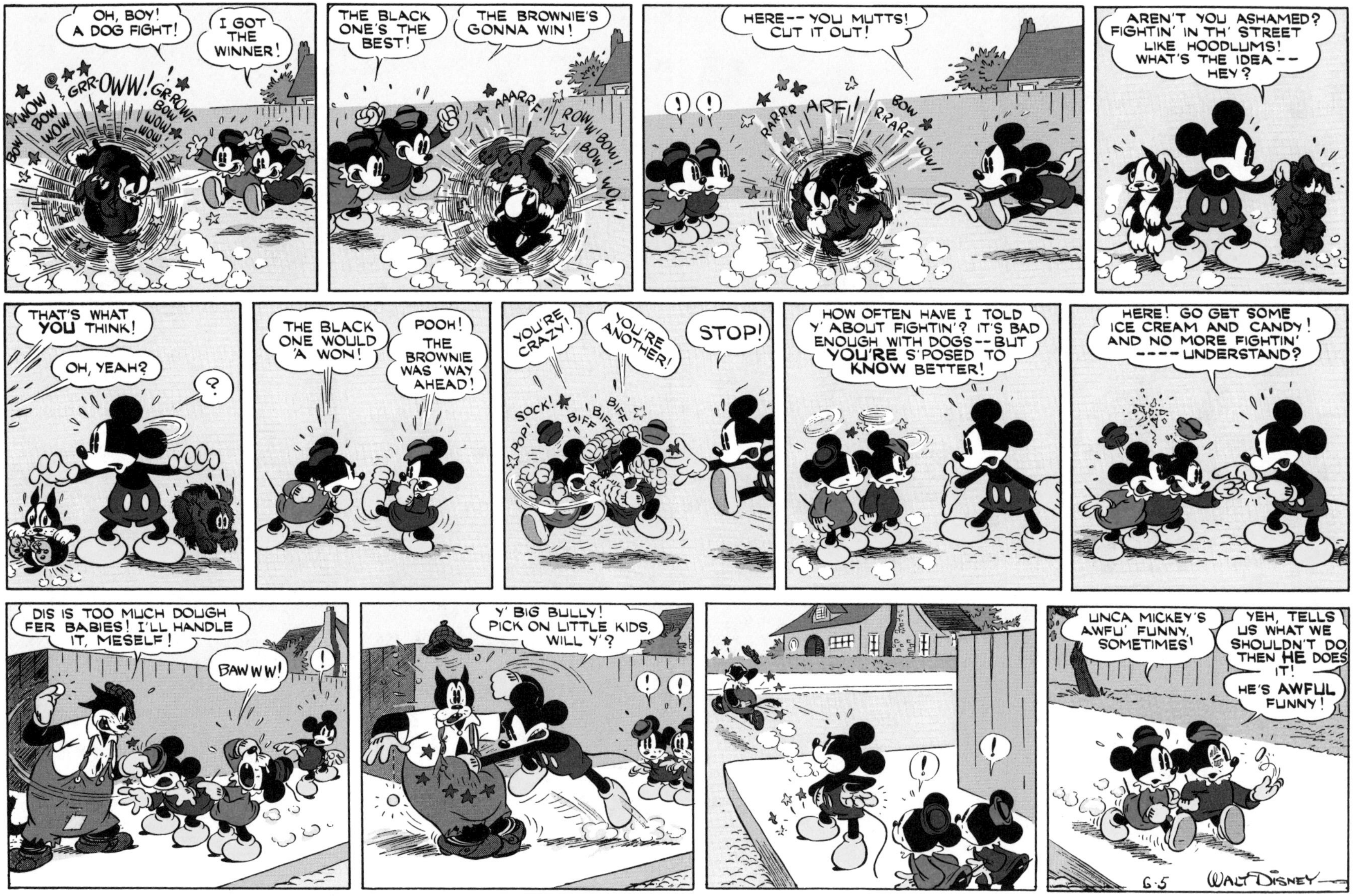
OH, BOY! A DOG FIGHT!
I GOT THE WINNER!
GRR-OWW! GR-ROWF
THE BLACK ONE'S THE BEST!
THE BROWNIE'S GONNA WIN!
AAARRF! ROWW BOW BOW WOW
HERE-- YOU MUTTS! CUT IT OUT!
RARRR ARF! BOW RRARF WOW
AREN'T YOU ASHAMED? FIGHTIN' IN TH' STREET LIKE HOODLUMS! WHAT'S THE IDEA -- HEY?
THAT'S WHAT YOU THINK!
OH, YEAH?
?
THE BLACK ONE WOULD 'A WON!
POOH! THE BROWNIE WAS 'WAY AHEAD!
YOU'RE CRAZY!
YOU'RE ANOTHER!
STOP!
SOCK! POP! BIFF BIFF BIFF
HOW OFTEN HAVE I TOLD Y' ABOUT FIGHTIN'? IT'S BAD ENOUGH WITH DOGS -- BUT YOU'RE S'POSED TO KNOW BETTER!
HERE! GO GET SOME ICE CREAM AND CANDY! AND NO MORE FIGHTIN' ---- UNDERSTAND?
DIS IS TOO MUCH DOUGH FER BABIES! I'LL HANDLE IT, MESELF!
BAWWW!
Y' BIG BULLY! PICK ON LITTLE KIDS, WILL Y'?
UNCA MICKEY'S AWFU' FUNNY, SOMETIMES!
YEH, TELLS US WHAT WE SHOULDN'T DO, THEN HE DOES IT!
HE'S AWFUL FUNNY!
6-5
WALT DISNEY

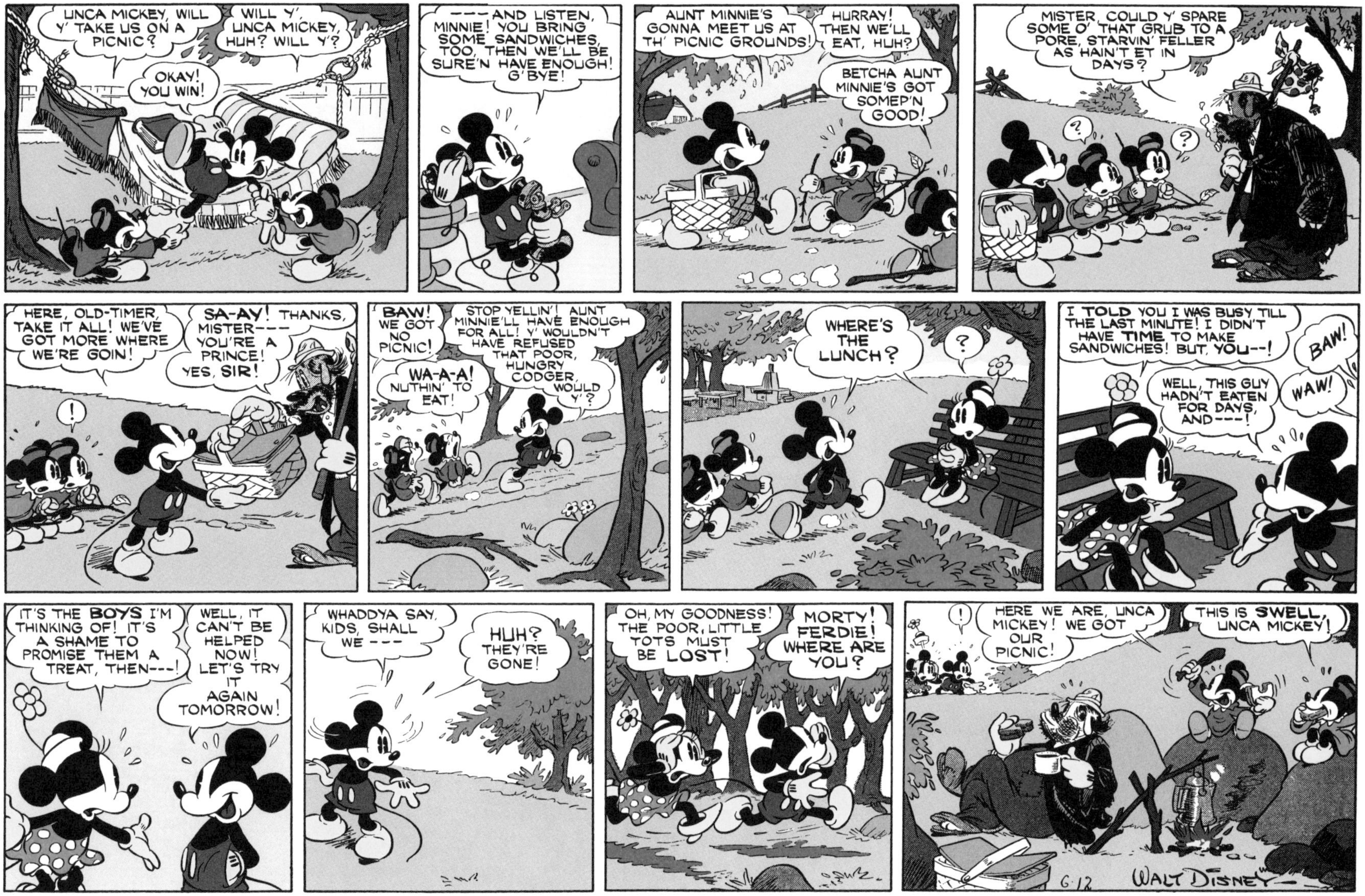
UNCA MICKEY, WILL Y' TAKE US ON A PICNIC?
WILL Y', UNCA MICKEY, HUH? WILL Y'?
OKAY! YOU WIN!
---AND LISTEN, MINNIE! YOU BRING SOME SANDWICHES, TOO, THEN WE'LL BE SURE'N HAVE ENOUGH! G'BYE!
AUNT MINNIE'S GONNA MEET US AT TH' PICNIC GROUNDS!
HURRAY! THEN WE'LL EAT, HUH?
BETCHA AUNT MINNIE'S GOT SOMEP'N GOOD!
MISTER, COULD Y' SPARE SOME O' THAT GRUB TO A PORE, STARVIN' FELLER AS HAIN'T ET IN DAYS?
?
?
HERE, OLD-TIMER, TAKE IT ALL! WE'VE GOT MORE WHERE WE'RE GOIN!
SA-AY! THANKS, MISTER--- YOU'RE A PRINCE! YES, SIR!
!
BAW! WE GOT NO PICNIC!
STOP YELLIN'! AUNT MINNIE'LL HAVE ENOUGH FOR ALL! Y' WOULDN'T HAVE REFUSED THAT POOR, HUNGRY CODGER, WOULD Y'?
WA-A-A! NUTHIN' TO EAT!
WHERE'S THE LUNCH?
?
I TOLD YOU I WAS BUSY TILL THE LAST MINUTE! I DIDN'T HAVE TIME TO MAKE SANDWICHES! BUT, YOU--!
WELL, THIS GUY HADN'T EATEN FOR DAYS, AND---!
BAW!
WAW!
IT'S THE BOYS I'M THINKING OF! IT'S A SHAME TO PROMISE THEM A TREAT, THEN---!
WELL, IT CAN'T BE HELPED NOW! LET'S TRY IT AGAIN TOMORROW!
WHADDYA SAY, KIDS, SHALL WE ---
HUH? THEY'RE GONE!
OH, MY GOODNESS! THE POOR, LITTLE TOTS MUST BE LOST!
MORTY! FERDIE! WHERE ARE YOU?
!
HERE WE ARE, UNCA MICKEY! WE GOT OUR PICNIC!
THIS IS SWELL, UNCA MICKEY!
6-12
WALT DISNEY

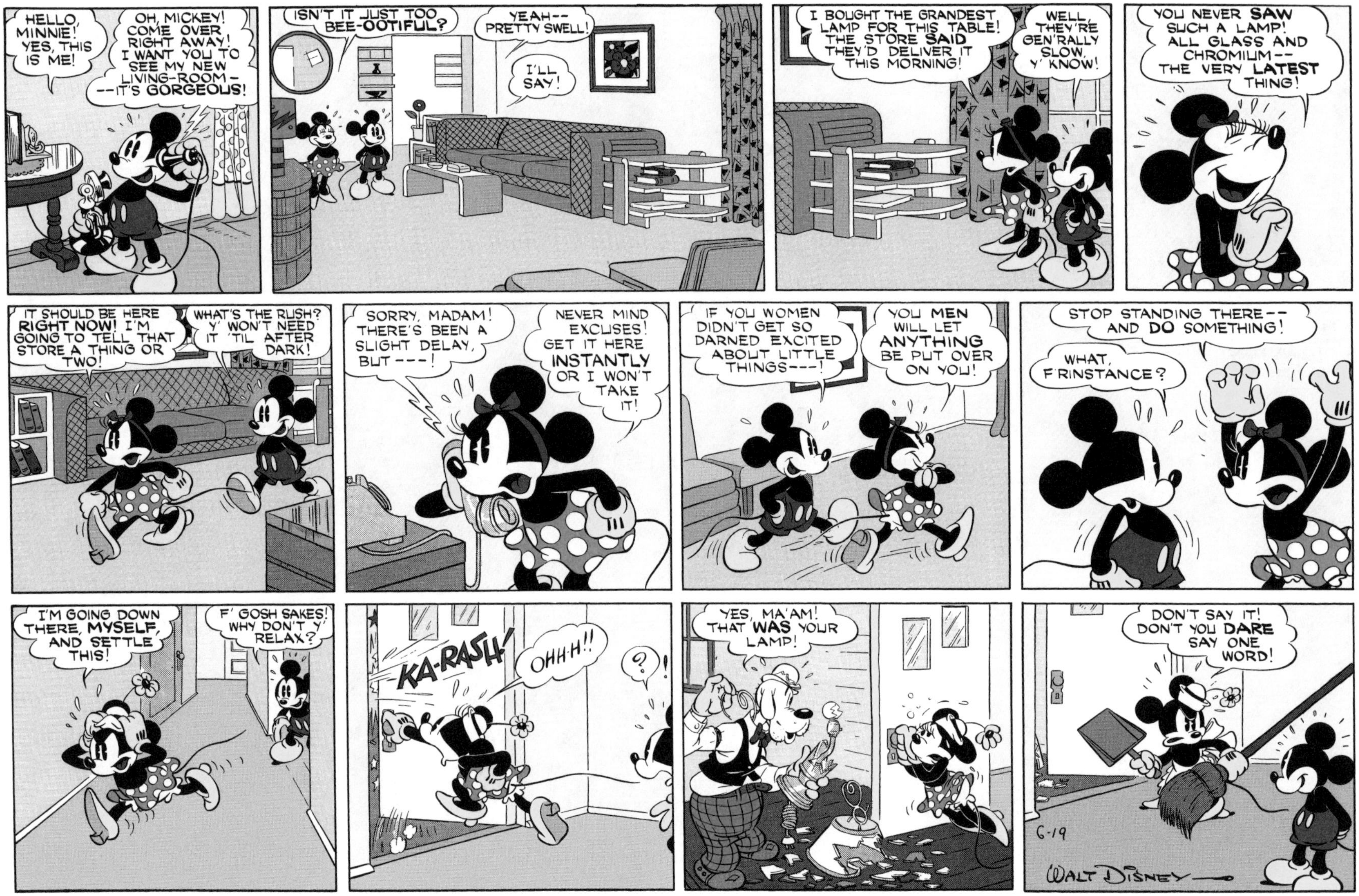

HELLO, MINNIE! YES, THIS IS ME!
OH, MICKEY! COME OVER RIGHT AWAY! I WANT YOU TO SEE MY NEW LIVING-ROOM--IT'S GORGEOUS!
ISN'T IT JUST TOO BEE-OOTIFUL?
YEAH-- PRETTY SWELL!
I'LL SAY!
I BOUGHT THE GRANDEST LAMP FOR THIS TABLE! THE STORE SAID THEY'D DELIVER IT THIS MORNING!
WELL, THEY'RE GEN'RALLY SLOW, Y' KNOW!
YOU NEVER SAW SUCH A LAMP! ALL GLASS AND CHROMIUM-- THE VERY LATEST THING!
IT SHOULD BE HERE RIGHT NOW! I'M GOING TO TELL THAT STORE A THING OR TWO!
WHAT'S THE RUSH? Y' WON'T NEED IT 'TIL AFTER DARK!
SORRY, MADAM! THERE'S BEEN A SLIGHT DELAY, BUT---!
NEVER MIND EXCUSES! GET IT HERE INSTANTLY OR I WON'T TAKE IT!
IF YOU WOMEN DIDN'T GET SO DARNED EXCITED ABOUT LITTLE THINGS---!
YOU MEN WILL LET ANYTHING BE PUT OVER ON YOU!
STOP STANDING THERE-- AND DO SOMETHING!
WHAT, F'RINSTANCE?
I'M GOING DOWN THERE, MYSELF, AND SETTLE THIS!
F' GOSH SAKES! WHY DON'T Y' RELAX?
KA-RASH!
OHH-H!!
?!
YES, MA'AM! THAT WAS YOUR LAMP!
DON'T SAY IT! DON'T YOU DARE SAY ONE WORD!
6-19
WALT DISNEY

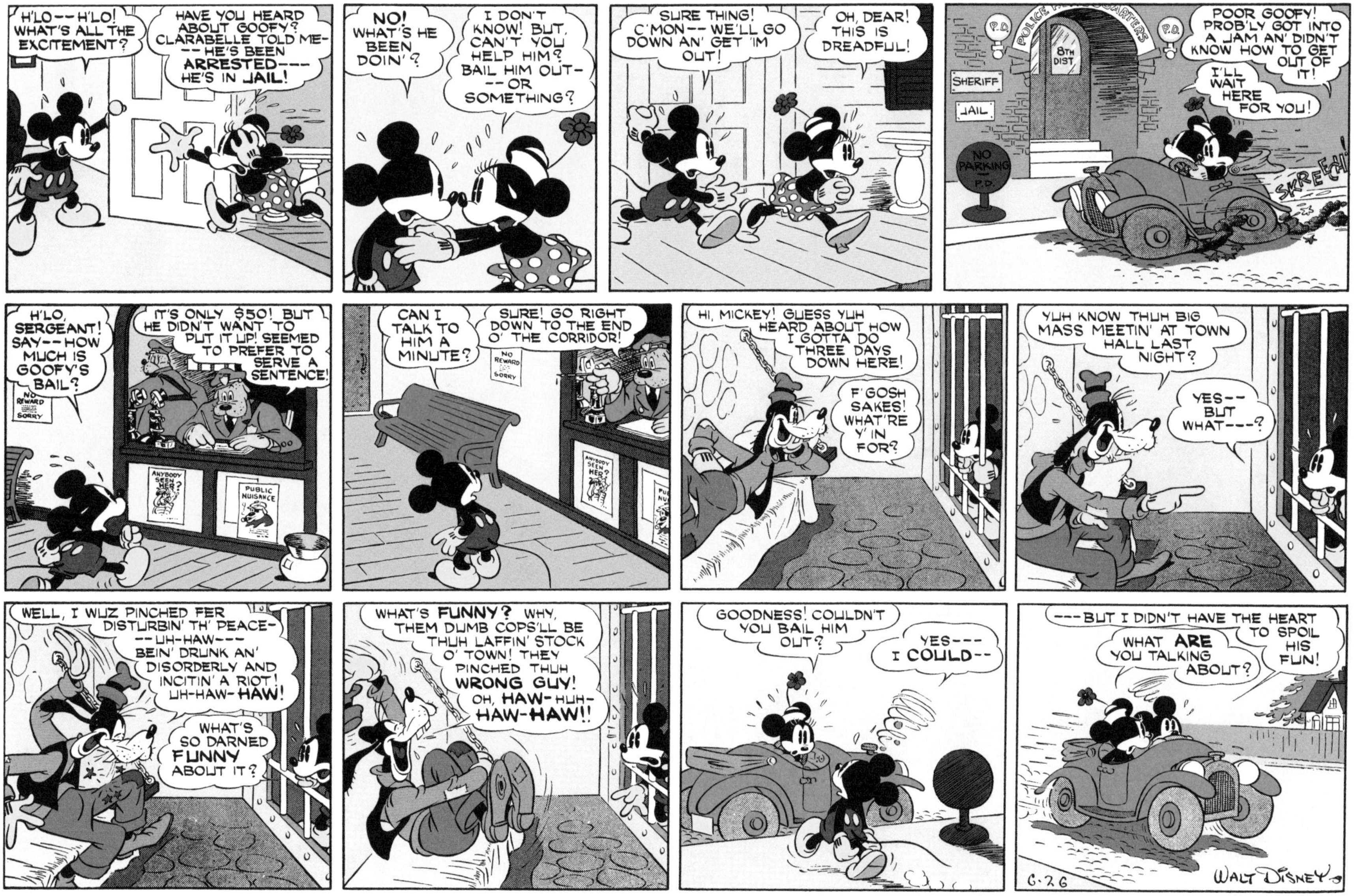
H'LO--H'LO! WHAT'S ALL THE EXCITEMENT?
HAVE YOU HEARD ABOUT GOOFY? CLARABELLE TOLD ME---HE'S BEEN ARRESTED---- HE'S IN JAIL!
NO! WHAT'S HE BEEN DOIN'?
I DON'T KNOW! BUT, CAN'T YOU HELP HIM? BAIL HIM OUT---OR SOMETHING?
SURE THING! C'MON--WE'LL GO DOWN AN' GET 'IM OUT!
OH, DEAR! THIS IS DREADFUL!
P.D.
8TH DIST.
P.D.
SHERIFF
JAIL
NO PARKING P.D.
POOR GOOFY! PROB'LY GOT INTO A JAM AN' DIDN'T KNOW HOW TO GET OUT OF IT!
I'LL WAIT HERE FOR YOU!
SKREECH!
H'LO, SERGEANT! SAY--HOW MUCH IS GOOFY'S BAIL?
IT'S ONLY $50! BUT HE DIDN'T WANT TO PUT IT UP! SEEMED TO PREFER TO SERVE A SENTENCE!
NO REWARD SORRY
ANYBODY SEEN HER?
PUBLIC NUISANCE
CAN I TALK TO HIM A MINUTE?
SURE! GO RIGHT DOWN TO THE END O' THE CORRIDOR!
NO REWARD SORRY
ANYBODY SEEN HER?
HI, MICKEY! GUESS YUH HEARD ABOUT HOW I GOTTA DO THREE DAYS DOWN HERE!
F'GOSH SAKES! WHAT'RE Y' IN FOR?
YUH KNOW THUH BIG MASS MEETIN' AT TOWN HALL LAST NIGHT?
YES-- BUT WHAT---?
WELL, I WUZ PINCHED FER DISTURBIN' TH' PEACE---UH-HAW--- BEIN' DRUNK AN' DISORDERLY AND INCITIN' A RIOT! UH-HAW-HAW!
WHAT'S SO DARNED FUNNY ABOUT IT?
WHAT'S FUNNY? WHY, THEM DUMB COPS'LL BE THUH LAFFIN' STOCK O' TOWN! THEY PINCHED THUH WRONG GUY!
OH, HAW-HUH-HAW-HAW!!
GOODNESS! COULDN'T YOU BAIL HIM OUT?
YES--- I COULD--
---BUT I DIDN'T HAVE THE HEART TO SPOIL HIS FUN!
WHAT ARE YOU TALKING ABOUT?
6·26
WALT DISNEY

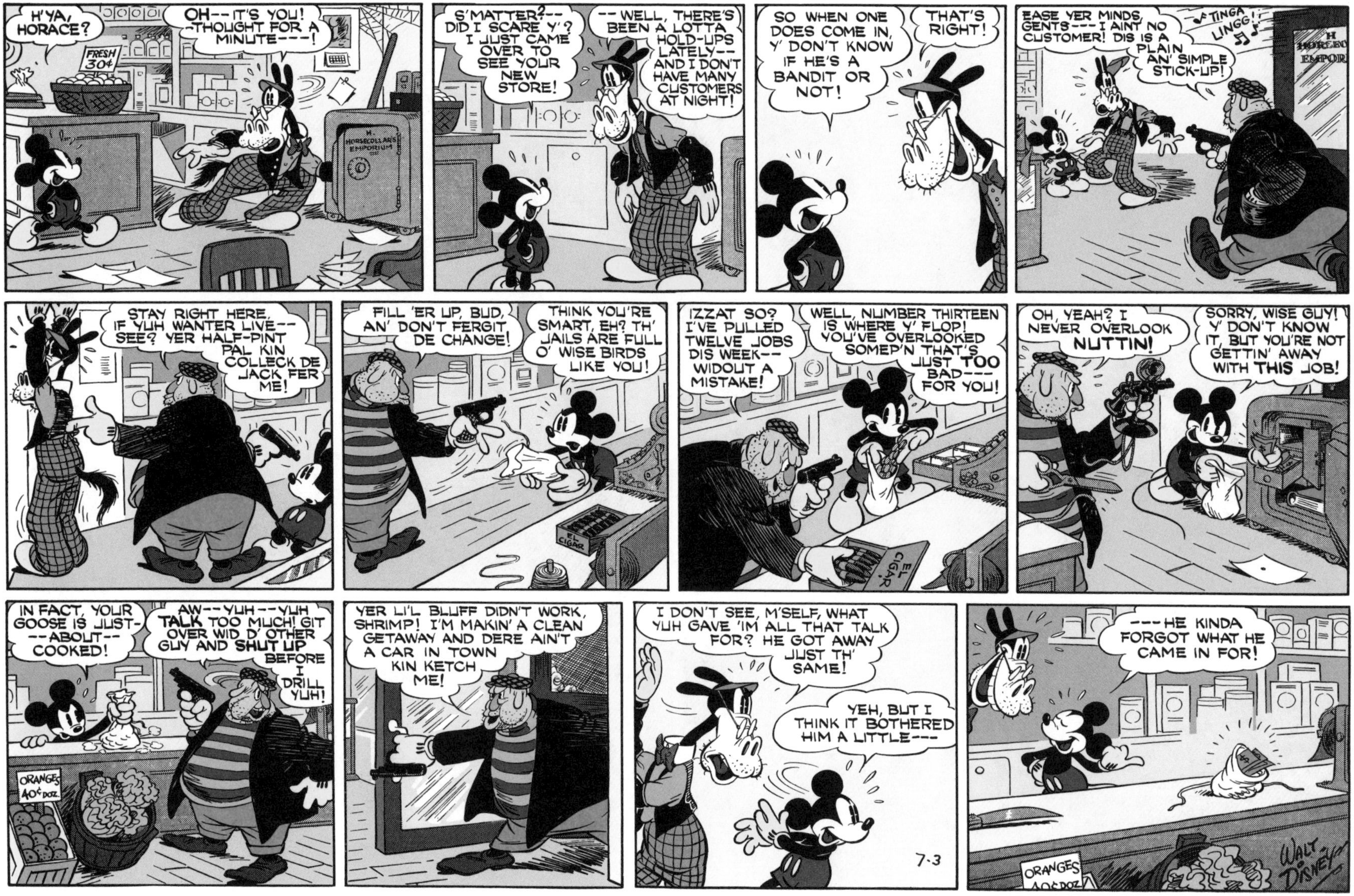
H'YA, HORACE?
OH-- IT'S YOU! -THOUGHT FOR A MINUTE---!
FRESH 30¢
S'MATTER?-- DID I SCARE Y'? I JUST CAME OVER TO SEE YOUR NEW STORE!
-- WELL, THERE'S BEEN A LOTTA HOLD-UPS LATELY-- AND I DON'T HAVE MANY CUSTOMERS AT NIGHT!
SO WHEN ONE DOES COME IN, Y' DON'T KNOW IF HE'S A BANDIT OR NOT!
THAT'S RIGHT!
EASE YER MINDS, GENTS--- I AINT NO CUSTOMER! DIS IS A PLAIN AN' SIMPLE STICK-UP!
TINGA LINGG!
STAY RIGHT HERE, IF YUH WANTER LIVE-- SEE? YER HALF-PINT PAL KIN COLLECK DE JACK FER ME!
FILL 'ER UP, BUD, AN' DON'T FERGIT DE CHANGE!
THINK YOU'RE SMART, EH? TH' JAILS ARE FULL O' WISE BIRDS LIKE YOU!
EL CIGAR
IZZAT SO? I'VE PULLED TWELVE JOBS DIS WEEK-- WIDOUT A MISTAKE!
WELL, NUMBER THIRTEEN IS WHERE Y' FLOP! YOU'VE OVERLOOKED SOMEP'N THAT'S JUST TOO BAD--- FOR YOU!
EL CIGAR
OH, YEAH? I NEVER OVERLOOK NUTTIN!
SORRY, WISE GUY! Y' DON'T KNOW IT, BUT YOU'RE NOT GETTIN' AWAY WITH THIS JOB!
IN FACT, YOUR GOOSE IS JUST- --ABOUT-- COOKED!
AW-- YUH --YUH TALK TOO MUCH! GIT OVER WID D' OTHER GUY AND SHUT UP BEFORE I DRILL YUH!
ORANGES 40¢ DOZ.
YER LI'L BLUFF DIDN'T WORK, SHRIMP! I'M MAKIN' A CLEAN GETAWAY AND DERE AIN'T A CAR IN TOWN KIN KETCH ME!
I DON'T SEE, M'SELF, WHAT YUH GAVE 'IM ALL THAT TALK FOR? HE GOT AWAY JUST TH' SAME!
YEH, BUT I THINK IT BOTHERED HIM A LITTLE---
7-3
---HE KINDA FORGOT WHAT HE CAME IN FOR!
ORANGES
WALT DISNEY

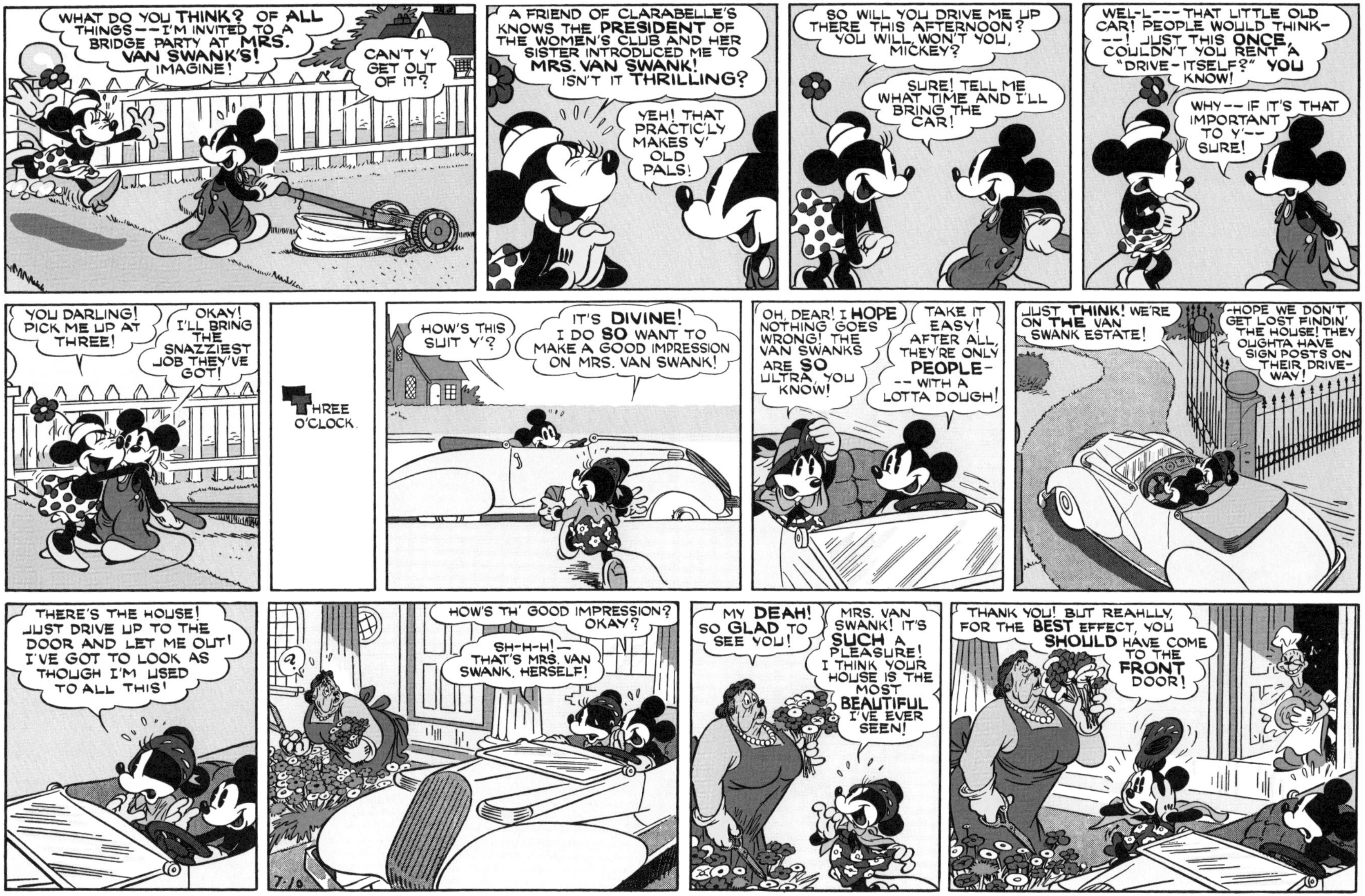
WHAT DO YOU THINK? OF ALL THINGS--I'M INVITED TO A BRIDGE PARTY AT MRS. VAN SWANK'S! IMAGINE!
CAN'T Y' GET OUT OF IT?
A FRIEND OF CLARABELLE'S KNOWS THE PRESIDENT OF THE WOMEN'S CLUB AND HER SISTER INTRODUCED ME TO MRS. VAN SWANK! ISN'T IT THRILLING?
YEH! THAT PRACTIC'LY MAKES Y' OLD PALS!
SO WILL YOU DRIVE ME UP THERE THIS AFTERNOON? YOU WILL, WON'T YOU, MICKEY?
SURE! TELL ME WHAT TIME AND I'LL BRING THE CAR!
WEL-L---THAT LITTLE OLD CAR! PEOPLE WOULD THINK---! JUST THIS ONCE, COULDN'T YOU RENT A "DRIVE-ITSELF?" YOU KNOW!
WHY--IF IT'S THAT IMPORTANT TO Y'--SURE!
YOU DARLING! PICK ME UP AT THREE!
OKAY! I'LL BRING THE SNAZZIEST JOB THEY'VE GOT!
THREE O'CLOCK.
HOW'S THIS SUIT Y'?
IT'S DIVINE! I DO SO WANT TO MAKE A GOOD IMPRESSION ON MRS. VAN SWANK!
OH, DEAR! I HOPE NOTHING GOES WRONG! THE VAN SWANKS ARE SO ULTRA, YOU KNOW!
TAKE IT EASY! AFTER ALL, THEY'RE ONLY PEOPLE--WITH A LOTTA DOUGH!
JUST THINK! WE'RE ON THE VAN SWANK ESTATE!
-HOPE WE DON'T GET LOST FINDIN' THE HOUSE! THEY OUGHTA HAVE SIGN POSTS ON THEIR DRIVE-WAY!
THERE'S THE HOUSE! JUST DRIVE UP TO THE DOOR AND LET ME OUT! I'VE GOT TO LOOK AS THOUGH I'M USED TO ALL THIS!
HOW'S TH' GOOD IMPRESSION? OKAY?
SH-H-H!—THAT'S MRS. VAN SWANK, HERSELF!
MY DEAH! SO GLAD TO SEE YOU!
MRS. VAN SWANK! IT'S SUCH A PLEASURE! I THINK YOUR HOUSE IS THE MOST BEAUTIFUL I'VE EVER SEEN!
THANK YOU! BUT REAHLLY, FOR THE BEST EFFECT, YOU SHOULD HAVE COME TO THE FRONT DOOR!

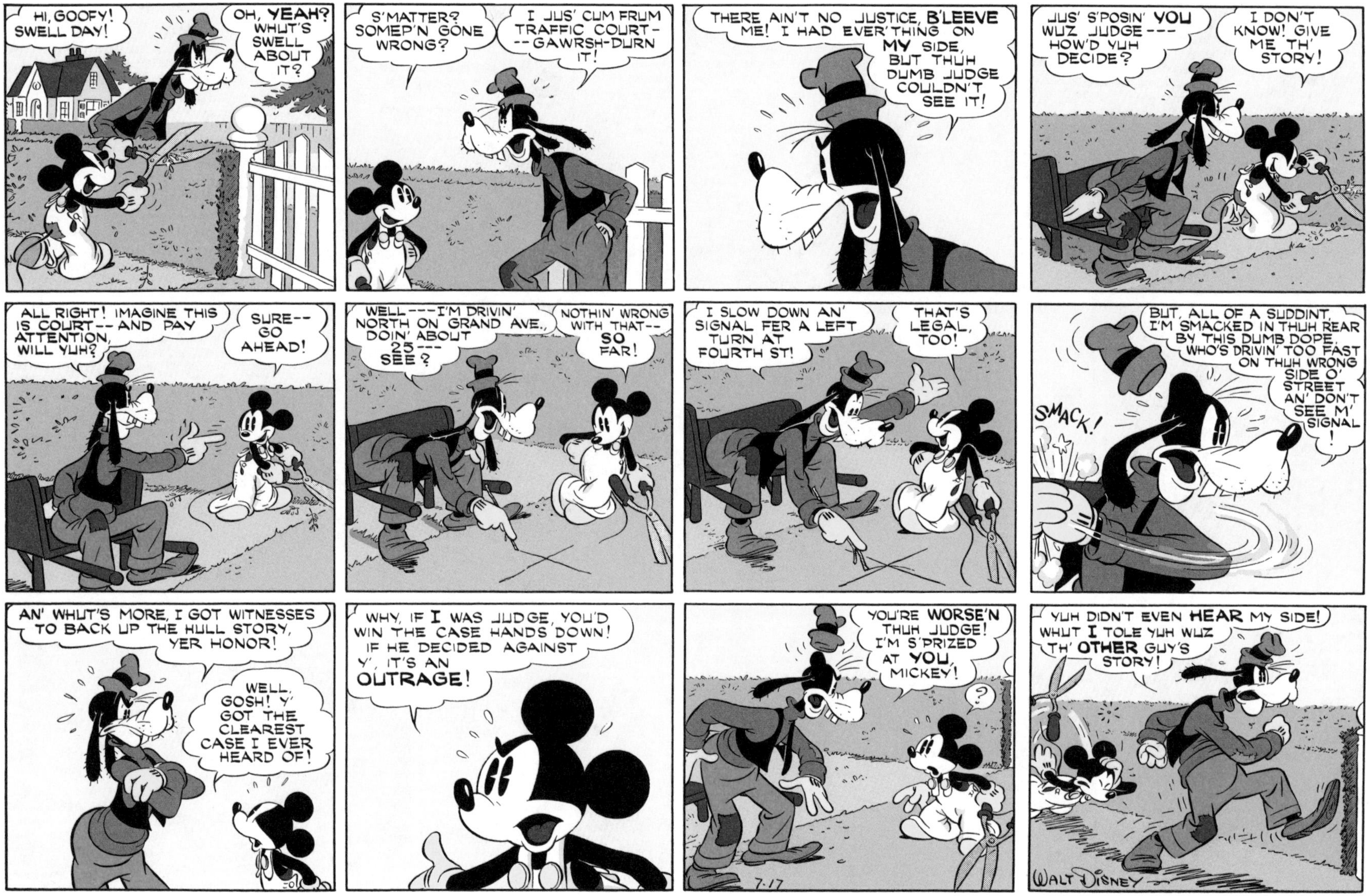
HI, GOOFY! SWELL DAY!
OH, YEAH? WHUT'S SWELL ABOUT IT?
S'MATTER? SOMEP'N GONE WRONG?
I JUS' CUM FRUM TRAFFIC COURT--GAWRSH-DURN IT!
THERE AIN'T NO JUSTICE, B'LEEVE ME! I HAD EVER'THING ON MY SIDE, BUT THUH DUMB JUDGE COULDN'T SEE IT!
JUS' S'POSIN' YOU WUZ JUDGE--- HOW'D YUH DECIDE?
I DON'T KNOW! GIVE ME TH' STORY!
ALL RIGHT! IMAGINE THIS IS COURT--AND PAY ATTENTION, WILL YUH?
SURE-- GO AHEAD!
WELL---I'M DRIVIN' NORTH ON GRAND AVE., DOIN' ABOUT 25--- SEE?
NOTHIN' WRONG WITH THAT-- SO FAR!
I SLOW DOWN AN' SIGNAL FER A LEFT TURN AT FOURTH ST!
THAT'S LEGAL, TOO!
BUT, ALL OF A SUDDINT, I'M SMACKED IN THUH REAR BY THIS DUMB DOPE, WHO'S DRIVIN' TOO FAST ON THUH WRONG SIDE O' STREET AN' DON'T SEE M' SIGNAL!
SMACK!
AN' WHUT'S MORE, I GOT WITNESSES TO BACK UP THE HULL STORY, YER HONOR!
WELL, GOSH! Y' GOT THE CLEAREST CASE I EVER HEARD OF!
WHY, IF I WAS JUDGE, YOU'D WIN THE CASE HANDS DOWN! IF HE DECIDED AGAINST Y', IT'S AN OUTRAGE!
YOU'RE WORSE'N THUH JUDGE! I'M S'PRIZED AT YOU, MICKEY!
?
7-17
YUH DIDN'T EVEN HEAR MY SIDE! WHUT I TOLE YUH WUZ TH' OTHER GUY'S STORY!
WALT DISNEY

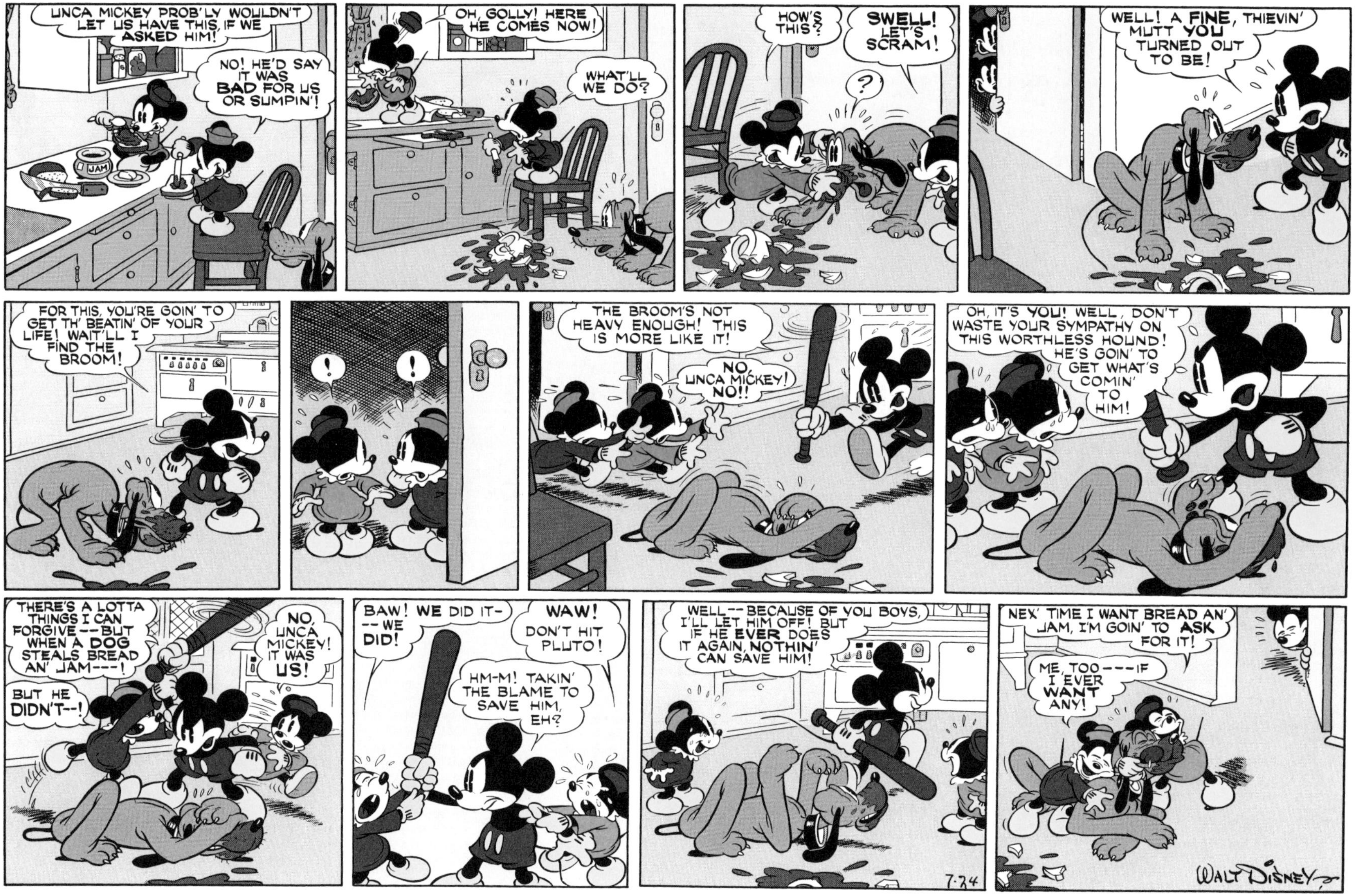

UNCA MICKEY PROB'LY WOULDN'T LET US HAVE THIS, IF WE ASKED HIM!
NO! HE'D SAY IT WAS BAD FOR US OR SUMPIN'!
JAM
OH, GOLLY! HERE HE COMES NOW!
WHAT'LL WE DO?
HOW'S THIS?
SWELL! LET'S SCRAM!
?
WELL! A FINE, THIEVIN' MUTT YOU TURNED OUT TO BE!
FOR THIS, YOU'RE GOIN' TO GET TH' BEATIN' OF YOUR LIFE! WAIT'LL I FIND THE BROOM!
!
!
THE BROOM'S NOT HEAVY ENOUGH! THIS IS MORE LIKE IT!
NO, UNCA MICKEY! NO!!
OH, IT'S YOU! WELL, DON'T WASTE YOUR SYMPATHY ON THIS WORTHLESS HOUND! HE'S GOIN' TO GET WHAT'S COMIN' TO HIM!
THERE'S A LOTTA THINGS I CAN FORGIVE--BUT WHEN A DOG STEALS BREAD AN' JAM---!
NO, UNCA MICKEY! IT WAS US!
BUT HE DIDN'T--!
BAW! WE DID IT---WE DID!
WAW! DON'T HIT PLUTO!
HM-M! TAKIN' THE BLAME TO SAVE HIM, EH?
WELL--BECAUSE OF YOU BOYS, I'LL LET HIM OFF! BUT IF HE EVER DOES IT AGAIN, NOTHIN' CAN SAVE HIM!
7·24
NEX' TIME I WANT BREAD AN' JAM, I'M GOIN' TO ASK FOR IT!
ME, TOO---IF I EVER WANT ANY!
WALT DISNEY

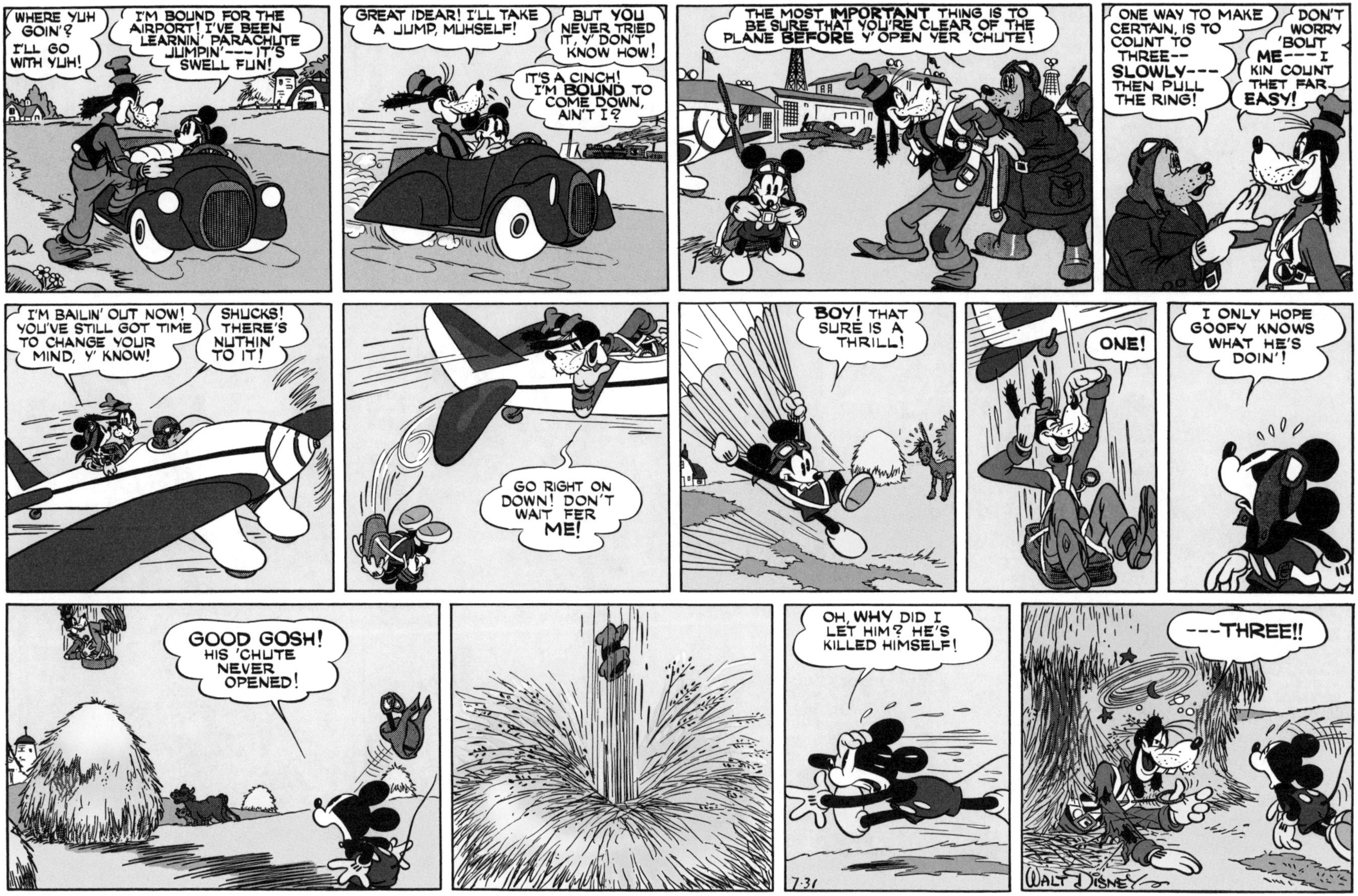
WHERE YUH GOIN'? I'LL GO WITH YUH!
I'M BOUND FOR THE AIRPORT! I'VE BEEN LEARNIN' PARACHUTE JUMPIN'--- IT'S SWELL FUN!
GREAT IDEAR! I'LL TAKE A JUMP, MUHSELF!
BUT YOU NEVER TRIED IT, Y' DON'T KNOW HOW!
IT'S A CINCH! I'M BOUND TO COME DOWN, AIN'T I?
THE MOST IMPORTANT THING IS TO BE SURE THAT YOU'RE CLEAR OF THE PLANE BEFORE Y' OPEN YER 'CHUTE!
ONE WAY TO MAKE CERTAIN, IS TO COUNT TO THREE-- SLOWLY--- THEN PULL THE RING!
DON'T WORRY 'BOUT ME--- I KIN COUNT THET FAR EASY!
I'M BAILIN' OUT NOW! YOU'VE STILL GOT TIME TO CHANGE YOUR MIND, Y' KNOW!
SHUCKS! THERE'S NUTHIN' TO IT!
GO RIGHT ON DOWN! DON'T WAIT FER ME!
BOY! THAT SURE IS A THRILL!
ONE!
I ONLY HOPE GOOFY KNOWS WHAT HE'S DOIN'!
GOOD GOSH! HIS 'CHUTE NEVER OPENED!
OH, WHY DID I LET HIM? HE'S KILLED HIMSELF!
7·31
---THREE!!
WALT DISNEY

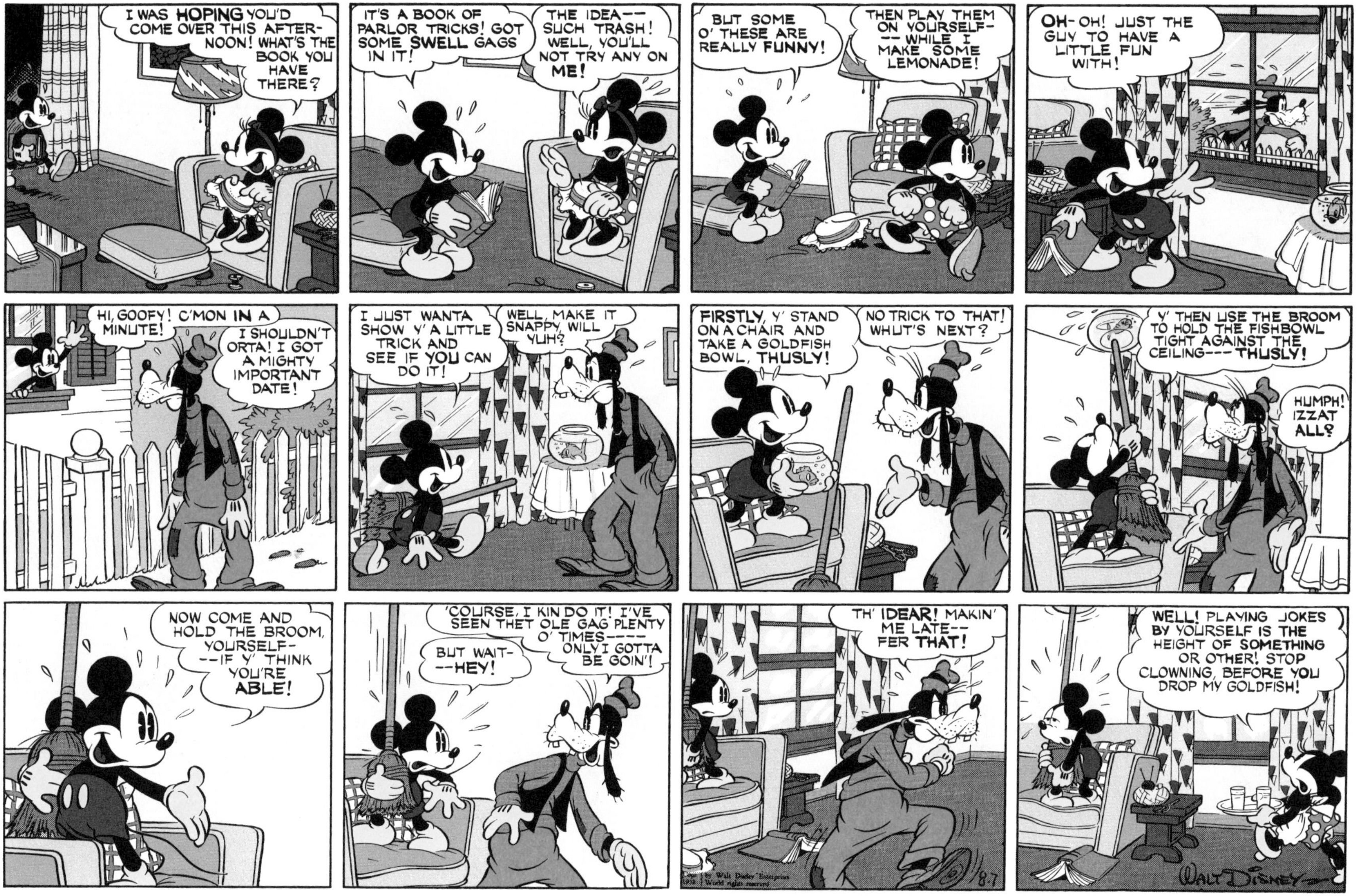
I WAS HOPING YOU'D COME OVER THIS AFTER-NOON! WHAT'S THE BOOK YOU HAVE THERE?
IT'S A BOOK OF PARLOR TRICKS! GOT SOME SWELL GAGS IN IT!
THE IDEA-- SUCH TRASH! WELL, YOU'LL NOT TRY ANY ON ME!
BUT SOME O' THESE ARE REALLY FUNNY!
THEN PLAY THEM ON YOURSELF- -- WHILE I MAKE SOME LEMONADE!
OH-OH! JUST THE GUY TO HAVE A LITTLE FUN WITH!
HI, GOOFY! C'MON IN A MINUTE!
I SHOULDN'T ORTA! I GOT A MIGHTY IMPORTANT DATE!
I JUST WANTA SHOW Y' A LITTLE TRICK AND SEE IF YOU CAN DO IT!
WELL, MAKE IT SNAPPY, WILL YUH?
FIRSTLY, Y' STAND ON A CHAIR AND TAKE A GOLDFISH BOWL, THUSLY!
NO TRICK TO THAT! WHUT'S NEXT?
Y' THEN USE THE BROOM TO HOLD THE FISHBOWL TIGHT AGAINST THE CEILING--- THUSLY!
HUMPH! IZZAT ALL?
NOW COME AND HOLD THE BROOM, YOURSELF- --IF Y' THINK YOU'RE ABLE!
'COURSE, I KIN DO IT! I'VE SEEN THET OLE GAG PLENTY O' TIMES---- ONLY I GOTTA BE GOIN'!
BUT WAIT- --HEY!
TH' IDEAR! MAKIN' ME LATE-- FER THAT!
Copr 1938 by Walt Disney Enterprises World rights reserved
8-7
WELL! PLAYING JOKES BY YOURSELF IS THE HEIGHT OF SOMETHING OR OTHER! STOP CLOWNING, BEFORE YOU DROP MY GOLDFISH!
WALT DISNEY

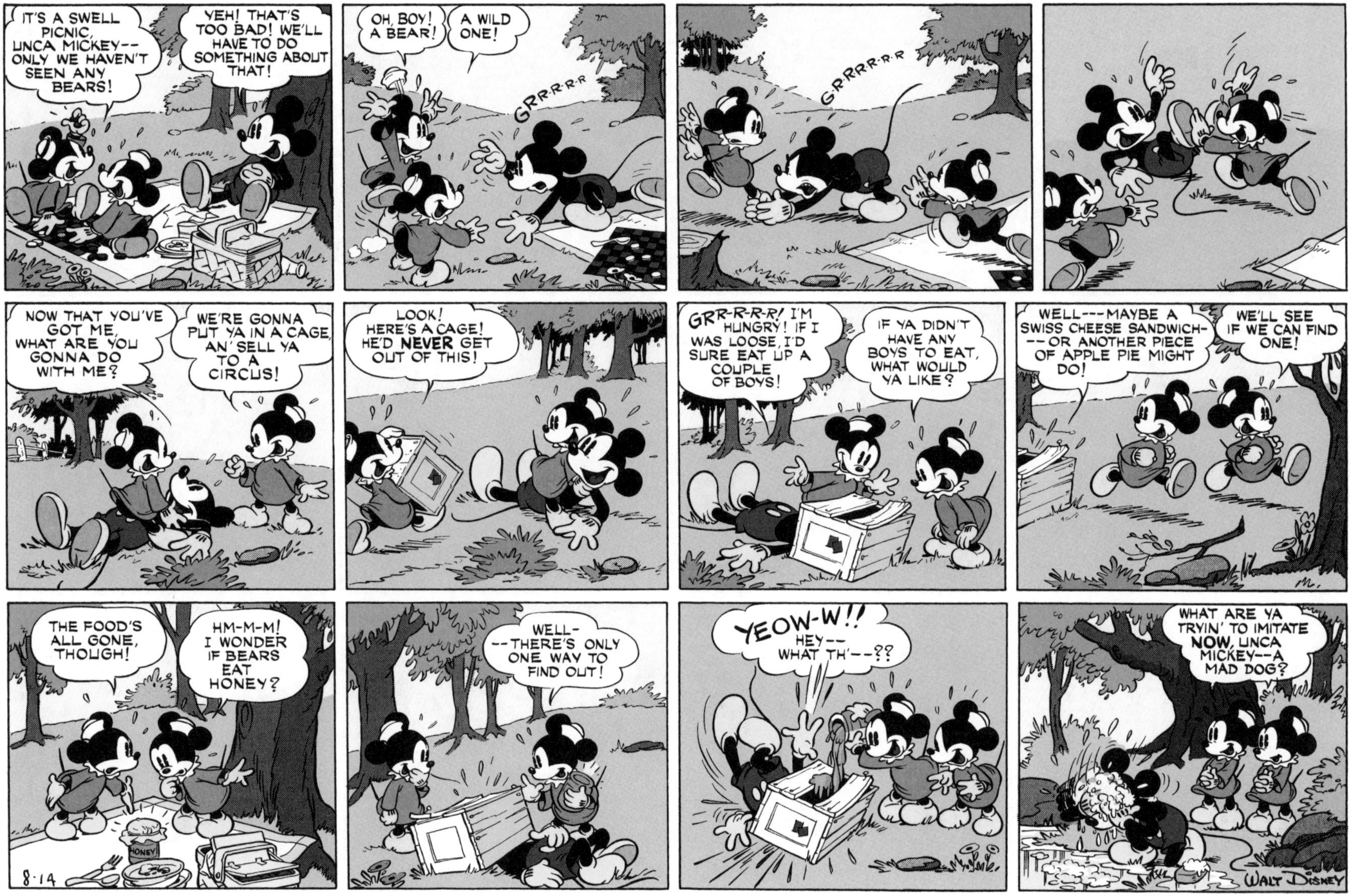
IT'S A SWELL PICNIC, UNCA MICKEY-- ONLY WE HAVEN'T SEEN ANY BEARS!
YEH! THAT'S TOO BAD! WE'LL HAVE TO DO SOMETHING ABOUT THAT!
OH, BOY! A BEAR!
A WILD ONE!
GRR-R-R-R
G-R-R-R-R-R-R
NOW THAT YOU'VE GOT ME, WHAT ARE YOU GONNA DO WITH ME?
WE'RE GONNA PUT YA IN A CAGE, AN' SELL YA TO A CIRCUS!
LOOK! HERE'S A CAGE! HE'D NEVER GET OUT OF THIS!
GRR-R-R-R! I'M HUNGRY! IF I WAS LOOSE, I'D SURE EAT UP A COUPLE OF BOYS!
IF YA DIDN'T HAVE ANY BOYS TO EAT, WHAT WOULD YA LIKE?
WELL---MAYBE A SWISS CHEESE SANDWICH- --OR ANOTHER PIECE OF APPLE PIE MIGHT DO!
WE'LL SEE IF WE CAN FIND ONE!
THE FOOD'S ALL GONE, THOUGH!
HM-M-M! I WONDER IF BEARS EAT HONEY?
HONEY
8·14
WELL- --THERE'S ONLY ONE WAY TO FIND OUT!
YEOW-W!!
HEY-- WHAT TH'--??
WHAT ARE YA TRYIN' TO IMITATE NOW, UNCA MICKEY--A MAD DOG?
WALT DISNEY

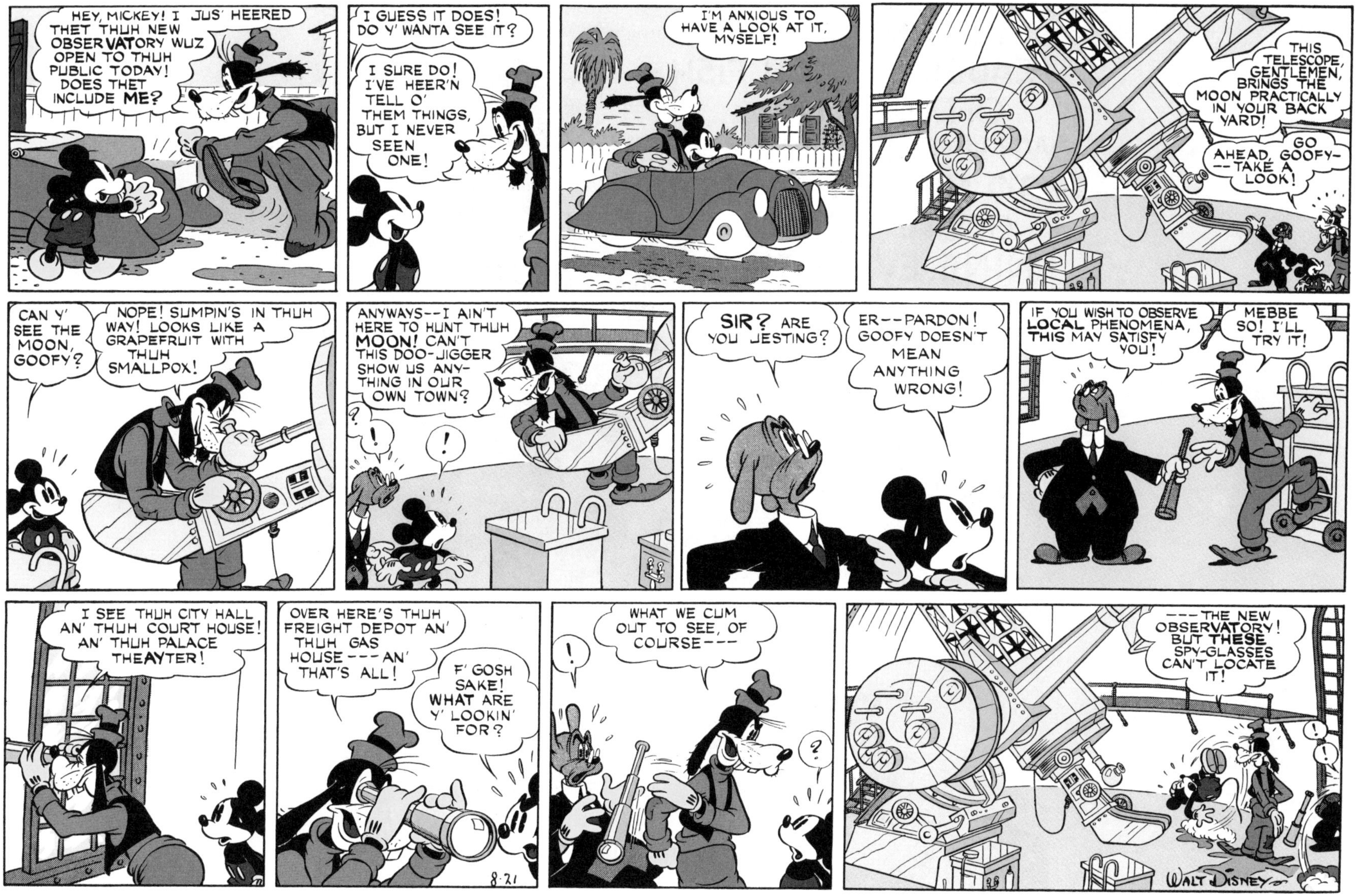
HEY, MICKEY! I JUS' HEERED THET THUH NEW OBSERVATORY WUZ OPEN TO THUH PUBLIC TODAY! DOES THET INCLUDE **ME?**
I GUESS IT DOES! DO Y' WANTA SEE IT?
I SURE DO! I'VE HEER'N TELL O' THEM THINGS, BUT I NEVER SEEN ONE!
I'M ANXIOUS TO HAVE A LOOK AT IT, MYSELF!
THIS TELESCOPE, GENTLEMEN, BRINGS THE MOON PRACTICALLY IN YOUR BACK YARD!
GO AHEAD, GOOFY-- TAKE A LOOK!
CAN Y' SEE THE MOON, GOOFY?
NOPE! SUMPIN'S IN THUH WAY! LOOKS LIKE A GRAPEFRUIT WITH THUH SMALLPOX!
ANYWAYS--I AIN'T HERE TO HUNT THUH **MOON!** CAN'T THIS DOO-JIGGER SHOW US ANYTHING IN OUR OWN TOWN?
?
!
!
SIR? ARE YOU JESTING?
ER--PARDON! GOOFY DOESN'T MEAN ANYTHING WRONG!
IF YOU WISH TO OBSERVE **LOCAL** PHENOMENA, **THIS** MAY SATISFY YOU!
MEBBE SO! I'LL TRY IT!
I SEE THUH CITY HALL AN' THUH COURT HOUSE! AN' THUH PALACE THEAYTER!
OVER HERE'S THUH FREIGHT DEPOT AN' THUH GAS HOUSE---AN' THAT'S ALL!
F' GOSH SAKE! **WHAT** ARE Y' LOOKIN' FOR?
8-21
!
WHAT WE CUM OUT TO SEE, OF COURSE---
?
---THE NEW OBSERVATORY! BUT **THESE** SPY-GLASSES CAN'T LOCATE IT!
!
!
WALT DISNEY

WHEN GOOFY GOES A FISHIN'

HUH, WHEN I GO FISHIN
I DO NO WISHIN'
CAUSE I CATCH FISH —
ON MY LINE
WITH THIS CONTRAPTION
TO MY SATISFACTION.
GOSH! I CATCH
NINE, EVERY TIME!

Goofy's talent for screwy inventions moved from comics to films in the mid-1930s (see page 267)—and also to Disney periodicals. This poem page from *Mickey Mouse Magazine* 59 (1940) caught the contemporary Gottfredson spirit. Art attributed to Bob Grant; image courtesy Walt Disney Photo Library. Original color recreated by David Gerstein.

THE BRAVE LITTLE TAILOR

AND

GAG STRIPS

AUGUST 28, 1938

–

DECEMBER 25, 1938

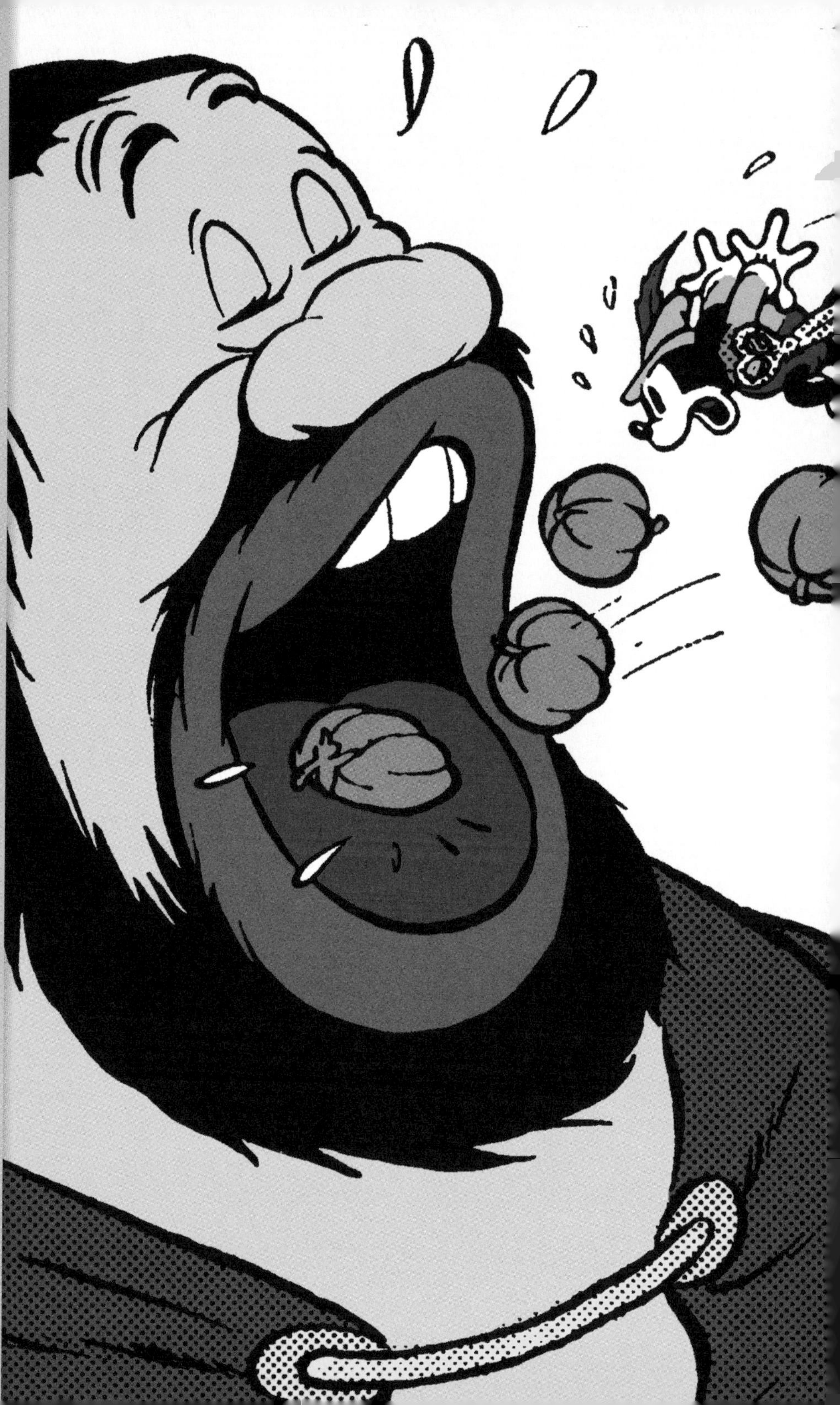

MICKEY MOUSE

REGISTERED U.S. PATENT OFFICE

TAILORING A BETTER MOUSE

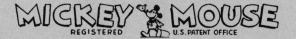

Mickey Mouse's movie star status was dwindling by 1938, with Pluto, Donald, and Goofy regularly stealing the spotlight in Mickey's own pictures. A starring role in his very own epic adventure, *Brave Little Tailor* (1938), proved to remedy that problem. Not only did an interesting characterization of Mickey once again take center stage; so did the strides that the Disney studio had made in the wake of *Snow White and the Seven Dwarfs* (1937), where compelling character animation and technical bravado were pulled off rather effortlessly.

It was only natural to promote a landmark short like *Tailor* as vigorously as possible, and what better place to do so than the *Mickey* Sunday strip? The newspaper Mickey stories would occasionally parallel the animated shorts, but this was the first time a strip continuity mirrored a film point-for-point, right down to reusing actual character poses.

The "Tailor" strip serial also marked a passing of the torch. Floyd Gottfredson only drew the framing strips for the start and end of the continuity. The strips adapting preexisting cartoon scenes were drawn by Manuel Gonzales, a Disney in-betweener and publicity artist up until that time. Gonzales was a natural choice to reinterpret Disney animation, given that he actually did animation work on a regular basis. It was only the beginning of Gonzales' decades-long association with the Disney comic strips.

To modern readers, the newsprint "Tailor" may shrivel in comparison to the animated cartoon. Indeed, a comparison illustrates the significance of animation's collaborative nature, and how ideas are specifically tailored for different media. Without the benefit of good timing, movement, music, and voice work, a potentially powerful visual sequence—like the one Frank Thomas animated on-screen, showing Mickey's embellishment of his fly-swatting deed—is reduced, in the 2 October 1938 strip, to merely static drawings.

Of course, the average Mickey Mouse fan in 1938 was surely not discerning enough to compare two mediums' strengths and weaknesses. Given that a sizable portion—or all—of the "Tailor" strip serial had appeared in print before the short was even released, the strip more than likely accomplished its job of getting readers excited about the cartoon debuting in theaters. The continuity also adds the clever framing device of Mickey taking a break from his "real-life" comics adventures to make an appearance in one of Mr. Disney's films. What better way to remind the public that Mickey was still a Hollywood superstar?

— Thad Komorowski

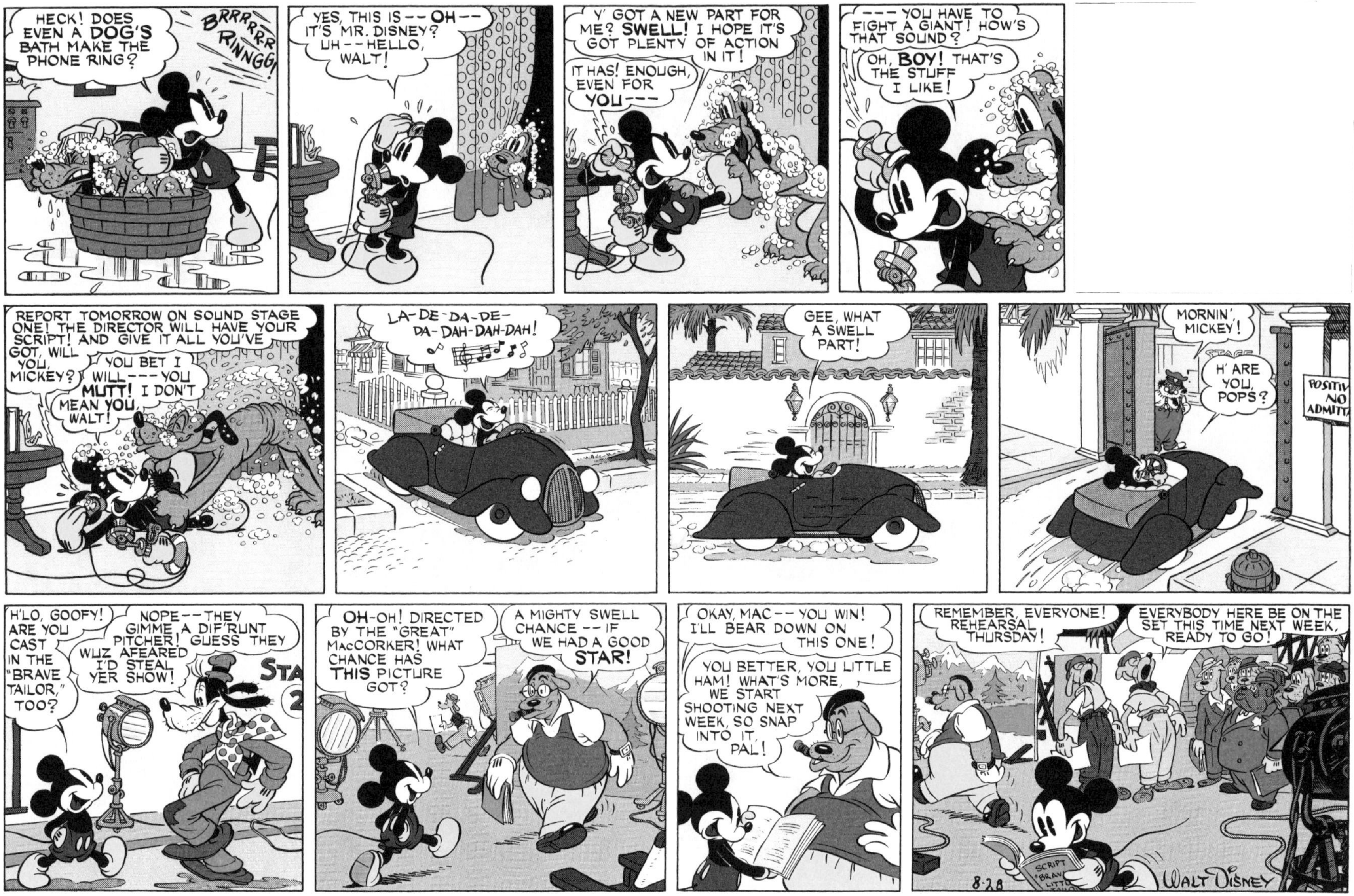
HECK! DOES EVEN A DOG'S BATH MAKE THE PHONE RING?
BRRRRRRR RINNGG!
YES, THIS IS --OH-- IT'S MR. DISNEY? UH--HELLO, WALT!
Y' GOT A NEW PART FOR ME? SWELL! I HOPE IT'S GOT PLENTY OF ACTION IN IT!
IT HAS! ENOUGH, EVEN FOR YOU---
---YOU HAVE TO FIGHT A GIANT! HOW'S THAT SOUND?
OH, BOY! THAT'S THE STUFF I LIKE!
REPORT TOMORROW ON SOUND STAGE ONE! THE DIRECTOR WILL HAVE YOUR SCRIPT! AND GIVE IT ALL YOU'VE GOT, WILL YOU, MICKEY?
YOU BET I WILL---YOU MUTT! I DON'T MEAN YOU, WALT!
LA-DE-DA-DE-DA-DAH-DAH-DAH!
GEE, WHAT A SWELL PART!
MORNIN', MICKEY!
H' ARE YOU, POPS?
H'LO, GOOFY! ARE YOU CAST IN THE "BRAVE TAILOR," TOO?
NOPE--THEY GIMME A DIF'RUNT PITCHER! GUESS THEY WUZ AFEARED I'D STEAL YER SHOW!
OH-OH! DIRECTED BY THE "GREAT" MacCORKER! WHAT CHANCE HAS THIS PICTURE GOT?
A MIGHTY SWELL CHANCE --IF WE HAD A GOOD STAR!
OKAY, MAC-- YOU WIN! I'LL BEAR DOWN ON THIS ONE!
YOU BETTER, YOU LITTLE HAM! WHAT'S MORE, WE START SHOOTING NEXT WEEK, SO SNAP INTO IT, PAL!
REMEMBER, EVERYONE! REHEARSAL THURSDAY!
EVERYBODY HERE BE ON THE SET THIS TIME NEXT WEEK, READY TO GO!
8-28
WALT DISNEY

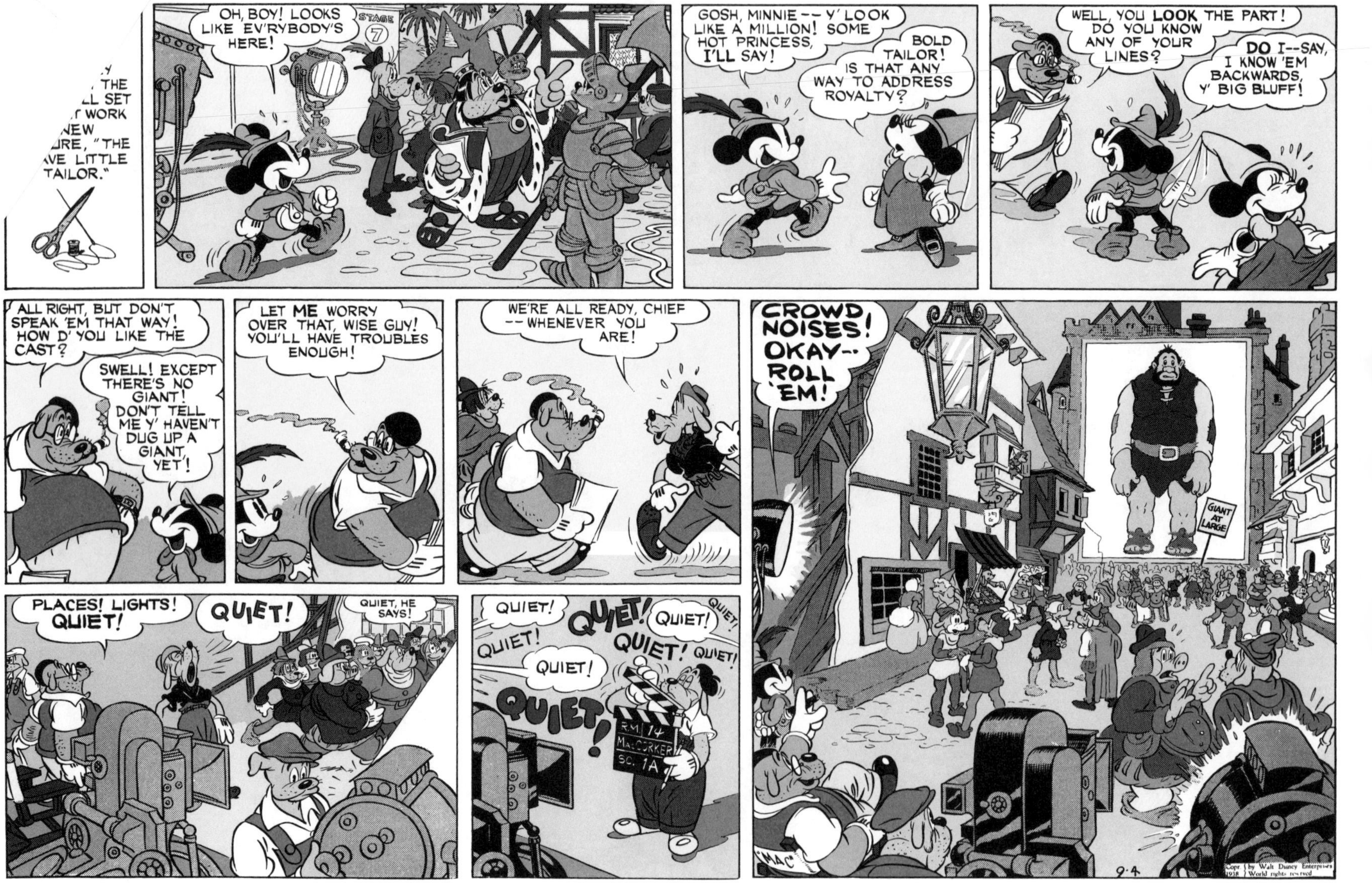
THE
WORK
NEW
"THE
LITTLE
TAILOR."
OH, BOY! LOOKS LIKE EV'RYBODY'S HERE!
STAGE 7
GOSH, MINNIE -- Y' LOOK LIKE A MILLION! SOME HOT PRINCESS, I'LL SAY!
BOLD TAILOR! IS THAT ANY WAY TO ADDRESS ROYALTY?
WELL, YOU LOOK THE PART! DO YOU KNOW ANY OF YOUR LINES?
DO I--SAY, I KNOW 'EM BACKWARDS, Y' BIG BLUFF!
ALL RIGHT, BUT DON'T SPEAK 'EM THAT WAY! HOW D' YOU LIKE THE CAST?
SWELL! EXCEPT THERE'S NO GIANT! DON'T TELL ME Y' HAVEN'T DUG UP A GIANT, YET!
LET ME WORRY OVER THAT, WISE GUY! YOU'LL HAVE TROUBLES ENOUGH!
WE'RE ALL READY, CHIEF -- WHENEVER YOU ARE!
CROWD NOISES! OKAY-- ROLL 'EM!
GIANT AT LARGE
PLACES! LIGHTS! QUIET!
QUIET!
QUIET, HE SAYS!
QUIET!
QUIET!
QUIET!
QUIET!
QUIET!
QUIET!
QUIET!
QUIET!
QUIET!
RM. 14
MacCORKER
SC. 1A
"MAC"
9-4
Copr 1938 by Walt Disney Enterprises World rights reserved

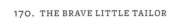

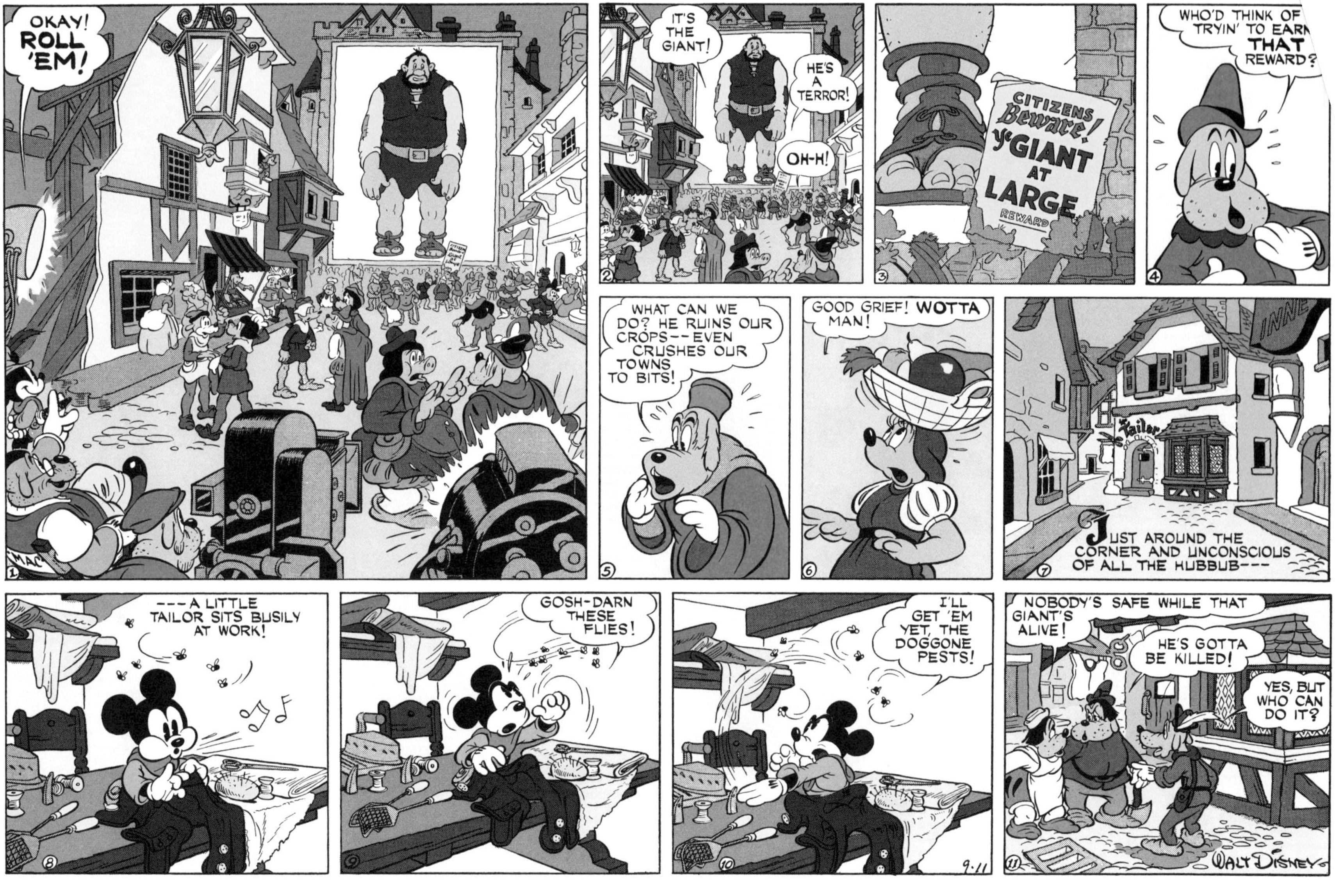

OKAY! ROLL 'EM!
MAC
IT'S THE GIANT!
HE'S A TERROR!
OH-H!
CITIZENS Beware! y' GIANT AT LARGE REWARD
WHO'D THINK OF TRYIN' TO EARN THAT REWARD?
WHAT CAN WE DO? HE RUINS OUR CROPS--EVEN CRUSHES OUR TOWNS TO BITS!
GOOD GRIEF! WOTTA MAN!
INNE
Tailor
JUST AROUND THE CORNER AND UNCONSCIOUS OF ALL THE HUBBUB---
---A LITTLE TAILOR SITS BUSILY AT WORK!
GOSH-DARN THESE FLIES!
I'LL GET 'EM YET, THE DOGGONE PESTS!
9-11
NOBODY'S SAFE WHILE THAT GIANT'S ALIVE!
HE'S GOTTA BE KILLED!
YES, BUT WHO CAN DO IT?
WALT DISNEY

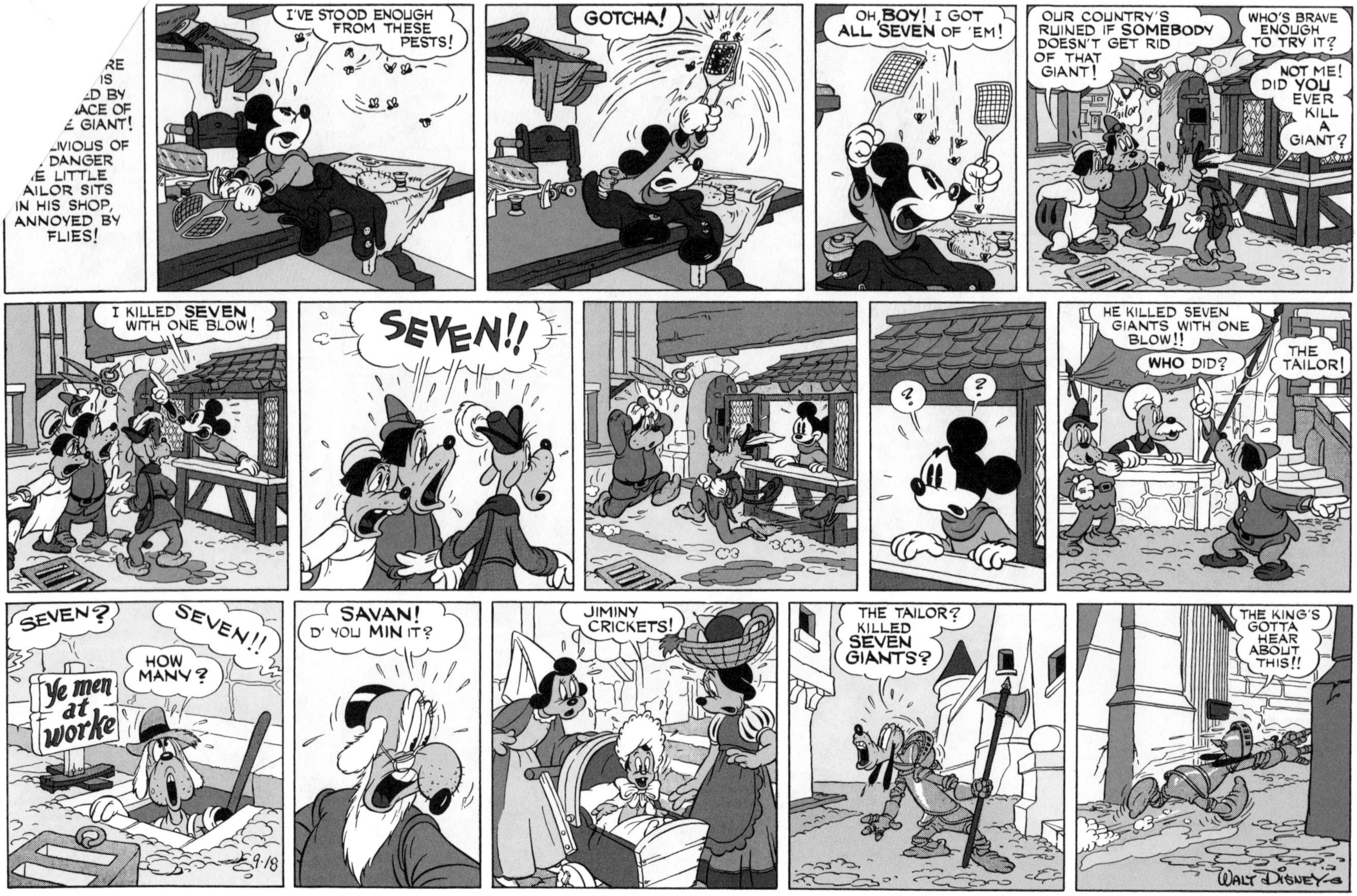
...RE
...IS
...ED BY
...NACE OF
...E GIANT!
...LIVIOUS OF
... DANGER
...E LITTLE
...AILOR SITS
IN HIS SHOP,
ANNOYED BY
FLIES!
I'VE STOOD ENOUGH FROM THESE PESTS!
GOTCHA!
OH, BOY! I GOT ALL SEVEN OF 'EM!
OUR COUNTRY'S RUINED IF SOMEBODY DOESN'T GET RID OF THAT GIANT!
WHO'S BRAVE ENOUGH TO TRY IT?
NOT ME! DID YOU EVER KILL A GIANT?
Ye Tailor
I KILLED SEVEN WITH ONE BLOW!
SEVEN!!
?
?
HE KILLED SEVEN GIANTS WITH ONE BLOW!!
WHO DID?
THE TAILOR!
SEVEN?
SEVEN!!
HOW MANY?
Ye men at worke
9-18
SAVAN! D' YOU MIN IT?
JIMINY CRICKETS!
THE TAILOR? KILLED SEVEN GIANTS?
THE KING'S GOTTA HEAR ABOUT THIS!!
WALT DISNEY

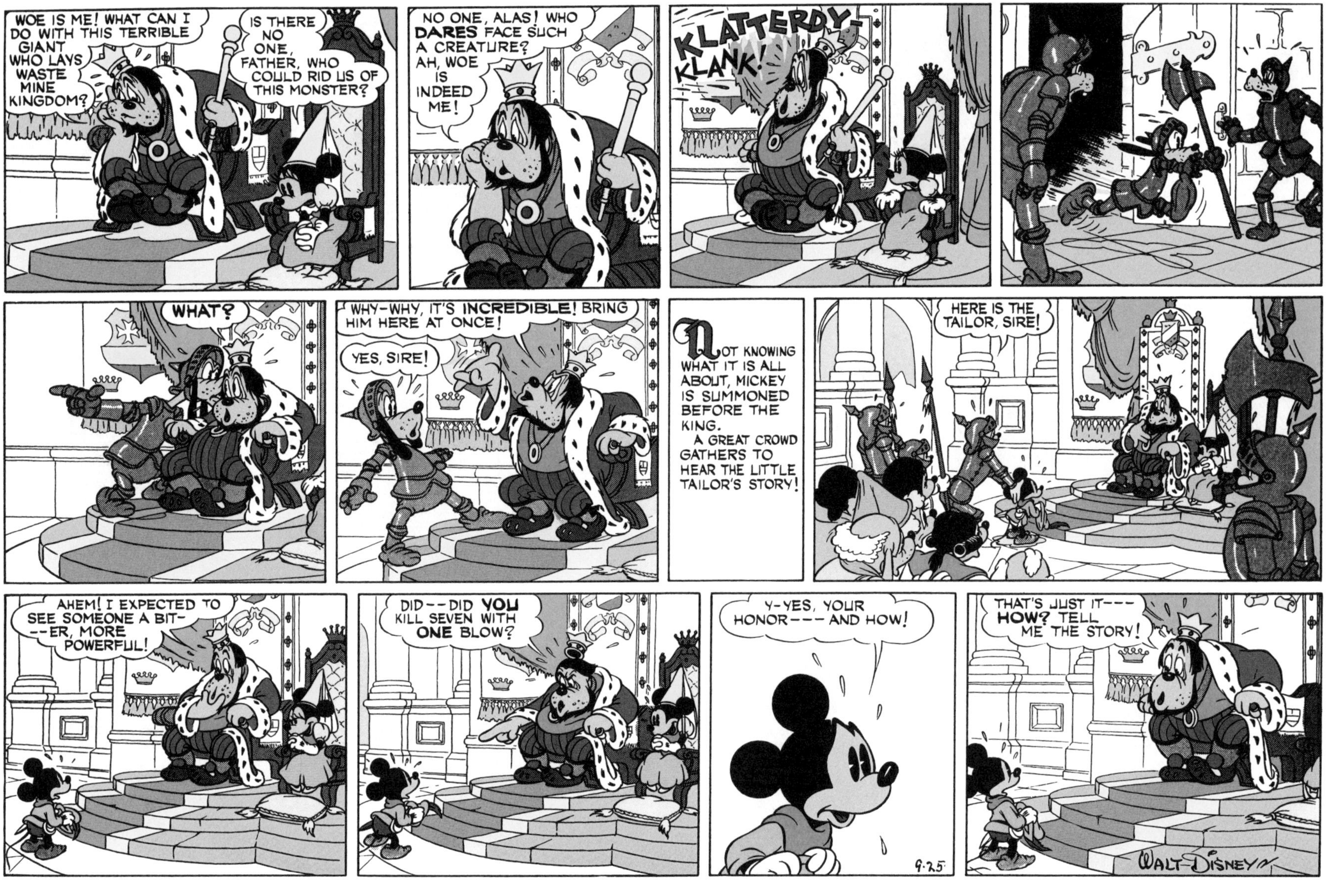
WOE IS ME! WHAT CAN I DO WITH THIS TERRIBLE GIANT WHO LAYS WASTE MINE KINGDOM?
IS THERE NO ONE, FATHER, WHO COULD RID US OF THIS MONSTER?
NO ONE, ALAS! WHO DARES FACE SUCH A CREATURE? AH, WOE IS INDEED ME!
KLATTERDY-KLANK!
WHAT?
WHY-WHY, IT'S INCREDIBLE! BRING HIM HERE AT ONCE!
YES, SIRE!
NOT KNOWING WHAT IT IS ALL ABOUT, MICKEY IS SUMMONED BEFORE THE KING. A GREAT CROWD GATHERS TO HEAR THE LITTLE TAILOR'S STORY!
HERE IS THE TAILOR, SIRE!
AHEM! I EXPECTED TO SEE SOMEONE A BIT- --ER, MORE POWERFUL!
DID--DID YOU KILL SEVEN WITH ONE BLOW?
Y-YES, YOUR HONOR--- AND HOW!
9·25
THAT'S JUST IT--- HOW? TELL ME THE STORY!
WALT DISNEY

ABOVE: The start of a several-week sequence in which Mickey is briefly given a flesh-tone face. Perhaps it was thought that he would more closely resemble his on-screen *Tailor* counterpart, though the conceit misses the start (and end!) of the movie plotline by a couple of weeks.

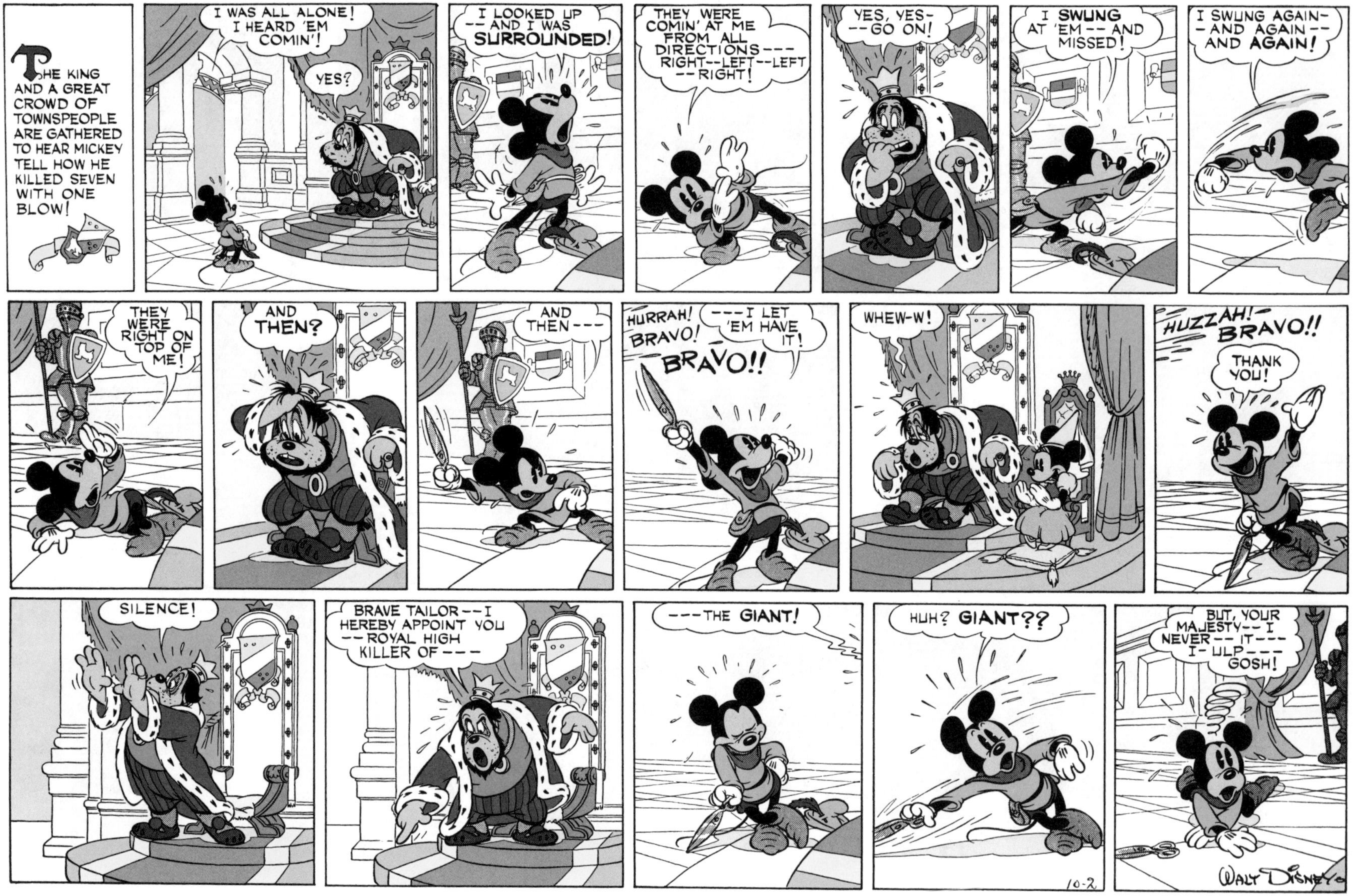
THE KING AND A GREAT CROWD OF TOWNSPEOPLE ARE GATHERED TO HEAR MICKEY TELL HOW HE KILLED SEVEN WITH ONE BLOW!
I WAS ALL ALONE! I HEARD 'EM COMIN'!
YES?
I LOOKED UP -- AND I WAS SURROUNDED!
THEY WERE COMIN' AT ME FROM ALL DIRECTIONS --- RIGHT--LEFT--LEFT --RIGHT!
YES, YES- --GO ON!
I SWUNG AT 'EM -- AND MISSED!
I SWUNG AGAIN- -AND AGAIN-- AND AGAIN!
THEY WERE RIGHT ON TOP OF ME!
AND THEN?
AND THEN---
HURRAH! BRAVO!
---I LET 'EM HAVE IT!
BRAVO!!
WHEW-W!
HUZZAH! BRAVO!!
THANK YOU!
SILENCE!
BRAVE TAILOR--I HEREBY APPOINT YOU --ROYAL HIGH KILLER OF---
---THE GIANT!
HUH? GIANT??
BUT, YOUR MAJESTY-- I NEVER-- IT--- I- ULP--- GOSH!
10-2
WALT DISNEY

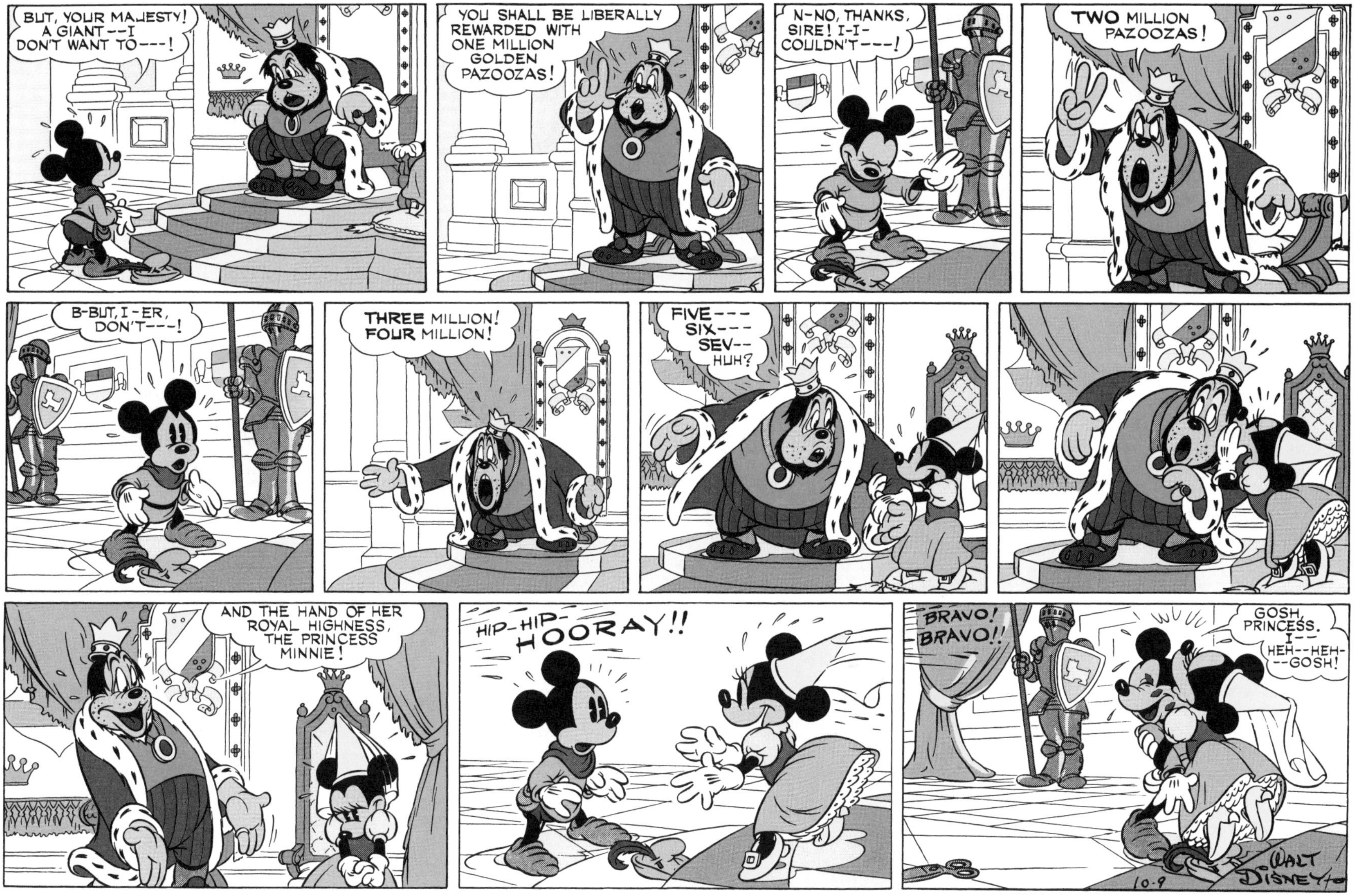

BUT, YOUR MAJESTY! A GIANT--I DON'T WANT TO---!
YOU SHALL BE LIBERALLY REWARDED WITH ONE MILLION GOLDEN PAZOOZAS!
N-NO, THANKS, SIRE! I-I-COULDN'T---!
TWO MILLION PAZOOZAS!
B-BUT, I-ER, DON'T---!
THREE MILLION! FOUR MILLION!
FIVE--- SIX--- SEV-- HUH?
AND THE HAND OF HER ROYAL HIGHNESS, THE PRINCESS MINNIE!
HIP-HIP-HOORAY!!
BRAVO! BRAVO!!
GOSH, PRINCESS. I-- HEH--HEH--GOSH!
10-9
WALT DISNEY

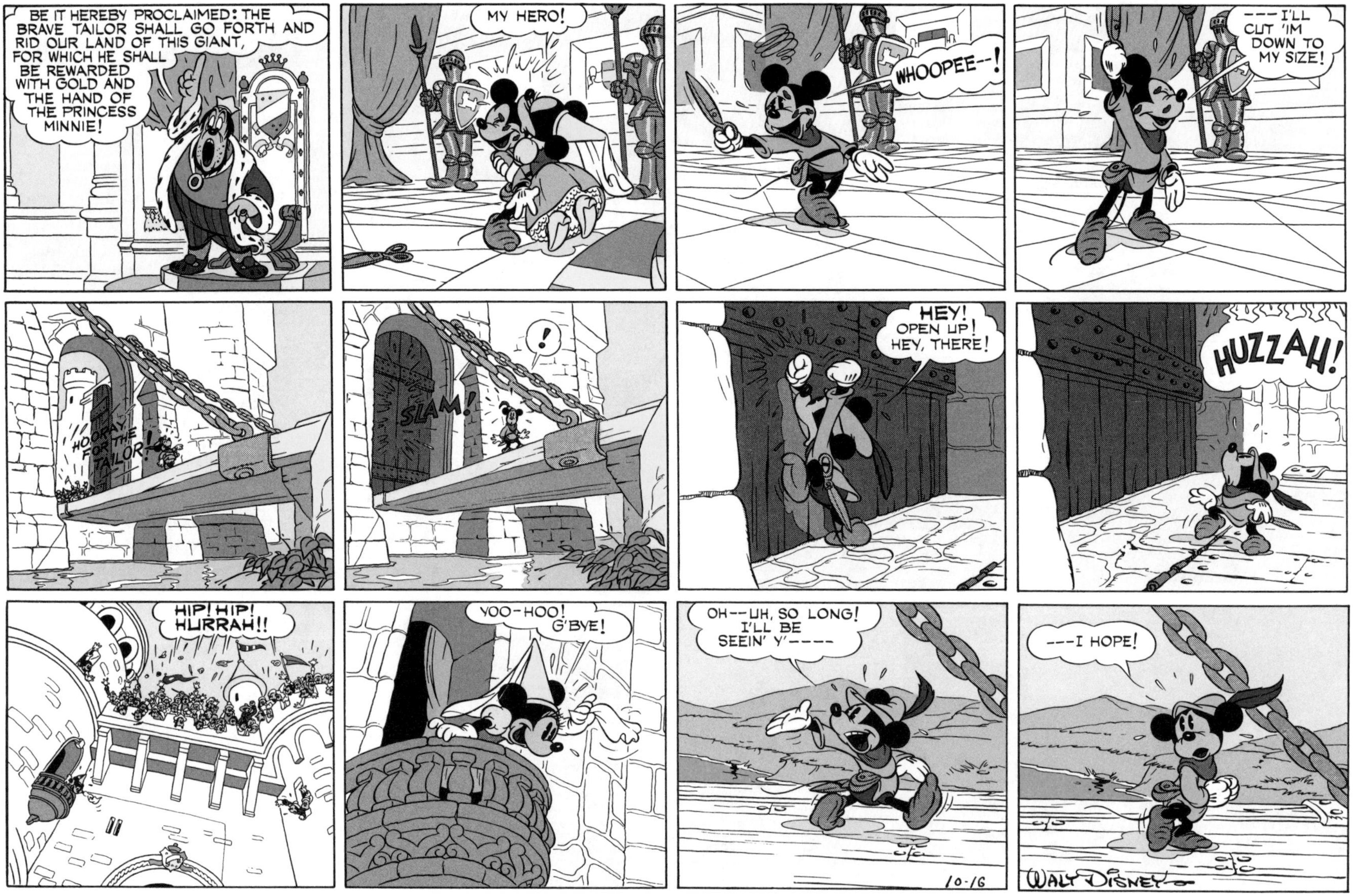

BE IT HEREBY PROCLAIMED: THE BRAVE TAILOR SHALL GO FORTH AND RID OUR LAND OF THIS GIANT, FOR WHICH HE SHALL BE REWARDED WITH GOLD AND THE HAND OF THE PRINCESS MINNIE!
MY HERO!
WHOOPEE--!
---I'LL CUT 'IM DOWN TO MY SIZE!
HOORAY FOR THE TAILOR!
SLAM!
!
HEY! OPEN UP! HEY, THERE!
HUZZAH!
HIP! HIP! HURRAH!!
YOO-HOO! G'BYE!
OH--UH, SO LONG! I'LL BE SEEIN' Y'----
10-16
---I HOPE!
WALT DISNEY

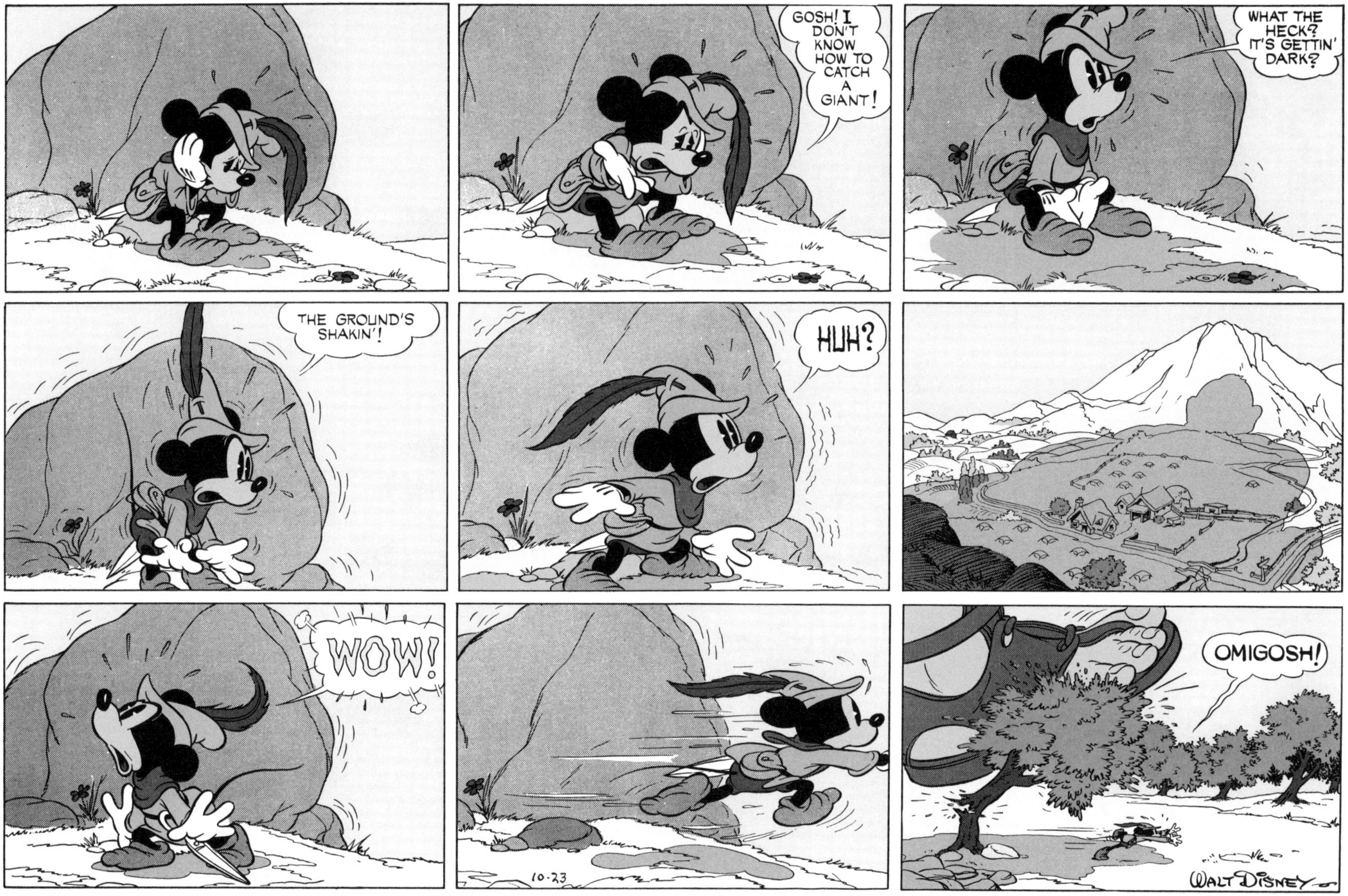
GOSH! I DON'T KNOW HOW TO CATCH A GIANT!
WHAT THE HECK? IT'S GETTIN' DARK?
THE GROUND'S SHAKIN'!
HUH?
WOW!
10-23
OMIGOSH!
WALT DISNEY

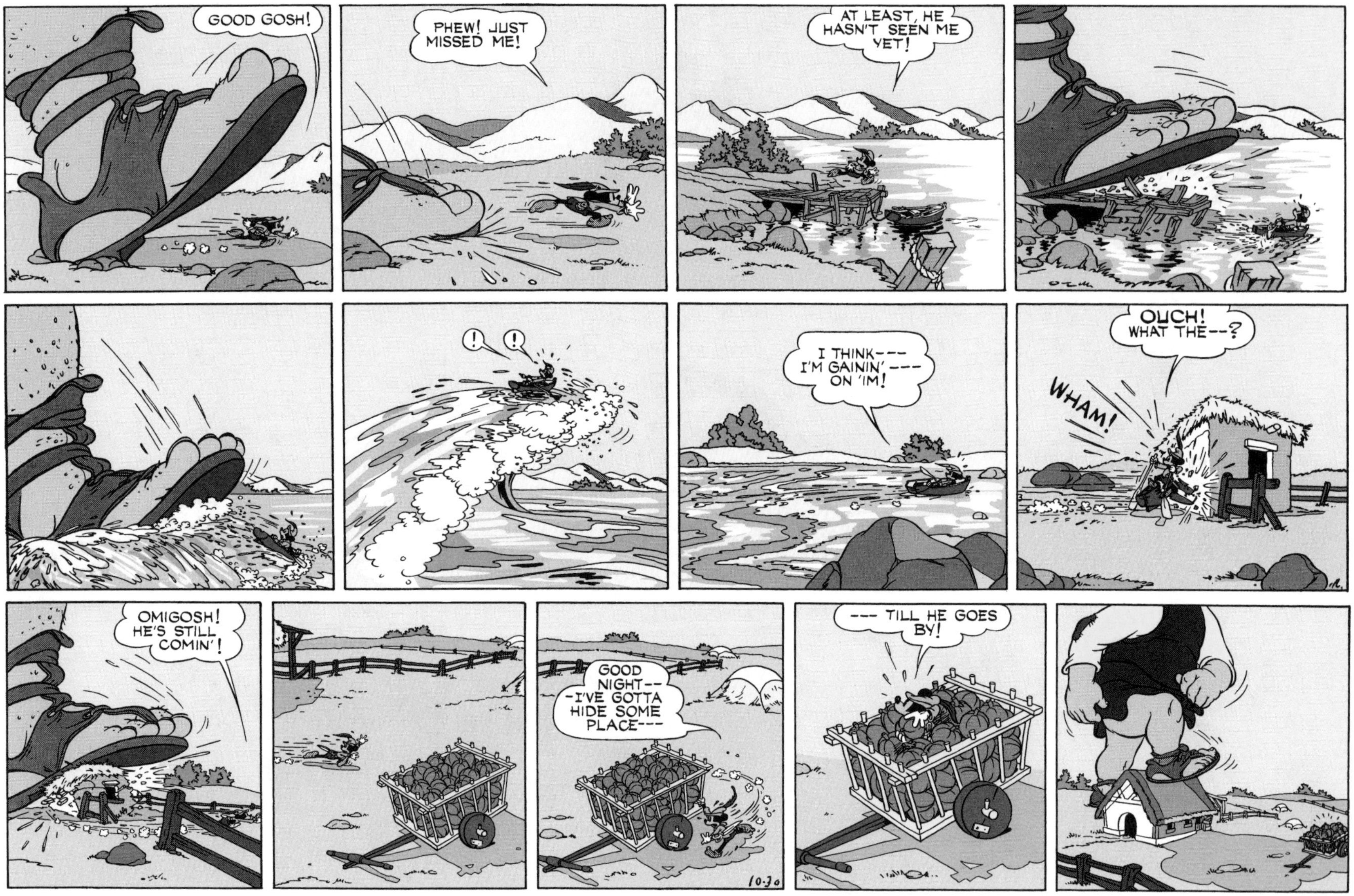
GOOD GOSH!
PHEW! JUST MISSED ME!
AT LEAST, HE HASN'T SEEN ME YET!
! !
I THINK--- I'M GAININ' --- ON 'IM!
WHAM!
OUCH! WHAT THE--?
OMIGOSH! HE'S STILL COMIN'!
GOOD NIGHT-- -I'VE GOTTA HIDE SOME PLACE---
10-30
--- TILL HE GOES BY!

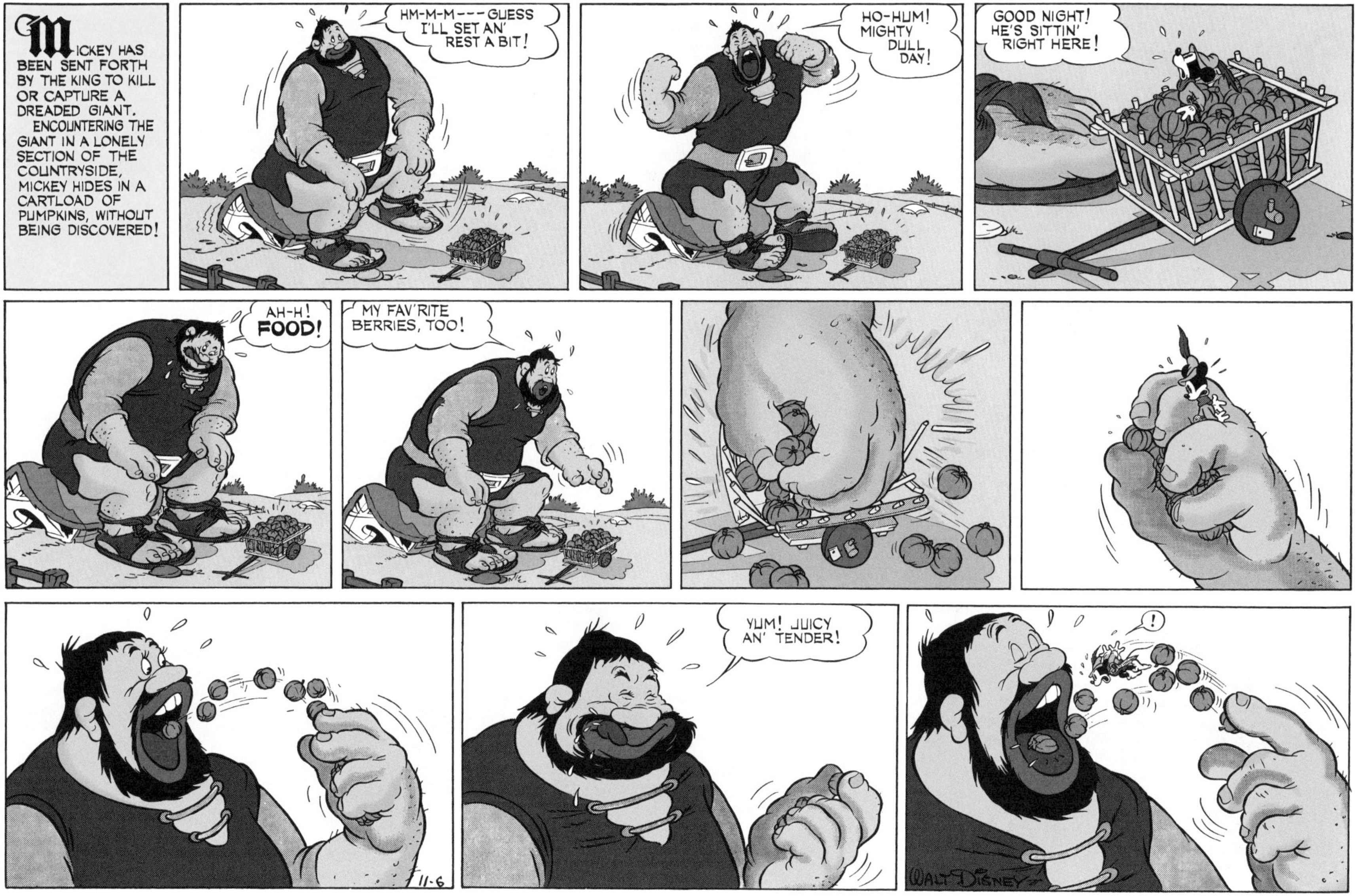

MICKEY HAS BEEN SENT FORTH BY THE KING TO KILL OR CAPTURE A DREADED GIANT.
ENCOUNTERING THE GIANT IN A LONELY SECTION OF THE COUNTRYSIDE, MICKEY HIDES IN A CARTLOAD OF PUMPKINS, WITHOUT BEING DISCOVERED!
HM-M-M--- GUESS I'LL SET AN' REST A BIT!
HO-HUM! MIGHTY DULL DAY!
GOOD NIGHT! HE'S SITTIN' RIGHT HERE!
AH-H! FOOD!
MY FAV'RITE BERRIES, TOO!
YUM! JUICY AN' TENDER!
!
11-6
WALT DISNEY

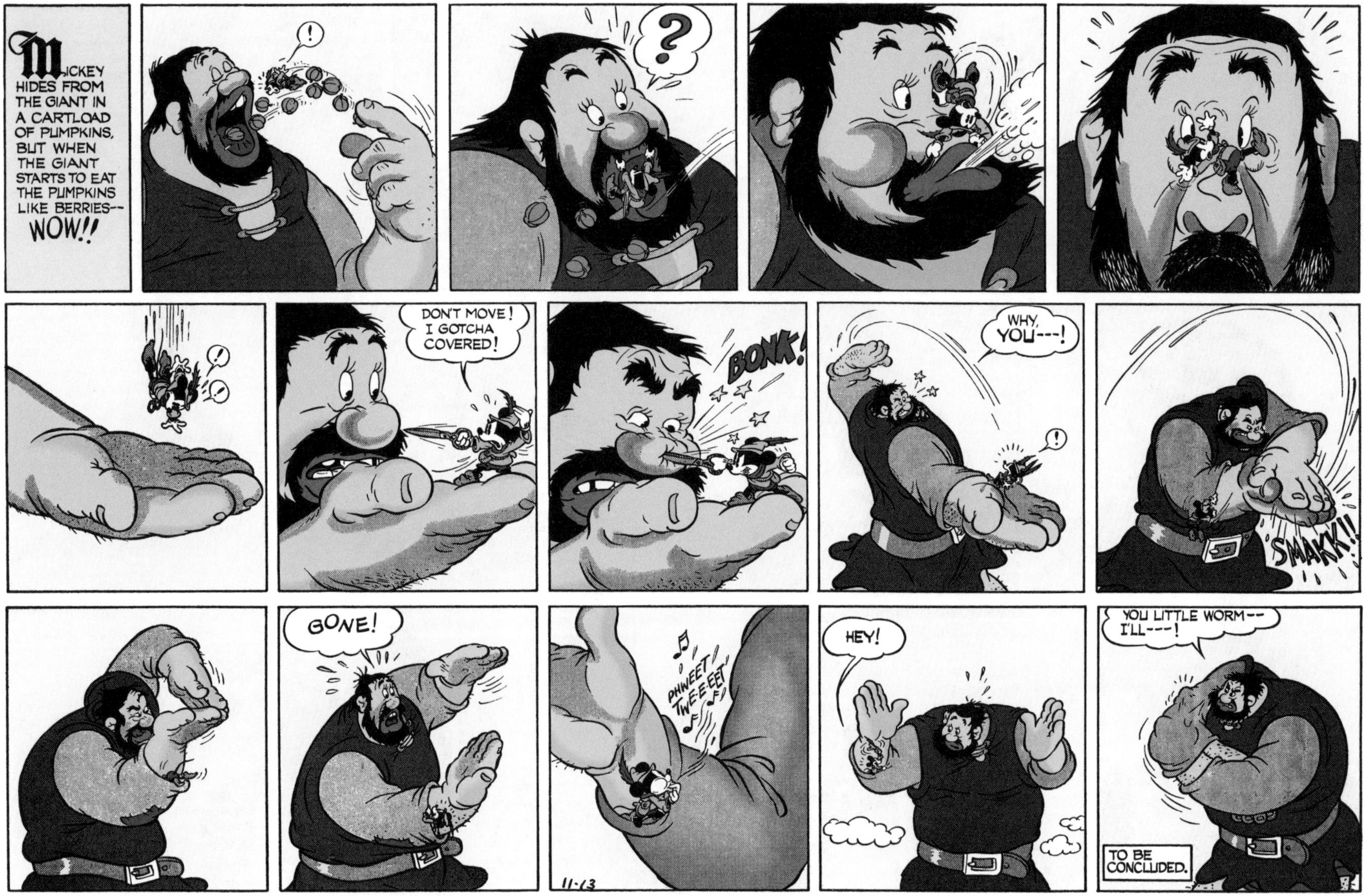
MICKEY HIDES FROM THE GIANT IN A CARTLOAD OF PUMPKINS, BUT WHEN THE GIANT STARTS TO EAT THE PUMPKINS LIKE BERRIES--
WOW!!
!
?
!
!
DON'T MOVE! I GOTCHA COVERED!
BONK!
WHY, YOU---!
!
SMAKK!!
GONE!
PHWEET TWE-E-EET
11-13
HEY!
YOU LITTLE WORM-- I'LL---!
TO BE CONCLUDED.

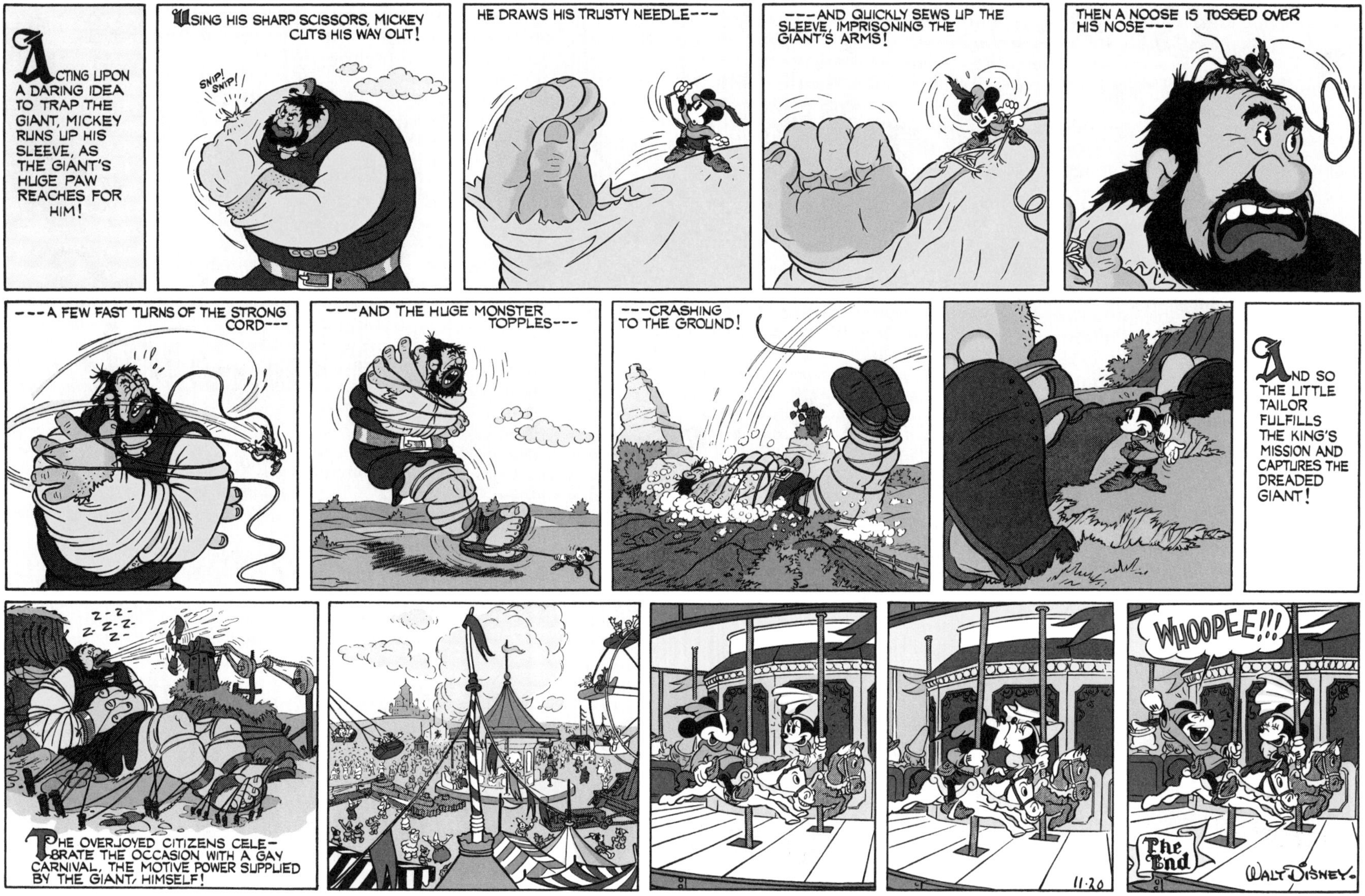

ACTING UPON A DARING IDEA TO TRAP THE GIANT, MICKEY RUNS UP HIS SLEEVE, AS THE GIANT'S HUGE PAW REACHES FOR HIM!
USING HIS SHARP SCISSORS, MICKEY CUTS HIS WAY OUT!
SNIP! SNIP!
HE DRAWS HIS TRUSTY NEEDLE---
---AND QUICKLY SEWS UP THE SLEEVE, IMPRISONING THE GIANT'S ARMS!
THEN A NOOSE IS TOSSED OVER HIS NOSE---
---A FEW FAST TURNS OF THE STRONG CORD---
---AND THE HUGE MONSTER TOPPLES---
---CRASHING TO THE GROUND!
AND SO THE LITTLE TAILOR FULFILLS THE KING'S MISSION AND CAPTURES THE DREADED GIANT!
Z-Z- Z-Z-Z- Z-
THE OVERJOYED CITIZENS CELEBRATE THE OCCASION WITH A GAY CARNIVAL, THE MOTIVE POWER SUPPLIED BY THE GIANT, HIMSELF!
11-20
WHOOPEE!!!
The End
WALT DISNEY

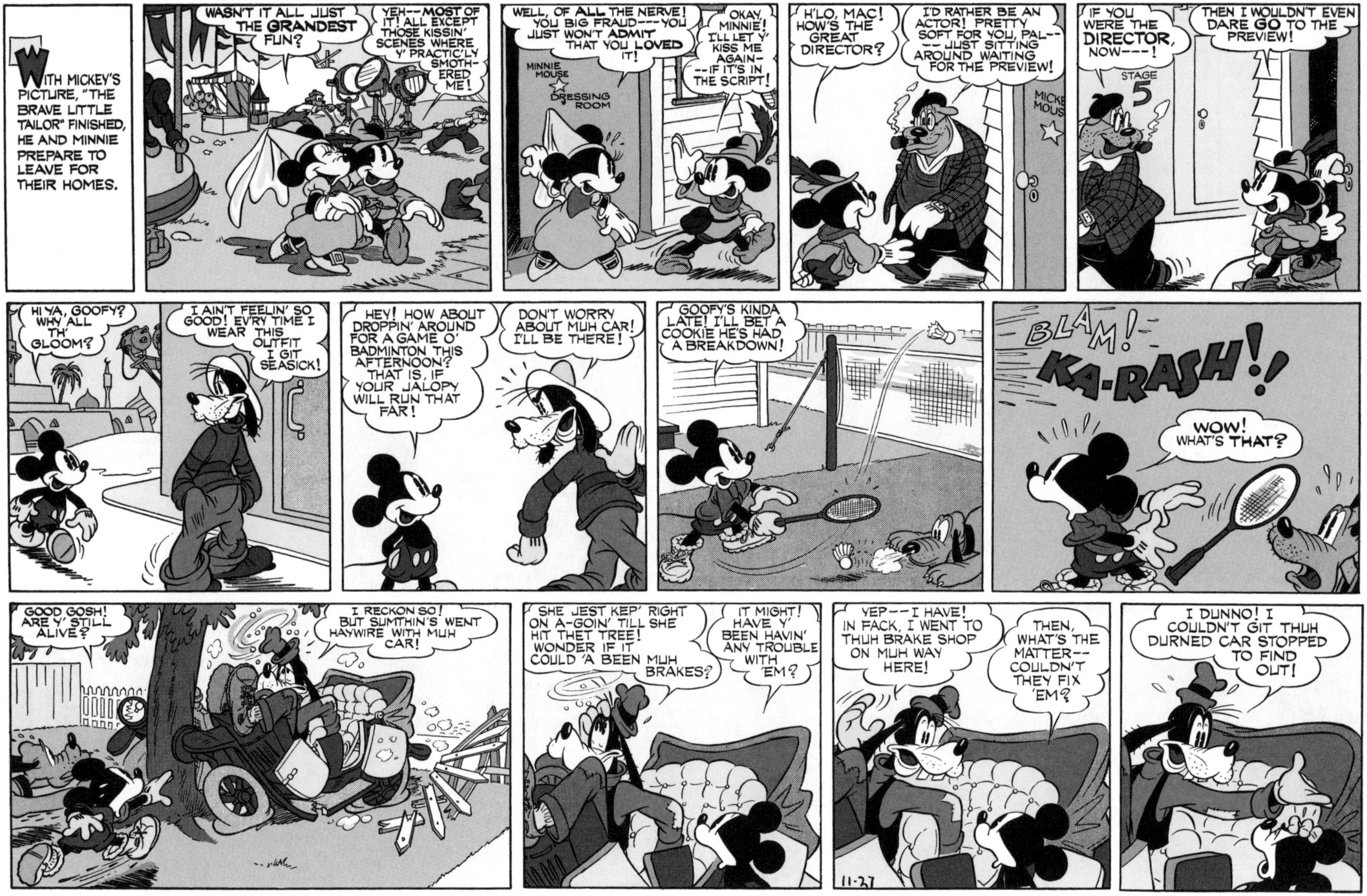
WITH MICKEY'S PICTURE, "THE BRAVE LITTLE TAILOR" FINISHED, HE AND MINNIE PREPARE TO LEAVE FOR THEIR HOMES.
WASN'T IT ALL JUST THE GRANDEST FUN?
YEH--MOST OF IT! ALL EXCEPT THOSE KISSIN' SCENES WHERE Y' PRACTIC'LY SMOTHERED ME!
WELL, OF ALL THE NERVE! YOU BIG FRAUD---YOU JUST WON'T ADMIT THAT YOU LOVED IT!
MINNIE MOUSE DRESSING ROOM
OKAY, MINNIE! I'LL LET Y' KISS ME AGAIN--IF IT'S IN THE SCRIPT!
H'LO, MAC! HOW'S THE GREAT DIRECTOR?
I'D RATHER BE AN ACTOR! PRETTY SOFT FOR YOU, PAL----JUST SITTING AROUND WAITING FOR THE PREVIEW!
IF YOU WERE THE DIRECTOR, NOW---!
STAGE 5
THEN I WOULDN'T EVEN DARE GO TO THE PREVIEW!
HI YA, GOOFY? WHY ALL TH' GLOOM?
I AIN'T FEELIN' SO GOOD! EV'RY TIME I WEAR THIS OUTFIT I GIT SEASICK!
HEY! HOW ABOUT DROPPIN' AROUND FOR A GAME O' BADMINTON THIS AFTERNOON? THAT IS, IF YOUR JALOPY WILL RUN THAT FAR!
DON'T WORRY ABOUT MUH CAR! I'LL BE THERE!
GOOFY'S KINDA LATE! I'LL BET A COOKIE HE'S HAD A BREAKDOWN!
BLAM!
KA-RASH!!
WOW! WHAT'S THAT?
GOOD GOSH! ARE Y' STILL ALIVE?
I RECKON SO! BUT SUMTHIN'S WENT HAYWIRE WITH MUH CAR!
SHE JEST KEP' RIGHT ON A-GOIN' TILL SHE HIT THET TREE! WONDER IF IT COULD 'A BEEN MUH BRAKES?
IT MIGHT! HAVE Y' BEEN HAVIN' ANY TROUBLE WITH 'EM?
YEP--I HAVE! IN FACK, I WENT TO THUH BRAKE SHOP ON MUH WAY HERE!
THEN, WHAT'S THE MATTER--COULDN'T THEY FIX 'EM?
11-27
I DUNNO! I COULDN'T GIT THUH DURNED CAR STOPPED TO FIND OUT!

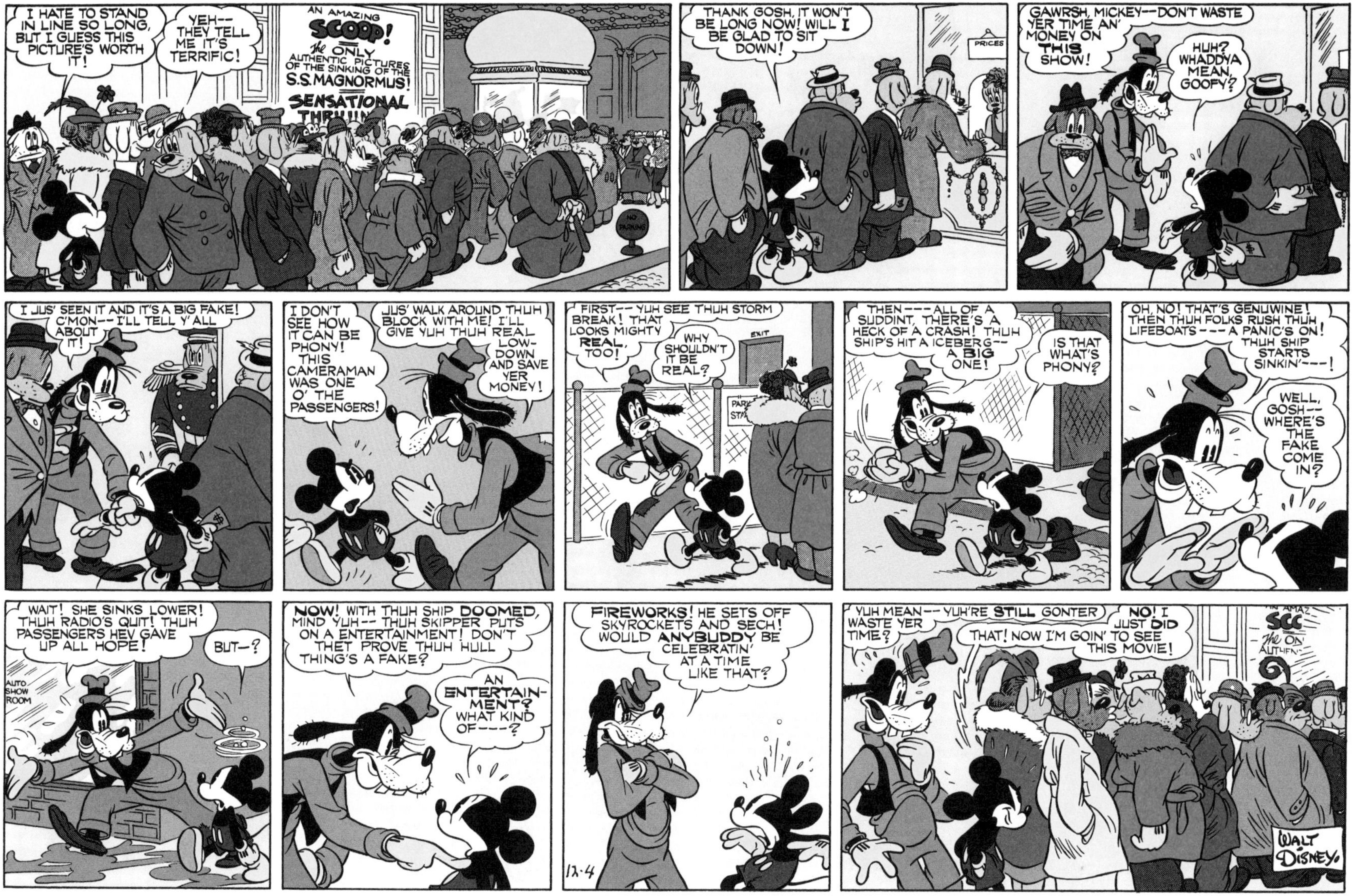

I HATE TO STAND IN LINE SO LONG, BUT I GUESS THIS PICTURE'S WORTH IT!
YEH-- THEY TELL ME IT'S TERRIFIC!
AN AMAZING SCOOP! the ONLY AUTHENTIC PICTURES OF THE SINKING OF THE S.S. MAGNORMUS!
SENSATIONAL
THANK GOSH, IT WON'T BE LONG NOW! WILL I BE GLAD TO SIT DOWN!
PRICES
GAWRSH, MICKEY--DON'T WASTE YER TIME AN' MONEY ON THIS SHOW!
HUH? WHADDYA MEAN, GOOFY?
I JUS' SEEN IT AND IT'S A BIG FAKE! C'MON-- I'LL TELL Y'ALL ABOUT IT!
I DON'T SEE HOW IT CAN BE PHONY! THIS CAMERAMAN WAS ONE O' THE PASSENGERS!
JUS' WALK AROUND THUH BLOCK WITH ME! I'LL GIVE YUH THUH REAL LOW-DOWN AND SAVE YER MONEY!
FIRST-- YUH SEE THUH STORM BREAK! THAT LOOKS MIGHTY REAL, TOO!
WHY SHOULDN'T IT BE REAL?
EXIT
THEN---ALL OF A SUDDINT, THERE'S A HECK OF A CRASH! THUH SHIP'S HIT A ICEBERG-- A BIG ONE!
IS THAT WHAT'S PHONY?
OH, NO! THAT'S GENUWINE! THEN THUH FOLKS RUSH THUH LIFEBOATS---A PANIC'S ON! THUH SHIP STARTS SINKIN'---!
WELL, GOSH-- WHERE'S THE FAKE COME IN?
WAIT! SHE SINKS LOWER! THUH RADIO'S QUIT! THUH PASSENGERS HEV GAVE UP ALL HOPE!
BUT--?
AUTO SHOW ROOM
NOW! WITH THUH SHIP DOOMED, MIND YUH-- THUH SKIPPER PUTS ON A ENTERTAINMENT! DON'T THET PROVE THUH HULL THING'S A FAKE?
AN ENTERTAIN-MENT? WHAT KIND OF---?
FIREWORKS! HE SETS OFF SKYROCKETS AND SECH! WOULD ANYBUDDY BE CELEBRATIN' AT A TIME LIKE THAT?
12·4
YUH MEAN-- YUH'RE STILL GONTER WASTE YER TIME?
NO! I JUST DID THAT! NOW I'M GOIN' TO SEE THIS MOVIE!
WALT DISNEY

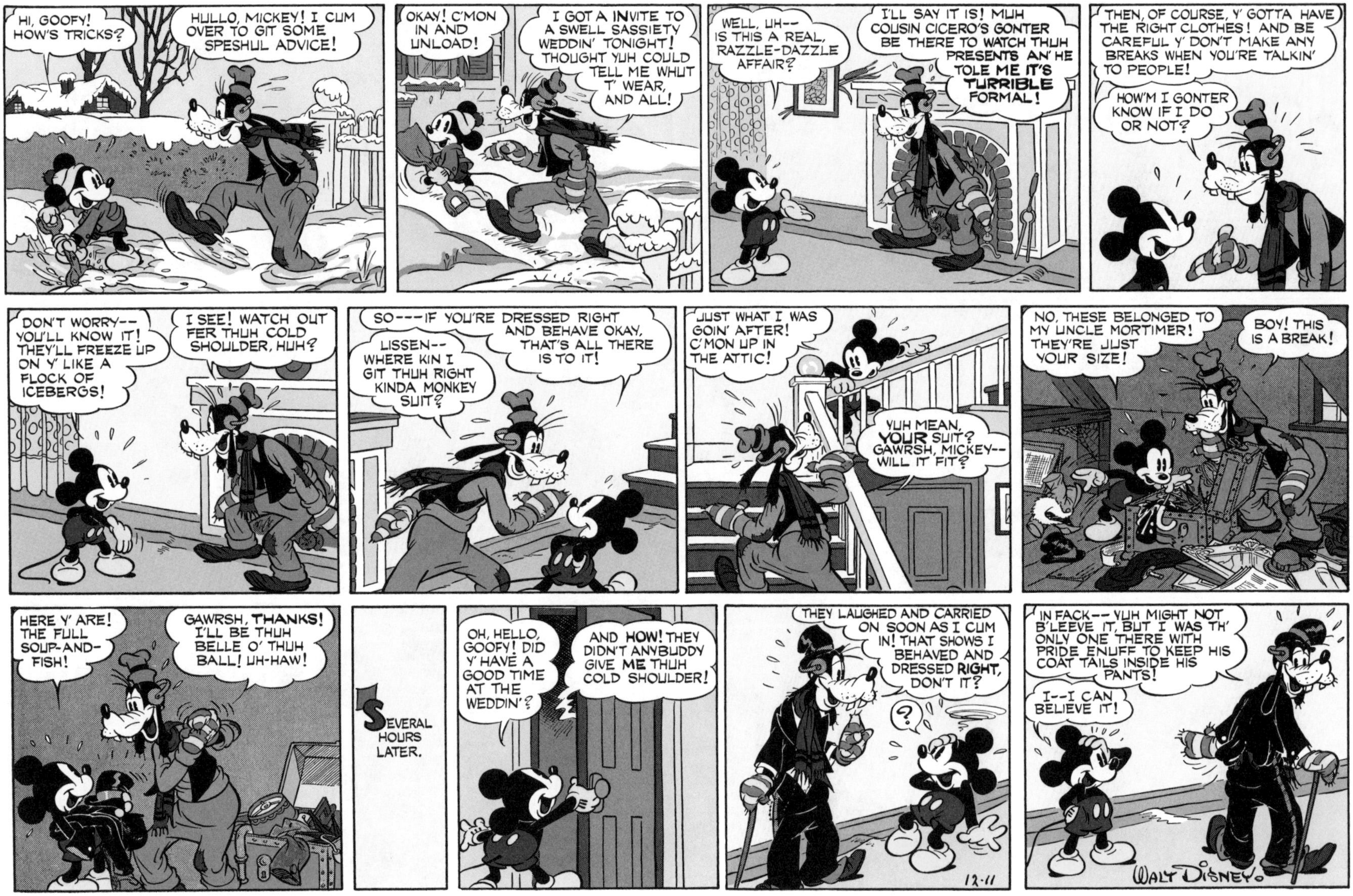
HI, GOOFY! HOW'S TRICKS?
HULLO, MICKEY! I CUM OVER TO GIT SOME SPESHUL ADVICE!
OKAY! C'MON IN AND UNLOAD!
I GOT A INVITE TO A SWELL SASSIETY WEDDIN' TONIGHT! THOUGHT YUH COULD TELL ME WHUT T' WEAR, AND ALL!
WELL, UH-- IS THIS A REAL, RAZZLE-DAZZLE AFFAIR?
I'LL SAY IT IS! MUH COUSIN CICERO'S GONTER BE THERE TO WATCH THUH PRESENTS AN' HE TOLE ME IT'S TURRIBLE FORMAL!
THEN, OF COURSE, Y' GOTTA HAVE THE RIGHT CLOTHES! AND BE CAREFUL Y' DON'T MAKE ANY BREAKS WHEN YOU'RE TALKIN' TO PEOPLE!
HOW'M I GONTER KNOW IF I DO OR NOT?
DON'T WORRY-- YOU'LL KNOW IT! THEY'LL FREEZE UP ON Y' LIKE A FLOCK OF ICEBERGS!
I SEE! WATCH OUT FER THUH COLD SHOULDER, HUH?
SO---IF YOU'RE DRESSED RIGHT AND BEHAVE OKAY, THAT'S ALL THERE IS TO IT!
LISSEN-- WHERE KIN I GIT THUH RIGHT KINDA MONKEY SUIT?
JUST WHAT I WAS GOIN' AFTER! C'MON UP IN THE ATTIC!
YUH MEAN, YOUR SUIT? GAWRSH, MICKEY-- WILL IT FIT?
NO, THESE BELONGED TO MY UNCLE MORTIMER! THEY'RE JUST YOUR SIZE!
BOY! THIS IS A BREAK!
HERE Y' ARE! THE FULL SOUP-AND-FISH!
GAWRSH, THANKS! I'LL BE THUH BELLE O' THUH BALL! UH-HAW!
SEVERAL HOURS LATER.
OH, HELLO, GOOFY! DID Y' HAVE A GOOD TIME AT THE WEDDIN'?
AND HOW! THEY DIDN'T ANYBUDDY GIVE ME THUH COLD SHOULDER!
THEY LAUGHED AND CARRIED ON SOON AS I CUM IN! THAT SHOWS I BEHAVED AND DRESSED RIGHT, DON'T IT?
?
12-11
IN FACK-- YUH MIGHT NOT B'LEEVE IT, BUT I WAS TH' ONLY ONE THERE WITH PRIDE ENUFF TO KEEP HIS COAT TAILS INSIDE HIS PANTS!
I--I CAN BELIEVE IT!
WALT DISNEY

184. GOOFY AMUSED THEM WITH HIS TAILS

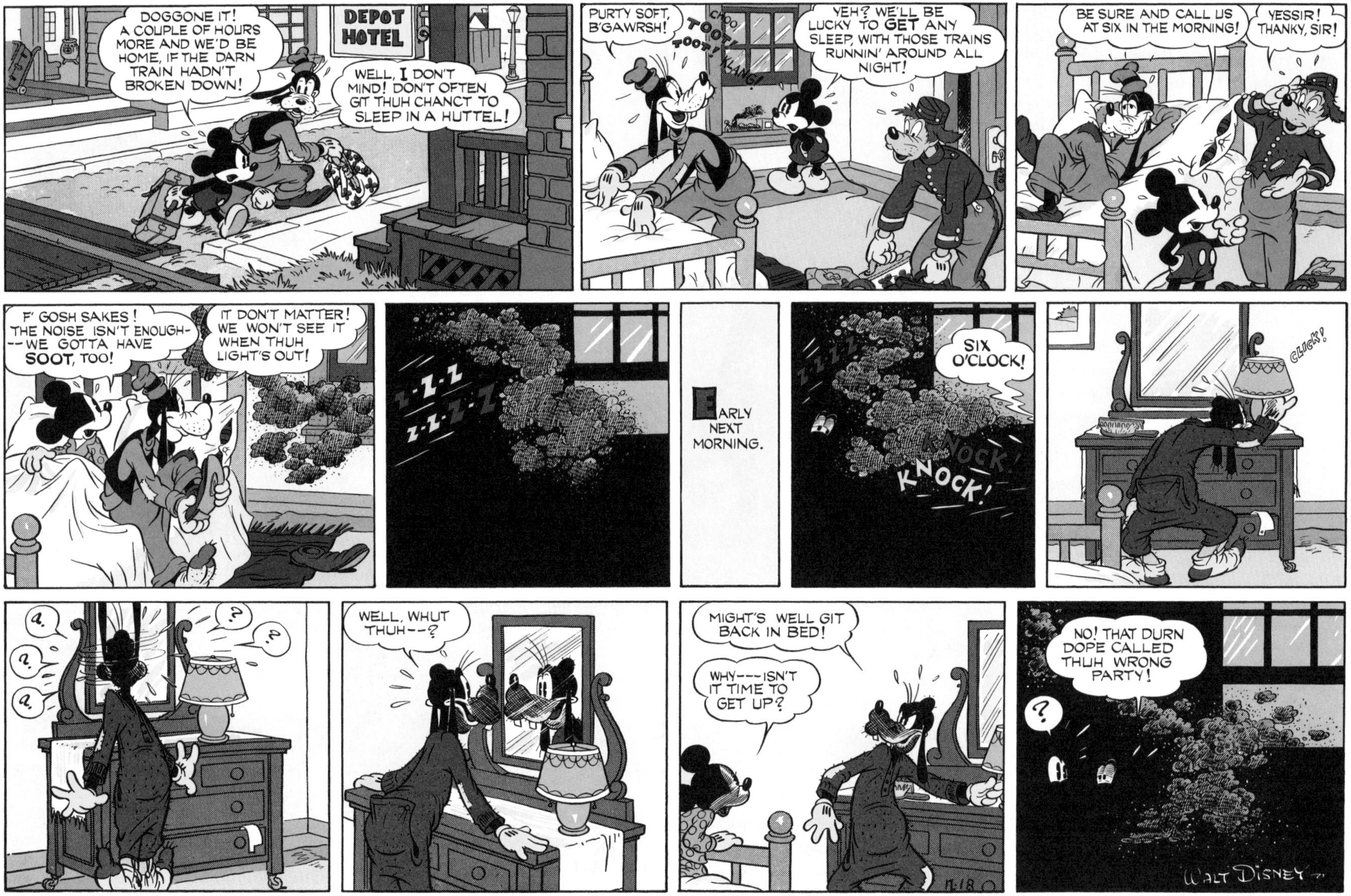

DOGGONE IT! A COUPLE OF HOURS MORE AND WE'D BE HOME, IF THE DARN TRAIN HADN'T BROKEN DOWN!
DEPOT HOTEL
WELL, I DON'T MIND! DON'T OFTEN GIT THUH CHANCT TO SLEEP IN A HUTTEL!
PURTY SOFT, B'GAWRSH!
TOOT! TOOT!
YEH? WE'LL BE LUCKY TO GET ANY SLEEP, WITH THOSE TRAINS RUNNIN' AROUND ALL NIGHT!
BE SURE AND CALL US AT SIX IN THE MORNING!
YESSIR! THANKY, SIR!
F' GOSH SAKES! THE NOISE ISN'T ENOUGH--WE GOTTA HAVE SOOT, TOO!
IT DON'T MATTER! WE WON'T SEE IT WHEN THUH LIGHT'S OUT!
Z-Z-Z
Z-Z-Z-Z
EARLY NEXT MORNING.
SIX O'CLOCK!
KNOCK! KNOCK!
CLICK!
WELL, WHUT THUH--?
MIGHT'S WELL GIT BACK IN BED!
WHY---ISN'T IT TIME TO GET UP?
NO! THAT DURN DOPE CALLED THUH WRONG PARTY!
WALT DISNEY

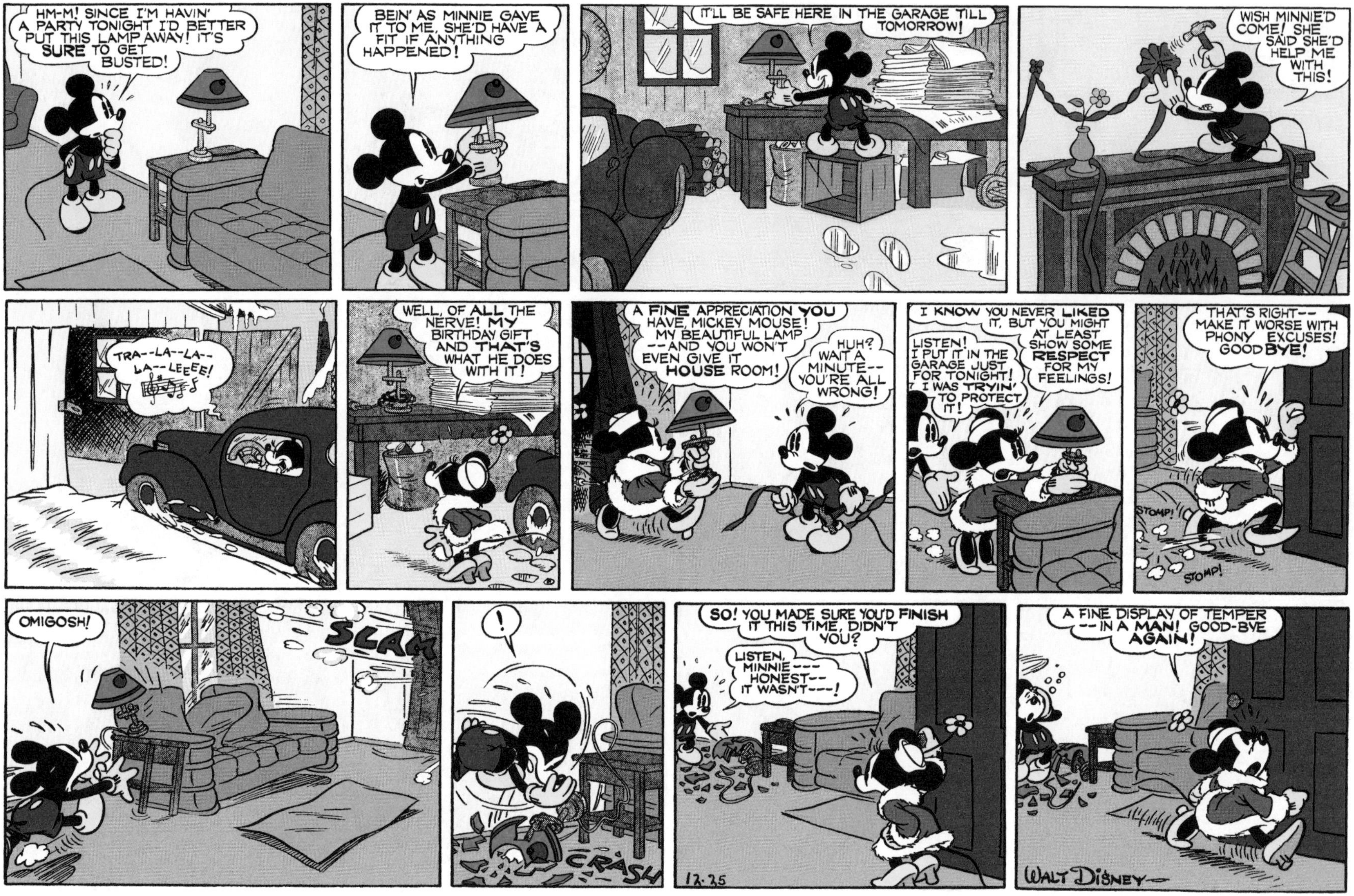
HM-M! SINCE I'M HAVIN' A PARTY TONIGHT I'D BETTER PUT THIS LAMP AWAY! IT'S SURE TO GET BUSTED!
BEIN' AS MINNIE GAVE IT TO ME, SHE'D HAVE A FIT IF ANYTHING HAPPENED!
IT'LL BE SAFE HERE IN THE GARAGE TILL TOMORROW!
WISH MINNIE'D COME! SHE SAID SHE'D HELP ME WITH THIS!
TRA--LA--LA--LA--LEEEE!
WELL, OF ALL THE NERVE! MY BIRTHDAY GIFT AND THAT'S WHAT HE DOES WITH IT!
A FINE APPRECIATION YOU HAVE, MICKEY MOUSE! MY BEAUTIFUL LAMP --AND YOU WON'T EVEN GIVE IT HOUSE ROOM!
HUH? WAIT A MINUTE-- YOU'RE ALL WRONG!
I KNOW YOU NEVER LIKED IT, BUT YOU MIGHT AT LEAST SHOW SOME RESPECT FOR MY FEELINGS!
LISTEN! I PUT IT IN THE GARAGE JUST FOR TONIGHT! I WAS TRYIN' TO PROTECT IT!
THAT'S RIGHT-- MAKE IT WORSE WITH PHONY EXCUSES! GOOD BYE!
STOMP!
STOMP!
OMIGOSH!
SLAM
!
CRASH
SO! YOU MADE SURE YOU'D FINISH IT THIS TIME, DIDN'T YOU?
LISTEN, MINNIE--- HONEST-- IT WASN'T---!
12-25
A FINE DISPLAY OF TEMPER --IN A MAN! GOOD-BYE AGAIN!
WALT DISNEY

LATER YEARS: GOTTFREDSON FILL-INS

JUNE 17, 1956

–

SEPTEMBER 19, 1976

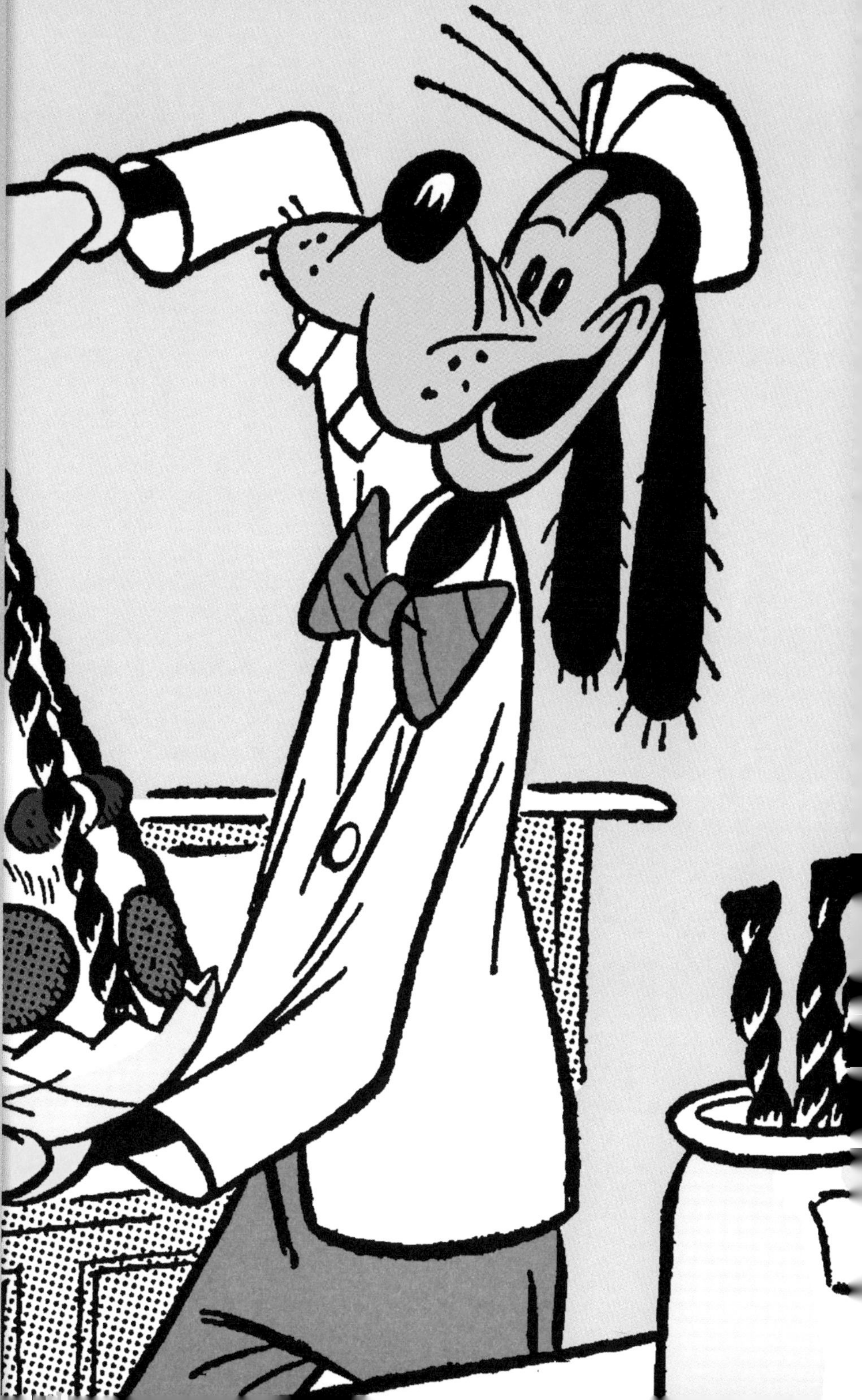

MICKEY MOUSE

REGISTERED U.S. PATENT OFFICE

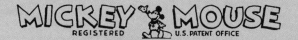

MOUSE SOUP

Floyd Gottfredson finished his ongoing *Mickey Mouse* Sunday work at the end of 1938, but his involvement with the series was hardly over. As Comic Strip Department manager, Gottfredson supervised Manuel Gonzales' Sunday *Mickey* work into the mid-1940s. Then later—after passing his managerial hat to Frank Reilly—Gottfredson had a little more time for special projects; among them, drawing occasional *Mickey* Sundays when Gonzales was not available.

One might hope to discover some lost classics among this later output; but while well-drawn, the post-golden-age Sundays are merely representative of their time: a "mouse soup" mixing great with average. The first few examples pair Gottfredson with Bill Walsh, his postwar writer on the *Mickey* daily—and feature plenty of Walsh's trademark screwball humor. While perhaps most ideally suited to Goofy, this comedy of the absurd provides Mickey with a different challenge: turning outrageous situations to his advantage. Sometimes Mickey succeeds; other times, he just ends up knee-deep in the hoopla.

Walsh was succeeded as *Mickey Mouse* writer by Roy Williams—previously the "Big Mooseketeer" on TV's *Mickey Mouse Club* (1955)—and Del Connell, an editor at Western Publishing. While Williams' and Connell's Goofy remained a delightful eccentric, their Mickey became "just another suburbanite family man," as Gottfredson described his relationship with Morty, Minnie, and Pluto.[1]

"This was the thing that I was never happy about myself," Gottfredson later recalled, "but [it] was the way Frank [Reilly] saw [Mickey], and apparently [King Features] Syndicate agreed with him. It would be nice if we could bring back Mickey's personality, with its foibles and idiosyncrasies, so that he can handle comedy again."

Luckily for us, bringing back Mickey's personality is as easy as rereading the earlier, greater Sunday strips already seen in this series. [DG]

1 Floyd Gottfredson to David R. Smith, *Mickey Mouse in Color* deluxe edition (Prescott: Another Rainbow, 1988), p. 165.

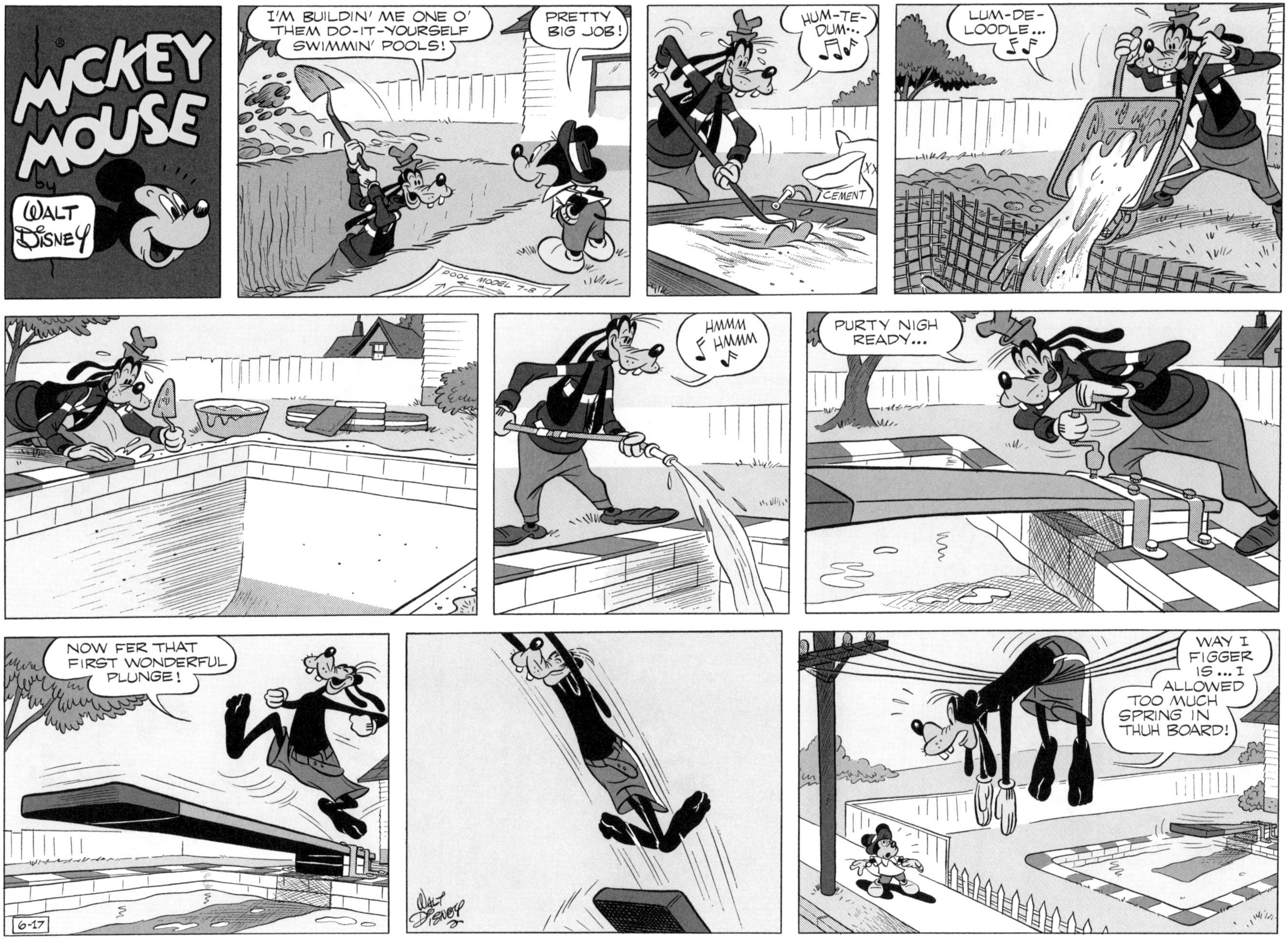
MICKEY MOUSE
by
WALT DISNEY
I'M BUILDIN' ME ONE O' THEM DO-IT-YOURSELF SWIMMIN' POOLS!
PRETTY BIG JOB!
POOL MODEL 7-8
HUM-TE-DUM...
CEMENT
LUM-DE-LOODLE...
HMMM HMMM
PURTY NIGH READY...
NOW FER THAT FIRST WONDERFUL PLUNGE!
6-17
WALT DISNEY
WAY I FIGGER IS... I ALLOWED TOO MUCH SPRING IN THUH BOARD!

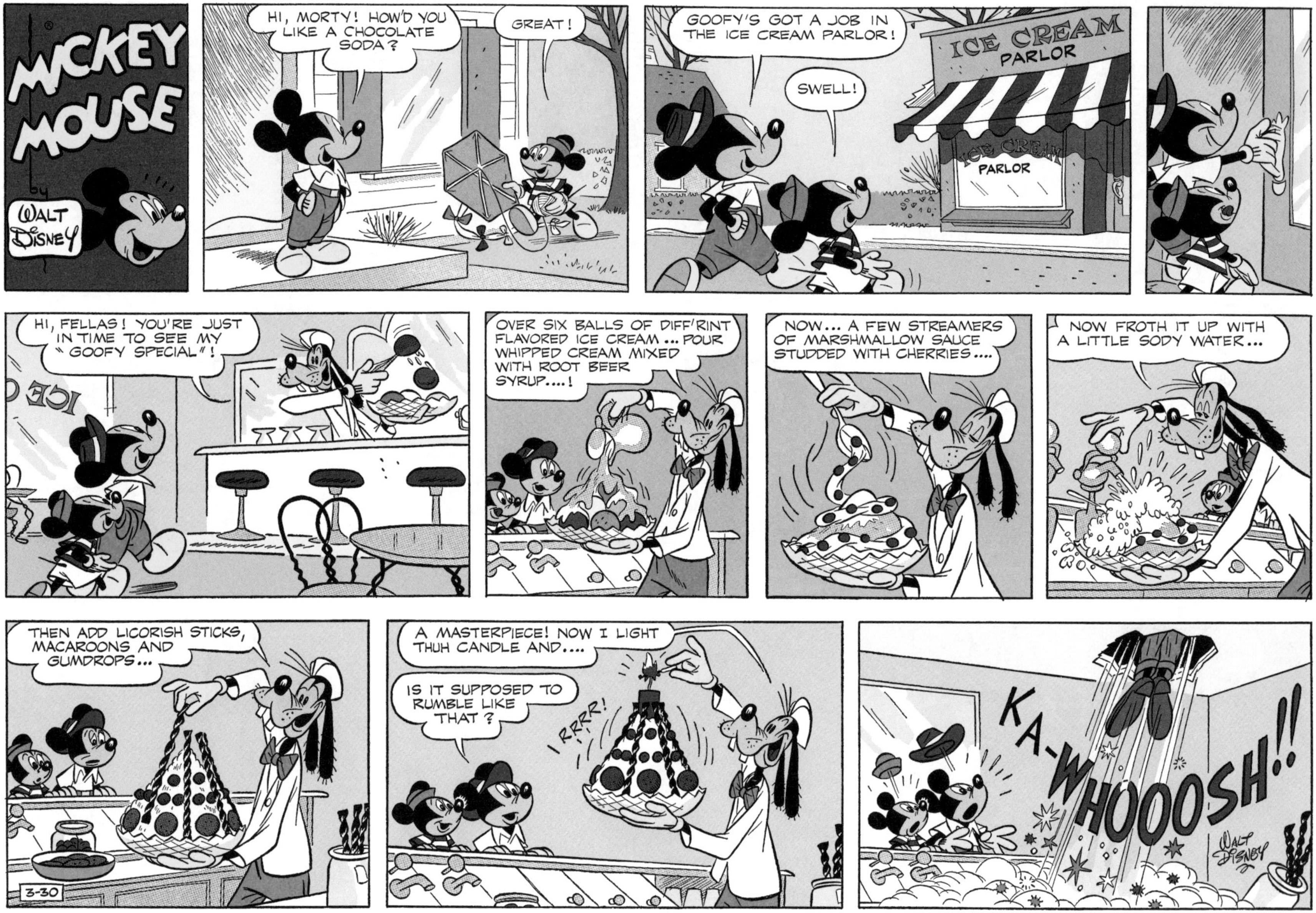
MICKEY MOUSE
by WALT DISNEY
HI, MORTY! HOW'D YOU LIKE A CHOCOLATE SODA?
GREAT!
GOOFY'S GOT A JOB IN THE ICE CREAM PARLOR!
SWELL!
ICE CREAM PARLOR
HI, FELLAS! YOU'RE JUST IN TIME TO SEE MY "GOOFY SPECIAL"!
OVER SIX BALLS OF DIFF'RINT FLAVORED ICE CREAM ... POUR WHIPPED CREAM MIXED WITH ROOT BEER SYRUP....!
NOW... A FEW STREAMERS OF MARSHMALLOW SAUCE STUDDED WITH CHERRIES....
NOW FROTH IT UP WITH A LITTLE SODY WATER...
THEN ADD LICORISH STICKS, MACAROONS AND GUMDROPS...
3-30
A MASTERPIECE! NOW I LIGHT THUH CANDLE AND....
IS IT SUPPOSED TO RUMBLE LIKE THAT?
RRRR!
KA-WHOOOSH!!
WALT DISNEY

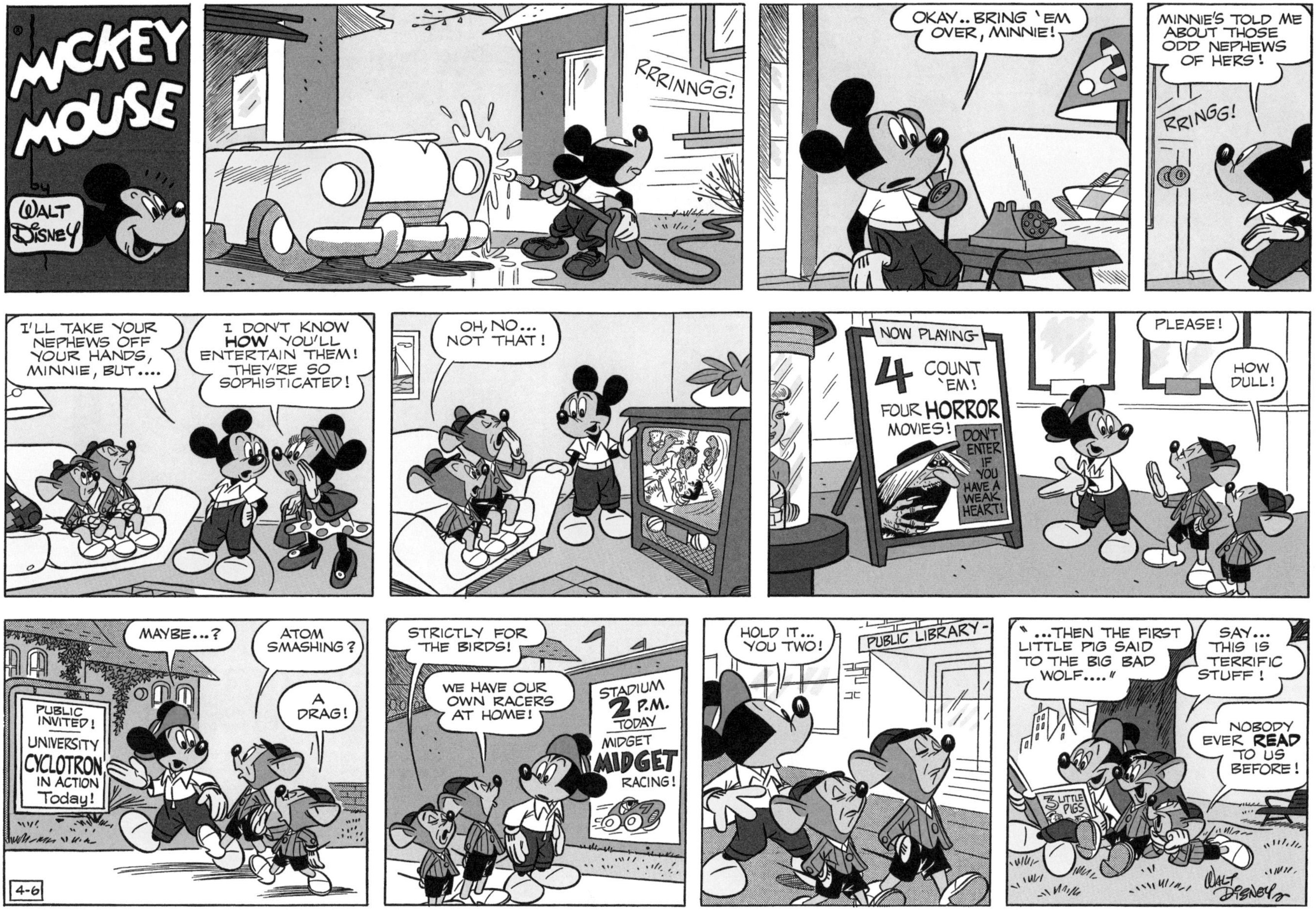
MICKEY MOUSE
by WALT DISNEY
RRRINNGG!
OKAY.. BRING 'EM OVER, MINNIE!
MINNIE'S TOLD ME ABOUT THOSE ODD NEPHEWS OF HERS!
RRINGG!
I'LL TAKE YOUR NEPHEWS OFF YOUR HANDS, MINNIE, BUT....
I DON'T KNOW **HOW** YOU'LL ENTERTAIN THEM! THEY'RE SO SOPHISTICATED!
OH, NO... NOT THAT!
NOW PLAYING
4 COUNT 'EM! FOUR HORROR MOVIES!
DON'T ENTER IF YOU HAVE A WEAK HEART!
PLEASE!
HOW DULL!
PUBLIC INVITED! UNIVERSITY CYCLOTRON IN ACTION Today!
MAYBE...?
ATOM SMASHING?
A DRAG!
4-6
STRICTLY FOR THE BIRDS!
WE HAVE OUR OWN RACERS AT HOME!
STADIUM 2 P.M. TODAY MIDGET MIDGET RACING!
PUBLIC LIBRARY
HOLD IT... YOU TWO!
"...THEN THE FIRST LITTLE PIG SAID TO THE BIG BAD WOLF...."
3 LITTLE PIGS
SAY... THIS IS TERRIFIC STUFF!
NOBODY EVER **READ** TO US BEFORE!
WALT DISNEY

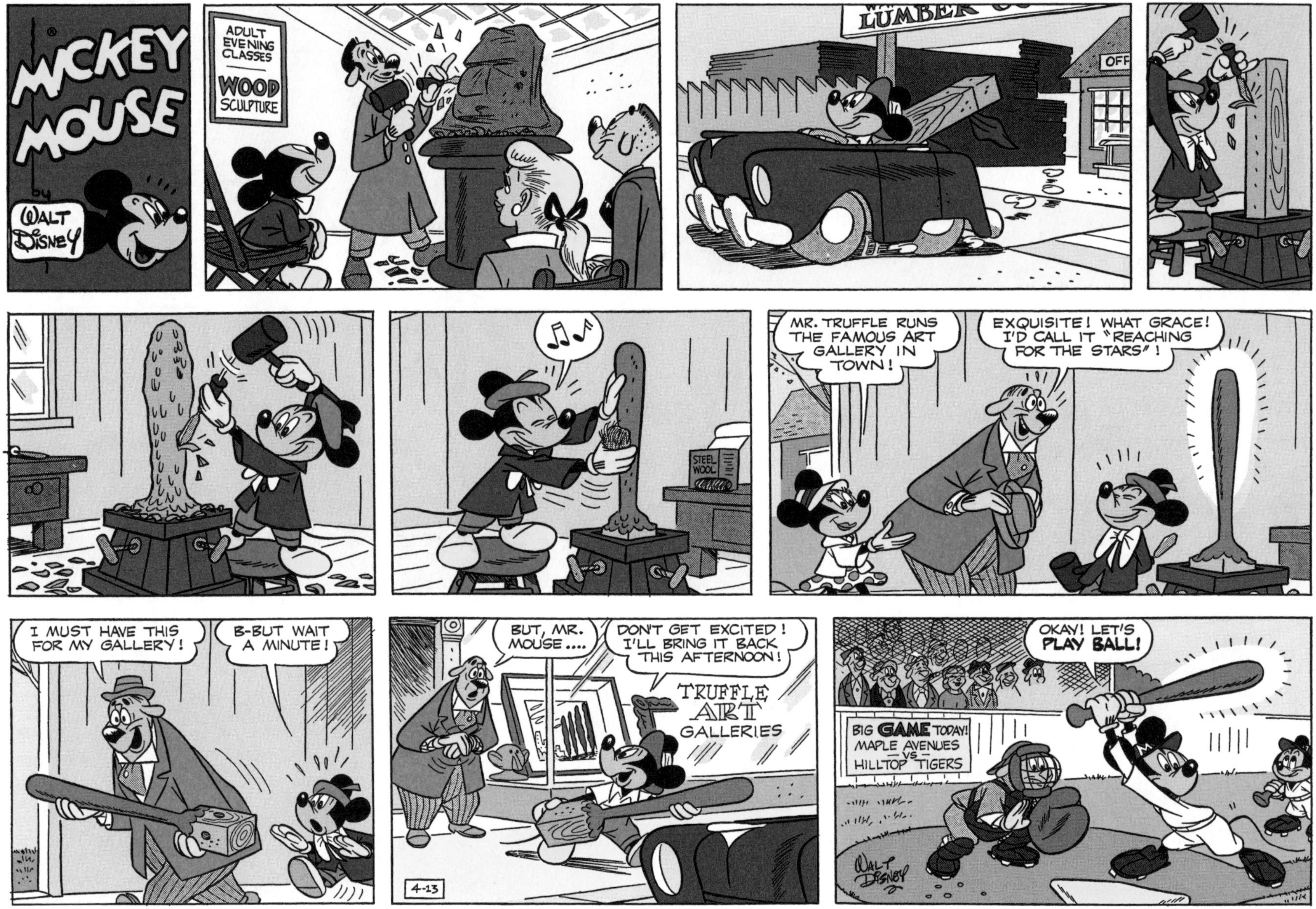
MICKEY MOUSE
by WALT DISNEY
ADULT EVENING CLASSES
WOOD SCULPTURE
LUMBER
OFF
STEEL WOOL
MR. TRUFFLE RUNS THE FAMOUS ART GALLERY IN TOWN!
EXQUISITE! WHAT GRACE! I'D CALL IT "REACHING FOR THE STARS"!
I MUST HAVE THIS FOR MY GALLERY!
B-BUT WAIT A MINUTE!
BUT, MR. MOUSE....
DON'T GET EXCITED! I'LL BRING IT BACK THIS AFTERNOON!
TRUFFLE ART GALLERIES
4-13
OKAY! LET'S PLAY BALL!
BIG GAME TODAY! MAPLE AVENUES —VS— HILLTOP TIGERS
WALT DISNEY

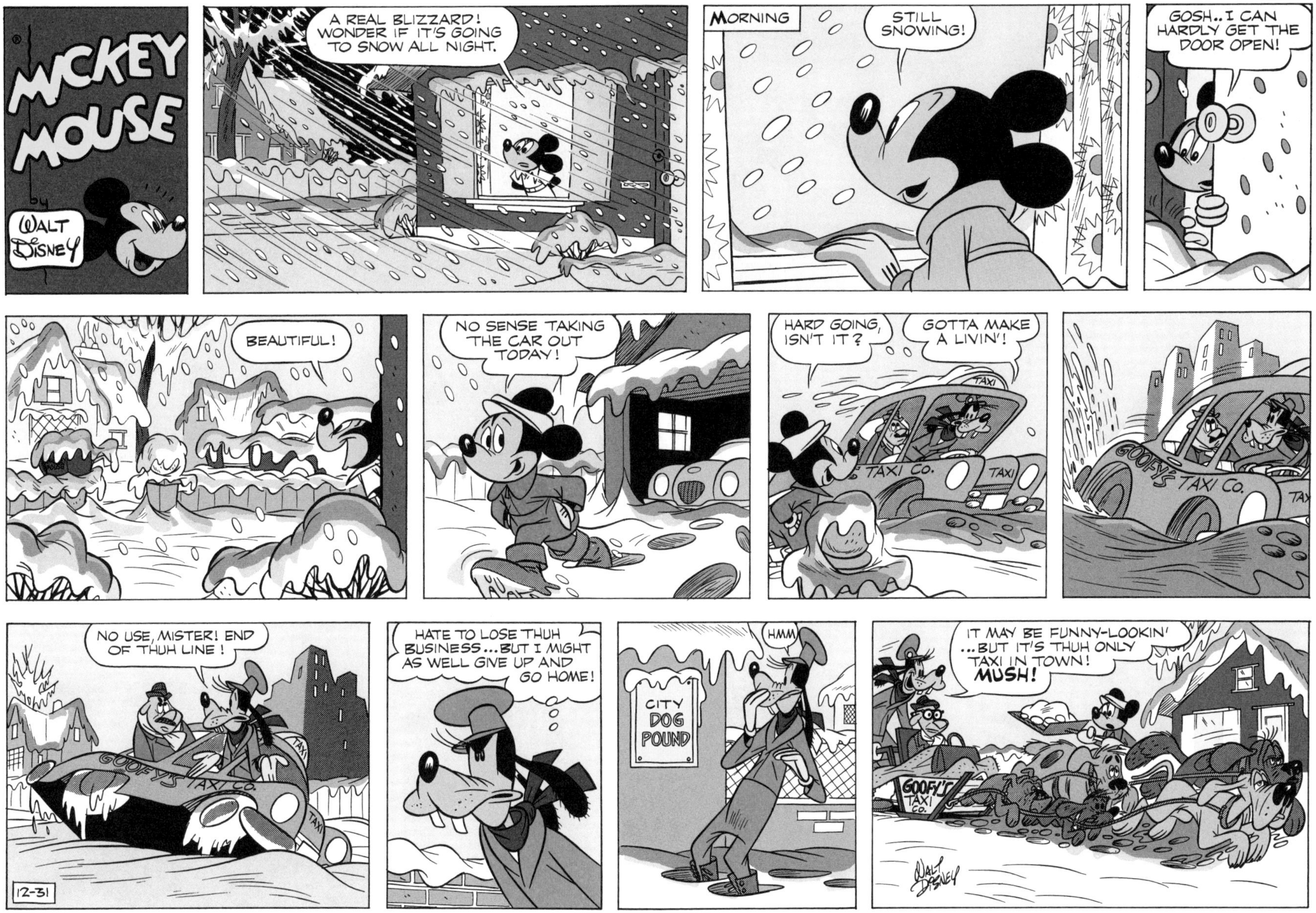
MICKEY MOUSE
by WALT DISNEY
A REAL BLIZZARD! WONDER IF IT'S GOING TO SNOW ALL NIGHT.
MORNING
STILL SNOWING!
GOSH.. I CAN HARDLY GET THE DOOR OPEN!
BEAUTIFUL!
NO SENSE TAKING THE CAR OUT TODAY!
HARD GOING, ISN'T IT?
GOTTA MAKE A LIVIN'!
TAXI
TAXI CO.
GOOFY'S TAXI CO.
NO USE, MISTER! END OF THUH LINE!
12-31
HATE TO LOSE THUH BUSINESS...BUT I MIGHT AS WELL GIVE UP AND GO HOME!
HMM
CITY DOG POUND
IT MAY BE FUNNY-LOOKIN' ...BUT IT'S THUH ONLY TAXI IN TOWN! MUSH!
GOOFY'S TAXI CO.
WALT DISNEY

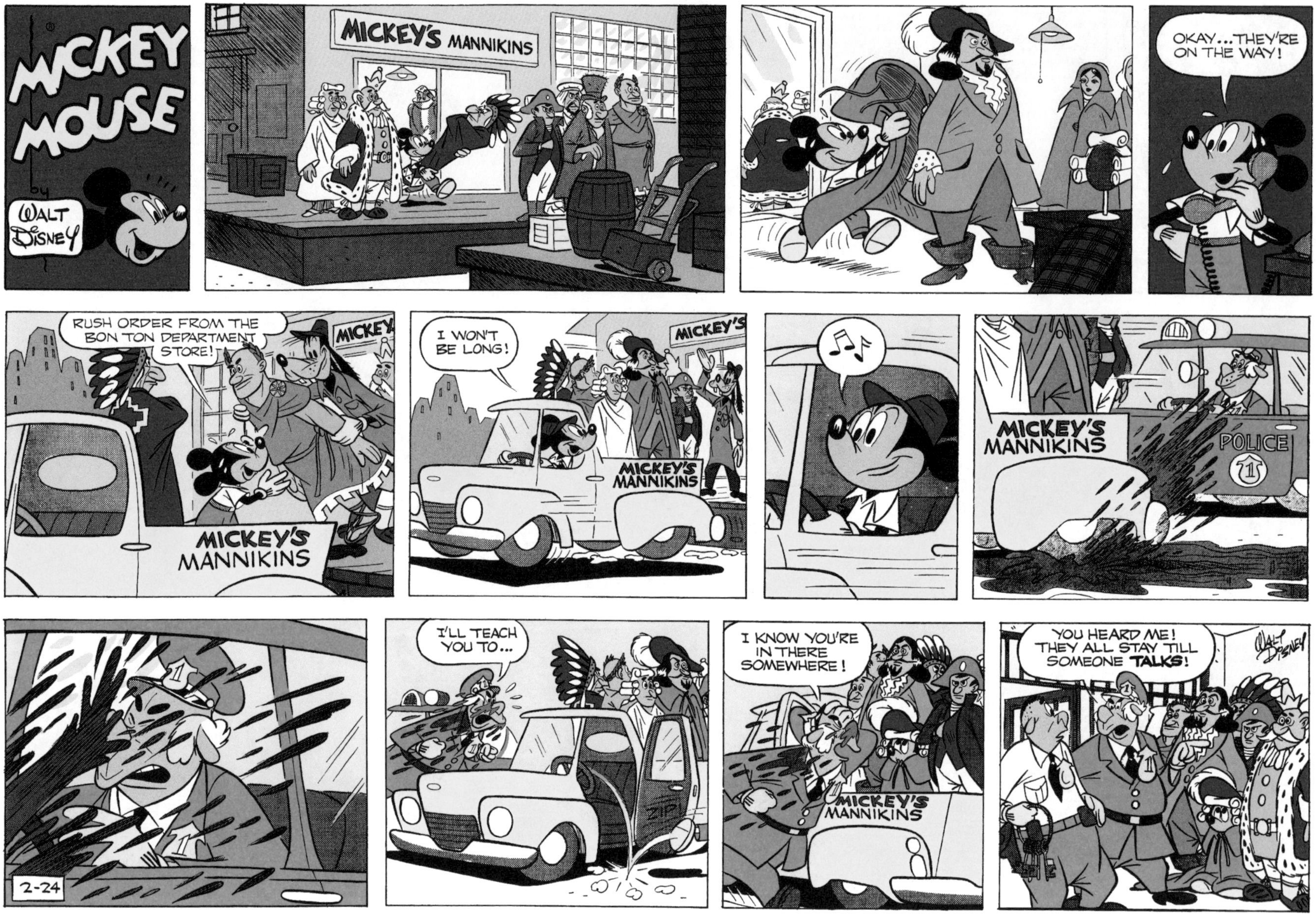
MICKEY MOUSE
by WALT DISNEY
MICKEY'S MANNIKINS
OKAY... THEY'RE ON THE WAY!
RUSH ORDER FROM THE BON TON DEPARTMENT STORE!
MICKEY'S MANNIKINS
I WON'T BE LONG!
MICKEY'S MANNIKINS
MICKEY'S MANNIKINS
POLICE
2-24
I'LL TEACH YOU TO...
ZIP!
I KNOW YOU'RE IN THERE SOMEWHERE!
MICKEY'S MANNIKINS
YOU HEARD ME! THEY ALL STAY TILL SOMEONE **TALKS**!
WALT DISNEY

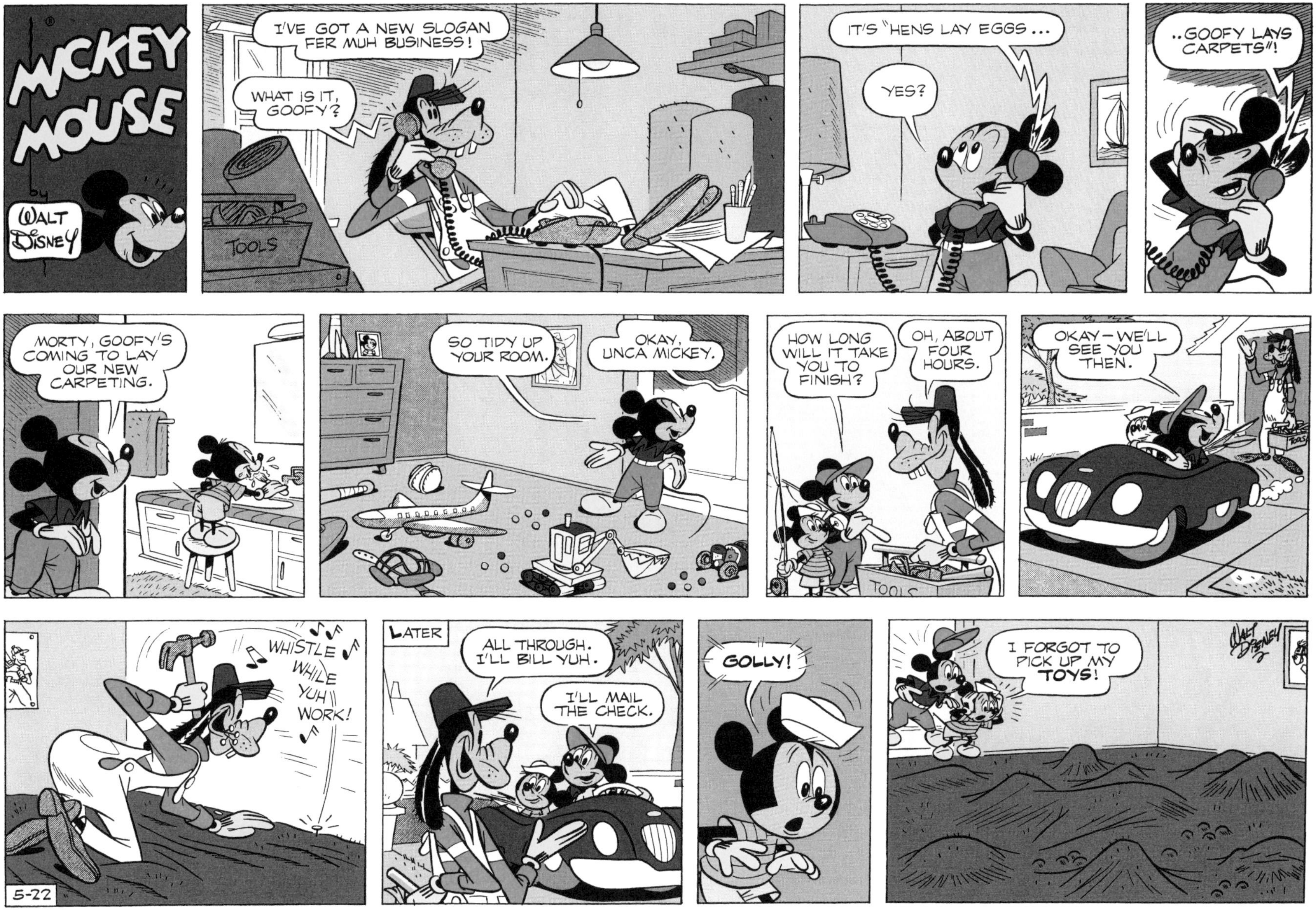
MICKEY MOUSE
by WALT DISNEY
I'VE GOT A NEW SLOGAN FER MUH BUSINESS!
WHAT IS IT, GOOFY?
TOOLS
IT'S "HENS LAY EGGS...
YES?
..GOOFY LAYS CARPETS"!
MORTY, GOOFY'S COMING TO LAY OUR NEW CARPETING.
SO TIDY UP YOUR ROOM.
OKAY, UNCA MICKEY.
HOW LONG WILL IT TAKE YOU TO FINISH?
OH, ABOUT FOUR HOURS.
TOOLS
OKAY—WE'LL SEE YOU THEN.
WHISTLE WHILE YUH WORK!
5-22
LATER
ALL THROUGH. I'LL BILL YUH.
I'LL MAIL THE CHECK.
GOLLY!
I FORGOT TO PICK UP MY TOYS!
WALT DISNEY

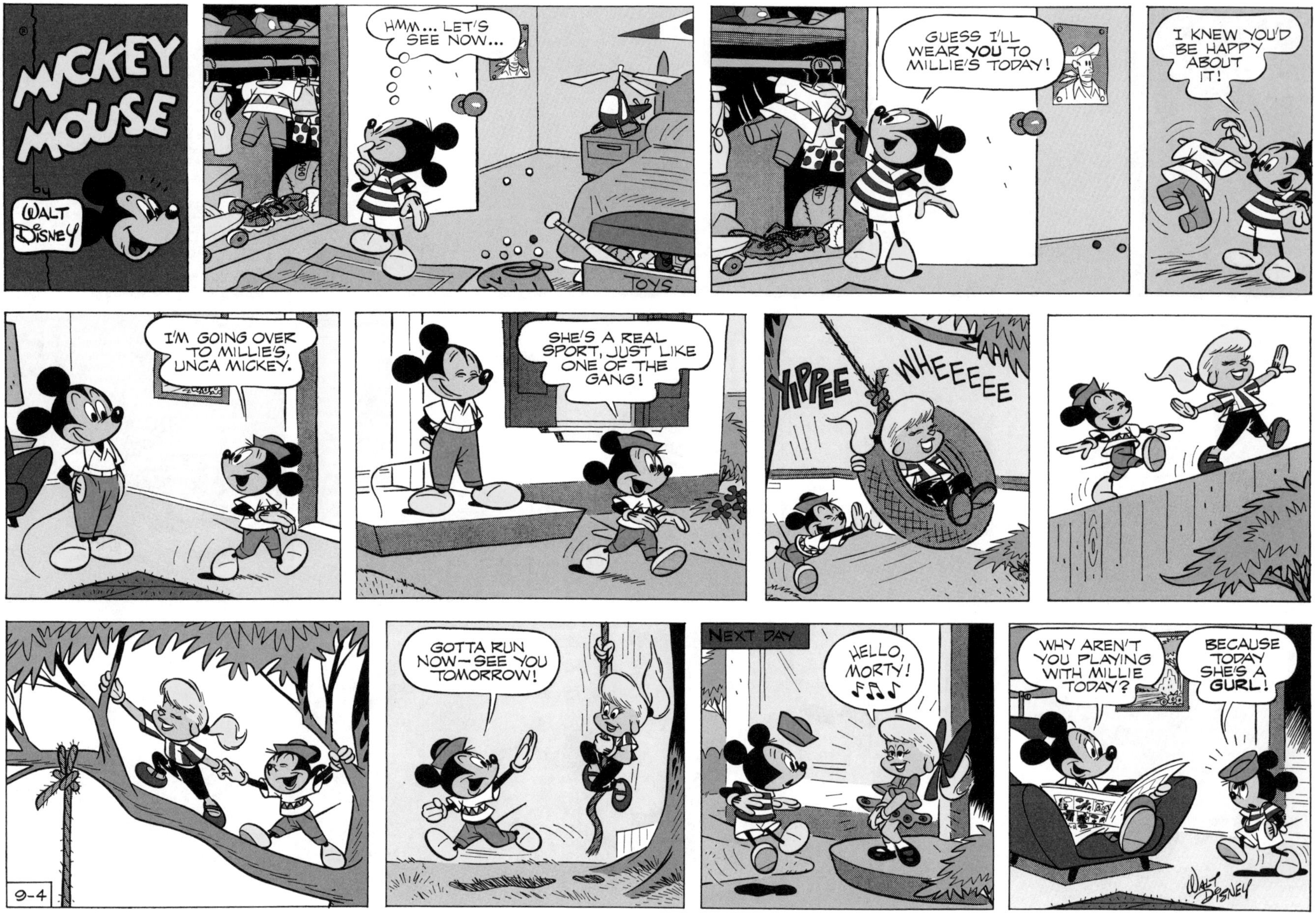
MICKEY MOUSE
by WALT DISNEY
HMM... LET'S SEE NOW...
TOYS
GUESS I'LL WEAR **YOU** TO MILLIE'S TODAY!
I KNEW YOU'D BE HAPPY ABOUT IT!
I'M GOING OVER TO MILLIE'S, UNCA MICKEY.
SHE'S A REAL SPORT, JUST LIKE ONE OF THE GANG!
YIPPEE
WHEEEEEE
9-4
GOTTA RUN NOW—SEE YOU TOMORROW!
NEXT DAY
HELLO, MORTY!
WHY AREN'T YOU PLAYING WITH MILLIE TODAY?
BECAUSE TODAY SHE'S A **GURL**!
WALT DISNEY

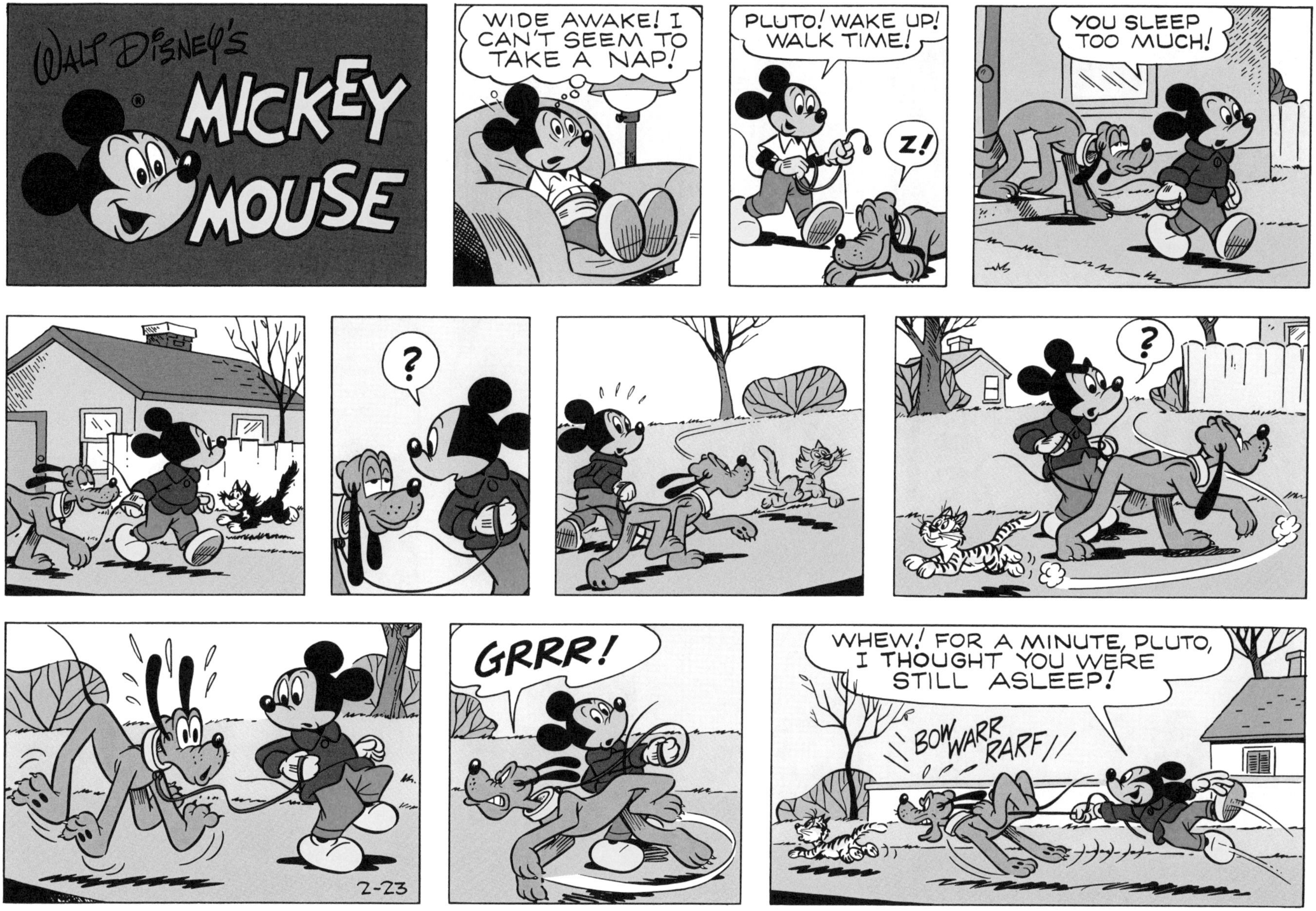
WALT DISNEY'S
MICKEY MOUSE
WIDE AWAKE! I CAN'T SEEM TO TAKE A NAP!
PLUTO! WAKE UP! WALK TIME!
Z!
YOU SLEEP TOO MUCH!
?
?
?
2-23
GRRR!
WHEW! FOR A MINUTE, PLUTO, I THOUGHT YOU WERE STILL ASLEEP!
BOW WARR RARF

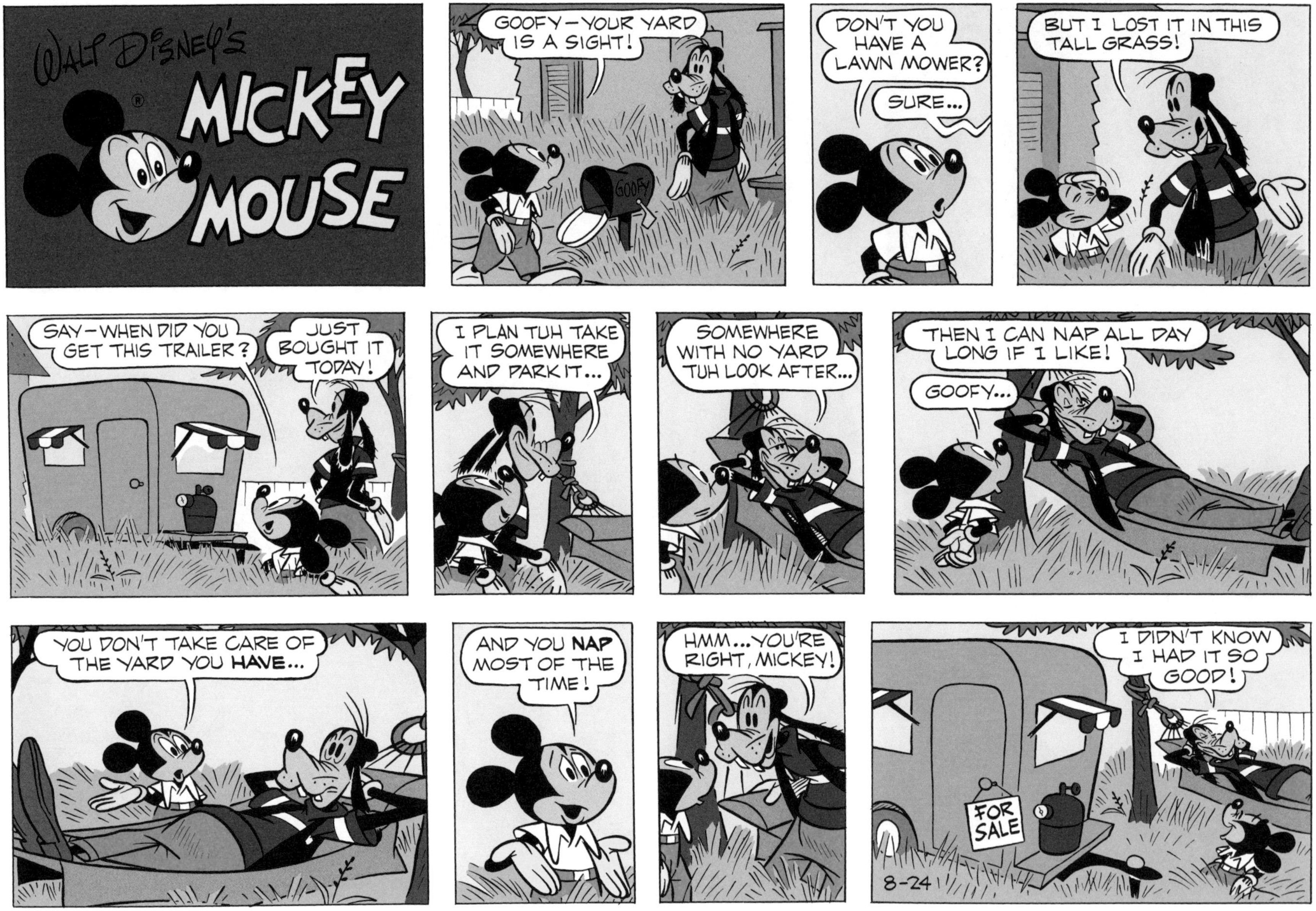

WALT DISNEY'S
MICKEY MOUSE
GOOFY—YOUR YARD IS A SIGHT!
GOOFY
DON'T YOU HAVE A LAWN MOWER?
SURE...
BUT I LOST IT IN THIS TALL GRASS!
SAY—WHEN DID YOU GET THIS TRAILER?
JUST BOUGHT IT TODAY!
I PLAN TUH TAKE IT SOMEWHERE AND PARK IT...
SOMEWHERE WITH NO YARD TUH LOOK AFTER...
THEN I CAN NAP ALL DAY LONG IF I LIKE!
GOOFY...
YOU DON'T TAKE CARE OF THE YARD YOU **HAVE**...
AND YOU **NAP** MOST OF THE TIME!
HMM...YOU'RE RIGHT, MICKEY!
I DIDN'T KNOW I HAD IT SO GOOD!
FOR SALE
8-24

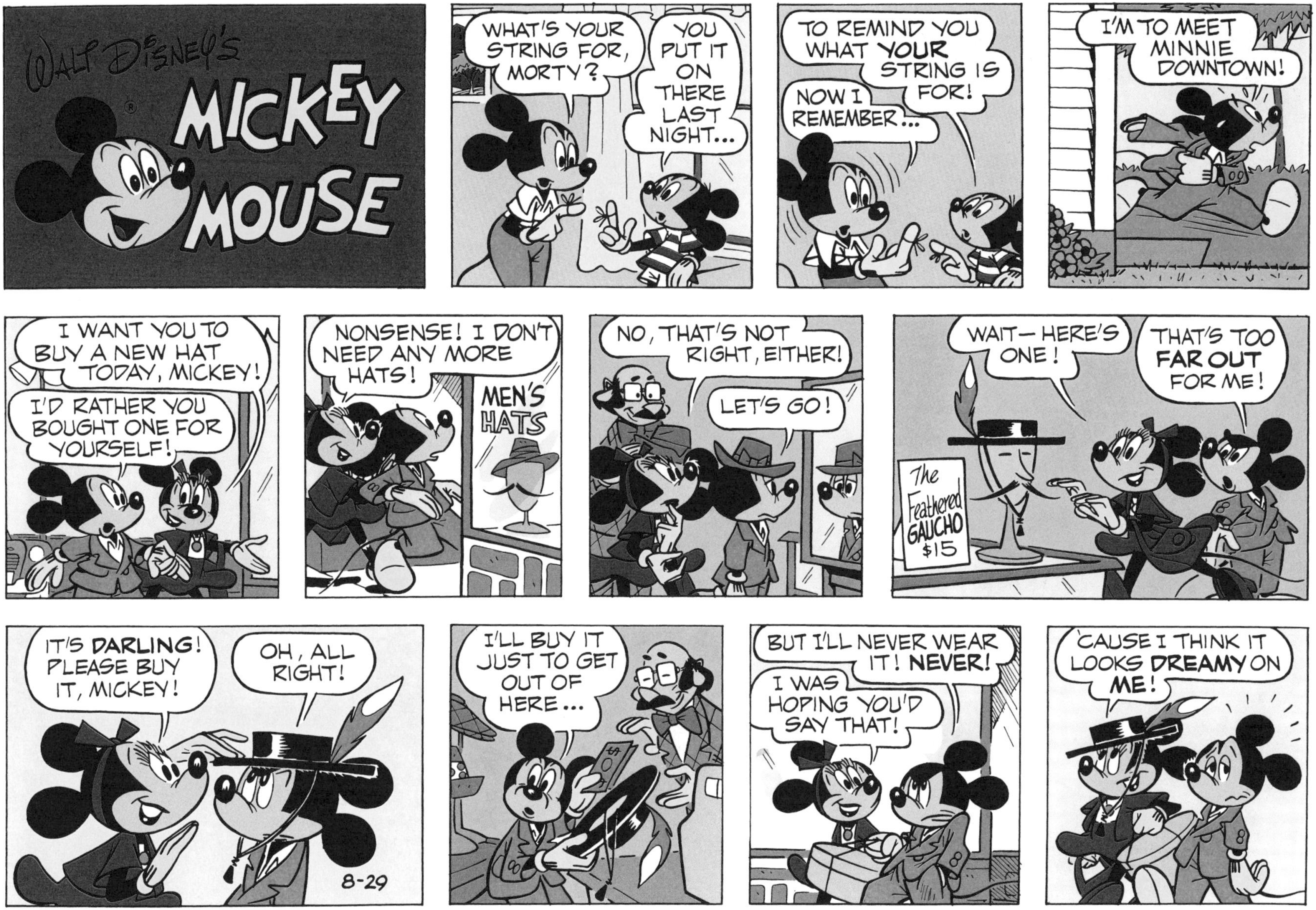
Walt Disney's
MICKEY MOUSE
WHAT'S YOUR STRING FOR, MORTY?
YOU PUT IT ON THERE LAST NIGHT...
TO REMIND YOU WHAT YOUR STRING IS FOR!
NOW I REMEMBER...
I'M TO MEET MINNIE DOWNTOWN!
I WANT YOU TO BUY A NEW HAT TODAY, MICKEY!
I'D RATHER YOU BOUGHT ONE FOR YOURSELF!
NONSENSE! I DON'T NEED ANY MORE HATS!
MEN'S HATS
NO, THAT'S NOT RIGHT, EITHER!
LET'S GO!
WAIT— HERE'S ONE!
THAT'S TOO FAR OUT FOR ME!
The Feathered GAUCHO $15
IT'S DARLING! PLEASE BUY IT, MICKEY!
OH, ALL RIGHT!
8-29
I'LL BUY IT JUST TO GET OUT OF HERE...
BUT I'LL NEVER WEAR IT! NEVER!
I WAS HOPING YOU'D SAY THAT!
'CAUSE I THINK IT LOOKS DREAMY ON ME!

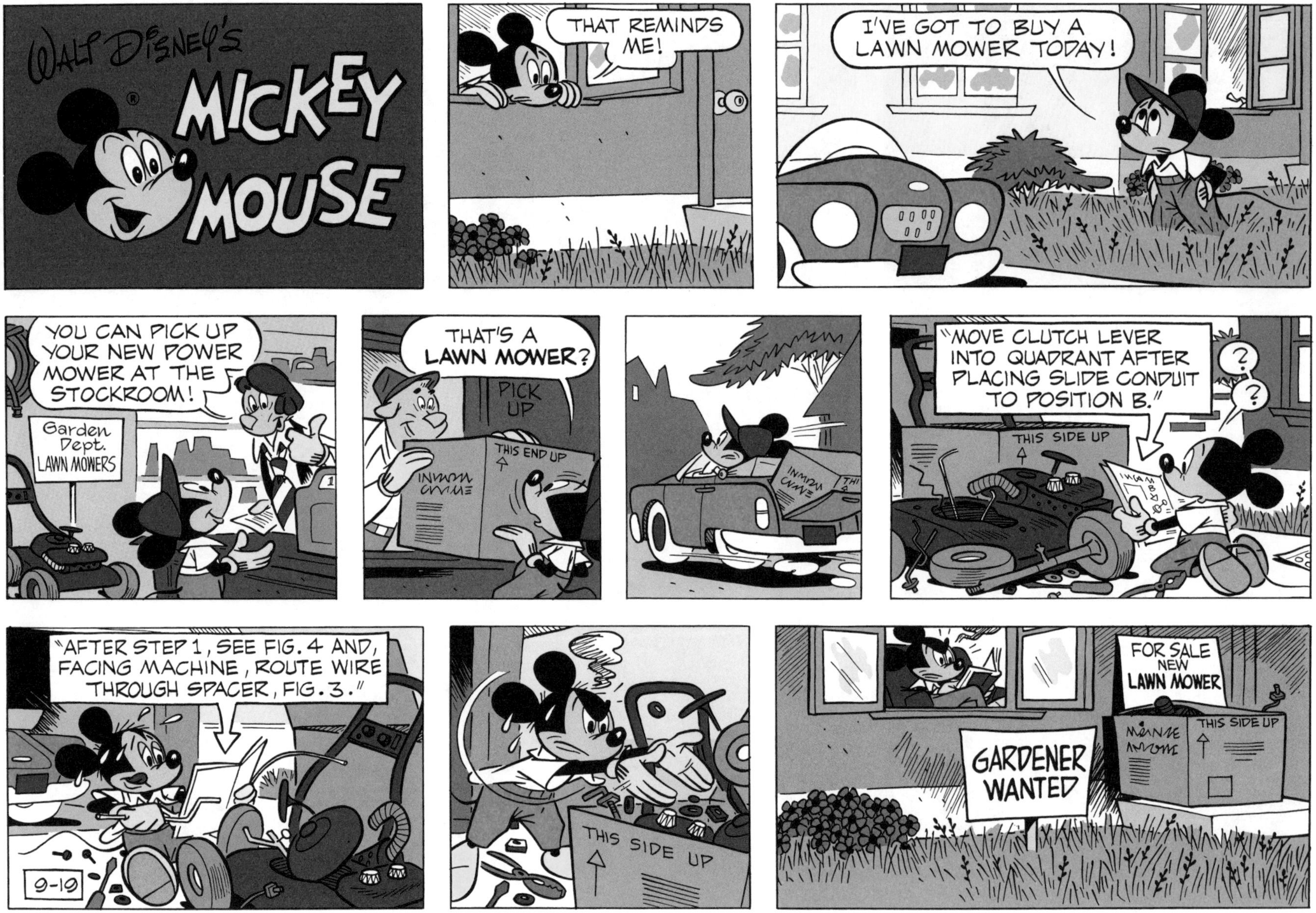
WALT DISNEY'S
MICKEY MOUSE
THAT REMINDS ME!
I'VE GOT TO BUY A LAWN MOWER TODAY!
YOU CAN PICK UP YOUR NEW POWER MOWER AT THE STOCKROOM!
Garden Dept. LAWN MOWERS
THAT'S A **LAWN MOWER**?
PICK UP
THIS END UP
"MOVE CLUTCH LEVER INTO QUADRANT AFTER PLACING SLIDE CONDUIT TO POSITION B."
THIS SIDE UP
"AFTER STEP 1, SEE FIG. 4 AND, FACING MACHINE, ROUTE WIRE THROUGH SPACER, FIG. 3."
9-19
THIS SIDE UP
FOR SALE NEW LAWN MOWER
GARDENER WANTED
THIS SIDE UP

GOTTFREDSON GUEST STARS:

DONALD DUCK

AND

TREASURY OF CLASSIC TALES

OCTOBER 3, 1937
–
MARCH 26, 1961

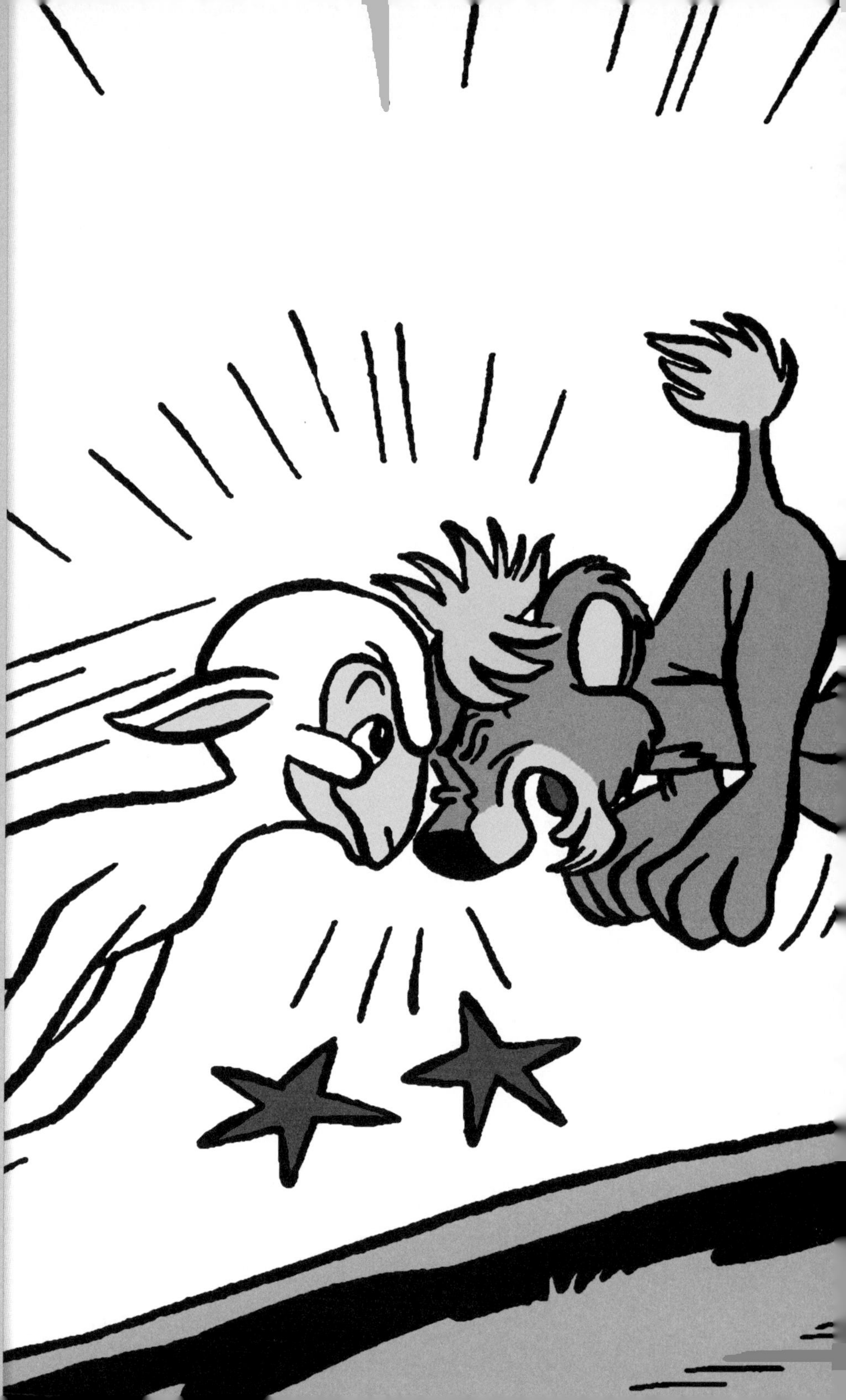

MICKEY MOUSE
REGISTERED U.S. PATENT OFFICE

CALLING ALL CHARACTERS!

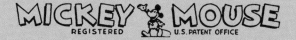

Mickey Mouse tales made up the vast majority of Floyd Gottfredson's Sunday oeuvre—but not quite *all* of it. In October 1937, Gottfredson inked two *Silly Symphony* Donald Duck strips for Al Taliaferro; perhaps to take the heat off Taliaferro as he fine-tuned Donald's nephews, who were to debut in the strips immediately following.

Then decades later, years after Gottfredson's regular *Mickey* Sunday gig ended, he got back in the full-color game for Disney's *Treasury of Classic Tales*, a serialized strip based on feature films and one-shot shorts.

At this late date, we're not sure how Gottfredson came to work on the *Classic Tales* series. Perhaps he just had extra time on his hands; perhaps other staffers had less on theirs. Between 1956 and 1961, Gottfredson scripted two *Tales* continuities, filling in for regular writer Frank Reilly. Then, with Reilly as writer, Gottfredson did art duty on a third serial and most of a fourth.

Reilly was manager of Disney's Comic Strip Department at the time. As such, in 1955, he had been ordered by King Features to transform *Mickey Mouse* from an adventure serial into a gag strip. It was a sad day at the office when Reilly passed the order to Gottfredson. Could *Classic Tales*, then, have been a kind of consolation prize: a make-do means of keeping Gottfredson in serials?

One thing was for sure: *Classic Tales* may have been a serial-format strip, but it was no *Mickey Mouse*. More specifically: since its huge stock company rotated constantly, there was no time to get comfy with any one group. Characters from one movie could return for an original sequel—Gottfredson's "Seven Dwarfs and the Witch-Queen" was one—but such events were highly uncommon. The basic aim was to adapt as many different stars, moods, and movie stories as possible.

What could be accomplished in such a shifting environment? "Lambert the Sheepish Lion," with scripter Reilly adapting the 1952 cartoon almost exactly, offered some of Gottfredson's finest art of the period. The bombastic cub Lambert was a perfect match for Gottfredson's art style—and as a grown lion, he resembled several earlier Gottfredson jungle cats. Gottfredson's layouts on "101 Dalmatians," meanwhile, were complex and expressive; but Reilly's storytelling bears little of the same depth.

This leaves Gottfredson's two script-only serials for analysis. While fun, they are memorable mainly for their echoes of Gottfredson's earlier, more famous work. Characters in "Sleeping Beauty" repeatedly talk about "fixing" each other, reflecting less medieval royalty than Mickey's 1930s mobster foes. "Witch-Queen," meanwhile, has a clever idea at its core—what if the Dwarfs, already little people, became even littler?—but the story's energy stops and starts. The Witch herself appears to be aware something's amiss; when she breaks the fourth wall to address readers directly, it seems a self-conscious effort to pick up the pace.

After 1955, Floyd Gottfredson arguably never recaptured the speed and energy of his greatest Mickey work. But it's fun to watch him try out these disparate Disney stars, as if one might have afforded him the chance. [DG]

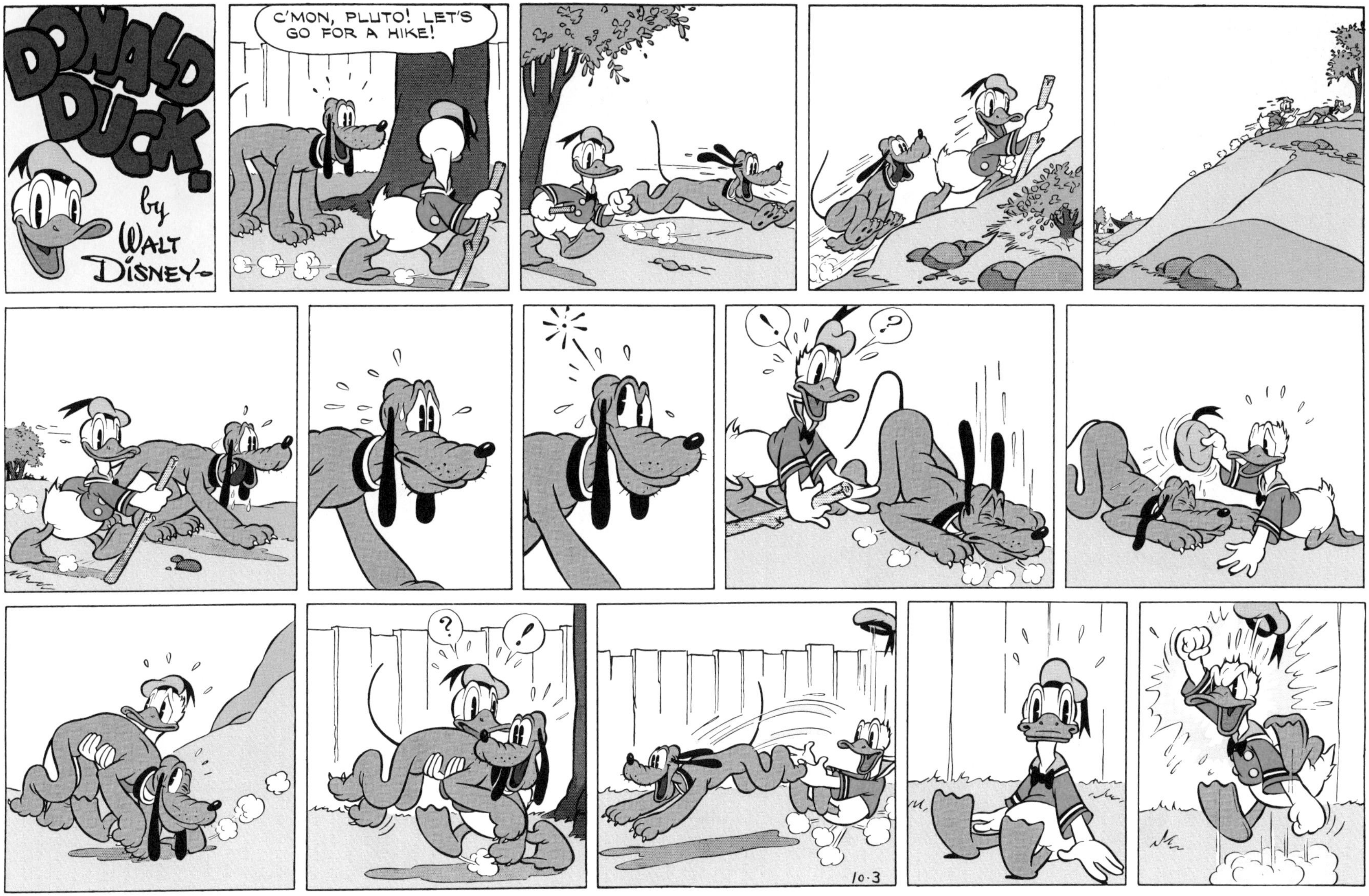
DONALD DUCK
by WALT DISNEY
C'MON, PLUTO! LET'S GO FOR A HIKE!
!
?
?
!
10·3

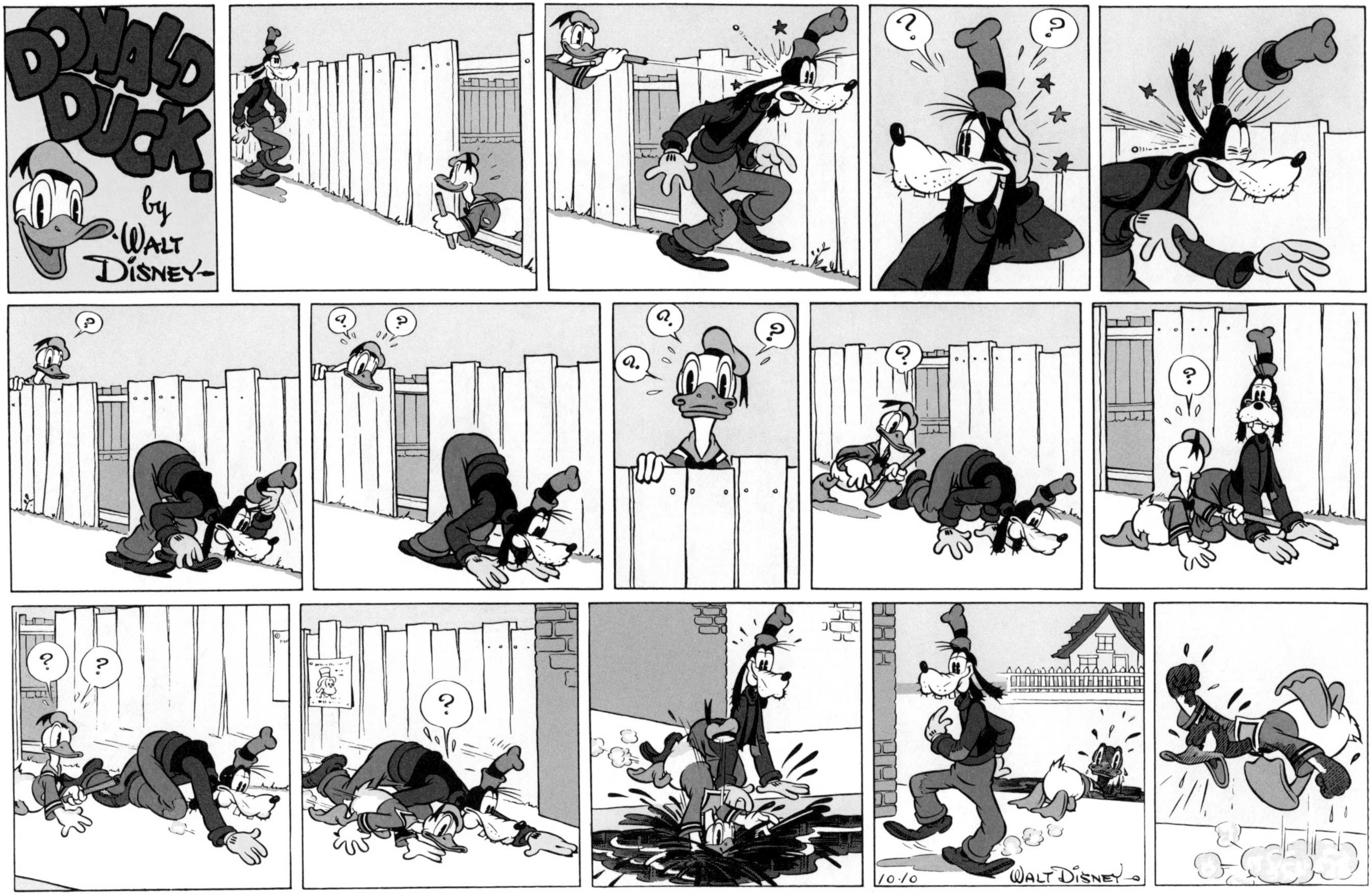
DONALD DUCK
by WALT DISNEY
?
?
?
?
?
?
?
?
?
?
?
?
?
10-10
WALT DISNEY

204. DONALD SCENTED FOUL PLAY

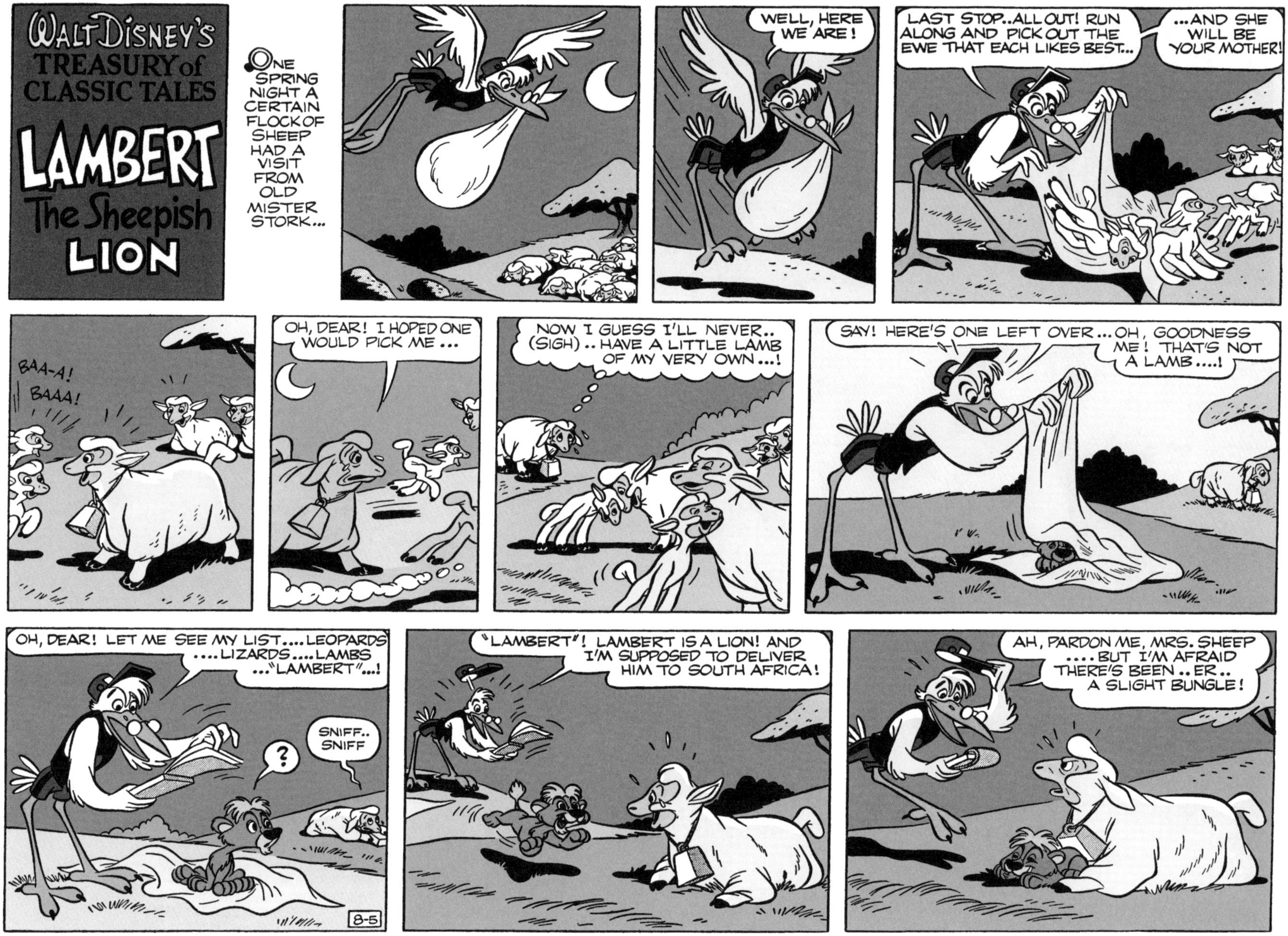
WALT DISNEY'S
TREASURY of CLASSIC TALES
LAMBERT The Sheepish LION
ONE SPRING NIGHT A CERTAIN FLOCK OF SHEEP HAD A VISIT FROM OLD MISTER STORK...
WELL, HERE WE ARE!
LAST STOP..ALL OUT! RUN ALONG AND PICK OUT THE EWE THAT EACH LIKES BEST...
...AND SHE WILL BE YOUR MOTHER!
BAA-A!
BAAA!
OH, DEAR! I HOPED ONE WOULD PICK ME...
NOW I GUESS I'LL NEVER.. (SIGH).. HAVE A LITTLE LAMB OF MY VERY OWN...!
SAY! HERE'S ONE LEFT OVER...OH, GOODNESS ME! THAT'S NOT A LAMB....!
OH, DEAR! LET ME SEE MY LIST....LEOPARDS ....LIZARDS....LAMBS ..."LAMBERT"...!
?
SNIFF.. SNIFF
8-5
"LAMBERT"! LAMBERT IS A LION! AND I'M SUPPOSED TO DELIVER HIM TO SOUTH AFRICA!
AH, PARDON ME, MRS. SHEEP ....BUT I'M AFRAID THERE'S BEEN..ER.. A SLIGHT BUNGLE!

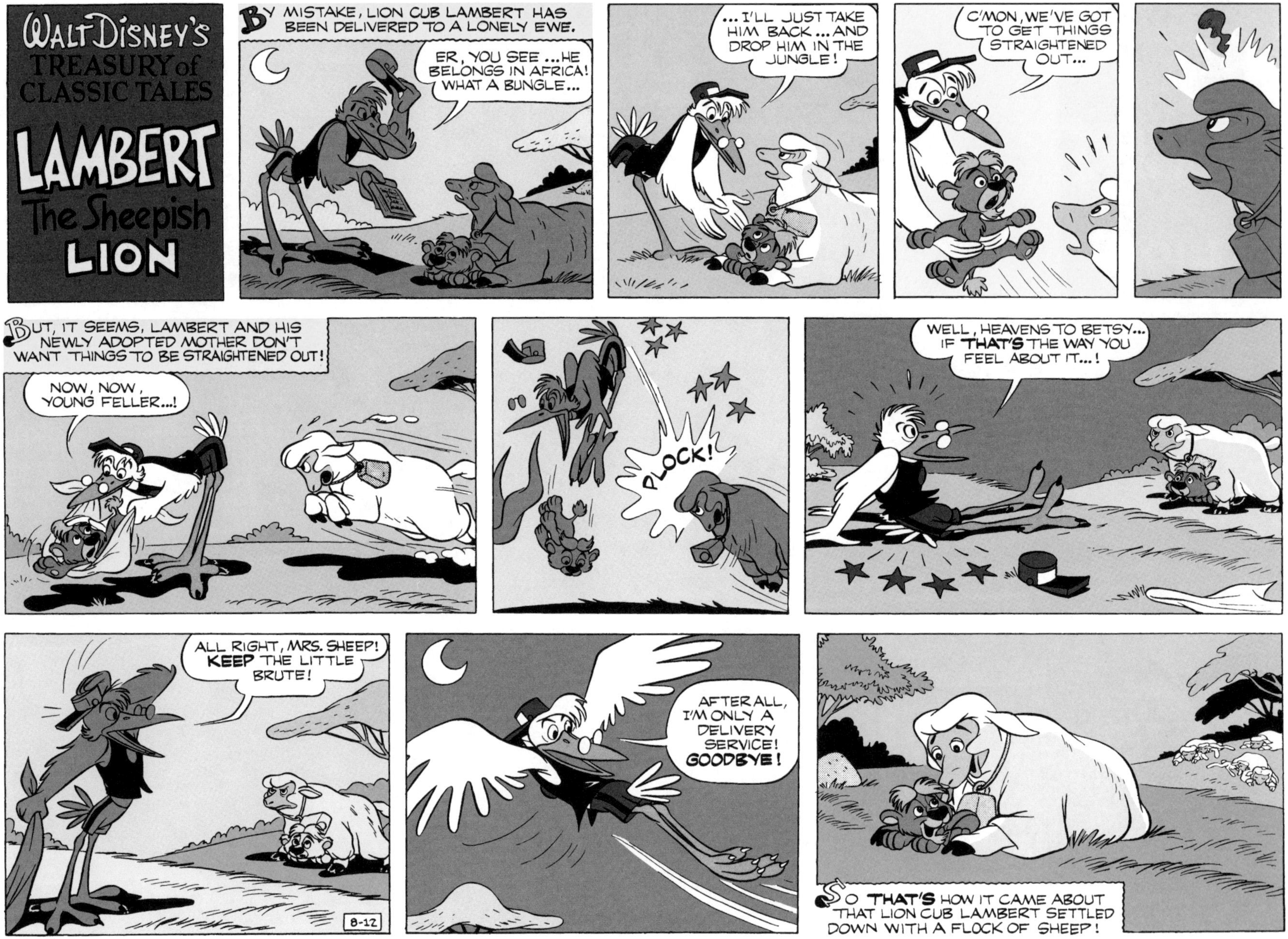
WALT DISNEY'S TREASURY of CLASSIC TALES
LAMBERT The Sheepish LION
BY MISTAKE, LION CUB LAMBERT HAS BEEN DELIVERED TO A LONELY EWE.
ER, YOU SEE ...HE BELONGS IN AFRICA! WHAT A BUNGLE...
... I'LL JUST TAKE HIM BACK ... AND DROP HIM IN THE JUNGLE!
C'MON, WE'VE GOT TO GET THINGS STRAIGHTENED OUT...
BUT, IT SEEMS, LAMBERT AND HIS NEWLY ADOPTED MOTHER DON'T WANT THINGS TO BE STRAIGHTENED OUT!
NOW, NOW, YOUNG FELLER...!
PLOCK!
WELL, HEAVENS TO BETSY... IF THAT'S THE WAY YOU FEEL ABOUT IT...!
ALL RIGHT, MRS. SHEEP! KEEP THE LITTLE BRUTE!
8-12
AFTER ALL, I'M ONLY A DELIVERY SERVICE! GOODBYE!
SO THAT'S HOW IT CAME ABOUT THAT LION CUB LAMBERT SETTLED DOWN WITH A FLOCK OF SHEEP!

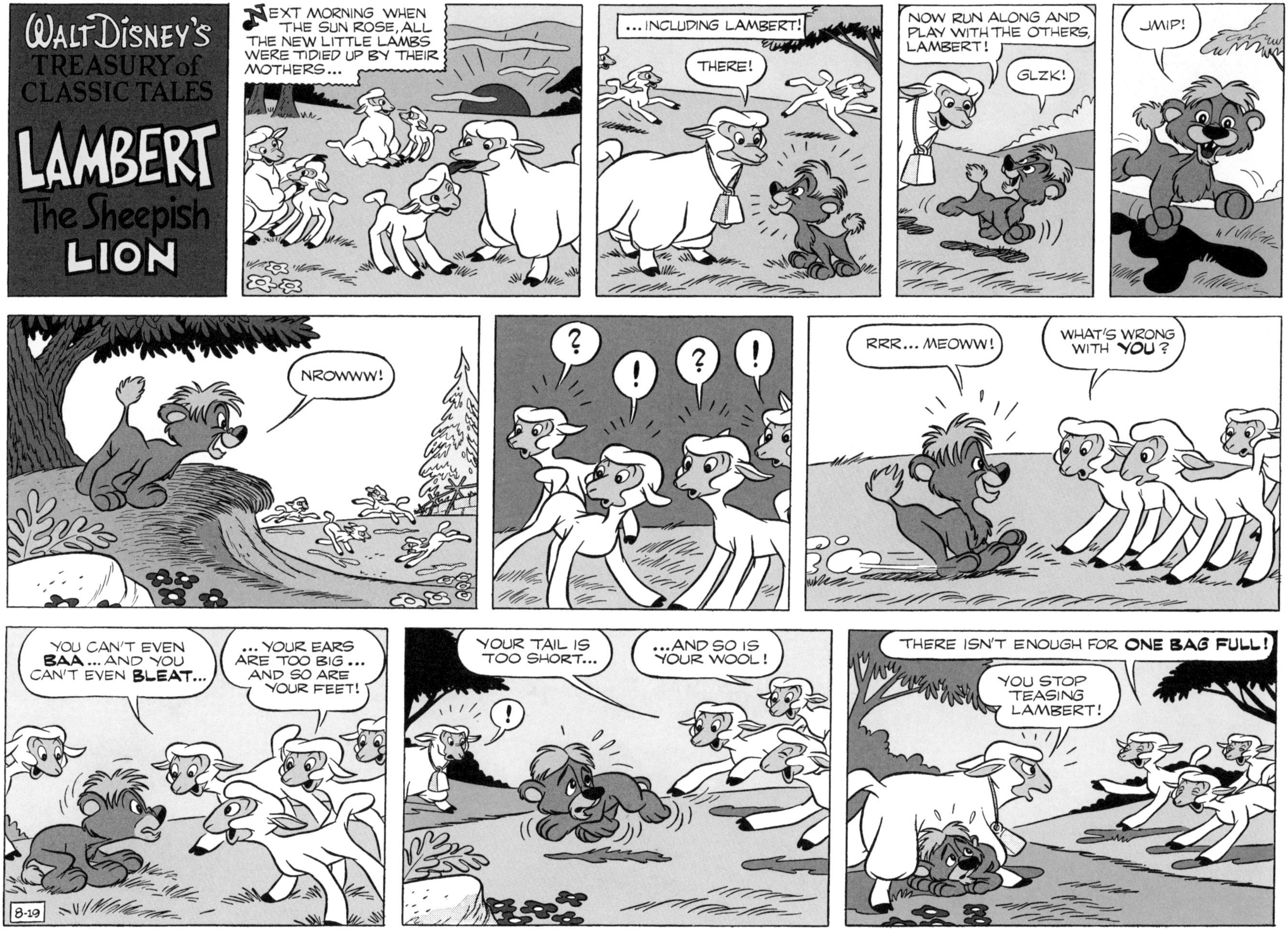
WALT DISNEY'S TREASURY of CLASSIC TALES
LAMBERT The Sheepish LION
NEXT MORNING WHEN THE SUN ROSE, ALL THE NEW LITTLE LAMBS WERE TIDIED UP BY THEIR MOTHERS...
...INCLUDING LAMBERT!
THERE!
NOW RUN ALONG AND PLAY WITH THE OTHERS, LAMBERT!
GLZK!
JMIP!
NROWWW!
?
!
?
!
RRR... MEOWW!
WHAT'S WRONG WITH YOU?
YOU CAN'T EVEN BAA... AND YOU CAN'T EVEN BLEAT...
... YOUR EARS ARE TOO BIG... AND SO ARE YOUR FEET!
8-19
YOUR TAIL IS TOO SHORT...
...AND SO IS YOUR WOOL!
!
THERE ISN'T ENOUGH FOR ONE BAG FULL!
YOU STOP TEASING LAMBERT!

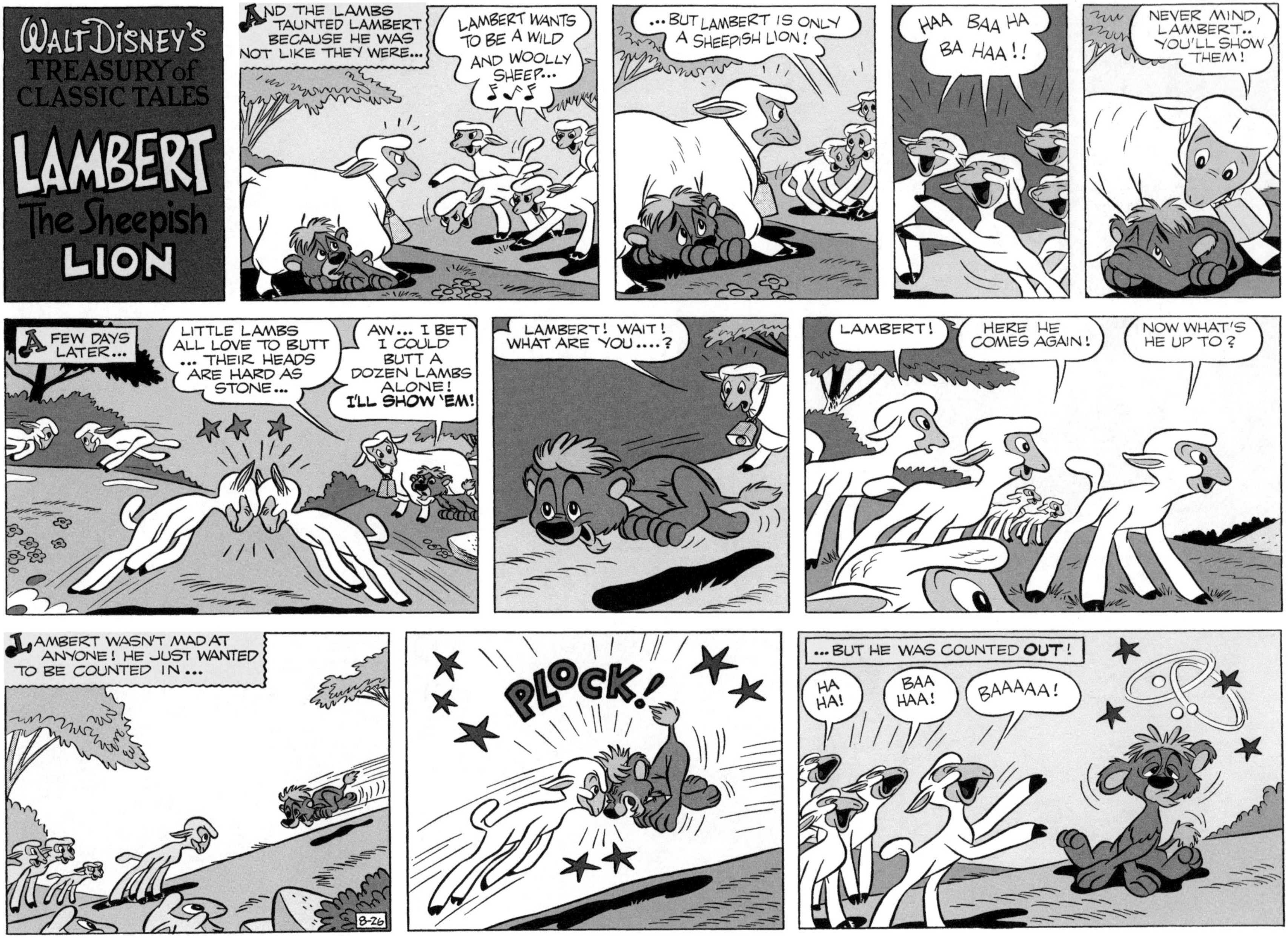
WALT DISNEY'S TREASURY of CLASSIC TALES
LAMBERT The Sheepish LION
AND THE LAMBS TAUNTED LAMBERT BECAUSE HE WAS NOT LIKE THEY WERE...
LAMBERT WANTS TO BE A WILD AND WOOLLY SHEEP...
...BUT LAMBERT IS ONLY A SHEEPISH LION!
HAA BAA HA BA HAA!!
NEVER MIND, LAMBERT.. YOU'LL SHOW THEM!
A FEW DAYS LATER...
LITTLE LAMBS ALL LOVE TO BUTT ... THEIR HEADS ARE HARD AS STONE...
AW... I BET I COULD BUTT A DOZEN LAMBS ALONE! I'LL SHOW 'EM!
LAMBERT! WAIT! WHAT ARE YOU....?
LAMBERT!
HERE HE COMES AGAIN!
NOW WHAT'S HE UP TO?
LAMBERT WASN'T MAD AT ANYONE! HE JUST WANTED TO BE COUNTED IN...
8-26
PLOCK!
...BUT HE WAS COUNTED OUT!
HA HA!
BAA HAA!
BAAAAA!

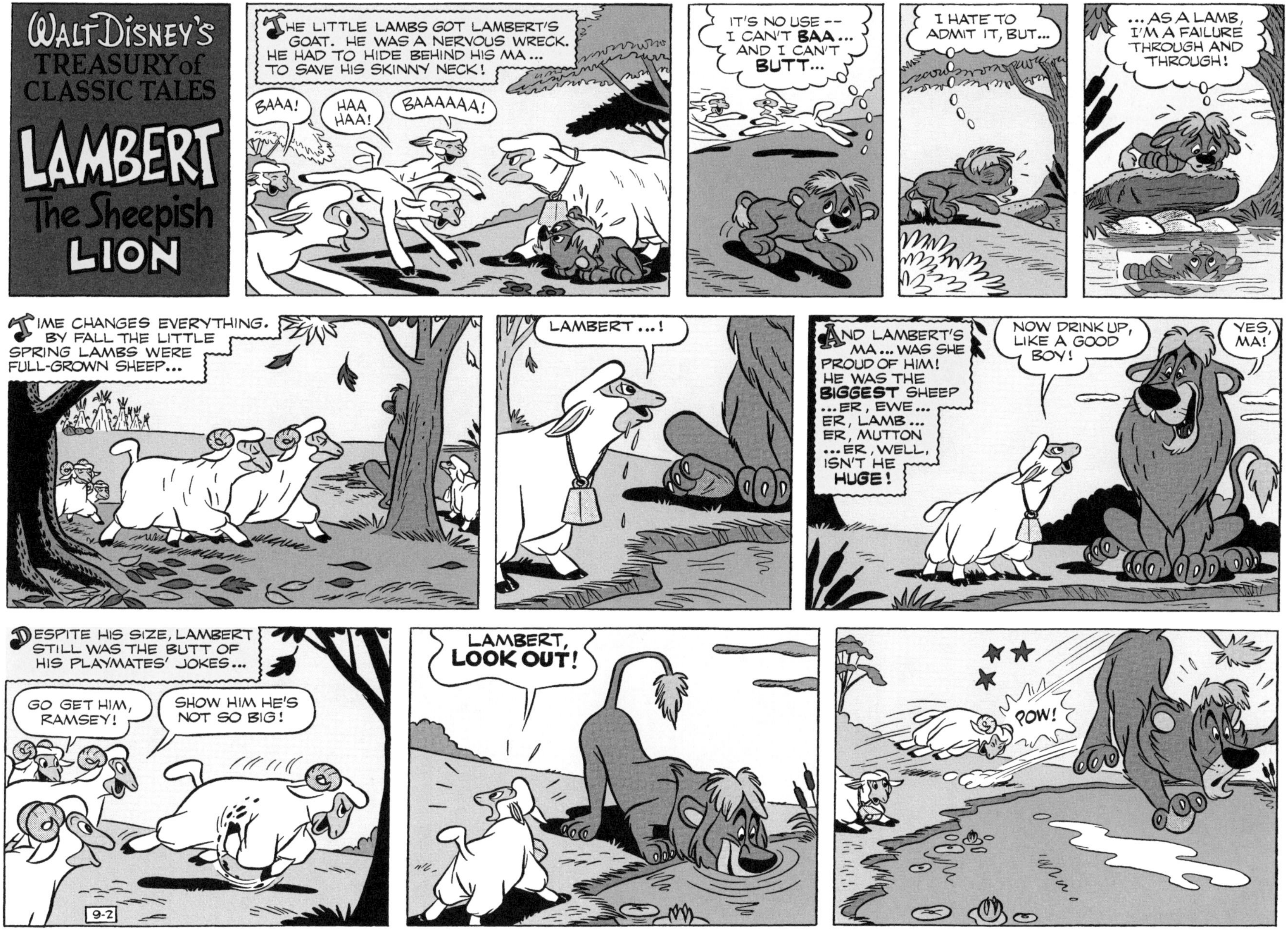

WALT DISNEY'S
TREASURY of CLASSIC TALES
LAMBERT The Sheepish LION
THE LITTLE LAMBS GOT LAMBERT'S GOAT. HE WAS A NERVOUS WRECK. HE HAD TO HIDE BEHIND HIS MA... TO SAVE HIS SKINNY NECK!
BAAA!
HAA HAA!
BAAAAAA!
IT'S NO USE -- I CAN'T BAA... AND I CAN'T BUTT...
I HATE TO ADMIT IT, BUT...
...AS A LAMB, I'M A FAILURE THROUGH AND THROUGH!
TIME CHANGES EVERYTHING. BY FALL THE LITTLE SPRING LAMBS WERE FULL-GROWN SHEEP...
LAMBERT...!
AND LAMBERT'S MA... WAS SHE PROUD OF HIM! HE WAS THE BIGGEST SHEEP ...ER, EWE... ER, LAMB... ER, MUTTON ...ER, WELL, ISN'T HE HUGE!
NOW DRINK UP, LIKE A GOOD BOY!
YES, MA!
DESPITE HIS SIZE, LAMBERT STILL WAS THE BUTT OF HIS PLAYMATES' JOKES...
GO GET HIM, RAMSEY!
SHOW HIM HE'S NOT SO BIG!
9-2
LAMBERT, LOOK OUT!
POW!

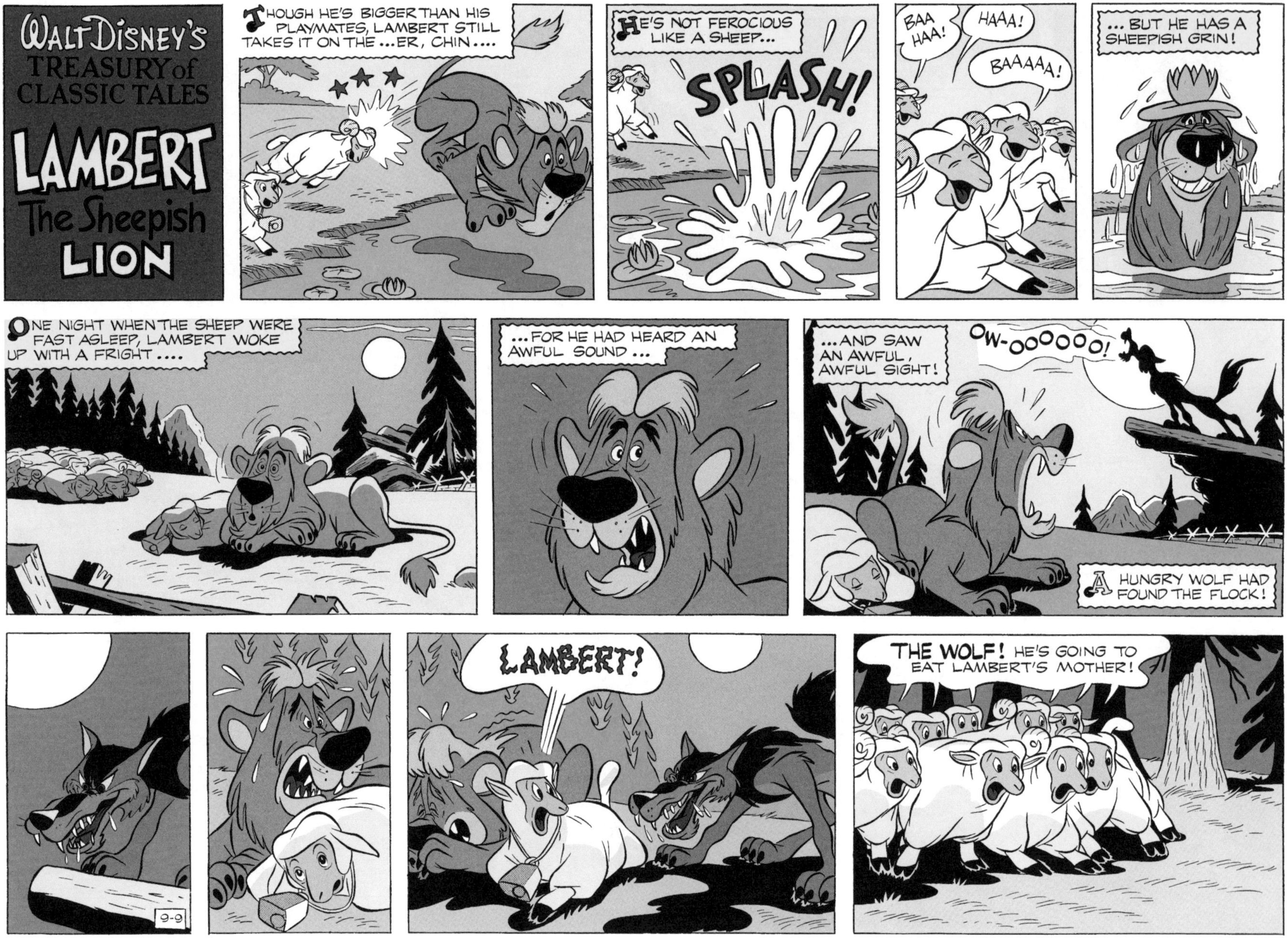
WALT DISNEY'S
TREASURY of CLASSIC TALES
LAMBERT The Sheepish LION
THOUGH HE'S BIGGER THAN HIS PLAYMATES, LAMBERT STILL TAKES IT ON THE ...ER, CHIN....
HE'S NOT FEROCIOUS LIKE A SHEEP...
SPLASH!
BAA HAA!
HAAA!
BAAAAA!
...BUT HE HAS A SHEEPISH GRIN!
ONE NIGHT WHEN THE SHEEP WERE FAST ASLEEP, LAMBERT WOKE UP WITH A FRIGHT....
...FOR HE HAD HEARD AN AWFUL SOUND...
...AND SAW AN AWFUL, AWFUL SIGHT!
OW-OOOOOO!
A HUNGRY WOLF HAD FOUND THE FLOCK!
9-9
LAMBERT!
THE WOLF! HE'S GOING TO EAT LAMBERT'S MOTHER!

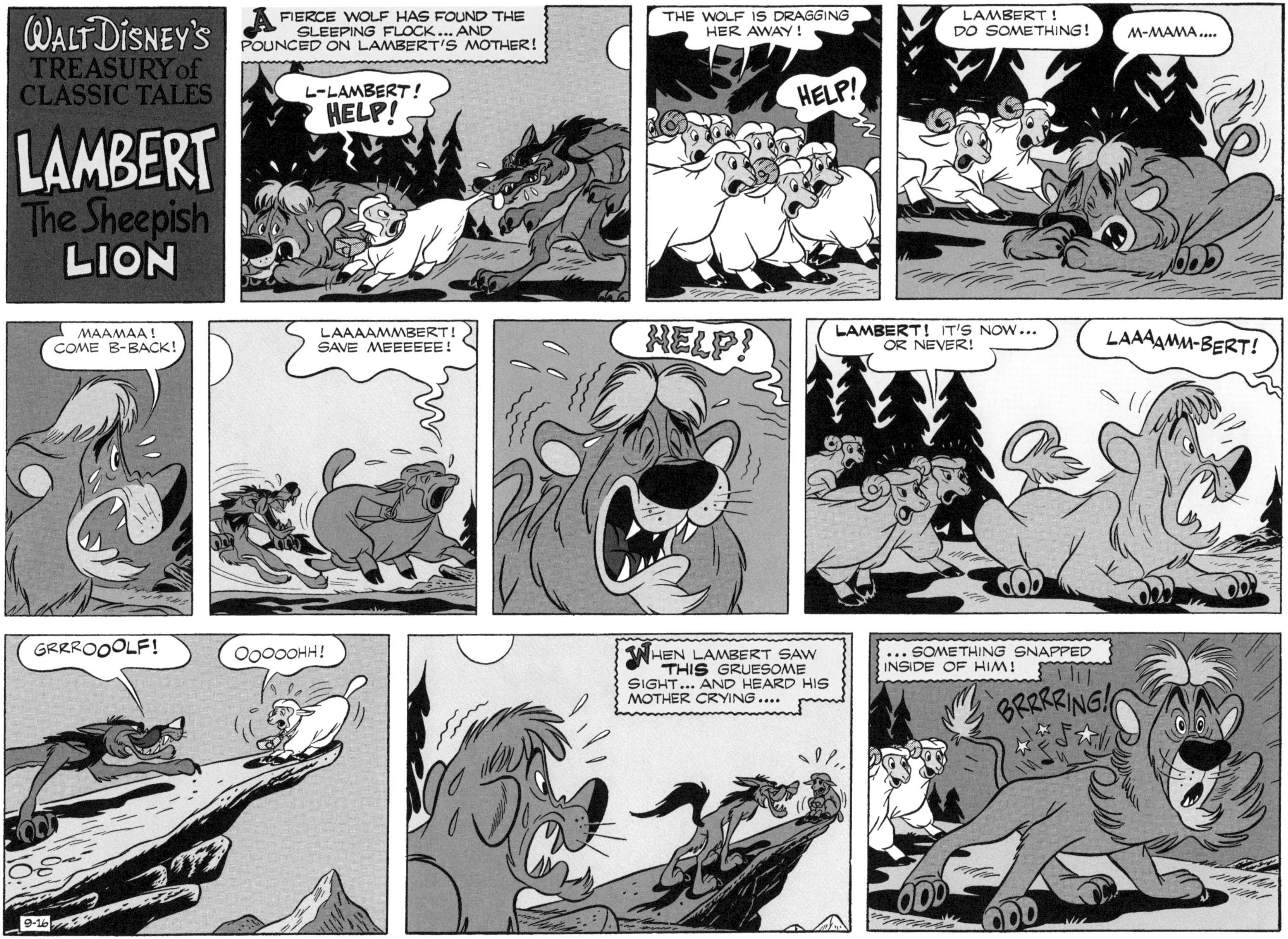
WALT DISNEY'S TREASURY of CLASSIC TALES
LAMBERT The Sheepish LION
A FIERCE WOLF HAS FOUND THE SLEEPING FLOCK... AND POUNCED ON LAMBERT'S MOTHER!
L-LAMBERT! HELP!
THE WOLF IS DRAGGING HER AWAY!
HELP!
LAMBERT! DO SOMETHING!
M-MAMA....
MAAMAA! COME B-BACK!
LAAAAMMBERT! SAVE MEEEEEE!
HELP!
LAMBERT! IT'S NOW... OR NEVER!
LAAAAMM-BERT!
GRRROOOLF!
OOOOOHH!
9-16
WHEN LAMBERT SAW THIS GRUESOME SIGHT... AND HEARD HIS MOTHER CRYING....
...SOMETHING SNAPPED INSIDE OF HIM!
BRRRRING!

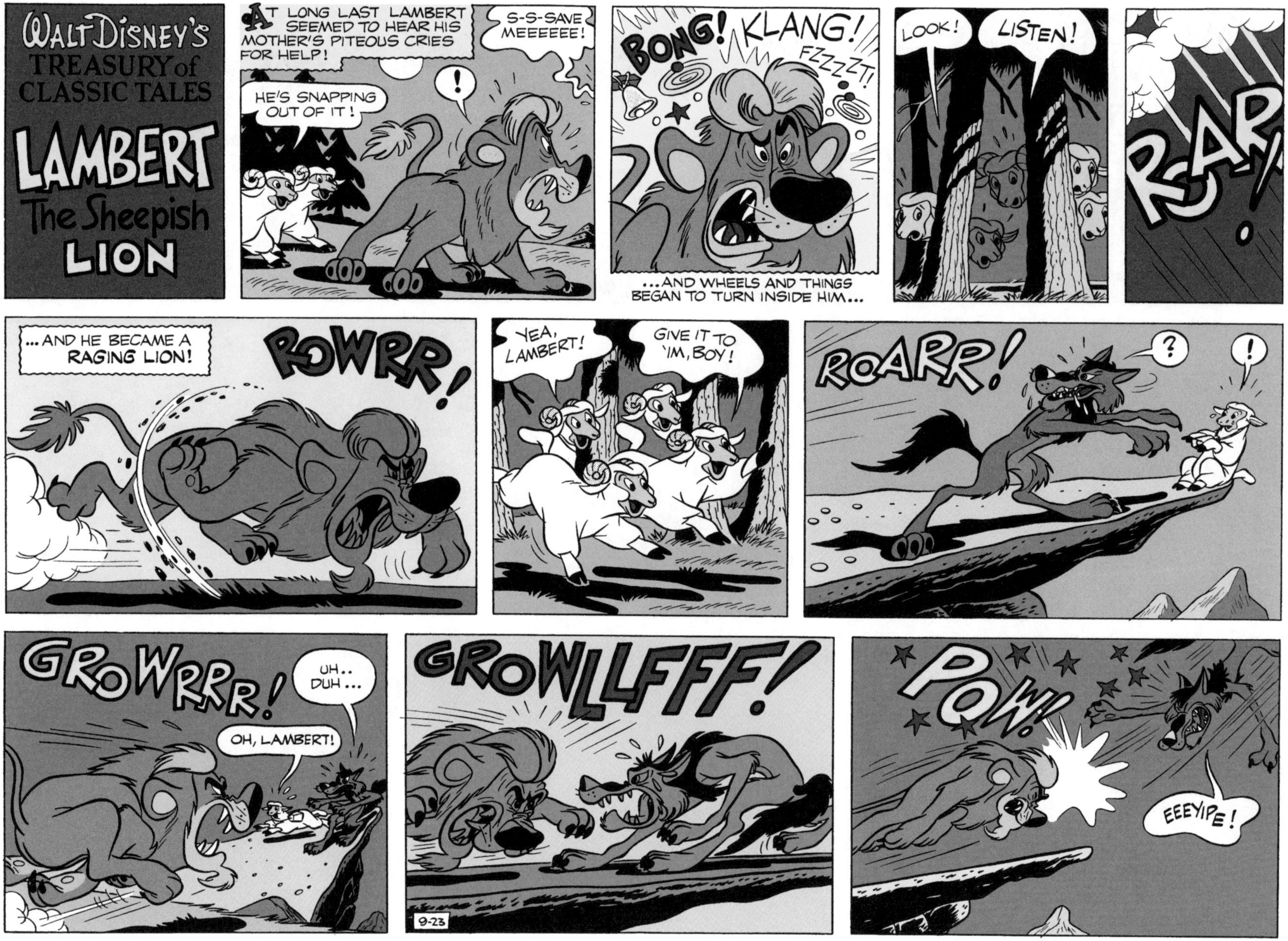
WALT DISNEY'S
TREASURY of CLASSIC TALES
LAMBERT The Sheepish LION
AT LONG LAST LAMBERT SEEMED TO HEAR HIS MOTHER'S PITEOUS CRIES FOR HELP!
S-S-SAVE MEEEEEE!
HE'S SNAPPING OUT OF IT!
!
BONG! KLANG! FZZZZT!
...AND WHEELS AND THINGS BEGAN TO TURN INSIDE HIM...
LOOK!
LISTEN!
ROAR!
...AND HE BECAME A RAGING LION!
ROWRR!
YEA, LAMBERT!
GIVE IT TO 'IM, BOY!
ROARR!
?
!
GROWRRR!
UH.. DUH...
OH, LAMBERT!
GROWLLFFF!
9-23
POW!
EEEYIPE!

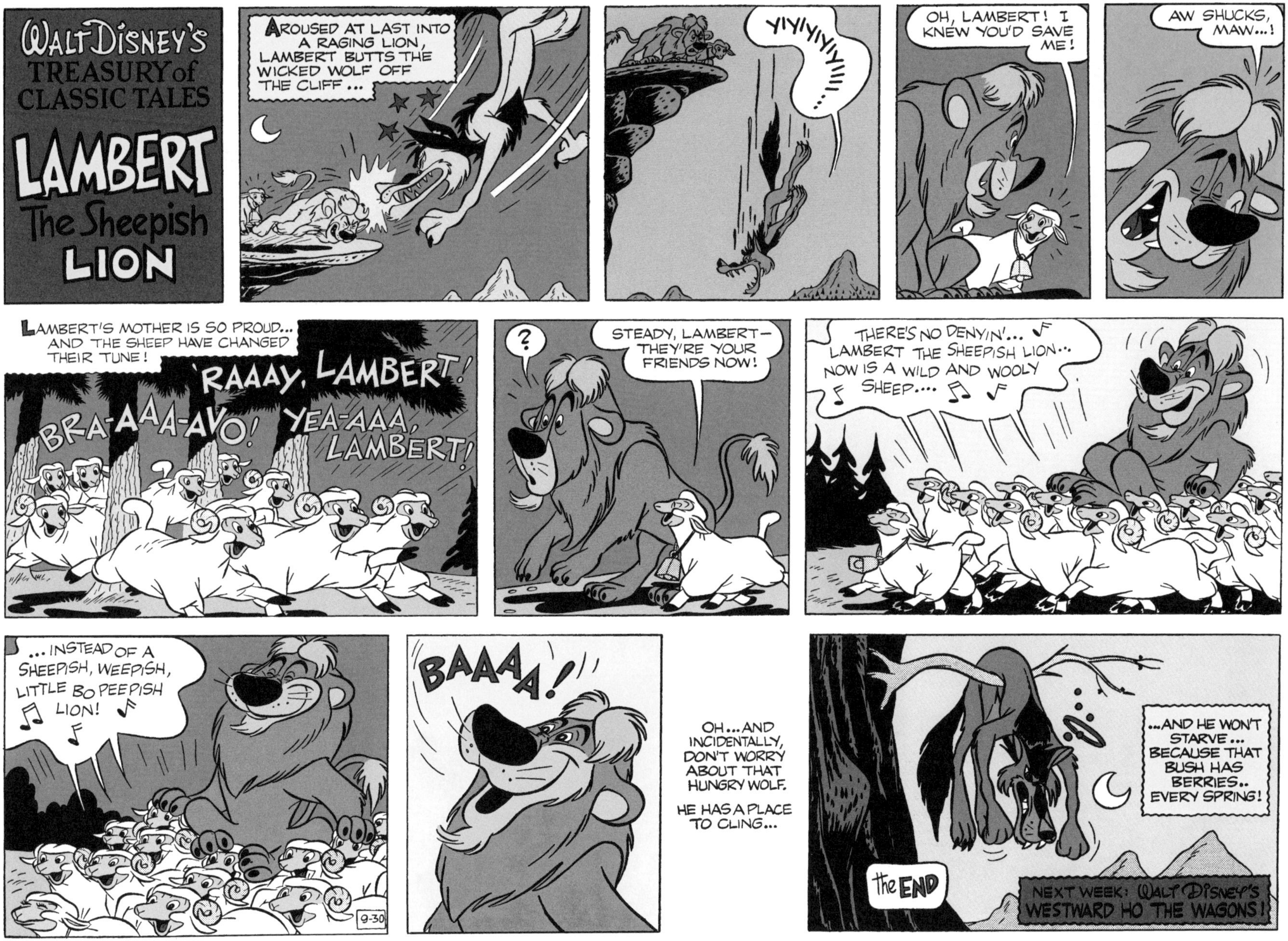
WALT DISNEY'S
TREASURY of CLASSIC TALES
LAMBERT The Sheepish LION
AROUSED AT LAST INTO A RAGING LION, LAMBERT BUTTS THE WICKED WOLF OFF THE CLIFF...
YIYIYIYIYI!!!...
OH, LAMBERT! I KNEW YOU'D SAVE ME!
AW SHUCKS, MAW...!
LAMBERT'S MOTHER IS SO PROUD... AND THE SHEEP HAVE CHANGED THEIR TUNE!
'RAAAY, LAMBERT!
BRA-AAA-AVO!
YEA-AAA, LAMBERT!
?
STEADY, LAMBERT— THEY'RE YOUR FRIENDS NOW!
THERE'S NO DENYIN'... LAMBERT THE SHEEPISH LION... NOW IS A WILD AND WOOLY SHEEP....
...INSTEAD OF A SHEEPISH, WEEPISH, LITTLE BO PEEPISH LION!
9-30
BAAAAA!
OH...AND INCIDENTALLY, DON'T WORRY ABOUT THAT HUNGRY WOLF.
HE HAS A PLACE TO CLING...
...AND HE WON'T STARVE... BECAUSE THAT BUSH HAS BERRIES.. EVERY SPRING!
the END
NEXT WEEK: WALT DISNEY'S WESTWARD HO THE WAGONS!

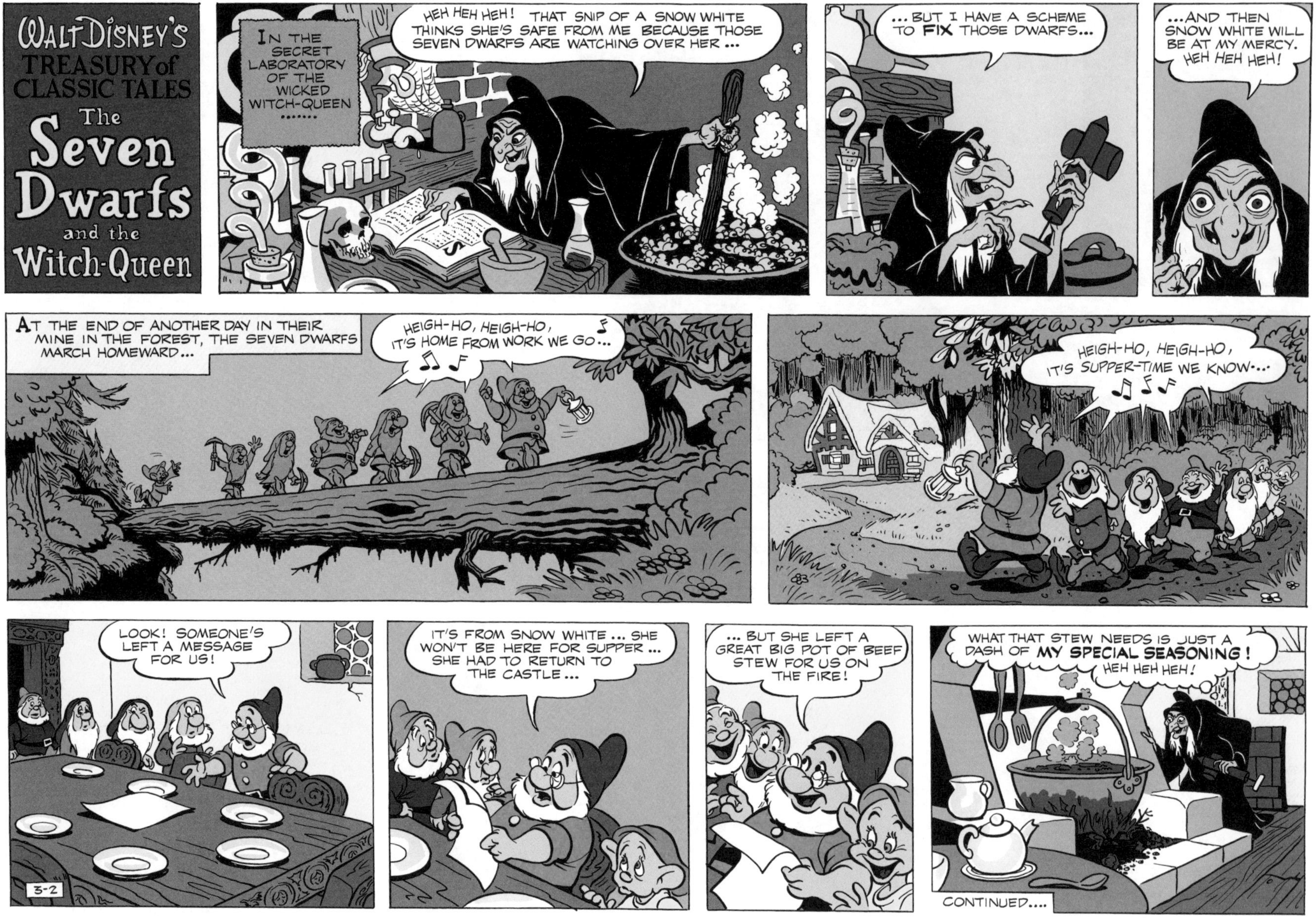

WALT DISNEY'S
TREASURY of CLASSIC TALES
The Seven Dwarfs and the Witch-Queen
IN THE SECRET LABORATORY OF THE WICKED WITCH-QUEEN ....
HEH HEH HEH! THAT SNIP OF A SNOW WHITE THINKS SHE'S SAFE FROM ME BECAUSE THOSE SEVEN DWARFS ARE WATCHING OVER HER ...
... BUT I HAVE A SCHEME TO FIX THOSE DWARFS...
...AND THEN SNOW WHITE WILL BE AT MY MERCY. HEH HEH HEH!
AT THE END OF ANOTHER DAY IN THEIR MINE IN THE FOREST, THE SEVEN DWARFS MARCH HOMEWARD...
HEIGH-HO, HEIGH-HO, IT'S HOME FROM WORK WE GO...
HEIGH-HO, HEIGH-HO, IT'S SUPPER-TIME WE KNOW...
LOOK! SOMEONE'S LEFT A MESSAGE FOR US!
3-2
IT'S FROM SNOW WHITE ... SHE WON'T BE HERE FOR SUPPER ... SHE HAD TO RETURN TO THE CASTLE ...
... BUT SHE LEFT A GREAT BIG POT OF BEEF STEW FOR US ON THE FIRE!
WHAT THAT STEW NEEDS IS JUST A DASH OF MY SPECIAL SEASONING! HEH HEH HEH!
CONTINUED....

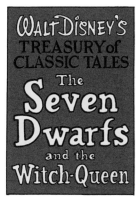

WALT DISNEY'S
TREASURY of CLASSIC TALES

The
Seven Dwarfs
and the
Witch-Queen

WASH TIME! NO SUPPER TILL YOUR HANDS AND FACES ARE CLEAN!

COME ON, GRUMPY! YOU'RE JUST AS SOOTY AS THE REST OF US!

HMPH!

WHILE THE DWARFS PREPARE FOR SUPPER...THE EVIL WITCH SLINKS INTO THEIR KITCHEN...

THOSE DRATTED DWARFS MUST BE HUNGRY AFTER A HARD DAY IN THE MINE ... HEH HEH HEH...

... SO I'LL JUST SPICE UP THIS STEW SNOW WHITE MADE FOR 'EM ... SO THEY'LL FINISH EVERY SPECK OF IT!

THERE! MY SEVEN SIMPLETONS! EAT HEARTY! HEH HEH HEH!

TONIGHT IT'S LITTLE DOPEY'S TURN TO WAIT ON TABLE...

3-9

HEIGH-HO!

WHEE!

YUM-MIE!

HURRY, DOPEY, AND GET YOUR BOWL-- SO WE CAN START EATING!

HEH HEH HEH!

DOPEY

CONTINUED....

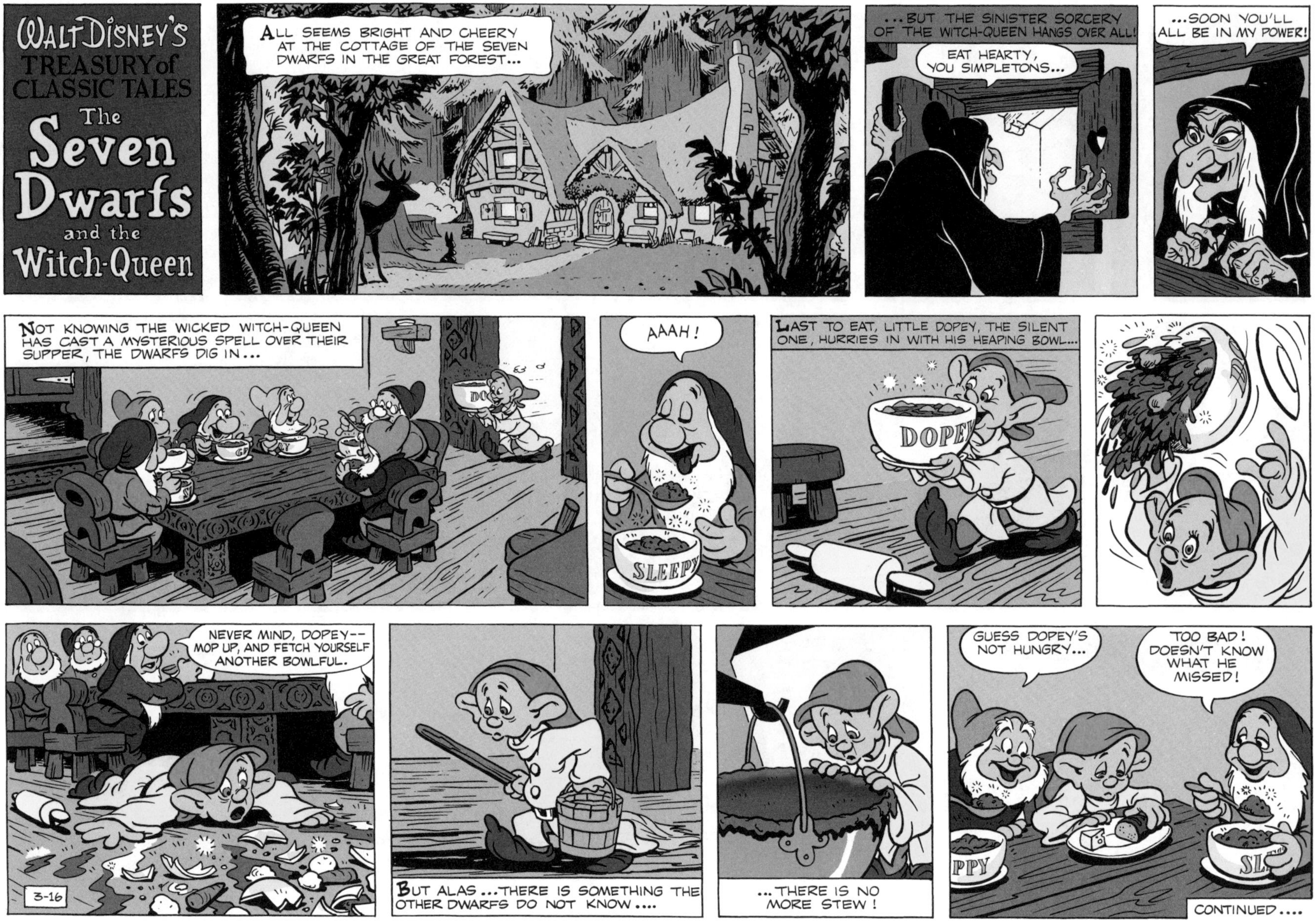
WALT DISNEY'S
TREASURY of CLASSIC TALES
The Seven Dwarfs and the Witch-Queen
ALL SEEMS BRIGHT AND CHEERY AT THE COTTAGE OF THE SEVEN DWARFS IN THE GREAT FOREST...
...BUT THE SINISTER SORCERY OF THE WITCH-QUEEN HANGS OVER ALL!
EAT HEARTY, YOU SIMPLETONS...
...SOON YOU'LL ALL BE IN MY POWER!
NOT KNOWING THE WICKED WITCH-QUEEN HAS CAST A MYSTERIOUS SPELL OVER THEIR SUPPER, THE DWARFS DIG IN...
AAAH!
SLEEPY
LAST TO EAT, LITTLE DOPEY, THE SILENT ONE, HURRIES IN WITH HIS HEAPING BOWL...
DOPEY
NEVER MIND, DOPEY-- MOP UP, AND FETCH YOURSELF ANOTHER BOWLFUL.
3-16
BUT ALAS...THERE IS SOMETHING THE OTHER DWARFS DO NOT KNOW....
...THERE IS NO MORE STEW!
GUESS DOPEY'S NOT HUNGRY...
TOO BAD! DOESN'T KNOW WHAT HE MISSED!
CONTINUED....

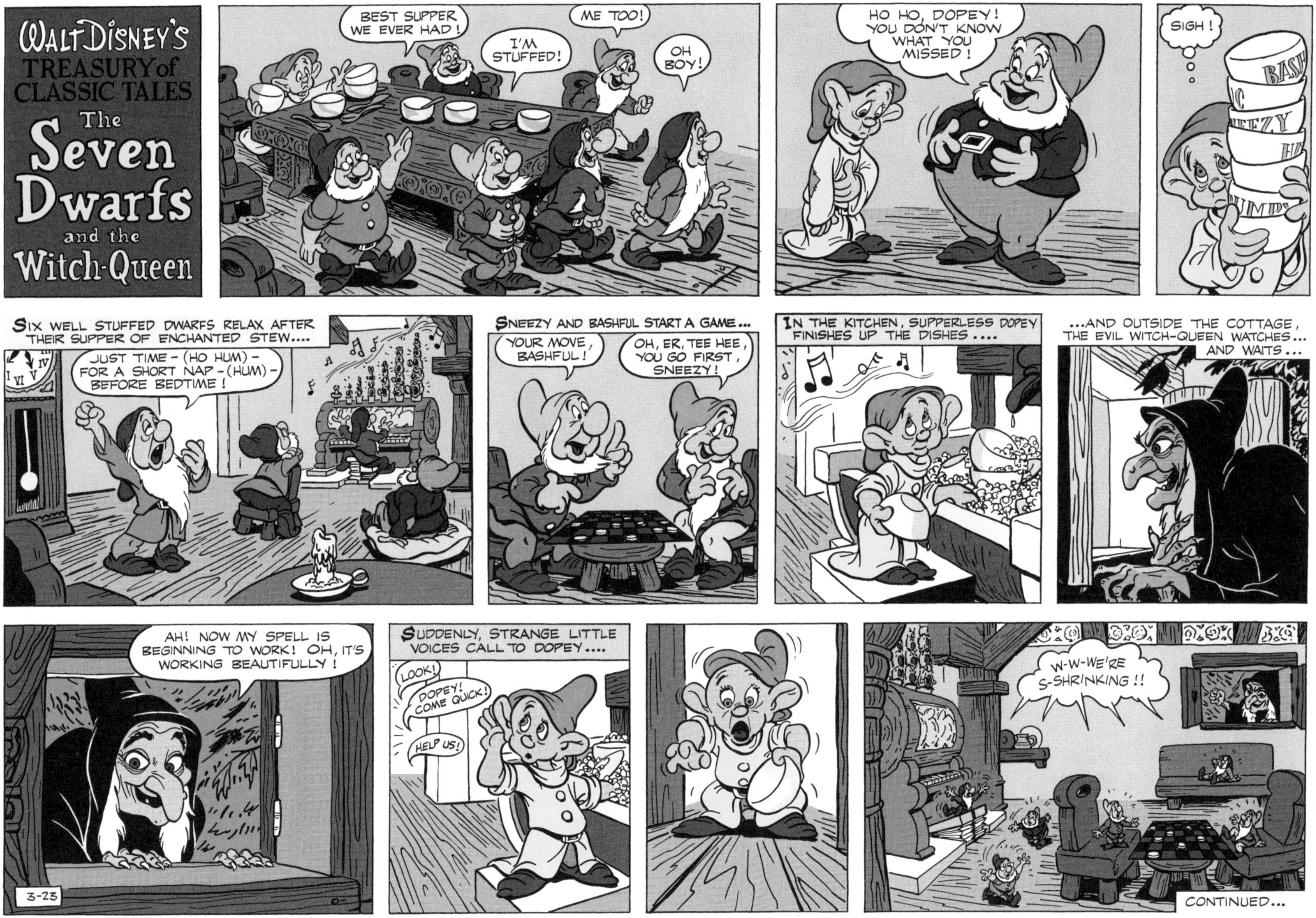

WALT DISNEY'S TREASURY of CLASSIC TALES
The Seven Dwarfs and the Witch-Queen
BEST SUPPER WE EVER HAD!
I'M STUFFED!
ME TOO!
OH BOY!
HO HO, DOPEY! YOU DON'T KNOW WHAT YOU MISSED!
SIGH!
SIX WELL STUFFED DWARFS RELAX AFTER THEIR SUPPER OF ENCHANTED STEW....
JUST TIME - (HO HUM) - FOR A SHORT NAP - (HUM) - BEFORE BEDTIME!
SNEEZY AND BASHFUL START A GAME...
YOUR MOVE, BASHFUL!
OH, ER, TEE HEE, YOU GO FIRST, SNEEZY!
IN THE KITCHEN, SUPPERLESS DOPEY FINISHES UP THE DISHES....
...AND OUTSIDE THE COTTAGE, THE EVIL WITCH-QUEEN WATCHES... AND WAITS...
AH! NOW MY SPELL IS BEGINNING TO WORK! OH, IT'S WORKING BEAUTIFULLY!
3-23
SUDDENLY, STRANGE LITTLE VOICES CALL TO DOPEY....
LOOK!
DOPEY! COME QUICK!
HELP US!
W-W-WE'RE S-SHRINKING!!
CONTINUED...

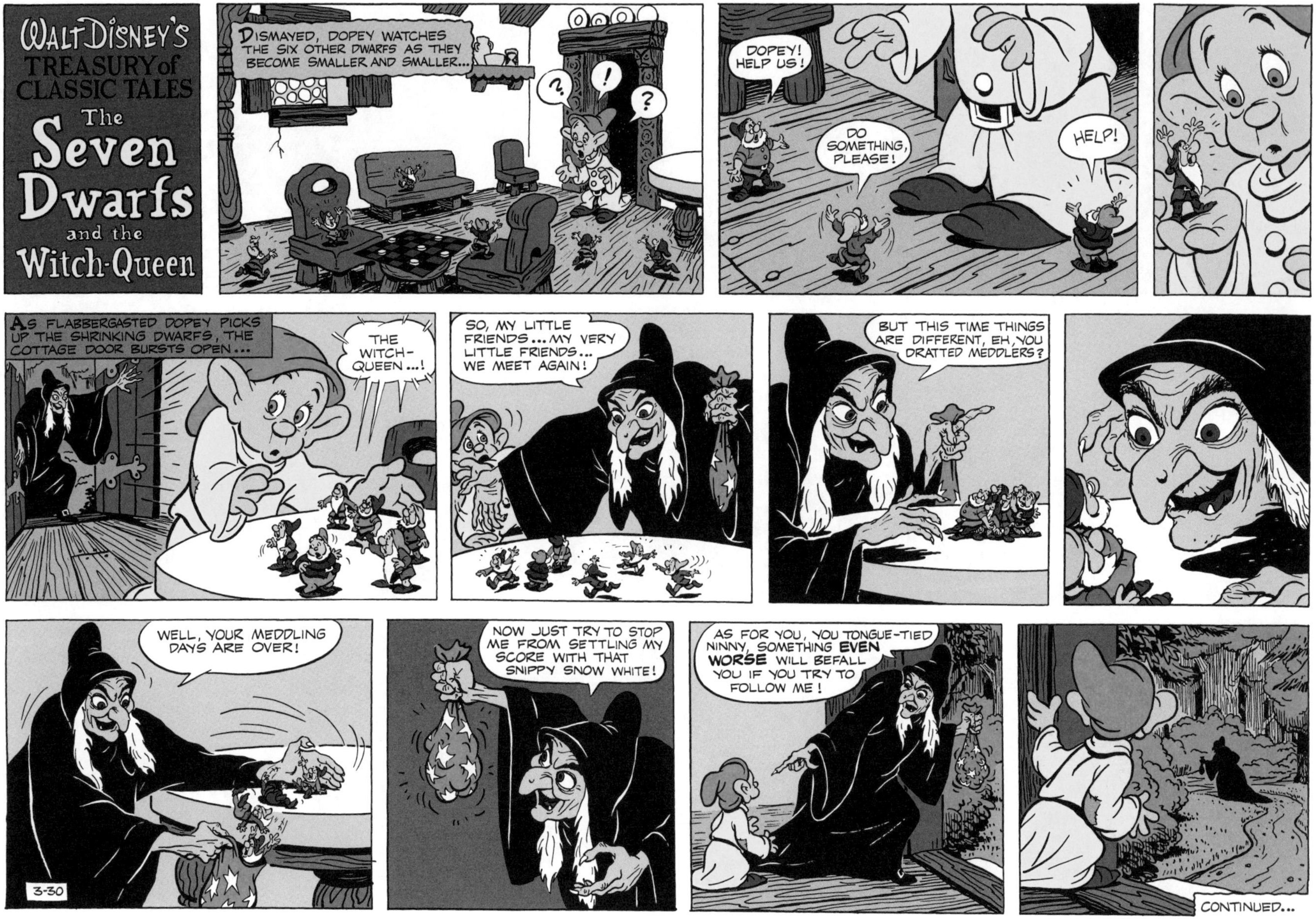

Walt Disney's Treasury of Classic Tales
The Seven Dwarfs and the Witch-Queen
DISMAYED, DOPEY WATCHES THE SIX OTHER DWARFS AS THEY BECOME SMALLER AND SMALLER...
?
!
?
DOPEY! HELP US!
DO SOMETHING, PLEASE!
HELP!
AS FLABBERGASTED DOPEY PICKS UP THE SHRINKING DWARFS, THE COTTAGE DOOR BURSTS OPEN...
THE WITCH-QUEEN...!
SO, MY LITTLE FRIENDS... MY VERY LITTLE FRIENDS... WE MEET AGAIN!
BUT THIS TIME THINGS ARE DIFFERENT, EH, YOU DRATTED MEDDLERS?
WELL, YOUR MEDDLING DAYS ARE OVER!
3-30
NOW JUST TRY TO STOP ME FROM SETTLING MY SCORE WITH THAT SNIPPY SNOW WHITE!
AS FOR YOU, YOU TONGUE-TIED NINNY, SOMETHING EVEN WORSE WILL BEFALL YOU IF YOU TRY TO FOLLOW ME!
CONTINUED...

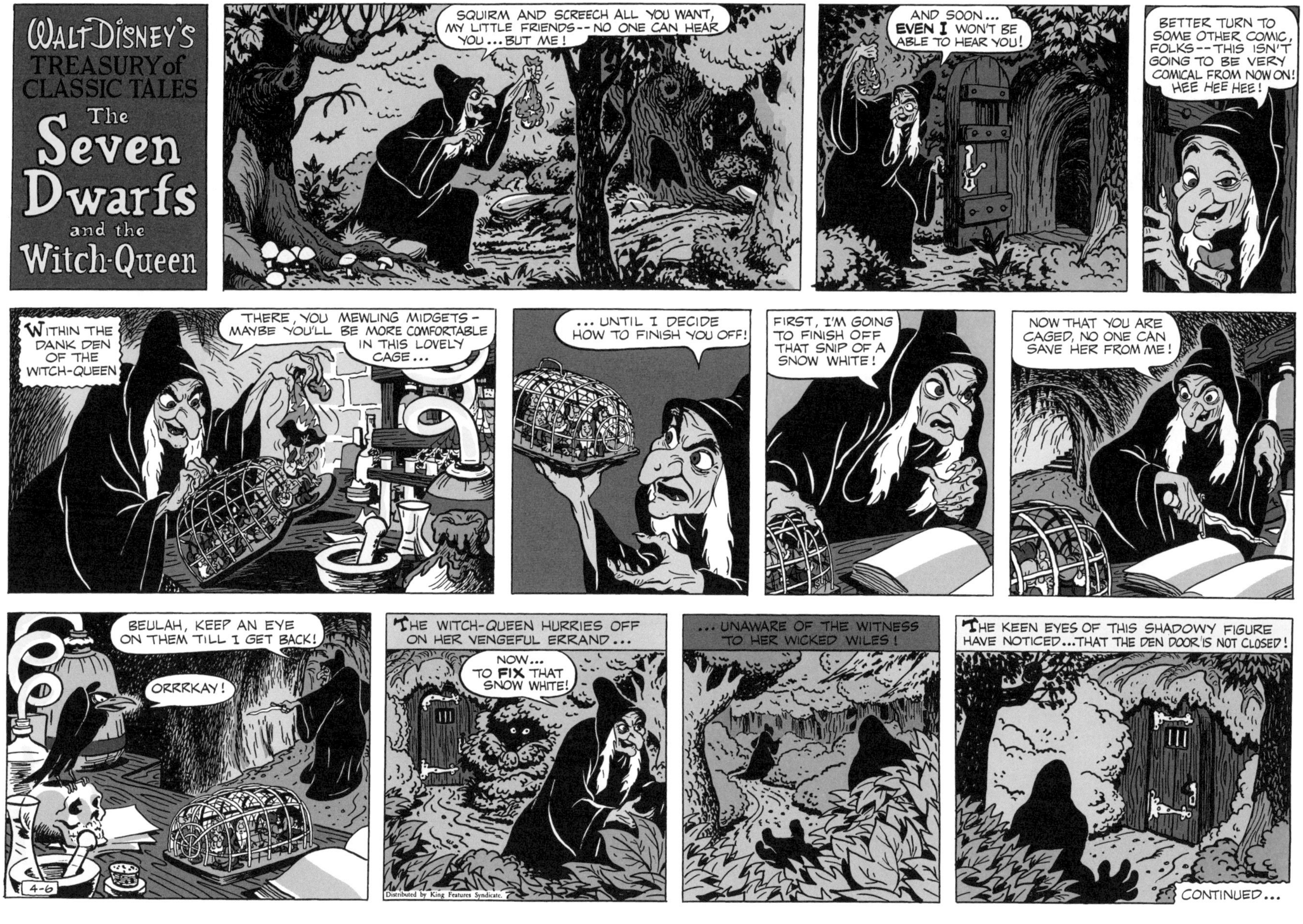

WALT DISNEY'S TREASURY of CLASSIC TALES
The Seven Dwarfs and the Witch-Queen
SQUIRM AND SCREECH ALL YOU WANT, MY LITTLE FRIENDS-- NO ONE CAN HEAR YOU... BUT ME!
AND SOON... EVEN I WON'T BE ABLE TO HEAR YOU!
BETTER TURN TO SOME OTHER COMIC, FOLKS--THIS ISN'T GOING TO BE VERY COMICAL FROM NOW ON! HEE HEE HEE!
WITHIN THE DANK DEN OF THE WITCH-QUEEN
THERE, YOU MEWLING MIDGETS-MAYBE YOU'LL BE MORE COMFORTABLE IN THIS LOVELY CAGE...
... UNTIL I DECIDE HOW TO FINISH YOU OFF!
FIRST, I'M GOING TO FINISH OFF THAT SNIP OF A SNOW WHITE!
NOW THAT YOU ARE CAGED, NO ONE CAN SAVE HER FROM ME!
BEULAH, KEEP AN EYE ON THEM TILL I GET BACK!
ORRRKAY!
4-6
THE WITCH-QUEEN HURRIES OFF ON HER VENGEFUL ERRAND...
NOW... TO FIX THAT SNOW WHITE!
Distributed by King Features Syndicate.
... UNAWARE OF THE WITNESS TO HER WICKED WILES!
THE KEEN EYES OF THIS SHADOWY FIGURE HAVE NOTICED...THAT THE DEN DOOR IS NOT CLOSED!
CONTINUED...

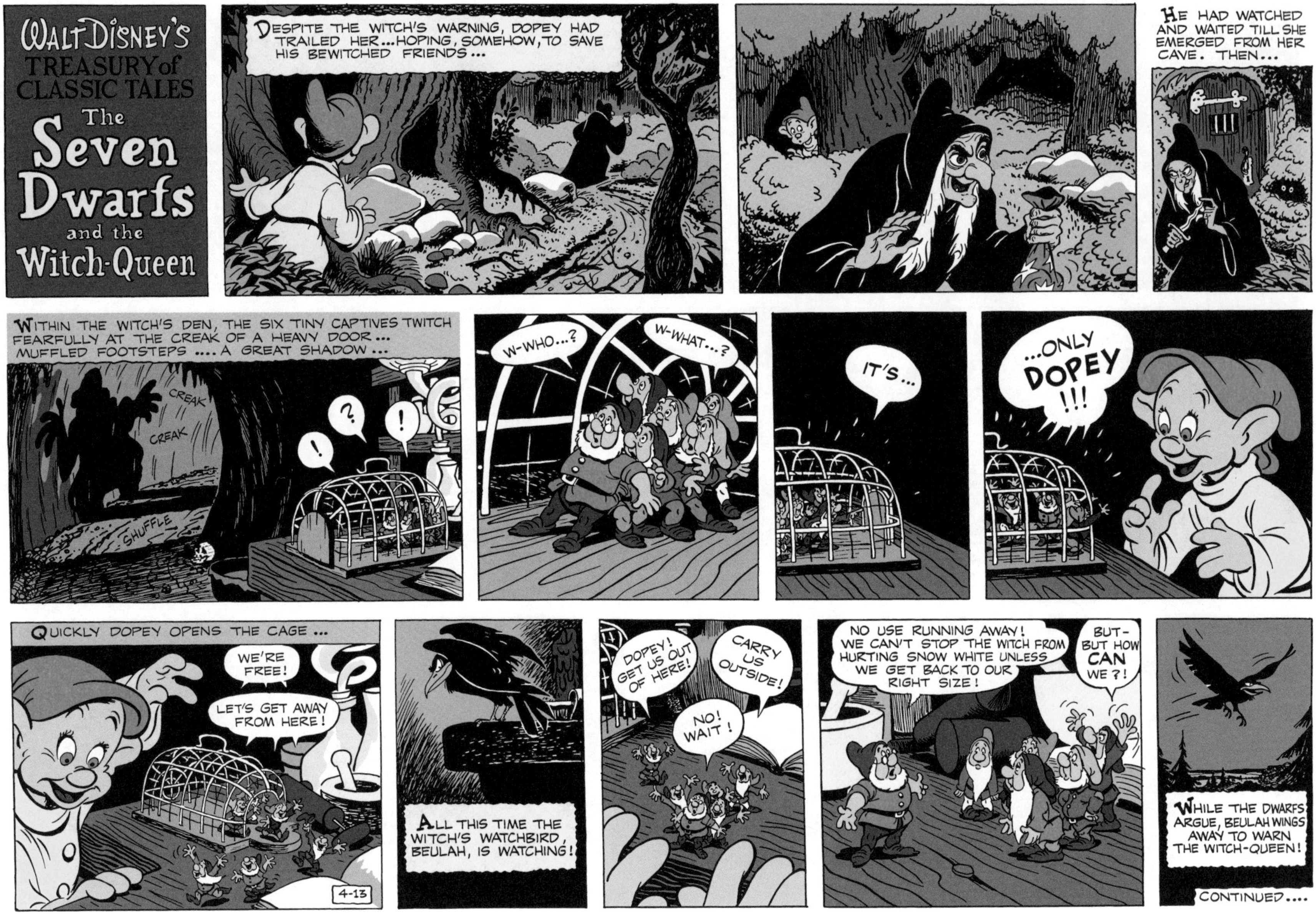

WALT DISNEY'S
TREASURY of CLASSIC TALES
The Seven Dwarfs and the Witch-Queen
DESPITE THE WITCH'S WARNING, DOPEY HAD TRAILED HER...HOPING, SOMEHOW, TO SAVE HIS BEWITCHED FRIENDS...
HE HAD WATCHED AND WAITED TILL SHE EMERGED FROM HER CAVE. THEN...
WITHIN THE WITCH'S DEN, THE SIX TINY CAPTIVES TWITCH FEARFULLY AT THE CREAK OF A HEAVY DOOR... MUFFLED FOOTSTEPS .... A GREAT SHADOW...
CREAK
CREAK
SHUFFLE
!
?
!
W-WHO...?
W-WHAT...?
IT'S...
...ONLY DOPEY !!!
QUICKLY DOPEY OPENS THE CAGE...
WE'RE FREE!
LET'S GET AWAY FROM HERE!
4-13
ALL THIS TIME THE WITCH'S WATCHBIRD, BEULAH, IS WATCHING!
DOPEY! GET US OUT OF HERE!
CARRY US OUTSIDE!
NO! WAIT!
NO USE RUNNING AWAY! WE CAN'T STOP THE WITCH FROM HURTING SNOW WHITE UNLESS WE GET BACK TO OUR RIGHT SIZE!
BUT- BUT HOW CAN WE?!
WHILE THE DWARFS ARGUE, BEULAH WINGS AWAY TO WARN THE WITCH-QUEEN!
CONTINUED....

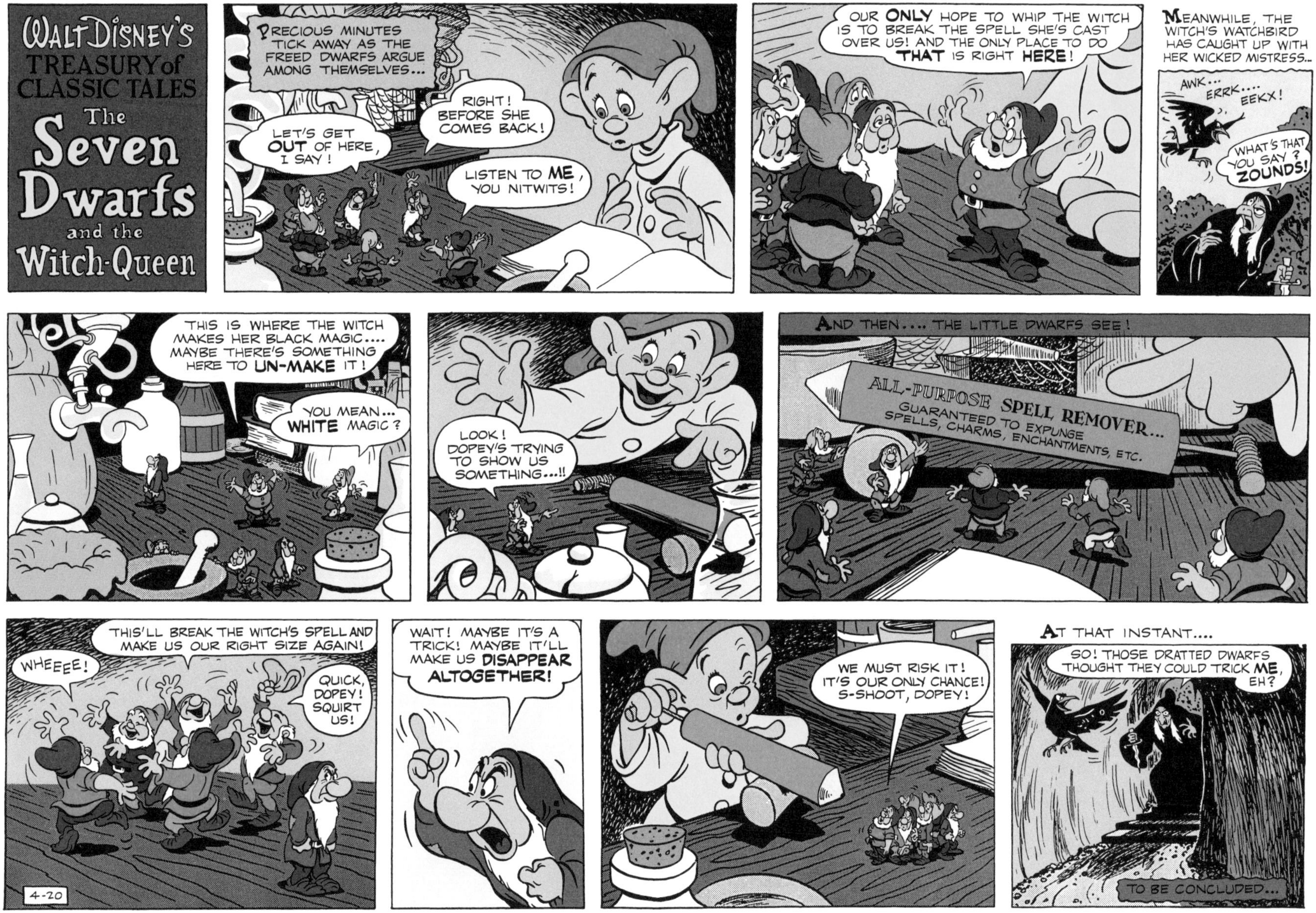
WALT DISNEY'S TREASURY of CLASSIC TALES
The Seven Dwarfs and the Witch-Queen
PRECIOUS MINUTES TICK AWAY AS THE FREED DWARFS ARGUE AMONG THEMSELVES...
LET'S GET OUT OF HERE, I SAY!
RIGHT! BEFORE SHE COMES BACK!
LISTEN TO ME, YOU NITWITS!
OUR ONLY HOPE TO WHIP THE WITCH IS TO BREAK THE SPELL SHE'S CAST OVER US! AND THE ONLY PLACE TO DO THAT IS RIGHT HERE!
MEANWHILE, THE WITCH'S WATCHBIRD HAS CAUGHT UP WITH HER WICKED MISTRESS...
AWK... ERRK.... EEKX!
WHAT'S THAT YOU SAY? ZOUNDS!
THIS IS WHERE THE WITCH MAKES HER BLACK MAGIC.... MAYBE THERE'S SOMETHING HERE TO UN-MAKE IT!
YOU MEAN... WHITE MAGIC?
LOOK! DOPEY'S TRYING TO SHOW US SOMETHING...!!
AND THEN.... THE LITTLE DWARFS SEE!
ALL-PURPOSE SPELL REMOVER... GUARANTEED TO EXPUNGE SPELLS, CHARMS, ENCHANTMENTS, ETC.
THIS'LL BREAK THE WITCH'S SPELL AND MAKE US OUR RIGHT SIZE AGAIN!
WHEEEEE!
QUICK, DOPEY! SQUIRT US!
4-20
WAIT! MAYBE IT'S A TRICK! MAYBE IT'LL MAKE US DISAPPEAR ALTOGETHER!
WE MUST RISK IT! IT'S OUR ONLY CHANCE! S-SHOOT, DOPEY!
AT THAT INSTANT....
SO! THOSE DRATTED DWARFS THOUGHT THEY COULD TRICK ME, EH?
TO BE CONCLUDED...

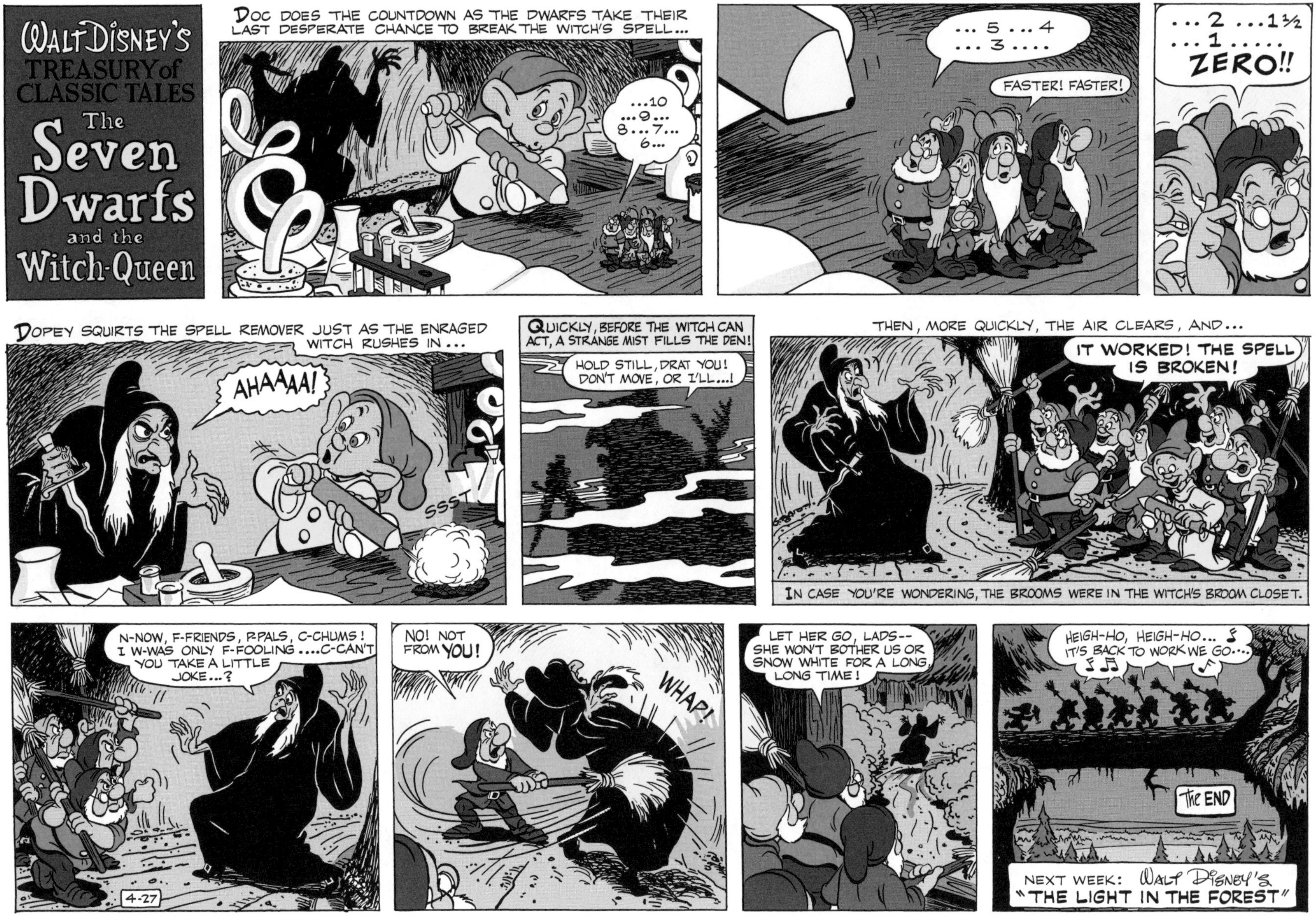
WALT DISNEY'S TREASURY of CLASSIC TALES
The Seven Dwarfs and the Witch-Queen
DOC DOES THE COUNTDOWN AS THE DWARFS TAKE THEIR LAST DESPERATE CHANCE TO BREAK THE WITCH'S SPELL...
...10 ...9... 8...7... 6...
... 5 ... 4 ... 3 ....
FASTER! FASTER!
... 2 ... 1½ ... 1 ..... ZERO!!
DOPEY SQUIRTS THE SPELL REMOVER JUST AS THE ENRAGED WITCH RUSHES IN ...
AHAAAA!
SSST
QUICKLY, BEFORE THE WITCH CAN ACT, A STRANGE MIST FILLS THE DEN!
HOLD STILL, DRAT YOU! DON'T MOVE, OR I'LL...!
THEN, MORE QUICKLY, THE AIR CLEARS, AND...
IT WORKED! THE SPELL IS BROKEN!
IN CASE YOU'RE WONDERING, THE BROOMS WERE IN THE WITCH'S BROOM CLOSET.
N-NOW, F-FRIENDS, P-PALS, C-CHUMS! I W-WAS ONLY F-FOOLING ....C-CAN'T YOU TAKE A LITTLE JOKE...?
4-27
NO! NOT FROM YOU!
WHAP!
LET HER GO, LADS-- SHE WON'T BOTHER US OR SNOW WHITE FOR A LONG, LONG TIME!
HEIGH-HO, HEIGH-HO... IT'S BACK TO WORK WE GO...
The END
NEXT WEEK: WALT DISNEY'S "THE LIGHT IN THE FOREST"

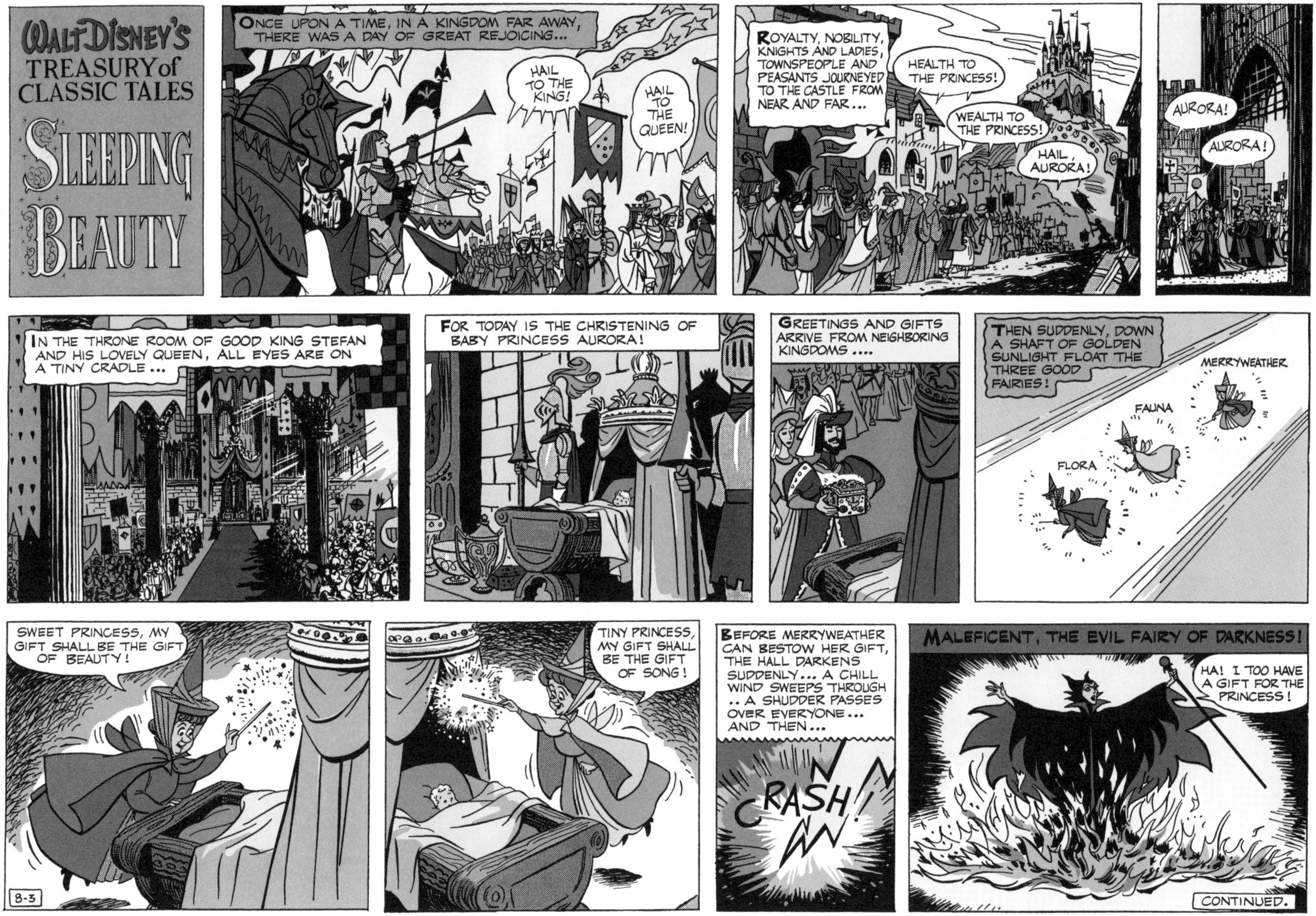
WALT DISNEY'S
TREASURY of CLASSIC TALES
SLEEPING BEAUTY
ONCE UPON A TIME, IN A KINGDOM FAR AWAY, THERE WAS A DAY OF GREAT REJOICING...
HAIL TO THE KING!
HAIL TO THE QUEEN!
ROYALTY, NOBILITY, KNIGHTS AND LADIES, TOWNSPEOPLE AND PEASANTS JOURNEYED TO THE CASTLE FROM NEAR AND FAR...
HEALTH TO THE PRINCESS!
WEALTH TO THE PRINCESS!
HAIL, AURORA!
AURORA!
AURORA!
IN THE THRONE ROOM OF GOOD KING STEFAN AND HIS LOVELY QUEEN, ALL EYES ARE ON A TINY CRADLE...
FOR TODAY IS THE CHRISTENING OF BABY PRINCESS AURORA!
GREETINGS AND GIFTS ARRIVE FROM NEIGHBORING KINGDOMS....
THEN SUDDENLY, DOWN A SHAFT OF GOLDEN SUNLIGHT FLOAT THE THREE GOOD FAIRIES!
MERRYWEATHER
FAUNA
FLORA
SWEET PRINCESS, MY GIFT SHALL BE THE GIFT OF BEAUTY!
8-3
TINY PRINCESS, MY GIFT SHALL BE THE GIFT OF SONG!
BEFORE MERRYWEATHER CAN BESTOW HER GIFT, THE HALL DARKENS SUDDENLY... A CHILL WIND SWEEPS THROUGH .. A SHUDDER PASSES OVER EVERYONE... AND THEN...
CRASH!
MALEFICENT, THE EVIL FAIRY OF DARKNESS!
HA! I TOO HAVE A GIFT FOR THE PRINCESS!
CONTINUED.

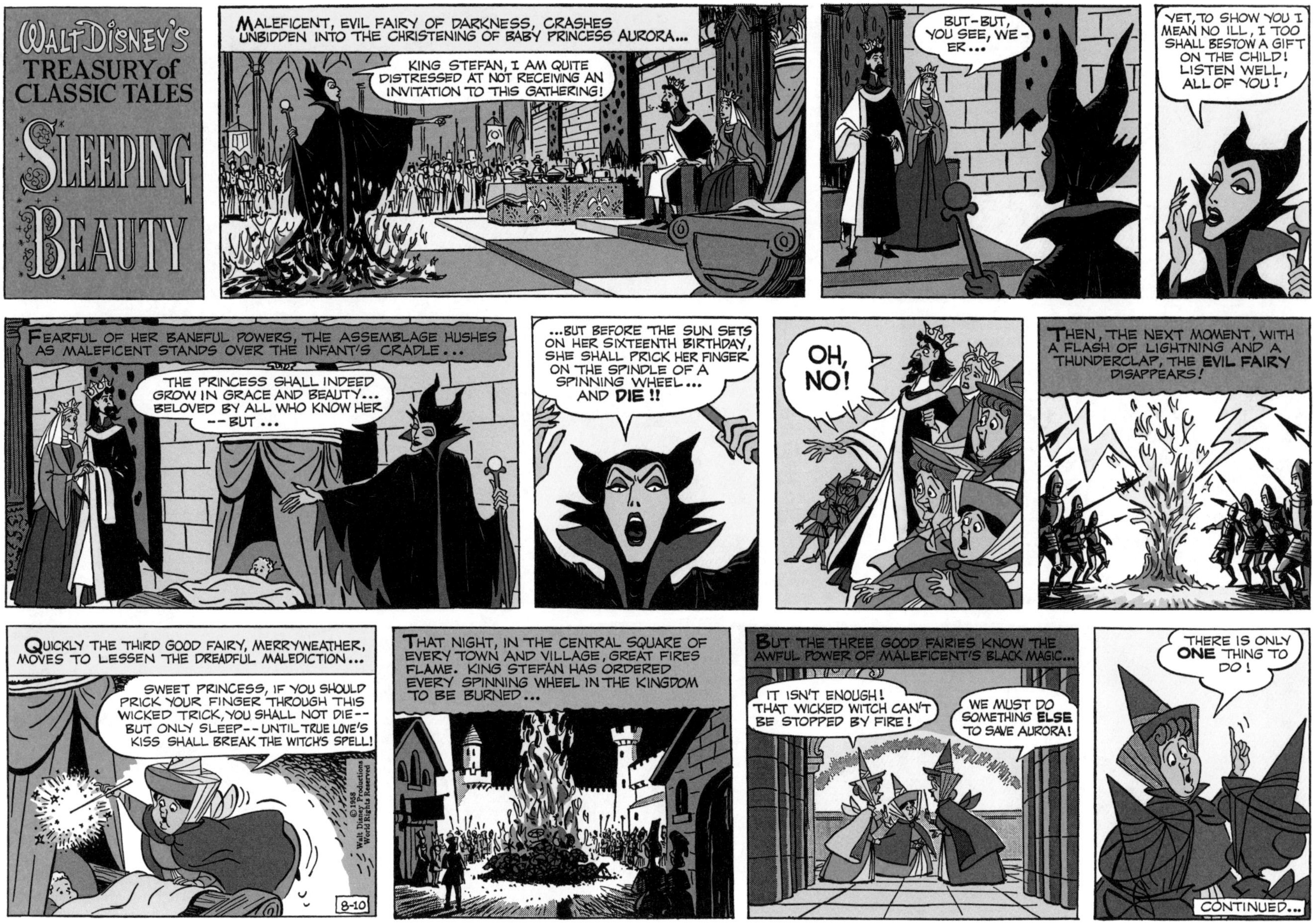
WALT DISNEY'S
TREASURY of CLASSIC TALES
SLEEPING BEAUTY
MALEFICENT, EVIL FAIRY OF DARKNESS, CRASHES UNBIDDEN INTO THE CHRISTENING OF BABY PRINCESS AURORA...
KING STEFAN, I AM QUITE DISTRESSED AT NOT RECEIVING AN INVITATION TO THIS GATHERING!
BUT-BUT, YOU SEE, WE-ER...
YET, TO SHOW YOU I MEAN NO ILL, I TOO SHALL BESTOW A GIFT ON THE CHILD! LISTEN WELL, ALL OF YOU!
FEARFUL OF HER BANEFUL POWERS, THE ASSEMBLAGE HUSHES AS MALEFICENT STANDS OVER THE INFANT'S CRADLE...
THE PRINCESS SHALL INDEED GROW IN GRACE AND BEAUTY... BELOVED BY ALL WHO KNOW HER --BUT...
...BUT BEFORE THE SUN SETS ON HER SIXTEENTH BIRTHDAY, SHE SHALL PRICK HER FINGER ON THE SPINDLE OF A SPINNING WHEEL... AND **DIE**!!
OH, NO!
THEN, THE NEXT MOMENT, WITH A FLASH OF LIGHTNING AND A THUNDERCLAP, THE **EVIL FAIRY** DISAPPEARS!
QUICKLY THE THIRD GOOD FAIRY, MERRYWEATHER, MOVES TO LESSEN THE DREADFUL MALEDICTION...
SWEET PRINCESS, IF YOU SHOULD PRICK YOUR FINGER THROUGH THIS WICKED TRICK, YOU SHALL NOT DIE-- BUT ONLY SLEEP--UNTIL TRUE LOVE'S KISS SHALL BREAK THE WITCH'S SPELL!
© 1958 Walt Disney Productions World Rights Reserved
8-10
THAT NIGHT, IN THE CENTRAL SQUARE OF EVERY TOWN AND VILLAGE, GREAT FIRES FLAME. KING STEFAN HAS ORDERED EVERY SPINNING WHEEL IN THE KINGDOM TO BE BURNED...
BUT THE THREE GOOD FAIRIES KNOW THE AWFUL POWER OF MALEFICENT'S BLACK MAGIC...
IT ISN'T ENOUGH! THAT WICKED WITCH CAN'T BE STOPPED BY FIRE!
WE MUST DO SOMETHING **ELSE** TO SAVE AURORA!
THERE IS ONLY **ONE** THING TO DO!
CONTINUED...

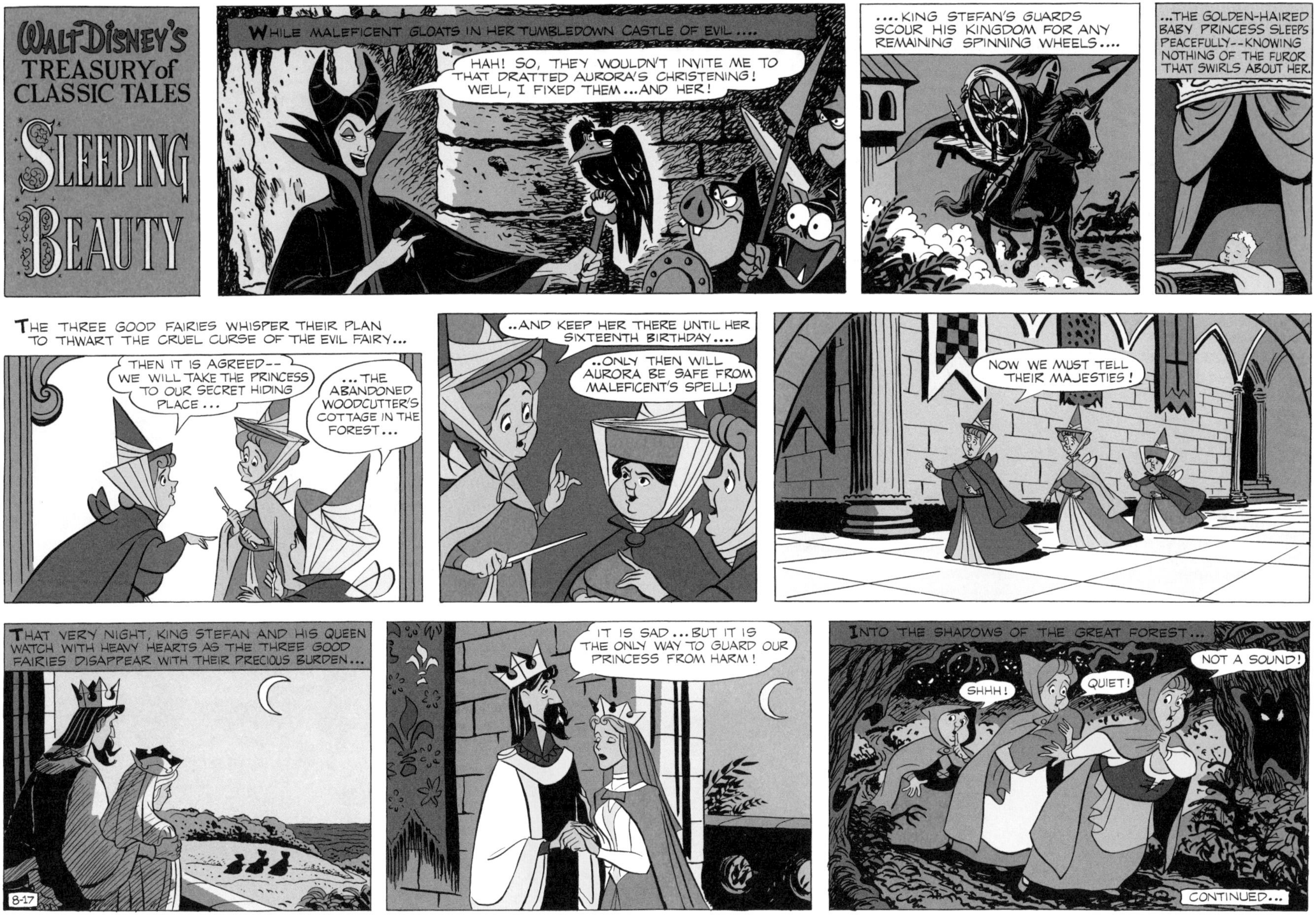

WALT DISNEY'S TREASURY of CLASSIC TALES
SLEEPING BEAUTY
WHILE MALEFICENT GLOATS IN HER TUMBLEDOWN CASTLE OF EVIL....
HAH! SO, THEY WOULDN'T INVITE ME TO THAT DRATTED AURORA'S CHRISTENING! WELL, I FIXED THEM...AND HER!
....KING STEFAN'S GUARDS SCOUR HIS KINGDOM FOR ANY REMAINING SPINNING WHEELS....
..THE GOLDEN-HAIRED BABY PRINCESS SLEEPS PEACEFULLY--KNOWING NOTHING OF THE FUROR THAT SWIRLS ABOUT HER.
THE THREE GOOD FAIRIES WHISPER THEIR PLAN TO THWART THE CRUEL CURSE OF THE EVIL FAIRY...
THEN IT IS AGREED-- WE WILL TAKE THE PRINCESS TO OUR SECRET HIDING PLACE...
...THE ABANDONED WOODCUTTER'S COTTAGE IN THE FOREST...
..AND KEEP HER THERE UNTIL HER SIXTEENTH BIRTHDAY....
..ONLY THEN WILL AURORA BE SAFE FROM MALEFICENT'S SPELL!
NOW WE MUST TELL THEIR MAJESTIES!
THAT VERY NIGHT, KING STEFAN AND HIS QUEEN WATCH WITH HEAVY HEARTS AS THE THREE GOOD FAIRIES DISAPPEAR WITH THEIR PRECIOUS BURDEN...
8-17
IT IS SAD...BUT IT IS THE ONLY WAY TO GUARD OUR PRINCESS FROM HARM!
INTO THE SHADOWS OF THE GREAT FOREST...
SHHH!
QUIET!
NOT A SOUND!
CONTINUED...

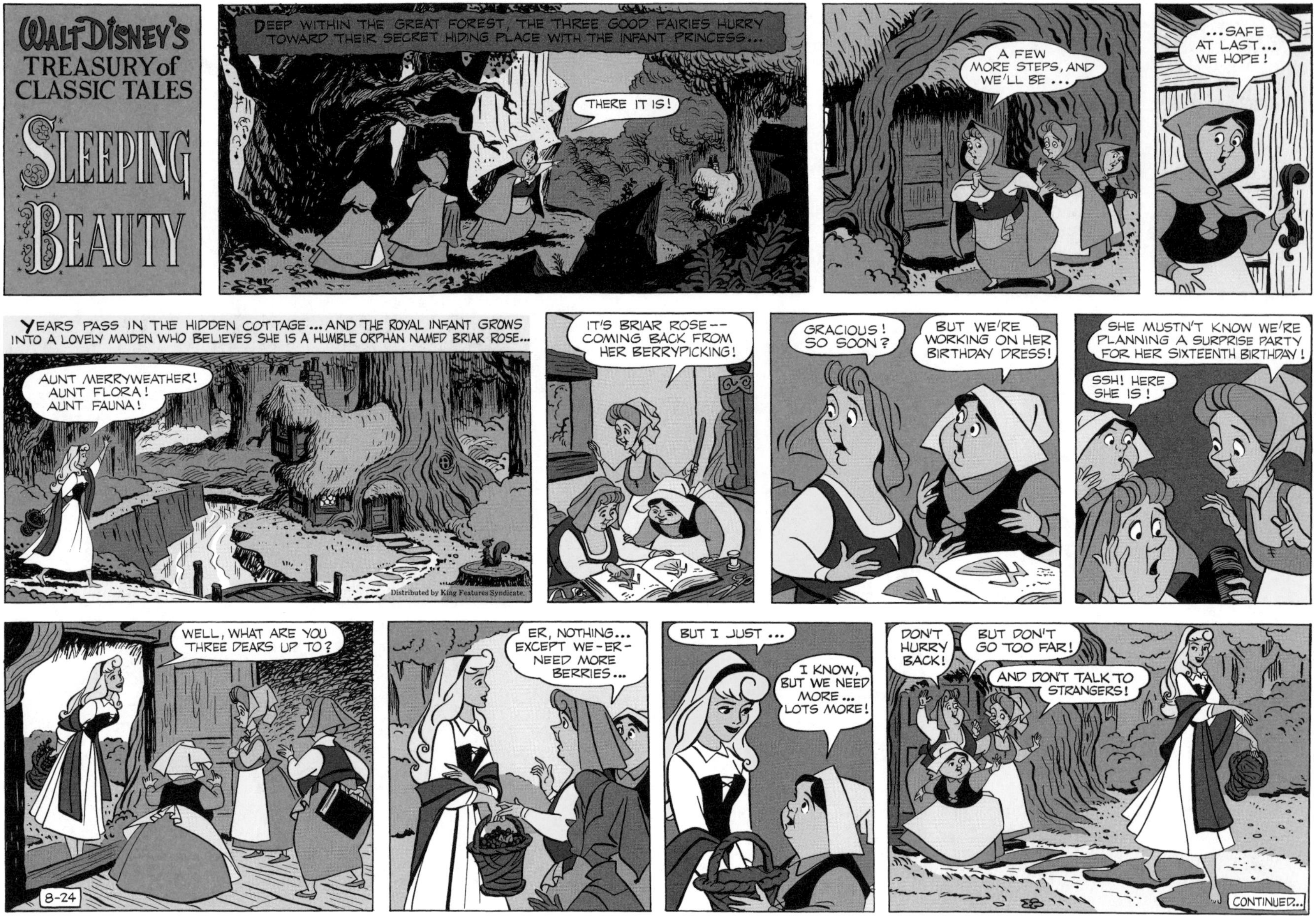
WALT DISNEY'S
TREASURY of CLASSIC TALES
SLEEPING BEAUTY
DEEP WITHIN THE GREAT FOREST, THE THREE GOOD FAIRIES HURRY TOWARD THEIR SECRET HIDING PLACE WITH THE INFANT PRINCESS...
THERE IT IS!
A FEW MORE STEPS, AND WE'LL BE...
...SAFE AT LAST... WE HOPE!
YEARS PASS IN THE HIDDEN COTTAGE... AND THE ROYAL INFANT GROWS INTO A LOVELY MAIDEN WHO BELIEVES SHE IS A HUMBLE ORPHAN NAMED BRIAR ROSE...
AUNT MERRYWEATHER! AUNT FLORA! AUNT FAUNA!
Distributed by King Features Syndicate.
IT'S BRIAR ROSE-- COMING BACK FROM HER BERRYPICKING!
GRACIOUS! SO SOON?
BUT WE'RE WORKING ON HER BIRTHDAY DRESS!
SHE MUSTN'T KNOW WE'RE PLANNING A SURPRISE PARTY FOR HER SIXTEENTH BIRTHDAY!
SSH! HERE SHE IS!
WELL, WHAT ARE YOU THREE DEARS UP TO?
8-24
ER, NOTHING... EXCEPT WE-ER- NEED MORE BERRIES...
BUT I JUST...
I KNOW, BUT WE NEED MORE... LOTS MORE!
DON'T HURRY BACK!
BUT DON'T GO TOO FAR!
AND DON'T TALK TO STRANGERS!
CONTINUED...

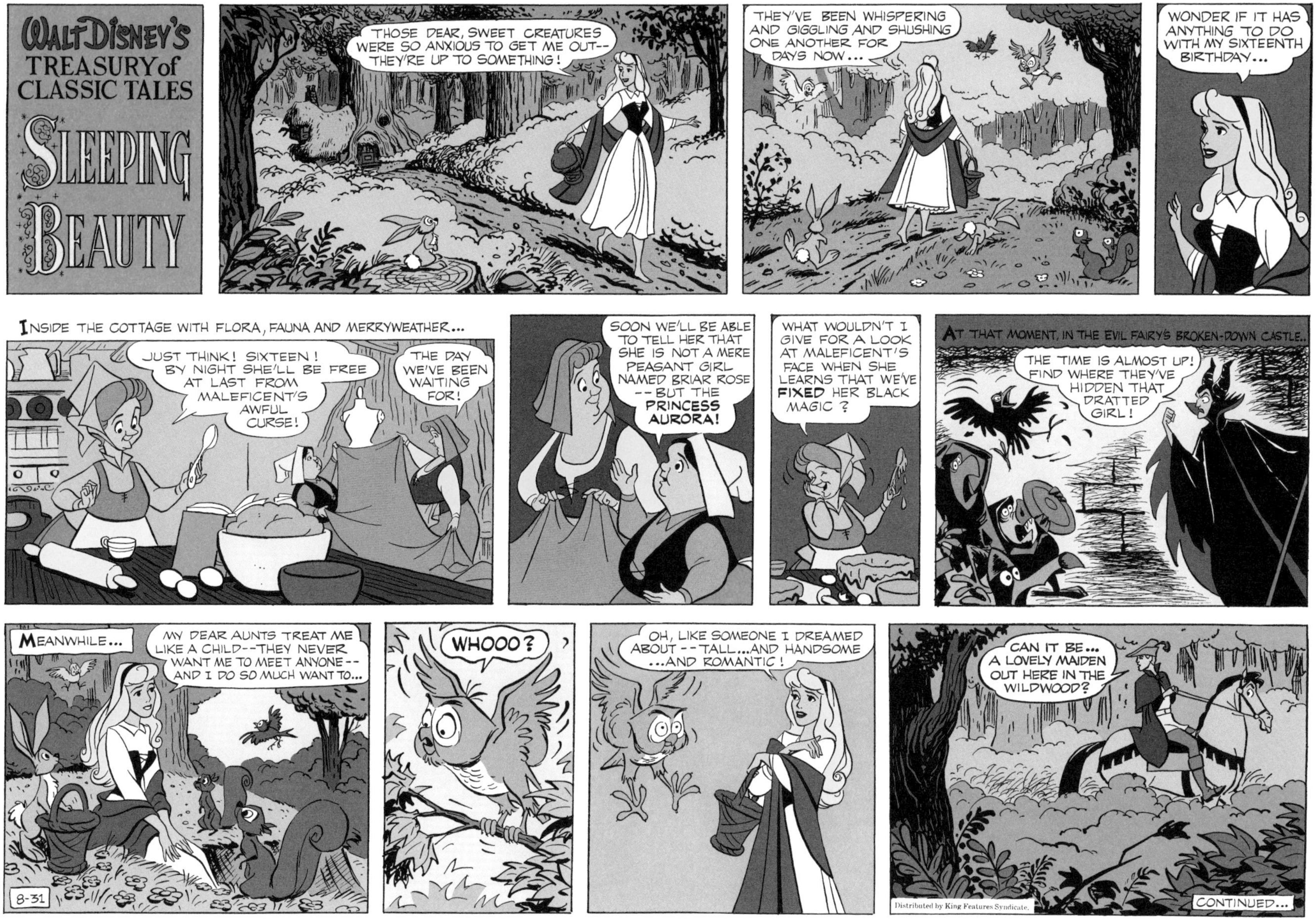
WALT DISNEY'S TREASURY of CLASSIC TALES
SLEEPING BEAUTY
THOSE DEAR, SWEET CREATURES WERE SO ANXIOUS TO GET ME OUT-- THEY'RE UP TO SOMETHING!
THEY'VE BEEN WHISPERING AND GIGGLING AND SHUSHING ONE ANOTHER FOR DAYS NOW...
WONDER IF IT HAS ANYTHING TO DO WITH MY SIXTEENTH BIRTHDAY...
INSIDE THE COTTAGE WITH FLORA, FAUNA AND MERRYWEATHER...
JUST THINK! SIXTEEN! BY NIGHT SHE'LL BE FREE AT LAST FROM MALEFICENT'S AWFUL CURSE!
THE DAY WE'VE BEEN WAITING FOR!
SOON WE'LL BE ABLE TO TELL HER THAT SHE IS NOT A MERE PEASANT GIRL NAMED BRIAR ROSE --BUT THE PRINCESS AURORA!
WHAT WOULDN'T I GIVE FOR A LOOK AT MALEFICENT'S FACE WHEN SHE LEARNS THAT WE'VE FIXED HER BLACK MAGIC?
AT THAT MOMENT, IN THE EVIL FAIRY'S BROKEN-DOWN CASTLE..
THE TIME IS ALMOST UP! FIND WHERE THEY'VE HIDDEN THAT DRATTED GIRL!
MEANWHILE...
MY DEAR AUNTS TREAT ME LIKE A CHILD--THEY NEVER WANT ME TO MEET ANYONE-- AND I DO SO MUCH WANT TO...
8-31
WHOOO?
OH, LIKE SOMEONE I DREAMED ABOUT --TALL...AND HANDSOME ...AND ROMANTIC!
CAN IT BE... A LOVELY MAIDEN OUT HERE IN THE WILDWOOD?
Distributed by King Features Syndicate.
CONTINUED...

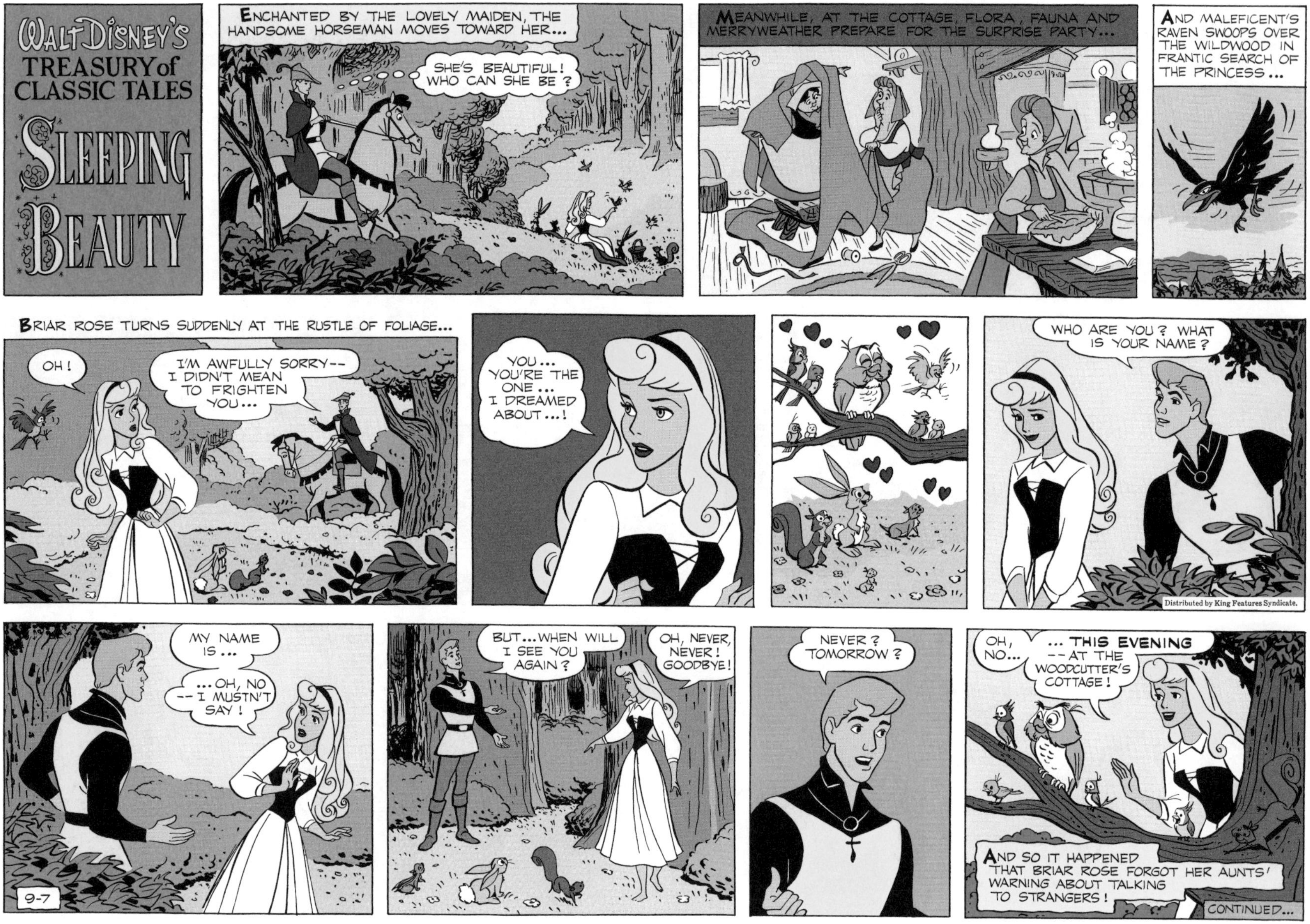
WALT DISNEY'S TREASURY of CLASSIC TALES
SLEEPING BEAUTY
ENCHANTED BY THE LOVELY MAIDEN, THE HANDSOME HORSEMAN MOVES TOWARD HER...
SHE'S BEAUTIFUL! WHO CAN SHE BE ?
MEANWHILE, AT THE COTTAGE, FLORA, FAUNA AND MERRYWEATHER PREPARE FOR THE SURPRISE PARTY...
AND MALEFICENT'S RAVEN SWOOPS OVER THE WILDWOOD IN FRANTIC SEARCH OF THE PRINCESS...
BRIAR ROSE TURNS SUDDENLY AT THE RUSTLE OF FOLIAGE...
OH !
I'M AWFULLY SORRY-- I DIDN'T MEAN TO FRIGHTEN YOU...
YOU... YOU'RE THE ONE... I DREAMED ABOUT...!
WHO ARE YOU ? WHAT IS YOUR NAME ?
Distributed by King Features Syndicate.
MY NAME IS...
...OH, NO -- I MUSTN'T SAY !
9-7
BUT...WHEN WILL I SEE YOU AGAIN ?
OH, NEVER, NEVER ! GOODBYE !
NEVER ? TOMORROW ?
OH, NO...
... THIS EVENING --AT THE WOODCUTTER'S COTTAGE !
AND SO IT HAPPENED THAT BRIAR ROSE FORGOT HER AUNTS' WARNING ABOUT TALKING TO STRANGERS !
CONTINUED...

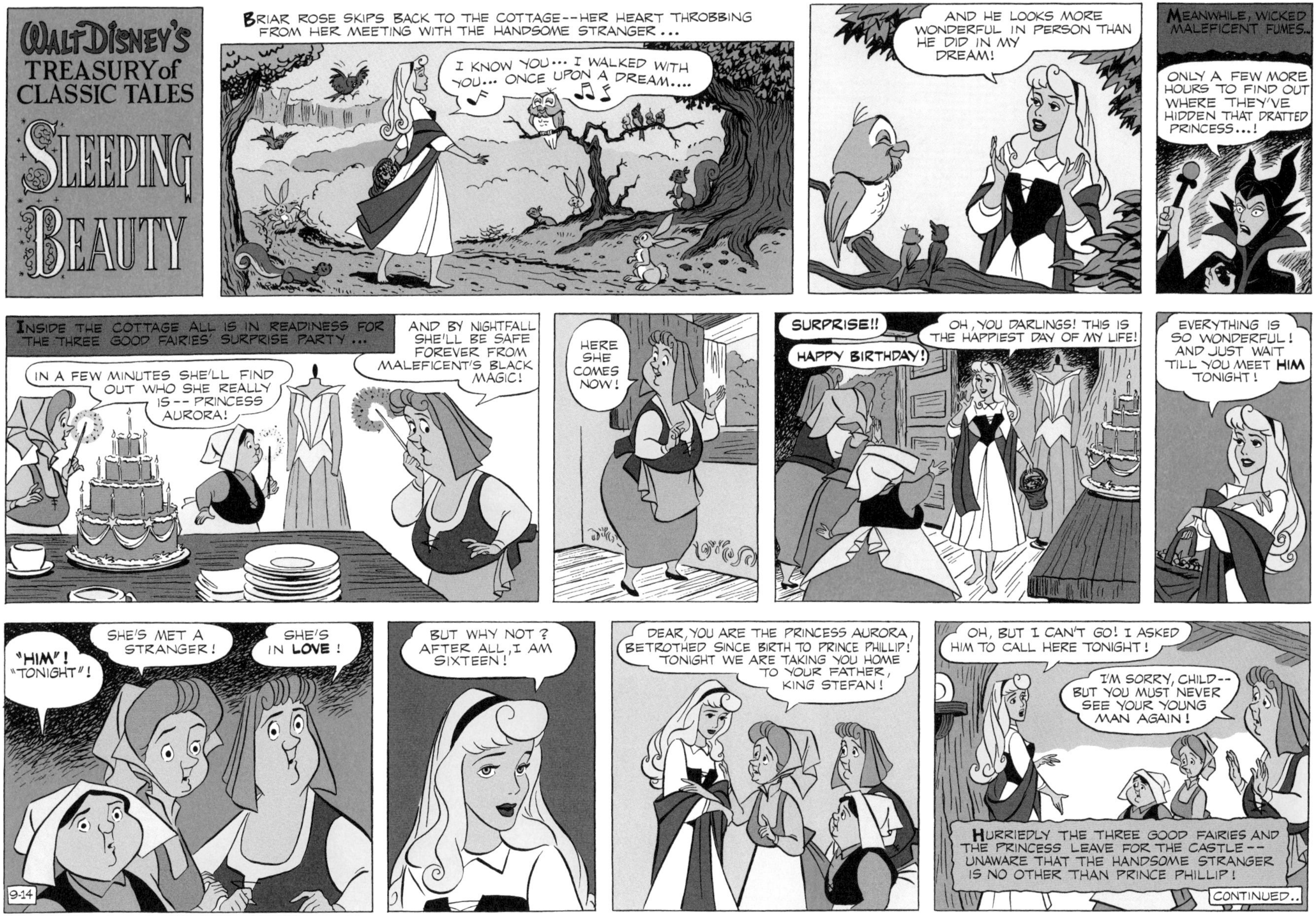

WALT DISNEY'S TREASURY of CLASSIC TALES
SLEEPING BEAUTY
BRIAR ROSE SKIPS BACK TO THE COTTAGE--HER HEART THROBBING FROM HER MEETING WITH THE HANDSOME STRANGER...
I KNOW YOU... I WALKED WITH YOU... ONCE UPON A DREAM....
AND HE LOOKS MORE WONDERFUL IN PERSON THAN HE DID IN MY DREAM!
MEANWHILE, WICKED MALEFICENT FUMES...
ONLY A FEW MORE HOURS TO FIND OUT WHERE THEY'VE HIDDEN THAT DRATTED PRINCESS...!
INSIDE THE COTTAGE ALL IS IN READINESS FOR THE THREE GOOD FAIRIES' SURPRISE PARTY...
IN A FEW MINUTES SHE'LL FIND OUT WHO SHE REALLY IS -- PRINCESS AURORA!
AND BY NIGHTFALL SHE'LL BE SAFE FOREVER FROM MALEFICENT'S BLACK MAGIC!
HERE SHE COMES NOW!
SURPRISE!!
HAPPY BIRTHDAY!
OH, YOU DARLINGS! THIS IS THE HAPPIEST DAY OF MY LIFE!
EVERYTHING IS SO WONDERFUL! AND JUST WAIT TILL YOU MEET HIM TONIGHT!
"HIM"! "TONIGHT"!
SHE'S MET A STRANGER!
SHE'S IN LOVE!
BUT WHY NOT? AFTER ALL, I AM SIXTEEN!
DEAR, YOU ARE THE PRINCESS AURORA, BETROTHED SINCE BIRTH TO PRINCE PHILLIP! TONIGHT WE ARE TAKING YOU HOME TO YOUR FATHER, KING STEFAN!
OH, BUT I CAN'T GO! I ASKED HIM TO CALL HERE TONIGHT!
I'M SORRY, CHILD-- BUT YOU MUST NEVER SEE YOUR YOUNG MAN AGAIN!
HURRIEDLY THE THREE GOOD FAIRIES AND THE PRINCESS LEAVE FOR THE CASTLE-- UNAWARE THAT THE HANDSOME STRANGER IS NO OTHER THAN PRINCE PHILLIP!
CONTINUED..
9-14

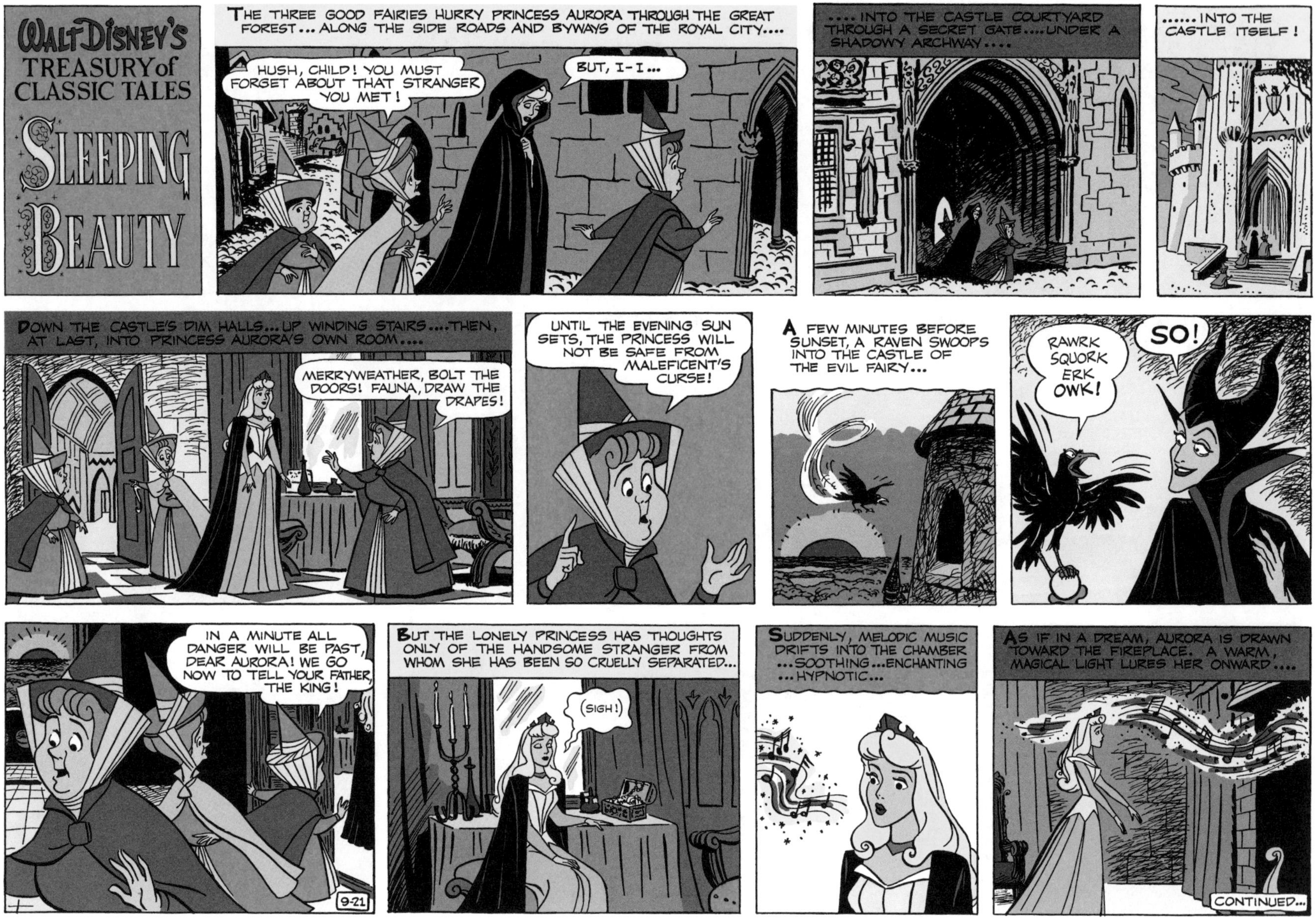

WALT DISNEY'S TREASURY of CLASSIC TALES
SLEEPING BEAUTY
THE THREE GOOD FAIRIES HURRY PRINCESS AURORA THROUGH THE GREAT FOREST... ALONG THE SIDE ROADS AND BYWAYS OF THE ROYAL CITY....
HUSH, CHILD! YOU MUST FORGET ABOUT THAT STRANGER YOU MET!
BUT, I-I...
....INTO THE CASTLE COURTYARD THROUGH A SECRET GATE....UNDER A SHADOWY ARCHWAY....
......INTO THE CASTLE ITSELF!
DOWN THE CASTLE'S DIM HALLS...UP WINDING STAIRS....THEN, AT LAST, INTO PRINCESS AURORA'S OWN ROOM....
MERRYWEATHER, BOLT THE DOORS! FAUNA, DRAW THE DRAPES!
UNTIL THE EVENING SUN SETS, THE PRINCESS WILL NOT BE SAFE FROM MALEFICENT'S CURSE!
A FEW MINUTES BEFORE SUNSET, A RAVEN SWOOPS INTO THE CASTLE OF THE EVIL FAIRY...
RAWRK SQUORK ERK OWK!
SO!
IN A MINUTE ALL DANGER WILL BE PAST, DEAR AURORA! WE GO NOW TO TELL YOUR FATHER, THE KING!
9-21
BUT THE LONELY PRINCESS HAS THOUGHTS ONLY OF THE HANDSOME STRANGER FROM WHOM SHE HAS BEEN SO CRUELLY SEPARATED...
(SIGH!)
SUDDENLY, MELODIC MUSIC DRIFTS INTO THE CHAMBER ...SOOTHING...ENCHANTING ...HYPNOTIC...
AS IF IN A DREAM, AURORA IS DRAWN TOWARD THE FIREPLACE. A WARM, MAGICAL LIGHT LURES HER ONWARD....
CONTINUED...

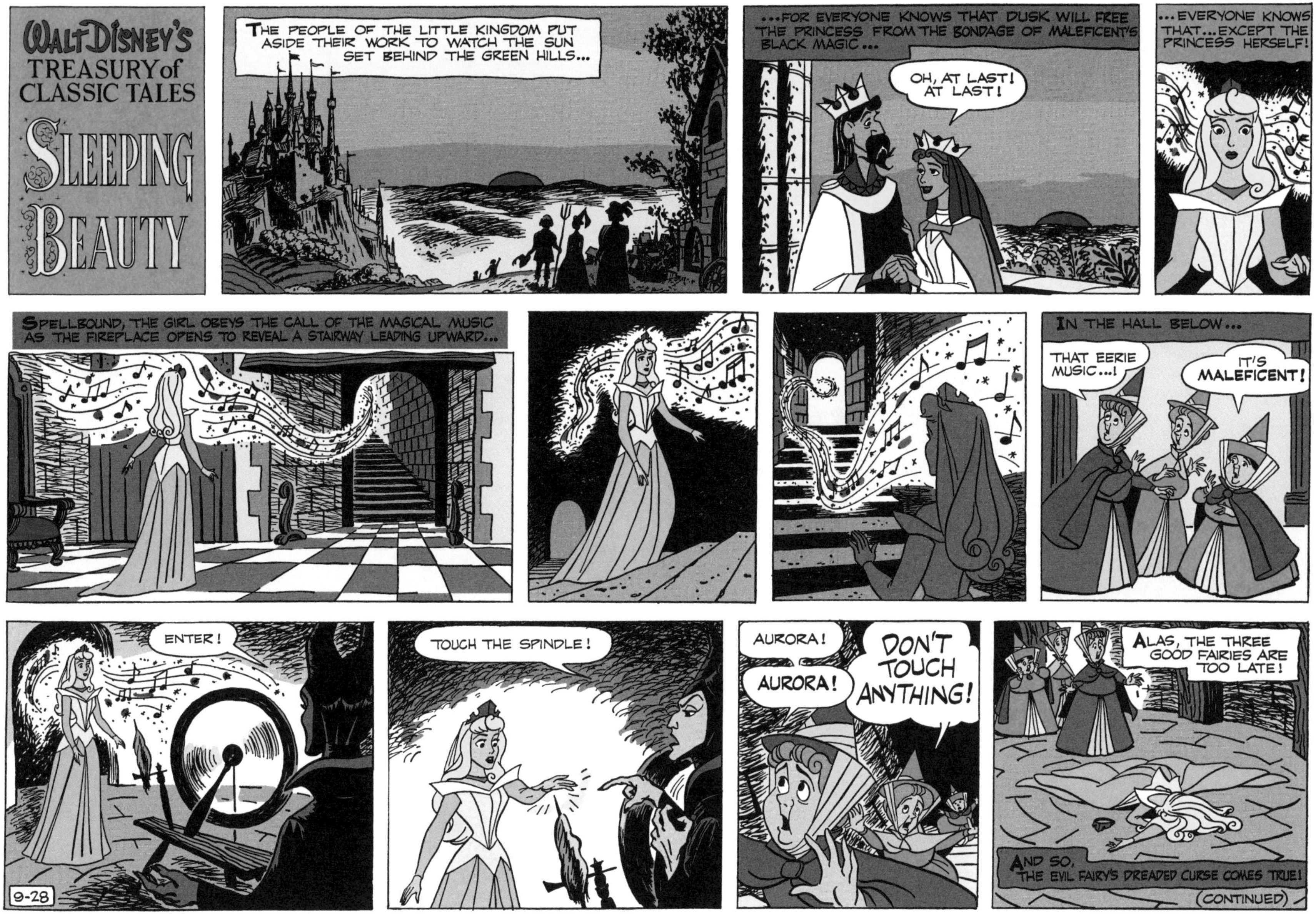
WALT DISNEY'S
TREASURY of CLASSIC TALES
SLEEPING BEAUTY
THE PEOPLE OF THE LITTLE KINGDOM PUT ASIDE THEIR WORK TO WATCH THE SUN SET BEHIND THE GREEN HILLS...
...FOR EVERYONE KNOWS THAT DUSK WILL FREE THE PRINCESS FROM THE BONDAGE OF MALEFICENT'S BLACK MAGIC...
OH, AT LAST! AT LAST!
...EVERYONE KNOWS THAT...EXCEPT THE PRINCESS HERSELF!
SPELLBOUND, THE GIRL OBEYS THE CALL OF THE MAGICAL MUSIC AS THE FIREPLACE OPENS TO REVEAL A STAIRWAY LEADING UPWARD...
IN THE HALL BELOW...
THAT EERIE MUSIC...!
IT'S MALEFICENT!
ENTER!
9-28
TOUCH THE SPINDLE!
AURORA!
AURORA!
DON'T TOUCH ANYTHING!
ALAS, THE THREE GOOD FAIRIES ARE TOO LATE!
AND SO, THE EVIL FAIRY'S DREADED CURSE COMES TRUE!
(CONTINUED)

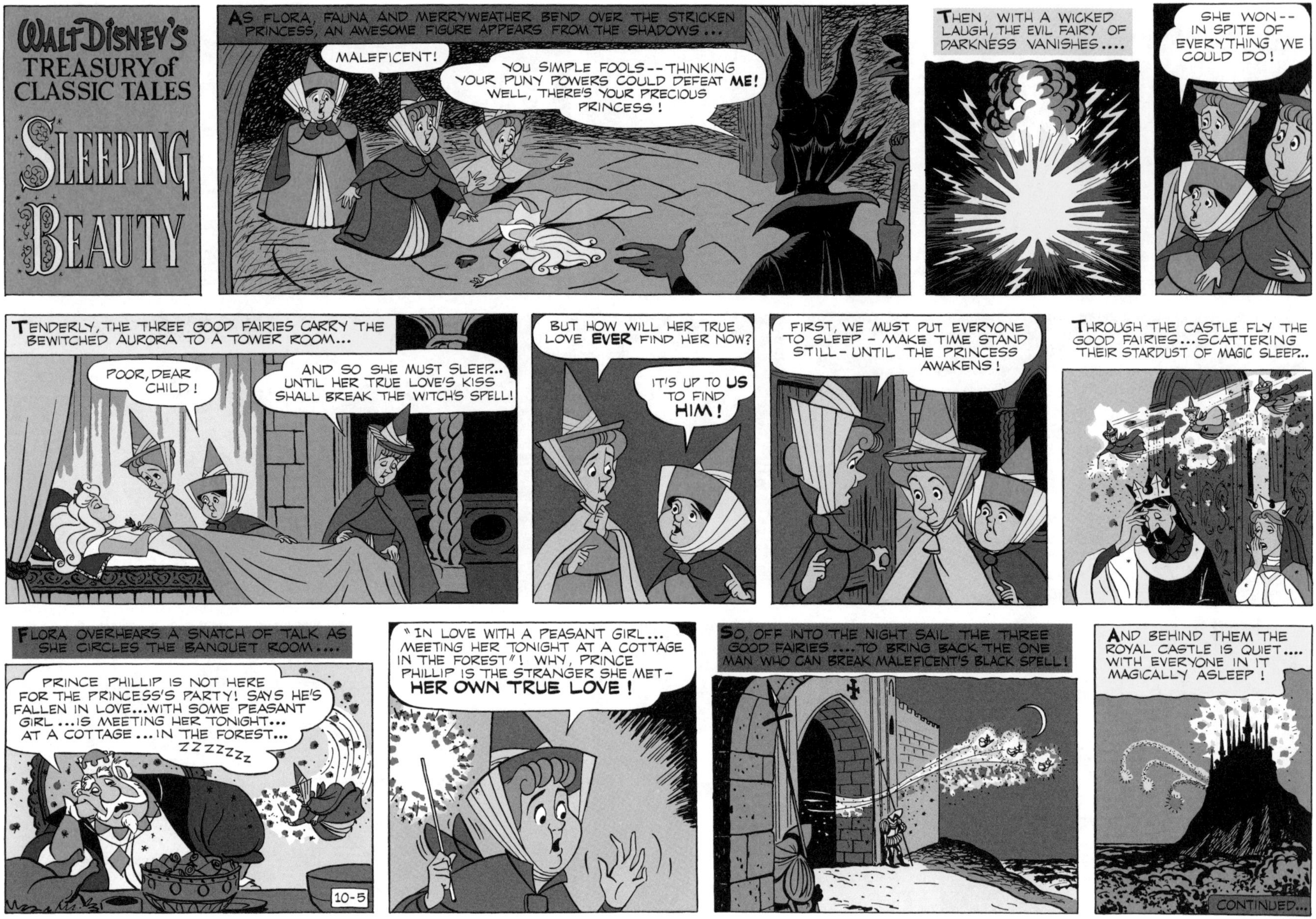
WALT DISNEY'S TREASURY of CLASSIC TALES
SLEEPING BEAUTY
AS FLORA, FAUNA AND MERRYWEATHER BEND OVER THE STRICKEN PRINCESS, AN AWESOME FIGURE APPEARS FROM THE SHADOWS...
MALEFICENT!
YOU SIMPLE FOOLS--THINKING YOUR PUNY POWERS COULD DEFEAT ME! WELL, THERE'S YOUR PRECIOUS PRINCESS!
THEN, WITH A WICKED LAUGH, THE EVIL FAIRY OF DARKNESS VANISHES....
SHE WON-- IN SPITE OF EVERYTHING WE COULD DO!
TENDERLY, THE THREE GOOD FAIRIES CARRY THE BEWITCHED AURORA TO A TOWER ROOM...
POOR, DEAR CHILD!
AND SO SHE MUST SLEEP.. UNTIL HER TRUE LOVE'S KISS SHALL BREAK THE WITCH'S SPELL!
BUT HOW WILL HER TRUE LOVE EVER FIND HER NOW?
IT'S UP TO US TO FIND HIM!
FIRST, WE MUST PUT EVERYONE TO SLEEP - MAKE TIME STAND STILL - UNTIL THE PRINCESS AWAKENS!
THROUGH THE CASTLE FLY THE GOOD FAIRIES...SCATTERING THEIR STARDUST OF MAGIC SLEEP...
FLORA OVERHEARS A SNATCH OF TALK AS SHE CIRCLES THE BANQUET ROOM....
PRINCE PHILLIP IS NOT HERE FOR THE PRINCESS'S PARTY! SAYS HE'S FALLEN IN LOVE...WITH SOME PEASANT GIRL...IS MEETING HER TONIGHT... AT A COTTAGE...IN THE FOREST... ZZZZZZZ
10-5
"IN LOVE WITH A PEASANT GIRL... MEETING HER TONIGHT AT A COTTAGE IN THE FOREST"! WHY, PRINCE PHILLIP IS THE STRANGER SHE MET- HER OWN TRUE LOVE!
SO, OFF INTO THE NIGHT SAIL THE THREE GOOD FAIRIES....TO BRING BACK THE ONE MAN WHO CAN BREAK MALEFICENT'S BLACK SPELL!
AND BEHIND THEM THE ROYAL CASTLE IS QUIET.... WITH EVERYONE IN IT MAGICALLY ASLEEP!
CONTINUED...

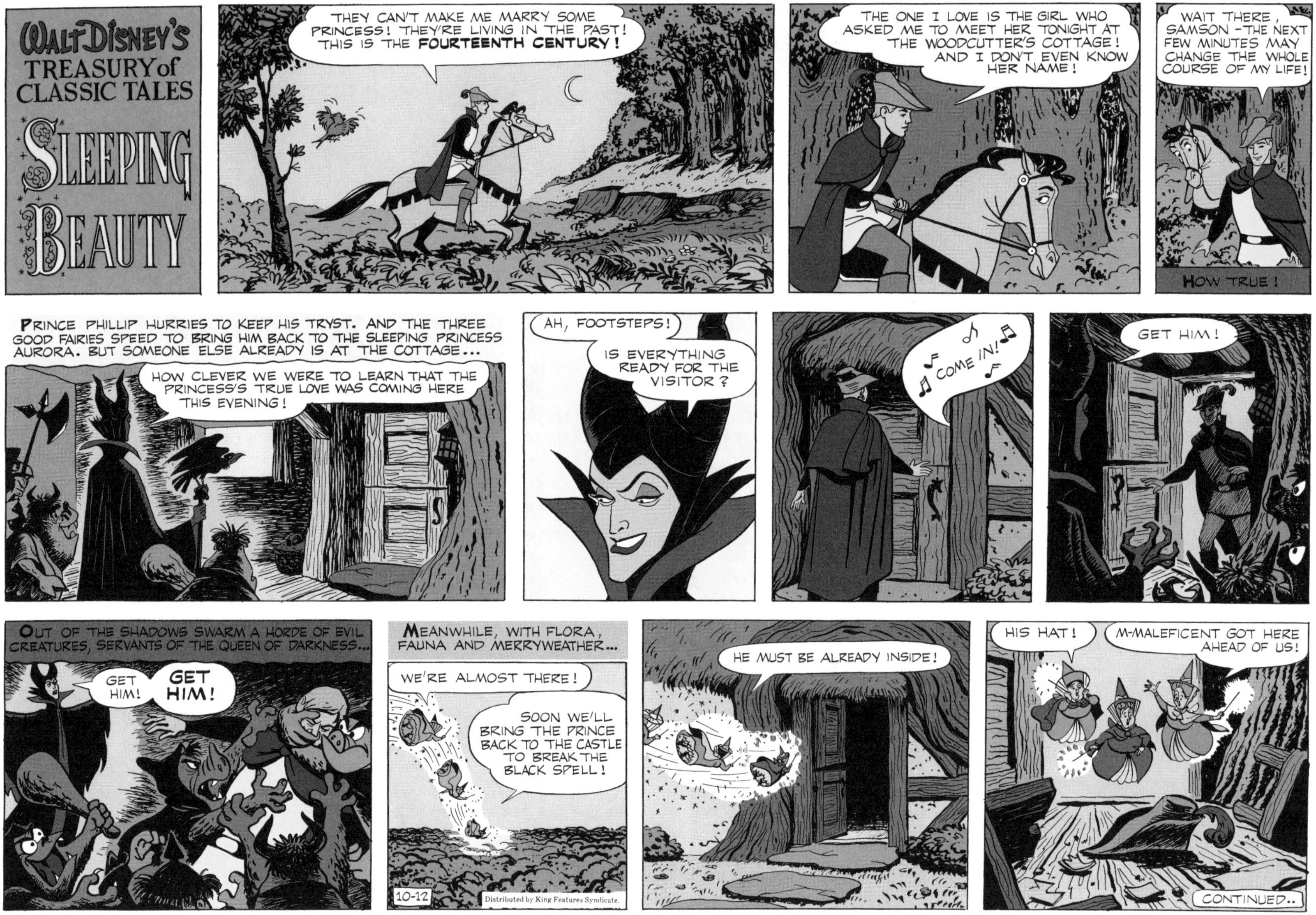
WALT DISNEY'S TREASURY of CLASSIC TALES
SLEEPING BEAUTY
THEY CAN'T MAKE ME MARRY SOME PRINCESS! THEY'RE LIVING IN THE PAST! THIS IS THE FOURTEENTH CENTURY!
THE ONE I LOVE IS THE GIRL WHO ASKED ME TO MEET HER TONIGHT AT THE WOODCUTTER'S COTTAGE! AND I DON'T EVEN KNOW HER NAME!
WAIT THERE, SAMSON –THE NEXT FEW MINUTES MAY CHANGE THE WHOLE COURSE OF MY LIFE!
HOW TRUE!
PRINCE PHILLIP HURRIES TO KEEP HIS TRYST. AND THE THREE GOOD FAIRIES SPEED TO BRING HIM BACK TO THE SLEEPING PRINCESS AURORA. BUT SOMEONE ELSE ALREADY IS AT THE COTTAGE...
HOW CLEVER WE WERE TO LEARN THAT THE PRINCESS'S TRUE LOVE WAS COMING HERE THIS EVENING!
AH, FOOTSTEPS!
IS EVERYTHING READY FOR THE VISITOR?
COME IN!
GET HIM!
OUT OF THE SHADOWS SWARM A HORDE OF EVIL CREATURES, SERVANTS OF THE QUEEN OF DARKNESS...
GET HIM!
GET HIM!
MEANWHILE, WITH FLORA, FAUNA AND MERRYWEATHER...
WE'RE ALMOST THERE!
SOON WE'LL BRING THE PRINCE BACK TO THE CASTLE TO BREAK THE BLACK SPELL!
10-12
Distributed by King Features Syndicate.
HE MUST BE ALREADY INSIDE!
HIS HAT!
M-MALEFICENT GOT HERE AHEAD OF US!
CONTINUED..

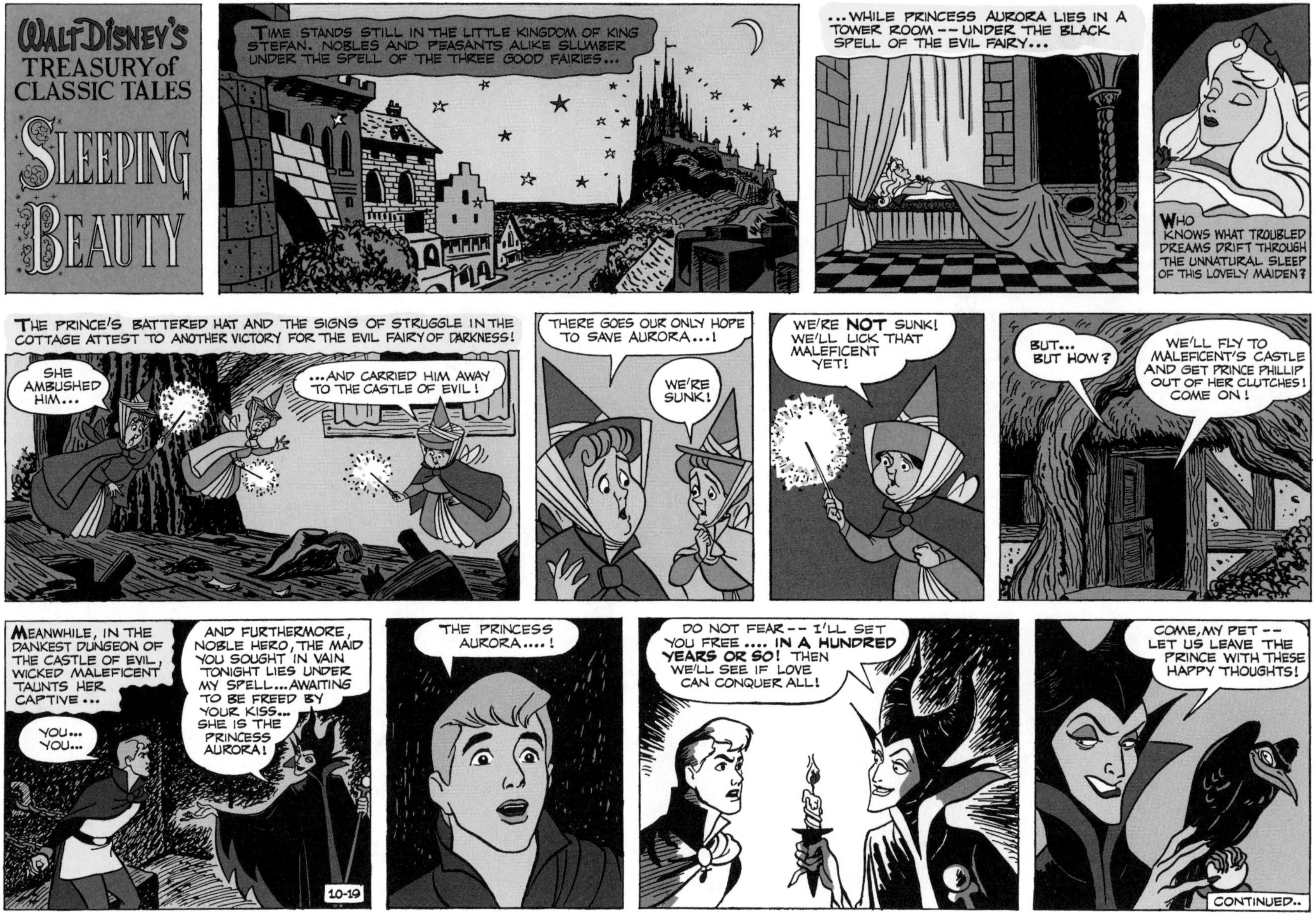

Walt Disney's Treasury of Classic Tales
Sleeping Beauty
Time stands still in the little kingdom of King Stefan. Nobles and peasants alike slumber under the spell of the three good fairies...
...while Princess Aurora lies in a tower room -- under the black spell of the evil fairy...
Who knows what troubled dreams drift through the unnatural sleep of this lovely maiden?
The prince's battered hat and the signs of struggle in the cottage attest to another victory for the evil fairy of darkness!
She ambushed him...
...and carried him away to the castle of evil!
There goes our only hope to save Aurora...!
We're sunk!
We're **not** sunk! We'll lick that Maleficent yet!
But... but how?
We'll fly to Maleficent's castle and get Prince Phillip out of her clutches! Come on!
Meanwhile, in the dankest dungeon of the castle of evil, wicked Maleficent taunts her captive...
You... you...
And furthermore, noble hero, the maid you sought in vain tonight lies under my spell... awaiting to be freed by your kiss... she is the Princess Aurora!
10-19
The Princess Aurora....!
Do not fear -- I'll set you free.... **in a hundred years or so!** Then we'll see if love can conquer all!
Come, my pet -- let us leave the prince with these happy thoughts!
Continued..

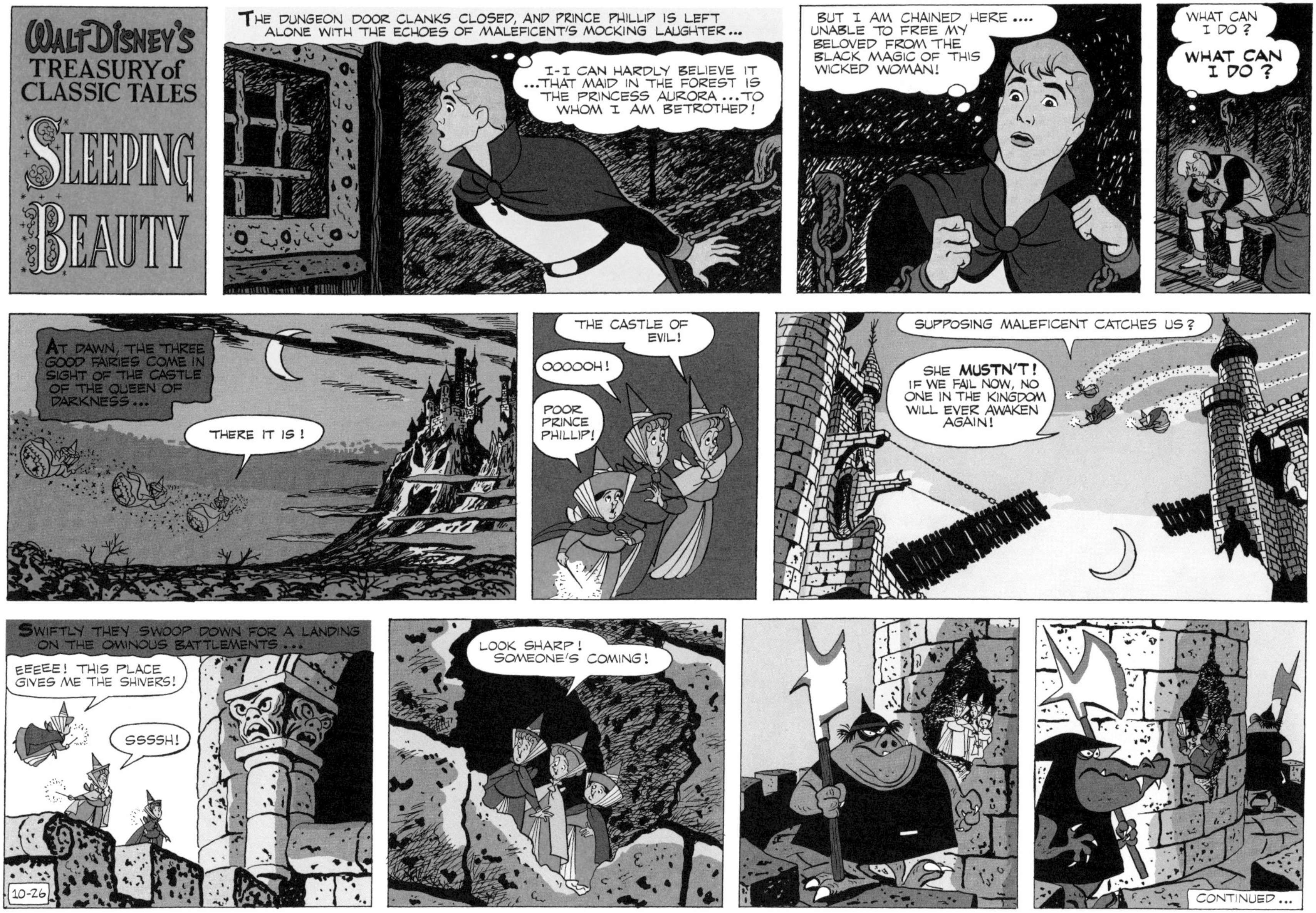

WALT DISNEY'S TREASURY of CLASSIC TALES
SLEEPING BEAUTY
THE DUNGEON DOOR CLANKS CLOSED, AND PRINCE PHILLIP IS LEFT ALONE WITH THE ECHOES OF MALEFICENT'S MOCKING LAUGHTER...
I-I CAN HARDLY BELIEVE IT ...THAT MAID IN THE FOREST IS THE PRINCESS AURORA ...TO WHOM I AM BETROTHED!
BUT I AM CHAINED HERE .... UNABLE TO FREE MY BELOVED FROM THE BLACK MAGIC OF THIS WICKED WOMAN!
WHAT CAN I DO?
WHAT CAN I DO?
AT DAWN, THE THREE GOOD FAIRIES COME IN SIGHT OF THE CASTLE OF THE QUEEN OF DARKNESS...
THERE IT IS!
THE CASTLE OF EVIL!
OOOOOH!
POOR PRINCE PHILLIP!
SUPPOSING MALEFICENT CATCHES US?
SHE MUSTN'T! IF WE FAIL NOW, NO ONE IN THE KINGDOM WILL EVER AWAKEN AGAIN!
SWIFTLY THEY SWOOP DOWN FOR A LANDING ON THE OMINOUS BATTLEMENTS...
EEEEE! THIS PLACE GIVES ME THE SHIVERS!
SSSSH!
10-26
LOOK SHARP! SOMEONE'S COMING!
CONTINUED...

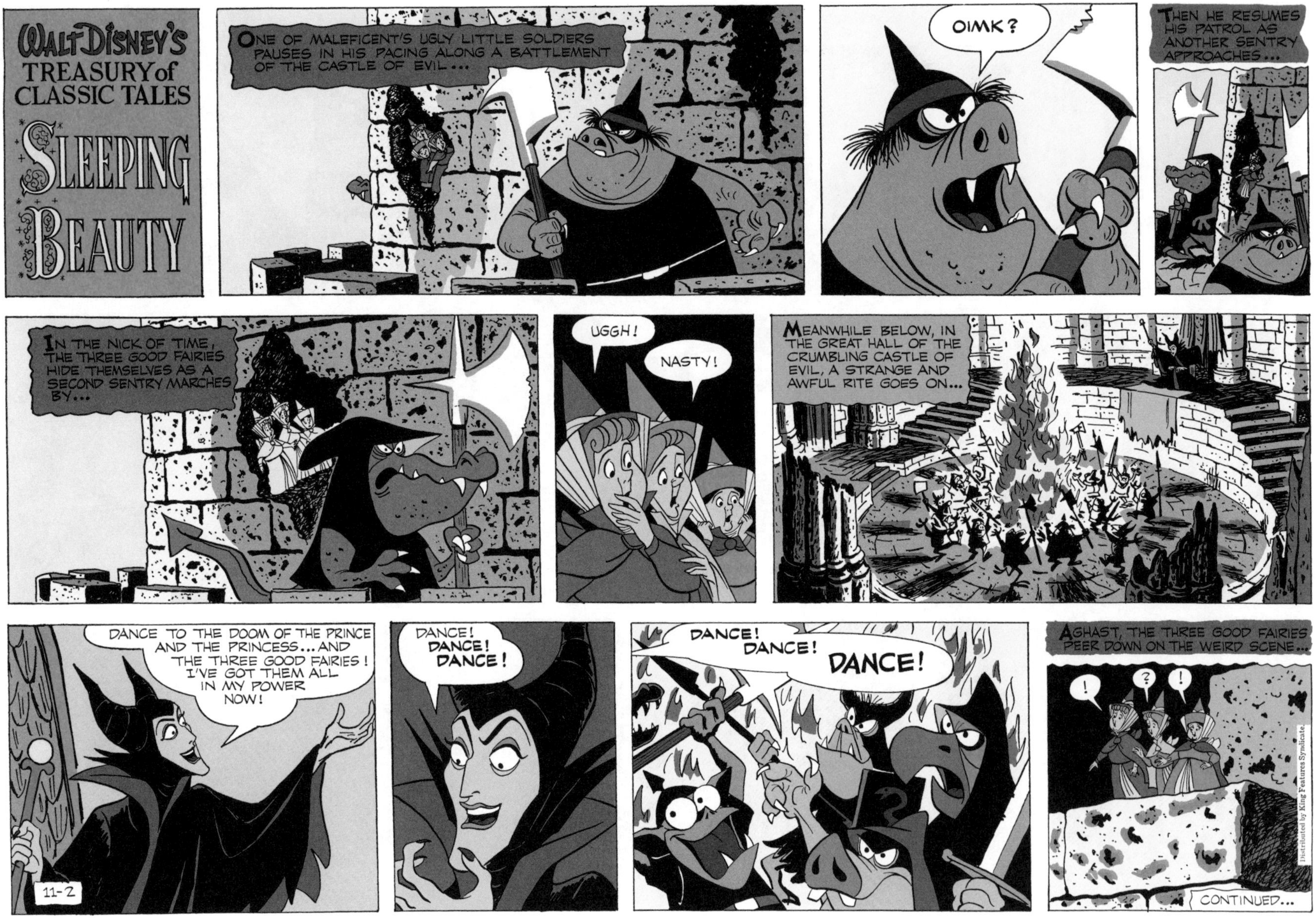
WALT DISNEY'S
TREASURY of CLASSIC TALES
SLEEPING BEAUTY
ONE OF MALEFICENT'S UGLY LITTLE SOLDIERS PAUSES IN HIS PACING ALONG A BATTLEMENT OF THE CASTLE OF EVIL...
OIMK?
THEN HE RESUMES HIS PATROL AS ANOTHER SENTRY APPROACHES...
IN THE NICK OF TIME, THE THREE GOOD FAIRIES HIDE THEMSELVES AS A SECOND SENTRY MARCHES BY...
UGGH!
NASTY!
MEANWHILE BELOW, IN THE GREAT HALL OF THE CRUMBLING CASTLE OF EVIL, A STRANGE AND AWFUL RITE GOES ON...
DANCE TO THE DOOM OF THE PRINCE AND THE PRINCESS... AND THE THREE GOOD FAIRIES! I'VE GOT THEM ALL IN MY POWER NOW!
11-2
DANCE! DANCE! DANCE!
DANCE! DANCE! DANCE!
AGHAST, THE THREE GOOD FAIRIES PEER DOWN ON THE WEIRD SCENE...
! ? !
Distributed by King Features Syndicate.
CONTINUED...

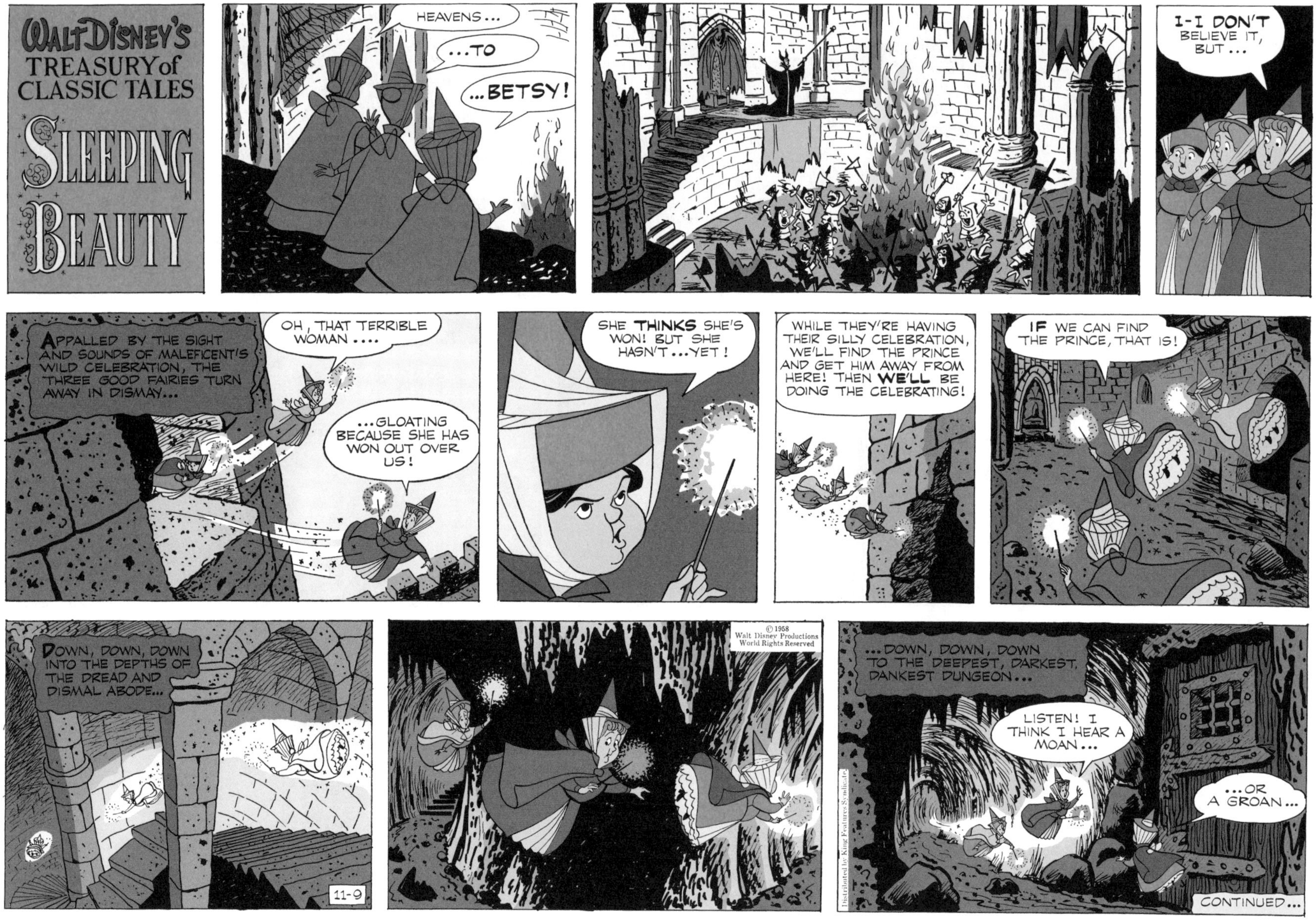

WALT DISNEY'S
TREASURY of CLASSIC TALES
SLEEPING BEAUTY
HEAVENS ...
...TO
...BETSY!
I-I DON'T BELIEVE IT, BUT ...
APPALLED BY THE SIGHT AND SOUNDS OF MALEFICENT'S WILD CELEBRATION, THE THREE GOOD FAIRIES TURN AWAY IN DISMAY...
OH, THAT TERRIBLE WOMAN ....
...GLOATING BECAUSE SHE HAS WON OUT OVER US!
SHE THINKS SHE'S WON! BUT SHE HASN'T ...YET!
WHILE THEY'RE HAVING THEIR SILLY CELEBRATION, WE'LL FIND THE PRINCE AND GET HIM AWAY FROM HERE! THEN WE'LL BE DOING THE CELEBRATING!
IF WE CAN FIND THE PRINCE, THAT IS!
DOWN, DOWN, DOWN INTO THE DEPTHS OF THE DREAD AND DISMAL ABODE...
11-9
© 1958 Walt Disney Productions World Rights Reserved
Distributed by King Features Syndicate
...DOWN, DOWN, DOWN TO THE DEEPEST, DARKEST, DANKEST DUNGEON...
LISTEN! I THINK I HEAR A MOAN...
...OR A GROAN...
CONTINUED...

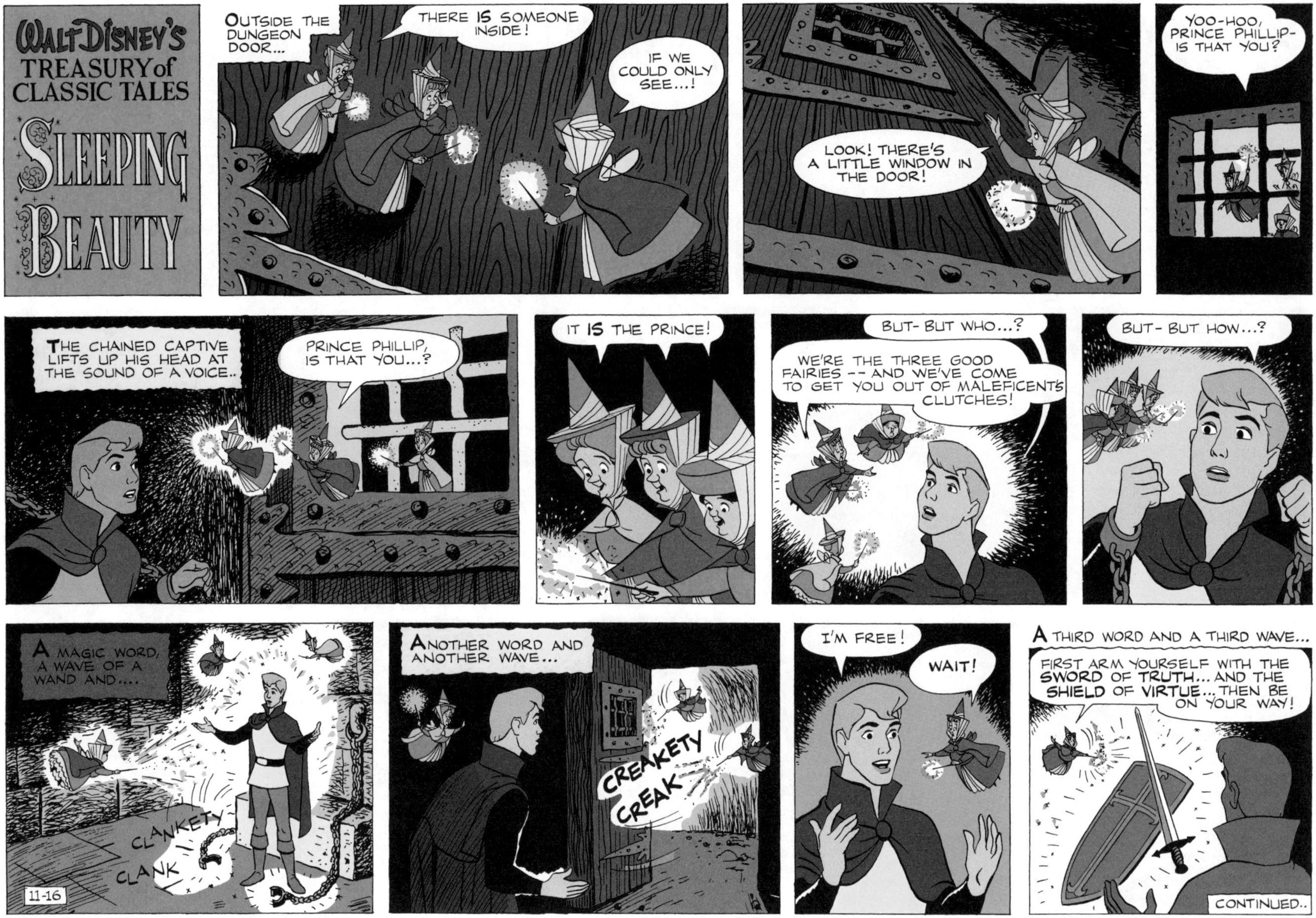
WALT DISNEY'S
TREASURY of CLASSIC TALES
SLEEPING BEAUTY
OUTSIDE THE DUNGEON DOOR...
THERE IS SOMEONE INSIDE!
IF WE COULD ONLY SEE...!
LOOK! THERE'S A LITTLE WINDOW IN THE DOOR!
YOO-HOO, PRINCE PHILLIP- IS THAT YOU?
THE CHAINED CAPTIVE LIFTS UP HIS HEAD AT THE SOUND OF A VOICE..
PRINCE PHILLIP, IS THAT YOU...?
IT IS THE PRINCE!
BUT- BUT WHO...?
WE'RE THE THREE GOOD FAIRIES -- AND WE'VE COME TO GET YOU OUT OF MALEFICENT'S CLUTCHES!
BUT- BUT HOW...?
A MAGIC WORD, A WAVE OF A WAND AND....
CLANKETY
CLANK
11-16
ANOTHER WORD AND ANOTHER WAVE...
CREAKETY
CREAK
I'M FREE!
WAIT!
A THIRD WORD AND A THIRD WAVE...
FIRST ARM YOURSELF WITH THE SWORD OF TRUTH... AND THE SHIELD OF VIRTUE... THEN BE ON YOUR WAY!
CONTINUED..

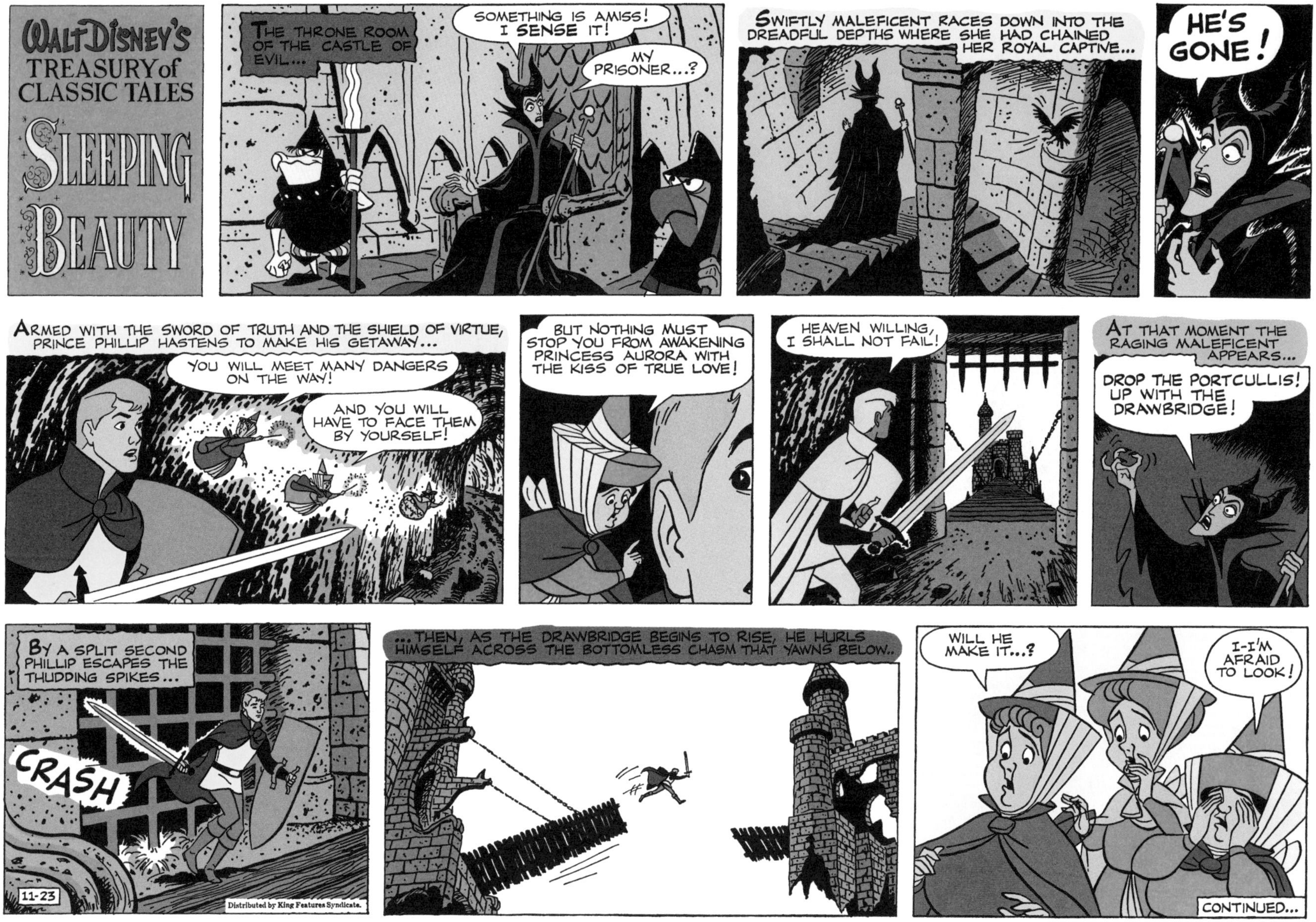
WALT DISNEY'S
TREASURY of CLASSIC TALES
SLEEPING BEAUTY
THE THRONE ROOM OF THE CASTLE OF EVIL...
SOMETHING IS AMISS! I SENSE IT!
MY PRISONER...?
SWIFTLY MALEFICENT RACES DOWN INTO THE DREADFUL DEPTHS WHERE SHE HAD CHAINED HER ROYAL CAPTIVE...
HE'S GONE!
ARMED WITH THE SWORD OF TRUTH AND THE SHIELD OF VIRTUE, PRINCE PHILLIP HASTENS TO MAKE HIS GETAWAY...
YOU WILL MEET MANY DANGERS ON THE WAY!
AND YOU WILL HAVE TO FACE THEM BY YOURSELF!
BUT NOTHING MUST STOP YOU FROM AWAKENING PRINCESS AURORA WITH THE KISS OF TRUE LOVE!
HEAVEN WILLING, I SHALL NOT FAIL!
AT THAT MOMENT THE RAGING MALEFICENT APPEARS...
DROP THE PORTCULLIS! UP WITH THE DRAWBRIDGE!
BY A SPLIT SECOND PHILLIP ESCAPES THE THUDDING SPIKES...
CRASH
11-23
Distributed by King Features Syndicate.
...THEN, AS THE DRAWBRIDGE BEGINS TO RISE, HE HURLS HIMSELF ACROSS THE BOTTOMLESS CHASM THAT YAWNS BELOW..
WILL HE MAKE IT...?
I-I'M AFRAID TO LOOK!
CONTINUED...

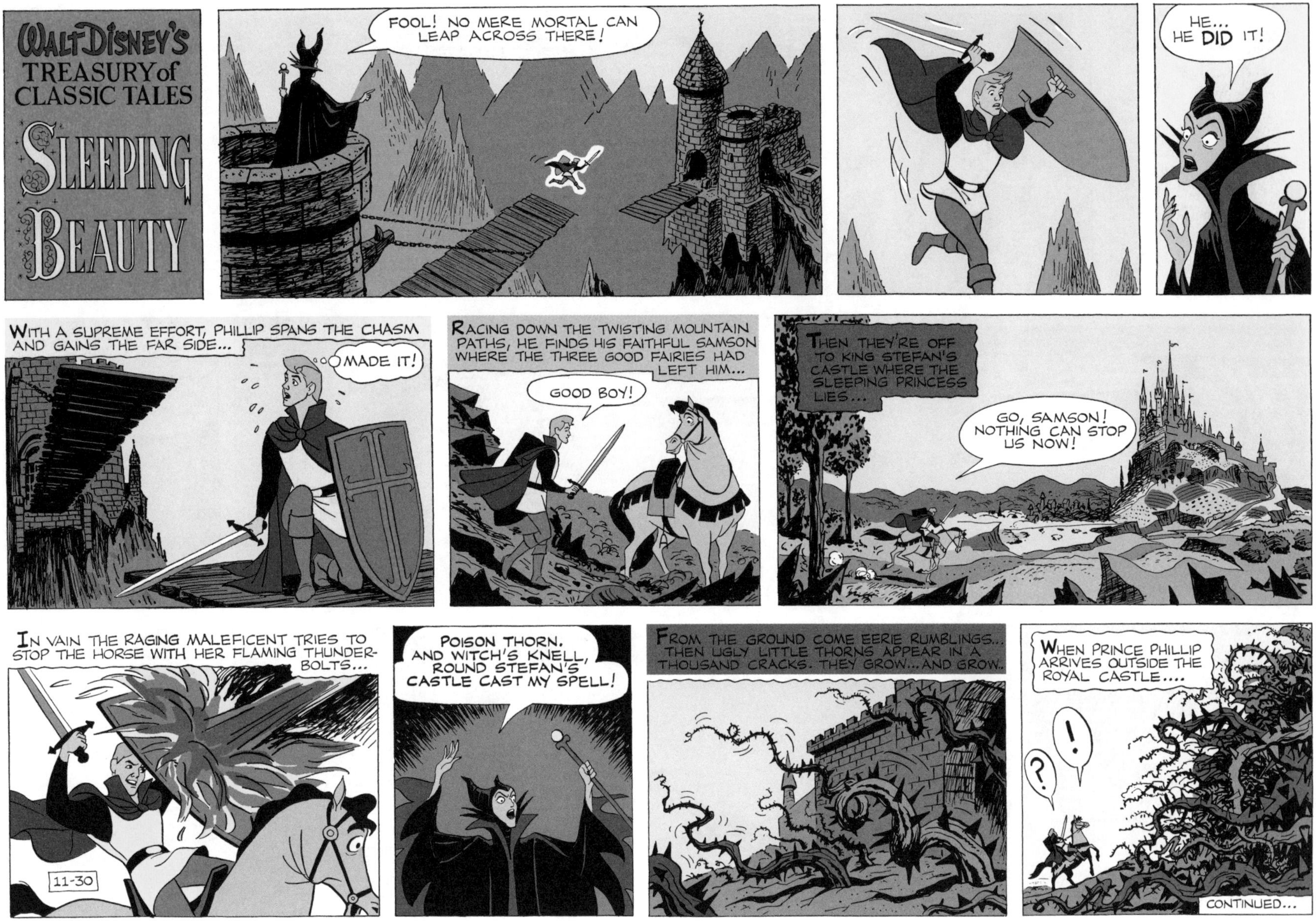
WALT DISNEY'S
TREASURY of CLASSIC TALES
SLEEPING BEAUTY
FOOL! NO MERE MORTAL CAN LEAP ACROSS THERE!
HE... HE DID IT!
WITH A SUPREME EFFORT, PHILLIP SPANS THE CHASM AND GAINS THE FAR SIDE...
MADE IT!
RACING DOWN THE TWISTING MOUNTAIN PATHS, HE FINDS HIS FAITHFUL SAMSON WHERE THE THREE GOOD FAIRIES HAD LEFT HIM...
GOOD BOY!
THEN THEY'RE OFF TO KING STEFAN'S CASTLE WHERE THE SLEEPING PRINCESS LIES...
GO, SAMSON! NOTHING CAN STOP US NOW!
IN VAIN THE RAGING MALEFICENT TRIES TO STOP THE HORSE WITH HER FLAMING THUNDER-BOLTS...
11-30
POISON THORN, AND WITCH'S KNELL, ROUND STEFAN'S CASTLE CAST MY SPELL!
FROM THE GROUND COME EERIE RUMBLINGS... THEN UGLY LITTLE THORNS APPEAR IN A THOUSAND CRACKS. THEY GROW... AND GROW..
WHEN PRINCE PHILLIP ARRIVES OUTSIDE THE ROYAL CASTLE....
?
!
CONTINUED...

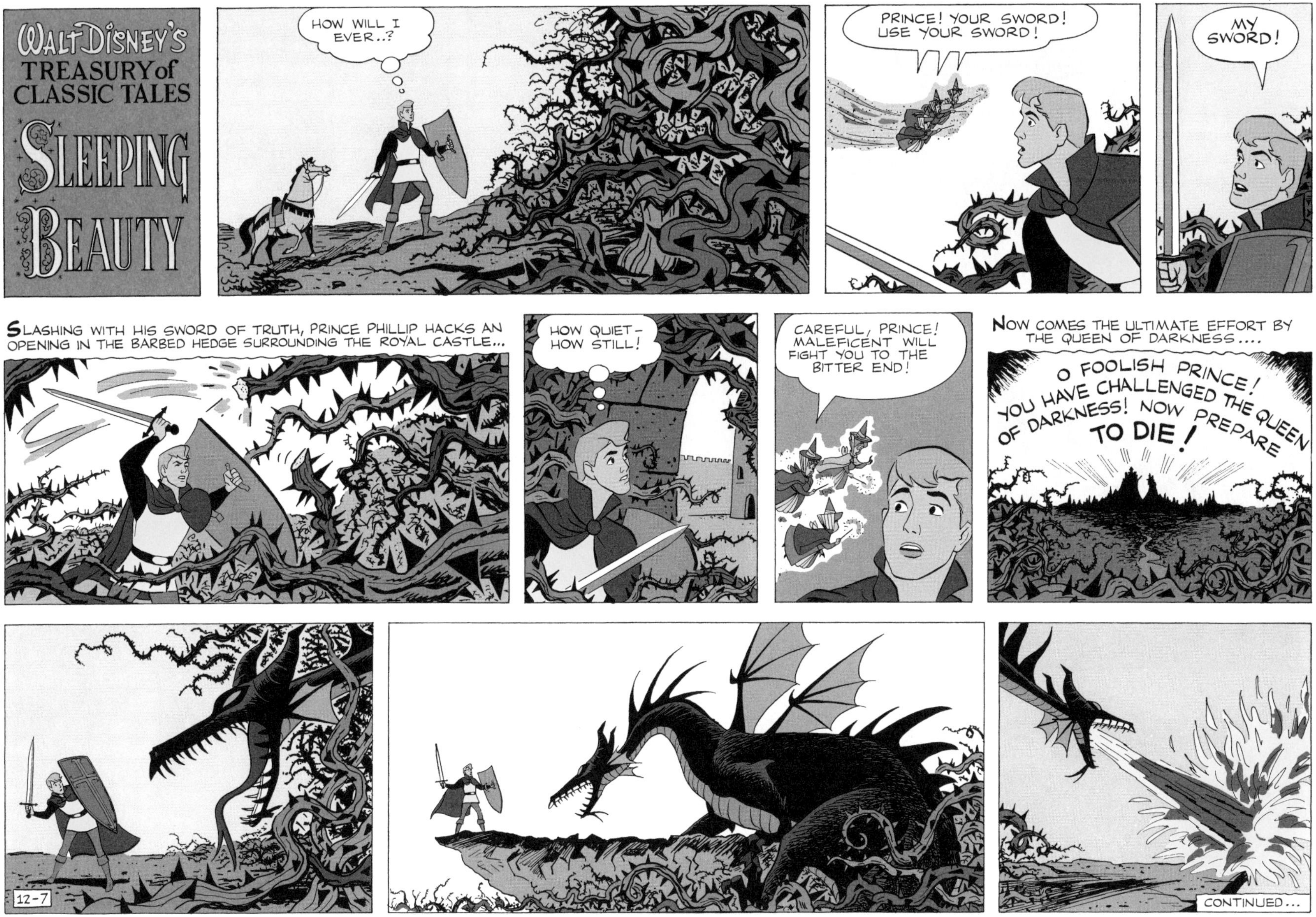
WALT DISNEY'S
TREASURY of CLASSIC TALES
SLEEPING BEAUTY
HOW WILL I EVER..?
PRINCE! YOUR SWORD! USE YOUR SWORD!
MY SWORD!
SLASHING WITH HIS SWORD OF TRUTH, PRINCE PHILLIP HACKS AN OPENING IN THE BARBED HEDGE SURROUNDING THE ROYAL CASTLE...
HOW QUIET– HOW STILL!
CAREFUL, PRINCE! MALEFICENT WILL FIGHT YOU TO THE BITTER END!
NOW COMES THE ULTIMATE EFFORT BY THE QUEEN OF DARKNESS....
O FOOLISH PRINCE! YOU HAVE CHALLENGED THE QUEEN OF DARKNESS! NOW PREPARE TO DIE!
12-7
CONTINUED...

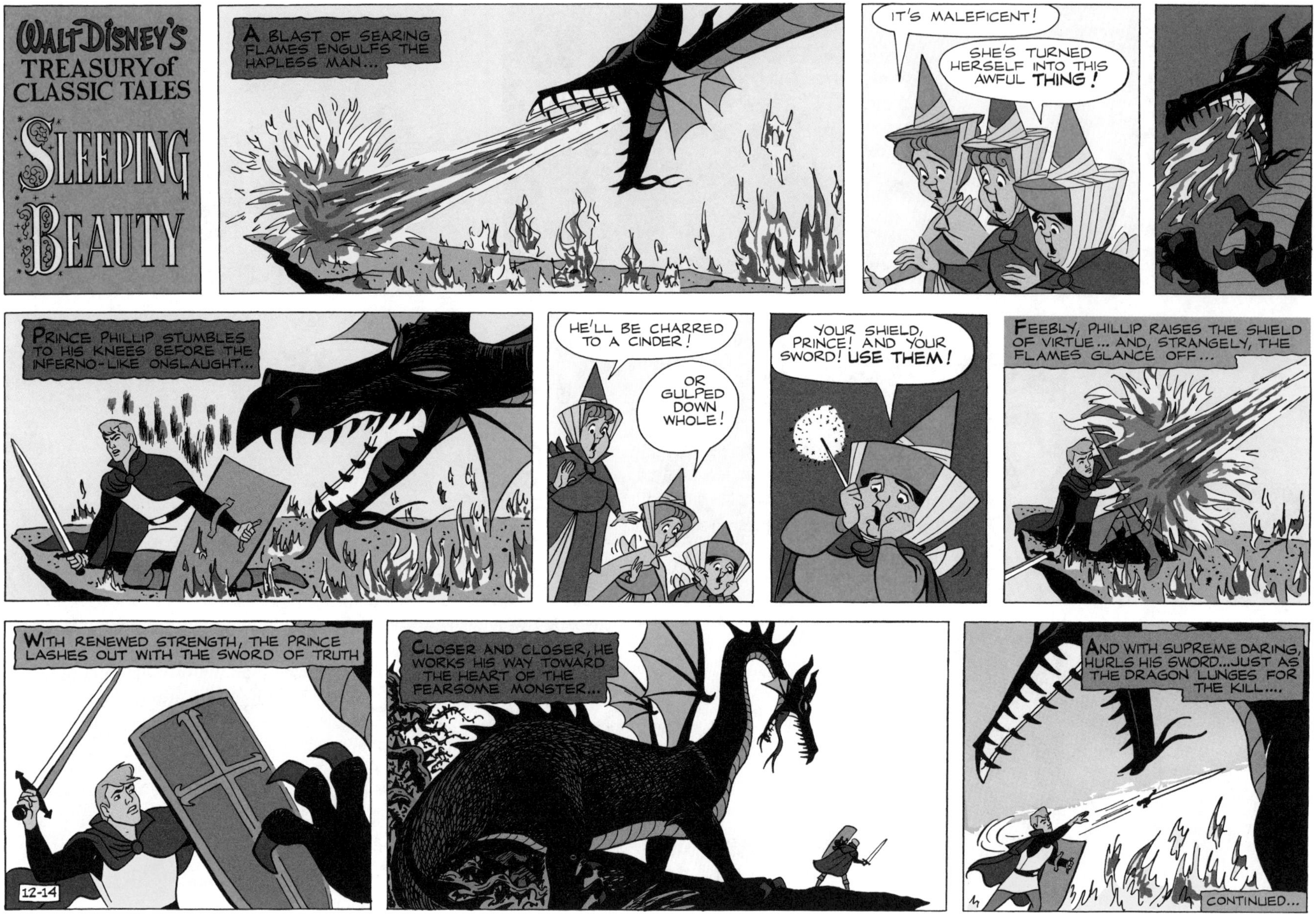

WALT DISNEY'S TREASURY of CLASSIC TALES
SLEEPING BEAUTY
A BLAST OF SEARING FLAMES ENGULFS THE HAPLESS MAN...
IT'S MALEFICENT!
SHE'S TURNED HERSELF INTO THIS AWFUL THING!
PRINCE PHILLIP STUMBLES TO HIS KNEES BEFORE THE INFERNO-LIKE ONSLAUGHT...
HE'LL BE CHARRED TO A CINDER!
OR GULPED DOWN WHOLE!
YOUR SHIELD, PRINCE! AND YOUR SWORD! USE THEM!
FEEBLY, PHILLIP RAISES THE SHIELD OF VIRTUE... AND, STRANGELY, THE FLAMES GLANCE OFF...
WITH RENEWED STRENGTH, THE PRINCE LASHES OUT WITH THE SWORD OF TRUTH
12-14
CLOSER AND CLOSER, HE WORKS HIS WAY TOWARD THE HEART OF THE FEARSOME MONSTER...
AND WITH SUPREME DARING, HURLS HIS SWORD...JUST AS THE DRAGON LUNGES FOR THE KILL....
CONTINUED...

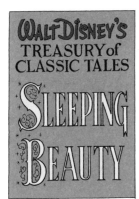

WALT DISNEY'S
TREASURY of
CLASSIC TALES

SLEEPING BEAUTY

WITH A PIERCING SCREAM, THE MONSTROUS CREATURE COLLAPSES...

IF IT HADN'T BEEN FOR THE SHIELD OF VIRTUE... AND THE SWORD OF TRUTH..!

OH, PRINCE PHILLIP --YOU DID IT!

THAT'S THE END OF MALEFICENT ...AND ALL HER BLACK MAGIC!

AND THE BEGINNING FOR AURORA AND ME!

FOR A MOMENT THE PRINCE STANDS OVER THE NOW LIFELESS MONSTER, THEN...

AND THE SUN IS SHINING AGAIN!

LOOK! THE HEDGE OF THORNS HAS DISAPPEARED!

NOW TO AWAKEN AURORA...AND THE REST OF THE CASTLE!

AURORA!

THROUGH THE SLEEPING CASTLE, UP THE TOWER STAIRS RACES THE PRINCE

SHE'S (PUFF) INSIDE HERE!

SHE IS EVEN MORE BEAUTIFUL THAN I REMEMBERED!

THE KISS! THE KISS OF TRUE LOVE!

12-21

W-WILL IT WORK...?

W-WILL SHE AWAKE...?

THEN, SLOWLY, THE LONG EYELASHES FLUTTER OPEN....

AURORA! IT IS YOUR PHILLIP!

PHILLIP!

TO BE CONCLUDED...

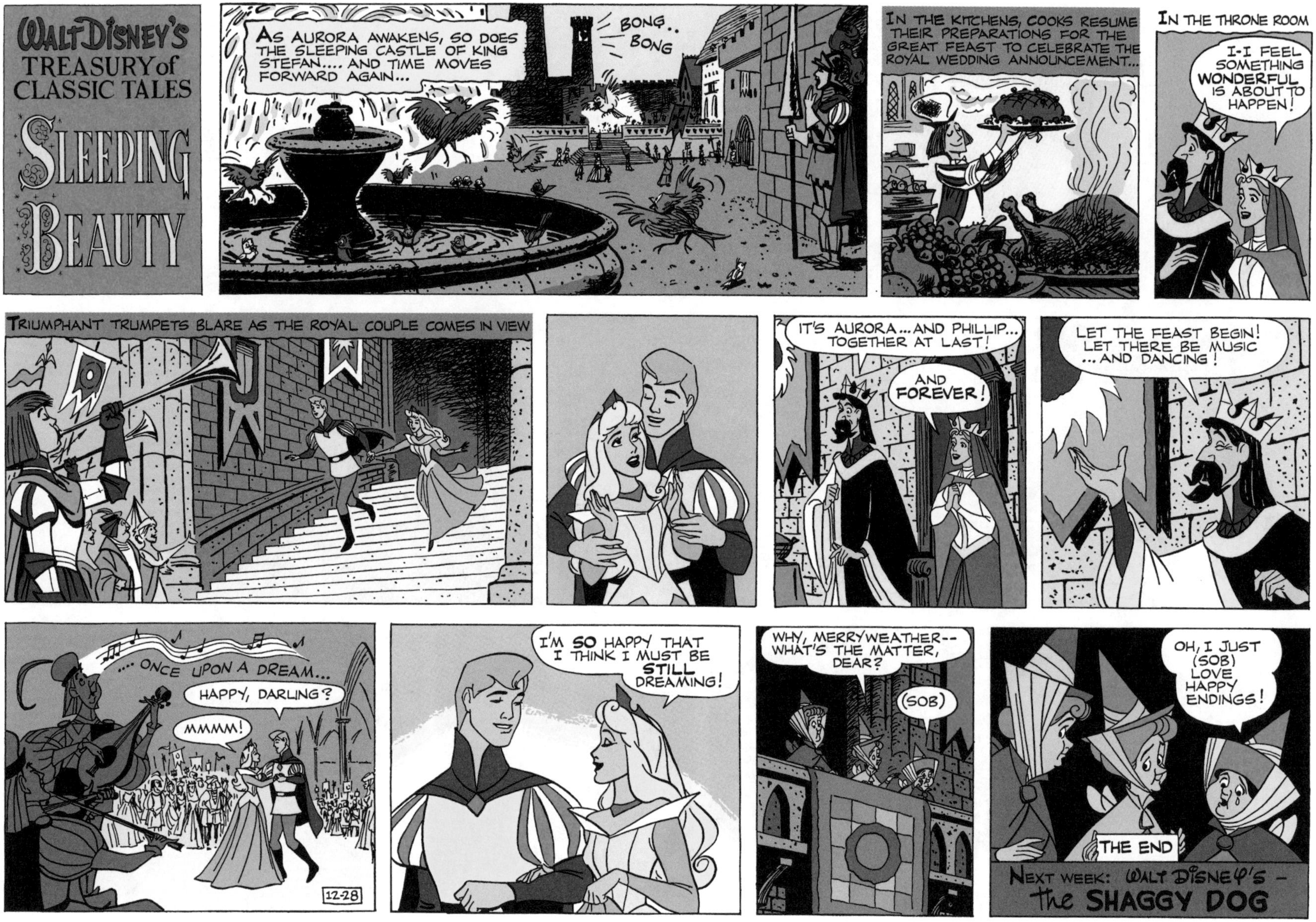

WALT DISNEY'S
TREASURY of CLASSIC TALES
SLEEPING BEAUTY
AS AURORA AWAKENS, SO DOES THE SLEEPING CASTLE OF KING STEFAN.... AND TIME MOVES FORWARD AGAIN...
BONG.. BONG
IN THE KITCHENS, COOKS RESUME THEIR PREPARATIONS FOR THE GREAT FEAST TO CELEBRATE THE ROYAL WEDDING ANNOUNCEMENT...
IN THE THRONE ROOM
I-I FEEL SOMETHING WONDERFUL IS ABOUT TO HAPPEN!
TRIUMPHANT TRUMPETS BLARE AS THE ROYAL COUPLE COMES IN VIEW
IT'S AURORA...AND PHILLIP... TOGETHER AT LAST!
AND FOREVER!
LET THE FEAST BEGIN! LET THERE BE MUSIC ...AND DANCING!
...ONCE UPON A DREAM...
HAPPY, DARLING?
MMMM!
12-28
I'M SO HAPPY THAT I THINK I MUST BE STILL DREAMING!
WHY, MERRYWEATHER-- WHAT'S THE MATTER, DEAR?
(SOB)
OH, I JUST (SOB) LOVE HAPPY ENDINGS!
THE END
NEXT WEEK: WALT DISNEY'S - the SHAGGY DOG

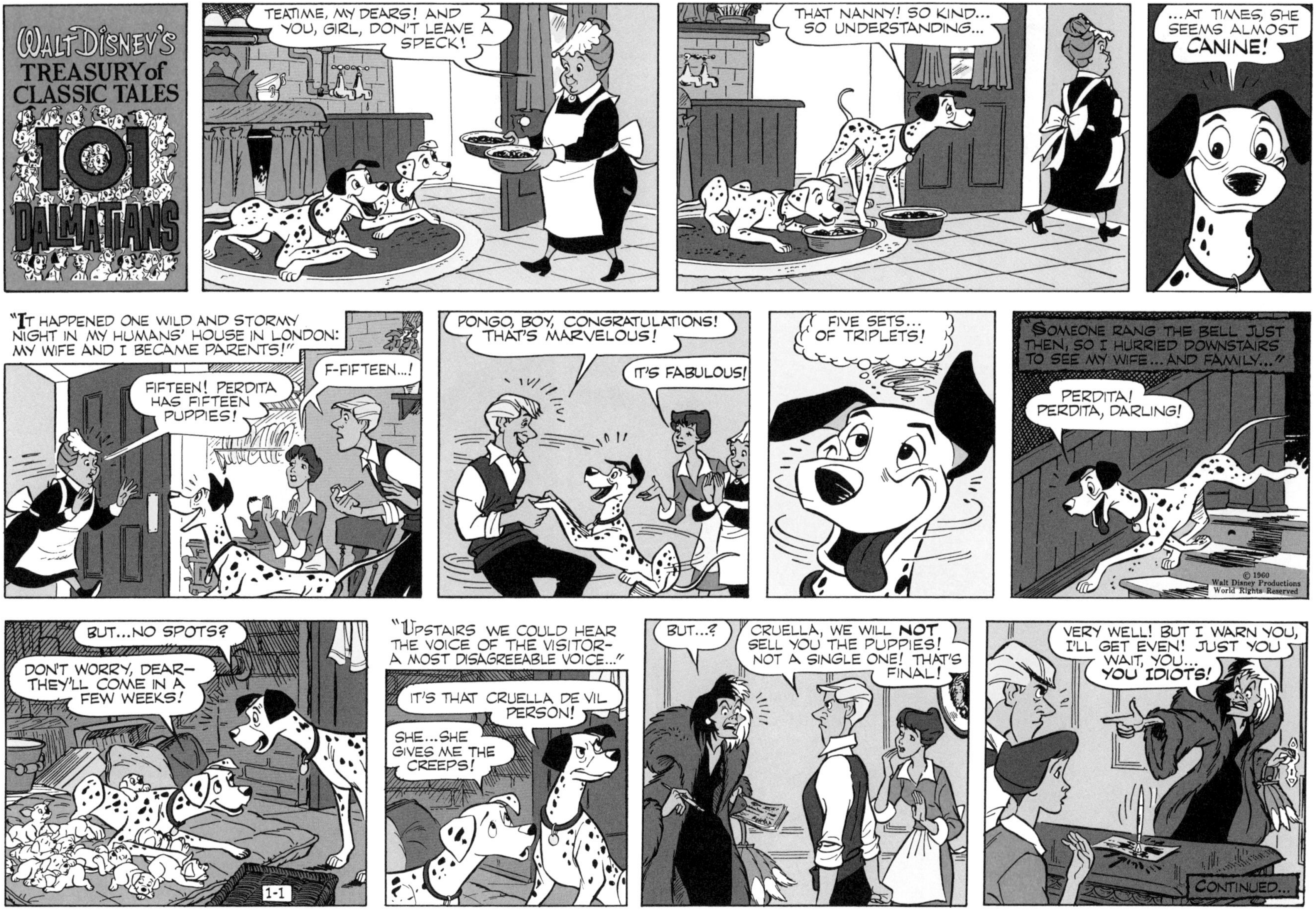
WALT DISNEY'S
TREASURY of CLASSIC TALES
101 DALMATIANS
TEATIME, MY DEARS! AND YOU, GIRL, DON'T LEAVE A SPECK!
THAT NANNY! SO KIND... SO UNDERSTANDING...
...AT TIMES, SHE SEEMS ALMOST CANINE!
"IT HAPPENED ONE WILD AND STORMY NIGHT IN MY HUMANS' HOUSE IN LONDON: MY WIFE AND I BECAME PARENTS!"
FIFTEEN! PERDITA HAS FIFTEEN PUPPIES!
F-FIFTEEN...!
PONGO, BOY, CONGRATULATIONS! THAT'S MARVELOUS!
IT'S FABULOUS!
FIVE SETS... OF TRIPLETS!
"SOMEONE RANG THE BELL JUST THEN, SO I HURRIED DOWNSTAIRS TO SEE MY WIFE... AND FAMILY..."
PERDITA! PERDITA, DARLING!
© 1960 Walt Disney Productions World Rights Reserved
BUT...NO SPOTS?
DON'T WORRY, DEAR— THEY'LL COME IN A FEW WEEKS!
1-1
"UPSTAIRS WE COULD HEAR THE VOICE OF THE VISITOR— A MOST DISAGREEABLE VOICE..."
IT'S THAT CRUELLA DE VIL PERSON!
SHE...SHE GIVES ME THE CREEPS!
BUT...?
CRUELLA, WE WILL NOT SELL YOU THE PUPPIES! NOT A SINGLE ONE! THAT'S FINAL!
VERY WELL! BUT I WARN YOU, I'LL GET EVEN! JUST YOU WAIT, YOU... YOU IDIOTS!
CONTINUED...

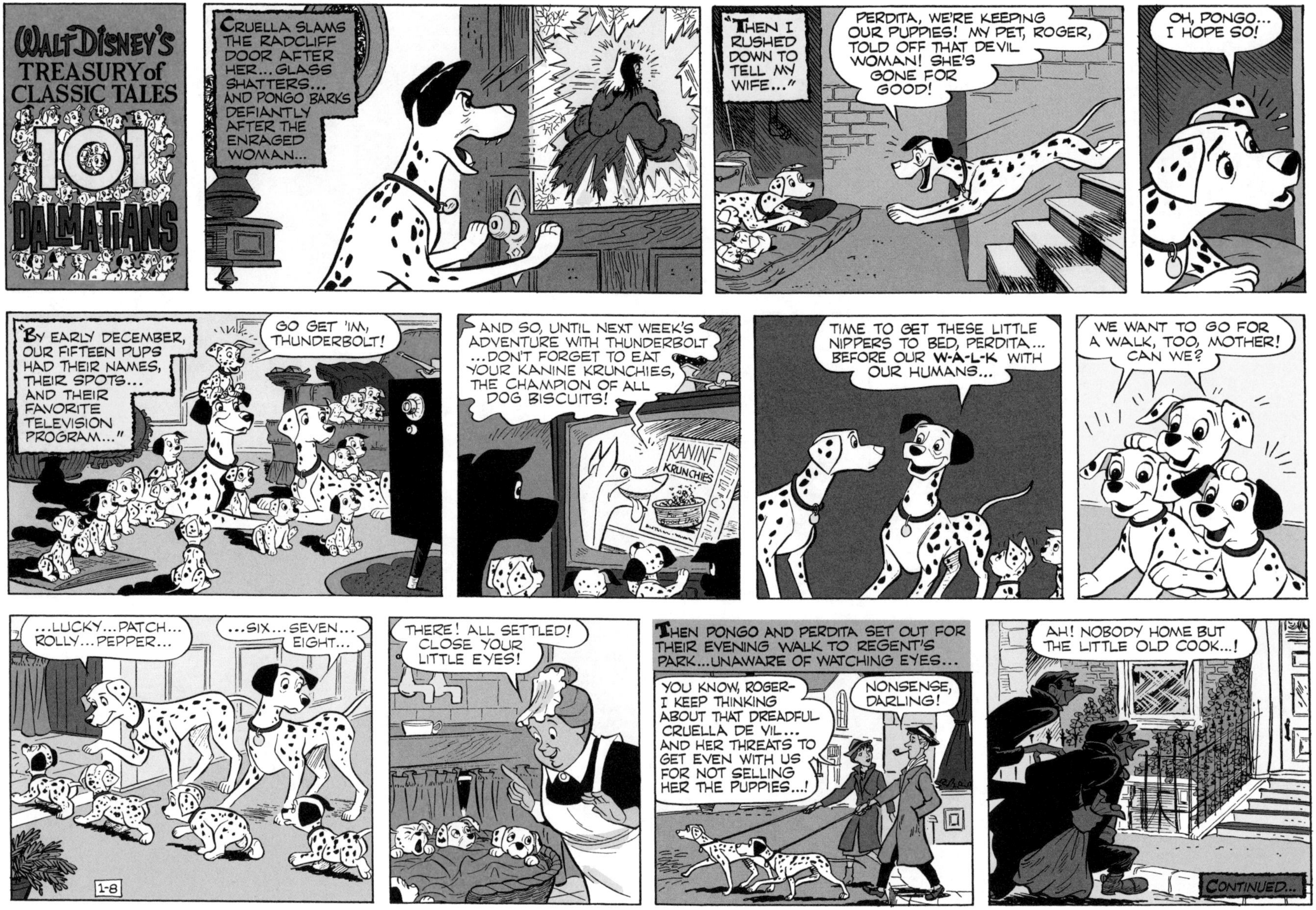
WALT DISNEY'S TREASURY of CLASSIC TALES
101 DALMATIANS
CRUELLA SLAMS THE RADCLIFF DOOR AFTER HER... GLASS SHATTERS... AND PONGO BARKS DEFIANTLY AFTER THE ENRAGED WOMAN...
"THEN I RUSHED DOWN TO TELL MY WIFE..."
PERDITA, WE'RE KEEPING OUR PUPPIES! MY PET, ROGER, TOLD OFF THAT DEVIL WOMAN! SHE'S GONE FOR GOOD!
OH, PONGO... I HOPE SO!
"BY EARLY DECEMBER, OUR FIFTEEN PUPS HAD THEIR NAMES, THEIR SPOTS... AND THEIR FAVORITE TELEVISION PROGRAM..."
GO GET 'IM, THUNDERBOLT!
AND SO, UNTIL NEXT WEEK'S ADVENTURE WITH THUNDERBOLT ...DON'T FORGET TO EAT YOUR KANINE KRUNCHIES, THE CHAMPION OF ALL DOG BISCUITS!
KANINE KRUNCHIES
TIME TO GET THESE LITTLE NIPPERS TO BED, PERDITA... BEFORE OUR W-A-L-K WITH OUR HUMANS...
WE WANT TO GO FOR A WALK, TOO, MOTHER! CAN WE?
...LUCKY...PATCH... ROLLY...PEPPER...
...SIX...SEVEN... EIGHT...
1-8
THERE! ALL SETTLED! CLOSE YOUR LITTLE EYES!
THEN PONGO AND PERDITA SET OUT FOR THEIR EVENING WALK TO REGENT'S PARK...UNAWARE OF WATCHING EYES...
YOU KNOW, ROGER-- I KEEP THINKING ABOUT THAT DREADFUL CRUELLA DE VIL... AND HER THREATS TO GET EVEN WITH US FOR NOT SELLING HER THE PUPPIES...!
NONSENSE, DARLING!
AH! NOBODY HOME BUT THE LITTLE OLD COOK...!
CONTINUED...

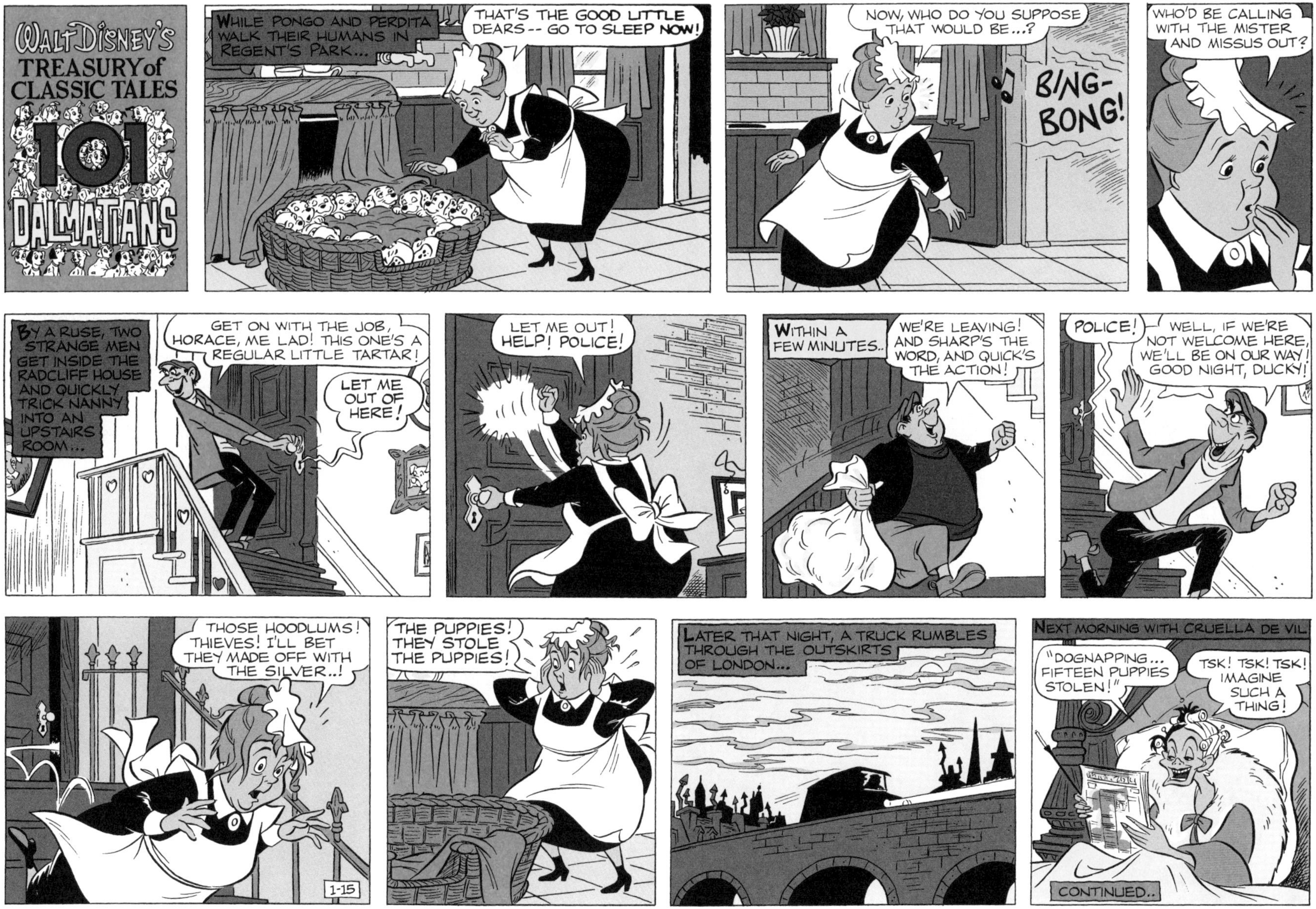
WALT DISNEY'S
TREASURY of CLASSIC TALES
101 DALMATIANS
WHILE PONGO AND PERDITA WALK THEIR HUMANS IN REGENT'S PARK...
THAT'S THE GOOD LITTLE DEARS -- GO TO SLEEP NOW!
NOW, WHO DO YOU SUPPOSE THAT WOULD BE...?
BING-BONG!
WHO'D BE CALLING WITH THE MISTER AND MISSUS OUT?
BY A RUSE, TWO STRANGE MEN GET INSIDE THE RADCLIFF HOUSE AND QUICKLY TRICK NANNY INTO AN UPSTAIRS ROOM...
GET ON WITH THE JOB, HORACE, ME LAD! THIS ONE'S A REGULAR LITTLE TARTAR!
LET ME OUT OF HERE!
LET ME OUT! HELP! POLICE!
WITHIN A FEW MINUTES..
WE'RE LEAVING! AND SHARP'S THE WORD, AND QUICK'S THE ACTION!
POLICE!
WELL, IF WE'RE NOT WELCOME HERE, WE'LL BE ON OUR WAY! GOOD NIGHT, DUCKY!
THOSE HOODLUMS! THIEVES! I'LL BET THEY MADE OFF WITH THE SILVER..!
1-15
THE PUPPIES! THEY STOLE THE PUPPIES!
LATER THAT NIGHT, A TRUCK RUMBLES THROUGH THE OUTSKIRTS OF LONDON...
NEXT MORNING WITH CRUELLA DE VIL
"DOGNAPPING... FIFTEEN PUPPIES STOLEN!"
TSK! TSK! TSK! IMAGINE SUCH A THING!
CONTINUED..

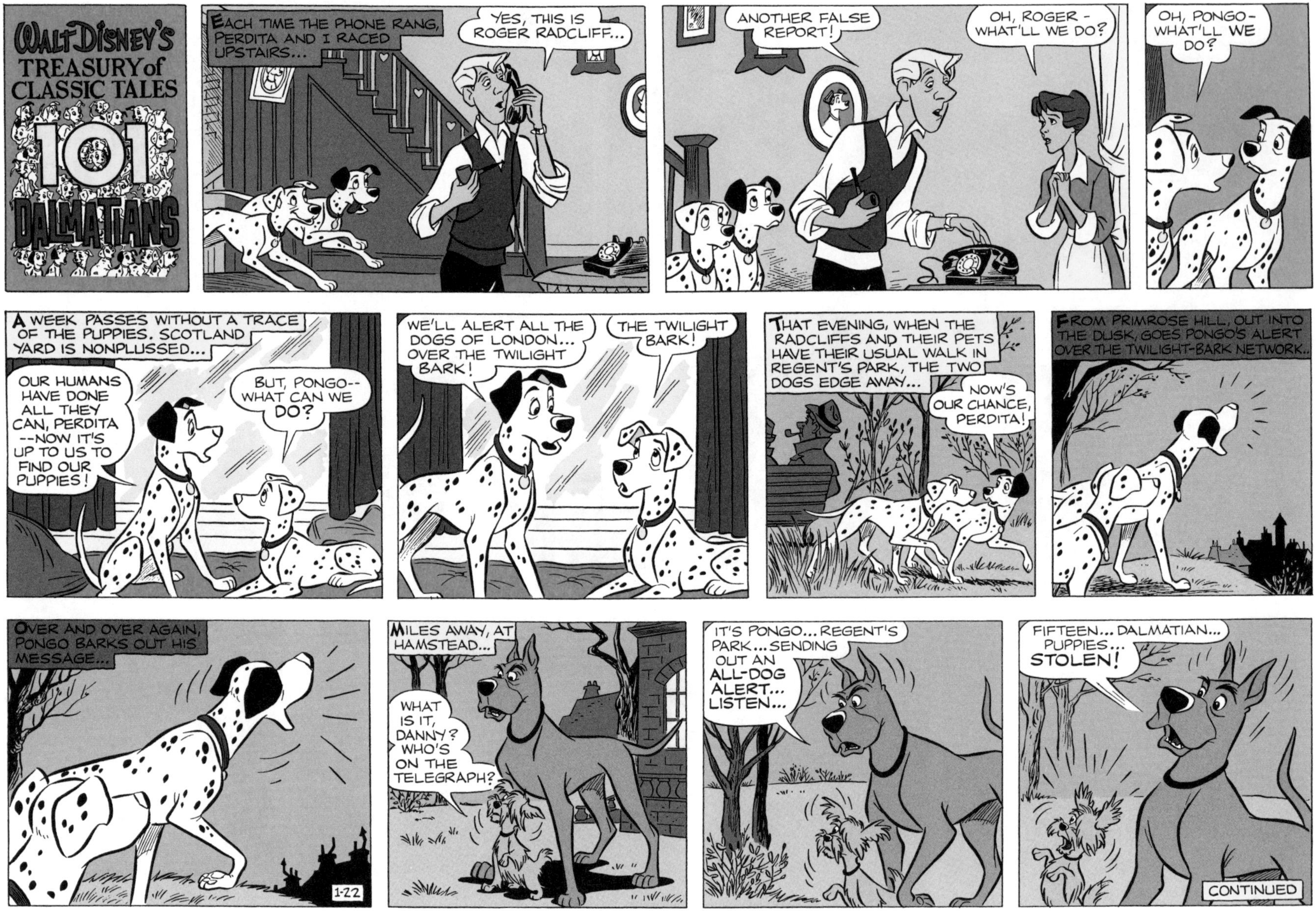
WALT DISNEY'S
TREASURY of CLASSIC TALES
101 DALMATIANS
EACH TIME THE PHONE RANG, PERDITA AND I RACED UPSTAIRS...
YES, THIS IS ROGER RADCLIFF...
ANOTHER FALSE REPORT!
OH, ROGER - WHAT'LL WE DO?
OH, PONGO - WHAT'LL WE DO?
A WEEK PASSES WITHOUT A TRACE OF THE PUPPIES. SCOTLAND YARD IS NONPLUSSED...
OUR HUMANS HAVE DONE ALL THEY CAN, PERDITA --NOW IT'S UP TO US TO FIND OUR PUPPIES!
BUT, PONGO-- WHAT CAN WE DO?
WE'LL ALERT ALL THE DOGS OF LONDON... OVER THE TWILIGHT BARK!
THE TWILIGHT BARK!
THAT EVENING, WHEN THE RADCLIFFS AND THEIR PETS HAVE THEIR USUAL WALK IN REGENT'S PARK, THE TWO DOGS EDGE AWAY...
NOW'S OUR CHANCE, PERDITA!
FROM PRIMROSE HILL, OUT INTO THE DUSK, GOES PONGO'S ALERT OVER THE TWILIGHT-BARK NETWORK...
OVER AND OVER AGAIN, PONGO BARKS OUT HIS MESSAGE...
1-22
MILES AWAY, AT HAMSTEAD...
WHAT IS IT, DANNY? WHO'S ON THE TELEGRAPH?
IT'S PONGO... REGENT'S PARK... SENDING OUT AN ALL-DOG ALERT... LISTEN...
FIFTEEN... DALMATIAN... PUPPIES... STOLEN!
CONTINUED

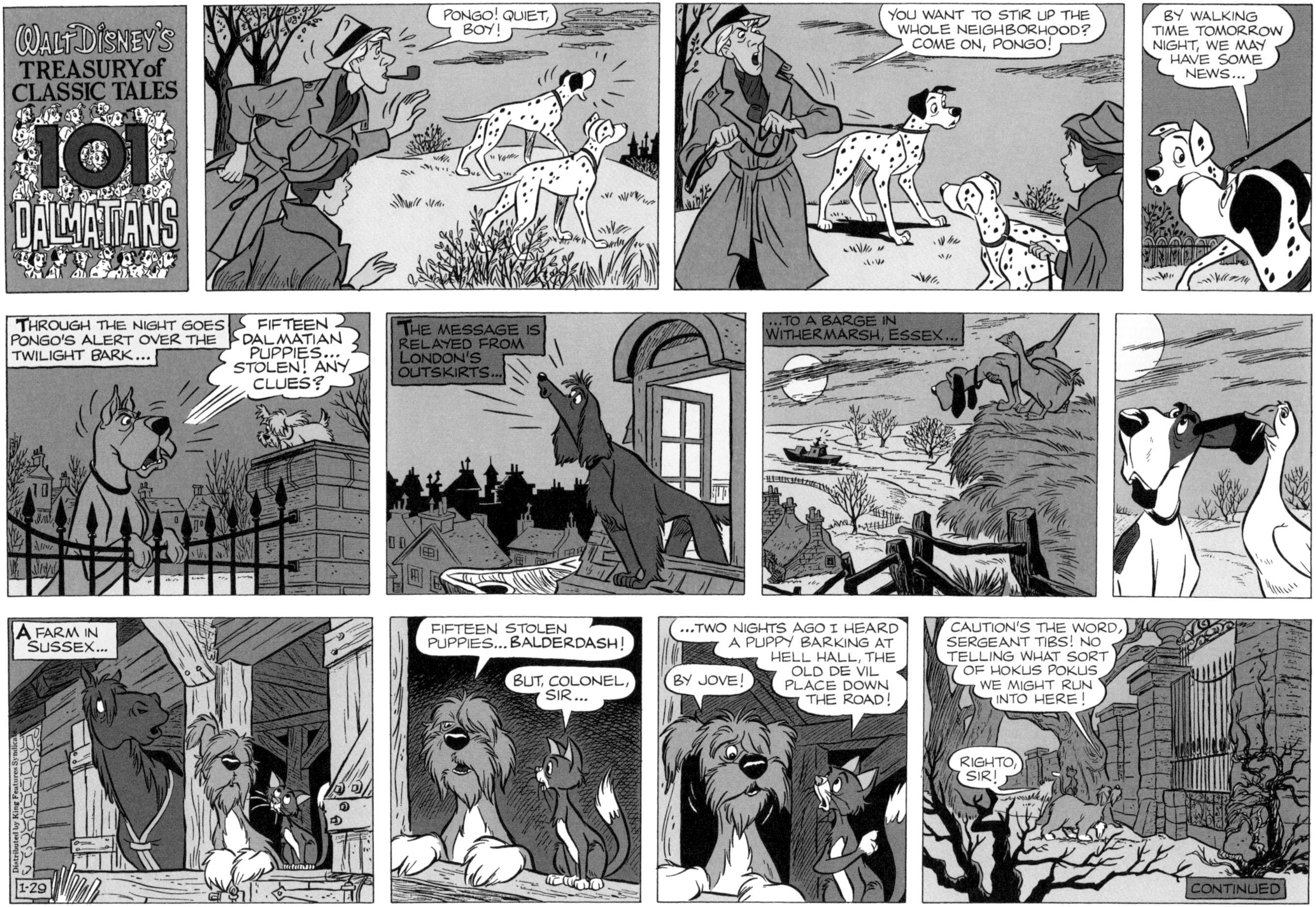
WALT DISNEY'S
TREASURY of CLASSIC TALES
101 DALMATIANS
PONGO! QUIET, BOY!
YOU WANT TO STIR UP THE WHOLE NEIGHBORHOOD? COME ON, PONGO!
BY WALKING TIME TOMORROW NIGHT, WE MAY HAVE SOME NEWS...
THROUGH THE NIGHT GOES PONGO'S ALERT OVER THE TWILIGHT BARK...
FIFTEEN DALMATIAN PUPPIES... STOLEN! ANY CLUES?
THE MESSAGE IS RELAYED FROM LONDON'S OUTSKIRTS...
...TO A BARGE IN WITHERMARSH, ESSEX...
A FARM IN SUSSEX...
1-29
FIFTEEN STOLEN PUPPIES... BALDERDASH!
BUT, COLONEL, SIR...
...TWO NIGHTS AGO I HEARD A PUPPY BARKING AT HELL HALL, THE OLD DE VIL PLACE DOWN THE ROAD!
BY JOVE!
CAUTION'S THE WORD, SERGEANT TIBS! NO TELLING WHAT SORT OF HOKUS POKUS WE MIGHT RUN INTO HERE!
RIGHTO, SIR!
CONTINUED

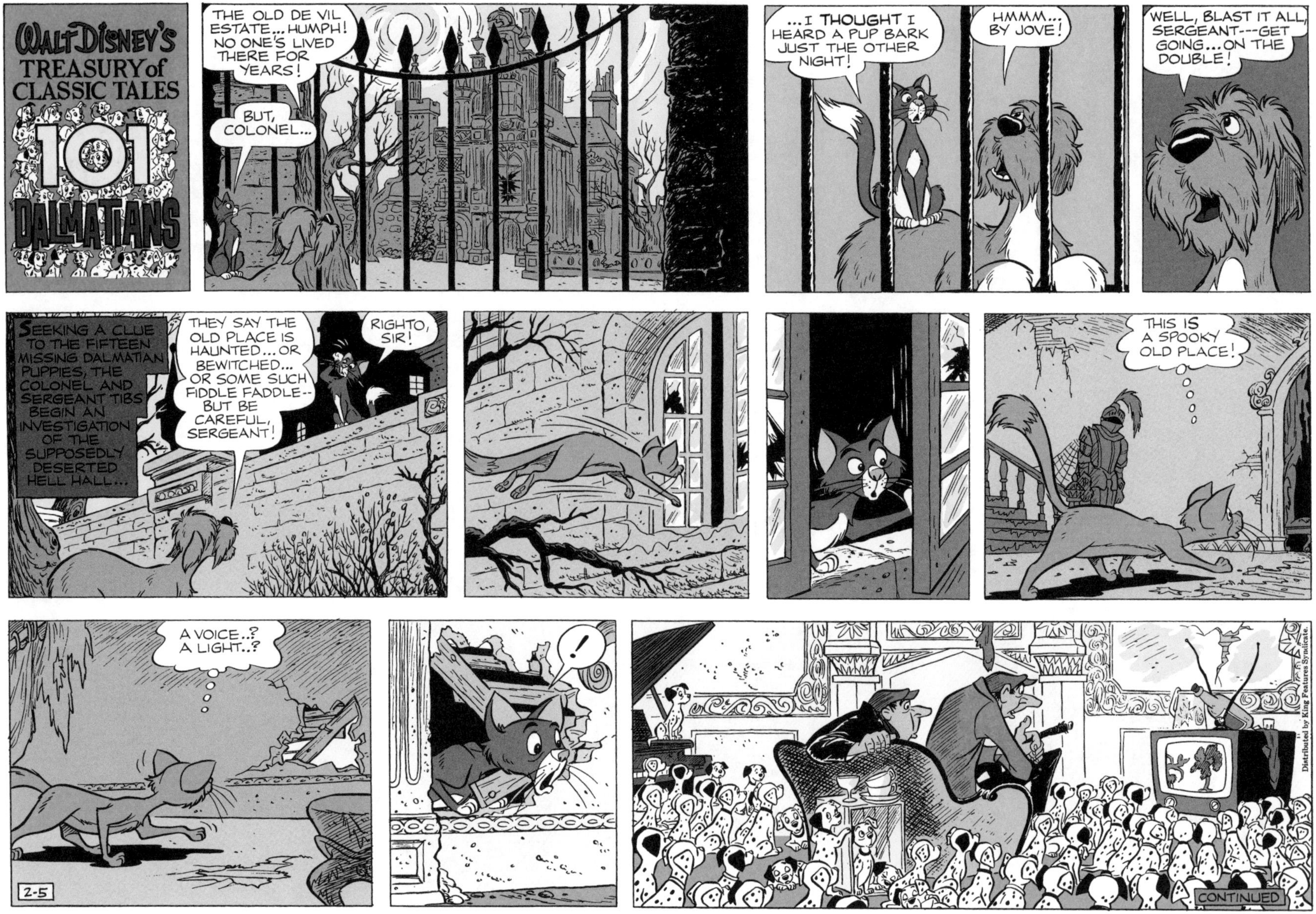
WALT DISNEY'S
TREASURY of CLASSIC TALES
101 DALMATIANS
THE OLD DE VIL ESTATE... HUMPH! NO ONE'S LIVED THERE FOR YEARS!
BUT, COLONEL...
...I THOUGHT I HEARD A PUP BARK JUST THE OTHER NIGHT!
HMMM... BY JOVE!
WELL, BLAST IT ALL, SERGEANT---GET GOING... ON THE DOUBLE!
SEEKING A CLUE TO THE FIFTEEN MISSING DALMATIAN PUPPIES, THE COLONEL AND SERGEANT TIBS BEGIN AN INVESTIGATION OF THE SUPPOSEDLY DESERTED HELL HALL...
THEY SAY THE OLD PLACE IS HAUNTED... OR BEWITCHED... OR SOME SUCH FIDDLE FADDLE-- BUT BE CAREFUL, SERGEANT!
RIGHTO, SIR!
THIS IS A SPOOKY OLD PLACE!
A VOICE..? A LIGHT..?
2-5
!
Distributed by King Features Syndicate.
CONTINUED

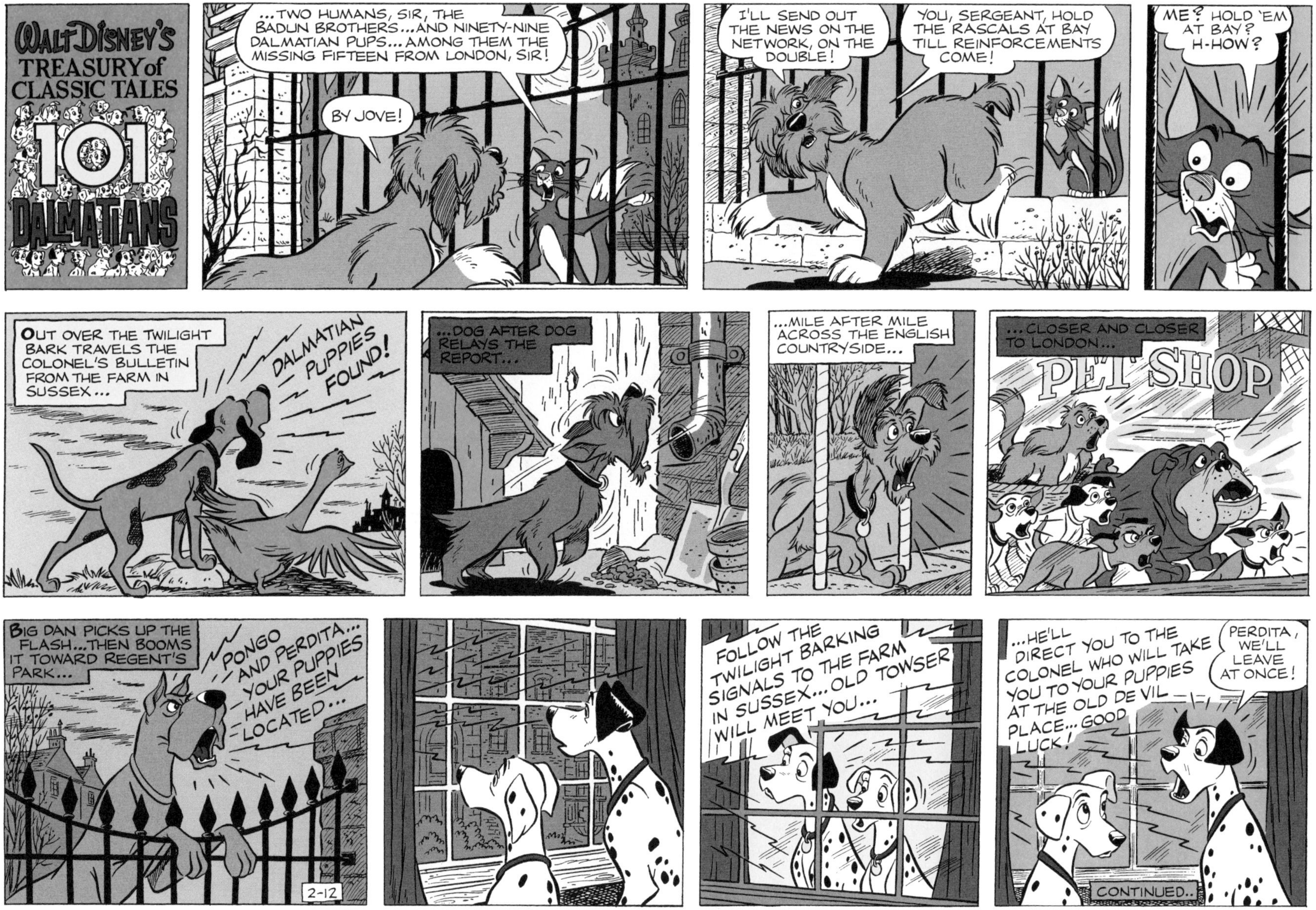
WALT DISNEY'S
TREASURY of CLASSIC TALES
101 DALMATIANS
...TWO HUMANS, SIR, THE BADUN BROTHERS...AND NINETY-NINE DALMATIAN PUPS...AMONG THEM THE MISSING FIFTEEN FROM LONDON, SIR!
BY JOVE!
I'LL SEND OUT THE NEWS ON THE NETWORK, ON THE DOUBLE!
YOU, SERGEANT, HOLD THE RASCALS AT BAY TILL REINFORCEMENTS COME!
ME? HOLD 'EM AT BAY? H-HOW?
OUT OVER THE TWILIGHT BARK TRAVELS THE COLONEL'S BULLETIN FROM THE FARM IN SUSSEX...
DALMATIAN PUPPIES FOUND!
...DOG AFTER DOG RELAYS THE REPORT...
...MILE AFTER MILE ACROSS THE ENGLISH COUNTRYSIDE...
...CLOSER AND CLOSER TO LONDON...
PET SHOP
BIG DAN PICKS UP THE FLASH...THEN BOOMS IT TOWARD REGENT'S PARK...
PONGO AND PERDITA... YOUR PUPPIES HAVE BEEN LOCATED...
2-12
FOLLOW THE TWILIGHT BARKING SIGNALS TO THE FARM IN SUSSEX...OLD TOWSER WILL MEET YOU...
...HE'LL DIRECT YOU TO THE COLONEL WHO WILL TAKE YOU TO YOUR PUPPIES AT THE OLD DE VIL PLACE...GOOD LUCK!
PERDITA, WE'LL LEAVE AT ONCE!
CONTINUED..

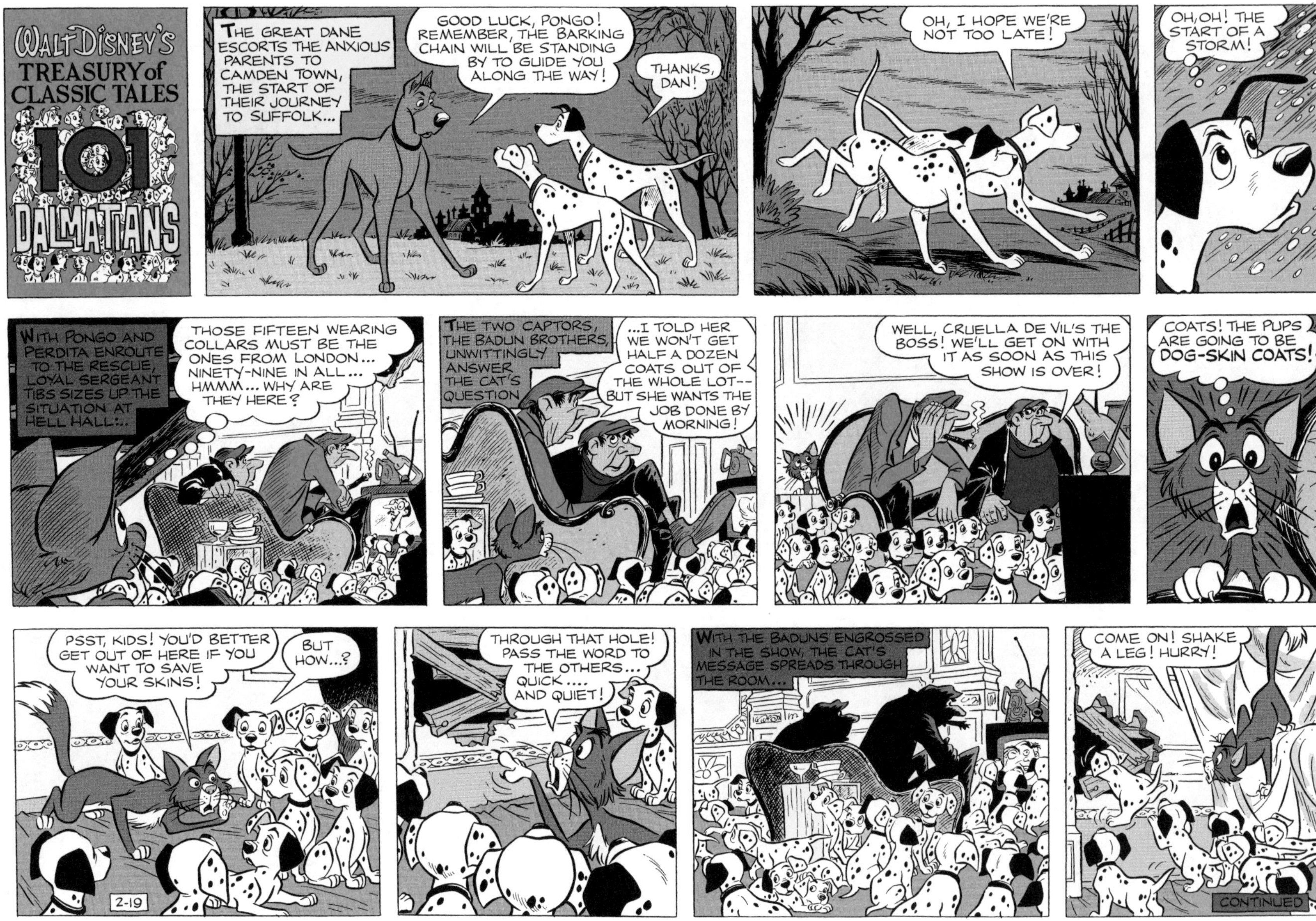
WALT DISNEY'S
TREASURY of CLASSIC TALES
101 DALMATIANS
THE GREAT DANE ESCORTS THE ANXIOUS PARENTS TO CAMDEN TOWN, THE START OF THEIR JOURNEY TO SUFFOLK...
GOOD LUCK, PONGO! REMEMBER, THE BARKING CHAIN WILL BE STANDING BY TO GUIDE YOU ALONG THE WAY!
THANKS, DAN!
OH, I HOPE WE'RE NOT TOO LATE!
OH, OH! THE START OF A STORM!
WITH PONGO AND PERDITA ENROUTE TO THE RESCUE, LOYAL SERGEANT TIBS SIZES UP THE SITUATION AT HELL HALL:..
THOSE FIFTEEN WEARING COLLARS MUST BE THE ONES FROM LONDON... NINETY-NINE IN ALL... HMMM... WHY ARE THEY HERE?
THE TWO CAPTORS, THE BADUN BROTHERS, UNWITTINGLY ANSWER THE CAT'S QUESTION
...I TOLD HER WE WON'T GET HALF A DOZEN COATS OUT OF THE WHOLE LOT-- BUT SHE WANTS THE JOB DONE BY MORNING!
WELL, CRUELLA DE VIL'S THE BOSS! WE'LL GET ON WITH IT AS SOON AS THIS SHOW IS OVER!
COATS! THE PUPS ARE GOING TO BE DOG-SKIN COATS!
PSST, KIDS! YOU'D BETTER GET OUT OF HERE IF YOU WANT TO SAVE YOUR SKINS!
BUT HOW...?
2-19
THROUGH THAT HOLE! PASS THE WORD TO THE OTHERS... QUICK... AND QUIET!
WITH THE BADUNS ENGROSSED IN THE SHOW, THE CAT'S MESSAGE SPREADS THROUGH THE ROOM...
COME ON! SHAKE A LEG! HURRY!
CONTINUED

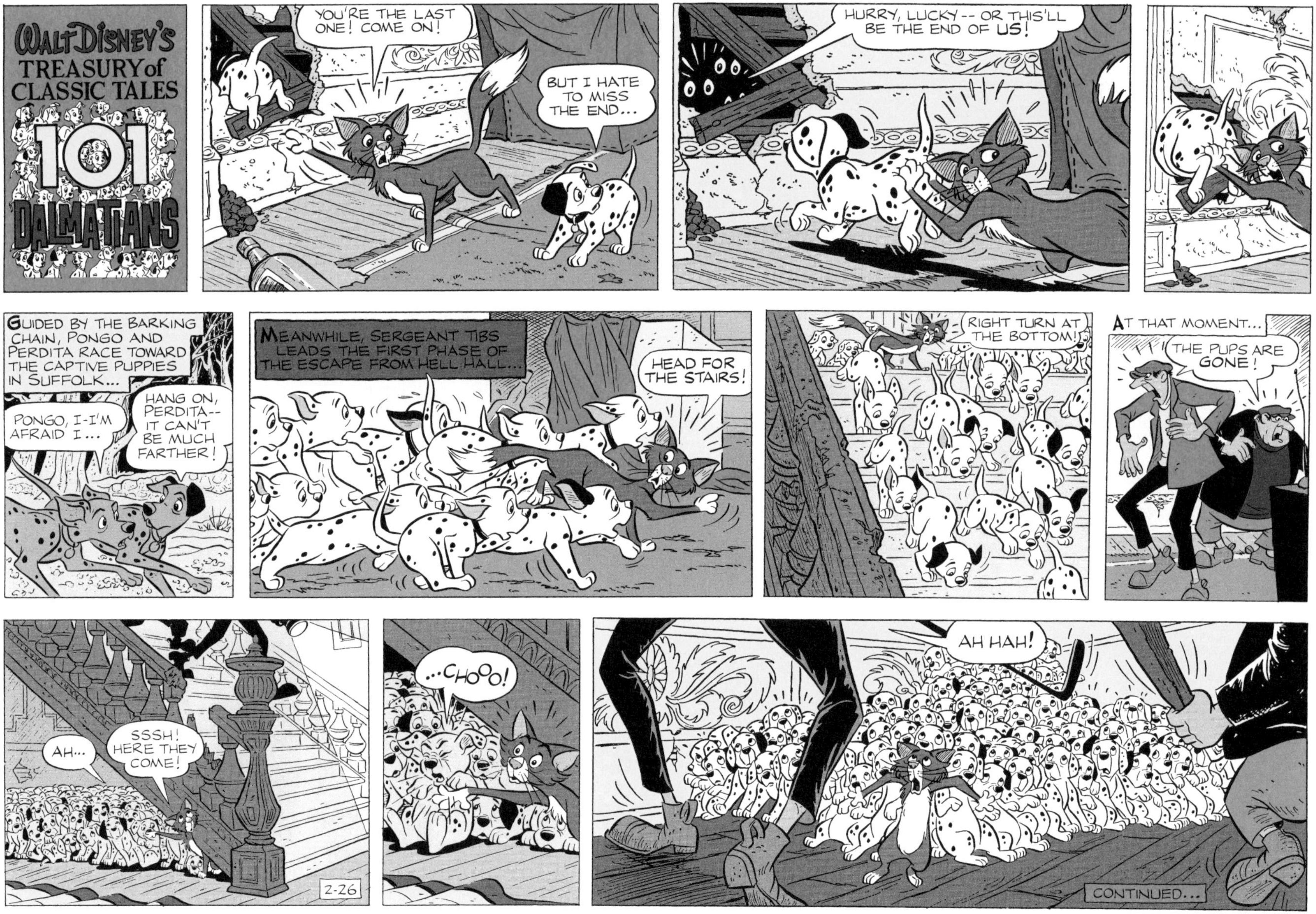
WALT DISNEY'S
TREASURY of CLASSIC TALES
101 DALMATIANS
YOU'RE THE LAST ONE! COME ON!
BUT I HATE TO MISS THE END...
HURRY, LUCKY -- OR THIS'LL BE THE END OF US!
GUIDED BY THE BARKING CHAIN, PONGO AND PERDITA RACE TOWARD THE CAPTIVE PUPPIES IN SUFFOLK...
PONGO, I-I'M AFRAID I...
HANG ON, PERDITA-- IT CAN'T BE MUCH FARTHER!
MEANWHILE, SERGEANT TIBS LEADS THE FIRST PHASE OF THE ESCAPE FROM HELL HALL...
HEAD FOR THE STAIRS!
RIGHT TURN AT THE BOTTOM!
AT THAT MOMENT...
THE PUPS ARE GONE!
AH...
SSSH! HERE THEY COME!
2-26
...CHOOO!
AH HAH!
CONTINUED...

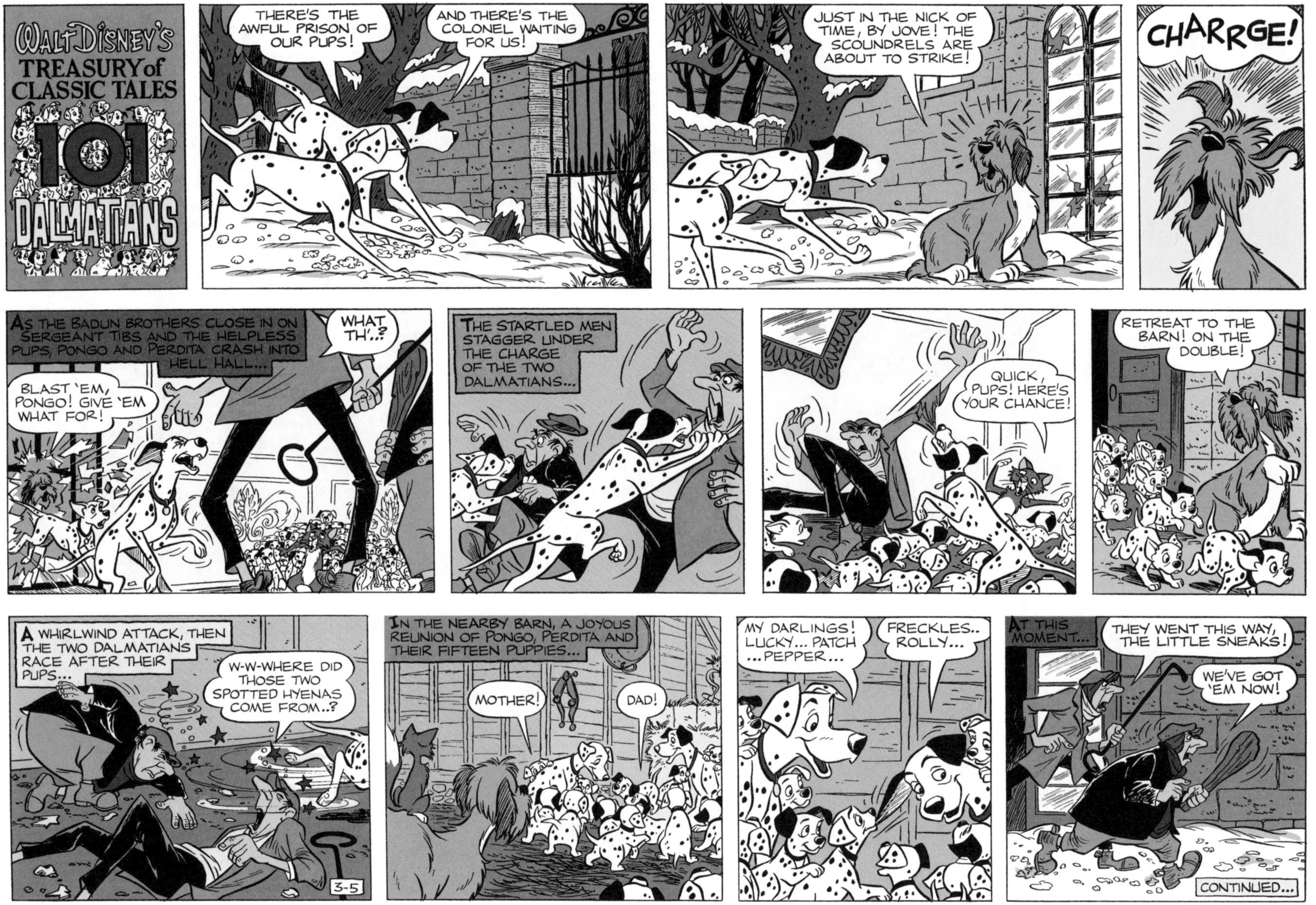

WALT DISNEY'S
TREASURY of CLASSIC TALES
101 DALMATIANS
THERE'S THE AWFUL PRISON OF OUR PUPS!
AND THERE'S THE COLONEL WAITING FOR US!
JUST IN THE NICK OF TIME, BY JOVE! THE SCOUNDRELS ARE ABOUT TO STRIKE!
CHARRGE!
AS THE BADUN BROTHERS CLOSE IN ON SERGEANT TIBS AND THE HELPLESS PUPS, PONGO AND PERDITA CRASH INTO HELL HALL...
WHAT TH'..?
BLAST 'EM, PONGO! GIVE 'EM WHAT FOR!
THE STARTLED MEN STAGGER UNDER THE CHARGE OF THE TWO DALMATIANS...
QUICK, PUPS! HERE'S YOUR CHANCE!
RETREAT TO THE BARN! ON THE DOUBLE!
A WHIRLWIND ATTACK, THEN THE TWO DALMATIANS RACE AFTER THEIR PUPS...
W-W-WHERE DID THOSE TWO SPOTTED HYENAS COME FROM..?
3-5
IN THE NEARBY BARN, A JOYOUS REUNION OF PONGO, PERDITA AND THEIR FIFTEEN PUPPIES...
MOTHER!
DAD!
MY DARLINGS! LUCKY... PATCH ...PEPPER...
FRECKLES.. ROLLY...
AT THIS MOMENT...
THEY WENT THIS WAY, THE LITTLE SNEAKS!
WE'VE GOT 'EM NOW!
CONTINUED...

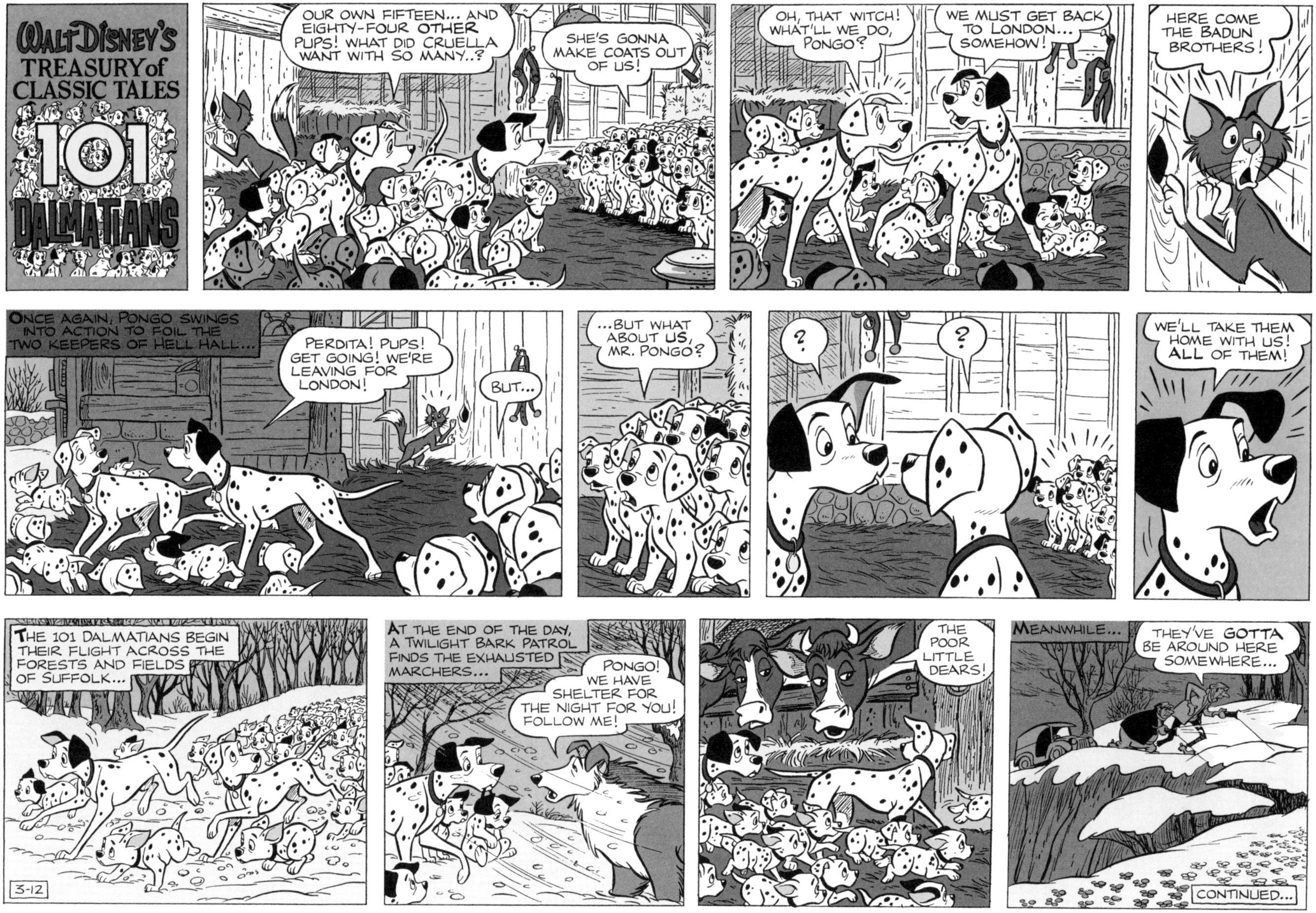
WALT DISNEY'S
TREASURY of CLASSIC TALES
101 DALMATIANS
OUR OWN FIFTEEN... AND EIGHTY-FOUR OTHER PUPS! WHAT DID CRUELLA WANT WITH SO MANY..?
SHE'S GONNA MAKE COATS OUT OF US!
OH, THAT WITCH! WHAT'LL WE DO, PONGO?
WE MUST GET BACK TO LONDON... SOMEHOW!
HERE COME THE BADUN BROTHERS!
ONCE AGAIN, PONGO SWINGS INTO ACTION TO FOIL THE TWO KEEPERS OF HELL HALL...
PERDITA! PUPS! GET GOING! WE'RE LEAVING FOR LONDON!
BUT...
...BUT WHAT ABOUT US, MR. PONGO?
?
?
WE'LL TAKE THEM HOME WITH US! ALL OF THEM!
THE 101 DALMATIANS BEGIN THEIR FLIGHT ACROSS THE FORESTS AND FIELDS OF SUFFOLK...
3-12
AT THE END OF THE DAY, A TWILIGHT BARK PATROL FINDS THE EXHAUSTED MARCHERS...
PONGO! WE HAVE SHELTER FOR THE NIGHT FOR YOU! FOLLOW ME!
THE POOR LITTLE DEARS!
MEANWHILE...
THEY'VE GOTTA BE AROUND HERE SOMEWHERE...
CONTINUED...

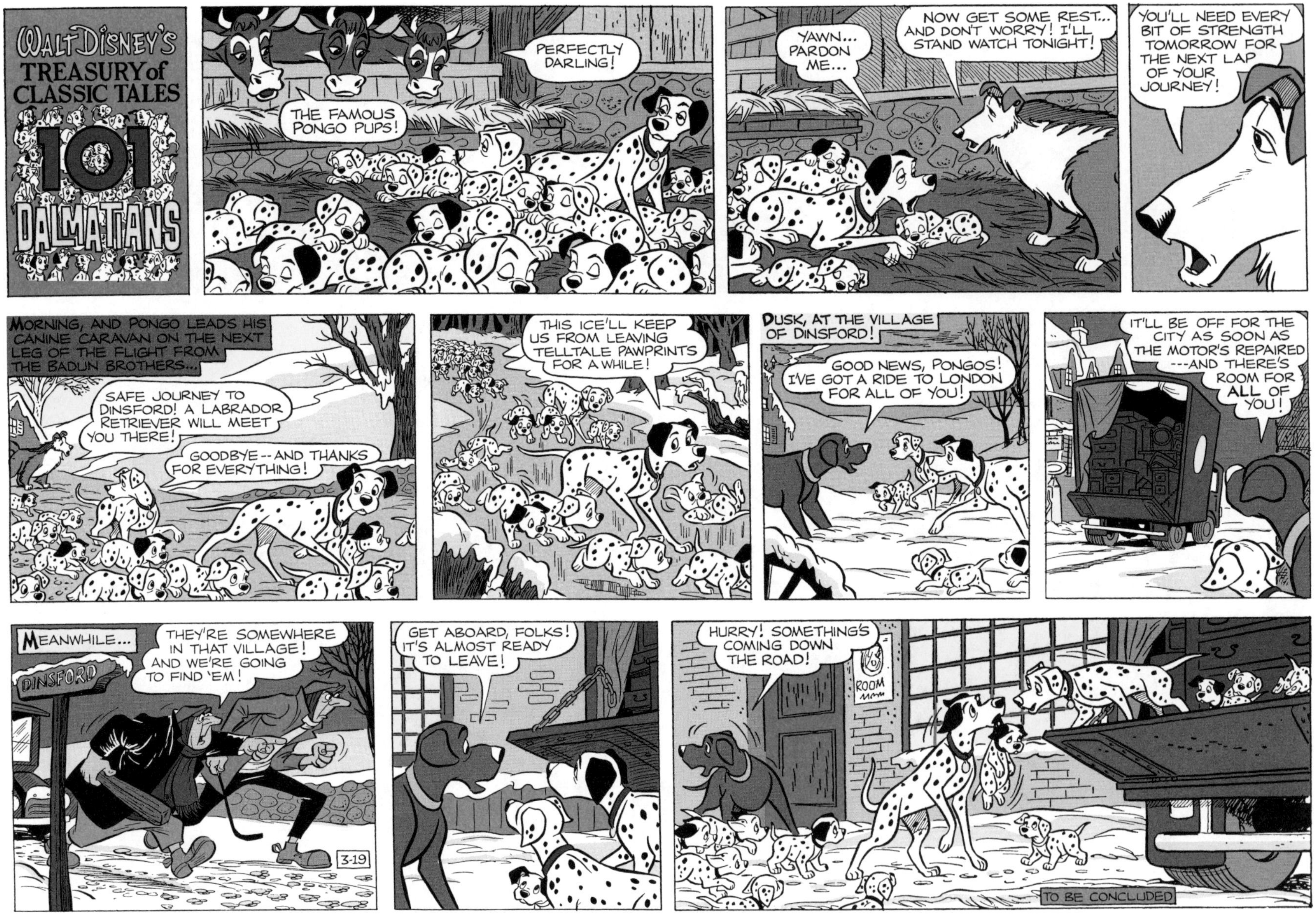
WALT DISNEY'S
TREASURY of CLASSIC TALES
101 DALMATIANS
PERFECTLY DARLING!
THE FAMOUS PONGO PUPS!
YAWN... PARDON ME...
NOW GET SOME REST... AND DON'T WORRY! I'LL STAND WATCH TONIGHT!
YOU'LL NEED EVERY BIT OF STRENGTH TOMORROW FOR THE NEXT LAP OF YOUR JOURNEY!
MORNING, AND PONGO LEADS HIS CANINE CARAVAN ON THE NEXT LEG OF THE FLIGHT FROM THE BADUN BROTHERS...
SAFE JOURNEY TO DINSFORD! A LABRADOR RETRIEVER WILL MEET YOU THERE!
GOODBYE -- AND THANKS FOR EVERYTHING!
THIS ICE'LL KEEP US FROM LEAVING TELLTALE PAWPRINTS FOR A WHILE!
DUSK, AT THE VILLAGE OF DINSFORD!
GOOD NEWS, PONGOS! I'VE GOT A RIDE TO LONDON FOR ALL OF YOU!
IT'LL BE OFF FOR THE CITY AS SOON AS THE MOTOR'S REPAIRED ---AND THERE'S ROOM FOR ALL OF YOU!
MEANWHILE...
THEY'RE SOMEWHERE IN THAT VILLAGE! AND WE'RE GOING TO FIND 'EM!
DINSFORD
3-19
GET ABOARD, FOLKS! IT'S ALMOST READY TO LEAVE!
HURRY! SOMETHING'S COMING DOWN THE ROAD!
ROOM
TO BE CONCLUDED

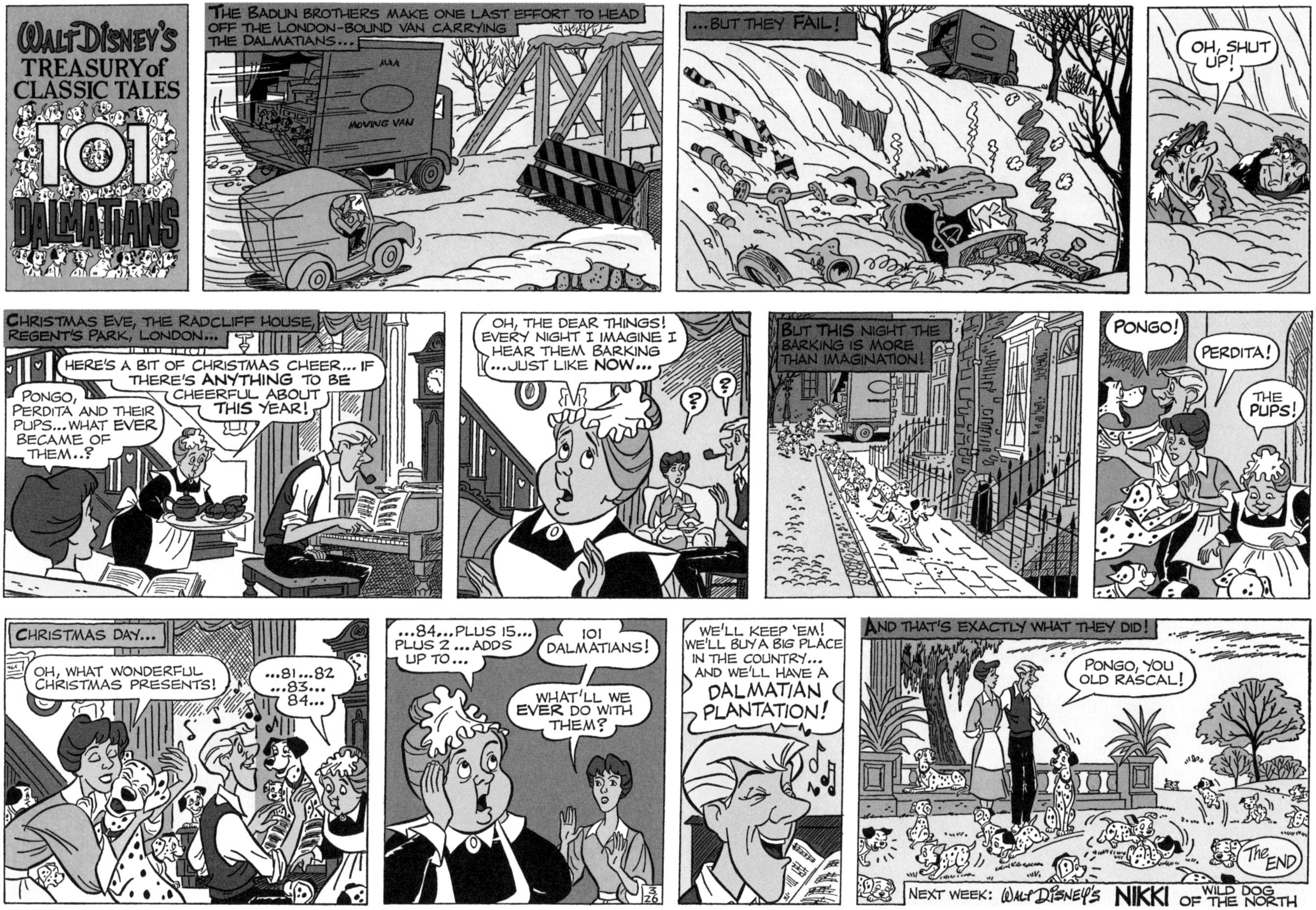
WALT DISNEY'S
TREASURY of CLASSIC TALES
101 DALMATIANS
THE BADUN BROTHERS MAKE ONE LAST EFFORT TO HEAD OFF THE LONDON-BOUND VAN CARRYING THE DALMATIANS...
MOVING VAN
...BUT THEY FAIL!
OH, SHUT UP!
CHRISTMAS EVE, THE RADCLIFF HOUSE, REGENT'S PARK, LONDON...
HERE'S A BIT OF CHRISTMAS CHEER... IF THERE'S ANYTHING TO BE CHEERFUL ABOUT THIS YEAR!
PONGO, PERDITA AND THEIR PUPS...WHAT EVER BECAME OF THEM..?
OH, THE DEAR THINGS! EVERY NIGHT I IMAGINE I HEAR THEM BARKING ...JUST LIKE NOW...
? ?
BUT THIS NIGHT THE BARKING IS MORE THAN IMAGINATION!
PONGO!
PERDITA!
THE PUPS!
CHRISTMAS DAY...
OH, WHAT WONDERFUL CHRISTMAS PRESENTS!
...81...82 ...83... 84...
...84...PLUS 15... PLUS 2...ADDS UP TO...
101 DALMATIANS!
WHAT'LL WE EVER DO WITH THEM?
WE'LL KEEP 'EM! WE'LL BUY A BIG PLACE IN THE COUNTRY... AND WE'LL HAVE A DALMATIAN PLANTATION!
AND THAT'S EXACTLY WHAT THEY DID!
PONGO, YOU OLD RASCAL!
The END
NEXT WEEK: WALT DISNEY'S NIKKI WILD DOG OF THE NORTH

MICKEY! I'M SO GLAD YOU'VE COME,-- THERE'S A GANG OF BURGLARS IN THE HOUSE !!!
©By Walter E. Disney, Great Britain rights reserved.
B-B-BE CAREFUL, MICKEY !!!
I'LL MAKE THEM WISH THEY'D NEVER BEEN BORN !!! YOU STAY OUTSIDE AND COUNT THEM AS I THROW THEM OUT !!!
MY HERO! I HOPE HE DOESN'T KILL ANYBODY !!!
WALT DISNEY
ONE!
STOP COUNTING DURN IT! IT'S ME !!!

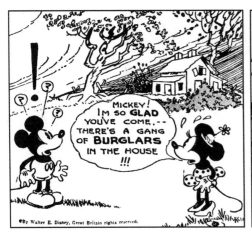

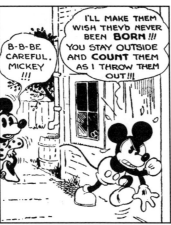

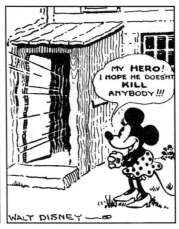

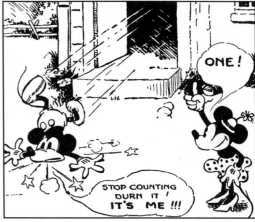

Back to the beginning. Before America saw a *Mickey Mouse* Sunday strip in color, it's a little-known fact that Disney produced eleven foreign-only *Mickey* Sunday strips in the black-and-white, four-panel daily strip format.

First seen July 13, 1930 in England's *Sunday Pictorial*, the special strips ran intermittently through December 28, switching off with regular *Mickey* dailies in the same slot. Each foreign-only Sunday consisted of preexisting character art rearranged atop new backgrounds, relettered to tell standalone jokes. Lettering was done by an as-yet-unidentified Disney staffer who also lettered some regular *Mickey* dailies in 1930.

These "extra" strips owed their existence to a timing snafu. Thanks to a promotional tie-up between the *Pictorial* and various weekday papers, the regular *Mickey* daily—a six-days-a-week affair in the USA—was running *seven* days per week in the UK. Extra content was needed to keep British papers from overtaking the American publication schedule.

The example seen above appeared in the *Pictorial* September 21, 1930. It recycles Mickey and Minnie poses drawn by Ub Iwerks and Win Smith for the January 13, March 26, April 3, and April 17 daily strips. The background in panel one comes from Gottfredson's May 13 daily.

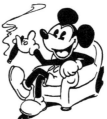

Both the daily *Mickey* and the foreign-only Sundays were advertised in Britain with the unique Win Smith-drawn vignette at right. Needless to say, Disney would not associate Mickey with tobacco products today. [DG]

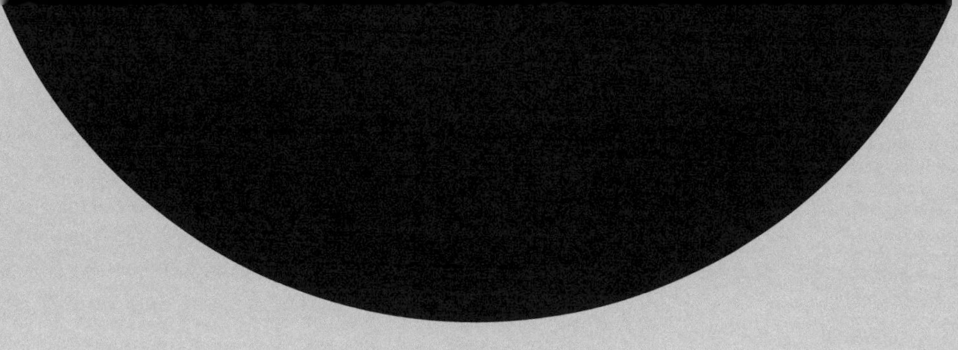

THE GOTTFREDSON ARCHIVES

Essays and Special Features

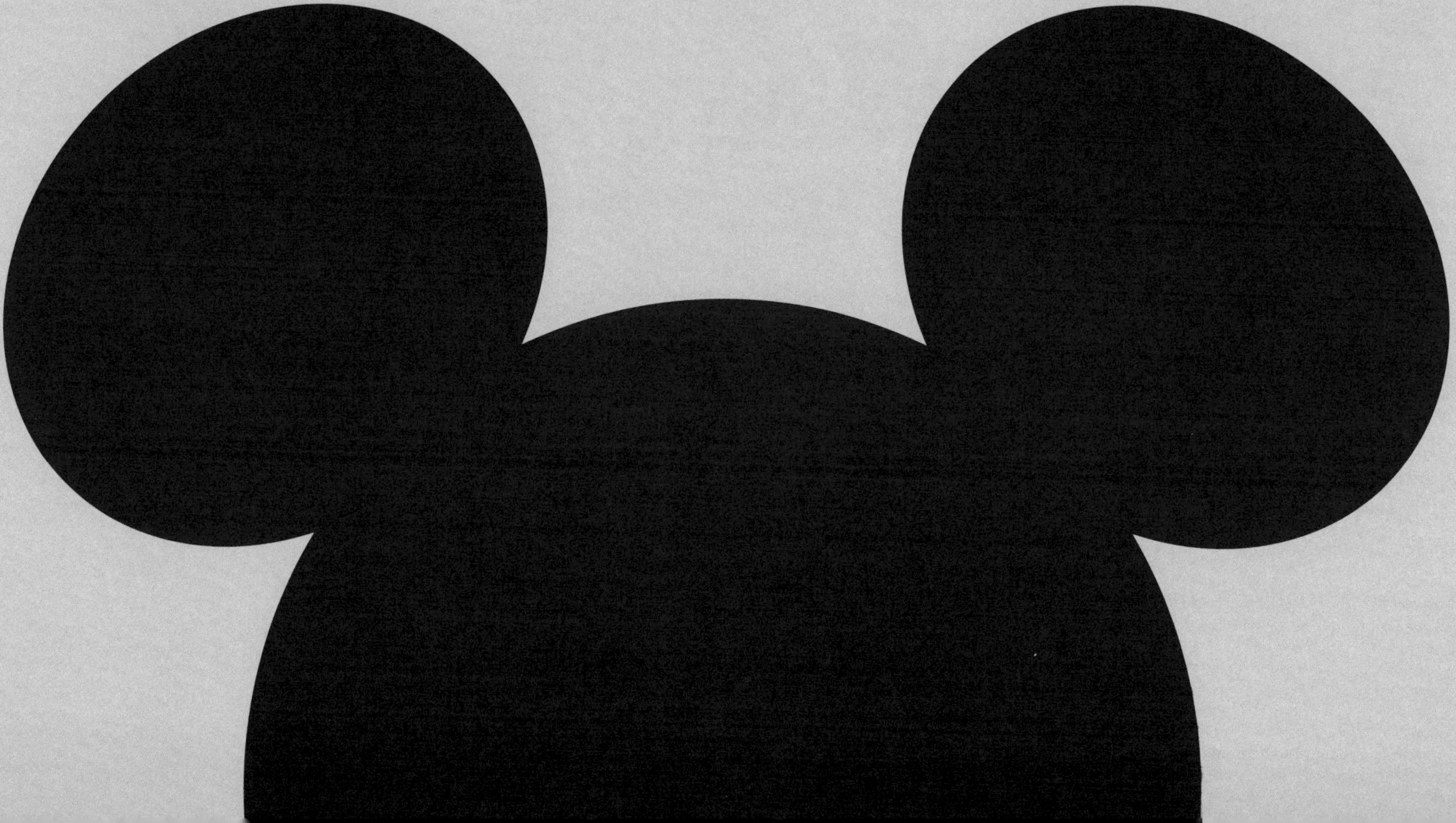

Every country that loves Mickey Mouse has had its own edition—or editions—of Floyd Gottfredson's epics. And each country's Disney comics publisher has tried to make its own version unique, usually by asking homegrown talent to create their own covers or vignettes based on the stories.

In this series we're proud to anthologize these images, both foreign and domestic, old and new—and give you a sense of how far Gottfredson's classic adventures have traveled over the years. Of course, when it comes to pesky Mortimer in "Mickey's Rival" and destructive Donald in "Helpless Helpers," Mickey thinks they *couldn't* travel far *enough*! [DG]

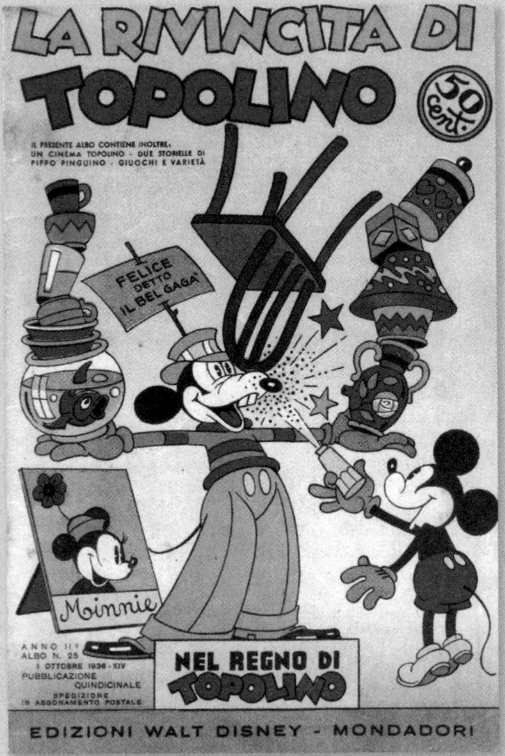
LA RIVINCITA DI
TOPOLINO
50 cent.
FELICE DETTO IL BEL GAGA'
Minnie
NEL REGNO DI
TOPOLINO
EDIZIONI WALT DISNEY - MONDADORI

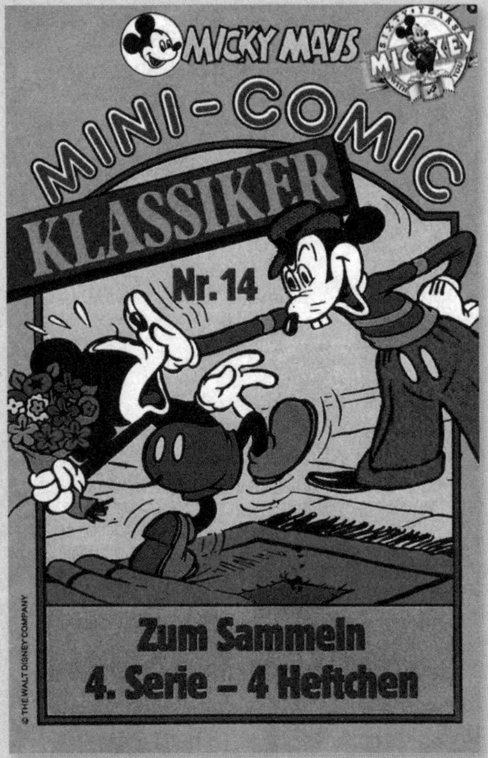
MICKY MAUS
MINI-COMIC
KLASSIKER
Nr. 14
Zum Sammeln
4. Serie – 4 Heftchen
© THE WALT DISNEY COMPANY

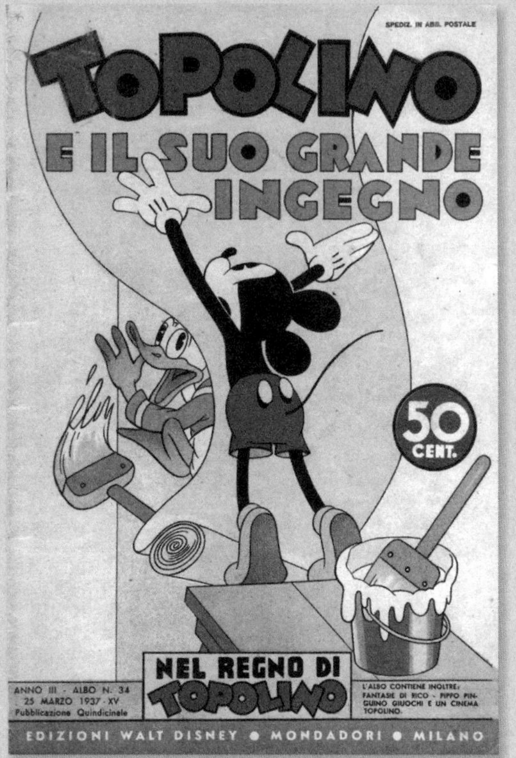
SPEDIZ. IN ABB. POSTALE
TOPOLINO
E IL SUO GRANDE INGEGNO
50 CENT.
NEL REGNO DI
TOPOLINO
EDIZIONI WALT DISNEY • MONDADORI • MILANO

LEFT: Italian *Nel Regno di Topolino* 25 (1936), illustrating "Mickey's Rival." Art by Antonio Rubino; image courtesy Leonardo Gori.

MIDDLE: German *Micky Maus Mini-Comic* 14 (1988), illustrating "Mickey's Rival." Art by Floyd Gottfredson; image courtesy Christoph Overberg.

RIGHT: Italian *Nel Regno di Topolino* 34 (1937), illustrating "Helpless Helpers." Art by Enrico Mauro Pinochi; image courtesy Leonardo Gori.

The Cast: MORTIMER

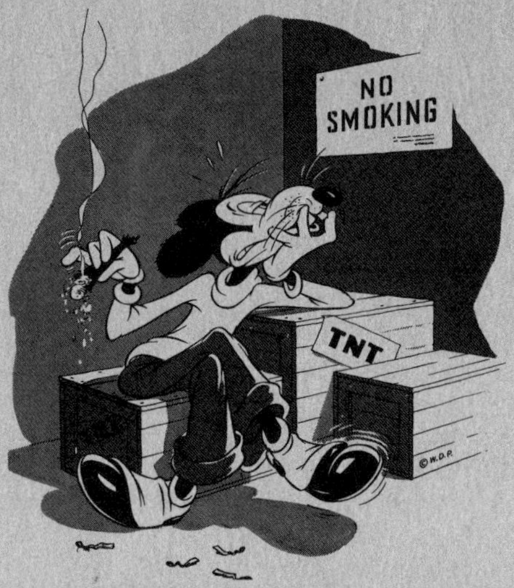
NO SMOKING
TNT

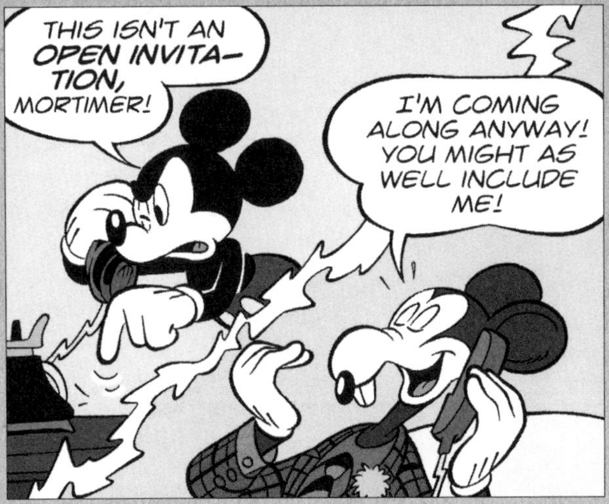
THIS ISN'T AN OPEN INVITATION, MORTIMER!
I'M COMING ALONG ANYWAY! YOU MIGHT AS WELL INCLUDE ME!

Mortimer's true debut, in both the *Mickey's Rival* (1936) cartoon and its associated Gottfredson comic, showed plain evidence of this. On-screen, the dirty rat spends less time flattering Minnie than humbling Mickey, counting on Mickey's embarrassment to postpone any counterattack. In the strip, similarly, Mortimer proclaims "Minnie's my girl from now on"; but the ensuing conflict turns less on Minnie than on Mickey—and on Mickey's mixed success rate not at wooing, but at practical joking.

Perhaps this was the rub: though romance was Mortimer's basic reason for conflict with Mickey, their personalities—and Minnie's—kept the rivalry from feeling very romantic in practice.

Hot-cha-cha! While every Mickey Mouse fan knows Pegleg Pete and the Phantom Blot, Mickey's third most famous foe is less often seen. Yet this doesn't make Mortimer Mouse less valuable as a character; it merely draws attention to the dynamics of personality and continuity in Disney comics.

The Mortimer Mouse story begins not with his debut in 1936, but with his prehistory: the appearance of a similar romantic rival a few years prior.[1] Mr. Slicker, in Gottfredson's "Mr. Slicker and the Egg Robbers" (1930), was a sporty, conniving dandy who seemed able to outdo Mickey at everything. But Slicker was also a crook, leading a gang of robbers and landing in jail at story's end. Not only did this decisive comedown scotch any future for Slicker as a love interest—but Minnie had renounced him *before* his criminality was revealed. "There [will] *never* be anyone for me," she tells her father only midway through the story, "but—well—er—well, anyway not Mr. Slicker!"

Minnie's change of heart revealed a trait that has stuck with her over time: as opposed to Daisy Duck (or, from the distaff perspective, Donald himself!), Gottfredson's Minnie was not a fickle lover. Any serious suitor would have to *work* to turn her head—and, significantly, work harder to make Mickey look bad than to make himself look good.

Was this why Gottfredson used the character so seldom? When Mortimer finally returned to the comics in "Love Trouble" (1941), it was under an alias, "Montmorency Rodent," to avoid confusion with Mickey's nephew Morty. And he was given an extra edge—temporary wealth—with which to interest Minnie; an implicit admission that without it, he had little to offer her. Even with it, his appeal is limited; before story's end, Minnie goes through a realistic disillusionment that would seem to preclude any future romances.

That said, we've seen a few; in part because Mortimer is such a dynamic, lovably annoying figure—and in part because it's just so much fun to watch the normally unflappable Mickey burn up!

In modern Disney comics and TV cartoons, including *House of Mouse*, Mortimer often returns; usually combining his original name with his 1941 Gottfredson design. Tellingly, however, Mortimer's modern contests with Mickey turn less often on romance than on other pursuits, from treasure hunting to Christmas decorating. It's just too hard to believe Minnie could take Mortimer seriously more than once in a blue moon.

Besides, we hear Daisy is single and looking at the moment. [DG]

LEFT: When Mortimer plays with fire, he's bound to get—blasted! Promotional drawing, 1942; art by Hank Porter, image courtesy Walt Disney Photo Library.

RIGHT: Mickey just can't get rid of him! From "King of the Bungaloos Strikes Back" (2006; version from *Walt Disney's Comics and Stories* 680, 2007). Story by Don Markstein, art by Cèsar Ferioli.

1 In some countries' Disney comics—notably France and Germany—Slicker and Mortimer are translated as the same character, leading to some modern fans perceiving them that way. They were not, however, originally intended as such.

Behind the Scenes: INTERIOR DECORATORS (AGAIN!)

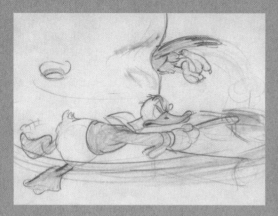

Disney's unfinished mid-1930s cartoon "Interior Decorators" had a symbiotic relationship with the comics. As we saw last volume, some gags were created for Gottfredson strips, then found their way into "Decorators." But other gags took the opposite route. The example on this page—pitting Donald against Clarabelle's wiseacre parrot—was created for the "Decorators" cartoon, then adapted as part of Gottfredson's "Helpless Helpers" serial (page 27). In the process, however, the parrot was thrown out.

How come? Perhaps due to the nature of the "Helpers" continuity. In it, Mickey is the sympathetic reader identification figure, while Donald and Goofy are pests who cause problems. Had the parrot—an even peskier beast—been the real culprit behind Donald's accidents, our sympathies might have shifted to Donald. Evidently, Gottfredson and Ted Osborne felt that in a *Mickey* strip, we should sympathize with Mickey!

Images courtesy Walt Disney Animation Research Library; special thanks to Fox Carney. [DG]

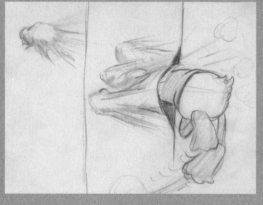

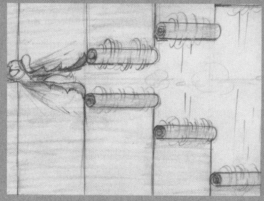

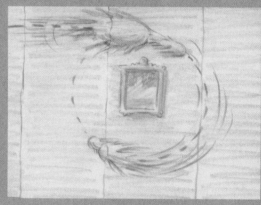

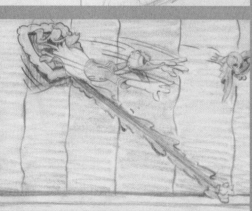

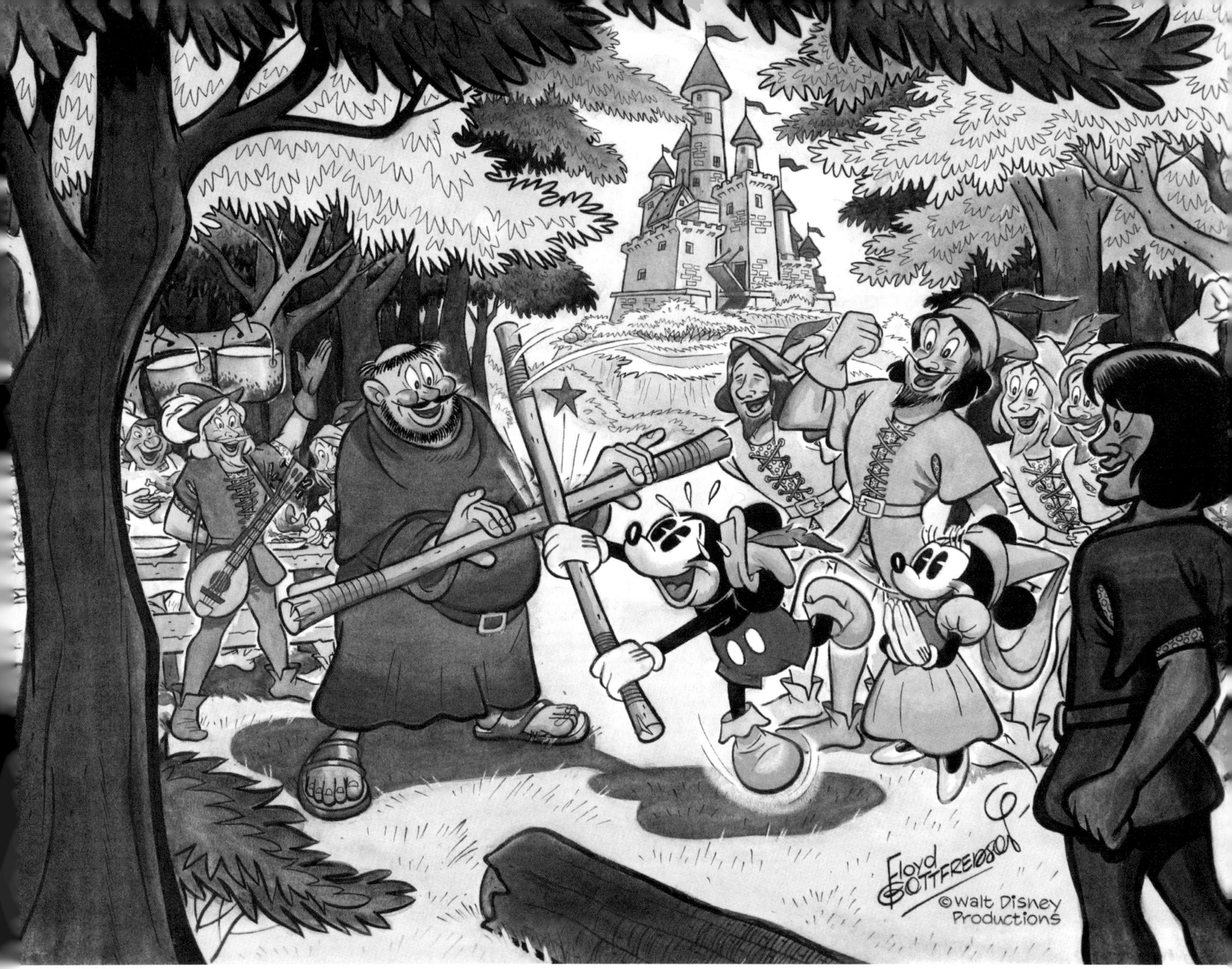
Floyd Gottfredson
©Walt Disney Productions

MICKEY MOUSE ADVENTURES WITH ROBIN HOOD. Painting by Floyd Gottfredson, February 1980 (based on "The Robin Hood Adventure"). Image courtesy Malcolm Willits.

Yoicks and away! As Gottfredson's most famous Sunday strip saga, "The Robin Hood Adventure" has received a king's bounty of rich, exciting international covers. Readers have had many chances to get lost in a book about Mickey—er, getting lost in a book! [DG]

МИКИЈЕВЕ НОВИНЕ
Год. II
БЕОГРАД, 1 ЈАНУАР 1937
Бр. 22
НЕОБИЧНИ САН МИКИ МАУСА
5 ДИНАРА

TOPOLINO
cent. 50
BATTE Robin Hood
MI DICHIARO VINTO!
GUARDA, ROBIN! HO PROPRIO INFILATO L'ANELLO!
NEL REGNO DI TOPOLINO
EDIZIONI WALT DISNEY - MONDADORI - Piazza Duse 2 - MILANO

TOPOLINO
cent. 50
E LA BELLA PRIGIONIERA
NEL REGNO DI TOPOLINO
EDIZIONI WALT DISNEY - MONDADORI - Piazza Duse 2 - MILANO

ALMANAQUE Disney
A LENDA DE ROBIN HOOD
O MUNDO FANTÁSTICO DE OZ

MICKEY
REVISTA MENSAL DE WALT DISNEY
APRESENTA
Robin Hood

CLOCKWISE: Yugoslavian *Mikijeve Novine* 22 (1937). Art reinked from Gottfredson by J. Milanovic; image courtesy Dejan Zivkovic.

Italian *Nel Regno di Topolino* 26 and 27 (1936). Art by Antonio Rubino; images courtesy Leonardo Gori.

Brazilian *Mickey* 16 (1954). Art by Álvaro de Moya; image courtesy Fernando Ventura.

Brazilian *Almanaque Disney* 176 (1986). Art by Moacir Rodrigues Soares; image courtesy Arthur Faria Jr.

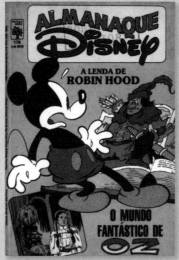

Behind the Scenes: MICKEY'S GARDEN

As J. B. Kaufman has noted earlier in this volume, Floyd Gottfredson's "Robin Hood Adventure" was inspired by various mid-1930s Mickey Mouse cartoons—*Mickey's Garden* (1935) not least among them. In it, chemist Mickey brews the perfect pesticide for veggie-munching bugs... and accidentally inhales some, leading to a wild hallucination!

In Mickey's fever dream, the pesticide becomes a growth tonic, turning bugs and garden plants into giants. In "The Robin Hood Adventure," of course, it's not a dream at all: the giantism is *really* going on! Mickey must fight for his waking life against a whomping weed and a fearless fly.

The story sketches and animation drawings on this page, created in the making of *Mickey's Garden*, show us what Floyd Gottfredson saw when the short was in development. How could he *not* want to spin a comic off of this?

Story sketch with tomato attributed to Earl Hurd; all images courtesy Walt Disney Animation Research Library. [DG]

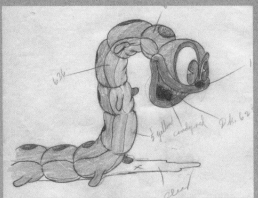
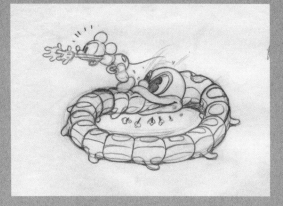

Gottfredson's World: GAGS OF 1936-38

Most Mickey fans associate Gottfredson-related comic book covers with Gottfredson *serials*: long, complicated stories that merit exciting, often intricate front page illustrations. But Gottfredson gag strips were also anthologized in the 1930s, and quite a few received dedicated covers, too. Ever-curious Mickey wants a peek—how about you? [DG]

WALT DISNEY'S STORY OF
MICKEY MOUSE
1066

WALT DISNEY'S
10¢
MICKEY MOUSE
with GOOFY and MICKEY'S NEPHEWS
A FAST-ACTION STORY

SPEDIZ. IN ABBON. POSTALE
TOPOLINO
E IL GRAN PIPPO
QUESTO ALBO CONTIENE 2 FIGURINE OMAGGIO TOPOLINO
60 CENT.
ANNO III - ALBO N. 41
25 LUGLIO 1937-XV
PUBBLICAZ. QUINDICINALE
NEL REGNO DI TOPOLINO
EDIZIONI WALT DISNEY • MONDADORI • MILANO

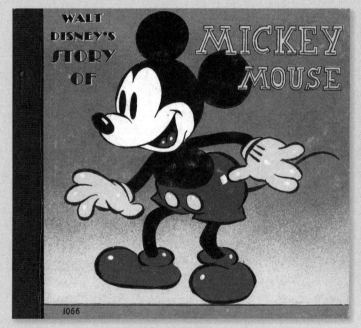

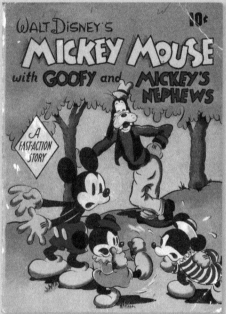

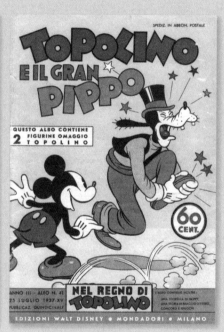

LEFT: From *Walt Disney Story Books* 1066 series (1938), collecting 1936-37 Sunday gag strips. Artist unknown; image courtesy Larry Lowery.

MIDDLE: From *Fast Action Story*, Set IV series (1938), illustrating the June 5, 1938 gag strip. Art reinked from Gottfredson by unknown talent; image courtesy Larry Lowery.

RIGHT: Italian *Nel Regno di Topolino* 41 (1937), illustrating the December 20, 1936 gag strip. Art reinked from Gottfredson by Michele Rubino, image courtesy Leonardo Gori.

The Inventive GOOF

» BY DAVID GERSTEIN

"EACH OBJECT OR PIECE of mechanism which to us is lifeless," said animator Art Babbitt in 1934, "has a soul and personality in the mind of the Goof."[1] In a short character analysis, Babbitt was clearly defining Goofy's thought processes for the first time. Initially named "Dippy Dawg," Mickey's friend had begun life as a dumb, amoral pest. From 1934, Babbitt's influence on film—and Floyd Gottfredson's in the comics—gradually turned Goofy into something else: a figure less amoral than naïve, less stupid than dreamily eccentric.

And the more eccentric, the better, or so Disney staffers felt. A prime expression of the vogue came in a new hobby for Goofy: inventing. What more perfect outlet for a screwball thinker than way-out solutions to problems?

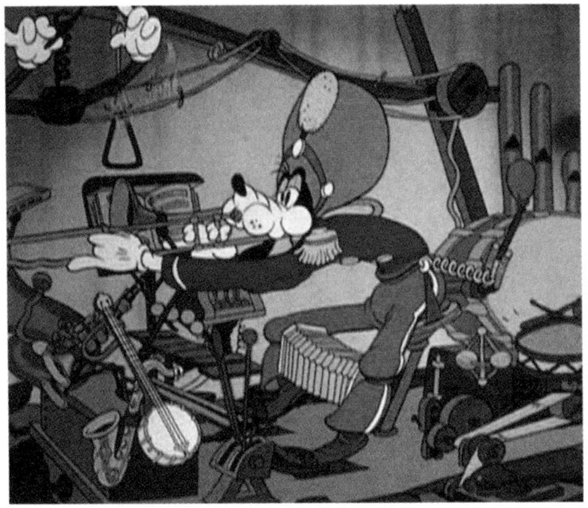

Gottfredson's comics seem to be where the theme got its start. As early as January 1935, Goofy invented "folding skis," which saved space on the climb up snowy slopes—but defeated their own purpose by requiring long boards to hold them straight!

Babbitt's cartoon Goof followed the inventive trend. In *On Ice* (1935), "goofy logic" created a new ice-fishing method: feed the fish tobacco, install a spittoon above the ice, hide nearby in camouflage—then club the fish when they come up to spit! The plan was both clever and silly at once... sillier because whenever Goofy tried to club the fish, he missed.

It was a short ways from silly hunting ingenuity to silly mechanical ingenuity. *Mickey's Amateurs* (1937) featured "Bandmaster Goofy... and his fifty-piece band," an infernal machine that *almost* played many horns at once—by trying to push them all at Goofy's mouth.

Sunday comics made a perfect venue for more Goofy inventions—in part because of the strips' pacing. The twelve-panel format lent itself to first the introduction, then the demo of a wacky contraption. In this book we see Goofy's malfunctioning "motor sled" (page 81) and his brakeless "compressed air auto" (page 121). And while Gottfredson ceased

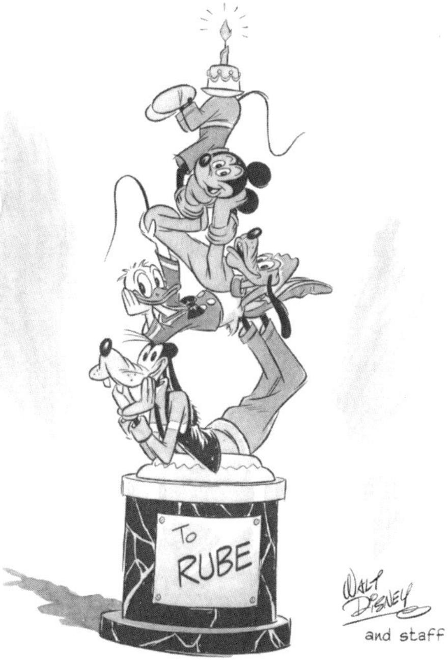

To
RUBE
Walt Disney
and staff

RIGHT: Special Gottfredson drawing for Rube Goldberg's 80th birthday luncheon, June 7, 1963. Image courtesy Disney Publishing Worldwide.

LEFT: Bandmaster Goofy invents electronic music in *Mickey's Amateurs* (1937). Animation by Art Babbitt.

drawing the strip after this, the gadgets continued—perhaps because Gottfredson remained in a managerial capacity. His fomer scripters had Goofy invent a burglar ejector, a turkey-flavored cologne, and even "a quick way to git out of a burnin' buildin' before thuh fire starts." The gag possibilities seemed limitless, as did the amount of complex effort Goofy could expend on simple tasks.

The theme of the simple made complex belied Disney comics' debt to Rube Goldberg (1883-1970), creator of classic invention-themed funnies in the 1910s. Goldberg was also the first president of the National Cartoonists' Society. For his 80th birthday in 1963, Gottfredson drew Goldberg a special tribute on Disney's behalf.

Goofy, needless to say, was present and accounted for. •

1 Art Babbitt, "Character Analysis of the Goof." Reprinted in Frank Thomas and Ollie Johnston, *The Illusion of Life: Disney Animation* (New York: Disney Editions, 1995), p. 561.

WALT DISNEY
Winnie the Pooh
and the blustery day
ACADEMY AWARD WINNER

JUST AS HE DIVVIED UP the *Mickey Mouse* authorial duties, Floyd Gottfredson shared the reins on Disney's *Treasury of Classic Tales*. For two celebrated serials in 1958, Gottfredson took scripting and lettering detail[1] while another prized Disney draftsman handled the visuals: Julius Svendsen.

Born January 3, 1919 in Kristiansand, Norway, Svendsen came to the USA in 1923 when his father, Captain Fredrik F. Svendsen, emigrated with his family.[2] Soon Julius was attending New York public schools, where he found early praise for his artistic talent. A full scholarship from the New York Society of Illustrators enabled the boy to study at the Pratt Institute of Art. His skill growing fast, Svendsen applied for work at Disney, was accepted, and moved to California in early 1940.

Svendsen started his job as an in-betweener on *Fantasia* (1940) and *Dumbo* (1941). But by taking special art classes that Walt provided to his staff, the new recruit swiftly rose to assistant animator rank.

Svendsen spent World War II with the Army Signal Corps in Canada; then returned to become a full-fledged animator, diving into Disney features like *Cinderella* (1950) and *Lady and the Tramp* (1954). But Svendsen also labored on many shorts and featurettes, including the modernistic TV milestone *Mars and Beyond* (1957).

Given this full plate, it's hard to imagine that Svendsen had time for more—but he did! "My dad's work and home life were inseparable," his daughter Julie recalled. First Svendsen moonlighted as a Disney book illustrator for Western Publishing. Then came in-studio comics work. Svendsen teamed with Gottfredson on their *Classic Tales* collaborations. He occasionally helped Gottfredson ink the *Mickey Mouse* daily. And, of course, Svendsen held up *his own* Mickey daily strip.

It's a little-known fact that Mickey Mouse had *two* daily strips from 1959 to 1962. One was Gottfredson's perennial. The other, *Mickey Mouse and His Friends*, was an all-pantomime gag strip; several months after its inception, Svendsen took over drawing it. Featuring a stylized look reminiscent of *Mars and Beyond*, the series was short-lived—but not for want of energetic art.

Undaunted, Svendsen soldiered onward with more Disney book work; more Disney film work—including script duty on Winnie the Pooh—and attempts at a non-Disney career. The children's books of family friend Bill Peet inspired Svendsen and wife Carol to create *Hulda*, the story of a spoiled kid, a bear, and a family of trolls.

By the time of *Hulda*'s publication, alas, Svendsen was already two years gone. On August 26, 1971, the prolific Disney talent passed away in a boating accident in Contra Costa County, California. Happily for his memory, however, Carol Svendsen brought *Hulda* into print in 1974. Several of Svendsen's Disney projects also appeared after his passing: story and animation work on *The Aristocats* (1971), and story work only on *Bedknobs and Broomsticks* (1971) and *Robin Hood* (1973).

The Svendsen connection to Disney has proudly marched on, with daughter Julie spending decades as a theme park artist/designer—and, today, creating freelance character art for varied licensees.

—Alberto Becattini and David Gerstein

1 Some earlier references list Gottfredson only as letterer, with Frank Reilly as writer. Carol and Julie Svendsen corrected the record in more recent years.

2 Most biographical details and quotes: Julie Svendsen to Jim Korkis and Didier Ghez, *Walt's People – Volume 9: Talking Disney with the Artists Who Knew Him* (Bloomington: Xlibris, 2010), pp. 371-375.

© 1960
Walt Disney Productions
World Rights Reserved
Distributed by King Features Syndicate.
WALT DISNEY
2-20

ABOVE: Julius Svendsen in 1969 alongside a poster for one of his later writing assignments, *Winnie the Pooh and the Blustery Day* (1968). Photo © and courtesy Julie Svendsen; used with permission.

RIGHT: Minnie meets an uncivilized relative in the *Mickey Mouse and His Friends* daily strip for February 20, 1960. Story by Roy Williams, art by Julius Svendsen.

Gottfredson's World: SHERIFF OF NUGGET GULCH

Mickey's pulse-pounding pow-wow with Pauncho Malarky has made for some ten-gallon covers over the years. You'd almost forget this was the story of a "sheriff" who needs shooting lessons from a crabby old lady—and a "deputy" who thinks bicycles are a breed of horse! [DG]

GLADSTONE
WALT DISNEY'S
MICKEY MOUSE
GLADSTONE COMIC ALBUM SERIES
22
SHERIFF OF NUGGET GULCH

MICKEY MOUSE
THE SHERIFF OF NUGGET GULCH
by WALT DISNEY
A FAST-ACTION STORY
10¢

WALT DISNEY
MICKEY ET MINNIE
HACHETTE

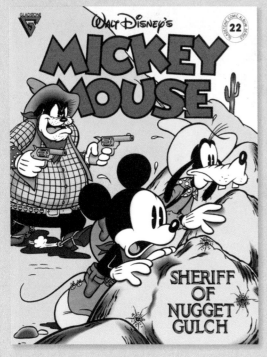

LEFT: *Gladstone Comic Album* 22 (1989). Art by Murad Gumen; image courtesy Mike Matei.

MIDDLE: From *Fast Action Story*, Set I series (1938). Art by Al Taliaferro; image courtesy Larry Lowery.

RIGHT: French *Albums Mickey* 24 (1950). A startling mix of 1930s Minnie and 1950s Mickey models—did somebody poison this artist's water hole? Image courtesy Gilles Garrigues.

Lights... camera... *Mickey*! Our marvelous Mouse's fairy-tale film made the jump to comics in 1938—and then to magazine reprints, many times over many years. In fact, rumor has it that even Gustav the giant was startled by the Brobdingnagian pile of printings! Let's check out six (with one blow!) of these comics colossuses. [DG]

TOPOLINO
AMMAZZASETTE
2 LIRE
GLI ALBI D'ORO
A.P.I. ANONIMA PERIODICI ITALIANI. MILANO

WALT DISNEY'S
DUMBO
THE FLYING ELEPHANT
10¢
No. 17
ALSO
DONALD DUCK
THE VILLAGE SMITHY
MICKEY MOUSE
in the Brave Little Tailor
PLUTO
THE PUP

WALT DISNEY'S
MICKEY MOUSE
YE REWARD FOR CAPTURE
The Brave Little Tailor

WALT DISNEY'S
COMICS
And Stories
64 PAGES

CLOCKWISE: Italian *Albi d'Oro* 23 (1938). Art by Michele Rubino; image courtesy Leonardo Gori.

Four Color 17 (series 1, 1941). Art by Irving Tripp; image courtesy Thomas Jensen.

Mickey Mouse 246 (1989). Art by Hank Porter from 1938 publicity drawing; image courtesy Thomas Jensen.

Walt Disney's Comics and Stories 580 (1993). Layout by Bob Foster, pencils by Jim Franzen, inks by Bruce Patterson; image courtesy Thomas Jensen.

Yugoslavian *Mickey* one-shot (1952). Art by Manuel Gonzales; image courtesy Dejan Zivkovic.

From *Walt Disney Story Books* 1058 series (1939). Art by Manuel Gonzales, image courtesy Larry Lowery.

The Brave Little Tailor
by WALT DISNEY.

МИКИ
Храбри кројач

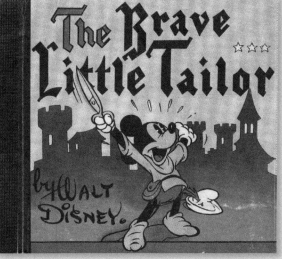

THE HEIRS OF GOTTFREDSON:

Manuel Gonzales

» BY TIMO RONKAINEN AND DAVID GERSTEIN

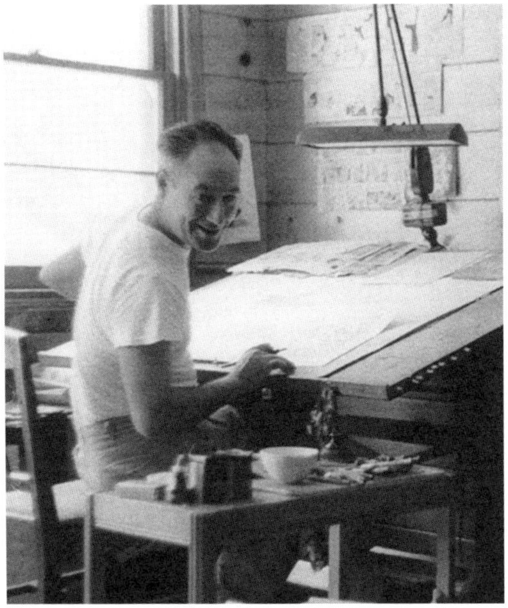

SOMETIMES A GREAT ARTIST is unaware of his greatness. Spanish-born Manuel Gonzales (1913-1993) was one such talent. A quiet and unassuming man, Gonzales seemed content merely to be known as Floyd Gottfredson's successor: "just" an artist who was "lucky to be able" to draw the *Mickey Mouse* Sunday page.[1] Yet while Gonzales may have started out as Gottfredson's understudy, he quickly became every bit the equal of his Disney colleagues. Gonzales' style grew in a uniquely new direction—and his skilled, expressive line complemented several fine scripters' funniest work.

Manuel Gonzales was born in Cabañas de Sayago, Zamora, Spain on March 3, 1913, but emigrated to the United States with his family just five years later.[2] He spent his later childhood in Westfield, Massachusetts; in the 1930s, he studied painting and the arts in New York City. But the art of Mickey Mouse eluded Gonzales at first. When his father brought him an "artists wanted" notice offering Disney job interviews, young Manuel admitted he had never heard of the studio. At the time, his highest hope was to become an illustrator with the *Saturday Evening Post*.

But in September 1936, Gonzales moved to California—and was soon a Disney in-betweener, learning the ropes of animation on *Snow White and the Seven Dwarfs* (1937). And his new job didn't stop there. When not in-betweening, "Gonzy"—his nickname at the studio—served as an ad artist under Publicity Department manager Tom Wood, creating pencil art for Wood's publicity drawings and *Good Housekeeping* Disney children's pages.[3]

Gonzales' publicity art, slick and accomplished from the start, drew the attention of Gottfredson, Wood's former superior. In mid-1938, Gottfredson fell ill and needed to lighten his workload. A fill-in artist was needed for the *Mickey Mouse* Sunday—and "Gonzy" was Johnny-on-the-spot. His trial run on *Mickey* found him assigned to draw several one-off gags and most of "The Brave Little Tailor" serial. Soon after, in 1939, Gonzales took over the Sunday *Mickey* permanently.

Gonzales, as a trained artist, was a virtuoso mimic; and at first, he tried hard to imitate the Gottfredson style. By the early 1940s, the two men's Mickeys were hard to tell apart; as scripted by Gottfredson's own Merrill de Maris, the early Gonzales Sunday strips even *sounded* the same.

On some level, the similarities simply reflected a group camaraderie in the Comic Strip Department, whose staff was becoming quite closely-knit—and closely connected to Walt Disney in the process. Son Dan Gonzales recounts how his father casually bought the same make of car as Walt:

> The first day my father drove his 1939 Packard to the studio, the guard directed him to [Walt's] parking area... probably not paying attention

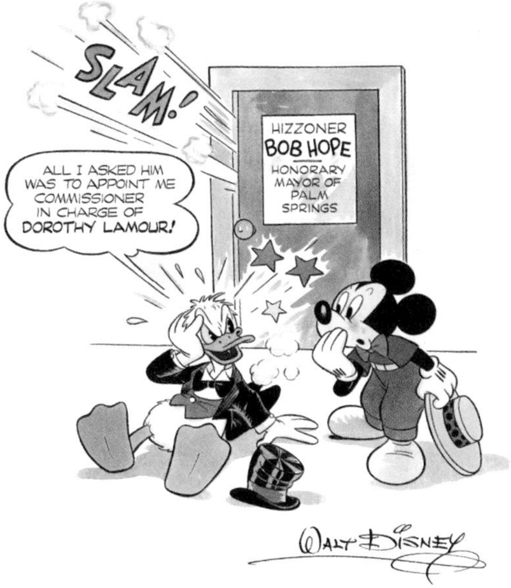
SLAM!
HIZZONER BOB HOPE HONORARY MAYOR OF PALM SPRINGS
ALL I ASKED HIM WAS TO APPOINT ME COMMISSIONER IN CHARGE OF DOROTHY LAMOUR!
WALT DISNEY

ABOVE: Manuel Gonzales at his Disney drawing board in 1955. Photo © Dan Gonzales; used with permission.

RIGHT: Special drawing by Manuel Gonzales to commemorate Bob Hope's honorary political title; March 18, 1948. Image courtesy Library of Congress, Bob Hope Collection; used with permission of Bob Hope Enterprises.

YESSIR - LADDIE! YOU SHOULD SAVE YOUR BONES FOR A RAINY DAY!
IT'S RAINING, UNCLE JOCK!

LEFT: Excerpt from *Scamp* Sunday strip; August 5, 1956. Story by Bill Berg, pencils by Bob Grant, inks by Manuel Gonzales.

> to the driver... Walt looked at my father's car and said to him with a sly smile, "I think I'm paying my animators too well." Walt was only joking and continued to tease my father about it for months to come, asking, "What kind of car should we buy next?"

World War II broke up the happy Comic Strip family; in 1942, Gonzales was drafted. For four years, the Spaniard worked on military films for the U. S. War Department; in his absence, the *Mickey* Sunday was covered by Bill Wright. When Gonzales returned to it in 1946, he found Comic Strip a changed place. A new staffer, Bill Walsh, had taken over writing *Mickey Mouse*. A veteran of radio, Walsh filled his scripts with excessive dialogue and elaborate visual detail. Gottfredson and Wright, both skilled writers themselves, were capable of editing and condensing Walsh's scripts as they drew them. Gonzales, with little experience in writing, was flummoxed.

OPPOSITE AND PAGES 274-278: selected *Mickey Mouse* Sunday strips penciled by Manuel Gonzales. In chronological order: August 25, 1940; August 10, 1941; September 27, 1942 (all: story by Merrill de Maris, inks by Bill Wright); November 30, 1947; April 2, 1950; February 18, 1951 (all: story by Bill Walsh, inks by Gonzales himself).

Rather than trimming the excesses of "Cecil B. DeWalsh," as Gonzales called him, Gonzales seems to have tried to draw as much of the requested detail as possible. Strip backgrounds became more complex; figures smaller and settings richer. Mickey and Goofy lost their Gottfredson streamlining and became subtly more humanlike in their manner. The overall effect was one of greater realism—which made Gonzales' art the perfect match for Walsh's surreal humor. Readers *expected* odd events in Gottfredson's bouncy, exaggerated Mouseton. By contrast, in Gonzales' richer, gentler world, the impossible never lost its ability to surprise.

Perhaps the greatest fruit of the Walsh/Gonzales partnership was an extraordinary new character. In late 1949 the pair introduced Ellsworth, Goofy's pet mynah bird—or *was* he a pet? Sometimes treated as an animal, sometimes as a "human," and openly aware of the distinction, the brainiac bird subverted every norm in Disney comics at the time.

Characteristically, Gonzales took little credit for his popular creation. "My father never made a big deal of [Ellsworth]," Dan Gonzales remembers.

> Whether it was Ellsworth or just some character that would only be used one time... my father would look through lots of books and other materials researching ideas, and then would go through several drafts developing characters [...] He was very much about precision and a well-developed drawing, but conveying an idea or emotion was most important to him.

Gonzales honed his ability by building up a vast dossier of art references at his home office. From the early 1950s, Gonzales worked almost exclusively at home—a peaceful existence that allowed him to take on extra assignments with ease. Starting in 1956 and continuing for 25 years, Gonzales supplemented his *Mickey* work by inking *Scamp*, a daily and Sunday *Lady and the Tramp* (1955) spin-off. Gonzales also found time to contribute to licensed Disney children's books and to *Treasury of Classic Tales*, the feature film-based Sunday strip on which Gottfredson also worked.

Ever shy and retiring, Manuel Gonzales never sought acclaim for his impressive output—but his studio colleagues gave it to him regardless. Not once, but twice did Gonzales receive the Mousecar, an Oscar-like bronze statue commemorating heroic service to Disney. Gonzales was also a hero to his family. "It was very cool," recounts Dan Gonzales, "to have a dad who could make amazing things magically appear at the end of his pen."

Generations of "Gonzy's" fans agree.

— Timo Ronkainen and David Gerstein

The authors wish to thank Dan Gonzales and Francois Willot for invaluable assistance.

1 All quotes and much background information: Dan Gonzales, e-mail message to Francois Willot, January 7, 2009.
2 Earlier references erroneously cite Fresnadillo a Cabañas, not Cabañas de Sayago, due to a misreading of Gonzales family data. The estate has corrected the record today.
3 Earlier references erroneously credit Wood with having done all his own pencils. In recent years, the Gonzales estate and collector Craig Englund have found and authenticated examples initialed by Manuel Gonzales.

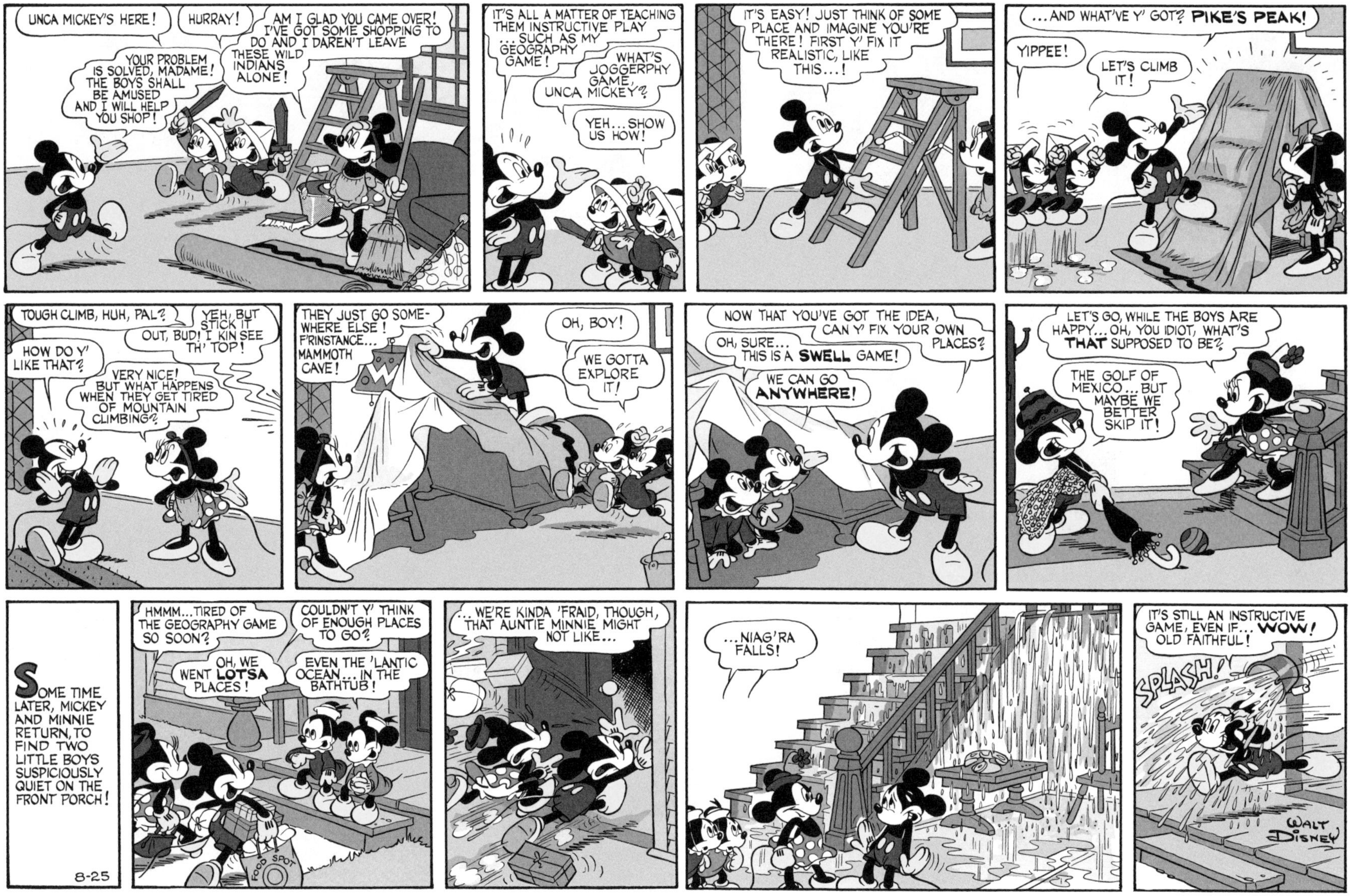
UNCA MICKEY'S HERE!
HURRAY!
AM I GLAD YOU CAME OVER! I'VE GOT SOME SHOPPING TO DO AND I DAREN'T LEAVE THESE WILD INDIANS ALONE!
YOUR PROBLEM IS SOLVED, MADAME! THE BOYS SHALL BE AMUSED AND I WILL HELP YOU SHOP!
IT'S ALL A MATTER OF TEACHING THEM INSTRUCTIVE PLAY ... SUCH AS MY GEOGRAPHY GAME!
WHAT'S JOGGERPHY GAME, UNCA MICKEY?
YEH... SHOW US HOW!
IT'S EASY! JUST THINK OF SOME PLACE AND IMAGINE YOU'RE THERE! FIRST Y' FIX IT REALISTIC, LIKE THIS...!
... AND WHAT'VE Y' GOT? PIKE'S PEAK!
YIPPEE!
LET'S CLIMB IT!
TOUGH CLIMB, HUH, PAL?
YEH, BUT STICK IT OUT, BUD! I KIN SEE TH' TOP!
HOW DO Y' LIKE THAT?
VERY NICE! BUT WHAT HAPPENS WHEN THEY GET TIRED OF MOUNTAIN CLIMBING?
THEY JUST GO SOMEWHERE ELSE! F'RINSTANCE... MAMMOTH CAVE!
OH, BOY!
WE GOTTA EXPLORE IT!
NOW THAT YOU'VE GOT THE IDEA, CAN Y' FIX YOUR OWN PLACES?
OH, SURE... THIS IS A SWELL GAME!
WE CAN GO ANYWHERE!
LET'S GO, WHILE THE BOYS ARE HAPPY... OH, YOU IDIOT, WHAT'S THAT SUPPOSED TO BE?
THE GOLF OF MEXICO... BUT MAYBE WE BETTER SKIP IT!
SOME TIME LATER, MICKEY AND MINNIE RETURN, TO FIND TWO LITTLE BOYS SUSPICIOUSLY QUIET ON THE FRONT PORCH!
8-25
HMMM... TIRED OF THE GEOGRAPHY GAME SO SOON?
COULDN'T Y' THINK OF ENOUGH PLACES TO GO?
OH, WE WENT LOTSA PLACES!
EVEN THE 'LANTIC OCEAN... IN THE BATHTUB!
FOOD SPOT
... WE'RE KINDA 'FRAID, THOUGH, THAT AUNTIE MINNIE MIGHT NOT LIKE...
... NIAG'RA FALLS!
IT'S STILL AN INSTRUCTIVE GAME, EVEN IF... WOW! OLD FAITHFUL!
SPLASH!
WALT DISNEY

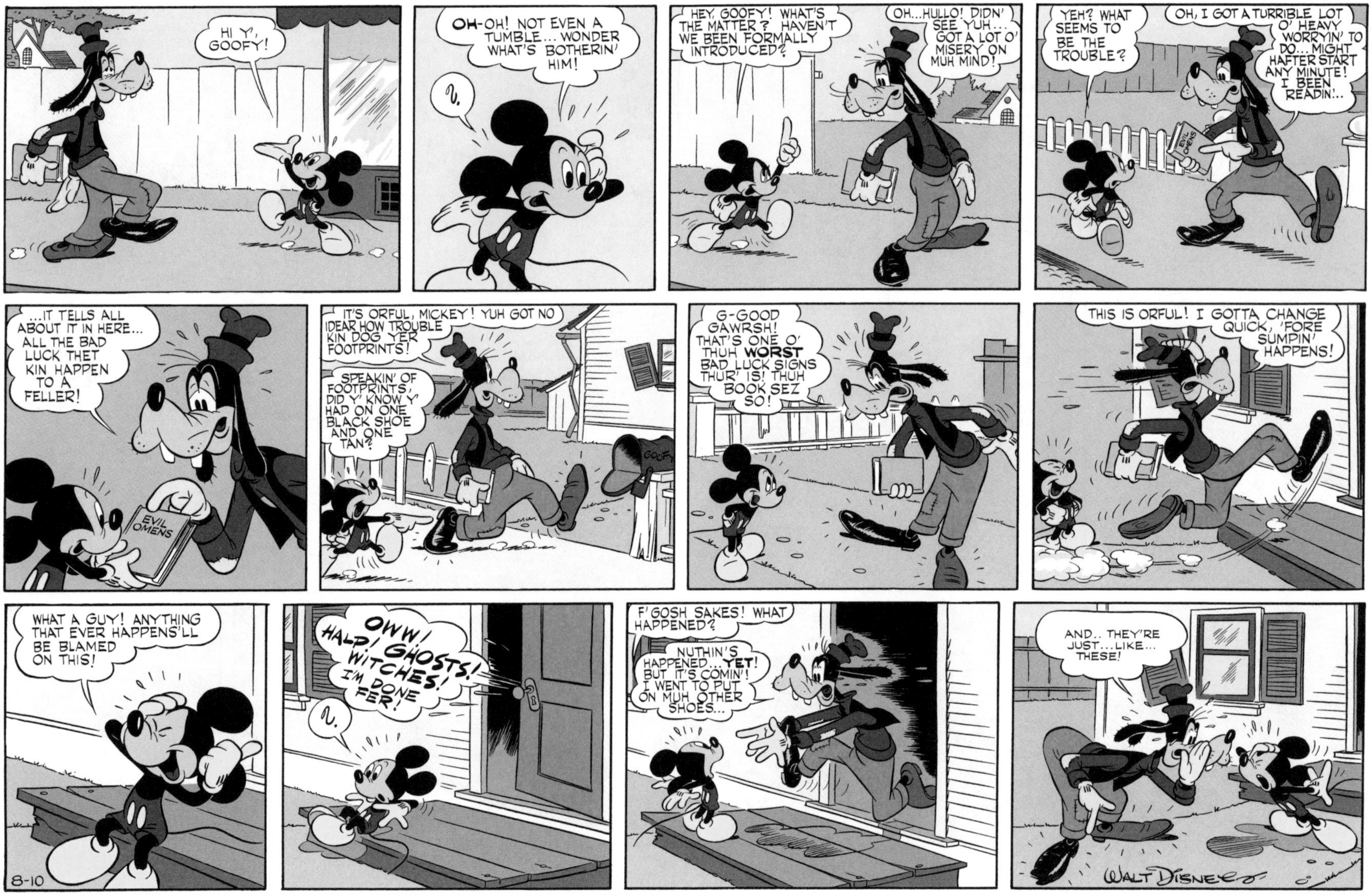
HI Y', GOOFY!
OH-OH! NOT EVEN A TUMBLE... WONDER WHAT'S BOTHERIN' HIM!
HEY, GOOFY! WHAT'S THE MATTER? HAVEN'T WE BEEN FORMALLY INTRODUCED?
OH...HULLO! DIDN' SEE YUH... GOT A LOT O' MISERY ON MUH MIND!
YEH? WHAT SEEMS TO BE THE TROUBLE?
OH, I GOT A TURRIBLE LOT O' HEAVY WORRYIN' TO DO... MIGHT HAFTER START ANY MINUTE! I BEEN READIN'..
EVIL OMENS
...IT TELLS ALL ABOUT IT IN HERE... ALL THE BAD LUCK THET KIN HAPPEN TO A FELLER!
EVIL OMENS
IT'S ORFUL, MICKEY! YUH GOT NO IDEAR HOW TROUBLE KIN DOG YER FOOTPRINTS!
SPEAKIN' OF FOOTPRINTS, DID Y' KNOW Y' HAD ON ONE BLACK SHOE AND ONE TAN?
GOOF
G-GOOD GAWRSH! THAT'S ONE O' THUH WORST BAD LUCK SIGNS THUR' IS! THUH BOOK SEZ SO!
THIS IS ORFUL! I GOTTA CHANGE QUICK, 'FORE SUMPIN' HAPPENS!
WHAT A GUY! ANYTHING THAT EVER HAPPENS'LL BE BLAMED ON THIS!
8-10
OWW! HALP! GHOSTS! WITCHES! I'M DONE FER!
F'GOSH SAKES! WHAT HAPPENED?
NUTHIN'S HAPPENED...YET! BUT IT'S COMIN'! I WENT TO PUT ON MUH OTHER SHOES...
AND.. THEY'RE JUST...LIKE... THESE!
WALT DISNEY

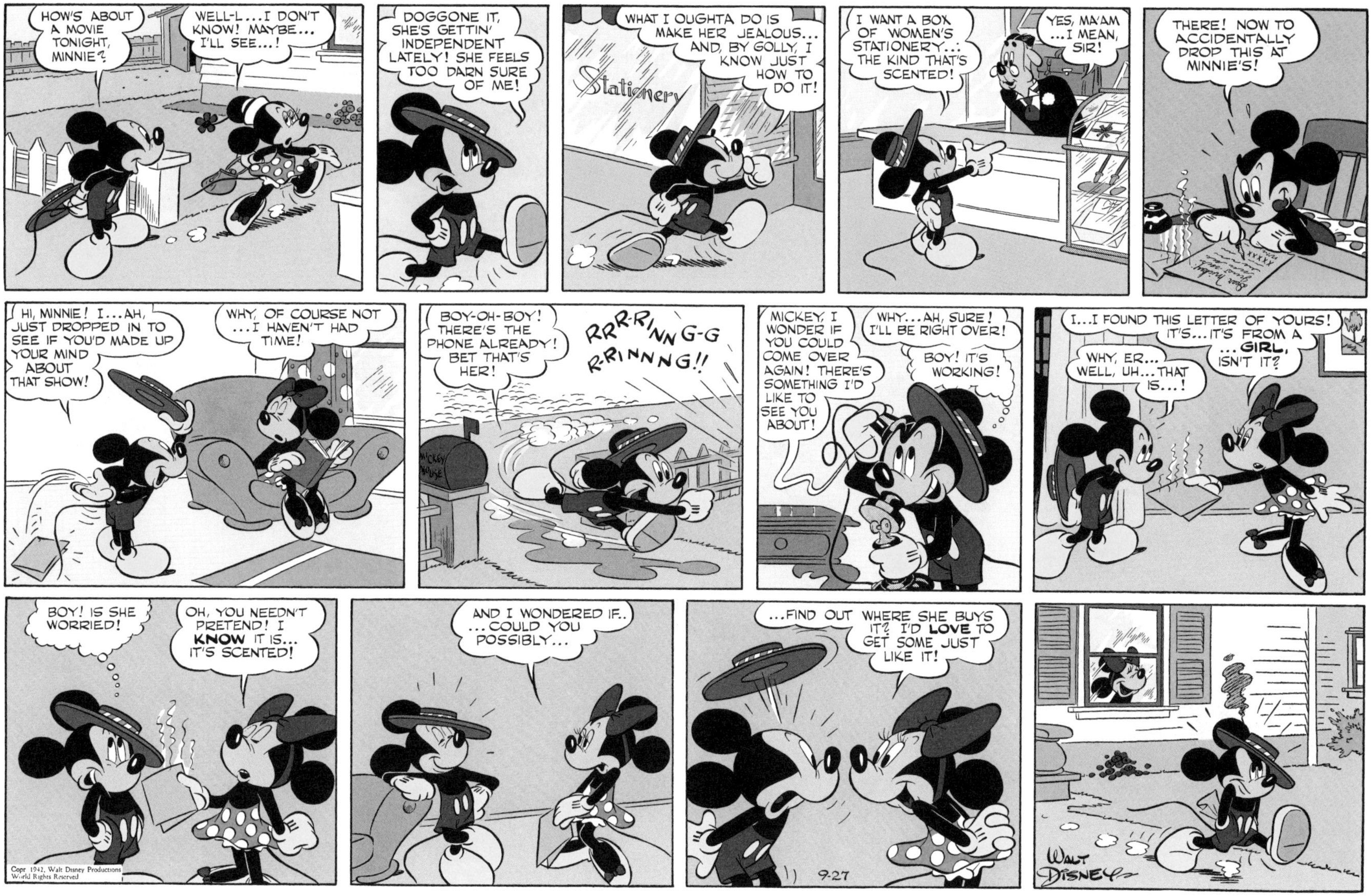
HOW'S ABOUT A MOVIE TONIGHT, MINNIE?
WELL-L...I DON'T KNOW! MAYBE... I'LL SEE...!
DOGGONE IT, SHE'S GETTIN' INDEPENDENT LATELY! SHE FEELS TOO DARN SURE OF ME!
WHAT I OUGHTA DO IS MAKE HER JEALOUS... AND, BY GOLLY, I KNOW JUST HOW TO DO IT!
Stationery
I WANT A BOX OF WOMEN'S STATIONERY...: THE KIND THAT'S SCENTED!
YES, MA'AM ...I MEAN, SIR!
THERE! NOW TO ACCIDENTALLY DROP THIS AT MINNIE'S!
HI, MINNIE! I...AH, JUST DROPPED IN TO SEE IF YOU'D MADE UP YOUR MIND ABOUT THAT SHOW!
WHY, OF COURSE NOT ...I HAVEN'T HAD TIME!
BOY-OH-BOY! THERE'S THE PHONE ALREADY! BET THAT'S HER!
RRR-RINN G-G R-RINNNG!!
MICKEY MOUSE
MICKEY, I WONDER IF YOU COULD COME OVER AGAIN! THERE'S SOMETHING I'D LIKE TO SEE YOU ABOUT!
WHY...AH, SURE! I'LL BE RIGHT OVER!
BOY! IT'S WORKING!
I...I FOUND THIS LETTER OF YOURS! IT'S...IT'S FROM A ...GIRL, ISN'T IT?
WHY, ER... WELL, UH...THAT IS...!
BOY! IS SHE WORRIED!
OH, YOU NEEDN'T PRETEND! I KNOW IT IS... IT'S SCENTED!
AND I WONDERED IF.. ...COULD YOU POSSIBLY...
...FIND OUT WHERE SHE BUYS IT? I'D LOVE TO GET SOME JUST LIKE IT!
9-27
WALT DISNEY
Copr 1942, Walt Disney Productions World Rights Reserved

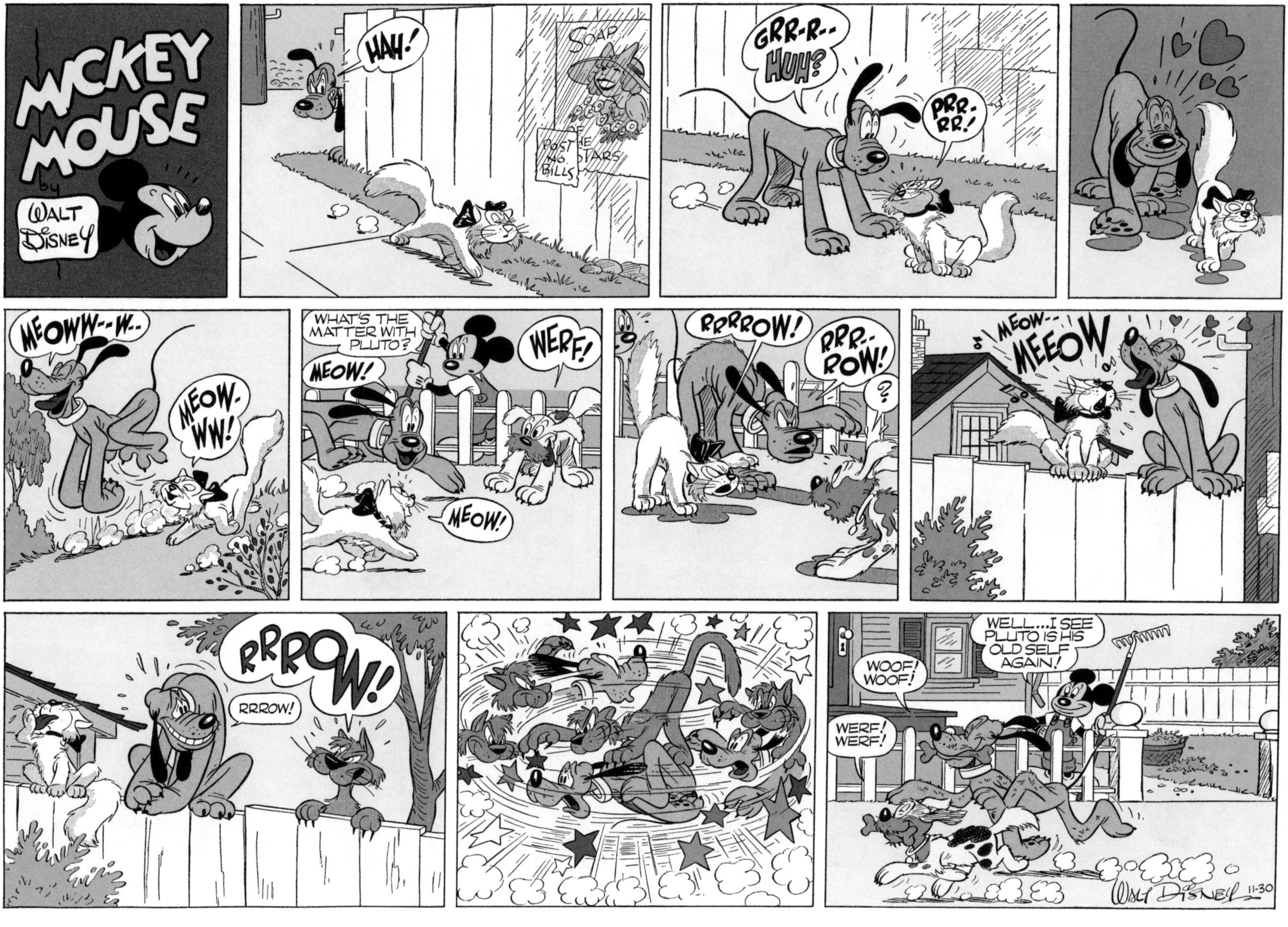
MICKEY MOUSE
by
WALT DISNEY
HAH!
SOAP
OF THE STARS
POST NO BILLS
GRR-R--
HUH?
PRR-RR!
MEOWW--W--
MEOW-WW!
WHAT'S THE MATTER WITH PLUTO?
MEOW!
WERF!
MEOW!
RRRROW!
RRR-ROW!
?
MEOW--
MEEOW
RRROW!
RRROW!
WELL...I SEE PLUTO IS HIS OLD SELF AGAIN!
WOOF! WOOF!
WERF! WERF!
WALT DISNEY 11-30

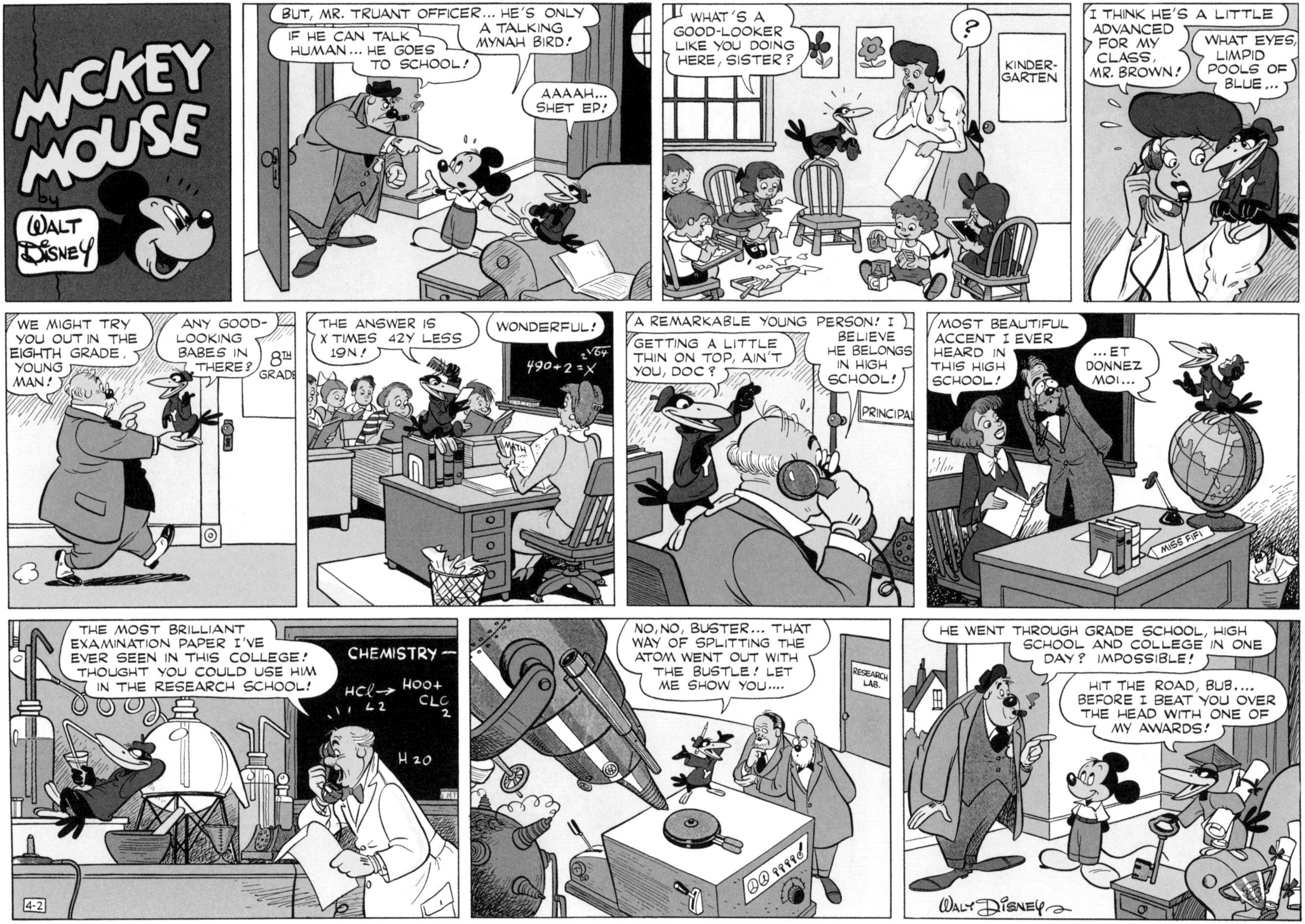
MICKEY MOUSE
by
WALT DISNEY
BUT, MR. TRUANT OFFICER... HE'S ONLY A TALKING MYNAH BIRD!
IF HE CAN TALK HUMAN... HE GOES TO SCHOOL!
AAAAH... SHET EP!
WHAT'S A GOOD-LOOKER LIKE YOU DOING HERE, SISTER?
?
KINDER-GARTEN
I THINK HE'S A LITTLE ADVANCED FOR MY CLASS, MR. BROWN!
WHAT EYES, LIMPID POOLS OF BLUE...
WE MIGHT TRY YOU OUT IN THE EIGHTH GRADE, YOUNG MAN!
ANY GOOD-LOOKING BABES IN THERE?
8TH GRADE
THE ANSWER IS X TIMES 42Y LESS 19N!
WONDERFUL!
490 + 2 = X
MATH
A REMARKABLE YOUNG PERSON! I BELIEVE HE BELONGS IN HIGH SCHOOL!
GETTING A LITTLE THIN ON TOP, AIN'T YOU, DOC?
PRINCIPAL
MOST BEAUTIFUL ACCENT I EVER HEARD IN THIS HIGH SCHOOL!
...ET DONNEZ MOI...
MISS FIFI
THE MOST BRILLIANT EXAMINATION PAPER I'VE EVER SEEN IN THIS COLLEGE! THOUGHT YOU COULD USE HIM IN THE RESEARCH SCHOOL!
CHEMISTRY
H 20
4-2
NO, NO, BUSTER... THAT WAY OF SPLITTING THE ATOM WENT OUT WITH THE BUSTLE! LET ME SHOW YOU....
RESEARCH LAB.
HE WENT THROUGH GRADE SCHOOL, HIGH SCHOOL AND COLLEGE IN ONE DAY? IMPOSSIBLE!
HIT THE ROAD, BUB.... BEFORE I BEAT YOU OVER THE HEAD WITH ONE OF MY AWARDS!
WALT DISNEY

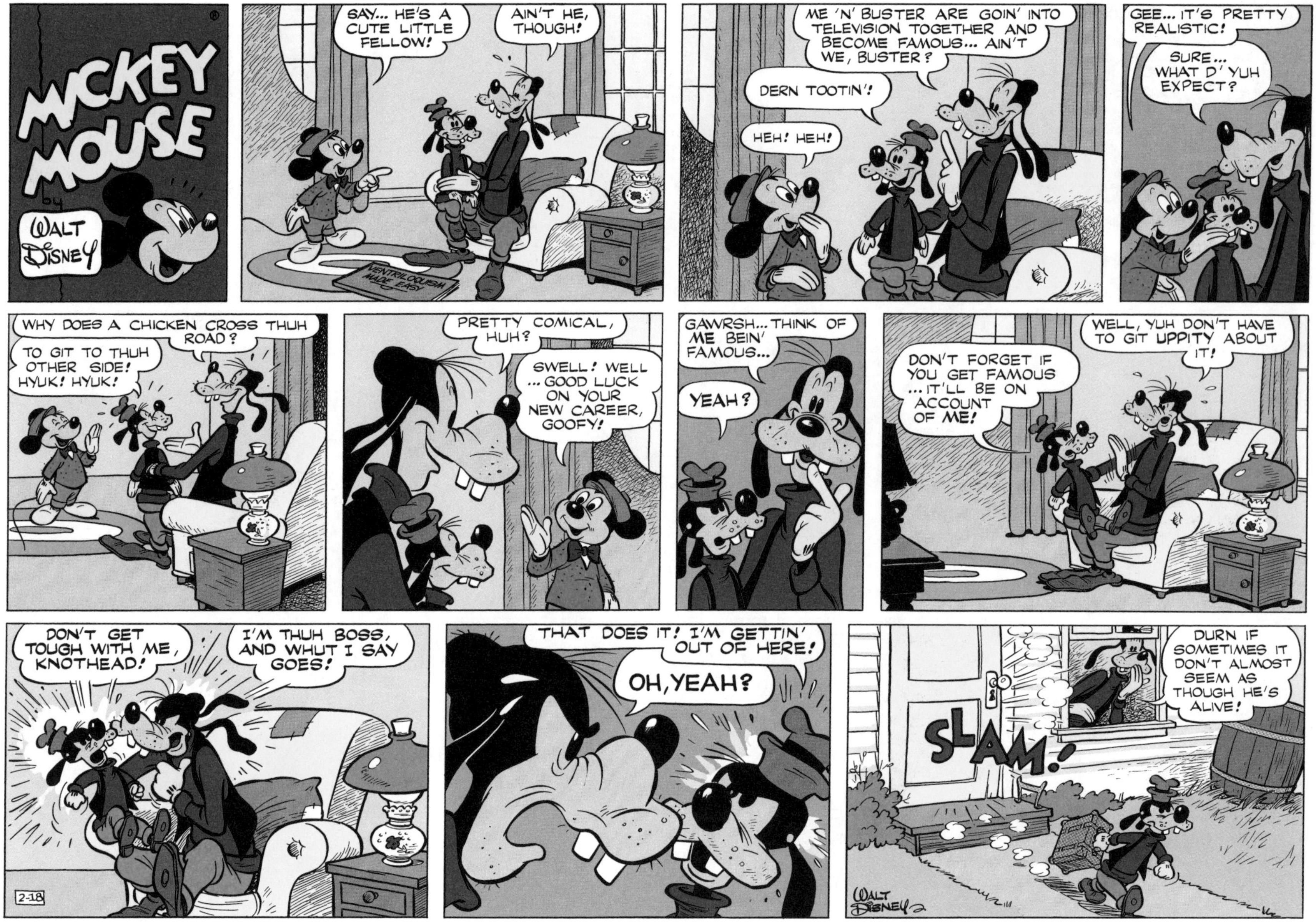

MICKEY MOUSE
by WALT DISNEY
SAY... HE'S A CUTE LITTLE FELLOW!
AIN'T HE, THOUGH!
VENTRILOQUISM MADE EASY
ME 'N' BUSTER ARE GOIN' INTO TELEVISION TOGETHER AND BECOME FAMOUS... AIN'T WE, BUSTER?
DERN TOOTIN'!
HEH! HEH!
GEE... IT'S PRETTY REALISTIC!
SURE... WHAT D' YUH EXPECT?
WHY DOES A CHICKEN CROSS THUH ROAD?
TO GIT TO THUH OTHER SIDE! HYUK! HYUK!
PRETTY COMICAL, HUH?
SWELL! WELL ... GOOD LUCK ON YOUR NEW CAREER, GOOFY!
GAWRSH... THINK OF ME BEIN' FAMOUS...
YEAH?
DON'T FORGET IF YOU GET FAMOUS ... IT'LL BE ON ACCOUNT OF ME!
WELL, YUH DON'T HAVE TO GIT UPPITY ABOUT IT!
DON'T GET TOUGH WITH ME, KNOTHEAD!
I'M THUH BOSS, AND WHUT I SAY GOES!
2-18
THAT DOES IT! I'M GETTIN' OUT OF HERE!
OH, YEAH?
SLAM!
DURN IF SOMETIMES IT DON'T ALMOST SEEM AS THOUGH HE'S ALIVE!
WALT DISNEY

"Al [Taliaferro] came to the Studio in '31... to ink my stuff on the strip... Al [would later] draw, ink and letter the Silly Symphonies. Al would also [pencil] an occasional [Mickey] Sunday page for me, when things got too hectic, because the department was slowly building now... Al was a pretty ambitious guy, hardworking and a fast worker, too."

— *Floyd Gottfredson to David R. Smith, 1975*

LEFT: Al Taliaferro, collaborator on many strips in this volume, departed from the Mickey Sunday before its *Brave Little Tailor* (1938) adaptation was created. But Taliaferro did draw this one *Tailor* sketch on a story outline for the cartoon.

Notably, Taliaferro's giant bears less resemblance to the movie's Gustav than to Rumplewatt, the bearded titan from the earlier short *Giantland* (1933)—and Gottfredson's Sunday strip adaptation ("Rumplewatt the Giant," 1934). Taliaferro's Mickey, meanwhile, rides his mule from the even earlier *Ye Olden Days* (1933). Image courtesy Walt Disney Archives.

California
Magazine of Pacific Business
March 1937 • 25 Cents
In Two Parts—PART ONE
Mickey Mouse—
Million
Dollar
Merchant
Imperial Valley • Quicksilver • Wild Flowers

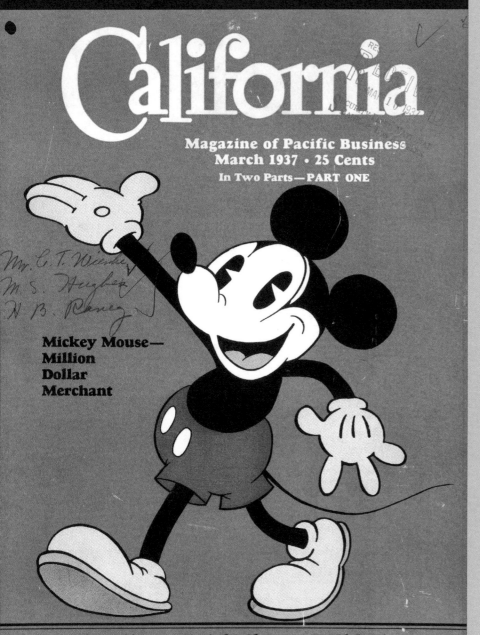

ABOUT THE EDITORS

DAVID GERSTEIN is an animation and comics researcher, writer, and editor working extensively with the Walt Disney Company and its licensees. Gerstein's published work includes *Mickey and the Gang: Classic Stories in Verse*; *Walt Disney Treasures – Disney Comics: 75 Years of Innovation*; and *The Katzenjammer Kids: 100 Years in Norway*. He has also worked with Disney to preserve the *Mickey Mouse* newspaper strips seen in this volume.

GARY GROTH co-founded Fantagraphics Books and *The Comics Journal* in 1976. And he is still at it.

J. B. KAUFMAN is a film historian on the staff of the Walt Disney Family Foundation. He is the author of *The Fairest One of All: The Making of Walt Disney's Snow White and the Seven Dwarfs* and *South of the Border With Disney*, and the coauthor—with Russell Merritt—of *Walt in Wonderland: The Silent Films of Walt Disney* and *Walt Disney's Silly Symphonies: A Companion to the Classic Cartoon Series*.

TOM NEELY is an artist living in Los Angeles. He is best known for the cult-hit indie comic book *Henry & Glenn Forever*. His self-published debut graphic novel, *The Blot* (2007), earned an Ignatz Award and was listed as one of *The Comics Journal's* "Best Graphic Novels of the Decade 2000-2010." His most recent painted novel, *The Wolf*, was released in 2011 to critical acclaim. He is currently working on a sequel to the *Henry & Glenn* saga, as well as making plans for his next graphic novel, *The Devil*.

JOE TORCIVIA is a comics historian renowned for decades of Disney, Warner Bros, Hanna-Barbera, and DC Comics scholarship. He has also worked as a dialogue writer for American editions of European Disney comics. He maintains the blog "The Issue At Hand" (*tiahblog.blogspot.com*), featuring a light-hearted look at pop culture. Torcivia has also read every retelling and/or redrawing of Gottfredson's "Island in the Sky"—and lived to tell about it.

STEFANO PRIARONE was born in northwestern Italy shortly before Floyd Gottfredson's retirement. Priarone was introduced to Gottfredson's work at just five years of age, when his Aunt Pinuccia read him an Italian collection of Mickey classics (including "Mickey Mouse Outwits the Phantom Blot"). Today Priarone writes about pop culture for many Italian newspapers and magazines.

FRANCESCO "Frank" STAJANO was imprinted on Disney comics at preschool age and never grew out of it: the walls of his house are covered in bookshelves and many of them hold comics. He has often written about Disney comics, particularly with Leonardo Gori. In real life he is an associate professor at the University of Cambridge in England.

LEONARDO GORI is a comics scholar and collector specializing in Italian Disney authors and syndicated 1930s newspaper strips. With Frank Stajano and others, he has written many books on Italian "fumetti" and American comics in Italy. He has also written thrillers, which have been translated into Spanish, Portuguese, and Korean.

THAD KOMOROWSKI began his professional association with Disney comics as a teenager, writing character dialogue for American editions of European *Uncle Scrooge* stories. Today a historian and archivist, Komorowski maintains the blog *whataboutthad.com*, devoted to the art of animation, comics, and live-action film. He is the author of *Sick Little Monkeys: The Unauthorized Ren & Stimpy Story*.

ALBERTO BECATTINI was born in Florence, Italy in 1955. He has been a high school teacher of English since 1983. Since 1978, he has written essays for Italian and US publications about comics, specializing in Disney characters and American comics generally, and since 1992 he has been a freelance writer and consultant for The Walt Disney Company Italia.

TIMO RONKAINEN is a Finnish cartoonist, graphic designer, and comics critic. He has published essays and criticism in newspapers, magazines, and local Disney comics anthologies as well as on the *kvaak.fi* website. He has also created his own comics for business communications and advertising projects. As editor of *Ankkalinnan Pamaus*, a fanzine focused on Disney comics, Timo is a proponent of pure Barksism—*but* allows himself to admire other artists, too.

LEFT: Cover by Floyd Gottfredson for a state economic journal, 1937 (image likely drawn circa 1933). Image courtesy Hake's Americana.

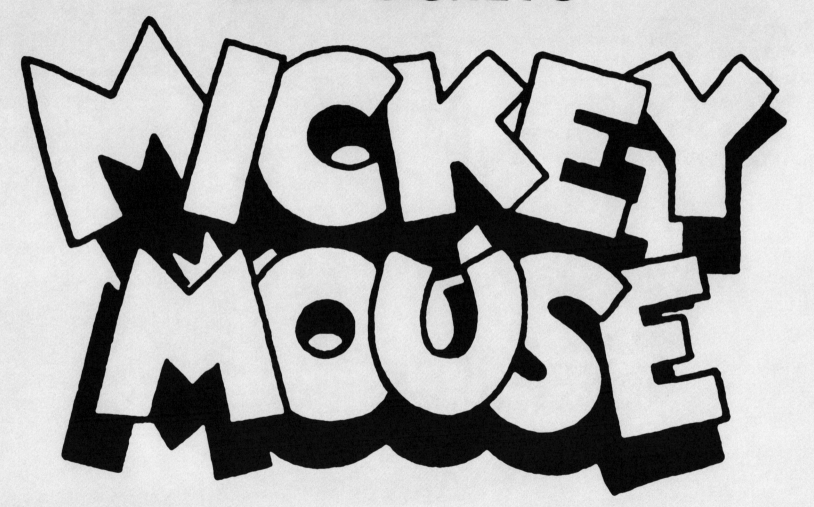

WALT DISNEY'S

MICKEY MOUSE

BY FLOYD GOTTFREDSON

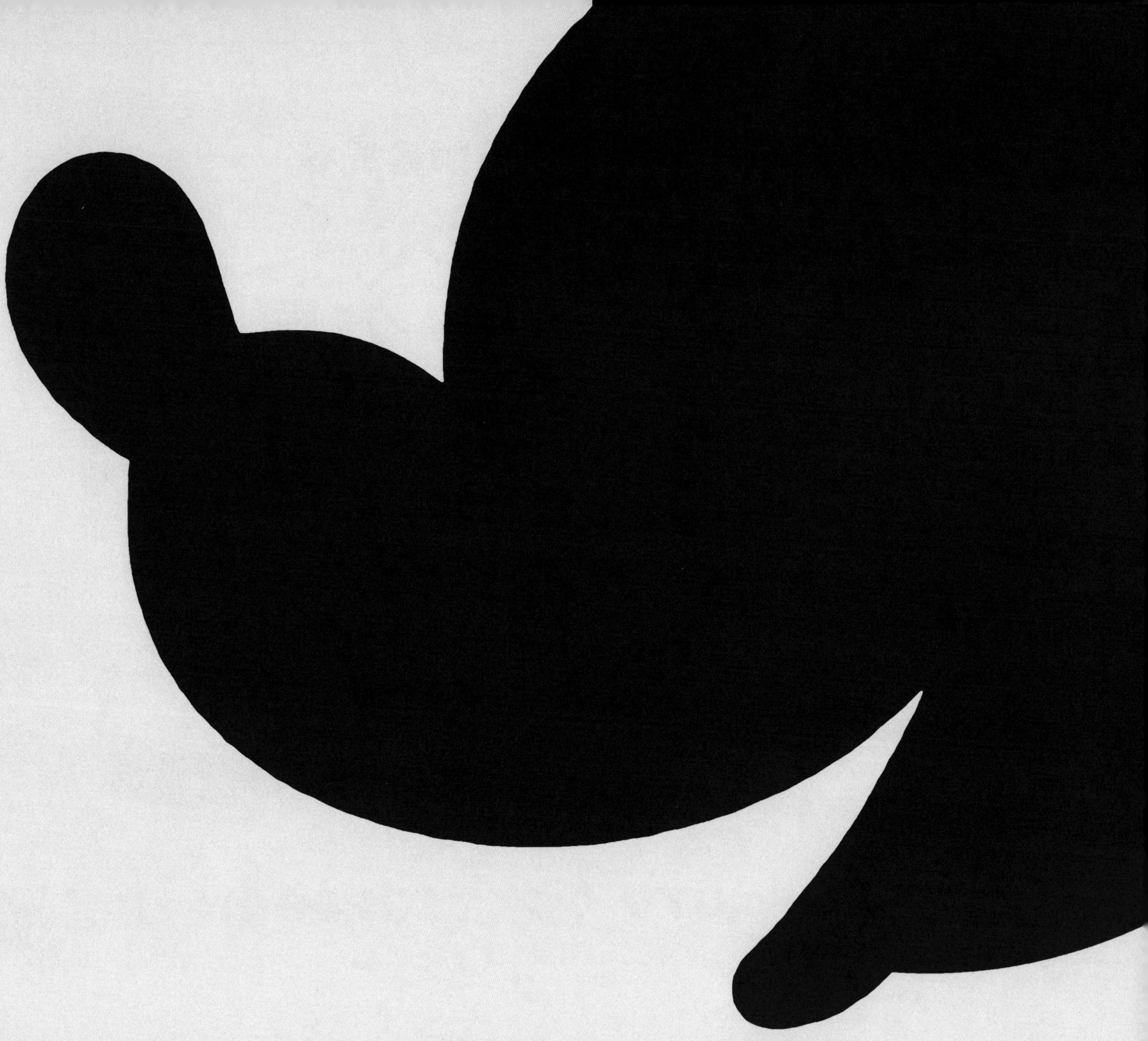

WALT DISNEY'S MICKEY MOUSE
BY FLOYD GOTTFREDSON

Color Sundays

"CALL OF THE WILD"

Series Editors: David Gerstein and Gary Groth

LEFT: when famed "Duck Man" Carl Barks (*Uncle Scrooge*) first applied for his job with Walt Disney in 1935, he submitted this drawing as one of several samples. Drawn with pen and ink and blue wash on board, it illustrates Floyd Gottfredson's "Lair of Wolf Barker," reprinted in this volume. Barks and Gottfredson would later become close friends.

The Floyd Gottfredson Library

Series Editors: DAVID GERSTEIN with GARY GROTH
Series Designers: JACOB COVEY and TONY ONG
Colorists: DIGIKORE STUDIOS with RICH TOMMASO
Production: PAUL BARESH
Associate Publisher: ERIC REYNOLDS
Publishers: GARY GROTH and KIM THOMPSON

To receive a free catalogue of graphic novels, newspaper strip reprints, prose novels, art books, cultural criticism and essays, and more, call 1-800-657-1100 or visit our website at Fantagraphics.com.

To receive a free catalogue of graphic novels, newspaper strip reprints, prose novels, art books, cultural criticism and essays, and more, call 1-800-657-1100 or visit our website at www.fantagraphics.com.

Second Printing: October, 2013

ISBN 978-1-60699-643-0

Printed in Singapore.

FLOYD GOTTFREDSON'S MICKEY MOUSE enters every battle like a trouper. He tells desperados he'll "break ya with my naked hands"; almost as if, with just enough bluff, the fight might prove easy. But it's easier to *talk* about subduing tough guys than to *do* it. Mickey only soldiers through because his grit won't quit.

Remastering the *Mickey Mouse* Sunday strip was also easier to talk about than to do. Line art sometimes had to be reseparated from printed pages; compiling color stats for reference was an elephant of a job. But strip collectors Thomas Andrae and Thomas Jensen, and restoration master Paul Baresh, proved that an elephant could fly.

Many others also merit thanks for this book's contents. Ken Shue, Disney Publishing Worldwide's Vice President of Global Art and Design Development, and his Secretary Iliana Lopez, moved mountains to make surviving Gottfredson line art negs available. Danny Saeva, DPW's Director of Licensing, North America, aided us with further cross-studio connections.

Numerous other scholars contributed artwork, essays, knowledge, and archival items. We're grateful to Director Rebecca Cline, Archivist Michael Buckhoff, Contractor Kevin Kern, and Senior Secretary Alesha Reyes at the Walt Disney Archives; also to Creative Director Lella Smith, Research Manager Fox Carney, and Researchers Ann Hansen and Jackie Vasquez at the Walt Disney Animation Research Library. I'd also like to thank Paul F. Anderson, Gunnar Andreassen, Garry Apgar, Geoffrey Blum, Massimo Bonura, Paolo Castagno, Robert Cowan, Dale Dietzman, Diane Disney Miller, Shernaaz Engineer, Fabio Gadducci, Didier Ghez, Leonardo Gori, the Hake's Americana staff (including Alex Winter, Terence Kean, and Deak Stagemeyer), Kevin Huizenga, Lars Jensen, Mark and Cole Johnson, Diego Jourdan Pereira, Thad Komorowski, Jim Korkis, Kosta Labropoulos, Sergio Lama, Jens Lindell, Mike Matei, Stefano Priarone, Frank Stajano, Ricky Turner, Germund Von Wowern, and Dejan Zivkovic.

Others, too, have provided crucial support and encouragement. First and foremost come my parents, Susan and Larry Gerstein, and my brother Ben. Then come friends including Céline and Stefan Allirol-Molin, Christopher and Nicky Barat, Jerry Beck, John Clark, César Ferioli, Jonathan Gray, Joakim Gunnarsson, Andy Hershberger, Nelson Hughes, Vincent Joseph, Mark Kausler, Carl Keil, Raquel Lopez, Jean Marie Metauten, Geoffrey Moses, Floyd Norman, KaJuan Osborne, Tarkan Rosenberg, Travis Seitler, Warren Spector, Tom Stathes, Kwongmei To, Joe and Esther Torcivia, and Wilbert Watts.

A last, special thanks goes to scholar and friend J. B. Kaufman, who gave this volume its sparkling Foreword—and discovered that Mickey's vow to "break ya with my naked hands" actually references *The Spoilers* (1914), a pivotal early adventure film. J. B.'s grit, like Mickey's, won't quit.

—David Gerstein
January 2013

TABLE of CONTENTS

Setting the Stage

The Sundays: Floyd Gottfredson's Mickey Mouse Stories With Introductory Notes

TABLE *of* CONTENTS

THE GOTTFREDSON ARCHIVES: ESSAYS AND SPECIAL FEATURES

MICKEY'S SUNDAY BEST

FLOYD GOTTFREDSON AND THE DISNEY COLOR COMICS

1932-1935: *A New Arena*

» *FOREWORD BY J. B. KAUFMAN*

NO "OVERNIGHT" SUCCESS ever really happens overnight; but to Mickey Mouse's many fans in the early 1930s, it must have seemed that their hero had burst into the public consciousness out of nowhere. Appearing sporadically on movie screens in 1928-29, elevated to greater national and international prominence by new distribution agreements in 1930, Mickey struck a responsive chord with audiences and quickly moved beyond the confines of the screen. By early 1932 he was everywhere: his grinning visage could be seen not only in the movies but in storybooks, on dolls and other toys—and in a daily black-and-white newspaper comic strip. A counterpart Sunday comic page in color must have seemed inevitable.

King Features, the comics syndicate handling the Mickey daily strip, evidently thought so. As comics legend Floyd Gottfredson later remembered it, the syndicate was eager for a Mickey Sunday page, and the feature might have started far earlier than it did if not for a simple lack of manpower. "King Features had been after Walt for, I guess, nearly a year to do a Sunday page," Gottfredson told Disney archivist Dave Smith. "Walt had thus been after me to do it, and I couldn't find the time."[1] In 1931 Gottfredson had his hands full writing and drawing the *Mickey* daily strip. But his department was gradually growing; and Earl Duvall, who had been hired to ink the dailies, had ambitions for bigger things. By the end of the year inker Al Taliaferro and scripter Ted Osborne had joined the team, relieving pressure on Gottfredson and Duvall and allowing them to devote some time to new projects. Early in 1932, Walt, King Features, and legions of Disney fans all got their wish: a fresh, delightful new Disney comics page in full color debuted in the Sunday papers.

RIGHT: Gottfredson self-caricature drawn for in-house use, c. 1933. Image courtesy The Walt Disney Company.

The new feature was an ambitious undertaking, occupying a full page in comic sections and offering *two* generous weekly servings of Disney art. The upper third of the page was devoted to a *Silly Symphony* top strip, initially written, drawn and inked by Duvall.[2] For the page's initial offering on 10 January 1932, Duvall was a true one-man show, performing all writing and artistic duties for both the *Silly Symphony* story *and* the *Mickey Mouse* episode—a somewhat odd one—that appeared on the bottom half of the page. Thereafter Gottfredson, the experienced hand, took over the *Mickey* series, launching what would become a long, rich body of work in its own right. The first four years of that remarkable series are collected in this volume for the first time in English.

In Fantagraphics' preceding *Mickey Mouse* daily strip books, David Gerstein and Thomas Andrae have already discussed the relationship between the Mickey theatrical cartoons and the daily newspaper comic strip— the fascinating process by which a central character, and a series of comic situations, were adapted from one medium into a very different medium with different demands. By early 1932 the relationship between film and comic-strip worlds was well established, and Gottfredson had begun to explore it in depth. But the advent of the Sunday page represented a new arena: a form unlike either of the others, with new challenges and opportunities all its own. The creative team began to experiment in ways that are endlessly intriguing today. At the most basic level, the format of the Sundays differed from that of the dailies in three important ways: the stories were longer, they appeared at weekly intervals, and they were in color.

Today, in hindsight, the color may seem like a non-issue, but it's important to remember that in early 1932 Mickey and his friends were still appearing in the movies in black and white, and would continue to do so for another three years. In some instances, audiences knew them only in their monochrome incarnations, and King Features' colorists were charged with introducing them in color for the first time. The decision to render Mickey's shorts in red would seem a predetermined choice, since by January 1932 he had already appeared in books and merchandise with red shorts;

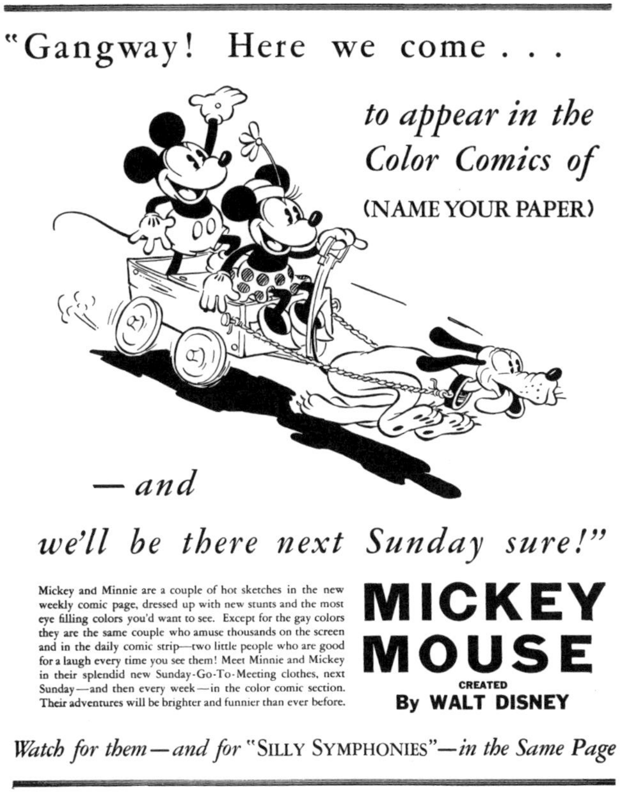
"Gangway! Here we come . . .
to appear in the Color Comics of
(NAME YOUR PAPER)
— and
we'll be there next Sunday sure!"
Mickey and Minnie are a couple of hot sketches in the new weekly comic page, dressed up with new stunts and the most eye filling colors you'd want to see. Except for the gay colors they are the same couple who amuse thousands on the screen and in the daily comic strip—two little people who are good for a laugh every time you see them! Meet Minnie and Mickey in their splendid new Sunday-Go-To-Meeting clothes, next Sunday—and then every week—in the color comic section. Their adventures will be brighter and funnier than ever before.
MICKEY MOUSE
CREATED
By WALT DISNEY
Watch for them—and for "SILLY SYMPHONIES"—in the Same Page

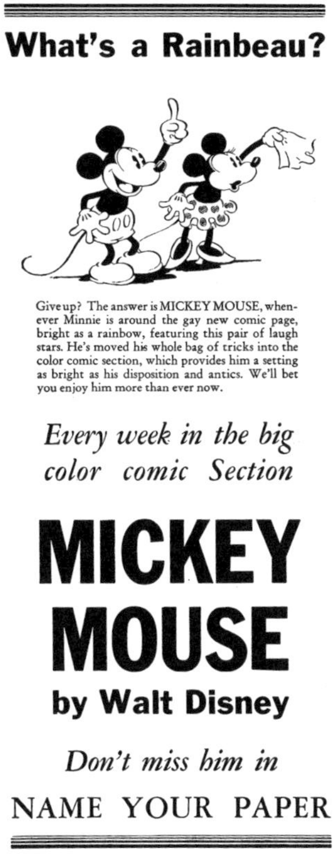
What's a Rainbeau?
Give up? The answer is MICKEY MOUSE, whenever Minnie is around the gay new comic page, bright as a rainbow, featuring this pair of laugh stars. He's moved his whole bag of tricks into the color comic section, which provides him a setting as bright as his disposition and antics. We'll bet you enjoy him more than ever now.
Every week in the big color comic Section
MICKEY MOUSE
by Walt Disney
Don't miss him in
NAME YOUR PAPER

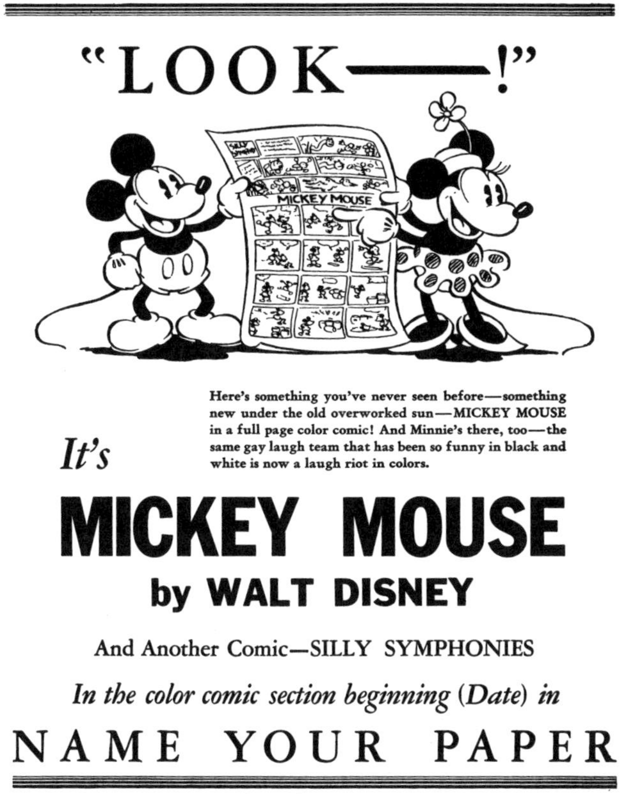
"LOOK——!"
MICKEY MOUSE
Here's something you've never seen before—something new under the old overworked sun—MICKEY MOUSE in a full page color comic! And Minnie's there, too—the same gay laugh team that has been so funny in black and white is now a laugh riot in colors.
It's
MICKEY MOUSE
by WALT DISNEY
And Another Comic—SILLY SYMPHONIES
In the color comic section beginning (Date) in
NAME YOUR PAPER

but even this was no certainty. In fact, the Mouse had sported *green* shorts in many early licensed items; and in November 1932, when he did first appear in a Technicolor cartoon—produced not for public consumption, but for the 1931-32 Academy Awards banquet—the shorts again were green.[3] No matter; the Sunday comics clothed Mickey in red from the beginning. By 1935, when the theatrical Mickey cartoons made their official jump to Technicolor, Mickey's red shorts had come to be accepted as the standard—thanks in no small part to the Sunday comics—and most later color films followed suit (no pun intended).

Mickey's and Minnie's gloves proved likewise variable. Today we tend to picture the gloves in basic white, but in fact the yellow gloves in Gottfredson's comics reappeared in many of Mickey's earliest color films. Other anomalies of color, some more surprising than others, pop up in the Sunday pages as King's colorists—presumably with Walt's blessing—experiment with the form. Note Mickey's and Minnie's facial coloring during the first few months of the page, with a white area for the eyes set off by a pinkish "skin tone" below, and Pluto's startling "albino" appearance at various times in 1932. Donald Duck received yellow feathers throughout 1935; long enough for the trend to spread into locally produced European Disney comics.

Far more than color, the other inherent properties of the Sunday page—the dimensions of Gottfredson's canvas, and its appearance at weekly intervals—determined his approach to story material. We've already seen in Volume 1 of Fantagraphics' daily strip series how the nature of the daily—the steady recurrence of short bursts of action—lent itself to a continuing narrative. Scarcely two weeks into its run in January 1930, the daily had already launched a continuing story, its adventurous course

ABOVE: Three original ad drawings (and surrounding text copy) from Disney's and King Features' Sunday strip launch pack, 1932. Art by Floyd Gottfredson; images courtesy Walt Disney Archives.

plotted by Walt Disney himself. Gottfredson, taking over the writing duties in mid-1930, had built on this precedent with increasingly extended and thrill-packed plotlines, and by early 1932 had established the direction he would follow in the *Mouse* dailies for the rest of his career. But the Sunday page was a different matter. Continuity stories were not unheard of in Sunday comics, but Gottfredson seems to have felt from the beginning that this larger, colorful, intermittent format might be better suited to other kinds of story material—perhaps self-contained stories or gags that didn't depend on the reader's familiarity with earlier installments. For the first six months of its existence, and at frequent intervals thereafter, the *Mickey Mouse* Sunday page featured these self-contained "gag-a-day" stories.

And what sort of stories were they? Thanks to the increased length of the Sunday strip, Gottfredson was free to plot more extended narratives than in individual episodes of the daily—but he didn't always use that freedom. Sometimes the extra space was used for other purposes. Twice in July 1933, the *Mickey* page tells an exceedingly simple story, but one packed by Gottfredson with an overabundance of drawings. The result is a remarkable simulation of movement, reminding us that Gottfredson had begun his Disney career as an animator. By contrast, on other Sundays, Gottfredson *does* use the extra panels to build up the narrative substance of the story, filling them with incident, gags, and dialogue.

As with the daily strip, Gottfredson drew much of his basic inspiration from contemporary Mickey Mouse theatrical films. If anything, the Sunday Mickey remained closer to his cinematic roots than did his daily counterpart. Some examples are obvious enough: in February 1932 Gottfredson recycles a horse-anchor gag from *The Barn Dance* (1928), the fourth Mickey cartoon, more or less verbatim; and a month later Mickey shoots a literally explosive flash photo of a flock of prize hens—a memorable episode from *Musical Farmer* (1932), then in production. Elsewhere Gottfredson uses his source material in less obvious ways, creatively mixing gags and characters from more than one film. One Mickey-Pluto hunting story in February 1932 combines hunting gags from *The Moose Hunt* (1931) and *The Duck Hunt* (1932) with a Wild West bit player from *Pioneer Days* (1930).

Silly Symphonies
by Walt Disney
BUCKY BUG WANDERS IN MOTHER GOOSE LAND, TO THE COURT OF KING COLE AND HIS MERRY BAND!
OLD KING COLE, YOU'RE A MERRY OLD SOUL, WHILE I AM JUST ONE OF THE MOB... SAD AND BLUE AND HUNGRY, TOO... AND LOOKING FOR A JOB
HA! HA! HO! HO! A JOB FOR YOU; AND FOR ME, A SHOW! FOR MANY YEARS I'VE LAUGHED AND SUNG AND DANCED THE WHOLE DAY THROUGH, AND I'VE FORGOTTEN HOW IT FEELS TO BE FORLORN AND BLUE!
'TWOULD REALLY BE A NOVELTY IF I WERE FEELING BAD, SO ALL THAT YOU WILL HAVE TO DO IS TRY TO MAKE ME SAD!
HURRY! DRESS UP FOR THE PART, BUT PLEASE DON'T BE MIS-LED! FOR EITHER YOU MUST MAKE ME CRY OR...OFF WILL COME YOUR HEAD!
OLD KING COLE IS A MERRY OLD SOUL! YEAH! FAR TOO MERRY IS HE! HE MAY BE THE LIFE OF A PARTY, BUT HE'LL BE THE DEATH OF ME!
TO BE CONTINUED

BEGINNING
"DON POOCHO"
FUNNY FILMS
CUT OUT STAGE AND FILM — MAKE SLITS ALONG DOTTED LINES ON THE SCREEN.
CHANGE HEADS BY MOVING THEM THROUGH SLITS — A NEW SHOW -EVERY WEEK-
MICKEY MOUSE MOVIES
BEGINNING
THE "BOYS ABOUT TOWN"
END
END

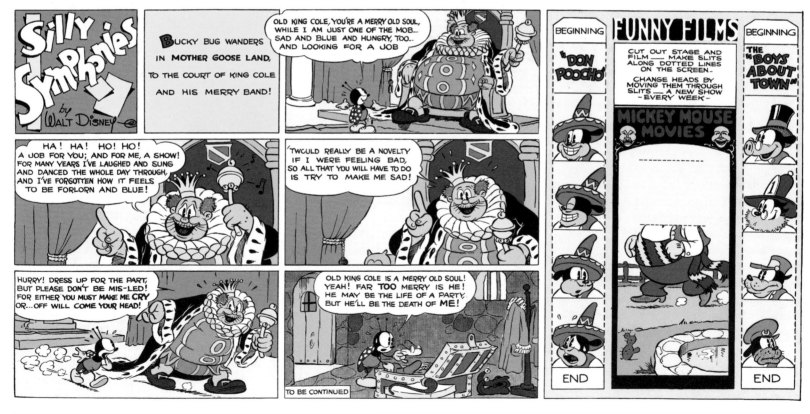

Sometimes, in fact, the relationship between the films and the comics became downright labyrinthine. In July 1933 the Disney story department circulated a story outline for a cartoon to be called "Spring Cleaning." This outline inspired so many gag and story ideas that it was split into two separate films, then three.[4] In the end "Spring Cleaning" kicked around the Disney studio for years without ever reaching the screen, although some of its component ideas did. In the meantime, three of those ideas—Mickey's attempt to patch a window screen, Pluto's misadventures with a garden hose, and Pluto's messy encounter with a package of flypaper—were borrowed for three separate installments of the Sunday comic strip in September-October 1933. By the following spring, all three of those gag ideas had also been absorbed into the theatrical short *Playful Pluto* (1934), and the last of the three would be forever enshrined in animation history as the legendary "flypaper sequence."

When the Sunday page did venture a continuing story, the results became even more fascinating. As a rule, the Sunday continuities were unlike those in the daily strip: less heroic adventure, more comedy and fantasy. Gottfredson set the tone in 1932 by plotting the page's first two continuities, filling them not with feats of derring-do but with gags, drama, and characters based loosely on two of the studio's current films. "Dan the Dogcatcher" starts with the last half of *The Mad Dog* (1932), then continues on a plot trajectory all its own. "Mickey's Nephews" may seem unconnected with any film, but Mickey's dream visions of wedding bells point unmistakably to *Mickey's Nightmare* (1932), which had climaxed with our hero's home overrun by mischievous little mice. In the strip—at Walt Disney's suggestion—Gottfredson singles out just two of those little hellions, personalizes them, and creates formative versions of two characters who will become familiar to later generations of comics fans.[5]

Early in 1933 Ted Osborne took over the writing duties for the Sunday page. As this volume demonstrates, Osborne's continuities followed Gottfredson's lead: stories based on current Disney pictures—with an offbeat twist. "Rumplewatt the Giant" pitted the giant from the Mickey short *Giantland* (1933) against the dwarfs from the Silly Symphony *Babes in the Woods* (1932), with Princess Minnie from *Ye Olden Days* (1933) thrown in for good measure. "Hoppy the Kangaroo," in 1935, starts like an obvious replay of that year's *Mickey's Kangaroo* (1935), then veers unexpectedly into story elements borrowed from the earlier *Mickey's Mechanical Man* (1933).

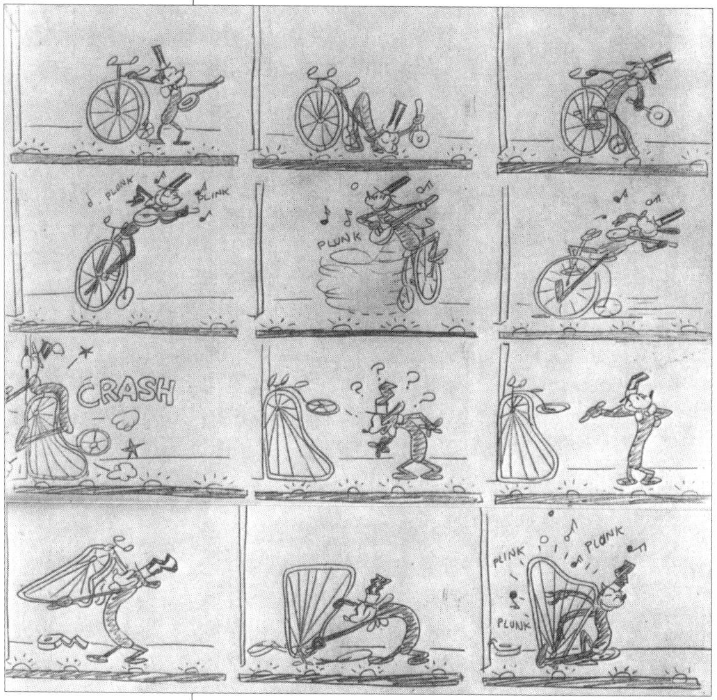
PLUNK
PLINK
PLUNK
CRASH
PLINK
PLONK
PLUNK

Even after surrendering the writing duties for the Sunday page, Gottfredson continued to plot the *Mickey* dailies. In effect, the daily and Sunday comics became two separate but parallel tracks, and Gottfredson seemed to revel in their relationship, creating a kind of subtle crosstalk between them. Sometimes this took the form of playful cross-references, inserted in the Sunday art as understated in-jokes. Readers of Fantagraphics' *Mickey* daily strip books will remember that, in April 1934, Gottfredson built a short daily serial around a character from an earlier Silly Symphony, *Just Dogs* (1932): an unnamed Boston terrier whom he dubbed "Terry." In *this* volume we can see that "Terry" had already been lurking around Gottfredson's Sunday comics for nearly two years by 1934—popping up unannounced as an occasional supporting character, as if to pave the way for his brief starring role in the dailies. Conversely, we've seen an extended daily continuity in June-October 1933 featuring "Mickey Mouse and His Horse Tanglefoot." Now we find that in the midst of that run, in August 1933, Tanglefoot made an unbilled guest appearance in the Sunday comics as well—testing the market, perhaps, before returning to Sundays the following spring in "Tanglefoot Pulls His Weight."

And what of the major characters? By and large, the world of the Sunday comics affected them

FACING PAGE: Sample *Silly Symphony* from September 24, 1933. By this time Al Taliaferro had supplanted Earl Duvall as sole artist on the strip. Taliaferro also drew the "Funny Films" extra feature, tied into Gottfredson's ongoing *Mickey* tales: the character of Don Jollio comes from this volume's "Lair of Wolf Barker" serial.

ABOVE: Gottfredson's strip for April 17, 1932 evolved from this unused storyboard sequence with Wienie the dachshund, perhaps intended at one time for *The Opry House* (1929). Art attributed to Ub Iwerks; image courtesy Walt Disney Archives.

SU

in varying ways. Horace Horsecollar and Clarabelle Cow, already well-established in early 1932 when the Sunday feature started, arrived in that world virtually unchanged. David Gerstein has written of an odd continuity lapse in the daily strips of 1932: the impending wedding of Horace and Clarabelle was announced, given an elaborate buildup, then apparently forgotten.[6] No matter; married or not, they behave like a stereotypical bickering married couple in Sunday continuities like "Dr. Oofgay's Secret Serum" and "Foray to Mt. Fishflake." Horace obnoxiously brags and brays; Clarabelle nags and criticizes. When Horace's life seems threatened by Dr. Oofgay's serum, Clarabelle calls him "the poor dear" and declares: "I always said there never was a finer character than old Horsecollar!" But no sooner is Horace cured than Clarabelle reverts to type, nagging him mercilessly.

Donald Duck, as introduced to movie audiences in *The Wise Little Hen* (1934), was notable for his laziness and greed—and a followup continuity in the *Silly Symphony* Sunday comics portrayed him in the same way.[7] But Donald soon migrated to the Mickey Mouse film series and to Mickey's half of the Sunday comics page, and now those traits were supplanted by a funnier one: his terrible temper. Osborne and Gottfredson were at pains to build up Donald's irascible nature: on his introduction in February 1935 Mickey comments that the Duck is "always scrappin' over somep'n," and in the last panel Donald assumes the fighting stance that he had introduced on the screen in *Orphans' Benefit* (1934).

Pluto, gradually introduced in both the movies and the daily strip during 1930-31, underwent an odd reentry process during the launch of the Sunday comics in 1932. In that first oddball Earl Duvall page, the hapless hound is unnamed, and Mickey seems never to have seen him before. It's not until Pluto's second appearance, a month later, that Mickey addresses him by name.

Dippy Dawg, the character who will evolve into Goofy, enters the Sunday page early in 1933—and, still being in a formative state, gives us a unique look at his early developmental process. (Note the "Dippy Dog" spelling in these earliest appearances, later replaced by the more familiar "Dawg.") Perhaps because the character was still so unformed and malleable, Osborne and Gottfredson felt free to take creative liberties with his personality. Dippy's outlandishly ingenious solutions to problems would become familiar on the screen soon enough, but his obsession with his "juice-harp," oblivious to the indifference or irritation of everyone around him, was an intriguing trait that could be found only in the comics.

It was Mickey himself, the star of the strip, who displayed the widest range of responses to its Sunday showcase. As the nature of the stories changed, Mickey's persona changed with it. For an adventure serial like "The Lair of Wolf Barker," he could be the same intrepid little daredevil as in the daily strip, but more benign settings and stories brought out

JOSEPH M. SCHENCK
PRESENTS
WALT DISNEY'S
MICKEY MOUSE
IN "MICKEY'S MECHANICAL MAN"
UNITED ARTISTS PICTURE
UMM-184

ABOVE: Some scenes in Gottfredson's "Rumplewatt the Giant" (1934) mimicked staging from the cartoon *Giantland* (1933): compare the film still with the Sunday strip for April 1, 1934. Animation by Hamilton Luske.

RIGHT: Gottfredson's "Hoppy the Kangaroo" (1935) featured the 'roo in a boxing match against a gorilla. On-screen, it was *Mickey's Mechanical Man* (1933) who fought the big ape in the ring.

FACING PAGE: Initial Sunday strip artist Earl Duvall also drew this 1930 box design for an unreleased card game. Image courtesy Hake's Americana; used with permission of the Walt Disney Family Foundation.

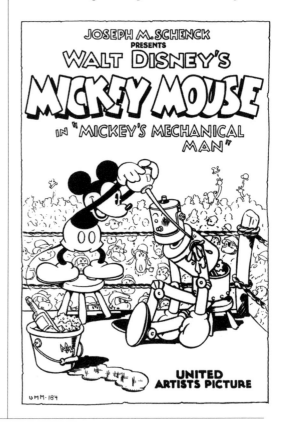

other facets of his personality. In some of the early Mickey films the Mouse had displayed a mischievous streak; in the Sunday page he became even more mischievous and was given to elaborate practical jokes. Sometimes, to be sure, those jokes backfired. In October 1934 Mickey pulls a prank on Minnie with a garden hose, only to be drenched himself; and in January 1933, after Minnie herself colludes with Mickey to throw a snowball at a top-hatted gent, both find themselves in frigid discomfort when their victim turns the tables on them. But just as often, Mickey's impish pranks are successful, and either way he usually prevails with a smile.

On and off the screen, the early Mickey loved music. In his films he occasionally sang, but more often was seen playing a piano or some other instrument. In the comics the proportions were reversed: Mickey might be seen playing instrumental music now and then, but was far more likely to lift his voice in song. "Minnie's Yoo Hoo," his theme song in the movies since 1929, was a favorite number in his comics repertoire as well; in one October 1932 page he performs a complete chorus—at intervals, pausing for various interruptions.

In the Sunday comics, in fact, Mickey takes his musical hobby a step further and tries his hand as a songwriter. Several installments find him actively endeavoring to write a love song for Minnie. On one of these occasions, in November 1932, his playful streak gets the better of him and he ends the song with a mischievous insult, bringing down Minnie's wrath and beating a retreat amidst a hail of cookware and other missiles. (In a later episode, playing Cyrano to Horace's Christian de Neuvillette, Mickey pulls a similar reversal on Clarabelle.) Elsewhere, in another variation, Mickey can sometimes be seen improvising a verse about events that have just taken place.

But Mickey is not always clever or mischievous. If the story calls for it, he can fill any number of other roles. In some pages he's simply a well-meaning good citizen whose earnest efforts to clean house, fix

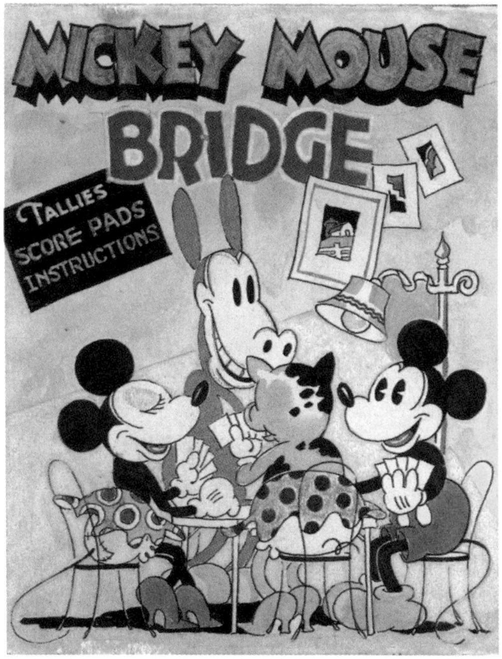
MICKEY MOUSE
BRIDGE
TALLIES
SCORE PADS
INSTRUCTIONS

a kitchen drain, or perform some other simple task lead to comic disaster. Yet again, even when he's not in a particularly mischievous mood, he may be simply a youngster bursting with energy and high spirits.

In his 1935 character analysis, Disney story department head Ted Sears would write: "Mickey is not a clown... he is neither silly nor dumb."[8] Not dumb, certainly, but in fact Mickey *had* already clowned around in a number of his films, indulging in silly hijinks just for the fun of it. Nor did this

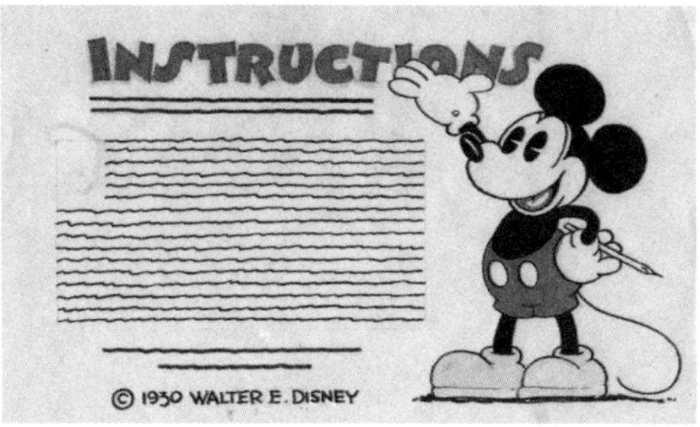
INSTRUCTIONS
© 1930 WALTER E. DISNEY

playful side disappear from Mickey's persona as he matured; his well-loved exploits in "The Sorcerer's Apprentice," appearing on the screen as late as 1940, were yet another expression of his boyish, unbounded enthusiasm. And that side of his persona continued to appear in the Sunday comics as well—sometimes with the same calamitous consequences.

Daring adventurer, hapless clown, songster, high-spirited mischief maker; these and other traits can easily be absorbed in Mickey Mouse's persona. It's a tribute to his versatility, and to the skill of Gottfredson and his collaborators, that one character can display all these facets and yet remain consistently a recognizable, distinct individual—a Mouse for all seasons. The early Sunday comics provide Mickey with a splendid stage; the years afterward, as we shall see in the next volume, will offer him a whole new set of challenges and innovations. •

1 Floyd Gottfredson to David R. Smith, *Mickey Mouse in Color* deluxe edition (Prescott: Another Rainbow, 1988), p. 159.

2 This and other credits information: Gottfredson to Smith, pp. 159-161.

3 See *Parade of the Award Nominees* (1932) on *Walt Disney Treasures: Mickey Mouse in Living Color* (Disney DVD, 2001).

4 The additional shorts were the "autumn cleaning" cartoon *Playful Pluto* (1934) and the unproduced "Interior Decorators" (in and out of production from 1936-38).

5 Gottfredson to Smith, p. 166. Gottfredson incorrectly recalled the source cartoon as *Orphans' Benefit* (1934), a much later appearance by the crowd of kids.

6 David Gerstein, "The Cast: Horace, Clarabelle... and Dippy," in *Walt Disney's Mickey Mouse: Trapped on Treasure Island* (Vol. 2 of Fantagraphics' companion daily strip series), p. 243.

7 "The Wise Little Hen" comics adaptation, September 16-December 16, 1934.

8 Ted Sears, "Mickey Mouse." Character analysis, 1935, p. 1.

A Brief Essay About FLOYD GOTTFREDSON

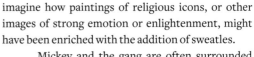

» *Appreciation by Kevin Huizenga*

I FIRST CAME ACROSS Floyd Gottfredson's work in *Mickey Mouse Best Comics*, the big white 1978 book that collected many of his 1930s strips in bright colors. I didn't know that the color wasn't original or that the stories were condensed. But I still checked the book out of the library many times as a teenager, back when reprints of old strips were much harder to come by.

Gottfredson's strips appealed to me in part because of the canonical 1930s cartoon style—that mix of pleasant liveliness and weirdly unsettling energy—but also because the storytelling was so straightforward. Mickey and the gang were mostly the same size from panel to panel, and the "camera angle" stayed sensibly steady. It was a breath of fresh air for me after all the "dynamic" layouts of modern superhero comics.

The other thing that amazed me about Gottfredson's work was his habit of drawing sweat droplets bursting from characters' heads. So many! Gottfredson drew *Mickey Mouse* for forty-five years, and some years are drier than others, but during the rainy seasons there are sometimes more panels with bursts of sweat (or tears) than not!

When I started work at a small design and illustration company, I learned to call these small droplets of liquid "sweatles" (pronounced "swet-tels"). The term first showed up in the comic strip *Bloom County* in 1987. But the sweatle itself is older, one of cartooning's great contributions to the vocabulary of art. Like a visual metaphor, the sweatle externalizes a subjective state; like the word balloon and the thought balloon, it is an intuitive and satisfying symbol that has passed into common use. One can imagine how paintings of religious icons, or other images of strong emotion or enlightenment, might have been enriched with the addition of sweatles.

Mickey and the gang are often surrounded by halos of water, shining from their heads like rays. It's clear Gottfredson knew that these droplets made a lot of subtle effects available to a cartoonist. One need only measure out the right amount of droplets, the right shape, and the trajectory which best fit not only the characters' internal states, but also the composition of each panel.

Other cartoonists—George Herriman (*Krazy Kat*), for instance—who also use a high volume of droplets often show gravity's curving effect on the water. Gottfredson's sweatles usually shoot off at a higher velocity, though there are a wide variety of forms and speeds for the connoisseur to find.

The effect of these thousands of sweatles is that Gottfredson's already-lively Mickey seems even more expressive and alive on the page. Not only do we see his expertly controlled expression and posture—but our glance picks up the sweatles in flight, signaling that this is the very moment that panic, or surprise, or joy is striking him. Mickey has feelings so strong that they actually produce a kind of kinetic energy. This is the same force that pushes cartoon hats up in the air. Gottfredson used it to open up shortcuts into our brains.

Some years ago I filled some space in my comic book *Or Else* with a visual tribute to Floyd Gottfredson (reprinted opposite)—and his supreme mastery of the sweatle. I also tried to answer the question: where do Mickey's sweatles *go*? •

જોયું કે મીની! આપુને છેક મુંબઈ માંબી યાદ કરેછ. આય જામે જમશેદ વાંચ.
Walt Disney

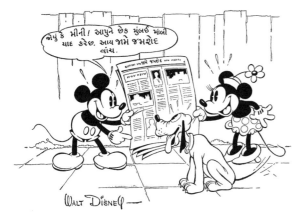

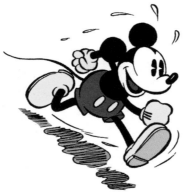

LEFT: Gottfredson's "sweatles" (detail from August 20, 1933) were such a trademark that his assistants mimicked them when creating ad art for the strip. Tom Wood drew the present example for a newspaper in India (March 21, 1934). Mickey's Gujarati voice balloon says, "Have you seen, Minnie? They know us all the way out in Mumbai! Read *Jam-e-Jamshed* and see for yourself!" Image from Walt Disney Archives; reprinted courtesy of Shernaaz Engineer, editor *Jam-e-Jamshed.*

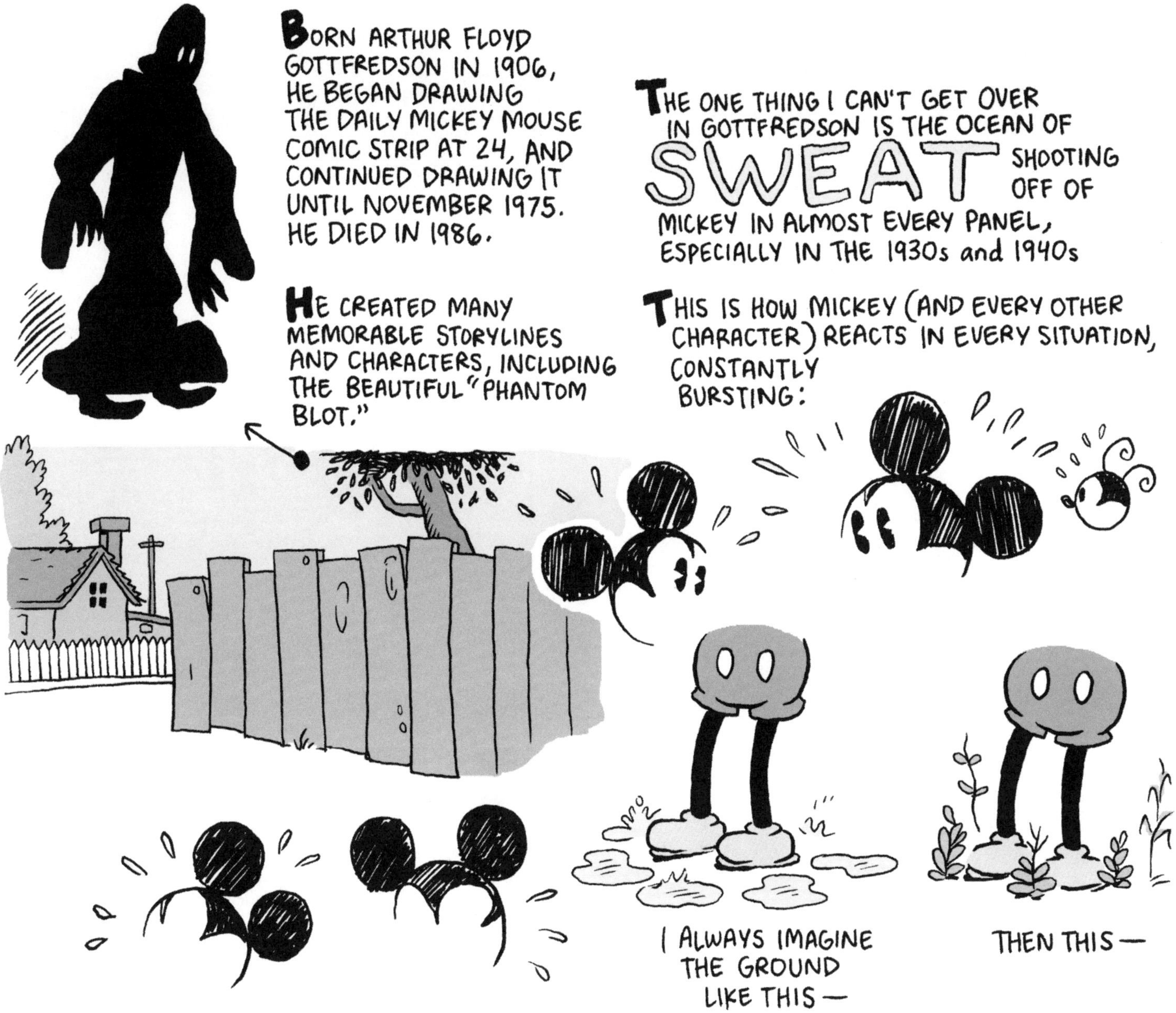
BORN ARTHUR FLOYD GOTTFREDSON IN 1906, HE BEGAN DRAWING THE DAILY MICKEY MOUSE COMIC STRIP AT 24, AND CONTINUED DRAWING IT UNTIL NOVEMBER 1975. HE DIED IN 1986.
HE CREATED MANY MEMORABLE STORYLINES AND CHARACTERS, INCLUDING THE BEAUTIFUL "PHANTOM BLOT."
THE ONE THING I CAN'T GET OVER IN GOTTFREDSON IS THE OCEAN OF SWEAT SHOOTING OFF OF MICKEY IN ALMOST EVERY PANEL, ESPECIALLY IN THE 1930s and 1940s
THIS IS HOW MICKEY (AND EVERY OTHER CHARACTER) REACTS IN EVERY SITUATION, CONSTANTLY BURSTING:
I ALWAYS IMAGINE THE GROUND LIKE THIS —
THEN THIS —

From *Or Else* 3 (1999). Art © and courtesy Kevin Huizenga.

IN THE BEGINNING: GAG STRIPS

JANUARY 10, 1932

–

JULY 24, 1932

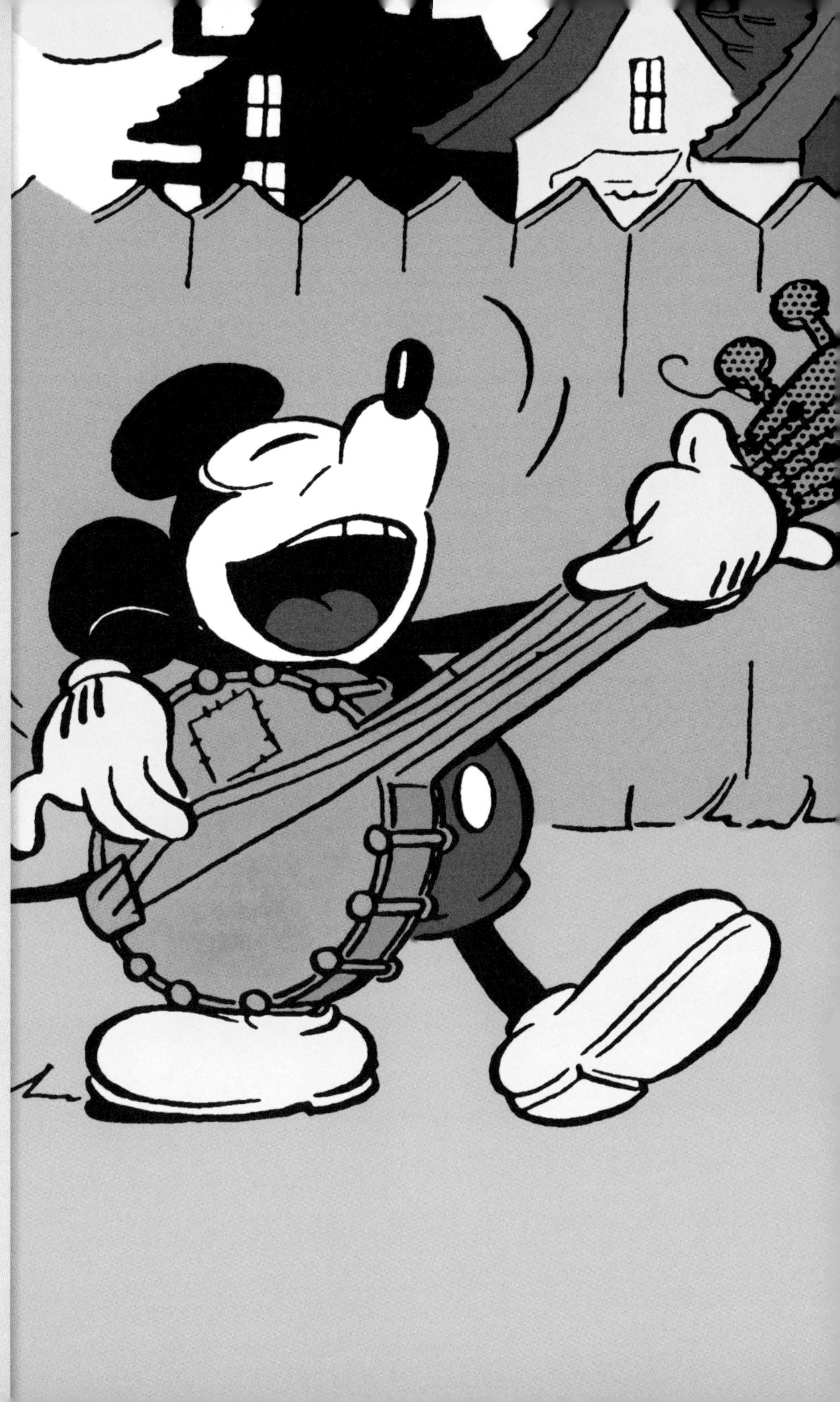

MICKEY MOUSE

REGISTERED U.S. PATENT OFFICE

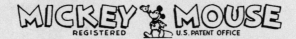

SUNDAY STORYTELLING

While Mickey Mouse successfully entered comics in 1930, the tone of his animated shorts did not. The earliest *Mickey* daily gags tried to mimic cartoon slapstick; but the daily strip, limited to four or five panels per instalment, could only carry slapstick so far. At such a short length, the form felt simple and repetitive. Under Floyd Gottfredson's guiding hand, the daily soon evolved into an adventure serial—and rarely looked back at its cartoony origins.

But there was still a comics canvas where slapstick made sense; where intricate visual gags and extended cartoony situations had more breathing room to develop naturally. This canvas was the *Mickey* Sunday strip. In it, Gottfredson birthed an entirely different animal from the daily; but that in its difference, pioneered several classic storytelling techniques.

One technique involved more sophisticated pacing. Short daily strips had limited space per day to advance their plots; by contrast, Sunday strips had room to let the action stop and start. After setting up a plotline, Gottfredson could pause for comedic—or dramatic—tension as Mickey went about a task, unaware of what lay ahead. He could spend several panels happily stunting on ice, not noticing danger; he might be singing as he worked, unaware of an impending pratfall. The effect was fundamentally cartoonish; many a film short had used lulls to build up to a dramatic climax. But the effect also made for good comics storytelling; a kind that had been spatially impossible before.

A related Sunday-only technique was the gag that escalated. Prefigured, again, by similar structures in animation, the *Mickey* Sunday often involved an activity that got increasingly silly or comically frustrating as it continued; a hard concept to communicate in four panels, but easy to express in twelve. Mickey's setup of a farmyard photoshoot might involve increasing numbers of interfering animals. Mickey's effort to fix Minnie's pipes might extend to the point of enlisting wrench, plunger, pump and hose.

A third cartoon-like technique—often following on an escalating gag—was the final twist. Mickey or another character would attempt to accomplish some goal in an elaborate manner; multiple panels would show complex or frenzied action. But then, with victory or failure seemingly imminent, events would comically reverse themselves. Minnie's pipes might not have the problem Mickey thought they did. The photoshoot, after laborious prep work, might unexpectedly end in embarrassment.

Let's jump into the earliest Floyd Gottfredson Sunday strips—and Earl Duvall's one-time-only predecessor, with its taller aspect ratio–and see how these cartoonish techniques were explored.

(One final cartoonish technique we should note, by the way, is the occasional use of dated content: exaggerated ethnic characters, for instance, or gags about gunplay and smoking. Needless to say, Mickey wouldn't mix it up with these elements today; we include them here, as in our past volumes, with the understanding that they reflect a bygone era.) [DG]

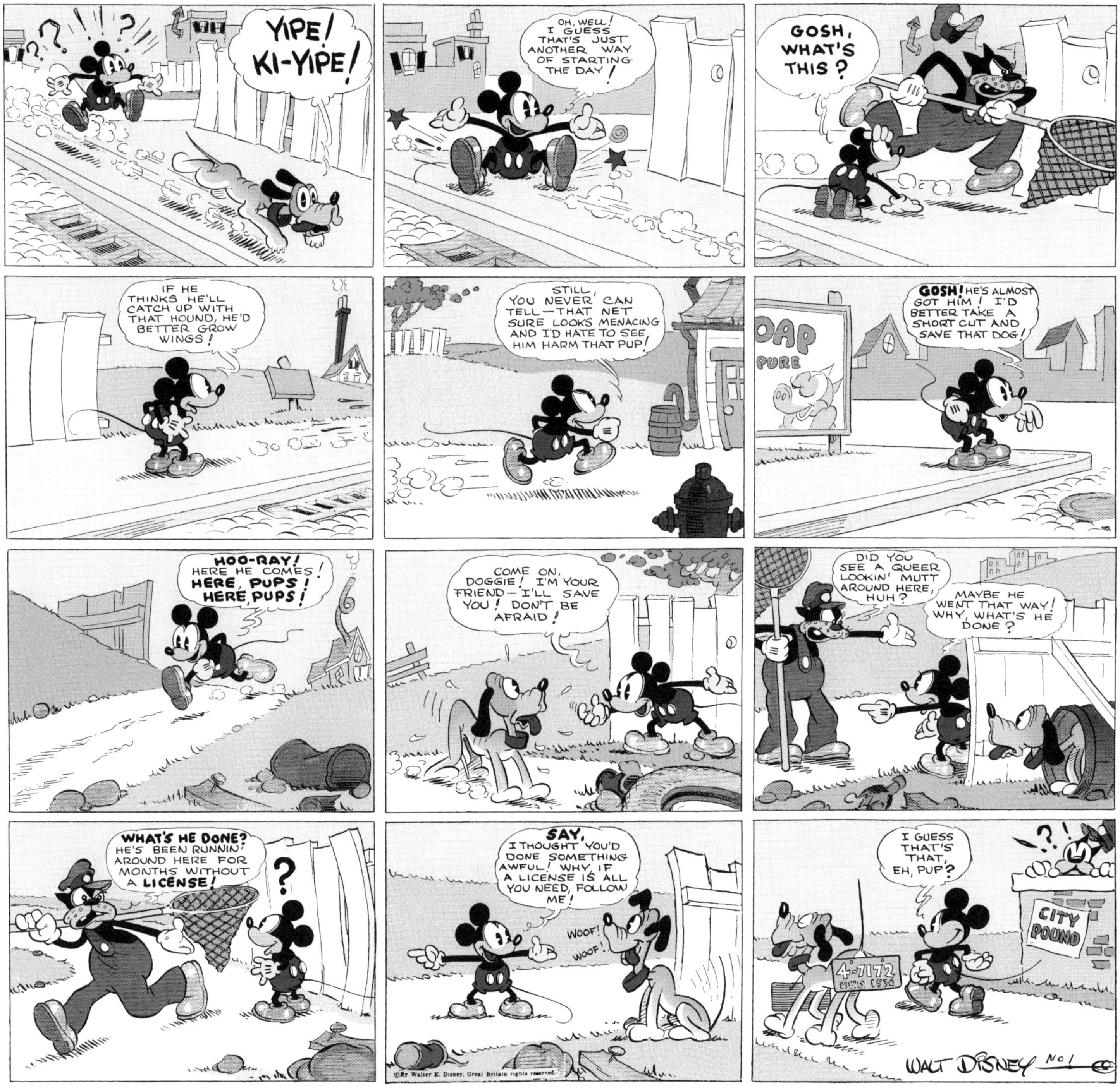
YIPE! KI-YIPE!
OH, WELL! I GUESS THAT'S JUST ANOTHER WAY OF STARTING THE DAY!
GOSH, WHAT'S THIS?
IF HE THINKS HE'LL CATCH UP WITH THAT HOUND, HE'D BETTER GROW WINGS!
STILL, YOU NEVER CAN TELL—THAT NET SURE LOOKS MENACING AND I'D HATE TO SEE HIM HARM THAT PUP!
GOSH! HE'S ALMOST GOT HIM! I'D BETTER TAKE A SHORT CUT AND SAVE THAT DOG!
HOO-RAY! HERE HE COMES! HERE, PUPS! HERE, PUPS!
COME ON, DOGGIE! I'M YOUR FRIEND—I'LL SAVE YOU! DON'T BE AFRAID!
DID YOU SEE A QUEER LOOKIN' MUTT AROUND HERE, HUH?
MAYBE HE WENT THAT WAY! WHY, WHAT'S HE DONE?
WHAT'S HE DONE? HE'S BEEN RUNNIN' AROUND HERE FOR MONTHS WITHOUT A LICENSE!
?
SAY, I THOUGHT YOU'D DONE SOMETHING AWFUL! WHY, IF A LICENSE IS ALL YOU NEED, FOLLOW ME!
WOOF! WOOF!
©By Walter E. Disney, Great Britain rights reserved.
I GUESS THAT'S THAT, EH, PUP?
CITY POUND
4-7172
WALT DISNEY

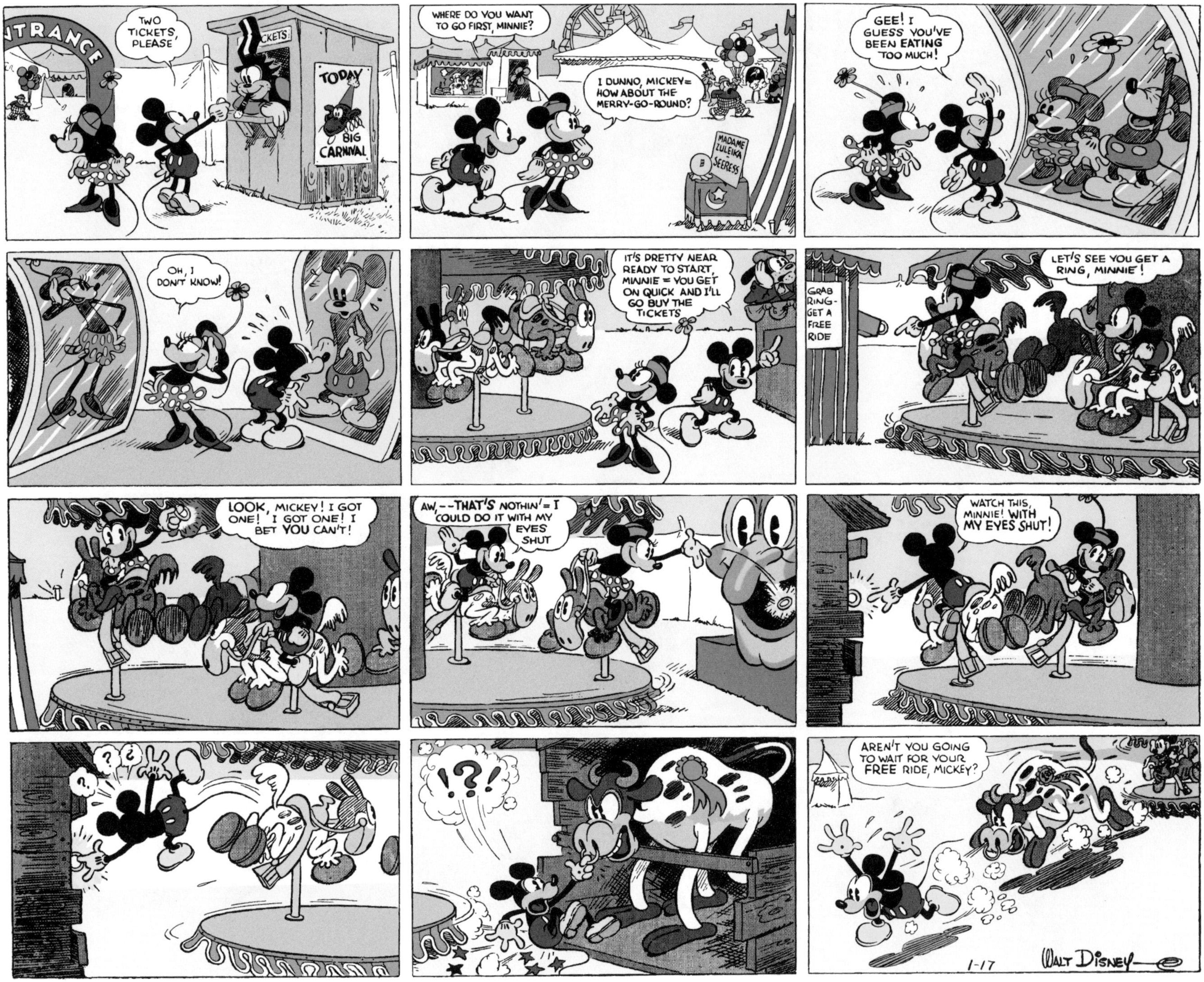

ENTRANCE
TWO TICKETS, PLEASE
TICKETS
TODAY BIG CARNIVAL
WHERE DO YOU WANT TO GO FIRST, MINNIE?
I DUNNO, MICKEY= HOW ABOUT THE MERRY-GO-ROUND?
MADAME ZULEIKA SEERESS
GEE! I GUESS YOU'VE BEEN EATING TOO MUCH!
OH, I DON'T KNOW!
IT'S PRETTY NEAR READY TO START, MINNIE = YOU GET ON QUICK AND I'LL GO BUY THE TICKETS
GRAB RING- GET A FREE RIDE
LET'S SEE YOU GET A RING, MINNIE!
LOOK, MICKEY! I GOT ONE! I GOT ONE! I BET YOU CAN'T!
AW, --THAT'S NOTHIN'= I COULD DO IT WITH MY EYES SHUT
WATCH THIS, MINNIE! WITH MY EYES SHUT!
? ¿ ?
!?!
AREN'T YOU GOING TO WAIT FOR YOUR FREE RIDE, MICKEY?
1-17
WALT DISNEY

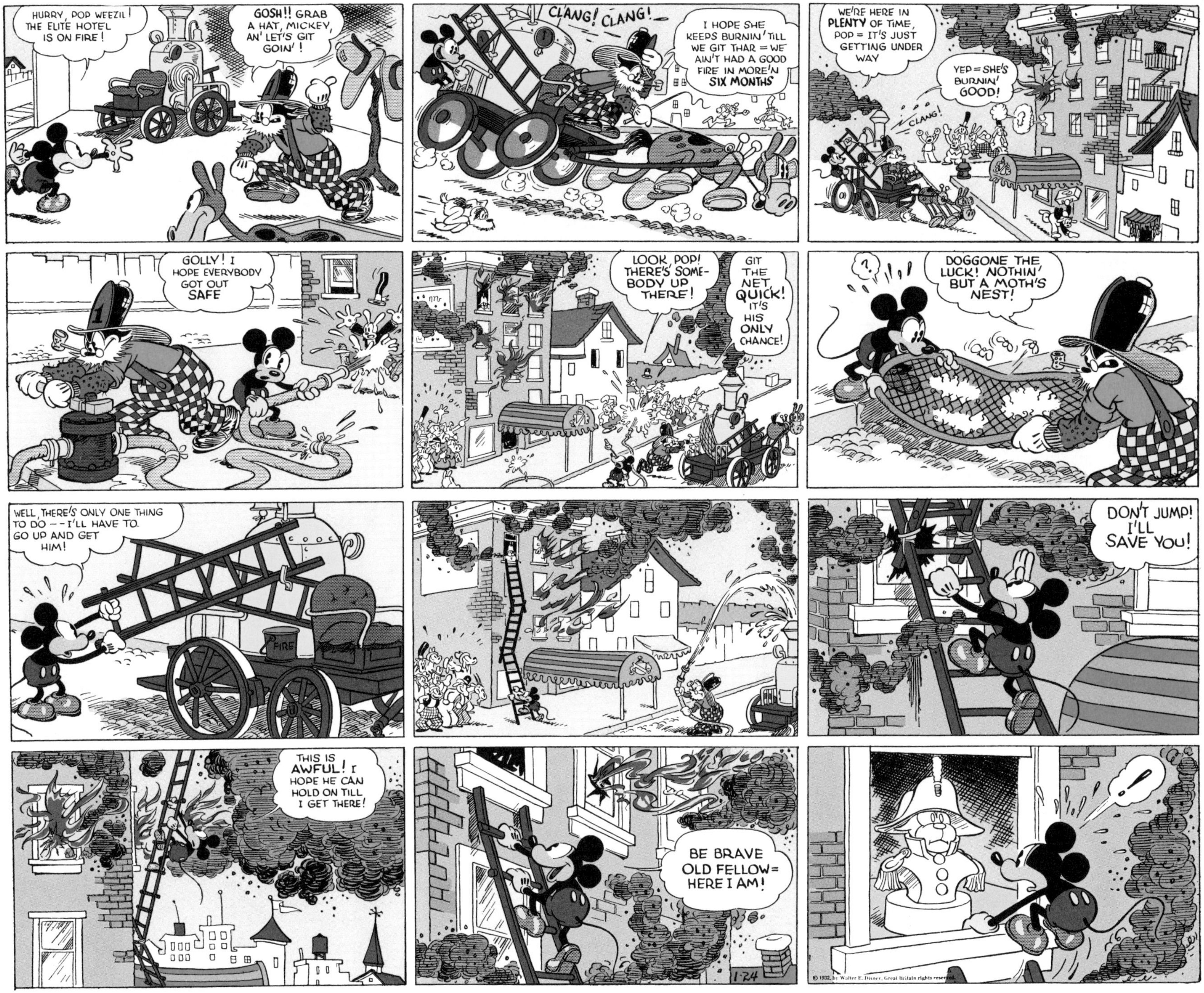

HURRY, POP WEEZIL! THE ELITE HOTEL IS ON FIRE!
GOSH!! GRAB A HAT, MICKEY, AN' LET'S GIT GOIN'!
CLANG! CLANG!
I HOPE SHE KEEPS BURNIN' TILL WE GIT THAR = WE AIN'T HAD A GOOD FIRE IN MORE'N SIX MONTHS
WE'RE HERE IN PLENTY OF TIME, POP = IT'S JUST GETTING UNDER WAY
YEP = SHE'S BURNIN' GOOD!
CLANG!
GOLLY! I HOPE EVERYBODY GOT OUT SAFE
LOOK, POP! THERE'S SOMEBODY UP THERE!
GIT THE NET QUICK! IT'S HIS ONLY CHANCE!
DOGGONE THE LUCK! NOTHIN' BUT A MOTH'S NEST!
WELL, THERE'S ONLY ONE THING TO DO - - I'LL HAVE TO GO UP AND GET HIM!
FIRE
DON'T JUMP! I'LL SAVE YOU!
THIS IS AWFUL! I HOPE HE CAN HOLD ON TILL I GET THERE!
BE BRAVE OLD FELLOW = HERE I AM!
1-24
© 1932, by Walter E. Disney, Great Britain rights reserved.

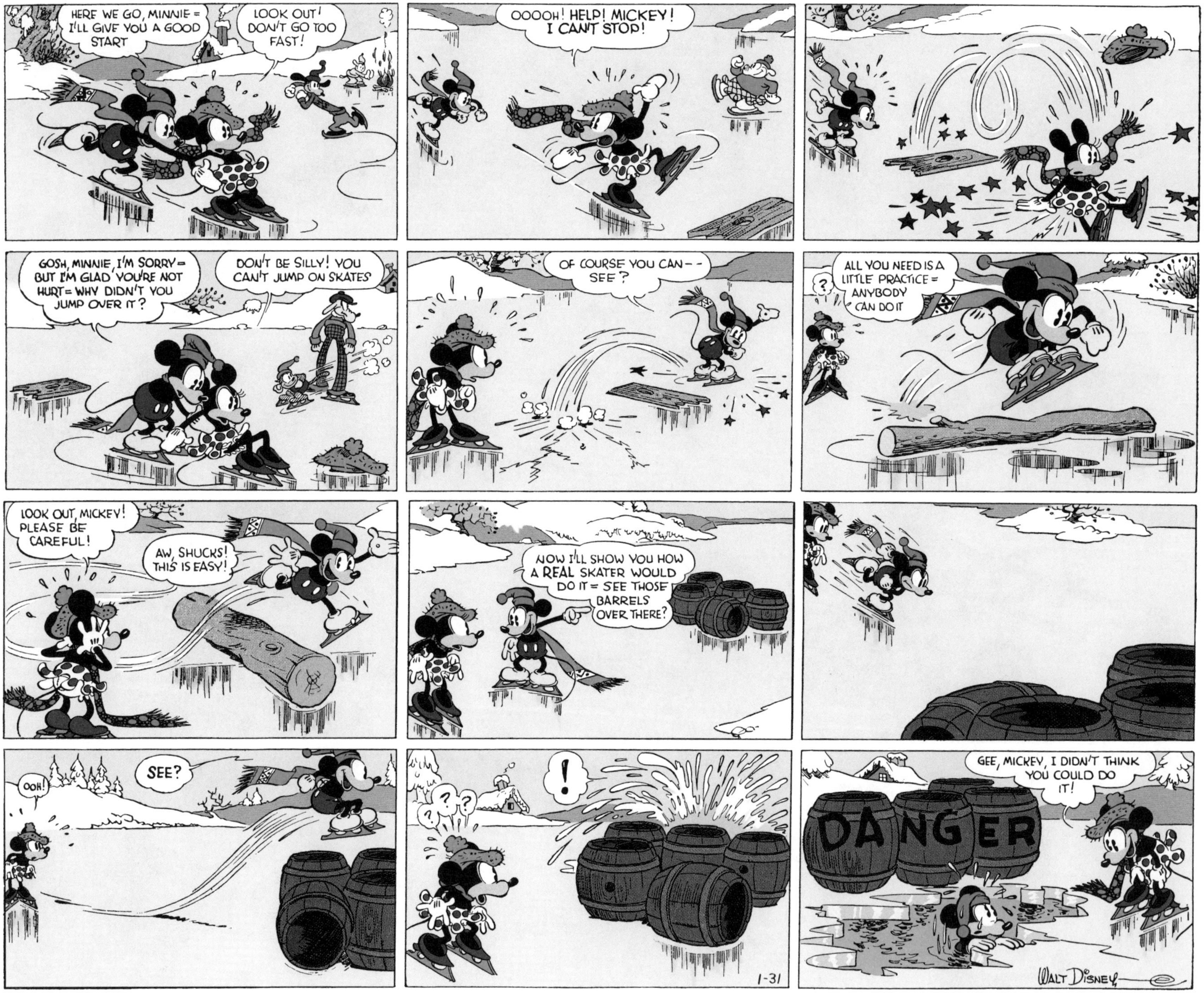
HERE WE GO, MINNIE = I'LL GIVE YOU A GOOD START
LOOK OUT! DON'T GO TOO FAST!
OOOOH! HELP! MICKEY! I CAN'T STOP!
GOSH, MINNIE, I'M SORRY = BUT I'M GLAD YOU'RE NOT HURT = WHY DIDN'T YOU JUMP OVER IT?
DON'T BE SILLY! YOU CAN'T JUMP ON SKATES
OF COURSE YOU CAN - - SEE?
?
ALL YOU NEED IS A LITTLE PRACTICE = ANYBODY CAN DO IT
LOOK OUT, MICKEY! PLEASE BE CAREFUL!
AW, SHUCKS! THIS IS EASY!
NOW I'LL SHOW YOU HOW A REAL SKATER WOULD DO IT = SEE THOSE BARRELS OVER THERE?
OOH!
SEE?
? ? ?
!
1-31
DANGER
GEE, MICKEY, I DIDN'T THINK YOU COULD DO IT!
WALT DISNEY

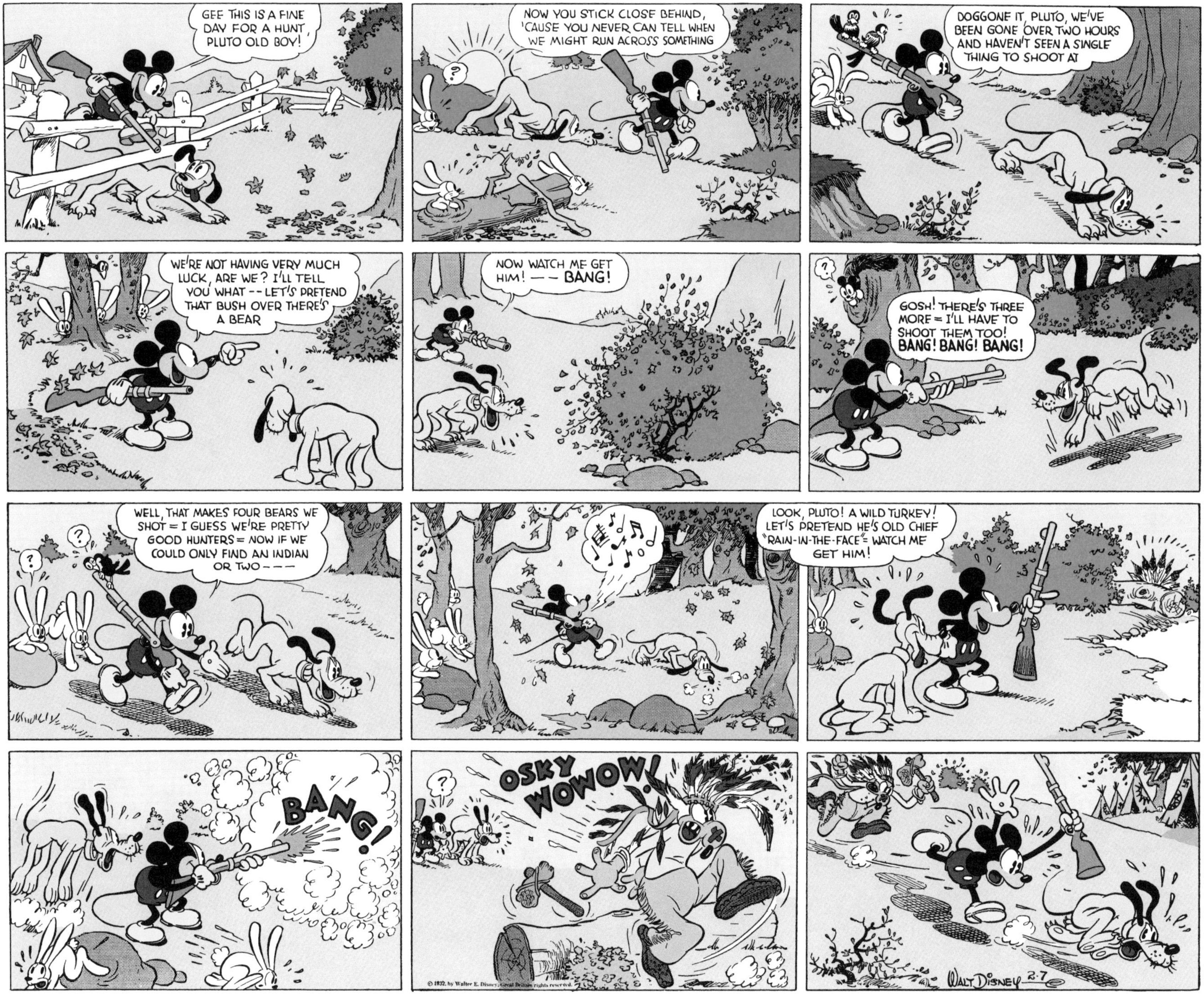

GEE THIS IS A FINE DAY FOR A HUNT PLUTO OLD BOY!
NOW YOU STICK CLOSE BEHIND, 'CAUSE YOU NEVER CAN TELL WHEN WE MIGHT RUN ACROSS SOMETHING
?
DOGGONE IT, PLUTO, WE'VE BEEN GONE OVER TWO HOURS AND HAVEN'T SEEN A SINGLE THING TO SHOOT AT
WE'RE NOT HAVING VERY MUCH LUCK, ARE WE? I'LL TELL YOU WHAT -- LET'S PRETEND THAT BUSH OVER THERE'S A BEAR
NOW WATCH ME GET HIM! --- BANG!
?
GOSH! THERE'S THREE MORE = I'LL HAVE TO SHOOT THEM TOO! BANG! BANG! BANG!
?
?
WELL, THAT MAKES FOUR BEARS WE SHOT = I GUESS WE'RE PRETTY GOOD HUNTERS = NOW IF WE COULD ONLY FIND AN INDIAN OR TWO ---
LOOK, PLUTO! A WILD TURKEY! LET'S PRETEND HE'S OLD CHIEF "RAIN-IN-THE-FACE" = WATCH ME GET HIM!
BANG!
?
OSKY WOWOW!
© 1932, by Walter E. Disney, Great Britain rights reserved.
WALT DISNEY 2-7

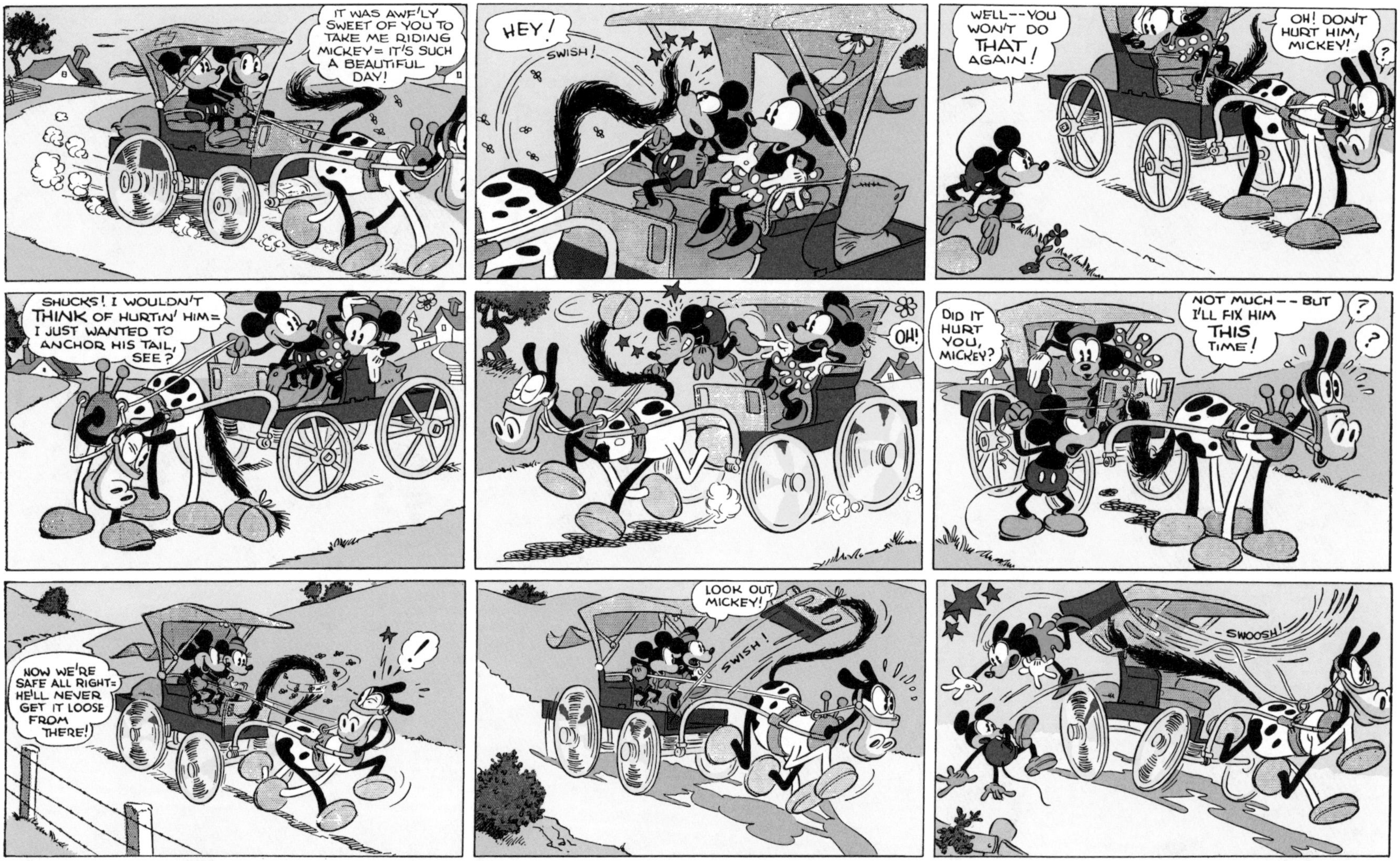
IT WAS AWF'LY SWEET OF YOU TO TAKE ME RIDING MICKEY= IT'S SUCH A BEAUTIFUL DAY!
HEY!
SWISH!
WELL--YOU WON'T DO THAT AGAIN!
OH! DON'T HURT HIM, MICKEY!
?
SHUCKS! I WOULDN'T THINK OF HURTIN' HIM= I JUST WANTED TO ANCHOR HIS TAIL, SEE?
OH!
DID IT HURT YOU, MICKEY?
NOT MUCH--BUT I'LL FIX HIM THIS TIME!
?
?
NOW WE'RE SAFE ALL RIGHT= HE'LL NEVER GET IT LOOSE FROM THERE!
!
LOOK OUT, MICKEY!
SWISH!
-SWOOSH!
WELL, DOGGONE IT, I'M TIRED OF FOOLING AROUND= YOU'VE HIT ME FOR THE LAST TIME!
THERE!
2-14
WALT DISNEY ©

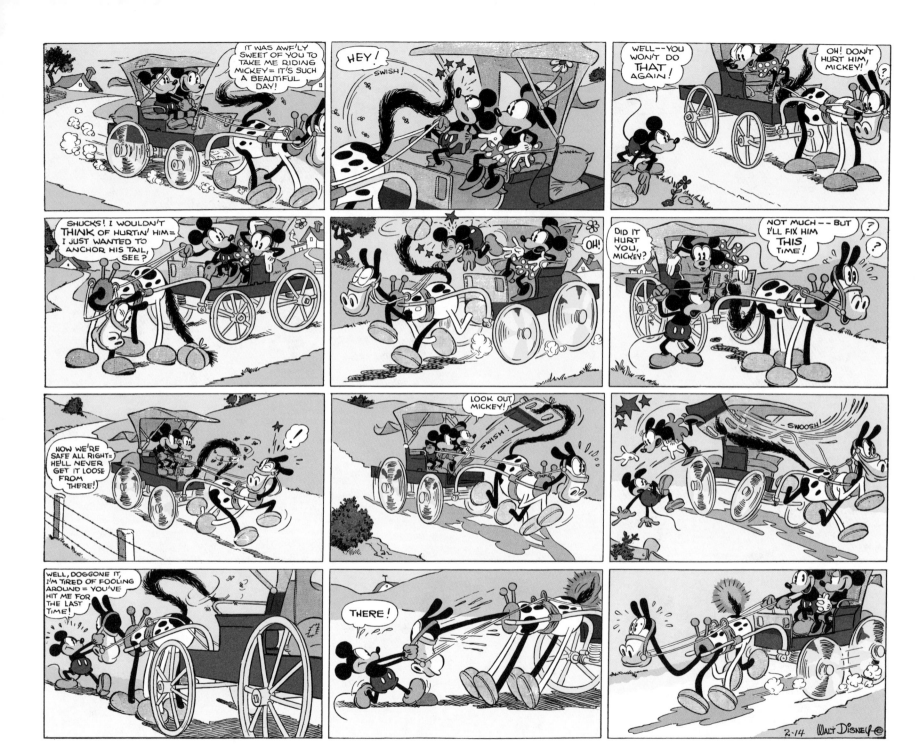

24. RUBBERNECKER

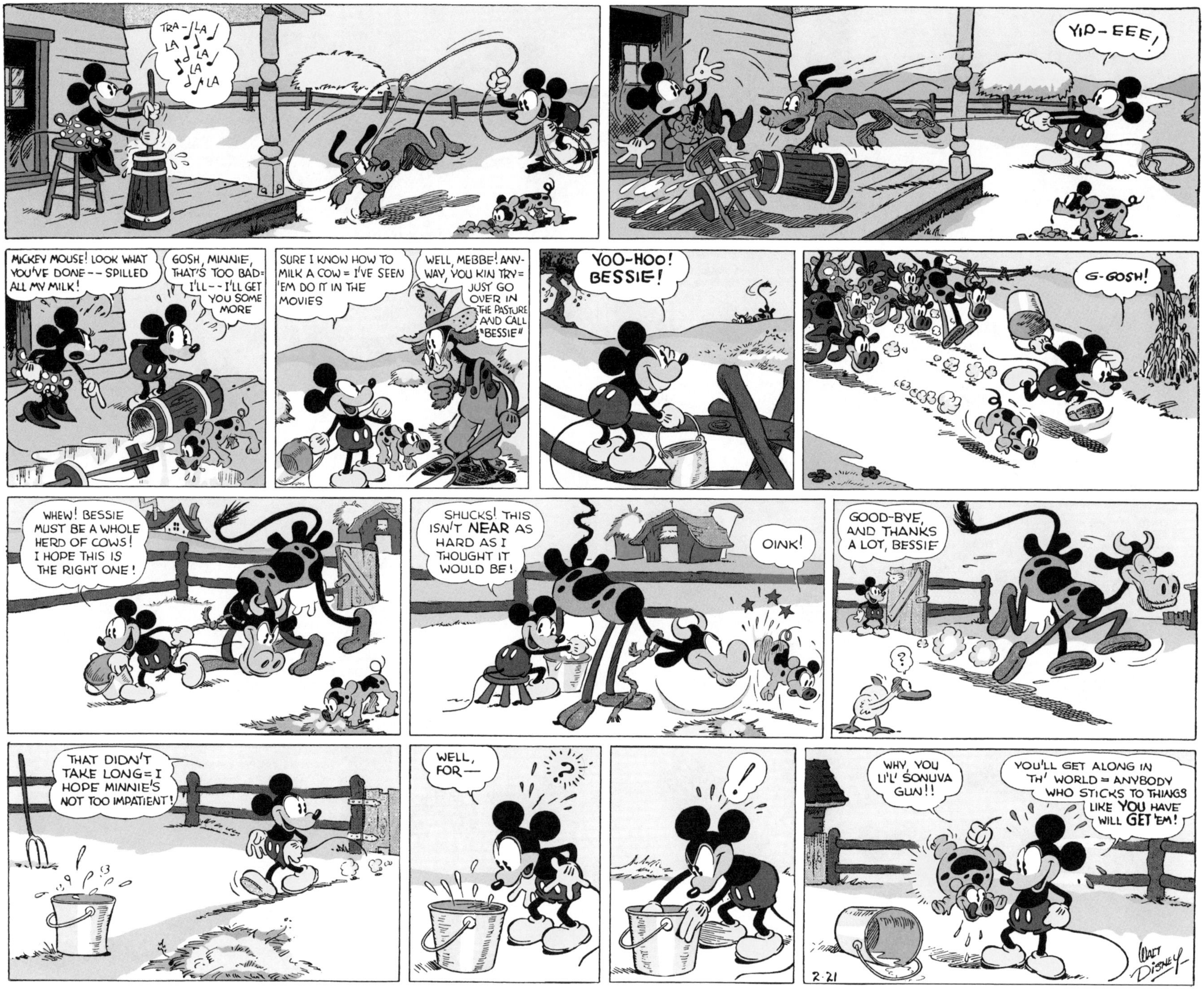
TRA-LA LA LA LA LA
YIP-EEE!
MICKEY MOUSE! LOOK WHAT YOU'VE DONE--SPILLED ALL MY MILK!
GOSH, MINNIE, THAT'S TOO BAD= I'LL--I'LL GET YOU SOME MORE
SURE I KNOW HOW TO MILK A COW= I'VE SEEN 'EM DO IT IN THE MOVIES
WELL, MEBBE! ANY-WAY, YOU KIN TRY= JUST GO OVER IN THE PASTURE AND CALL "BESSIE"
YOO-HOO! BESSIE!
G-GOSH!
WHEW! BESSIE MUST BE A WHOLE HERD OF COWS! I HOPE THIS IS THE RIGHT ONE!
SHUCKS! THIS ISN'T NEAR AS HARD AS I THOUGHT IT WOULD BE!
OINK!
GOOD-BYE, AND THANKS A LOT, BESSIE
?
THAT DIDN'T TAKE LONG= I HOPE MINNIE'S NOT TOO IMPATIENT!
WELL, FOR—
?
!
WHY, YOU LI'L' SONUVA GUN!!
YOU'LL GET ALONG IN TH' WORLD= ANYBODY WHO STICKS TO THINGS LIKE YOU HAVE WILL GET 'EM!
2-21
WALT DISNEY

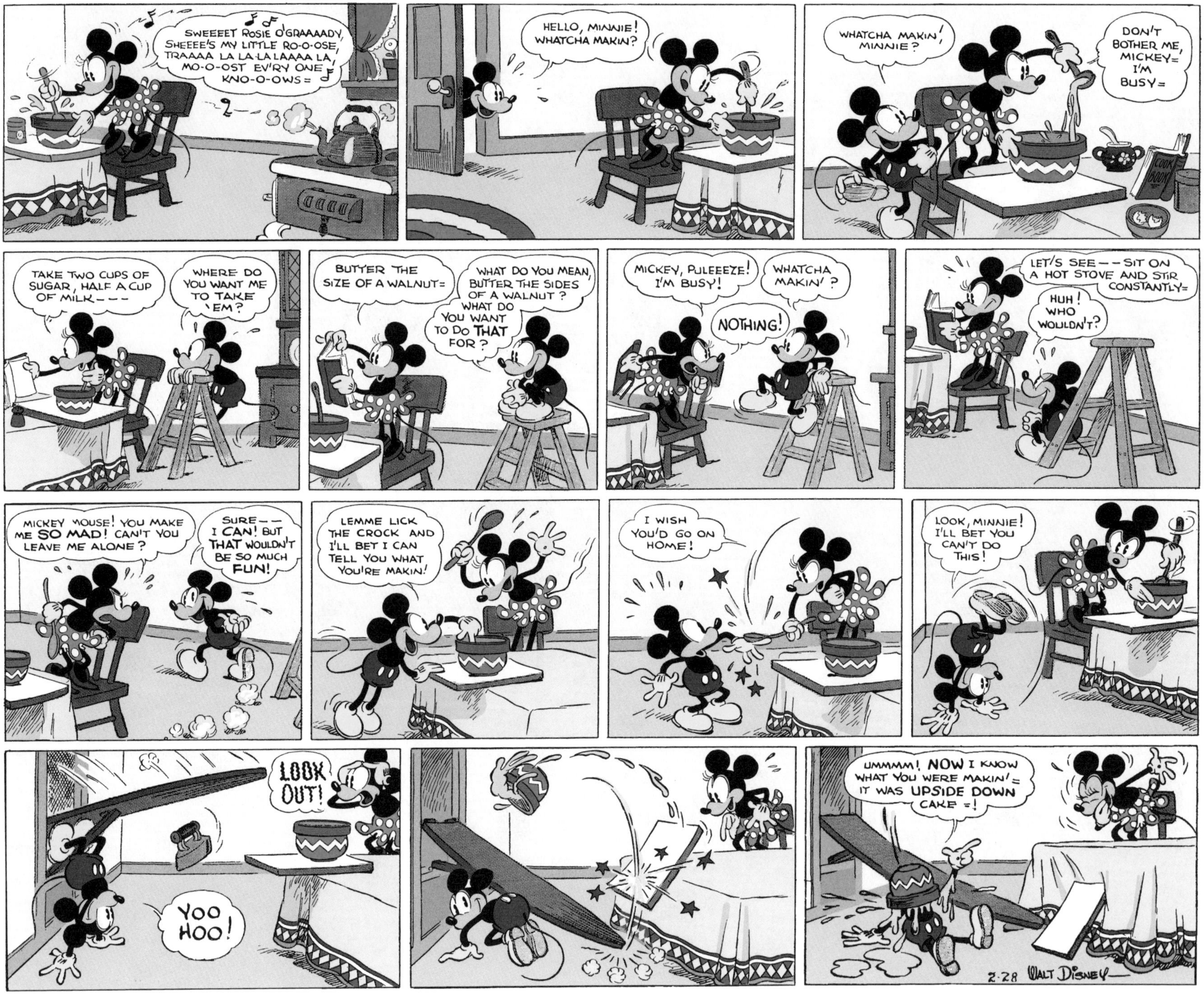
SWEEEET ROSIE O'GRAAAADY, SHEEEE'S MY LITTLE RO-O-OSE, TRAAAA LA LA-LA LAAAA LA MO-O-OST EV'RY ONE KNO-O-OWS=
HELLO, MINNIE! WHATCHA MAKIN?
WHATCHA MAKIN', MINNIE?
DON'T BOTHER ME, MICKEY= I'M BUSY=
TAKE TWO CUPS OF SUGAR, HALF A CUP OF MILK---
WHERE DO YOU WANT ME TO TAKE 'EM?
BUTTER THE SIZE OF A WALNUT=
WHAT DO YOU MEAN, BUTTER THE SIDES OF A WALNUT? WHAT DO YOU WANT TO DO THAT FOR?
MICKEY, PULEEEEZE! I'M BUSY!
WHATCHA MAKIN'?
NOTHING!
LET'S SEE--SIT ON A HOT STOVE AND STIR CONSTANTLY=
HUH! WHO WOULDN'T?
MICKEY MOUSE! YOU MAKE ME SO MAD! CAN'T YOU LEAVE ME ALONE?
SURE-- I CAN! BUT THAT WOULDN'T BE SO MUCH FUN!
LEMME LICK THE CROCK AND I'LL BET I CAN TELL YOU WHAT YOU'RE MAKIN'!
I WISH YOU'D GO ON HOME!
LOOK, MINNIE! I'LL BET YOU CAN'T DO THIS!
LOOK OUT!
YOO HOO!
UMMMM! NOW I KNOW WHAT YOU WERE MAKIN'= IT WAS UPSIDE DOWN CAKE =!
2-28 WALT DISNEY

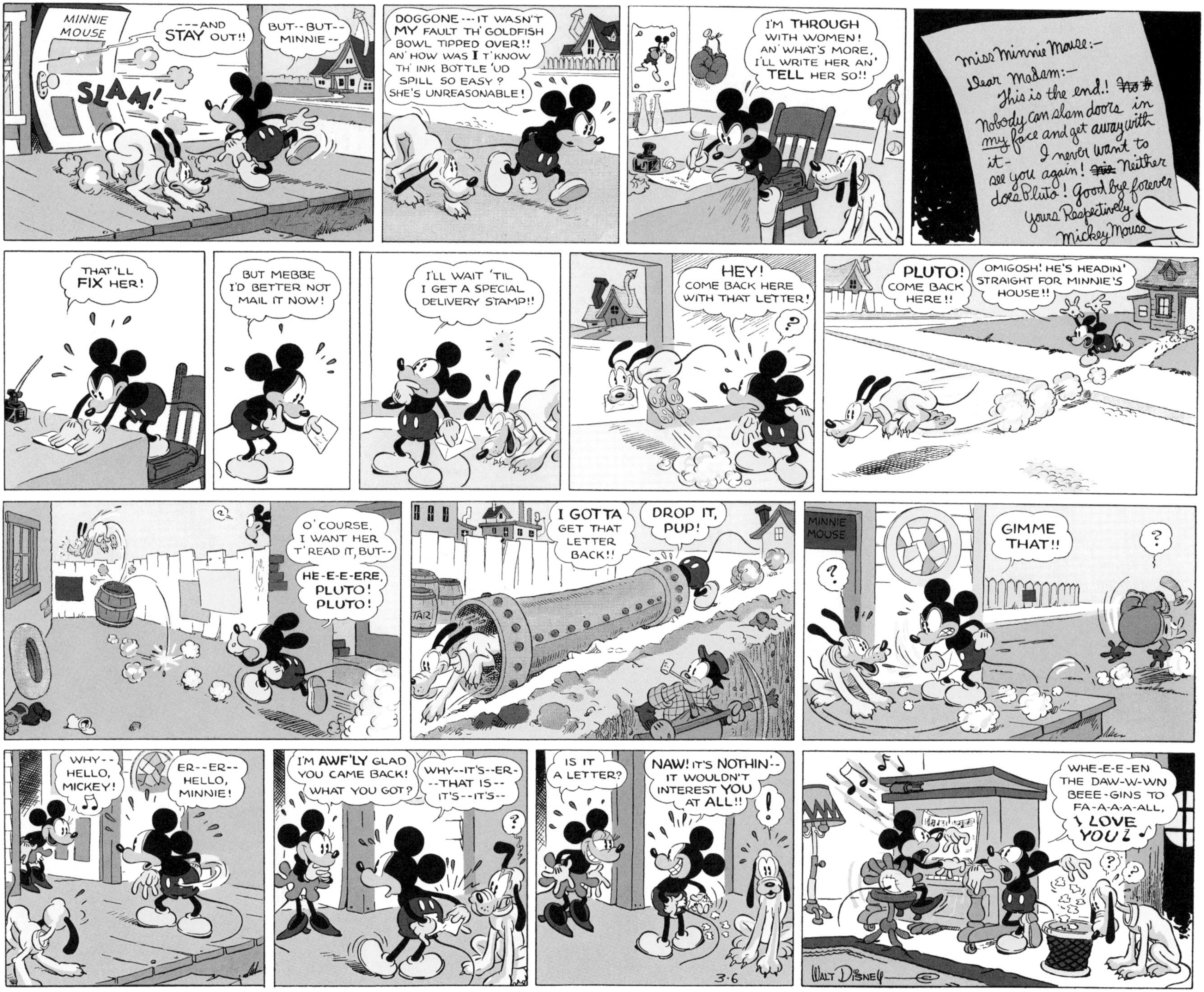

MINNIE MOUSE
---AND STAY OUT!!
SLAM!
BUT--BUT--MINNIE--
DOGGONE---IT WASN'T MY FAULT TH' GOLDFISH BOWL TIPPED OVER!! AN' HOW WAS I T'KNOW TH' INK BOTTLE 'UD SPILL SO EASY? SHE'S UNREASONABLE!
I'M THROUGH WITH WOMEN! AN' WHAT'S MORE, I'LL WRITE HER AN' TELL HER SO!!
Miss Minnie Mouse:-
Dear Madam:-
This is the end.!
Nobody can slam doors in my face and get away with it- I never want to see you again! Neither does Pluto! Good bye forever
Yours Respectively
Mickey Mouse
THAT'LL FIX HER!
BUT MEBBE I'D BETTER NOT MAIL IT NOW!
I'LL WAIT 'TIL I GET A SPECIAL DELIVERY STAMP!!
HEY! COME BACK HERE WITH THAT LETTER!
PLUTO! COME BACK HERE!!
OMIGOSH! HE'S HEADIN' STRAIGHT FOR MINNIE'S HOUSE!!
O' COURSE, I WANT HER T' READ IT, BUT--
HE-E-E-ERE, PLUTO! PLUTO!
I GOTTA GET THAT LETTER BACK!!
DROP IT, PUP!
TAR
MINNIE MOUSE
GIMME THAT!!
WHY--HELLO, MICKEY!
ER--ER--HELLO, MINNIE!
I'M AWF'LY GLAD YOU CAME BACK! WHAT YOU GOT?
WHY--IT'S--ER--THAT IS--IT'S--IT'S--
IS IT A LETTER?
NAW! IT'S NOTHIN'--IT WOULDN'T INTEREST YOU AT ALL!!
3·6
WHE-E-E-EN THE DAW-W-WN BEEE-GINS TO FA-A-A-A-ALL, I LOVE YOU!
WALT DISNEY

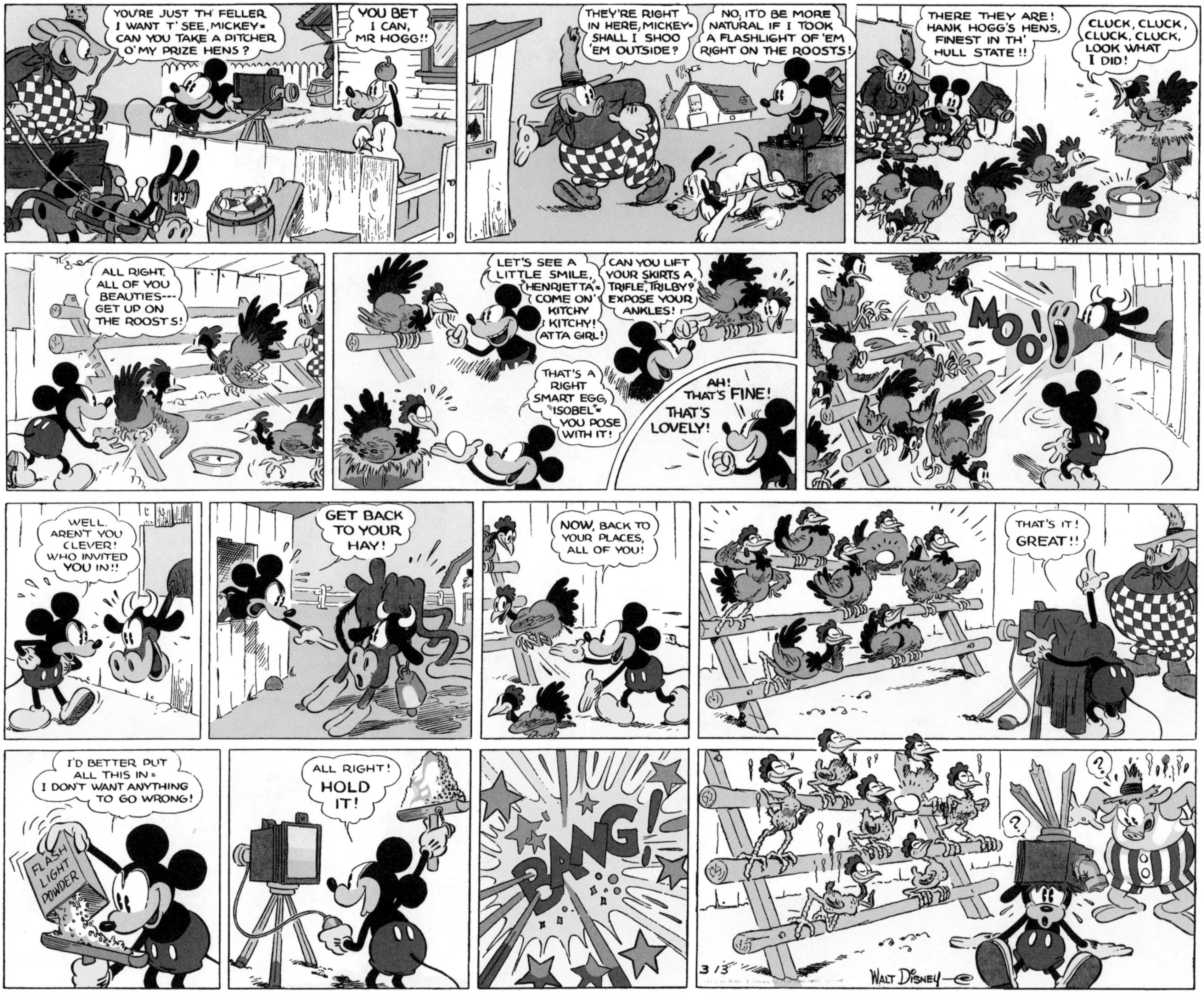

YOU'RE JUST TH' FELLER I WANT T' SEE, MICKEY= CAN YOU TAKE A PITCHER O' MY PRIZE HENS ?
YOU BET I CAN, MR HOGG!!
THEY'RE RIGHT IN HERE, MICKEY= SHALL I SHOO 'EM OUTSIDE?
NO, IT'D BE MORE NATURAL IF I TOOK A FLASHLIGHT OF 'EM RIGHT ON THE ROOSTS!
THERE THEY ARE! HANK HOGG'S HENS, FINEST IN TH' HULL STATE!!
CLUCK, CLUCK, CLUCK, CLUCK, LOOK WHAT I DID!
ALL RIGHT, ALL OF YOU BEAUTIES--- GET UP ON THE ROOSTS!
LET'S SEE A LITTLE SMILE, "HENRIETTA"= COME ON' KITCHY KITCHY! ATTA GIRL!
CAN YOU LIFT YOUR SKIRTS A TRIFLE, "TRILBY"? EXPOSE YOUR ANKLES!
THAT'S A RIGHT SMART EGG, "ISOBEL"= YOU POSE WITH IT!
AH! THAT'S FINE!
THAT'S LOVELY!
MOO!
WELL, AREN'T YOU CLEVER! WHO INVITED YOU IN!!
GET BACK TO YOUR HAY!
NOW, BACK TO YOUR PLACES, ALL OF YOU!
THAT'S IT! GREAT!!
I'D BETTER PUT ALL THIS IN= I DON'T WANT ANYTHING TO GO WRONG!
FLASH LIGHT POWDER
ALL RIGHT! HOLD IT!
BANG!
3/13
WALT DISNEY

28. MICKEY EGGS 'EM ON

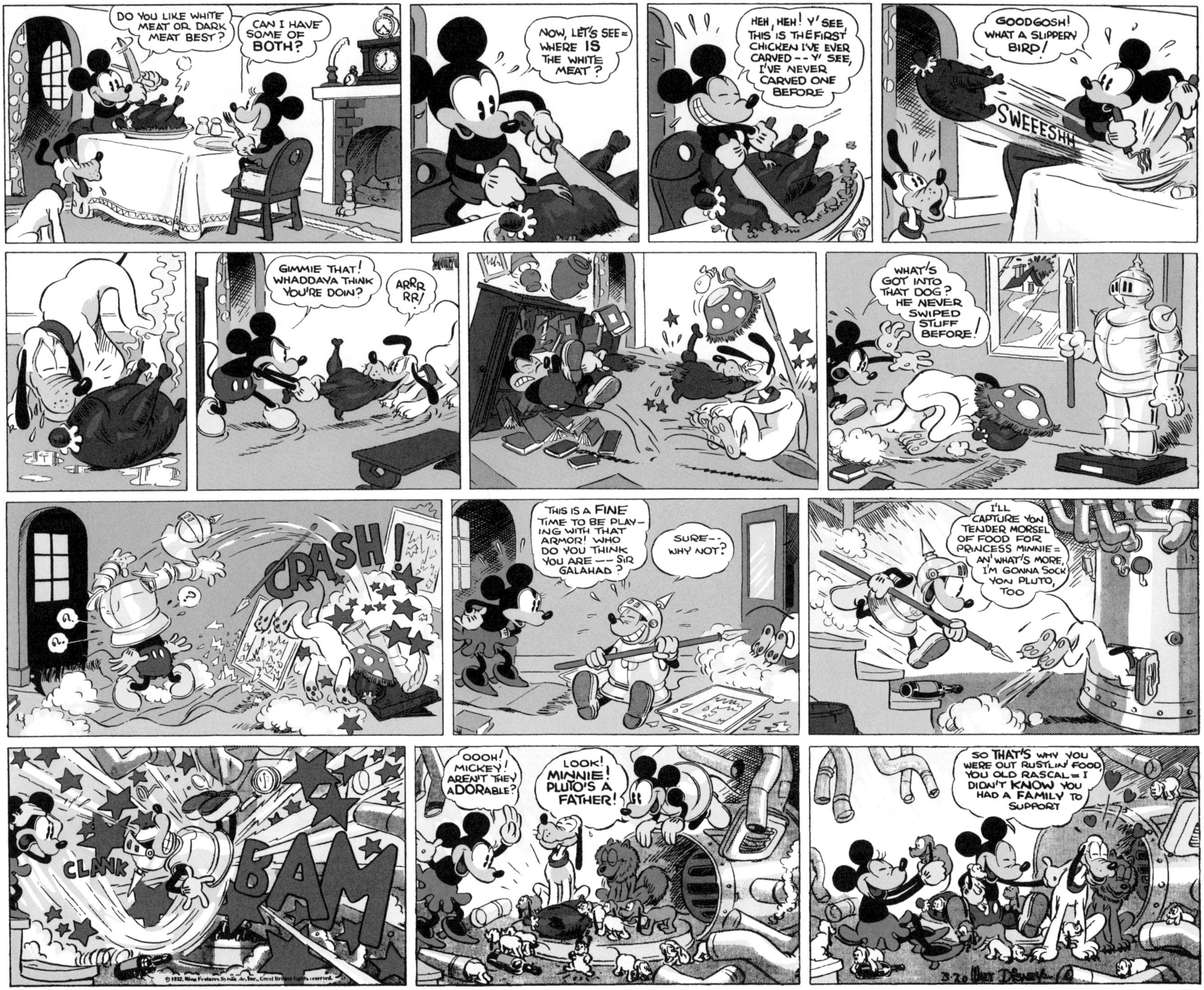
DO YOU LIKE WHITE MEAT OR DARK MEAT BEST?
CAN I HAVE SOME OF BOTH?
NOW, LET'S SEE = WHERE IS THE WHITE MEAT?
HEH, HEH! Y' SEE, THIS IS THE FIRST CHICKEN I'VE EVER CARVED -- Y' SEE, I'VE NEVER CARVED ONE BEFORE
GOOD GOSH! WHAT A SLIPPERY BIRD!
SWEEESHH
GIMMIE THAT! WHADDAYA THINK YOU'RE DOIN?
ARRR RR!
WHAT'S GOT INTO THAT DOG? HE NEVER SWIPED STUFF BEFORE!
CRASH!
THIS IS A FINE TIME TO BE PLAYING WITH THAT ARMOR! WHO DO YOU THINK YOU ARE -- SIR GALAHAD?
SURE -- WHY NOT?
I'LL CAPTURE YON TENDER MORSEL OF FOOD FOR PRINCESS MINNIE = AN' WHAT'S MORE, I'M GONNA SOCK YON PLUTO, TOO
CLANK
BAM
© 1932, King Features Syndicate, Inc., Great Britain rights reserved.
OOOH! MICKEY! AREN'T THEY ADORABLE?
LOOK! MINNIE! PLUTO'S A FATHER!
SO THAT'S WHY YOU WERE OUT RUSTLIN' FOOD, YOU OLD RASCAL = I DIDN'T KNOW YOU HAD A FAMILY TO SUPPORT
3-20 WALT DISNEY

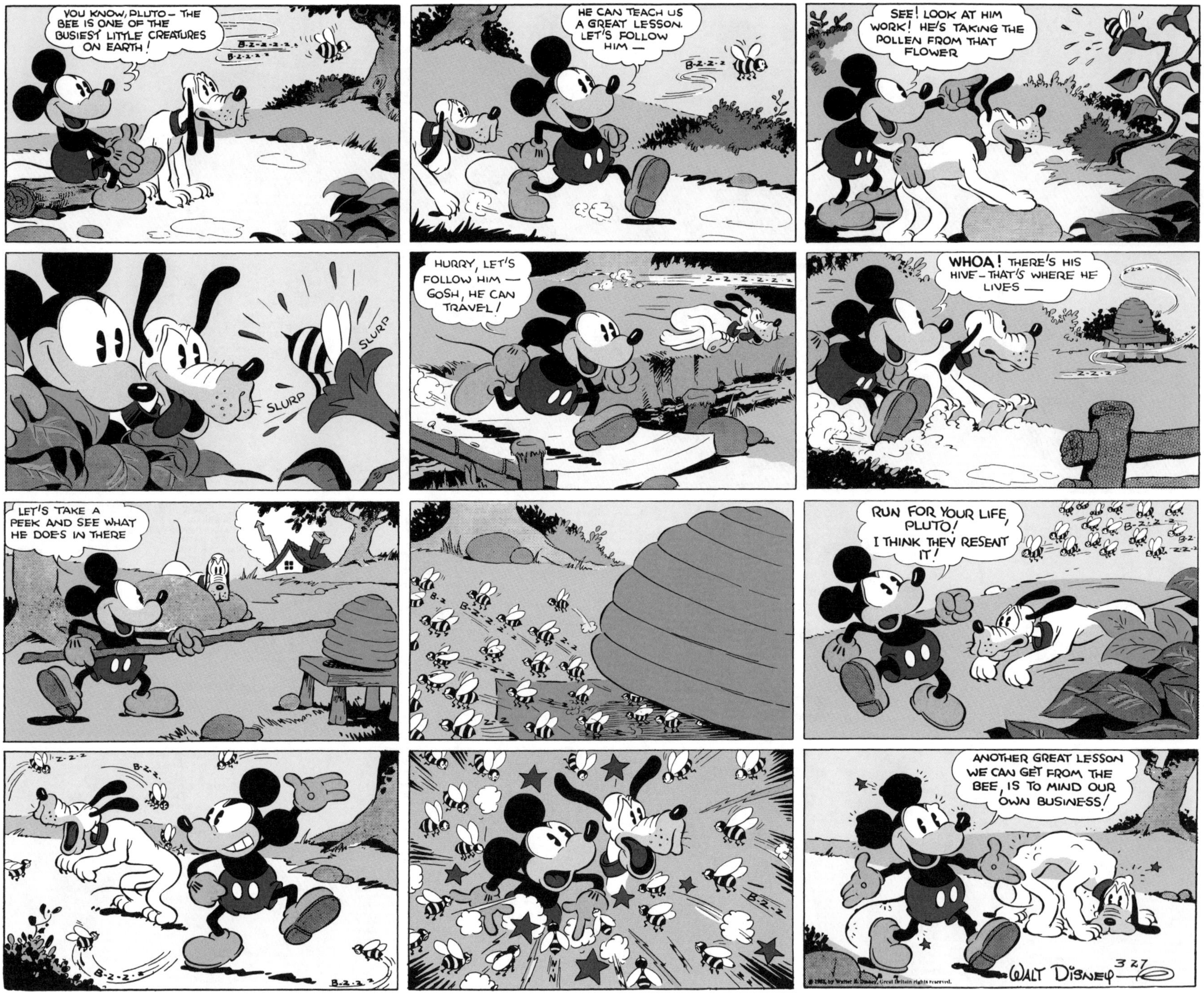
YOU KNOW, PLUTO – THE BEE IS ONE OF THE BUSIEST LITTLE CREATURES ON EARTH!
B-Z-Z-Z-Z
B-Z-Z-Z
HE CAN TEACH US A GREAT LESSON. LET'S FOLLOW HIM —
B-Z-Z-Z
SEE! LOOK AT HIM WORK! HE'S TAKING THE POLLEN FROM THAT FLOWER
SLURP
SLURP
HURRY, LET'S FOLLOW HIM — GOSH, HE CAN TRAVEL!
Z-Z-Z-Z-Z-Z-Z
WHOA! THERE'S HIS HIVE – THAT'S WHERE HE LIVES —
Z-Z-Z
LET'S TAKE A PEEK AND SEE WHAT HE DOES IN THERE
RUN FOR YOUR LIFE, PLUTO! I THINK THEY RESENT IT!
B-Z-Z-Z
Z-Z-Z
B-Z-Z
B-Z-Z-Z
B-Z-Z-Z
B-Z-Z
ANOTHER GREAT LESSON WE CAN GET FROM THE BEE, IS TO MIND OUR OWN BUSINESS!
WALT DISNEY
3-27

30. TO BEE OR NOT TO BEE

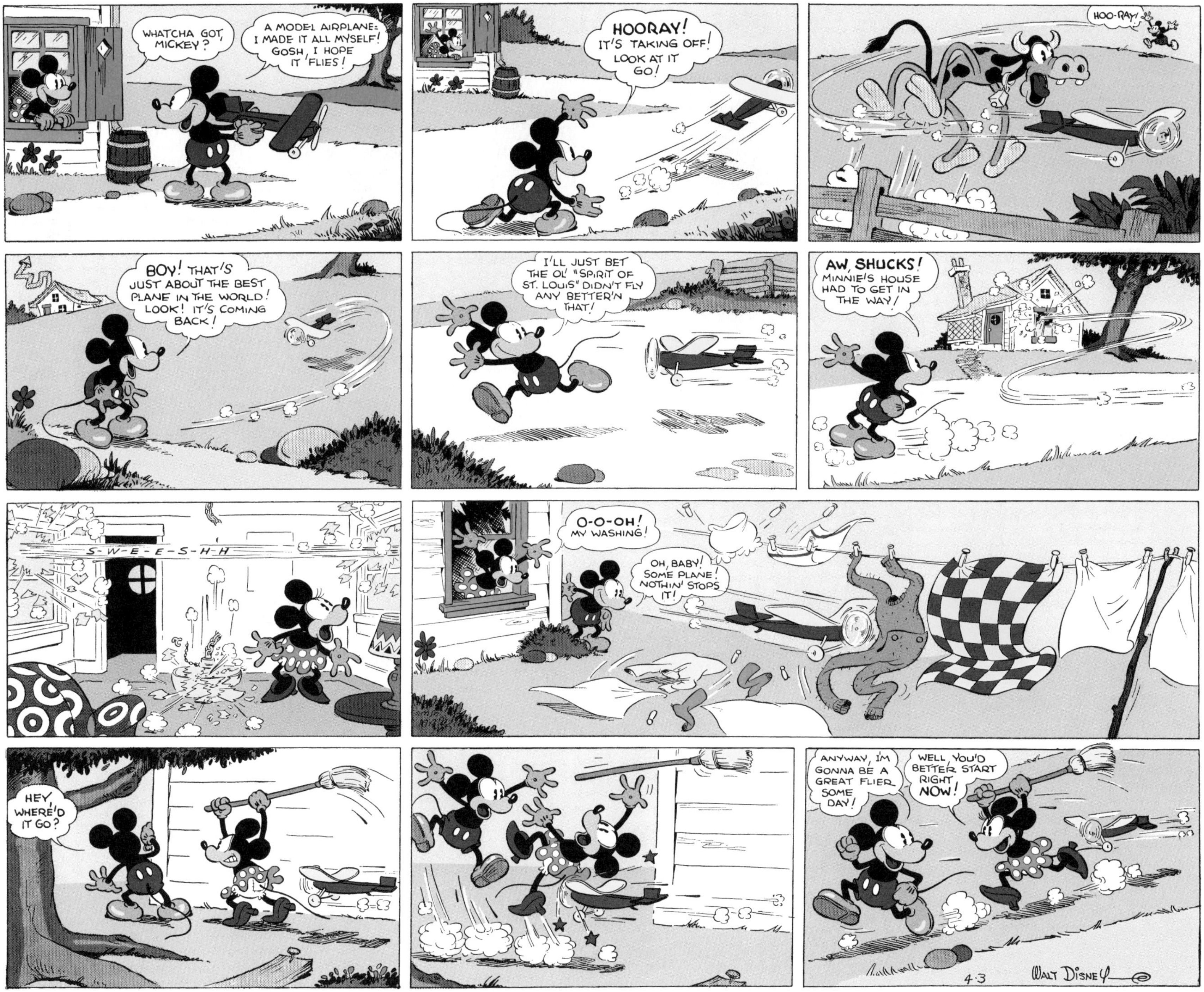

WHATCHA GOT, MICKEY?
A MODEL AIRPLANE - I MADE IT ALL MYSELF! GOSH, I HOPE IT FLIES!
HOORAY! IT'S TAKING OFF! LOOK AT IT GO!
HOO-RAY!
BOY! THAT'S JUST ABOUT THE BEST PLANE IN THE WORLD! LOOK! IT'S COMING BACK!
I'LL JUST BET THE OL' "SPIRIT OF ST. LOUIS" DIDN'T FLY ANY BETTER'N THAT!
AW, SHUCKS! MINNIE'S HOUSE HAD TO GET IN THE WAY!
S-W-E-E-S-H-H
O-O-OH! MY WASHING!
OH, BABY! SOME PLANE! NOTHIN' STOPS IT!
HEY, WHERE'D IT GO?
ANYWAY, I'M GONNA BE A GREAT FLIER SOME DAY!
WELL, YOU'D BETTER START RIGHT NOW!
4-3
WALT DISNEY

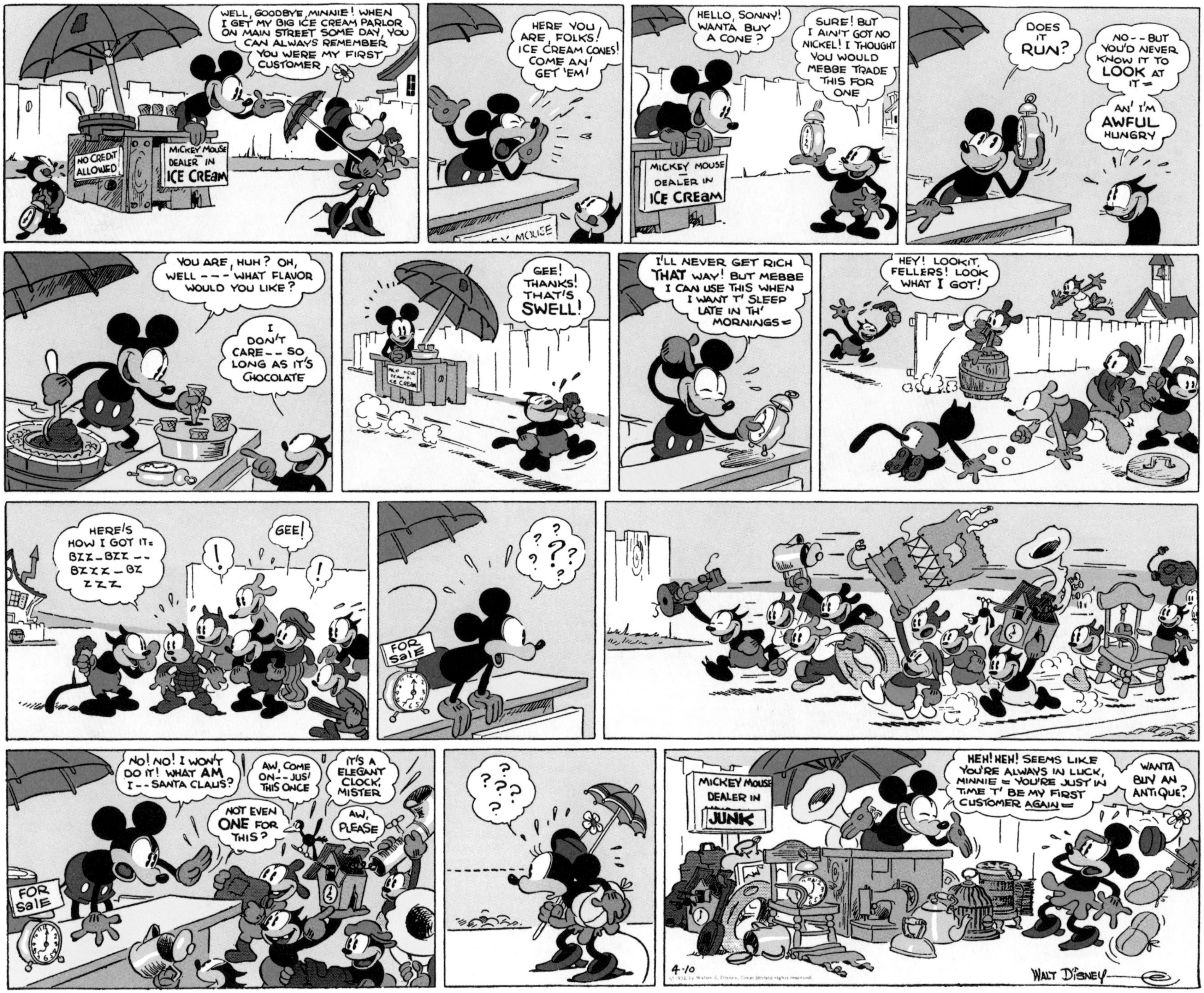
WELL, GOODBYE, MINNIE! WHEN I GET MY BIG ICE CREAM PARLOR ON MAIN STREET SOME DAY, YOU CAN ALWAYS REMEMBER YOU WERE MY FIRST CUSTOMER
NO CREDIT ALLOWED
MICKEY MOUSE DEALER IN ICE CREAM
HERE YOU ARE, FOLKS! ICE CREAM CONES! COME AN' GET 'EM!
HELLO, SONNY! WANTA BUY A CONE?
SURE! BUT I AIN'T GOT NO NICKEL! I THOUGHT YOU WOULD MEBBE TRADE THIS FOR ONE
MICKEY MOUSE DEALER IN ICE CREAM
DOES IT RUN?
NO-- BUT YOU'D NEVER KNOW IT TO LOOK AT IT =
AN' I'M AWFUL HUNGRY
YOU ARE, HUH? OH, WELL --- WHAT FLAVOR WOULD YOU LIKE?
I DON'T CARE-- SO LONG AS IT'S CHOCOLATE
GEE! THANKS! THAT'S SWELL!
I'LL NEVER GET RICH THAT WAY! BUT MEBBE I CAN USE THIS WHEN I WANT T' SLEEP LATE IN TH' MORNINGS =
HEY! LOOKIT, FELLERS! LOOK WHAT I GOT!
HERE'S HOW I GOT IT= BZZ_BZZ -- BZZZ_BZ ZZZ
!
GEE!
!
FOR SALE
NO! NO! I WON'T DO IT! WHAT AM I--SANTA CLAUS?
AW, COME ON--JUS' THIS ONCE
IT'S A ELEGANT CLOCK, MISTER
NOT EVEN ONE FOR THIS?
AW, PLEASE
FOR SALE
MICKEY MOUSE DEALER IN JUNK
HEH! HEH! SEEMS LIKE YOU'RE ALWAYS IN LUCK, MINNIE = YOU'RE JUST IN TIME T' BE MY FIRST CUSTOMER AGAIN =
WANTA BUY AN ANTIQUE?
4-10
WALT DISNEY

32. TRADE SECRET

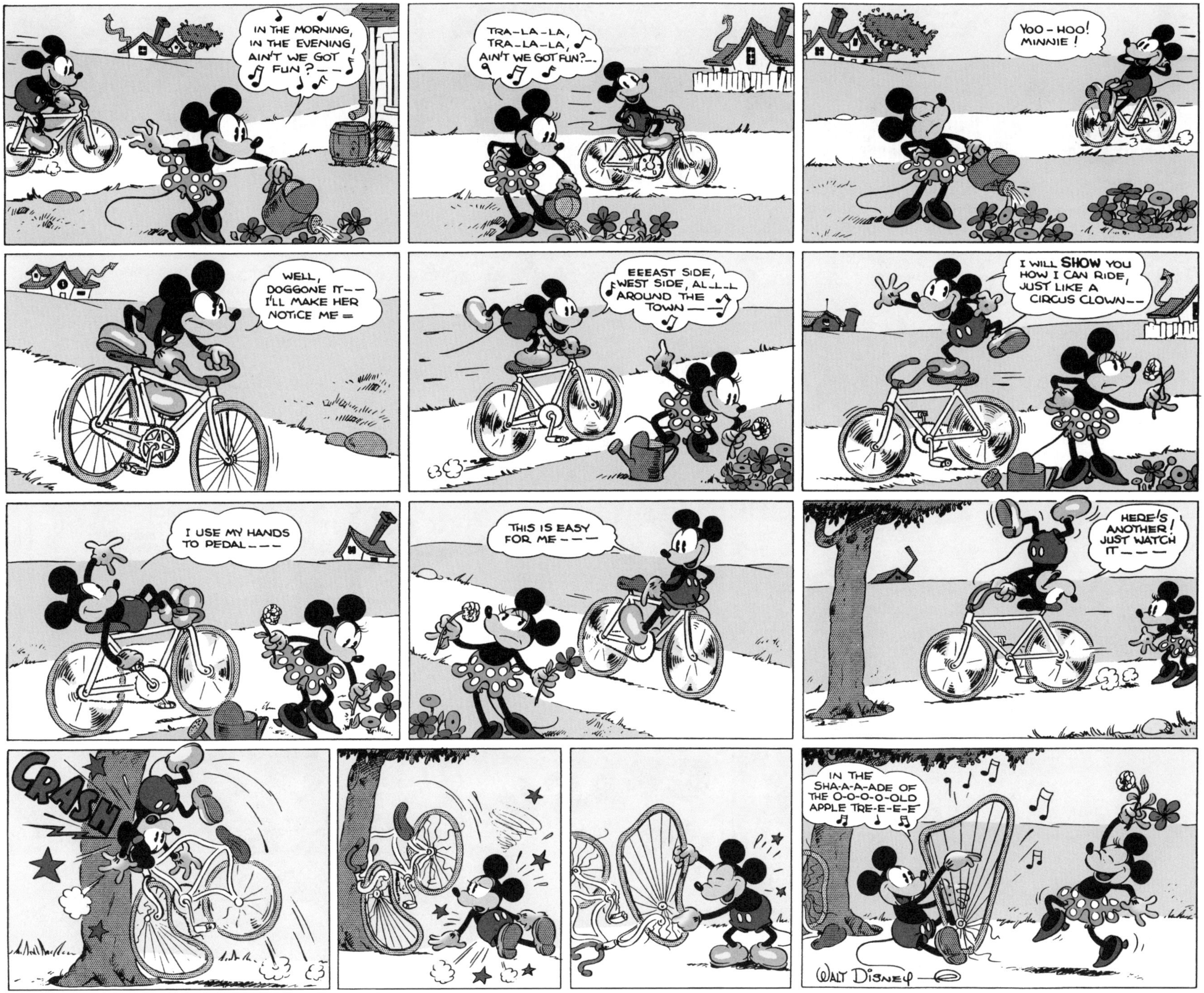

IN THE MORNING, IN THE EVENING, AIN'T WE GOT FUN? — — —
TRA-LA-LA, TRA-LA-LA, AIN'T WE GOT FUN?—
YOO-HOO! MINNIE!
WELL, DOGGONE IT— — I'LL MAKE HER NOTICE ME =
EEEAST SIDE, WEST SIDE, AL-L-L AROUND THE TOWN — —
I WILL SHOW YOU HOW I CAN RIDE, JUST LIKE A CIRCUS CLOWN— —
I USE MY HANDS TO PEDAL— — —
THIS IS EASY FOR ME — — —
HERE'S ANOTHER! JUST WATCH IT — — —
CRASH
IN THE SHA-A-A-ADE OF THE O-O-O-O-OLD APPLE TRE-E-E-E
WALT DISNEY

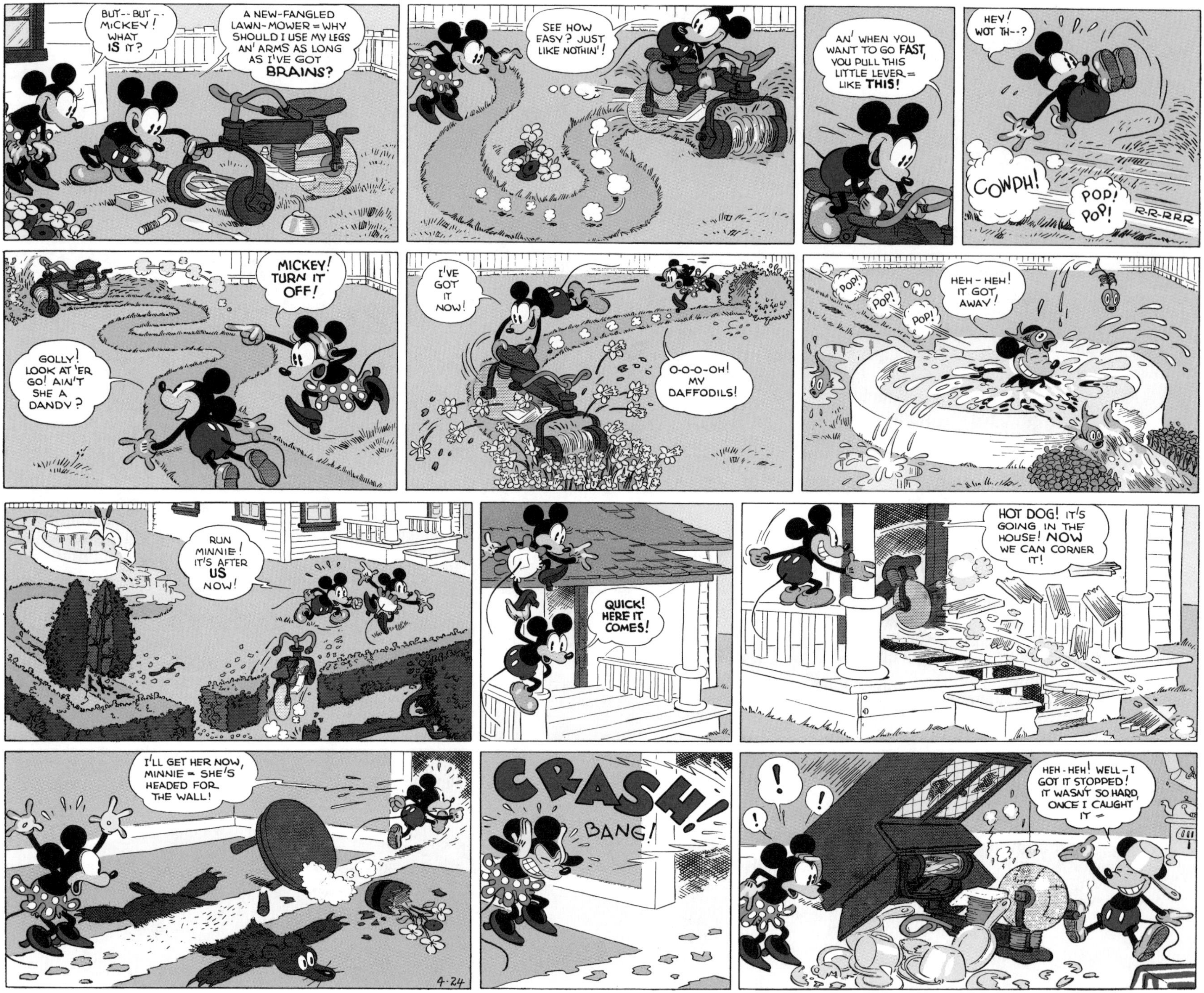
BUT-- BUT -- MICKEY! WHAT IS IT?
A NEW-FANGLED LAWN-MOWER = WHY SHOULD I USE MY LEGS AN' ARMS AS LONG AS I'VE GOT BRAINS?
SEE HOW EASY? JUST LIKE NOTHIN'!
AN' WHEN YOU WANT TO GO FAST, YOU PULL THIS LITTLE LEVER = LIKE THIS!
HEY! WOT TH--?
COWPH!
POP! POP!
R-R-RRR
MICKEY! TURN IT OFF!
GOLLY! LOOK AT 'ER GO! AIN'T SHE A DANDY?
I'VE GOT IT NOW!
O-O-O-OH! MY DAFFODILS!
POP! POP! POP!
HEH - HEH! IT GOT AWAY!
RUN MINNIE! IT'S AFTER US NOW!
QUICK! HERE IT COMES!
HOT DOG! IT'S GOING IN THE HOUSE! NOW WE CAN CORNER IT!
I'LL GET HER NOW, MINNIE = SHE'S HEADED FOR THE WALL!
4-24
CRASH!
BANG!
! ! !
HEH-HEH! WELL-I GOT IT STOPPED! IT WASN'T SO HARD, ONCE I CAUGHT IT =

34. INVENTION OF THE YEAR

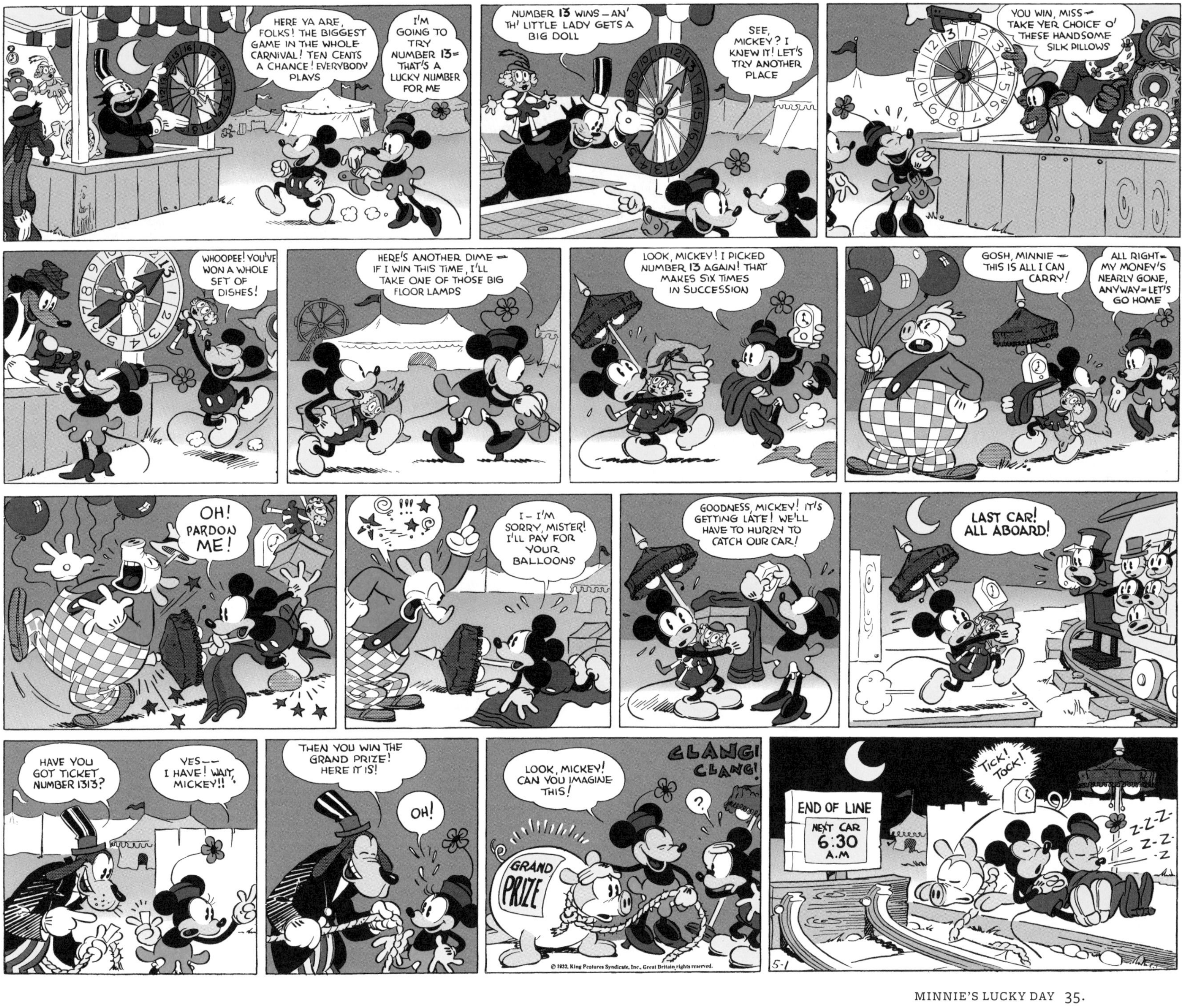

HERE YA ARE, FOLKS! THE BIGGEST GAME IN THE WHOLE CARNIVAL! TEN CENTS A CHANCE! EVERYBODY PLAYS
I'M GOING TO TRY NUMBER 13= THAT'S A LUCKY NUMBER FOR ME
NUMBER 13 WINS—AN' TH' LITTLE LADY GETS A BIG DOLL
SEE, MICKEY? I KNEW IT! LET'S TRY ANOTHER PLACE
YOU WIN, MISS— TAKE YER CHOICE O' THESE HANDSOME SILK PILLOWS
WHOOPEE! YOU'VE WON A WHOLE SET OF DISHES!
HERE'S ANOTHER DIME— IF I WIN THIS TIME, I'LL TAKE ONE OF THOSE BIG FLOOR LAMPS
LOOK, MICKEY! I PICKED NUMBER 13 AGAIN! THAT MAKES SIX TIMES IN SUCCESSION
GOSH, MINNIE— THIS IS ALL I CAN CARRY!
ALL RIGHT— MY MONEY'S NEARLY GONE, ANYWAY= LET'S GO HOME
OH! PARDON ME!
!!!
I-I'M SORRY, MISTER! I'LL PAY FOR YOUR BALLOONS
GOODNESS, MICKEY! IT'S GETTING LATE! WE'LL HAVE TO HURRY TO CATCH OUR CAR!
LAST CAR! ALL ABOARD!
HAVE YOU GOT TICKET NUMBER 1313?
YES— I HAVE! WAIT, MICKEY!!
THEN YOU WIN THE GRAND PRIZE! HERE IT IS!
OH!
LOOK, MICKEY! CAN YOU IMAGINE THIS!
CLANG! CLANG!
?
GRAND PRIZE
END OF LINE
NEXT CAR 6:30 A.M
TICK! TOCK!
Z-Z-Z- Z-Z- -Z
© 1932, King Features Syndicate, Inc., Great Britain rights reserved.
5-1

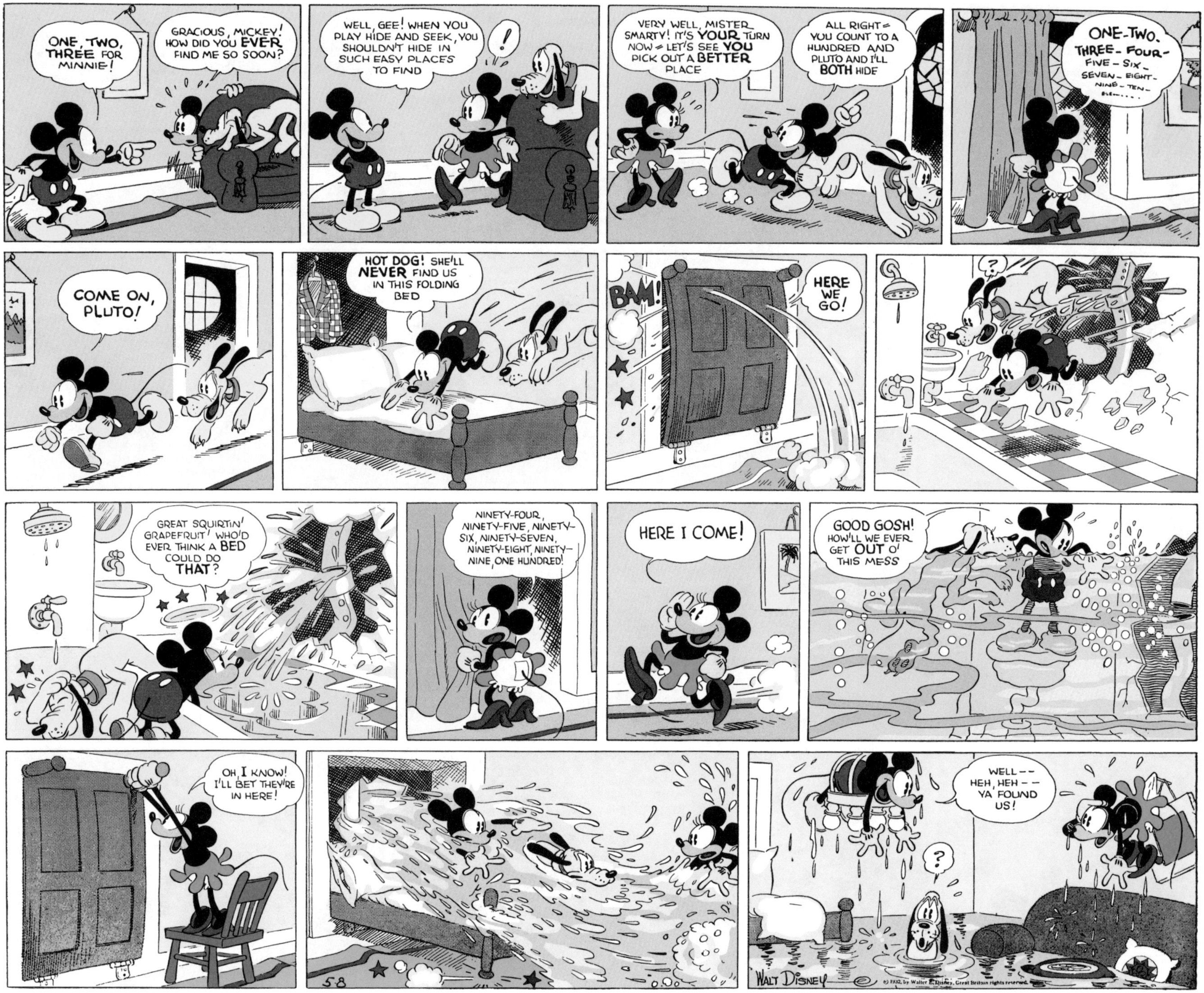
ONE, TWO, THREE FOR MINNIE!
GRACIOUS, MICKEY! HOW DID YOU EVER FIND ME SO SOON?
WELL, GEE! WHEN YOU PLAY HIDE AND SEEK, YOU SHOULDN'T HIDE IN SUCH EASY PLACES TO FIND
!
VERY WELL, MISTER SMARTY! IT'S YOUR TURN NOW = LET'S SEE YOU PICK OUT A BETTER PLACE
ALL RIGHT = YOU COUNT TO A HUNDRED AND PLUTO AND I'LL BOTH HIDE
ONE-TWO-THREE-FOUR-FIVE-SIX-SEVEN-EIGHT-NINE-TEN-
COME ON, PLUTO!
HOT DOG! SHE'LL NEVER FIND US IN THIS FOLDING BED
BAM!
HERE WE GO!
?
GREAT SQUIRTIN' GRAPEFRUIT! WHO'D EVER THINK A BED COULD DO THAT?
NINETY-FOUR, NINETY-FIVE, NINETY-SIX, NINETY-SEVEN, NINETY-EIGHT, NINETY-NINE, ONE HUNDRED!
HERE I COME!
GOOD GOSH! HOW'LL WE EVER GET OUT O' THIS MESS
OH, I KNOW! I'LL BET THEY'RE IN HERE!
5-8
WELL-- HEH, HEH -- YA FOUND US!
?
WALT DISNEY
© 1932, by Walter E. Disney, Great Britain rights reserved.

36. HIDE AND FOUND

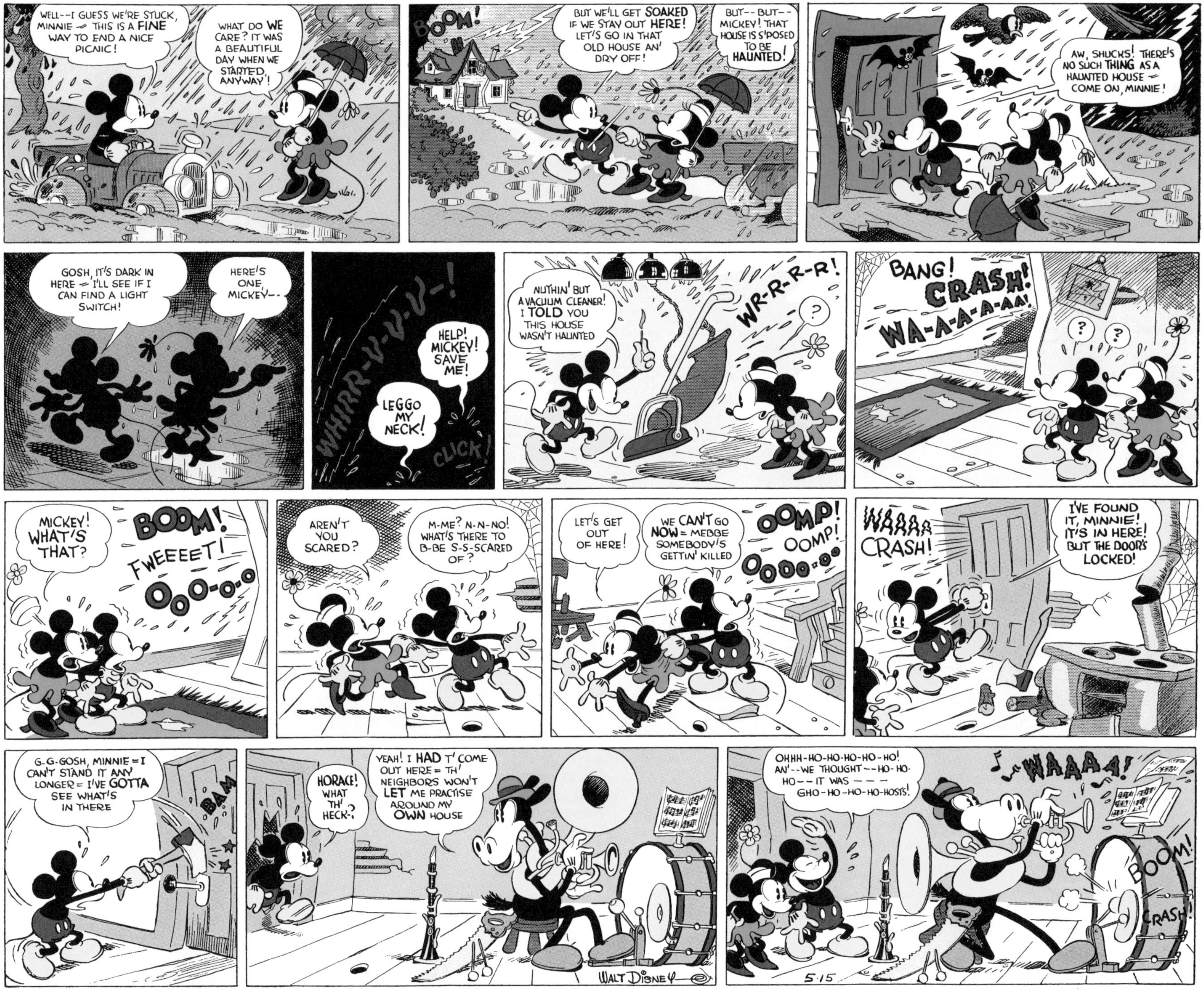
WELL--I GUESS WE'RE STUCK, MINNIE = THIS IS A FINE WAY TO END A NICE PICNIC!
WHAT DO WE CARE? IT WAS A BEAUTIFUL DAY WHEN WE STARTED, ANYWAY!
BOOM!
BUT WE'LL GET SOAKED IF WE STAY OUT HERE! LET'S GO IN THAT OLD HOUSE AN' DRY OFF!
BUT-- BUT-- MICKEY! THAT HOUSE IS S'POSED TO BE HAUNTED!
AW, SHUCKS! THERE'S NO SUCH THING AS A HAUNTED HOUSE = COME ON, MINNIE!
GOSH, IT'S DARK IN HERE = I'LL SEE IF I CAN FIND A LIGHT SWITCH!
HERE'S ONE, MICKEY--
WHIRR-V-V-V-!
HELP! MICKEY! SAVE ME!
LEGGO MY NECK!
CLICK!
NUTHIN' BUT A VACUUM CLEANER! I TOLD YOU THIS HOUSE WASN'T HAUNTED
WR-R-R-R!
?
BANG!
CRASH!
WA-A-A-A-AA!
? ?
MICKEY! WHAT'S THAT?
BOOM!
FWEEEET!
OOO-O-O
AREN'T YOU SCARED?
M-ME? N-N-NO! WHAT'S THERE TO B-BE S-S-SCARED OF?
LET'S GET OUT OF HERE!
WE CAN'T GO NOW = MEBBE SOMEBODY'S GETTIN' KILLED
OOMP! OOMP!
OOOO-O-O
WAAAA
CRASH!
I'VE FOUND IT, MINNIE! IT'S IN HERE! BUT THE DOOR'S LOCKED!
G-G-GOSH, MINNIE = I CAN'T STAND IT ANY LONGER = I'VE GOTTA SEE WHAT'S IN THERE
BAM
HORACE! WHAT TH' HECK-?
YEAH! I HAD T' COME OUT HERE = TH' NEIGHBORS WON'T LET ME PRACTISE AROUND MY OWN HOUSE
WALT DISNEY
OHHH-HO-HO-HO-HO-HO! AN'--WE THOUGHT--HO-HO-HO--IT WAS --- GHO-HO-HO-HO-HOSTS!
WAAAA!
BOOM!
CRASH!
5-15

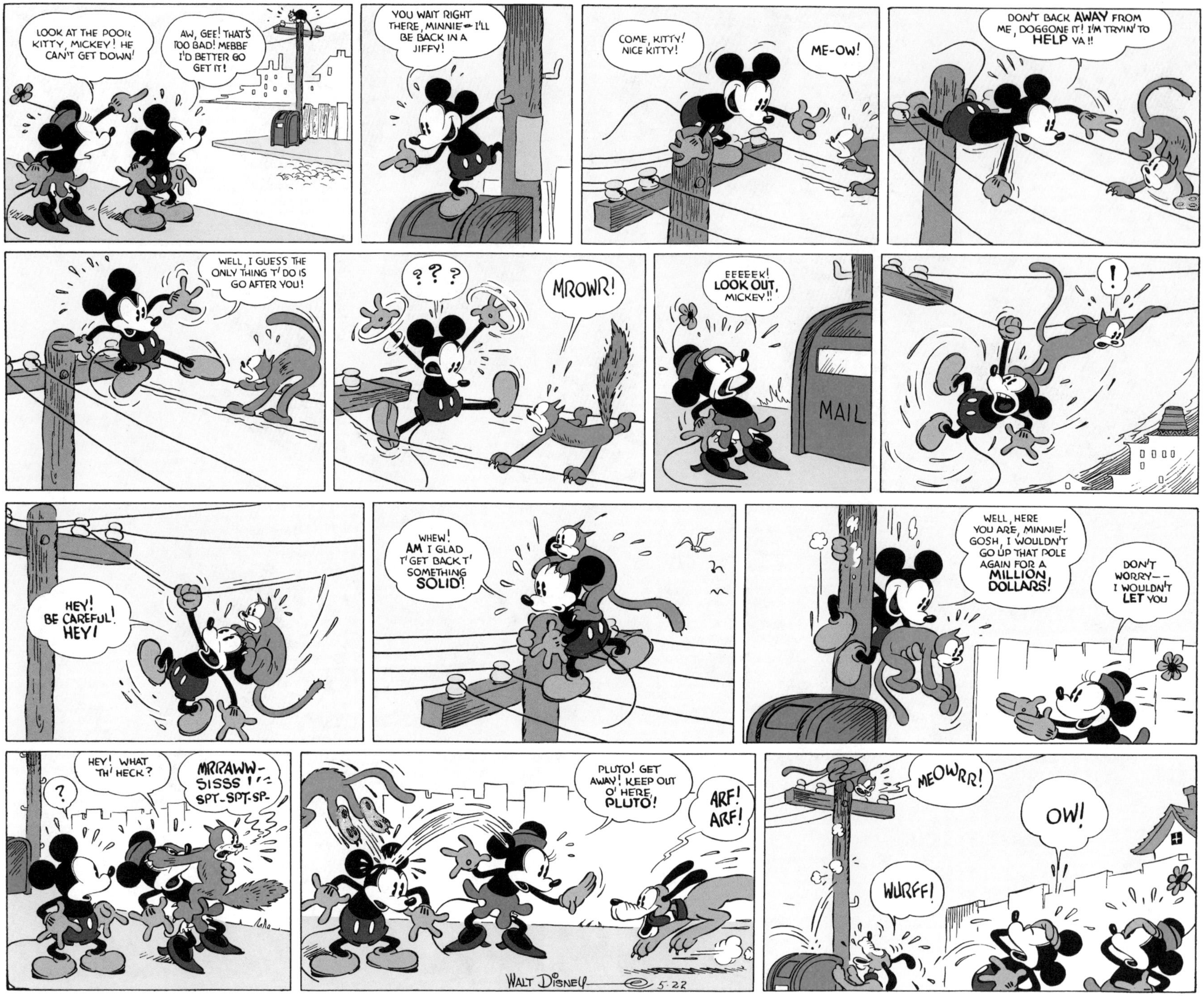

LOOK AT THE POOR KITTY, MICKEY! HE CAN'T GET DOWN!
AW, GEE! THAT'S TOO BAD! MEBBE I'D BETTER GO GET IT!
YOU WAIT RIGHT THERE, MINNIE — I'LL BE BACK IN A JIFFY!
COME, KITTY! NICE KITTY!
ME-OW!
DON'T BACK AWAY FROM ME, DOGGONE IT! I'M TRYIN' TO HELP YA!!
WELL, I GUESS THE ONLY THING T' DO IS GO AFTER YOU!
? ? ?
MROWR!
EEEEEK! LOOK OUT, MICKEY!!
MAIL
!
HEY! BE CAREFUL! HEY!
WHEW! AM I GLAD T' GET BACK T' SOMETHING SOLID!
WELL, HERE YOU ARE, MINNIE! GOSH, I WOULDN'T GO UP THAT POLE AGAIN FOR A MILLION DOLLARS!
DON'T WORRY— — I WOULDN'T LET YOU
?
HEY! WHAT TH' HECK?
MRRAWW-SISSS! SPT-SPT-SP-
PLUTO! GET AWAY! KEEP OUT O' HERE, PLUTO!
ARF! ARF!
WALT DISNEY 5-22
MEOWRR!
OW!
WURFF!

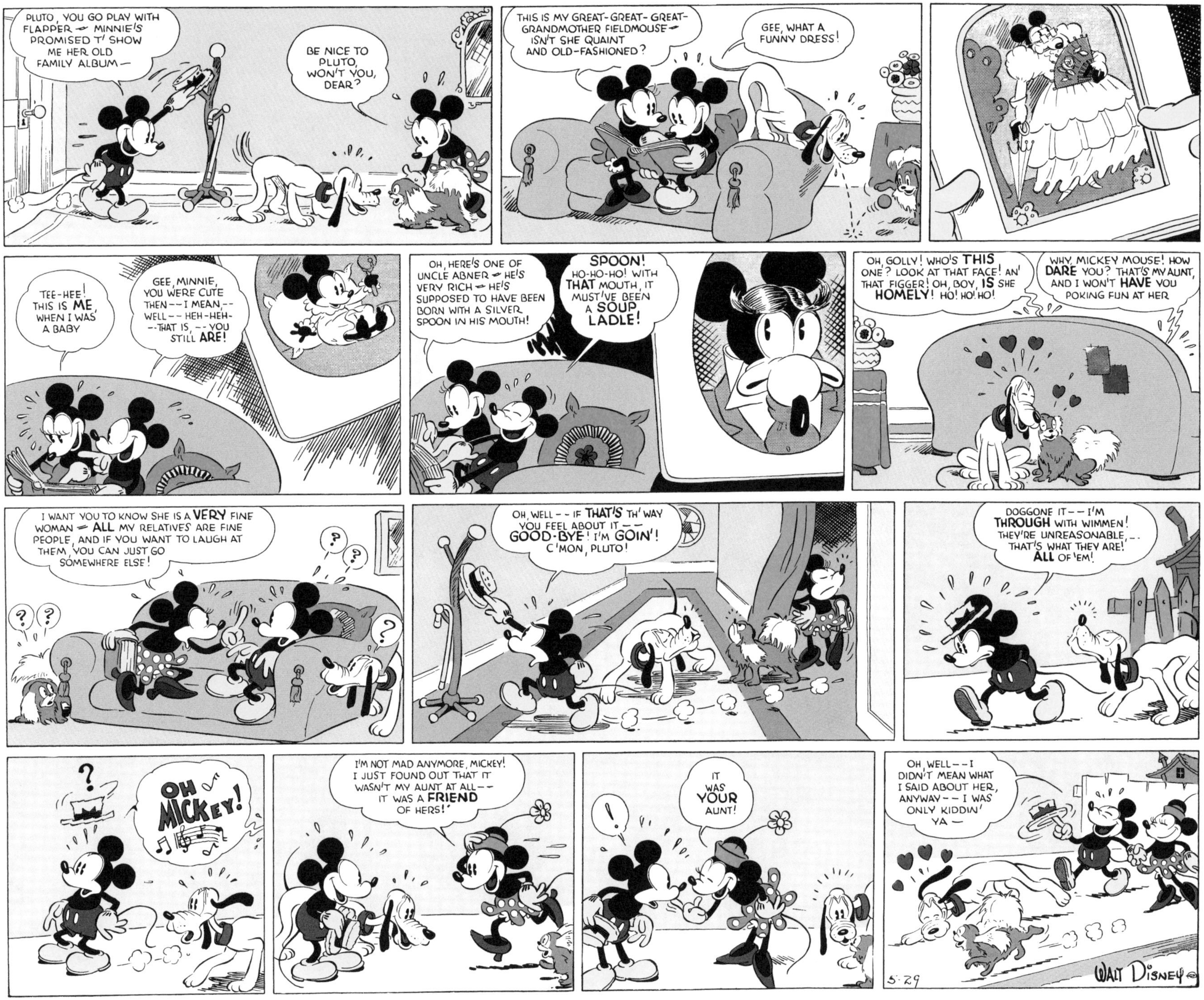
PLUTO, YOU GO PLAY WITH FLAPPER — MINNIE'S PROMISED T' SHOW ME HER OLD FAMILY ALBUM —
BE NICE TO PLUTO, WON'T YOU, DEAR?
THIS IS MY GREAT-GREAT-GREAT-GRANDMOTHER FIELDMOUSE — ISN'T SHE QUAINT AND OLD-FASHIONED?
GEE, WHAT A FUNNY DRESS!
TEE-HEE! THIS IS ME, WHEN I WAS A BABY
GEE, MINNIE, YOU WERE CUTE THEN -- I MEAN, -- WELL -- HEH-HEH- -THAT IS, -- YOU STILL ARE!
OH, HERE'S ONE OF UNCLE ABNER — HE'S VERY RICH — HE'S SUPPOSED TO HAVE BEEN BORN WITH A SILVER SPOON IN HIS MOUTH!
SPOON! HO-HO-HO! WITH THAT MOUTH, IT MUST'VE BEEN A SOUP LADLE!
OH, GOLLY! WHO'S THIS ONE? LOOK AT THAT FACE! AN' THAT FIGGER! OH, BOY, IS SHE HOMELY! HO! HO! HO!
WHY, MICKEY MOUSE! HOW DARE YOU? THAT'S MY AUNT, AND I WON'T HAVE YOU POKING FUN AT HER
I WANT YOU TO KNOW SHE IS A VERY FINE WOMAN — ALL MY RELATIVES ARE FINE PEOPLE, AND IF YOU WANT TO LAUGH AT THEM, YOU CAN JUST GO SOMEWHERE ELSE!
OH, WELL -- IF THAT'S TH' WAY YOU FEEL ABOUT IT -- GOOD-BYE! I'M GOIN'! C'MON, PLUTO!
DOGGONE IT -- I'M THROUGH WITH WIMMEN! THEY'RE UNREASONABLE, -- THAT'S WHAT THEY ARE! ALL OF 'EM!
OH MICKEY!
I'M NOT MAD ANYMORE, MICKEY! I JUST FOUND OUT THAT IT WASN'T MY AUNT AT ALL -- IT WAS A FRIEND OF HERS!
IT WAS YOUR AUNT!
OH, WELL -- I DIDN'T MEAN WHAT I SAID ABOUT HER, ANYWAY -- I WAS ONLY KIDDIN' YA —
5-29
WALT DISNEY

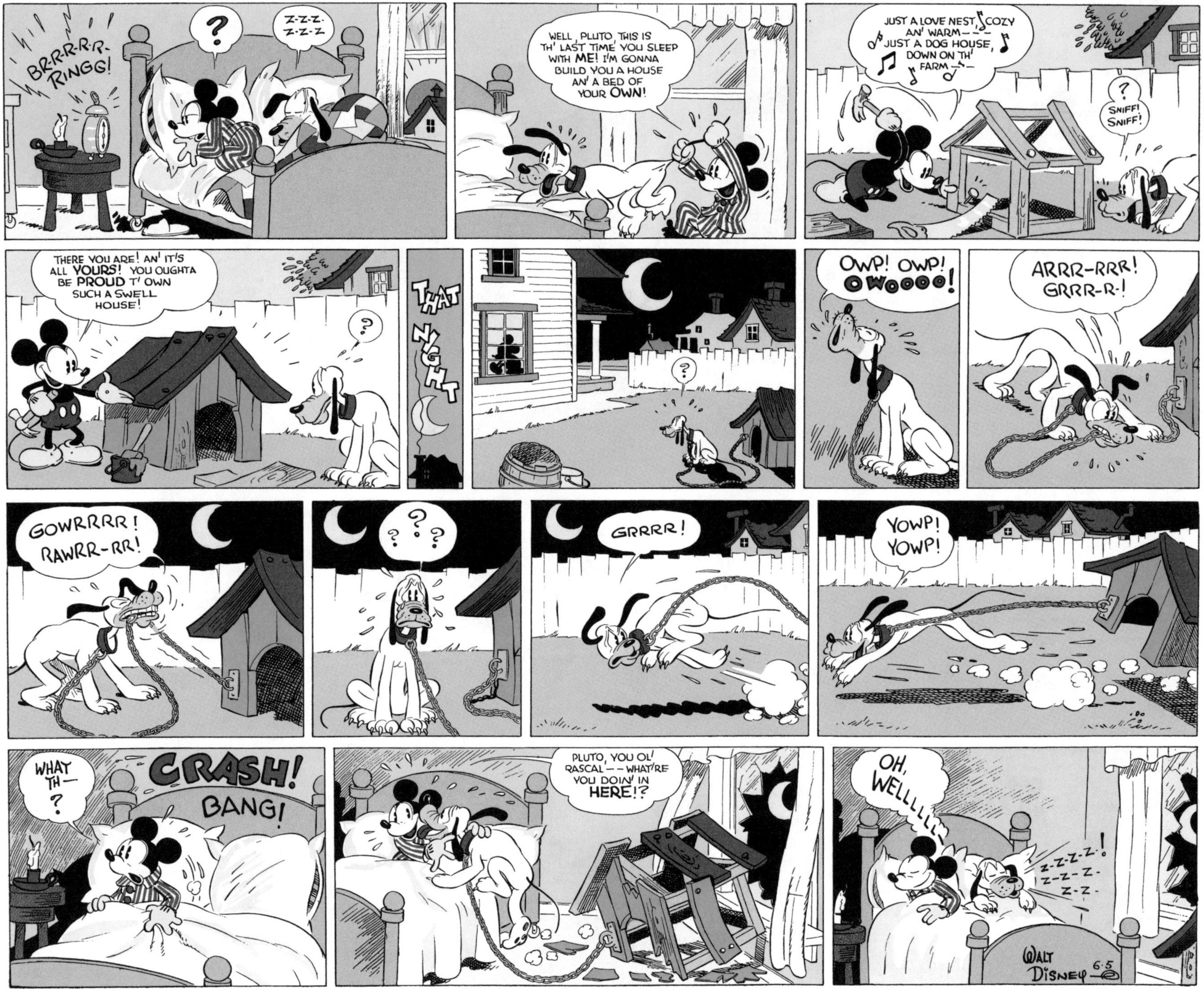
BR-R-R-R-R-RINGG!
?
Z-Z-Z. Z-Z-Z
WELL, PLUTO, THIS IS TH' LAST TIME YOU SLEEP WITH ME! I'M GONNA BUILD YOU A HOUSE AN' A BED OF YOUR OWN!
JUST A LOVE NEST COZY AN' WARM--- JUST A DOG HOUSE, DOWN ON TH' FARM--
?
SNIFF! SNIFF!
THERE YOU ARE! AN' IT'S ALL YOURS! YOU OUGHTA BE PROUD T' OWN SUCH A SWELL HOUSE!
?
THAT NIGHT
?
OWP! OWP! OWOOOO!
ARRR-RRR! GRRR-R-!
GOWRRRR! RAWRR-RR!
? ? ?
GRRRR!
YOWP! YOWP!
WHAT TH— ?
CRASH!
BANG!
PLUTO, YOU OL' RASCAL-- WHAT'RE YOU DOIN' IN HERE!?
OH, WELLLLLL
Z-Z-Z-Z-! Z-Z-Z- Z-Z-
WALT DISNEY 6-5

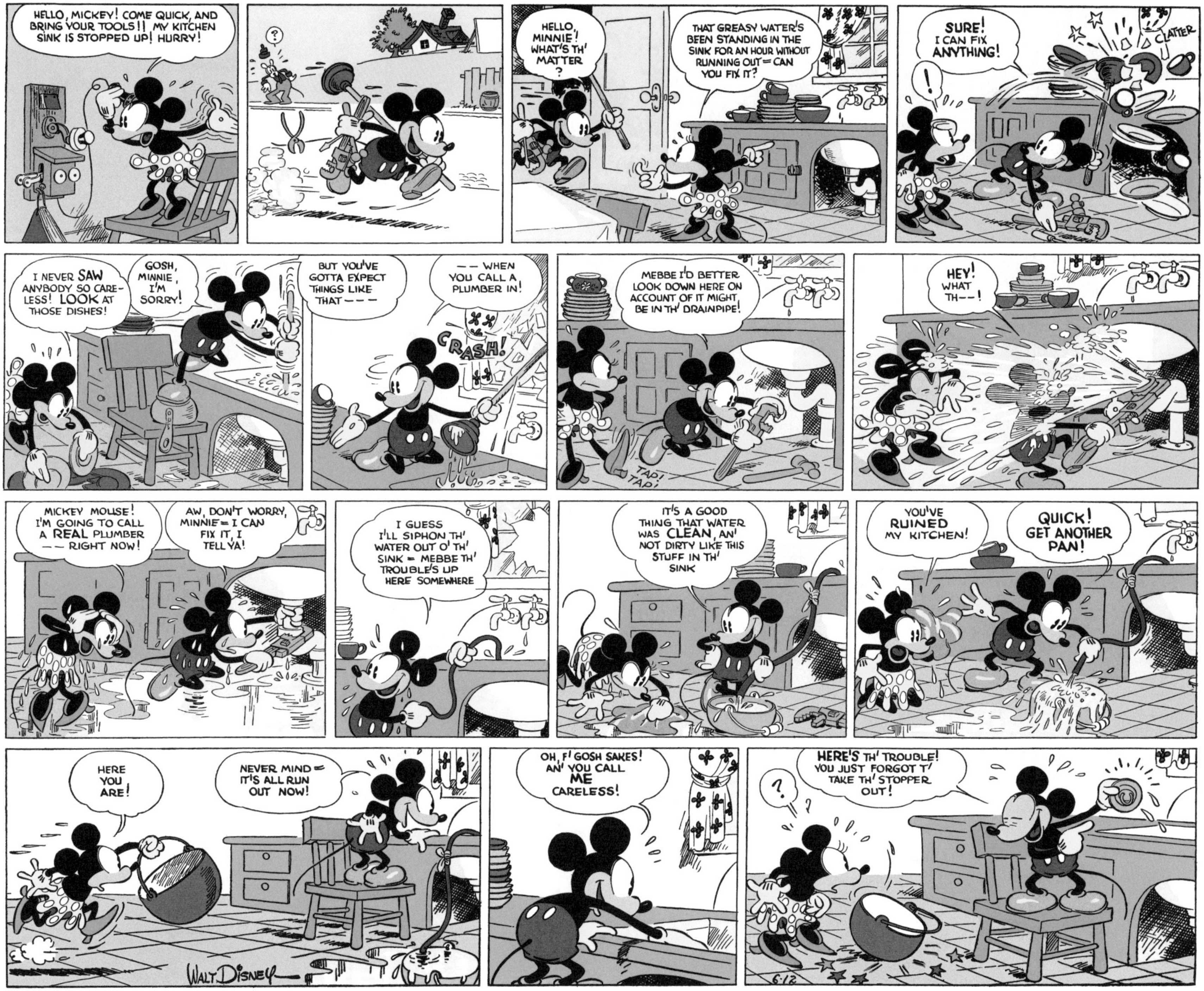
HELLO, MICKEY! COME QUICK, AND BRING YOUR TOOLS!! MY KITCHEN SINK IS STOPPED UP! HURRY!
?
HELLO, MINNIE! WHAT'S TH' MATTER?
THAT GREASY WATER'S BEEN STANDING IN THE SINK FOR AN HOUR WITHOUT RUNNING OUT = CAN YOU FIX IT?
SURE! I CAN FIX ANYTHING!
!
CLATTER
I NEVER SAW ANYBODY SO CARELESS! LOOK AT THOSE DISHES!
GOSH, MINNIE, I'M SORRY!
BUT YOU'VE GOTTA EXPECT THINGS LIKE THAT - - -
- - WHEN YOU CALL A PLUMBER IN!
CRASH!
MEBBE I'D BETTER LOOK DOWN HERE ON ACCOUNT OF IT MIGHT BE IN TH' DRAINPIPE!
TAP! TAP!
HEY! WHAT TH- -!
MICKEY MOUSE! I'M GOING TO CALL A REAL PLUMBER - - RIGHT NOW!
AW, DON'T WORRY, MINNIE = I CAN FIX IT, I TELL YA!
I GUESS I'LL SIPHON TH' WATER OUT O' TH' SINK = MEBBE TH' TROUBLE'S UP HERE SOMEWHERE
IT'S A GOOD THING THAT WATER WAS CLEAN, AN' NOT DIRTY LIKE THIS STUFF IN TH' SINK
YOU'VE RUINED MY KITCHEN!
QUICK! GET ANOTHER PAN!
HERE YOU ARE!
NEVER MIND = IT'S ALL RUN OUT NOW!
WALT DISNEY
OH, F' GOSH SAKES! AN' YOU CALL ME CARELESS!
? ?
HERE'S TH' TROUBLE! YOU JUST FORGOT T' TAKE TH' STOPPER OUT!
6-12

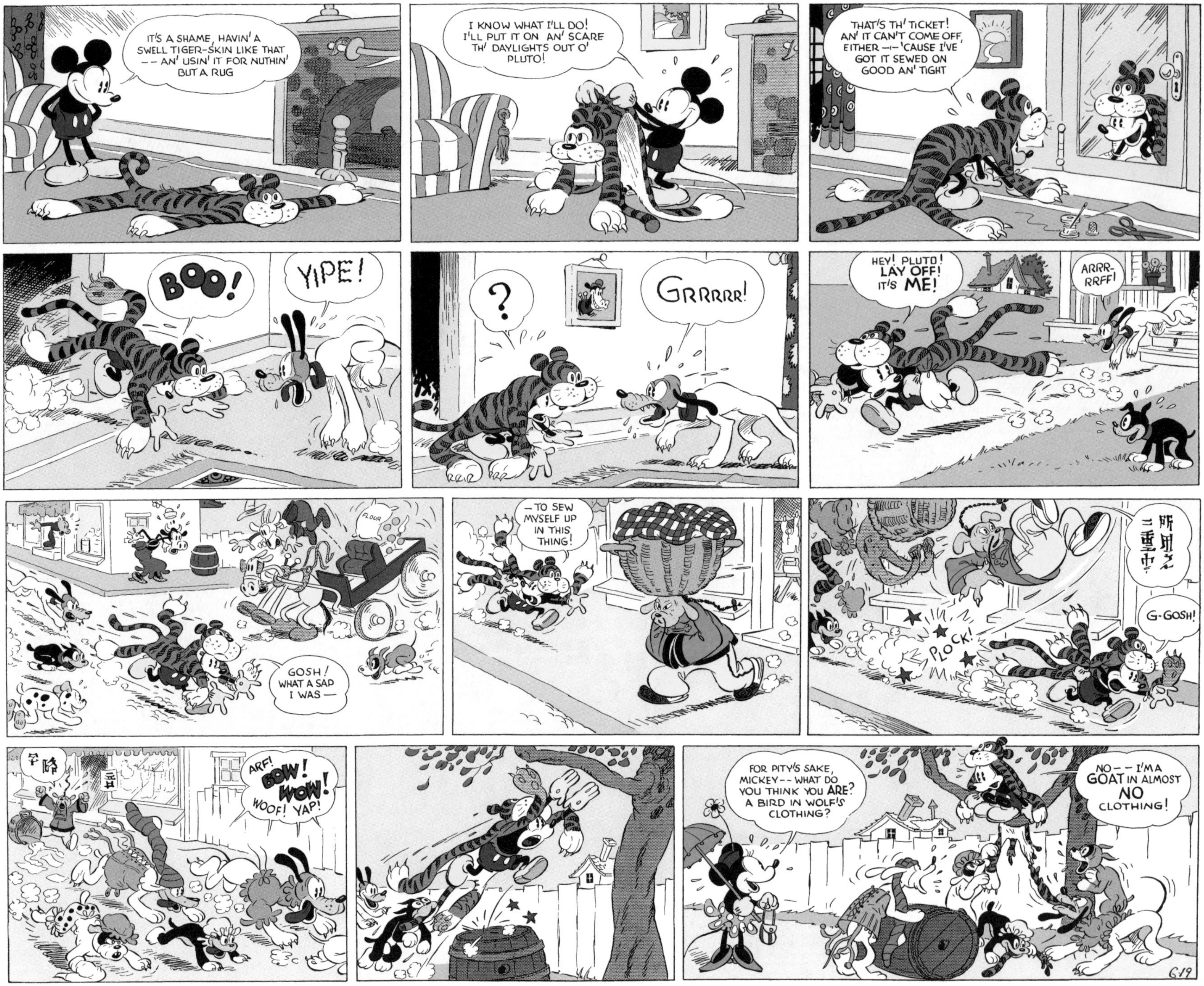
IT'S A SHAME, HAVIN' A SWELL TIGER-SKIN LIKE THAT -- AN' USIN' IT FOR NUTHIN' BUT A RUG
I KNOW WHAT I'LL DO! I'LL PUT IT ON AN' SCARE TH' DAYLIGHTS OUT O' PLUTO!
THAT'S TH' TICKET! AN' IT CAN'T COME OFF, EITHER --- 'CAUSE I'VE GOT IT SEWED ON GOOD AN' TIGHT
BOO!
YIPE!
?
GRRRRRR!
HEY! PLUTO! LAY OFF! IT'S ME!
ARRR-RRFF!
FLOUR
GOSH! WHAT A SAP I WAS—
—TO SEW MYSELF UP IN THIS THING!
PLOCK!
G-GOSH!
ARF! BOW! WOW! WOOF! YAP!
FOR PITY'S SAKE, MICKEY-- WHAT DO YOU THINK YOU ARE? A BIRD IN WOLF'S CLOTHING?
NO-- I'M A GOAT IN ALMOST NO CLOTHING!
6-19

42. HOLD THAT TIGER!

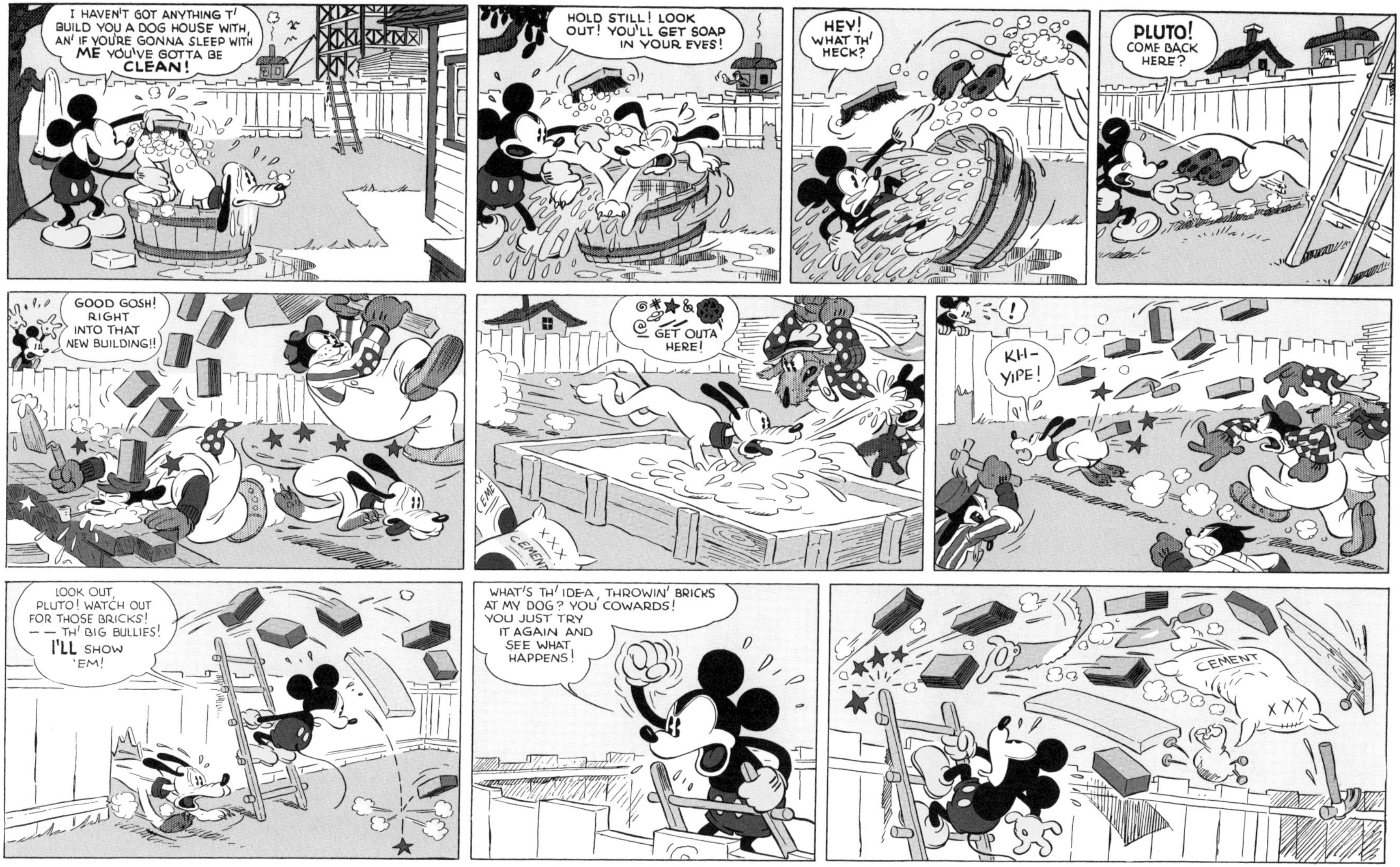

I HAVEN'T GOT ANYTHING T' BUILD YOU A DOG HOUSE WITH, AN' IF YOU'RE GONNA SLEEP WITH ME YOU'VE GOTTA BE CLEAN!
HOLD STILL! LOOK OUT! YOU'LL GET SOAP IN YOUR EYES!
HEY! WHAT TH' HECK?
PLUTO! COME BACK HERE?
GOOD GOSH! RIGHT INTO THAT NEW BUILDING!!
GET OUTA HERE!
CEMENT
!
KI-YIPE!
LOOK OUT, PLUTO! WATCH OUT FOR THOSE BRICKS! — — TH' BIG BULLIES! I'LL SHOW 'EM!
WHAT'S TH' IDEA, THROWIN' BRICKS AT MY DOG? YOU COWARDS! YOU JUST TRY IT AGAIN AND SEE WHAT HAPPENS!
CEMENT
SAY, YOU KNOW, I AIN'T SEEN THAT KID FOR TWO HOURS = WE MIGHT HAVE HURT HIM!
BY GOSH YO'RE RIGHT — WE BETTER GO SEE!
KEG O' NAILS
ATTA BOY, PLUTO! BRING ME ANOTHER BRICK! GOSH! WE'VE GOT ENOUGH MATERIAL NOW T' MAKE TWO DOG HOUSES!
CEMENT
WALT DISNEY 6-26

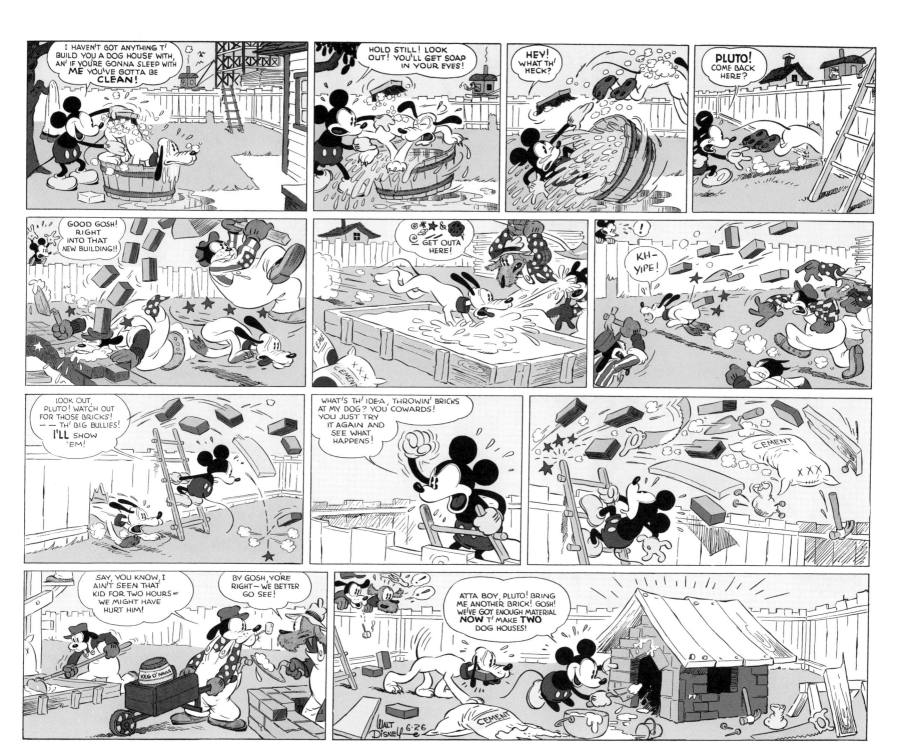

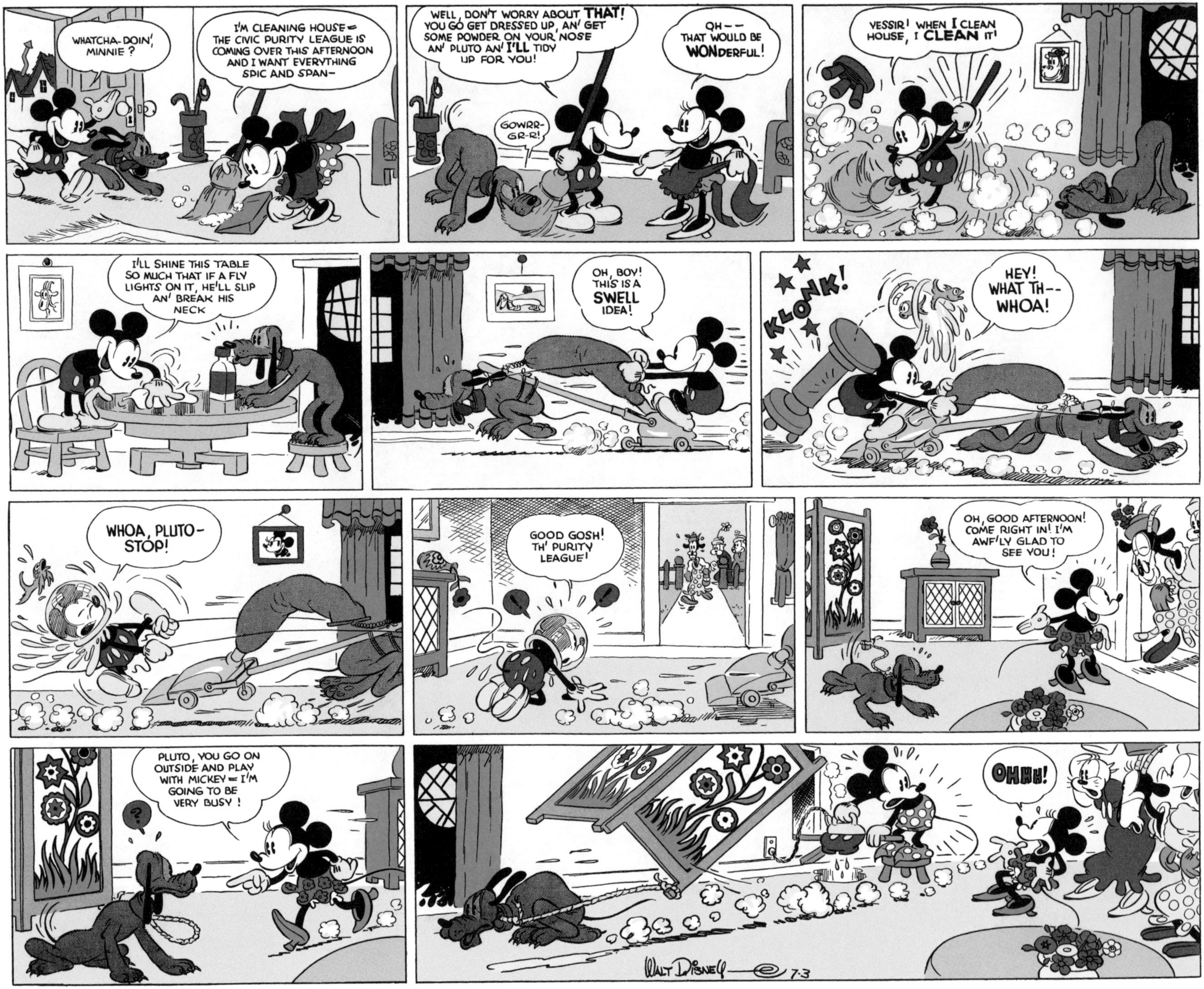

WHATCHA-DOIN', MINNIE ?
I'M CLEANING HOUSE— THE CIVIC PURITY LEAGUE IS COMING OVER THIS AFTERNOON AND I WANT EVERYTHING SPIC AND SPAN—
WELL, DON'T WORRY ABOUT THAT! YOU GO GET DRESSED UP, AN' GET SOME POWDER ON YOUR NOSE AN' PLUTO AN' I'LL TIDY UP FOR YOU!
GOWRR-GR-R!
OH—— THAT WOULD BE WONDERFUL!
YESSIR! WHEN I CLEAN HOUSE, I CLEAN IT!
I'LL SHINE THIS TABLE SO MUCH THAT IF A FLY LIGHTS ON IT, HE'LL SLIP AN' BREAK HIS NECK
OH, BOY! THIS IS A SWELL IDEA!
KLONK!
HEY! WHAT TH-- WHOA!
WHOA, PLUTO-STOP!
GOOD GOSH! TH' PURITY LEAGUE!
OH, GOOD AFTERNOON! COME RIGHT IN! I'M AWF'LY GLAD TO SEE YOU!
PLUTO, YOU GO ON OUTSIDE AND PLAY WITH MICKEY— I'M GOING TO BE VERY BUSY !
OHHH!
WALT DISNEY © 7-3

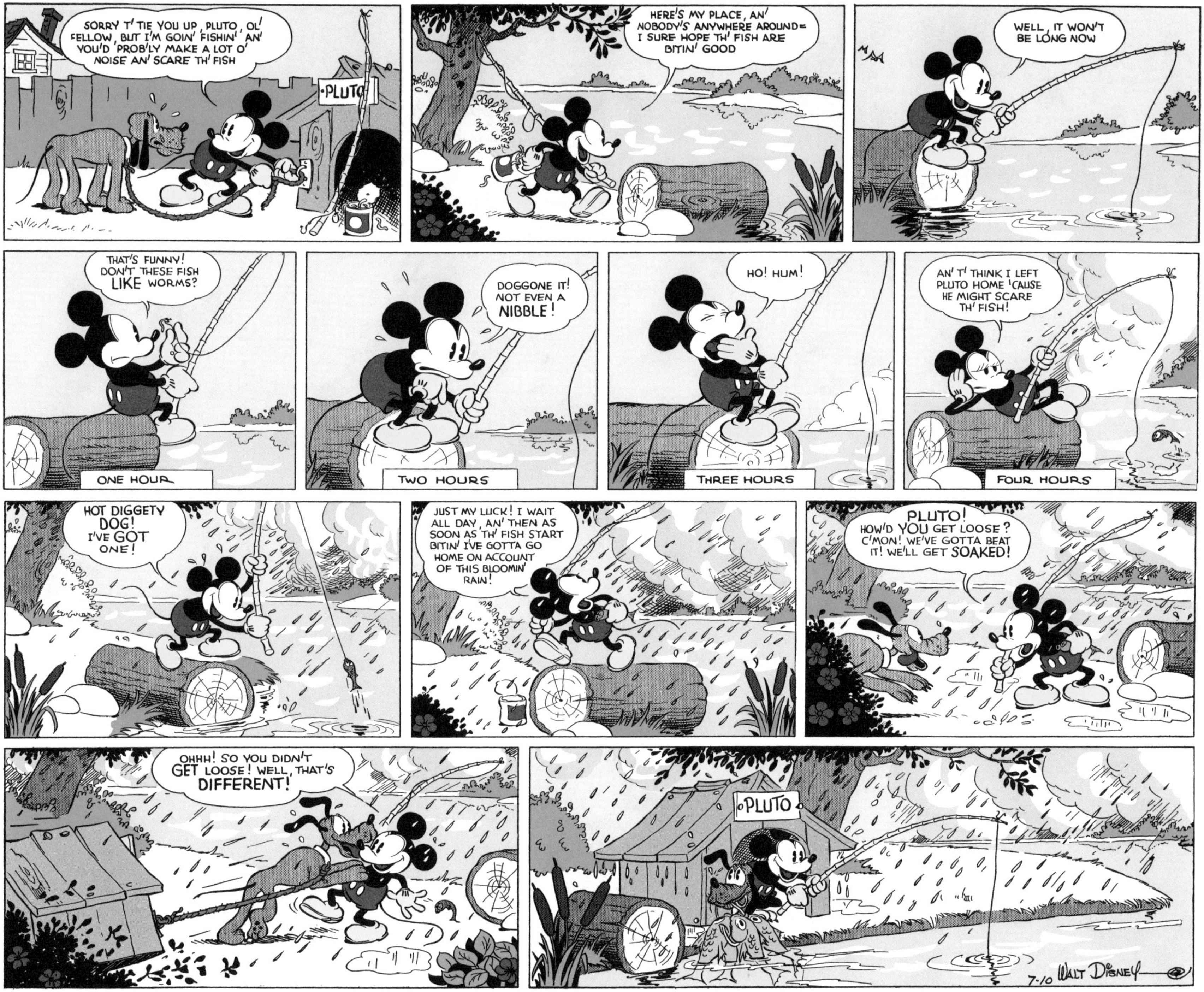

SORRY T' TIE YOU UP, PLUTO, OL' FELLOW, BUT I'M GOIN' FISHIN' AN' YOU'D PROB'LY MAKE A LOT O' NOISE AN' SCARE TH' FISH
PLUTO
HERE'S MY PLACE, AN' NOBODY'S ANYWHERE AROUND= I SURE HOPE TH' FISH ARE BITIN' GOOD
WELL, IT WON'T BE LONG NOW
THAT'S FUNNY! DON'T THESE FISH LIKE WORMS?
ONE HOUR
DOGGONE IT! NOT EVEN A NIBBLE!
TWO HOURS
HO! HUM!
THREE HOURS
AN' T' THINK I LEFT PLUTO HOME 'CAUSE HE MIGHT SCARE TH' FISH!
FOUR HOURS
HOT DIGGETY DOG! I'VE GOT ONE!
JUST MY LUCK! I WAIT ALL DAY, AN' THEN AS SOON AS TH' FISH START BITIN' I'VE GOTTA GO HOME ON ACCOUNT OF THIS BLOOMIN' RAIN!
PLUTO! HOW'D YOU GET LOOSE? C'MON! WE'VE GOTTA BEAT IT! WE'LL GET SOAKED!
OHHH! SO YOU DIDN'T GET LOOSE! WELL, THAT'S DIFFERENT!
PLUTO
7-10 WALT DISNEY

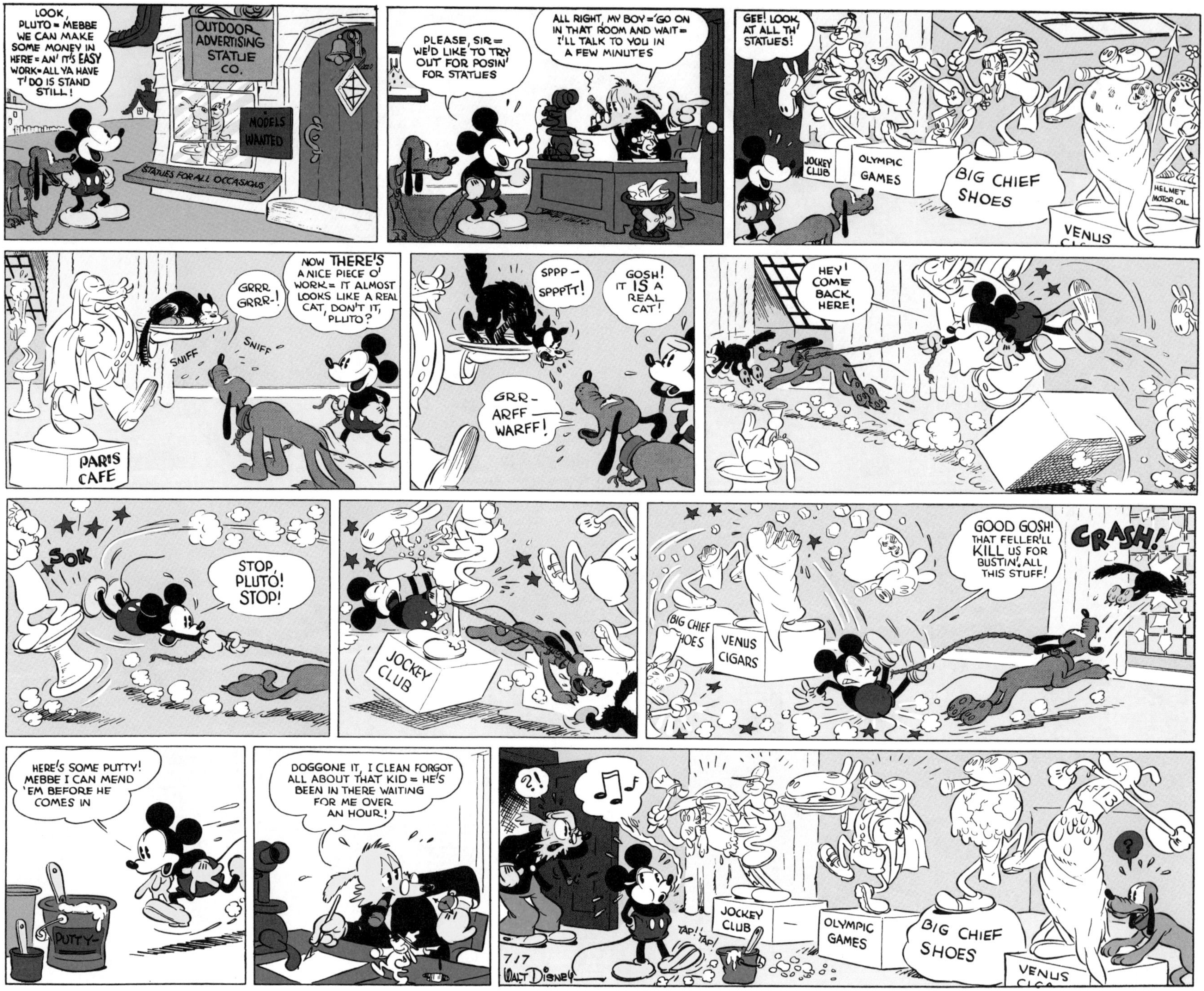
LOOK, PLUTO = MEBBE WE CAN MAKE SOME MONEY IN HERE = AN' IT'S EASY WORK = ALL YA HAVE T' DO IS STAND STILL!
OUTDOOR ADVERTISING STATUE CO.
MODELS WANTED
STATUES FOR ALL OCCASIONS
PLEASE, SIR = WE'D LIKE TO TRY OUT FOR POSIN' FOR STATUES
ALL RIGHT, MY BOY = GO ON IN THAT ROOM AND WAIT = I'LL TALK TO YOU IN A FEW MINUTES
GEE! LOOK AT ALL TH' STATUES!
JOCKEY CLUB
OLYMPIC GAMES
BIG CHIEF SHOES
HELMET MOTOR OIL
VENUS
GRRR GRRR-!
NOW THERE'S A NICE PIECE O' WORK = IT ALMOST LOOKS LIKE A REAL CAT, DON'T IT, PLUTO?
SNIFF
SNIFF
PARIS CAFE
SPPP - SPPPTT!
GOSH! IT IS A REAL CAT!
GRR - ARFF - WARFF!
HEY! COME BACK HERE!
SOK
STOP, PLUTO! STOP!
JOCKEY CLUB
CRASH!
GOOD GOSH! THAT FELLER'LL KILL US FOR BUSTIN' ALL THIS STUFF!
BIG CHIEF SHOES
VENUS CIGARS
HERE'S SOME PUTTY! MEBBE I CAN MEND 'EM BEFORE HE COMES IN
PUTTY
DOGGONE IT, I CLEAN FORGOT ALL ABOUT THAT KID = HE'S BEEN IN THERE WAITING FOR ME OVER AN HOUR!
?!
TAP! TAP!
JOCKEY CLUB
OLYMPIC GAMES
BIG CHIEF SHOES
VENUS
?
7/7
WALT DISNEY

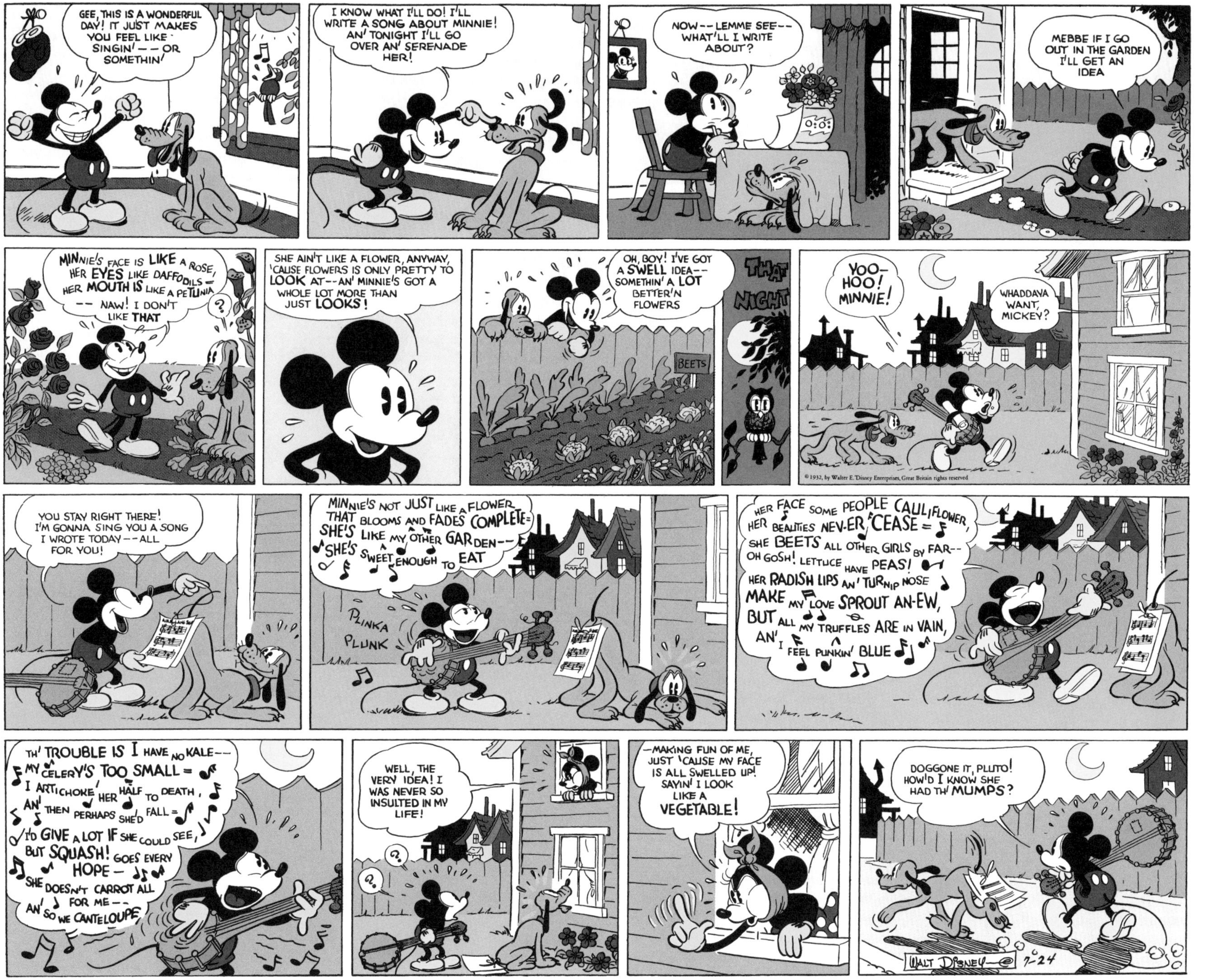
GEE, THIS IS A WONDERFUL DAY! IT JUST MAKES YOU FEEL LIKE SINGIN' -- OR SOMETHIN'
I KNOW WHAT I'LL DO! I'LL WRITE A SONG ABOUT MINNIE! AN' TONIGHT I'LL GO OVER AN' SERENADE HER!
NOW -- LEMME SEE -- WHAT'LL I WRITE ABOUT?
MEBBE IF I GO OUT IN THE GARDEN I'LL GET AN IDEA
MINNIE'S FACE IS LIKE A ROSE, HER EYES LIKE DAFFODILS = HER MOUTH IS LIKE A PETUNIA -- NAW! I DON'T LIKE THAT
?
SHE AIN'T LIKE A FLOWER, ANYWAY, 'CAUSE FLOWERS IS ONLY PRETTY TO LOOK AT -- AN' MINNIE'S GOT A WHOLE LOT MORE THAN JUST LOOKS!
OH, BOY! I'VE GOT A SWELL IDEA -- SOMETHIN' A LOT BETTER'N FLOWERS
BEETS
THAT NIGHT
YOO-HOO! MINNIE!
WHADDAYA WANT, MICKEY?
© 1932, by Walter E. Disney Enterprises, Great Britain rights reserved
YOU STAY RIGHT THERE! I'M GONNA SING YOU A SONG I WROTE TODAY -- ALL FOR YOU!
MINNIE'S NOT JUST LIKE A FLOWER THAT BLOOMS AND FADES COMPLETE = SHE'S LIKE MY OTHER GARDEN -- SHE'S SWEET ENOUGH TO EAT
PLINKA PLUNK
HER FACE SOME PEOPLE CAULIFLOWER, HER BEAUTIES NEV-ER CEASE = SHE BEETS ALL OTHER GIRLS BY FAR -- OH GOSH! LETTUCE HAVE PEAS! HER RADISH LIPS AN' TURNIP NOSE MAKE MY LOVE SPROUT AN-EW, BUT ALL MY TRUFFLES ARE IN VAIN, AN' I FEEL PUNKIN' BLUE
TH' TROUBLE IS I HAVE NO KALE -- MY CELERY'S TOO SMALL = I ARTICHOKE HER HALF TO DEATH, AN' THEN PERHAPS SHE'D FALL = I'D GIVE A LOT IF SHE COULD SEE, BUT SQUASH! HOPE GOES EVERY SHE DOESN'T CARROT ALL FOR ME -- AN' SO WE CANTELOUPE
WELL, THE VERY IDEA! I WAS NEVER SO INSULTED IN MY LIFE!
?
?
-- MAKING FUN OF ME, JUST 'CAUSE MY FACE IS ALL SWELLED UP! SAYIN' I LOOK LIKE A VEGETABLE!
DOGGONE IT, PLUTO! HOW'D I KNOW SHE HAD TH' MUMPS?
WALT DISNEY 7-24

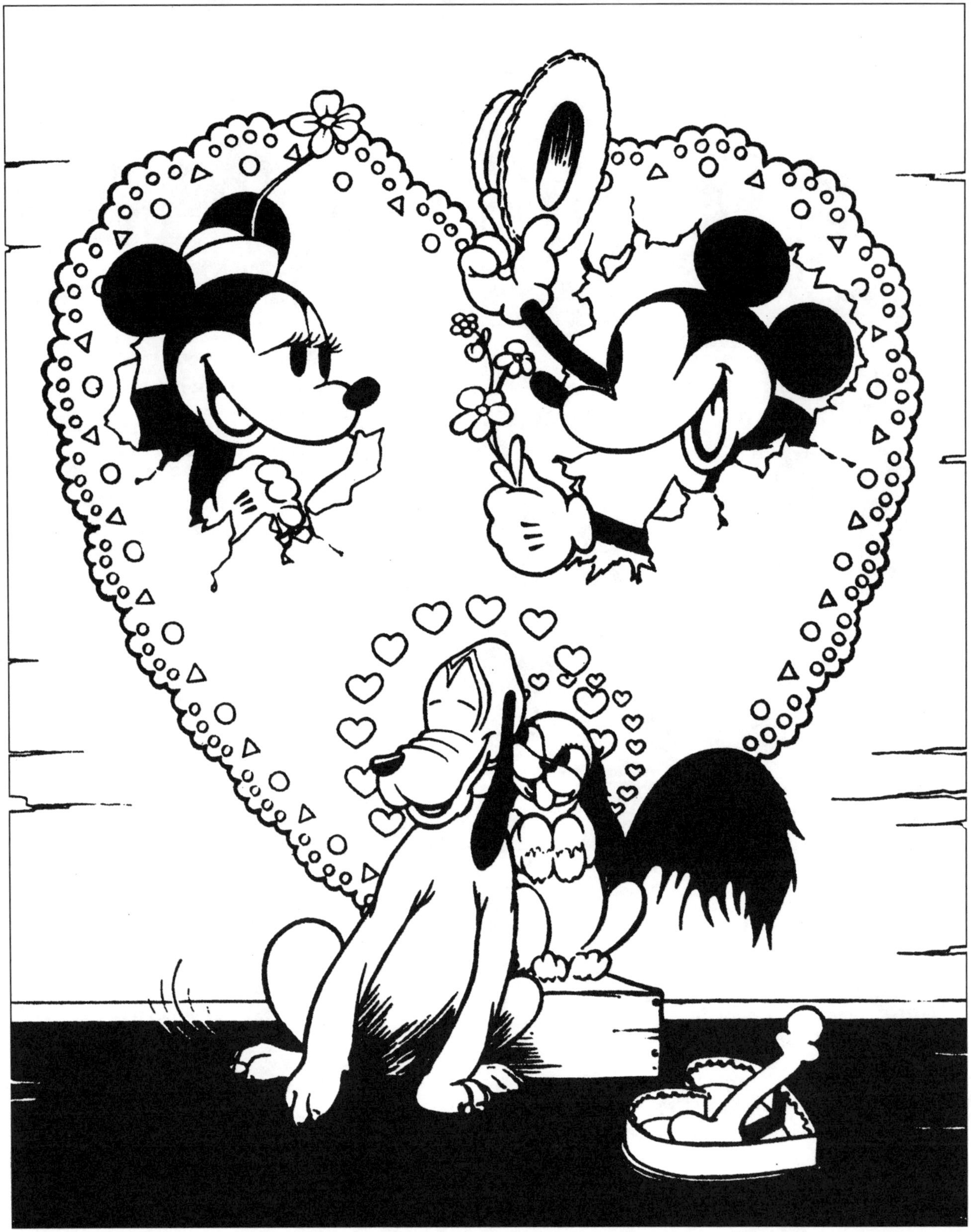

Yowp! Pluto and Mickey would a-wooing go in *Puppy Love* (1933), a classic cartoon short adapted roughly from Gottfredson's May 29, 1932 Sunday strip. Poster art from theatrical release; artist unknown. Image courtesy Walt Disney Archives.

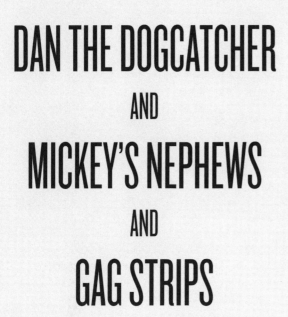

DAN THE DOGCATCHER
AND
MICKEY'S NEPHEWS
AND
GAG STRIPS

JULY 31, 1932
–
JANUARY 22, 1933

MICKEY MOUSE
REGISTERED U.S. PATENT OFFICE

THE PETER PRINCIPLE

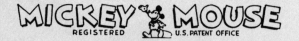

Floyd Gottfredson was not one to rest on his laurels. After mastering several kinds of Sunday gag strip storytelling, how else could he improve his new feature? Perhaps by introducing continuity—though not yet the semi-serious, high adventure continuity that characterized the *Mickey* daily strip.

Gottfredson's first Sunday serials were firmly comedies, often loosely inspired by concurrent cartoons. But this didn't make them lightweight in Gottfredson's mind. He evidently took care to make sure that they integrated sensibly with the continuity of their daily counterparts.

What did this mean in practice? It meant that when *The Mad Dog* (1932), a new Mickey cartoon short, featured a comedy storyline that begged for Sunday adaptation, Gottfredson hopped right to it. Action-packed battles between Mickey and a misunderstanding dogcatcher—as shown in the cartoon—were obvious fodder for a long-form, multi-week scenario. But there was a problem: in the cartoon, this dogcatcher—the voice of law and order—was "played" by Pegleg Pete. And in Gottfredson's ongoing daily strip serials, Pegleg Pete was consistently a crook: "the most perennial heavy of all time," as Gottfredson described him.[1] Could *Mickey Mouse* comics fans make sense of seeing Pete as a lawbreaker during the week, and a law-and-order city official on Sunday? Perhaps not. So how to avoid confusion?

Gottfredson's "out" seems to have been the fact that in *The Mad Dog* cartoon, Pete's physique differed slightly from past incarnations. *Dog* gave Pete a fatter figure and more slovenly demeanor than in earlier *Mickey* shorts—and earlier Gottfredson strips. At the time, Gottfredson drew Pete as a top-heavy, barrel-chested strongman, not a fat slob; and Gottfredson decided to continue that way for the moment. The *Mad Dog* slob design could instead become a somewhat Petelike, but ultimately different peg-legged cat. Exit Pete; enter "Dan the Dogcatcher," fat feline lawman, who starred in both the eponymous 1932 Sunday story and the short 1933 daily serial, "Pluto and the Dogcatcher" (see Volume 2 of our daily strip series).

Of course, time wounds all heels. Several cartoons later, it became clear that Disney's Animation Department would be *keeping* the animated Pete in his new fatter form. What to do now? Gottfredson's cast numbered a Pete who no longer looked like the cartoon Pete—and a Dan who did.

The answer was to blubber up the comics Pete, which Gottfredson did in 1934, and surreptitiously remove Dan from the cast for awhile. In much later 1940s strips, the catfaced dogcatcher eventually reappeared, fat figure and all. But in a nod to perfectionism, Dan now had gray fur or a shaven chin, just to make sure readers still knew he wasn't Pete.

Continuity makes perfect. [DG]

1 Floyd Gottfredson, *Walt Disney Best Comics—Mickey Mouse* (New York: Abbeville Press, Inc., 1978), p. 12.

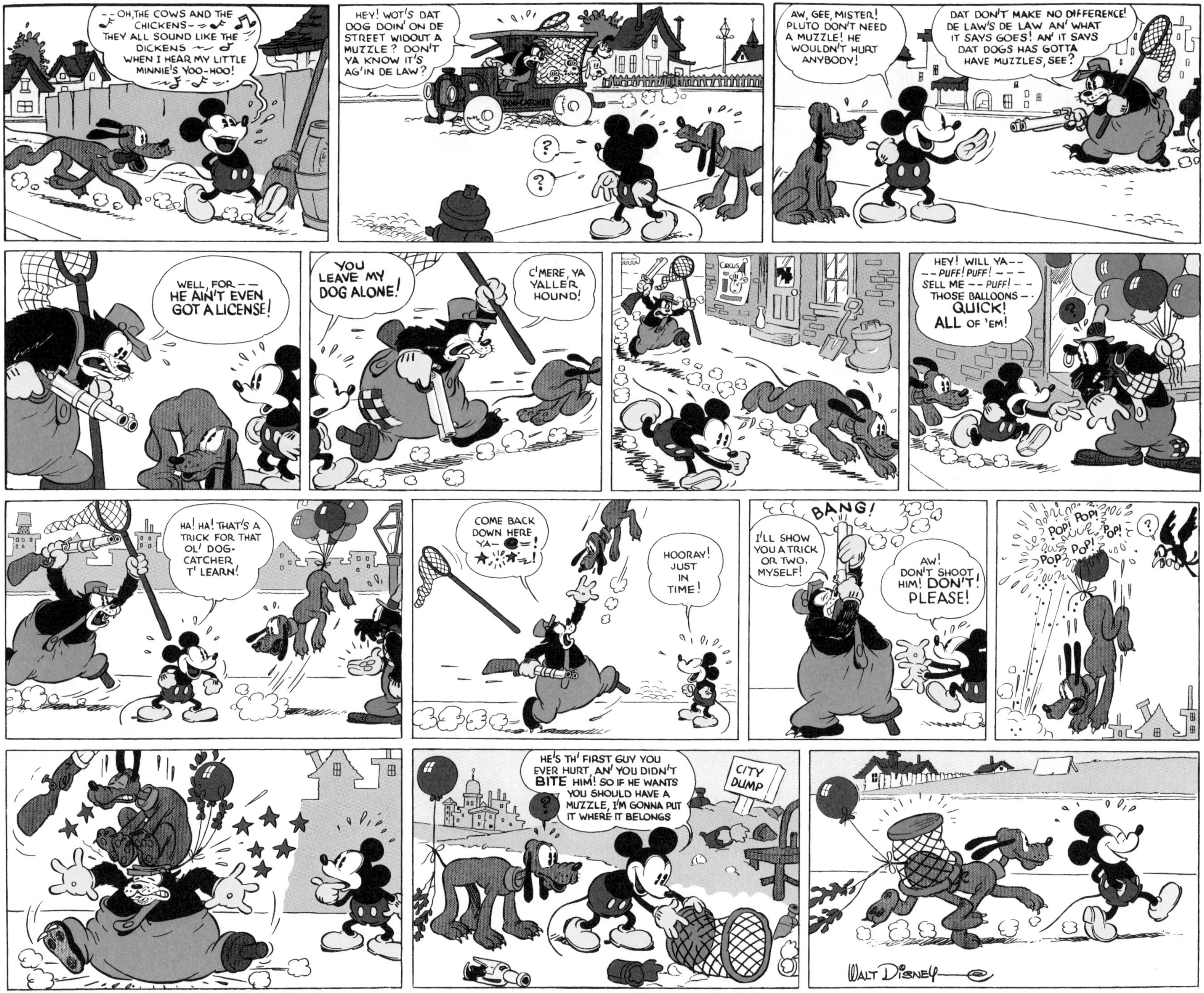
--OH, THE COWS AND THE CHICKENS-- THEY ALL SOUND LIKE THE DICKENS WHEN I HEAR MY LITTLE MINNIE'S YOO-HOO!
HEY! WOT'S DAT DOG DOIN' ON DE STREET WIDOUT A MUZZLE? DON'T YA KNOW IT'S AG'IN DE LAW?
DOG-CATCHER
AW, GEE, MISTER! PLUTO DON'T NEED A MUZZLE! HE WOULDN'T HURT ANYBODY!
DAT DON'T MAKE NO DIFFERENCE! DE LAW'S DE LAW AN' WHAT IT SAYS GOES! AN' IT SAYS DAT DOGS HAS GOTTA HAVE MUZZLES, SEE?
WELL, FOR-- HE AIN'T EVEN GOT A LICENSE!
YOU LEAVE MY DOG ALONE!
C'MERE, YA YALLER HOUND!
CIRCUS
HEY! WILL YA-- --PUFF! PUFF!-- SELL ME --PUFF!-- THOSE BALLOONS-- QUICK! ALL OF 'EM!
HA! HA! THAT'S A TRICK FOR THAT OL' DOG-CATCHER T' LEARN!
COME BACK DOWN HERE YA--
HOORAY! JUST IN TIME!
BANG!
I'LL SHOW YOU A TRICK OR TWO, MYSELF!
AW! DON'T SHOOT HIM! DON'T! PLEASE!
POP! POP! POP! POP! POP!
HE'S TH' FIRST GUY YOU EVER HURT, AN' YOU DIDN'T BITE HIM! SO IF HE WANTS YOU SHOULD HAVE A MUZZLE, I'M GONNA PUT IT WHERE IT BELONGS
CITY DUMP
WALT DISNEY

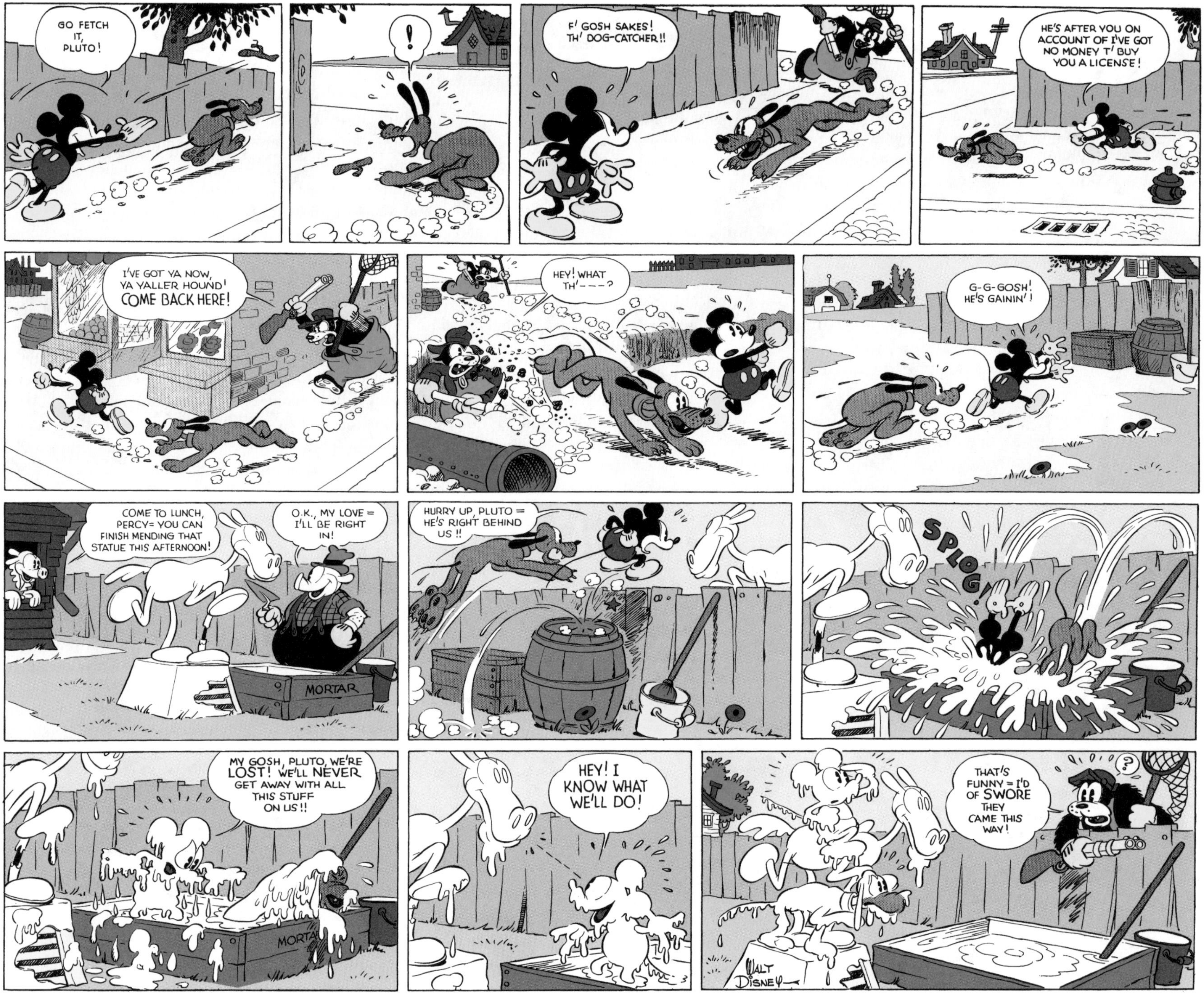

GO FETCH IT, PLUTO!
!
F' GOSH SAKES! TH' DOG-CATCHER!!
HE'S AFTER YOU ON ACCOUNT OF I'VE GOT NO MONEY T' BUY YOU A LICENSE!
I'VE GOT YA NOW, YA YALLER HOUND! COME BACK HERE!
HEY! WHAT TH'---?
G-G-GOSH! HE'S GAININ'!
COME TO LUNCH, PERCY= YOU CAN FINISH MENDING THAT STATUE THIS AFTERNOON!
O.K., MY LOVE = I'LL BE RIGHT IN!
MORTAR
HURRY UP, PLUTO = HE'S RIGHT BEHIND US!!
SPLOG!
MY GOSH, PLUTO, WE'RE LOST! WE'LL NEVER GET AWAY WITH ALL THIS STUFF ON US!!
MORTA
HEY! I KNOW WHAT WE'LL DO!
?
THAT'S FUNNY = I'D OF SWORE THEY CAME THIS WAY!
WALT DISNEY

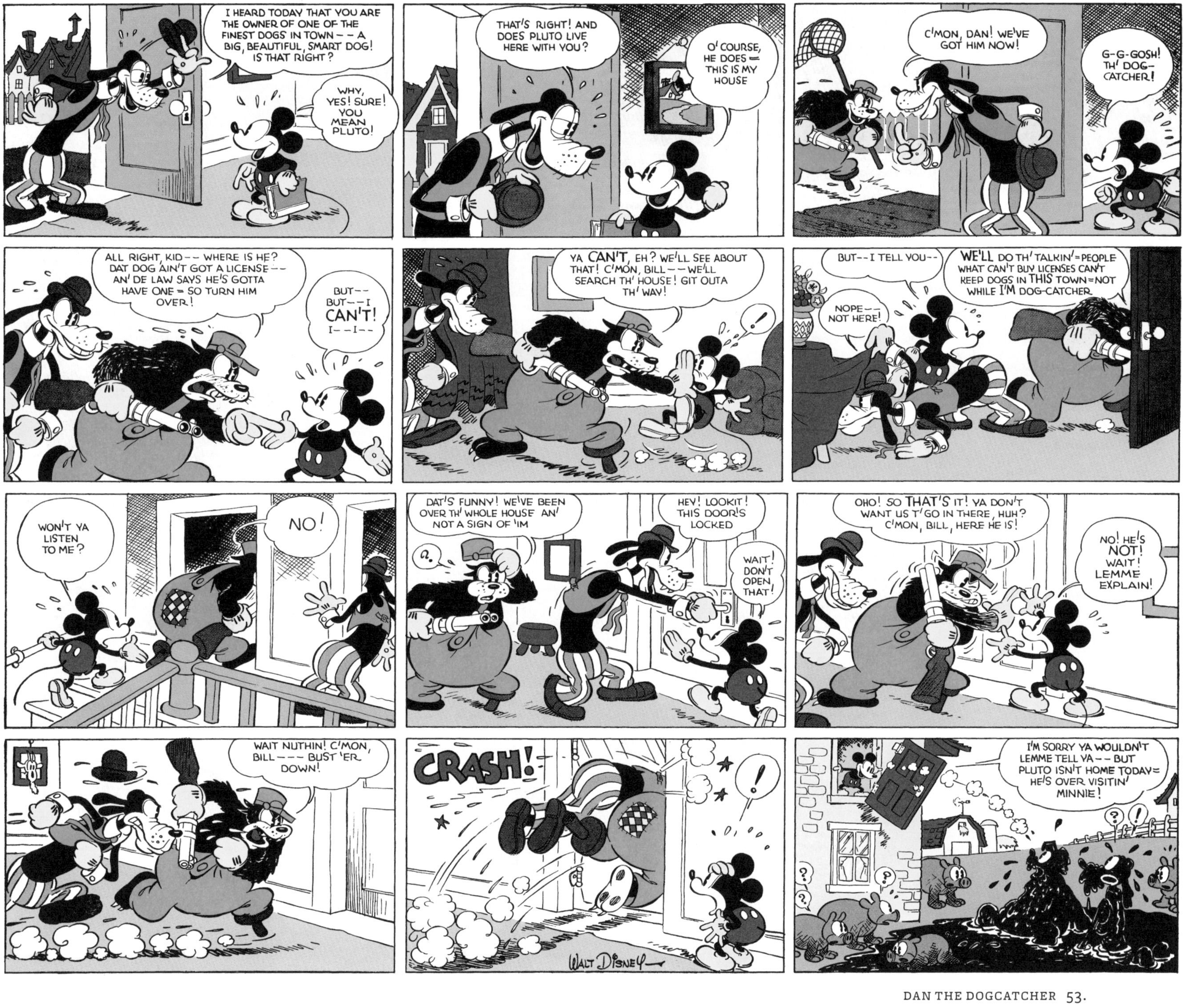
I HEARD TODAY THAT YOU ARE THE OWNER OF ONE OF THE FINEST DOGS IN TOWN -- A BIG, BEAUTIFUL, SMART DOG! IS THAT RIGHT?
WHY, YES! SURE! YOU MEAN PLUTO!
THAT'S RIGHT! AND DOES PLUTO LIVE HERE WITH YOU?
O' COURSE, HE DOES = THIS IS MY HOUSE
C'MON, DAN! WE'VE GOT HIM NOW!
G-G-GOSH! TH' DOG-CATCHER!
ALL RIGHT, KID -- WHERE IS HE? DAT DOG AIN'T GOT A LICENSE -- AN' DE LAW SAYS HE'S GOTTA HAVE ONE = SO TURN HIM OVER!
BUT-- BUT--I CAN'T! I--I--
YA CAN'T, EH? WE'LL SEE ABOUT THAT! C'MON, BILL -- WE'LL SEARCH TH' HOUSE! GIT OUTA TH' WAY!
!
BUT--I TELL YOU--
WE'LL DO TH' TALKIN' = PEOPLE WHAT CAN'T BUY LICENSES CAN'T KEEP DOGS IN THIS TOWN = NOT WHILE I'M DOG-CATCHER
NOPE-- NOT HERE!
WON'T YA LISTEN TO ME?
NO!
DAT'S FUNNY! WE'VE BEEN OVER TH' WHOLE HOUSE AN' NOT A SIGN OF 'IM
HEY! LOOKIT! THIS DOOR'S LOCKED
WAIT! DON'T OPEN THAT!
OHO! SO THAT'S IT! YA DON'T WANT US T' GO IN THERE, HUH? C'MON, BILL, HERE HE IS!
NO! HE'S NOT! WAIT! LEMME EXPLAIN!
WAIT NUTHIN! C'MON, BILL --- BUST 'ER DOWN!
CRASH!
!
WALT DISNEY
I'M SORRY YA WOULDN'T LEMME TELL YA -- BUT PLUTO ISN'T HOME TODAY = HE'S OVER VISITIN' MINNIE!

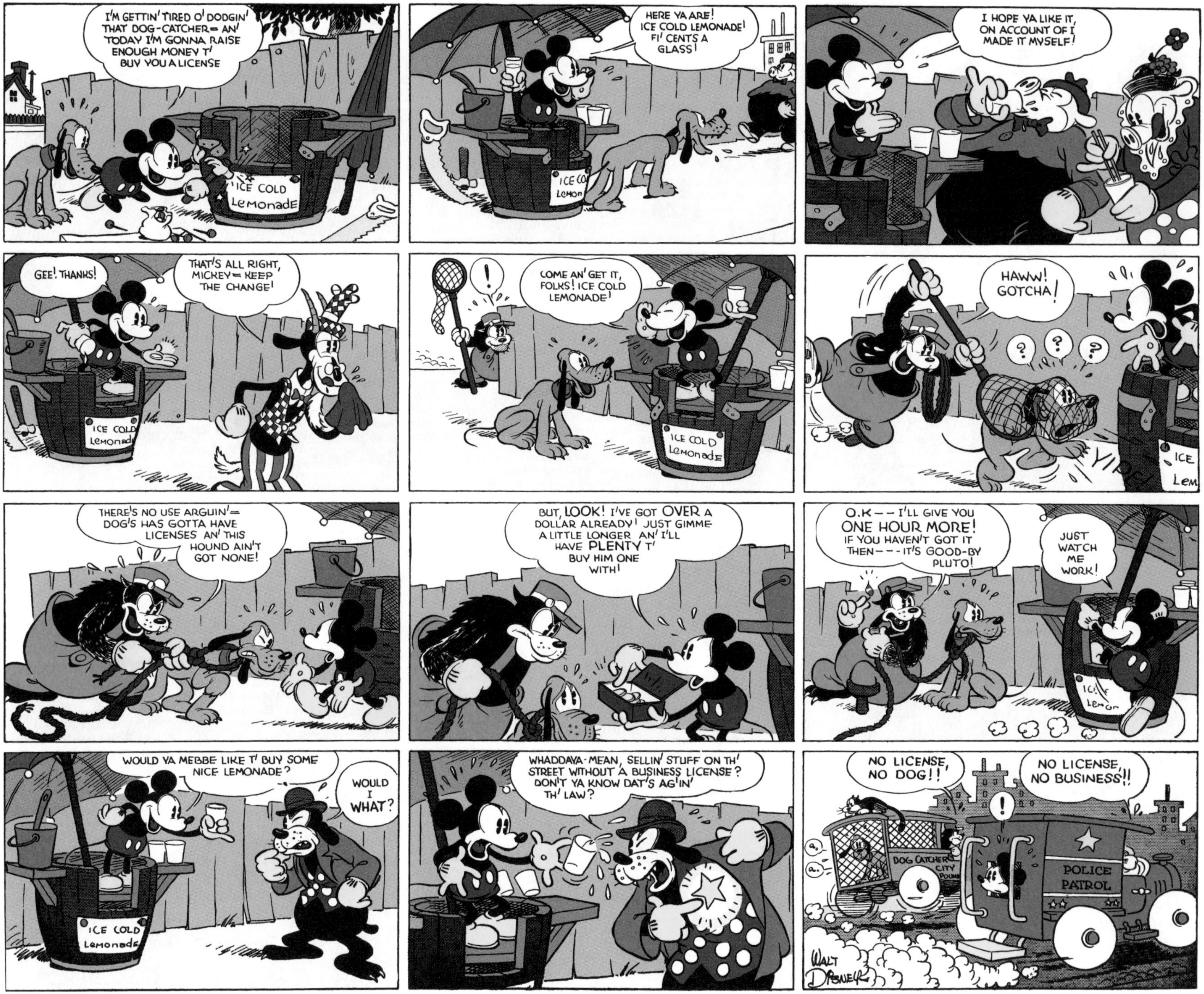

I'M GETTIN' TIRED O' DODGIN' THAT DOG-CATCHER= AN' TODAY I'M GONNA RAISE ENOUGH MONEY T' BUY YOU A LICENSE
ICE COLD Lemonade
HERE YA ARE! ICE COLD LEMONADE! FI' CENTS A GLASS!
ICE COLD Lemon
I HOPE YA LIKE IT, ON ACCOUNT OF I MADE IT MYSELF!
GEE! THANKS!
THAT'S ALL RIGHT, MICKEY= KEEP THE CHANGE!
ICE COLD Lemonade
!
COME AN' GET IT, FOLKS! ICE COLD LEMONADE!
ICE COLD Lemonade
HAWW! GOTCHA!
? ? ?
YIPE!
ICE Lem
THERE'S NO USE ARGUIN'= DOG'S HAS GOTTA HAVE LICENSES AN' THIS HOUND AIN'T GOT NONE!
BUT, LOOK! I'VE GOT OVER A DOLLAR ALREADY! JUST GIMME A LITTLE LONGER AN' I'LL HAVE PLENTY T' BUY HIM ONE WITH!
O.K -- I'LL GIVE YOU ONE HOUR MORE! IF YOU HAVEN'T GOT IT THEN --- IT'S GOOD-BY PLUTO!
JUST WATCH ME WORK!
WOULD YA MEBBE LIKE T' BUY SOME NICE LEMONADE?
WOULD I WHAT?
ICE COLD Lemonade
WHADDAYA-MEAN, SELLIN' STUFF ON TH' STREET WITHOUT A BUSINESS LICENSE? DON'T YA KNOW DAT'S AG'IN' TH' LAW?
NO LICENSE, NO DOG!!
NO LICENSE, NO BUSINESS!!
!
DOG CATCHER CITY POUND
POLICE PATROL
WALT DISNEY

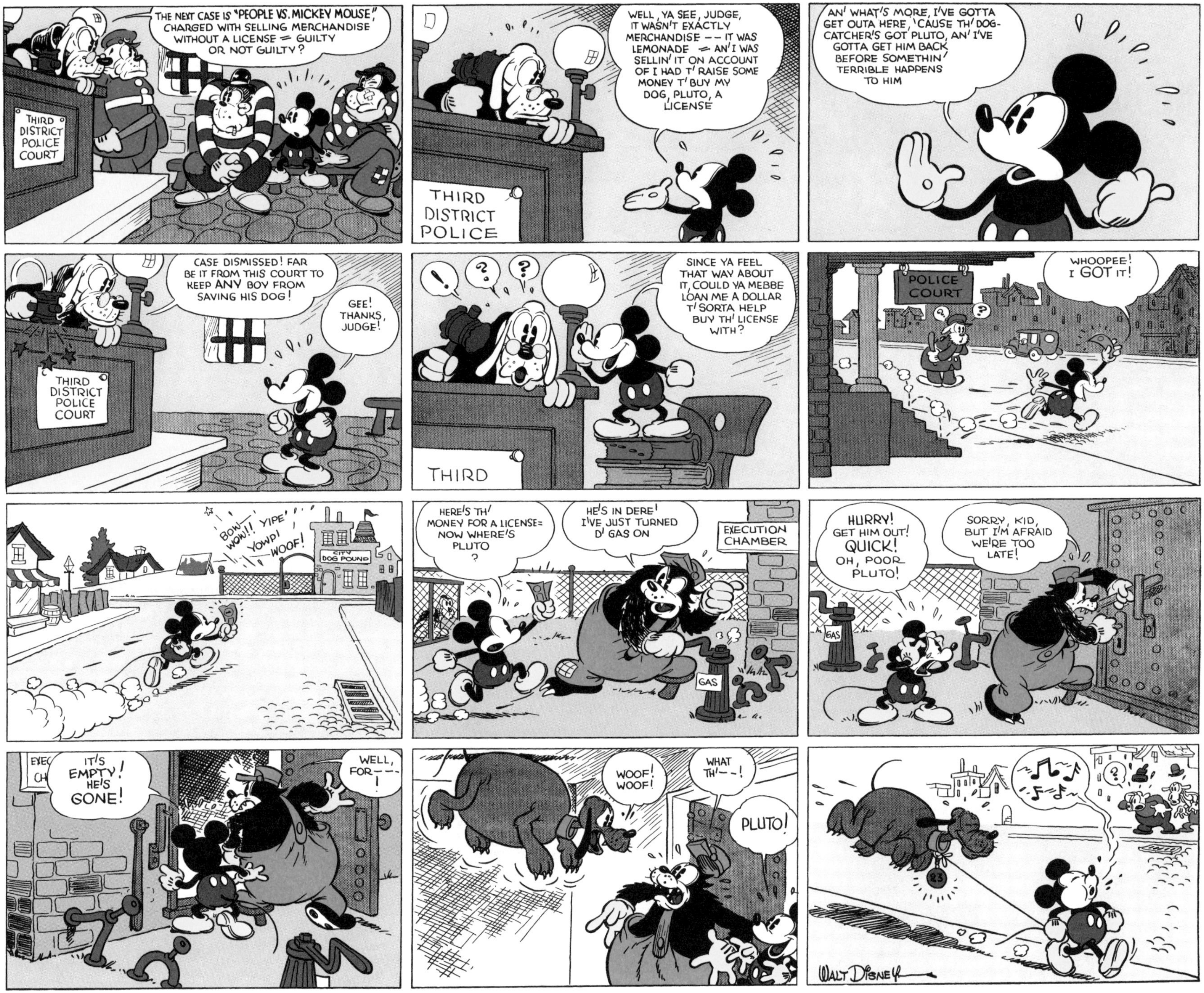
THE NEXT CASE IS "PEOPLE VS. MICKEY MOUSE," CHARGED WITH SELLING MERCHANDISE WITHOUT A LICENSE = GUILTY OR NOT GUILTY?
THIRD DISTRICT POLICE COURT
WELL, YA SEE, JUDGE, IT WASN'T EXACTLY MERCHANDISE -- IT WAS LEMONADE = AN' I WAS SELLIN' IT ON ACCOUNT OF I HAD T' RAISE SOME MONEY T' BUY MY DOG, PLUTO, A LICENSE
THIRD DISTRICT POLICE
AN' WHAT'S MORE, I'VE GOTTA GET OUTA HERE, 'CAUSE TH' DOG-CATCHER'S GOT PLUTO, AN' I'VE GOTTA GET HIM BACK BEFORE SOMETHIN' TERRIBLE HAPPENS TO HIM
CASE DISMISSED! FAR BE IT FROM THIS COURT TO KEEP ANY BOY FROM SAVING HIS DOG!
GEE! THANKS, JUDGE!
THIRD DISTRICT POLICE COURT
!
?
?
SINCE YA FEEL THAT WAY ABOUT IT, COULD YA MEBBE LOAN ME A DOLLAR T' SORTA HELP BUY TH' LICENSE WITH?
THIRD
POLICE COURT
WHOOPEE! I GOT IT!
BOW-WOW!! YIPE! YOWP! WOOF!
CITY DOG POUND
HERE'S TH' MONEY FOR A LICENSE= NOW WHERE'S PLUTO ?
HE'S IN DERE! I'VE JUST TURNED D' GAS ON
EXECUTION CHAMBER
GAS
HURRY! GET HIM OUT! QUICK! OH, POOR PLUTO!
SORRY, KID, BUT I'M AFRAID WE'RE TOO LATE!
GAS
IT'S EMPTY! HE'S GONE!
WELL, FOR---!
WOOF! WOOF!
WHAT TH'--!
PLUTO!
?
WALT DISNEY

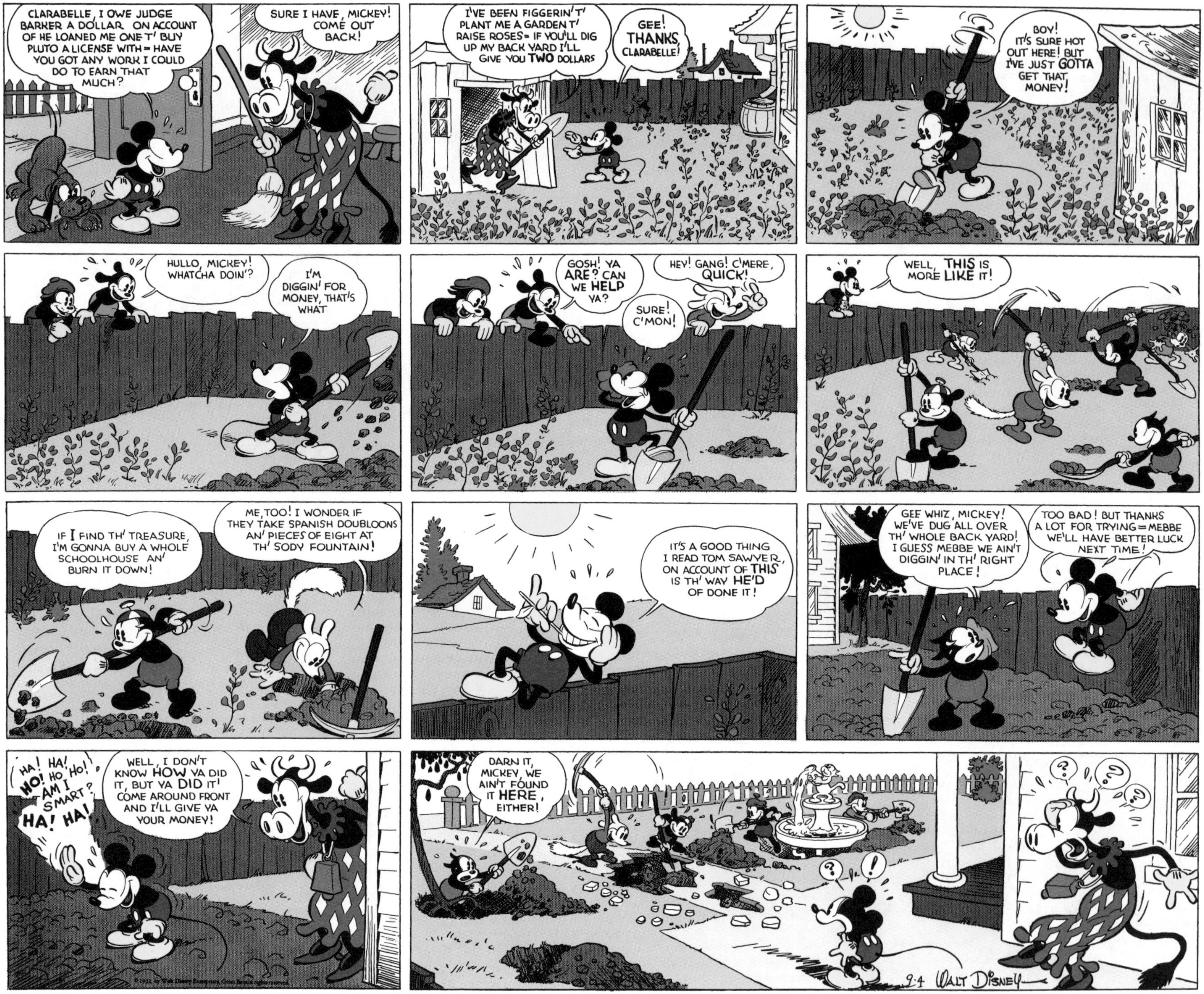
CLARABELLE, I OWE JUDGE BARKER A DOLLAR ON ACCOUNT OF HE LOANED ME ONE T' BUY PLUTO A LICENSE WITH = HAVE YOU GOT ANY WORK I COULD DO TO EARN THAT MUCH?
SURE I HAVE, MICKEY! COME OUT BACK!
I'VE BEEN FIGGERIN' T' PLANT ME A GARDEN T' RAISE ROSES = IF YOU'LL DIG UP MY BACK YARD I'LL GIVE YOU TWO DOLLARS
GEE! THANKS, CLARABELLE!
BOY! IT'S SURE HOT OUT HERE! BUT I'VE JUST GOTTA GET THAT MONEY!
HULLO, MICKEY! WHATCHA DOIN'?
I'M DIGGIN' FOR MONEY, THAT'S WHAT
GOSH! YA ARE? CAN WE HELP YA?
HEY! GANG! C'MERE, QUICK!
SURE! C'MON!
WELL, THIS IS MORE LIKE IT!
IF I FIND TH' TREASURE, I'M GONNA BUY A WHOLE SCHOOLHOUSE AN' BURN IT DOWN!
ME, TOO! I WONDER IF THEY TAKE SPANISH DOUBLOONS AN' PIECES OF EIGHT AT TH' SODY FOUNTAIN!
IT'S A GOOD THING I READ TOM SAWYER, ON ACCOUNT OF THIS IS TH' WAY HE'D OF DONE IT!
GEE WHIZ, MICKEY! WE'VE DUG ALL OVER TH' WHOLE BACK YARD! I GUESS MEBBE WE AIN'T DIGGIN' IN TH' RIGHT PLACE!
TOO BAD! BUT THANKS A LOT FOR TRYING = MEBBE WE'LL HAVE BETTER LUCK NEXT TIME!
HA! HA! HO! HO! HO! AM I SMART? HA! HA!
WELL, I DON'T KNOW HOW YA DID IT, BUT YA DID IT! COME AROUND FRONT AND I'LL GIVE YA YOUR MONEY!
DARN IT, MICKEY, WE AIN'T FOUND IT HERE, EITHER!
? !
9-4 WALT DISNEY

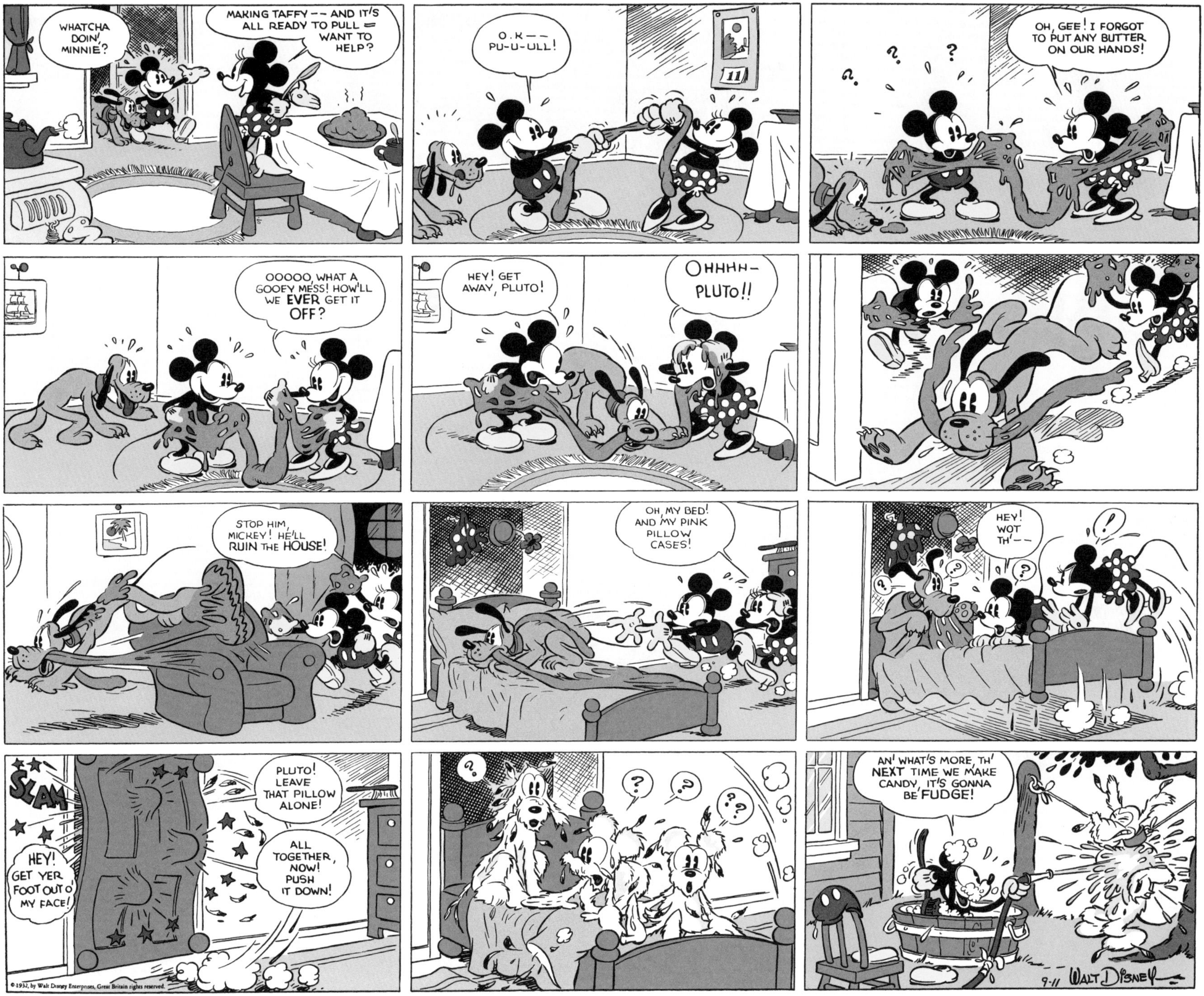
WHATCHA DOIN', MINNIE?
MAKING TAFFY -- AND IT'S ALL READY TO PULL = WANT TO HELP?
O.K. -- PU-U-ULL!
11
OH, GEE! I FORGOT TO PUT ANY BUTTER ON OUR HANDS!
OOOOO, WHAT A GOOEY MESS! HOW'LL WE EVER GET IT OFF?
HEY! GET AWAY, PLUTO!
OHHHH- PLUTO!!
STOP HIM, MICKEY! HE'LL RUIN THE HOUSE!
OH, MY BED! AND MY PINK PILLOW CASES!
HEY! WOT TH'--
SLAM
HEY! GET YER FOOT OUT O' MY FACE!
PLUTO! LEAVE THAT PILLOW ALONE!
ALL TOGETHER, NOW! PUSH IT DOWN!
AN' WHAT'S MORE, TH' NEXT TIME WE MAKE CANDY, IT'S GONNA BE FUDGE!
9-11 WALT DISNEY
© 1932, by Walt Disney Enterprises, Great Britain rights reserved.

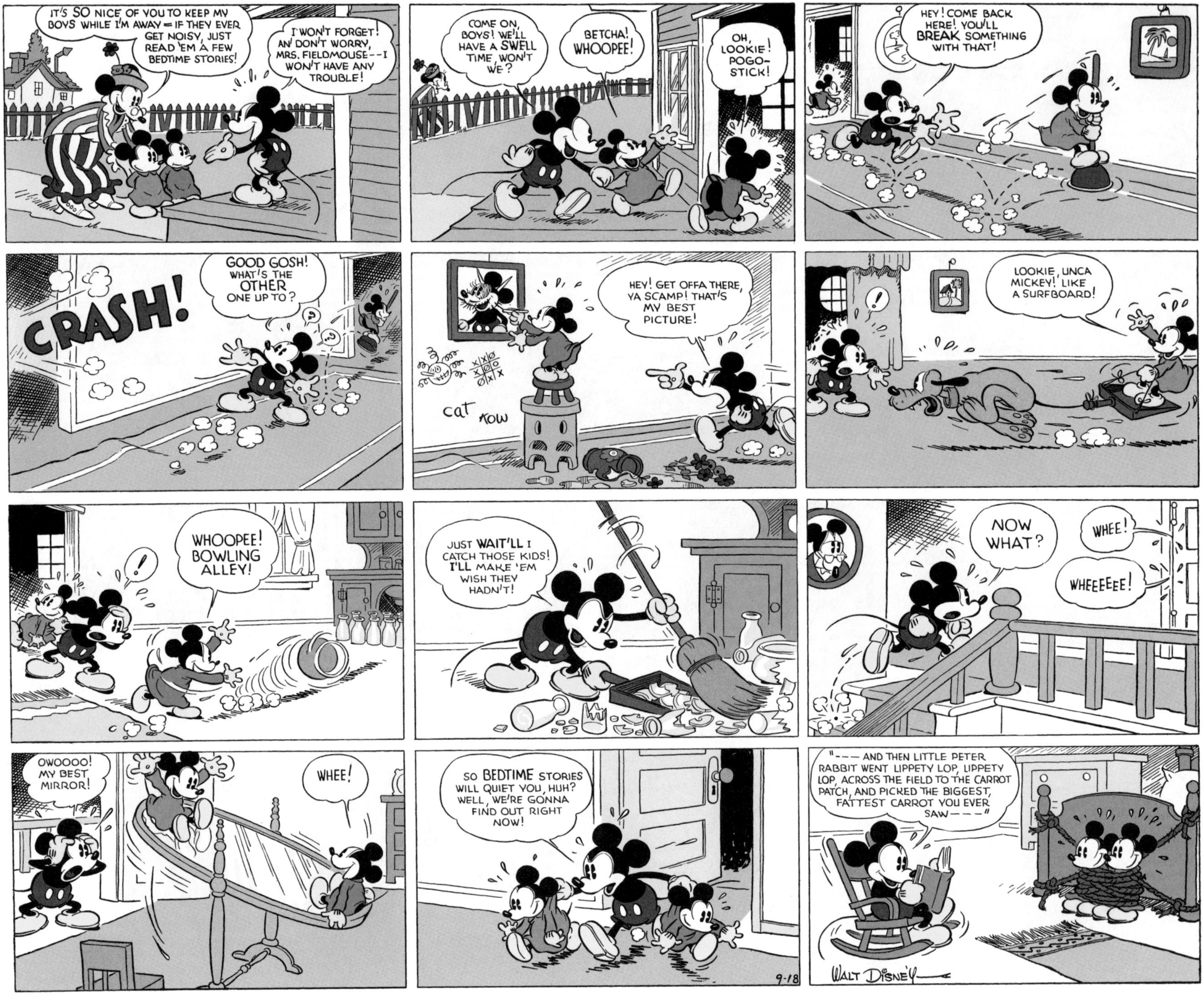

IT'S SO NICE OF YOU TO KEEP MY BOYS WHILE I'M AWAY = IF THEY EVER GET NOISY, JUST READ 'EM A FEW BEDTIME STORIES!
I WON'T FORGET! AN' DON'T WORRY, MRS. FIELDMOUSE--I WON'T HAVE ANY TROUBLE!
COME ON, BOYS! WE'LL HAVE A SWELL TIME, WON'T WE?
BETCHA! WHOOPEE!
OH, LOOKIE! POGO-STICK!
HEY! COME BACK HERE! YOU'LL BREAK SOMETHING WITH THAT!
CRASH!
GOOD GOSH! WHAT'S THE OTHER ONE UP TO?
HEY! GET OFFA THERE, YA SCAMP! THAT'S MY BEST PICTURE!
CAT
KOW
LOOKIE, UNCA MICKEY! LIKE A SURFBOARD!
WHOOPEE! BOWLING ALLEY!
JUST WAIT'LL I CATCH THOSE KIDS! I'LL MAKE 'EM WISH THEY HADN'T!
NOW WHAT?
WHEE!
WHEEEEEE!
OWOOOO! MY BEST MIRROR!
WHEE!
SO BEDTIME STORIES WILL QUIET YOU, HUH? WELL, WE'RE GONNA FIND OUT RIGHT NOW!
9-18
"--- AND THEN LITTLE PETER RABBIT WENT LIPPETY LOP, LIPPETY LOP, ACROSS THE FIELD TO THE CARROT PATCH, AND PICKED THE BIGGEST, FATTEST CARROT YOU EVER SAW---"
WALT DISNEY

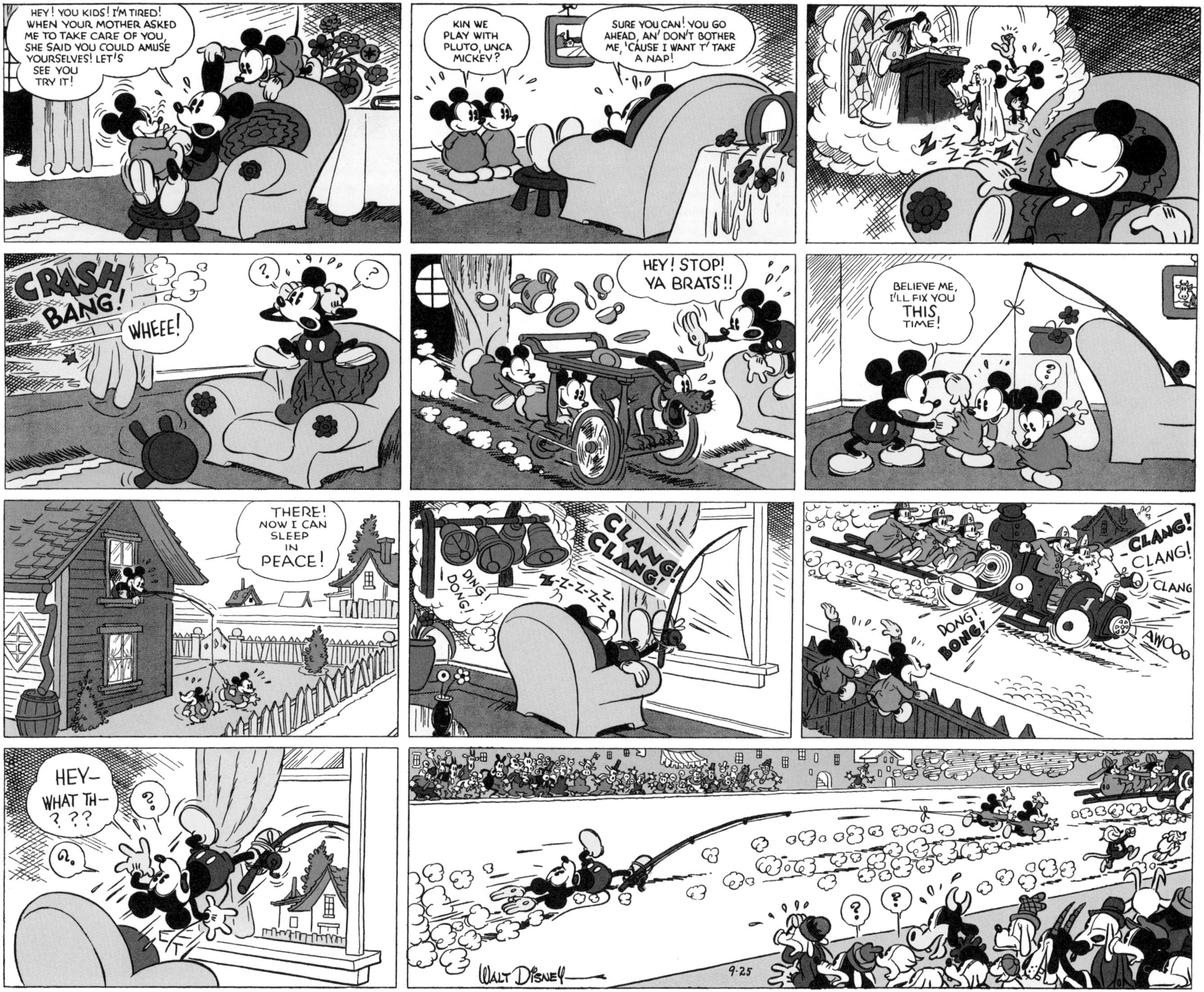
HEY! YOU KIDS! I'M TIRED! WHEN YOUR MOTHER ASKED ME TO TAKE CARE OF YOU, SHE SAID YOU COULD AMUSE YOURSELVES! LET'S SEE YOU TRY IT!
KIN WE PLAY WITH PLUTO, UNCA MICKEY?
SURE YOU CAN! YOU GO AHEAD, AN' DON'T BOTHER ME, 'CAUSE I WANT T' TAKE A NAP!
Z-Z-Z-Z
CRASH
BANG!
WHEEE!
?
?
HEY! STOP! YA BRATS!!
BELIEVE ME, I'LL FIX YOU THIS TIME!
?
THERE! NOW I CAN SLEEP IN PEACE!
DING! DONG!
Z-Z-Z-Z-Z
CLANG! CLANG!
CLANG!
CLANG!
CLANG
DONG! BONG!
AWOOO
HEY— WHAT TH— ? ??
?
?
?
?
WALT DISNEY
9·25

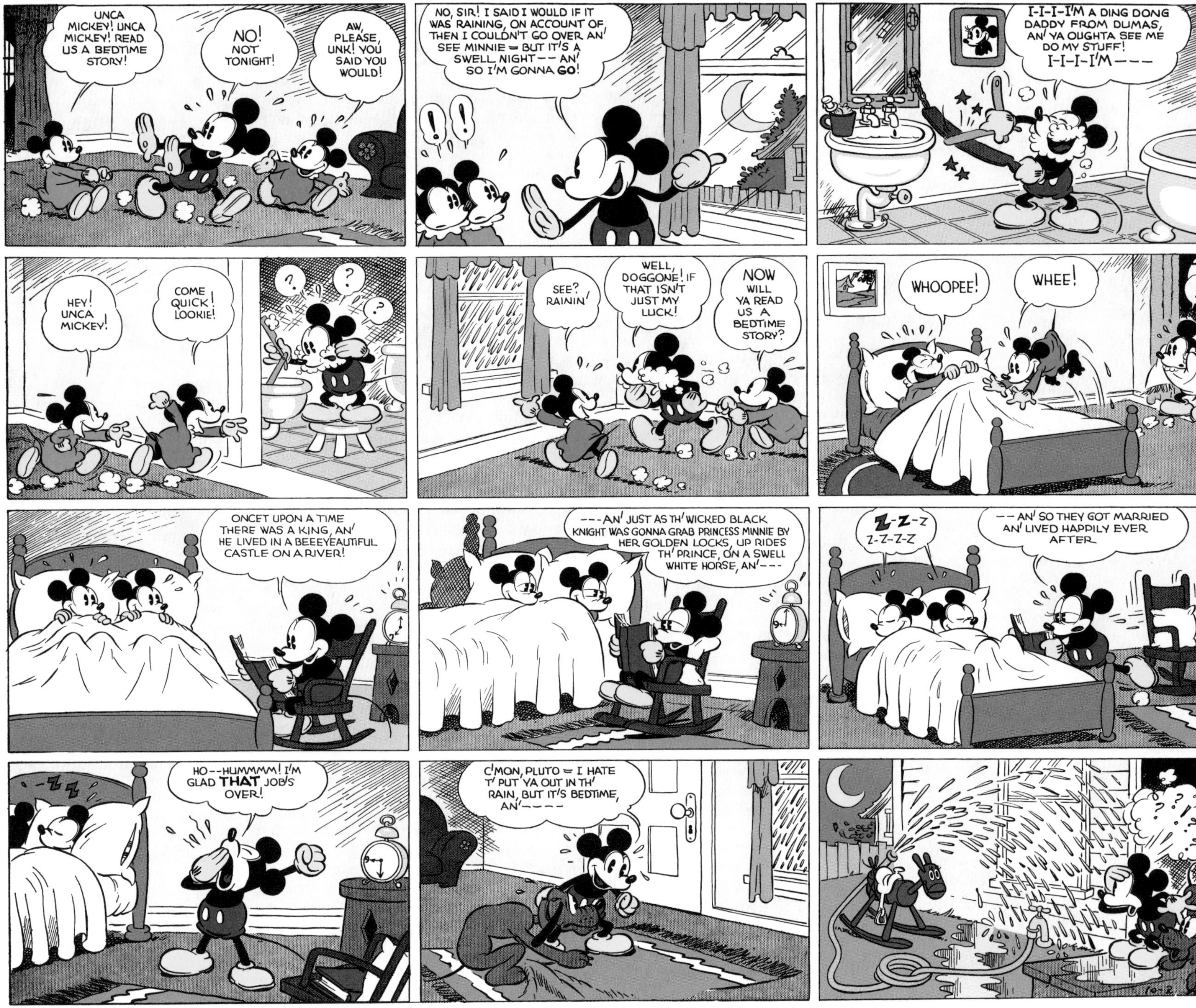
UNCA MICKEY! UNCA MICKEY! READ US A BEDTIME STORY!
NO! NOT TONIGHT!
AW, PLEASE, UNK! YOU SAID YOU WOULD!
NO, SIR! I SAID I WOULD IF IT WAS RAINING, ON ACCOUNT OF THEN I COULDN'T GO OVER AN' SEE MINNIE — BUT IT'S A SWELL NIGHT — — AN' SO I'M GONNA GO!
! !
I-I-I-I'M A DING DONG DADDY FROM DUMAS, AN' YA OUGHTA SEE ME DO MY STUFF! I-I-I-I'M — — —
HEY! UNCA MICKEY!
COME QUICK! LOOKIE!
? ? ?
SEE? RAININ'
WELL, DOGGONE! IF THAT ISN'T JUST MY LUCK!
NOW WILL YA READ US A BEDTIME STORY?
WHOOPEE!
WHEE!
!
ONCET UPON A TIME THERE WAS A KING, AN' HE LIVED IN A BEEEYEAUTIFUL CASTLE ON A RIVER!
— — — AN' JUST AS TH' WICKED BLACK KNIGHT WAS GONNA GRAB PRINCESS MINNIE BY HER GOLDEN LOCKS, UP RIDES TH' PRINCE, ON A SWELL WHITE HORSE, AN' — — —
Z-Z-Z Z-Z-Z-Z
— — AN' SO THEY GOT MARRIED AN' LIVED HAPPILY EVER AFTER
Z Z
HO — — HUMMMM! I'M GLAD THAT JOB'S OVER!
C'MON, PLUTO — I HATE T' PUT YA OUT IN TH' RAIN, BUT IT'S BEDTIME, AN' — — — —
? ! ?
10-2

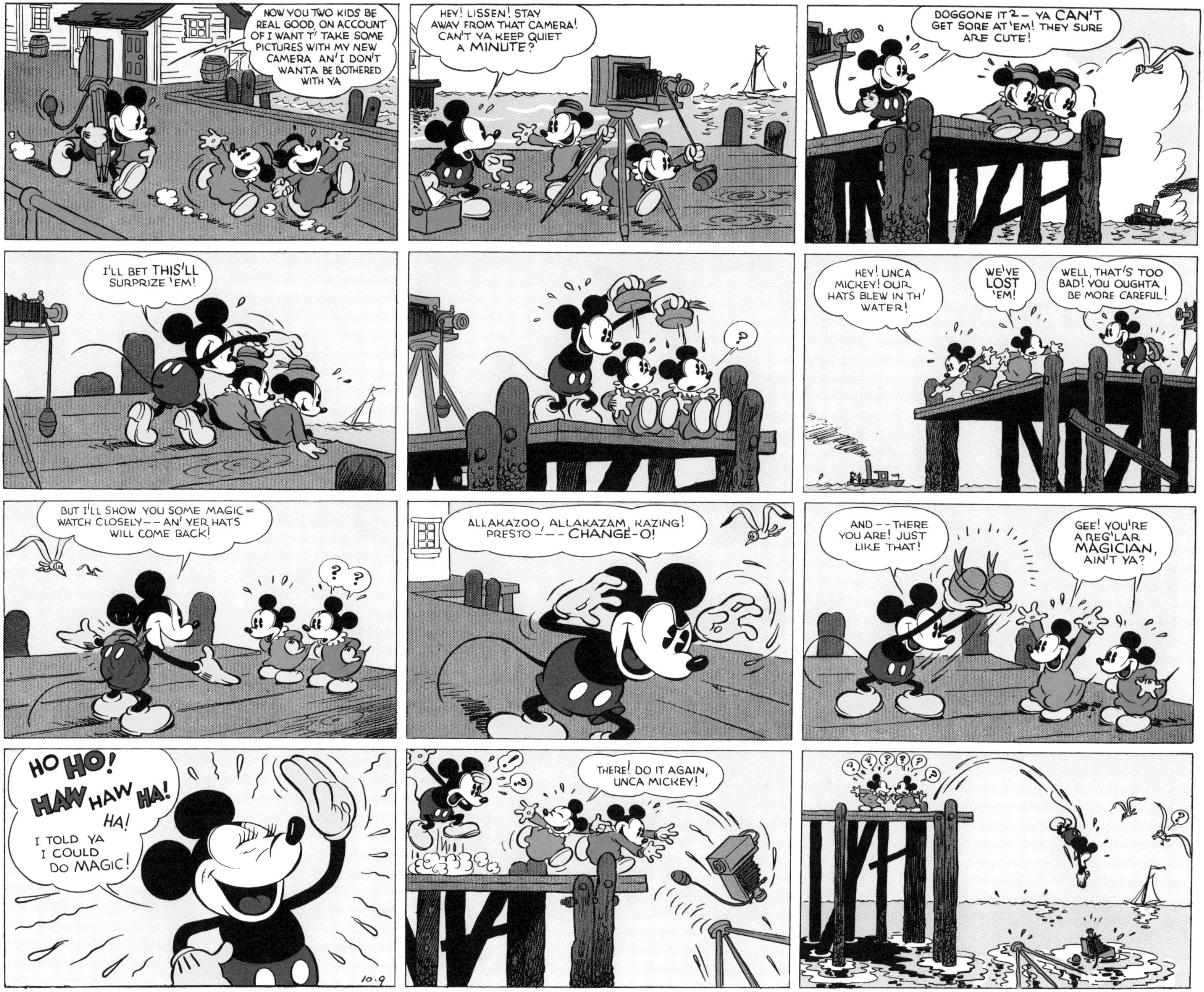
NOW YOU TWO KIDS BE REAL GOOD, ON ACCOUNT OF I WANT T' TAKE SOME PICTURES WITH MY NEW CAMERA AN' I DON'T WANTA BE BOTHERED WITH YA
HEY! LISSEN! STAY AWAY FROM THAT CAMERA! CAN'T YA KEEP QUIET A MINUTE?
DOGGONE IT ?-- YA CAN'T GET SORE AT 'EM! THEY SURE ARE CUTE!
I'LL BET THIS'LL SURPRIZE 'EM!
HEY! UNCA MICKEY! OUR HATS BLEW IN TH' WATER!
WE'VE LOST 'EM!
WELL, THAT'S TOO BAD! YOU OUGHTA BE MORE CAREFUL!
BUT I'LL SHOW YOU SOME MAGIC = WATCH CLOSELY--- AN' YER HATS WILL COME BACK!
ALLAKAZOO, ALLAKAZAM, KAZING! PRESTO --- CHANGE-O!
AND -- THERE YOU ARE! JUST LIKE THAT!
GEE! YOU'RE A REG'LAR MAGICIAN, AIN'T YA?
HO HO! HAW HAW HA! HA!
I TOLD YA I COULD DO MAGIC!
10.9
THERE! DO IT AGAIN, UNCA MICKEY!

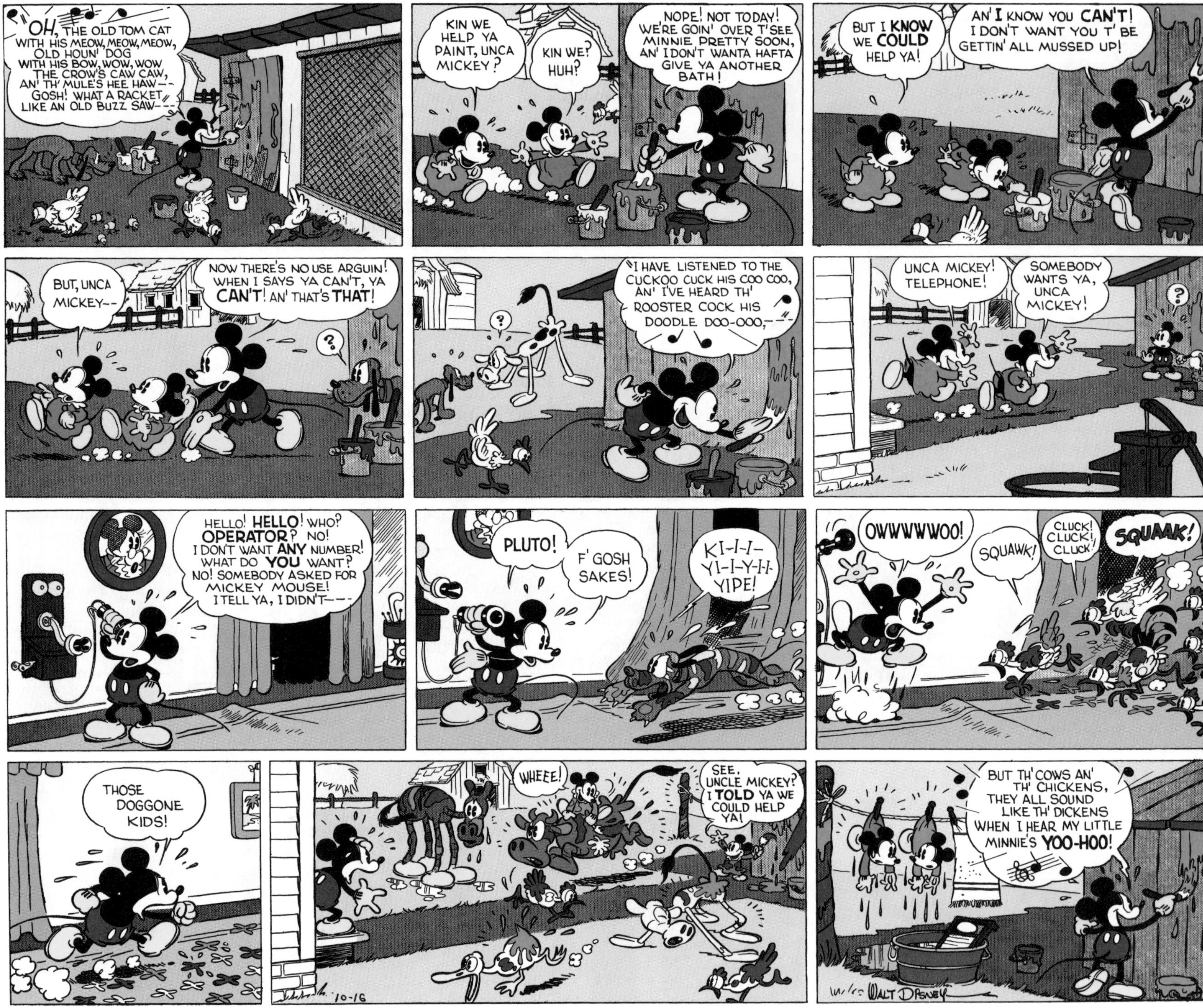
OH, THE OLD TOM CAT WITH HIS MEOW, MEOW, MEOW, OLD HOUN' DOG WITH HIS BOW, WOW, WOW THE CROW'S CAW CAW, AN' TH' MULE'S HEE HAW-- GOSH! WHAT A RACKET LIKE AN OLD BUZZ SAW---
KIN WE HELP YA PAINT, UNCA MICKEY?
KIN WE? HUH?
NOPE! NOT TODAY! WE'RE GOIN' OVER T'SEE MINNIE PRETTY SOON, AN' I DON'T WANTA HAFTA GIVE YA ANOTHER BATH!
BUT I KNOW WE COULD HELP YA!
AN' I KNOW YOU CAN'T! I DON'T WANT YOU T' BE GETTIN' ALL MUSSED UP!
BUT, UNCA MICKEY--
NOW THERE'S NO USE ARGUIN! WHEN I SAYS YA CAN'T, YA CAN'T! AN' THAT'S THAT!
?
?
I HAVE LISTENED TO THE CUCKOO CUCK HIS COO COO, AN' I'VE HEARD TH' ROOSTER COCK HIS DOODLE DOO-OOO,---
UNCA MICKEY! TELEPHONE!
SOMEBODY WANTS YA, UNCA MICKEY!
?
HELLO! HELLO! WHO? OPERATOR? NO! I DON'T WANT ANY NUMBER! WHAT DO YOU WANT? NO! SOMEBODY ASKED FOR MICKEY MOUSE! I TELL YA, I DIDN'T---
PLUTO!
F' GOSH SAKES!
KI-I-I-YI-I-Y-I-I-YIPE!
OWWWWWOO!
SQUAWK!
CLUCK! CLUCK! CLUCK!
SQUAAK!
THOSE DOGGONE KIDS!
WHEEE!
SEE, UNCLE MICKEY? I TOLD YA WE COULD HELP YA!
10-16
BUT TH' COWS AN' TH' CHICKENS, THEY ALL SOUND LIKE TH' DICKENS WHEN I HEAR MY LITTLE MINNIE'S YOO-HOO!
WALT DISNEY

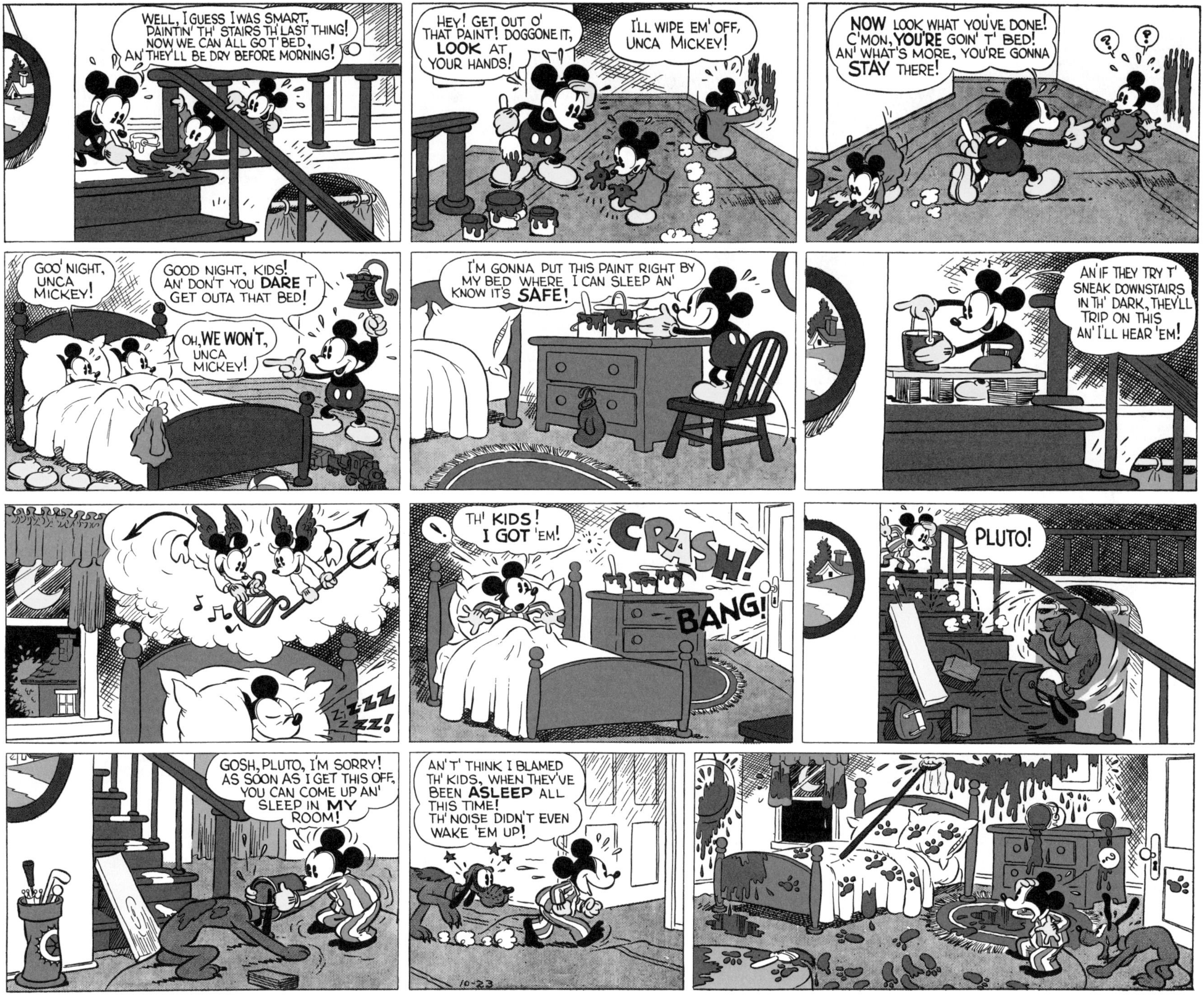

WELL, I GUESS I WAS SMART, PAINTIN' TH' STAIRS TH' LAST THING! NOW WE CAN ALL GO T' BED, AN' THEY'LL BE DRY BEFORE MORNING!
HEY! GET OUT O' THAT PAINT! DOGGONE IT, LOOK AT YOUR HANDS!
I'LL WIPE EM' OFF, UNCA MICKEY!
NOW LOOK WHAT YOU'VE DONE! C'MON, YOU'RE GOIN' T' BED! AN' WHAT'S MORE, YOU'RE GONNA STAY THERE!
?
?
GOO' NIGHT, UNCA MICKEY!
GOOD NIGHT, KIDS! AN' DON'T YOU DARE T' GET OUTA THAT BED!
OH, WE WON'T, UNCA MICKEY!
I'M GONNA PUT THIS PAINT RIGHT BY MY BED WHERE I CAN SLEEP AN' KNOW IT'S SAFE!
AN' IF THEY TRY T' SNEAK DOWNSTAIRS IN TH' DARK, THEY'LL TRIP ON THIS AN' I'LL HEAR 'EM!
ZZZZ ZZZ!
!
TH' KIDS! I GOT 'EM!
CRASH!
BANG!
PLUTO!
GOSH, PLUTO, I'M SORRY! AS SOON AS I GET THIS OFF, YOU CAN COME UP AN' SLEEP IN MY ROOM!
AN' T' THINK I BLAMED TH' KIDS, WHEN THEY'VE BEEN ASLEEP ALL THIS TIME! TH' NOISE DIDN'T EVEN WAKE 'EM UP!
10-23
?

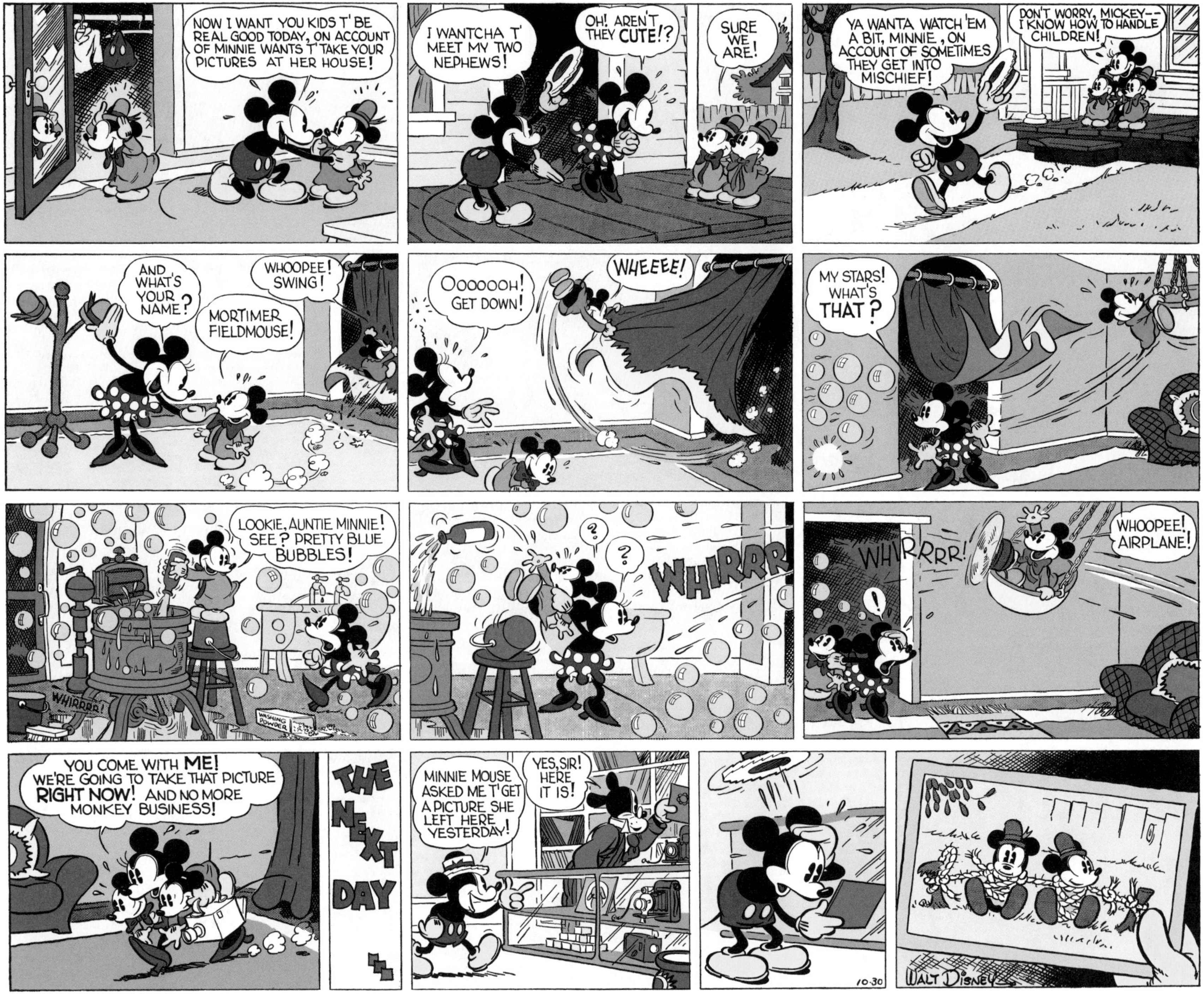

NOW I WANT YOU KIDS T' BE REAL GOOD TODAY, ON ACCOUNT OF MINNIE WANTS T' TAKE YOUR PICTURES AT HER HOUSE!
I WANTCHA T' MEET MY TWO NEPHEWS!
OH! AREN'T THEY CUTE!?
SURE WE ARE!
YA WANTA WATCH 'EM A BIT, MINNIE, ON ACCOUNT OF SOMETIMES THEY GET INTO MISCHIEF!
DON'T WORRY, MICKEY-- I KNOW HOW TO HANDLE CHILDREN!
AND WHAT'S YOUR NAME?
MORTIMER FIELDMOUSE!
WHOOPEE! SWING!
OOOOOOH! GET DOWN!
WHEEEE!
MY STARS! WHAT'S THAT?
LOOKIE, AUNTIE MINNIE! SEE? PRETTY BLUE BUBBLES!
WHIRRRR!
WASHING POWDER
WHIRRR
WHIRRRR!
WHOOPEE! AIRPLANE!
YOU COME WITH ME! WE'RE GOING TO TAKE THAT PICTURE RIGHT NOW! AND NO MORE MONKEY BUSINESS!
THE NEXT DAY
MINNIE MOUSE ASKED ME T' GET A PICTURE SHE LEFT HERE YESTERDAY!
YES, SIR! HERE IT IS!
10-30
WALT DISNEY

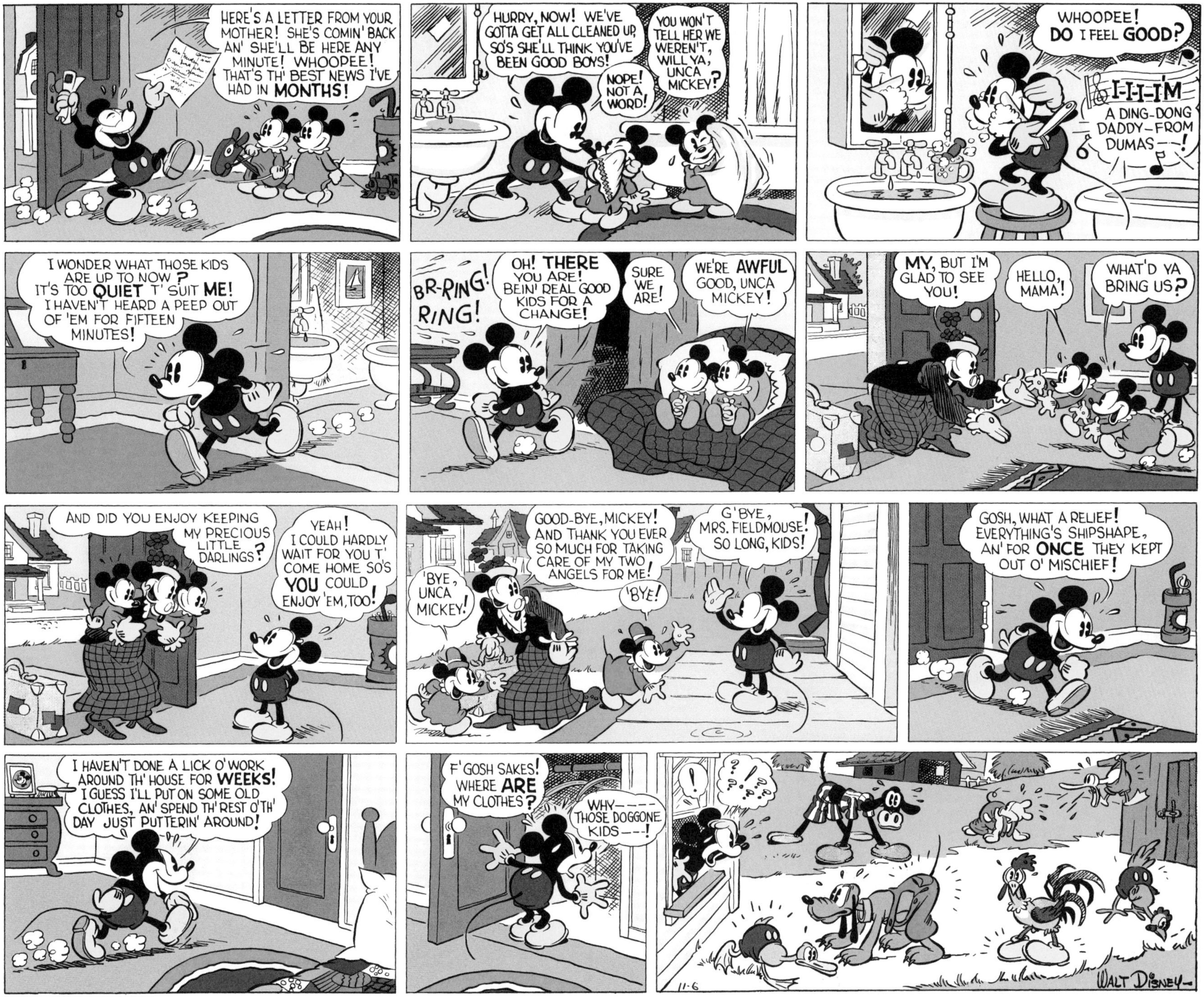
HERE'S A LETTER FROM YOUR MOTHER! SHE'S COMIN' BACK AN' SHE'LL BE HERE ANY MINUTE! WHOOPEE! THAT'S TH' BEST NEWS I'VE HAD IN MONTHS!
HURRY, NOW! WE'VE GOTTA GET ALL CLEANED UP, SO'S SHE'LL THINK YOU'VE BEEN GOOD BOYS!
YOU WON'T TELL HER WE WEREN'T, WILL YA, UNCA MICKEY?
NOPE! NOT A WORD!
WHOOPEE! DO I FEEL GOOD?
I-I-I-I'M
A DING-DONG DADDY—FROM DUMAS——!
I WONDER WHAT THOSE KIDS ARE UP TO NOW? IT'S TOO QUIET T' SUIT ME! I HAVEN'T HEARD A PEEP OUT OF 'EM FOR FIFTEEN MINUTES!
BR-RING! RING!
OH! THERE YOU ARE! BEIN' REAL GOOD KIDS FOR A CHANGE!
SURE WE ARE!
WE'RE AWFUL GOOD, UNCA MICKEY!
MY, BUT I'M GLAD TO SEE YOU!
HELLO, MAMA!
WHAT'D YA BRING US?
AND DID YOU ENJOY KEEPING MY PRECIOUS LITTLE DARLINGS?
YEAH! I COULD HARDLY WAIT FOR YOU T' COME HOME SO'S YOU COULD ENJOY 'EM, TOO!
GOOD-BYE, MICKEY! AND THANK YOU EVER SO MUCH FOR TAKING CARE OF MY TWO ANGELS FOR ME!
'BYE, UNCA MICKEY!
'BYE!
G'BYE, MRS. FIELDMOUSE! SO LONG, KIDS!
GOSH, WHAT A RELIEF! EVERYTHING'S SHIPSHAPE, AN' FOR ONCE THEY KEPT OUT O' MISCHIEF!
I HAVEN'T DONE A LICK O' WORK AROUND TH' HOUSE FOR WEEKS! I GUESS I'LL PUT ON SOME OLD CLOTHES, AN' SPEND TH' REST O' TH' DAY JUST PUTTERIN' AROUND!
F' GOSH SAKES! WHERE ARE MY CLOTHES?
WHY———— THOSE DOGGONE KIDS———!
11-6
WALT DISNEY

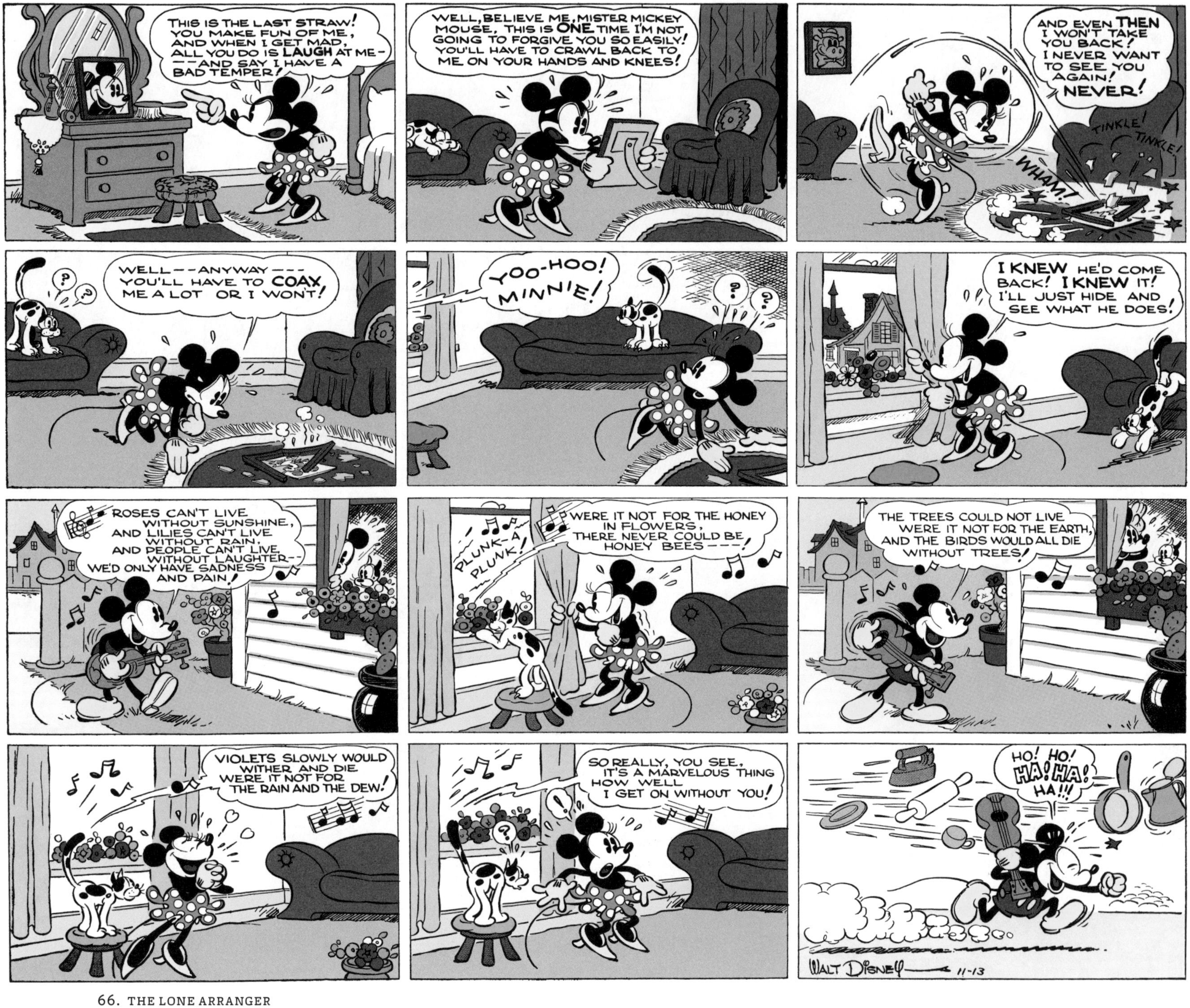
THIS IS THE LAST STRAW! YOU MAKE FUN OF ME, AND WHEN I GET MAD, ALL YOU DO IS LAUGH AT ME---AND SAY I HAVE A BAD TEMPER!
WELL, BELIEVE ME, MISTER MICKEY MOUSE, THIS IS ONE TIME I'M NOT GOING TO FORGIVE YOU SO EASILY! YOU'LL HAVE TO CRAWL BACK TO ME ON YOUR HANDS AND KNEES!
AND EVEN THEN I WON'T TAKE YOU BACK! I NEVER WANT TO SEE YOU AGAIN! NEVER!
TINKLE! TINKLE!
WHAM!
WELL--ANYWAY--- YOU'LL HAVE TO COAX ME A LOT OR I WON'T!
YOO-HOO! MINNIE!
I KNEW HE'D COME BACK! I KNEW IT! I'LL JUST HIDE AND SEE WHAT HE DOES!
ROSES CAN'T LIVE WITHOUT SUNSHINE, AND LILIES CAN'T LIVE WITHOUT RAIN, AND PEOPLE CAN'T LIVE WITHOUT LAUGHTER-- WE'D ONLY HAVE SADNESS AND PAIN!
PLUNK-A PLUNK!
WERE IT NOT FOR THE HONEY IN FLOWERS, THERE NEVER COULD BE HONEY BEES---!
THE TREES COULD NOT LIVE WERE IT NOT FOR THE EARTH, AND THE BIRDS WOULD ALL DIE WITHOUT TREES!
VIOLETS SLOWLY WOULD WITHER AND DIE WERE IT NOT FOR THE RAIN AND THE DEW!
SO REALLY, YOU SEE, IT'S A MARVELOUS THING HOW WELL I GET ON WITHOUT YOU!
HO! HO! HA! HA! HA!!!
WALT DISNEY 11-13

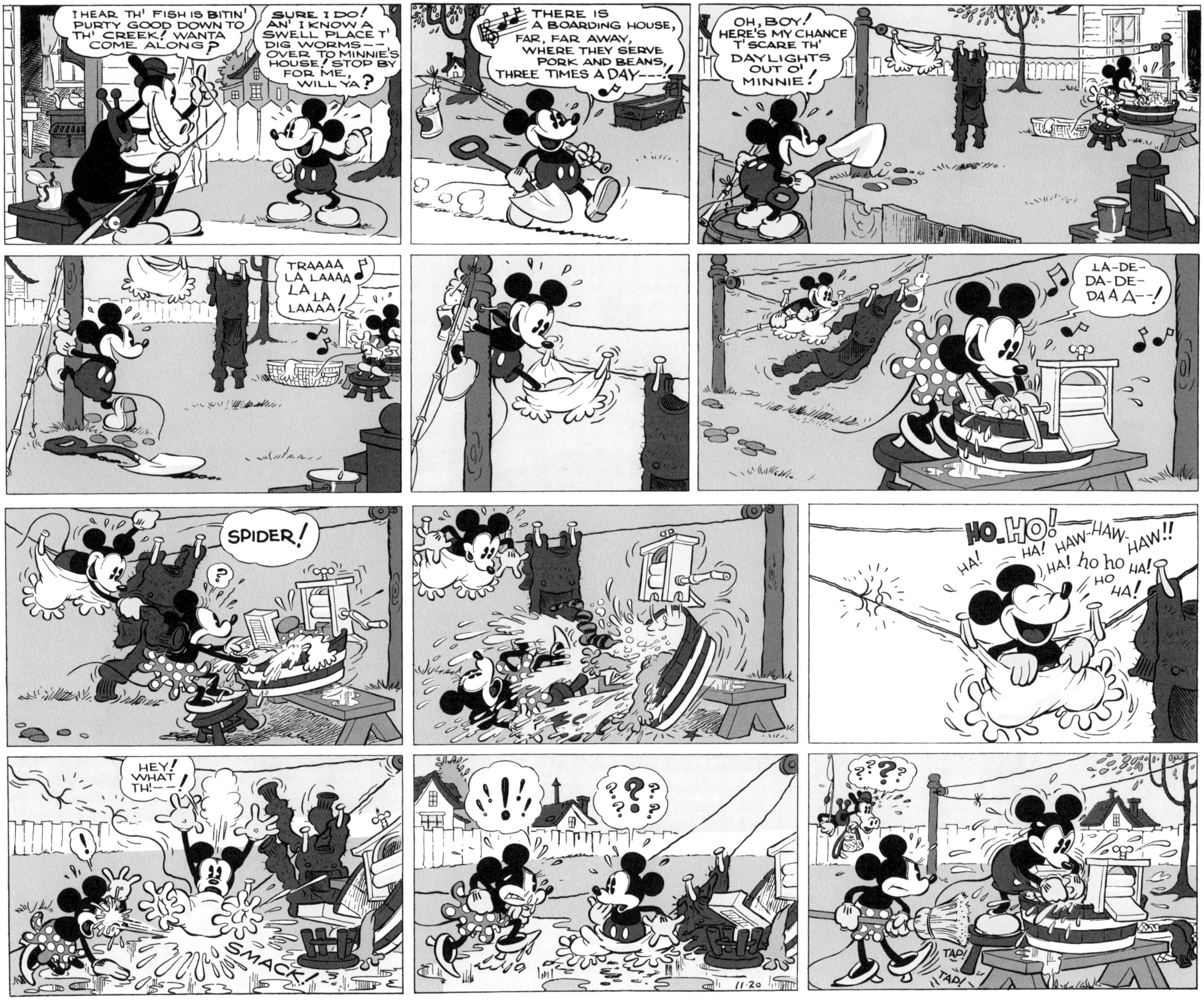

I HEAR TH' FISH IS BITIN' PURTY GOOD DOWN TO TH' CREEK! WANTA COME ALONG?
SURE I DO! AN' I KNOW A SWELL PLACE T' DIG WORMS-- OVER TO MINNIE'S HOUSE! STOP BY FOR ME, WILL YA?
THERE IS A BOARDING HOUSE, FAR, FAR AWAY, WHERE THEY SERVE PORK AND BEANS, THREE TIMES A DAY---!
OH, BOY! HERE'S MY CHANCE T' SCARE TH' DAYLIGHTS OUT O' MINNIE!
TRAAAA LA LAAAA LA LA LAAAA!
LA-DE-DA-DE-DA A A--!
SPIDER!
?
HO-HO! HA! HA! HAW-HAW-HAW!! HA! ho ho HA! HO HA!
!
HEY! WHAT TH'--!
SMACK!
!!!
???
11·20
???
TAP!
TAP!

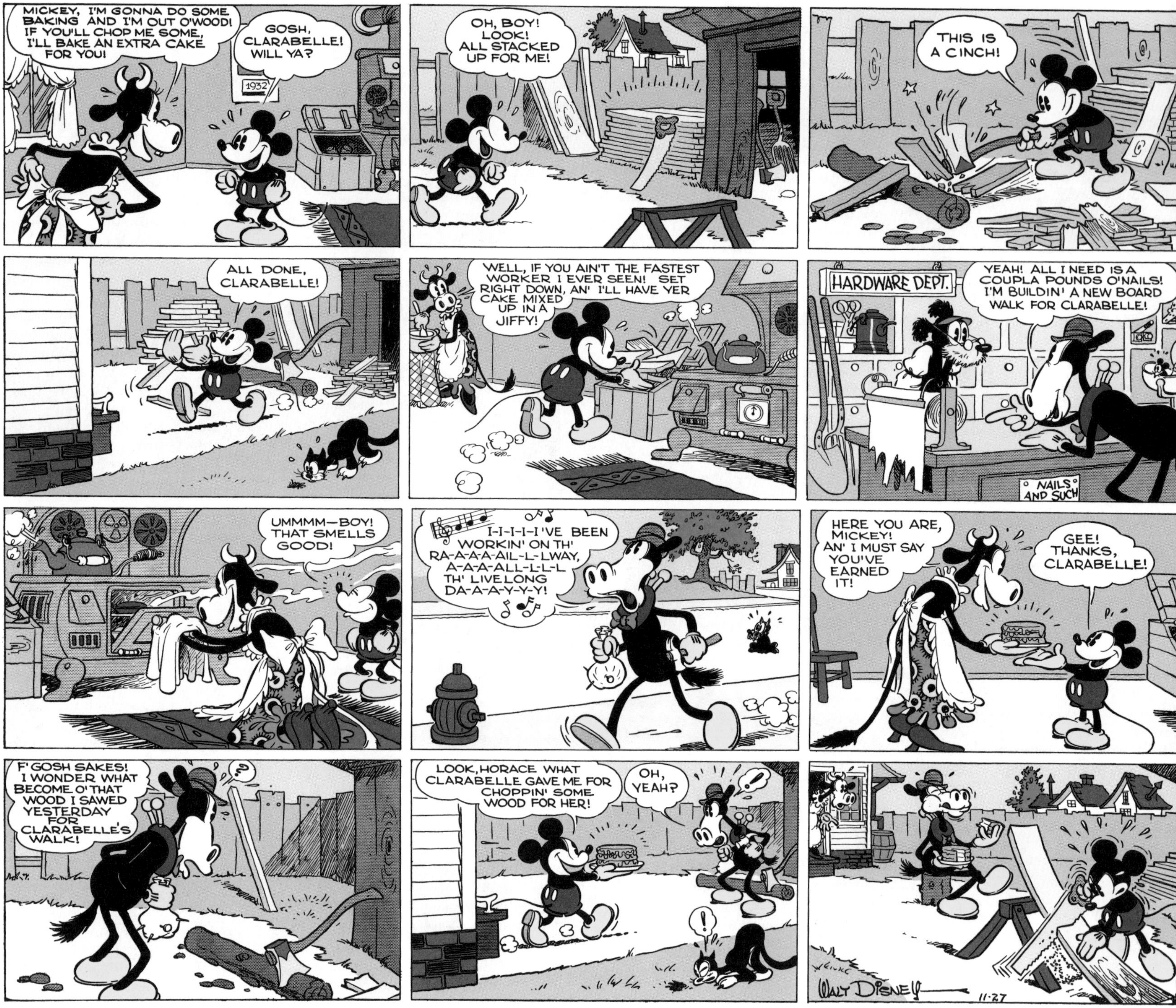
MICKEY, I'M GONNA DO SOME BAKING AND I'M OUT O'WOOD! IF YOU'LL CHOP ME SOME, I'LL BAKE AN EXTRA CAKE FOR YOU!
GOSH, CLARABELLE! WILL YA?
1932
OH, BOY! LOOK! ALL STACKED UP FOR ME!
THIS IS A CINCH!
ALL DONE, CLARABELLE!
WELL, IF YOU AIN'T THE FASTEST WORKER I EVER SEEN! SET RIGHT DOWN, AN' I'LL HAVE YER CAKE MIXED UP IN A JIFFY!
HARDWARE DEPT.
YEAH! ALL I NEED IS A COUPLA POUNDS O'NAILS! I'M BUILDIN' A NEW BOARD WALK FOR CLARABELLE!
NAILS AND SUCH
UMMMM—BOY! THAT SMELLS GOOD!
I-I-I-I'VE BEEN WORKIN' ON TH' RA-A-A-AIL-L-LWAY, A-A-A-ALL-L-L-L TH' LIVELONG DA-A-A-Y-Y-Y!
HERE YOU ARE, MICKEY! AN' I MUST SAY YOU'VE EARNED IT!
GEE! THANKS, CLARABELLE!
F'GOSH SAKES! I WONDER WHAT BECOME O'THAT WOOD I SAWED YESTERDAY FOR CLARABELLE'S WALK!
?
LOOK, HORACE WHAT CLARABELLE GAVE ME FOR CHOPPIN' SOME WOOD FOR HER!
OH, YEAH?
!
!
WALT DISNEY
11-27

68. CUT THE WOOD

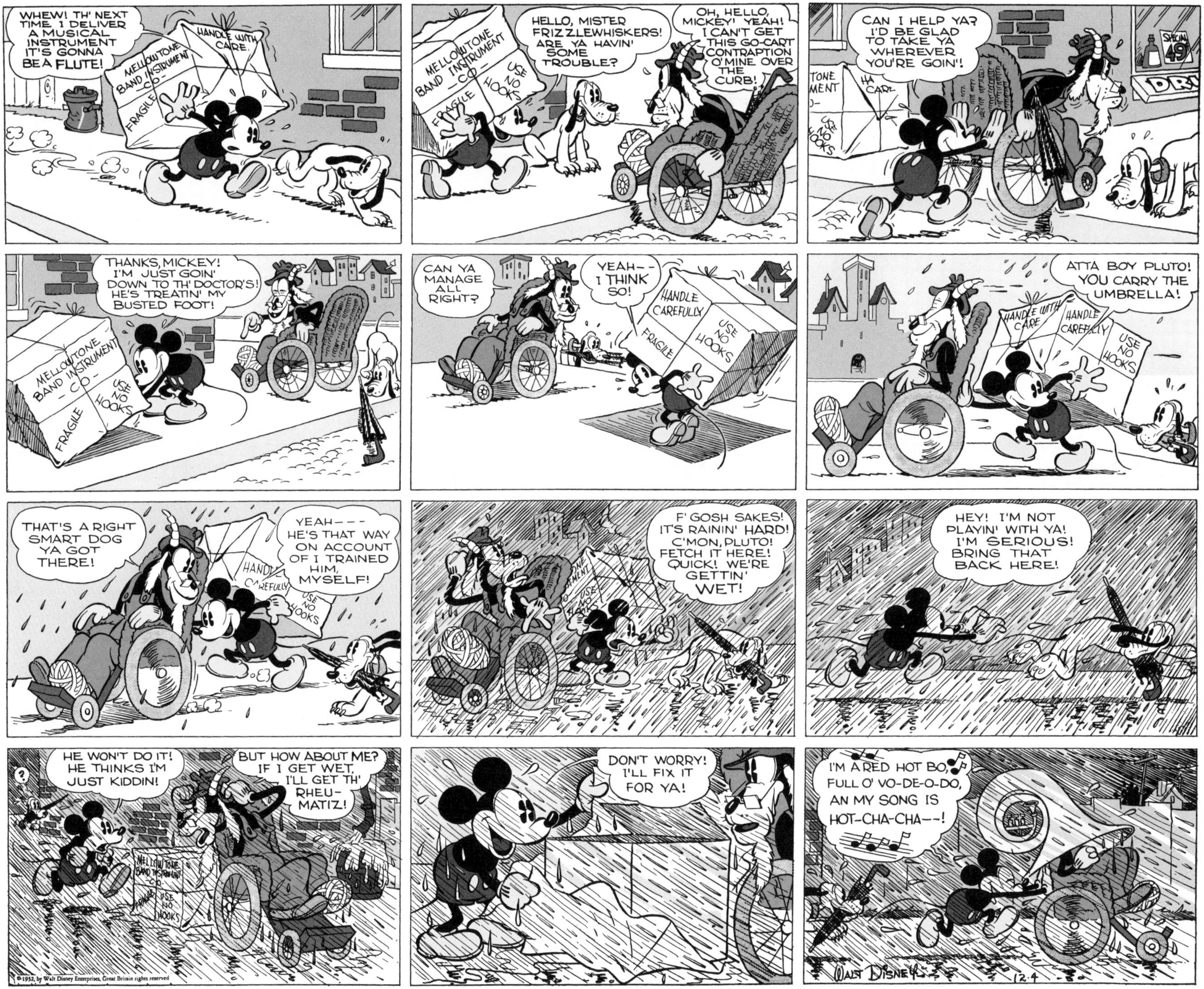

WHEW! TH' NEXT TIME I DELIVER A MUSICAL INSTRUMENT IT'S GONNA BE A FLUTE!
MELLOWTONE BAND INSTRUMENT -CO-
FRAGILE
HANDLE WITH CARE
HELLO, MISTER FRIZZLEWHISKERS! ARE YA HAVIN' SOME TROUBLE?
OH, HELLO, MICKEY! YEAH! I CAN'T GET THIS GO-CART CONTRAPTION O'MINE OVER THE CURB!
MELLOWTONE BAND INSTRUMENT -CO-
FRAGILE
USE NO HOOKS
CAN I HELP YA? I'D BE GLAD TO TAKE YA WHEREVER YOU'RE GOIN'!
49¢
THANKS, MICKEY! I'M JUST GOIN' DOWN TO TH' DOCTOR'S! HE'S TREATIN' MY BUSTED FOOT!
MELLOWTONE BAND INSTRUMENT -CO-
FRAGILE
USE NO HOOKS
CAN YA MANAGE ALL RIGHT?
YEAH-- I THINK SO!
HANDLE CAREFULLY
FRAGILE
USE NO HOOKS
ATTA BOY PLUTO! YOU CARRY THE UMBRELLA!
HANDLE WITH CARE
HANDLE CAREFULLY
USE NO HOOKS
THAT'S A RIGHT SMART DOG YA GOT THERE!
YEAH--- HE'S THAT WAY ON ACCOUNT OF I TRAINED HIM, MYSELF!
HANDLE CAREFULLY
USE NO HOOKS
F' GOSH SAKES! IT'S RAININ' HARD! C'MON, PLUTO! FETCH IT HERE! QUICK! WE'RE GETTIN' WET!
HEY! I'M NOT PLAYIN' WITH YA! I'M SERIOUS! BRING THAT BACK HERE!
?
HE WON'T DO IT! HE THINKS I'M JUST KIDDIN!
BUT HOW ABOUT ME? IF I GET WET, I'LL GET TH' RHEU-MATIZ!
MELLOWTONE BAND INSTRUMENT -CO-
USE NO HOOKS
DON'T WORRY! I'LL FIX IT FOR YA!
I'M A RED HOT BO, FULL O' VO-DE-O-DO, AN MY SONG IS HOT-CHA-CHA--!
WALT DISNEY
12-4

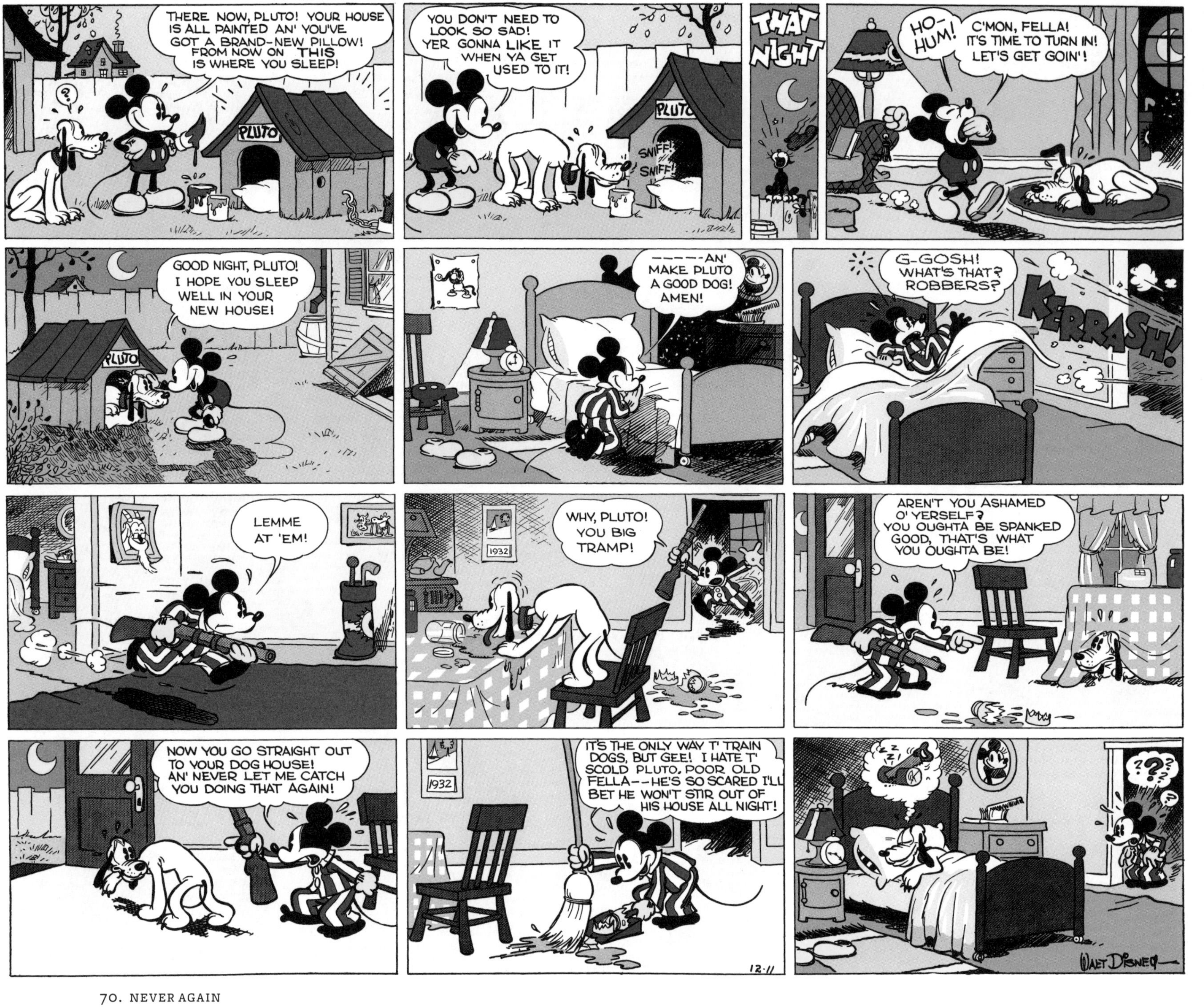

?
THERE NOW, PLUTO! YOUR HOUSE IS ALL PAINTED AN' YOU'VE GOT A BRAND-NEW PILLOW! FROM NOW ON THIS IS WHERE YOU SLEEP!
PLUTO
YOU DON'T NEED TO LOOK SO SAD! YER GONNA LIKE IT WHEN YA GET USED TO IT!
PLUTO
SNIFF! SNIFF!
THAT NIGHT
HO-HUM!
C'MON, FELLA! IT'S TIME TO TURN IN! LET'S GET GOIN'!
GOOD NIGHT, PLUTO! I HOPE YOU SLEEP WELL IN YOUR NEW HOUSE!
PLUTO
-----AN' MAKE PLUTO A GOOD DOG! AMEN!
G-GOSH! WHAT'S THAT? ROBBERS?
KERRASH!
LEMME AT 'EM!
1932
WHY, PLUTO! YOU BIG TRAMP!
AREN'T YOU ASHAMED O' YERSELF? YOU OUGHTA BE SPANKED GOOD, THAT'S WHAT YOU OUGHTA BE!
NOW YOU GO STRAIGHT OUT TO YOUR DOG HOUSE! AN' NEVER LET ME CATCH YOU DOING THAT AGAIN!
1932
IT'S THE ONLY WAY T' TRAIN DOGS, BUT GEE! I HATE T' SCOLD PLUTO. POOR OLD FELLA--HE'S SO SCARED I'LL BET HE WON'T STIR OUT OF HIS HOUSE ALL NIGHT!
12-11
Z Z Z
? ? ? ?
?
WALT DISNEY

70. NEVER AGAIN

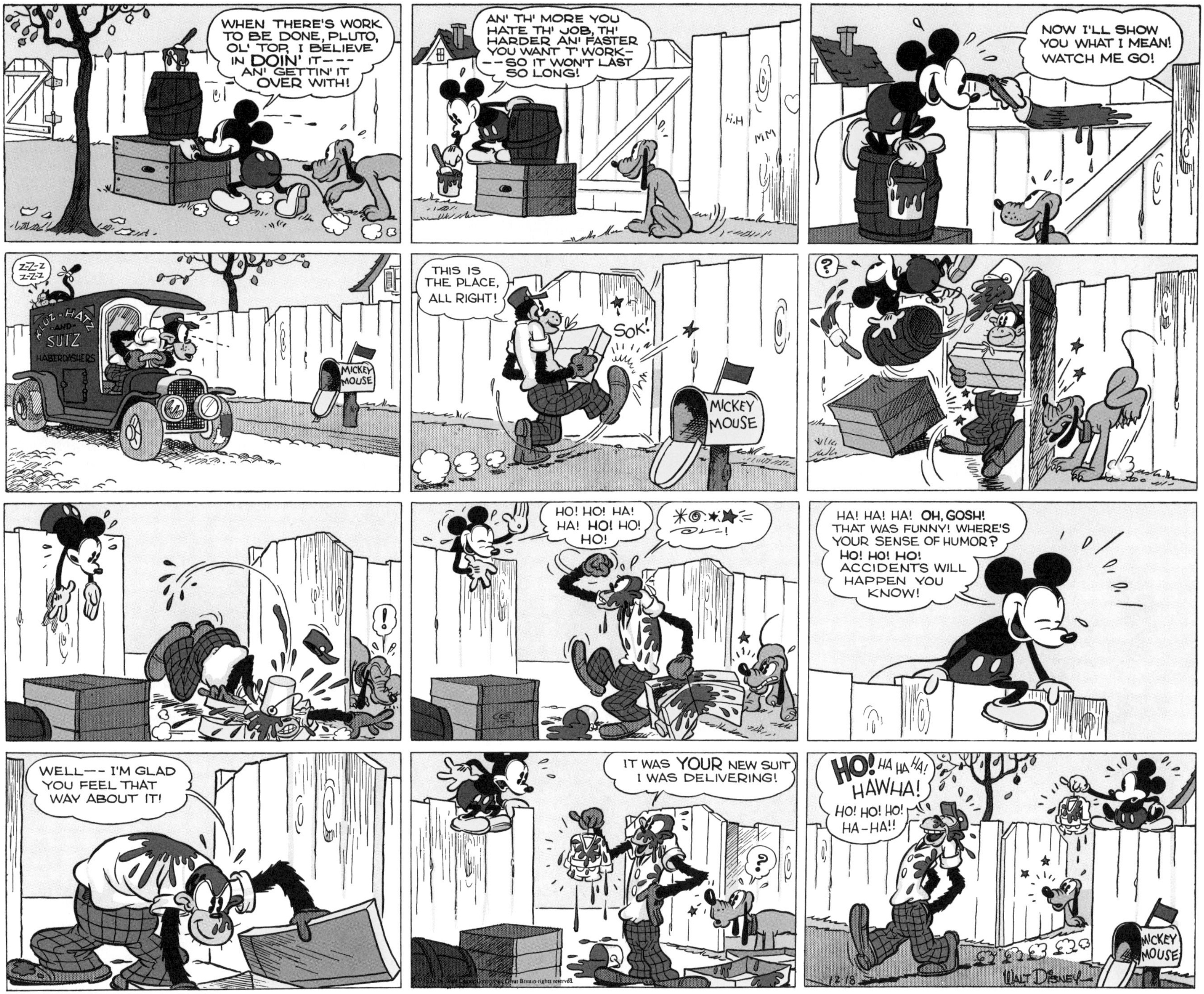
WHEN THERE'S WORK TO BE DONE, PLUTO, OL' TOP, I BELIEVE IN DOIN' IT--- AN' GETTIN' IT OVER WITH!
AN' TH' MORE YOU HATE TH' JOB, TH' HARDER AN' FASTER YOU WANT T' WORK- --SO IT WON'T LAST SO LONG!
H.H
MM
NOW I'LL SHOW YOU WHAT I MEAN! WATCH ME GO!
Z-Z-Z Z-Z-Z
KLOZ-HATZ AND SUTZ HABERDASHERS
MICKEY MOUSE
THIS IS THE PLACE, ALL RIGHT!
SOK!
MICKEY MOUSE
?
!
HO! HO! HA! HA! HO! HO! HO!
HA! HA! HA! OH, GOSH! THAT WAS FUNNY! WHERE'S YOUR SENSE OF HUMOR? HO! HO! HO! ACCIDENTS WILL HAPPEN YOU KNOW!
WELL-- I'M GLAD YOU FEEL THAT WAY ABOUT IT!
IT WAS YOUR NEW SUIT I WAS DELIVERING!
?
Great Britain rights reserved.
HO! HA HA HA! HAWHA! HO! HO! HO! HA-HA!!
MICKEY MOUSE
12/18
WALT DISNEY

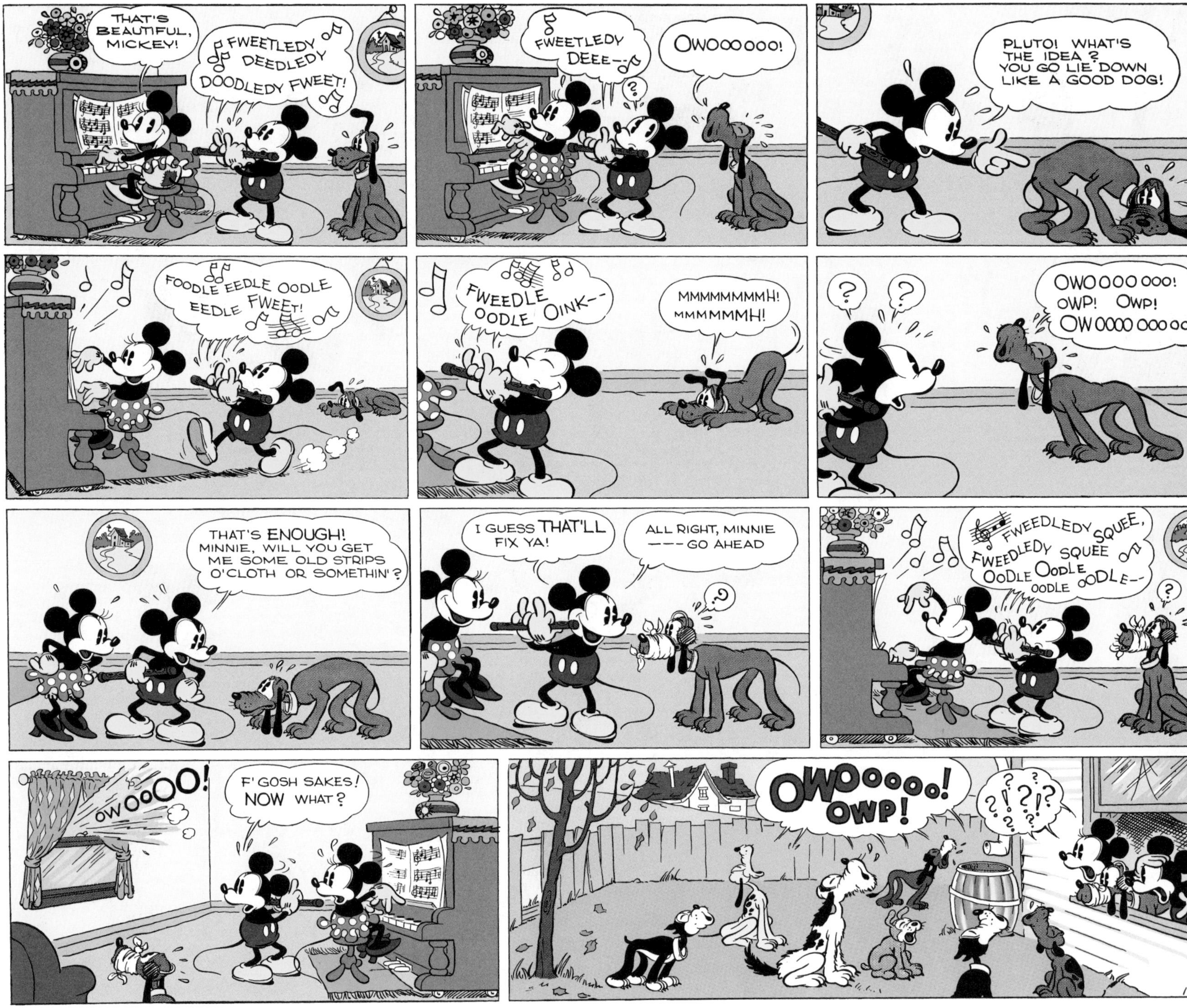
THAT'S BEAUTIFUL, MICKEY!
FWEETLEDY DEEDLEDY DOODLEDY FWEET!
FWEETLEDY DEEE--
?
OWOOOOOO!
PLUTO! WHAT'S THE IDEA? YOU GO LIE DOWN LIKE A GOOD DOG!
FOODLE EEDLE OODLE EEDLE FWEET!
FWEEDLE OODLE OINK--
MMMMMMMMH! MMMMMMH!
? ?
OWOOOOOOO! OWP! OWP! OWOOOOOOOOOO!
THAT'S ENOUGH! MINNIE, WILL YOU GET ME SOME OLD STRIPS O'CLOTH OR SOMETHIN'?
I GUESS THAT'LL FIX YA!
ALL RIGHT, MINNIE --- GO AHEAD
?
FWEEDLEDY SQUEE, FWEEDLEDY SQUEE OODLE OODLE OODLE OODLE--
? ?
OWOoOO!
F' GOSH SAKES! NOW WHAT?
OWOooooo! OWP!
?!?!?
12.25

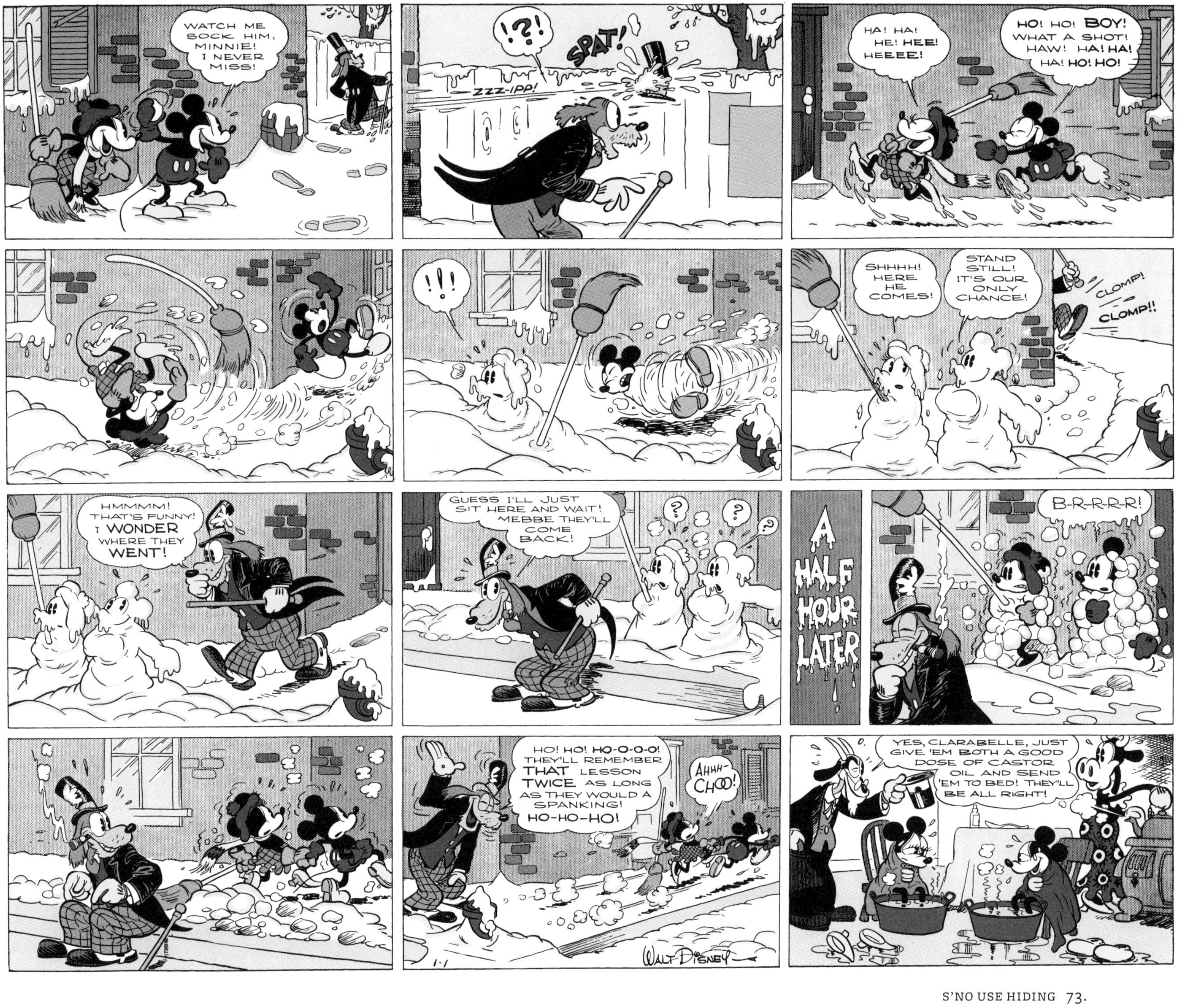
WATCH ME SOCK HIM, MINNIE! I NEVER MISS!
!?!
SPAT!
ZZZ-IPP!
HA! HA! HE! HEE! HEEEE!
HO! HO! BOY! WHAT A SHOT! HAW! HA! HA! HA! HO! HO!
!!!
SHHHH! HERE HE COMES!
STAND STILL! IT'S OUR ONLY CHANCE!
CLOMP!
CLOMP!!
HMMMM! THAT'S FUNNY! I WONDER WHERE THEY WENT!
GUESS I'LL JUST SIT HERE AND WAIT! MEBBE THEY'LL COME BACK!
?
?
?
A HALF HOUR LATER
B-R-R-R-R!
HO! HO! HO-O-O-O! THEY'LL REMEMBER THAT LESSON TWICE AS LONG AS THEY WOULD A SPANKING! HO-HO-HO!
AHHH-CHOO!
1-1
WALT DISNEY
YES, CLARABELLE, JUST GIVE 'EM BOTH A GOOD DOSE OF CASTOR OIL AND SEND 'EM TO BED! THEY'LL BE ALL RIGHT!

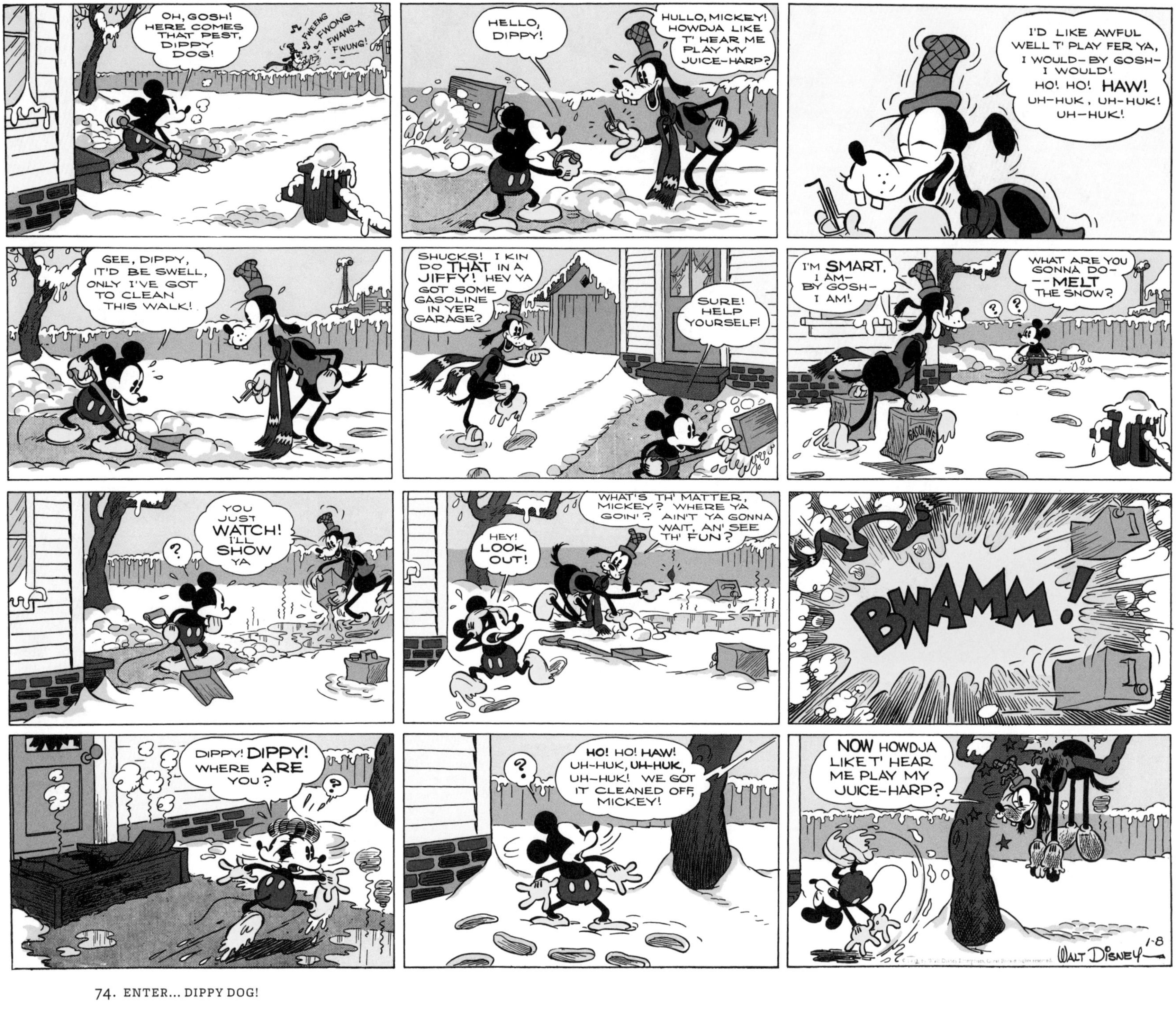
OH, GOSH! HERE COMES THAT PEST, DIPPY DOG!
FWEENG FWONG FWANG-A FWUNG!
HELLO, DIPPY!
HULLO, MICKEY! HOWDJA LIKE T' HEAR ME PLAY MY JUICE-HARP?
I'D LIKE AWFUL WELL T' PLAY FER YA, I WOULD-BY GOSH-I WOULD! HO! HO! HAW! UH-HUK, UH-HUK! UH-HUK!
GEE, DIPPY, IT'D BE SWELL, ONLY I'VE GOT TO CLEAN THIS WALK!
SHUCKS! I KIN DO THAT IN A JIFFY! HEV YA GOT SOME GASOLINE IN YER GARAGE?
SURE! HELP YOURSELF!
I'M SMART, I AM-BY GOSH-I AM!
?
?
WHAT ARE YOU GONNA DO--MELT THE SNOW?
GASOLINE
?
YOU JUST WATCH! I'LL SHOW YA
HEY! LOOK OUT!
WHAT'S TH' MATTER, MICKEY? WHERE YA GOIN'? AIN'T YA GONNA WAIT, AN' SEE TH' FUN?
BWAMM!
DIPPY! DIPPY! WHERE ARE YOU?
?
?
HO! HO! HAW! UH-HUK, UH-HUK, UH-HUK! WE GOT IT CLEANED OFF, MICKEY!
NOW HOWDJA LIKE T' HEAR ME PLAY MY JUICE-HARP?
WALT DISNEY 1-8

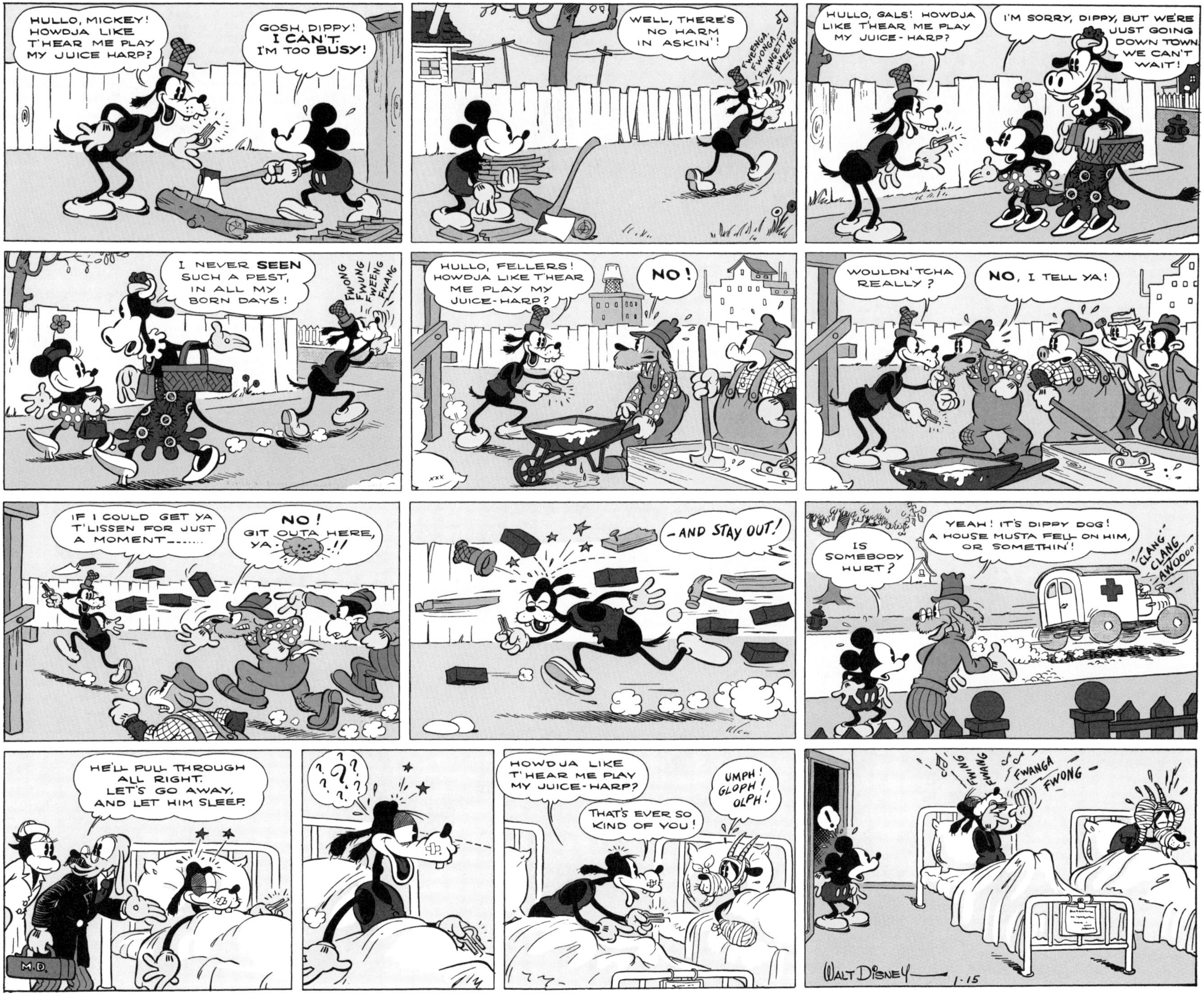

HULLO, MICKEY! HOWDJA LIKE T'HEAR ME PLAY MY JUICE HARP?
GOSH, DIPPY! I CAN'T. I'M TOO BUSY!
WELL, THERE'S NO HARM IN ASKIN'!
FWEENGA FWONGA FWANGETTY FWEENG
HULLO, GALS! HOWDJA LIKE T'HEAR ME PLAY MY JUICE-HARP?
I'M SORRY, DIPPY, BUT WE'RE JUST GOING DOWN TOWN. WE CAN'T WAIT!
I NEVER SEEN SUCH A PEST, IN ALL MY BORN DAYS!
FWONG FWUNG FWEENG FWANG
HULLO, FELLERS! HOWDJA LIKE T'HEAR ME PLAY MY JUICE-HARP?
NO!
WOULDN'TCHA REALLY?
NO, I TELL YA!
IF I COULD GET YA T'LISSEN FOR JUST A MOMENT.......
NO! GIT OUTA HERE, YA !!
-AND STAY OUT!
IS SOMEBODY HURT?
YEAH! IT'S DIPPY DOG! A HOUSE MUSTA FELL ON HIM, OR SOMETHIN'!
CLANG CLANG AWOOO
HE'LL PULL THROUGH ALL RIGHT. LET'S GO AWAY, AND LET HIM SLEEP.
M.D.
HOWDJA LIKE T'HEAR ME PLAY MY JUICE-HARP?
THAT'S EVER SO KIND OF YOU!
UMPH! GLOPH! OLPH!
FWING FWANG FWANGA FWONG
WALT DISNEY 1-15

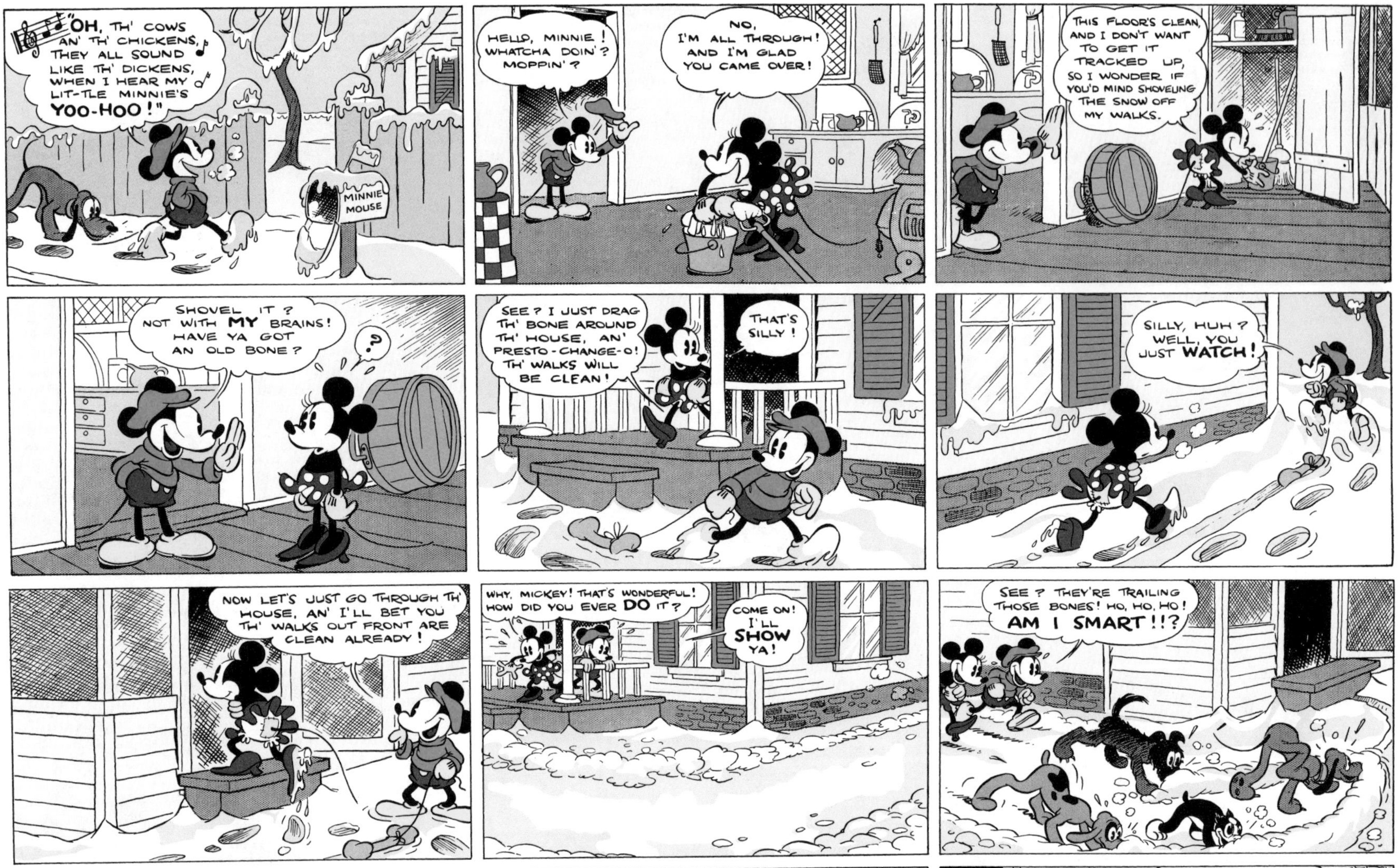
"OH, TH' COWS AN' TH' CHICKENS, THEY ALL SOUND LIKE TH' DICKENS, WHEN I HEAR MY LIT-TLE MINNIE'S YOO-HOO!"
MINNIE MOUSE
HELLO, MINNIE! WHATCHA DOIN'? MOPPIN'?
NO, I'M ALL THROUGH! AND I'M GLAD YOU CAME OVER!
THIS FLOOR'S CLEAN, AND I DON'T WANT TO GET IT TRACKED UP, SO I WONDER IF YOU'D MIND SHOVELING THE SNOW OFF MY WALKS.
SHOVEL IT? NOT WITH MY BRAINS! HAVE YA GOT AN OLD BONE?
?
SEE? I JUST DRAG TH' BONE AROUND TH' HOUSE, AN' PRESTO-CHANGE-O! TH' WALKS WILL BE CLEAN!
THAT'S SILLY!
SILLY, HUH? WELL, YOU JUST WATCH!
NOW LET'S JUST GO THROUGH TH' HOUSE, AN' I'LL BET YOU TH' WALKS OUT FRONT ARE CLEAN ALREADY!
WHY, MICKEY! THAT'S WONDERFUL! HOW DID YOU EVER DO IT?
COME ON! I'LL SHOW YA!
SEE? THEY'RE TRAILING THOSE BONES! HO, HO, HO! AM I SMART!!?
ARF! ARF!
YIPE! YIPE!
GOOD GOSH! I FORGOT TO SHUT TH' DOOR!
YOWP!
?
OHHHHHHHHHH! MY SPOTLESS FLOOR!
WELL..... ANYWAY..... IT WAS A SWELL IDEA, EVEN IF IT DIDN'T WORK!
WALT DISNEY
1-22

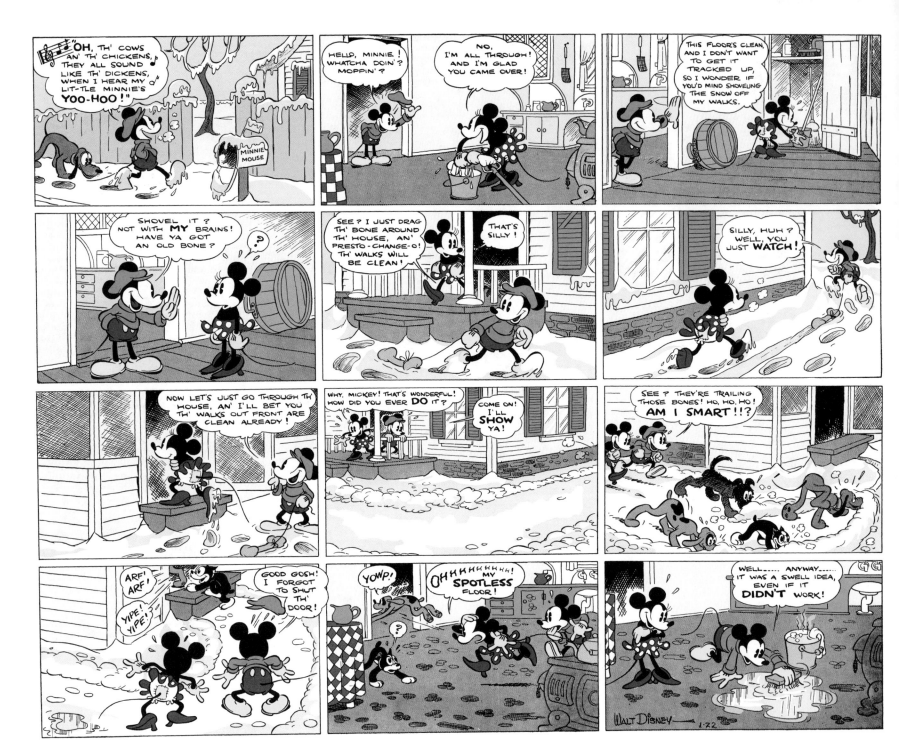

THE LAIR OF WOLF BARKER AND GAG STRIPS

JANUARY 29, 1933
–
MARCH 4, 1934

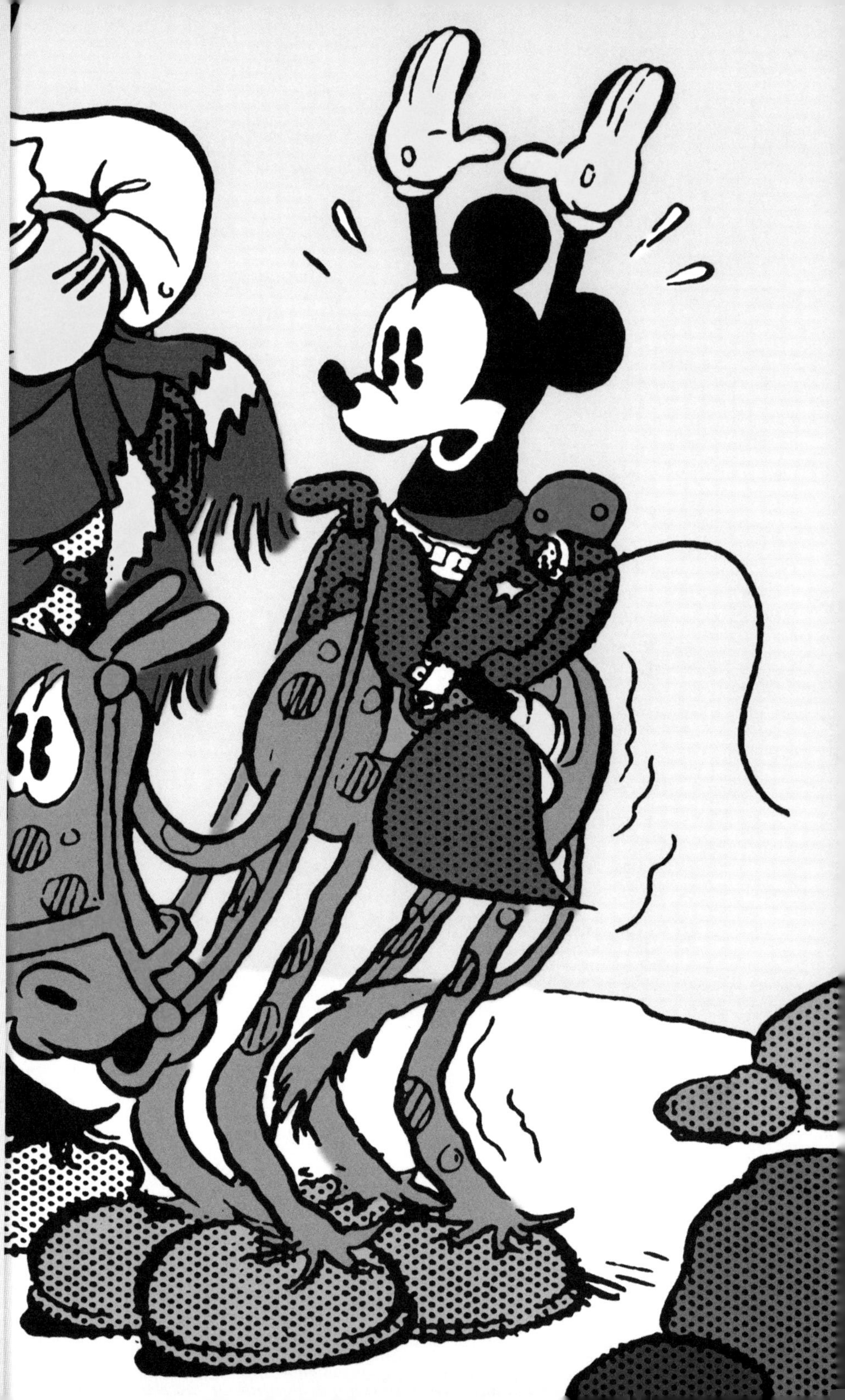

MICKEY MOUSE
REGISTERED U.S. PATENT OFFICE

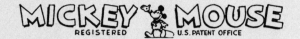

MICKEY'S DELAYED DRAMA

Once again, a letter with a plea for help calls Mickey and friends to action. But this time the "action" is not quite a grand adventure in some exotic locale. It's merely a task, looking after Uncle Mortimer's cattle ranch in his absence—and, despite a definite change of scenery, this particular "Far West" doesn't actually feel that far from home; certainly not when compared to, say, Treasure Island or other daily strip locales.

The first few scene-setting weeks of "Wolf Barker" are full of cartoon-like humor. Dippy Dog continues to upset everyone with his noisy juice-harp. Horace attempts to look cool in his cowboy outfit, but his misplaced pride hilariously backfires. Don Poocho, the fat foreman with the Hispanic accent, is instantly made funny by his plump looks and overly laidback attitude—and funnier still when a mouthful of Tabasco sauce puts an abrupt stop to his musical performance. We also smile at Poocho's quick wits, as when he tricks and deters Wolf Barker's bandits by demonstrating Mickey's alleged sharpshooting prowess.

It's all a laugh; especially when Minnie, not to be outdone by Mickey's tracking skill, discovers a "cow's nest" with delightful naïveté. Even the gangsters that stop the stagecoach—with the intention of robbing the passengers and kidnapping the girl—cannot be taken too seriously; they are scared away by a walking luggage-trunk.

In the end, though, our suspension of disbelief gets turned up a couple of notches—from a "Sunday strip mood" to a "daily strip mood," one might say—and we do get our dose of proper adventure. Once again we see Gottfredson's classic Mickey leitmotivs: the glorious Horatio Alger hero; the conflict between David and Goliath; and the victory of intelligence over brute force, particularly at the climax of the fight between Mickey and Wolf Barker in a dilapidated cabin.

It is fascinating to note the evolution of Mickey's partners in his escapades. In 1933, Dippy has yet to morph into the more well-rounded character of Goofy: he is not merely simpleminded—as when he hands over his friends' luggage to a junk dealer—but peskily mischievous, as when he stows away in Clarabelle's trunk, throwing out her clothes in the process. Dippy is mostly part of the story for comic relief: it is still Horace who plays the role of Mickey's buddy during the actual rustler-chasing adventure, as he did in the contemporary daily serial "Blaggard Castle" (1932-33). The resourceful Horace Horsecollar can serenade his girl (albeit with dubious results) and is capable of wielding a revolver (well, almost), while the dimwitted Dippy Dog is not capable of handling much more than his annoying juice-harp.

But just give it a few more years. Once Dippy matures into Goofy, he will take over Horace's buddy role, causing the humanized horse to all but disappear from the strip.

—LEONARDO GORI AND FRANCESCO STAJANO

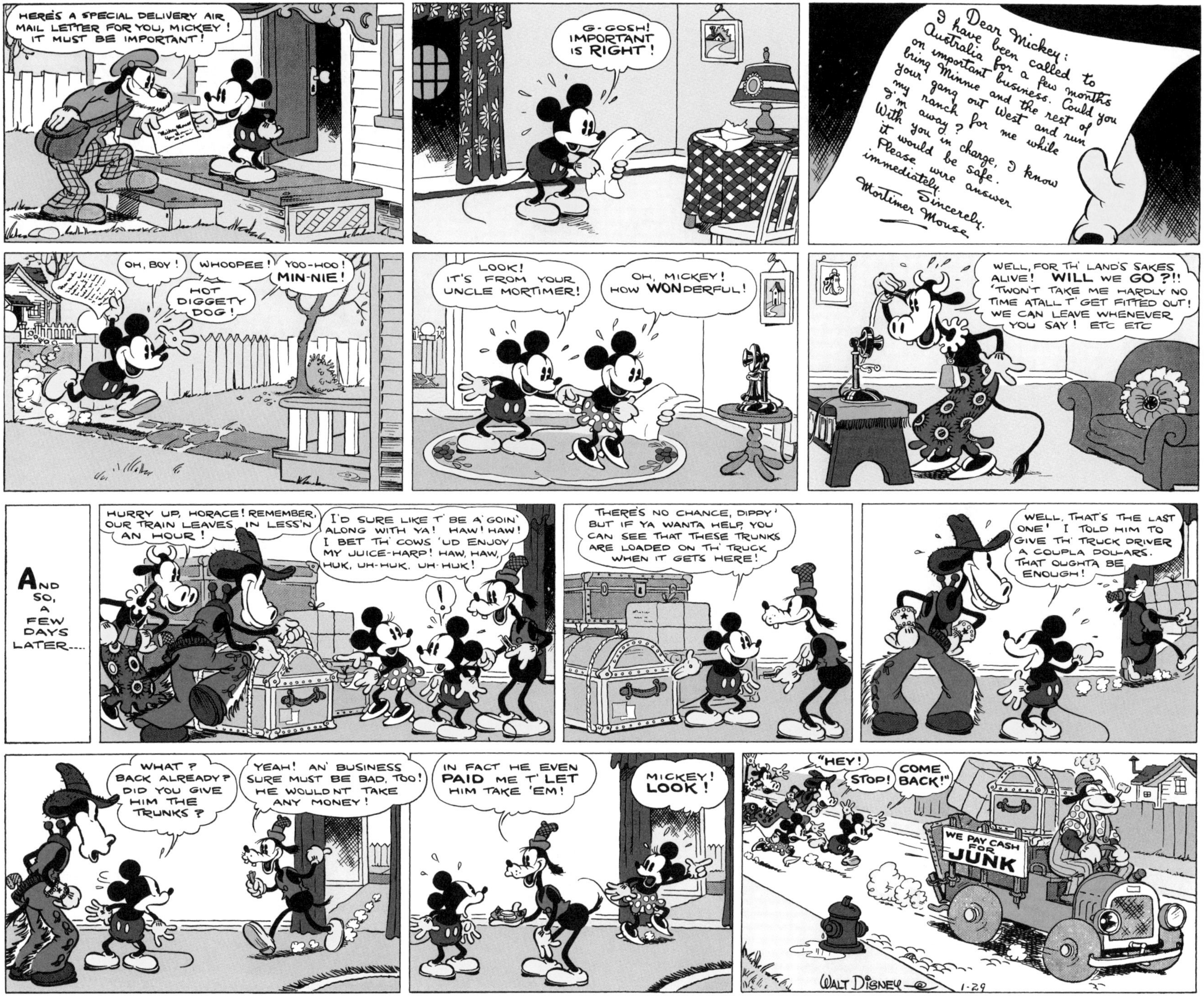
HERE'S A SPECIAL DELIVERY AIR MAIL LETTER FOR YOU, MICKEY! IT MUST BE IMPORTANT!
G-GOSH! IMPORTANT IS RIGHT!
Dear Mickey:
I have been called to Australia for a few months on important business. Could you bring Minnie and the rest of your gang out West and run my ranch for me while I'm away?
With you in charge, I know it would be safe.
Please wire answer immediately.
Sincerely,
Mortimer Mouse
OH, BOY!
WHOOPEE!
YOO-HOO! MIN-NIE!
HOT DIGGETY DOG!
LOOK! IT'S FROM YOUR UNCLE MORTIMER!
OH, MICKEY! HOW WONDERFUL!
WELL, FOR TH' LAND'S SAKES ALIVE! WILL WE GO?!! 'TWON'T TAKE ME HARDLY NO TIME ATALL T' GET FITTED OUT! WE CAN LEAVE WHENEVER YOU SAY! ETC ETC
AND SO, A FEW DAYS LATER----
HURRY UP, HORACE! REMEMBER, OUR TRAIN LEAVES IN LESS'N AN HOUR!
I'D SURE LIKE T' BE A' GOIN' ALONG WITH YA! HAW! HAW! I BET TH' COWS 'UD ENJOY MY JUICE-HARP! HAW, HAW, HUK, UH-HUK, UH-HUK!
!
THERE'S NO CHANCE, DIPPY! BUT IF YA WANTA HELP, YOU CAN SEE THAT THESE TRUNKS ARE LOADED ON TH' TRUCK WHEN IT GETS HERE!
WELL, THAT'S THE LAST ONE! I TOLD HIM TO GIVE TH' TRUCK DRIVER A COUPLA DOLLARS. THAT OUGHTA BE ENOUGH!
WHAT? BACK ALREADY? DID YOU GIVE HIM THE TRUNKS?
YEAH! AN' BUSINESS SURE MUST BE BAD, TOO! HE WOULDN'T TAKE ANY MONEY!
IN FACT HE EVEN PAID ME T' LET HIM TAKE 'EM!
MICKEY! LOOK!
"HEY!
STOP!
COME BACK!"
WE PAY CASH FOR JUNK
WALT DISNEY
1-29

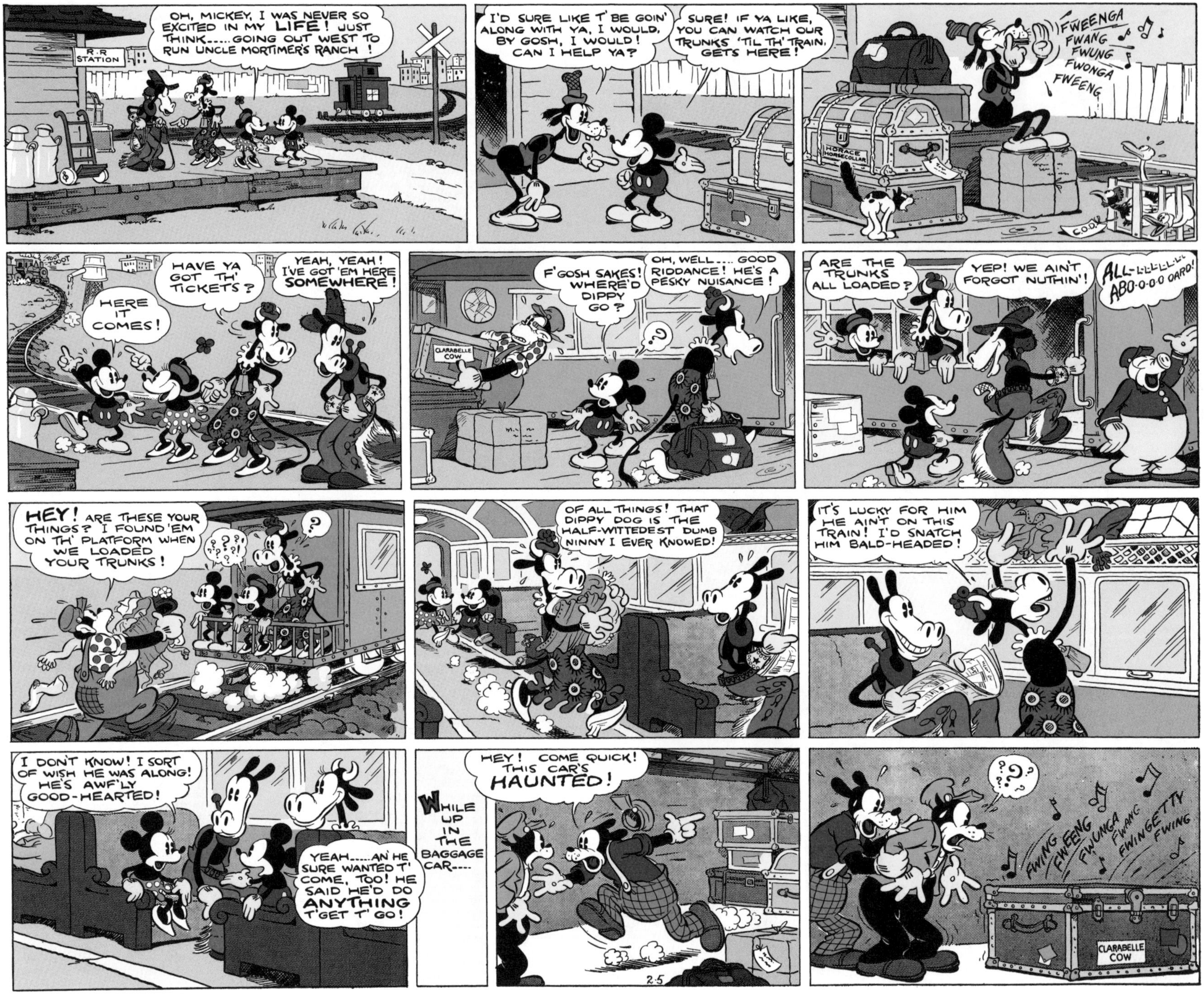
OH, MICKEY, I WAS NEVER SO EXCITED IN MY LIFE! JUST THINK.....GOING OUT WEST TO RUN UNCLE MORTIMER'S RANCH!
R.R STATION
I'D SURE LIKE T' BE GOIN' ALONG WITH YA, I WOULD, BY GOSH, I WOULD! CAN I HELP YA?
SURE! IF YA LIKE, YOU CAN WATCH OUR TRUNKS 'TIL TH' TRAIN GETS HERE!
FWEENGA FWANG FWUNG FWONGA FWEENG
HORACE HORSECOLLAR
C.O.D.
TOOT TOOOT
HERE IT COMES!
HAVE YA GOT TH' TICKETS?
YEAH, YEAH! I'VE GOT 'EM HERE SOMEWHERE!
CLARABELLE COW
F'GOSH SAKES! WHERE'D DIPPY GO?
OH, WELL.... GOOD RIDDANCE! HE'S A PESKY NUISANCE!
ARE THE TRUNKS ALL LOADED?
YEP! WE AIN'T FORGOT NUTHIN'!
ALL-LLLLLL ABO-O-O-O OARD!
HEY! ARE THESE YOUR THINGS? I FOUND 'EM ON TH' PLATFORM WHEN WE LOADED YOUR TRUNKS!
OF ALL THINGS! THAT DIPPY DOG IS THE HALF-WITTEDEST DUMB NINNY I EVER KNOWED!
IT'S LUCKY FOR HIM HE AIN'T ON THIS TRAIN! I'D SNATCH HIM BALD-HEADED!
I DON'T KNOW! I SORT OF WISH HE WAS ALONG! HE'S AWF'LY GOOD-HEARTED!
YEAH.....AN' HE SURE WANTED T' COME, TOO! HE SAID HE'D DO ANYTHING T'GET T' GO!
WHILE UP IN THE BAGGAGE CAR----
HEY! COME QUICK! THIS CAR'S HAUNTED!
2-5
FWING FWEENG FWUNGA FWANG FWINGETTY FWING
CLARABELLE COW

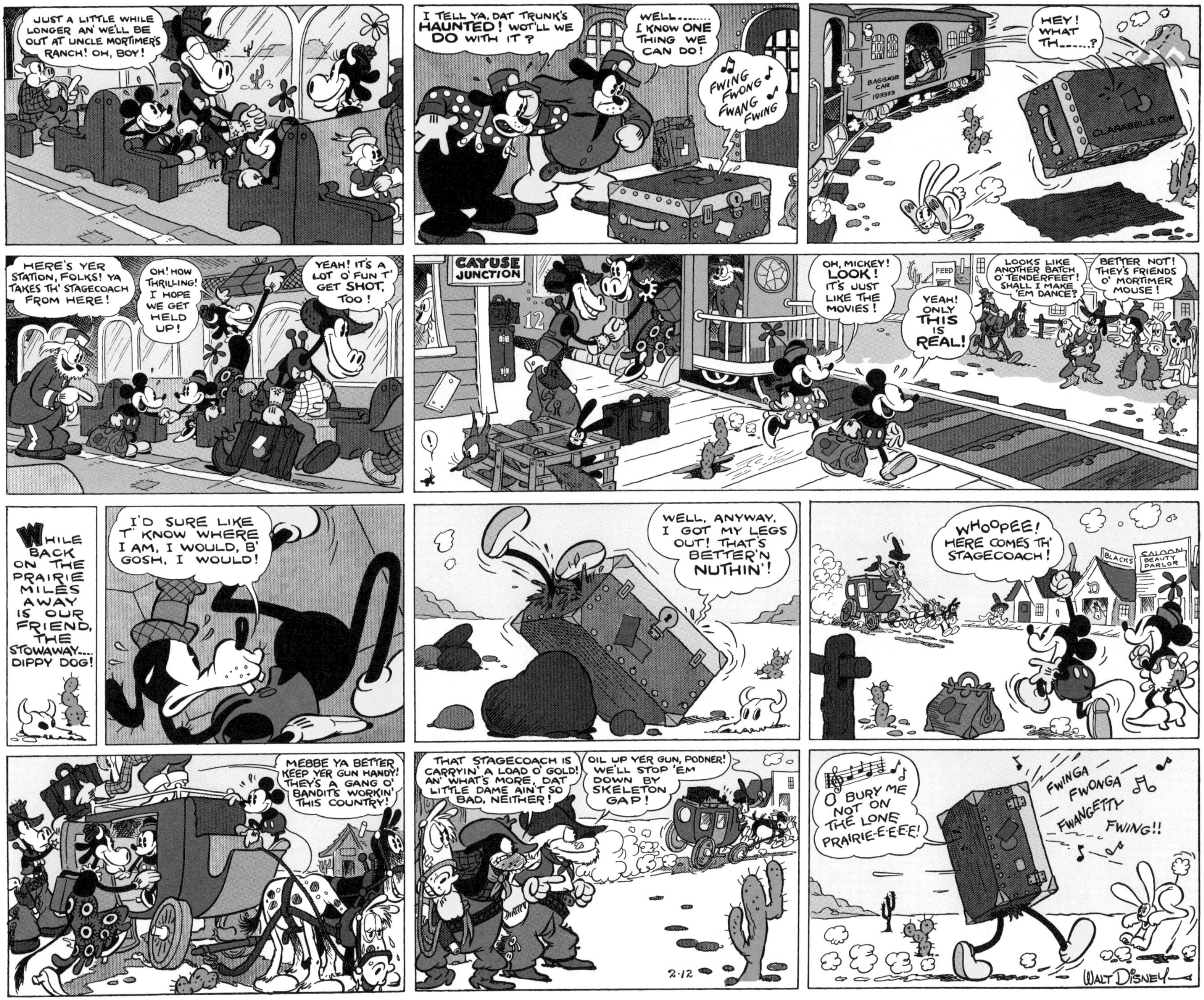
JUST A LITTLE WHILE LONGER AN' WE'LL BE OUT AT UNCLE MORTIMER'S RANCH! OH, BOY!
I TELL YA, DAT TRUNK'S HAUNTED! WOT'LL WE DO WITH IT?
WELL....... I KNOW ONE THING WE CAN DO!
FWING FWONG FWANG FWING
BAGGAGE CAR 103333
HEY! WHAT TH.....?
CLARABELLE COW
HERE'S YER STATION, FOLKS! YA TAKES TH' STAGECOACH FROM HERE!
OH! HOW THRILLING! I HOPE WE GET HELD UP!
YEAH! IT'S A LOT O' FUN T' GET SHOT, TOO!
CAYUSE JUNCTION
FEED
OH, MICKEY! LOOK! IT'S JUST LIKE THE MOVIES!
YEAH! ONLY THIS IS REAL!
LOOKS LIKE ANOTHER BATCH O' TENDERFEET! SHALL I MAKE 'EM DANCE?
BETTER NOT! THEY'S FRIENDS O' MORTIMER MOUSE!
WHILE BACK ON THE PRAIRIE MILES AWAY IS OUR FRIEND, THE STOWAWAY.... DIPPY DOG!
I'D SURE LIKE T' KNOW WHERE I AM, I WOULD, B' GOSH, I WOULD!
WELL, ANYWAY, I GOT MY LEGS OUT! THAT'S BETTER'N NUTHIN'!
WHOOPEE! HERE COMES TH' STAGECOACH!
BLACKS
SALOON
BEAUTY PARLOR
MEBBE YA BETTER KEEP YER GUN HANDY! THEY'S A GANG O' BANDITS WORKIN' THIS COUNTRY!
THAT STAGECOACH IS CARRYIN' A LOAD O' GOLD! AN' WHAT'S MORE, DAT LITTLE DAME AIN'T SO BAD, NEITHER!
OIL UP YER GUN, PODNER! WE'LL STOP 'EM DOWN BY SKELETON GAP!
2-12
O BURY ME NOT ON THE LONE PRAIRIE-E-EEE!
FWINGA FWONGA FWANGETTY FWING!!
WALT DISNEY

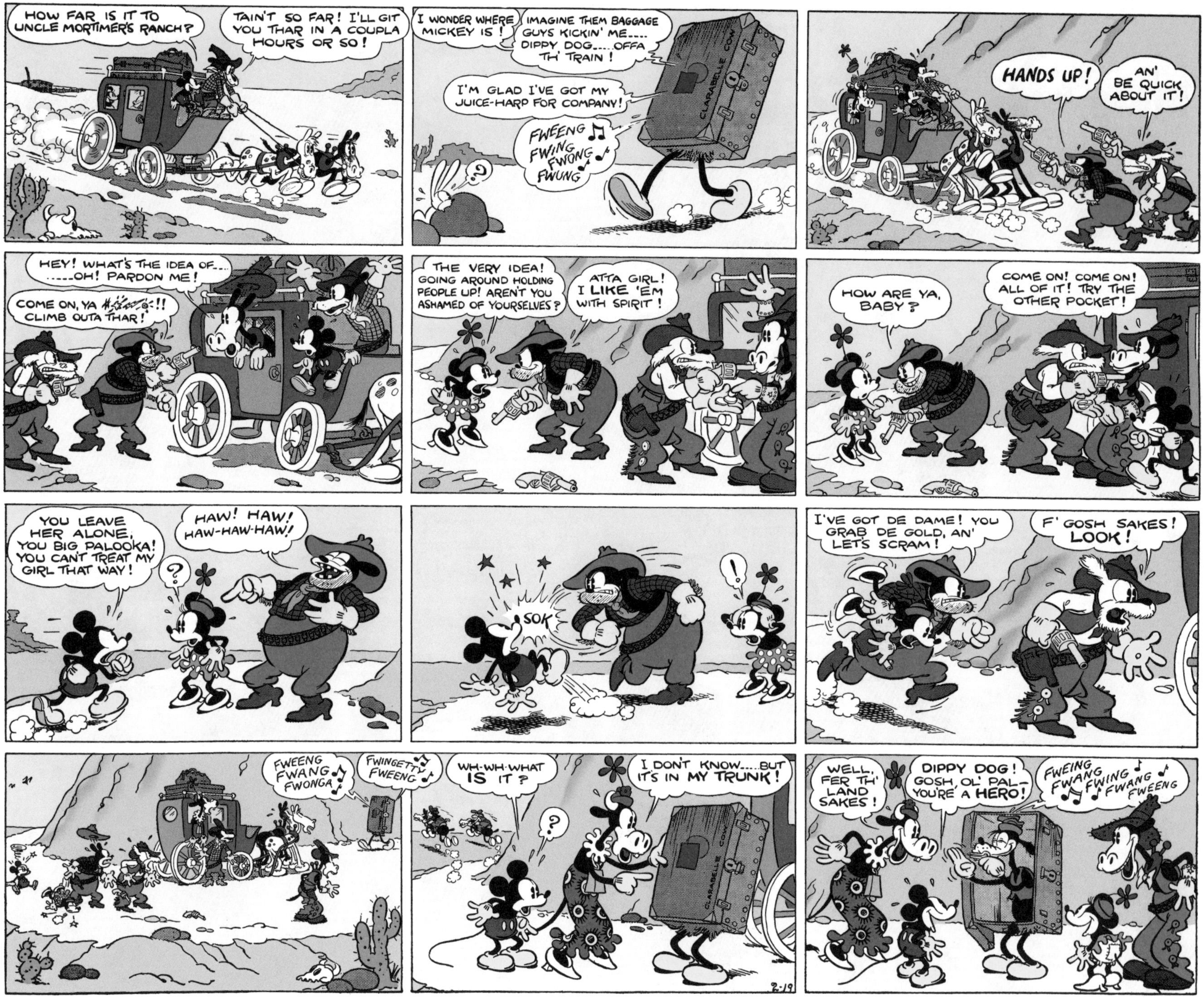

HOW FAR IS IT TO UNCLE MORTIMER'S RANCH?
TAIN'T SO FAR! I'LL GIT YOU THAR IN A COUPLA HOURS OR SO!
I WONDER WHERE MICKEY IS!
IMAGINE THEM BAGGAGE GUYS KICKIN' ME.... DIPPY DOG.....OFFA TH' TRAIN!
I'M GLAD I'VE GOT MY JUICE-HARP FOR COMPANY!
FWEENG FWING FWONG FWUNG
CLARABELLE COW
?
HANDS UP!
AN' BE QUICK ABOUT IT!
HEY! WHAT'S THE IDEA OF.... .....OH! PARDON ME!
COME ON, YA #!!
CLIMB OUTA THAR!
THE VERY IDEA! GOING AROUND HOLDING PEOPLE UP! AREN'T YOU ASHAMED OF YOURSELVES?
ATTA GIRL! I LIKE 'EM WITH SPIRIT!
HOW ARE YA, BABY?
COME ON! COME ON! ALL OF IT! TRY THE OTHER POCKET!
YOU LEAVE HER ALONE, YOU BIG PALOOKA! YOU CAN'T TREAT MY GIRL THAT WAY!
?
HAW! HAW! HAW-HAW-HAW!
SOK
!
I'VE GOT DE DAME! YOU GRAB DE GOLD, AN' LET'S SCRAM!
F' GOSH SAKES! LOOK!
FWEENG FWANG FWONGA
FWINGETTY FWEENG
WH-WH-WHAT IS IT?
?
I DON'T KNOW....BUT IT'S IN MY TRUNK!
CLARABELLE COW
2-19
WELL, FER TH' LAND SAKES!
DIPPY DOG! GOSH, OL' PAL—YOU'RE A HERO!
FWEING FWANG FWING FWANG FWEENG

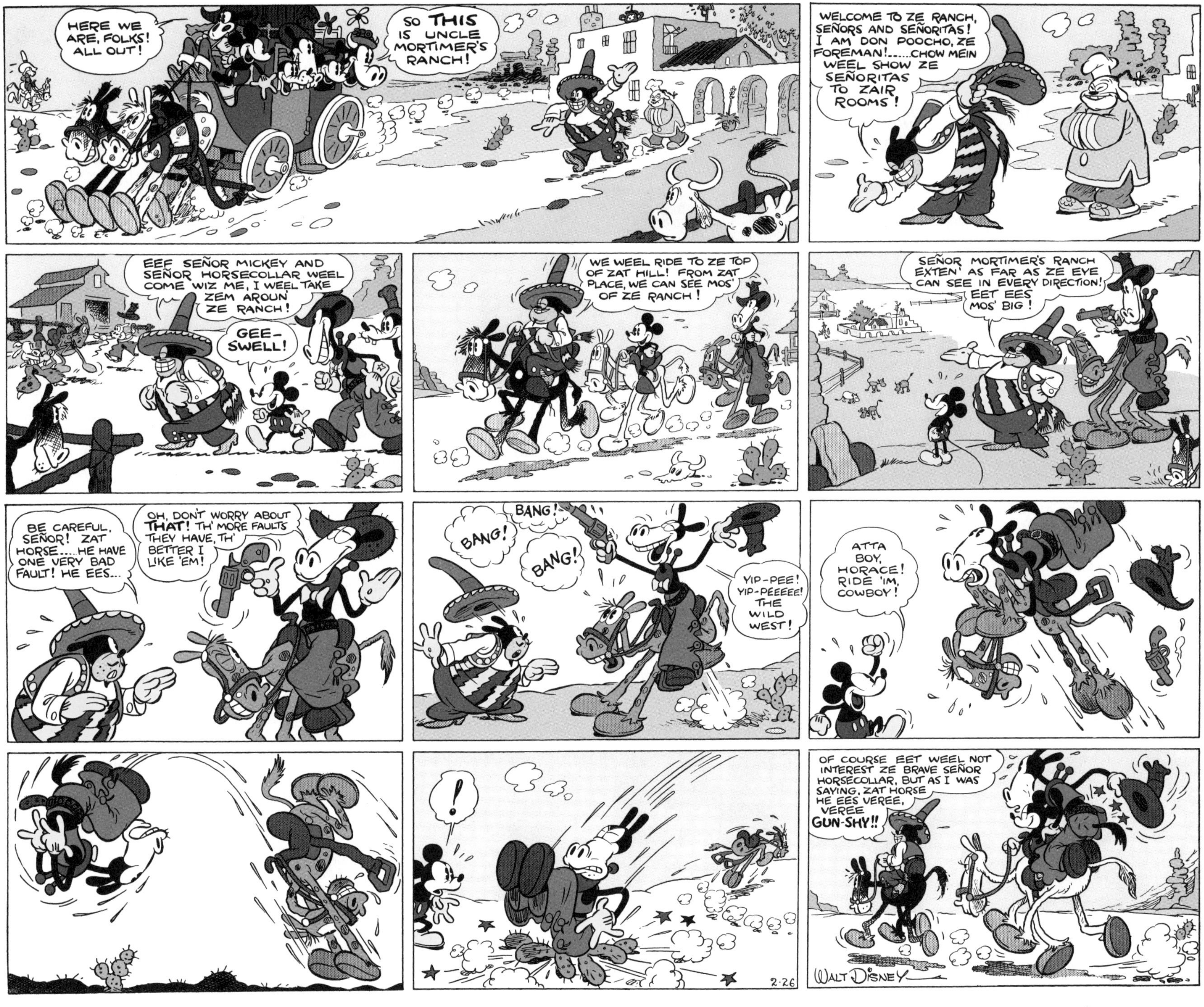

HERE WE ARE, FOLKS! ALL OUT!
SO THIS IS UNCLE MORTIMER'S RANCH!
WELCOME TO ZE RANCH, SEÑORS AND SEÑORITAS! I AM DON POOCHO, ZE FOREMAN!......CHOW MEIN WEEL SHOW ZE SEÑORITAS TO ZAIR ROOMS!
EEF SEÑOR MICKEY AND SEÑOR HORSECOLLAR WEEL COME WIZ ME, I WEEL TAKE ZEM AROUN' ZE RANCH!
GEE-SWELL!
WE WEEL RIDE TO ZE TOP OF ZAT HILL! FROM ZAT PLACE, WE CAN SEE MOS' OF ZE RANCH!
SEÑOR MORTIMER'S RANCH EXTEN' AS FAR AS ZE EYE CAN SEE IN EVERY DIRECTION! EET EES MOS' BIG!
BE CAREFUL, SEÑOR! ZAT HORSE.....HE HAVE ONE VERY BAD FAULT! HE EES...
OH, DON'T WORRY ABOUT THAT! TH' MORE FAULTS THEY HAVE, TH' BETTER I LIKE 'EM!
BANG!
BANG!
BANG!
YIP-PEE! YIP-PEEEEE! THE WILD WEST!
ATTA BOY, HORACE! RIDE 'IM, COWBOY!
!
2·26
OF COURSE EET WEEL NOT INTEREST ZE BRAVE SEÑOR HORSECOLLAR, BUT AS I WAS SAYING, ZAT HORSE HE EES VEREE, VEREE GUN-SHY!!
WALT DISNEY

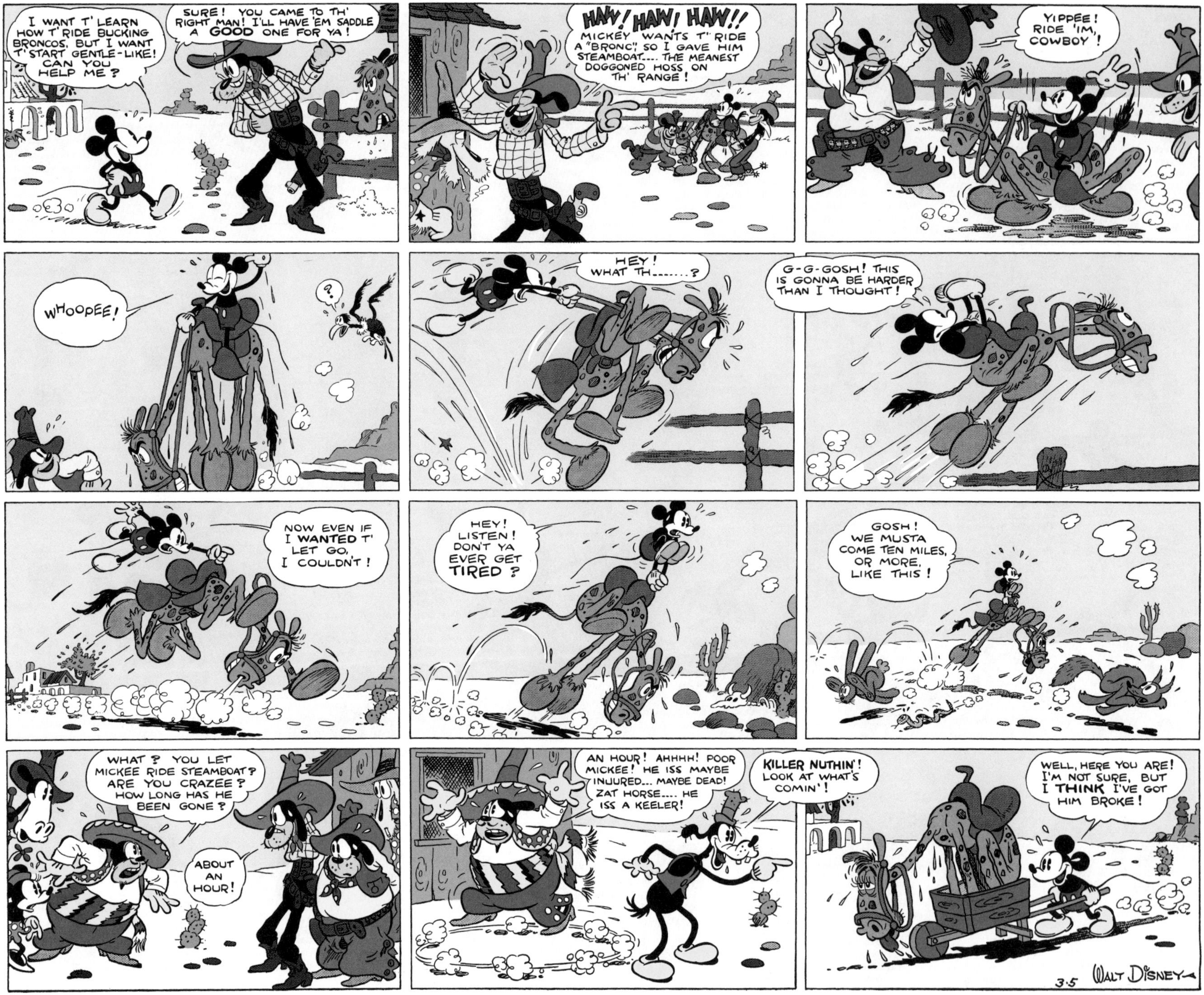

I WANT T' LEARN HOW T' RIDE BUCKING BRONCOS, BUT I WANT T' START GENTLE-LIKE! CAN YOU HELP ME?
SURE! YOU CAME TO TH' RIGHT MAN! I'LL HAVE 'EM SADDLE A GOOD ONE FOR YA!
HAW! HAW! HAW!!
MICKEY WANTS T' RIDE A "BRONC", SO I GAVE HIM STEAMBOAT.... THE MEANEST DOGGONED HOSS ON TH' RANGE!
YIPPEE! RIDE 'IM, COWBOY!
WHOOPEE!
?
HEY! WHAT TH.......?
G-G-GOSH! THIS IS GONNA BE HARDER THAN I THOUGHT!
NOW EVEN IF I WANTED T' LET GO, I COULDN'T!
HEY! LISTEN! DON'T YA EVER GET TIRED?
GOSH! WE MUSTA COME TEN MILES, OR MORE, LIKE THIS!
WHAT? YOU LET MICKEE RIDE STEAMBOAT? ARE YOU CRAZEE? HOW LONG HAS HE BEEN GONE?
ABOUT AN HOUR!
AN HOUR! AHHHH! POOR MICKEE! HE ISS MAYBE INJURED... MAYBE DEAD! ZAT HORSE.... HE ISS A KEELER!
KILLER NUTHIN'! LOOK AT WHAT'S COMIN'!
WELL, HERE YOU ARE! I'M NOT SURE, BUT I THINK I'VE GOT HIM BROKE!
3·5
WALT DISNEY

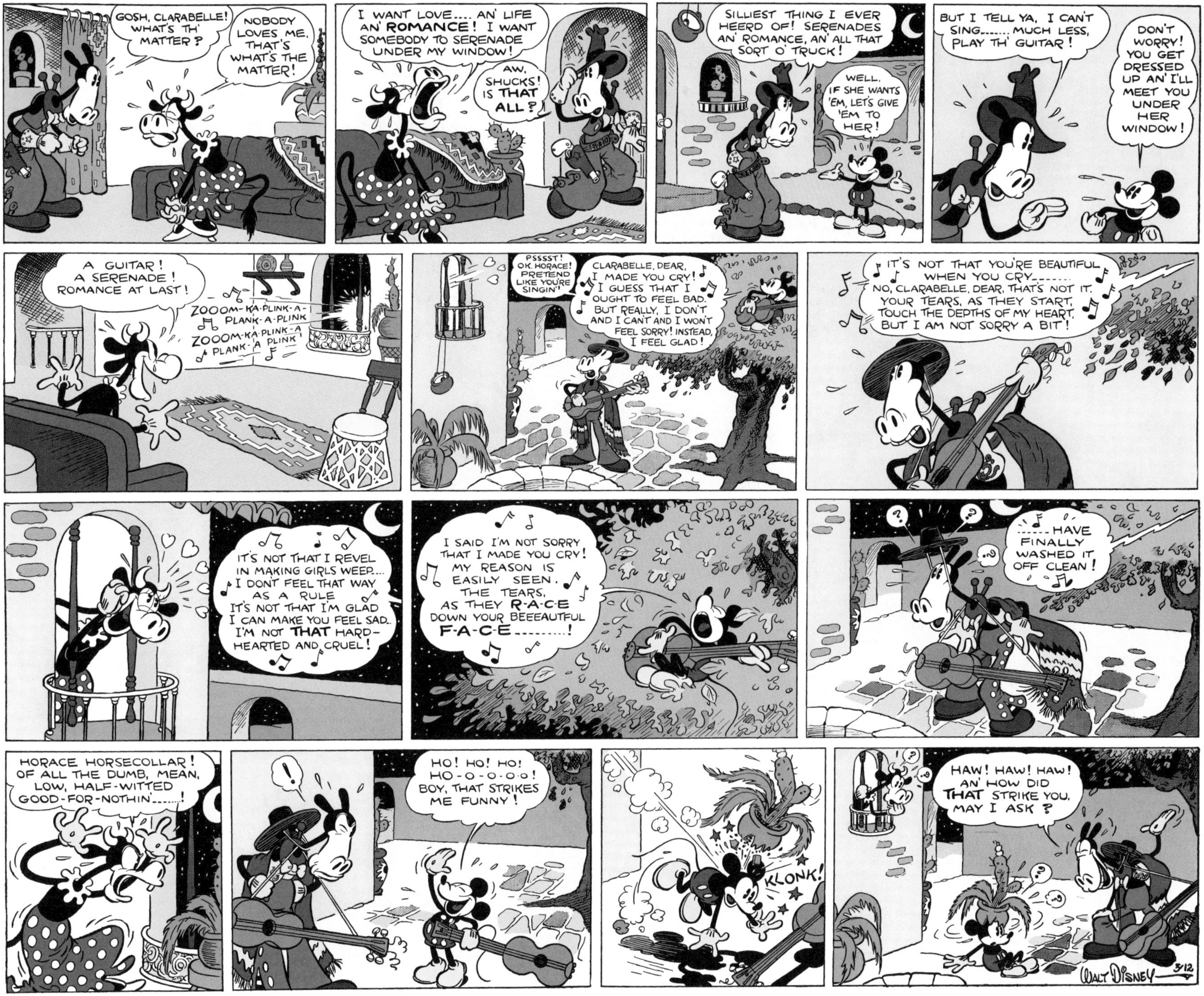
GOSH, CLARABELLE! WHAT'S TH' MATTER?
NOBODY LOVES ME, THAT'S WHAT'S THE MATTER!
I WANT LOVE.... AN' LIFE AN' **ROMANCE**! I WANT SOMEBODY TO SERENADE UNDER MY WINDOW!
AW, SHUCKS! IS **THAT** ALL?
SILLIEST THING I EVER HEERD OF! SERENADES AN' ROMANCE, AN' ALL THAT SORT O' TRUCK!
WELL, IF SHE WANTS 'EM, LET'S GIVE 'EM TO HER!
BUT I TELL YA, I CAN'T SING....... MUCH LESS, PLAY TH' GUITAR!
DON'T WORRY! YOU GET DRESSED UP AN' I'LL MEET YOU UNDER HER WINDOW!
A GUITAR! A SERENADE! ROMANCE AT LAST!
ZOOOM-KA-PLINK-A-PLANK-A-PLINK ZOOOM-KA-PLINK-A PLANK-A PLINK
PSSSST! OK, HORACE! PRETEND LIKE YOU'RE SINGIN'!
CLARABELLE, DEAR, I MADE YOU CRY! I GUESS THAT I OUGHT TO FEEL BAD. BUT REALLY, I DON'T AND I CAN'T AND I WON'T FEEL SORRY! INSTEAD, I FEEL GLAD!
IT'S NOT THAT YOU'RE BEAUTIFUL WHEN YOU CRY------- NO, CLARABELLE, DEAR, THAT'S NOT IT. YOUR TEARS, AS THEY START, TOUCH THE DEPTHS OF MY HEART, BUT I AM NOT SORRY A BIT!
IT'S NOT THAT I REVEL IN MAKING GIRLS WEEP... I DON'T FEEL THAT WAY AS A RULE IT'S NOT THAT I'M GLAD I CAN MAKE YOU FEEL SAD.. I'M NOT **THAT** HARD-HEARTED AND CRUEL!
I SAID I'M NOT SORRY THAT I MADE YOU CRY! MY REASON IS EASILY SEEN. THE TEARS, AS THEY **R-A-C-E** DOWN YOUR BEEEAUTFUL **F-A-C-E**---------!
------HAVE FINALLY WASHED IT OFF CLEAN!
HORACE HORSECOLLAR! OF ALL THE DUMB, MEAN, LOW, HALF-WITTED GOOD-FOR-NOTHIN'.......!
!
HO! HO! HO! HO-O-O-O-O! BOY, THAT STRIKES ME FUNNY!
KLONK!
HAW! HAW! HAW! AN' HOW DID **THAT** STRIKE YOU, MAY I ASK?
WALT DISNEY 3/12

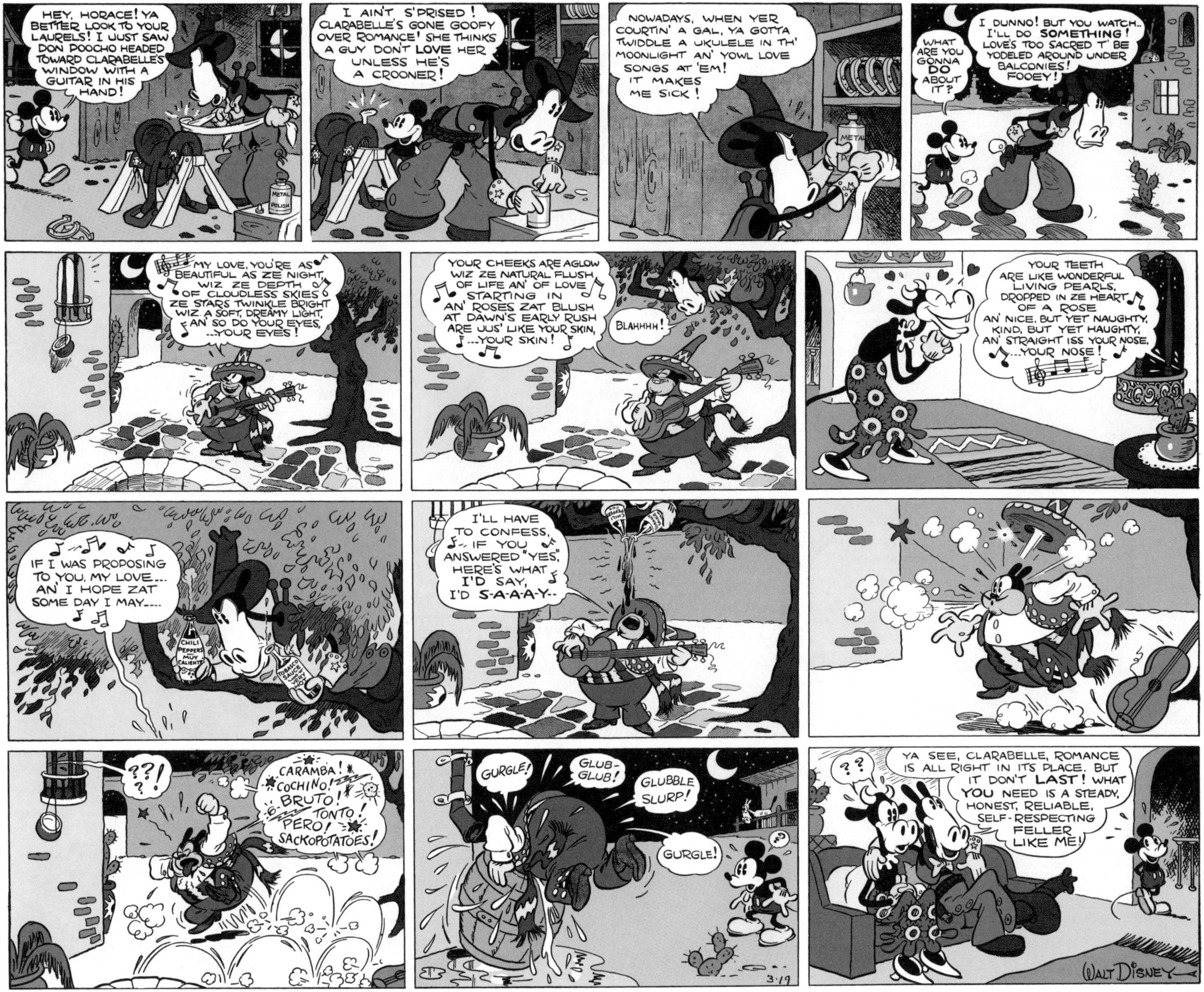
HEY, HORACE! YA BETTER LOOK TO YOUR LAURELS! I JUST SAW DON POOCHO HEADED TOWARD CLARABELLE'S WINDOW WITH A GUITAR IN HIS HAND!
METAL POLISH
I AIN'T S'PRISED! CLARABELLE'S GONE GOOFY OVER ROMANCE! SHE THINKS A GUY DON'T **LOVE** HER UNLESS HE'S A CROONER!
NOWADAYS, WHEN YER COURTIN' A GAL, YA GOTTA TWIDDLE A UKULELE IN TH' MOONLIGHT AN' YOWL LOVE SONGS AT 'EM! IT MAKES ME SICK!
WHAT ARE YOU GONNA **DO** ABOUT IT?
I DUNNO! BUT YOU WATCH.. I'LL DO **SOMETHING**! LOVE'S TOO SACRED T' BE YODELED AROUND UNDER BALCONIES! FOOEY!
MY LOVE, YOU'RE AS BEAUTIFUL AS ZE NIGHT, WIZ ZE DEPTH OF CLOUDLESS SKIES ZE STARS TWINKLE BRIGHT WIZ A SOFT, DREAMY LIGHT, AN' SO DO YOUR EYES, ..YOUR EYES!
YOUR CHEEKS ARE AGLOW WIZ ZE NATURAL FLUSH OF LIFE AN' OF LOVE STARTING IN AN' ROSES ZAT BLUSH AT DAWN'S EARLY RUSH ARE JUS' LIKE YOUR SKIN, ...YOUR SKIN!
BLAHHHH!
YOUR TEETH ARE LIKE WONDERFUL LIVING PEARLS, DROPPED IN ZE HEART OF A ROSE AN' NICE, BUT YET NAUGHTY, KIND, BUT YET HAUGHTY, AN' STRAIGHT ISS YOUR NOSE, ...YOUR NOSE!
IF I WAS PROPOSING TO YOU, MY LOVE... AN' I HOPE ZAT SOME DAY I MAY....
CHILI PEPPERS MUY CALIENTE
I'LL HAVE TO CONFESS, IF YOU ANSWERED "YES," HERE'S WHAT **I'D** SAY, I'D **S-A-A-A-Y--**
??!
CARAMBA! COCHINO! BRUTO! TONTO! PERO! SACKOPOTATOES!
GURGLE!
GLUB-GLUB!
GLUBBLE SLURP!
GURGLE!
3·19
??
YA SEE, CLARABELLE, ROMANCE IS ALL RIGHT IN ITS PLACE. BUT IT DON'T **LAST**! WHAT **YOU** NEED IS A STEADY, HONEST, RELIABLE, SELF-RESPECTING FELLER **LIKE ME**!
WALT DISNEY

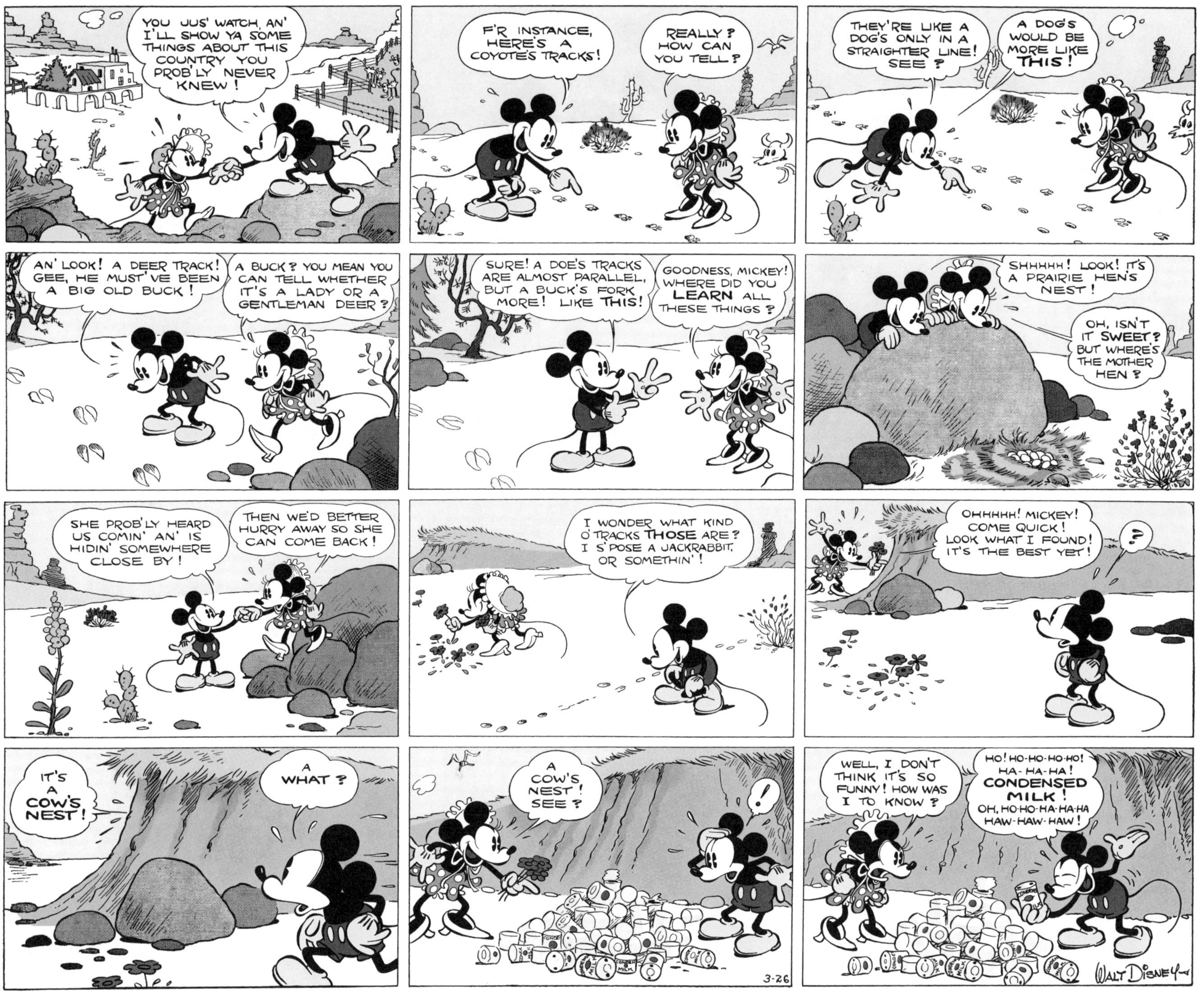

YOU JUS' WATCH, AN' I'LL SHOW YA SOME THINGS ABOUT THIS COUNTRY YOU PROB'LY NEVER KNEW!
F'R INSTANCE, HERE'S A COYOTE'S TRACKS!
REALLY? HOW CAN YOU TELL?
THEY'RE LIKE A DOG'S ONLY IN A STRAIGHTER LINE! SEE?
A DOG'S WOULD BE MORE LIKE THIS!
AN' LOOK! A DEER TRACK! GEE, HE MUST'VE BEEN A BIG OLD BUCK!
A BUCK? YOU MEAN YOU CAN TELL WHETHER IT'S A LADY OR A GENTLEMAN DEER?
SURE! A DOE'S TRACKS ARE ALMOST PARALLEL, BUT A BUCK'S FORK MORE! LIKE THIS!
GOODNESS, MICKEY! WHERE DID YOU LEARN ALL THESE THINGS?
SHHHHH! LOOK! IT'S A PRAIRIE HEN'S NEST!
OH, ISN'T IT SWEET? BUT WHERE'S THE MOTHER HEN?
SHE PROB'LY HEARD US COMIN' AN' IS HIDIN' SOMEWHERE CLOSE BY!
THEN WE'D BETTER HURRY AWAY SO SHE CAN COME BACK!
I WONDER WHAT KIND O' TRACKS THOSE ARE? I S'POSE A JACKRABBIT, OR SOMETHIN'!
OHHHHH! MICKEY! COME QUICK! LOOK WHAT I FOUND! IT'S THE BEST YET!
?
IT'S A COW'S NEST!
A WHAT?
A COW'S NEST! SEE?
!
WELL, I DON'T THINK IT'S SO FUNNY! HOW WAS I TO KNOW?
HO! HO-HO-HO-HO! HA-HA-HA! CONDENSED MILK! OH, HO-HO-HA-HA-HA HAW-HAW-HAW!
3-26
WALT DISNEY

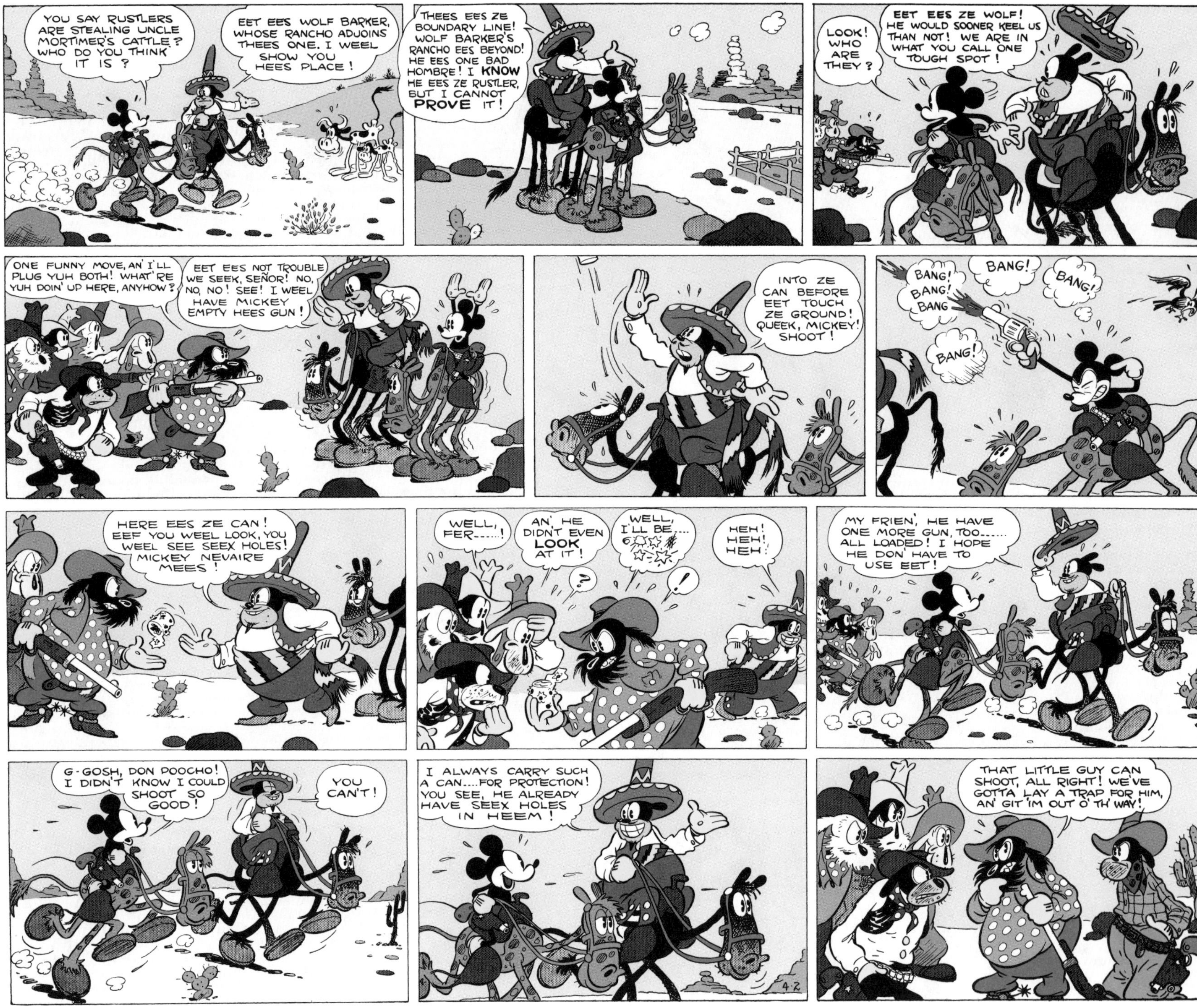
YOU SAY RUSTLERS ARE STEALING UNCLE MORTIMER'S CATTLE? WHO DO YOU THINK IT IS?
EET EES WOLF BARKER, WHOSE RANCHO ADJOINS THEES ONE. I WEEL SHOW YOU HEES PLACE!
THEES EES ZE BOUNDARY LINE! WOLF BARKER'S RANCHO EES BEYOND! HE EES ONE BAD HOMBRE! I KNOW HE EES ZE RUSTLER, BUT I CANNOT PROVE IT!
LOOK! WHO ARE THEY?
EET EES ZE WOLF! HE WOULD SOONER KEEL US THAN NOT! WE ARE IN WHAT YOU CALL ONE TOUGH SPOT!
ONE FUNNY MOVE, AN' I'LL PLUG YUH BOTH! WHAT'RE YUH DOIN' UP HERE, ANYHOW?
EET EES NOT TROUBLE WE SEEK, SEÑOR! NO, NO! SEE! I WEEL HAVE MICKEY EMPTY HEES GUN!
INTO ZE CAN BEFORE EET TOUCH ZE GROUND! QUEEK, MICKEY! SHOOT!
BANG! BANG! BANG
BANG!
BANG!
BANG!
HERE EES ZE CAN! EEF YOU WEEL LOOK, YOU WEEL SEE SEEX HOLES! MICKEY NEVAIRE MEES!
WELL, FER----!
AN' HE DIDN'T EVEN LOOK AT IT!
WELL, I'LL BE....
HEH! HEH! HEH!
MY FRIEN', HE HAVE ONE MORE GUN, TOO...... ALL LOADED! I HOPE HE DON' HAVE TO USE EET!
G-GOSH, DON POOCHO! I DIDN'T KNOW I COULD SHOOT SO GOOD!
YOU CAN'T!
I ALWAYS CARRY SUCH A CAN....FOR PROTECTION! YOU SEE, HE ALREADY HAVE SEEX HOLES IN HEEM!
THAT LITTLE GUY CAN SHOOT, ALL RIGHT! WE'VE GOTTA LAY A TRAP FOR HIM, AN' GIT 'IM OUT O' TH' WAY!

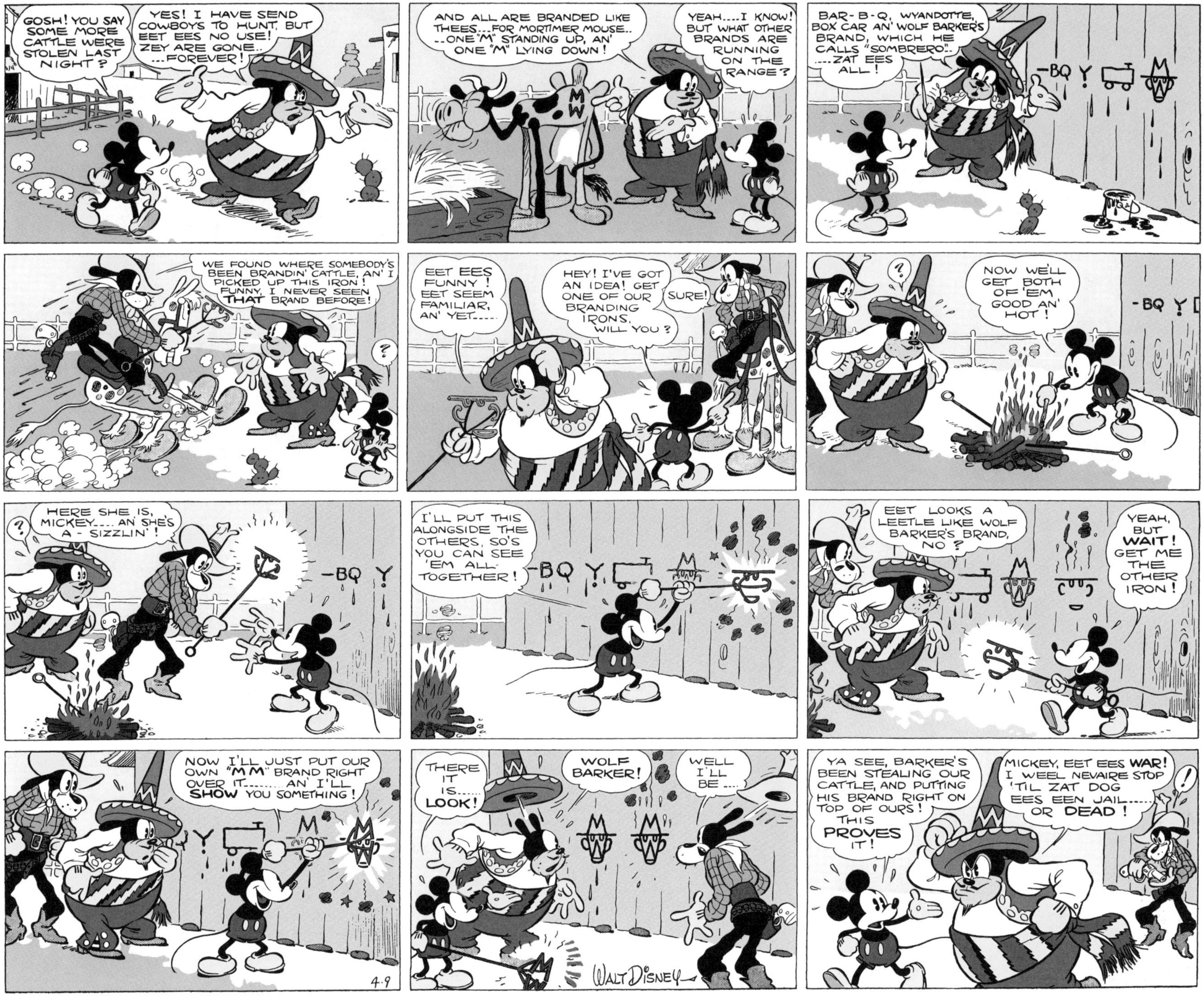
GOSH! YOU SAY SOME MORE CATTLE WERE STOLEN LAST NIGHT?
YES! I HAVE SEND COWBOYS TO HUNT, BUT EET EES NO USE! ZEY ARE GONE.. ...FOREVER!
AND ALL ARE BRANDED LIKE THEES...FOR MORTIMER MOUSE.. ..ONE "M" STANDING UP, AN' ONE "M" LYING DOWN!
YEAH....I KNOW! BUT WHAT OTHER BRANDS ARE RUNNING ON THE RANGE?
BAR-B-Q, WYANDOTTE, BOX CAR AN' WOLF BARKER'S BRAND, WHICH HE CALLS "SOMBRERO".. ....ZAT EES ALL!
WE FOUND WHERE SOMEBODY'S BEEN BRANDIN' CATTLE, AN' I PICKED UP THIS IRON! FUNNY, I NEVER SEEN THAT BRAND BEFORE!
?
EET EES FUNNY! EET SEEM FAMILIAR, AN' YET.....
HEY! I'VE GOT AN IDEA! GET ONE OF OUR BRANDING IRONS, WILL YOU?
SURE!
?
NOW WE'LL GET BOTH OF 'EM GOOD AN' HOT!
?
HERE SHE IS, MICKEY.... AN' SHE'S A-SIZZLIN'!
I'LL PUT THIS ALONGSIDE THE OTHERS, SO'S YOU CAN SEE 'EM ALL TOGETHER!
EET LOOKS A LEETLE LIKE WOLF BARKER'S BRAND, NO?
YEAH, BUT WAIT! GET ME THE OTHER IRON!
NOW I'LL JUST PUT OUR OWN "MM" BRAND RIGHT OVER IT....... AN' I'LL SHOW YOU SOMETHING!
4-9
THERE IT IS..... LOOK!
WOLF BARKER!
WELL I'LL BE....
WALT DISNEY
YA SEE, BARKER'S BEEN STEALING OUR CATTLE, AND PUTTING HIS BRAND RIGHT ON TOP OF OURS! THIS PROVES IT!
MICKEY, EET EES WAR! I WEEL NEVAIRE STOP 'TIL ZAT DOG EES EEN JAIL..... OR DEAD!
!

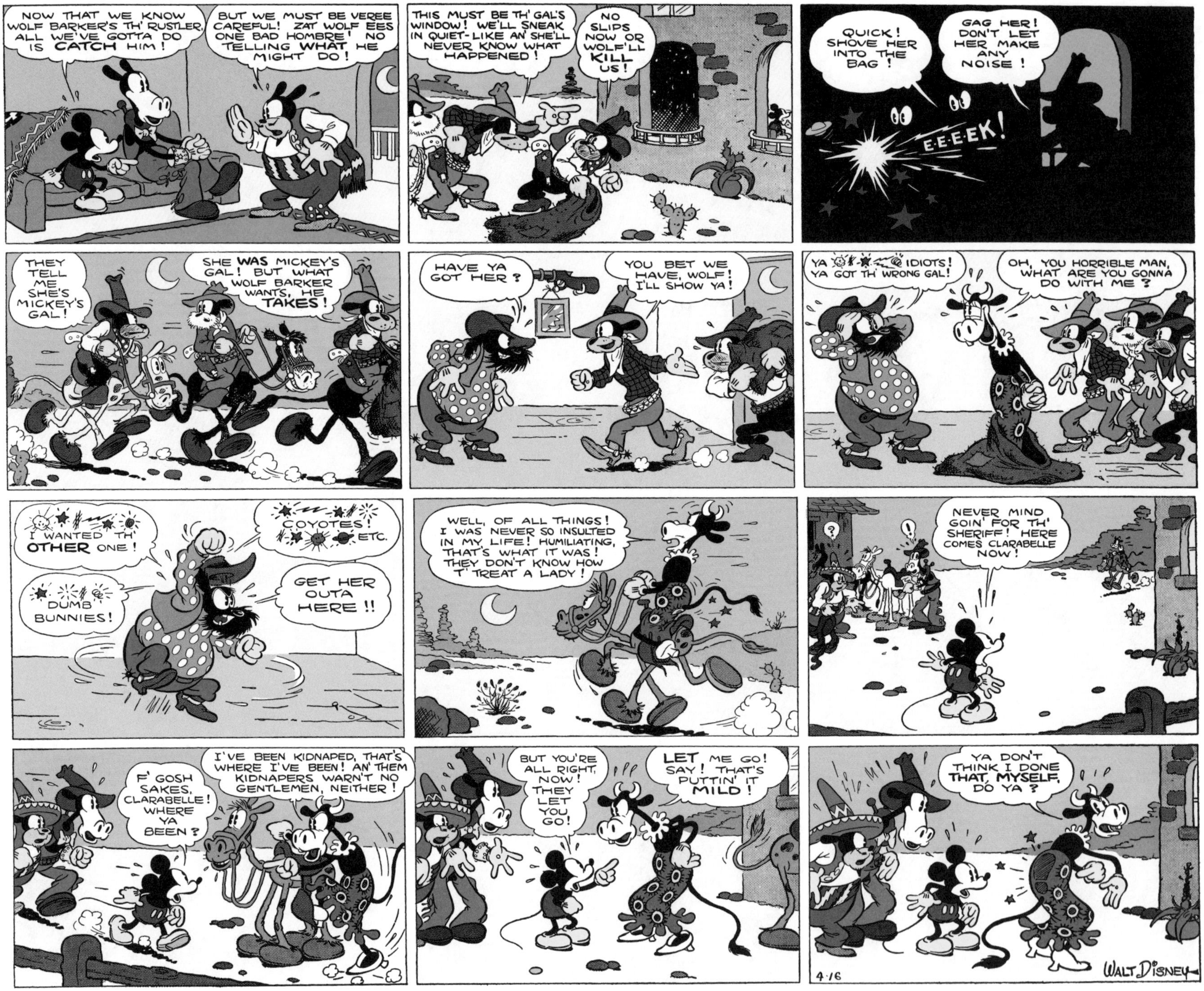
NOW THAT WE KNOW WOLF BARKER'S TH' RUSTLER, ALL WE'VE GOTTA DO IS CATCH HIM!
BUT WE MUST BE VEREE CAREFUL! ZAT WOLF EES ONE BAD HOMBRE! NO TELLING WHAT HE MIGHT DO!
THIS MUST BE TH' GAL'S WINDOW! WE'LL SNEAK IN QUIET-LIKE AN' SHE'LL NEVER KNOW WHAT HAPPENED!
NO SLIPS NOW OR WOLF'LL KILL US!
QUICK! SHOVE HER INTO THE BAG!
GAG HER! DON'T LET HER MAKE ANY NOISE!
E-E-E-EK!
THEY TELL ME SHE'S MICKEY'S GAL!
SHE WAS MICKEY'S GAL! BUT WHAT WOLF BARKER WANTS, HE TAKES!
HAVE YA GOT HER?
YOU BET WE HAVE, WOLF! I'LL SHOW YA!
YA IDIOTS! YA GOT TH' WRONG GAL!
OH, YOU HORRIBLE MAN, WHAT ARE YOU GONNA DO WITH ME?
I WANTED TH' OTHER ONE!
COYOTES! ETC.
DUMB BUNNIES!
GET HER OUTA HERE!!
WELL, OF ALL THINGS! I WAS NEVER SO INSULTED IN MY LIFE! HUMILIATING, THAT'S WHAT IT WAS! THEY DON'T KNOW HOW T' TREAT A LADY!
NEVER MIND GOIN' FOR TH' SHERIFF! HERE COMES CLARABELLE NOW!
F' GOSH SAKES, CLARABELLE! WHERE YA BEEN?
I'VE BEEN KIDNAPED, THAT'S WHERE I'VE BEEN! AN' THEM KIDNAPERS WARN'T NO GENTLEMEN, NEITHER!
BUT YOU'RE ALL RIGHT, NOW! THEY LET YOU GO!
LET ME GO! SAY! THAT'S PUTTIN' IT MILD!
YA DON'T THINK I DONE THAT, MYSELF, DO YA?
4-16
WALT DISNEY

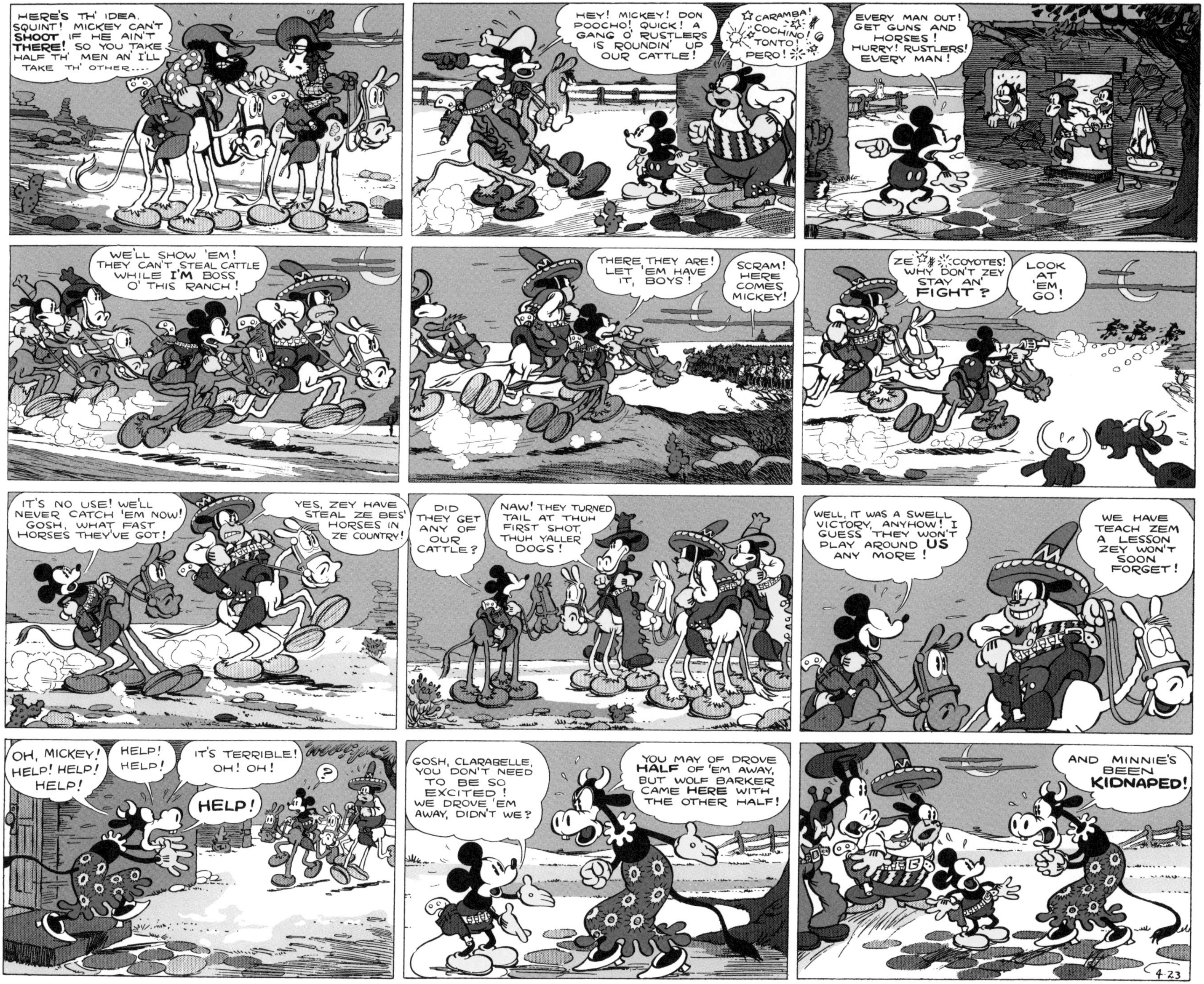
HERE'S TH' IDEA. SQUINT! MICKEY CAN'T SHOOT IF HE AIN'T THERE! SO YOU TAKE HALF TH' MEN AN' I'LL TAKE TH' OTHER....
HEY! MICKEY! DON POOCHO! QUICK! A GANG O' RUSTLERS IS ROUNDIN' UP OUR CATTLE!
CARAMBA! COCHINO! TONTO! PERO!
EVERY MAN OUT! GET GUNS AND HORSES! HURRY! RUSTLERS! EVERY MAN!
WE'LL SHOW 'EM! THEY CAN'T STEAL CATTLE WHILE I'M BOSS O' THIS RANCH!
THERE THEY ARE! LET 'EM HAVE IT, BOYS!
SCRAM! HERE COMES MICKEY!
ZE COYOTES! WHY DON'T ZEY STAY AN' FIGHT?
LOOK AT 'EM GO!
IT'S NO USE! WE'LL NEVER CATCH 'EM NOW! GOSH, WHAT FAST HORSES THEY'VE GOT!
YES, ZEY HAVE STEAL ZE BES' HORSES IN ZE COUNTRY!
DID THEY GET ANY OF OUR CATTLE?
NAW! THEY TURNED TAIL AT THUH FIRST SHOT, THUH YALLER DOGS!
WELL, IT WAS A SWELL VICTORY, ANYHOW! I GUESS THEY WON'T PLAY AROUND US ANY MORE!
WE HAVE TEACH ZEM A LESSON ZEY WON'T SOON FORGET!
OH, MICKEY! HELP! HELP! HELP!
HELP! HELP!
IT'S TERRIBLE! OH! OH!
HELP!
?
GOSH, CLARABELLE, YOU DON'T NEED TO BE SO EXCITED! WE DROVE 'EM AWAY, DIDN'T WE?
YOU MAY OF DROVE HALF OF 'EM AWAY, BUT WOLF BARKER CAME HERE WITH THE OTHER HALF!
AND MINNIE'S BEEN KIDNAPED!
4-23

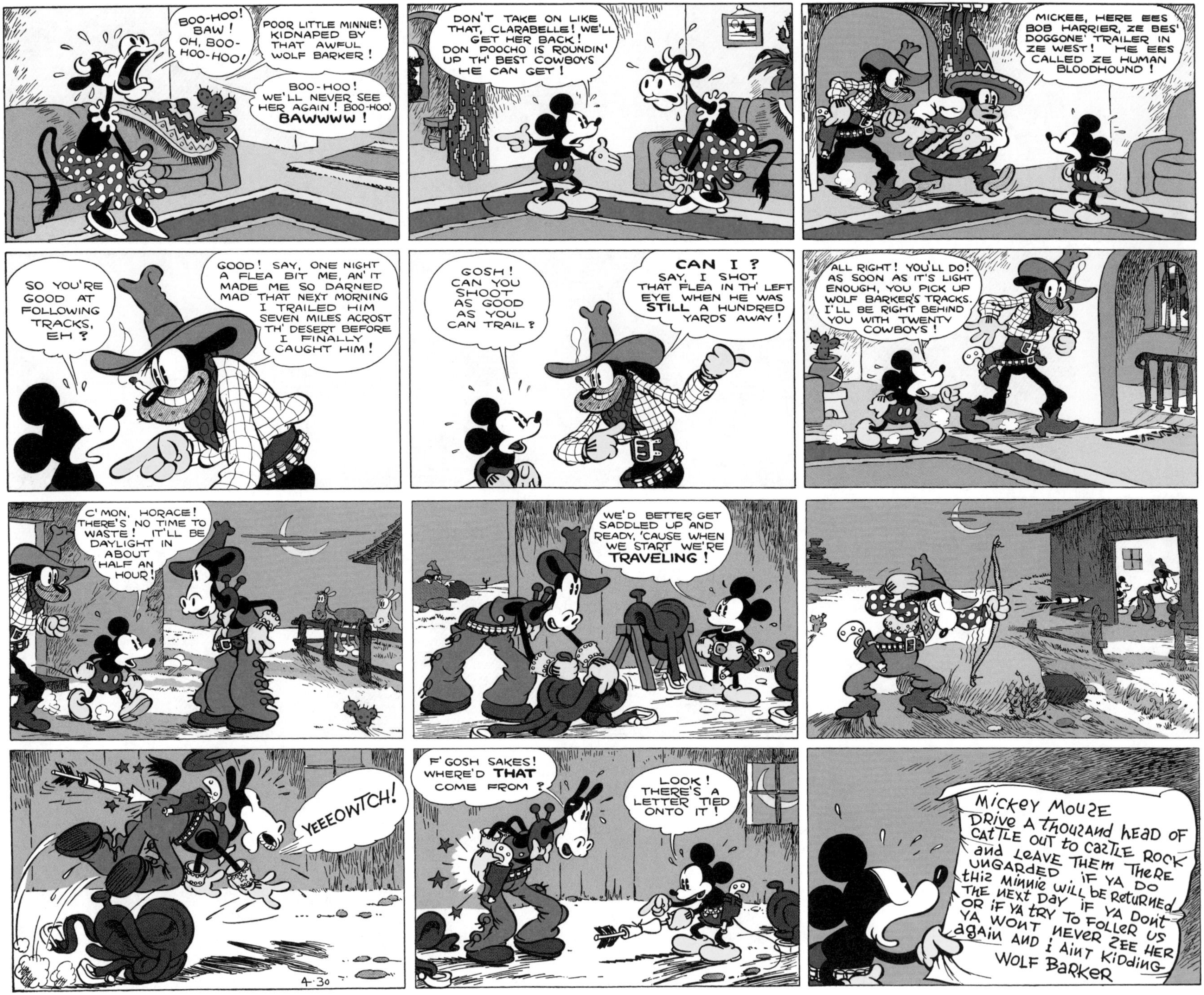
BOO-HOO! BAW! OH, BOO-HOO-HOO!
POOR LITTLE MINNIE! KIDNAPED BY THAT AWFUL WOLF BARKER!
BOO-HOO! WE'LL NEVER SEE HER AGAIN! BOO-HOO! BAWWWW!
DON'T TAKE ON LIKE THAT, CLARABELLE! WE'LL GET HER BACK! DON POOCHO IS ROUNDIN' UP TH' BEST COWBOYS HE CAN GET!
MICKEE, HERE EES BOB HARRIER, ZE BES' DOGGONE' TRAILER IN ZE WEST! HE EES CALLED ZE HUMAN BLOODHOUND!
SO YOU'RE GOOD AT FOLLOWING TRACKS, EH?
GOOD! SAY, ONE NIGHT A FLEA BIT ME, AN' IT MADE ME SO DARNED MAD THAT NEXT MORNING I TRAILED HIM SEVEN MILES ACROST TH' DESERT BEFORE I FINALLY CAUGHT HIM!
GOSH! CAN YOU SHOOT AS GOOD AS YOU CAN TRAIL?
CAN I? SAY, I SHOT THAT FLEA IN TH' LEFT EYE WHEN HE WAS STILL A HUNDRED YARDS AWAY!
ALL RIGHT! YOU'LL DO! AS SOON AS IT'S LIGHT ENOUGH, YOU PICK UP WOLF BARKER'S TRACKS. I'LL BE RIGHT BEHIND YOU WITH TWENTY COWBOYS!
C'MON, HORACE! THERE'S NO TIME TO WASTE! IT'LL BE DAYLIGHT IN ABOUT HALF AN HOUR!
WE'D BETTER GET SADDLED UP AND READY, 'CAUSE WHEN WE START WE'RE TRAVELING!
YEEEOWTCH!
4-30
F' GOSH SAKES! WHERE'D THAT COME FROM?
LOOK! THERE'S A LETTER TIED ONTO IT!
MICKEY MOUZE
DRIVE A THOUZAND HEAD OF CATTLE OUT TO CAZTLE ROCK AND LEAVE THEM THERE UNGARDED. IF YA DO THIS MINNIE WILL BE RETURNED THE NEXT DAY IF YA DONT OR IF YA TRY TO FOLLER US YA WONT NEVER ZEE HER AGAIN AND I AINT KIDDING-
WOLF BARKER

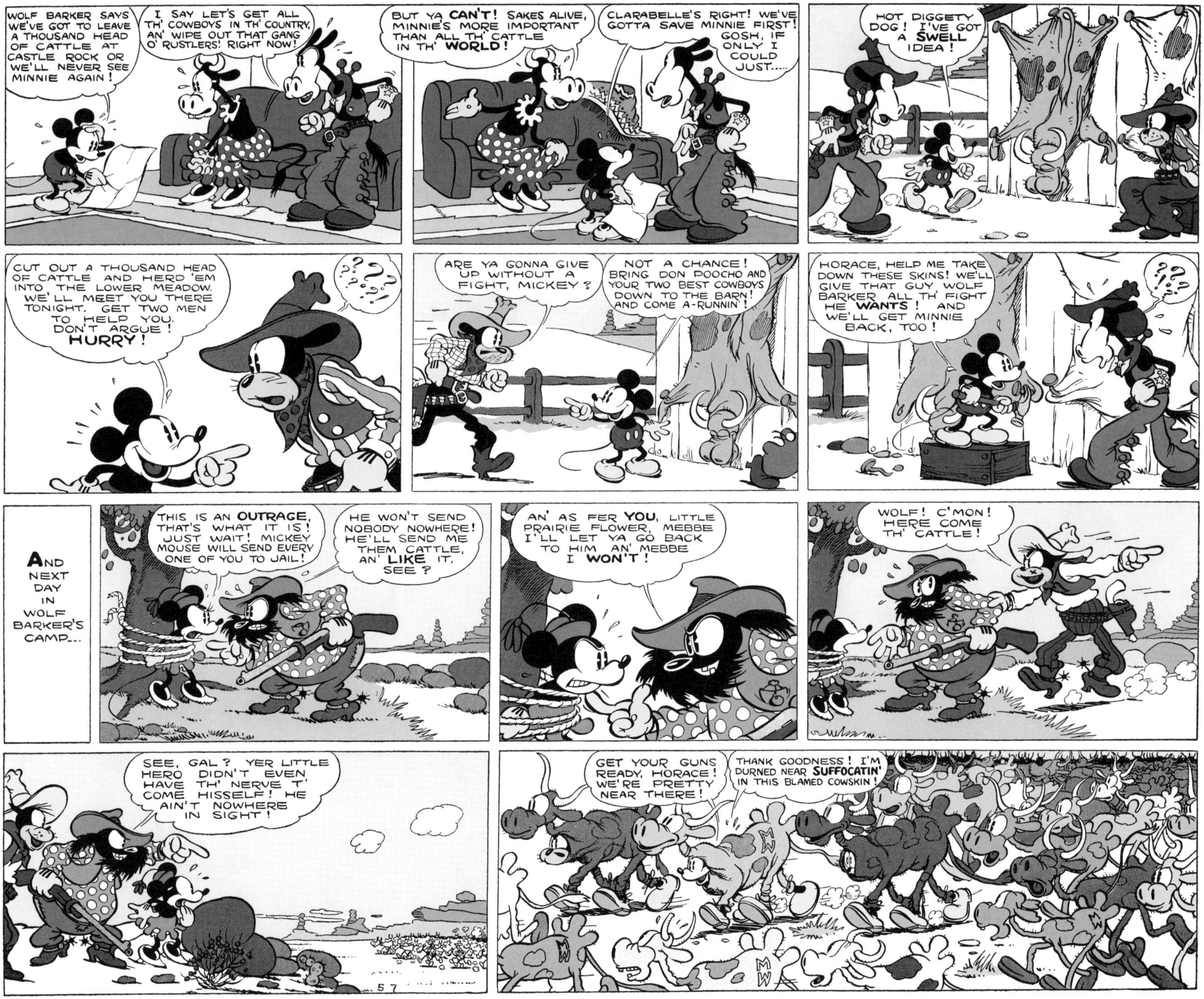

WOLF BARKER SAYS WE'VE GOT TO LEAVE A THOUSAND HEAD OF CATTLE AT CASTLE ROCK OR WE'LL NEVER SEE MINNIE AGAIN!
I SAY LET'S GET ALL TH' COWBOYS IN TH' COUNTRY, AN' WIPE OUT THAT GANG O' RUSTLERS! RIGHT NOW!
BUT YA CAN'T! SAKES ALIVE, MINNIE'S MORE IMPORTANT THAN ALL TH' CATTLE IN TH' WORLD!
CLARABELLE'S RIGHT! WE'VE GOTTA SAVE MINNIE FIRST!
GOSH, IF ONLY I COULD JUST.....
HOT DIGGETY DOG! I'VE GOT A SWELL IDEA!
CUT OUT A THOUSAND HEAD OF CATTLE AND HERD 'EM INTO THE LOWER MEADOW. WE'LL MEET YOU THERE TONIGHT. GET TWO MEN TO HELP YOU. DON'T ARGUE! HURRY!
ARE YA GONNA GIVE UP WITHOUT A FIGHT, MICKEY?
NOT A CHANCE! BRING DON POOCHO AND YOUR TWO BEST COWBOYS DOWN TO THE BARN! AND COME A-RUNNIN'!
HORACE, HELP ME TAKE DOWN THESE SKINS! WE'LL GIVE THAT GUY WOLF BARKER ALL TH' FIGHT HE WANTS! AND WE'LL GET MINNIE BACK, TOO!
AND NEXT DAY IN WOLF BARKER'S CAMP...
THIS IS AN OUTRAGE, THAT'S WHAT IT IS! JUST WAIT! MICKEY MOUSE WILL SEND EVERY ONE OF YOU TO JAIL!
HE WON'T SEND NOBODY NOWHERE! HE'LL SEND ME THEM CATTLE, AN' LIKE IT, SEE?
AN' AS FER YOU, LITTLE PRAIRIE FLOWER, MEBBE I'LL LET YA GO BACK TO HIM AN' MEBBE I WON'T!
WOLF! C'MON! HERE COME TH' CATTLE!
SEE, GAL? YER LITTLE HERO DIDN'T EVEN HAVE TH' NERVE T' COME HISSELF! HE AIN'T NOWHERE IN SIGHT!
GET YOUR GUNS READY, HORACE! WE'RE PRETTY NEAR THERE!
THANK GOODNESS! I'M DURNED NEAR SUFFOCATIN' IN THIS BLAMED COWSKIN!

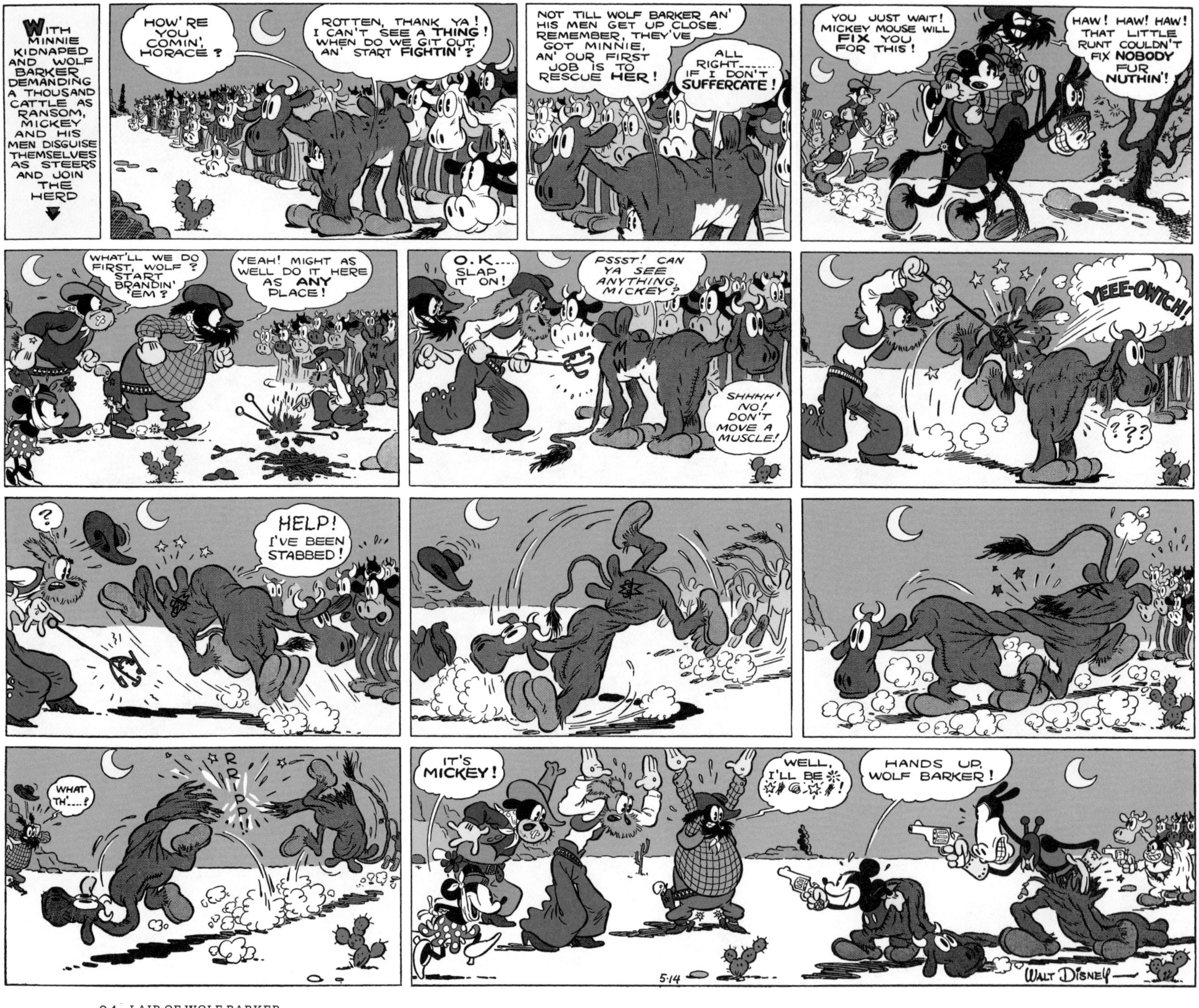
WITH MINNIE KIDNAPED AND WOLF BARKER DEMANDING A THOUSAND CATTLE AS RANSOM, MICKEY AND HIS MEN DISGUISE THEMSELVES AS STEERS AND JOIN THE HERD
HOW'RE YOU COMIN', HORACE?
ROTTEN, THANK YA! I CAN'T SEE A THING! WHEN DO WE GIT OUT, AN' START FIGHTIN'?
NOT TILL WOLF BARKER AN' HIS MEN GET UP CLOSE. REMEMBER, THEY'VE GOT MINNIE, AN' OUR FIRST JOB IS TO RESCUE HER!
ALL RIGHT...... IF I DON'T SUFFERCATE!
YOU JUST WAIT! MICKEY MOUSE WILL FIX YOU FOR THIS!
HAW! HAW! HAW! THAT LITTLE RUNT COULDN'T FIX NOBODY FUR NUTHIN'!
WHAT'LL WE DO FIRST, WOLF? START BRANDIN' 'EM?
YEAH! MIGHT AS WELL DO IT HERE AS ANY PLACE!
O.K.... SLAP IT ON!
PSSST! CAN YA SEE ANYTHING, MICKEY?
SHHHH! NO! DON'T MOVE A MUSCLE!
YEEE-OWTCH!
???
?
HELP! I'VE BEEN STABBED!
WHAT TH'....?
RRRIPP!
IT'S MICKEY!
WELL, I'LL BE
HANDS UP, WOLF BARKER!
5·14
WALT DISNEY

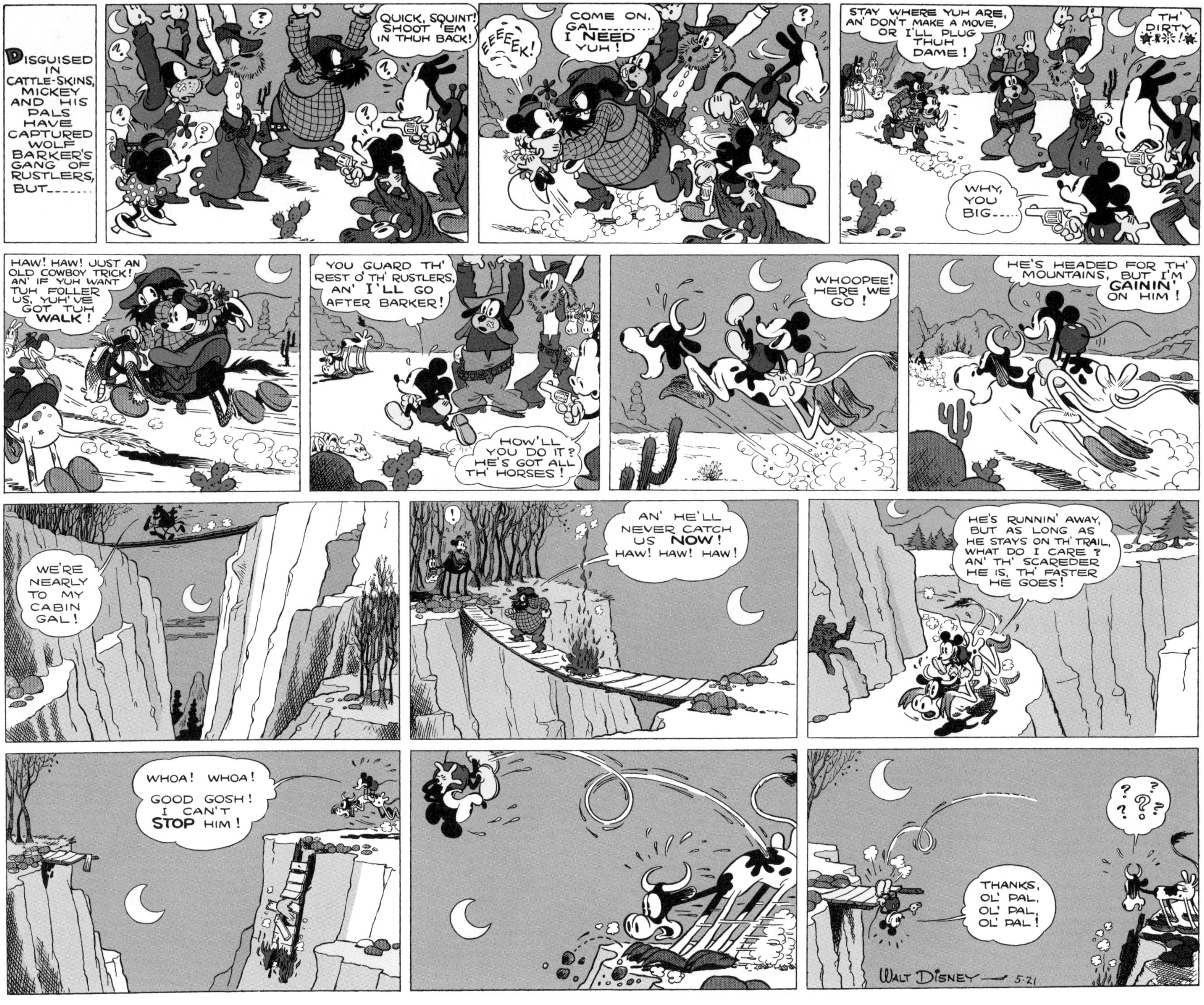
DISGUISED IN CATTLE-SKINS, MICKEY AND HIS PALS HAVE CAPTURED WOLF BARKER'S GANG OF RUSTLERS, BUT______
QUICK, SQUINT! SHOOT 'EM IN THUH BACK!
EEEEEEK!
COME ON, GAL________ I NEED YUH!
STAY WHERE YUH ARE, AN' DON'T MAKE A MOVE, OR I'LL PLUG THUH DAME!
TH' DIRTY ✱✱✱!✱
WHY, YOU BIG_____
HAW! HAW! JUST AN OLD COWBOY TRICK! AN' IF YUH WANT TUH FOLLER US, YUH'VE GOT TUH WALK!
YOU GUARD TH' REST O' TH' RUSTLERS, AN' I'LL GO AFTER BARKER!
HOW'LL YOU DO IT? HE'S GOT ALL TH' HORSES!
WHOOPEE! HERE WE GO!
HE'S HEADED FOR TH' MOUNTAINS, BUT I'M GAININ' ON HIM!
WE'RE NEARLY TO MY CABIN GAL!
AN' HE'LL NEVER CATCH US NOW! HAW! HAW! HAW!
HE'S RUNNIN' AWAY, BUT AS LONG AS HE STAYS ON TH' TRAIL, WHAT DO I CARE? AN' TH' SCAREDER HE IS, TH' FASTER HE GOES!
WHOA! WHOA! GOOD GOSH! I CAN'T STOP HIM!
THANKS, OL' PAL, OL' PAL, OL' PAL!
WALT DISNEY 5-21

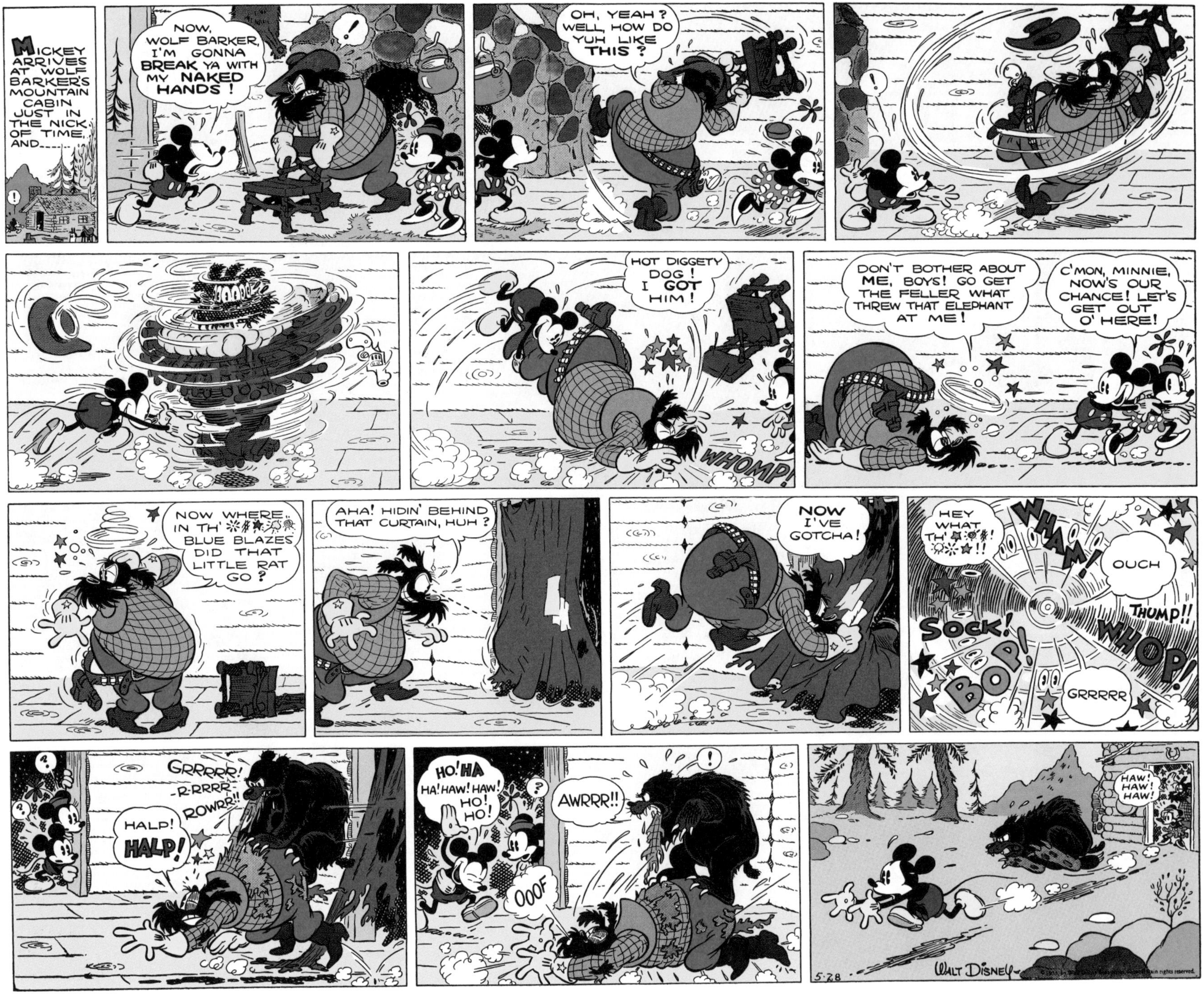
MICKEY ARRIVES AT WOLF BARKER'S MOUNTAIN CABIN JUST IN THE NICK OF TIME, AND.....
!
NOW, WOLF BARKER, I'M GONNA BREAK YA WITH MY NAKED HANDS !
!
OH, YEAH ? WELL, HOW DO YUH LIKE THIS ?
!
HOT DIGGETY DOG ! I GOT HIM !
WHOMP!
DON'T BOTHER ABOUT ME, BOYS! GO GET THE FELLER WHAT THREW THAT ELEPHANT AT ME!
C'MON, MINNIE, NOW'S OUR CHANCE! LET'S GET OUT O' HERE!
NOW WHERE IN TH' BLUE BLAZES DID THAT LITTLE RAT GO ?
AHA! HIDIN' BEHIND THAT CURTAIN, HUH ?
NOW I'VE GOTCHA !
HEY WHAT TH' !!
WHAM!
OUCH
THUMP!!
SOCK!
BOP!
WHOP!
GRRRRR
?
?
GRRRRR! -R-RRRR ROWRR!!
HALP! HALP!
!
HO! HA HA! HAW! HAW! HO! HO!
?
AWRRR!!
OOOF
HAW! HAW! HAW!
5-28
WALT DISNEY

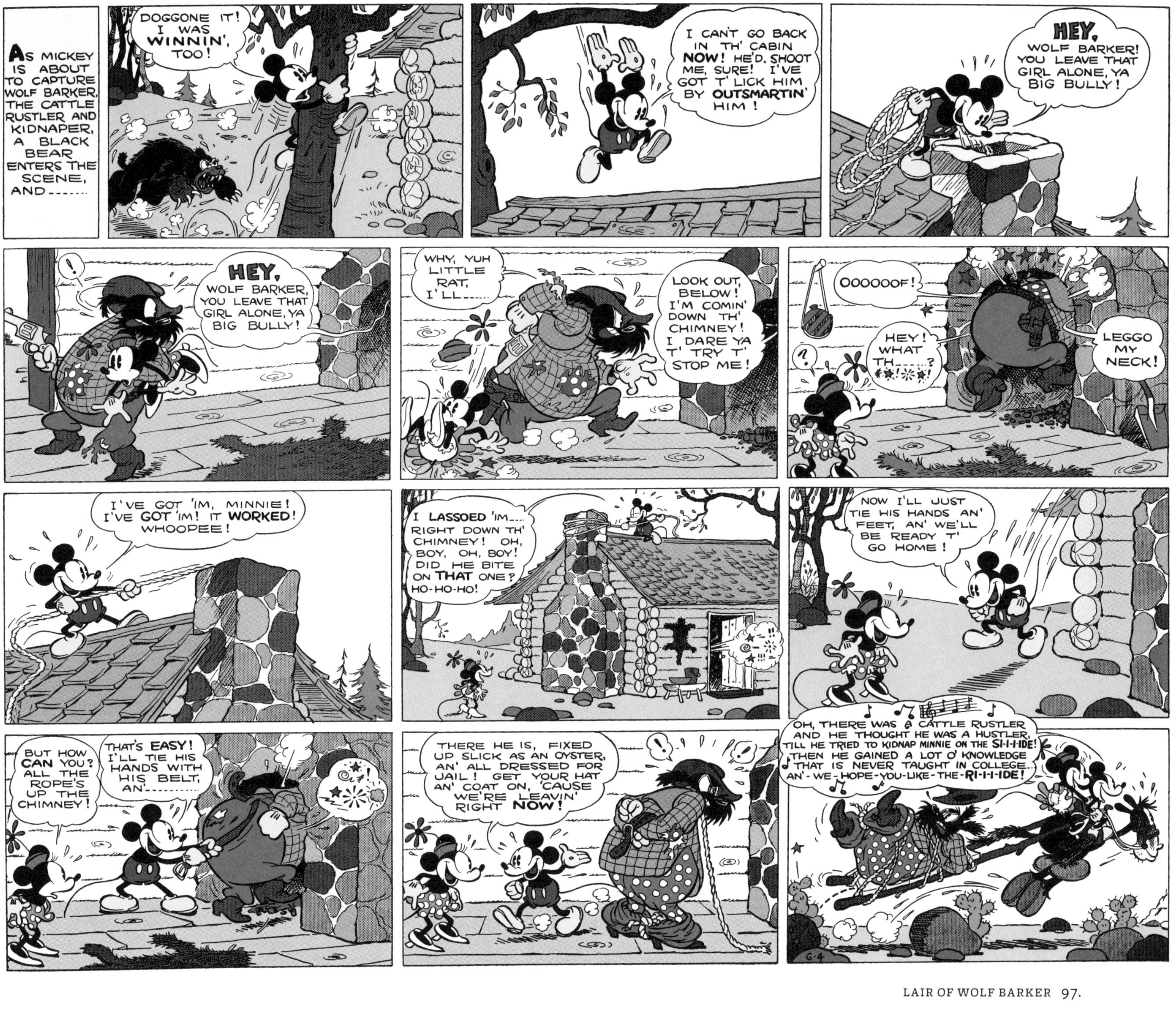
AS MICKEY IS ABOUT TO CAPTURE WOLF BARKER, THE CATTLE RUSTLER AND KIDNAPER, A BLACK BEAR ENTERS THE SCENE, AND.......
DOGGONE IT! I WAS WINNIN', TOO!
I CAN'T GO BACK IN TH' CABIN NOW! HE'D SHOOT ME, SURE! I'VE GOT T' LICK HIM BY OUTSMARTIN' HIM!
HEY, WOLF BARKER! YOU LEAVE THAT GIRL ALONE, YA BIG BULLY!
HEY, WOLF BARKER, YOU LEAVE THAT GIRL ALONE, YA BIG BULLY!
WHY, YUH LITTLE RAT, I'LL......
LOOK OUT, BELOW! I'M COMIN' DOWN TH' CHIMNEY! I DARE YA T' TRY T' STOP ME!
OOOOOOF!
HEY! WHAT TH.....?
LEGGO MY NECK!
I'VE GOT 'IM, MINNIE! I'VE GOT 'IM! IT WORKED! WHOOPEE!
I LASSOED 'IM.... RIGHT DOWN TH' CHIMNEY! OH, BOY, OH, BOY! DID HE BITE ON THAT ONE? HO-HO-HO!
NOW I'LL JUST TIE HIS HANDS AN' FEET, AN' WE'LL BE READY T' GO HOME!
BUT HOW CAN YOU? ALL THE ROPE'S UP THE CHIMNEY!
THAT'S EASY! I'LL TIE HIS HANDS WITH HIS BELT, AN'..........
THERE HE IS, FIXED UP SLICK AS AN OYSTER, AN' ALL DRESSED FOR JAIL! GET YOUR HAT AN' COAT ON, 'CAUSE WE'RE LEAVIN' RIGHT NOW!
OH, THERE WAS A CATTLE RUSTLER AND HE THOUGHT HE WAS A HUSTLER, TILL HE TRIED TO KIDNAP MINNIE ON THE SI-I-I-IDE! THEN HE GAINED A LOT O' KNOWLEDGE THAT IS NEVER TAUGHT IN COLLEGE... AN'-WE-HOPE-YOU-LIKE-THE-RI-I-I-IDE!

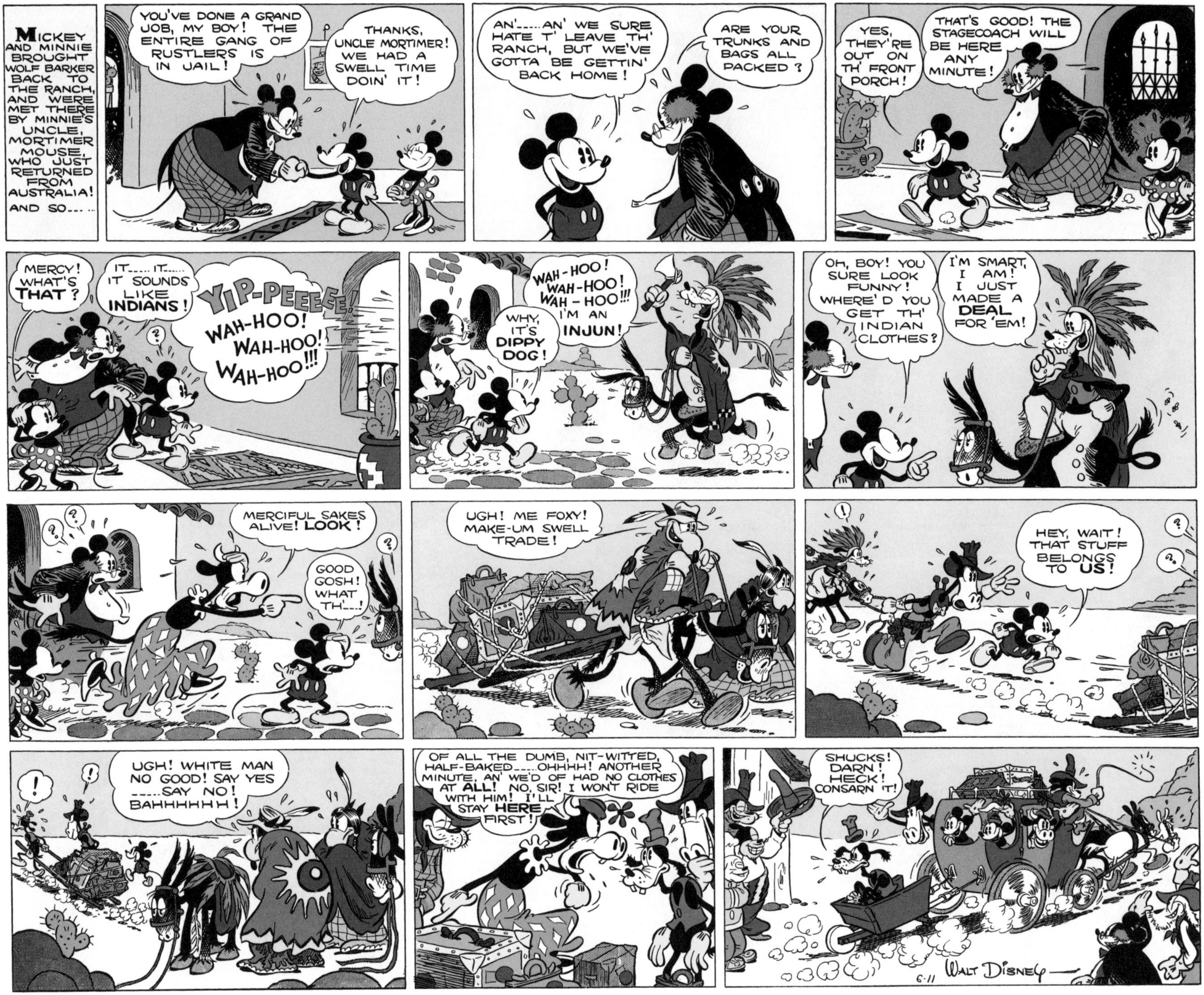
MICKEY AND MINNIE BROUGHT WOLF BARKER BACK TO THE RANCH, AND WERE MET THERE BY MINNIE'S UNCLE, MORTIMER MOUSE, WHO JUST RETURNED FROM AUSTRALIA! AND SO.....
YOU'VE DONE A GRAND JOB, MY BOY! THE ENTIRE GANG OF RUSTLERS IS IN JAIL!
THANKS, UNCLE MORTIMER! WE HAD A SWELL TIME DOIN' IT!
AN'.....AN' WE SURE HATE T' LEAVE TH' RANCH, BUT WE'VE GOTTA BE GETTIN' BACK HOME!
ARE YOUR TRUNKS AND BAGS ALL PACKED?
YES, THEY'RE OUT ON TH' FRONT PORCH!
THAT'S GOOD! THE STAGECOACH WILL BE HERE ANY MINUTE!
MERCY! WHAT'S THAT?
IT..... IT...... IT SOUNDS LIKE INDIANS!
YIP-PEEEEEE! WAH-HOO! WAH-HOO! WAH-HOO!!!
WHY, IT'S DIPPY DOG!
WAH-HOO! WAH-HOO! WAH - HOO!!! I'M AN INJUN!
OH, BOY! YOU SURE LOOK FUNNY! WHERE'D YOU GET TH' INDIAN CLOTHES?
I'M SMART, I AM! I JUST MADE A DEAL FOR 'EM!
MERCIFUL SAKES ALIVE! LOOK!
GOOD GOSH! WHAT TH'...!
UGH! ME FOXY! MAKE-UM SWELL TRADE!
HEY, WAIT! THAT STUFF BELONGS TO US!
UGH! WHITE MAN NO GOOD! SAY YES .....SAY NO! BAHHHHHHH!
OF ALL THE DUMB, NIT-WITTED, HALF-BAKED.....OHHHHH! ANOTHER MINUTE, AN' WE'D OF HAD NO CLOTHES AT ALL! NO, SIR! I WON'T RIDE WITH HIM! I'LL STAY HERE FIRST!
SHUCKS! DARN! HECK! CONSARN IT!
6-11
WALT DISNEY

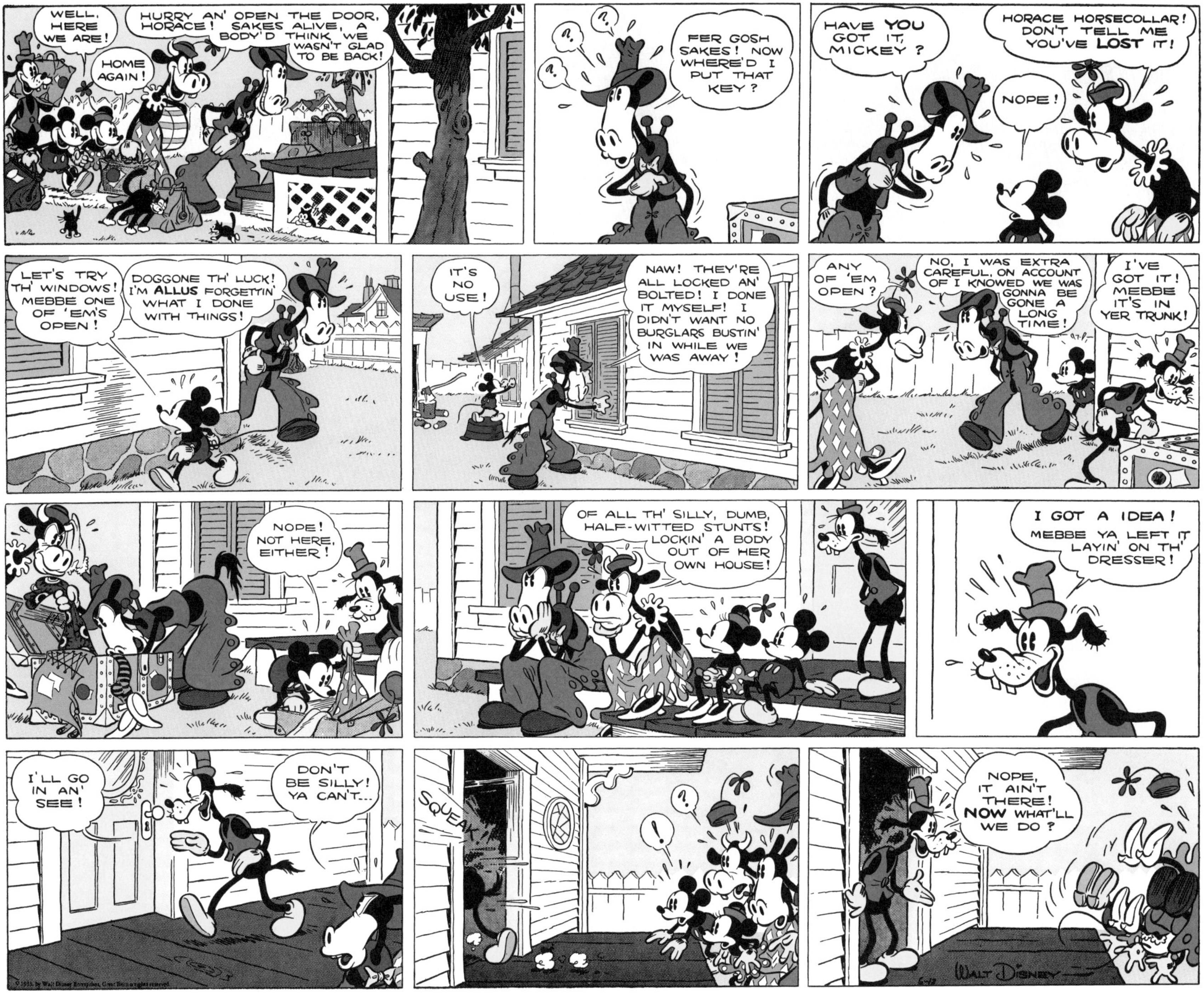
WELL, HERE WE ARE!
HURRY AN' OPEN THE DOOR, HORACE! SAKES ALIVE, A BODY'D THINK WE WASN'T GLAD TO BE BACK!
HOME AGAIN!
FER GOSH SAKES! NOW WHERE'D I PUT THAT KEY?
HAVE YOU GOT IT, MICKEY?
NOPE!
HORACE HORSECOLLAR! DON'T TELL ME YOU'VE LOST IT!
LET'S TRY TH' WINDOWS! MEBBE ONE OF 'EM'S OPEN!
DOGGONE TH' LUCK! I'M ALLUS FORGETTIN' WHAT I DONE WITH THINGS!
IT'S NO USE!
NAW! THEY'RE ALL LOCKED AN' BOLTED! I DONE IT MYSELF! I DIDN'T WANT NO BURGLARS BUSTIN' IN WHILE WE WAS AWAY!
ANY OF 'EM OPEN?
NO, I WAS EXTRA CAREFUL, ON ACCOUNT OF I KNOWED WE WAS GONNA BE GONE A LONG TIME!
I'VE GOT IT! MEBBE IT'S IN YER TRUNK!
NOPE! NOT HERE, EITHER!
OF ALL TH' SILLY, DUMB, HALF-WITTED STUNTS! LOCKIN' A BODY OUT OF HER OWN HOUSE!
I GOT A IDEA! MEBBE YA LEFT IT LAYIN' ON TH' DRESSER!
I'LL GO IN AN' SEE!
DON'T BE SILLY! YA CAN'T...
SQUEAK
NOPE, IT AIN'T THERE! NOW WHAT'LL WE DO?
WALT DISNEY

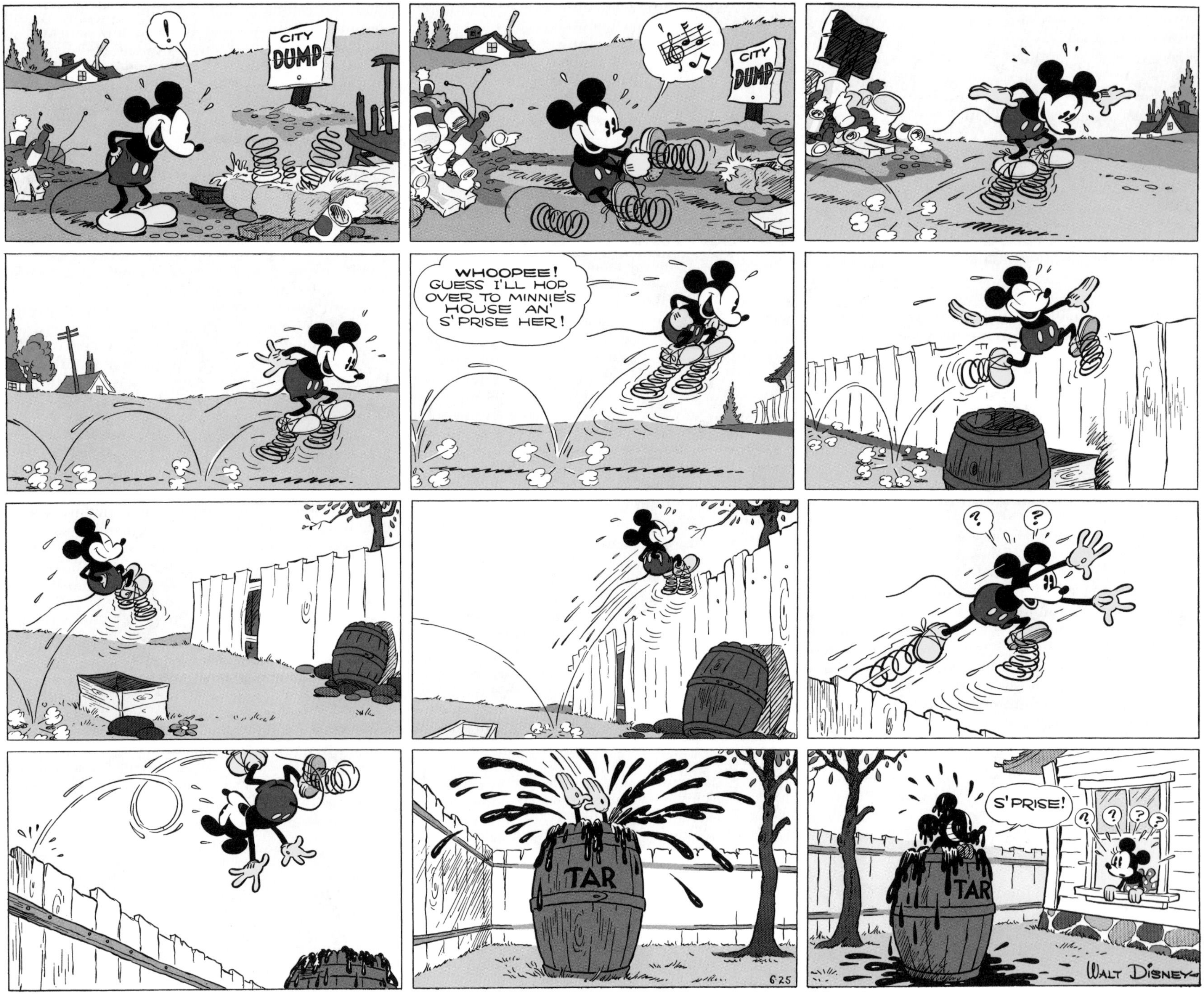
!
CITY DUMP
CITY DUMP
WHOOPEE! GUESS I'LL HOP OVER TO MINNIE'S HOUSE AN' S'PRISE HER!
? ?
TAR
6-25
S'PRISE!
? ? ? ?
TAR
WALT DISNEY

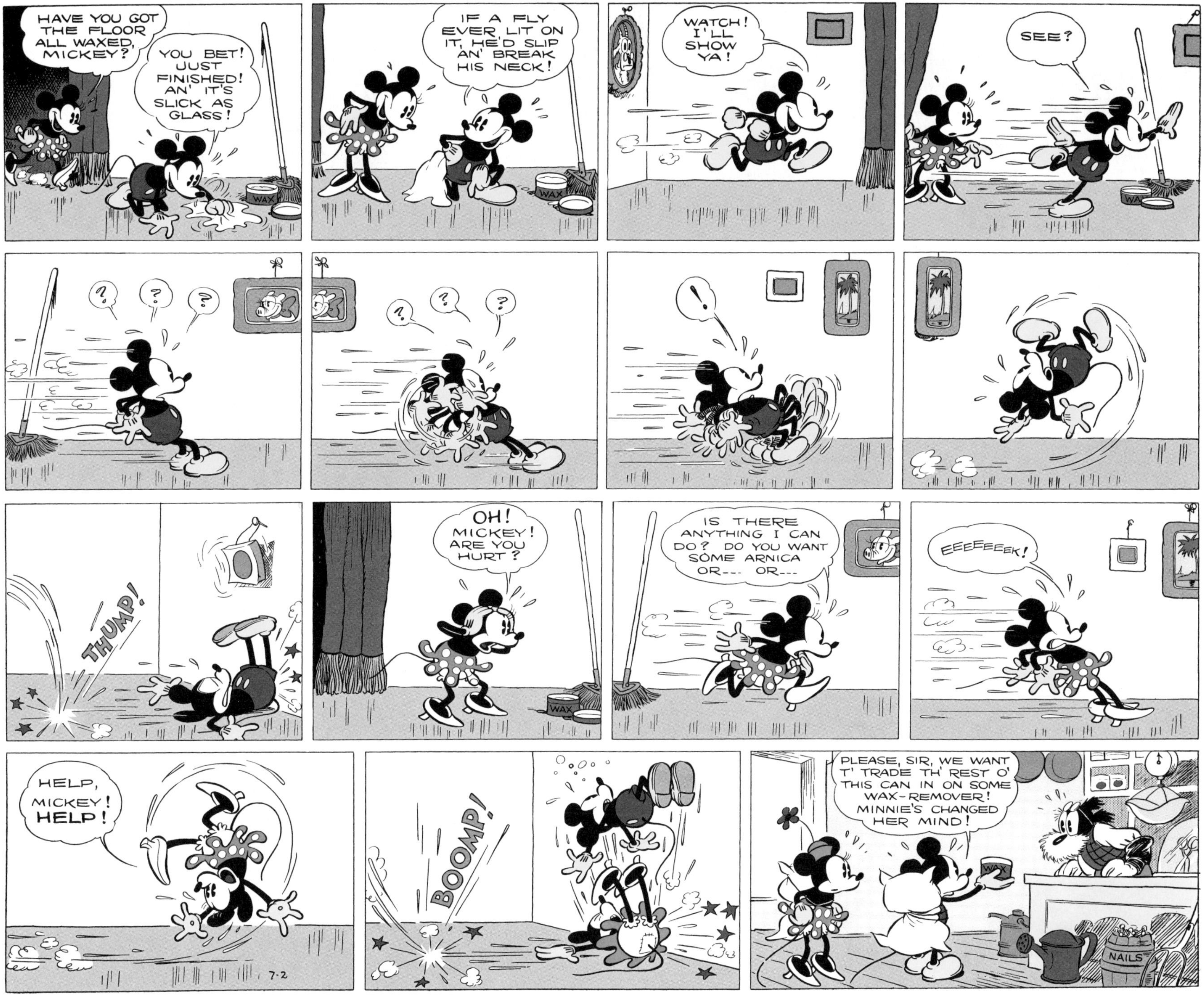
HAVE YOU GOT THE FLOOR ALL WAXED, MICKEY?
YOU BET! JUST FINISHED! AN' IT'S SLICK AS GLASS!
WAX
IF A FLY EVER LIT ON IT, HE'D SLIP AN' BREAK HIS NECK!
WAX
WATCH! I'LL SHOW YA!
SEE?
WAX
?
?
?
?
?
?
!
THUMP!
OH! MICKEY! ARE YOU HURT?
WAX
IS THERE ANYTHING I CAN DO? DO YOU WANT SOME ARNICA OR--- OR---
EEEEEEEEK!
HELP, MICKEY! HELP!
7-2
BOOMP!
PLEASE, SIR, WE WANT T' TRADE TH' REST O' THIS CAN IN ON SOME WAX-REMOVER! MINNIE'S CHANGED HER MIND!
WAX
NAILS

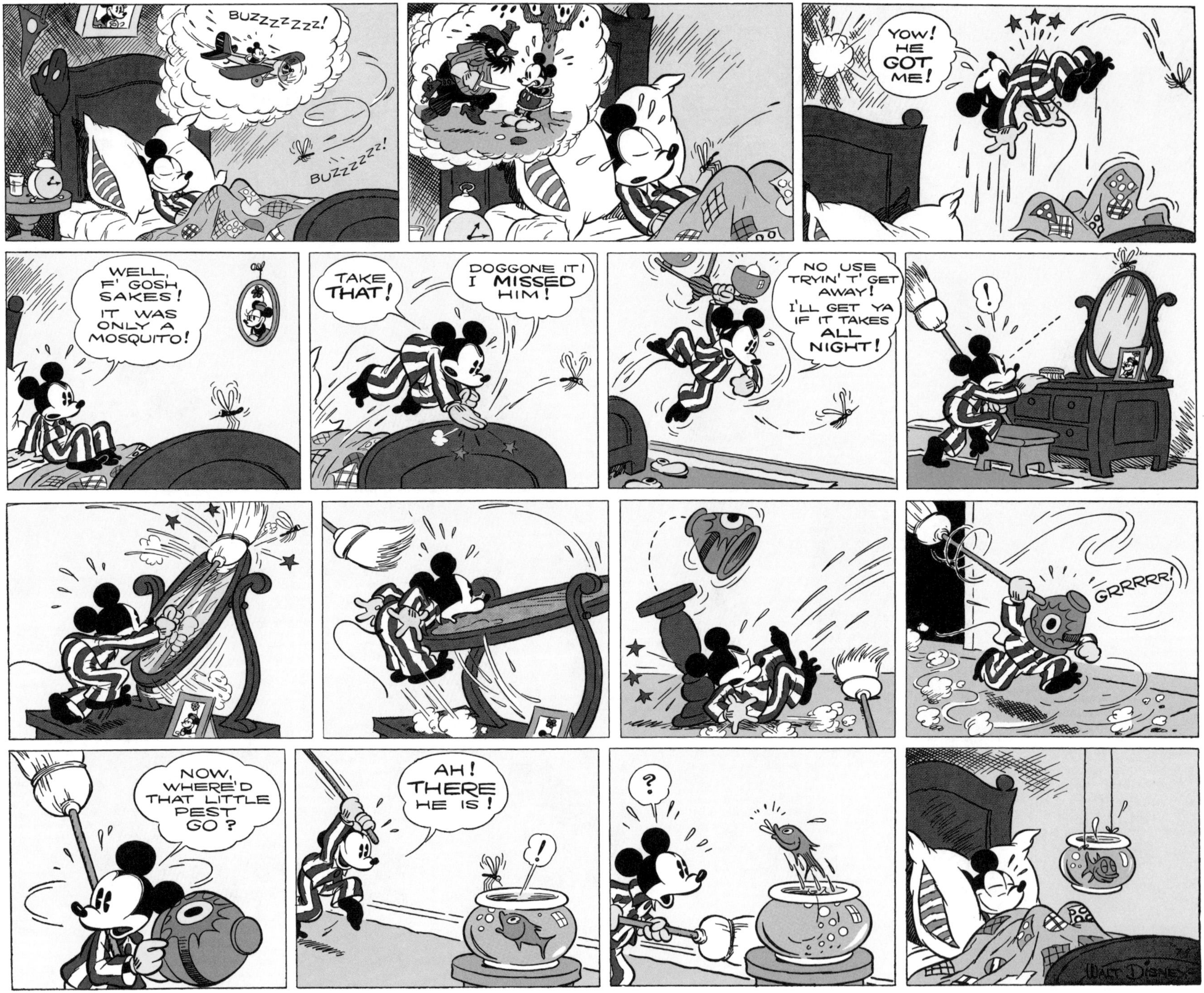
BUZZZZZZZ!
BUZZZZZZ!
YOW! HE GOT ME!
WELL, F' GOSH SAKES! IT WAS ONLY A MOSQUITO!
TAKE THAT!
DOGGONE IT! I MISSED HIM!
NO USE TRYIN' T' GET AWAY! I'LL GET YA IF IT TAKES ALL NIGHT!
!
GRRRRR!
NOW, WHERE'D THAT LITTLE PEST GO?
AH! THERE HE IS!
!
?
WALT DISNEY

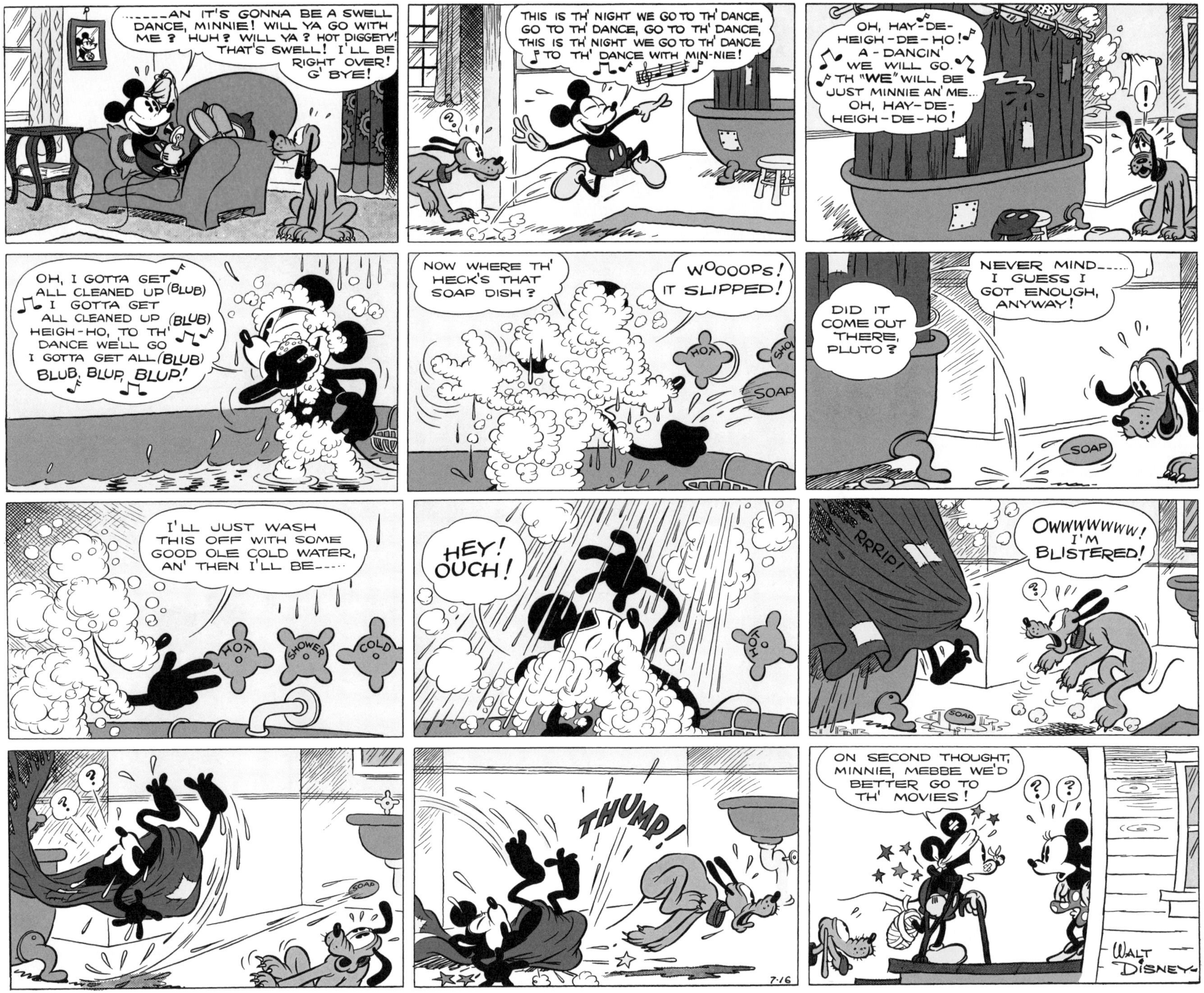
------AN IT'S GONNA BE A SWELL DANCE, MINNIE! WILL YA GO WITH ME? HUH? WILL YA? HOT DIGGETY! THAT'S SWELL! I'LL BE RIGHT OVER! G'BYE!
THIS IS TH' NIGHT WE GO TO TH' DANCE, GO TO TH' DANCE, GO TO TH' DANCE, THIS IS TH' NIGHT WE GO TO TH' DANCE TO TH' DANCE WITH MIN-NIE!
OH, HAY-DE-HEIGH-DE-HO! A-DANCIN' WE WILL GO. TH "WE" WILL BE JUST MINNIE AN' ME... OH, HAY-DE-HEIGH-DE-HO!
OH, I GOTTA GET ALL CLEANED UP (BLUB) I GOTTA GET ALL CLEANED UP (BLUB) HEIGH-HO, TO TH' DANCE WE'LL GO I GOTTA GET ALL (BLUB) BLUB, BLUP, BLUP!
NOW WHERE TH' HECK'S THAT SOAP DISH?
WOOOOPS! IT SLIPPED!
HOT
SOAP
DID IT COME OUT THERE, PLUTO?
NEVER MIND------ I GUESS I GOT ENOUGH, ANYWAY!
SOAP
I'LL JUST WASH THIS OFF WITH SOME GOOD OLE COLD WATER, AN' THEN I'LL BE-----
HOT
SHOWER
COLD
HEY! OUCH!
HOT
RRRIP!
OWWWWWWW! I'M BLISTERED!
SOAP
SOAP
THUMP!
7-16
ON SECOND THOUGHT, MINNIE, MEBBE WE'D BETTER GO TO TH' MOVIES!
WALT DISNEY

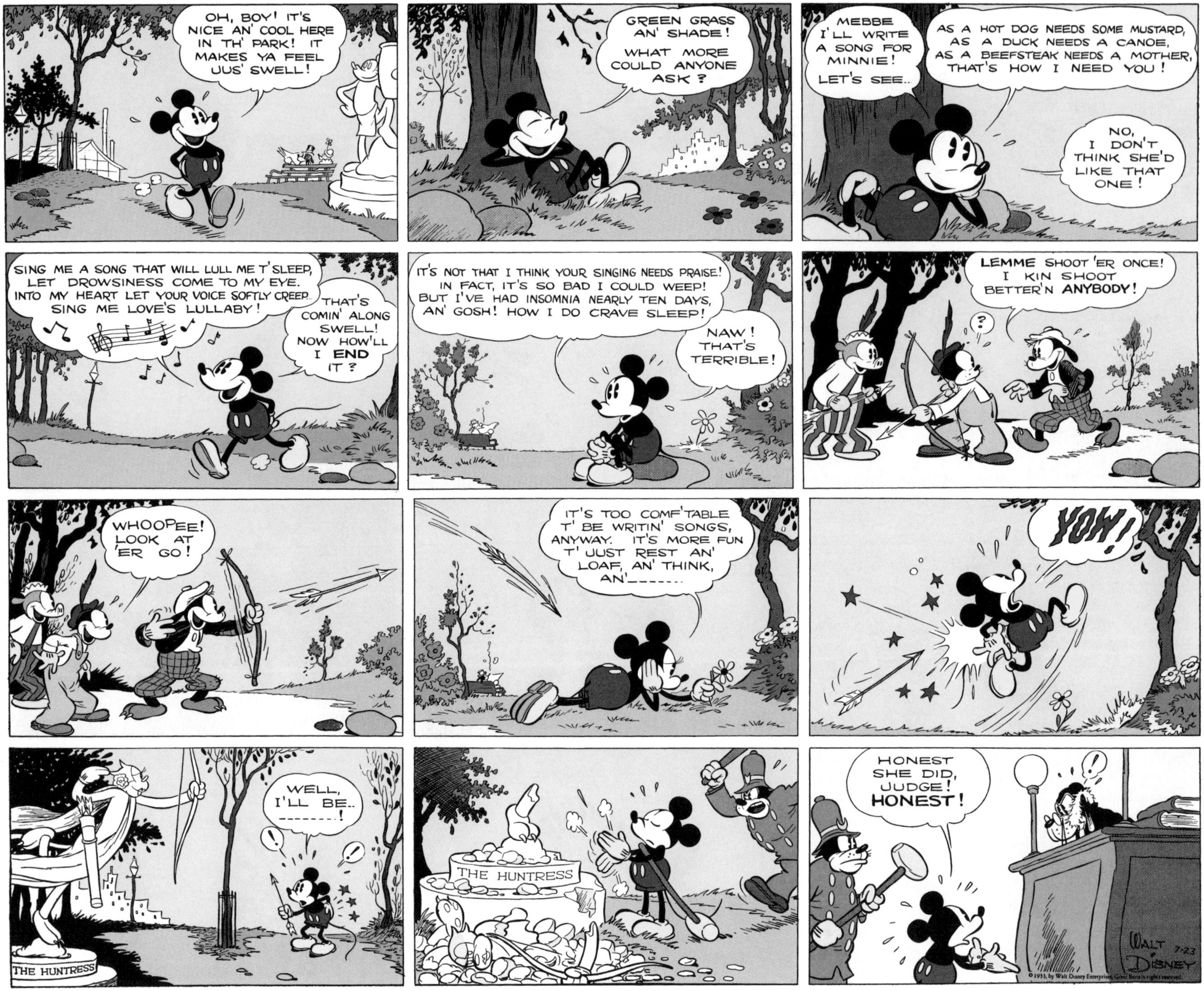
OH, BOY! IT'S NICE AN' COOL HERE IN TH' PARK! IT MAKES YA FEEL UUS' SWELL!
GREEN GRASS AN' SHADE! WHAT MORE COULD ANYONE ASK?
MEBBE I'LL WRITE A SONG FOR MINNIE! LET'S SEE...
AS A HOT DOG NEEDS SOME MUSTARD, AS A DUCK NEEDS A CANOE, AS A BEEFSTEAK NEEDS A MOTHER, THAT'S HOW I NEED YOU!
NO, I DON'T THINK SHE'D LIKE THAT ONE!
SING ME A SONG THAT WILL LULL ME T'SLEEP, LET DROWSINESS COME TO MY EYE. INTO MY HEART LET YOUR VOICE SOFTLY CREEP... SING ME LOVE'S LULLABY!
THAT'S COMIN' ALONG SWELL! NOW HOW'LL I **END** IT?
IT'S NOT THAT I THINK YOUR SINGING NEEDS PRAISE! IN FACT, IT'S SO BAD I COULD WEEP! BUT I'VE HAD INSOMNIA NEARLY TEN DAYS, AN' GOSH! HOW I DO CRAVE SLEEP!
NAW! THAT'S TERRIBLE!
LEMME SHOOT 'ER ONCE! I KIN SHOOT BETTER'N **ANYBODY**!
?
WHOOPEE! LOOK AT 'ER GO!
IT'S TOO COMF'TABLE T' BE WRITIN' SONGS, ANYWAY. IT'S MORE FUN T' UUST REST AN' LOAF, AN' THINK, AN'-------
YOW!
WELL, I'LL BE.. --------!
!
!
THE HUNTRESS
THE HUNTRESS
HONEST SHE DID, JUDGE! **HONEST**!
!
WALT DISNEY 7-23
© 1933, by Walt Disney Enterprises

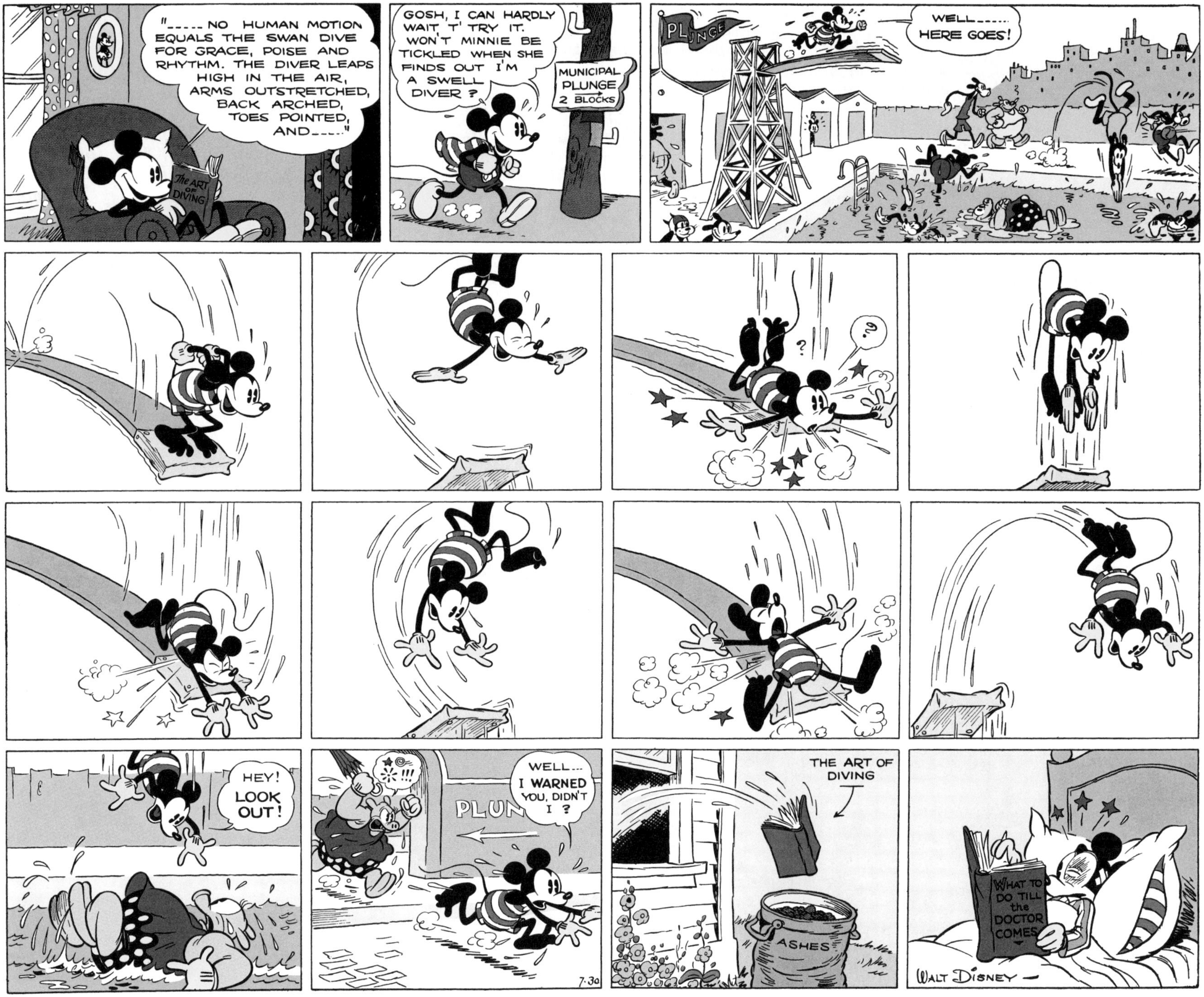
"----- NO HUMAN MOTION EQUALS THE SWAN DIVE FOR GRACE, POISE AND RHYTHM. THE DIVER LEAPS HIGH IN THE AIR, ARMS OUTSTRETCHED, BACK ARCHED, TOES POINTED, AND----."
The ART of DIVING
GOSH, I CAN HARDLY WAIT T' TRY IT. WON'T MINNIE BE TICKLED WHEN SHE FINDS OUT I'M A SWELL DIVER ?
MUNICIPAL PLUNGE 2 BLOCKS
PLUNGE
WELL...... HERE GOES!
HEY! LOOK OUT!
PLUN
WELL... I WARNED YOU, DIDN'T I ?
7.30
THE ART OF DIVING
ASHES
WHAT TO DO TILL the DOCTOR COMES
WALT DISNEY

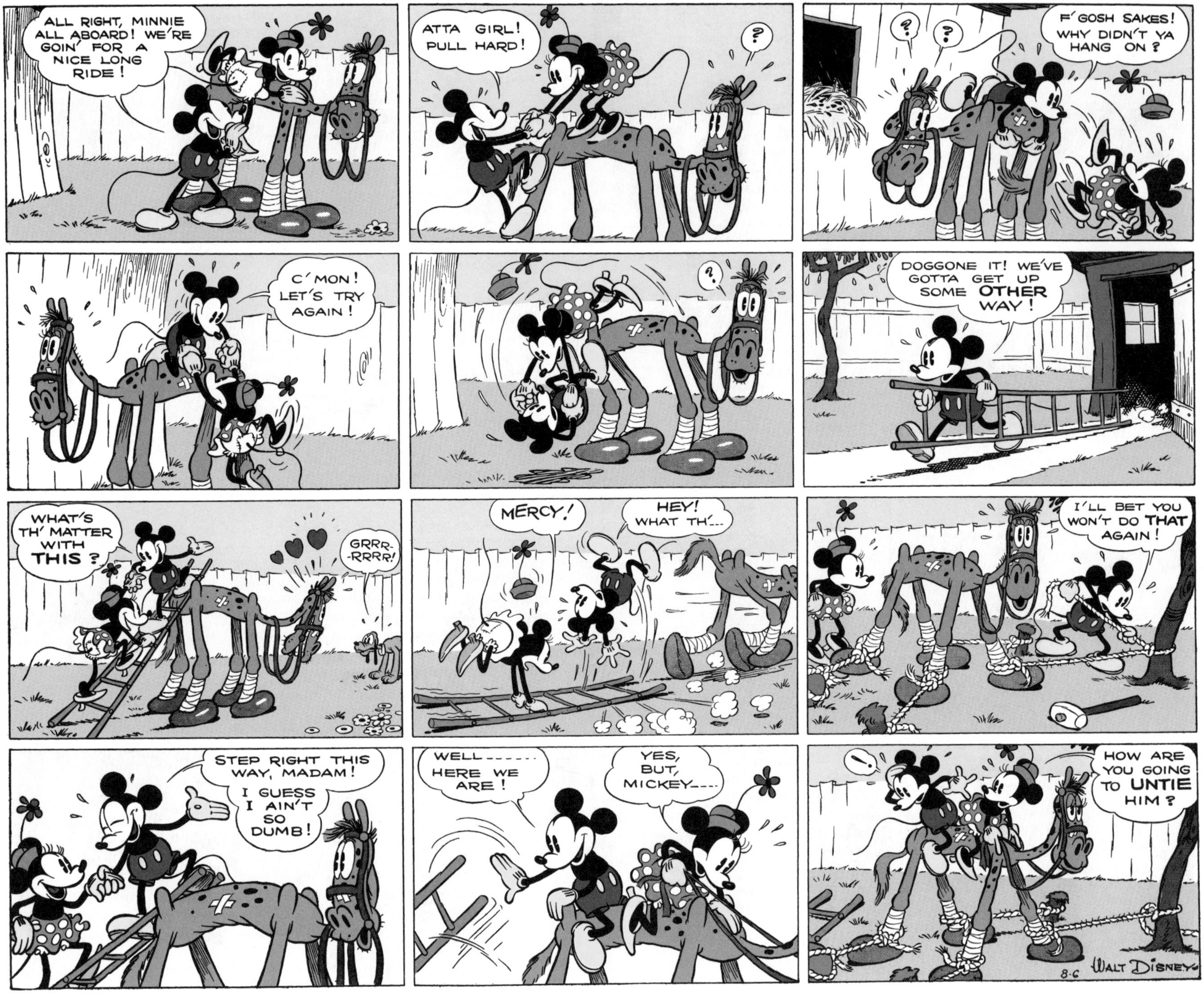
ALL RIGHT, MINNIE ALL ABOARD! WE'RE GOIN' FOR A NICE LONG RIDE!
ATTA GIRL! PULL HARD!
?
?
?
F'GOSH SAKES! WHY DIDN'T YA HANG ON?
C'MON! LET'S TRY AGAIN!
?
DOGGONE IT! WE'VE GOTTA GET UP SOME OTHER WAY!
WHAT'S TH' MATTER WITH THIS?
GRRR-RRRR!
MERCY!
HEY! WHAT TH'---
I'LL BET YOU WON'T DO THAT AGAIN!
STEP RIGHT THIS WAY, MADAM!
I GUESS I AIN'T SO DUMB!
WELL------ HERE WE ARE!
YES, BUT, MICKEY----
!
HOW ARE YOU GOING TO UNTIE HIM?
8-6
WALT DISNEY

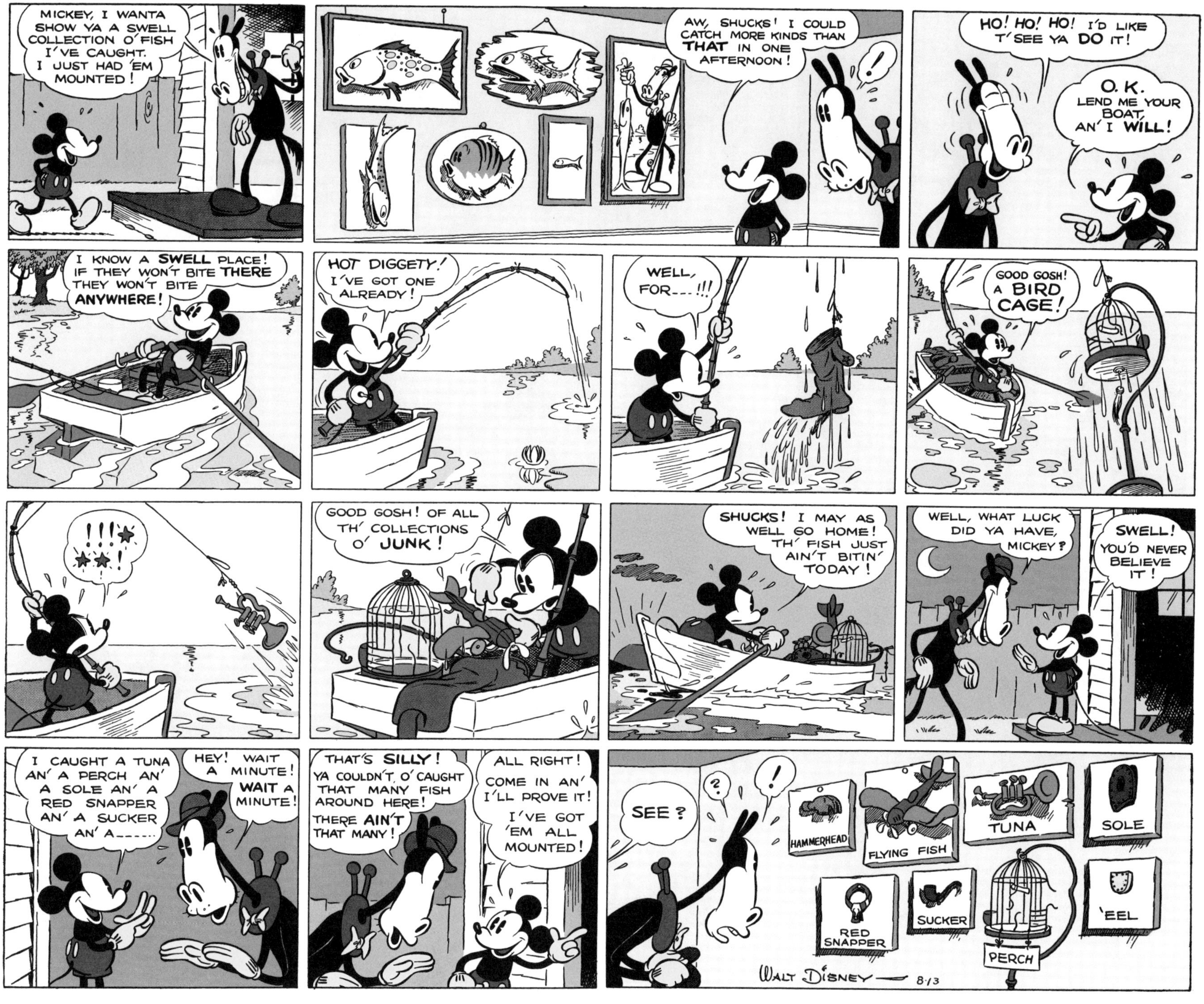
MICKEY, I WANTA SHOW YA A SWELL COLLECTION O' FISH I'VE CAUGHT. I JUST HAD 'EM MOUNTED!
AW, SHUCKS! I COULD CATCH MORE KINDS THAN **THAT** IN ONE AFTERNOON!
!
HO! HO! HO! I'D LIKE T' SEE YA **DO** IT!
O.K. LEND ME YOUR BOAT, AN' I **WILL**!
I KNOW A **SWELL** PLACE! IF THEY WON'T BITE **THERE** THEY WON'T BITE **ANYWHERE**!
HOT DIGGETY! I'VE GOT ONE ALREADY!
WELL, FOR---!!!
GOOD GOSH! A **BIRD CAGE**!
!!! !
GOOD GOSH! OF ALL TH' COLLECTIONS O' **JUNK**!
SHUCKS! I MAY AS WELL GO HOME! TH' FISH JUST AIN'T BITIN' TODAY!
WELL, WHAT LUCK DID YA HAVE, MICKEY?
SWELL! YOU'D NEVER BELIEVE IT!
I CAUGHT A TUNA AN' A PERCH AN' A SOLE AN' A RED SNAPPER AN' A SUCKER AN' A-----
HEY! WAIT A MINUTE! **WAIT** A MINUTE!
THAT'S **SILLY**! YA COULDN'T O' CAUGHT THAT MANY FISH AROUND HERE!
THERE **AIN'T** THAT MANY!
ALL RIGHT! COME IN AN' I'LL PROVE IT!
I'VE GOT 'EM ALL MOUNTED!
SEE?
?
!
HAMMERHEAD
FLYING FISH
TUNA
SOLE
RED SNAPPER
SUCKER
'EEL
PERCH
WALT DISNEY 8-13

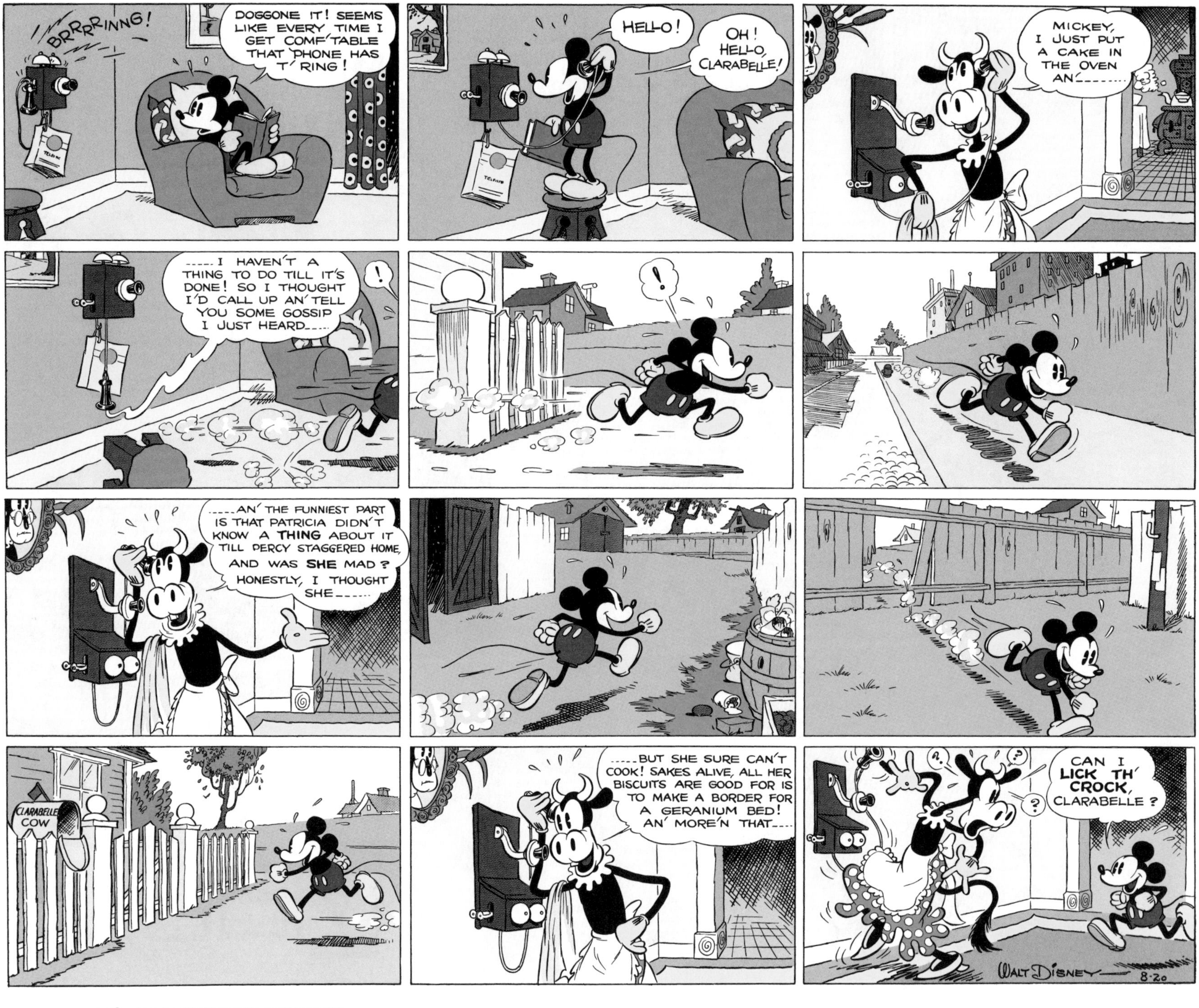
BRRRRINNG!
DOGGONE IT! SEEMS LIKE EVERY TIME I GET COMF'TABLE THAT 'PHONE HAS T' RING!
HELLO!
OH! HELLO, CLARABELLE!
MICKEY, I JUST PUT A CAKE IN THE OVEN AN'------
-----I HAVEN'T A THING TO DO TILL IT'S DONE! SO I THOUGHT I'D CALL UP AN' TELL YOU SOME GOSSIP I JUST HEARD-----
!
!
-----AN' THE FUNNIEST PART IS THAT PATRICIA DIDN'T KNOW A THING ABOUT IT TILL PERCY STAGGERED HOME, AND WAS SHE MAD? HONESTLY, I THOUGHT SHE------
CLARABELLE COW
-----BUT SHE SURE CAN'T COOK! SAKES ALIVE, ALL HER BISCUITS ARE GOOD FOR IS TO MAKE A BORDER FOR A GERANIUM BED! AN' MORE'N THAT----
?
CAN I LICK TH' CROCK, CLARABELLE?
WALT DISNEY
8-20

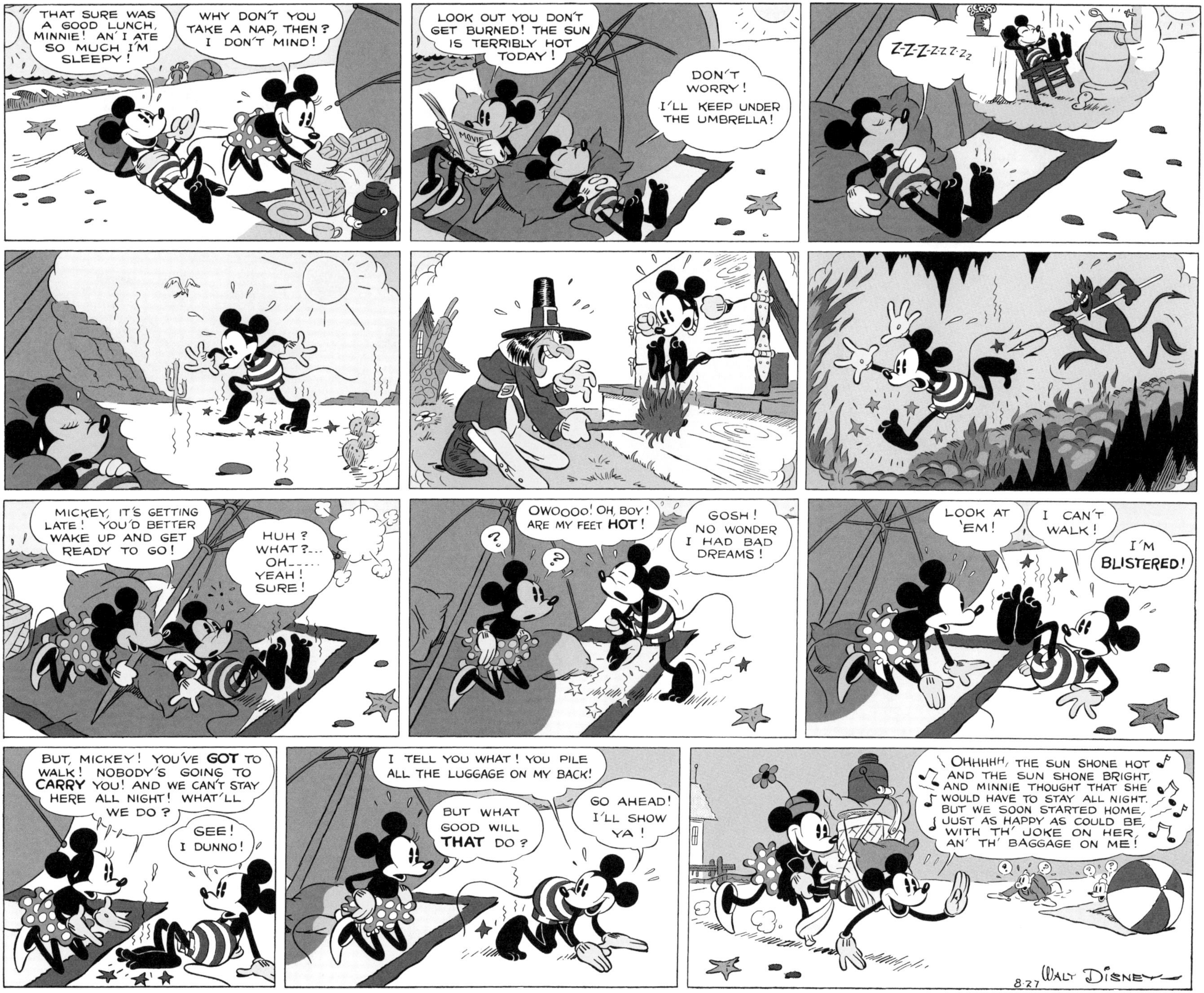

THAT SURE WAS A GOOD LUNCH, MINNIE! AN' I ATE SO MUCH I'M SLEEPY!
WHY DON'T YOU TAKE A NAP, THEN? I DON'T MIND!
LOOK OUT YOU DON'T GET BURNED! THE SUN IS TERRIBLY HOT TODAY!
MOVIE
DON'T WORRY! I'LL KEEP UNDER THE UMBRELLA!
Z-Z-Z-Z-Z-Z-Z-Z
MICKEY, IT'S GETTING LATE! YOU'D BETTER WAKE UP AND GET READY TO GO!
HUH? WHAT?... OH..... YEAH! SURE!
OWOOOO! OH, BOY! ARE MY FEET **HOT**!
GOSH! NO WONDER I HAD BAD DREAMS!
LOOK AT 'EM!
I CAN'T WALK!
I'M **BLISTERED**!
BUT, MICKEY! YOU'VE **GOT** TO WALK! NOBODY'S GOING TO **CARRY** YOU! AND WE CAN'T STAY HERE ALL NIGHT! WHAT'LL WE DO?
GEE! I DUNNO!
I TELL YOU WHAT! YOU PILE ALL THE LUGGAGE ON MY BACK!
BUT WHAT GOOD WILL **THAT** DO?
GO AHEAD! I'LL SHOW YA!
OHHHHH, THE SUN SHONE HOT AND THE SUN SHONE BRIGHT, AND MINNIE THOUGHT THAT SHE WOULD HAVE TO STAY ALL NIGHT. BUT WE SOON STARTED HOME, JUST AS HAPPY AS COULD BE, WITH TH' JOKE ON HER, AN' TH' BAGGAGE ON ME!
8-27 WALT DISNEY

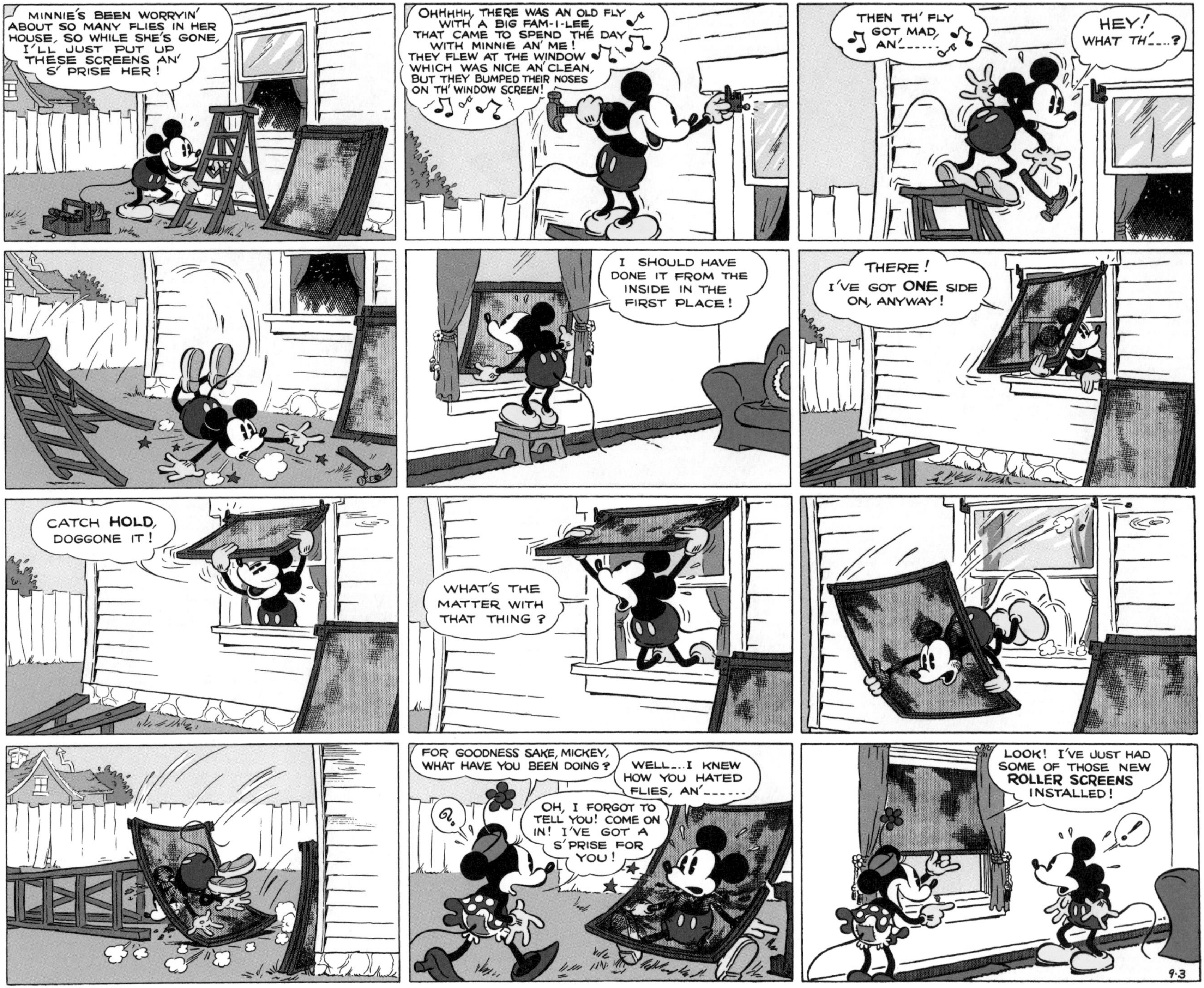

MINNIE'S BEEN WORRYIN' ABOUT SO MANY FLIES IN HER HOUSE, SO WHILE SHE'S GONE, I'LL JUST PUT UP THESE SCREENS AN' S'PRISE HER!
OHHHHH, THERE WAS AN OLD FLY WITH A BIG FAM-I-LEE, THAT CAME TO SPEND THE DAY WITH MINNIE AN' ME! THEY FLEW AT THE WINDOW WHICH WAS NICE AN' CLEAN, BUT THEY BUMPED THEIR NOSES ON TH' WINDOW SCREEN!
THEN TH' FLY GOT MAD, AN'-----
HEY! WHAT TH'---?
I SHOULD HAVE DONE IT FROM THE INSIDE IN THE FIRST PLACE!
THERE! I'VE GOT ONE SIDE ON, ANYWAY!
CATCH HOLD, DOGGONE IT!
WHAT'S THE MATTER WITH THAT THING?
FOR GOODNESS SAKE, MICKEY, WHAT HAVE YOU BEEN DOING?
WELL...I KNEW HOW YOU HATED FLIES, AN'------
OH, I FORGOT TO TELL YOU! COME ON IN! I'VE GOT A S'PRISE FOR YOU!
LOOK! I'VE JUST HAD SOME OF THOSE NEW ROLLER SCREENS INSTALLED!
9-3

110. WINDOW PAIN

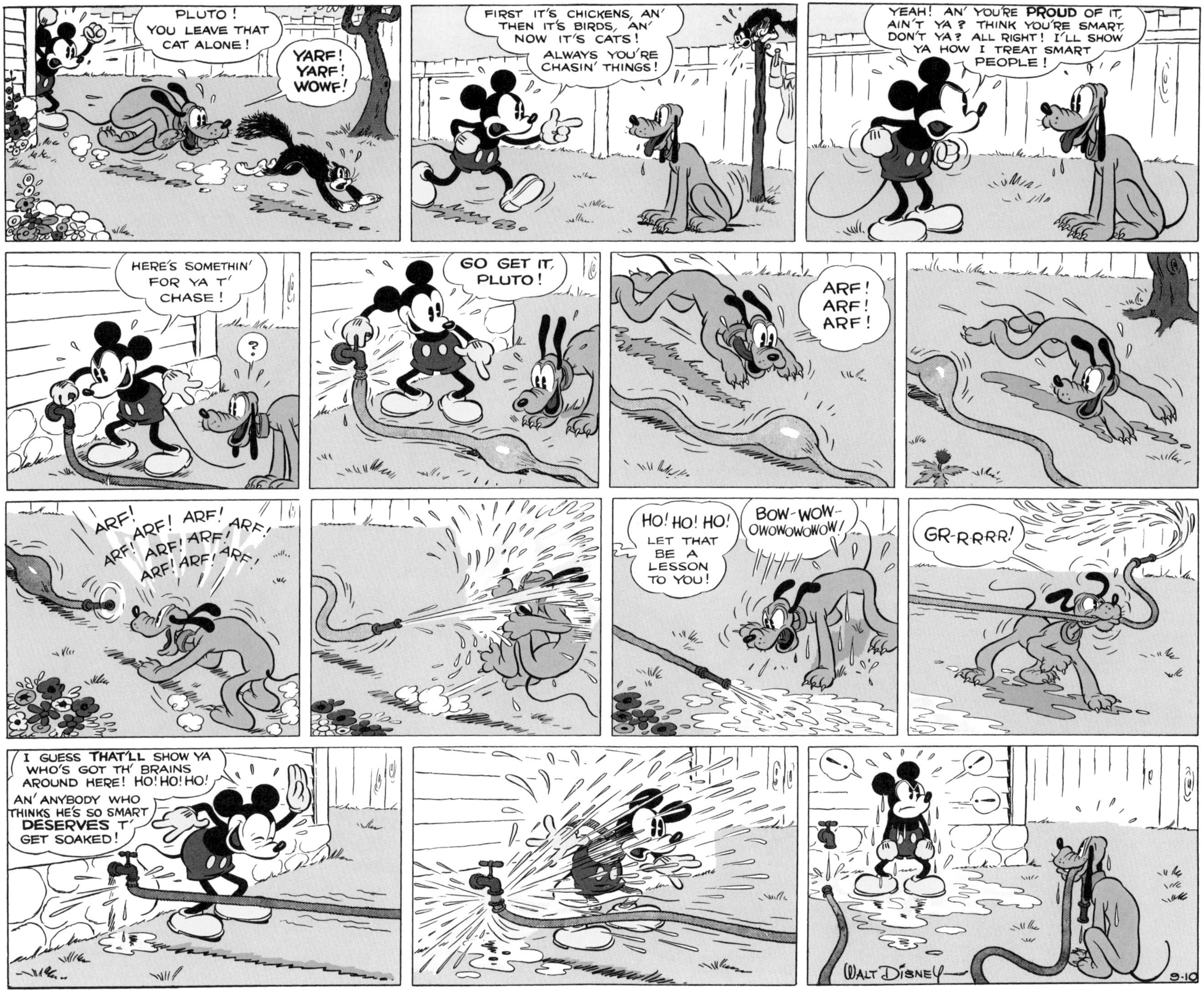
PLUTO! YOU LEAVE THAT CAT ALONE!
YARF! YARF! WOWF!
FIRST IT'S CHICKENS, AN' THEN IT'S BIRDS, AN' NOW IT'S CATS!
ALWAYS YOU'RE CHASIN' THINGS!
YEAH! AN' YOU'RE PROUD OF IT, AIN'T YA? THINK YOU'RE SMART, DON'T YA? ALL RIGHT! I'LL SHOW YA HOW I TREAT SMART PEOPLE!
HERE'S SOMETHIN' FOR YA T' CHASE!
?
GO GET IT, PLUTO!
ARF! ARF! ARF!
ARF! ARF! ARF! ARF! ARF! ARF! ARF! ARF! ARF! ARF!
HO! HO! HO! LET THAT BE A LESSON TO YOU!
BOW-WOW-OWOWOWOWOW!
GR-R-R-R-R!
I GUESS THAT'LL SHOW YA WHO'S GOT TH' BRAINS AROUND HERE! HO! HO! HO!
AN' ANYBODY WHO THINKS HE'S SO SMART DESERVES T' GET SOAKED!
!
!
!
WALT DISNEY
9-10

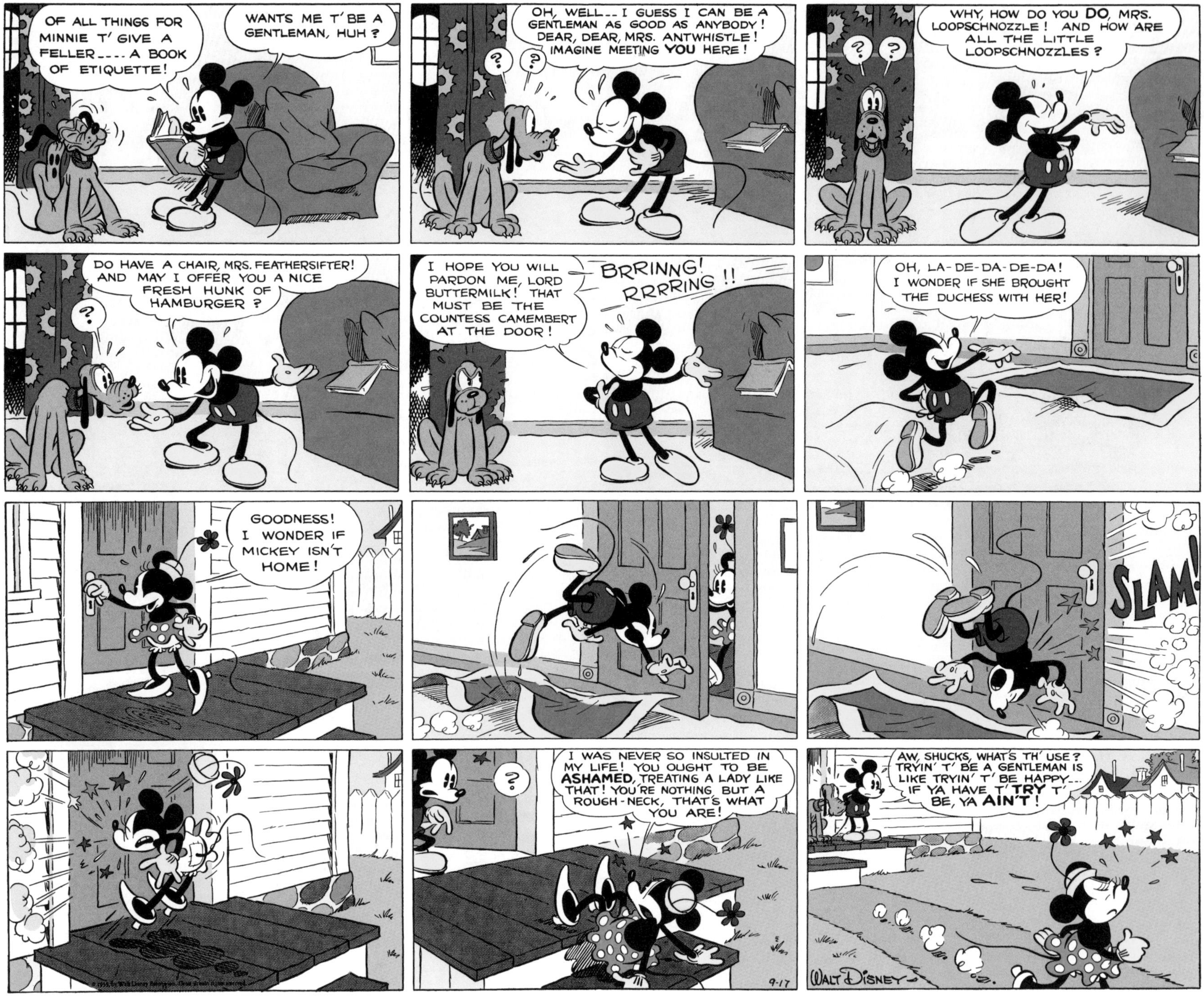
OF ALL THINGS FOR MINNIE T' GIVE A FELLER---- A BOOK OF ETIQUETTE!
WANTS ME T' BE A GENTLEMAN, HUH ?
?
?
OH, WELL-- I GUESS I CAN BE A GENTLEMAN AS GOOD AS ANYBODY! DEAR, DEAR, MRS. ANTWHISTLE! IMAGINE MEETING YOU HERE!
?
?
WHY, HOW DO YOU DO, MRS. LOOPSCHNOZZLE! AND HOW ARE ALL THE LITTLE LOOPSCHNOZZLES ?
?
DO HAVE A CHAIR, MRS. FEATHERSIFTER! AND MAY I OFFER YOU A NICE FRESH HUNK OF HAMBURGER ?
I HOPE YOU WILL PARDON ME, LORD BUTTERMILK! THAT MUST BE THE COUNTESS CAMEMBERT AT THE DOOR!
BRRINNG! RRRRING!!
OH, LA-DE-DA-DE-DA! I WONDER IF SHE BROUGHT THE DUCHESS WITH HER!
GOODNESS! I WONDER IF MICKEY ISN'T HOME!
SLAM!
?
I WAS NEVER SO INSULTED IN MY LIFE! YOU OUGHT TO BE ASHAMED, TREATING A LADY LIKE THAT! YOU'RE NOTHING BUT A ROUGH-NECK, THAT'S WHAT YOU ARE!
9-17
AW, SHUCKS, WHAT'S TH' USE? TRYIN' T' BE A GENTLEMAN IS LIKE TRYIN' T' BE HAPPY... IF YA HAVE T' TRY T' BE, YA AIN'T!
WALT DISNEY

112. OF MICE AND MANNERS

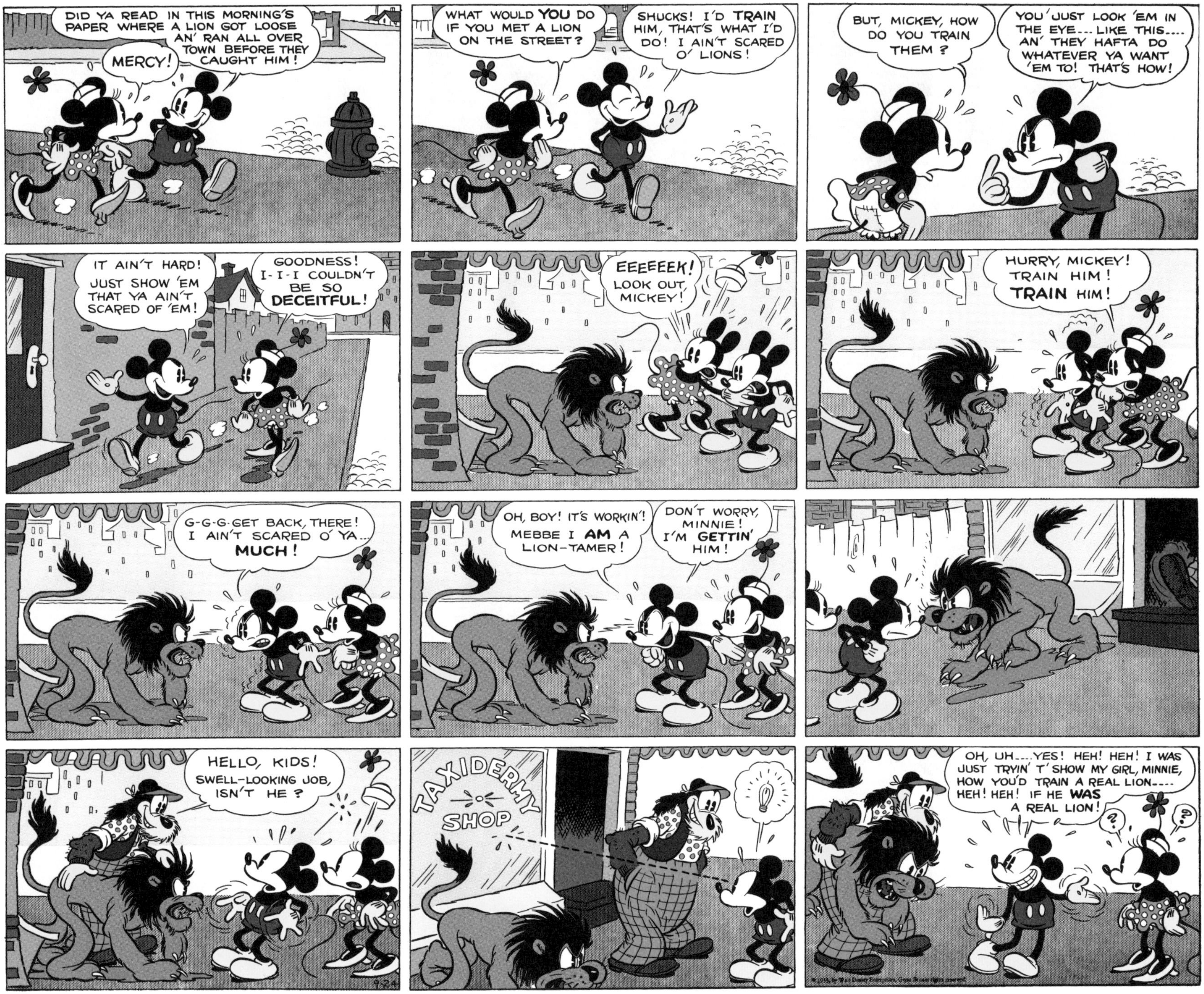
DID YA READ IN THIS MORNING'S PAPER WHERE A LION GOT LOOSE AN' RAN ALL OVER TOWN BEFORE THEY CAUGHT HIM!
MERCY!
WHAT WOULD YOU DO IF YOU MET A LION ON THE STREET?
SHUCKS! I'D TRAIN HIM, THAT'S WHAT I'D DO! I AIN'T SCARED O' LIONS!
BUT, MICKEY, HOW DO YOU TRAIN THEM?
YOU JUST LOOK 'EM IN THE EYE--- LIKE THIS---- AN' THEY HAFTA DO WHATEVER YA WANT 'EM TO! THAT'S HOW!
IT AIN'T HARD! JUST SHOW 'EM THAT YA AIN'T SCARED OF 'EM!
GOODNESS! I-I-I COULDN'T BE SO DECEITFUL!
EEEEEEK! LOOK OUT, MICKEY!
HURRY, MICKEY! TRAIN HIM! TRAIN HIM!
G-G-G-GET BACK, THERE! I AIN'T SCARED O' YA... MUCH!
OH, BOY! IT'S WORKIN'! MEBBE I AM A LION-TAMER!
DON'T WORRY, MINNIE! I'M GETTIN' HIM!
HELLO, KIDS! SWELL-LOOKING JOB, ISN'T HE?
TAXIDERMY SHOP
OH, UH----YES! HEH! HEH! I WAS JUST TRYIN' T' SHOW MY GIRL, MINNIE, HOW YOU'D TRAIN A REAL LION---- HEH! HEH! IF HE WAS A REAL LION!
?
?

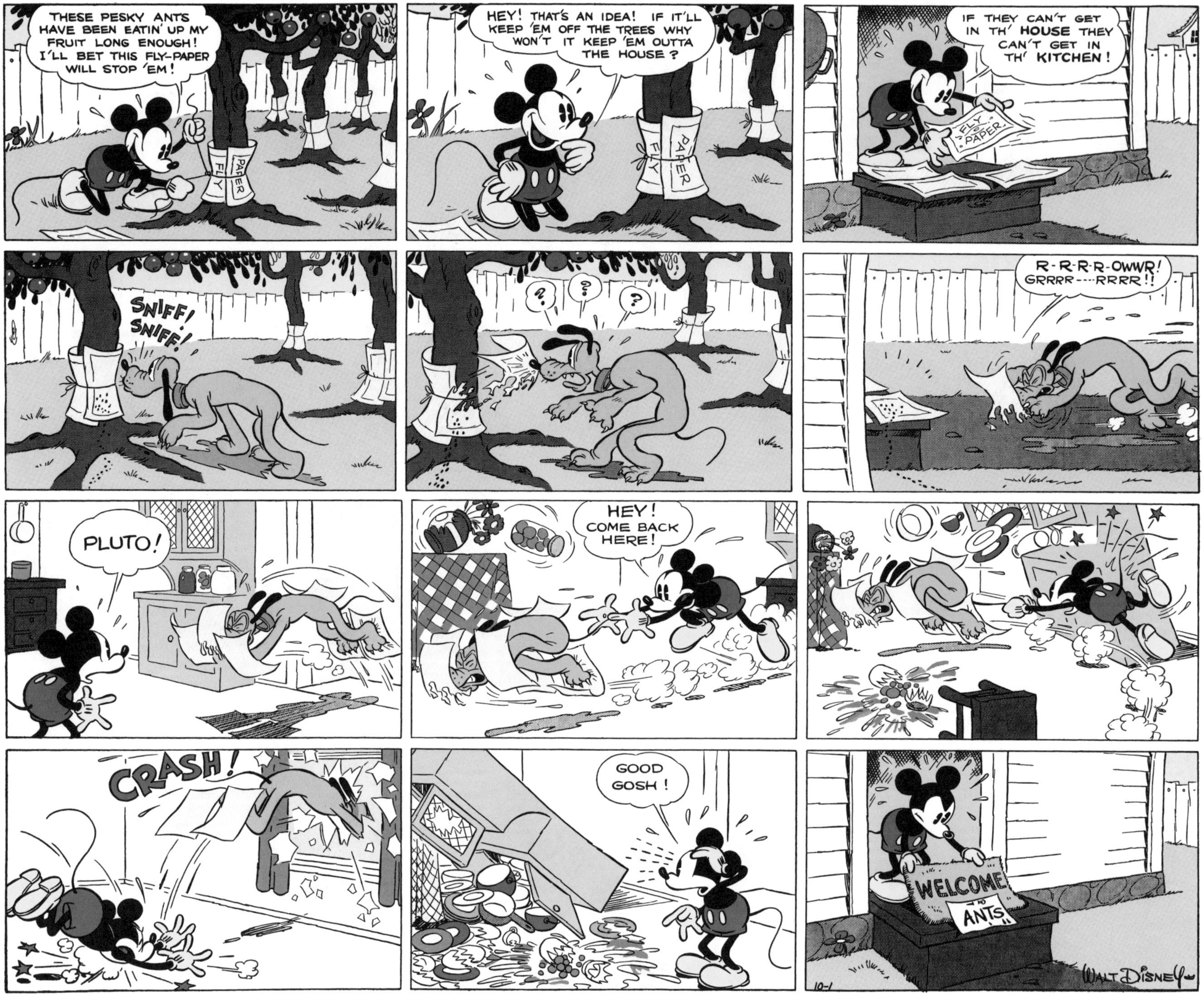
THESE PESKY ANTS HAVE BEEN EATIN' UP MY FRUIT LONG ENOUGH! I'LL BET THIS FLY-PAPER WILL STOP 'EM!
FLY PAPER
HEY! THAT'S AN IDEA! IF IT'LL KEEP 'EM OFF THE TREES WHY WON'T IT KEEP 'EM OUTTA THE HOUSE?
FLY PAPER
IF THEY CAN'T GET IN TH' HOUSE THEY CAN'T GET IN TH' KITCHEN!
FLY PAPER
SNIFF! SNIFF!
?
?
?
R-R-R-R-OWWR! GRRRR----RRRR!!
PLUTO!
HEY! COME BACK HERE!
CRASH!
GOOD GOSH!
WELCOME TO ANTS
10-1
WALT DISNEY

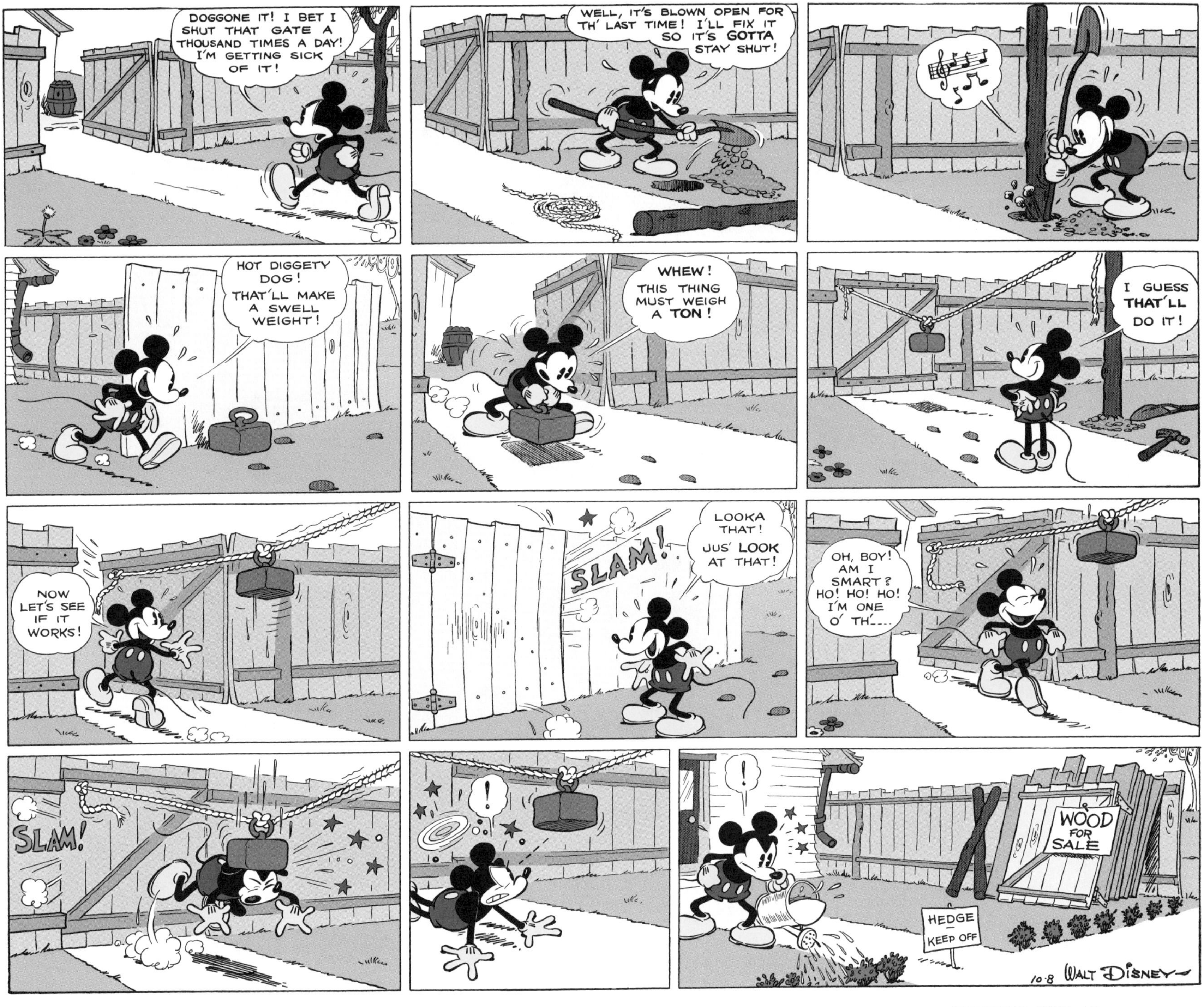
DOGGONE IT! I BET I SHUT THAT GATE A THOUSAND TIMES A DAY! I'M GETTING SICK OF IT!
WELL, IT'S BLOWN OPEN FOR TH' LAST TIME! I'LL FIX IT SO IT'S GOTTA STAY SHUT!
HOT DIGGETY DOG! THAT'LL MAKE A SWELL WEIGHT!
WHEW! THIS THING MUST WEIGH A TON!
I GUESS THAT'LL DO IT!
NOW LET'S SEE IF IT WORKS!
SLAM!
LOOKA THAT! JUS' LOOK AT THAT!
OH, BOY! AM I SMART? HO! HO! HO! I'M ONE O' TH'___
SLAM!
!
!
WOOD FOR SALE
HEDGE KEEP OFF
10·8
WALT DISNEY

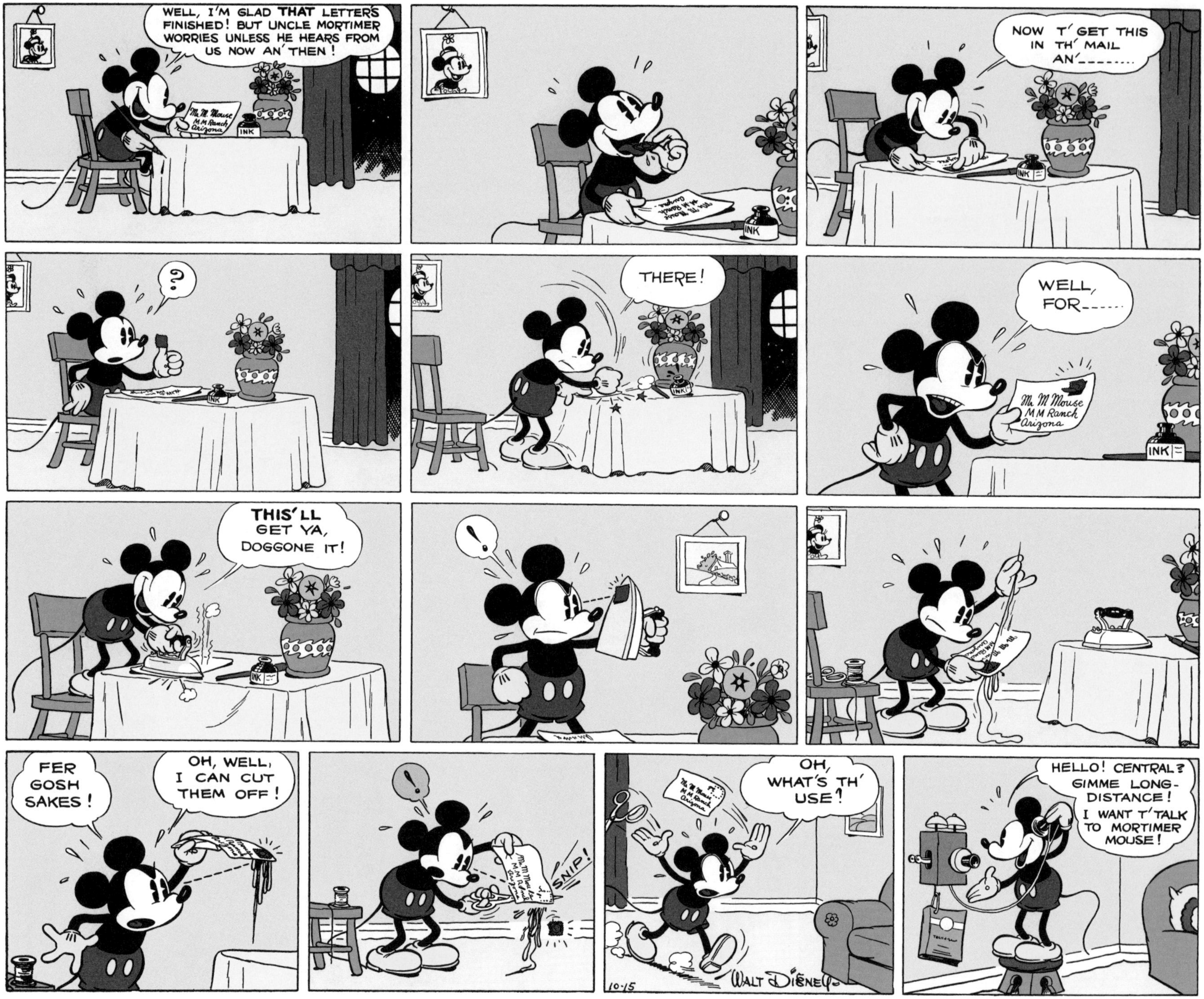

WELL, I'M GLAD THAT LETTER'S FINISHED! BUT UNCLE MORTIMER WORRIES UNLESS HE HEARS FROM US NOW AN' THEN!
M. M. Mouse M M Ranch Arizona
INK
NOW T' GET THIS IN TH' MAIL AN'-------
?
THERE!
WELL, FOR------
M. M Mouse M M Ranch Arizona
INK
THIS'LL GET YA, DOGGONE IT!
!
FER GOSH SAKES!
OH, WELL, I CAN CUT THEM OFF!
!
SNIP!
OH, WHAT'S TH' USE!
HELLO! CENTRAL? GIMME LONG-DISTANCE! I WANT T' TALK TO MORTIMER MOUSE!
10-15
WALT DISNEY

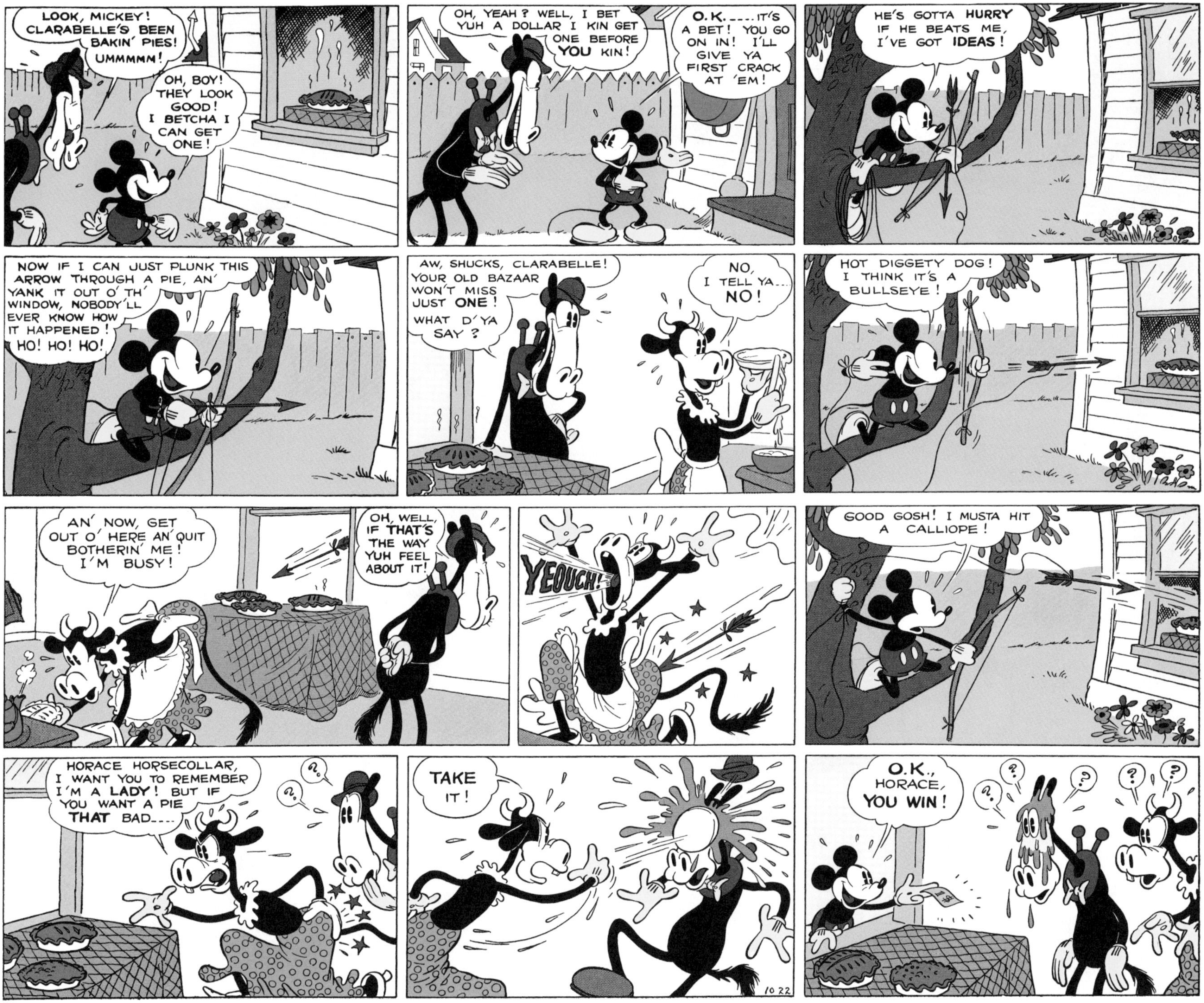

LOOK, MICKEY! CLARABELLE'S BEEN BAKIN' PIES! UMMMMM!
OH, BOY! THEY LOOK GOOD! I BETCHA I CAN GET ONE!
OH, YEAH? WELL, I BET YUH A DOLLAR I KIN GET ONE BEFORE YOU KIN!
O.K.____IT'S A BET! YOU GO ON IN! I'LL GIVE YA FIRST CRACK AT 'EM!
HE'S GOTTA HURRY IF HE BEATS ME, I'VE GOT IDEAS!
NOW IF I CAN JUST PLUNK THIS ARROW THROUGH A PIE, AN' YANK IT OUT O' TH' WINDOW, NOBODY'LL EVER KNOW HOW IT HAPPENED! HO! HO! HO!
AW, SHUCKS, CLARABELLE! YOUR OLD BAZAAR WON'T MISS JUST ONE! WHAT D'YA SAY?
NO, I TELL YA... NO!
HOT DIGGETY DOG! I THINK IT'S A BULLSEYE!
AN' NOW, GET OUT O' HERE AN' QUIT BOTHERIN' ME! I'M BUSY!
OH, WELL, IF THAT'S THE WAY YUH FEEL ABOUT IT!
YEOUCH!
GOOD GOSH! I MUSTA HIT A CALLIOPE!
HORACE HORSECOLLAR, I WANT YOU TO REMEMBER I'M A LADY! BUT IF YOU WANT A PIE THAT BAD....
?
?
TAKE IT!
10 22
O.K., HORACE, YOU WIN!
?
?
?
?
?

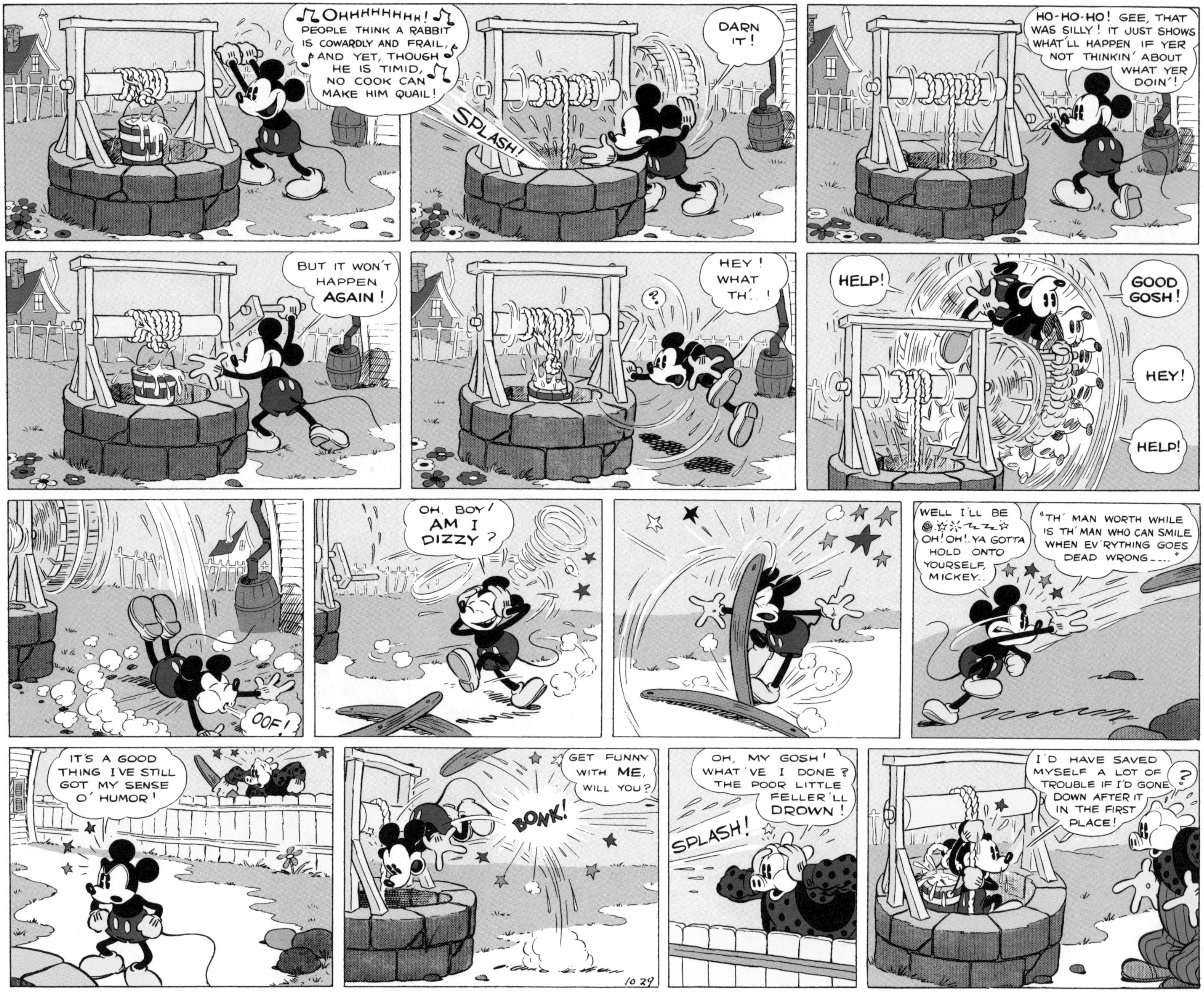
OHHHHHHHH! PEOPLE THINK A RABBIT IS COWARDLY AND FRAIL, AND YET, THOUGH HE IS TIMID, NO COOK CAN MAKE HIM QUAIL!
SPLASH!
DARN IT!
HO-HO-HO! GEE, THAT WAS SILLY! IT JUST SHOWS WHAT'LL HAPPEN IF YER NOT THINKIN' ABOUT WHAT YER DOIN'!
BUT IT WON'T HAPPEN AGAIN!
HEY! WHAT TH'..!
HELP!
GOOD GOSH!
HEY!
HELP!
OOF!
OH, BOY! AM I DIZZY?
WELL I'LL BE
OH! OH!.. YA GOTTA HOLD ONTO YOURSELF, MICKEY..
"TH' MAN WORTH WHILE IS TH' MAN WHO CAN SMILE WHEN EV'RYTHING GOES DEAD WRONG...."
IT'S A GOOD THING I'VE STILL GOT MY SENSE O' HUMOR!
GET FUNNY WITH ME, WILL YOU?
BONK!
10 29
OH, MY GOSH! WHAT'VE I DONE? THE POOR LITTLE FELLER'LL DROWN!
SPLASH!
I'D HAVE SAVED MYSELF A LOT OF TROUBLE IF I'D GONE DOWN AFTER IT IN THE FIRST PLACE!
?

118. WELL HEELED

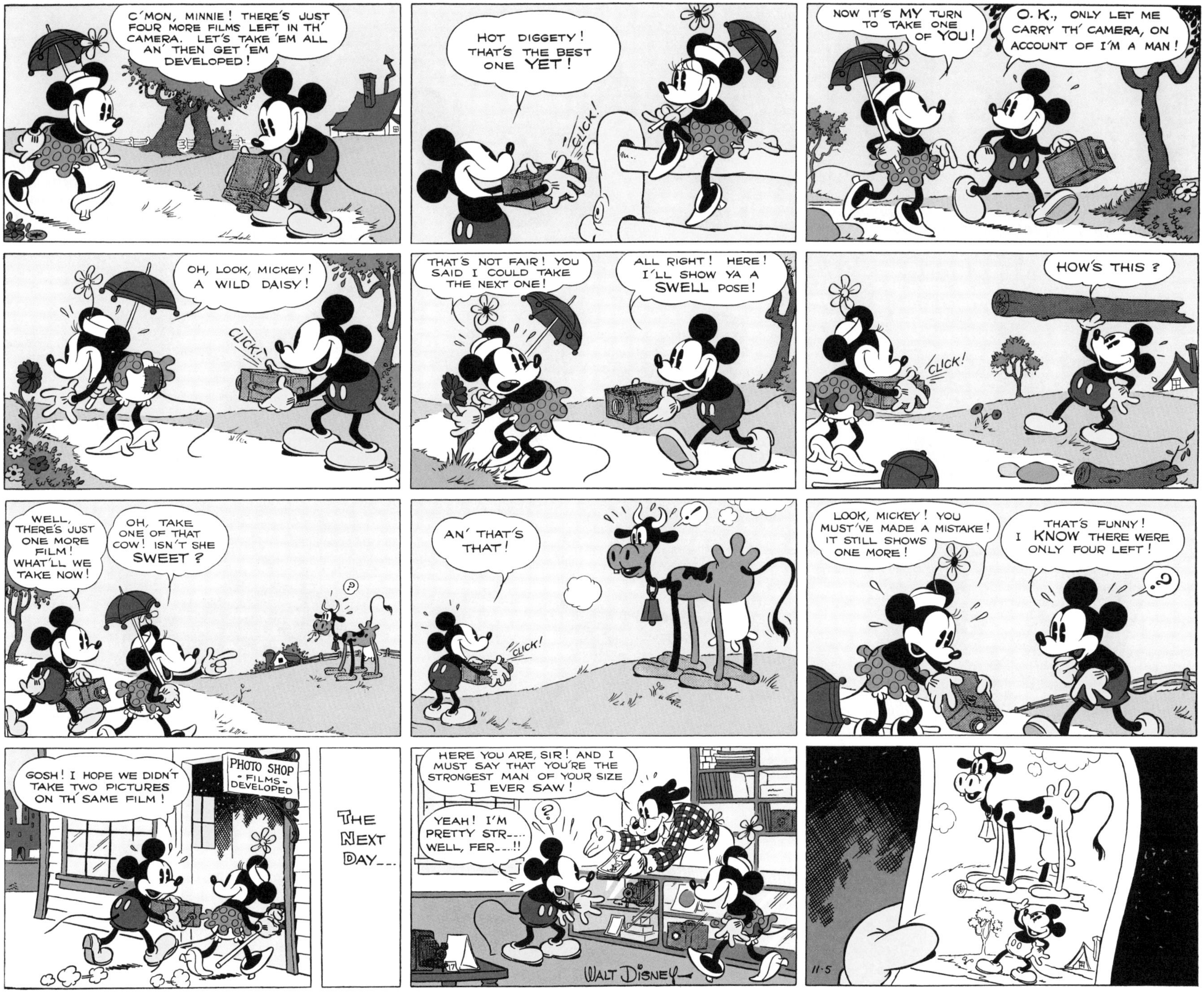
C'MON, MINNIE! THERE'S JUST FOUR MORE FILMS LEFT IN TH' CAMERA. LET'S TAKE 'EM ALL AN' THEN GET 'EM DEVELOPED!
HOT DIGGETY! THAT'S THE BEST ONE YET!
CLICK!
NOW IT'S MY TURN TO TAKE ONE OF YOU!
O. K., ONLY LET ME CARRY TH' CAMERA, ON ACCOUNT OF I'M A MAN!
OH, LOOK, MICKEY! A WILD DAISY!
CLICK!
THAT'S NOT FAIR! YOU SAID I COULD TAKE THE NEXT ONE!
ALL RIGHT! HERE! I'LL SHOW YA A SWELL POSE!
HOW'S THIS?
CLICK!
WELL, THERE'S JUST ONE MORE FILM! WHAT'LL WE TAKE NOW!
OH, TAKE ONE OF THAT COW! ISN'T SHE SWEET?
AN' THAT'S THAT!
CLICK!
LOOK, MICKEY! YOU MUST'VE MADE A MISTAKE! IT STILL SHOWS ONE MORE!
THAT'S FUNNY! I KNOW THERE WERE ONLY FOUR LEFT!
GOSH! I HOPE WE DIDN'T TAKE TWO PICTURES ON TH' SAME FILM!
PHOTO SHOP • FILMS • DEVELOPED
THE NEXT DAY ---
HERE YOU ARE, SIR! AND I MUST SAY THAT YOU'RE THE STRONGEST MAN OF YOUR SIZE I EVER SAW!
YEAH! I'M PRETTY STR---. WELL, FER---!!
WALT DISNEY
11-5

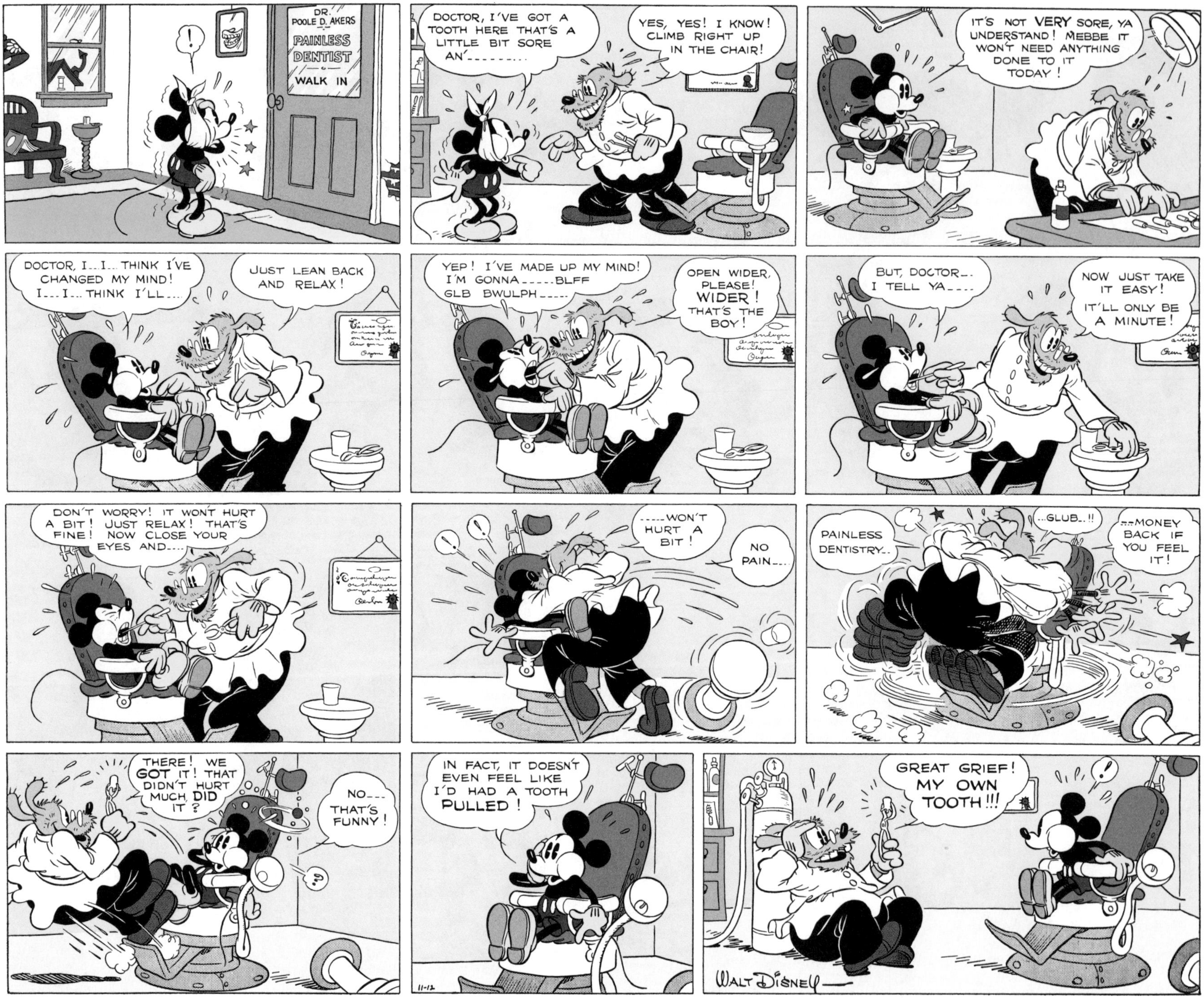

DR. POOLE D. AKERS
PAINLESS DENTIST
WALK IN
!
DOCTOR, I'VE GOT A TOOTH HERE THAT'S A LITTLE BIT SORE AN'--------
YES, YES! I KNOW! CLIMB RIGHT UP IN THE CHAIR!
IT'S NOT VERY SORE, YA UNDERSTAND! MEBBE IT WON'T NEED ANYTHING DONE TO IT TODAY!
DOCTOR, I--I--THINK I'VE CHANGED MY MIND! I---I---THINK I'LL----
JUST LEAN BACK AND RELAX!
YEP! I'VE MADE UP MY MIND! I'M GONNA-----BLFF GLB BWULPH-----
OPEN WIDER, PLEASE! WIDER! THAT'S THE BOY!
BUT, DOCTOR--I TELL YA----
NOW JUST TAKE IT EASY! IT'LL ONLY BE A MINUTE!
DON'T WORRY! IT WON'T HURT A BIT! JUST RELAX! THAT'S FINE! NOW CLOSE YOUR EYES AND----
!
!
-----WON'T HURT A BIT!
NO PAIN----
PAINLESS DENTISTRY--
...GLUB..!!
--MONEY BACK IF YOU FEEL IT!
THERE! WE GOT IT! THAT DIDN'T HURT MUCH, DID IT?
NO--- THAT'S FUNNY!
IN FACT, IT DOESN'T EVEN FEEL LIKE I'D HAD A TOOTH PULLED!
11-12
GREAT GRIEF! MY OWN TOOTH!!!
!
WALT DISNEY

120. A TOUGH PULL

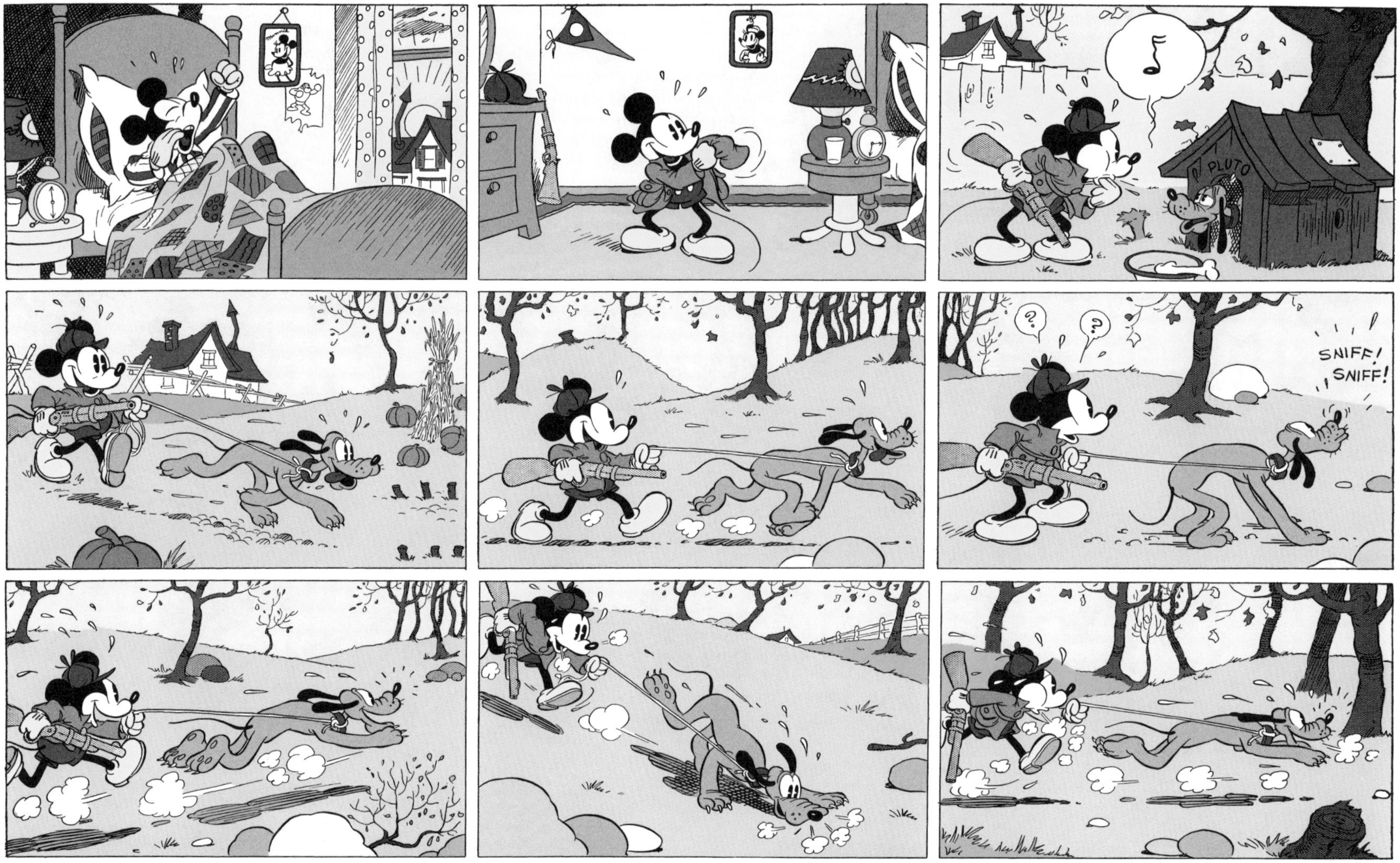
PLUTO
SNIFF! SNIFF!
?
!
11-19
WALT DISNEY

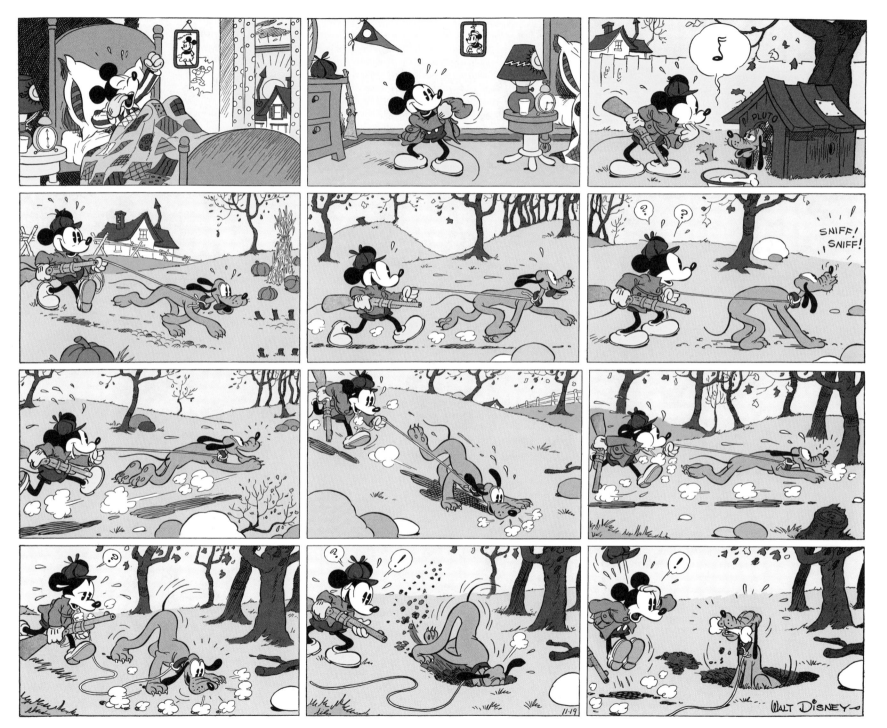

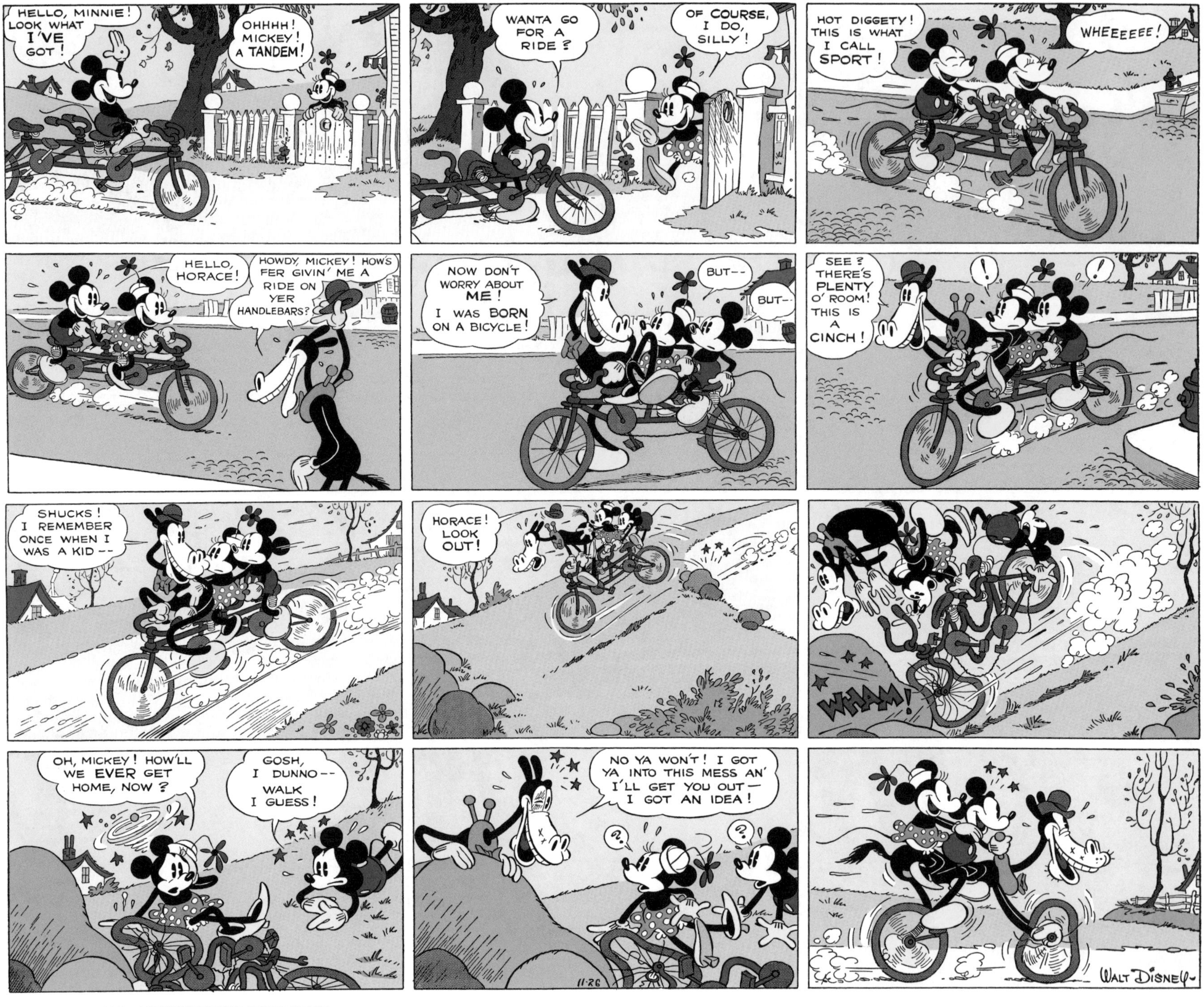
HELLO, MINNIE! LOOK WHAT I'VE GOT!
OHHHH! MICKEY! A TANDEM!
WANTA GO FOR A RIDE?
OF COURSE, I DO, SILLY!
HOT DIGGETY! THIS IS WHAT I CALL SPORT!
WHEEEEEE!
HELLO, HORACE!
HOWDY, MICKEY! HOW'S FER GIVIN' ME A RIDE ON YER HANDLEBARS?
NOW DON'T WORRY ABOUT ME! I WAS BORN ON A BICYCLE!
BUT--
BUT--
SEE? THERE'S PLENTY O' ROOM! THIS IS A CINCH!
!
!
SHUCKS! I REMEMBER ONCE WHEN I WAS A KID --
HORACE! LOOK OUT!
WHAM!
OH, MICKEY! HOW'LL WE EVER GET HOME, NOW?
GOSH, I DUNNO -- WALK I GUESS!
NO YA WON'T! I GOT YA INTO THIS MESS AN' I'LL GET YOU OUT — I GOT AN IDEA!
?
?
11-26
WALT DISNEY

122. A BICYCLE BUILT FOR THREE

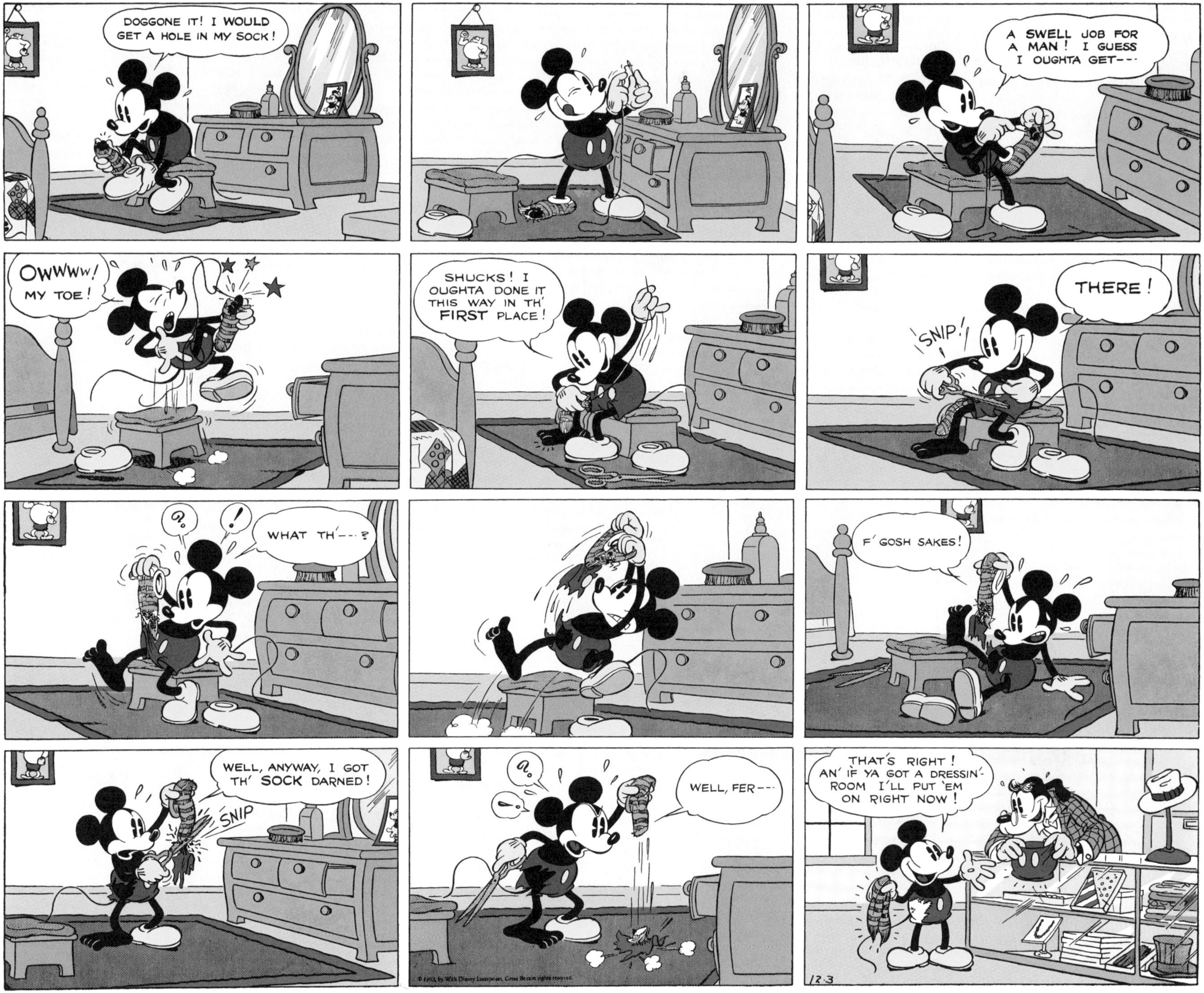
DOGGONE IT! I WOULD GET A HOLE IN MY SOCK!
A SWELL JOB FOR A MAN! I GUESS I OUGHTA GET---
OWWWW! MY TOE!
SHUCKS! I OUGHTA DONE IT THIS WAY IN TH' FIRST PLACE!
SNIP!
THERE!
?
!
WHAT TH'---?
F' GOSH SAKES!
WELL, ANYWAY, I GOT TH' SOCK DARNED!
SNIP
WELL, FER---
THAT'S RIGHT! AN' IF YA GOT A DRESSIN' ROOM I'LL PUT 'EM ON RIGHT NOW!
12-3

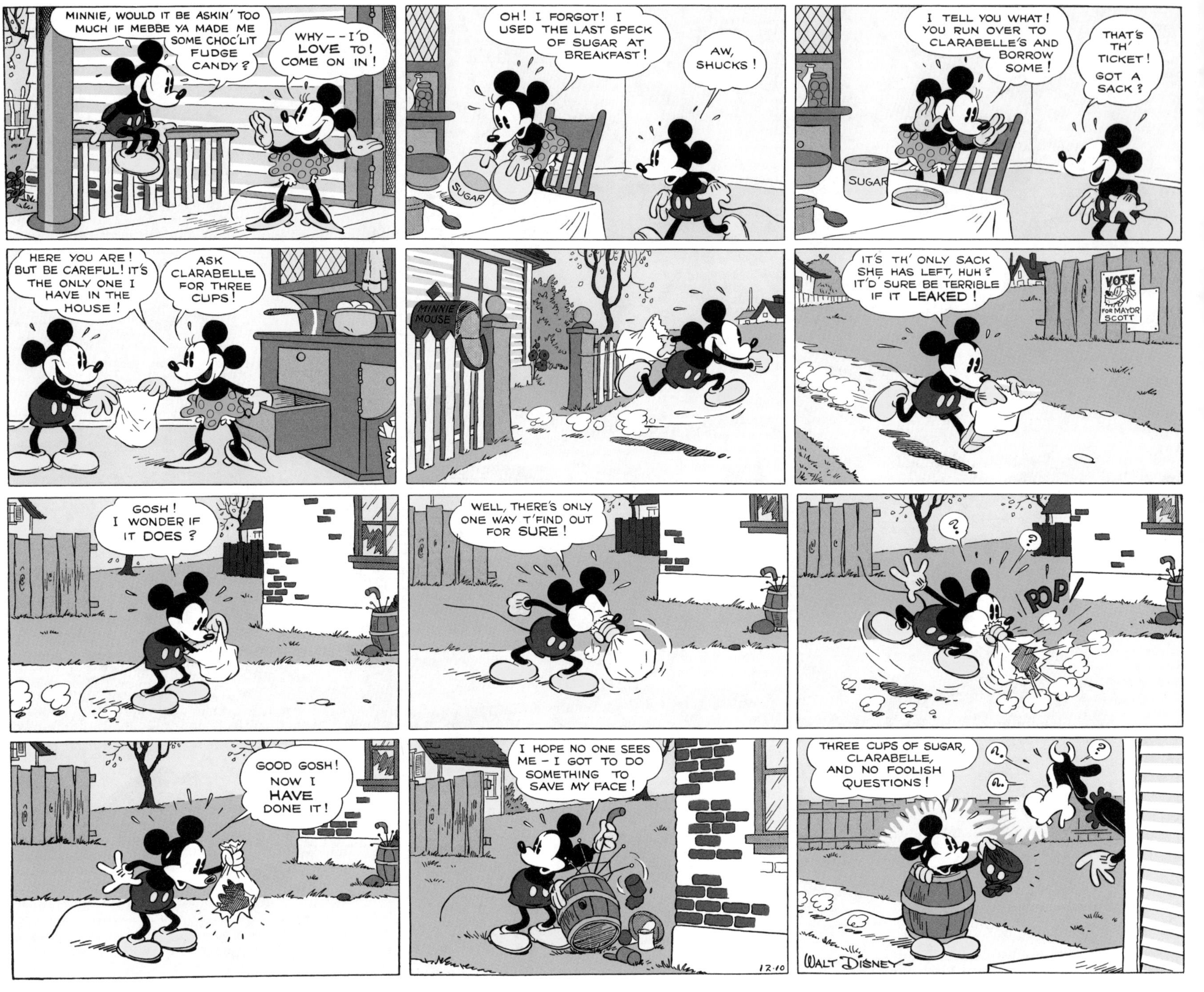

MINNIE, WOULD IT BE ASKIN' TOO MUCH IF MEBBE YA MADE ME SOME CHOC'LIT FUDGE CANDY?
WHY--I'D LOVE TO! COME ON IN!
OH! I FORGOT! I USED THE LAST SPECK OF SUGAR AT BREAKFAST!
AW, SHUCKS!
SUGAR
I TELL YOU WHAT! YOU RUN OVER TO CLARABELLE'S AND BORROW SOME!
THAT'S TH' TICKET! GOT A SACK?
SUGAR
HERE YOU ARE! BUT BE CAREFUL! IT'S THE ONLY ONE I HAVE IN THE HOUSE!
ASK CLARABELLE FOR THREE CUPS!
MINNIE MOUSE
IT'S TH' ONLY SACK SHE HAS LEFT, HUH? IT'D SURE BE TERRIBLE IF IT LEAKED!
VOTE
FOR MAYOR SCOTT
GOSH! I WONDER IF IT DOES?
WELL, THERE'S ONLY ONE WAY T'FIND OUT FOR SURE!
POP!
GOOD GOSH! NOW I HAVE DONE IT!
I HOPE NO ONE SEES ME - I GOT TO DO SOMETHING TO SAVE MY FACE!
12·10
THREE CUPS OF SUGAR, CLARABELLE, AND NO FOOLISH QUESTIONS!
WALT DISNEY

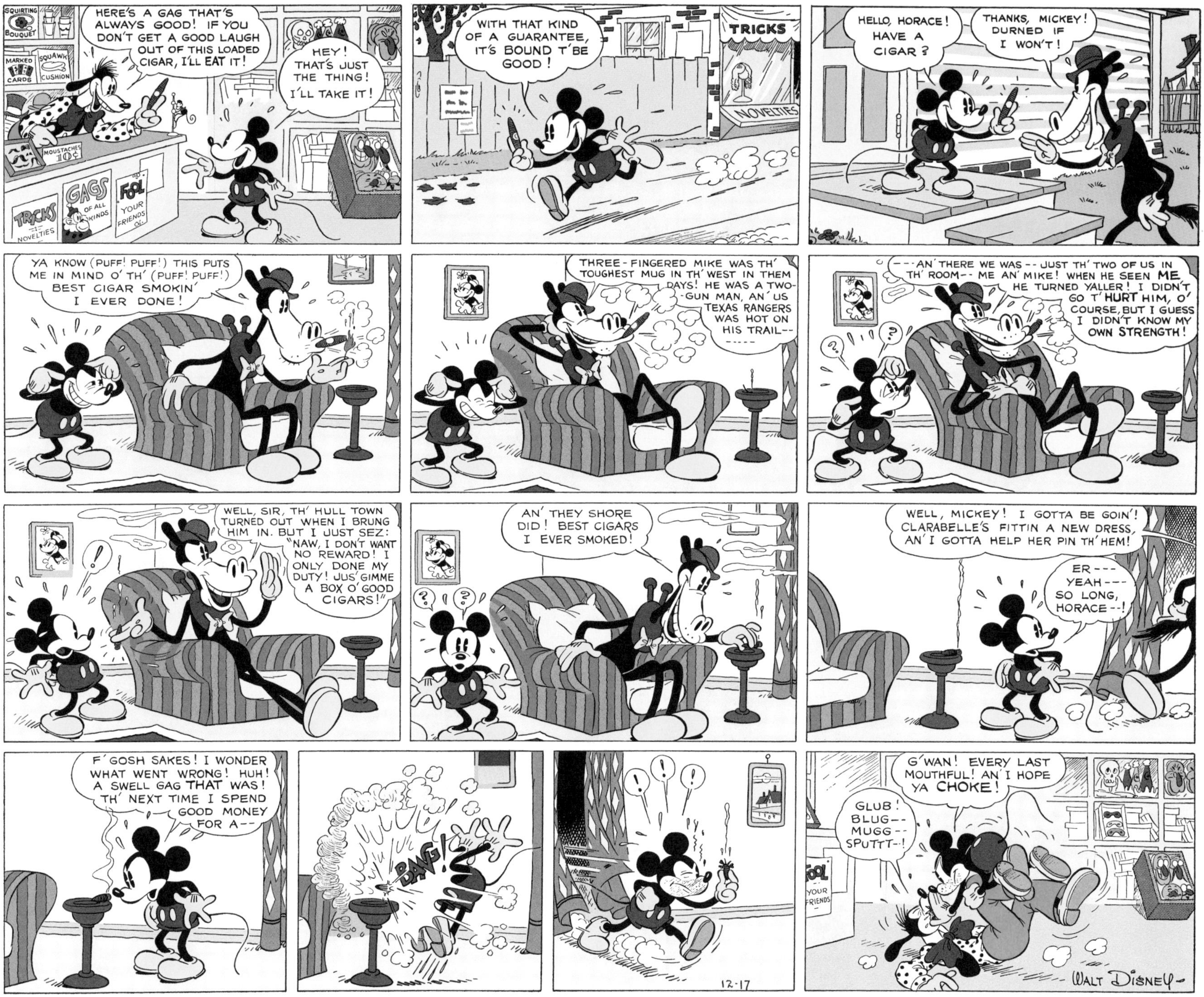
SQUIRTING BOUQUET
MARKED CARDS
SQUAWK CUSHION
HERE'S A GAG THAT'S ALWAYS GOOD! IF YOU DON'T GET A GOOD LAUGH OUT OF THIS LOADED CIGAR, I'LL EAT IT!
HEY! THAT'S JUST THE THING! I'LL TAKE IT!
MOUSTACHES 10¢
TRICKS NOVELTIES
GAGS OF ALL KINDS
FOOL YOUR FRIENDS
WITH THAT KIND OF A GUARANTEE, IT'S BOUND T'BE GOOD!
TRICKS
NOVELTIES
HELLO, HORACE! HAVE A CIGAR?
THANKS, MICKEY! DURNED IF I WON'T!
YA KNOW (PUFF! PUFF!) THIS PUTS ME IN MIND O' TH' (PUFF! PUFF!) BEST CIGAR SMOKIN' I EVER DONE!
THREE-FINGERED MIKE WAS TH' TOUGHEST MUG IN TH' WEST IN THEM DAYS! HE WAS A TWO-GUN MAN, AN' US TEXAS RANGERS WAS HOT ON HIS TRAIL-- ----
--AN' THERE WE WAS--JUST TH' TWO OF US IN TH' ROOM-- ME AN' MIKE! WHEN HE SEEN ME, HE TURNED YALLER! I DIDN'T GO T' HURT HIM, O' COURSE, BUT I GUESS I DIDN'T KNOW MY OWN STRENGTH!
WELL, SIR, TH' HULL TOWN TURNED OUT WHEN I BRUNG HIM IN. BUT I JUST SEZ: "NAW, I DON'T WANT NO REWARD! I ONLY DONE MY DUTY! JUS' GIMME A BOX O' GOOD CIGARS!"
AN' THEY SHORE DID! BEST CIGARS I EVER SMOKED!
WELL, MICKEY! I GOTTA BE GOIN'! CLARABELLE'S FITTIN A NEW DRESS, AN' I GOTTA HELP HER PIN TH' HEM!
ER--- YEAH--- SO LONG, HORACE--!
F' GOSH SAKES! I WONDER WHAT WENT WRONG! HUH! A SWELL GAG THAT WAS! TH' NEXT TIME I SPEND GOOD MONEY FOR A--
BANG!
12-17
G'WAN! EVERY LAST MOUTHFUL! AN' I HOPE YA CHOKE!
GLUB! BLUG-- MUGG-- SPUTTT-!
FOOL YOUR FRIENDS
WALT DISNEY

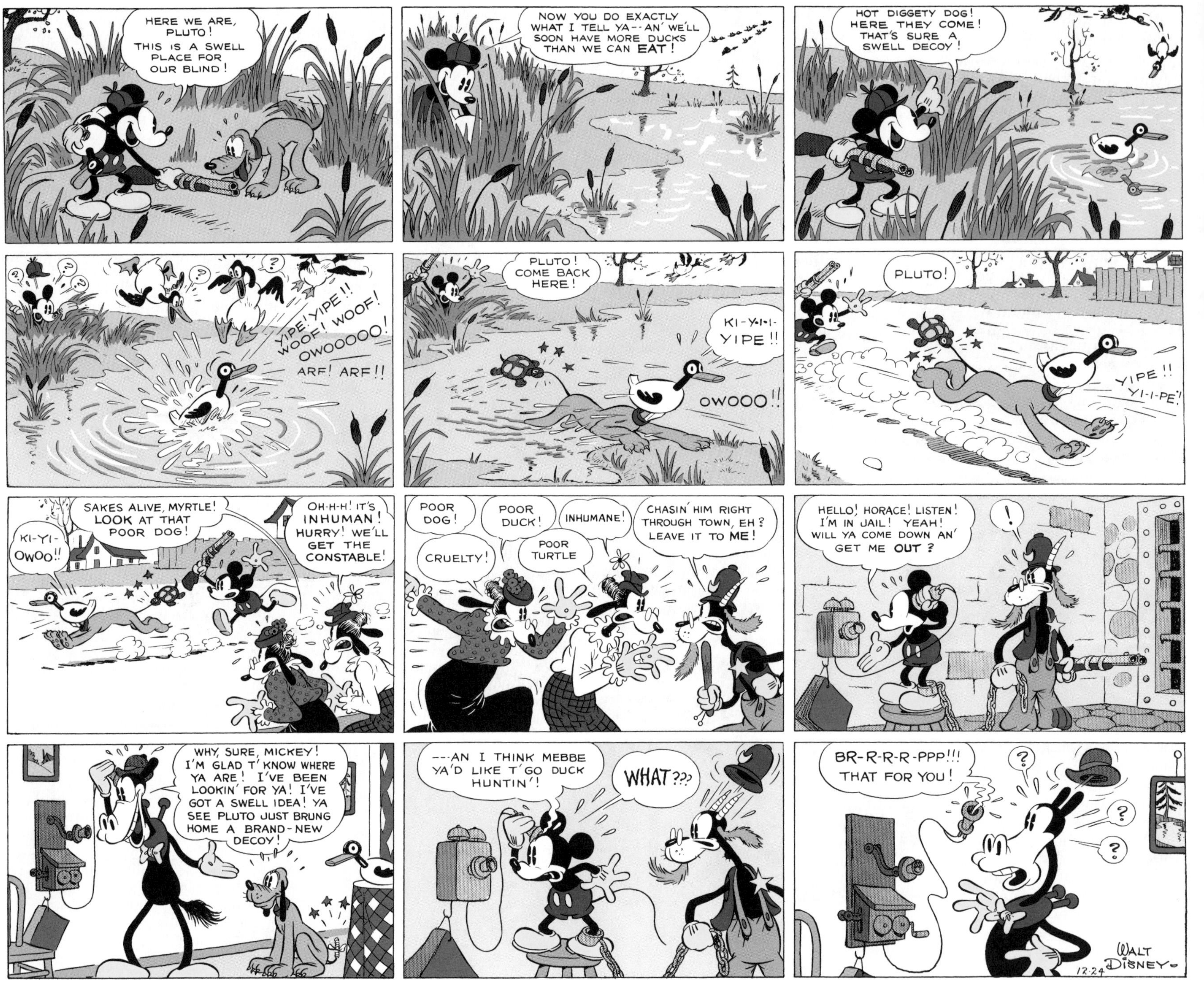
HERE WE ARE, PLUTO! THIS IS A SWELL PLACE FOR OUR BLIND!
NOW YOU DO EXACTLY WHAT I TELL YA--AN' WE'LL SOON HAVE MORE DUCKS THAN WE CAN EAT!
HOT DIGGETY DOG! HERE THEY COME! THAT'S SURE A SWELL DECOY!
YIPE! YIPE!! WOOF! WOOF! OWOOOOO! ARF! ARF!!
PLUTO! COME BACK HERE!
KI-Y-I-I-YIPE!!
OWOOO!!
PLUTO!
YIPE!! YI-I-PE!
KI-YI-OWOO!!
SAKES ALIVE, MYRTLE! LOOK AT THAT POOR DOG!
OH-H-H! IT'S INHUMAN! HURRY! WE'LL GET THE CONSTABLE!
POOR DOG!
POOR DUCK!
INHUMANE!
CHASIN' HIM RIGHT THROUGH TOWN, EH? LEAVE IT TO ME!
CRUELTY!
POOR TURTLE
HELLO, HORACE! LISTEN! I'M IN JAIL! YEAH! WILL YA COME DOWN AN' GET ME OUT?
!
WHY, SURE, MICKEY! I'M GLAD T' KNOW WHERE YA ARE! I'VE BEEN LOOKIN' FOR YA! I'VE GOT A SWELL IDEA! YA SEE PLUTO JUST BRUNG HOME A BRAND-NEW DECOY!
---AN I THINK MEBBE YA'D LIKE T' GO DUCK HUNTIN'!
WHAT???
BR-R-R-R-PPP!!! THAT FOR YOU!
?
?
?
WALT DISNEY
12-24

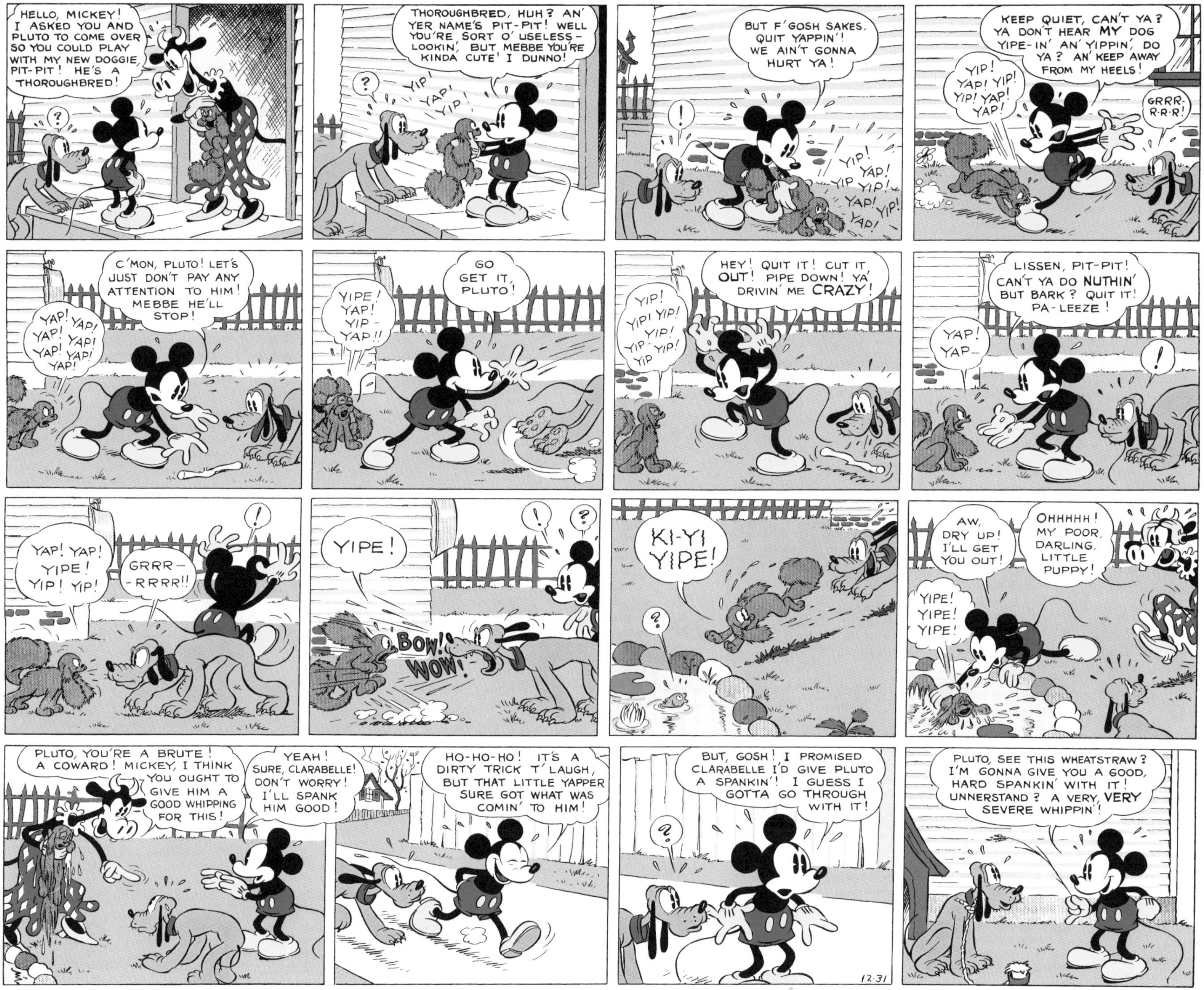
HELLO, MICKEY! I ASKED YOU AND PLUTO TO COME OVER SO YOU COULD PLAY WITH MY NEW DOGGIE, PIT-PIT! HE'S A THOROUGHBRED!
?
THOROUGHBRED, HUH? AN' YER NAME'S PIT-PIT! WELL YOU'RE SORT O' USELESS-LOOKIN', BUT MEBBE YOU'RE KINDA CUTE! I DUNNO!
?
YIP! YAP! YIP!
BUT F'GOSH SAKES, QUIT YAPPIN'! WE AIN'T GONNA HURT YA!
!
YIP! YAP! YIP YIP! YAP! YAP! YIP!
KEEP QUIET, CAN'T YA? YA DON'T HEAR MY DOG YIPE-IN' AN' YIPPIN', DO YA? AN' KEEP AWAY FROM MY HEELS!
YIP! YAP! YIP! YIP! YAP! YAP!
GRRR-R-R-R!
C'MON, PLUTO! LET'S JUST DON'T PAY ANY ATTENTION TO HIM! MEBBE HE'LL STOP!
YAP! YAP! YAP! YAP! YAP! YAP! YAP!
GO GET IT, PLUTO!
YIPE! YAP! YIP-YAP!!
HEY! QUIT IT! CUT IT OUT! PIPE DOWN! YA' DRIVIN' ME CRAZY!
YIP! YIP! YIP! YIP! YIP-YIP! YIP YIP!
LISSEN, PIT-PIT! CAN'T YA DO NUTHIN' BUT BARK? QUIT IT! PA-LEEZE!
YAP! YAP–
!
YAP! YAP! YIPE! YIP! YIP!
GRRR--RRRR!!
!
YIPE!
BOW! WOW!
!
?
KI-YI YIPE!
?
AW, DRY UP! I'LL GET YOU OUT!
OHHHHH! MY POOR, DARLING, LITTLE PUPPY!
YIPE! YIPE! YIPE!
PLUTO, YOU'RE A BRUTE! A COWARD! MICKEY, I THINK YOU OUGHT TO GIVE HIM A GOOD WHIPPING FOR THIS!
YEAH! SURE, CLARABELLE! DON'T WORRY! I'LL SPANK HIM GOOD!
HO-HO-HO! IT'S A DIRTY TRICK T' LAUGH, BUT THAT LITTLE YAPPER SURE GOT WHAT WAS COMIN' TO HIM!
BUT, GOSH! I PROMISED CLARABELLE I'D GIVE PLUTO A SPANKIN'! I GUESS I GOTTA GO THROUGH WITH IT!
?
12·31
PLUTO, SEE THIS WHEATSTRAW? I'M GONNA GIVE YOU A GOOD, HARD SPANKIN' WITH IT! UNNERSTAND? A VERY, VERY SEVERE WHIPPIN'!

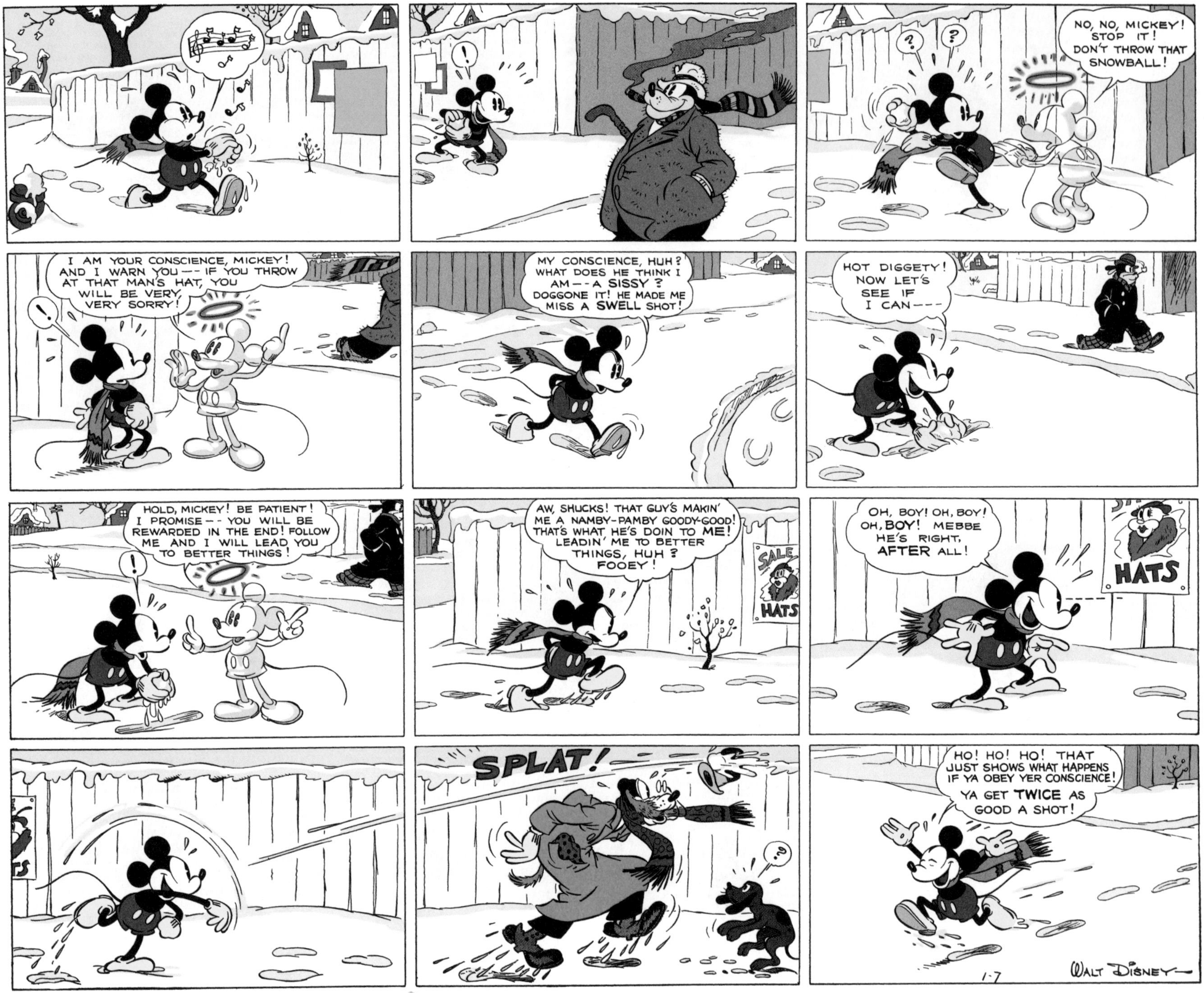

NO, NO, MICKEY! STOP IT! DON'T THROW THAT SNOWBALL!
I AM YOUR CONSCIENCE, MICKEY! AND I WARN YOU -- IF YOU THROW AT THAT MAN'S HAT, YOU WILL BE VERY, VERY SORRY!
MY CONSCIENCE, HUH? WHAT DOES HE THINK I AM -- A SISSY? DOGGONE IT! HE MADE ME MISS A SWELL SHOT!
HOT DIGGETY! NOW LET'S SEE IF I CAN ---
HOLD, MICKEY! BE PATIENT! I PROMISE -- YOU WILL BE REWARDED IN THE END! FOLLOW ME AND I WILL LEAD YOU TO BETTER THINGS!
AW, SHUCKS! THAT GUY'S MAKIN' ME A NAMBY-PAMBY GOODY-GOOD! THAT'S WHAT HE'S DOIN TO ME! LEADIN' ME TO BETTER THINGS, HUH? FOOEY!
SALE
HATS
OH, BOY! OH, BOY! OH, BOY! MEBBE HE'S RIGHT, AFTER ALL!
HATS
SPLAT!
HO! HO! HO! THAT JUST SHOWS WHAT HAPPENS IF YA OBEY YER CONSCIENCE!
YA GET TWICE AS GOOD A SHOT!
1-7
WALT DISNEY

128. PATIENCE IS REWARDED

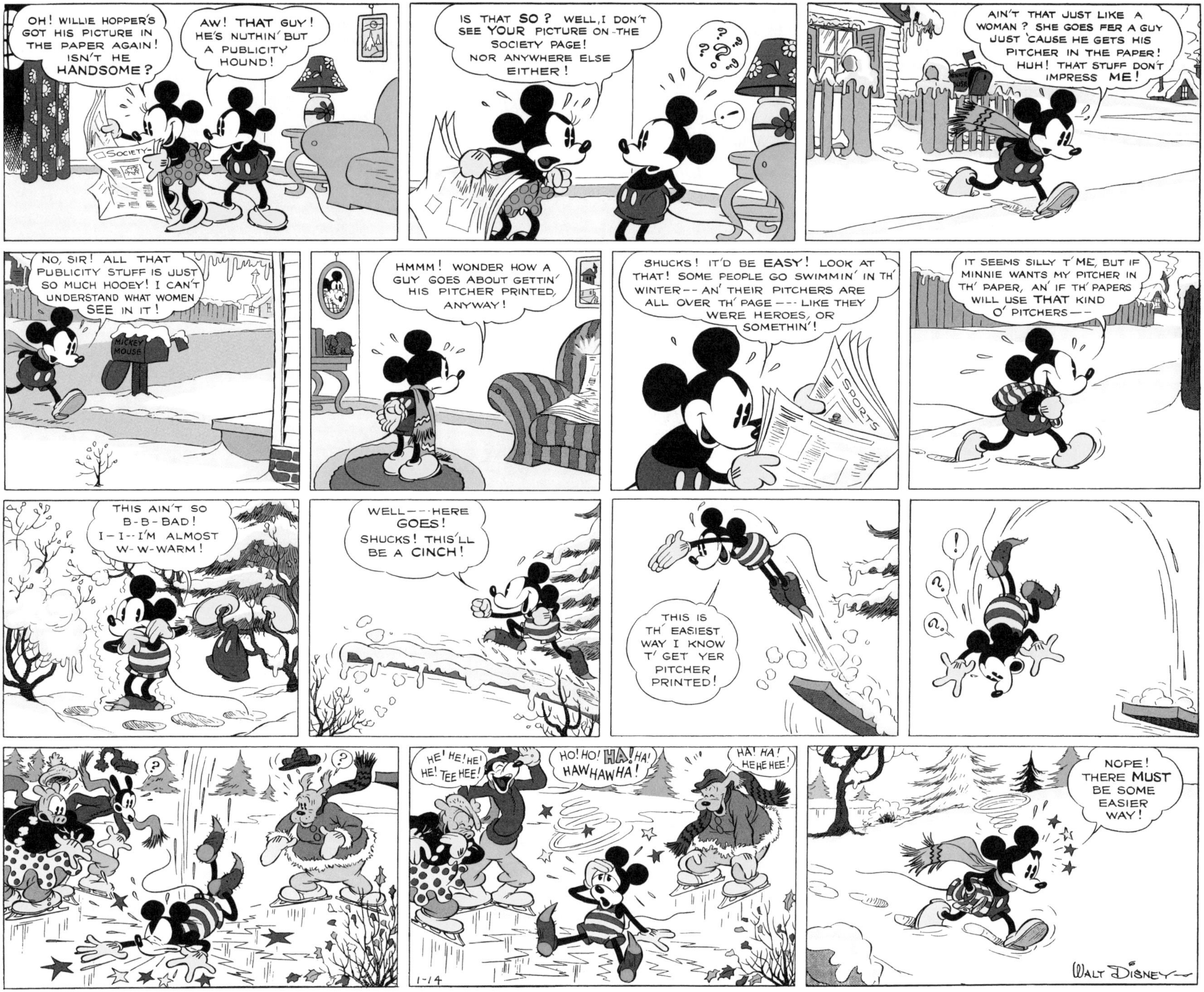

OH! WILLIE HOPPER'S GOT HIS PICTURE IN THE PAPER AGAIN! ISN'T HE HANDSOME?
AW! THAT GUY! HE'S NUTHIN' BUT A PUBLICITY HOUND!
SOCIETY
IS THAT SO? WELL, I DON'T SEE YOUR PICTURE ON THE SOCIETY PAGE! NOR ANYWHERE ELSE EITHER!
AIN'T THAT JUST LIKE A WOMAN? SHE GOES FER A GUY JUST 'CAUSE HE GETS HIS PITCHER IN THE PAPER! HUH! THAT STUFF DON'T IMPRESS ME!
NO, SIR! ALL THAT PUBLICITY STUFF IS JUST SO MUCH HOOEY! I CAN'T UNDERSTAND WHAT WOMEN SEE IN IT!
MICKEY MOUSE
HMMM! WONDER HOW A GUY GOES ABOUT GETTIN' HIS PITCHER PRINTED, ANYWAY!
SHUCKS! IT'D BE EASY! LOOK AT THAT! SOME PEOPLE GO SWIMMIN' IN TH' WINTER-- AN' THEIR PITCHERS ARE ALL OVER TH' PAGE--- LIKE THEY WERE HEROES, OR SOMETHIN'!
SPORTS
IT SEEMS SILLY T' ME, BUT IF MINNIE WANTS MY PITCHER IN TH' PAPER, AN' IF TH' PAPERS WILL USE THAT KIND O' PITCHERS--
THIS AIN'T SO B-B-BAD! I-I--I'M ALMOST W-W-WARM!
WELL---HERE GOES! SHUCKS! THIS'LL BE A CINCH!
THIS IS TH' EASIEST WAY I KNOW T' GET YER PITCHER PRINTED!
HE! HE! HE! HE! TEE HEE!
HO! HO! HA! HA! HAW HAW HA!
HA! HA! HE HE HEE!
NOPE! THERE MUST BE SOME EASIER WAY!
1-14
WALT DISNEY

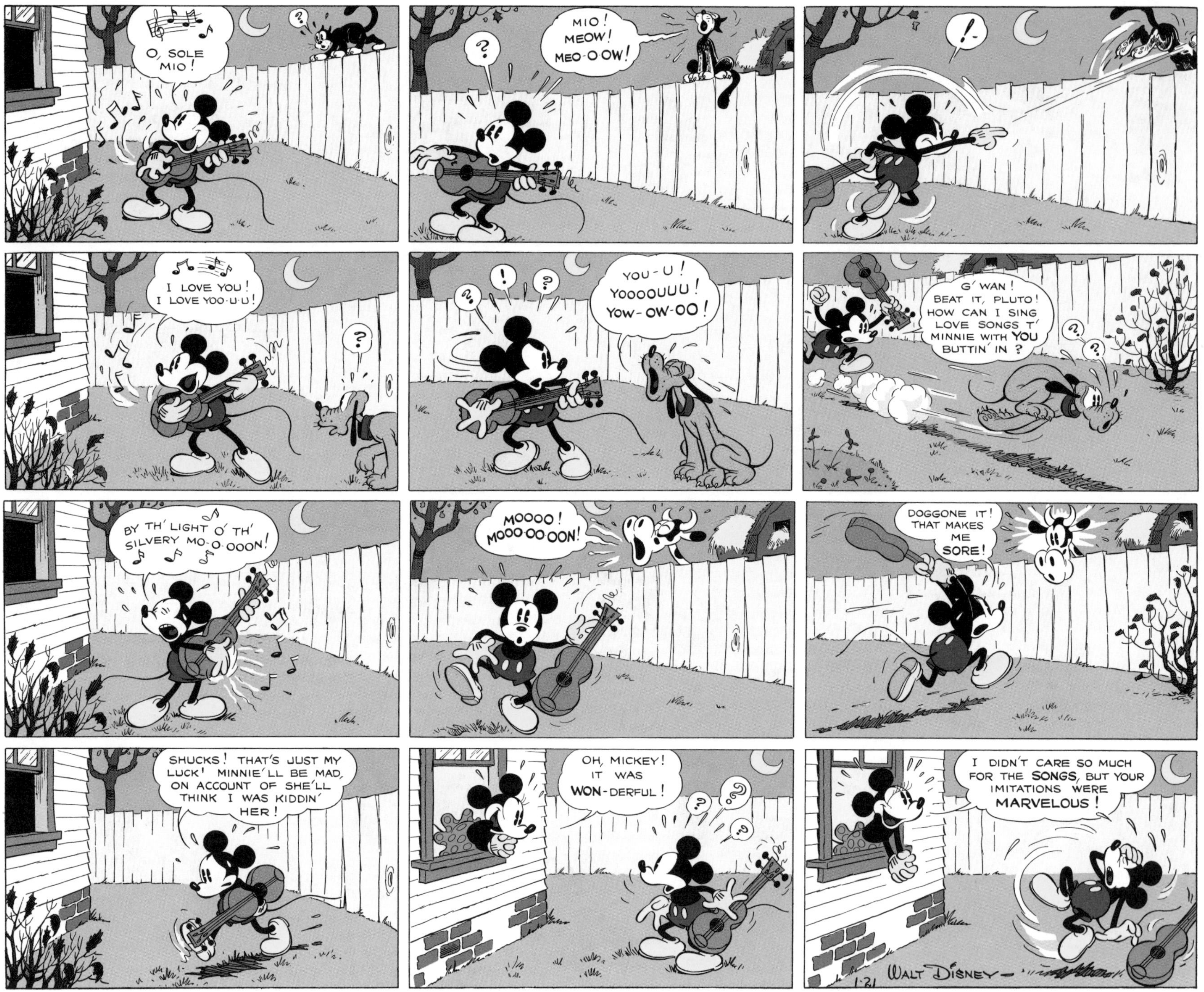
O, SOLE MIO!
MIO! MEOW! MEO-O-OW!
I LOVE YOU! I LOVE YOO-U-U!
YOU-U! YOOOOUUU! YOW-OW-OO!
G' WAN! BEAT IT, PLUTO! HOW CAN I SING LOVE SONGS T' MINNIE WITH YOU BUTTIN' IN?
BY TH' LIGHT O' TH' SILVERY MO-O-OOON!
MOOOO! MOOO-OO OON!
DOGGONE IT! THAT MAKES ME SORE!
SHUCKS! THAT'S JUST MY LUCK! MINNIE'LL BE MAD, ON ACCOUNT OF SHE'LL THINK I WAS KIDDIN' HER!
OH, MICKEY! IT WAS WON-DERFUL!
I DIDN'T CARE SO MUCH FOR THE SONGS, BUT YOUR IMITATIONS WERE MARVELOUS!
1-31
WALT DISNEY

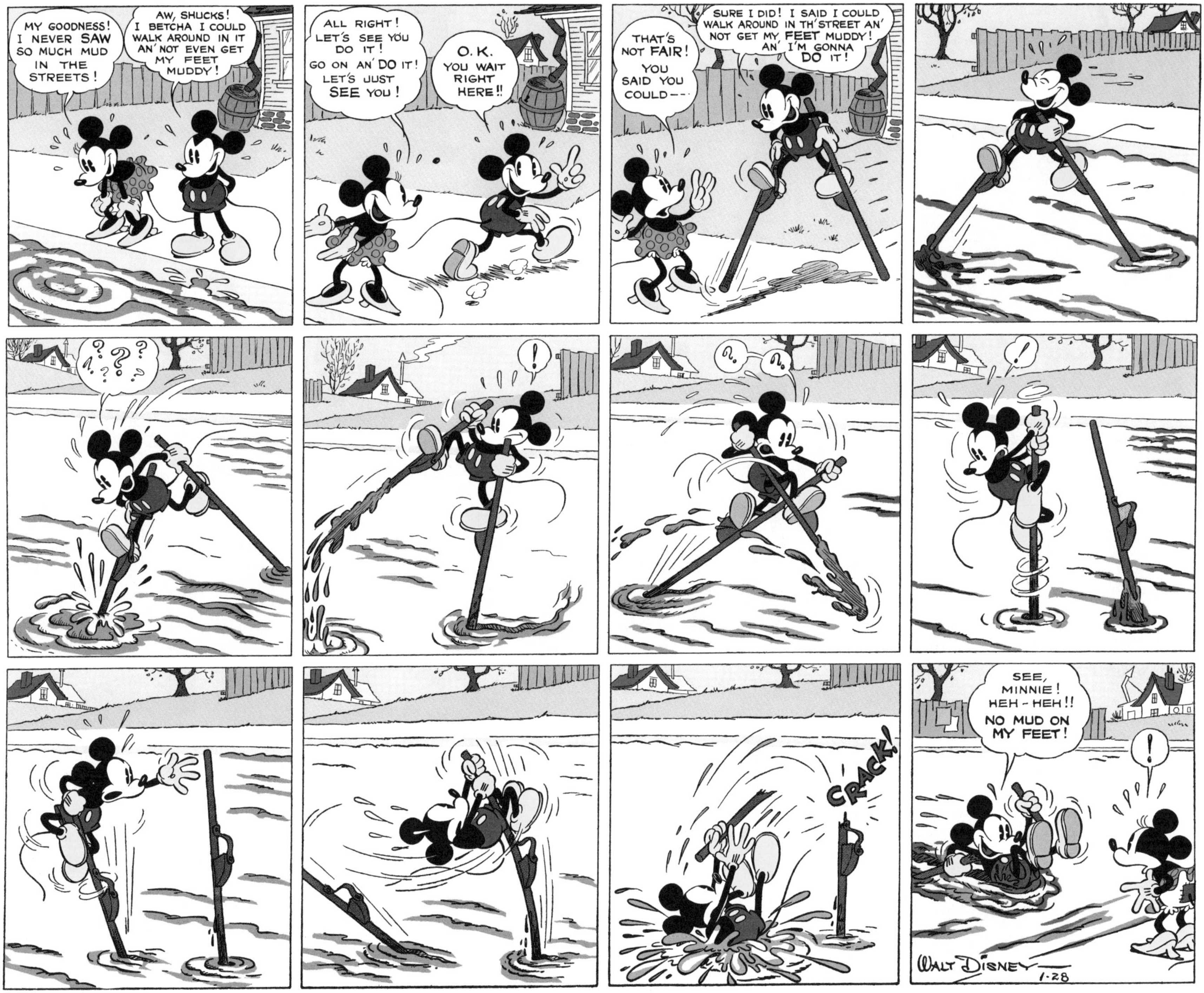
MY GOODNESS! I NEVER SAW SO MUCH MUD IN THE STREETS!
AW, SHUCKS! I BETCHA I COULD WALK AROUND IN IT AN' NOT EVEN GET MY FEET MUDDY!
ALL RIGHT! LET'S SEE YOU DO IT! GO ON AN' DO IT! LET'S JUST SEE YOU!
O.K. YOU WAIT RIGHT HERE!!
THAT'S NOT FAIR! YOU SAID YOU COULD---
SURE I DID! I SAID I COULD WALK AROUND IN TH' STREET AN' NOT GET MY FEET MUDDY! AN' I'M GONNA DO IT!
?? ? ? ?
!
?? ?
!
CRACK!
SEE, MINNIE! HEH-HEH!! NO MUD ON MY FEET!
!
WALT DISNEY
1-28

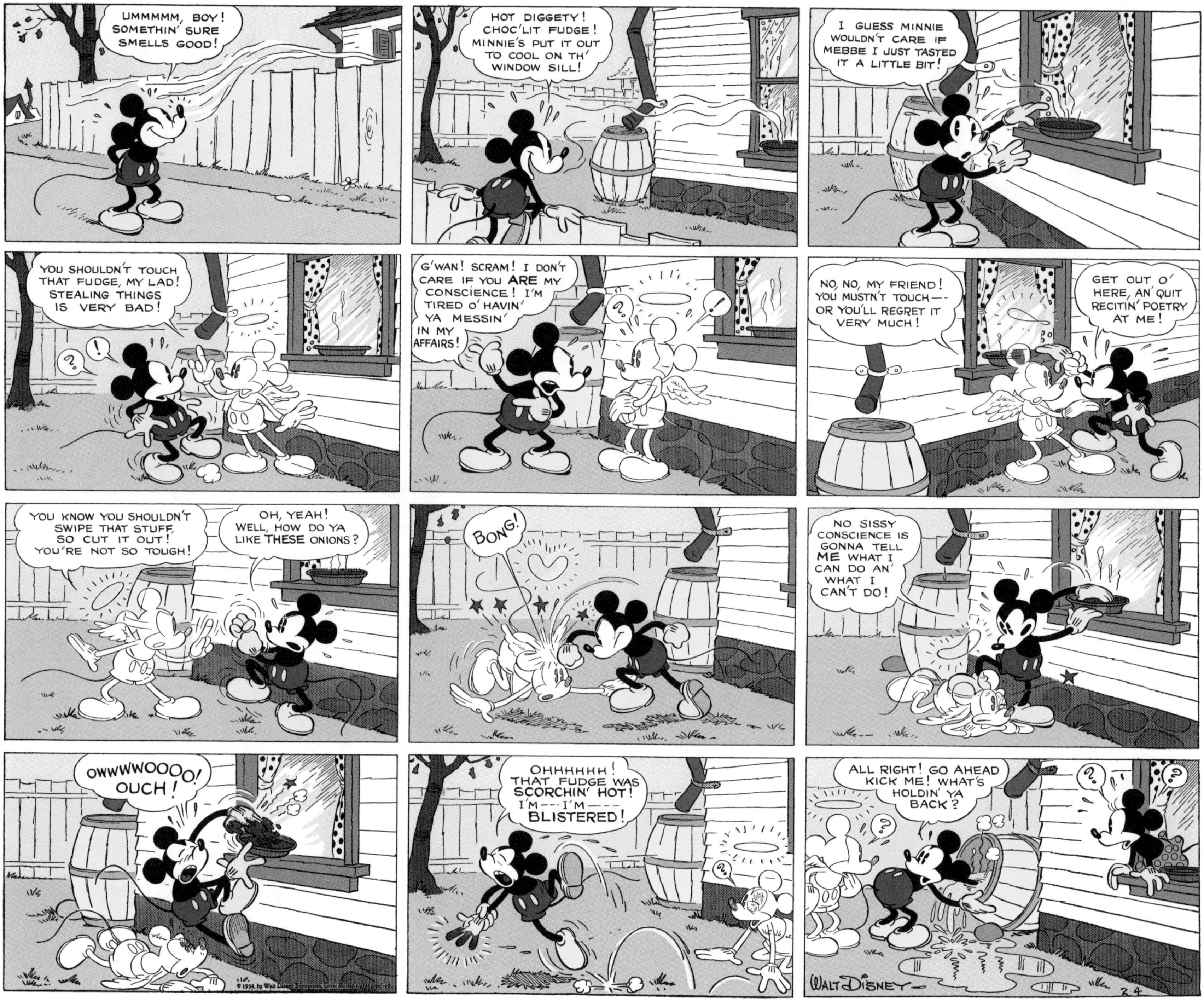
UMMMMM, BOY! SOMETHIN' SURE SMELLS GOOD!
HOT DIGGETY! CHOC'LIT FUDGE! MINNIE'S PUT IT OUT TO COOL ON TH' WINDOW SILL!
I GUESS MINNIE WOULDN'T CARE IF MEBBE I JUST TASTED IT A LITTLE BIT!
YOU SHOULDN'T TOUCH THAT FUDGE, MY LAD! STEALING THINGS IS VERY BAD!
G'WAN! SCRAM! I DON'T CARE IF YOU ARE MY CONSCIENCE! I'M TIRED O' HAVIN' YA MESSIN' IN MY AFFAIRS!
NO, NO, MY FRIEND! YOU MUSTN'T TOUCH—OR YOU'LL REGRET IT VERY MUCH!
GET OUT O' HERE, AN' QUIT RECITIN' POETRY AT ME!
YOU KNOW YOU SHOULDN'T SWIPE THAT STUFF, SO CUT IT OUT! YOU'RE NOT SO TOUGH!
OH, YEAH! WELL, HOW DO YA LIKE THESE ONIONS?
BONG!
NO SISSY CONSCIENCE IS GONNA TELL ME WHAT I CAN DO AN' WHAT I CAN'T DO!
OWWWWOOOOO! OUCH!
OHHHHHH! THAT FUDGE WAS SCORCHIN' HOT! I'M---I'M---BLISTERED!
ALL RIGHT! GO AHEAD KICK ME! WHAT'S HOLDIN' YA BACK?
WALT DISNEY
3-4

132. AW, FUDGE

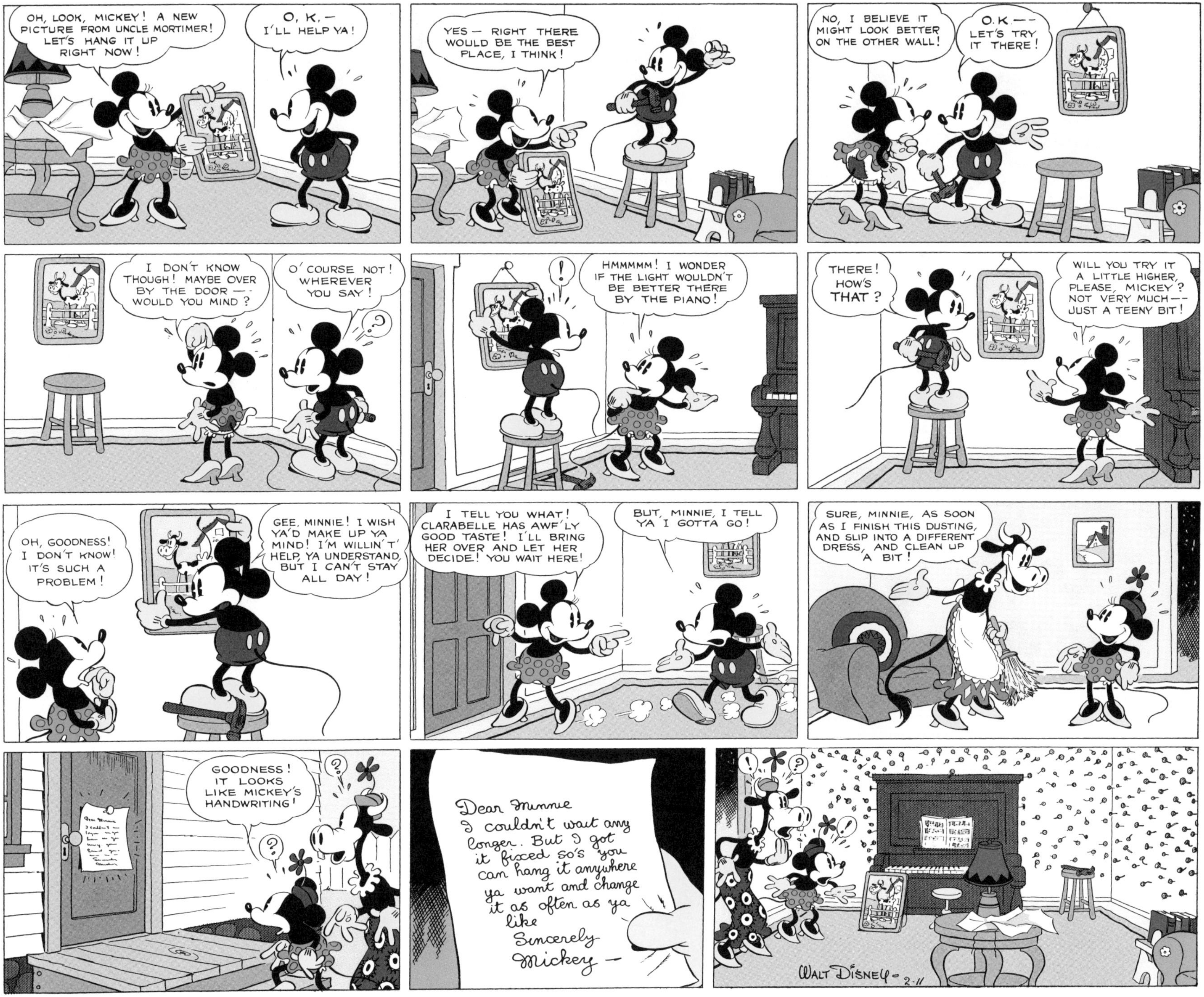
OH, LOOK, MICKEY! A NEW PICTURE FROM UNCLE MORTIMER! LET'S HANG IT UP RIGHT NOW!
O. K. — I'LL HELP YA!
YES — RIGHT THERE WOULD BE THE BEST PLACE, I THINK!
NO, I BELIEVE IT MIGHT LOOK BETTER ON THE OTHER WALL!
O. K — — LET'S TRY IT THERE!
I DON'T KNOW THOUGH! MAYBE OVER BY THE DOOR — - WOULD YOU MIND?
O' COURSE NOT! WHEREVER YOU SAY!
!
HMMMMM! I WONDER IF THE LIGHT WOULDN'T BE BETTER THERE BY THE PIANO!
THERE! HOW'S THAT?
WILL YOU TRY IT A LITTLE HIGHER, PLEASE, MICKEY? NOT VERY MUCH — — JUST A TEENY BIT!
OH, GOODNESS! I DON'T KNOW! IT'S SUCH A PROBLEM!
GEE, MINNIE! I WISH YA'D MAKE UP YA MIND! I'M WILLIN' T' HELP, YA UNDERSTAND, BUT I CAN'T STAY ALL DAY!
I TELL YOU WHAT! CLARABELLE HAS AWF'LY GOOD TASTE! I'LL BRING HER OVER AND LET HER DECIDE! YOU WAIT HERE!
BUT, MINNIE, I TELL YA I GOTTA GO!
SURE, MINNIE, AS SOON AS I FINISH THIS DUSTING, AND SLIP INTO A DIFFERENT DRESS, AND CLEAN UP A BIT!
GOODNESS! IT LOOKS LIKE MICKEY'S HANDWRITING!
Dear Minnie
I couldn't wait any longer. But I got it fixed so's you can hang it anywhere ya want and change it as often as ya like
Sincerely
Mickey —
WALT DISNEY 2-11

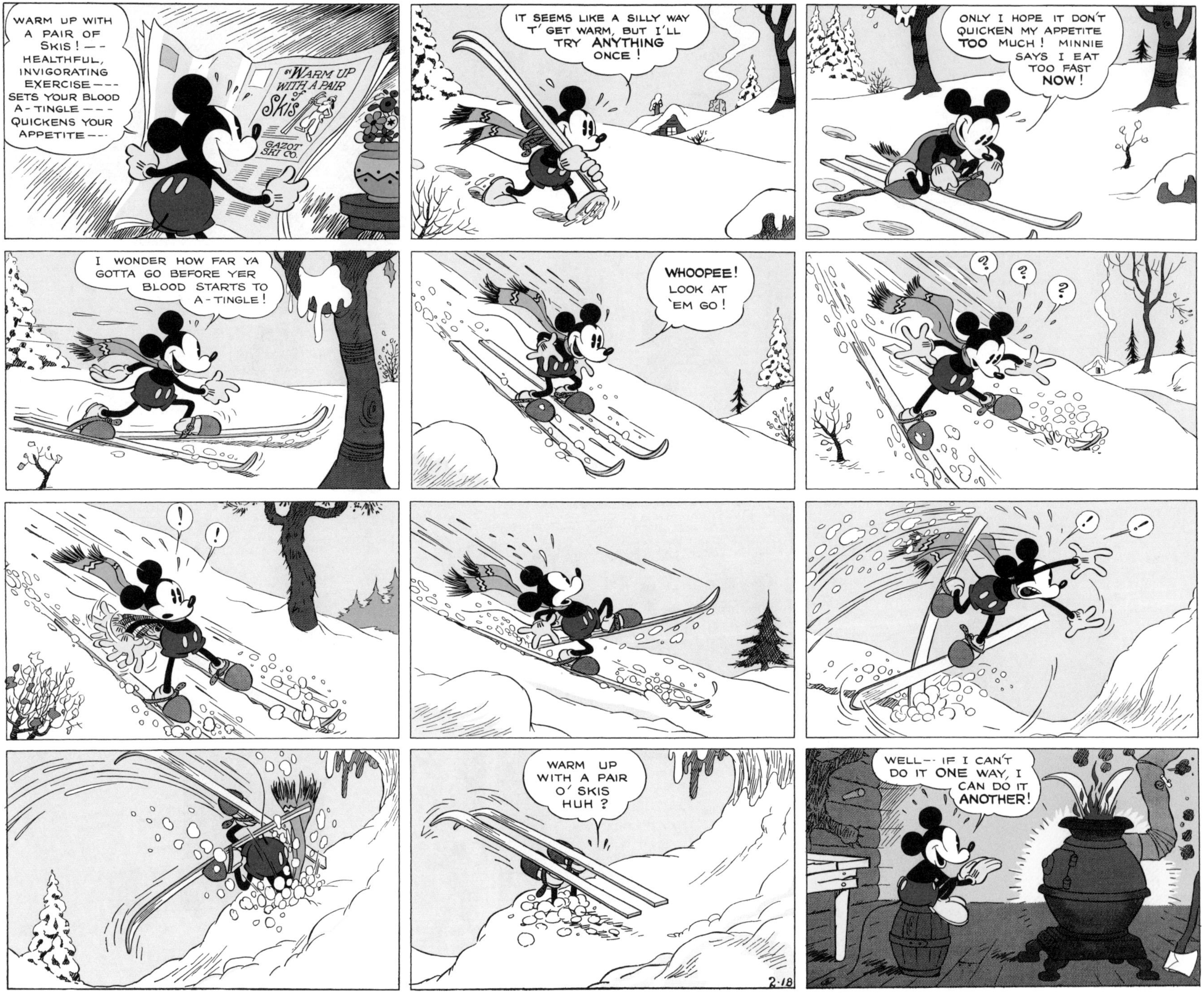
WARM UP WITH A PAIR OF SKIS! -- HEALTHFUL, INVIGORATING EXERCISE --- SETS YOUR BLOOD A-TINGLE --- QUICKENS YOUR APPETITE ---
WARM UP WITH A PAIR of SKIS
GAZOT SKI CO.
IT SEEMS LIKE A SILLY WAY T' GET WARM, BUT I'LL TRY ANYTHING ONCE!
ONLY I HOPE IT DON'T QUICKEN MY APPETITE TOO MUCH! MINNIE SAYS I EAT TOO FAST NOW!
I WONDER HOW FAR YA GOTTA GO BEFORE YER BLOOD STARTS TO A-TINGLE!
WHOOPEE! LOOK AT 'EM GO!
?
?
?
!
!
!
!
WARM UP WITH A PAIR O' SKIS HUH ?
2-18
WELL-- IF I CAN'T DO IT ONE WAY, I CAN DO IT ANOTHER!

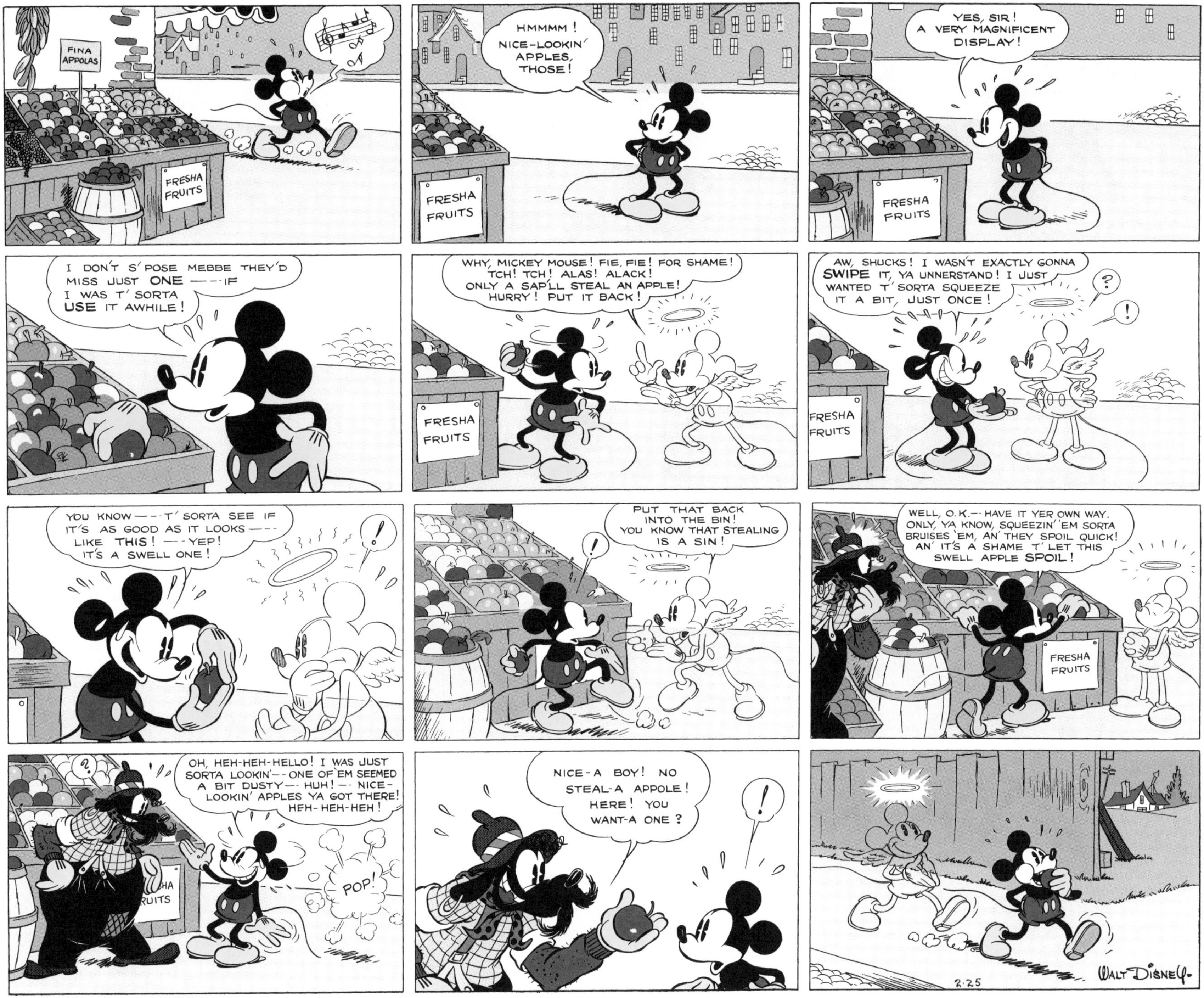

FINA APPOLAS
FRESHA FRUITS
HMMMM! NICE-LOOKIN' APPLES, THOSE!
FRESHA FRUITS
YES, SIR! A VERY MAGNIFICENT DISPLAY!
FRESHA FRUITS
I DON'T S'POSE MEBBE THEY'D MISS JUST ONE ---IF I WAS T' SORTA USE IT AWHILE!
WHY, MICKEY MOUSE! FIE, FIE! FOR SHAME! TCH! TCH! ALAS! ALACK! ONLY A SAP'LL STEAL AN APPLE! HURRY! PUT IT BACK!
FRESHA FRUITS
AW, SHUCKS! I WASN'T EXACTLY GONNA SWIPE IT, YA UNNERSTAND! I JUST WANTED T' SORTA SQUEEZE IT A BIT, JUST ONCE!
?
!
FRESHA FRUITS
YOU KNOW---T' SORTA SEE IF IT'S AS GOOD AS IT LOOKS--- LIKE THIS! ---YEP! IT'S A SWELL ONE!
!
PUT THAT BACK INTO THE BIN! YOU KNOW THAT STEALING IS A SIN!
!
WELL, O.K.-- HAVE IT YER OWN WAY. ONLY, YA KNOW, SQUEEZIN' 'EM SORTA BRUISES 'EM, AN' THEY SPOIL QUICK! AN' IT'S A SHAME T' LET THIS SWELL APPLE SPOIL!
FRESHA FRUITS
?
OH, HEH-HEH-HELLO! I WAS JUST SORTA LOOKIN'-- ONE OF 'EM SEEMED A BIT DUSTY-- HUH! -- NICE-LOOKIN' APPLES YA GOT THERE! HEH-HEH-HEH!
POP!
NICE-A BOY! NO STEAL-A APPOLE! HERE! YOU WANT-A ONE?
!
2.25
WALT DISNEY

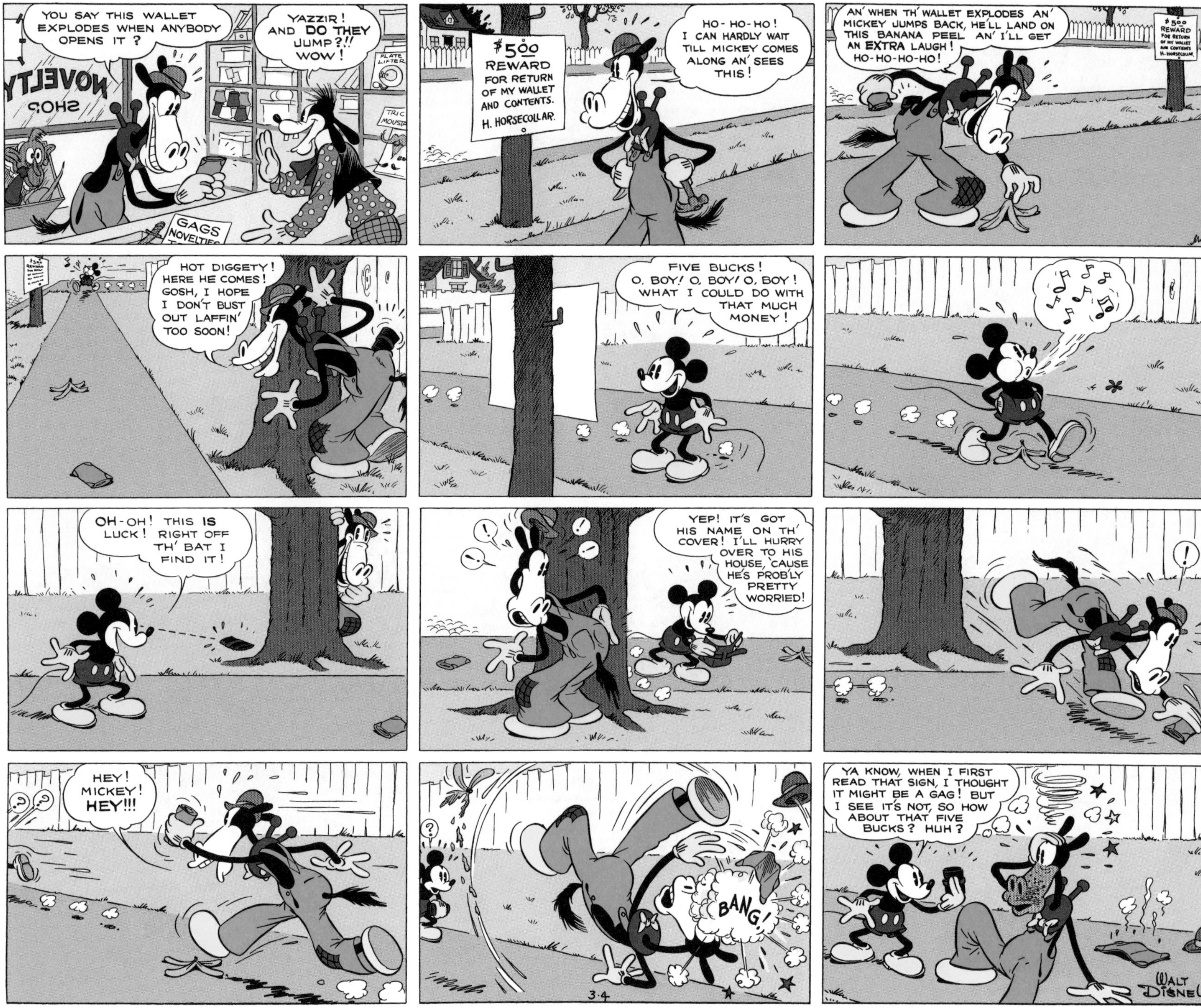
YOU SAY THIS WALLET EXPLODES WHEN ANYBODY OPENS IT?
YAZZIR! AND DO THEY JUMP?!! WOW!
NOVELTY SHOP
PLATE LIFTER
GAGS NOVELTIES
$5.00 REWARD FOR RETURN OF MY WALLET AND CONTENTS. H. HORSECOLLAR.
HO-HO-HO! I CAN HARDLY WAIT TILL MICKEY COMES ALONG AN' SEES THIS!
AN' WHEN TH' WALLET EXPLODES AN' MICKEY JUMPS BACK, HE'LL LAND ON THIS BANANA PEEL AN' I'LL GET AN EXTRA LAUGH! HO-HO-HO-HO!
HOT DIGGETY! HERE HE COMES! GOSH, I HOPE I DON'T BUST OUT LAFFIN' TOO SOON!
FIVE BUCKS! O, BOY! O, BOY! O, BOY! WHAT I COULD DO WITH THAT MUCH MONEY!
OH-OH! THIS IS LUCK! RIGHT OFF TH' BAT I FIND IT!
YEP! IT'S GOT HIS NAME ON TH' COVER! I'LL HURRY OVER TO HIS HOUSE, 'CAUSE HE'S PROB'LY PRETTY WORRIED!
HEY! MICKEY! HEY!!!
BANG!
YA KNOW, WHEN I FIRST READ THAT SIGN, I THOUGHT IT MIGHT BE A GAG! BUT I SEE IT'S NOT, SO HOW ABOUT THAT FIVE BUCKS? HUH?
3-4
WALT DISNEY

136. HE FAW DOWN AN' GO BOOM

RUMPLEWATT THE GIANT

AND

TANGLEFOOT PULLS HIS WEIGHT

MARCH 11, 1934
–
JUNE 10, 1934

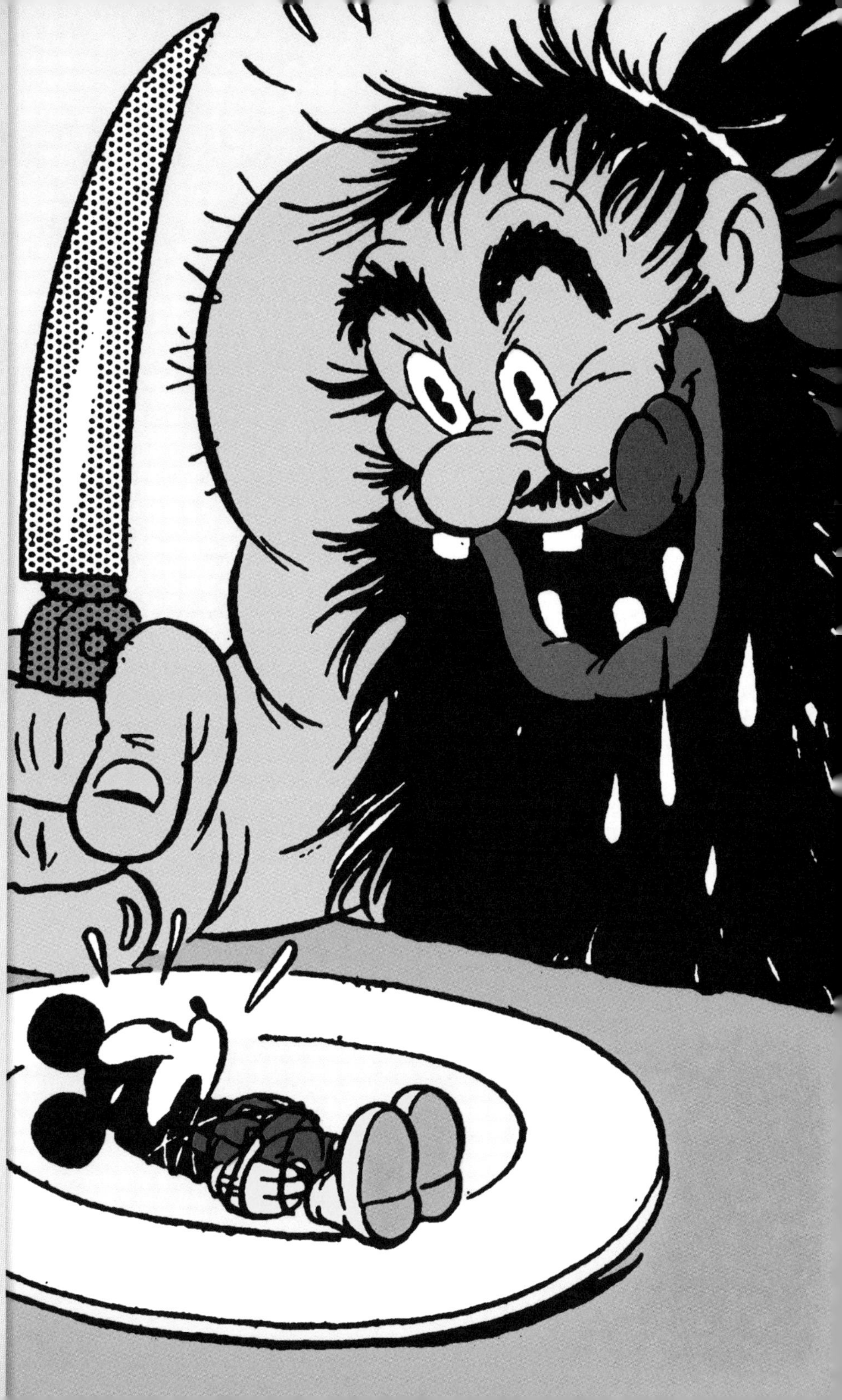

MICKEY MOUSE
REGISTERED U.S. PATENT OFFICE

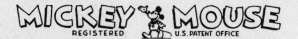

THE LONGEST SHORT STORY EVER TOLD!

The Mickey Mouse of the comics is known for being many things: brave, scrappy, determined, spunky, empathetic—and possessing an extraordinary amount of what bygone generations once called "moxie."

Yes, Mickey embodies many endearing character traits... but long-windedness has never been one of them. At least not until Mickey was provided with a receptive audience of about a dozen identical, nightshirted mouselings to hang on his every word. The Sunday continuity now known as "Rumplewatt the Giant" was based upon the Mickey Mouse cartoon short *Giantland* (1933). The crowd of young listeners was carried over from the cartoon—but the seven-minute runtime was not.

Vastly expanded for comics, Mickey's tall-tale of a tall adversary now unfolded over eight Sunday strips. Encountering it in one "dose," without weekly gaps between installments, the modern reader might fail to grasp exactly how long-winded Mickey's wily whopper actually is. But our "munchausing" Mouse acknowledges the epic length of the tale to come—and comes close to breaking the fourth wall (truly a rarity for a 1930s Disney strip)—when he ends the first installment with: "Th' story's too long t' finish now! You come back next week, an' I'll tell ya more!" Clearly, Mickey's announcement is intended for *us* as well as the mini-mice.

True to his word, Mickey does indeed continue the story "next week" with the March 18 installment. Three more Sundays are spent in Mickey's living room as the tale unfolds. But by April 15, we find Mickey continuing his epic adventure tale as a *bedtime* story—meaning that he has likely gone on *all day* and into the evening with his giant-sized saga! Even if all previous installments are to be considered as taking place over the course of a single day, we have the inescapable "overnight aspect" to consider, when measuring the windy effort from start to finish.

April 22 finds our tale-teller and his tell-ees back in the living room. Finally, on April 29, Mickey wraps up a lengthy storytelling effort that would shame Scheherazade—perhaps making "Rumplewatt" the longest short story ever told!

With Mickey suddenly given to so much talk, we might jokingly claim to have uncovered the reason why the busy Mr. Disney eventually ceased voicing his creation on-screen... he might have worried that one day he would be required to tell a story as lengthy as this! After all, more giants—in both *The Brave Little Tailor* (1938) and the "Mickey and the Beanstalk" segment of *Fun and Fancy Free* (1947)—were still to come, each rife with the possibility of its own embellished comics adaptation.

—JOE TORCIVIA

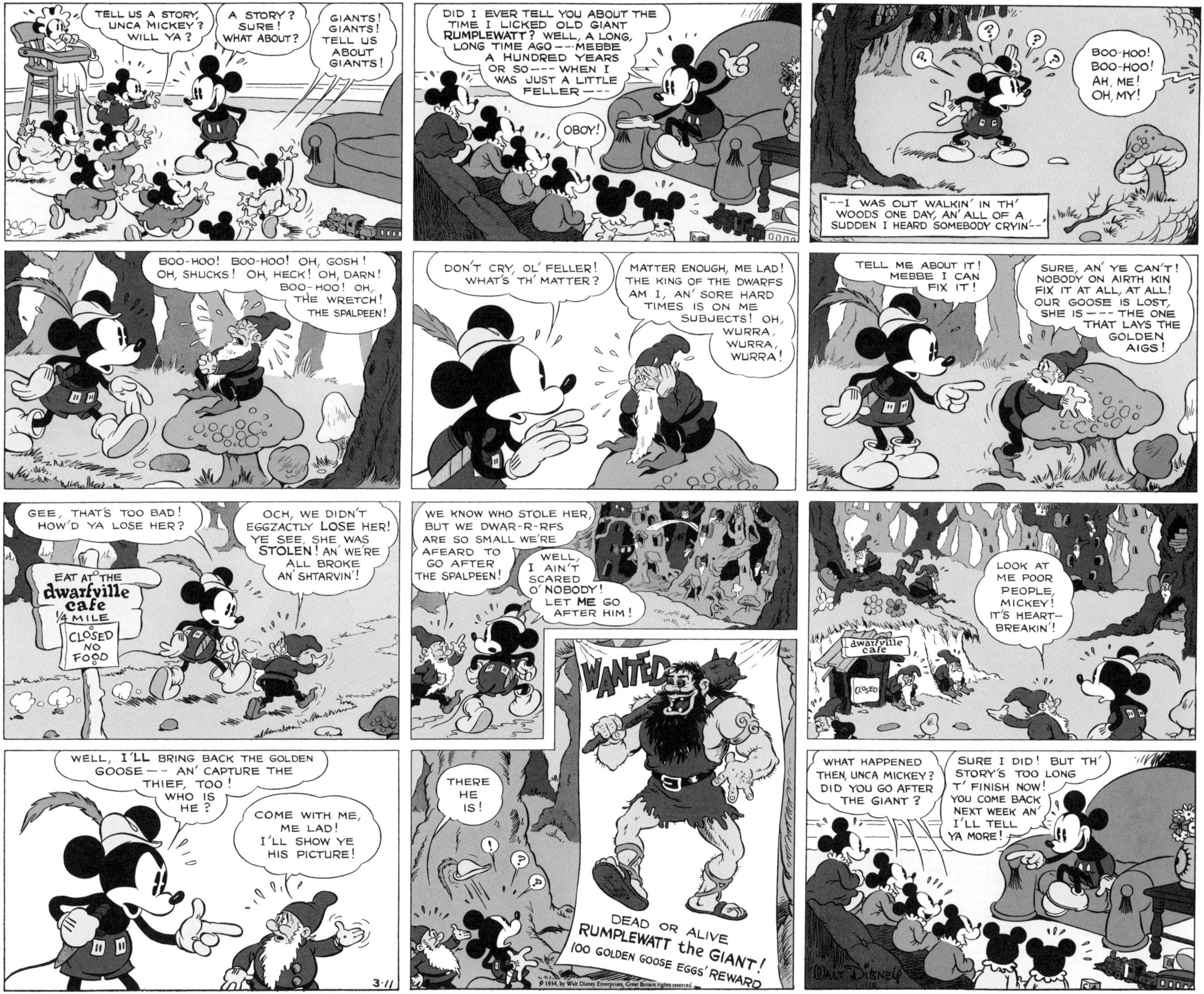
TELL US A STORY, UNCA MICKEY? WILL YA?
A STORY? SURE! WHAT ABOUT?
GIANTS! GIANTS! TELL US ABOUT GIANTS!
DID I EVER TELL YOU ABOUT THE TIME I LICKED OLD GIANT RUMPLEWATT? WELL, A LONG, LONG TIME AGO---MEBBE A HUNDRED YEARS OR SO--- WHEN I WAS JUST A LITTLE FELLER---
OBOY!
"--I WAS OUT WALKIN' IN TH' WOODS ONE DAY, AN' ALL OF A SUDDEN I HEARD SOMEBODY CRYIN'--"
BOO-HOO! BOO-HOO! AH, ME! OH, MY!
BOO-HOO! BOO-HOO! OH, GOSH! OH, SHUCKS! OH, HECK! OH, DARN! BOO-HOO! OH, THE WRETCH! THE SPALPEEN!
DON'T CRY, OL' FELLER! WHAT'S TH' MATTER?
MATTER ENOUGH, ME LAD! THE KING OF THE DWARFS AM I, AN' SORE HARD TIMES IS ON ME SUBJECTS! OH, WURRA, WURRA, WURRA!
TELL ME ABOUT IT! MEBBE I CAN FIX IT!
SURE, AN' YE CAN'T! NOBODY ON AIRTH KIN FIX IT AT ALL, AT ALL! OUR GOOSE IS LOST, SHE IS--- THE ONE THAT LAYS THE GOLDEN AIGS!
GEE, THAT'S TOO BAD! HOW'D YA LOSE HER?
OCH, WE DIDN'T EGGZACTLY LOSE HER! YE SEE, SHE WAS STOLEN! AN' WE'RE ALL BROKE AN' SHTARVIN'!
EAT AT THE dwarfville cafe 1/4 MILE
CLOSED NO FOOD
WE KNOW WHO STOLE HER, BUT WE DWAR-R-RFS ARE SO SMALL WE'RE AFEARD TO GO AFTER THE SPALPEEN!
WELL, I AIN'T SCARED O' NOBODY! LET ME GO AFTER HIM!
LOOK AT ME POOR PEOPLE, MICKEY! IT'S HEART-BREAKIN'!
dwarfville cafe
CLOSED
WELL, I'LL BRING BACK THE GOLDEN GOOSE-- AN' CAPTURE THE THIEF, TOO! WHO IS HE?
COME WITH ME, ME LAD! I'LL SHOW YE HIS PICTURE!
3·11
THERE HE IS!
WANTED
DEAD OR ALIVE RUMPLEWATT the GIANT! 100 GOLDEN GOOSE EGGS' REWARD
© 1934, by Walt Disney Enterprises, Great Britain rights reserved
WHAT HAPPENED THEN, UNCA MICKEY? DID YOU GO AFTER THE GIANT?
SURE I DID! BUT TH' STORY'S TOO LONG T' FINISH NOW! YOU COME BACK NEXT WEEK AN' I'LL TELL YA MORE!
WALT DISNEY

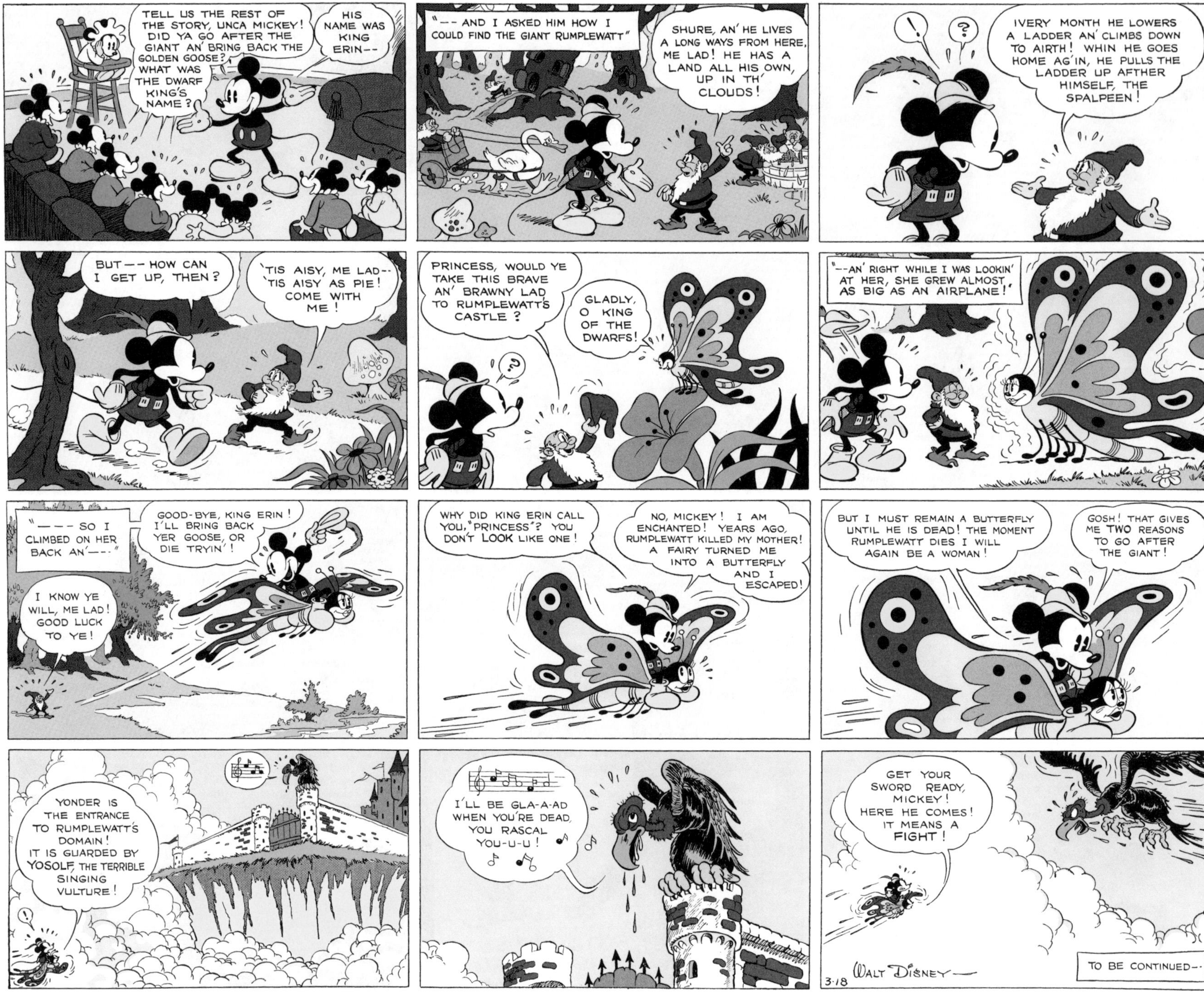
TELL US THE REST OF THE STORY, UNCA MICKEY! DID YA GO AFTER THE GIANT AN' BRING BACK THE GOLDEN GOOSE?
WHAT WAS THE DWARF KING'S NAME?
HIS NAME WAS KING ERIN--
"-- AND I ASKED HIM HOW I COULD FIND THE GIANT RUMPLEWATT"
SHURE, AN' HE LIVES A LONG WAYS FROM HERE, ME LAD! HE HAS A LAND ALL HIS OWN, UP IN TH' CLOUDS!
!
?
IVERY MONTH HE LOWERS A LADDER AN' CLIMBS DOWN TO AIRTH! WHIN HE GOES HOME AG'IN, HE PULLS THE LADDER UP AFTHER HIMSELF, THE SPALPEEN!
BUT -- HOW CAN I GET UP, THEN?
'TIS AISY, ME LAD-- 'TIS AISY AS PIE! COME WITH ME!
PRINCESS, WOULD YE TAKE THIS BRAVE AN' BRAWNY LAD TO RUMPLEWATT'S CASTLE?
?
GLADLY, O KING OF THE DWARFS!
"--AN' RIGHT WHILE I WAS LOOKIN' AT HER, SHE GREW ALMOST AS BIG AS AN AIRPLANE!"
"--- SO I CLIMBED ON HER BACK AN'---"
GOOD-BYE, KING ERIN! I'LL BRING BACK YER GOOSE, OR DIE TRYIN'!
I KNOW YE WILL, ME LAD! GOOD LUCK TO YE!
WHY DID KING ERIN CALL YOU, "PRINCESS"? YOU DON'T LOOK LIKE ONE!
NO, MICKEY! I AM ENCHANTED! YEARS AGO, RUMPLEWATT KILLED MY MOTHER! A FAIRY TURNED ME INTO A BUTTERFLY AND I ESCAPED!
BUT I MUST REMAIN A BUTTERFLY UNTIL HE IS DEAD! THE MOMENT RUMPLEWATT DIES I WILL AGAIN BE A WOMAN!
GOSH! THAT GIVES ME TWO REASONS TO GO AFTER THE GIANT!
YONDER IS THE ENTRANCE TO RUMPLEWATT'S DOMAIN! IT IS GUARDED BY YOSOLF, THE TERRIBLE SINGING VULTURE!
!
I'LL BE GLA-A-AD WHEN YOU'RE DEAD, YOU RASCAL YOU-U-U!
GET YOUR SWORD READY, MICKEY! HERE HE COMES! IT MEANS A FIGHT!
3-18
WALT DISNEY
TO BE CONTINUED--

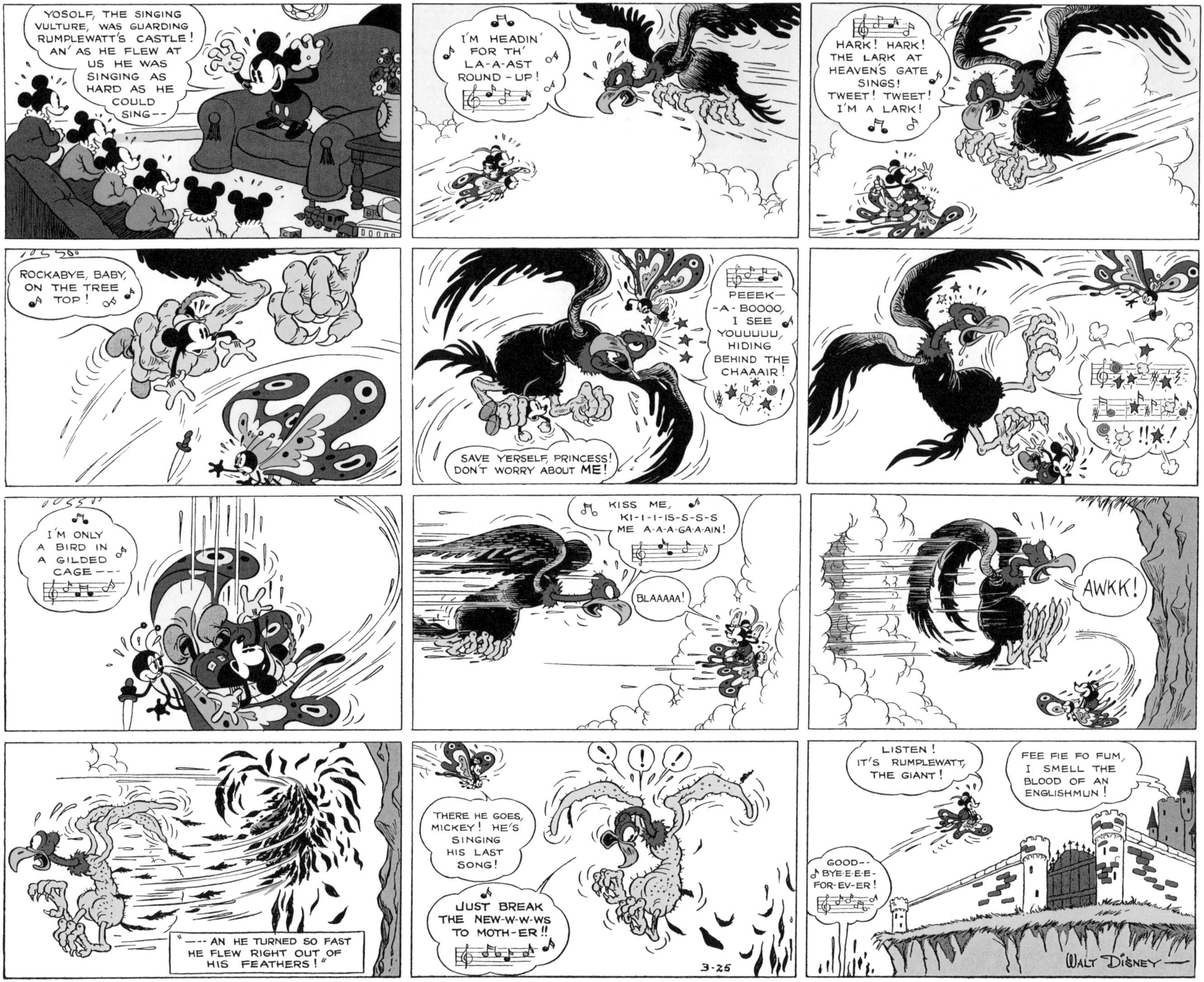
YOSOLF, THE SINGING VULTURE, WAS GUARDING RUMPLEWATT'S CASTLE! AN' AS HE FLEW AT US HE WAS SINGING AS HARD AS HE COULD SING--
I'M HEADIN' FOR TH' LA-A-AST ROUND-UP!
HARK! HARK! THE LARK AT HEAVEN'S GATE SINGS! TWEET! TWEET! I'M A LARK!
ROCKABYE, BABY, ON THE TREE TOP!
PEEEK--A-BOOOO, I SEE YOUUUUU, HIDING BEHIND THE CHAAAIR!
SAVE YERSELF, PRINCESS! DON'T WORRY ABOUT ME!
I'M ONLY A BIRD IN A GILDED CAGE---
KISS ME, KI-I-I-IS-S-S-S ME A-A-A-GA-A-AIN!
BLAAAAA!
AWKK!
"---AN HE TURNED SO FAST HE FLEW RIGHT OUT OF HIS FEATHERS!"
THERE HE GOES, MICKEY! HE'S SINGING HIS LAST SONG!
JUST BREAK THE NEW-W-W-WS TO MOTH-ER!!
3-25
LISTEN! IT'S RUMPLEWATT, THE GIANT!
FEE FIE FO FUM, I SMELL THE BLOOD OF AN ENGLISHMUN!
GOOD--BYE-E-E-E FOR-EV-ER!
WALT DISNEY

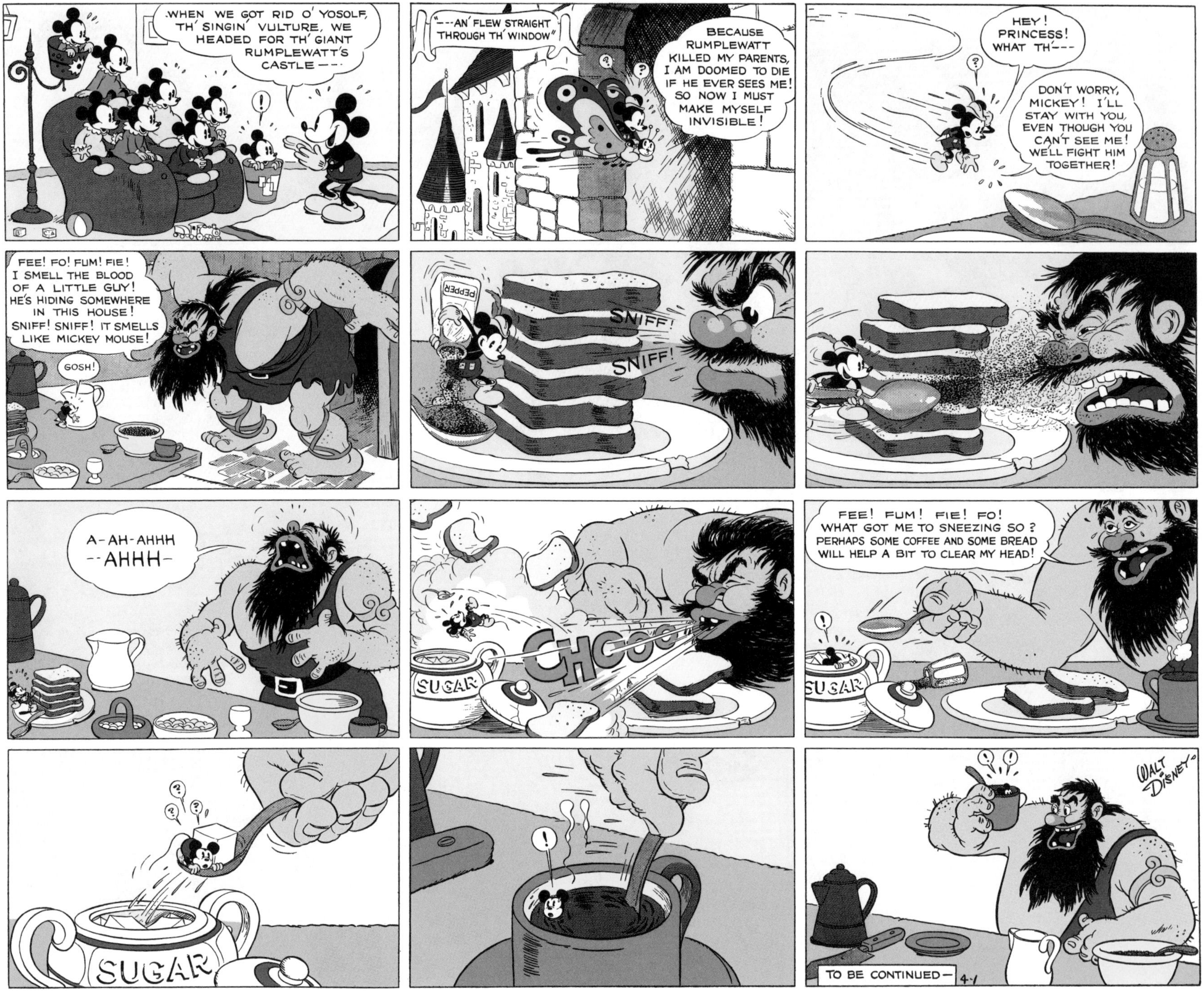

.WHEN WE GOT RID O' YOSOLF, TH' SINGIN' VULTURE, WE HEADED FOR TH' GIANT RUMPLEWATT'S CASTLE---
"---AN' FLEW STRAIGHT THROUGH TH' WINDOW"
BECAUSE RUMPLEWATT KILLED MY PARENTS, I AM DOOMED TO DIE IF HE EVER SEES ME! SO NOW I MUST MAKE MYSELF INVISIBLE!
HEY! PRINCESS! WHAT TH'---
DON'T WORRY, MICKEY! I'LL STAY WITH YOU, EVEN THOUGH YOU CAN'T SEE ME! WE'LL FIGHT HIM TOGETHER!
FEE! FO! FUM! FIE! I SMELL THE BLOOD OF A LITTLE GUY! HE'S HIDING SOMEWHERE IN THIS HOUSE! SNIFF! SNIFF! IT SMELLS LIKE MICKEY MOUSE!
GOSH!
PEPPER
SNIFF!
SNIFF!
A-AH-AHHH --AHHH-
CHOOO
SUGAR
FEE! FUM! FIE! FO! WHAT GOT ME TO SNEEZING SO? PERHAPS SOME COFFEE AND SOME BREAD WILL HELP A BIT TO CLEAR MY HEAD!
SUGAR
SUGAR
WALT DISNEY
TO BE CONTINUED— 4-1

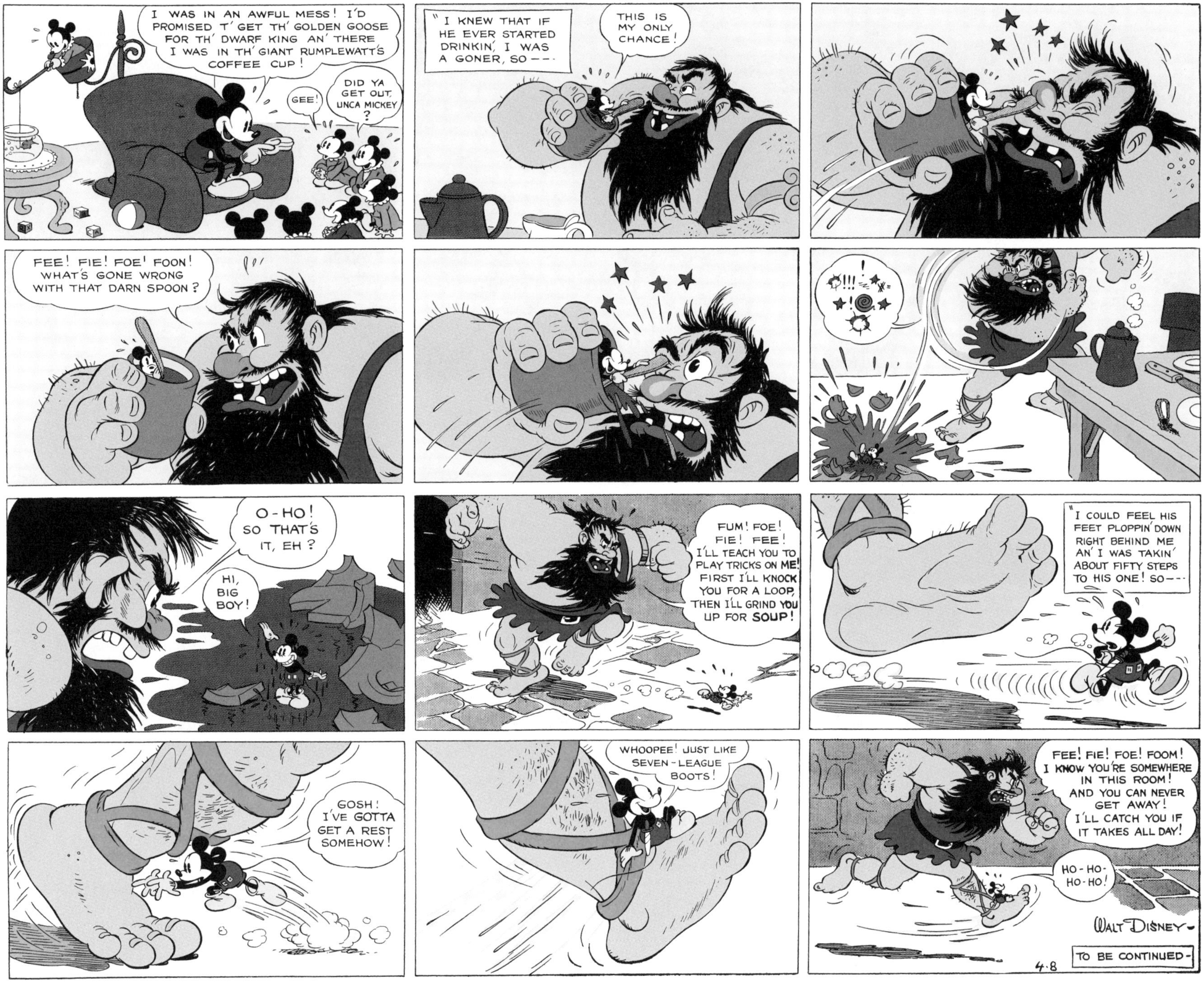
I WAS IN AN AWFUL MESS! I'D PROMISED T' GET TH' GOLDEN GOOSE FOR TH' DWARF KING AN' THERE I WAS IN TH' GIANT RUMPLEWATT'S COFFEE CUP!
GEE!
DID YA GET OUT, UNCA MICKEY?
"I KNEW THAT IF HE EVER STARTED DRINKIN', I WAS A GONER, SO---
THIS IS MY ONLY CHANCE!
FEE! FIE! FOE! FOON! WHAT'S GONE WRONG WITH THAT DARN SPOON?
O-HO! SO THAT'S IT, EH?
HI, BIG BOY!
FUM! FOE! FIE! FEE! I'LL TEACH YOU TO PLAY TRICKS ON ME! FIRST I'LL KNOCK YOU FOR A LOOP, THEN I'LL GRIND YOU UP FOR SOUP!
"I COULD FEEL HIS FEET PLOPPIN' DOWN RIGHT BEHIND ME AN' I WAS TAKIN' ABOUT FIFTY STEPS TO HIS ONE! SO---
GOSH! I'VE GOTTA GET A REST SOMEHOW!
WHOOPEE! JUST LIKE SEVEN-LEAGUE BOOTS!
FEE! FIE! FOE! FOOM! I KNOW YOU'RE SOMEWHERE IN THIS ROOM! AND YOU CAN NEVER GET AWAY! I'LL CATCH YOU IF IT TAKES ALL DAY!
HO-HO-HO-HO!
WALT DISNEY
TO BE CONTINUED
4-8

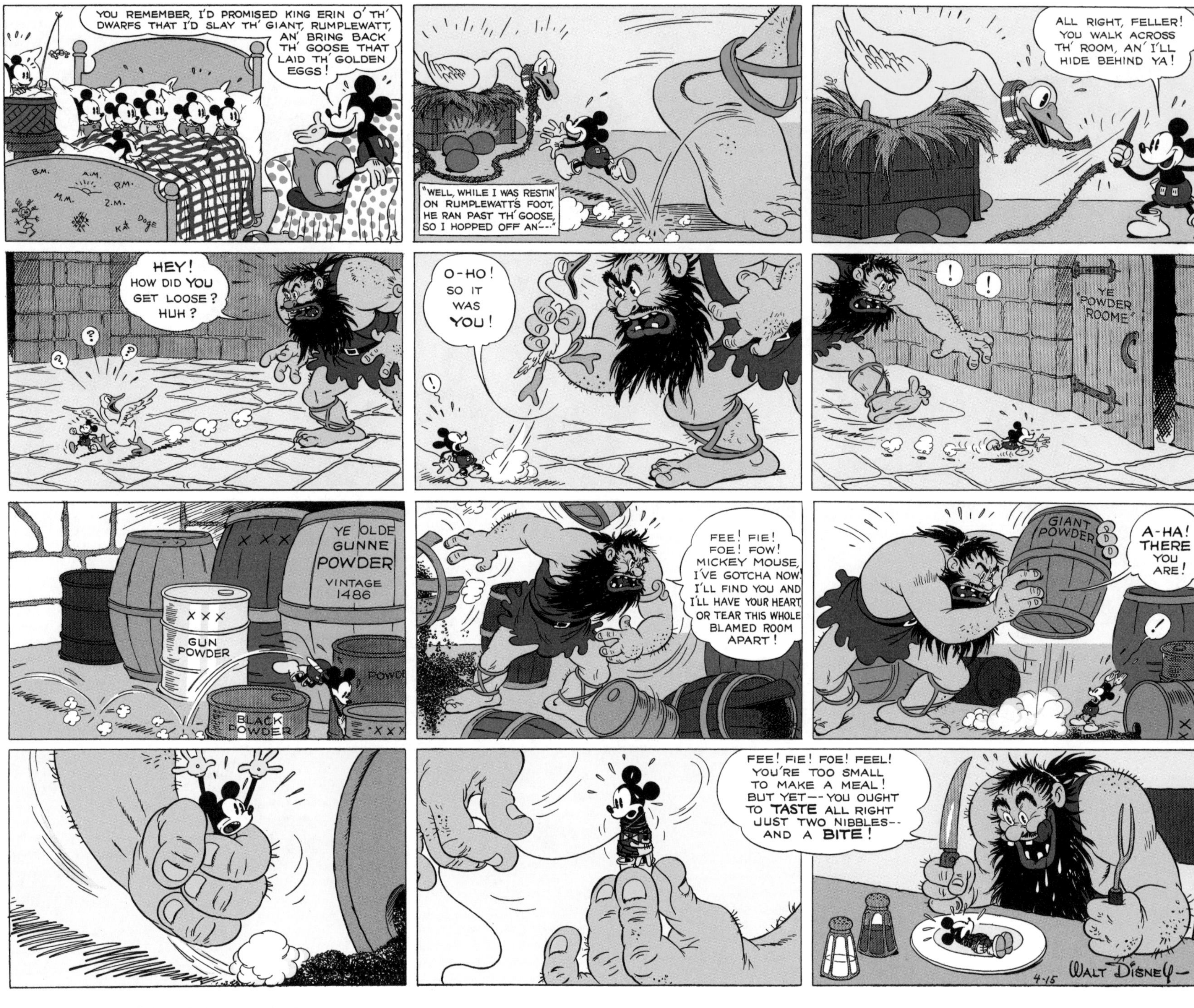
YOU REMEMBER, I'D PROMISED KING ERIN O' TH' DWARFS THAT I'D SLAY TH' GIANT, RUMPLEWATT, AN' BRING BACK TH' GOOSE THAT LAID TH' GOLDEN EGGS!
B.M.
A.M.
P.M.
M.M.
Z.M.
KAT
DOGE
"WELL, WHILE I WAS RESTIN' ON RUMPLEWATT'S FOOT, HE RAN PAST TH' GOOSE, SO I HOPPED OFF AN--"
ALL RIGHT, FELLER! YOU WALK ACROSS TH' ROOM, AN' I'LL HIDE BEHIND YA!
HEY! HOW DID YOU GET LOOSE? HUH?
O-HO! SO IT WAS YOU!
YE "POWDER ROOME"
YE OLDE GUNNE POWDER VINTAGE 1486
XXX
XXX GUN POWDER
BLACK POWDER
FEE! FIE! FOE! FOW! MICKEY MOUSE, I'VE GOTCHA NOW! I'LL FIND YOU AND I'LL HAVE YOUR HEART, OR TEAR THIS WHOLE BLAMED ROOM APART!
GIANT POWDER
A-HA! THERE YOU ARE!
FEE! FIE! FOE! FEEL! YOU'RE TOO SMALL TO MAKE A MEAL! BUT YET-- YOU OUGHT TO TASTE ALL RIGHT JUST TWO NIBBLES-- AND A BITE!
4-15
WALT DISNEY

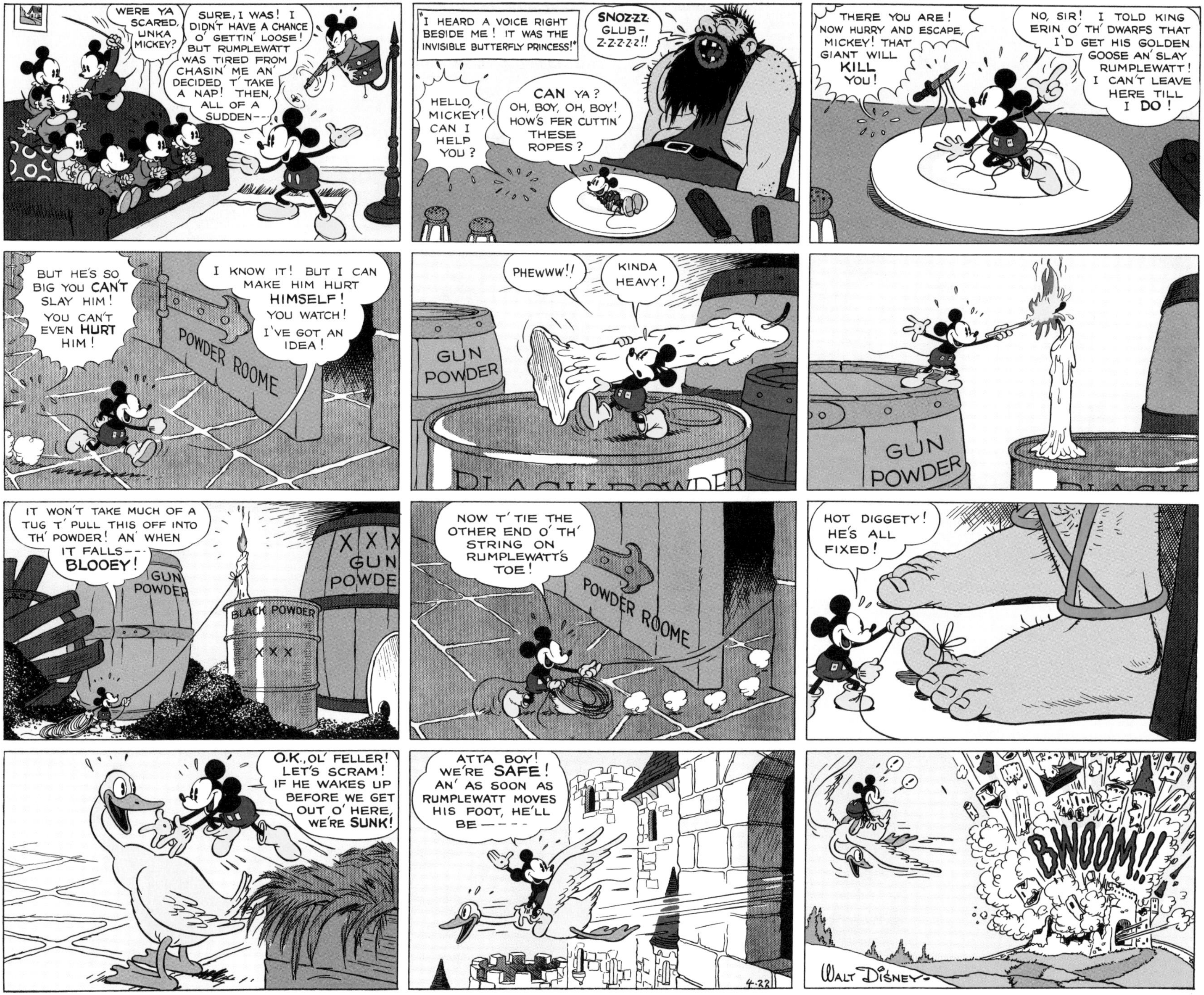
WERE YA SCARED, UNKA MICKEY?
SURE, I WAS! I DIDN'T HAVE A CHANCE O' GETTIN' LOOSE! BUT RUMPLEWATT WAS TIRED FROM CHASIN' ME AN' DECIDED T' TAKE A NAP! THEN, ALL OF A SUDDEN---
"I HEARD A VOICE RIGHT BESIDE ME! IT WAS THE INVISIBLE BUTTERFLY PRINCESS!"
SNOZZZ GLUB-Z-Z-Z-Z-Z!!
HELLO, MICKEY! CAN I HELP YOU?
CAN YA? OH, BOY, OH, BOY! HOW'S FER CUTTIN' THESE ROPES?
THERE YOU ARE! NOW HURRY AND ESCAPE, MICKEY! THAT GIANT WILL KILL YOU!
NO, SIR! I TOLD KING ERIN O' TH' DWARFS THAT I'D GET HIS GOLDEN GOOSE AN' SLAY RUMPLEWATT! I CAN'T LEAVE HERE TILL I DO!
BUT HE'S SO BIG YOU CAN'T SLAY HIM! YOU CAN'T EVEN HURT HIM!
I KNOW IT! BUT I CAN MAKE HIM HURT HIMSELF! YOU WATCH! I'VE GOT AN IDEA!
POWDER ROOME
PHEWWW!!
KINDA HEAVY!
GUN POWDER
GUN POWDER
IT WON'T TAKE MUCH OF A TUG T' PULL THIS OFF INTO TH' POWDER! AN' WHEN IT FALLS--- BLOOEY!
GUN POWDER
X X X GUN POWDE
BLACK POWDER
X X X
NOW T' TIE THE OTHER END O' TH' STRING ON RUMPLEWATT'S TOE!
POWDER ROOME
HOT DIGGETY! HE'S ALL FIXED!
O.K., OL' FELLER! LET'S SCRAM! IF HE WAKES UP BEFORE WE GET OUT O' HERE, WE'RE SUNK!
ATTA BOY! WE'RE SAFE! AN' AS SOON AS RUMPLEWATT MOVES HIS FOOT, HE'LL BE ----
4-22
BWOOM!!
WALT DISNEY

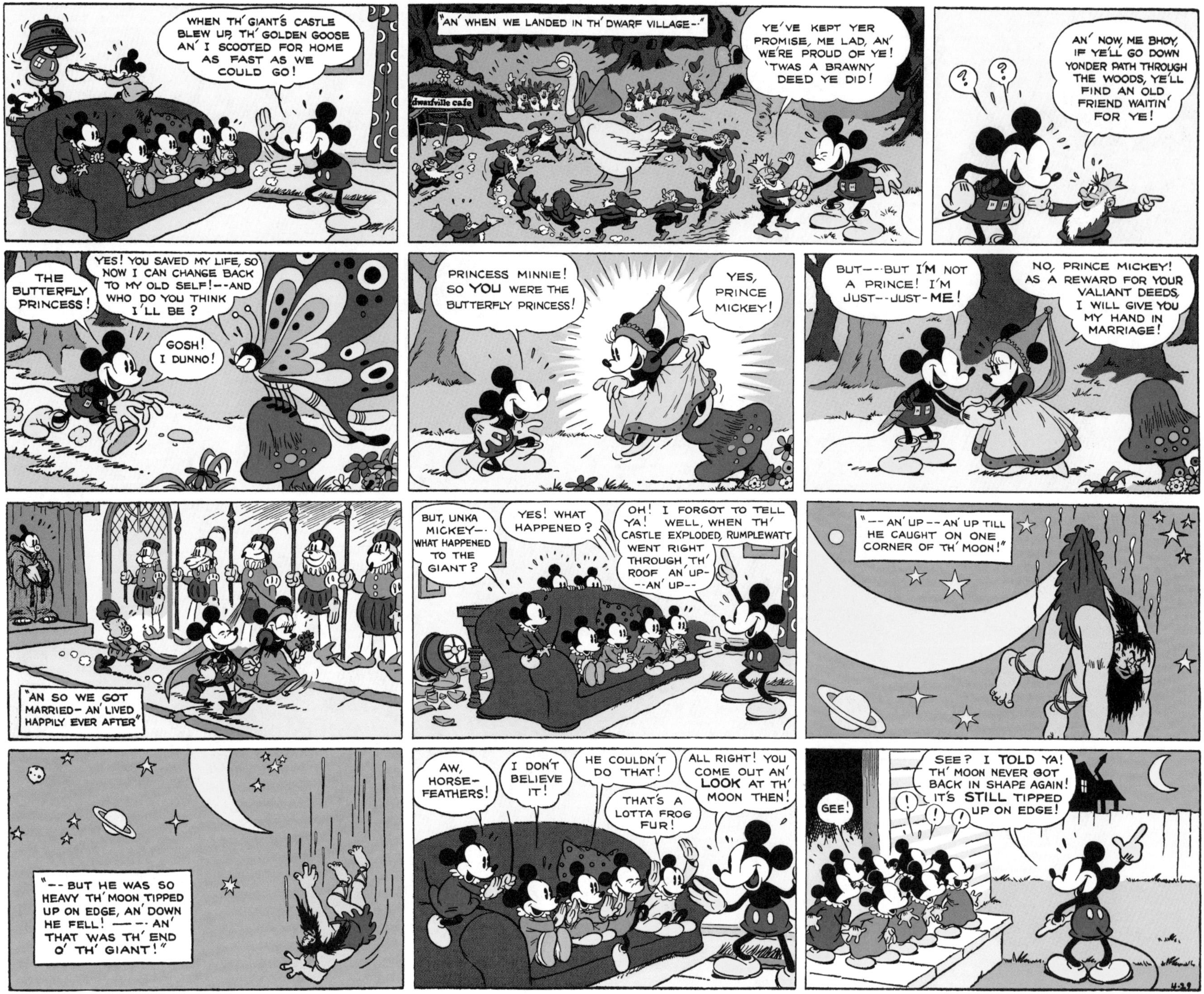
WHEN TH' GIANT'S CASTLE BLEW UP, TH' GOLDEN GOOSE AN' I SCOOTED FOR HOME AS FAST AS WE COULD GO!
"AN' WHEN WE LANDED IN TH' DWARF VILLAGE--"
dwarfville cafe
YE'VE KEPT YER PROMISE, ME LAD, AN' WE'RE PROUD OF YE! 'TWAS A BRAWNY DEED YE DID!
?
?
AN' NOW, ME BHOY, IF YE'LL GO DOWN YONDER PATH THROUGH THE WOODS, YE'LL FIND AN OLD FRIEND WAITIN' FOR YE!
THE BUTTERFLY PRINCESS!
YES! YOU SAVED MY LIFE, SO NOW I CAN CHANGE BACK TO MY OLD SELF!--AND WHO DO YOU THINK I'LL BE?
GOSH! I DUNNO!
PRINCESS MINNIE! SO YOU WERE THE BUTTERFLY PRINCESS!
YES, PRINCE MICKEY!
BUT---BUT I'M NOT A PRINCE! I'M JUST--JUST-ME!
NO, PRINCE MICKEY! AS A REWARD FOR YOUR VALIANT DEEDS, I WILL GIVE YOU MY HAND IN MARRIAGE!
"AN SO WE GOT MARRIED- AN' LIVED HAPPILY EVER AFTER"
BUT, UNKA MICKEY-- WHAT HAPPENED TO THE GIANT?
YES! WHAT HAPPENED?
OH! I FORGOT TO TELL YA! WELL, WHEN TH' CASTLE EXPLODED, RUMPLEWATT WENT RIGHT THROUGH TH' ROOF AN' UP- --AN' UP--
"--AN' UP--AN' UP TILL HE CAUGHT ON ONE CORNER OF TH' MOON!"
"--BUT HE WAS SO HEAVY TH' MOON TIPPED UP ON EDGE, AN' DOWN HE FELL! ---AN' THAT WAS TH' END O' TH' GIANT!"
AW, HORSE-FEATHERS!
I DON'T BELIEVE IT!
HE COULDN'T DO THAT!
THAT'S A LOTTA FROG FUR!
ALL RIGHT! YOU COME OUT AN' LOOK AT TH' MOON THEN!
GEE!
!
!
!
SEE? I TOLD YA! TH' MOON NEVER GOT BACK IN SHAPE AGAIN! IT'S STILL TIPPED UP ON EDGE!
4-29

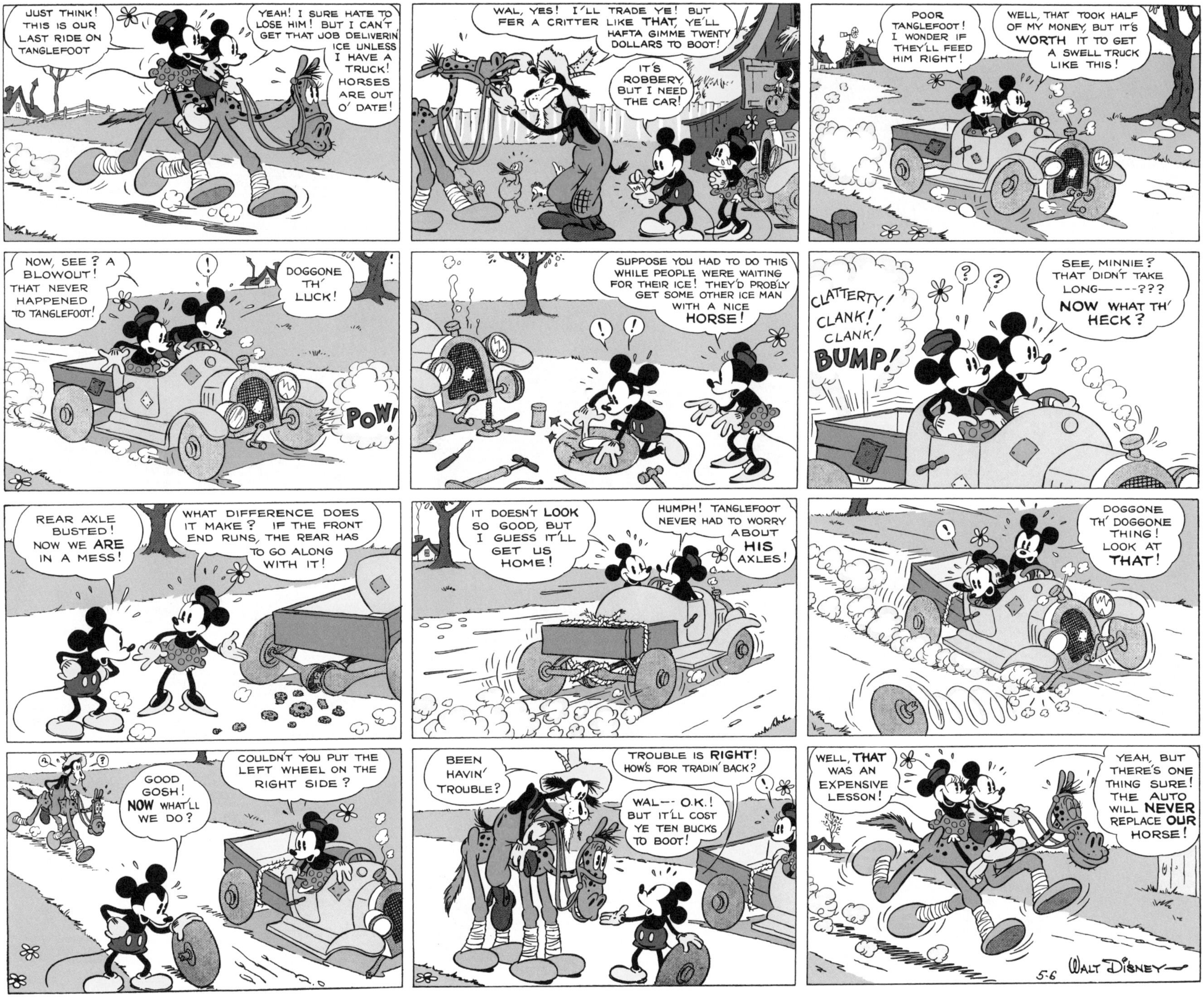
JUST THINK! THIS IS OUR LAST RIDE ON TANGLEFOOT!
YEAH! I SURE HATE TO LOSE HIM! BUT I CAN'T GET THAT JOB DELIVERIN' ICE UNLESS I HAVE A TRUCK! HORSES ARE OUT O' DATE!
WAL, YES! I'LL TRADE YE! BUT FER A CRITTER LIKE THAT, YE'LL HAFTA GIMME TWENTY DOLLARS TO BOOT!
IT'S ROBBERY, BUT I NEED THE CAR!
POOR TANGLEFOOT! I WONDER IF THEY'LL FEED HIM RIGHT!
WELL, THAT TOOK HALF OF MY MONEY, BUT IT'S WORTH IT TO GET A SWELL TRUCK LIKE THIS!
NOW, SEE? A BLOWOUT! THAT NEVER HAPPENED TO TANGLEFOOT!
DOGGONE TH' LUCK!
POW!
SUPPOSE YOU HAD TO DO THIS WHILE PEOPLE WERE WAITING FOR THEIR ICE! THEY'D PROB'LY GET SOME OTHER ICE MAN WITH A NICE HORSE!
CLATTERTY! CLANK! CLANK! BUMP!
SEE, MINNIE? THAT DIDN'T TAKE LONG----??? NOW WHAT TH' HECK?
REAR AXLE BUSTED! NOW WE ARE IN A MESS!
WHAT DIFFERENCE DOES IT MAKE? IF THE FRONT END RUNS, THE REAR HAS TO GO ALONG WITH IT!
IT DOESN'T LOOK SO GOOD, BUT I GUESS IT'LL GET US HOME!
HUMPH! TANGLEFOOT NEVER HAD TO WORRY ABOUT HIS AXLES!
DOGGONE TH' DOGGONE THING! LOOK AT THAT!
GOOD GOSH! NOW WHAT'LL WE DO?
COULDN'T YOU PUT THE LEFT WHEEL ON THE RIGHT SIDE?
BEEN HAVIN' TROUBLE?
TROUBLE IS RIGHT! HOW'S FOR TRADIN' BACK?
WAL-- O.K.! BUT IT'LL COST YE TEN BUCKS TO BOOT!
WELL, THAT WAS AN EXPENSIVE LESSON!
YEAH, BUT THERE'S ONE THING SURE! THE AUTO WILL NEVER REPLACE OUR HORSE!
5-6 WALT DISNEY

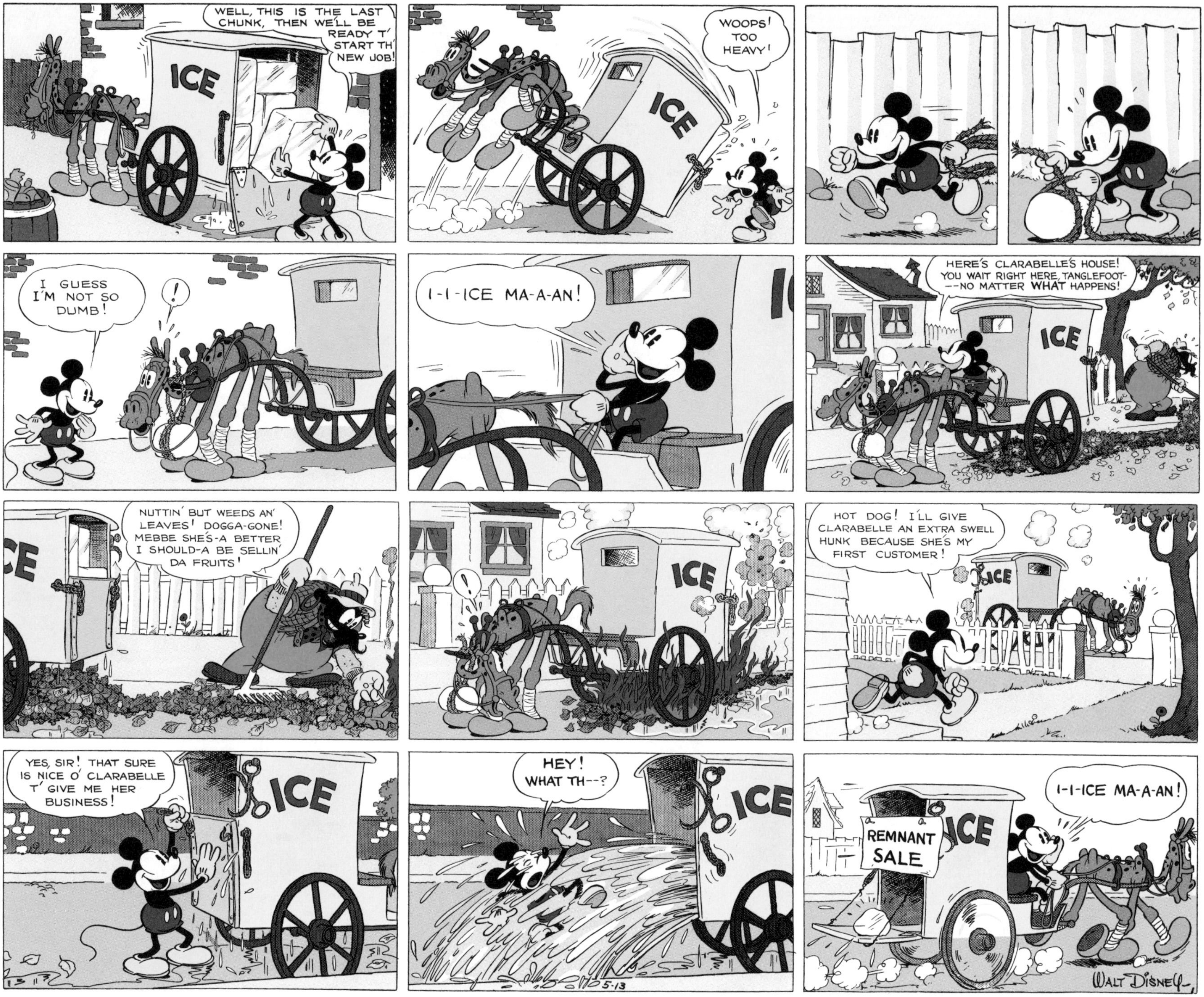
WELL, THIS IS THE LAST CHUNK, THEN WE'LL BE READY T' START TH' NEW JOB!
ICE
WOOPS! TOO HEAVY!
ICE
I GUESS I'M NOT SO DUMB!
!
I-I-ICE MA-A-AN!
HERE'S CLARABELLE'S HOUSE! YOU WAIT RIGHT HERE, TANGLEFOOT--NO MATTER WHAT HAPPENS!
ICE
NUTTIN' BUT WEEDS AN' LEAVES! DOGGA-GONE! MEBBE SHE'S-A BETTER I SHOULD-A BE SELLIN' DA FRUITS!
!
ICE
HOT DOG! I'LL GIVE CLARABELLE AN EXTRA SWELL HUNK BECAUSE SHE'S MY FIRST CUSTOMER!
ICE
YES, SIR! THAT SURE IS NICE O' CLARABELLE T' GIVE ME HER BUSINESS!
ICE
HEY! WHAT TH--?
ICE
5-13
I-I-ICE MA-A-AN!
REMNANT SALE
ICE
WALT DISNEY

148. TANGLEFOOT PULLS HIS WEIGHT

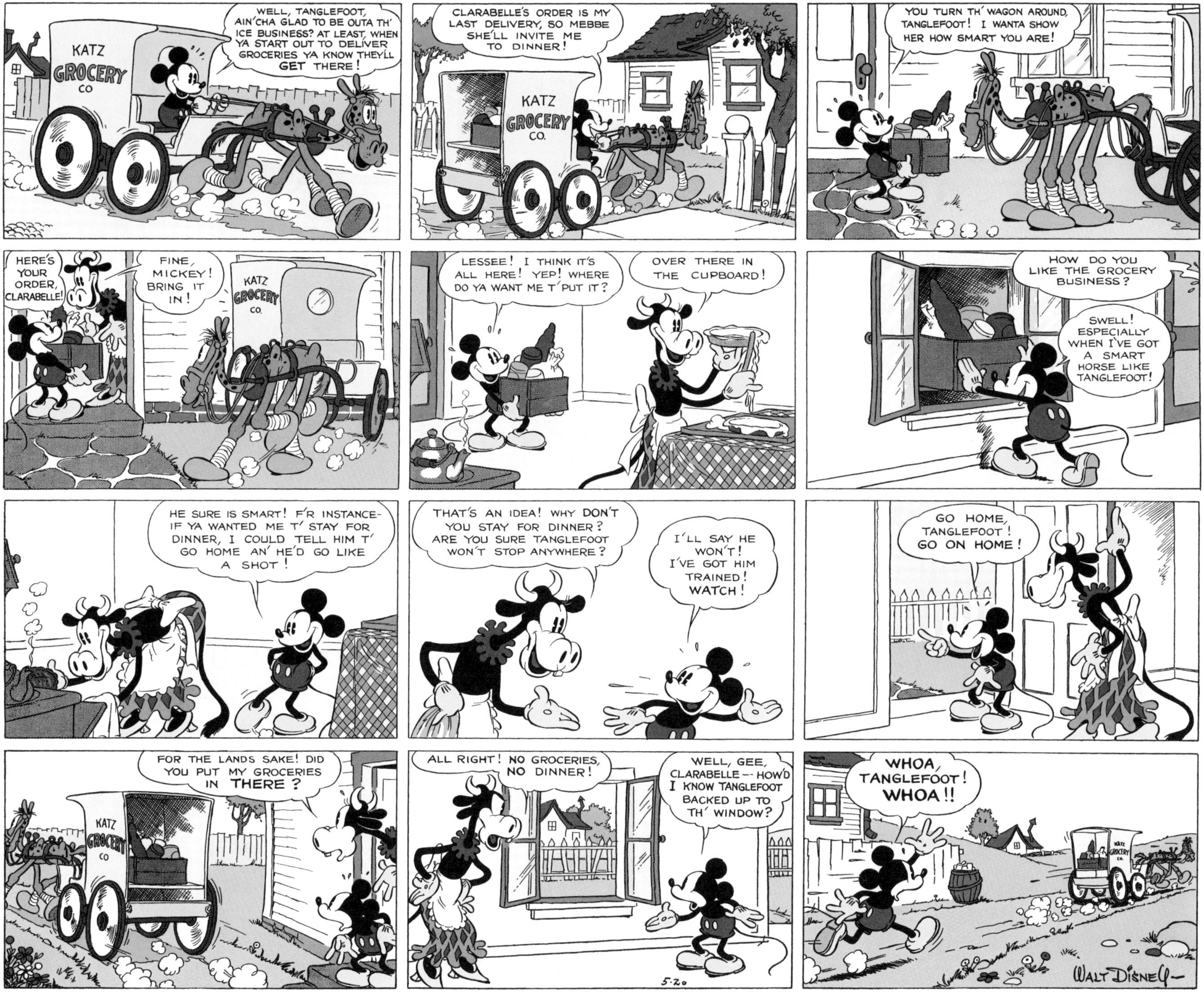
KATZ GROCERY CO
WELL, TANGLEFOOT, AIN'CHA GLAD TO BE OUTA TH' ICE BUSINESS? AT LEAST, WHEN YA START OUT TO DELIVER GROCERIES YA KNOW THEY'LL GET THERE!
CLARABELLE'S ORDER IS MY LAST DELIVERY, SO MEBBE SHE'LL INVITE ME TO DINNER!
KATZ GROCERY CO.
YOU TURN TH' WAGON AROUND, TANGLEFOOT! I WANTA SHOW HER HOW SMART YOU ARE!
HERE'S YOUR ORDER, CLARABELLE!
FINE, MICKEY! BRING IT IN!
KATZ GROCERY CO.
LESSEE! I THINK IT'S ALL HERE! YEP! WHERE DO YA WANT ME T' PUT IT?
OVER THERE IN THE CUPBOARD!
HOW DO YOU LIKE THE GROCERY BUSINESS?
SWELL! ESPECIALLY WHEN I'VE GOT A SMART HORSE LIKE TANGLEFOOT!
HE SURE IS SMART! F'R INSTANCE- IF YA WANTED ME T' STAY FOR DINNER, I COULD TELL HIM T' GO HOME AN' HE'D GO LIKE A SHOT!
THAT'S AN IDEA! WHY DON'T YOU STAY FOR DINNER? ARE YOU SURE TANGLEFOOT WON'T STOP ANYWHERE?
I'LL SAY HE WON'T! I'VE GOT HIM TRAINED! WATCH!
GO HOME, TANGLEFOOT! GO ON HOME!
FOR THE LANDS SAKE! DID YOU PUT MY GROCERIES IN THERE?
KATZ GROCERY CO
ALL RIGHT! NO GROCERIES, NO DINNER!
WELL, GEE, CLARABELLE-- HOW'D I KNOW TANGLEFOOT BACKED UP TO TH' WINDOW?
5-20
WHOA, TANGLEFOOT! WHOA!!
KATZ GROCERY CO.
WALT DISNEY

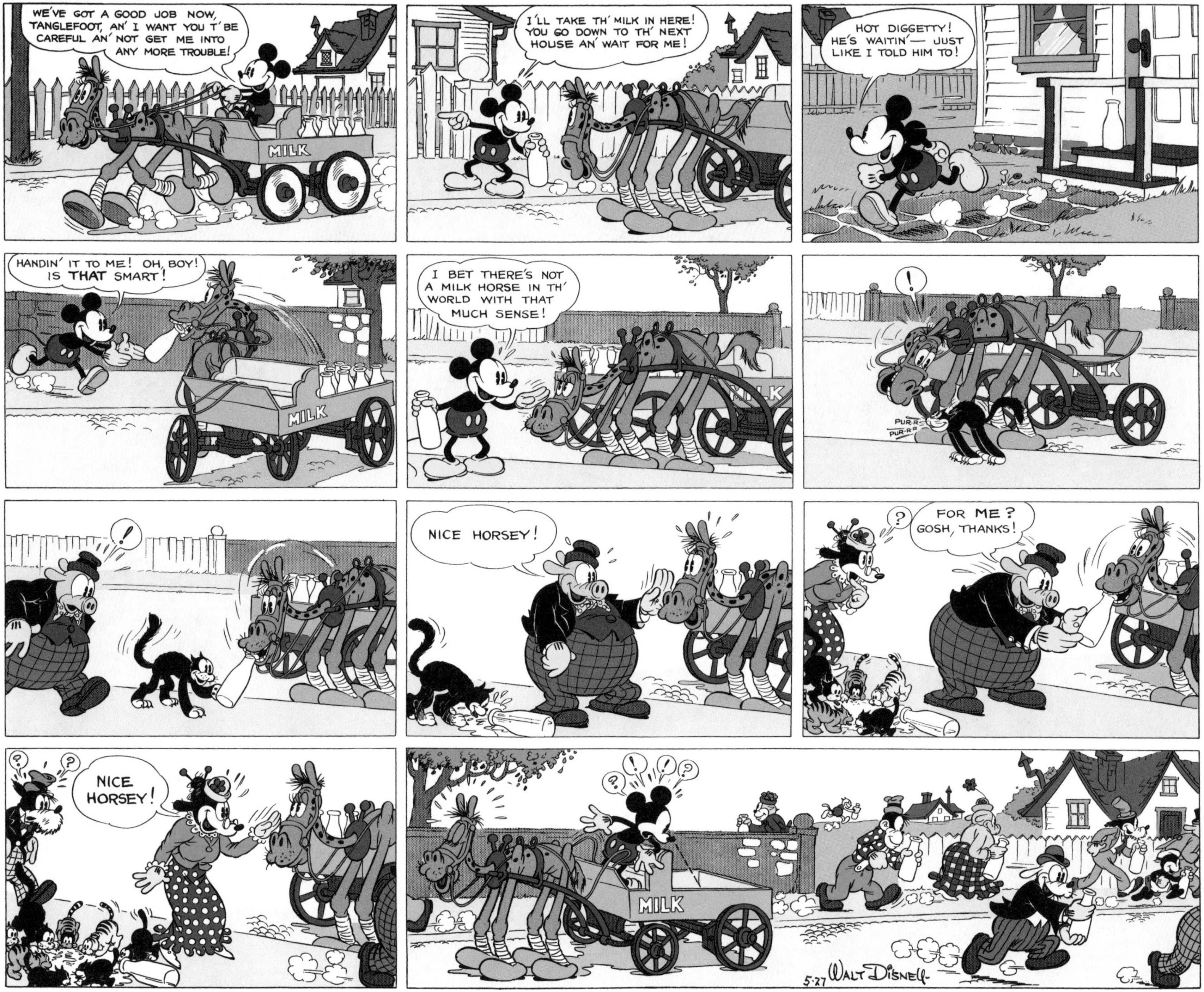
WE'VE GOT A GOOD JOB NOW, TANGLEFOOT, AN' I WANT YOU T' BE CAREFUL AN' NOT GET ME INTO ANY MORE TROUBLE!
MILK
I'LL TAKE TH' MILK IN HERE! YOU GO DOWN TO TH' NEXT HOUSE AN' WAIT FOR ME!
HOT DIGGETTY! HE'S WAITIN'— JUST LIKE I TOLD HIM TO!
HANDIN' IT TO ME! OH, BOY! IS THAT SMART!
MILK
I BET THERE'S NOT A MILK HORSE IN TH' WORLD WITH THAT MUCH SENSE!
MILK
!
PUR-R-R PUR-R-R
MILK
!
NICE HORSEY!
?
FOR ME? GOSH, THANKS!
NICE HORSEY!
MILK
5·27 WALT DISNEY

150. TANGLEFOOT PULLS HIS WEIGHT

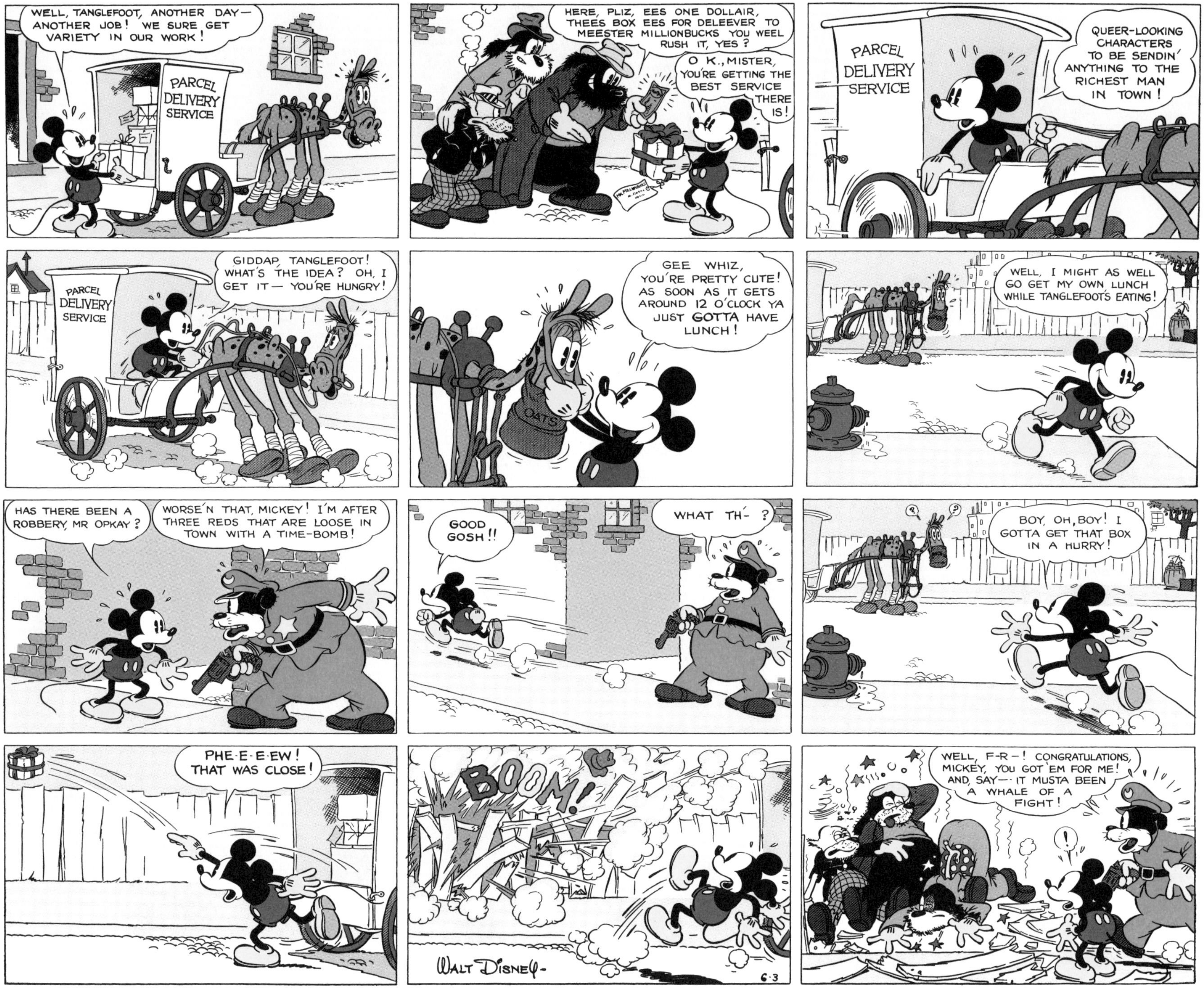
WELL, TANGLEFOOT, ANOTHER DAY— ANOTHER JOB! WE SURE GET VARIETY IN OUR WORK!
PARCEL DELIVERY SERVICE
HERE, PLIZ, EES ONE DOLLAIR, THEES BOX EES FOR DELEEVER TO MEESTER MILLIONBUCKS YOU WEEL RUSH IT, YES?
O K., MISTER, YOU'RE GETTING THE BEST SERVICE THERE IS!
PARCEL DELIVERY SERVICE
QUEER-LOOKING CHARACTERS TO BE SENDIN' ANYTHING TO THE RICHEST MAN IN TOWN!
PARCEL DELIVERY SERVICE
GIDDAP, TANGLEFOOT! WHAT'S THE IDEA? OH, I GET IT— YOU'RE HUNGRY!
OATS
GEE WHIZ, YOU'RE PRETTY CUTE! AS SOON AS IT GETS AROUND 12 O'CLOCK YA JUST GOTTA HAVE LUNCH!
WELL, I MIGHT AS WELL GO GET MY OWN LUNCH WHILE TANGLEFOOT'S EATING!
HAS THERE BEEN A ROBBERY, MR OPKAY?
WORSE'N THAT, MICKEY! I'M AFTER THREE REDS THAT ARE LOOSE IN TOWN WITH A TIME-BOMB!
GOOD GOSH!!
WHAT TH- ?
BOY, OH, BOY! I GOTTA GET THAT BOX IN A HURRY!
PHE-E-E-EW! THAT WAS CLOSE!
BOOM!
WALT DISNEY
6·3
WELL, F-R-! CONGRATULATIONS, MICKEY, YOU GOT 'EM FOR ME! AND, SAY— IT MUSTA BEEN A WHALE OF A FIGHT!

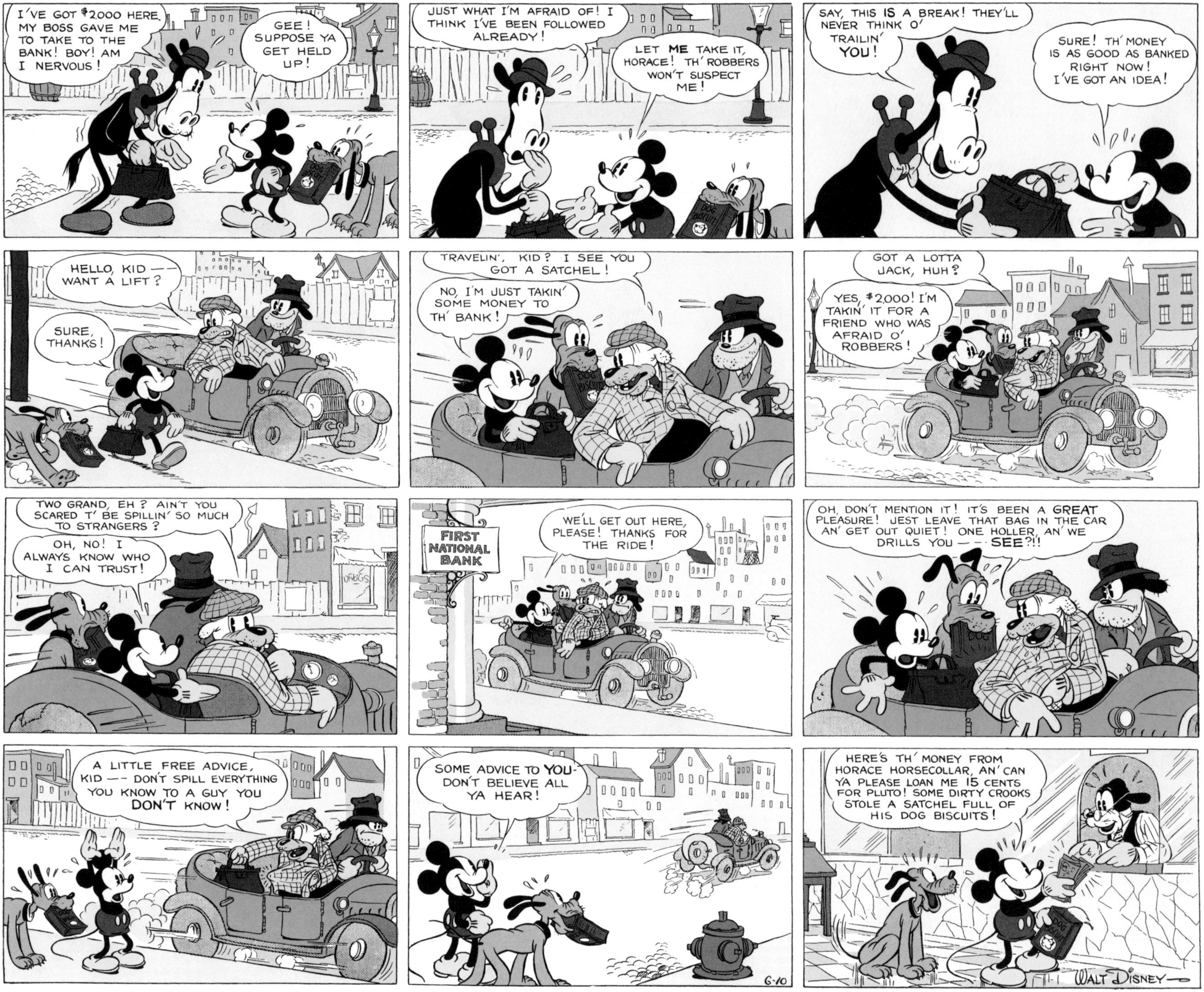
I'VE GOT $2000 HERE. MY BOSS GAVE ME TO TAKE TO THE BANK! BOY! AM I NERVOUS!
GEE! SUPPOSE YA GET HELD UP!
JUST WHAT I'M AFRAID OF! I THINK I'VE BEEN FOLLOWED ALREADY!
LET ME TAKE IT, HORACE! TH' ROBBERS WON'T SUSPECT ME!
SAY, THIS IS A BREAK! THEY'LL NEVER THINK O' TRAILIN' YOU!
SURE! TH' MONEY IS AS GOOD AS BANKED RIGHT NOW! I'VE GOT AN IDEA!
HELLO, KID — WANT A LIFT?
SURE, THANKS!
TRAVELIN', KID? I SEE YOU GOT A SATCHEL!
NO, I'M JUST TAKIN' SOME MONEY TO TH' BANK!
GOT A LOTTA JACK, HUH?
YES, $2,000! I'M TAKIN' IT FOR A FRIEND WHO WAS AFRAID O' ROBBERS!
TWO GRAND, EH? AIN'T YOU SCARED T' BE SPILLIN' SO MUCH TO STRANGERS?
OH, NO! I ALWAYS KNOW WHO I CAN TRUST!
DRUGS
FIRST NATIONAL BANK
WE'LL GET OUT HERE, PLEASE! THANKS FOR THE RIDE!
OH, DON'T MENTION IT! IT'S BEEN A GREAT PLEASURE! JUST LEAVE THAT BAG IN THE CAR AN' GET OUT QUIET! ONE HOLLER, AN' WE DRILLS YOU — — SEE?!!
A LITTLE FREE ADVICE, KID — DON'T SPILL EVERYTHING YOU KNOW TO A GUY YOU DON'T KNOW!
SOME ADVICE TO YOU- DON'T BELIEVE ALL YA HEAR!
6-10
HERE'S TH' MONEY FROM HORACE HORSECOLLAR, AN' CAN YA PLEASE LOAN ME 15 CENTS FOR PLUTO! SOME DIRTY CROOKS STOLE A SATCHEL FULL OF HIS DOG BISCUITS!
WALT DISNEY

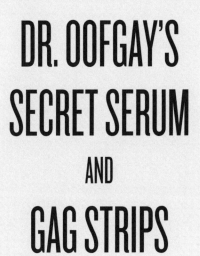

DR. OOFGAY'S
SECRET SERUM
AND
GAG STRIPS

JUNE 17, 1934

–

DECEMBER 2, 1934

MICKEY MOUSE
REGISTERED U.S. PATENT OFFICE

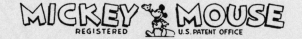

CALL OF THE WILD

Ah, anthropomorphism; how we take you for granted! The attribution of human characteristics to animals far predates the art of print and animated cartooning, but perhaps found its greatest sanctuary at the Walt Disney Studio. How many times have you heard people questioning why Mickey *Mouse* owns Pluto, a full-sized dog? Or: "Why does Goofy get to drive a car, while Pluto has to sleep outside, if they're both dogs?" To paraphrase *Mystery Science Theater 3000*, the answer is: "It's just a cartoon—relax."

Our cover story would not dare be so blasé. In "Dr. Oofgay's Secret Serum," we are only introduced to the titular mad scientist deep into the thirteen-week continuity. During the gang's camping trip to Dusty Lake, Mickey and Minnie stumble upon a mountain lion who is mysteriously "gentle as a lamb." After seven weeks of gags involving genuine, often dangerous wild animals, the reader would not be satisfied with simple cartoon license as an explanation. Enter Dr. Oofgay, who reveals that the lion has been given one of his marvelous serums. One chemical compound will tame even the wildest animal; the other will revert the beast to its wild state. Horace Horsecollar accidentally sits on the doctor's "wild" needle and becomes a rowdy, uncivilized brute. Of course, Clarabelle Cow—depending on her mood—might argue that there is little difference either way.

And that brings us to the real centerpiece of this very funny story: the dynamic between Horace and Clarabelle, a couple whose everyday routine normally involves a feigned damsel-in-distress act and an inept rescue attempt. The Horace-Clarabelle relationship was one of Floyd Gottfredson's funnier creations in the first half of the 1930s, a time when he helmed a strong supporting cast that would later prove interesting and workable in stories sans Mickey.

While in later years, Goofy has often posed as a suitor for Clarabelle, it has always been clear that the pompous, know-it-all "jackass" Horsecollar was made for the vain, gossipy bovine. During their darkest hours—as when Horace, hypnotized by Oofgay's serum, is howling at the moon—Clarabelle is the only person to voice genuine concern about her "poor Horace" and what a "noble character" he once was.

One might say Clarabelle and Horace are Ethel and Fred to Minnie and Mickey's Lucy and Desi, if the mice ever exhibited such rowdiness and energy. But doesn't Horace and Clarabelle's sheer instability more than make up for anyone else's normalcy?

— THAD KOMOROWSKI

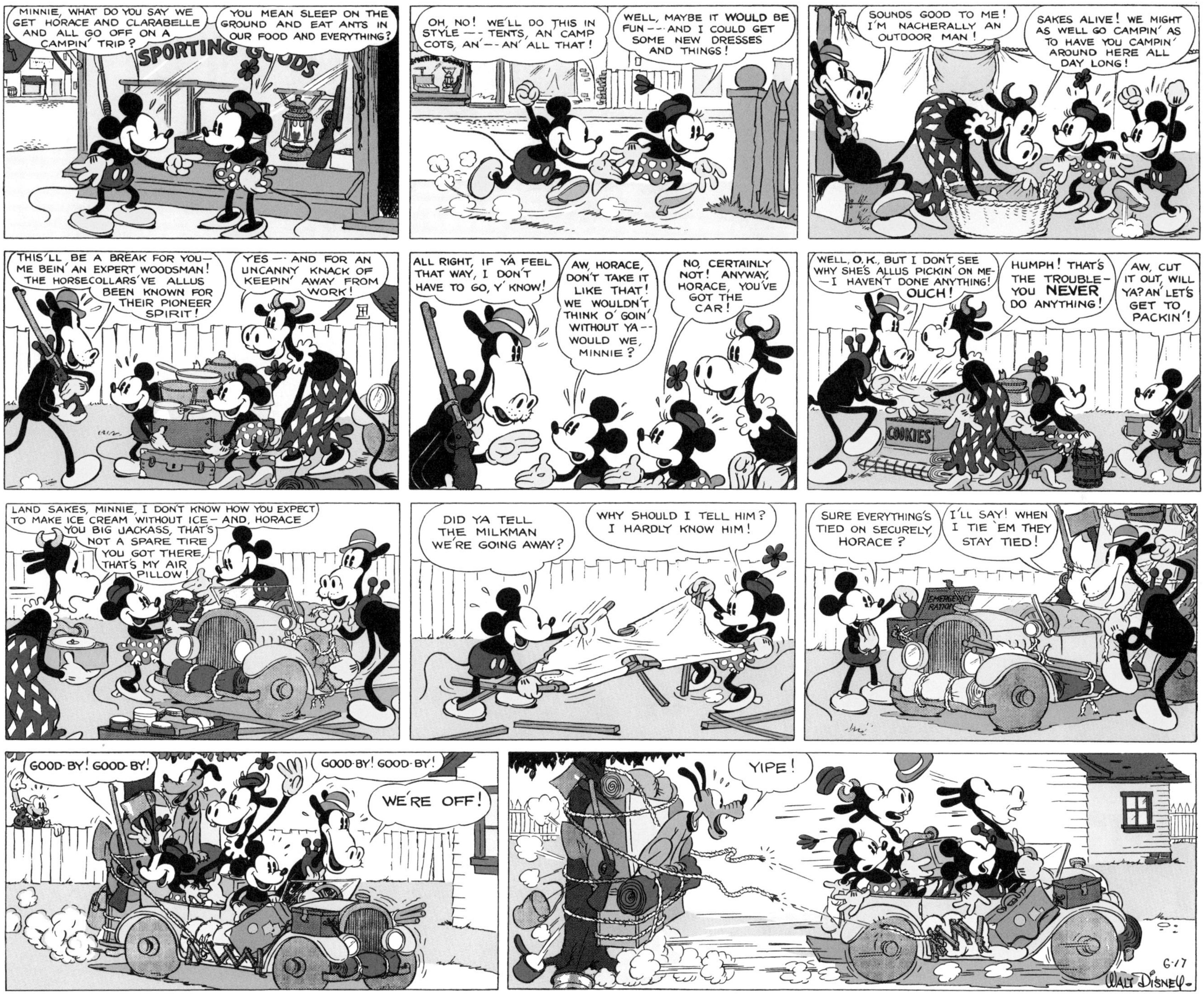

MINNIE, WHAT DO YOU SAY WE GET HORACE AND CLARABELLE AND ALL GO OFF ON A CAMPIN' TRIP?
YOU MEAN SLEEP ON THE GROUND AND EAT ANTS IN OUR FOOD AND EVERYTHING?
SPORTING GOODS
OH, NO! WE'LL DO THIS IN STYLE -- TENTS, AN CAMP COTS, AN'-- AN' ALL THAT!
WELL, MAYBE IT WOULD BE FUN -- AND I COULD GET SOME NEW DRESSES AND THINGS!
SOUNDS GOOD TO ME! I'M NACHERALLY AN OUTDOOR MAN!
SAKES ALIVE! WE MIGHT AS WELL GO CAMPIN' AS TO HAVE YOU CAMPIN' AROUND HERE ALL DAY LONG!
THIS'LL BE A BREAK FOR YOU— ME BEIN' AN EXPERT WOODSMAN! THE HORSECOLLARS'VE ALLUS BEEN KNOWN FOR THEIR PIONEER SPIRIT!
YES— AND FOR AN UNCANNY KNACK OF KEEPIN' AWAY FROM WORK!
ALL RIGHT, IF YA FEEL THAT WAY, I DON'T HAVE TO GO, Y'KNOW!
AW, HORACE, DON'T TAKE IT LIKE THAT! WE WOULDN'T THINK O' GOIN' WITHOUT YA-- WOULD WE, MINNIE?
NO, CERTAINLY NOT! ANYWAY, HORACE, YOU'VE GOT THE CAR!
WELL, O.K., BUT I DON'T SEE WHY SHE'S ALLUS PICKIN' ON ME— I HAVEN'T DONE ANYTHING! OUCH!
HUMPH! THAT'S THE TROUBLE— YOU NEVER DO ANYTHING!
AW, CUT IT OUT, WILL YA? AN' LET'S GET TO PACKIN'!
COOKIES
LAND SAKES, MINNIE, I DON'T KNOW HOW YOU EXPECT TO MAKE ICE CREAM WITHOUT ICE— AND, HORACE YOU BIG JACKASS, THAT'S NOT A SPARE TIRE YOU GOT THERE, THAT'S MY AIR PILLOW!
DID YA TELL THE MILKMAN WE'RE GOING AWAY?
WHY SHOULD I TELL HIM? I HARDLY KNOW HIM!
SURE EVERYTHING'S TIED ON SECURELY, HORACE?
I'LL SAY! WHEN I TIE 'EM THEY STAY TIED!
GOOD-BY! GOOD-BY!
GOOD-BY! GOOD-BY!
WE'RE OFF!
YIPE!
6-17
WALT DISNEY

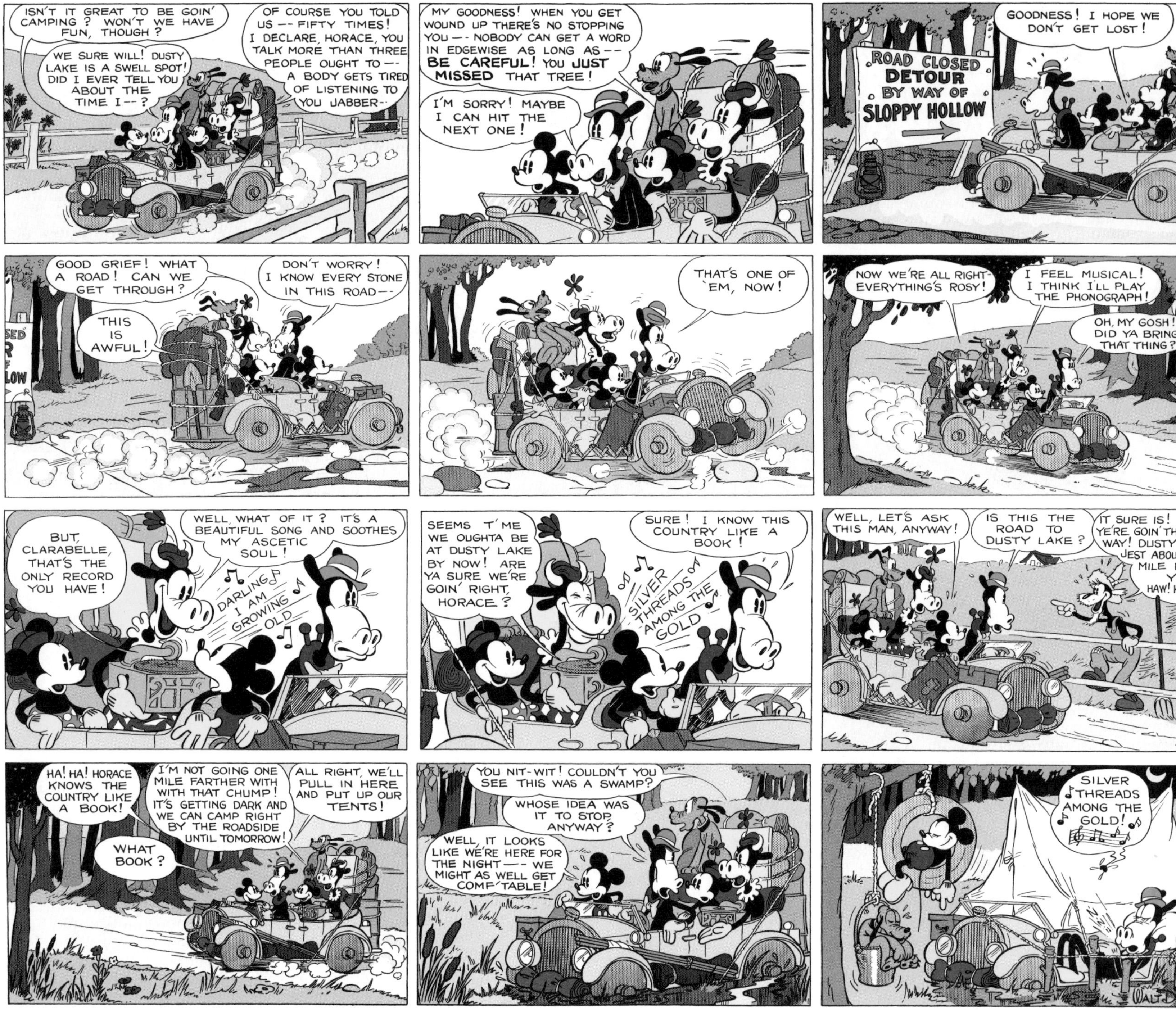

ISN'T IT GREAT TO BE GOIN' CAMPING? WON'T WE HAVE FUN, THOUGH?
WE SURE WILL! DUSTY LAKE IS A SWELL SPOT! DID I EVER TELL YOU ABOUT THE TIME I--?
OF COURSE YOU TOLD US -- FIFTY TIMES! I DECLARE, HORACE, YOU TALK MORE THAN THREE PEOPLE OUGHT TO -- A BODY GETS TIRED OF LISTENING TO YOU JABBER--
MY GOODNESS! WHEN YOU GET WOUND UP THERE'S NO STOPPING YOU -- NOBODY CAN GET A WORD IN EDGEWISE AS LONG AS -- BE CAREFUL! YOU JUST MISSED THAT TREE!
I'M SORRY! MAYBE I CAN HIT THE NEXT ONE!
ROAD CLOSED
DETOUR
BY WAY OF
SLOPPY HOLLOW
GOODNESS! I HOPE WE DON'T GET LOST!
GOOD GRIEF! WHAT A ROAD! CAN WE GET THROUGH?
DON'T WORRY! I KNOW EVERY STONE IN THIS ROAD--
THIS IS AWFUL!
THAT'S ONE OF 'EM, NOW!
NOW WE'RE ALL RIGHT-EVERYTHING'S ROSY!
I FEEL MUSICAL! I THINK I'LL PLAY THE PHONOGRAPH!
OH, MY GOSH! DID YA BRING THAT THING?
6-24
BUT, CLARABELLE, THAT'S THE ONLY RECORD YOU HAVE!
WELL, WHAT OF IT? IT'S A BEAUTIFUL SONG AND SOOTHES MY ASCETIC SOUL!
DARLING I AM GROWING OLD
SEEMS T' ME WE OUGHTA BE AT DUSTY LAKE BY NOW! ARE YA SURE WE'RE GOIN' RIGHT, HORACE?
SURE! I KNOW THIS COUNTRY LIKE A BOOK!
SILVER THREADS AMONG THE GOLD
WELL, LET'S ASK THIS MAN, ANYWAY!
IS THIS THE ROAD TO DUSTY LAKE?
IT SURE IS! ONLY YE'RE GOIN' TH' WRONG WAY! DUSTY LAKE'S JEST ABOUT NINETY MILE BEHIND YE! HAW! HAW! HAW!
HA! HA! HORACE KNOWS THE COUNTRY LIKE A BOOK!
WHAT BOOK?
I'M NOT GOING ONE MILE FARTHER WITH WITH THAT CHUMP! IT'S GETTING DARK AND WE CAN CAMP RIGHT BY THE ROADSIDE UNTIL TOMORROW!
ALL RIGHT, WE'LL PULL IN HERE AND PUT UP OUR TENTS!
YOU NIT-WIT! COULDN'T YOU SEE THIS WAS A SWAMP?
WHOSE IDEA WAS IT TO STOP ANYWAY?
WELL, IT LOOKS LIKE WE'RE HERE FOR THE NIGHT -- WE MIGHT AS WELL GET COMF'TABLE!
SILVER THREADS AMONG THE GOLD!
WALT DISNEY

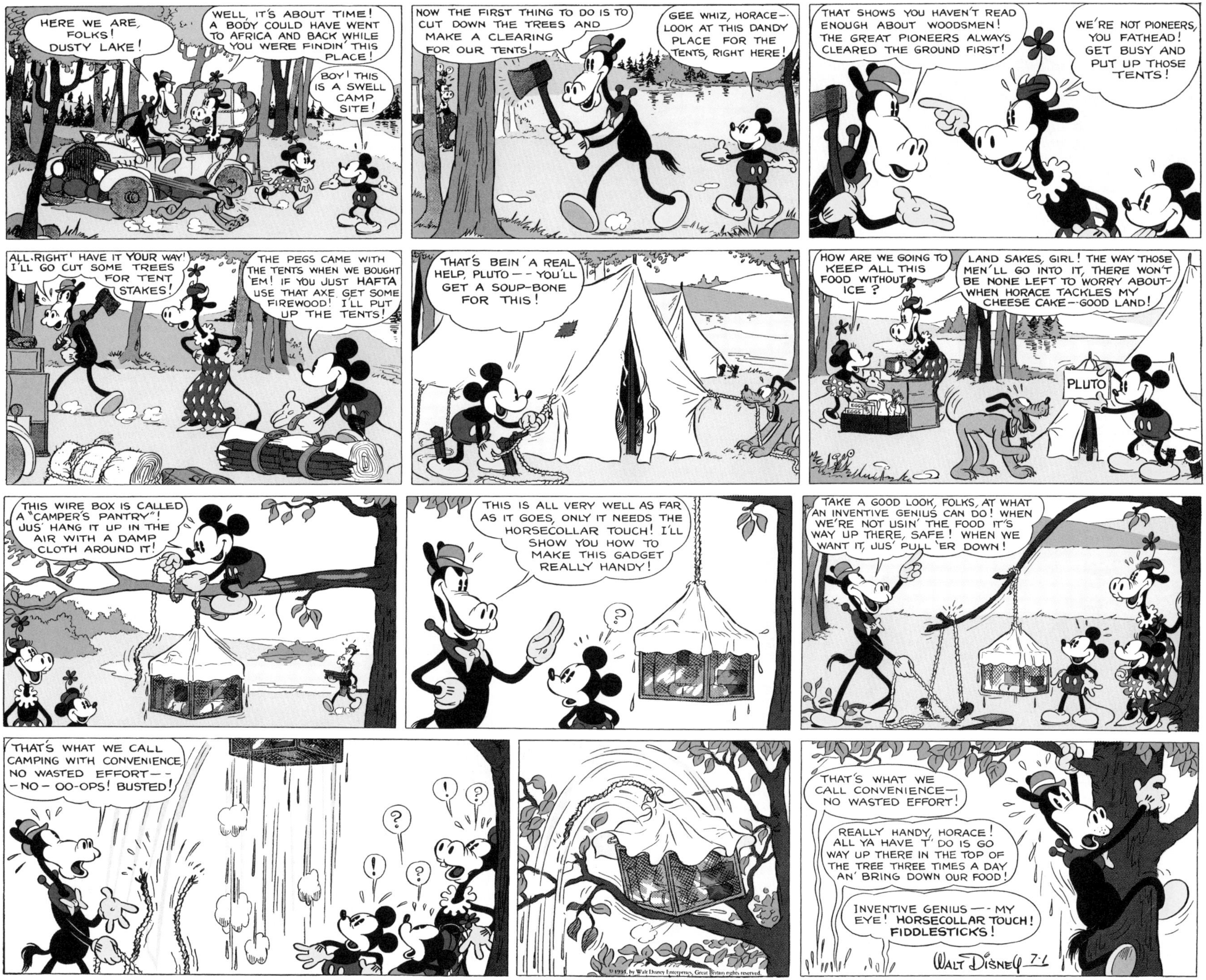
HERE WE ARE, FOLKS! DUSTY LAKE!
WELL, IT'S ABOUT TIME! A BODY COULD HAVE WENT TO AFRICA AND BACK WHILE YOU WERE FINDIN' THIS PLACE!
BOY! THIS IS A SWELL CAMP SITE!
NOW THE FIRST THING TO DO IS TO CUT DOWN THE TREES AND MAKE A CLEARING FOR OUR TENTS!
GEE WHIZ, HORACE— LOOK AT THIS DANDY PLACE FOR THE TENTS, RIGHT HERE!
THAT SHOWS YOU HAVEN'T READ ENOUGH ABOUT WOODSMEN! THE GREAT PIONEERS ALWAYS CLEARED THE GROUND FIRST!
WE'RE NOT PIONEERS, YOU FATHEAD! GET BUSY AND PUT UP THOSE TENTS!
ALL RIGHT! HAVE IT YOUR WAY! I'LL GO CUT SOME TREES FOR TENT STAKES!
THE PEGS CAME WITH THE TENTS WHEN WE BOUGHT 'EM! IF YOU JUST HAFTA USE THAT AXE, GET SOME FIREWOOD! I'LL PUT UP THE TENTS!
THAT'S BEIN' A REAL HELP, PLUTO — — YOU'LL GET A SOUP-BONE FOR THIS!
HOW ARE WE GOING TO KEEP ALL THIS FOOD WITHOUT ICE ?
LAND SAKES, GIRL! THE WAY THOSE MEN'LL GO INTO IT, THERE WON'T BE NONE LEFT TO WORRY ABOUT— WHEN HORACE TACKLES MY CHEESE CAKE — GOOD LAND!
PLUTO
THIS WIRE BOX IS CALLED A "CAMPER'S PANTRY"! JUS' HANG IT UP IN THE AIR WITH A DAMP CLOTH AROUND IT!
THIS IS ALL VERY WELL AS FAR AS IT GOES, ONLY IT NEEDS THE HORSECOLLAR TOUCH! I'LL SHOW YOU HOW TO MAKE THIS GADGET REALLY HANDY!
?
TAKE A GOOD LOOK, FOLKS, AT WHAT AN INVENTIVE GENIUS CAN DO! WHEN WE'RE NOT USIN' THE FOOD IT'S WAY UP THERE, SAFE! WHEN WE WANT IT, JUS' PULL 'ER DOWN!
THAT'S WHAT WE CALL CAMPING WITH CONVENIENCE, NO WASTED EFFORT— — NO — OO-OPS! BUSTED!
! ? ? ! ?
THAT'S WHAT WE CALL CONVENIENCE— NO WASTED EFFORT!
REALLY HANDY, HORACE! ALL YA HAVE T' DO IS GO WAY UP THERE IN THE TOP OF THE TREE THREE TIMES A DAY AN' BRING DOWN OUR FOOD!
INVENTIVE GENIUS — — MY EYE! HORSECOLLAR TOUCH! FIDDLESTICKS!
WALT DISNEY 7-1

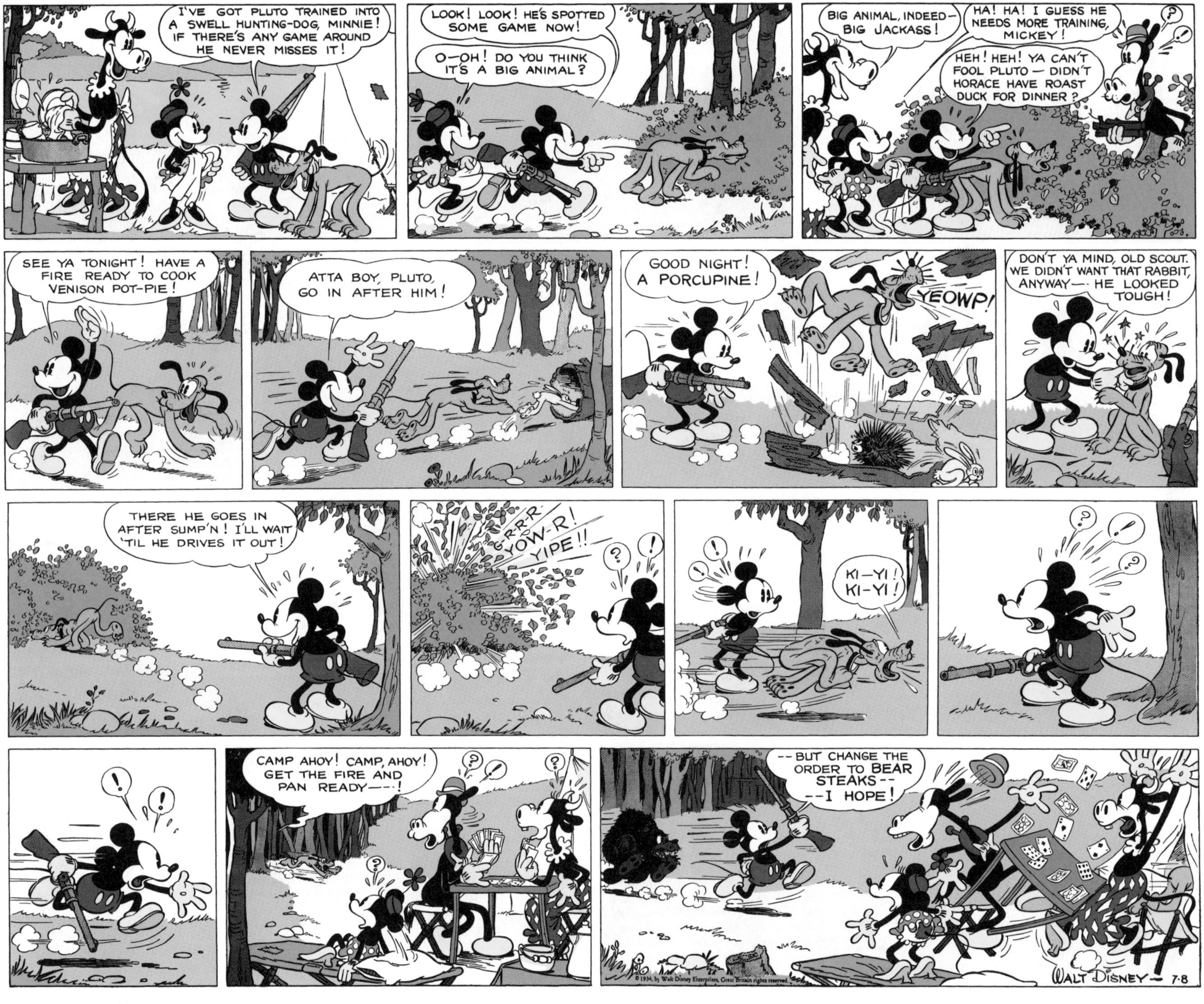
I'VE GOT PLUTO TRAINED INTO A SWELL HUNTING-DOG, MINNIE! IF THERE'S ANY GAME AROUND HE NEVER MISSES IT!
LOOK! LOOK! HE'S SPOTTED SOME GAME NOW!
O-OH! DO YOU THINK IT'S A BIG ANIMAL?
BIG ANIMAL, INDEED- BIG JACKASS!
HA! HA! I GUESS HE NEEDS MORE TRAINING, MICKEY!
HEH! HEH! YA CAN'T FOOL PLUTO — DIDN'T HORACE HAVE ROAST DUCK FOR DINNER?
?
!
SEE YA TONIGHT! HAVE A FIRE READY TO COOK VENISON POT-PIE!
ATTA BOY, PLUTO, GO IN AFTER HIM!
GOOD NIGHT! A PORCUPINE!
YEOWP!
DON'T YA MIND, OLD SCOUT. WE DIDN'T WANT THAT RABBIT, ANYWAY—- HE LOOKED TOUGH!
THERE HE GOES IN AFTER SUMP'N! I'LL WAIT 'TIL HE DRIVES IT OUT!
G-R-R-R!
YOW-R!
YIPE!!
?
!
!
!
KI-YI! KI-YI!
?
!
?
!
!
CAMP AHOY! CAMP, AHOY! GET THE FIRE AND PAN READY—-!
?
!
?
?
--BUT CHANGE THE ORDER TO BEAR STEAKS-- --I HOPE!
© 1934, by Walt Disney Enterprises, Great Britain rights reserved.
WALT DISNEY — 7·8

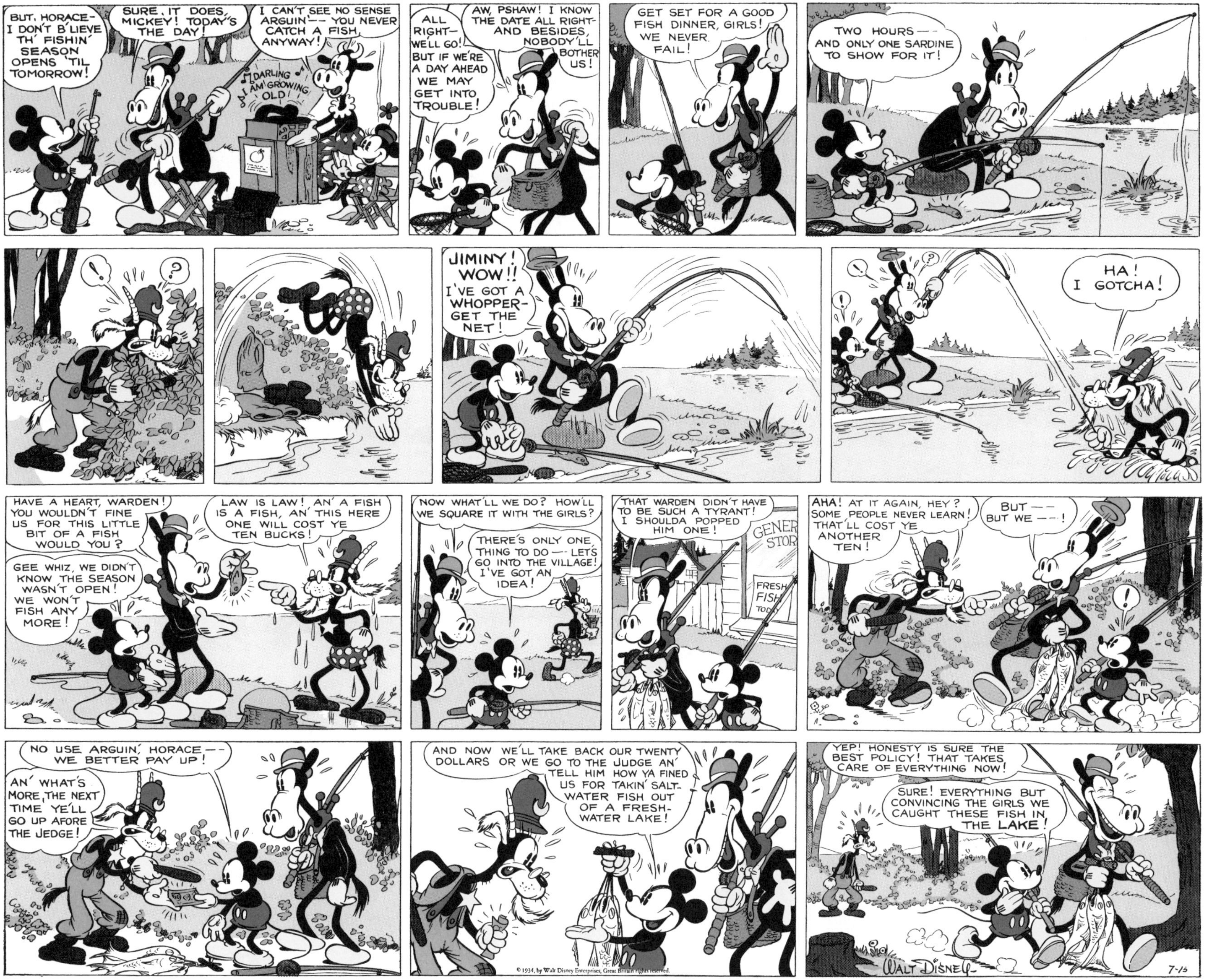
BUT, HORACE- I DON'T B'LIEVE TH' FISHIN' SEASON OPENS 'TIL TOMORROW!
SURE, IT DOES, MICKEY! TODAY'S THE DAY!
I CAN'T SEE NO SENSE ARGUIN'-- YOU NEVER CATCH A FISH, ANYWAY!
DARLING I AM GROWING OLD!
ALL RIGHT- WE'LL GO! BUT IF WE'RE A DAY AHEAD WE MAY GET INTO TROUBLE!
AW, PSHAW! I KNOW THE DATE ALL RIGHT- AND BESIDES, NOBODY'LL BOTHER US!
GET SET FOR A GOOD FISH DINNER, GIRLS! WE NEVER FAIL!
TWO HOURS--- AND ONLY ONE SARDINE TO SHOW FOR IT!
!
?
JIMINY! WOW!! I'VE GOT A WHOPPER- GET THE NET!
!
!
?
HA! I GOTCHA!
HAVE A HEART, WARDEN! YOU WOULDN'T FINE US FOR THIS LITTLE BIT OF A FISH WOULD YOU?
LAW IS LAW! AN' A FISH IS A FISH, AN' THIS HERE ONE WILL COST YE TEN BUCKS!
GEE WHIZ, WE DIDN'T KNOW THE SEASON WASN'T OPEN! WE WON'T FISH ANY MORE!
NOW WHAT'LL WE DO? HOW'LL WE SQUARE IT WITH THE GIRLS?
THERE'S ONLY ONE THING TO DO--- LET'S GO INTO THE VILLAGE! I'VE GOT AN IDEA!
THAT WARDEN DIDN'T HAVE TO BE SUCH A TYRANT! I SHOULDA POPPED HIM ONE!
FRESH FISH
AHA! AT IT AGAIN, HEY? SOME PEOPLE NEVER LEARN! THAT'LL COST YE ANOTHER TEN!
BUT--- BUT WE---!
NO USE ARGUIN', HORACE--- WE BETTER PAY UP!
AN' WHAT'S MORE, THE NEXT TIME YE'LL GO UP AFORE THE JEDGE!
AND NOW WE'LL TAKE BACK OUR TWENTY DOLLARS OR WE GO TO THE JUDGE AN' TELL HIM HOW YA FINED US FOR TAKIN' SALT-WATER FISH OUT OF A FRESH-WATER LAKE!
© 1934, by Walt Disney Enterprises, Great Britain rights reserved.
YEP! HONESTY IS SURE THE BEST POLICY! THAT TAKES CARE OF EVERYTHING NOW!
SURE! EVERYTHING BUT CONVINCING THE GIRLS WE CAUGHT THESE FISH IN THE LAKE!
WALT DISNEY
7-15

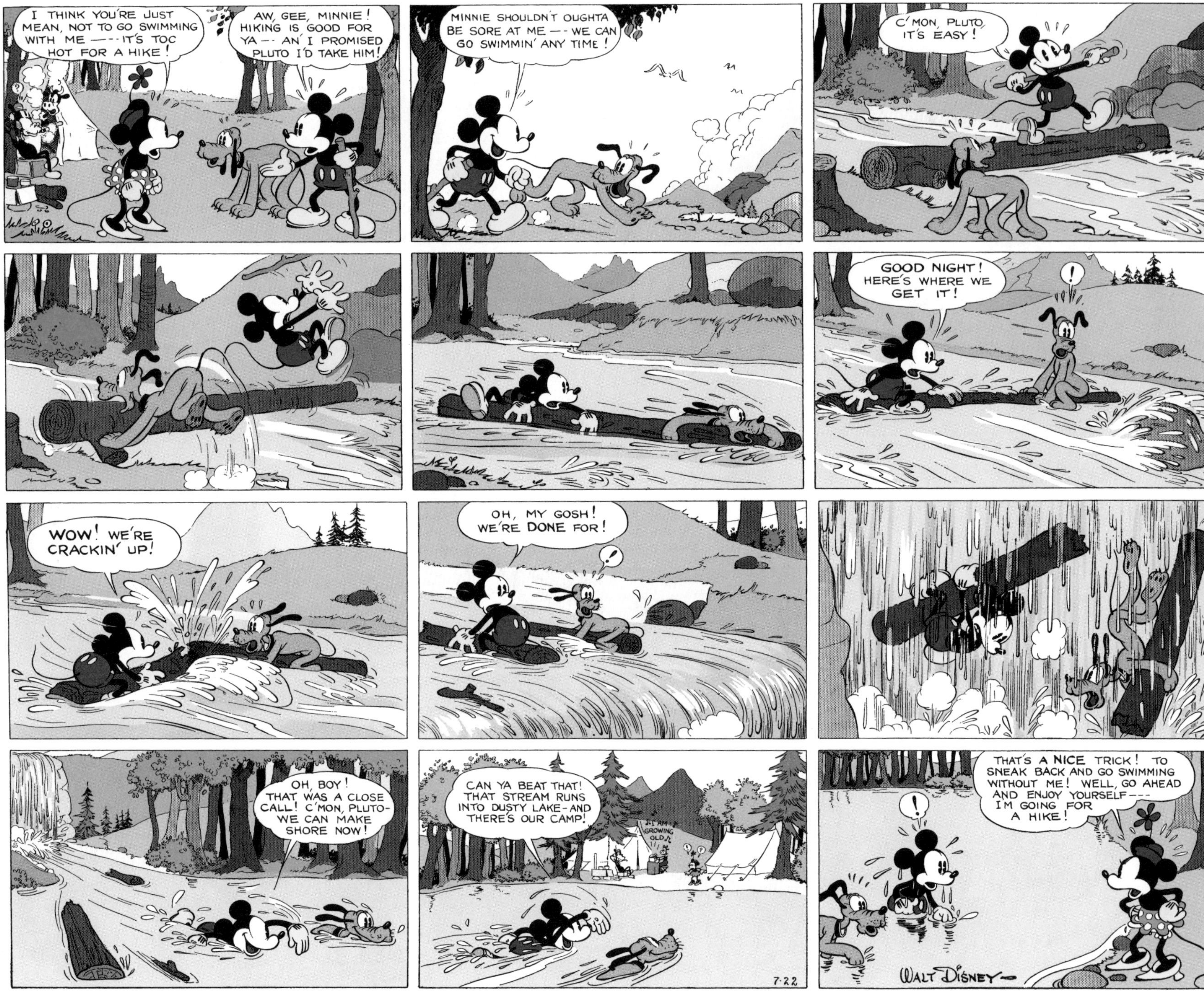

I THINK YOU'RE JUST MEAN, NOT TO GO SWIMMING WITH ME — - IT'S TOO HOT FOR A HIKE!
AW, GEE, MINNIE! HIKING IS GOOD FOR YA — AN' I PROMISED PLUTO I'D TAKE HIM!
MINNIE SHOULDN'T OUGHTA BE SORE AT ME — - WE CAN GO SWIMMIN' ANY TIME!
C'MON, PLUTO, IT'S EASY!
GOOD NIGHT! HERE'S WHERE WE GET IT!
WOW! WE'RE CRACKIN' UP!
OH, MY GOSH! WE'RE DONE FOR!
OH, BOY! THAT WAS A CLOSE CALL! C'MON, PLUTO- WE CAN MAKE SHORE NOW!
CAN YA BEAT THAT! THAT STREAM RUNS INTO DUSTY LAKE-AND THERE'S OUR CAMP!
7·22
THAT'S A NICE TRICK! TO SNEAK BACK AND GO SWIMMING WITHOUT ME! WELL, GO AHEAD AND ENJOY YOURSELF— — I'M GOING FOR A HIKE!
WALT DISNEY

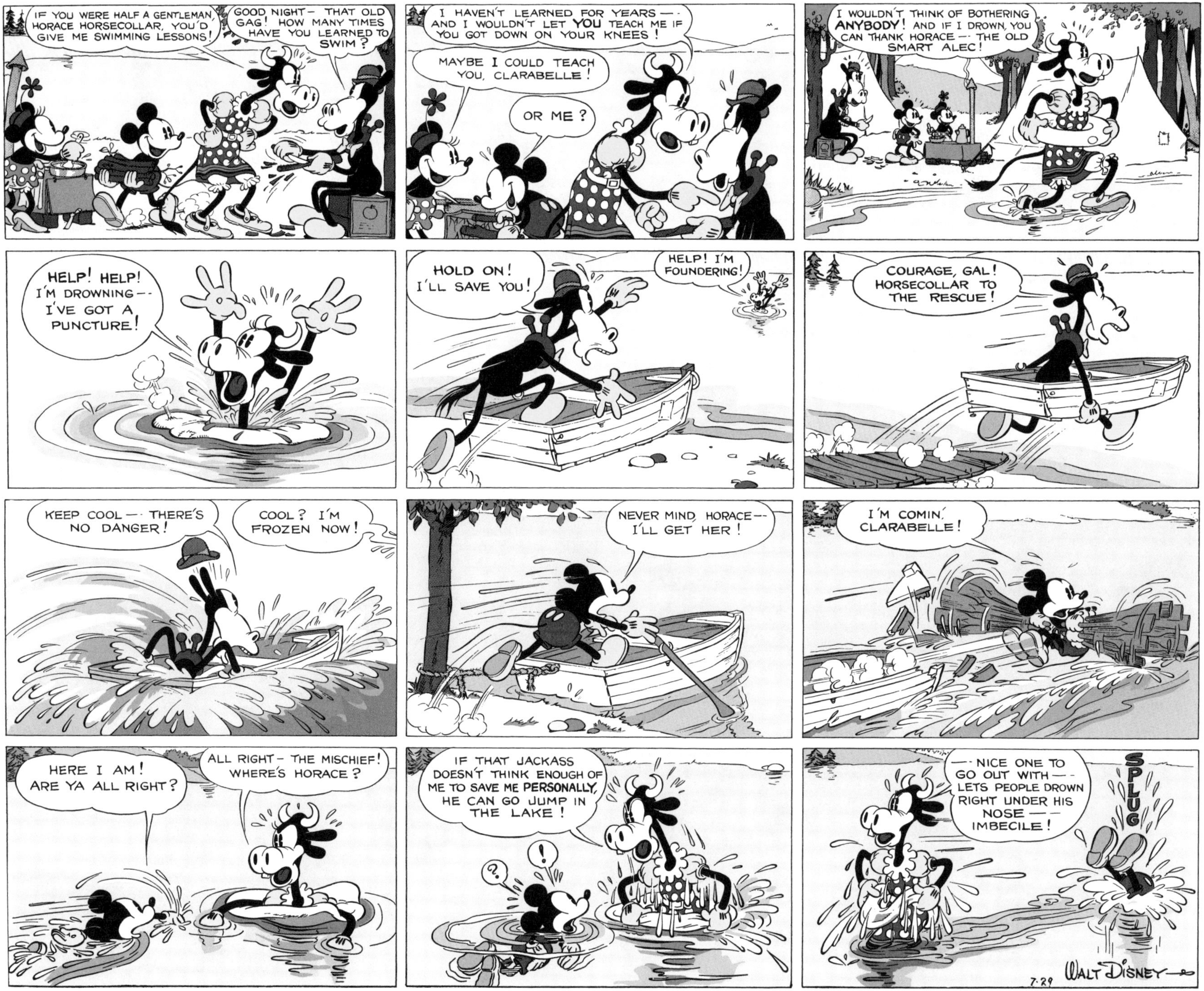
IF YOU WERE HALF A GENTLEMAN, HORACE HORSECOLLAR, YOU'D GIVE ME SWIMMING LESSONS!
GOOD NIGHT— THAT OLD GAG! HOW MANY TIMES HAVE YOU LEARNED TO SWIM?
I HAVEN'T LEARNED FOR YEARS— AND I WOULDN'T LET YOU TEACH ME IF YOU GOT DOWN ON YOUR KNEES!
MAYBE I COULD TEACH YOU, CLARABELLE!
OR ME?
I WOULDN'T THINK OF BOTHERING ANYBODY! AND IF I DROWN, YOU CAN THANK HORACE— THE OLD SMART ALEC!
HELP! HELP! I'M DROWNING— I'VE GOT A PUNCTURE!
HOLD ON! I'LL SAVE YOU!
HELP! I'M FOUNDERING!
COURAGE, GAL! HORSECOLLAR TO THE RESCUE!
KEEP COOL— THERE'S NO DANGER!
COOL? I'M FROZEN NOW!
NEVER MIND, HORACE— I'LL GET HER!
I'M COMIN', CLARABELLE!
HERE I AM! ARE YA ALL RIGHT?
ALL RIGHT— THE MISCHIEF! WHERE'S HORACE?
IF THAT JACKASS DOESN'T THINK ENOUGH OF ME TO SAVE ME PERSONALLY, HE CAN GO JUMP IN THE LAKE!
?
!
—NICE ONE TO GO OUT WITH— LETS PEOPLE DROWN RIGHT UNDER HIS NOSE— IMBECILE!
SPLUG
7·29
WALT DISNEY

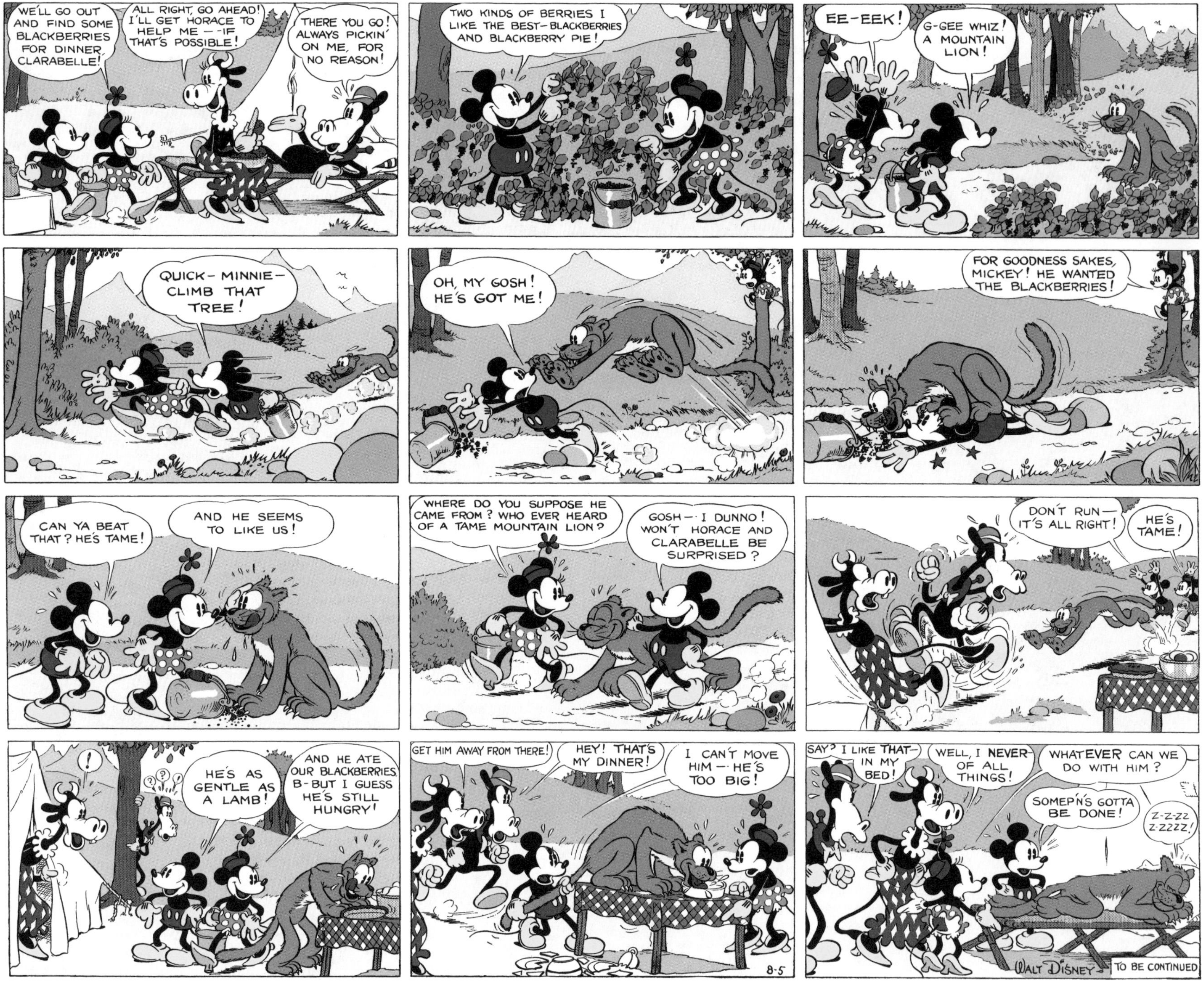
WE'LL GO OUT AND FIND SOME BLACKBERRIES FOR DINNER, CLARABELLE!
ALL RIGHT, GO AHEAD! I'LL GET HORACE TO HELP ME — IF THAT'S POSSIBLE!
THERE YOU GO! ALWAYS PICKIN' ON ME, FOR NO REASON!
TWO KINDS OF BERRIES I LIKE THE BEST- BLACKBERRIES AND BLACKBERRY PIE!
EE-EEK!
G-GEE WHIZ! A MOUNTAIN LION!
QUICK- MINNIE- CLIMB THAT TREE!
OH, MY GOSH! HE'S GOT ME!
FOR GOODNESS SAKES, MICKEY! HE WANTED THE BLACKBERRIES!
CAN YA BEAT THAT? HE'S TAME!
AND HE SEEMS TO LIKE US!
WHERE DO YOU SUPPOSE HE CAME FROM? WHO EVER HEARD OF A TAME MOUNTAIN LION?
GOSH — I DUNNO! WON'T HORACE AND CLARABELLE BE SURPRISED?
DON'T RUN — IT'S ALL RIGHT!
HE'S TAME!
!
HE'S AS GENTLE AS A LAMB!
AND HE ATE OUR BLACKBERRIES. B-BUT I GUESS HE'S STILL HUNGRY!
GET HIM AWAY FROM THERE!
HEY! THAT'S MY DINNER!
I CAN'T MOVE HIM — HE'S TOO BIG!
8-5
SAY? I LIKE THAT — IN MY BED!
WELL, I NEVER — OF ALL THINGS!
WHATEVER CAN WE DO WITH HIM?
SOMEP'N'S GOTTA BE DONE!
Z-Z-ZZ Z-ZZZZ!
WALT DISNEY
TO BE CONTINUED

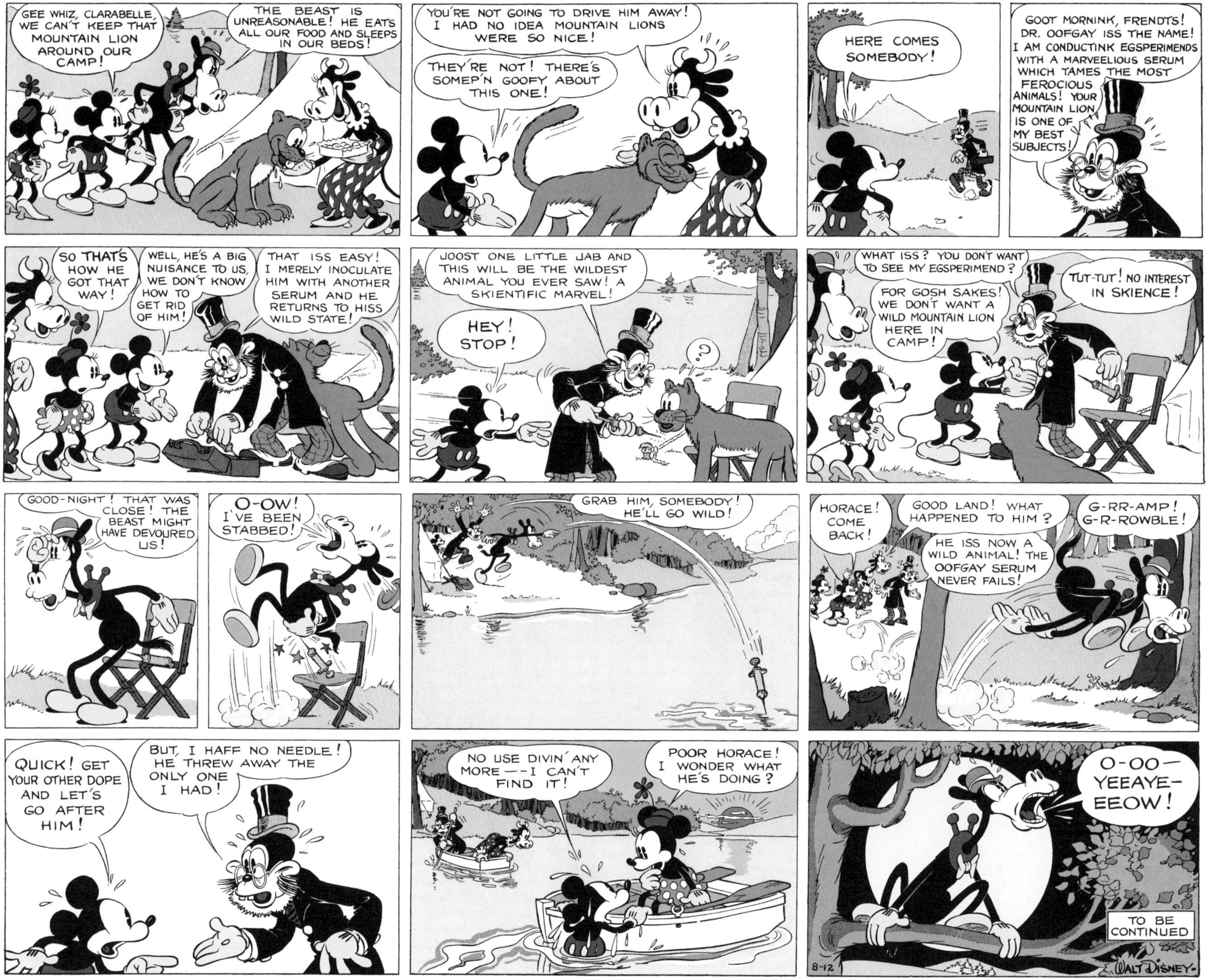
GEE WHIZ, CLARABELLE, WE CAN'T KEEP THAT MOUNTAIN LION AROUND OUR CAMP!
THE BEAST IS UNREASONABLE! HE EATS ALL OUR FOOD AND SLEEPS IN OUR BEDS!
YOU'RE NOT GOING TO DRIVE HIM AWAY! I HAD NO IDEA MOUNTAIN LIONS WERE SO NICE!
THEY'RE NOT! THERE'S SOMEP'N GOOFY ABOUT THIS ONE!
HERE COMES SOMEBODY!
GOOT MORNINK, FRENDTS! DR. OOFGAY ISS THE NAME! I AM CONDUCTINK EGSPERIMENDS WITH A MARVEELIOUS SERUM WHICH TAMES THE MOST FEROCIOUS ANIMALS! YOUR MOUNTAIN LION IS ONE OF MY BEST SUBJECTS!
SO THAT'S HOW HE GOT THAT WAY!
WELL, HE'S A BIG NUISANCE TO US, WE DON'T KNOW HOW TO GET RID OF HIM!
THAT ISS EASY! I MERELY INOCULATE HIM WITH ANOTHER SERUM AND HE RETURNS TO HISS WILD STATE!
JOOST ONE LITTLE JAB AND THIS WILL BE THE WILDEST ANIMAL YOU EVER SAW! A SKIENTIFIC MARVEL!
HEY! STOP!
?
WHAT ISS? YOU DON'T WANT TO SEE MY EGSPERIMEND?
FOR GOSH SAKES! WE DON'T WANT A WILD MOUNTAIN LION HERE IN CAMP!
TUT-TUT! NO INTEREST IN SKIENCE!
GOOD-NIGHT! THAT WAS CLOSE! THE BEAST MIGHT HAVE DEVOURED US!
O-OW! I'VE BEEN STABBED!
GRAB HIM, SOMEBODY! HE'LL GO WILD!
HORACE! COME BACK!
GOOD LAND! WHAT HAPPENED TO HIM?
HE ISS NOW A WILD ANIMAL! THE OOFGAY SERUM NEVER FAILS!
G-RR-AMP! G-R-ROWBLE!
QUICK! GET YOUR OTHER DOPE AND LET'S GO AFTER HIM!
BUT, I HAFF NO NEEDLE! HE THREW AWAY THE ONLY ONE I HAD!
NO USE DIVIN' ANY MORE --I CAN'T FIND IT!
POOR HORACE! I WONDER WHAT HE'S DOING?
O-OO— YEEAYE— EEOW!
TO BE CONTINUED
8-12
WALT DISNEY

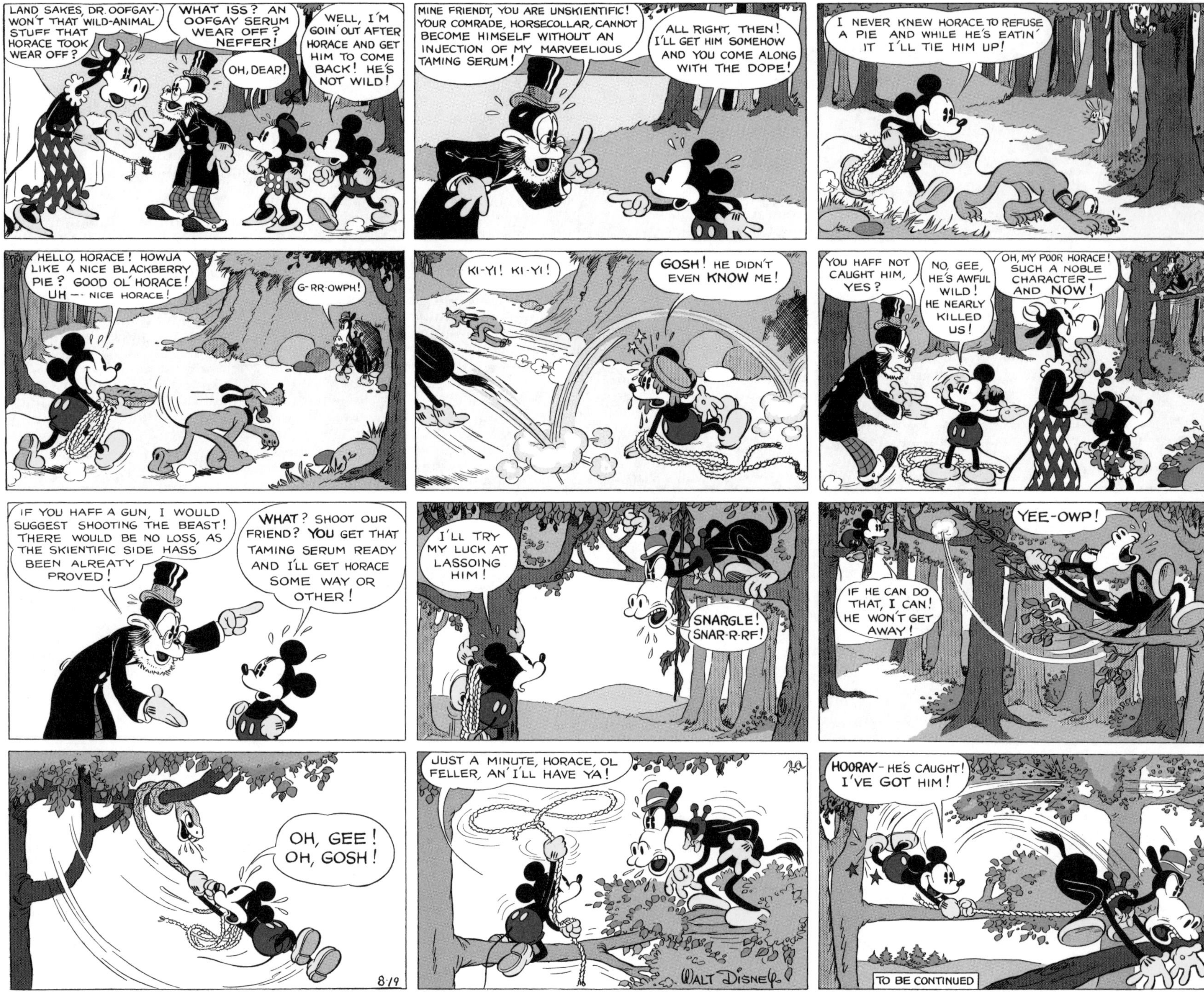

LAND SAKES, DR. OOFGAY—WON'T THAT WILD-ANIMAL STUFF THAT HORACE TOOK WEAR OFF?
WHAT ISS? AN OOFGAY SERUM WEAR OFF? NEFFER!
OH, DEAR!
WELL, I'M GOIN' OUT AFTER HORACE AND GET HIM TO COME BACK! HE'S NOT WILD!
MINE FRIENDT, YOU ARE UNSKIENTIFIC! YOUR COMRADE, HORSECOLLAR, CANNOT BECOME HIMSELF WITHOUT AN INJECTION OF MY MARVEELIOUS TAMING SERUM!
ALL RIGHT, THEN! I'LL GET HIM SOMEHOW AND YOU COME ALONG WITH THE DOPE!
I NEVER KNEW HORACE TO REFUSE A PIE AND WHILE HE'S EATIN' IT I'LL TIE HIM UP!
HELLO, HORACE! HOWJA LIKE A NICE BLACKBERRY PIE? GOOD OL' HORACE! UH -- NICE HORACE!
G-RR-OWPH!
KI-YI! KI-YI!
GOSH! HE DIDN'T EVEN KNOW ME!
YOU HAFF NOT CAUGHT HIM, YES?
NO, GEE, HE'S AWFUL WILD! HE NEARLY KILLED US!
OH, MY POOR HORACE! SUCH A NOBLE CHARACTER— AND NOW!
IF YOU HAFF A GUN, I WOULD SUGGEST SHOOTING THE BEAST! THERE WOULD BE NO LOSS, AS THE SKIENTIFIC SIDE HASS BEEN ALREATY PROVED!
WHAT? SHOOT OUR FRIEND? YOU GET THAT TAMING SERUM READY AND I'LL GET HORACE SOME WAY OR OTHER!
I'LL TRY MY LUCK AT LASSOING HIM!
SNARGLE! SNAR-R-RF!
YEE-OWP!
IF HE CAN DO THAT, I CAN! HE WON'T GET AWAY!
OH, GEE! OH, GOSH!
8·19
JUST A MINUTE, HORACE, OL FELLER, AN' I'LL HAVE YA!
WALT DISNEY
HOORAY- HE'S CAUGHT! I'VE GOT HIM!
TO BE CONTINUED

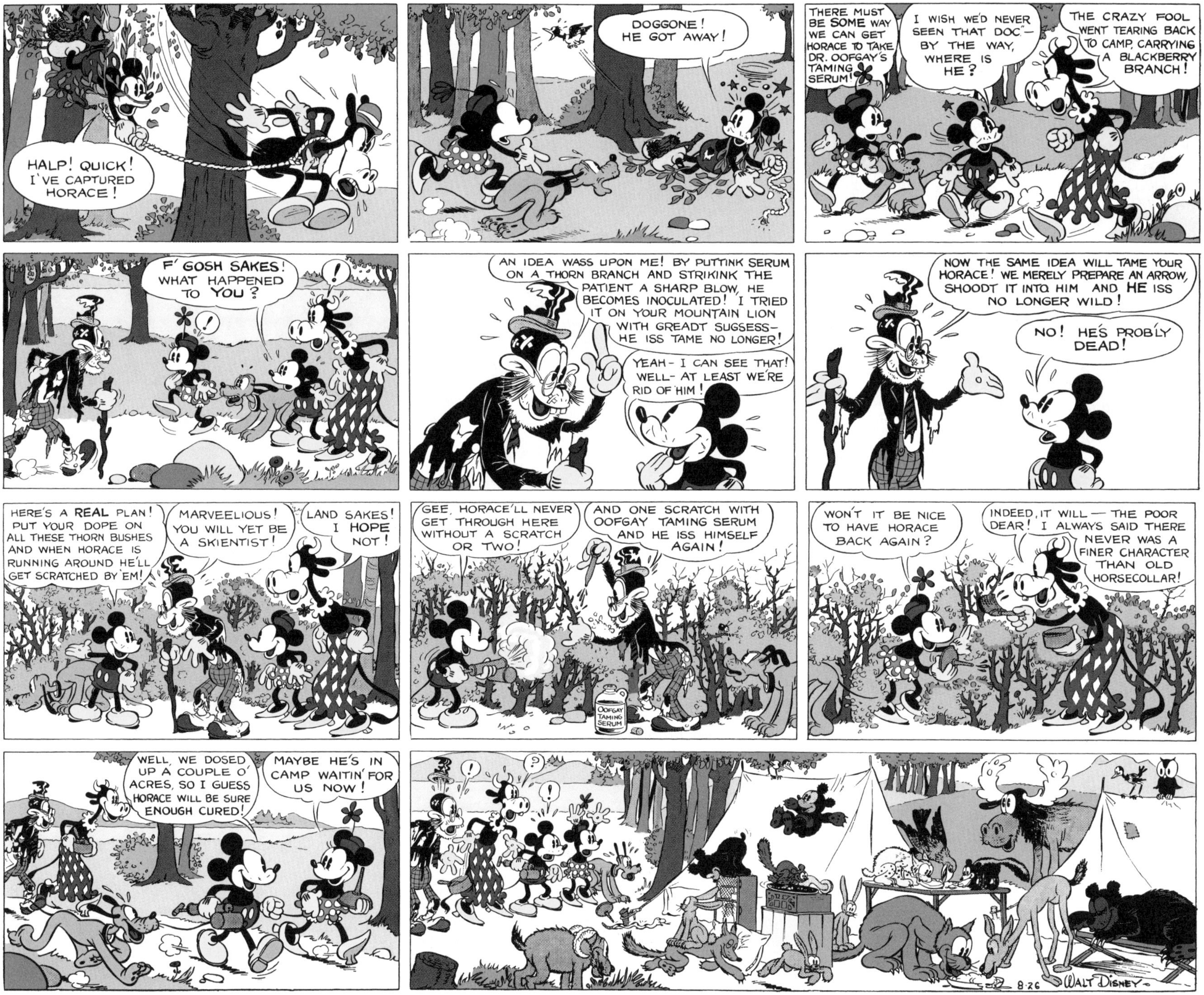
HALP! QUICK! I'VE CAPTURED HORACE!
DOGGONE! HE GOT AWAY!
THERE MUST BE SOME WAY WE CAN GET HORACE TO TAKE DR. OOFGAY'S TAMING SERUM!
I WISH WE'D NEVER SEEN THAT DOC"— BY THE WAY, WHERE IS HE?
THE CRAZY FOOL WENT TEARING BACK TO CAMP, CARRYING A BLACKBERRY BRANCH!
F' GOSH SAKES! WHAT HAPPENED TO YOU?
!
!
AN IDEA WASS UPON ME! BY PUTTINK SERUM ON A THORN BRANCH AND STRIKINK THE PATIENT A SHARP BLOW, HE BECOMES INOCULATED! I TRIED IT ON YOUR MOUNTAIN LION WITH GREADT SUGSESS— HE ISS TAME NO LONGER!
YEAH- I CAN SEE THAT! WELL- AT LEAST WE'RE RID OF HIM!
NOW THE SAME IDEA WILL TAME YOUR HORACE! WE MERELY PREPARE AN ARROW, SHOODT IT INTO HIM AND HE ISS NO LONGER WILD!
NO! HE'S PROB'LY DEAD!
HERE'S A REAL PLAN! PUT YOUR DOPE ON ALL THESE THORN BUSHES AND WHEN HORACE IS RUNNING AROUND HE'LL GET SCRATCHED BY 'EM!
MARVEELIOUS! YOU WILL YET BE A SKIENTIST!
LAND SAKES! I HOPE NOT!
GEE, HORACE'LL NEVER GET THROUGH HERE WITHOUT A SCRATCH OR TWO!
AND ONE SCRATCH WITH OOFGAY TAMING SERUM AND HE ISS HIMSELF AGAIN!
OOFGAY TAMING SERUM
WON'T IT BE NICE TO HAVE HORACE BACK AGAIN?
INDEED, IT WILL — THE POOR DEAR! I ALWAYS SAID THERE NEVER WAS A FINER CHARACTER THAN OLD HORSECOLLAR!
WELL, WE DOSED UP A COUPLE O' ACRES, SO I GUESS HORACE WILL BE SURE ENOUGH CURED!
MAYBE HE'S IN CAMP WAITIN' FOR US NOW!
!
?
!
8·26
WALT DISNEY

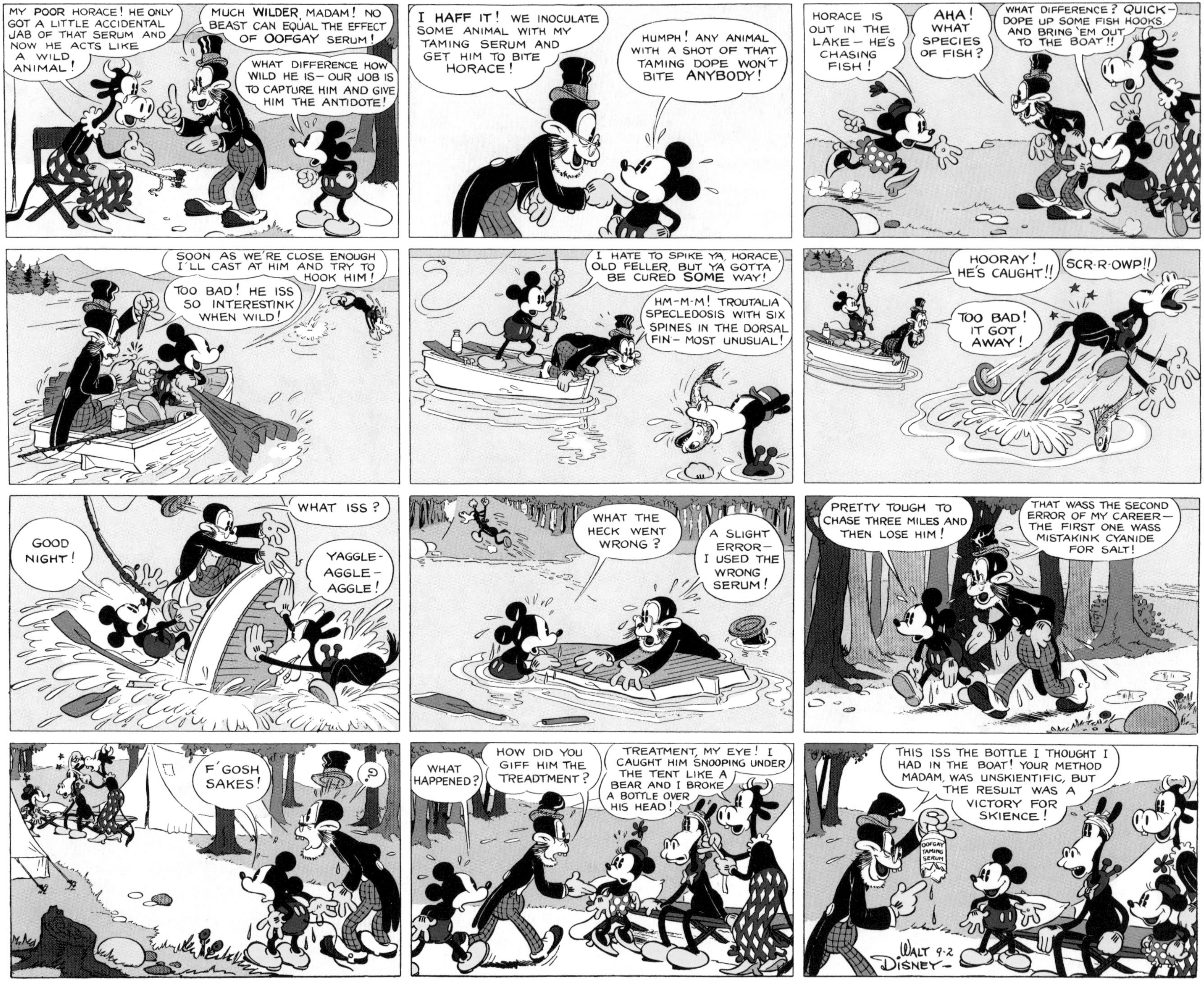
MY POOR HORACE! HE ONLY GOT A LITTLE ACCIDENTAL JAB OF THAT SERUM AND NOW HE ACTS LIKE A WILD ANIMAL!
MUCH WILDER, MADAM! NO BEAST CAN EQUAL THE EFFECT OF OOFGAY SERUM!
WHAT DIFFERENCE HOW WILD HE IS– OUR JOB IS TO CAPTURE HIM AND GIVE HIM THE ANTIDOTE!
I HAFF IT! WE INOCULATE SOME ANIMAL WITH MY TAMING SERUM AND GET HIM TO BITE HORACE!
HUMPH! ANY ANIMAL WITH A SHOT OF THAT TAMING DOPE WON'T BITE ANYBODY!
HORACE IS OUT IN THE LAKE– HE'S CHASING FISH!
AHA! WHAT SPECIES OF FISH?
WHAT DIFFERENCE? QUICK– DOPE UP SOME FISH HOOKS AND BRING 'EM OUT TO THE BOAT!!
SOON AS WE'RE CLOSE ENOUGH I'LL CAST AT HIM AND TRY TO HOOK HIM!
TOO BAD! HE ISS SO INTERESTINK WHEN WILD!
I HATE TO SPIKE YA, HORACE, OLD FELLER, BUT YA GOTTA BE CURED SOME WAY!
HM-M-M! TROUTALIA SPECLEDOSIS WITH SIX SPINES IN THE DORSAL FIN– MOST UNUSUAL!
HOORAY! HE'S CAUGHT!!
SCR-R-OWP!!
TOO BAD! IT GOT AWAY!
GOOD NIGHT!
WHAT ISS?
YAGGLE-AGGLE-AGGLE!
WHAT THE HECK WENT WRONG?
A SLIGHT ERROR– I USED THE WRONG SERUM!
PRETTY TOUGH TO CHASE THREE MILES AND THEN LOSE HIM!
THAT WASS THE SECOND ERROR OF MY CAREER– THE FIRST ONE WASS MISTAKINK CYANIDE FOR SALT!
F'GOSH SAKES!
?
WHAT HAPPENED?
HOW DID YOU GIFF HIM THE TREADTMENT?
TREATMENT, MY EYE! I CAUGHT HIM SNOOPING UNDER THE TENT LIKE A BEAR AND I BROKE A BOTTLE OVER HIS HEAD!
THIS ISS THE BOTTLE I THOUGHT I HAD IN THE BOAT! YOUR METHOD MADAM, WAS UNSKIENTIFIC, BUT THE RESULT WAS A VICTORY FOR SKIENCE!
OOFGAY TAMING SERUM
WALT DISNEY 9-2

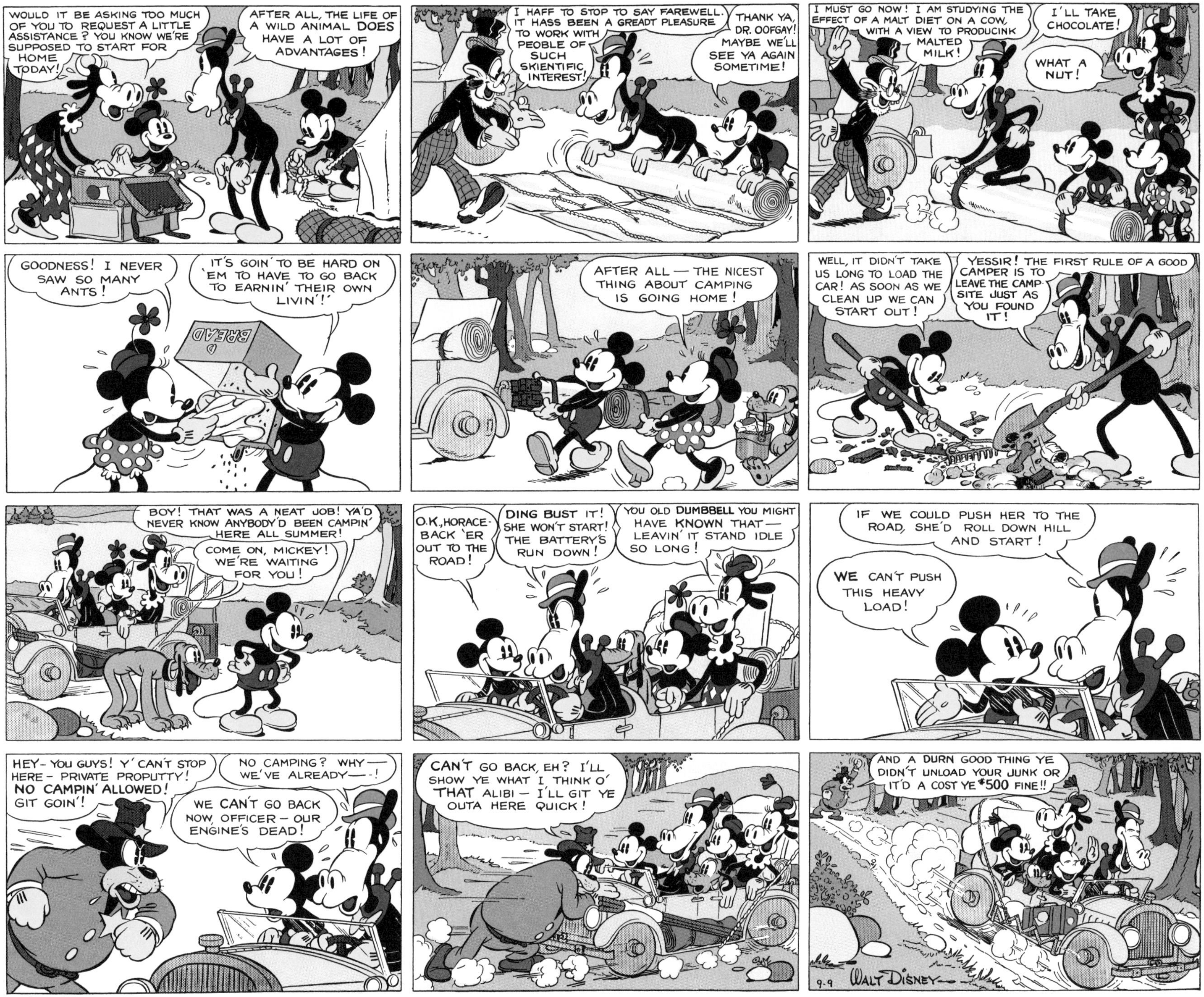
WOULD IT BE ASKING TOO MUCH OF YOU TO REQUEST A LITTLE ASSISTANCE? YOU KNOW WE'RE SUPPOSED TO START FOR HOME TODAY!
AFTER ALL, THE LIFE OF A WILD ANIMAL DOES HAVE A LOT OF ADVANTAGES!
I HAFF TO STOP TO SAY FAREWELL. IT HASS BEEN A GREADT PLEASURE TO WORK WITH PEOBLE OF SUCH SKIENTIFIC INTEREST!
THANK YA, DR. OOFGAY! MAYBE WE'LL SEE YA AGAIN SOMETIME!
I MUST GO NOW! I AM STUDYING THE EFFECT OF A MALT DIET ON A COW, WITH A VIEW TO PRODUCINK MALTED MILK!
I'LL TAKE CHOCOLATE!
WHAT A NUT!
GOODNESS! I NEVER SAW SO MANY ANTS!
IT'S GOIN' TO BE HARD ON 'EM TO HAVE TO GO BACK TO EARNIN' THEIR OWN LIVIN'!
BREAD
AFTER ALL — THE NICEST THING ABOUT CAMPING IS GOING HOME!
WELL, IT DIDN'T TAKE US LONG TO LOAD THE CAR! AS SOON AS WE CLEAN UP WE CAN START OUT!
YESSIR! THE FIRST RULE OF A GOOD CAMPER IS TO LEAVE THE CAMP SITE JUST AS YOU FOUND IT!
BOY! THAT WAS A NEAT JOB! YA'D NEVER KNOW ANYBODY'D BEEN CAMPIN' HERE ALL SUMMER!
COME ON, MICKEY! WE'RE WAITING FOR YOU!
O.K., HORACE-BACK 'ER OUT TO THE ROAD!
DING BUST IT! SHE WON'T START! THE BATTERY'S RUN DOWN!
YOU OLD DUMBBELL YOU MIGHT HAVE KNOWN THAT— LEAVIN' IT STAND IDLE SO LONG!
IF WE COULD PUSH HER TO THE ROAD, SHE'D ROLL DOWN HILL AND START!
WE CAN'T PUSH THIS HEAVY LOAD!
HEY- YOU GUYS! Y' CAN'T STOP HERE- PRIVATE PROPUTTY! NO CAMPIN' ALLOWED! GIT GOIN'!
NO CAMPING? WHY— WE'VE ALREADY—!
WE CAN'T GO BACK NOW, OFFICER- OUR ENGINE'S DEAD!
CAN'T GO BACK, EH? I'LL SHOW YE WHAT I THINK O' THAT ALIBI - I'LL GIT YE OUTA HERE QUICK!
AND A DURN GOOD THING YE DIDN'T UNLOAD YOUR JUNK OR IT'D A COST YE $500 FINE!!
9-9
WALT DISNEY

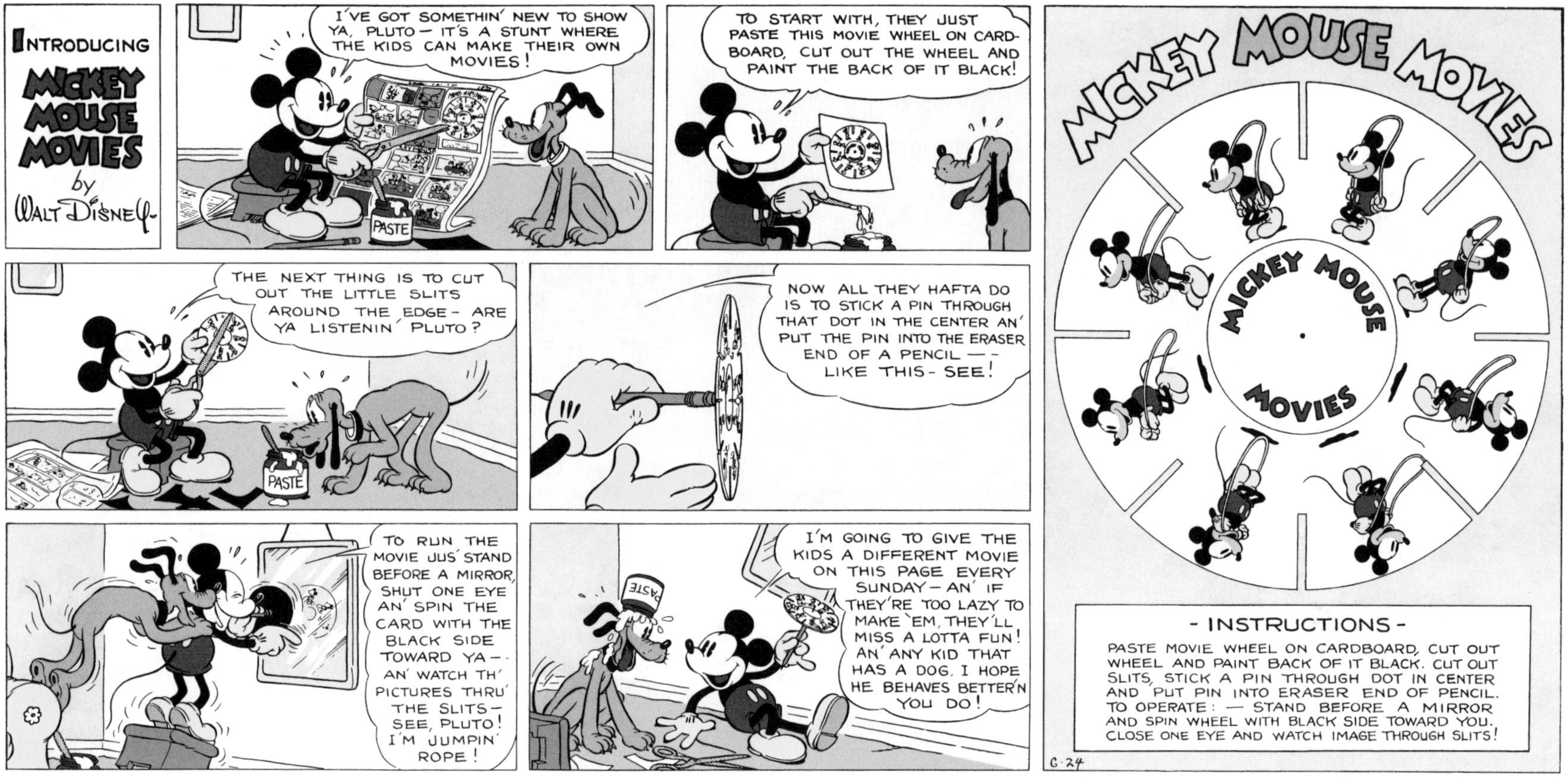

INTRODUCING
MICKEY MOUSE MOVIES
by
WALT DISNEY
I'VE GOT SOMETHIN' NEW TO SHOW YA, PLUTO — IT'S A STUNT WHERE THE KIDS CAN MAKE THEIR OWN MOVIES!
PASTE
TO START WITH, THEY JUST PASTE THIS MOVIE WHEEL ON CARDBOARD, CUT OUT THE WHEEL AND PAINT THE BACK OF IT BLACK!
THE NEXT THING IS TO CUT OUT THE LITTLE SLITS AROUND THE EDGE - ARE YA LISTENIN' PLUTO?
PASTE
NOW ALL THEY HAFTA DO IS TO STICK A PIN THROUGH THAT DOT IN THE CENTER AN' PUT THE PIN INTO THE ERASER END OF A PENCIL — - LIKE THIS - SEE!
TO RUN THE MOVIE JUS' STAND BEFORE A MIRROR, SHUT ONE EYE AN' SPIN THE CARD WITH THE BLACK SIDE TOWARD YA — AN' WATCH TH' PICTURES THRU' THE SLITS — SEE, PLUTO! I'M JUMPIN' ROPE!
PASTE
I'M GOING TO GIVE THE KIDS A DIFFERENT MOVIE ON THIS PAGE EVERY SUNDAY — AN' IF THEY'RE TOO LAZY TO MAKE 'EM, THEY'LL MISS A LOTTA FUN! AN' ANY KID THAT HAS A DOG, I HOPE HE BEHAVES BETTER'N YOU DO!
MICKEY MOUSE MOVIES
MICKEY MOUSE MOVIES
- INSTRUCTIONS -
PASTE MOVIE WHEEL ON CARDBOARD, CUT OUT WHEEL AND PAINT BACK OF IT BLACK. CUT OUT SLITS, STICK A PIN THROUGH DOT IN CENTER AND PUT PIN INTO ERASER END OF PENCIL. TO OPERATE: — STAND BEFORE A MIRROR AND SPIN WHEEL WITH BLACK SIDE TOWARD YOU. CLOSE ONE EYE AND WATCH IMAGE THROUGH SLITS!
6·24

ABOVE: Gottfredson's Sunday *Mickey Mouse* was usually accompanied by a *Silly Symphony* top strip. But for one time only—on June 24, 1934—Mickey starred in his own special topper, announcing a new "premium" that would accompany subsequent Sunday pages.

While Gottfredson penciled this introductory strip, the actual "Mickey Mouse Movies" phenakistocope wheels were drawn by others. The "Movies" appeared on and off alongside the *Silly Symphony* strip through March 24, 1935.

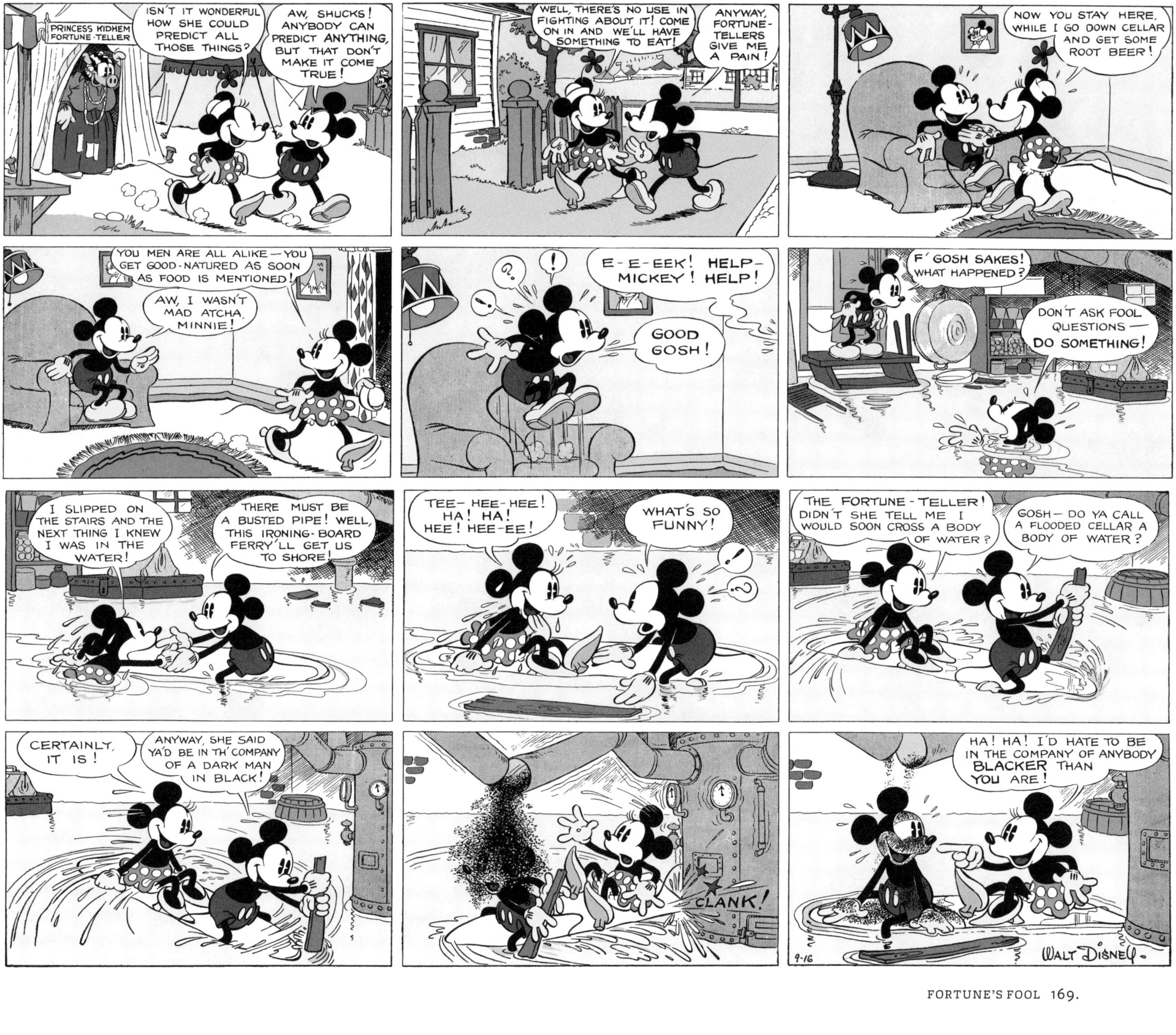

PRINCESS KIDHEM FORTUNE-TELLER
ISN'T IT WONDERFUL HOW SHE COULD PREDICT ALL THOSE THINGS?
AW, SHUCKS! ANYBODY CAN PREDICT ANYTHING, BUT THAT DON'T MAKE IT COME TRUE!
WELL, THERE'S NO USE IN FIGHTING ABOUT IT! COME ON IN AND WE'LL HAVE SOMETHING TO EAT!
ANYWAY, FORTUNE-TELLERS GIVE ME A PAIN!
NOW YOU STAY HERE, WHILE I GO DOWN CELLAR AND GET SOME ROOT BEER!
YOU MEN ARE ALL ALIKE — YOU GET GOOD-NATURED AS SOON AS FOOD IS MENTIONED!
AW, I WASN'T MAD ATCHA, MINNIE!
E-E-EEK! HELP-MICKEY! HELP!
GOOD GOSH!
F' GOSH SAKES! WHAT HAPPENED?
DON'T ASK FOOL QUESTIONS — DO SOMETHING!
I SLIPPED ON THE STAIRS AND THE NEXT THING I KNEW I WAS IN THE WATER!
THERE MUST BE A BUSTED PIPE! WELL, THIS IRONING-BOARD FERRY'LL GET US TO SHORE!
TEE-HEE-HEE! HA! HA! HEE! HEE-EE!
WHAT'S SO FUNNY!
THE FORTUNE-TELLER! DIDN'T SHE TELL ME I WOULD SOON CROSS A BODY OF WATER?
GOSH — DO YA CALL A FLOODED CELLAR A BODY OF WATER?
CERTAINLY, IT IS!
ANYWAY, SHE SAID YA'D BE IN TH' COMPANY OF A DARK MAN IN BLACK!
CLANK!
HA! HA! I'D HATE TO BE IN THE COMPANY OF ANYBODY BLACKER THAN YOU ARE!
9-16
WALT DISNEY

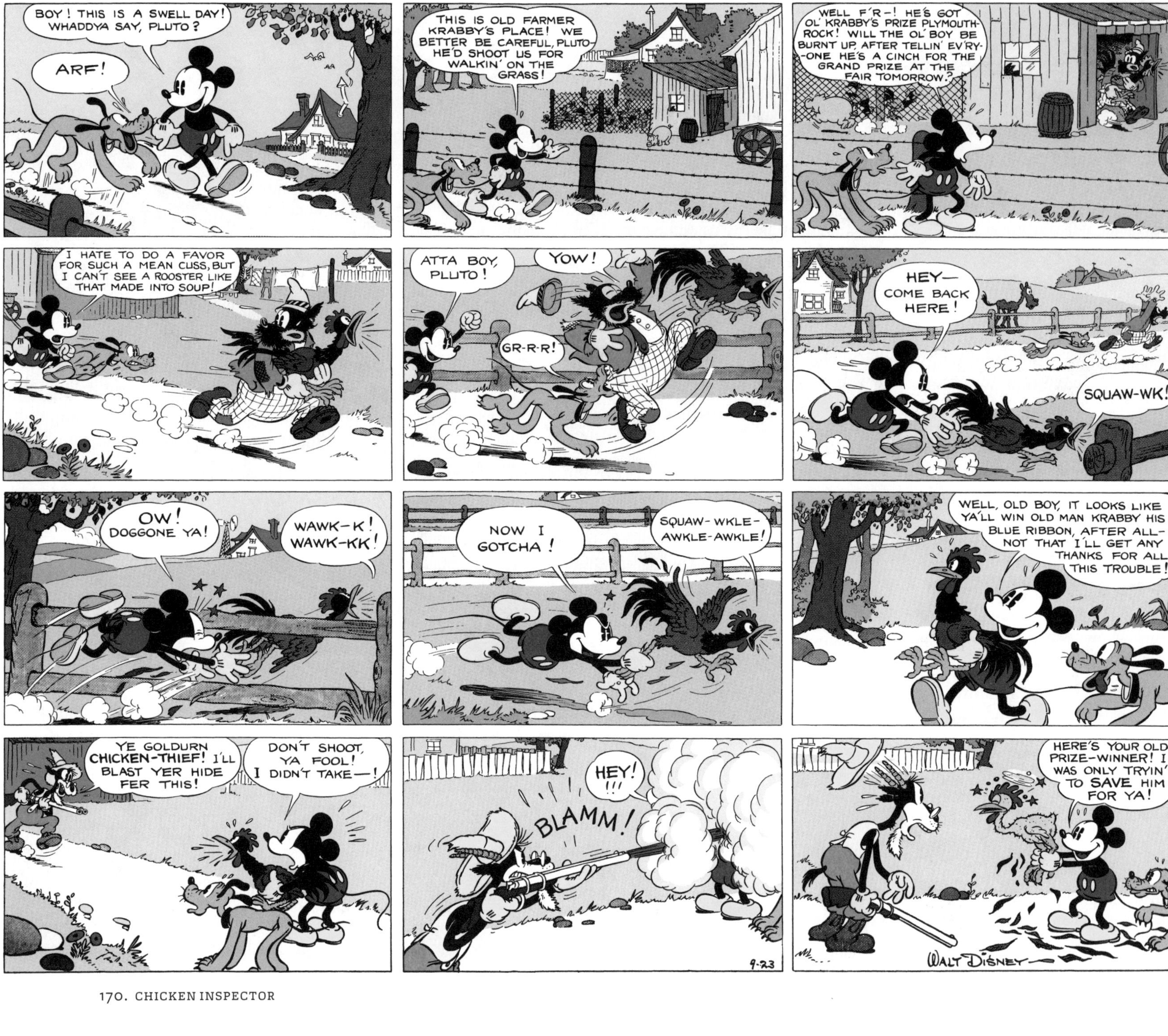
BOY! THIS IS A SWELL DAY! WHADDYA SAY, PLUTO?
ARF!
THIS IS OLD FARMER KRABBY'S PLACE! WE BETTER BE CAREFUL, PLUTO— HE'D SHOOT US FOR WALKIN' ON THE GRASS!
WELL F'R—! HE'S GOT OL' KRABBY'S PRIZE PLYMOUTH-ROCK! WILL THE OL' BOY BE BURNT UP, AFTER TELLIN' EV'RY-ONE HE'S A CINCH FOR THE GRAND PRIZE AT THE FAIR TOMORROW?
I HATE TO DO A FAVOR FOR SUCH A MEAN CUSS, BUT I CAN'T SEE A ROOSTER LIKE THAT MADE INTO SOUP!
ATTA BOY, PLUTO!
YOW!
GR-R-R!
HEY— COME BACK HERE!
SQUAW-WK!
OW! DOGGONE YA!
WAWK-K! WAWK-KK!
NOW I GOTCHA!
SQUAW-WKLE-AWKLE-AWKLE!
WELL, OLD BOY, IT LOOKS LIKE YA'LL WIN OLD MAN KRABBY HIS BLUE RIBBON, AFTER ALL— NOT THAT I'LL GET ANY THANKS FOR ALL THIS TROUBLE!
YE GOLDURN CHICKEN-THIEF! I'LL BLAST YER HIDE FER THIS!
DON'T SHOOT, YA FOOL! I DIDN'T TAKE—!
HEY! !!!
BLAMM!
9-23
HERE'S YOUR OLD PRIZE-WINNER! I WAS ONLY TRYIN' TO SAVE HIM FOR YA!
WALT DISNEY

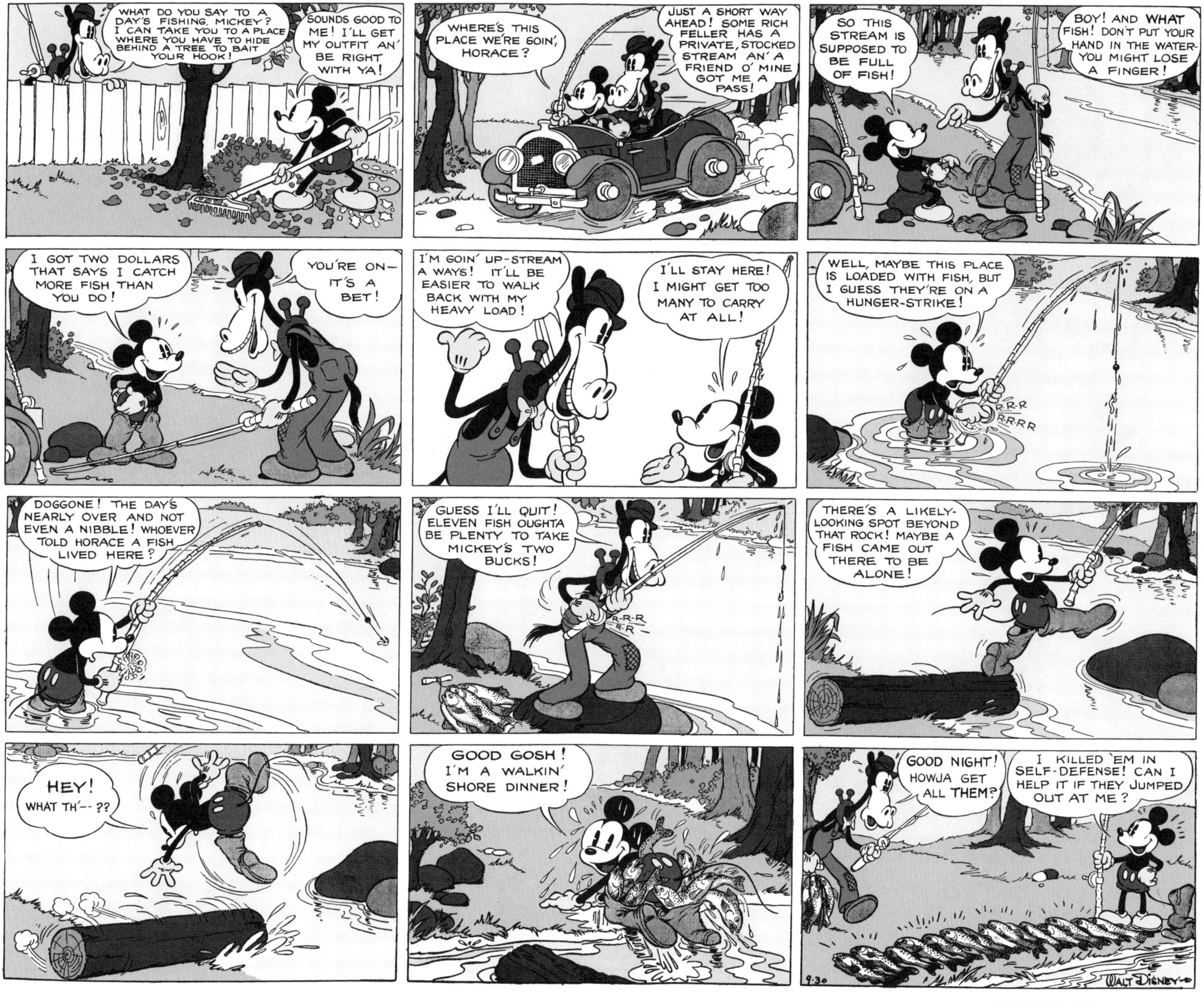
WHAT DO YOU SAY TO A DAY'S FISHING, MICKEY? I CAN TAKE YOU TO A PLACE WHERE YOU HAVE TO HIDE BEHIND A TREE TO BAIT YOUR HOOK!
SOUNDS GOOD TO ME! I'LL GET MY OUTFIT AN' BE RIGHT WITH YA!
WHERE'S THIS PLACE WE'RE GOIN', HORACE?
JUST A SHORT WAY AHEAD! SOME RICH FELLER HAS A PRIVATE, STOCKED STREAM AN' A FRIEND O' MINE GOT ME A PASS!
SO THIS STREAM IS SUPPOSED TO BE FULL OF FISH!
BOY! AND WHAT FISH! DON'T PUT YOUR HAND IN THE WATER-YOU MIGHT LOSE A FINGER!
I GOT TWO DOLLARS THAT SAYS I CATCH MORE FISH THAN YOU DO!
YOU'RE ON-IT'S A BET!
I'M GOIN' UP-STREAM A WAYS! IT'LL BE EASIER TO WALK BACK WITH MY HEAVY LOAD!
I'LL STAY HERE! I MIGHT GET TOO MANY TO CARRY AT ALL!
WELL, MAYBE THIS PLACE IS LOADED WITH FISH, BUT I GUESS THEY'RE ON A HUNGER-STRIKE!
R-R-R R-R-RR
DOGGONE! THE DAY'S NEARLY OVER AND NOT EVEN A NIBBLE! WHOEVER TOLD HORACE A FISH LIVED HERE?
GUESS I'LL QUIT! ELEVEN FISH OUGHTA BE PLENTY TO TAKE MICKEY'S TWO BUCKS!
R-R-R R-R
THERE'S A LIKELY-LOOKING SPOT BEYOND THAT ROCK! MAYBE A FISH CAME OUT THERE TO BE ALONE!
HEY! WHAT TH'--??
GOOD GOSH! I'M A WALKIN' SHORE DINNER!
GOOD NIGHT! HOWJA GET ALL THEM?
I KILLED 'EM IN SELF-DEFENSE! CAN I HELP IT IF THEY JUMPED OUT AT ME?
9-30
WALT DISNEY

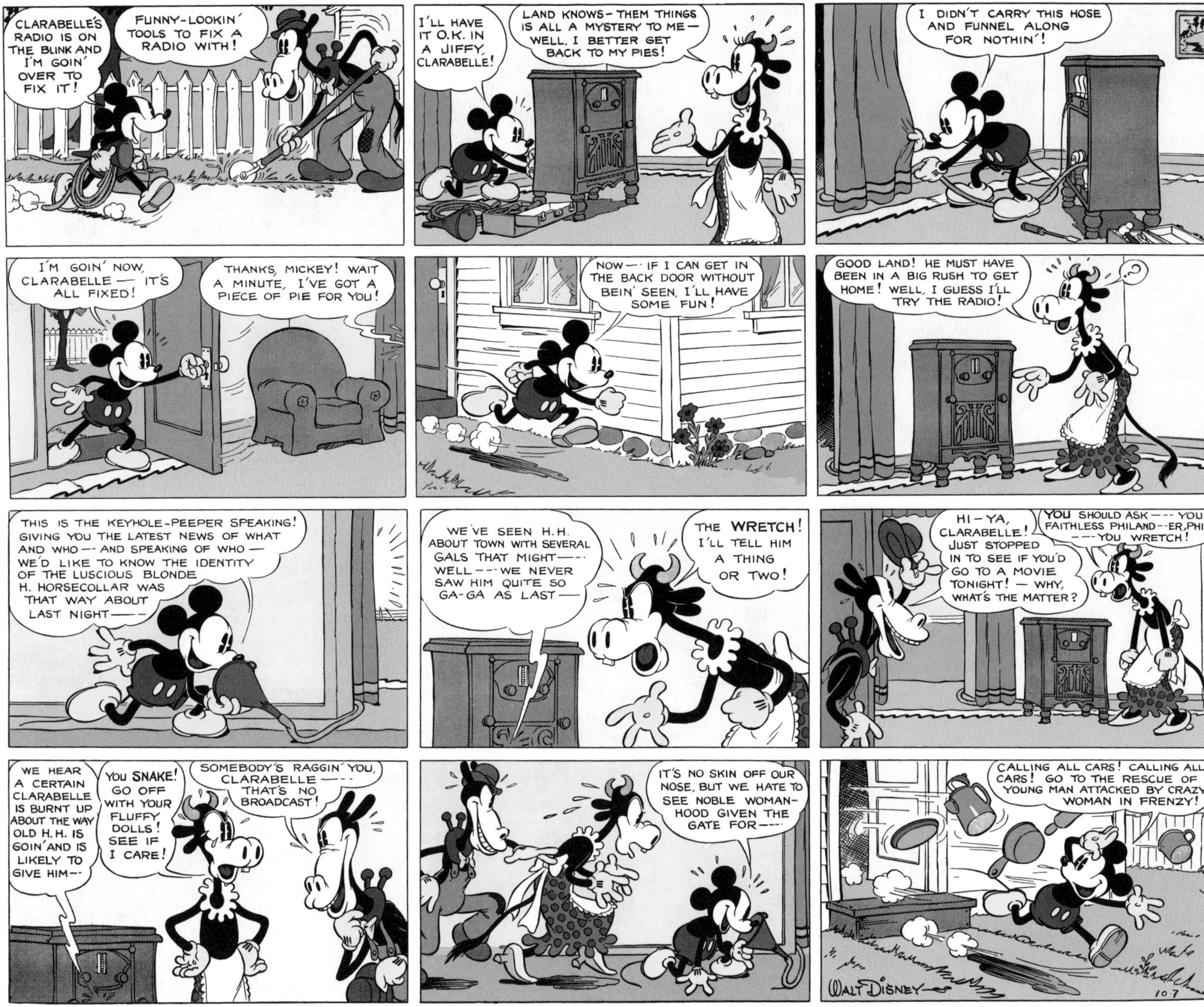
CLARABELLE'S RADIO IS ON THE BLINK AND I'M GOIN' OVER TO FIX IT!
FUNNY-LOOKIN' TOOLS TO FIX A RADIO WITH!
I'LL HAVE IT O.K. IN A JIFFY, CLARABELLE!
LAND KNOWS - THEM THINGS IS ALL A MYSTERY TO ME - WELL, I BETTER GET BACK TO MY PIES!
I DIDN'T CARRY THIS HOSE AND FUNNEL ALONG FOR NOTHIN'!
I'M GOIN' NOW, CLARABELLE — IT'S ALL FIXED!
THANKS, MICKEY! WAIT A MINUTE, I'VE GOT A PIECE OF PIE FOR YOU!
NOW — IF I CAN GET IN THE BACK DOOR WITHOUT BEIN' SEEN, I'LL HAVE SOME FUN!
GOOD LAND! HE MUST HAVE BEEN IN A BIG RUSH TO GET HOME! WELL, I GUESS I'LL TRY THE RADIO!
THIS IS THE KEYHOLE-PEEPER SPEAKING! GIVING YOU THE LATEST NEWS OF WHAT AND WHO — AND SPEAKING OF WHO — WE'D LIKE TO KNOW THE IDENTITY OF THE LUSCIOUS BLONDE H. HORSECOLLAR WAS THAT WAY ABOUT LAST NIGHT ——
WE'VE SEEN H.H. ABOUT TOWN WITH SEVERAL GALS THAT MIGHT — WELL — WE NEVER SAW HIM QUITE SO GA-GA AS LAST —
THE WRETCH! I'LL TELL HIM A THING OR TWO!
HI-YA, CLARABELLE! JUST STOPPED IN TO SEE IF YOU'D GO TO A MOVIE TONIGHT! — WHY, WHAT'S THE MATTER?
YOU SHOULD ASK — YOU FAITHLESS PHILAND — ER, PHIL — YOU WRETCH!
WE HEAR A CERTAIN CLARABELLE IS BURNT UP ABOUT THE WAY OLD H.H. IS GOIN' AND IS LIKELY TO GIVE HIM --
YOU SNAKE! GO OFF WITH YOUR FLUFFY DOLLS! SEE IF I CARE!
SOMEBODY'S RAGGIN' YOU, CLARABELLE — THAT'S NO BROADCAST!
IT'S NO SKIN OFF OUR NOSE, BUT WE HATE TO SEE NOBLE WOMANHOOD GIVEN THE GATE FOR —
CALLING ALL CARS! CALLING ALL CARS! GO TO THE RESCUE OF YOUNG MAN ATTACKED BY CRAZY WOMAN IN FRENZY!
WALT DISNEY
10·7

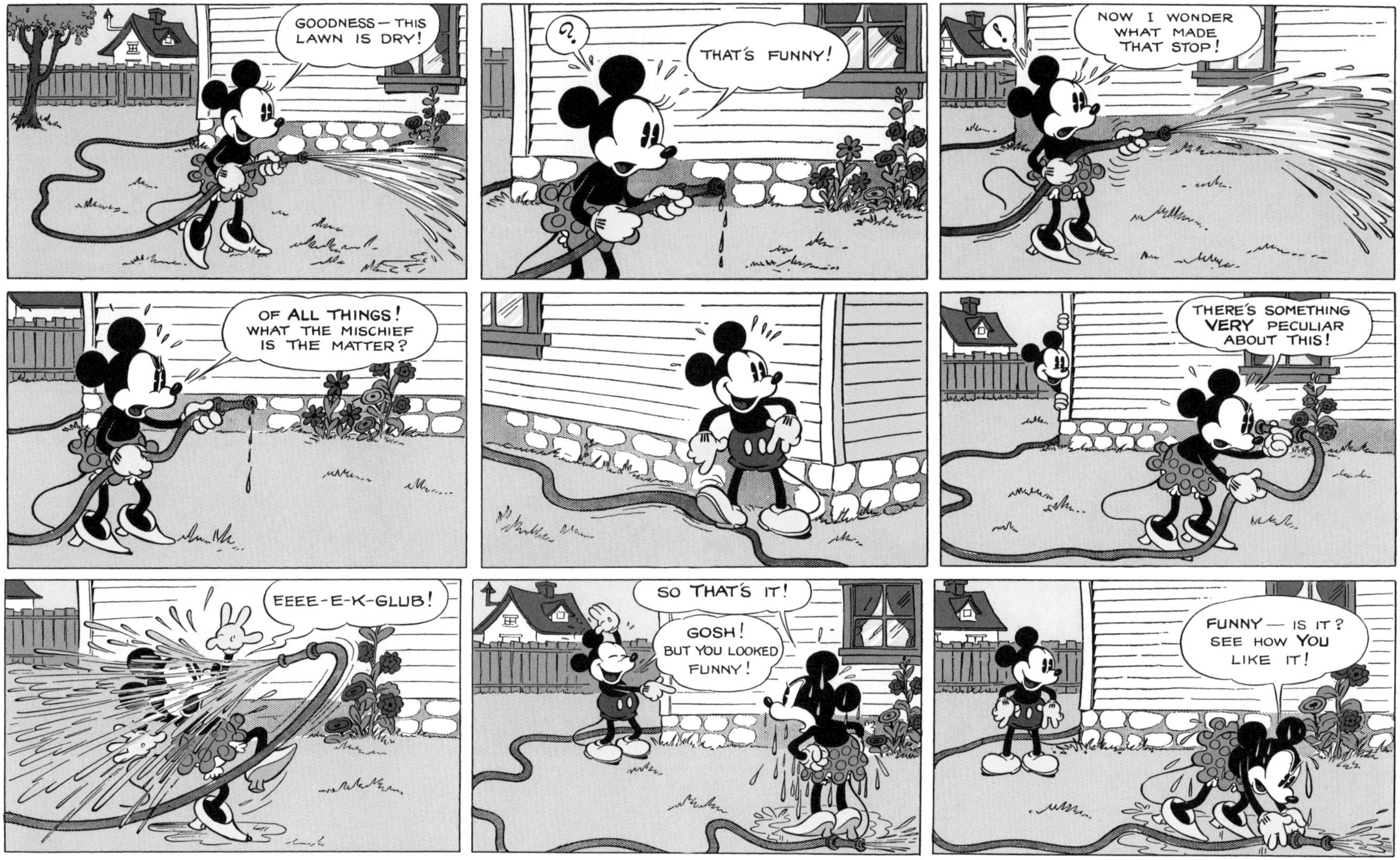
GOODNESS—THIS LAWN IS DRY!
THAT'S FUNNY!
NOW I WONDER WHAT MADE THAT STOP!
OF ALL THINGS! WHAT THE MISCHIEF IS THE MATTER?
THERE'S SOMETHING VERY PECULIAR ABOUT THIS!
EEEE-E-K-GLUB!
SO THAT'S IT!
GOSH! BUT YOU LOOKED FUNNY!
FUNNY—IS IT? SEE HOW YOU LIKE IT!
HA! HA! TOO SMART FOR YA, MINNIE!
WOW!
HA! HA! TOO SMART FOR YOUR OWN GOOD!
AND DON'T MISS ONE INCH OF THAT LAWN, EITHER! IT'S BEEN NEEDING WATER FOR A LONG TIME!
WALT DISNEY
10-14

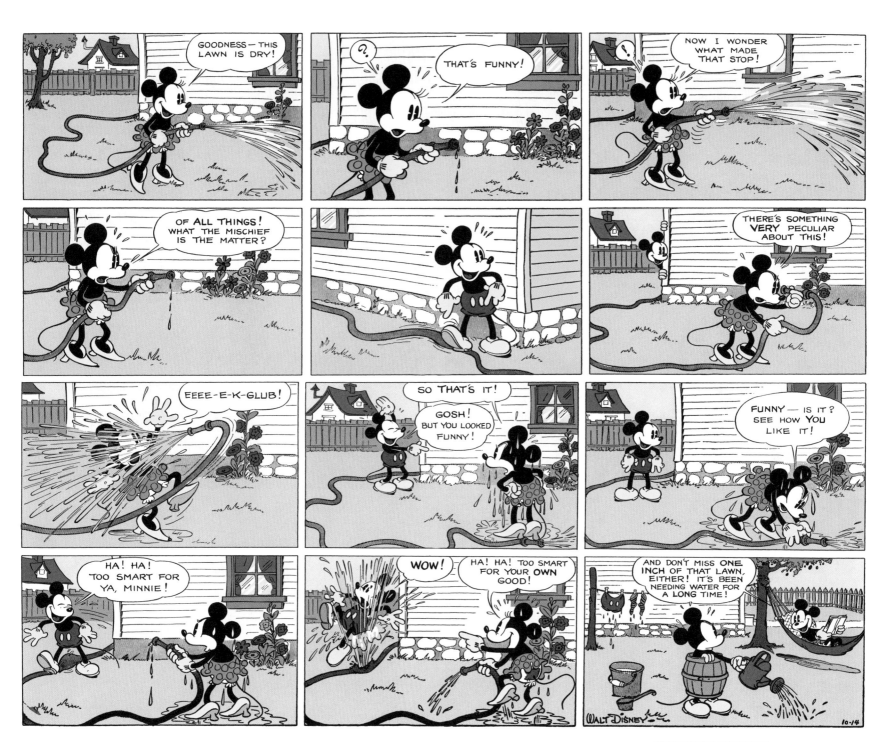

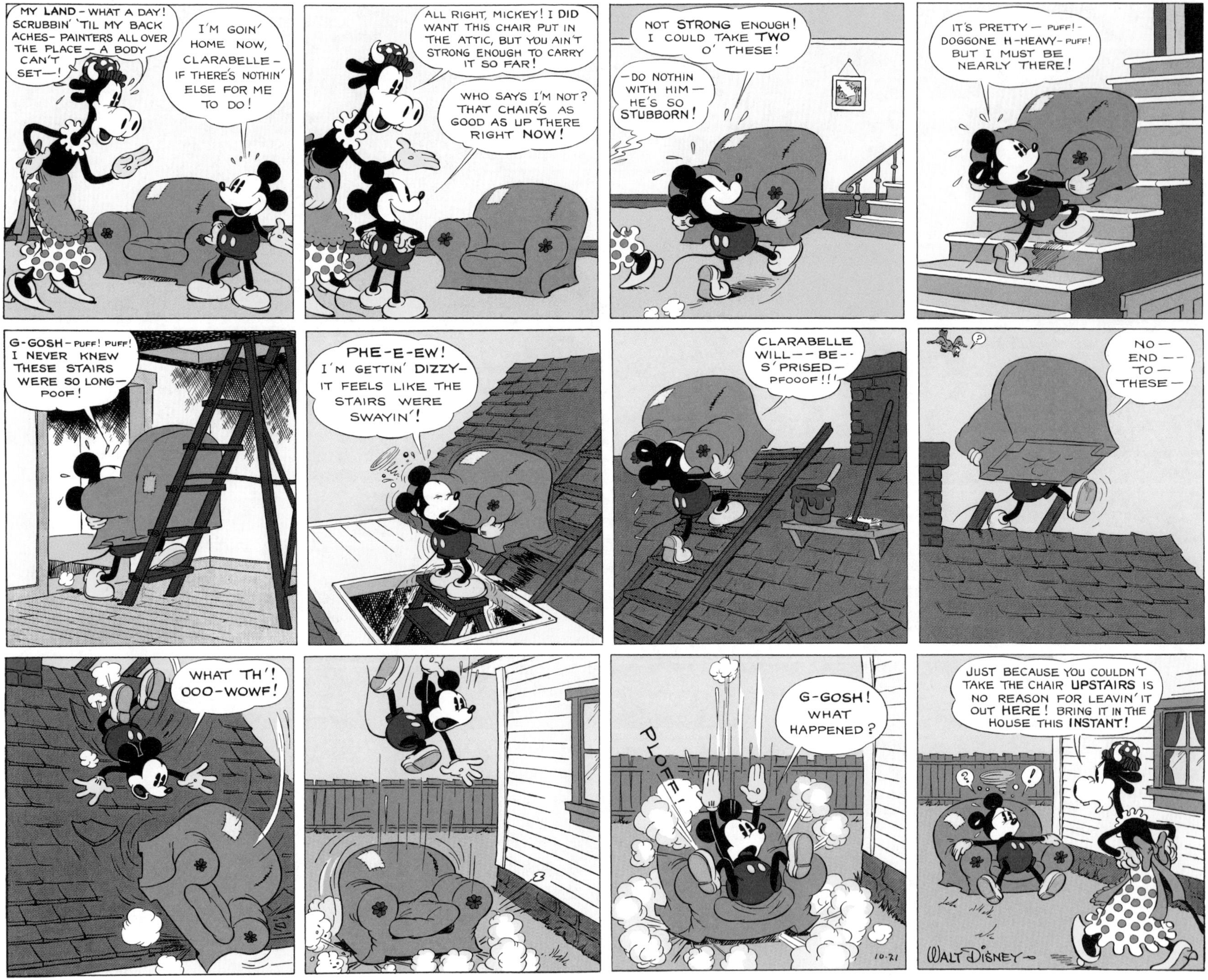
MY LAND - WHAT A DAY! SCRUBBIN' 'TIL MY BACK ACHES- PAINTERS ALL OVER THE PLACE - A BODY CAN'T SET—!
I'M GOIN' HOME NOW, CLARABELLE - IF THERE'S NOTHIN' ELSE FOR ME TO DO!
ALL RIGHT, MICKEY! I DID WANT THIS CHAIR PUT IN THE ATTIC, BUT YOU AIN'T STRONG ENOUGH TO CARRY IT SO FAR!
WHO SAYS I'M NOT? THAT CHAIR'S AS GOOD AS UP THERE RIGHT NOW!
NOT STRONG ENOUGH! I COULD TAKE TWO O' THESE!
-DO NOTHIN WITH HIM - HE'S SO STUBBORN!
IT'S PRETTY — PUFF! - DOGGONE H-HEAVY- PUFF! BUT I MUST BE NEARLY THERE!
G-GOSH - PUFF! PUFF! I NEVER KNEW THESE STAIRS WERE SO LONG- POOF!
PHE-E-EW! I'M GETTIN' DIZZY- IT FEELS LIKE THE STAIRS WERE SWAYIN'!
CLARABELLE WILL-- BE-- S'PRISED- PFOOOF!!!
NO — END -- TO — THESE —
WHAT TH'! OOO-WOWF!
PLOFF!
G-GOSH! WHAT HAPPENED?
JUST BECAUSE YOU COULDN'T TAKE THE CHAIR UPSTAIRS IS NO REASON FOR LEAVIN' IT OUT HERE! BRING IT IN THE HOUSE THIS INSTANT!
10-21
WALT DISNEY

174. "CHAIR" DID IT GO?

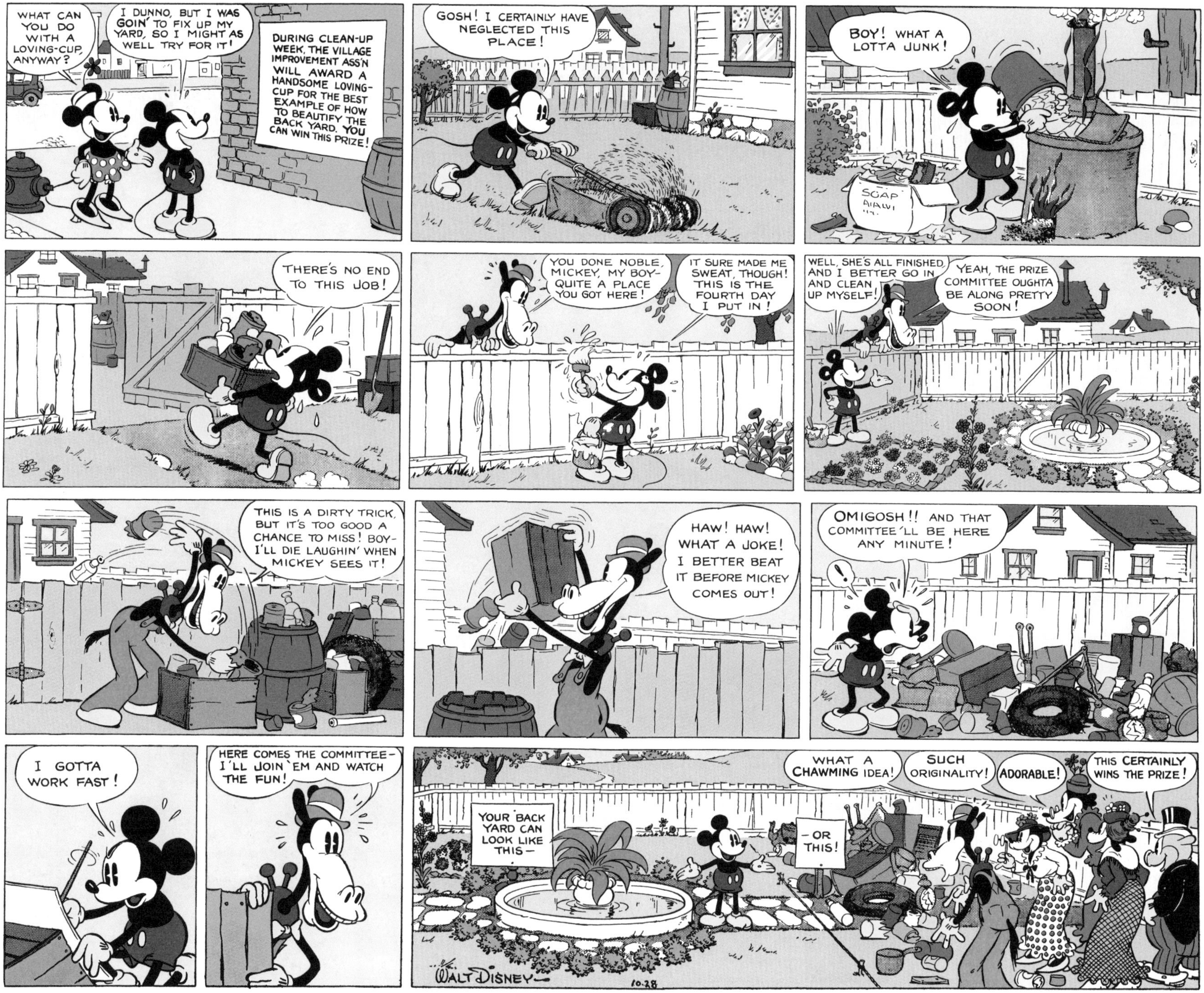
WHAT CAN YOU DO WITH A LOVING-CUP, ANYWAY?
I DUNNO, BUT I WAS GOIN' TO FIX UP MY YARD, SO I MIGHT AS WELL TRY FOR IT!
DURING CLEAN-UP WEEK, THE VILLAGE IMPROVEMENT ASS'N WILL AWARD A HANDSOME LOVING-CUP FOR THE BEST EXAMPLE OF HOW TO BEAUTIFY THE BACK YARD. YOU CAN WIN THIS PRIZE!
GOSH! I CERTAINLY HAVE NEGLECTED THIS PLACE!
BOY! WHAT A LOTTA JUNK!
SOAP
THERE'S NO END TO THIS JOB!
YOU DONE NOBLE, MICKEY, MY BOY-QUITE A PLACE YOU GOT HERE!
IT SURE MADE ME SWEAT, THOUGH! THIS IS THE FOURTH DAY I PUT IN!
WELL, SHE'S ALL FINISHED, AND I BETTER GO IN AND CLEAN UP MYSELF!
YEAH, THE PRIZE COMMITTEE OUGHTA BE ALONG PRETTY SOON!
THIS IS A DIRTY TRICK, BUT IT'S TOO GOOD A CHANCE TO MISS! BOY-I'LL DIE LAUGHIN' WHEN MICKEY SEES IT!
HAW! HAW! WHAT A JOKE! I BETTER BEAT IT BEFORE MICKEY COMES OUT!
OMIGOSH!! AND THAT COMMITTEE'LL BE HERE ANY MINUTE!
!
I GOTTA WORK FAST!
HERE COMES THE COMMITTEE-I'LL JOIN 'EM AND WATCH THE FUN!
YOUR BACK YARD CAN LOOK LIKE THIS-
-OR THIS!
WHAT A CHAWMING IDEA!
SUCH ORIGINALITY!
ADORABLE!
THIS CERTAINLY WINS THE PRIZE!
WALT DISNEY
10.28

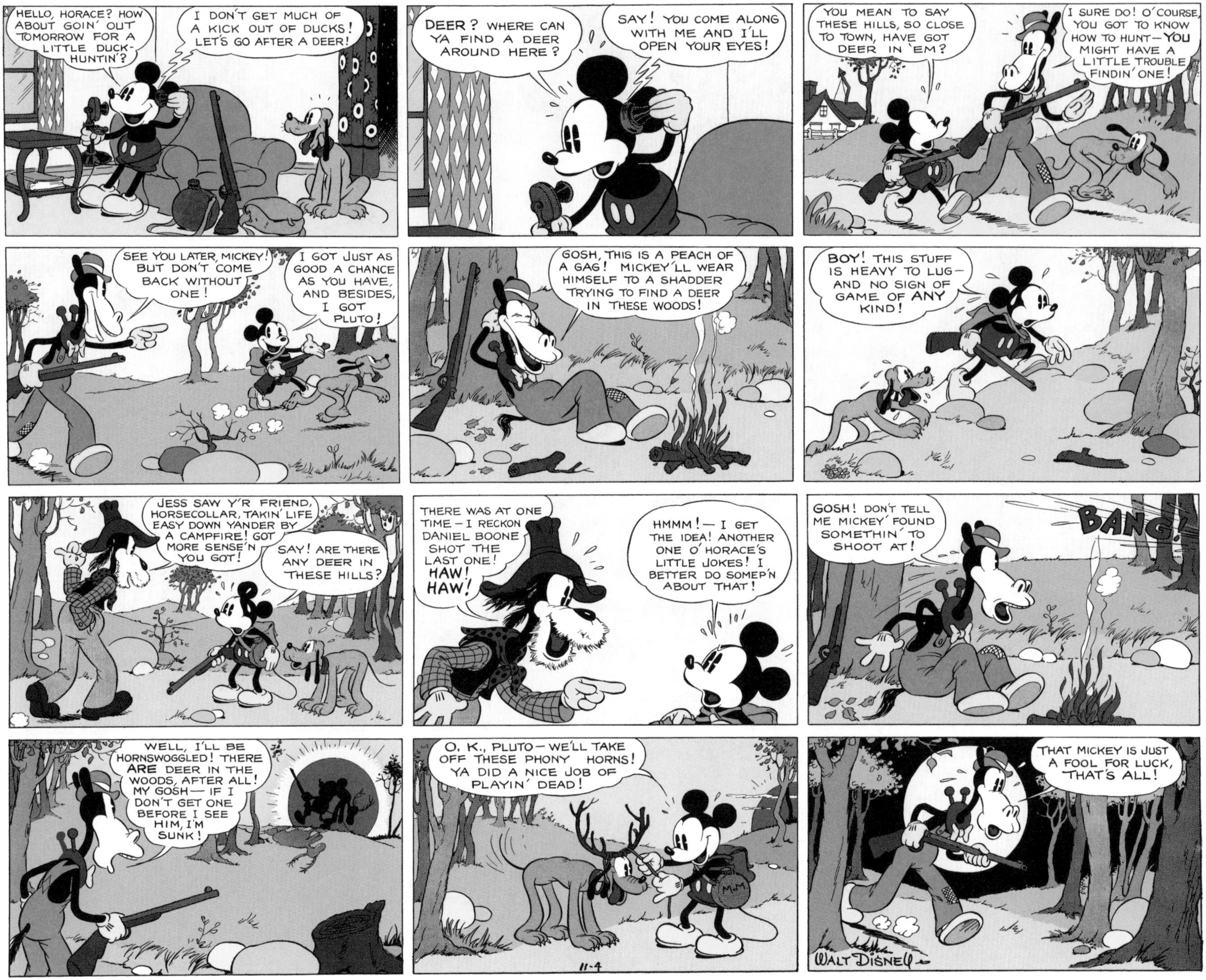
HELLO, HORACE? HOW ABOUT GOIN' OUT TOMORROW FOR A LITTLE DUCK-HUNTIN'?
I DON'T GET MUCH OF A KICK OUT OF DUCKS! LET'S GO AFTER A DEER!
DEER? WHERE CAN YA FIND A DEER AROUND HERE?
SAY! YOU COME ALONG WITH ME AND I'LL OPEN YOUR EYES!
YOU MEAN TO SAY THESE HILLS, SO CLOSE TO TOWN, HAVE GOT DEER IN 'EM?
I SURE DO! O'COURSE, YOU GOT TO KNOW HOW TO HUNT—YOU MIGHT HAVE A LITTLE TROUBLE FINDIN' ONE!
SEE YOU LATER, MICKEY! BUT DON'T COME BACK WITHOUT ONE!
I GOT JUST AS GOOD A CHANCE AS YOU HAVE, AND BESIDES, I GOT PLUTO!
GOSH, THIS IS A PEACH OF A GAG! MICKEY'LL WEAR HIMSELF TO A SHADDER TRYING TO FIND A DEER IN THESE WOODS!
BOY! THIS STUFF IS HEAVY TO LUG—AND NO SIGN OF GAME OF ANY KIND!
JESS SAW Y'R FRIEND, HORSECOLLAR, TAKIN' LIFE EASY DOWN YANDER BY A CAMPFIRE! GOT MORE SENSE'N YOU GOT!
SAY! ARE THERE ANY DEER IN THESE HILLS?
THERE WAS AT ONE TIME—I RECKON DANIEL BOONE SHOT THE LAST ONE! HAW! HAW!
HMMM!—I GET THE IDEA! ANOTHER ONE O' HORACE'S LITTLE JOKES! I BETTER DO SOMEP'N ABOUT THAT!
GOSH! DON'T TELL ME MICKEY FOUND SOMETHIN' TO SHOOT AT!
BANG!
WELL, I'LL BE HORNSWOGGLED! THERE ARE DEER IN THE WOODS, AFTER ALL! MY GOSH—IF I DON'T GET ONE BEFORE I SEE HIM, I'M SUNK!
O. K., PLUTO—WE'LL TAKE OFF THESE PHONY HORNS! YA DID A NICE JOB OF PLAYIN' DEAD!
M.M.
11-4
THAT MICKEY IS JUST A FOOL FOR LUCK, THAT'S ALL!
WALT DISNEY

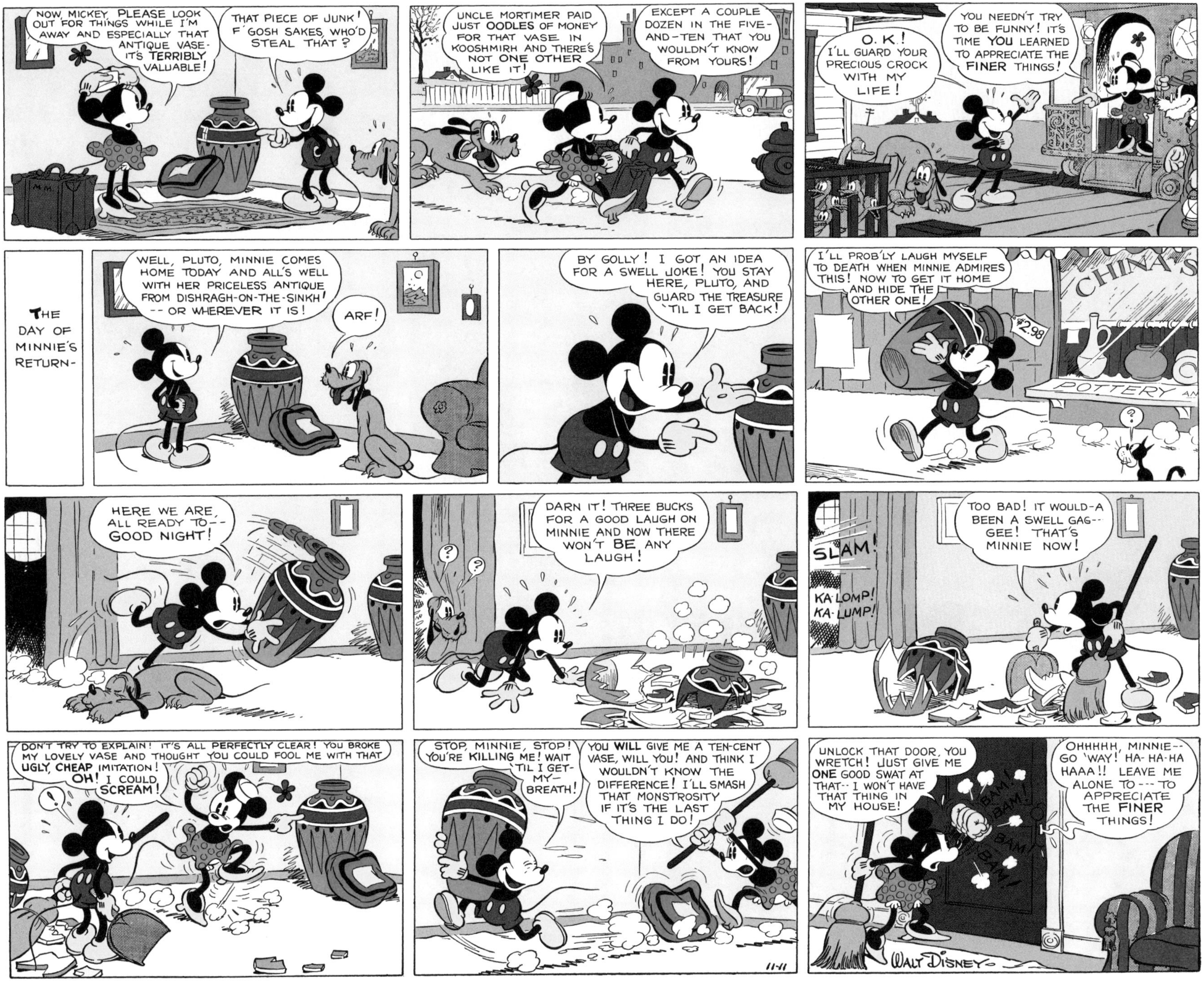
NOW, MICKEY, PLEASE LOOK OUT FOR THINGS WHILE I'M AWAY AND ESPECIALLY THAT ANTIQUE VASE- IT'S TERRIBLY VALUABLE!
THAT PIECE OF JUNK! F'GOSH SAKES, WHO'D STEAL THAT?
M.M.
UNCLE MORTIMER PAID JUST OODLES OF MONEY FOR THAT VASE IN KOOSHMIRH AND THERE'S NOT ONE OTHER LIKE IT!
EXCEPT A COUPLE DOZEN IN THE FIVE-AND-TEN THAT YOU WOULDN'T KNOW FROM YOURS!
O.K.! I'LL GUARD YOUR PRECIOUS CROCK WITH MY LIFE!
YOU NEEDN'T TRY TO BE FUNNY! IT'S TIME YOU LEARNED TO APPRECIATE THE FINER THINGS!
THE DAY OF MINNIE'S RETURN-
WELL, PLUTO, MINNIE COMES HOME TODAY AND ALL'S WELL WITH HER PRICELESS ANTIQUE FROM DISHRAGH-ON-THE-SINKH! -- OR WHEREVER IT IS!
ARF!
BY GOLLY! I GOT AN IDEA FOR A SWELL JOKE! YOU STAY HERE, PLUTO, AND GUARD THE TREASURE 'TIL I GET BACK!
I'LL PROB'LY LAUGH MYSELF TO DEATH WHEN MINNIE ADMIRES THIS! NOW TO GET IT HOME AND HIDE THE OTHER ONE!
CHINA'S
$2.98
POTTERY AN
HERE WE ARE, ALL READY TO-- GOOD NIGHT!
DARN IT! THREE BUCKS FOR A GOOD LAUGH ON MINNIE AND NOW THERE WON'T BE ANY LAUGH!
TOO BAD! IT WOULD-A BEEN A SWELL GAG-- GEE! THAT'S MINNIE NOW!
SLAM!
KA-LOMP! KA-LUMP!
DON'T TRY TO EXPLAIN! IT'S ALL PERFECTLY CLEAR! YOU BROKE MY LOVELY VASE AND THOUGHT YOU COULD FOOL ME WITH THAT UGLY, CHEAP IMITATION! OH! I COULD SCREAM!
STOP, MINNIE, STOP! YOU'RE KILLING ME! WAIT 'TIL I GET- MY- BREATH!
YOU WILL GIVE ME A TEN-CENT VASE, WILL YOU! AND THINK I WOULDN'T KNOW THE DIFFERENCE! I'LL SMASH THAT MONSTROSITY IF IT'S THE LAST THING I DO!
11-11
UNLOCK THAT DOOR, YOU WRETCH! JUST GIVE ME ONE GOOD SWAT AT THAT-- I WON'T HAVE THAT THING IN MY HOUSE!
OHHHHH, MINNIE-- GO 'WAY! HA-HA-HA HAAA!! LEAVE ME ALONE TO--- TO APPRECIATE THE FINER THINGS!
BAM! BAM! BAM! BAM!
WALT DISNEY

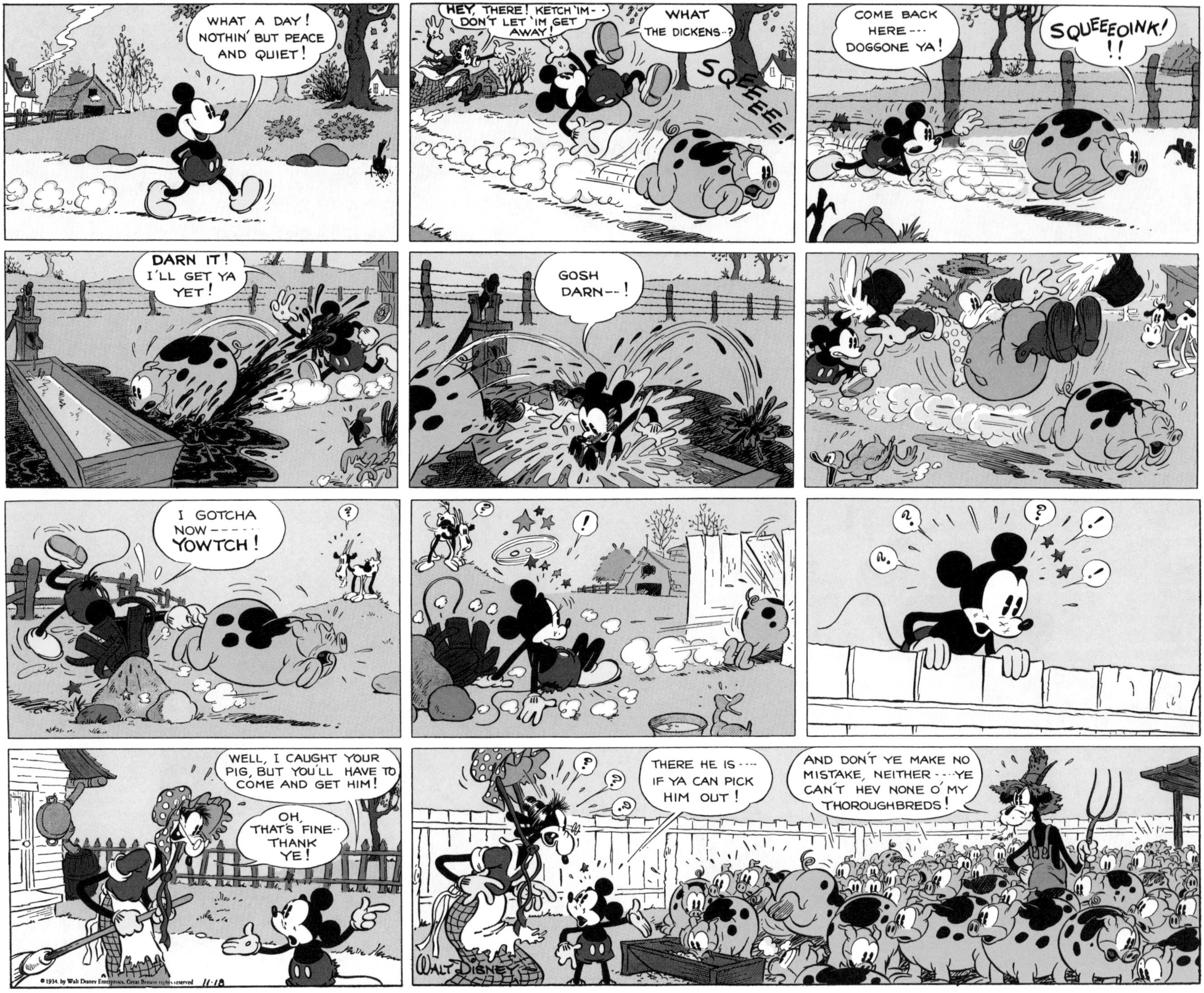
WHAT A DAY! NOTHIN' BUT PEACE AND QUIET!
HEY, THERE! KETCH 'IM-- DON'T LET 'IM GET AWAY!
WHAT THE DICKENS--?
SQEEEEE!
COME BACK HERE--- DOGGONE YA!
SQUEEEEOINK! !!
DARN IT! I'LL GET YA YET!
GOSH DARN--!
I GOTCHA NOW----- YOWTCH!
?
!
?
?
!
!
WELL, I CAUGHT YOUR PIG, BUT YOU'LL HAVE TO COME AND GET HIM!
OH, THAT'S FINE-- THANK YE!
© 1934, by Walt Disney Enterprises, Great Britain rights reserved
11-18
THERE HE IS---- IF YA CAN PICK HIM OUT!
AND DON'T YE MAKE NO MISTAKE, NEITHER----YE CAN'T HEV NONE O' MY THOROUGHBREDS!
WALT DISNEY

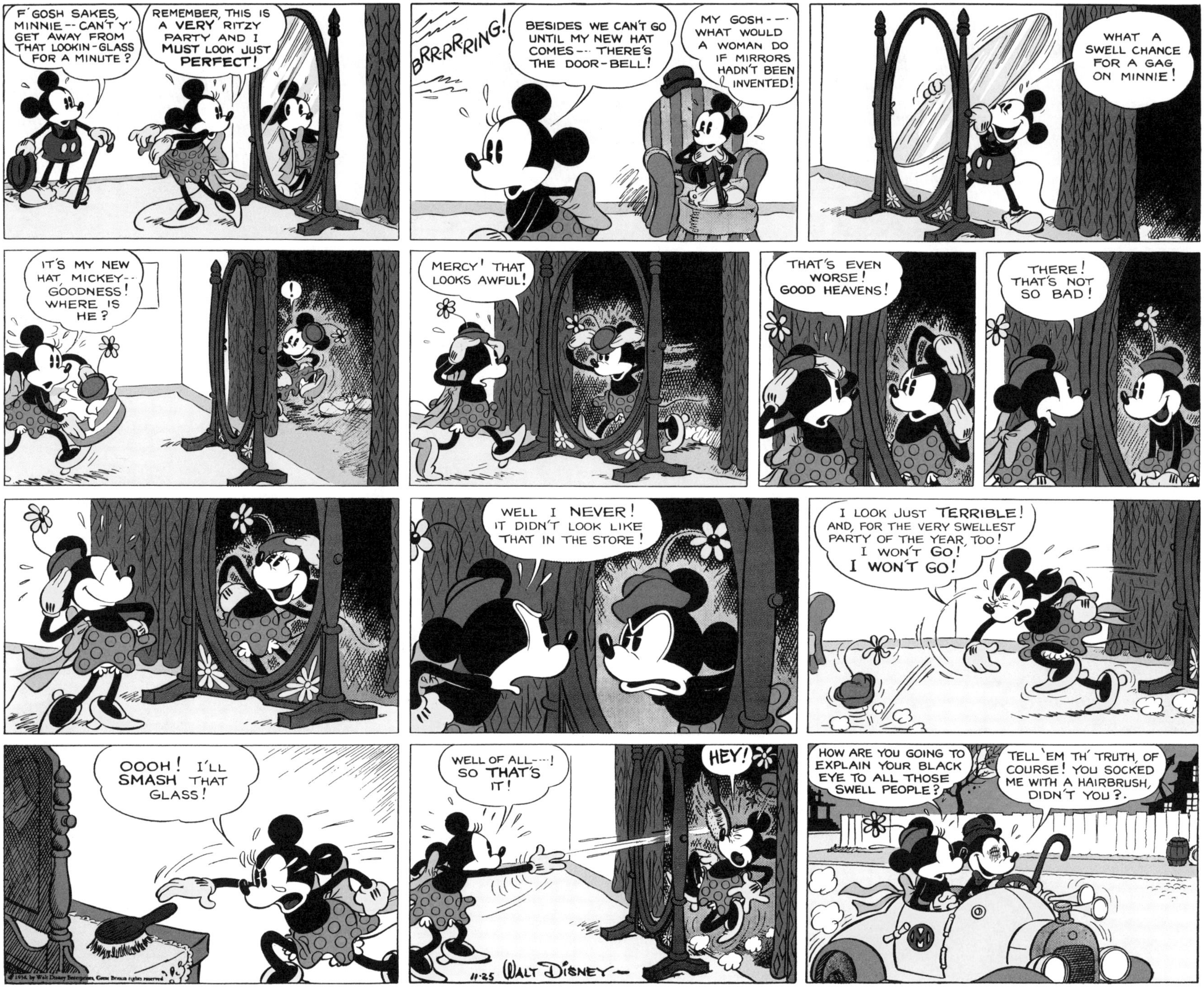
F'GOSH SAKES, MINNIE -- CAN'T Y' GET AWAY FROM THAT LOOKIN-GLASS FOR A MINUTE?
REMEMBER, THIS IS A VERY RITZY PARTY AND I MUST LOOK JUST PERFECT!
BRR-R-R-RING!
BESIDES WE CAN'T GO UNTIL MY NEW HAT COMES -- THERE'S THE DOOR-BELL!
MY GOSH -- WHAT WOULD A WOMAN DO IF MIRRORS HADN'T BEEN INVENTED!
WHAT A SWELL CHANCE FOR A GAG ON MINNIE!
IT'S MY NEW HAT, MICKEY -- GOODNESS! WHERE IS HE?
!
MERCY! THAT LOOKS AWFUL!
THAT'S EVEN WORSE! GOOD HEAVENS!
THERE! THAT'S NOT SO BAD!
WELL I NEVER! IT DIDN'T LOOK LIKE THAT IN THE STORE!
I LOOK JUST TERRIBLE! AND, FOR THE VERY SWELLEST PARTY OF THE YEAR, TOO! I WON'T GO! I WON'T GO!
OOOH! I'LL SMASH THAT GLASS!
WELL OF ALL---! SO THAT'S IT!
HEY!
HOW ARE YOU GOING TO EXPLAIN YOUR BLACK EYE TO ALL THOSE SWELL PEOPLE?
TELL 'EM TH' TRUTH, OF COURSE! YOU SOCKED ME WITH A HAIRBRUSH, DIDN'T YOU?.
11-25 WALT DISNEY

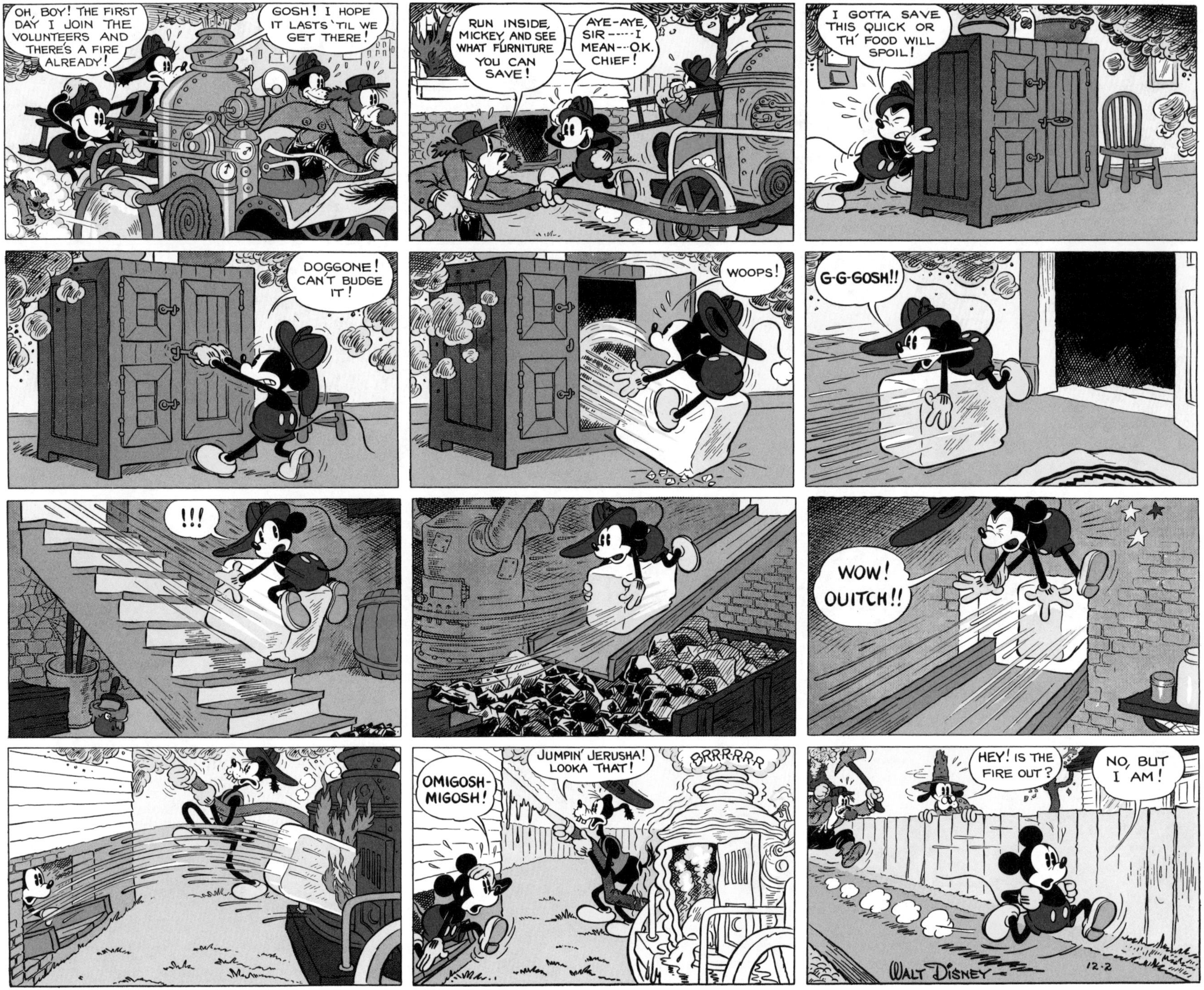

OH, BOY! THE FIRST DAY I JOIN THE VOLUNTEERS AND THERE'S A FIRE ALREADY!
GOSH! I HOPE IT LASTS 'TIL WE GET THERE!
RUN INSIDE, MICKEY, AND SEE WHAT FURNITURE YOU CAN SAVE!
AYE-AYE, SIR ----- I MEAN --- O.K. CHIEF!
I GOTTA SAVE THIS QUICK OR TH' FOOD WILL SPOIL!
DOGGONE! CAN'T BUDGE IT!
WOOPS!
G-G-GOSH!!
!!!
WOW! OUITCH!!
OMIGOSH-MIGOSH!
JUMPIN' JERUSHA! LOOKA THAT!
BRRRRRR
HEY! IS THE FIRE OUT?
NO, BUT I AM!
WALT DISNEY
12-2

FORAY TO MT. FISHFLAKE

AND

GAG STRIPS

DECEMBER 9, 1934
–
FEBRUARY 10, 1935

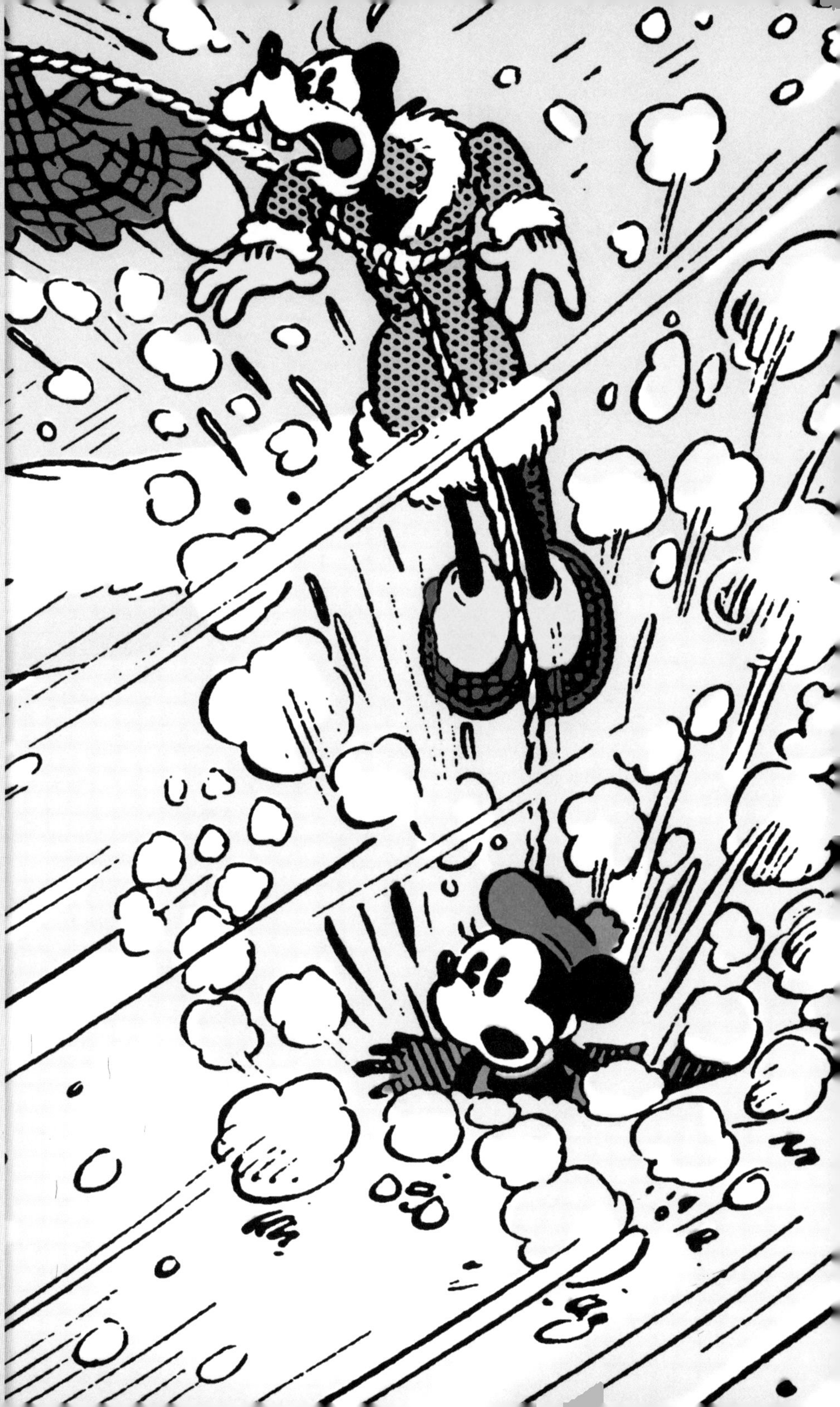

MICKEY MOUSE
REGISTERED U.S. PATENT OFFICE

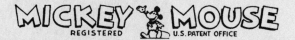

DEATH KNOCKS, FATE PESTERS

"Disaster capitalism," a common term in the modern political dialogue, describes what happens when powerful, cynical oligarchs want to force profitable but unpopular ideas on their communities. Under normal conditions, one cannot easily make average citizens accept a war, a tax hike, or the privatization of public services. But in situations of duress—like a financial panic or an attack from abroad—pundits and talking heads might agree that "sacrifices" are needed, and some desperate common folk can be persuaded to accept the cynical oligarchs' ideas as answers.

The cynicism is redoubled when some oligarchs use their economic clout to create situations of duress on purpose. Induce a disaster, then push a "solution" that conveniently allows you to capitalize; from Nazis to factory bosses, many opportunistic power brokers have gone this route.

Floyd Gottfredson was no despot, but in the mid-1930s, he used something like disaster capitalism—however unwittingly—as a means of shaking up Mickey Mouse's comics world. For Mickey's other world, his world on screen, was changing. Once dominated by musicales with Horace Horsecollar and Clarabelle, Mickey's cartoon universe was becoming one ruled by Goofy, Donald Duck, and crisis-based comedy.

Late 1934's "Foray to Mount Fishflake" uses nothing less than a natural disaster to transform Mickey's strip environment accordingly. When Mickey, Minnie, Horace, and Clarabelle set out to climb a mountain, the atmosphere is reminiscent of the earlier "Dr. Oofgay's Secret Serum": two close-knit couples, bickering like family, are heading off on a grand adventure. When Dippy Dawg joins them, he takes the role of an intruder: much as in the earlier "Lair of Wolf Barker," he is a tagalong pest whose company is often unwanted. But in a telling change, Mickey wants Dippy this time—and in an even more interesting shift, a dark, dangerous night physically separates Mickey and Dippy from the rest of their cohorts. What began as a family escapade for Mickey and his older buddies becomes a pulse-pounding, one-on-one quest for Mickey and a newer friend; facing deadly peril, Mickey and Dippy grow closer together.

We are witness as Gottfredson uses his own kind of fabricated disaster to change the status quo: no lesser duress could force headstrong Horace and Clarabelle from their key co-star positions.

While Goofy—as Dippy would soon be renamed—still had some maturing to do, the seeds of his later buddy relationship were now firmly planted; the lights were literally turned out on the mood of the earlier stories. The profiting party in this feat of "comics disaster capitalism" may not have fully understood how he capitalized; but then, Goofy's understanding of things always was a bit eccentric.

As the Goof slowly became less a pest, more a pal, another pest arrived on the scene. in February 1935, an obstreperous Duck flew in with a lot of fuss and feathers—feathers oddly colored yellow at first! Turn the pages and watch as Disney history hatches before our eyes. [DG]

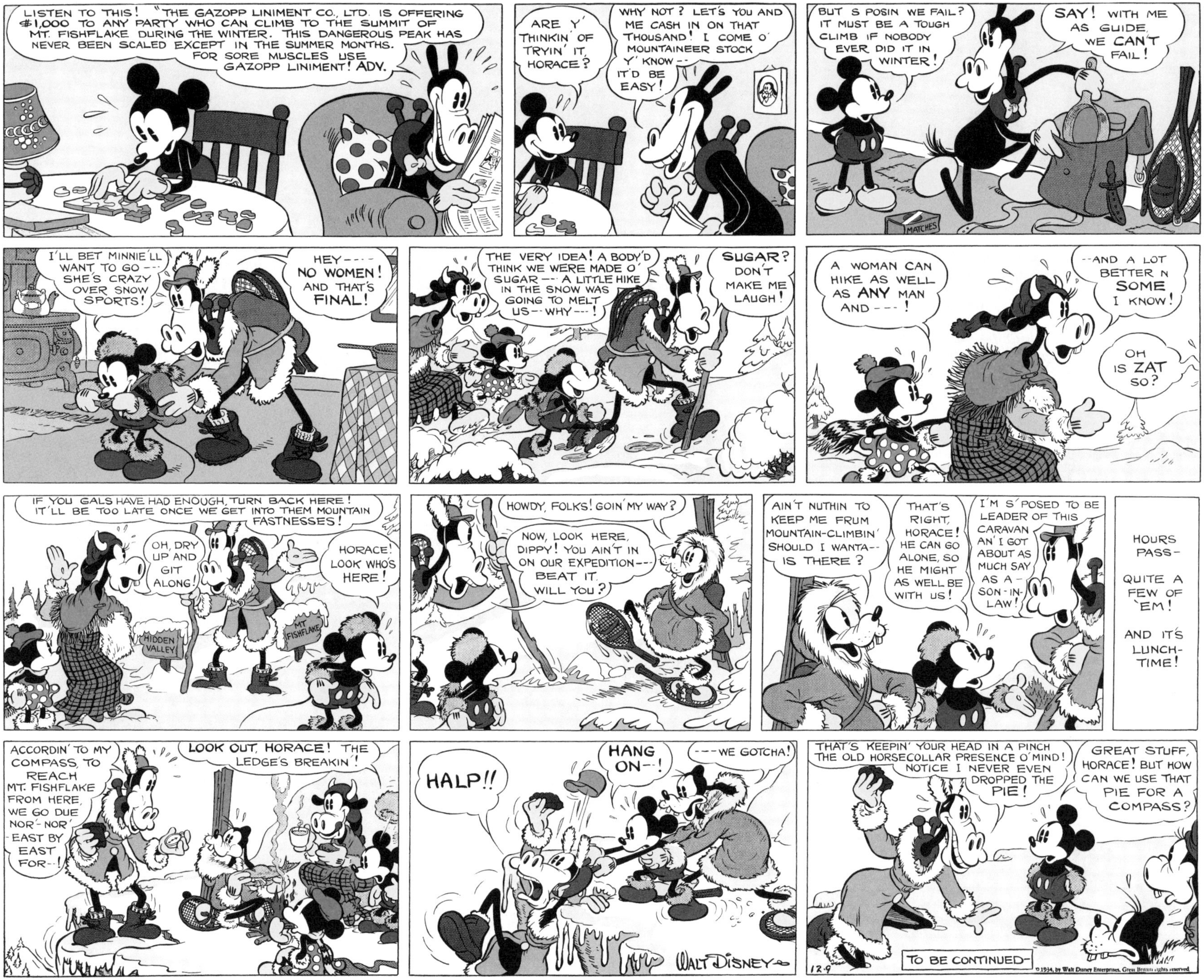
LISTEN TO THIS! "THE GAZOPP LINIMENT CO., LTD. IS OFFERING $1,000 TO ANY PARTY WHO CAN CLIMB TO THE SUMMIT OF MT. FISHFLAKE DURING THE WINTER. THIS DANGEROUS PEAK HAS NEVER BEEN SCALED EXCEPT IN THE SUMMER MONTHS. FOR SORE MUSCLES USE GAZOPP LINIMENT! ADV.
ARE Y' THINKIN' OF TRYIN' IT, HORACE?
WHY NOT? LET'S YOU AND ME CASH IN ON THAT THOUSAND! I COME O' MOUNTAINEER STOCK Y' KNOW-- IT'D BE EASY!
BUT S'POSIN WE FAIL? IT MUST BE A TOUGH CLIMB IF NOBODY EVER DID IT IN WINTER!
SAY! WITH ME AS GUIDE, WE CAN'T FAIL!
MATCHES
I'LL BET MINNIE'LL WANT TO GO--- SHE'S CRAZY OVER SNOW SPORTS!
HEY---- NO WOMEN! AND THAT'S FINAL!
THE VERY IDEA! A BODY'D THINK WE WERE MADE O' SUGAR--- A LITTLE HIKE IN THE SNOW WAS GOING TO MELT US--WHY---!
SUGAR? DON'T MAKE ME LAUGH!
A WOMAN CAN HIKE AS WELL AS ANY MAN AND---!
--AND A LOT BETTER'N SOME I KNOW!
OH IS ZAT SO?
IF YOU GALS HAVE HAD ENOUGH, TURN BACK HERE! IT'LL BE TOO LATE ONCE WE GET INTO THEM MOUNTAIN FASTNESSES!
OH, DRY UP AND GIT ALONG!
HORACE! LOOK WHO'S HERE!
HIDDEN VALLEY
MT FISHFLAKE
HOWDY, FOLKS! GOIN' MY WAY?
NOW, LOOK HERE, DIPPY! YOU AIN'T IN ON OUR EXPEDITION--- BEAT IT, WILL YOU?
AIN'T NUTHIN TO KEEP ME FRUM MOUNTAIN-CLIMBIN' SHOULD I WANTA-- IS THERE?
THAT'S RIGHT, HORACE! HE CAN GO ALONE, SO HE MIGHT AS WELL BE WITH US!
I'M S'POSED TO BE LEADER OF THIS CARAVAN AN' I GOT ABOUT AS MUCH SAY AS A SON-IN-LAW!
HOURS PASS- QUITE A FEW OF 'EM! AND IT'S LUNCH-TIME!
ACCORDIN' TO MY COMPASS, TO REACH MT. FISHFLAKE FROM HERE, WE GO DUE NOR'-NOR'-EAST BY EAST FOR--!
LOOK OUT, HORACE! THE LEDGE'S BREAKIN'!
HALP!!
HANG ON--!
---WE GOTCHA!
THAT'S KEEPIN' YOUR HEAD IN A PINCH THE OLD HORSECOLLAR PRESENCE O' MIND! NOTICE I NEVER EVEN DROPPED THE PIE!
GREAT STUFF, HORACE! BUT HOW CAN WE USE THAT PIE FOR A COMPASS?
WALT DISNEY
12-9
TO BE CONTINUED-
© 1934, by Walt Disney Enterprises, Great Britain rights reserved

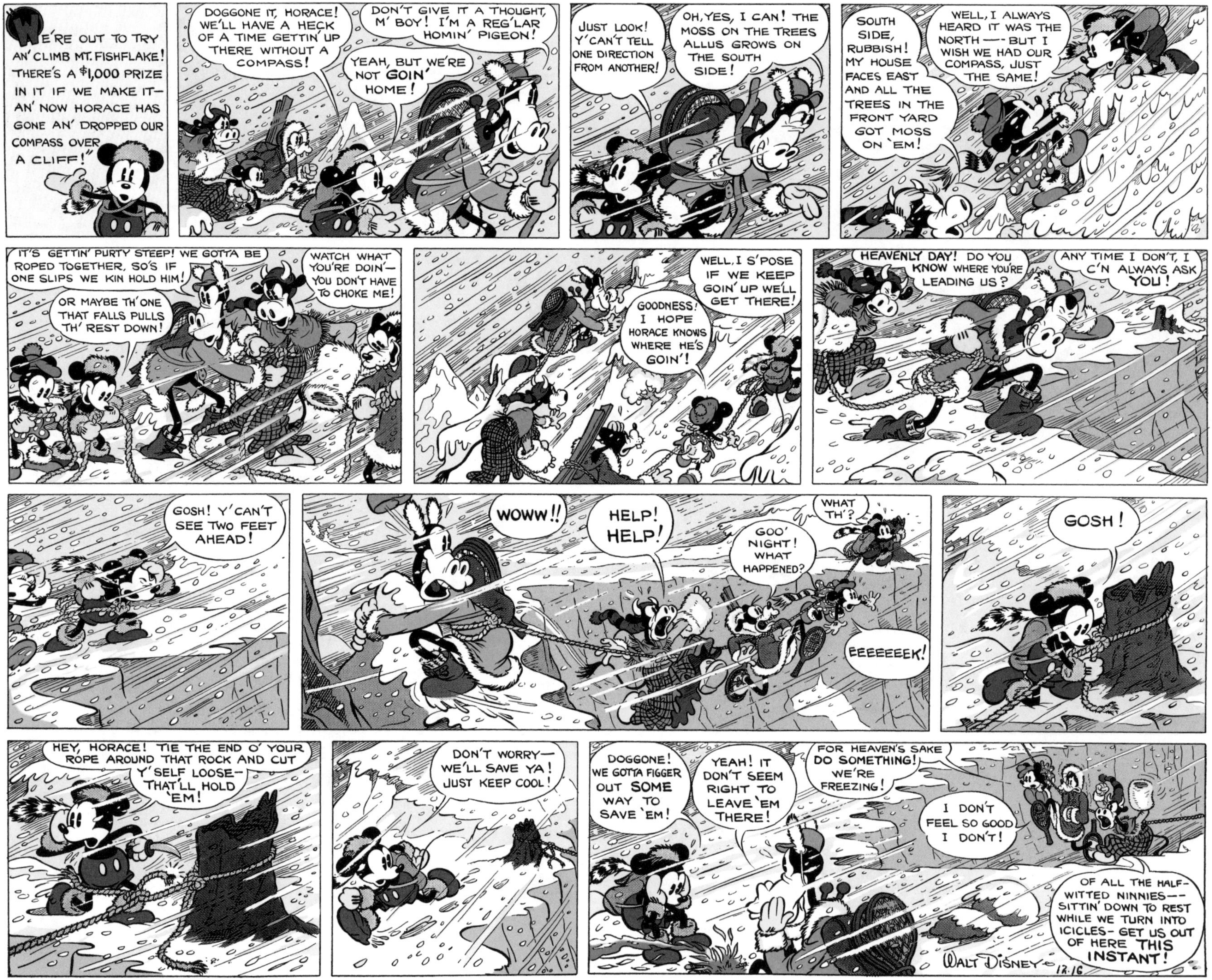

WE'RE OUT TO TRY AN' CLIMB MT. FISHFLAKE! THERE'S A $1,000 PRIZE IN IT IF WE MAKE IT— AN' NOW HORACE HAS GONE AN' DROPPED OUR COMPASS OVER A CLIFF!"
DOGGONE IT, HORACE! WE'LL HAVE A HECK OF A TIME GETTIN' UP THERE WITHOUT A COMPASS!
DON'T GIVE IT A THOUGHT, M' BOY! I'M A REG'LAR HOMIN' PIGEON!
YEAH, BUT WE'RE NOT GOIN' HOME!
JUST LOOK! Y'CAN'T TELL ONE DIRECTION FROM ANOTHER!
OH, YES, I CAN! THE MOSS ON THE TREES ALLUS GROWS ON THE SOUTH SIDE!
SOUTH SIDE, RUBBISH! MY HOUSE FACES EAST AND ALL THE TREES IN THE FRONT YARD GOT MOSS ON 'EM!
WELL, I ALWAYS HEARD IT WAS THE NORTH — BUT I WISH WE HAD OUR COMPASS, JUST THE SAME!
IT'S GETTIN' PURTY STEEP! WE GOTTA BE ROPED TOGETHER, SO'S IF ONE SLIPS WE KIN HOLD HIM!
OR MAYBE TH' ONE THAT FALLS PULLS TH' REST DOWN!
WATCH WHAT YOU'RE DOIN'— YOU DON'T HAVE TO CHOKE ME!
WELL, I S'POSE IF WE KEEP GOIN' UP WE'LL GET THERE!
GOODNESS! I HOPE HORACE KNOWS WHERE HE'S GOIN'!
HEAVENLY DAY! DO YOU KNOW WHERE YOU'RE LEADING US?
ANY TIME I DON'T, I C'N ALWAYS ASK YOU!
GOSH! Y'CAN'T SEE TWO FEET AHEAD!
WOWW!!
HELP! HELP!
WHAT TH'?
GOO' NIGHT! WHAT HAPPENED?
EEEEEEEK!
GOSH!
HEY, HORACE! TIE THE END O' YOUR ROPE AROUND THAT ROCK AND CUT Y'SELF LOOSE— THAT'LL HOLD 'EM!
DON'T WORRY— WE'LL SAVE YA! JUST KEEP COOL!
DOGGONE! WE GOTTA FIGGER OUT SOME WAY TO SAVE 'EM!
YEAH! IT DON'T SEEM RIGHT TO LEAVE 'EM THERE!
FOR HEAVEN'S SAKE DO SOMETHING! WE'RE FREEZING!
I DON'T FEEL SO GOOD I DON'T!
OF ALL THE HALF-WITTED NINNIES— SITTIN' DOWN TO REST WHILE WE TURN INTO ICICLES— GET US OUT OF HERE THIS INSTANT!
WALT DISNEY 12.16

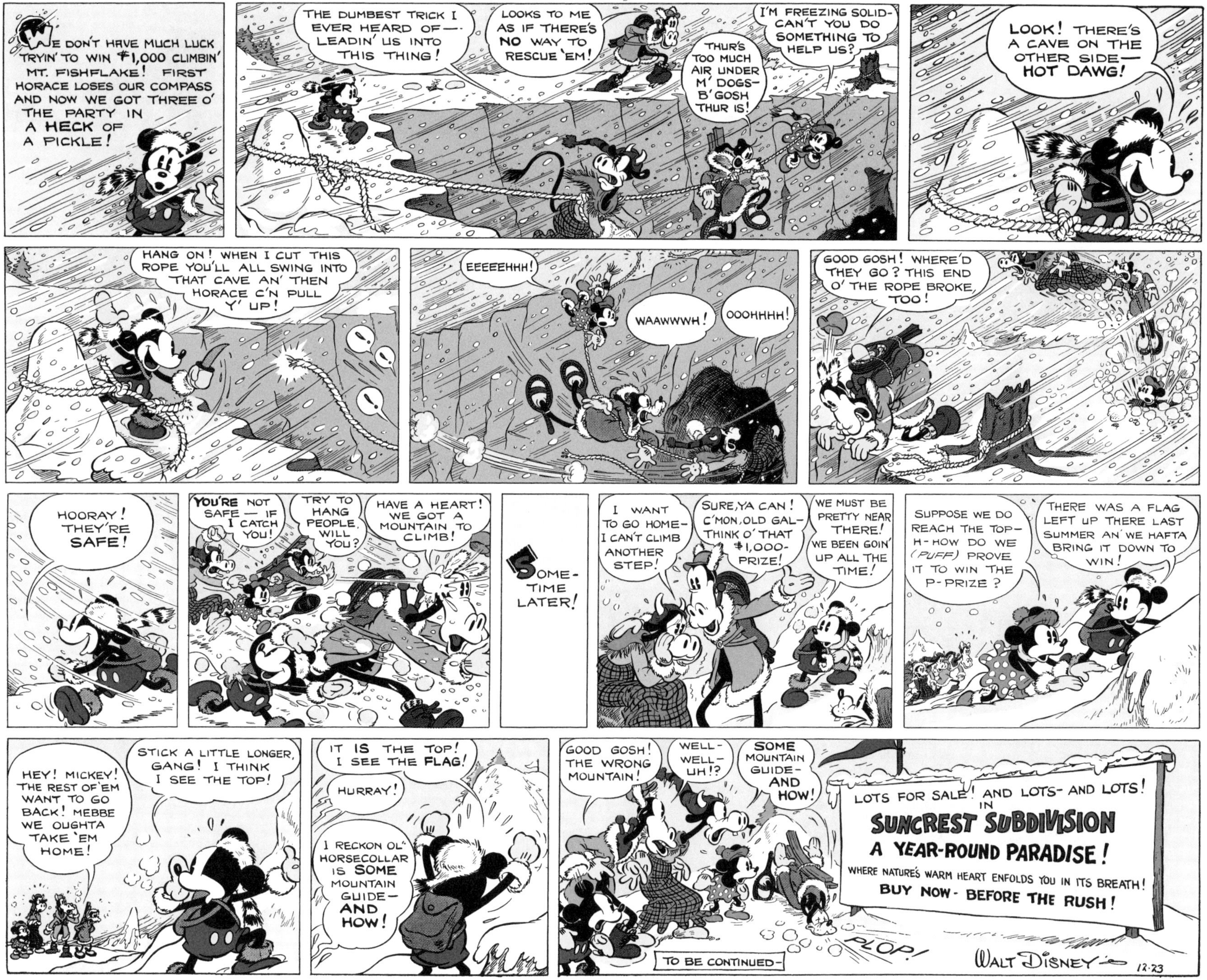
WE DON'T HAVE MUCH LUCK TRYIN' TO WIN $1,000 CLIMBIN' MT. FISHFLAKE! FIRST HORACE LOSES OUR COMPASS AND NOW WE GOT THREE O' THE PARTY IN A HECK OF A PICKLE!
THE DUMBEST TRICK I EVER HEARD OF — LEADIN' US INTO THIS THING!
LOOKS TO ME AS IF THERE'S NO WAY TO RESCUE 'EM!
THUR'S TOO MUCH AIR UNDER M' DOGS- B' GOSH THUR IS!
I'M FREEZING SOLID- CAN'T YOU DO SOMETHING TO HELP US?
LOOK! THERE'S A CAVE ON THE OTHER SIDE— HOT DAWG!
HANG ON! WHEN I CUT THIS ROPE YOU'LL ALL SWING INTO THAT CAVE AN' THEN HORACE C'N PULL Y' UP!
EEEEEHHH!
WAAWWWH!
OOOHHHH!
GOOD GOSH! WHERE'D THEY GO? THIS END O' THE ROPE BROKE, TOO!
HOORAY! THEY'RE SAFE!
YOU'RE NOT SAFE — IF I CATCH YOU!
TRY TO HANG PEOPLE, WILL YOU?
HAVE A HEART! WE GOT A MOUNTAIN TO CLIMB!
SOME-TIME LATER!
I WANT TO GO HOME- I CAN'T CLIMB ANOTHER STEP!
SURE, YA CAN! C'MON, OLD GAL- THINK O' THAT $1,000- PRIZE!
WE MUST BE PRETTY NEAR THERE! WE BEEN GOIN' UP ALL THE TIME!
SUPPOSE WE DO REACH THE TOP- H-HOW DO WE (PUFF) PROVE IT TO WIN THE P-PRIZE?
THERE WAS A FLAG LEFT UP THERE LAST SUMMER AN' WE HAFTA BRING IT DOWN TO WIN!
HEY! MICKEY! THE REST OF 'EM WANT TO GO BACK! MEBBE WE OUGHTA TAKE 'EM HOME!
STICK A LITTLE LONGER, GANG! I THINK I SEE THE TOP!
IT IS THE TOP! I SEE THE FLAG!
HURRAY!
I RECKON OL' HORSECOLLAR IS SOME MOUNTAIN GUIDE— AND HOW!
GOOD GOSH! THE WRONG MOUNTAIN!
WELL- WELL- UH!?
SOME MOUNTAIN GUIDE- AND HOW!
LOTS FOR SALE! AND LOTS- AND LOTS! IN
SUNCREST SUBDIVISION
A YEAR-ROUND PARADISE!
WHERE NATURE'S WARM HEART ENFOLDS YOU IN ITS BREATH!
BUY NOW- BEFORE THE RUSH!
PLOP!
TO BE CONTINUED-
WALT DISNEY
12-23

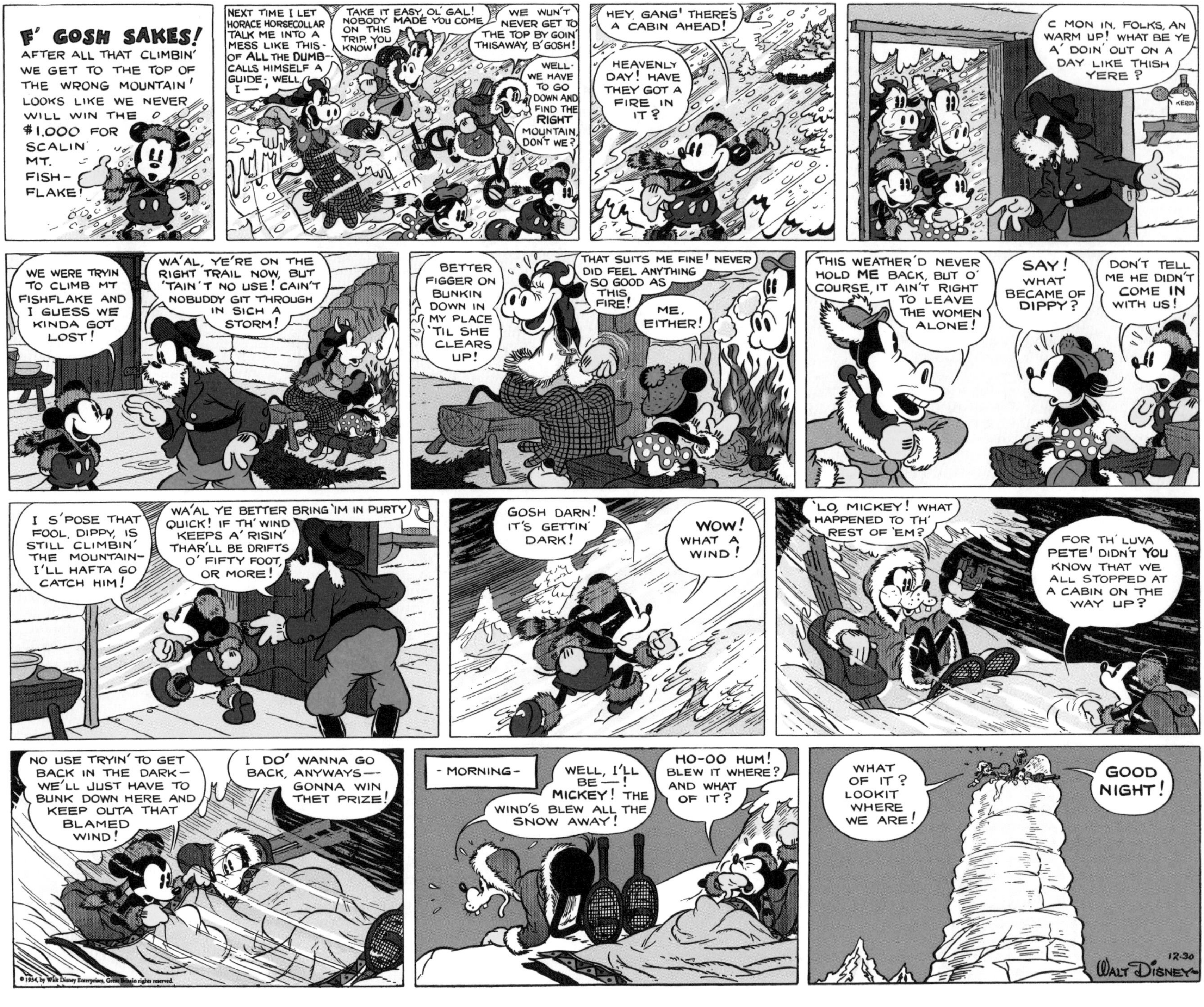
F' GOSH SAKES! AFTER ALL THAT CLIMBIN' WE GET TO THE TOP OF THE WRONG MOUNTAIN' LOOKS LIKE WE NEVER WILL WIN THE $1,000 FOR SCALIN' MT. FISH-FLAKE!
NEXT TIME I LET HORACE HORSECOLLAR TALK ME INTO A MESS LIKE THIS - OF ALL THE DUMB - CALLS HIMSELF A GUIDE - WELL I —
TAKE IT EASY, OL' GAL! NOBODY MADE YOU COME ON THIS TRIP, YOU KNOW!
WE WUN'T NEVER GET TO THE TOP BY GOIN' THISAWAY, B'GOSH!
WELL - WE HAVE TO GO DOWN AND FIND THE RIGHT MOUNTAIN, DON'T WE?
HEY, GANG! THERE'S A CABIN AHEAD!
HEAVENLY DAY! HAVE THEY GOT A FIRE IN IT?
C'MON IN, FOLKS, AN WARM UP! WHAT BE YE A' DOIN' OUT ON A DAY LIKE THISH YERE?
KEROS
WE WERE TRYIN TO CLIMB MT FISHFLAKE AND I GUESS WE KINDA GOT LOST!
WA'AL, YE'RE ON THE RIGHT TRAIL NOW, BUT 'TAIN'T NO USE! CAIN'T NOBUDDY GIT THROUGH IN SICH A STORM!
BETTER FIGGER ON BUNKIN DOWN IN MY PLACE 'TIL SHE CLEARS UP!
THAT SUITS ME FINE! NEVER DID FEEL ANYTHING SO GOOD AS THIS FIRE!
ME, EITHER!
THIS WEATHER'D NEVER HOLD ME BACK, BUT O' COURSE, IT AIN'T RIGHT TO LEAVE THE WOMEN ALONE!
SAY! WHAT BECAME OF DIPPY?
DON'T TELL ME HE DIDN'T COME IN WITH US!
I S'POSE THAT FOOL, DIPPY, IS STILL CLIMBIN' THE MOUNTAIN - I'LL HAFTA GO CATCH HIM!
WA'AL YE BETTER BRING 'IM IN PURTY QUICK! IF TH' WIND KEEPS A' RISIN' THAR'LL BE DRIFTS O' FIFTY FOOT, OR MORE!
GOSH DARN! IT'S GETTIN' DARK!
WOW! WHAT A WIND!
'LO, MICKEY! WHAT HAPPENED TO TH' REST OF 'EM?
FOR TH' LUVA PETE! DIDN'T YOU KNOW THAT WE ALL STOPPED AT A CABIN ON THE WAY UP?
NO USE TRYIN' TO GET BACK IN THE DARK - WE'LL JUST HAVE TO BUNK DOWN HERE AND KEEP OUTA THAT BLAMED WIND!
I DO' WANNA GO BACK, ANYWAYS — GONNA WIN THET PRIZE!
- MORNING -
WELL, I'LL BE —! MICKEY! THE WIND'S BLEW ALL THE SNOW AWAY!
HO-OO HUM! BLEW IT WHERE? AND WHAT OF IT?
WHAT OF IT? LOOKIT WHERE WE ARE!
GOOD NIGHT!
12-30
WALT DISNEY
© 1934, by Walt Disney Enterprises, Great Britain rights reserved.

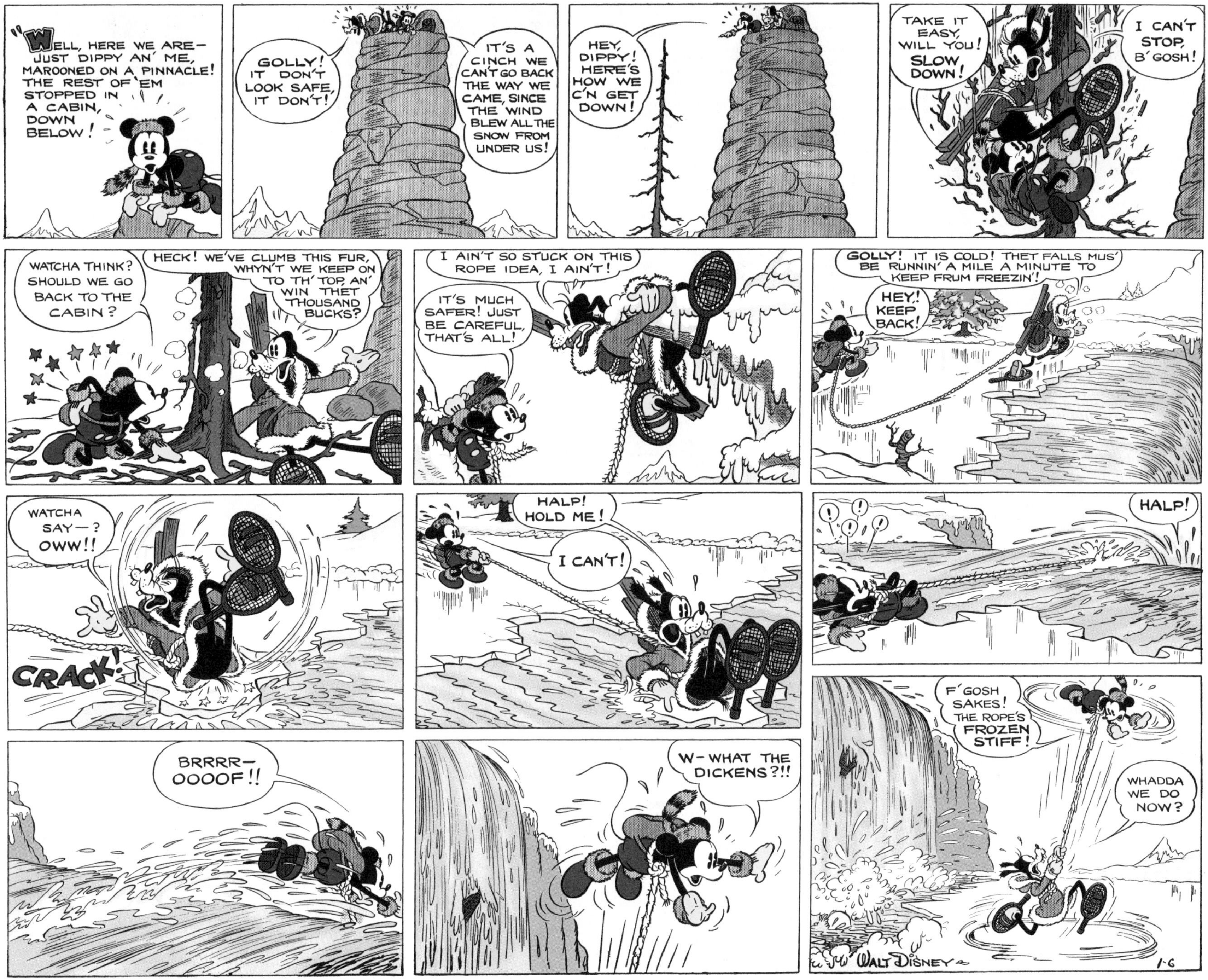

"WELL, HERE WE ARE— JUST DIPPY AN' ME, MAROONED ON A PINNACLE! THE REST OF 'EM STOPPED IN A CABIN, DOWN BELOW!
GOLLY! IT DON'T LOOK SAFE, IT DON'T!
IT'S A CINCH WE CAN'T GO BACK THE WAY WE CAME, SINCE THE WIND BLEW ALL THE SNOW FROM UNDER US!
HEY, DIPPY! HERE'S HOW WE C'N GET DOWN!
TAKE IT EASY, WILL YOU! SLOW DOWN!
I CAN'T STOP, B'GOSH!
WATCHA THINK? SHOULD WE GO BACK TO THE CABIN?
HECK! WE'VE CLUMB THIS FUR, WHYN'T WE KEEP ON TO TH' TOP, AN' WIN THET THOUSAND BUCKS?
I AIN'T SO STUCK ON THIS ROPE IDEA, I AIN'T!
IT'S MUCH SAFER! JUST BE CAREFUL, THAT'S ALL!
GOLLY! IT IS COLD! THET FALLS MUS' BE RUNNIN' A MILE A MINUTE TO KEEP FRUM FREEZIN'!
HEY! KEEP BACK!
WATCHA SAY—? OWW!!
CRACK!
HALP! HOLD ME!
I CAN'T!
HALP!
BRRRR— OOOOF!!
W-WHAT THE DICKENS?!!
F'GOSH SAKES! THE ROPE'S FROZEN STIFF!
WHADDA WE DO NOW?
WALT DISNEY
1-6

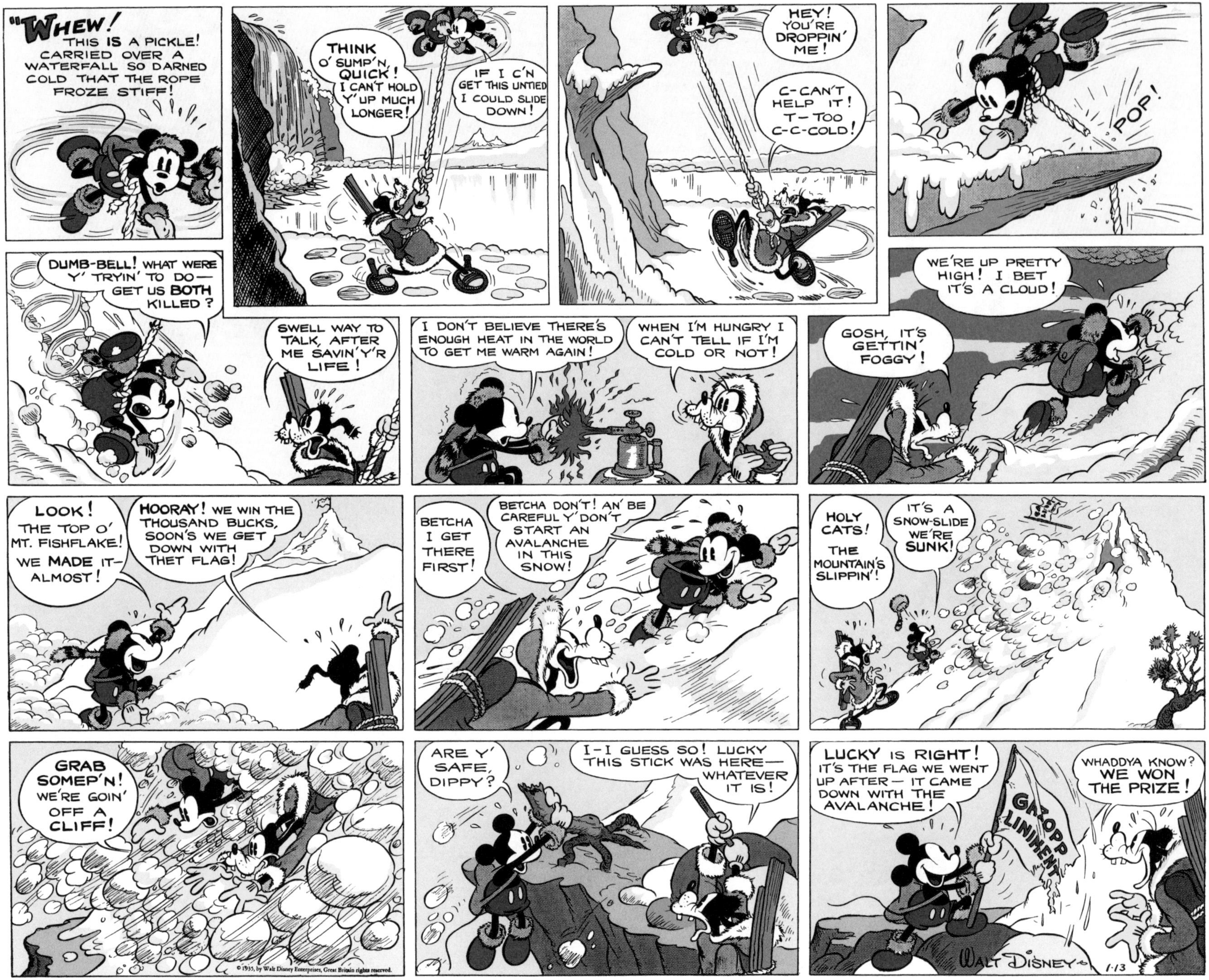
"WHEW! THIS IS A PICKLE! CARRIED OVER A WATERFALL SO DARNED COLD THAT THE ROPE FROZE STIFF!
THINK O' SUMP'N, QUICK! I CAN'T HOLD Y' UP MUCH LONGER!
IF I C'N GET THIS UNTIED I COULD SLIDE DOWN!
HEY! YOU'RE DROPPIN' ME!
C-CAN'T HELP IT! T-TOO C-C-COLD!
POP!
DUMB-BELL! WHAT WERE Y' TRYIN' TO DO— GET US BOTH KILLED?
SWELL WAY TO TALK, AFTER ME SAVIN' Y'R LIFE!
I DON'T BELIEVE THERE'S ENOUGH HEAT IN THE WORLD TO GET ME WARM AGAIN!
WHEN I'M HUNGRY I CAN'T TELL IF I'M COLD OR NOT!
WE'RE UP PRETTY HIGH! I BET IT'S A CLOUD!
GOSH, IT'S GETTIN' FOGGY!
LOOK! THE TOP O' MT. FISHFLAKE! WE MADE IT— ALMOST!
HOORAY! WE WIN THE THOUSAND BUCKS, SOON'S WE GET DOWN WITH THET FLAG!
BETCHA I GET THERE FIRST!
BETCHA DON'T! AN' BE CAREFUL Y' DON'T START AN AVALANCHE IN THIS SNOW!
HOLY CATS! THE MOUNTAIN'S SLIPPIN'!
IT'S A SNOW-SLIDE WE'RE SUNK!
GRAB SOMEP'N! WE'RE GOIN' OFF A CLIFF!
© 1935, by Walt Disney Enterprises, Great Britain rights reserved.
ARE Y' SAFE, DIPPY?
I-I GUESS SO! LUCKY THIS STICK WAS HERE— WHATEVER IT IS!
LUCKY IS RIGHT! IT'S THE FLAG WE WENT UP AFTER— IT CAME DOWN WITH THE AVALANCHE!
GAZOPP LINIMENT
WHADDYA KNOW? WE WON THE PRIZE!
WALT DISNEY
1-13

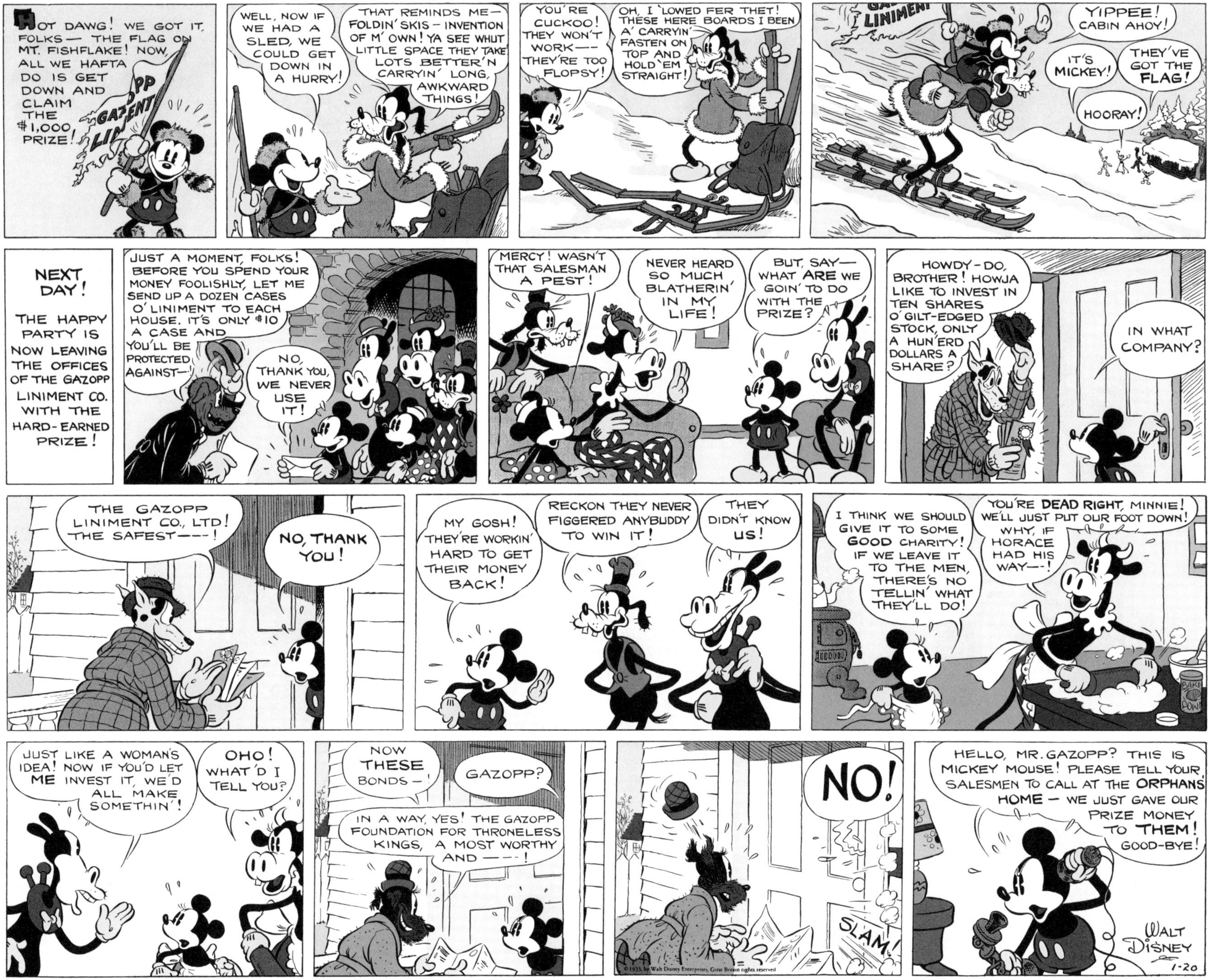
HOT DAWG! WE GOT IT, FOLKS— THE FLAG ON MT. FISHFLAKE! NOW, ALL WE HAFTA DO IS GET DOWN AND CLAIM THE $1,000 PRIZE!
WELL, NOW IF WE HAD A SLED, WE COULD GET DOWN IN A HURRY!
THAT REMINDS ME— FOLDIN' SKIS – INVENTION OF M' OWN! YA SEE WHUT LITTLE SPACE THEY TAKE! LOTS BETTER'N CARRYIN' LONG, AWKWARD THINGS!
YOU'RE CUCKOO! THEY WON'T WORK—— THEY'RE TOO FLOPSY!
OH, I 'LOWED FER THET! THESE HERE BOARDS I BEEN A' CARRYIN' FASTEN ON TOP AND HOLD 'EM STRAIGHT!
LINIMENT
YIPPEE! CABIN AHOY!
IT'S MICKEY!
THEY'VE GOT THE FLAG!
HOORAY!
NEXT DAY! THE HAPPY PARTY IS NOW LEAVING THE OFFICES OF THE GAZOPP LINIMENT CO. WITH THE HARD-EARNED PRIZE!
JUST A MOMENT, FOLKS! BEFORE YOU SPEND YOUR MONEY FOOLISHLY, LET ME SEND UP A DOZEN CASES O' LINIMENT TO EACH HOUSE. IT'S ONLY $10 A CASE AND YOU'LL BE PROTECTED AGAINST—!
NO, THANK YOU, WE NEVER USE IT!
MERCY! WASN'T THAT SALESMAN A PEST!
NEVER HEARD SO MUCH BLATHERIN' IN MY LIFE!
BUT, SAY— WHAT ARE WE GOIN' TO DO WITH THE PRIZE?
HOWDY-DO, BROTHER! HOWJA LIKE TO INVEST IN TEN SHARES O' GILT-EDGED STOCK, ONLY A HUN'ERD DOLLARS A SHARE?
IN WHAT COMPANY?
THE GAZOPP LINIMENT CO., LTD! THE SAFEST———!
NO, THANK YOU!
MY GOSH! THEY'RE WORKIN' HARD TO GET THEIR MONEY BACK!
RECKON THEY NEVER FIGGERED ANYBUDDY TO WIN IT!
THEY DIDN'T KNOW US!
I THINK WE SHOULD GIVE IT TO SOME GOOD CHARITY! IF WE LEAVE IT TO THE MEN, THERE'S NO TELLIN' WHAT THEY'LL DO!
YOU'RE DEAD RIGHT, MINNIE! WE'LL JUST PUT OUR FOOT DOWN! WHY, IF HORACE HAD HIS WAY—!
JUST LIKE A WOMAN'S IDEA! NOW IF YOU'D LET ME INVEST IT, WE'D ALL MAKE SOMETHIN'!
OHO! WHAT'D I TELL YOU?
NOW THESE BONDS—!
GAZOPP?
IN A WAY, YES! THE GAZOPP FOUNDATION FOR THRONELESS KINGS, A MOST WORTHY AND———!
NO!
SLAM!
© 1933, by Walt Disney Enterprises, Great Britain rights reserved
HELLO, MR. GAZOPP? THIS IS MICKEY MOUSE! PLEASE TELL YOUR SALESMEN TO CALL AT THE ORPHANS' HOME – WE JUST GAVE OUR PRIZE MONEY TO THEM! GOOD-BYE!
WALT DISNEY
1-20

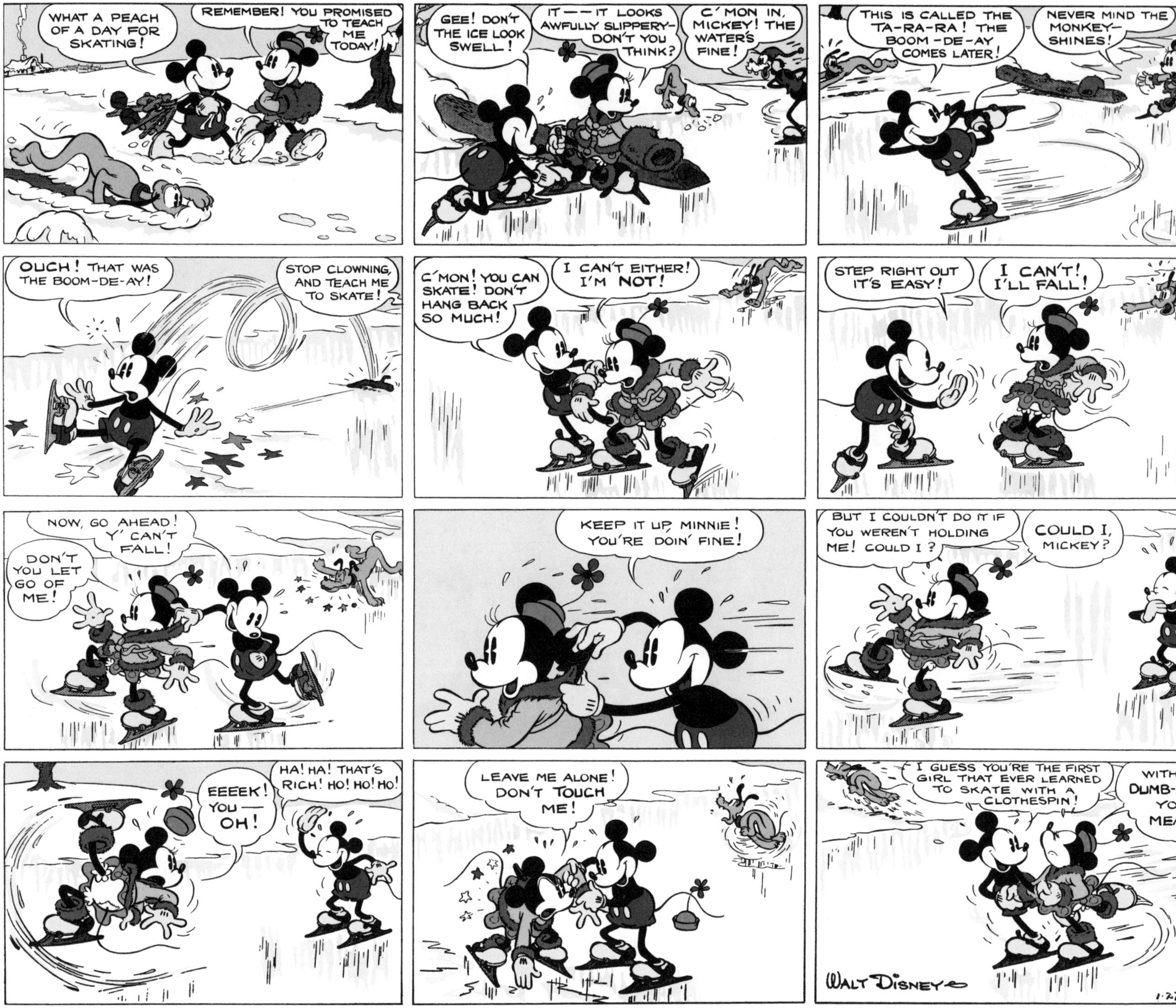

WHAT A PEACH OF A DAY FOR SKATING!
REMEMBER! YOU PROMISED TO TEACH ME TODAY!
GEE! DON'T THE ICE LOOK SWELL!
IT — — IT LOOKS AWFULLY SLIPPERY- DON'T YOU THINK?
C'MON IN, MICKEY! THE WATER'S FINE!
THIS IS CALLED THE TA-RA-RA! THE BOOM-DE-AY COMES LATER!
NEVER MIND THE MONKEY-SHINES!
OUCH! THAT WAS THE BOOM-DE-AY!
STOP CLOWNING, AND TEACH ME TO SKATE!
C'MON! YOU CAN SKATE! DON'T HANG BACK SO MUCH!
I CAN'T EITHER! I'M NOT!
STEP RIGHT OUT IT'S EASY!
I CAN'T! I'LL FALL!
NOW, GO AHEAD! Y' CAN'T FALL!
DON'T YOU LET GO OF ME!
KEEP IT UP, MINNIE! YOU'RE DOIN' FINE!
BUT I COULDN'T DO IT IF YOU WEREN'T HOLDING ME! COULD I?
COULD I, MICKEY?
EEEEK! YOU — OH!
HA! HA! THAT'S RICH! HO! HO! HO!
LEAVE ME ALONE! DON'T TOUCH ME!
I GUESS YOU'RE THE FIRST GIRL THAT EVER LEARNED TO SKATE WITH A CLOTHESPIN!
WITH A DUMB-BELL, YOU MEAN!
WALT DISNEY
1-27

190. MINNIE TAKES MICKEY DOWN A PEG

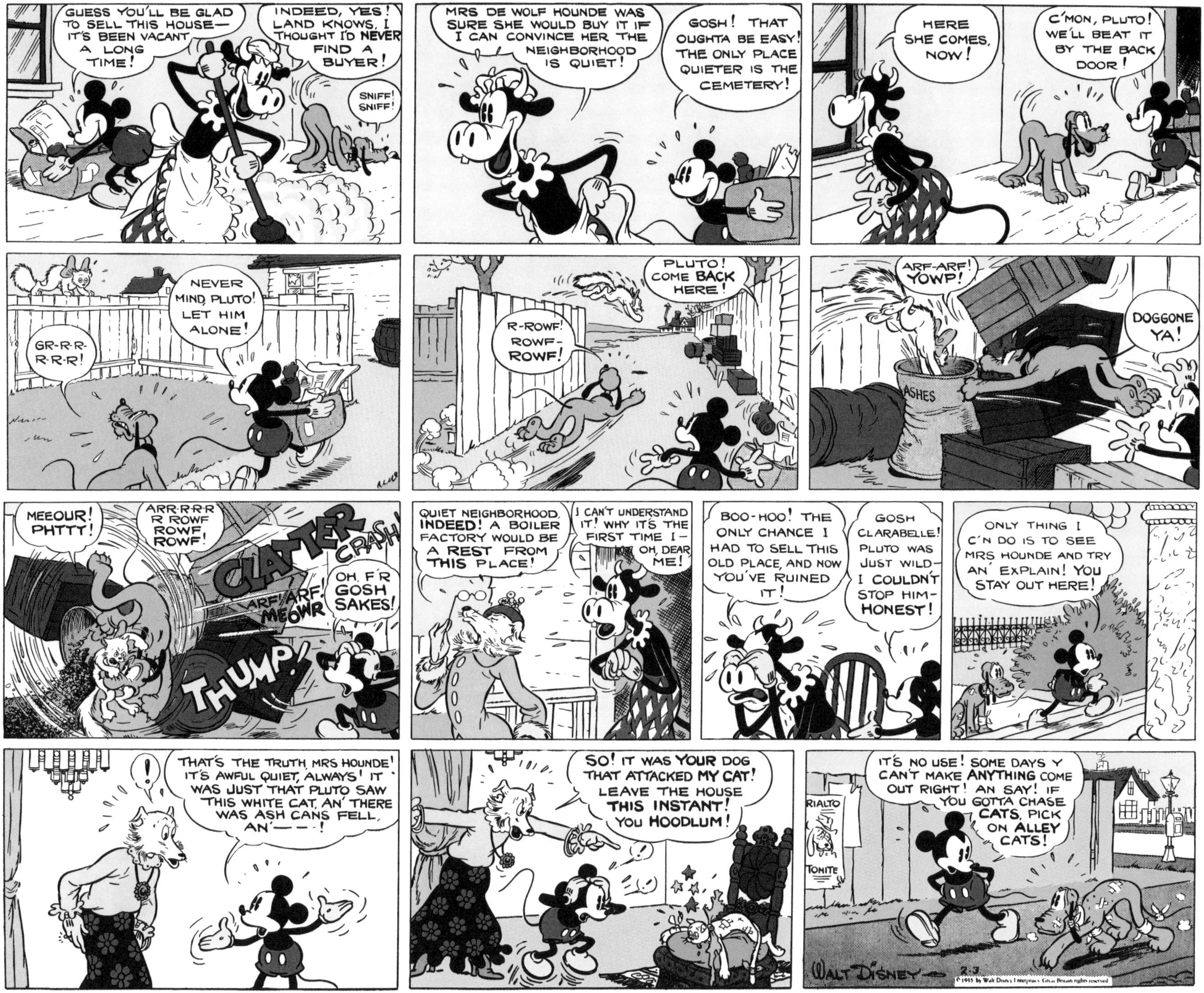
GUESS YOU'LL BE GLAD TO SELL THIS HOUSE— IT'S BEEN VACANT A LONG TIME!
INDEED, YES! LAND KNOWS, I THOUGHT I'D NEVER FIND A BUYER!
SNIFF! SNIFF!
MRS DE WOLF HOUNDE WAS SURE SHE WOULD BUY IT IF I CAN CONVINCE HER THE NEIGHBORHOOD IS QUIET!
GOSH! THAT OUGHTA BE EASY! THE ONLY PLACE QUIETER IS THE CEMETERY!
HERE SHE COMES, NOW!
C'MON, PLUTO! WE'LL BEAT IT BY THE BACK DOOR!
NEVER MIND, PLUTO! LET HIM ALONE!
GR-R-R-R-R-R!
PLUTO! COME BACK HERE!
R-ROWF! ROWF-ROWF!
ARF-ARF! YOWP!
DOGGONE YA!
ASHES
MEEOUR! PHTTT!
ARR-R-R-R R ROWF ROWF, ROWF!
CLATTER
CRASH!
ARF! ARF! MEOWR
OH, F'R GOSH SAKES!
THUMP!
QUIET NEIGHBORHOOD, INDEED! A BOILER FACTORY WOULD BE A REST FROM THIS PLACE!
I CAN'T UNDERSTAND IT! WHY IT'S THE FIRST TIME I—
OH, DEAR ME!
BOO-HOO! THE ONLY CHANCE I HAD TO SELL THIS OLD PLACE, AND NOW YOU'VE RUINED IT!
GOSH CLARABELLE! PLUTO WAS JUST WILD— I COULDN'T STOP HIM— HONEST!
ONLY THING I C'N DO IS TO SEE MRS HOUNDE AND TRY AN' EXPLAIN! YOU STAY OUT HERE!
!
THAT'S THE TRUTH, MRS HOUNDE! IT'S AWFUL QUIET, ALWAYS! IT WAS JUST THAT PLUTO SAW THIS WHITE CAT, AN' THERE WAS ASH CANS FELL, AN'— — —!
SO! IT WAS YOUR DOG THAT ATTACKED MY CAT! LEAVE THE HOUSE THIS INSTANT! YOU HOODLUM!
RIALTO
TONITE
IT'S NO USE! SOME DAYS Y CAN'T MAKE ANYTHING COME OUT RIGHT! AN SAY! IF YOU GOTTA CHASE CATS, PICK ON ALLEY CATS!
WALT DISNEY
2-3

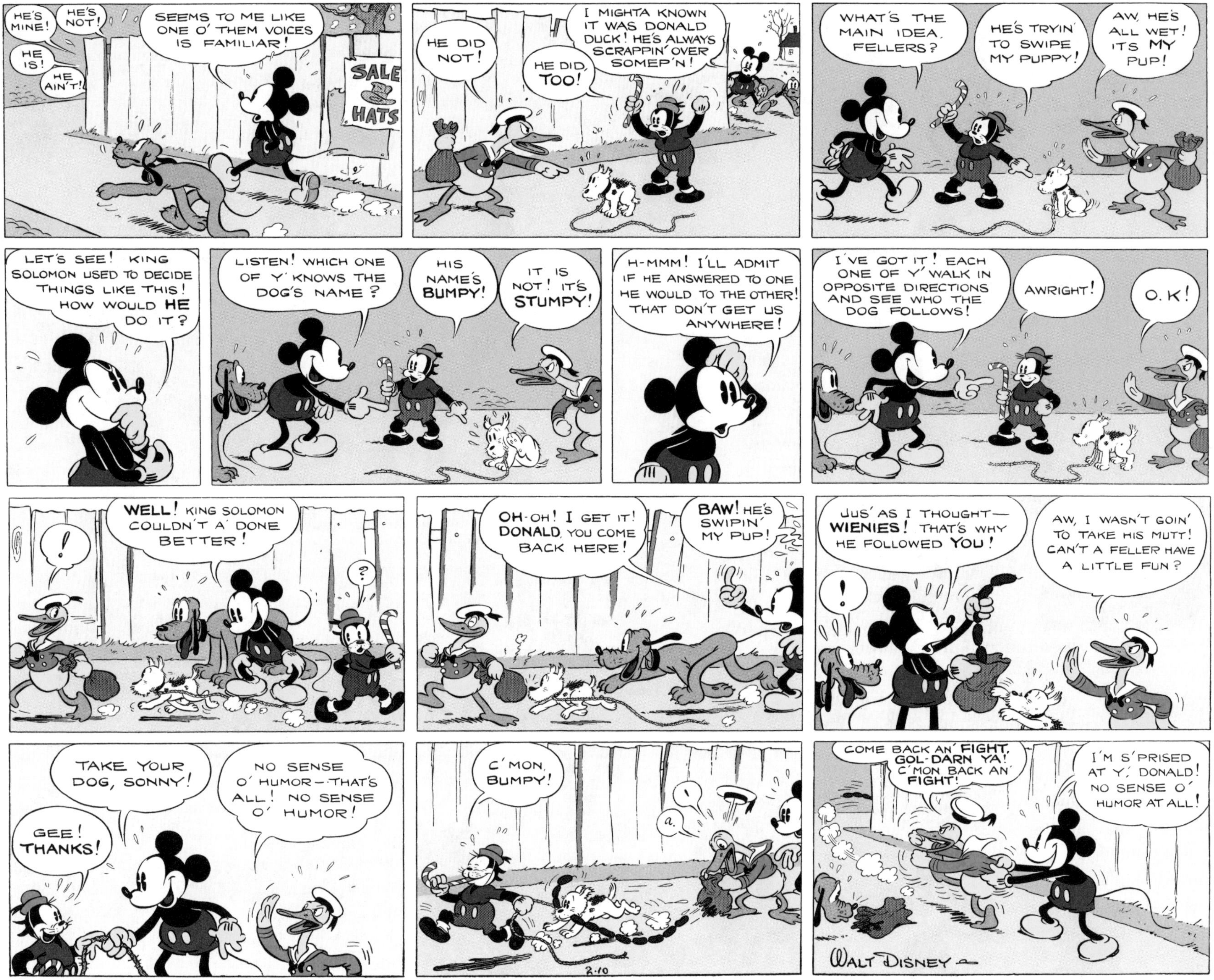
HE'S MINE!
HE'S NOT!
HE IS!
HE AIN'T!
SEEMS TO ME LIKE ONE O' THEM VOICES IS FAMILIAR!
SALE HATS
HE DID NOT!
HE DID, TOO!
I MIGHTA KNOWN IT WAS DONALD DUCK! HE'S ALWAYS SCRAPPIN' OVER SOMEP'N!
WHAT'S THE MAIN IDEA, FELLERS?
HE'S TRYIN' TO SWIPE MY PUPPY!
AW, HE'S ALL WET! IT'S MY PUP!
LET'S SEE! KING SOLOMON USED TO DECIDE THINGS LIKE THIS! HOW WOULD HE DO IT?
LISTEN! WHICH ONE OF Y' KNOWS THE DOG'S NAME?
HIS NAME'S BUMPY!
IT IS NOT! IT'S STUMPY!
H-MMM! I'LL ADMIT IF HE ANSWERED TO ONE HE WOULD TO THE OTHER! THAT DON'T GET US ANYWHERE!
I'VE GOT IT! EACH ONE OF Y' WALK IN OPPOSITE DIRECTIONS AND SEE WHO THE DOG FOLLOWS!
AWRIGHT!
O.K!
!
WELL! KING SOLOMON COULDN'T A' DONE BETTER!
?
OH-OH! I GET IT! DONALD, YOU COME BACK HERE!
BAW! HE'S SWIPIN' MY PUP!
!
JUS' AS I THOUGHT— WIENIES! THAT'S WHY HE FOLLOWED YOU!
AW, I WASN'T GOIN' TO TAKE HIS MUTT! CAN'T A FELLER HAVE A LITTLE FUN?
GEE! THANKS!
TAKE YOUR DOG, SONNY!
NO SENSE O' HUMOR—THAT'S ALL! NO SENSE O' HUMOR!
C'MON, BUMPY!
COME BACK AN' FIGHT, GOL-DARN YA! C'MON BACK AN' FIGHT!
I'M S'PRISED AT Y', DONALD! NO SENSE O' HUMOR AT ALL!
2-10
WALT DISNEY

192. DONALD THINKS IT'S A DOG'S LIFE

THE CASE OF
THE VANISHING COATS
AND
GAG STRIPS

FEBRUARY 17, 1935
–
JULY 21, 1935

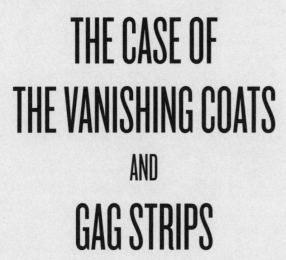

MICKEY MOUSE
REGISTERED U.S. PATENT OFFICE

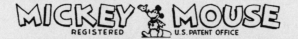

BENEATH THE OVERCOAT

Nothin' doin!" Donald shouts at Mickey. "I ain't nobody's uncle, I ain't!" Donald is abashed at the very idea of a non-relation treating him as family. But that doesn't stop Morty and Ferdie from coining the phrase "Unca Donald" in the strip for April 7, 1935. Indeed, Donald himself is not above childishly branding Mr. Zoup—his de facto landlord—with the familial pet name "Uncle Amos."

An immature duck dominates Donald's early gag strip appearances, and the same portrayal takes center stage in "The Case of the Vanishing Coats." Donald had only made his screen debut one year previous, so some infantile behavior seems appropriate. His fluctuation between schoolboy prankster and stubborn adult was simply part of the Disney developmental process—"growing pains," so to speak, as artists determined what kind of character they wanted this mallard to be.

Donald's rowdiness would gradually be toned down as he became the regular central character of the *Silly Symphony* Sunday feature and his own daily strip. In time, Donald would acquire his own biological nephews—though social scientists would likely argue that they did little to improve his behavior or personality.

"Vanishing Coats" itself is played for light-hearted laughs, showcasing the ineptitude of Donald's detective antics; but a bit of sinister seriousness seems to cross over from the grittier Mickey daily strip. As we are reminded each week, the thieving of Uncle Amos' coat supply is ruining his livelihood. He'll have to close shop if the perpetrator isn't caught. But the police consider Amos' woes a joke; Pluto lets the burglar get away; and even Mickey's shrewdness isn't providing any leads. After nearly five weeks of thievery, all Mickey can surmise is that "there's somep'n *mighty* peculiar about how these clothes get away!"

Had "Vanishing Coats" been a daily continuity, Gottfredson might have enlarged upon the potential of this psychological mystery. Indeed, the secret behind the coats' disappearance is a dilemma "for which there is no scientific cure." So what is the solution? Naturally, Mickey uses a remedy that is comically *unscientific*—even crass, by 1935 standards—to save Uncle Amos and his store.

After "Vanishing Coats'" swift, happy conclusion, there still remains one unsolved mystery: at story's start, who blackjacked Amos to steal the very first coat, and why the blazes *was* he so desperate? Perhaps this is an even darker scenario than we thought...

— THAD KOMOROWSKI

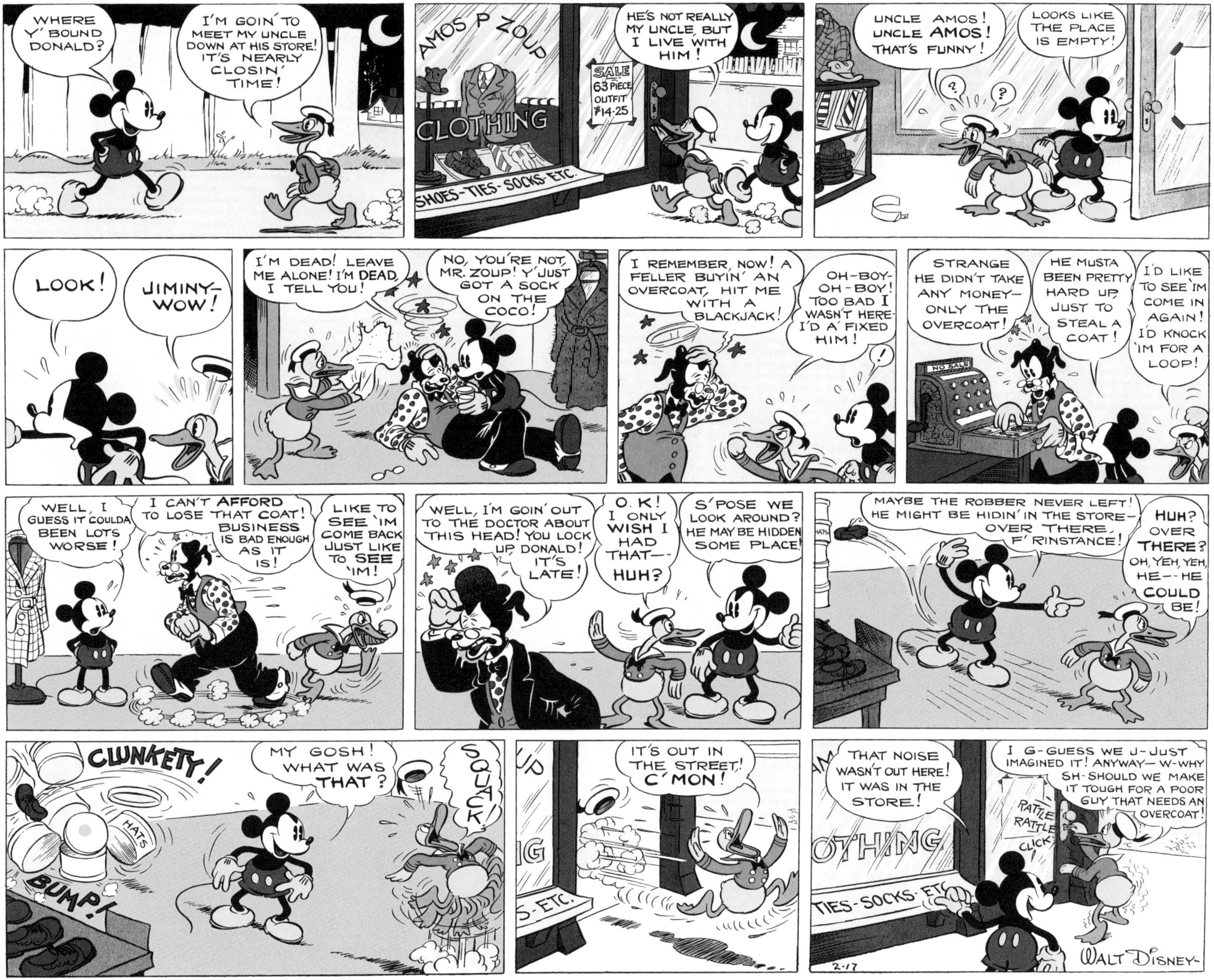

WHERE Y' BOUND DONALD?
I'M GOIN' TO MEET MY UNCLE DOWN AT HIS STORE! IT'S NEARLY CLOSIN' TIME!
AMOS P ZOUP
CLOTHING
SHOES-TIES-SOCKS-ETC.
SALE 63 PIECE OUTFIT $14.25
HE'S NOT REALLY MY UNCLE, BUT I LIVE WITH HIM!
UNCLE AMOS! UNCLE AMOS! THAT'S FUNNY!
LOOKS LIKE THE PLACE IS EMPTY!
LOOK!
JIMINY-WOW!
I'M DEAD! LEAVE ME ALONE! I'M DEAD, I TELL YOU!
NO, YOU'RE NOT, MR. ZOUP! Y' JUST GOT A SOCK ON THE COCO!
I REMEMBER, NOW! A FELLER BUYIN' AN OVERCOAT, HIT ME WITH A BLACKJACK!
OH-BOY-OH-BOY! TOO BAD I WASN'T HERE- I'D A' FIXED HIM!
!
STRANGE HE DIDN'T TAKE ANY MONEY- ONLY THE OVERCOAT!
NO SALE
HE MUSTA BEEN PRETTY HARD UP, JUST TO STEAL A COAT!
I'D LIKE TO SEE 'IM COME IN AGAIN! I'D KNOCK 'IM FOR A LOOP!
WELL, I GUESS IT COULDA BEEN LOTS WORSE!
I CAN'T AFFORD TO LOSE THAT COAT! BUSINESS IS BAD ENOUGH AS IT IS!
LIKE TO SEE 'IM COME BACK JUST LIKE TO SEE 'IM!
WELL, I'M GOIN' OUT TO THE DOCTOR ABOUT THIS HEAD! YOU LOCK UP, DONALD! IT'S LATE!
O.K! I ONLY WISH I HAD THAT--
HUH?
S'POSE WE LOOK AROUND? HE MAY BE HIDDEN SOME PLACE!
MAYBE THE ROBBER NEVER LEFT! HE MIGHT BE HIDIN' IN THE STORE- OVER THERE, F'RINSTANCE!
HUH? OVER THERE? OH, YEH, YEH, HE--HE COULD BE!
HATS
CLUNKETY!
BUMP!
HATS
MY GOSH! WHAT WAS THAT?
SQUACK!
IT'S OUT IN THE STREET! C'MON!
THAT NOISE WASN'T OUT HERE! IT WAS IN THE STORE!
I G-GUESS WE J-JUST IMAGINED IT! ANYWAY- W-WHY SH-SHOULD WE MAKE IT TOUGH FOR A POOR GUY THAT NEEDS AN OVERCOAT!
RATTLE RATTLE CLICK!
OTHING
TIES-SOCKS-ETC
2-17
WALT DISNEY

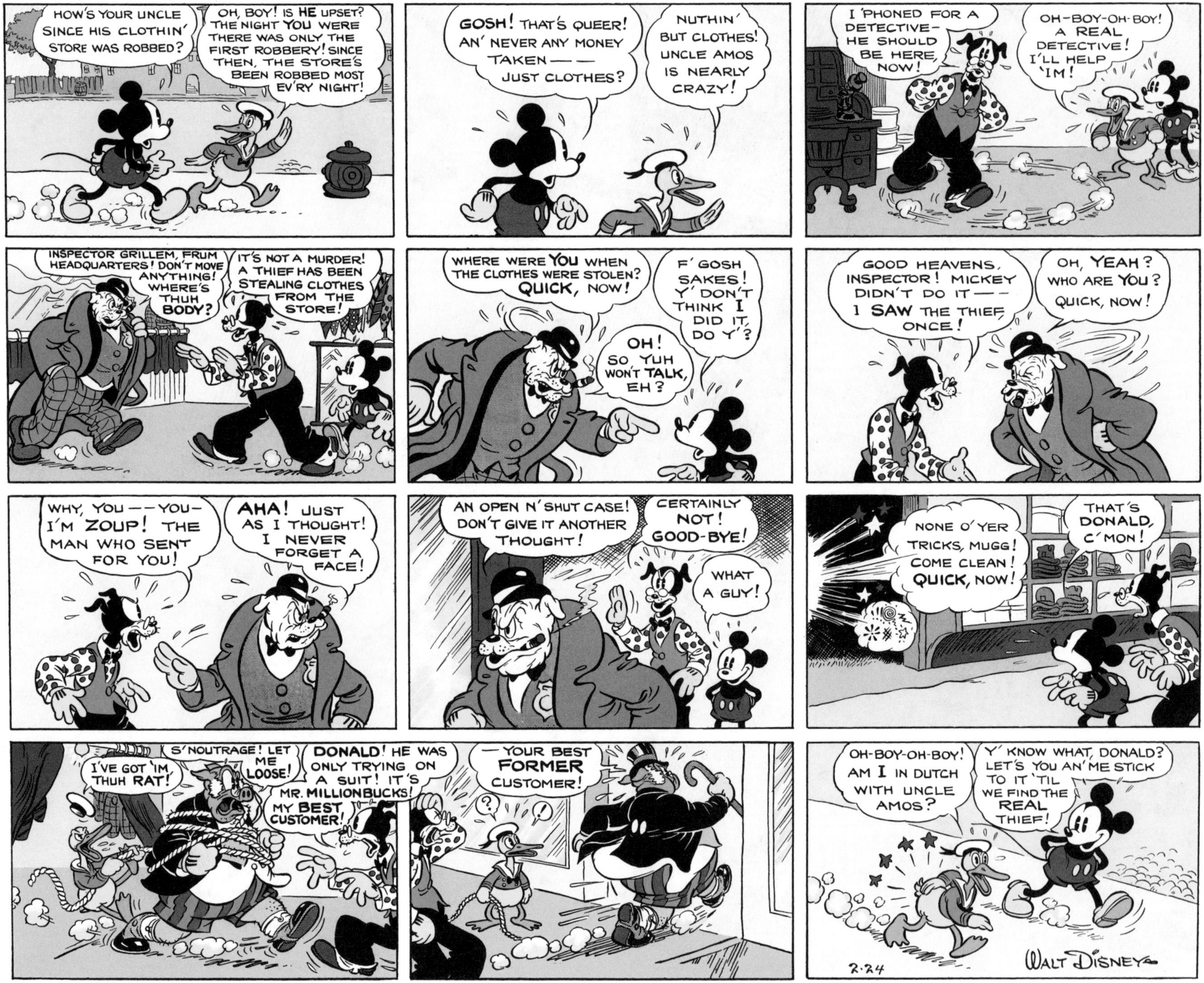
HOW'S YOUR UNCLE SINCE HIS CLOTHIN' STORE WAS ROBBED?
OH, BOY! IS HE UPSET? THE NIGHT YOU WERE THERE WAS ONLY THE FIRST ROBBERY! SINCE THEN, THE STORE'S BEEN ROBBED MOST EV'RY NIGHT!
GOSH! THAT'S QUEER! AN' NEVER ANY MONEY TAKEN —— JUST CLOTHES?
NUTHIN' BUT CLOTHES! UNCLE AMOS IS NEARLY CRAZY!
I 'PHONED FOR A DETECTIVE— HE SHOULD BE HERE, NOW!
OH-BOY-OH-BOY! A REAL DETECTIVE! I'LL HELP 'IM!
INSPECTOR GRILLEM, FRUM HEADQUARTERS! DON'T MOVE ANYTHING! WHERE'S THUH BODY?
IT'S NOT A MURDER! A THIEF HAS BEEN STEALING CLOTHES FROM THE STORE!
WHERE WERE YOU WHEN THE CLOTHES WERE STOLEN? QUICK, NOW!
F' GOSH SAKES! Y' DON'T THINK I DID IT, DO Y'?
OH! SO YUH WON'T TALK, EH?
GOOD HEAVENS, INSPECTOR! MICKEY DIDN'T DO IT —— I SAW THE THIEF ONCE!
OH, YEAH? WHO ARE YOU? QUICK, NOW!
WHY, YOU —— YOU— I'M ZOUP! THE MAN WHO SENT FOR YOU!
AHA! JUST AS I THOUGHT! I NEVER FORGET A FACE!
AN OPEN N' SHUT CASE! DON'T GIVE IT ANOTHER THOUGHT!
CERTAINLY NOT! GOOD-BYE!
WHAT A GUY!
NONE O' YER TRICKS, MUGG! COME CLEAN! QUICK, NOW!
THAT'S DONALD, C'MON!
I'VE GOT 'IM, THUH RAT!
S' NOUTRAGE! LET ME LOOSE!
DONALD! HE WAS ONLY TRYING ON A SUIT! IT'S MR. MILLIONBUCKS! MY BEST CUSTOMER!
— YOUR BEST FORMER CUSTOMER!
OH-BOY-OH-BOY! AM I IN DUTCH WITH UNCLE AMOS?
Y' KNOW WHAT, DONALD? LET'S YOU AN' ME STICK TO IT 'TIL WE FIND THE REAL THIEF!
2-24
WALT DISNEY

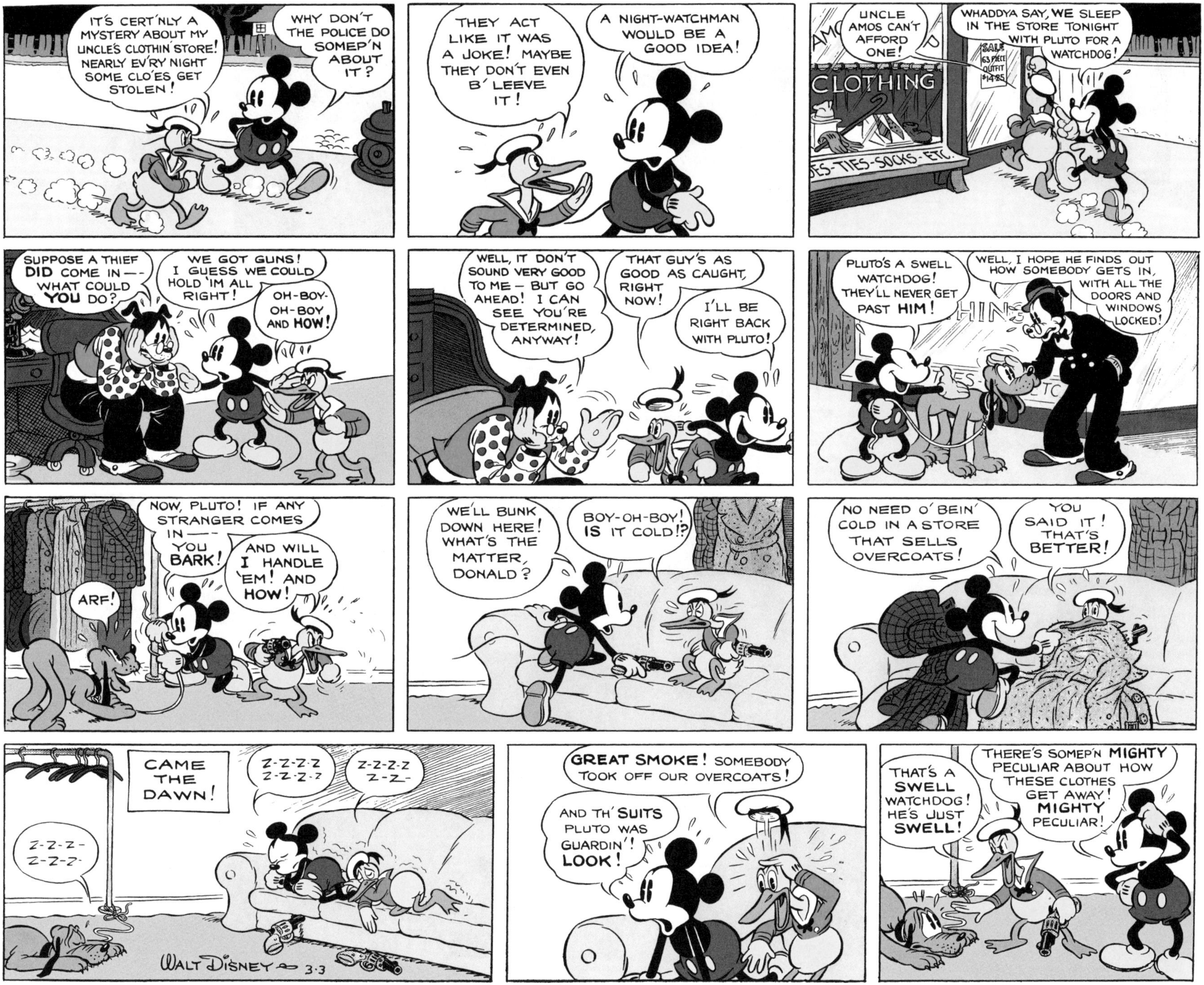
IT'S CERT'NLY A MYSTERY ABOUT MY UNCLE'S CLOTHIN' STORE! NEARLY EV'RY NIGHT SOME CLO'ES GET STOLEN!
WHY DON'T THE POLICE DO SOMEP'N ABOUT IT?
THEY ACT LIKE IT WAS A JOKE! MAYBE THEY DON'T EVEN B'LEEVE IT!
A NIGHT-WATCHMAN WOULD BE A GOOD IDEA!
UNCLE AMOS CAN'T AFFORD ONE!
WHADDYA SAY, WE SLEEP IN THE STORE TONIGHT WITH PLUTO FOR A WATCHDOG!
CLOTHING
SALE 63 PIECE OUTFIT $14.85
ES-TIES-SOCKS-ETC.
SUPPOSE A THIEF DID COME IN—WHAT COULD YOU DO?
WE GOT GUNS! I GUESS WE COULD HOLD 'IM ALL RIGHT!
OH-BOY-OH-BOY AND HOW!
WELL, IT DON'T SOUND VERY GOOD TO ME – BUT GO AHEAD! I CAN SEE YOU'RE DETERMINED, ANYWAY!
THAT GUY'S AS GOOD AS CAUGHT, RIGHT NOW!
I'LL BE RIGHT BACK WITH PLUTO!
PLUTO'S A SWELL WATCHDOG! THEY'LL NEVER GET PAST HIM!
WELL, I HOPE HE FINDS OUT HOW SOMEBODY GETS IN, WITH ALL THE DOORS AND WINDOWS LOCKED!
NOW, PLUTO! IF ANY STRANGER COMES IN— YOU BARK!
AND WILL I HANDLE 'EM! AND HOW!
ARF!
WE'LL BUNK DOWN HERE! WHAT'S THE MATTER, DONALD?
BOY-OH-BOY! IS IT COLD!?
NO NEED O' BEIN' COLD IN A STORE THAT SELLS OVERCOATS!
YOU SAID IT! THAT'S BETTER!
CAME THE DAWN!
Z-Z-Z-Z Z-Z-Z-Z
Z-Z-Z-Z Z-Z-
Z-Z-Z- Z-Z-Z-
WALT DISNEY 3·3
GREAT SMOKE! SOMEBODY TOOK OFF OUR OVERCOATS!
AND TH' SUITS PLUTO WAS GUARDIN'! LOOK!
THAT'S A SWELL WATCHDOG! HE'S JUST SWELL!
THERE'S SOMEP'N MIGHTY PECULIAR ABOUT HOW THESE CLOTHES GET AWAY! MIGHTY PECULIAR!

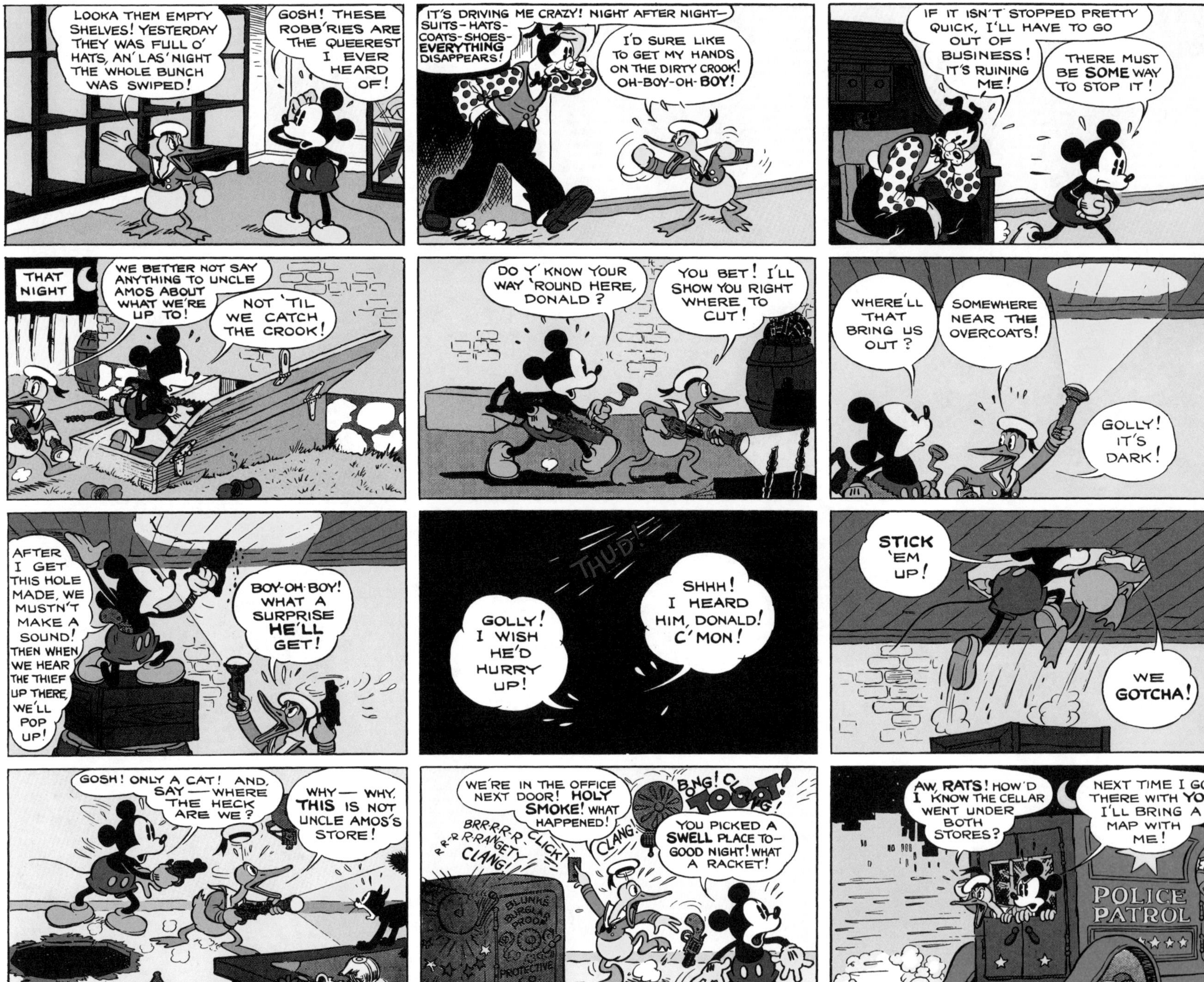

LOOKA THEM EMPTY SHELVES! YESTERDAY THEY WAS FULL O' HATS, AN' LAS' NIGHT THE WHOLE BUNCH WAS SWIPED!
GOSH! THESE ROBB'RIES ARE THE QUEEREST I EVER HEARD OF!
IT'S DRIVING ME CRAZY! NIGHT AFTER NIGHT— SUITS-HATS-COATS-SHOES- **EVERYTHING** DISAPPEARS!
I'D SURE LIKE TO GET MY HANDS ON THE DIRTY CROOK! OH-BOY-OH-**BOY**!
IF IT ISN'T STOPPED PRETTY QUICK, I'LL HAVE TO GO OUT OF BUSINESS! IT'S RUINING ME!
THERE MUST BE **SOME** WAY TO STOP IT!
THAT NIGHT
WE BETTER NOT SAY ANYTHING TO UNCLE AMOS ABOUT WHAT WE'RE UP TO!
NOT 'TIL WE CATCH THE CROOK!
DO Y' KNOW YOUR WAY 'ROUND HERE, DONALD?
YOU BET! I'LL SHOW YOU RIGHT WHERE TO CUT!
WHERE'LL THAT BRING US OUT?
SOMEWHERE NEAR THE OVERCOATS!
GOLLY! IT'S DARK!
AFTER I GET THIS HOLE MADE, WE MUSTN'T MAKE A SOUND! THEN WHEN WE HEAR THE THIEF UP THERE, WE'LL POP UP!
BOY-OH-BOY! WHAT A SURPRISE **HE'LL** GET!
THUD!
GOLLY! I WISH HE'D HURRY UP!
SHHH! I HEARD HIM, DONALD! **C'MON**!
STICK 'EM UP!
WE **GOTCHA**!
GOSH! ONLY A CAT! AND, SAY— WHERE THE HECK ARE WE?
WHY— WHY, **THIS** IS NOT UNCLE AMOS'S STORE!
3-10
WE'RE IN THE OFFICE NEXT DOOR! **HOLY SMOKE**! WHAT HAPPENED!
BRR-R-R-R-R-R-R-R-RANGETY CLICK!
CLANG!
CLANG!
BONG! CLANG!
YOU PICKED A **SWELL** PLACE TO— GOOD NIGHT! WHAT A RACKET!
PROTECTIVE CO.
AW, **RATS**! HOW'D **I** KNOW THE CELLAR WENT UNDER BOTH STORES?
NEXT TIME I GO THERE WITH **YOU** I'LL BRING A MAP WITH ME!
POLICE PATROL

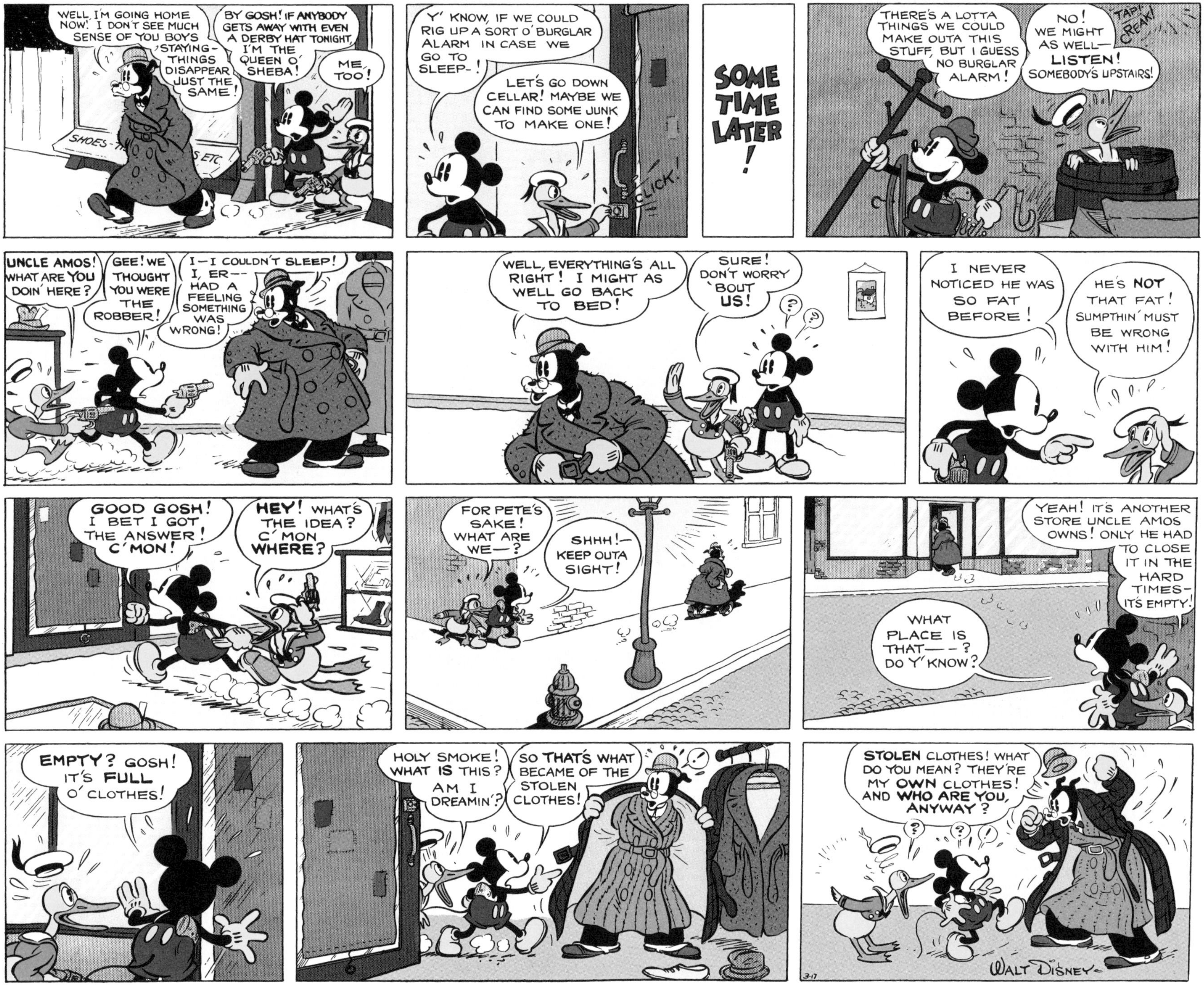

WELL, I'M GOING HOME NOW! I DON'T SEE MUCH SENSE OF YOU BOYS STAYING—THINGS DISAPPEAR JUST THE SAME!
BY GOSH! IF ANYBODY GETS AWAY WITH EVEN A DERBY HAT TONIGHT, I'M THE QUEEN O' SHEBA!
ME, TOO!
Y' KNOW, IF WE COULD RIG UP A SORT O' BURGLAR ALARM IN CASE WE GO TO SLEEP—!
LET'S GO DOWN CELLAR! MAYBE WE CAN FIND SOME JUNK TO MAKE ONE!
CLICK!
SOME TIME LATER!
THERE'S A LOTTA THINGS WE COULD MAKE OUTA THIS STUFF, BUT I GUESS NO BURGLAR ALARM!
NO! WE MIGHT AS WELL— LISTEN! SOMEBODY'S UPSTAIRS!
TAP! CREAK!
UNCLE AMOS! WHAT ARE YOU DOIN' HERE?
GEE! WE THOUGHT YOU WERE THE ROBBER!
I—I COULDN'T SLEEP! I, ER— HAD A FEELING SOMETHING WAS WRONG!
WELL, EVERYTHING'S ALL RIGHT! I MIGHT AS WELL GO BACK TO BED!
SURE! DON'T WORRY 'BOUT US!
?
?
I NEVER NOTICED HE WAS SO FAT BEFORE!
HE'S NOT THAT FAT! SUMPTHIN' MUST BE WRONG WITH HIM!
GOOD GOSH! I BET I GOT THE ANSWER! C'MON!
HEY! WHAT'S THE IDEA? C'MON WHERE?
FOR PETE'S SAKE! WHAT ARE WE—?
SHHH!— KEEP OUTA SIGHT!
WHAT PLACE IS THAT—? DO Y' KNOW?
YEAH! IT'S ANOTHER STORE UNCLE AMOS OWNS! ONLY HE HAD TO CLOSE IT IN THE HARD TIMES— IT'S EMPTY!
EMPTY? GOSH! IT'S FULL O' CLOTHES!
HOLY SMOKE! WHAT IS THIS? AM I DREAMIN'?
SO THAT'S WHAT BECAME OF THE STOLEN CLOTHES!
!
STOLEN CLOTHES! WHAT DO YOU MEAN? THEY'RE MY OWN CLOTHES! AND WHO ARE YOU, ANYWAY?
?
?
!
3-17
WALT DISNEY

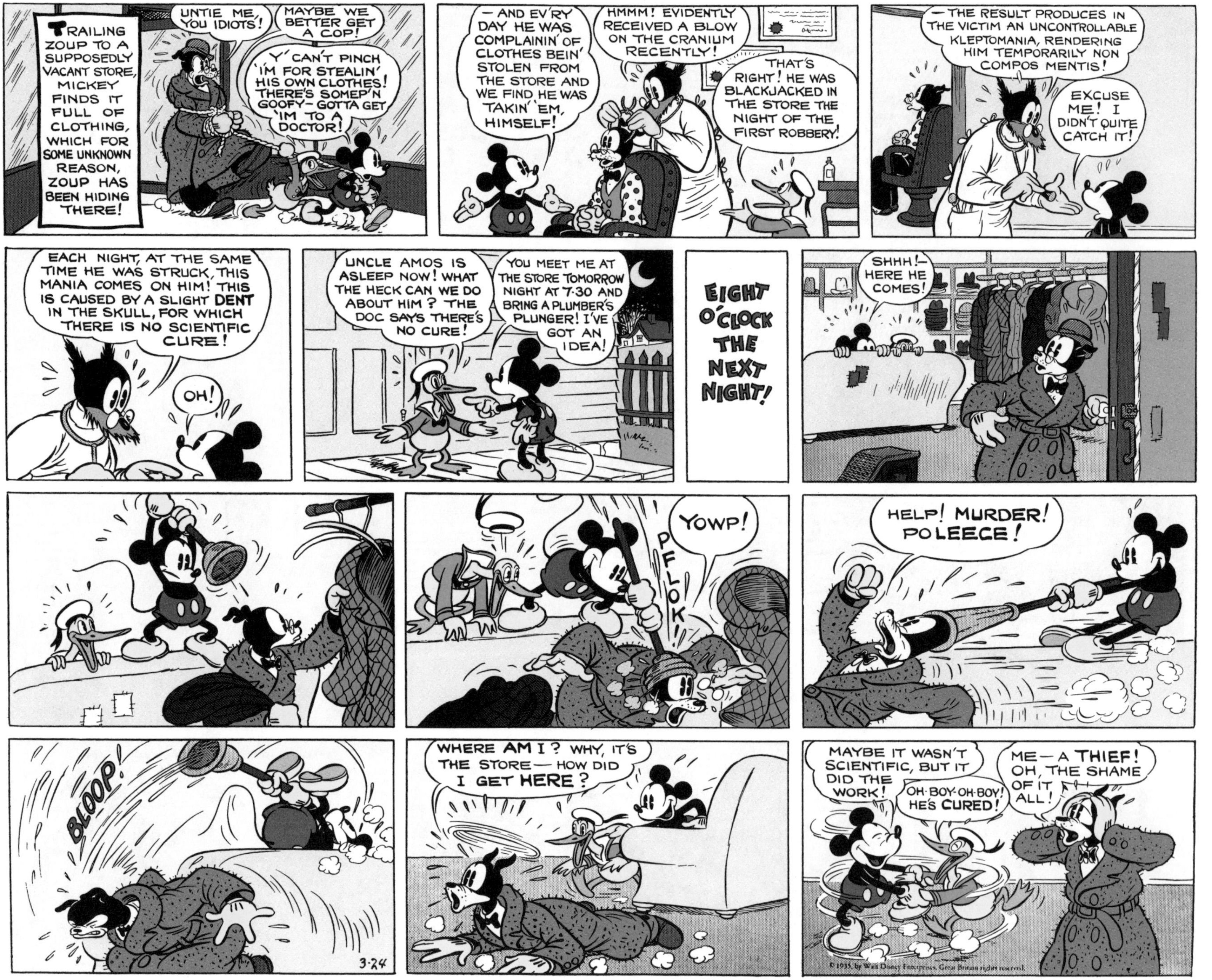

TRAILING ZOUP TO A SUPPOSEDLY VACANT STORE, MICKEY FINDS IT FULL OF CLOTHING, WHICH FOR SOME UNKNOWN REASON, ZOUP HAS BEEN HIDING THERE!
UNTIE ME, YOU IDIOTS!
MAYBE WE BETTER GET A COP!
Y' CAN'T PINCH 'IM FOR STEALIN' HIS OWN CLOTHES! THERE'S SOMEP'N GOOFY– GOTTA GET 'IM TO A DOCTOR!
—AND EV'RY DAY HE WAS COMPLAININ' OF CLOTHES BEIN' STOLEN FROM THE STORE AND WE FIND HE WAS TAKIN' 'EM, HIMSELF!
HMMM! EVIDENTLY RECEIVED A BLOW ON THE CRANIUM RECENTLY!
THAT'S RIGHT! HE WAS BLACKJACKED IN THE STORE THE NIGHT OF THE FIRST ROBBERY!
—THE RESULT PRODUCES IN THE VICTIM AN UNCONTROLLABLE KLEPTOMANIA, RENDERING HIM TEMPORARILY NON COMPOS MENTIS!
EXCUSE ME! I DIDN'T QUITE CATCH IT!
EACH NIGHT, AT THE SAME TIME HE WAS STRUCK, THIS MANIA COMES ON HIM! THIS IS CAUSED BY A SLIGHT DENT IN THE SKULL, FOR WHICH THERE IS NO SCIENTIFIC CURE!
OH!
UNCLE AMOS IS ASLEEP NOW! WHAT THE HECK CAN WE DO ABOUT HIM? THE DOC SAYS THERE'S NO CURE!
YOU MEET ME AT THE STORE TOMORROW NIGHT AT 7·30 AND BRING A PLUMBER'S PLUNGER! I'VE GOT AN IDEA!
EIGHT O'CLOCK THE NEXT NIGHT!
SHHH!— HERE HE COMES!
YOWP!
PFLOK
HELP! MURDER! POLEECE!
BLOOP!
3·24
WHERE AM I? WHY, IT'S THE STORE— HOW DID I GET HERE?
MAYBE IT WASN'T SCIENTIFIC, BUT IT DID THE WORK!
OH·BOY·OH·BOY! HE'S CURED!
ME—A THIEF! OH, THE SHAME OF IT ALL!
© 1935, by Walt Disney Enterprises. Great Britain rights reserved.

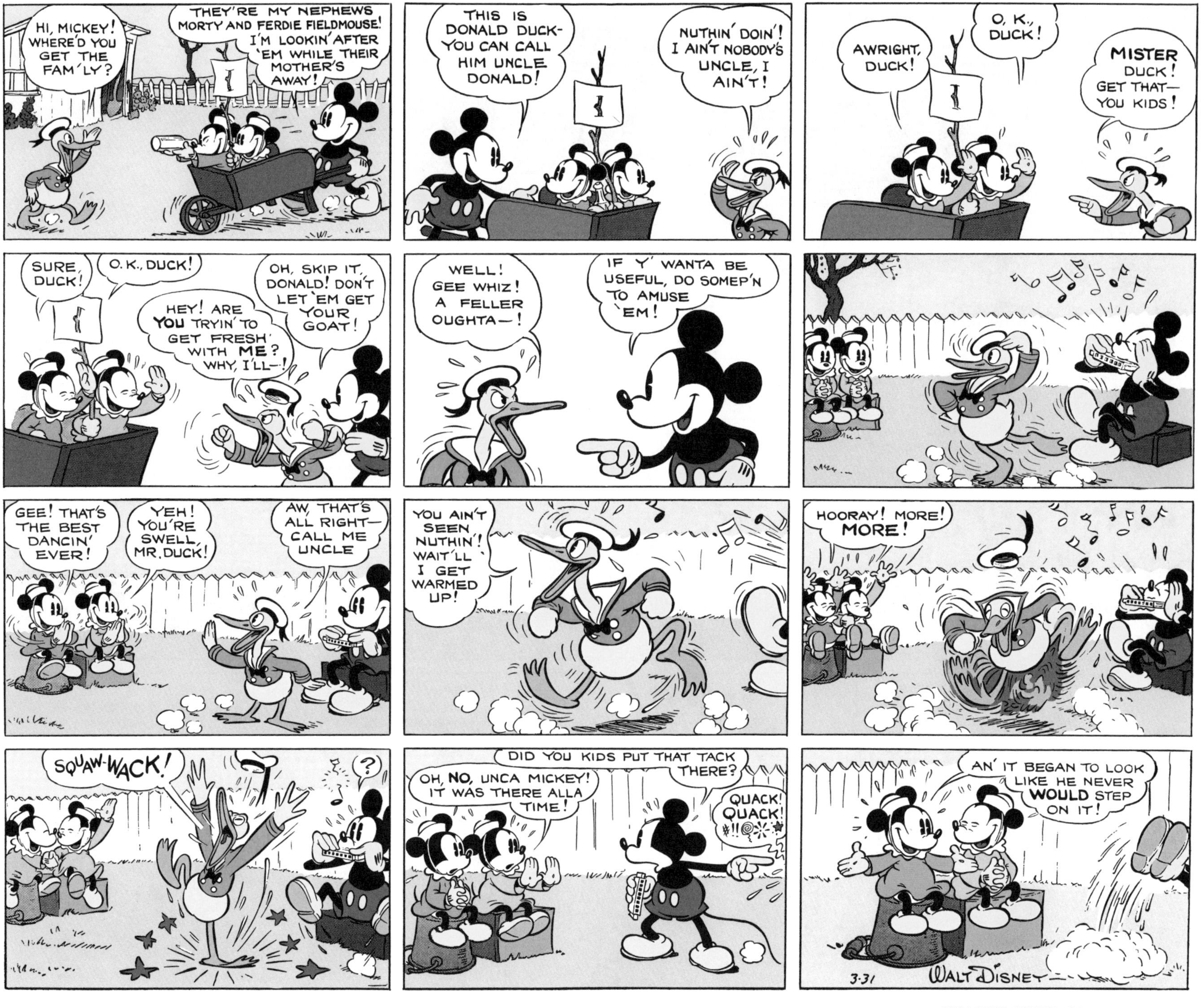
HI, MICKEY! WHERE'D YOU GET THE FAM'LY?
THEY'RE MY NEPHEWS MORTY AND FERDIE FIELDMOUSE! I'M LOOKIN' AFTER 'EM WHILE THEIR MOTHER'S AWAY!
THIS IS DONALD DUCK- YOU CAN CALL HIM UNCLE DONALD!
NUTHIN' DOIN'! I AIN'T NOBODY'S UNCLE, I AIN'T!
AWRIGHT, DUCK!
O, K., DUCK!
MISTER DUCK! GET THAT— YOU KIDS!
SURE, DUCK!
O. K., DUCK!
HEY! ARE YOU TRYIN' TO GET FRESH WITH ME? WHY, I'LL—!
OH, SKIP IT, DONALD! DON'T LET 'EM GET YOUR GOAT!
WELL! GEE WHIZ! A FELLER OUGHTA—!
IF Y' WANTA BE USEFUL, DO SOMEP'N TO AMUSE 'EM!
GEE! THAT'S THE BEST DANCIN' EVER!
YEH! YOU'RE SWELL, MR. DUCK!
AW, THAT'S ALL RIGHT— CALL ME UNCLE
YOU AIN'T SEEN NUTHIN'! WAIT'LL I GET WARMED UP!
HOORAY! MORE! MORE!
SQUAW-WACK!
?
DID YOU KIDS PUT THAT TACK THERE?
OH, NO, UNCA MICKEY! IT WAS THERE ALLA TIME!
QUACK! QUACK!
AN' IT BEGAN TO LOOK LIKE HE NEVER WOULD STEP ON IT!
3·31
WALT DISNEY

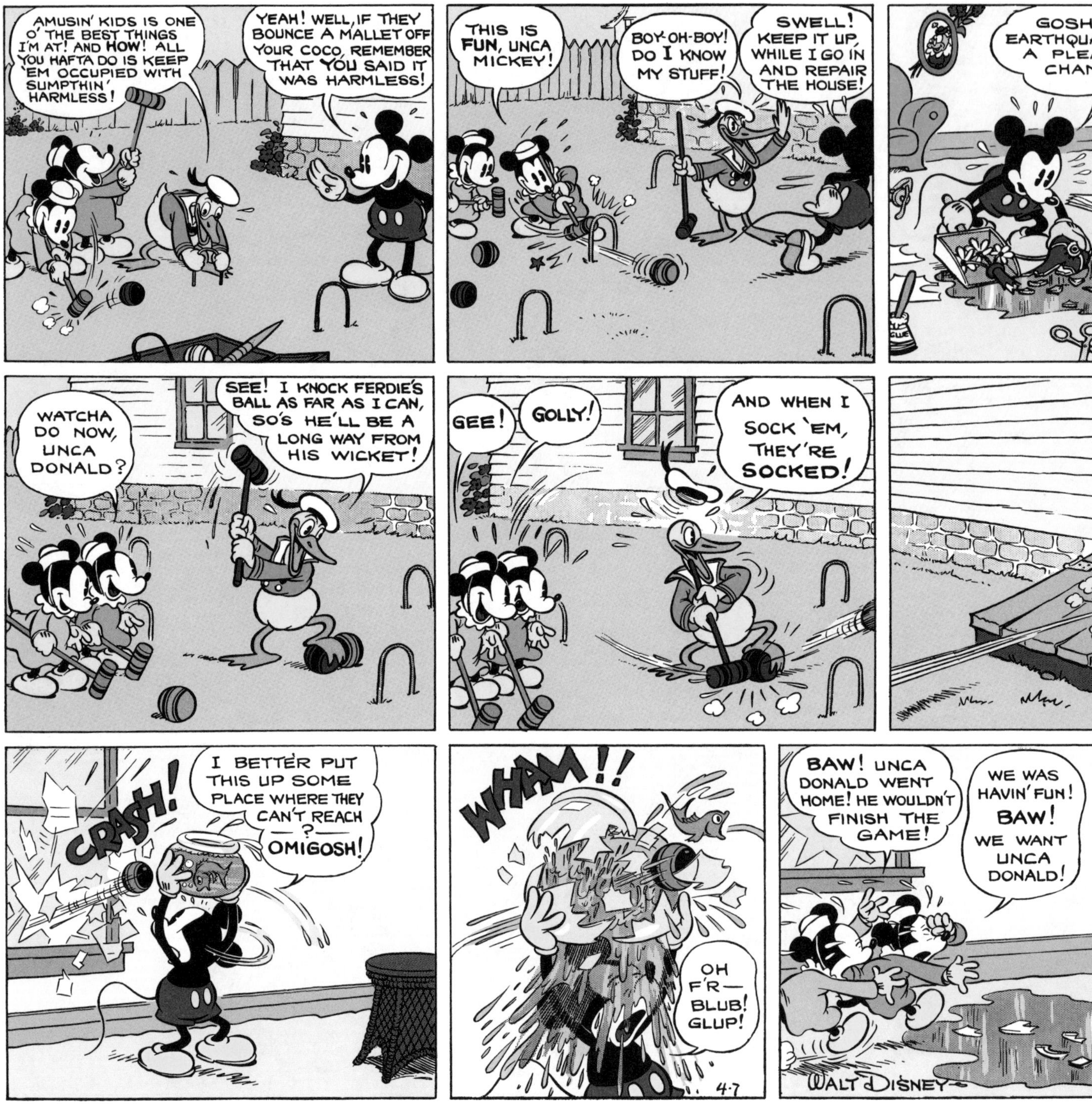
AMUSIN' KIDS IS ONE O' THE BEST THINGS I'M AT! AND HOW! ALL YOU HAFTA DO IS KEEP 'EM OCCUPIED WITH SUMPTHIN' HARMLESS!
YEAH! WELL, IF THEY BOUNCE A MALLET OFF YOUR COCO, REMEMBER THAT YOU SAID IT WAS HARMLESS!
THIS IS FUN, UNCA MICKEY!
BOY-OH-BOY! DO I KNOW MY STUFF!
SWELL! KEEP IT UP, WHILE I GO IN AND REPAIR THE HOUSE!
GOSH! AN EARTHQUAKE'D BE A PLEASANT CHANGE!
WATCHA DO NOW, UNCA DONALD?
SEE! I KNOCK FERDIE'S BALL AS FAR AS I CAN, SO'S HE'LL BE A LONG WAY FROM HIS WICKET!
GEE!
GOLLY!
AND WHEN I SOCK 'EM, THEY'RE SOCKED!
CRASH!
I BETTER PUT THIS UP SOME PLACE WHERE THEY CAN'T REACH —?— OMIGOSH!
WHAM!!
OH F'R— BLUB! GLUP!
4-7
BAW! UNCA DONALD WENT HOME! HE WOULDN'T FINISH THE GAME!
WE WAS HAVIN' FUN! BAW! WE WANT UNCA DONALD!
SO DO I— GOSH DARN HIS HIDE!
WALT DISNEY

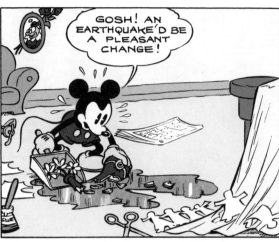

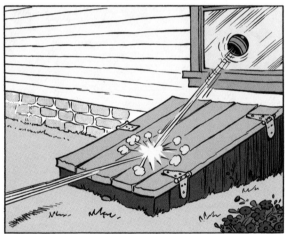

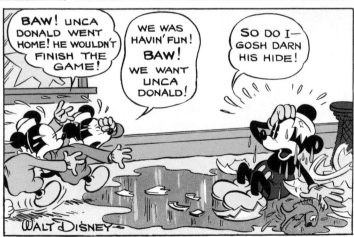

202. A "WICKET" HIT

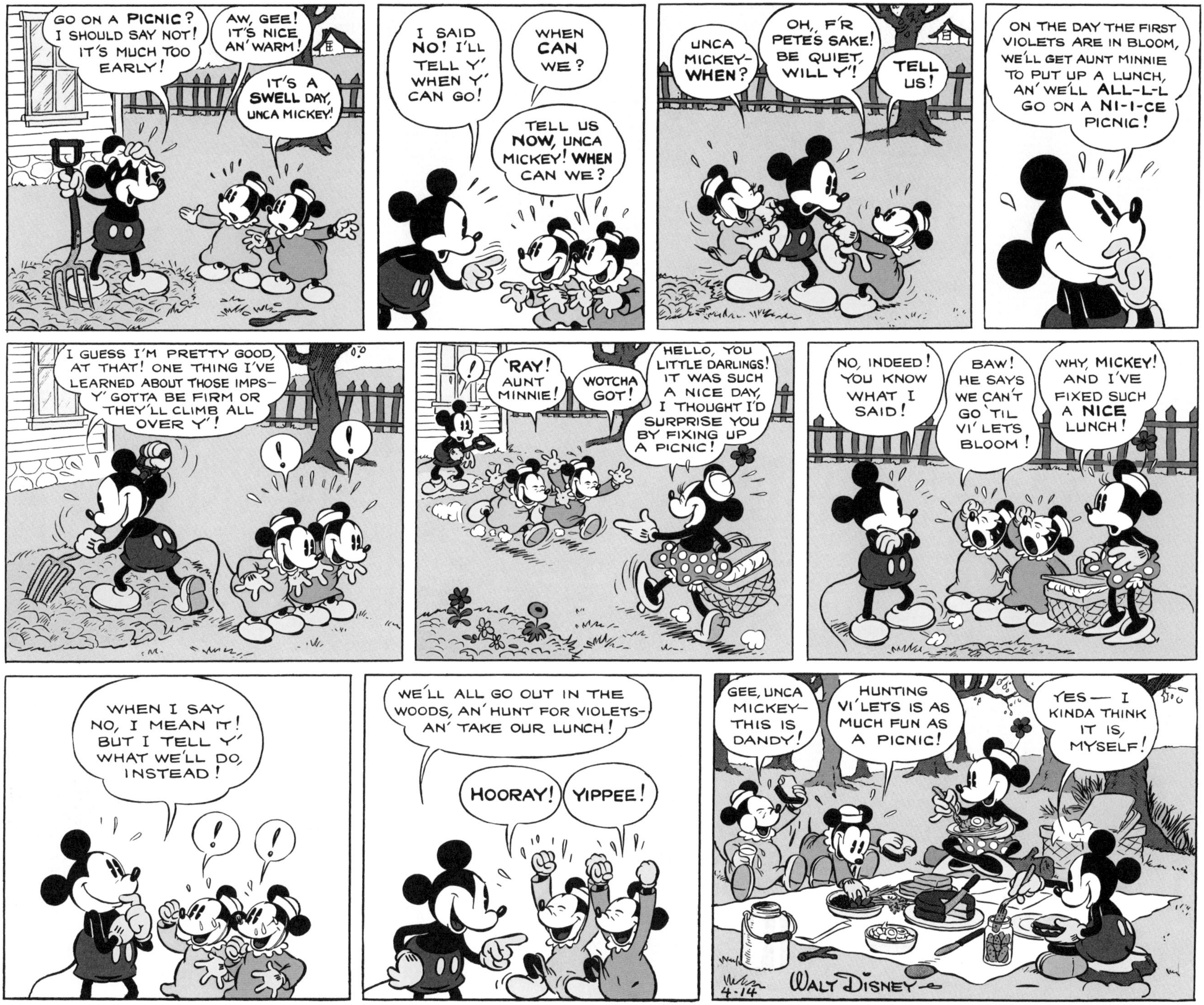
GO ON A PICNIC? I SHOULD SAY NOT! IT'S MUCH TOO EARLY!
AW, GEE! IT'S NICE AN' WARM!
IT'S A SWELL DAY, UNCA MICKEY!
I SAID NO! I'LL TELL Y' WHEN Y' CAN GO!
WHEN CAN WE?
TELL US NOW, UNCA MICKEY! WHEN CAN WE?
UNCA MICKEY— WHEN?
OH,, F'R PETE'S SAKE! BE QUIET WILL Y'!
TELL US!
ON THE DAY THE FIRST VIOLETS ARE IN BLOOM, WE'LL GET AUNT MINNIE TO PUT UP A LUNCH, AN' WE'LL ALL-L-L GO ON A NI-I-CE PICNIC!
I GUESS I'M PRETTY GOOD, AT THAT! ONE THING I'VE LEARNED ABOUT THOSE IMPS— Y' GOTTA BE FIRM OR THEY'LL CLIMB ALL OVER Y'!
!
!
!
'RAY! AUNT MINNIE!
WOTCHA GOT!
HELLO, YOU LITTLE DARLINGS! IT WAS SUCH A NICE DAY, I THOUGHT I'D SURPRISE YOU BY FIXING UP A PICNIC!
NO, INDEED! YOU KNOW WHAT I SAID!
BAW! HE SAYS WE CAN'T GO 'TIL VI'LETS BLOOM!
WHY, MICKEY! AND I'VE FIXED SUCH A NICE LUNCH!
WHEN I SAY NO, I MEAN IT! BUT I TELL Y' WHAT WE'LL DO, INSTEAD!
!
!
WE'LL ALL GO OUT IN THE WOODS, AN' HUNT FOR VIOLETS— AN' TAKE OUR LUNCH!
HOORAY!
YIPPEE!
GEE, UNCA MICKEY— THIS IS DANDY!
HUNTING VI'LETS IS AS MUCH FUN AS A PICNIC!
YES— I KINDA THINK IT IS, MYSELF!
4-14
WALT DISNEY

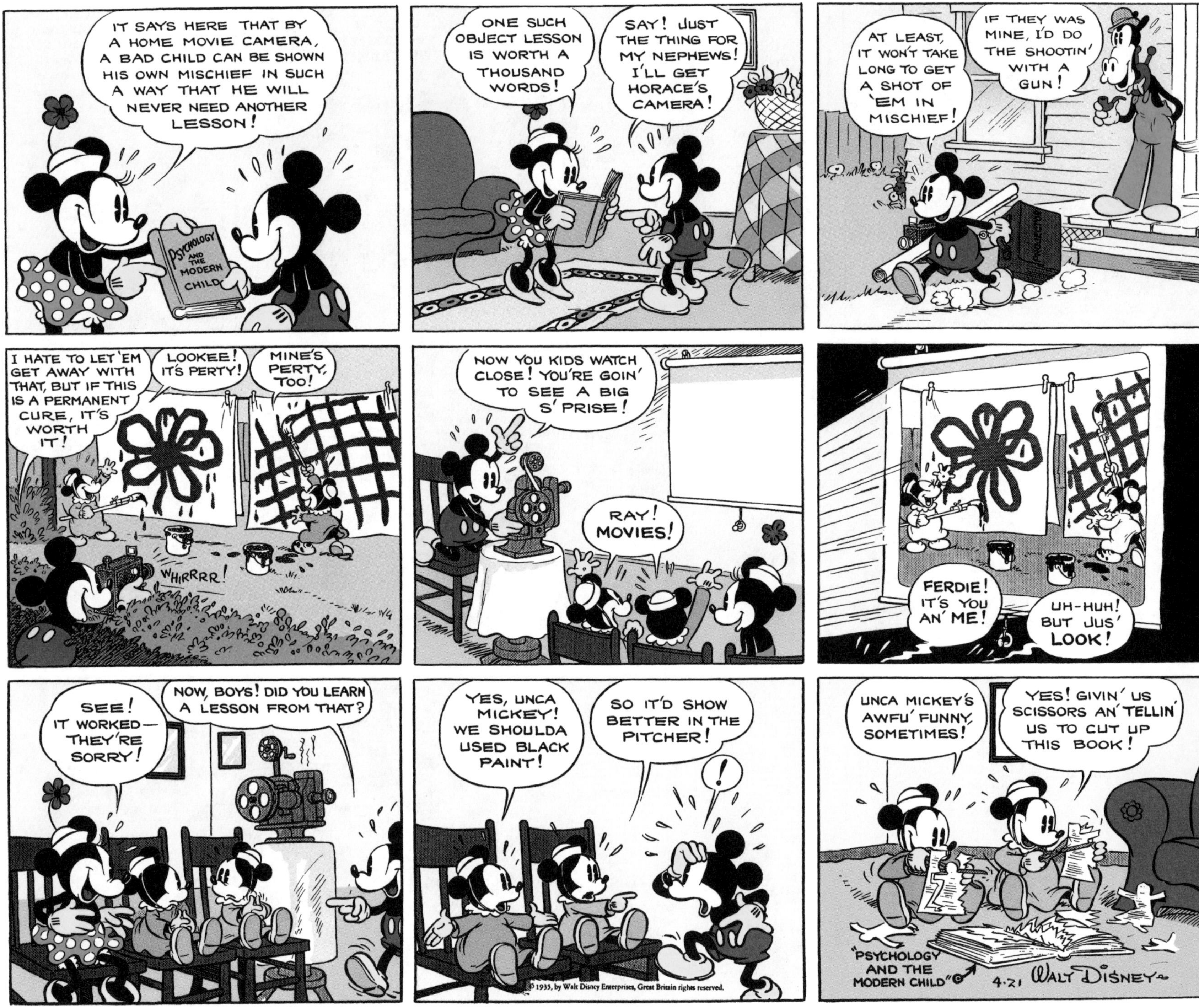
IT SAYS HERE THAT BY A HOME MOVIE CAMERA, A BAD CHILD CAN BE SHOWN HIS OWN MISCHIEF IN SUCH A WAY THAT HE WILL NEVER NEED ANOTHER LESSON!
PSYCHOLOGY AND THE MODERN CHILD
ONE SUCH OBJECT LESSON IS WORTH A THOUSAND WORDS!
SAY! JUST THE THING FOR MY NEPHEWS! I'LL GET HORACE'S CAMERA!
AT LEAST, IT WON'T TAKE LONG TO GET A SHOT OF 'EM IN MISCHIEF!
IF THEY WAS MINE, I'D DO THE SHOOTIN' WITH A GUN!
PROJECTOR
I HATE TO LET 'EM GET AWAY WITH THAT, BUT IF THIS IS A PERMANENT CURE, IT'S WORTH IT!
LOOKEE! IT'S PERTY!
MINE'S PERTY, TOO!
WHIRRRR!
NOW YOU KIDS WATCH CLOSE! YOU'RE GOIN' TO SEE A BIG S'PRISE!
RAY! MOVIES!
FERDIE! IT'S YOU AN' ME!
UH-HUH! BUT JUS' LOOK!
SEE! IT WORKED— THEY'RE SORRY!
NOW, BOYS! DID YOU LEARN A LESSON FROM THAT?
YES, UNCA MICKEY! WE SHOULDA USED BLACK PAINT!
SO IT'D SHOW BETTER IN THE PITCHER!
!
© 1935, by Walt Disney Enterprises, Great Britain rights reserved.
UNCA MICKEY'S AWFU' FUNNY, SOMETIMES!
YES! GIVIN' US SCISSORS AN' TELLIN' US TO CUT UP THIS BOOK!
"PSYCHOLOGY AND THE MODERN CHILD"
4·21 WALT DISNEY

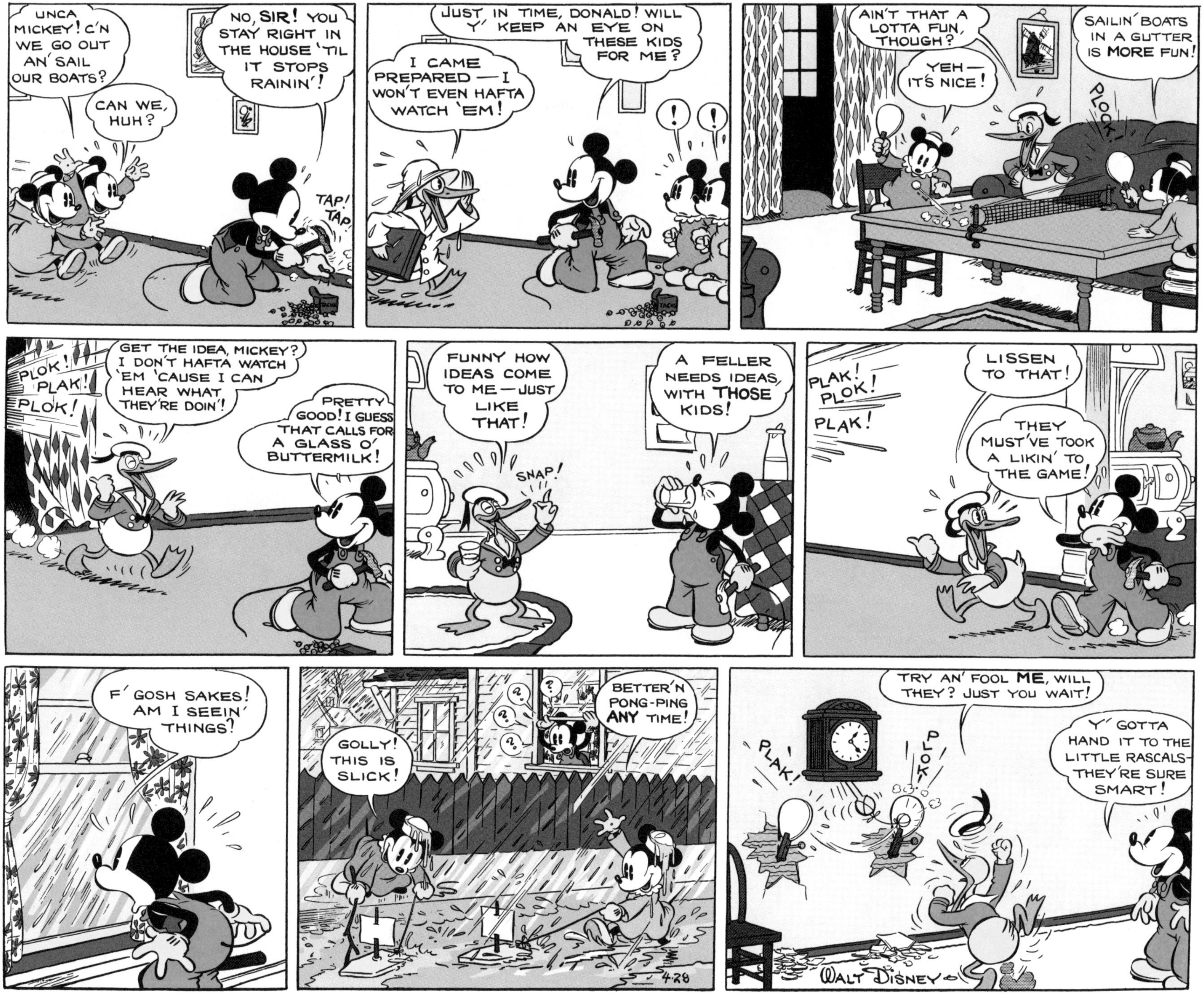

UNCA MICKEY! C'N WE GO OUT AN' SAIL OUR BOATS?
CAN WE, HUH?
NO, SIR! YOU STAY RIGHT IN THE HOUSE 'TIL IT STOPS RAININ'!
TAP! TAP!
JUST IN TIME, DONALD! WILL Y' KEEP AN EYE ON THESE KIDS FOR ME?
I CAME PREPARED — I WON'T EVEN HAFTA WATCH 'EM!
!
!
AIN'T THAT A LOTTA FUN, THOUGH?
YEH — IT'S NICE!
SAILIN' BOATS IN A GUTTER IS MORE FUN!
PLOCK!
PLOK! PLAK! PLOK!
GET THE IDEA, MICKEY? I DON'T HAFTA WATCH 'EM 'CAUSE I CAN HEAR WHAT THEY'RE DOIN'!
PRETTY GOOD! I GUESS THAT CALLS FOR A GLASS O' BUTTERMILK!
FUNNY HOW IDEAS COME TO ME — JUST LIKE THAT!
SNAP!
A FELLER NEEDS IDEAS WITH THOSE KIDS!
PLAK! PLOK! PLAK!
LISSEN TO THAT!
THEY MUST'VE TOOK A LIKIN' TO THE GAME!
F' GOSH SAKES! AM I SEEIN' THINGS?
GOLLY! THIS IS SLICK!
BETTER'N PONG-PING ANY TIME!
4-28
TRY AN' FOOL ME, WILL THEY? JUST YOU WAIT!
PLAK!
PLOK!
Y' GOTTA HAND IT TO THE LITTLE RASCALS — THEY'RE SURE SMART!
WALT DISNEY

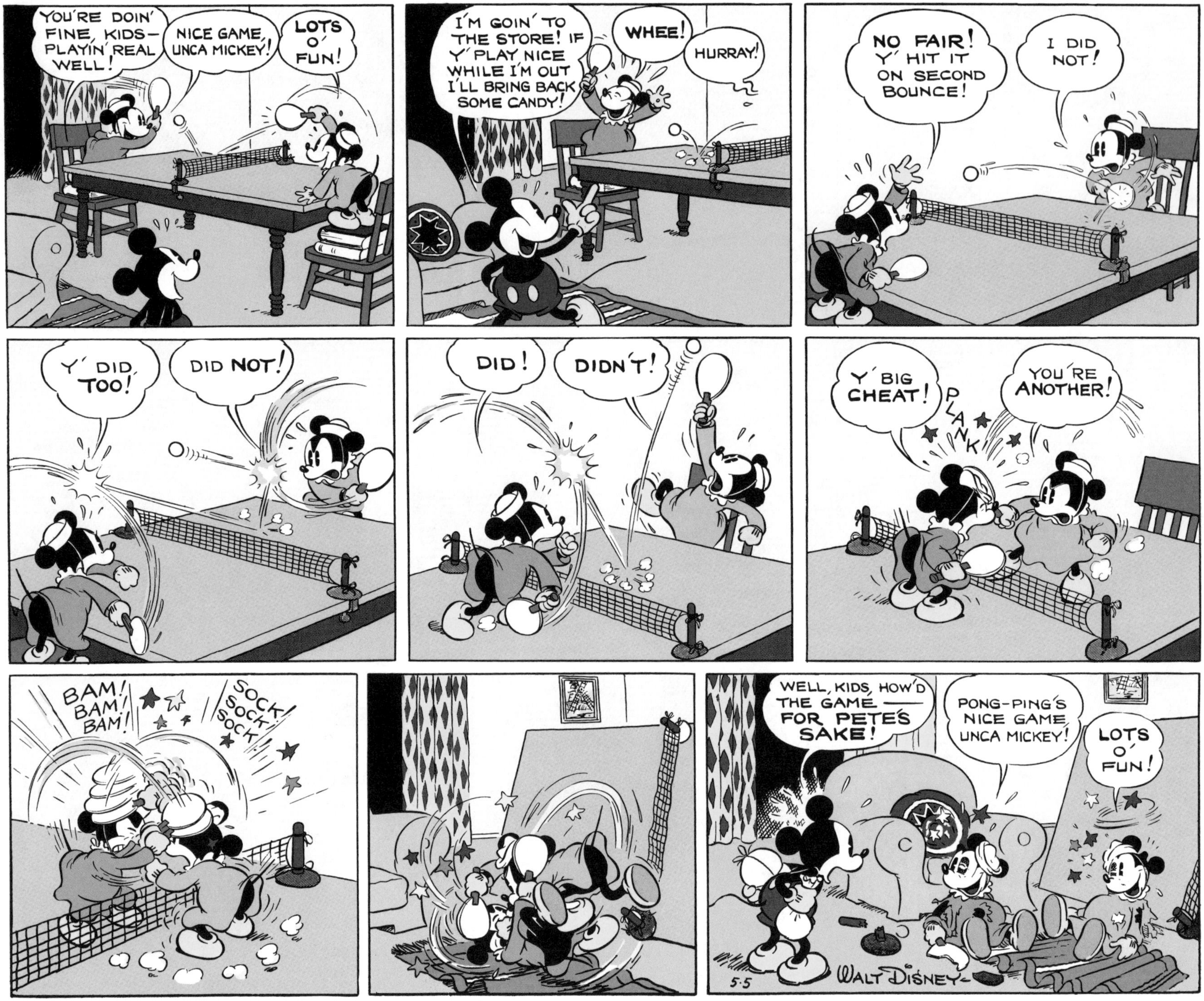

YOU'RE DOIN' FINE, KIDS— PLAYIN' REAL WELL!
NICE GAME, UNCA MICKEY!
LOTS O' FUN!
I'M GOIN' TO THE STORE! IF Y' PLAY NICE WHILE I'M OUT I'LL BRING BACK SOME CANDY!
WHEE!
HURRAY!
NO FAIR! Y' HIT IT ON SECOND BOUNCE!
I DID NOT!
Y' DID TOO!
DID NOT!
DID!
DIDN'T!
Y' BIG CHEAT!
PLANK
YOU'RE ANOTHER!
BAM! BAM! BAM!
SOCK! SOCK! SOCK!
WELL, KIDS, HOW'D THE GAME —— FOR PETE'S SAKE!
PONG-PING'S NICE GAME UNCA MICKEY!
LOTS O' FUN!
5·5
WALT DISNEY

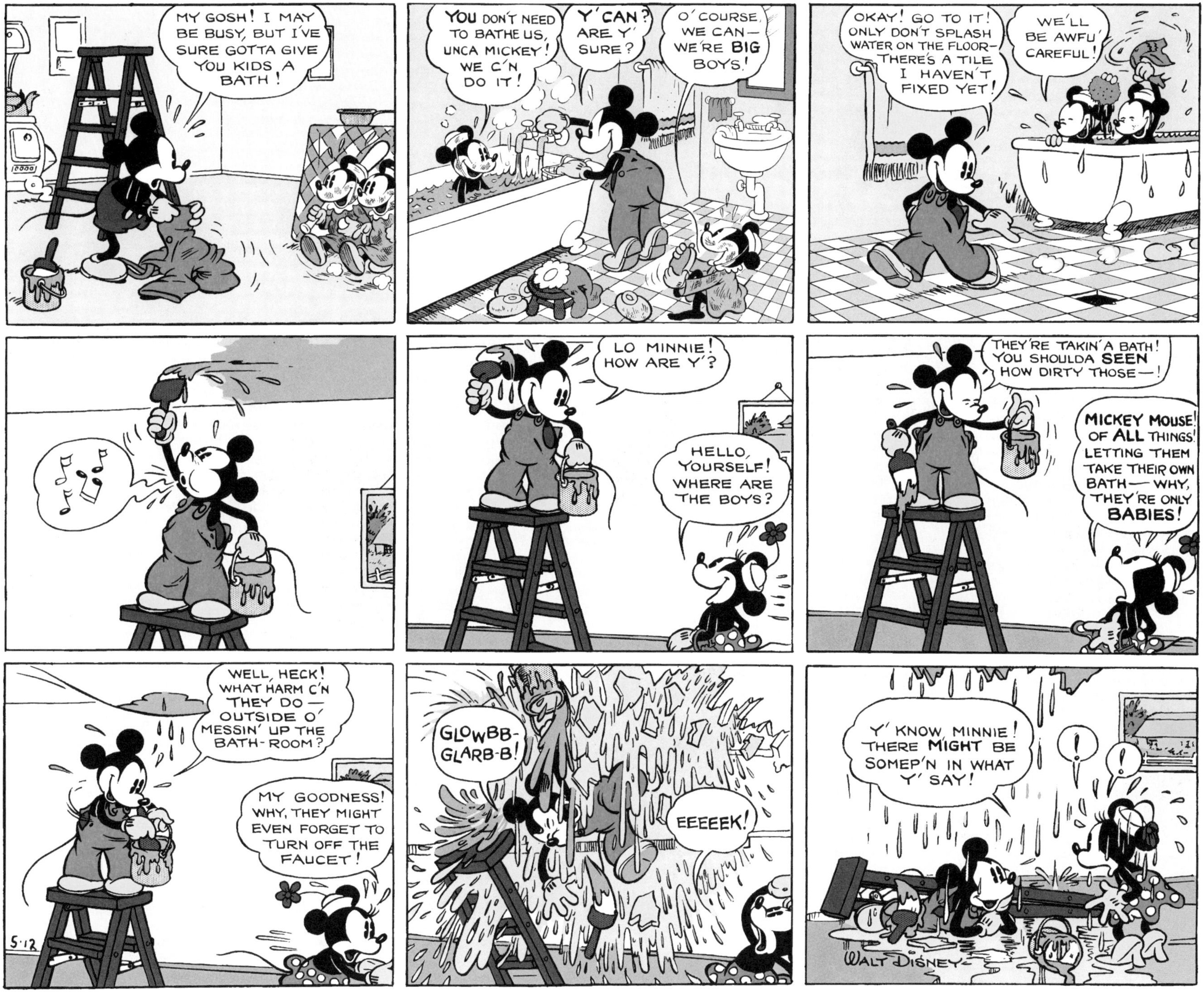
MY GOSH! I MAY BE BUSY, BUT I'VE SURE GOTTA GIVE YOU KIDS A BATH!
YOU DON'T NEED TO BATHE US, UNCA MICKEY! WE C'N DO IT!
Y'CAN? ARE Y' SURE?
O'COURSE, WE CAN— WE'RE BIG BOYS!
OKAY! GO TO IT! ONLY DON'T SPLASH WATER ON THE FLOOR— THERE'S A TILE I HAVEN'T FIXED YET!
WE'LL BE AWFU' CAREFUL!
LO MINNIE! HOW ARE Y'?
HELLO, YOURSELF! WHERE ARE THE BOYS?
THEY'RE TAKIN' A BATH! YOU SHOULDA SEEN HOW DIRTY THOSE—!
MICKEY MOUSE! OF ALL THINGS! LETTING THEM TAKE THEIR OWN BATH— WHY, THEY'RE ONLY BABIES!
WELL, HECK! WHAT HARM C'N THEY DO— OUTSIDE O' MESSIN' UP THE BATH-ROOM?
MY GOODNESS! WHY, THEY MIGHT EVEN FORGET TO TURN OFF THE FAUCET!
5·12
GLOWBB-GLARB-B!
EEEEEK!
Y' KNOW, MINNIE! THERE MIGHT BE SOMEP'N IN WHAT Y' SAY!
!
!
WALT DISNEY

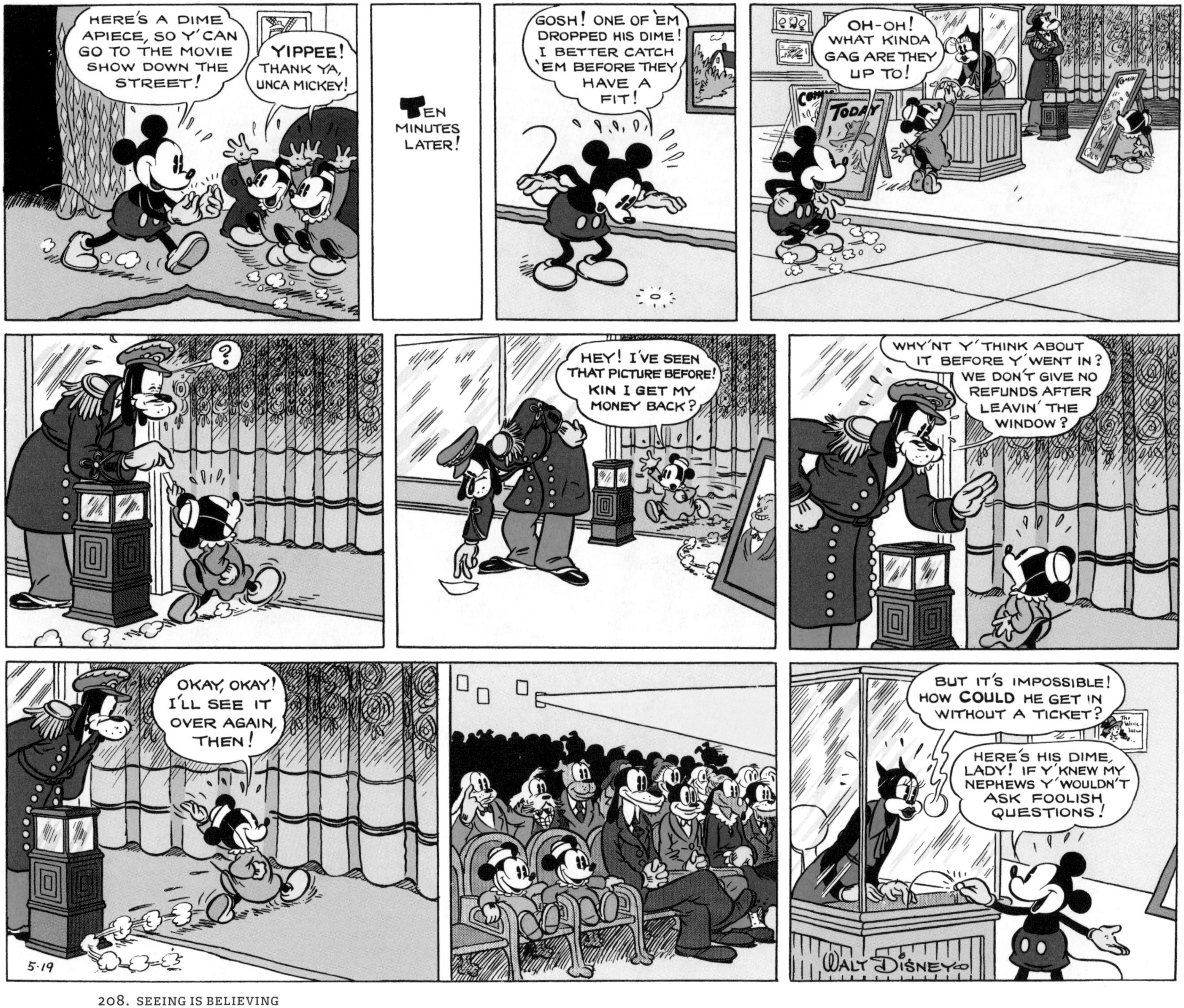
HERE'S A DIME APIECE, SO Y'CAN GO TO THE MOVIE SHOW DOWN THE STREET!
YIPPEE! THANK YA, UNCA MICKEY!
TEN MINUTES LATER!
GOSH! ONE OF 'EM DROPPED HIS DIME! I BETTER CATCH 'EM BEFORE THEY HAVE A FIT!
OH-OH! WHAT KINDA GAG ARE THEY UP TO!
TODAY
?
HEY! I'VE SEEN THAT PICTURE BEFORE! KIN I GET MY MONEY BACK?
WHY'NT Y'THINK ABOUT IT BEFORE Y'WENT IN? WE DON'T GIVE NO REFUNDS AFTER LEAVIN' THE WINDOW?
OKAY, OKAY! I'LL SEE IT OVER AGAIN, THEN!
5-19
BUT IT'S IMPOSSIBLE! HOW COULD HE GET IN WITHOUT A TICKET?
HERE'S HIS DIME, LADY! IF Y'KNEW MY NEPHEWS Y'WOULDN'T ASK FOOLISH QUESTIONS!
WALT DISNEY

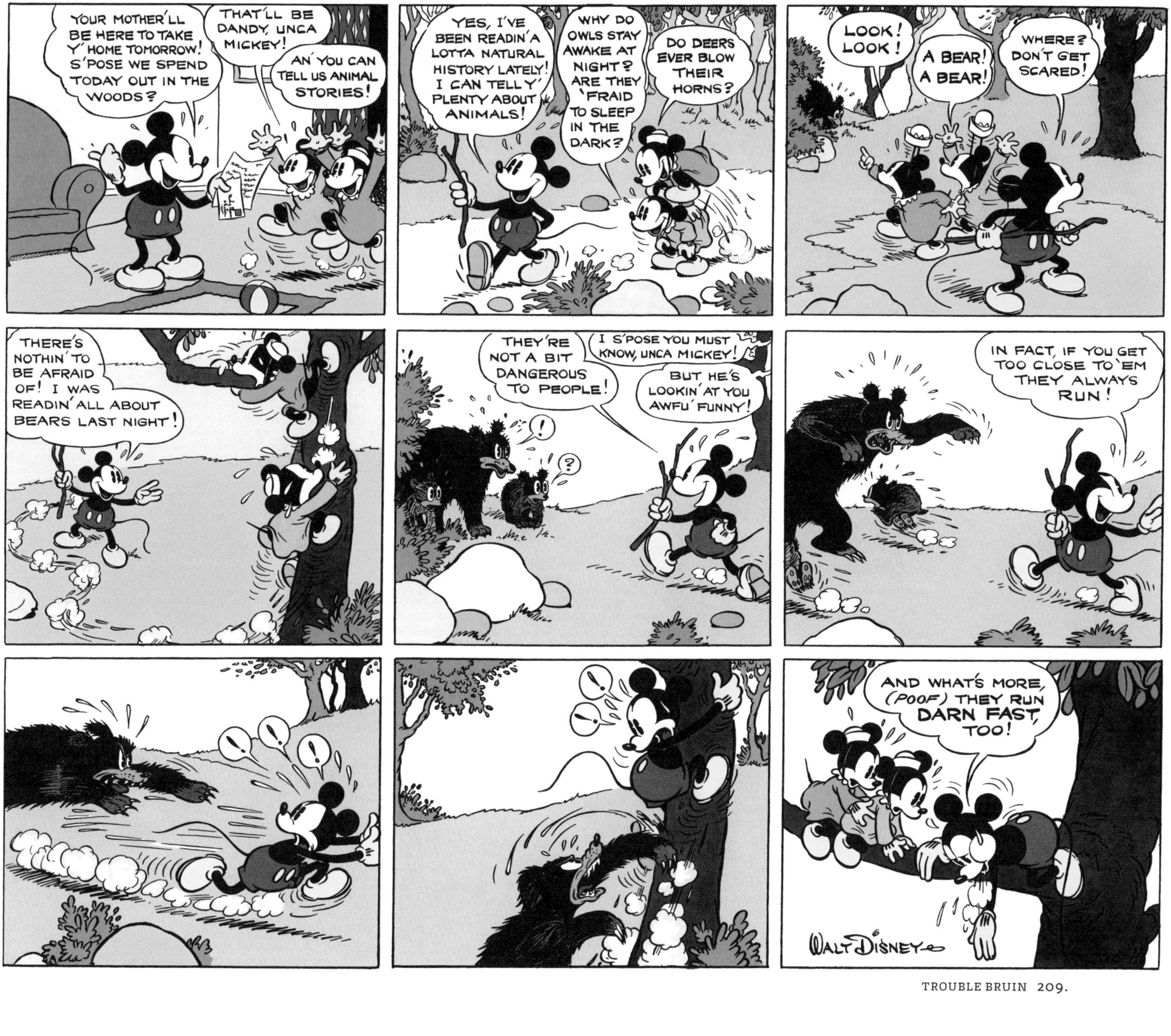
YOUR MOTHER'LL BE HERE TO TAKE Y' HOME TOMORROW! S'POSE WE SPEND TODAY OUT IN THE WOODS?
THAT'LL BE DANDY, UNCA MICKEY!
AN' YOU CAN TELL US ANIMAL STORIES!
YES, I'VE BEEN READIN' A LOTTA NATURAL HISTORY LATELY! I CAN TELL Y' PLENTY ABOUT ANIMALS!
WHY DO OWLS STAY AWAKE AT NIGHT? ARE THEY 'FRAID TO SLEEP IN THE DARK?
DO DEERS EVER BLOW THEIR HORNS?
LOOK! LOOK!
A BEAR! A BEAR!
WHERE? DON'T GET SCARED!
THERE'S NOTHIN' TO BE AFRAID OF! I WAS READIN' ALL ABOUT BEARS LAST NIGHT!
THEY'RE NOT A BIT DANGEROUS TO PEOPLE!
I S'POSE YOU MUST KNOW, UNCA MICKEY!
BUT HE'S LOOKIN' AT YOU AWFU' FUNNY!
!
?
IN FACT, IF YOU GET TOO CLOSE TO 'EM THEY ALWAYS RUN!
!
!
!
!
!
AND WHAT'S MORE, (POOF) THEY RUN DARN FAST, TOO!
WALT DISNEY

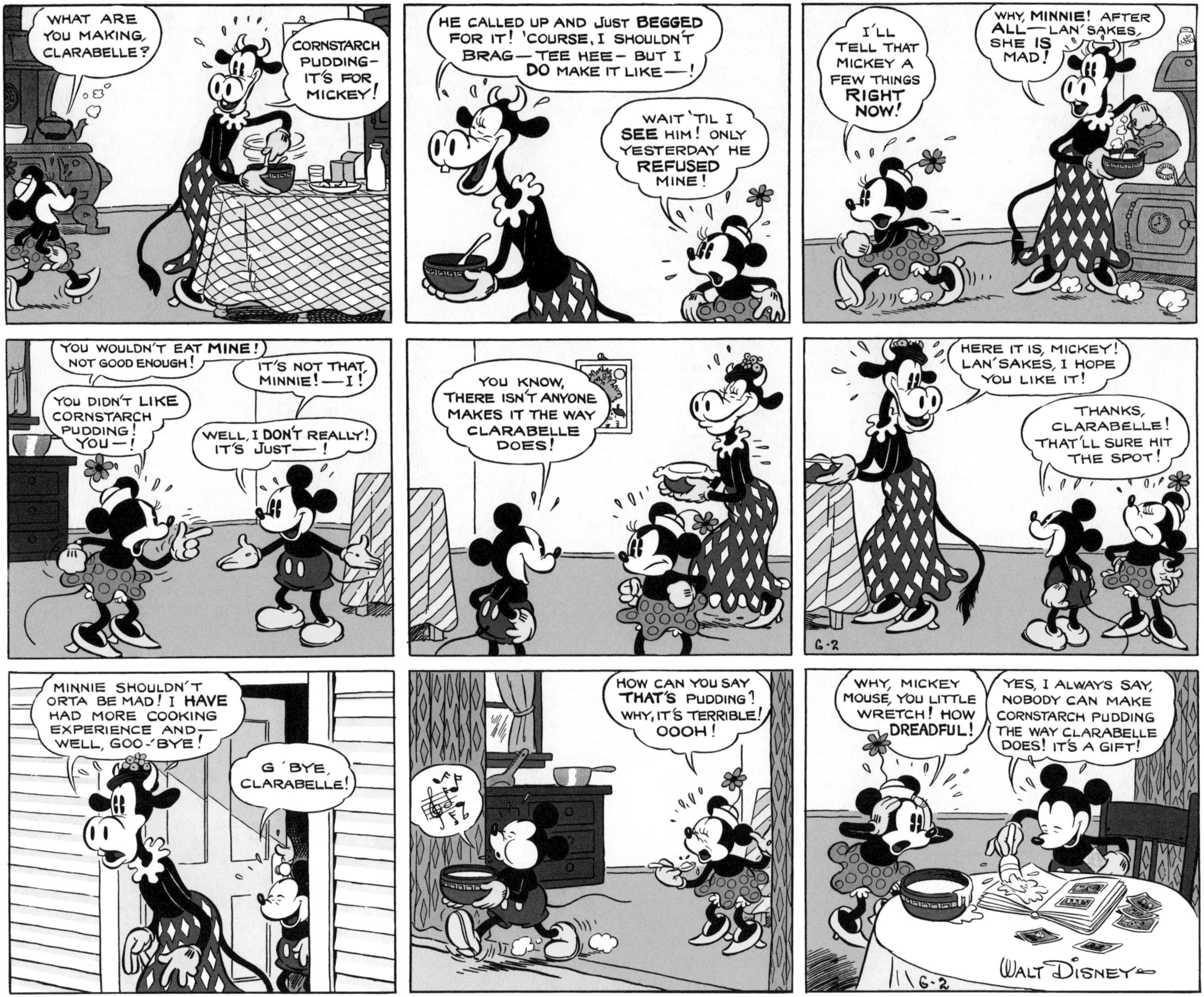
WHAT ARE YOU MAKING, CLARABELLE?
CORNSTARCH PUDDING— IT'S FOR MICKEY!
HE CALLED UP AND JUST BEGGED FOR IT! 'COURSE, I SHOULDN'T BRAG—TEE HEE—BUT I DO MAKE IT LIKE—!
WAIT 'TIL I SEE HIM! ONLY YESTERDAY HE REFUSED MINE!
I'LL TELL THAT MICKEY A FEW THINGS RIGHT NOW!
WHY, MINNIE! AFTER ALL—LAN'SAKES, SHE IS MAD!
YOU WOULDN'T EAT MINE! NOT GOOD ENOUGH!
YOU DIDN'T LIKE CORNSTARCH PUDDING! YOU—!
IT'S NOT THAT, MINNIE!—I!
WELL, I DON'T REALLY! IT'S JUST—!
YOU KNOW, THERE ISN'T ANYONE MAKES IT THE WAY CLARABELLE DOES!
HERE IT IS, MICKEY! LAN'SAKES, I HOPE YOU LIKE IT!
THANKS, CLARABELLE! THAT'LL SURE HIT THE SPOT!
6-2
MINNIE SHOULDN'T ORTA BE MAD! I HAVE HAD MORE COOKING EXPERIENCE AND—WELL, GOO-'BYE!
G'BYE, CLARABELLE!
HOW CAN YOU SAY THAT'S PUDDING? WHY, IT'S TERRIBLE! OOOH!
WHY, MICKEY MOUSE, YOU LITTLE WRETCH! HOW DREADFUL!
YES, I ALWAYS SAY, NOBODY CAN MAKE CORNSTARCH PUDDING THE WAY CLARABELLE DOES! IT'S A GIFT!
WALT DISNEY
6-2

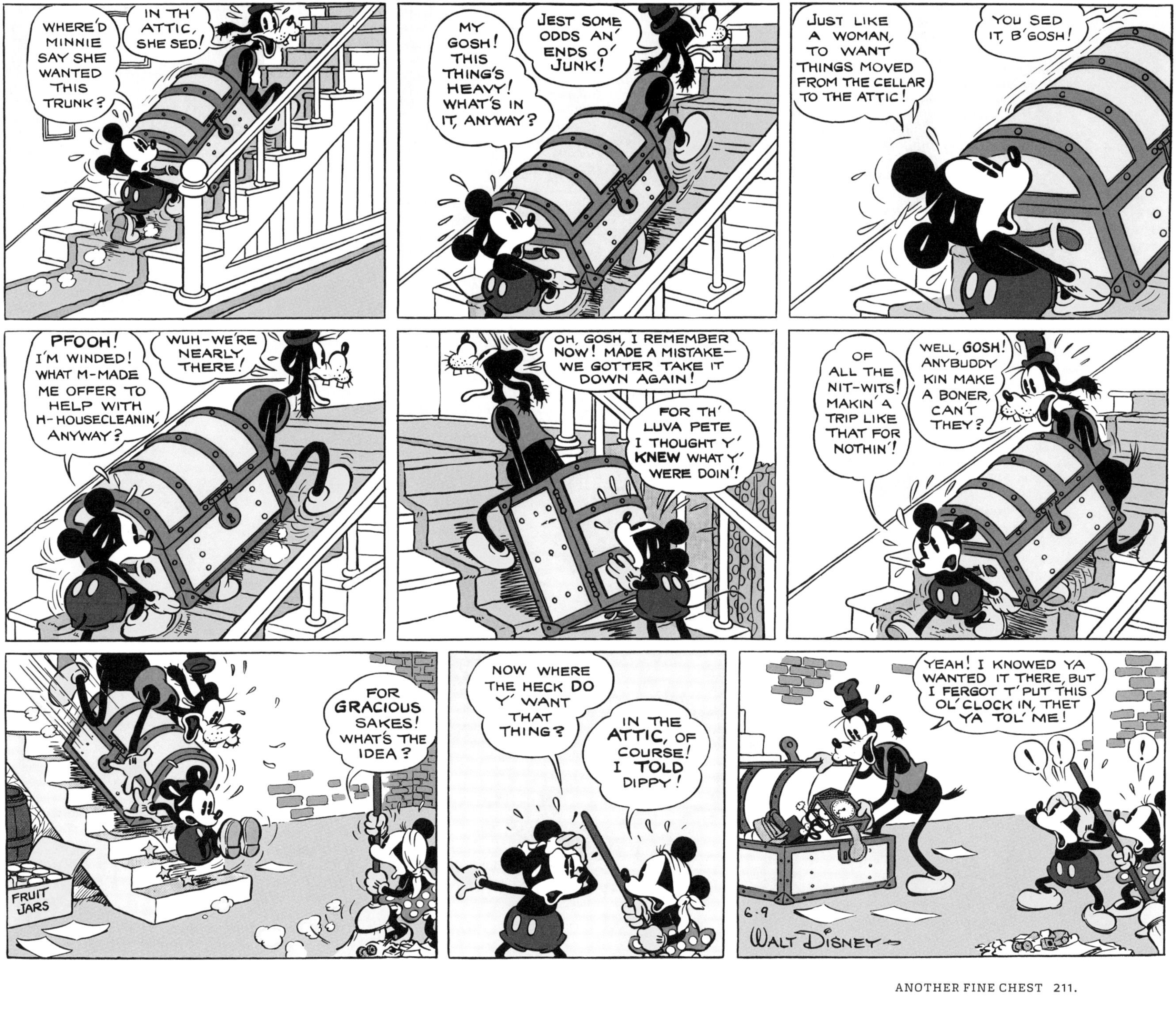
WHERE'D MINNIE SAY SHE WANTED THIS TRUNK?
IN TH' ATTIC, SHE SED!
MY GOSH! THIS THING'S HEAVY! WHAT'S IN IT, ANYWAY?
JEST SOME ODDS AN' ENDS O' JUNK!
JUST LIKE A WOMAN, TO WANT THINGS MOVED FROM THE CELLAR TO THE ATTIC!
YOU SED IT, B'GOSH!
PFOOH! I'M WINDED! WHAT M-MADE ME OFFER TO HELP WITH H-HOUSECLEANIN', ANYWAY?
WUH-WE'RE NEARLY THERE!
OH, GOSH, I REMEMBER NOW! MADE A MISTAKE— WE GOTTER TAKE IT DOWN AGAIN!
FOR TH' LUVA PETE I THOUGHT Y' KNEW WHAT Y' WERE DOIN'!
OF ALL THE NIT-WITS! MAKIN' A TRIP LIKE THAT FOR NOTHIN'!
WELL, GOSH! ANYBUDDY KIN MAKE A BONER, CAN'T THEY?
FOR GRACIOUS SAKES! WHAT'S THE IDEA?
FRUIT JARS
NOW WHERE THE HECK DO Y' WANT THAT THING?
IN THE ATTIC, OF COURSE! I TOLD DIPPY!
YEAH! I KNOWED YA WANTED IT THERE, BUT I FERGOT T'PUT THIS OL' CLOCK IN, THET YA TOL' ME!
!
!
!
6-9
WALT DISNEY

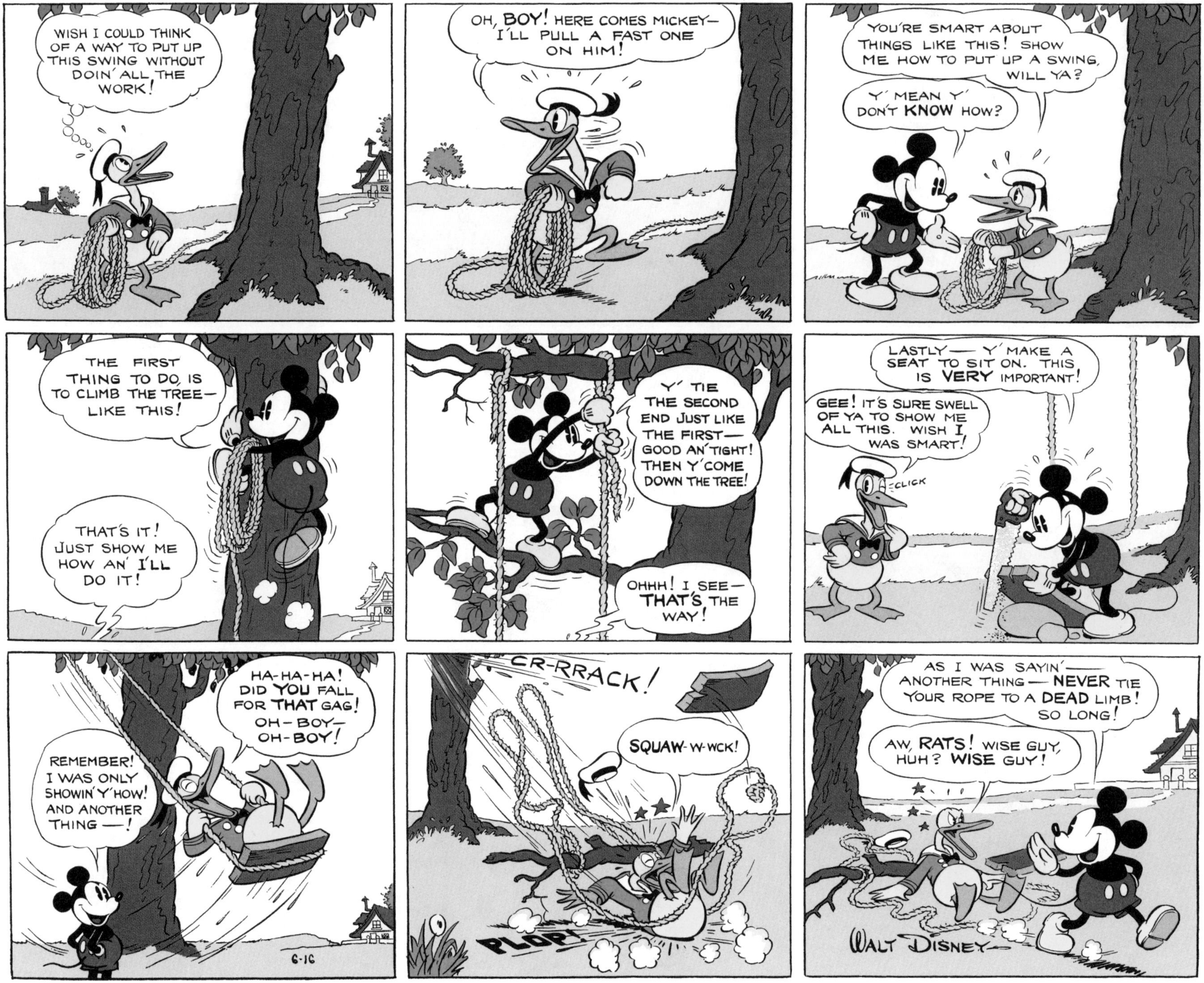
WISH I COULD THINK OF A WAY TO PUT UP THIS SWING WITHOUT DOIN' ALL THE WORK!
OH, BOY! HERE COMES MICKEY— I'LL PULL A FAST ONE ON HIM!
YOU'RE SMART ABOUT THINGS LIKE THIS! SHOW ME HOW TO PUT UP A SWING, WILL YA?
Y' MEAN Y' DON'T KNOW HOW?
THE FIRST THING TO DO, IS TO CLIMB THE TREE— LIKE THIS!
THAT'S IT! JUST SHOW ME HOW AN' I'LL DO IT!
Y' TIE THE SECOND END JUST LIKE THE FIRST— GOOD AN' TIGHT! THEN Y' COME DOWN THE TREE!
OHHH! I SEE— THAT'S THE WAY!
LASTLY— Y' MAKE A SEAT TO SIT ON. THIS IS VERY IMPORTANT!
GEE! IT'S SURE SWELL OF YA TO SHOW ME ALL THIS. WISH I WAS SMART!
CLICK
HA-HA-HA! DID YOU FALL FOR THAT GAG! OH-BOY- OH-BOY!
REMEMBER! I WAS ONLY SHOWIN' Y' HOW! AND ANOTHER THING—!
6-16
CR-RRACK!
SQUAW-W-WCK!
PLOP!
AS I WAS SAYIN'— ANOTHER THING— NEVER TIE YOUR ROPE TO A DEAD LIMB! SO LONG!
AW, RATS! WISE GUY, HUH? WISE GUY!
WALT DISNEY

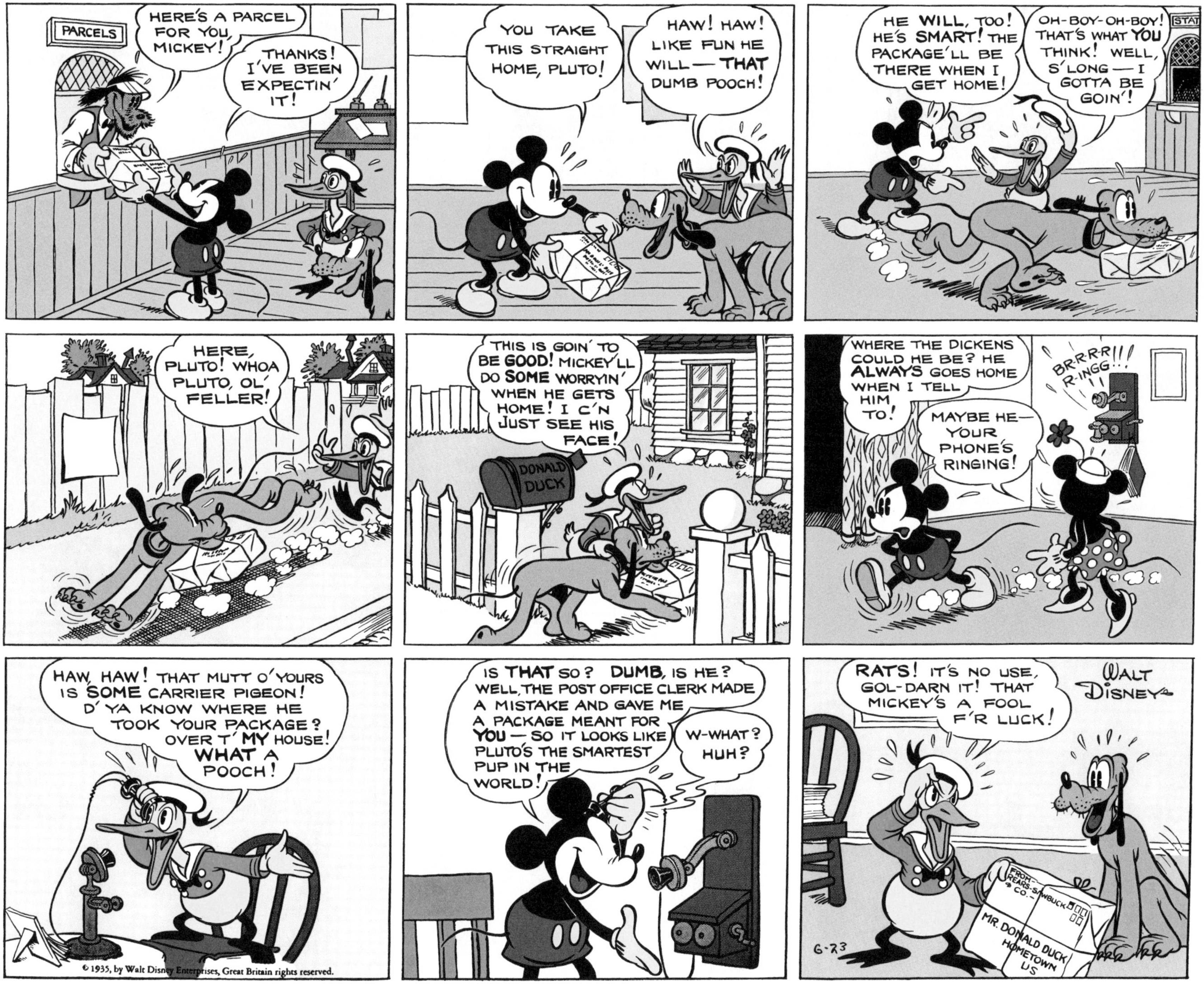
PARCELS
HERE'S A PARCEL FOR YOU, MICKEY!
THANKS! I'VE BEEN EXPECTIN' IT!
YOU TAKE THIS STRAIGHT HOME, PLUTO!
HAW! HAW! LIKE FUN HE WILL — THAT DUMB POOCH!
HE WILL, TOO! HE'S SMART! THE PACKAGE'LL BE THERE WHEN I GET HOME!
OH-BOY-OH-BOY! THAT'S WHAT YOU THINK! WELL, S'LONG — I GOTTA BE GOIN'!
HERE, PLUTO! WHOA PLUTO, OL' FELLER!
THIS IS GOIN' TO BE GOOD! MICKEY'LL DO SOME WORRYIN' WHEN HE GETS HOME! I C'N JUST SEE HIS FACE!
DONALD DUCK
WHERE THE DICKENS COULD HE BE? HE ALWAYS GOES HOME WHEN I TELL HIM TO!
BR-R-R-R R-INGG!!!
MAYBE HE— YOUR PHONE'S RINGING!
HAW, HAW! THAT MUTT O' YOURS IS SOME CARRIER PIGEON! D' YA KNOW WHERE HE TOOK YOUR PACKAGE? OVER T' MY HOUSE! WHAT A POOCH!
IS THAT SO? DUMB, IS HE? WELL, THE POST OFFICE CLERK MADE A MISTAKE AND GAVE ME A PACKAGE MEANT FOR YOU — SO IT LOOKS LIKE PLUTO'S THE SMARTEST PUP IN THE WORLD!
W-WHAT? HUH?
RATS! IT'S NO USE, GOL-DARN IT! THAT MICKEY'S A FOOL F'R LUCK!
WALT DISNEY
FROM SEARS-SAWBUCK & CO.
MR. DONALD DUCK HOMETOWN US
6-23

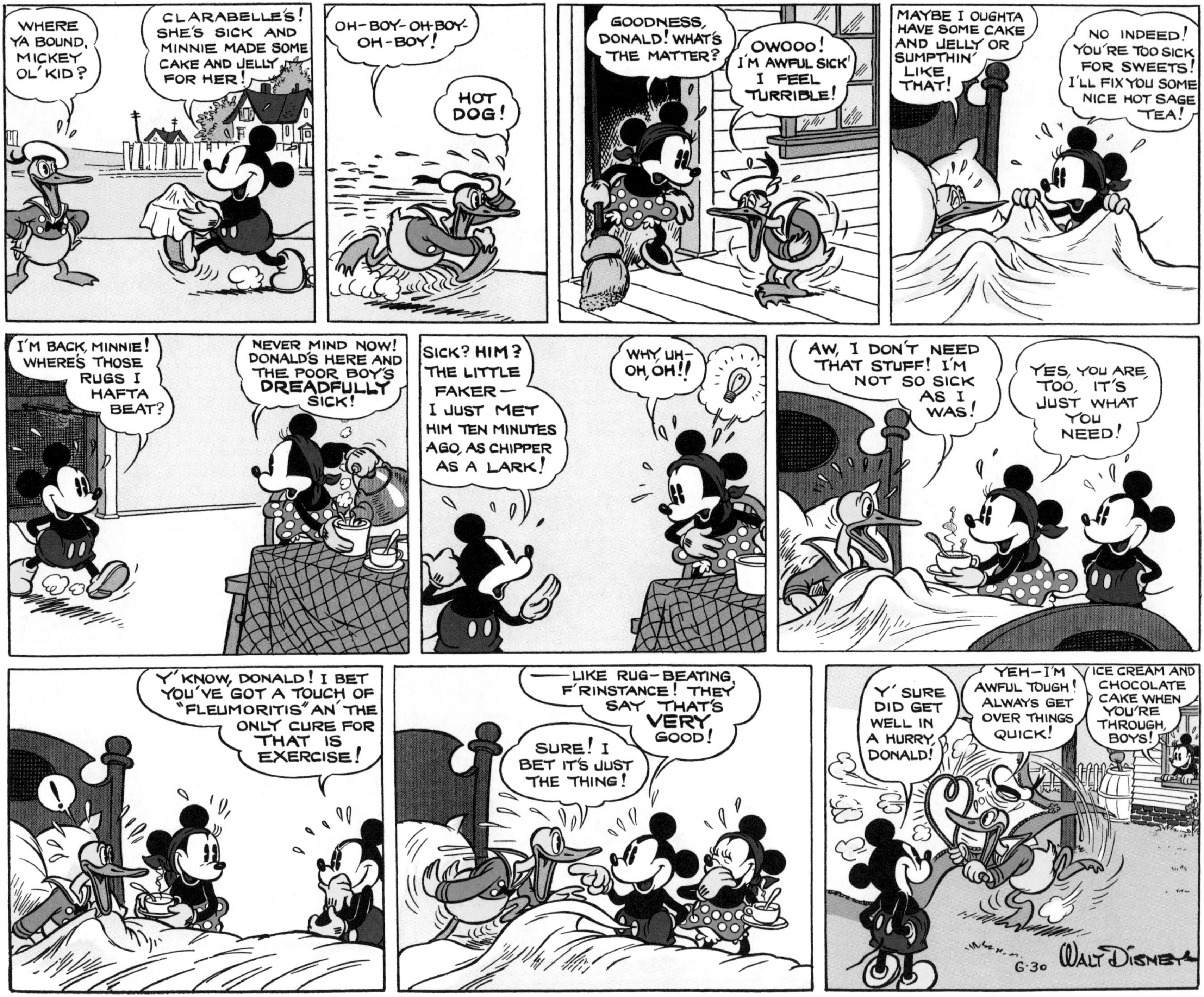
WHERE YA BOUND, MICKEY OL' KID?
CLARABELLE'S! SHE'S SICK AND MINNIE MADE SOME CAKE AND JELLY FOR HER!
OH-BOY-OH-BOY-OH-BOY!
HOT DOG!
GOODNESS, DONALD! WHAT'S THE MATTER?
OWOOO! I'M AWFUL SICK! I FEEL TURRIBLE!
MAYBE I OUGHTA HAVE SOME CAKE AND JELLY OR SUMPTHIN' LIKE THAT!
NO INDEED! YOU'RE TOO SICK FOR SWEETS! I'LL FIX YOU SOME NICE HOT SAGE TEA!
I'M BACK, MINNIE! WHERE'S THOSE RUGS I HAFTA BEAT?
NEVER MIND NOW! DONALD'S HERE AND THE POOR BOY'S DREADFULLY SICK!
SICK? HIM? THE LITTLE FAKER — I JUST MET HIM TEN MINUTES AGO, AS CHIPPER AS A LARK!
WHY, UH-OH, OH!!
AW, I DON'T NEED THAT STUFF! I'M NOT SO SICK AS I WAS!
YES, YOU ARE, TOO, IT'S JUST WHAT YOU NEED!
!
Y'KNOW, DONALD! I BET YOU'VE GOT A TOUCH OF "FLEUMORITIS" AN' THE ONLY CURE FOR THAT IS EXERCISE!
—LIKE RUG-BEATING, F'RINSTANCE! THEY SAY THAT'S VERY GOOD!
SURE! I BET IT'S JUST THE THING!
Y' SURE DID GET WELL IN A HURRY, DONALD!
YEH—I'M AWFUL TOUGH! ALWAYS GET OVER THINGS QUICK!
ICE CREAM AND CHOCOLATE CAKE WHEN YOU'RE THROUGH, BOYS!
6-30
WALT DISNEY

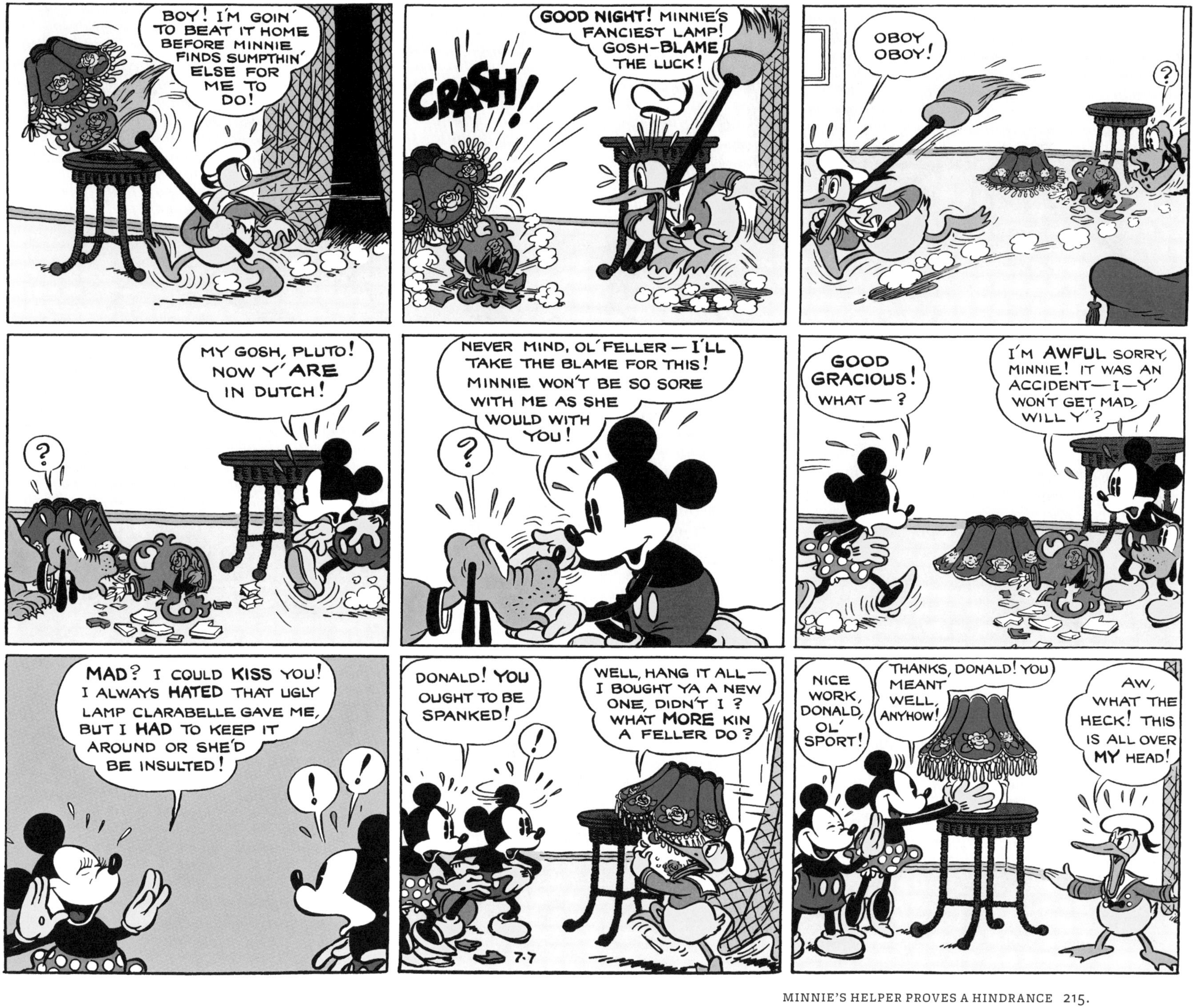

BOY! I'M GOIN' TO BEAT IT HOME BEFORE MINNIE FINDS SUMPTHIN' ELSE FOR ME TO DO!
CRASH!
GOOD NIGHT! MINNIE'S FANCIEST LAMP! GOSH-BLAME THE LUCK!
OBOY OBOY!
?
MY GOSH, PLUTO! NOW Y'ARE IN DUTCH!
?
NEVER MIND, OL' FELLER — I'LL TAKE THE BLAME FOR THIS! MINNIE WON'T BE SO SORE WITH ME AS SHE WOULD WITH YOU!
?
GOOD GRACIOUS! WHAT — ?
I'M AWFUL SORRY, MINNIE! IT WAS AN ACCIDENT — I — Y' WON'T GET MAD, WILL Y'?
MAD? I COULD KISS YOU! I ALWAYS HATED THAT UGLY LAMP CLARABELLE GAVE ME, BUT I HAD TO KEEP IT AROUND OR SHE'D BE INSULTED!
!
!
DONALD! YOU OUGHT TO BE SPANKED!
!
WELL, HANG IT ALL — I BOUGHT YA A NEW ONE, DIDN'T I? WHAT MORE KIN A FELLER DO?
7-7
NICE WORK, DONALD, OL' SPORT!
THANKS, DONALD! YOU MEANT WELL, ANYHOW!
AW, WHAT THE HECK! THIS IS ALL OVER MY HEAD!

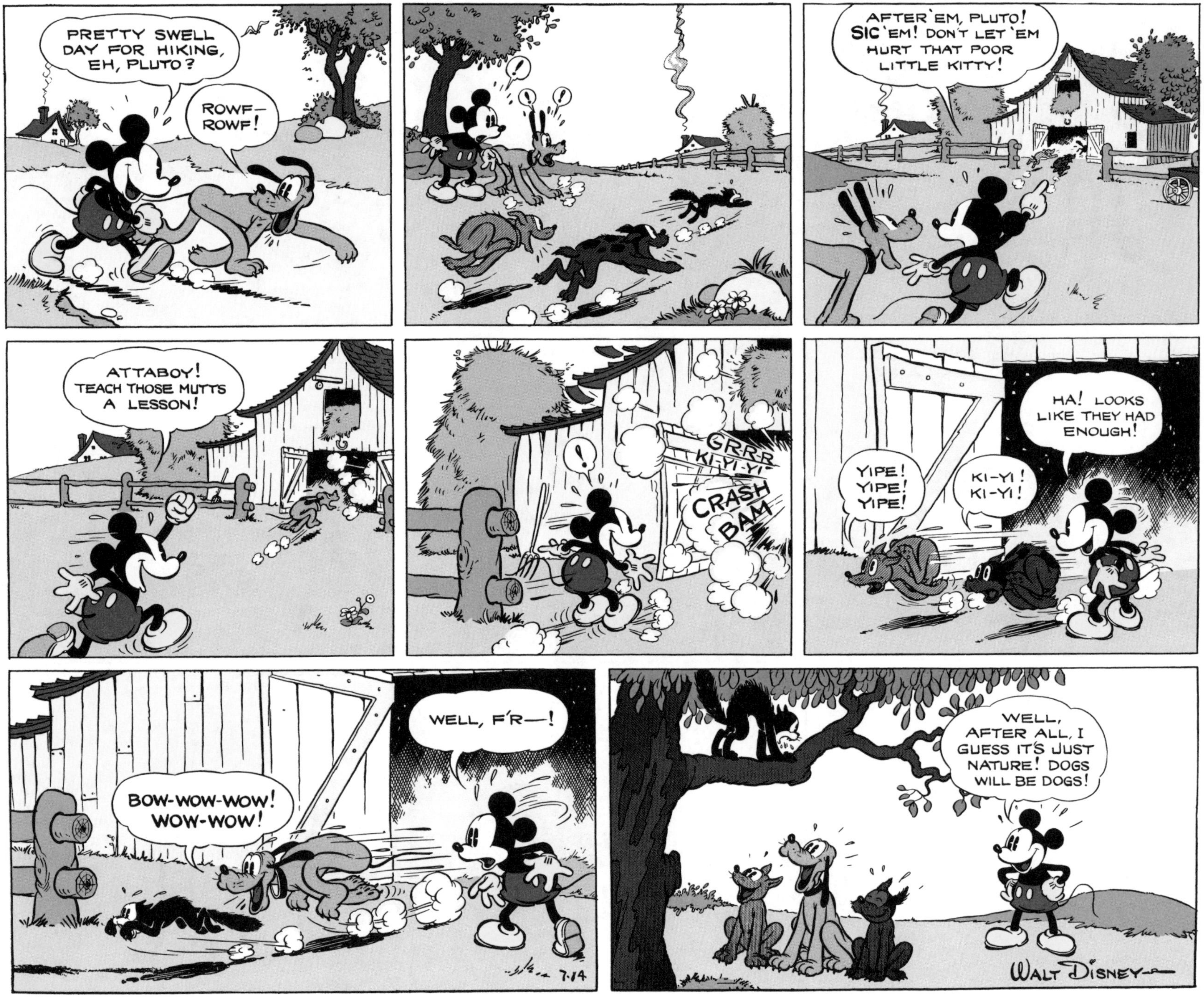
PRETTY SWELL DAY FOR HIKING, EH, PLUTO?
ROWF— ROWF!
!
!
!
AFTER 'EM, PLUTO! SIC 'EM! DON'T LET 'EM HURT THAT POOR LITTLE KITTY!
ATTABOY! TEACH THOSE MUTTS A LESSON!
!
GR-R-R
KI-YI-YI
CRASH
BAM
HA! LOOKS LIKE THEY HAD ENOUGH!
YIPE! YIPE! YIPE!
KI-YI! KI-YI!
WELL, F'R—!
BOW-WOW-WOW! WOW-WOW!
7.14
WELL, AFTER ALL, I GUESS IT'S JUST NATURE! DOGS WILL BE DOGS!
WALT DISNEY

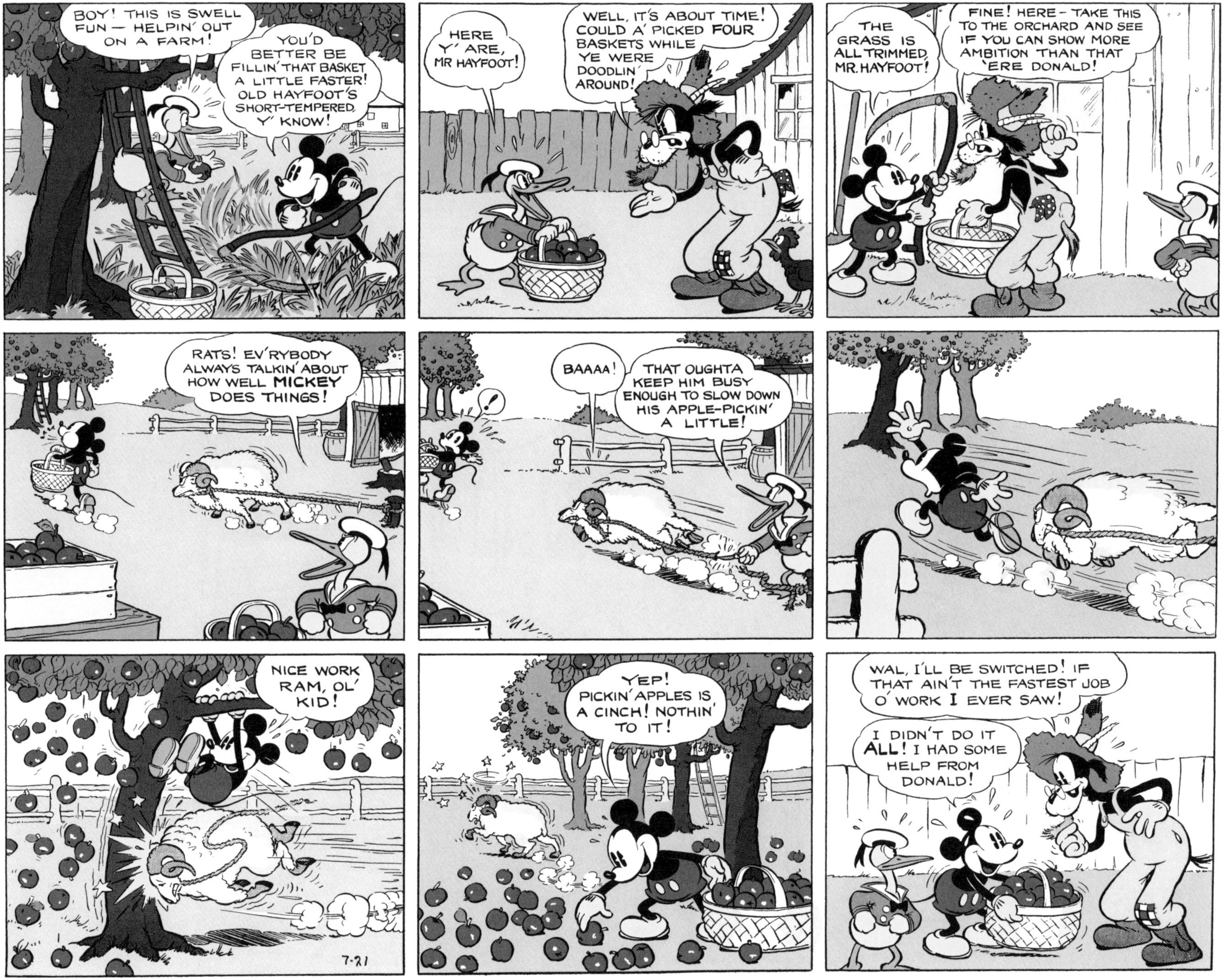
BOY! THIS IS SWELL FUN — HELPIN' OUT ON A FARM!
YOU'D BETTER BE FILLIN' THAT BASKET A LITTLE FASTER! OLD HAYFOOT'S SHORT-TEMPERED, Y' KNOW!
HERE Y' ARE, MR HAYFOOT!
WELL, IT'S ABOUT TIME! COULD A' PICKED FOUR BASKETS WHILE YE WERE DOODLIN' AROUND!
THE GRASS IS ALL TRIMMED, MR. HAYFOOT!
FINE! HERE - TAKE THIS TO THE ORCHARD AND SEE IF YOU CAN SHOW MORE AMBITION THAN THAT 'ERE DONALD!
RATS! EV'RYBODY ALWAYS TALKIN' ABOUT HOW WELL MICKEY DOES THINGS!
BAAAA!
THAT OUGHTA KEEP HIM BUSY ENOUGH TO SLOW DOWN HIS APPLE-PICKIN' A LITTLE!
NICE WORK RAM, OL' KID!
7-21
YEP! PICKIN' APPLES IS A CINCH! NOTHIN' TO IT!
WAL, I'LL BE SWITCHED! IF THAT AIN'T THE FASTEST JOB O' WORK I EVER SAW!
I DIDN'T DO IT ALL! I HAD SOME HELP FROM DONALD!

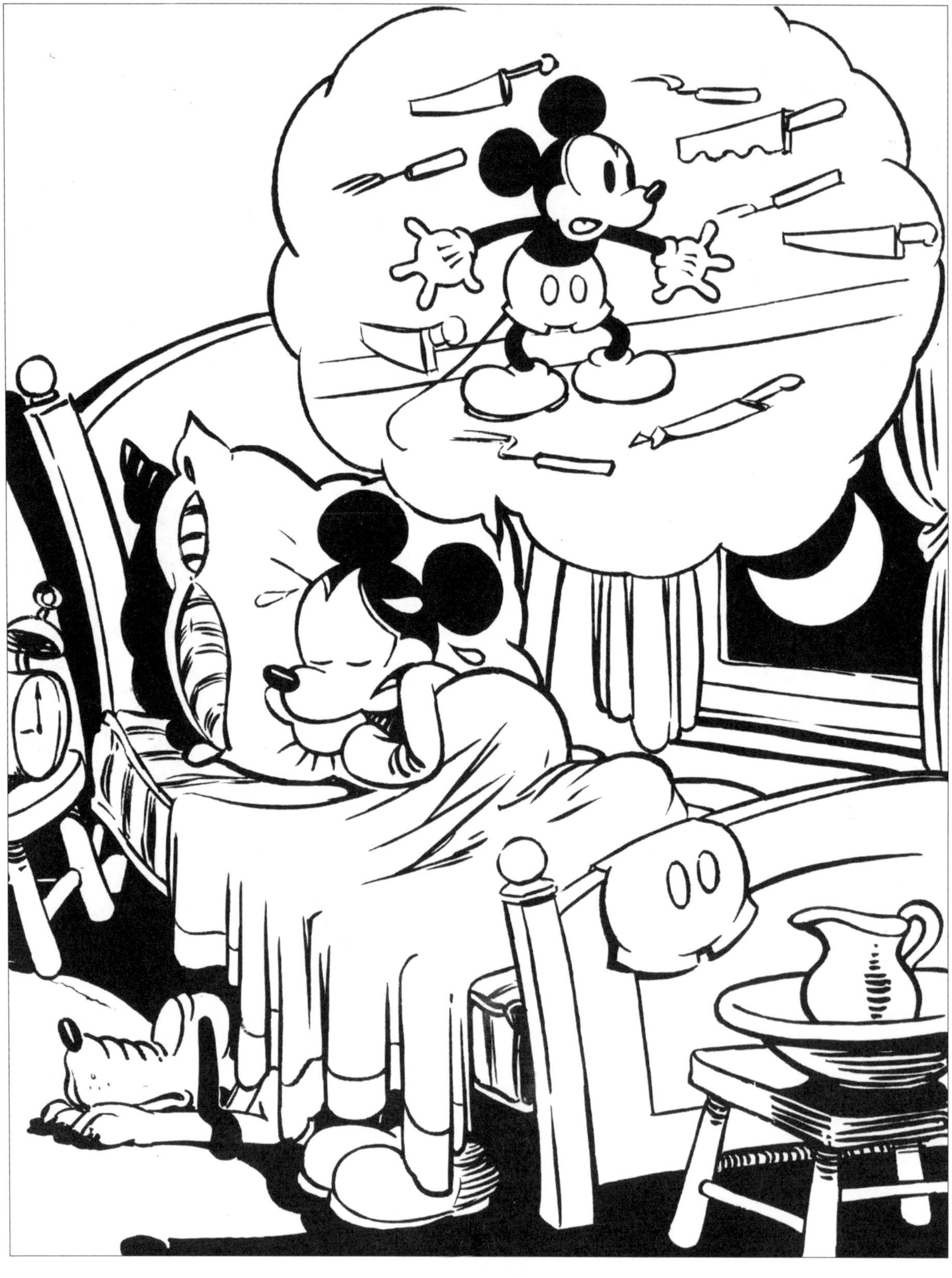

Mickey's nephews made Sunday strip mayhem in 1935—but not as much as Mickey faced from their "ancestors," the multiple mouselings in *Mickey's Nightmare* (1932; see page 253 for details). Poor Mickey envisions the kids' circus knife-throwing act in this *Nightmare* publicity drawing. Art attributed to Floyd Gottfredson (pencils) and Tom Wood (inks); image courtesy Walt Disney Photo Library.

HOPPY THE KANGAROO

AND

GAG STRIPS

JULY 28, 1935

–

DECEMBER 29, 1935

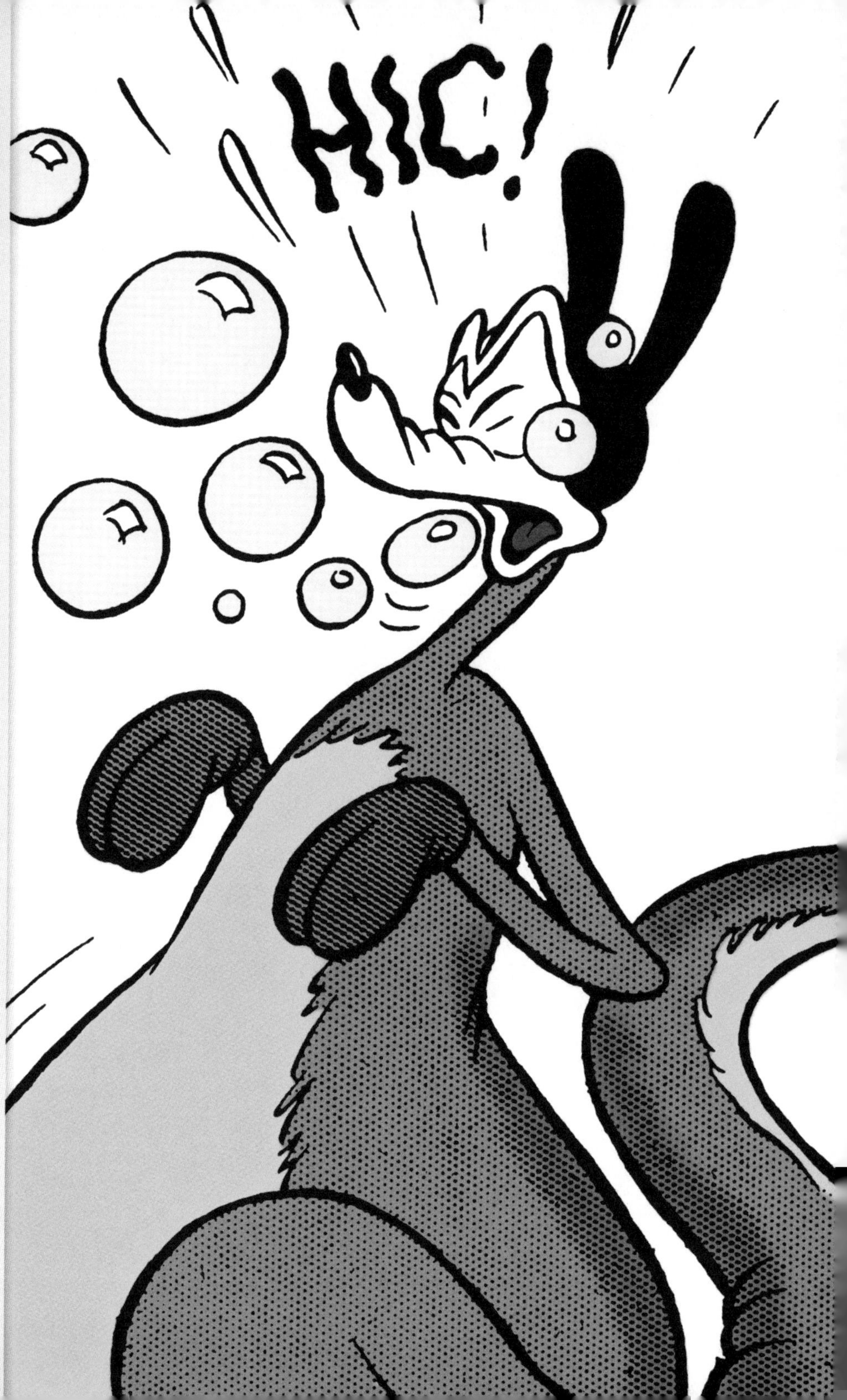
HIC!

MICKEY MOUSE
REGISTERED U.S. PATENT OFFICE

HOPPY THE AMBASSADOR

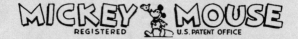

Numerous Mickey Mouse cartoons, comics, and marketing initiatives have been based on current events. Lindbergh's famous flight inspired the cartoon *Plane Crazy* (1928) and the comics continuity "Lost on a Desert Island" (1930). A national vogue for horse races led to the cartoon *The Steeplechase* (1933); the popularity of Depression-era science fiction inspired Gotfredson's "Island in the Sky" (1936-37).

"Hoppy the Kangaroo," on the other hand, was a whole different animal. Would you believe—a comics continuity inspired by a *wine tycoon*?

The "Hoppy" backstory began inauspiciously in early 1933, when the Disney studio circulated an outline for a proposed Mickey short called "The Station Agent." Mickey was to be "station master and freight agent of a one-horse depot," where he and Pluto would be pestered by a shipment of three boxing kangaroos.[1] It's easy to see why kangaroos seemed like ideal subjects for animation; with their jumping, fighting, and comical physiques, the animals would seem to be naturally funny. But perhaps the humor didn't flow as quickly as expected. After some on-and-off development, "Station Agent" evolved into the saga of a different big, bumptious critter—*Donald's Ostrich* (1937)—and kangaroos were left back out in the outback.

But not for long.

Mickey Mouse and Disney cartoons were popular from the start in Australia; and in August 1934, major Sydney wine exporter Leo Buring (1876-1961) decided to express his personal admiration. Buring sent a special gift to the Disney studio: three live wallabies, who—given the Marx Brothers-inspired names Poucho, Leapo, and Hoppo—spent awhile as popular office pets.[2] Their presence revived the notion of an Aussie-themed Mickey cartoon: *Mickey's Kangaroo* (1935) moved quickly into production.

No longer set at a train station, the plot was now staged at Mickey's home, to which two crated kangaroos were sent by Buring himself (!). Rather basic hijinks followed: Mickey boxed with mother 'roo Hoppy while Pluto battled her pouch-borne joey. The story was made unusual only by the technique of voicing Pluto's thoughts in a growly voice; otherwise, *Mickey's Kangaroo* offered little that was out of the ordinary.

In Australia, however, this didn't matter. The Down Under nation boasted little local animation presence; its greatest cartoon celebrity was expatriate Pat Sullivan, a New York-based producer who claimed to have created 1920s studio star Felix the Cat.[3] But since then, nothing, leaving *Mickey's Kangaroo* to fill a kind of vacuum. "This cartoon... will concentrate the minds of millions throughout the world on our portion of the globe," one Aussie newspaper gushed.[4]

Hoppy's tale didn't end there. Newspapers next had the honor of publishing Gottfredson's "Hoppy the Kangaroo" Sunday serial, in which the mama 'roo became a male; the baby was excised; and the cartoon's simple plot was spiced up immeasurably by the addition of Pegleg Pete and a gorilla. Formulaic conflict between Mouse and pets now became a classic grudge match between timeless foes.

We like to think Leo Buring raised his glass in a toast. [DG]

---

1 Walt Disney, et al. ""The Station Agent." Story outline, 1933.

2 Alice Pardoe West, "Drama Interest Kept Alive by Club's Activity." *The Ogden Standard-Examiner*, 12 August 1934. Buring only meant to send two animals, a grown male and female; but their baby was unexpectedly born in transit.

3 Decades later, after the Sullivan estate sold off the character, studio staffers could safely credit director Otto Messmer with Felix's creation.

4 "Mickey's Kangaroo." *The West Australian*, 12 July 1935.

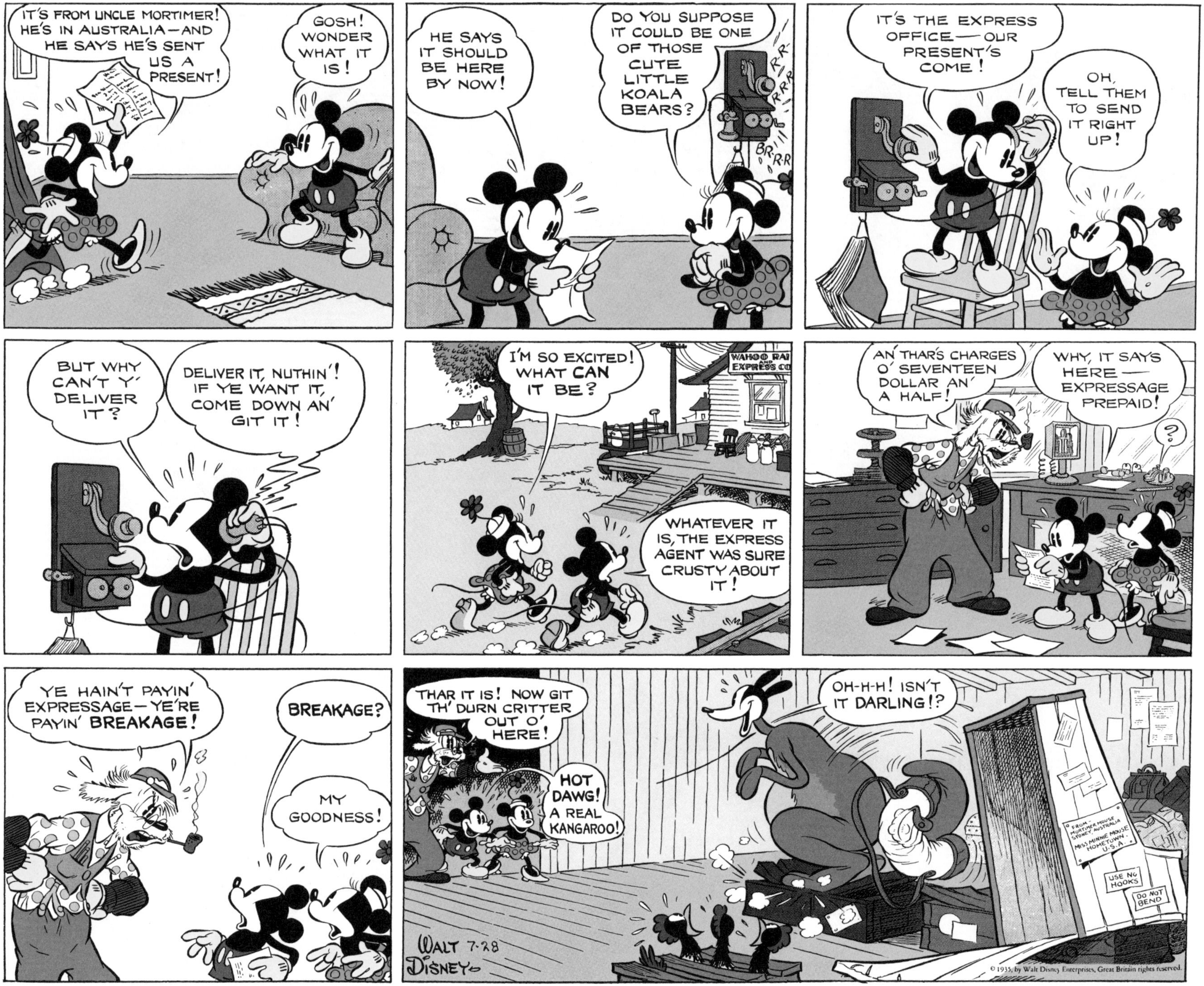

IT'S FROM UNCLE MORTIMER! HE'S IN AUSTRALIA—AND HE SAYS HE'S SENT US A PRESENT!
GOSH! WONDER WHAT IT IS!
HE SAYS IT SHOULD BE HERE BY NOW!
DO YOU SUPPOSE IT COULD BE ONE OF THOSE CUTE LITTLE KOALA BEARS?
R-R-R-R
BR-R-R
IT'S THE EXPRESS OFFICE—OUR PRESENT'S COME!
OH, TELL THEM TO SEND IT RIGHT UP!
BUT WHY CAN'T Y' DELIVER IT?
DELIVER IT, NUTHIN'! IF YE WANT IT, COME DOWN AN' GIT IT!
WAHOO RAI
EXPRESS CO
I'M SO EXCITED! WHAT CAN IT BE?
WHATEVER IT IS, THE EXPRESS AGENT WAS SURE CRUSTY ABOUT IT!
AN' THAR'S CHARGES O' SEVENTEEN DOLLAR AN' A HALF!
WHY, IT SAYS HERE—EXPRESSAGE PREPAID!
?
YE HAIN'T PAYIN' EXPRESSAGE—YE'RE PAYIN' BREAKAGE!
BREAKAGE?
MY GOODNESS!
THAR IT IS! NOW GIT TH' DURN CRITTER OUT O' HERE!
HOT DAWG! A REAL KANGAROO!
OH-H-H! ISN'T IT DARLING!?
FROM - MORTIMER MOUSE SYDNEY, AUSTRALIA
MISS MINNIE MOUSE - HOMETOWN - U.S.A
USE NO HOOKS
DO NOT BEND
WALT DISNEY 7-28
© 1933, by Walt Disney Enterprises, Great Britain rights reserved.

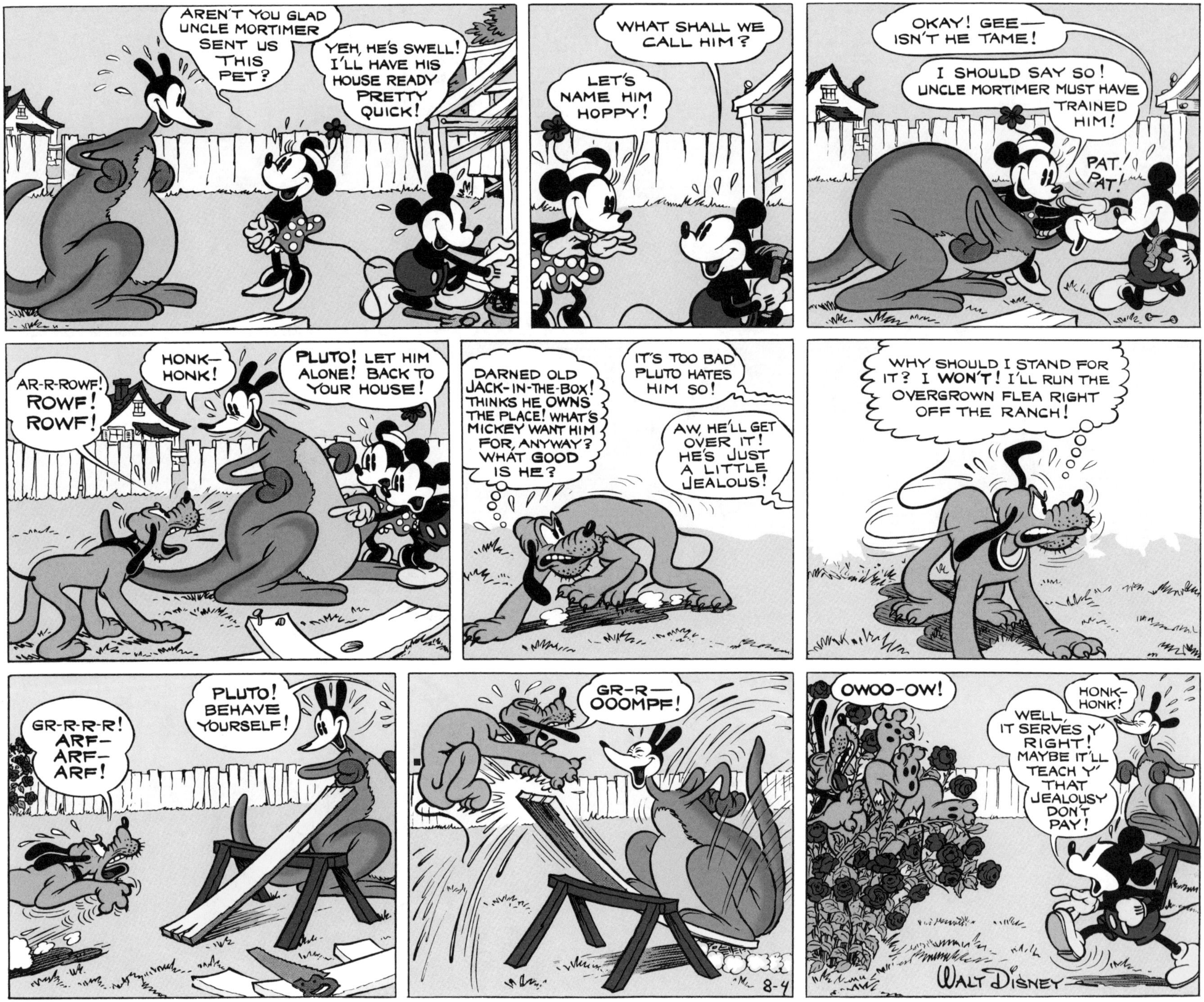

AREN'T YOU GLAD UNCLE MORTIMER SENT US THIS PET?
YEH, HE'S SWELL! I'LL HAVE HIS HOUSE READY PRETTY QUICK!
WHAT SHALL WE CALL HIM?
LET'S NAME HIM HOPPY!
OKAY! GEE— ISN'T HE TAME!
I SHOULD SAY SO! UNCLE MORTIMER MUST HAVE TRAINED HIM!
PAT! PAT!
AR-R-ROWF! ROWF! ROWF!
HONK— HONK!
PLUTO! LET HIM ALONE! BACK TO YOUR HOUSE!
DARNED OLD JACK-IN-THE-BOX! THINKS HE OWNS THE PLACE! WHAT'S MICKEY WANT HIM FOR, ANYWAY? WHAT GOOD IS HE?
IT'S TOO BAD PLUTO HATES HIM SO!
AW, HE'LL GET OVER IT! HE'S JUST A LITTLE JEALOUS!
WHY SHOULD I STAND FOR IT? I WON'T! I'LL RUN THE OVERGROWN FLEA RIGHT OFF THE RANCH!
GR-R-R-R! ARF- ARF- ARF!
PLUTO! BEHAVE YOURSELF!
GR-R— OOOMPF!
8-4
OWOO-OW!
HONK- HONK!
WELL, IT SERVES Y' RIGHT! MAYBE IT'LL TEACH Y' THAT JEALOUSY DON'T PAY!
WALT DISNEY

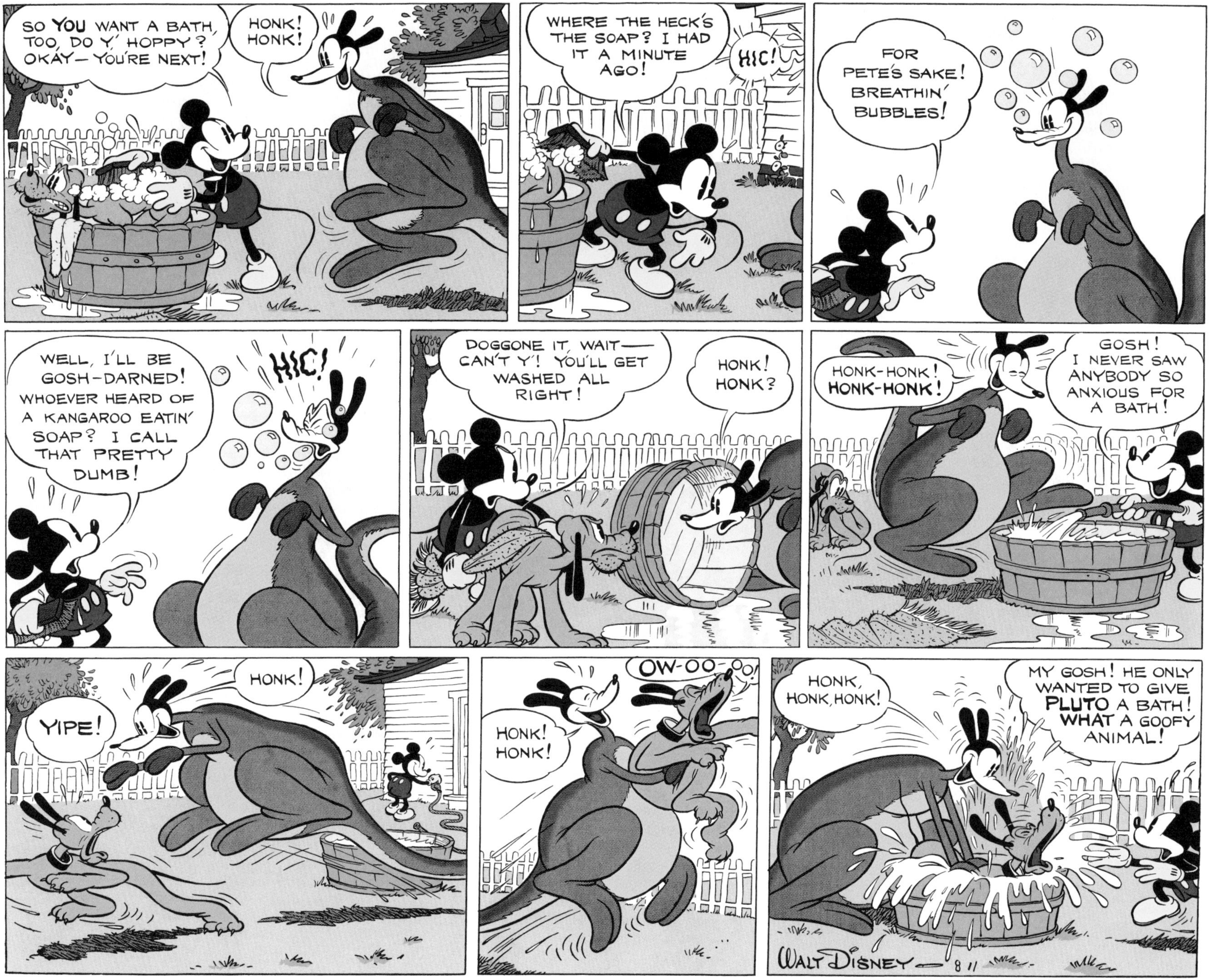
SO YOU WANT A BATH, TOO, DO Y' HOPPY? OKAY— YOU'RE NEXT!
HONK! HONK!
WHERE THE HECK'S THE SOAP? I HAD IT A MINUTE AGO!
HIC!
FOR PETE'S SAKE! BREATHIN' BUBBLES!
WELL, I'LL BE GOSH-DARNED! WHOEVER HEARD OF A KANGAROO EATIN' SOAP? I CALL THAT PRETTY DUMB!
HIC!
DOGGONE IT, WAIT— CAN'T Y'! YOU'LL GET WASHED ALL RIGHT!
HONK! HONK?
HONK-HONK! HONK-HONK!
GOSH! I NEVER SAW ANYBODY SO ANXIOUS FOR A BATH!
YIPE!
HONK!
HONK! HONK!
OW-OO-OO!
HONK, HONK, HONK!
MY GOSH! HE ONLY WANTED TO GIVE PLUTO A BATH! WHAT A GOOFY ANIMAL!
WALT DISNEY 8 11

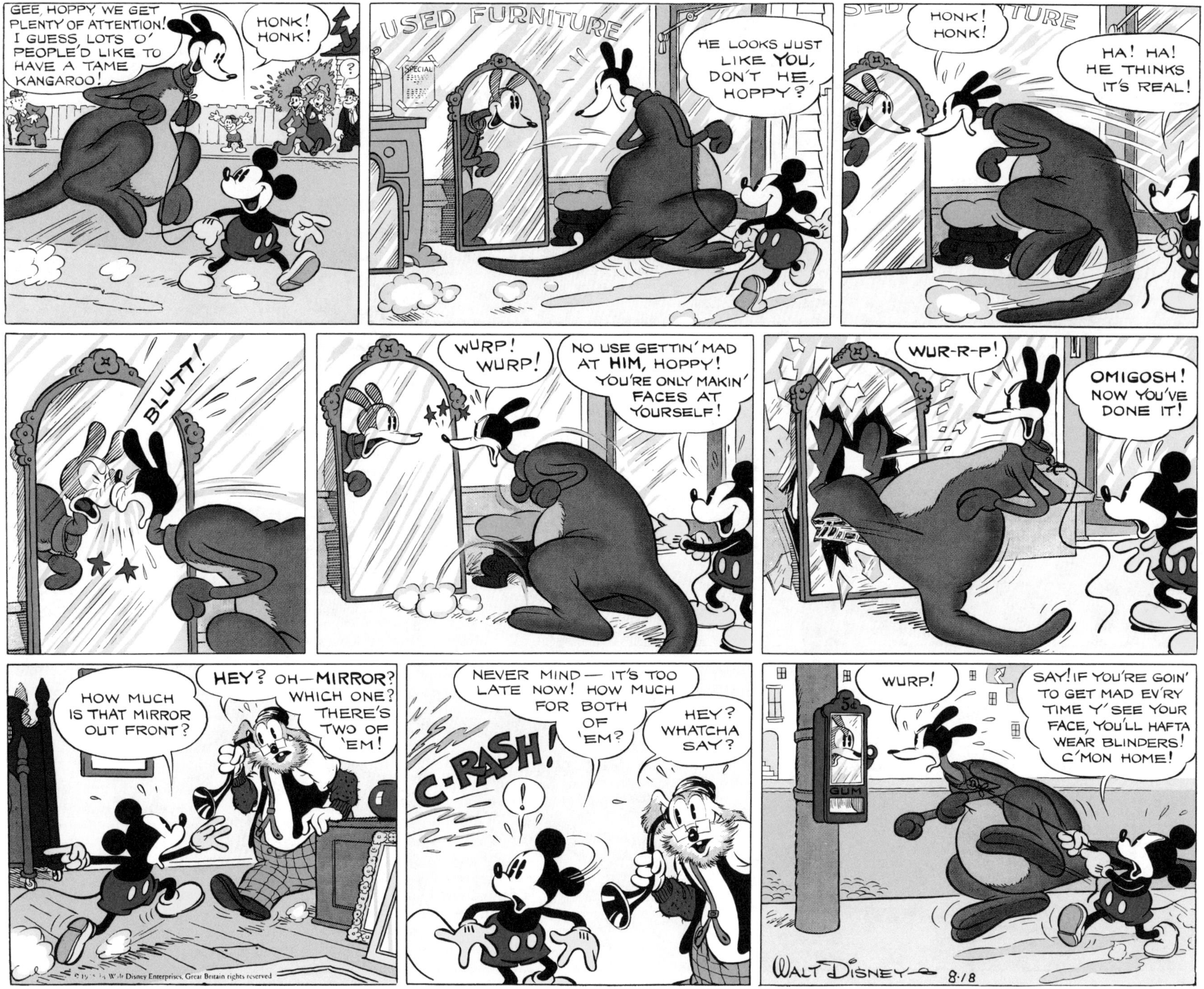
GEE, HOPPY, WE GET PLENTY OF ATTENTION! I GUESS LOTS O' PEOPLE'D LIKE TO HAVE A TAME KANGAROO!
HONK! HONK!
?
USED FURNITURE
SPECIAL
HE LOOKS JUST LIKE YOU, DON'T HE, HOPPY?
HONK! HONK!
HA! HA! HE THINKS IT'S REAL!
BLUTT!
WURP! WURP!
NO USE GETTIN' MAD AT HIM, HOPPY! YOU'RE ONLY MAKIN' FACES AT YOURSELF!
WUR-R-P!
OMIGOSH! NOW YOU'VE DONE IT!
HOW MUCH IS THAT MIRROR OUT FRONT?
HEY? OH—MIRROR? WHICH ONE? THERE'S TWO OF 'EM!
Walt Disney Enterprises, Great Britain rights reserved
C-RASH!
NEVER MIND— IT'S TOO LATE NOW! HOW MUCH FOR BOTH OF 'EM?
HEY? WHATCHA SAY?
!
WURP!
5¢
GUM
SAY! IF YOU'RE GOIN' TO GET MAD EV'RY TIME Y' SEE YOUR FACE, YOU'LL HAFTA WEAR BLINDERS! C'MON HOME!
WALT DISNEY 8-18

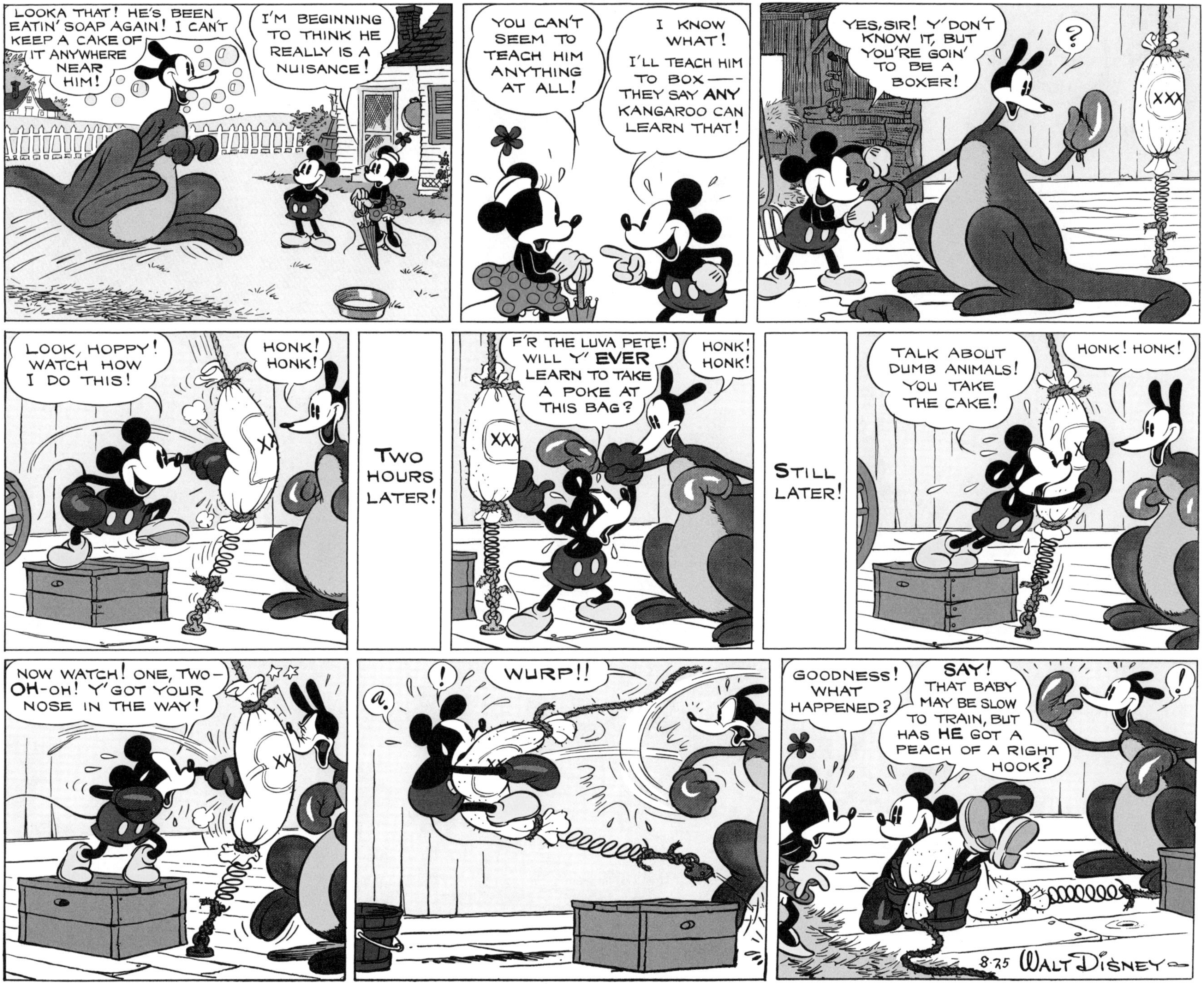
LOOKA THAT! HE'S BEEN EATIN' SOAP AGAIN! I CAN'T KEEP A CAKE OF IT ANYWHERE NEAR HIM!
I'M BEGINNING TO THINK HE REALLY IS A NUISANCE!
YOU CAN'T SEEM TO TEACH HIM ANYTHING AT ALL!
I KNOW WHAT! I'LL TEACH HIM TO BOX—— THEY SAY ANY KANGAROO CAN LEARN THAT!
YES, SIR! Y' DON'T KNOW IT, BUT YOU'RE GOIN' TO BE A BOXER!
?
XXX
LOOK, HOPPY! WATCH HOW I DO THIS!
HONK! HONK!
TWO HOURS LATER!
F'R THE LUVA PETE! WILL Y' EVER LEARN TO TAKE A POKE AT THIS BAG?
HONK! HONK!
STILL LATER!
TALK ABOUT DUMB ANIMALS! YOU TAKE THE CAKE!
HONK! HONK!
NOW WATCH! ONE, TWO- OH-OH! Y' GOT YOUR NOSE IN THE WAY!
WURP!!
!
GOODNESS! WHAT HAPPENED?
SAY! THAT BABY MAY BE SLOW TO TRAIN, BUT HAS HE GOT A PEACH OF A RIGHT HOOK?
!
8·25 WALT DISNEY

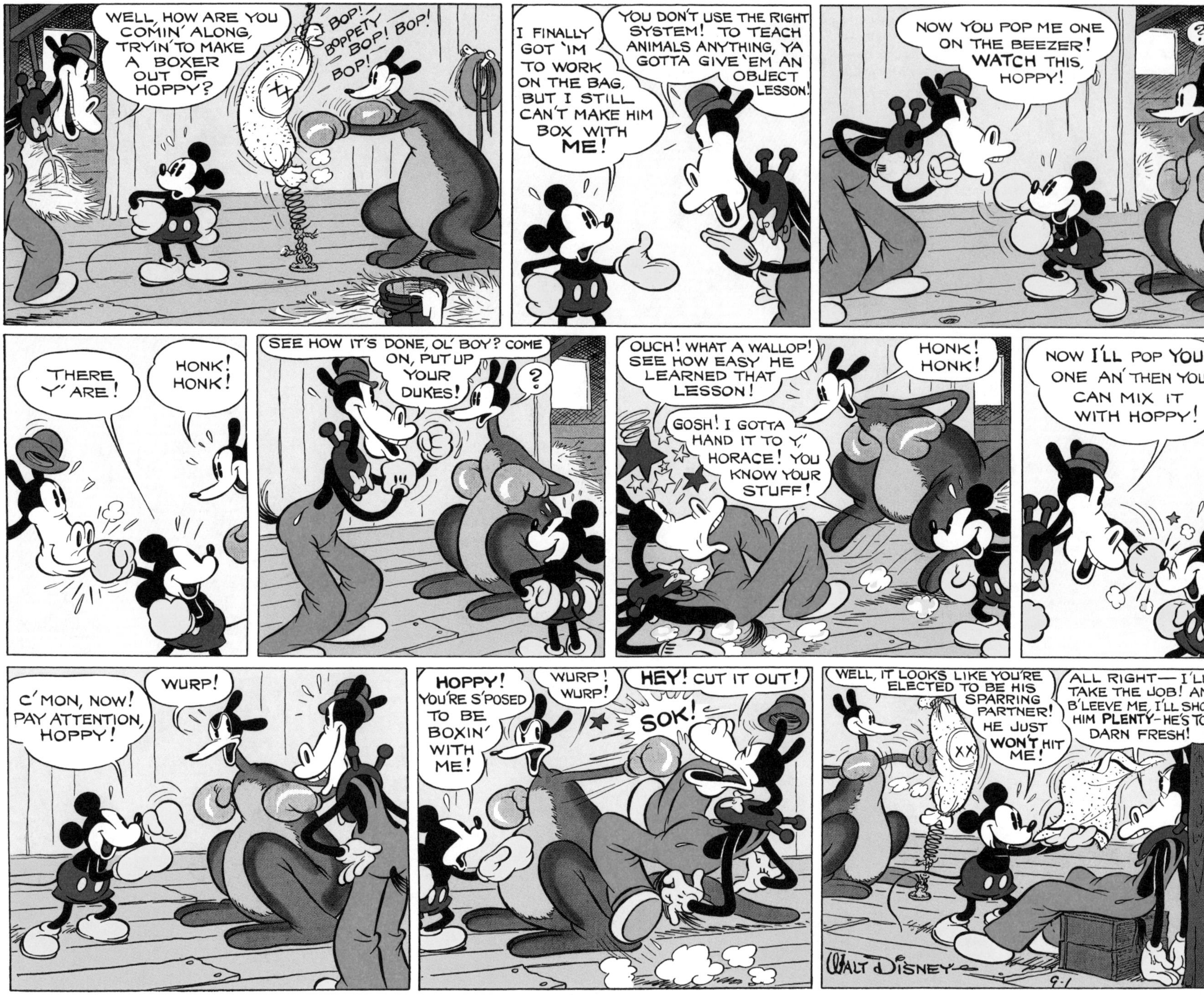

WELL, HOW ARE YOU COMIN' ALONG, TRYIN' TO MAKE A BOXER OUT OF HOPPY?
BOP! BOPPETY BOP! BOP! BOP! BOP!
I FINALLY GOT 'IM TO WORK ON THE BAG, BUT I STILL CAN'T MAKE HIM BOX WITH ME!
YOU DON'T USE THE RIGHT SYSTEM! TO TEACH ANIMALS ANYTHING, YA GOTTA GIVE 'EM AN OBJECT LESSON!
NOW YOU POP ME ONE ON THE BEEZER! WATCH THIS, HOPPY!
?
THERE Y' ARE!
HONK! HONK!
SEE HOW IT'S DONE, OL' BOY? COME ON, PUT UP YOUR DUKES!
?
OUCH! WHAT A WALLOP! SEE HOW EASY HE LEARNED THAT LESSON!
HONK! HONK!
GOSH! I GOTTA HAND IT TO Y', HORACE! YOU KNOW YOUR STUFF!
NOW I'LL POP YOU ONE AN' THEN YOU CAN MIX IT WITH HOPPY!
C'MON, NOW! PAY ATTENTION, HOPPY!
WURP!
HOPPY! YOU'RE S'POSED TO BE BOXIN' WITH ME!
WURP! WURP!
HEY! CUT IT OUT!
SOK!
WELL, IT LOOKS LIKE YOU'RE ELECTED TO BE HIS SPARRING PARTNER! HE JUST WON'T HIT ME!
ALL RIGHT— I'LL TAKE THE JOB! AN' B'LEEVE ME, I'LL SHOW HIM PLENTY— HE'S TOO DARN FRESH!
WALT DISNEY
9-1

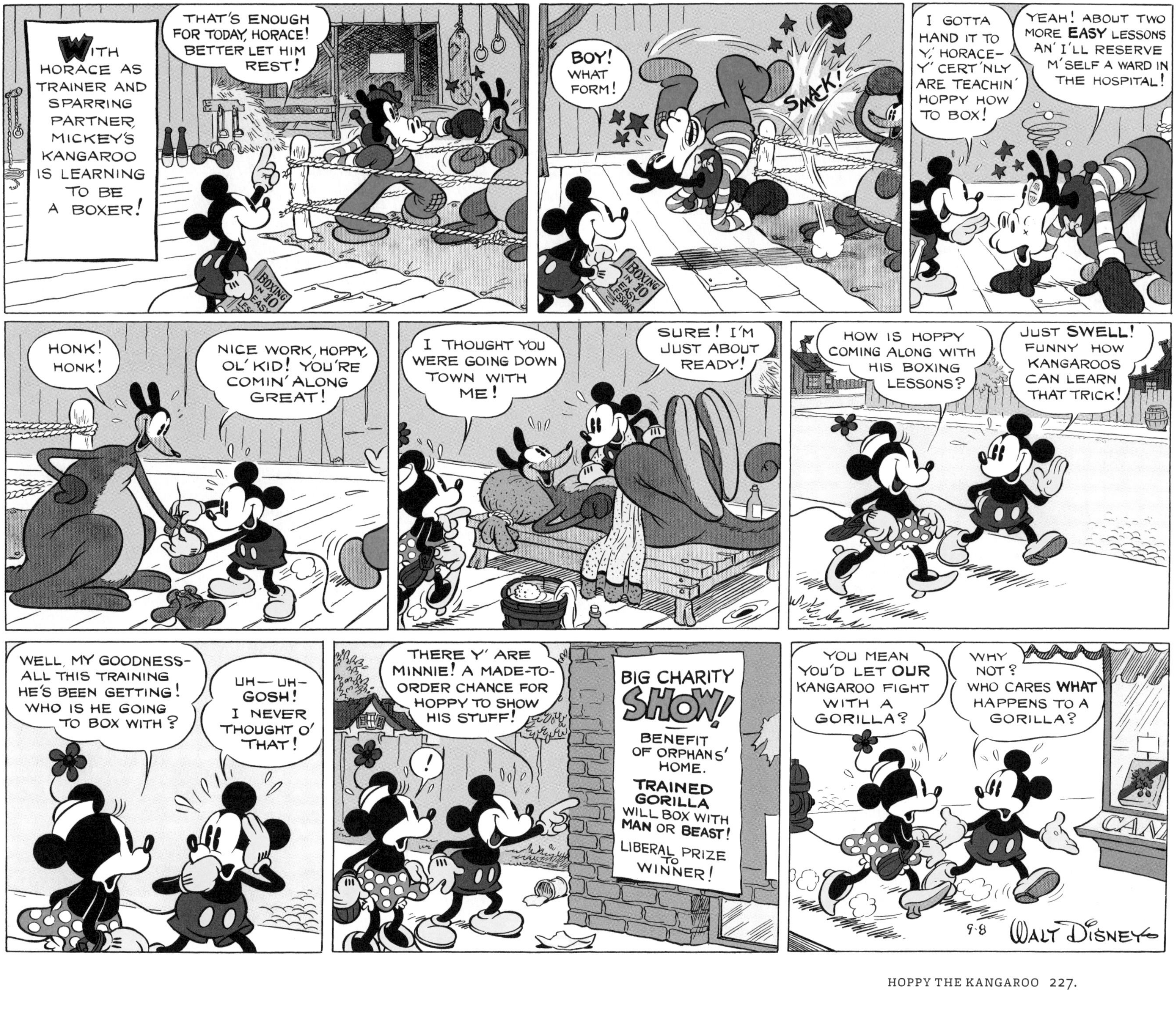

WITH HORACE AS TRAINER AND SPARRING PARTNER, MICKEY'S KANGAROO IS LEARNING TO BE A BOXER!
THAT'S ENOUGH FOR TODAY, HORACE! BETTER LET HIM REST!
BOXING IN 10 EASY LESSONS
BOY! WHAT FORM!
SMACK!
BOXING IN 10 EASY LESSONS
I GOTTA HAND IT TO Y', HORACE— Y' CERT'NLY ARE TEACHIN' HOPPY HOW TO BOX!
YEAH! ABOUT TWO MORE EASY LESSONS AN' I'LL RESERVE M'SELF A WARD IN THE HOSPITAL!
HONK! HONK!
NICE WORK, HOPPY, OL' KID! YOU'RE COMIN' ALONG GREAT!
I THOUGHT YOU WERE GOING DOWN TOWN WITH ME!
SURE! I'M JUST ABOUT READY!
HOW IS HOPPY COMING ALONG WITH HIS BOXING LESSONS?
JUST SWELL! FUNNY HOW KANGAROOS CAN LEARN THAT TRICK!
WELL, MY GOODNESS— ALL THIS TRAINING HE'S BEEN GETTING! WHO IS HE GOING TO BOX WITH?
UH—UH— GOSH! I NEVER THOUGHT O' THAT!
!
THERE Y' ARE MINNIE! A MADE-TO-ORDER CHANCE FOR HOPPY TO SHOW HIS STUFF!
BIG CHARITY SHOW! BENEFIT OF ORPHANS' HOME. TRAINED GORILLA WILL BOX WITH MAN OR BEAST! LIBERAL PRIZE TO WINNER!
YOU MEAN YOU'D LET OUR KANGAROO FIGHT WITH A GORILLA?
WHY NOT? WHO CARES WHAT HAPPENS TO A GORILLA?
9-8
WALT DISNEY

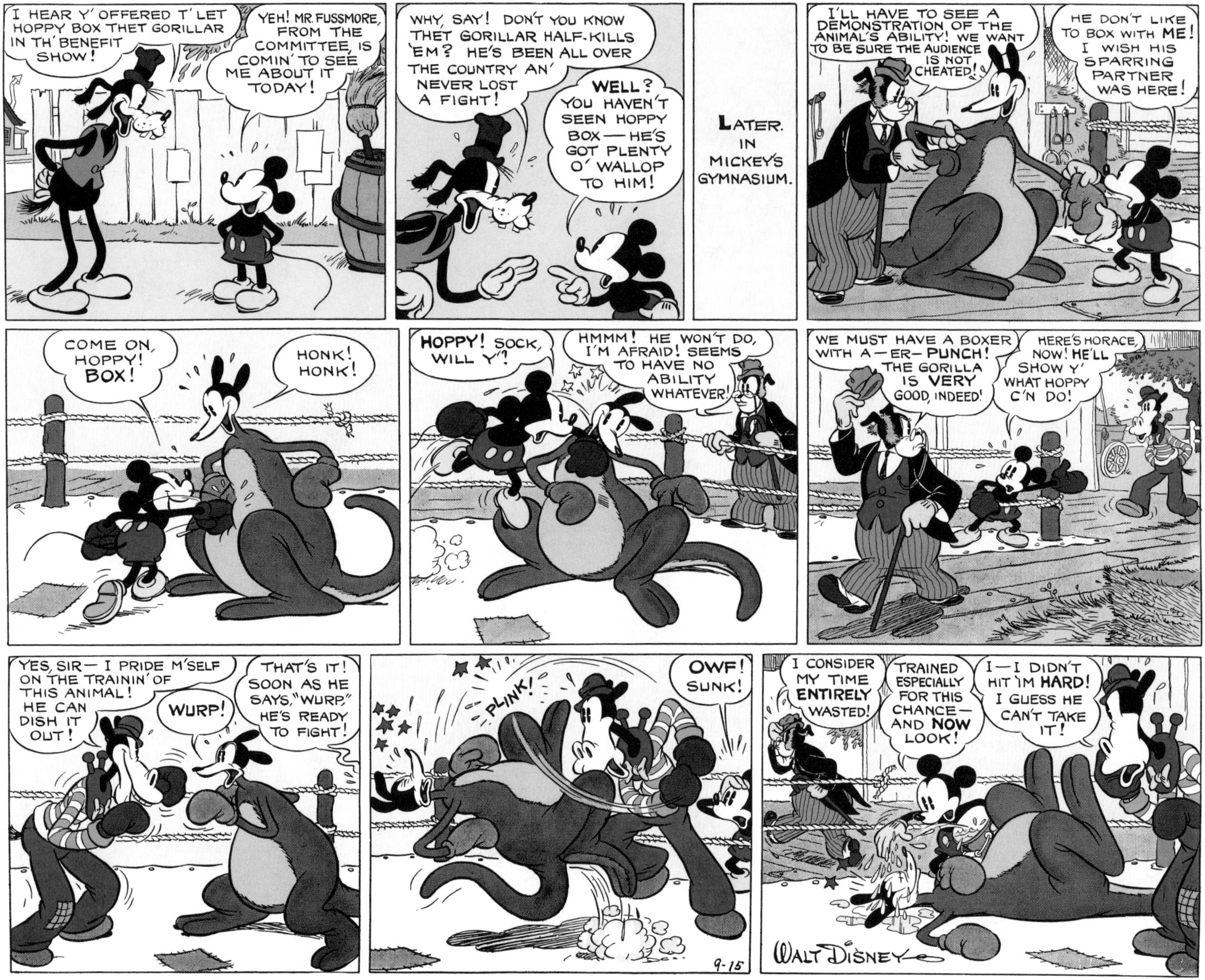
I HEAR Y' OFFERED T' LET HOPPY BOX THET GORILLAR IN TH' BENEFIT SHOW!
YEH! MR. FUSSMORE, FROM THE COMMITTEE, IS COMIN' TO SEE ME ABOUT IT TODAY!
WHY, SAY! DON'T YOU KNOW THET GORILLAR HALF-KILLS 'EM? HE'S BEEN ALL OVER THE COUNTRY AN' NEVER LOST A FIGHT!
WELL? YOU HAVEN'T SEEN HOPPY BOX — HE'S GOT PLENTY O' WALLOP TO HIM!
LATER. IN MICKEY'S GYMNASIUM.
I'LL HAVE TO SEE A DEMONSTRATION OF THE ANIMAL'S ABILITY! WE WANT TO BE SURE THE AUDIENCE IS NOT CHEATED!
HE DON'T LIKE TO BOX WITH ME! I WISH HIS SPARRING PARTNER WAS HERE!
COME ON, HOPPY! BOX!
HONK! HONK!
HOPPY! SOCK, WILL Y'?
HMMM! HE WON'T DO, I'M AFRAID! SEEMS TO HAVE NO ABILITY WHATEVER!
WE MUST HAVE A BOXER WITH A—ER—PUNCH! THE GORILLA IS VERY GOOD, INDEED!
HERE'S HORACE, NOW! HE'LL SHOW Y' WHAT HOPPY C'N DO!
YES, SIR— I PRIDE M'SELF ON THE TRAININ' OF THIS ANIMAL! HE CAN DISH IT OUT!
WURP!
THAT'S IT! SOON AS HE SAYS, "WURP," HE'S READY TO FIGHT!
PLINK!
OWF! SUNK!
9-15
I CONSIDER MY TIME ENTIRELY WASTED!
TRAINED ESPECIALLY FOR THIS CHANCE— AND NOW LOOK!
I—I DIDN'T HIT 'IM HARD! I GUESS HE CAN'T TAKE IT!
WALT DISNEY

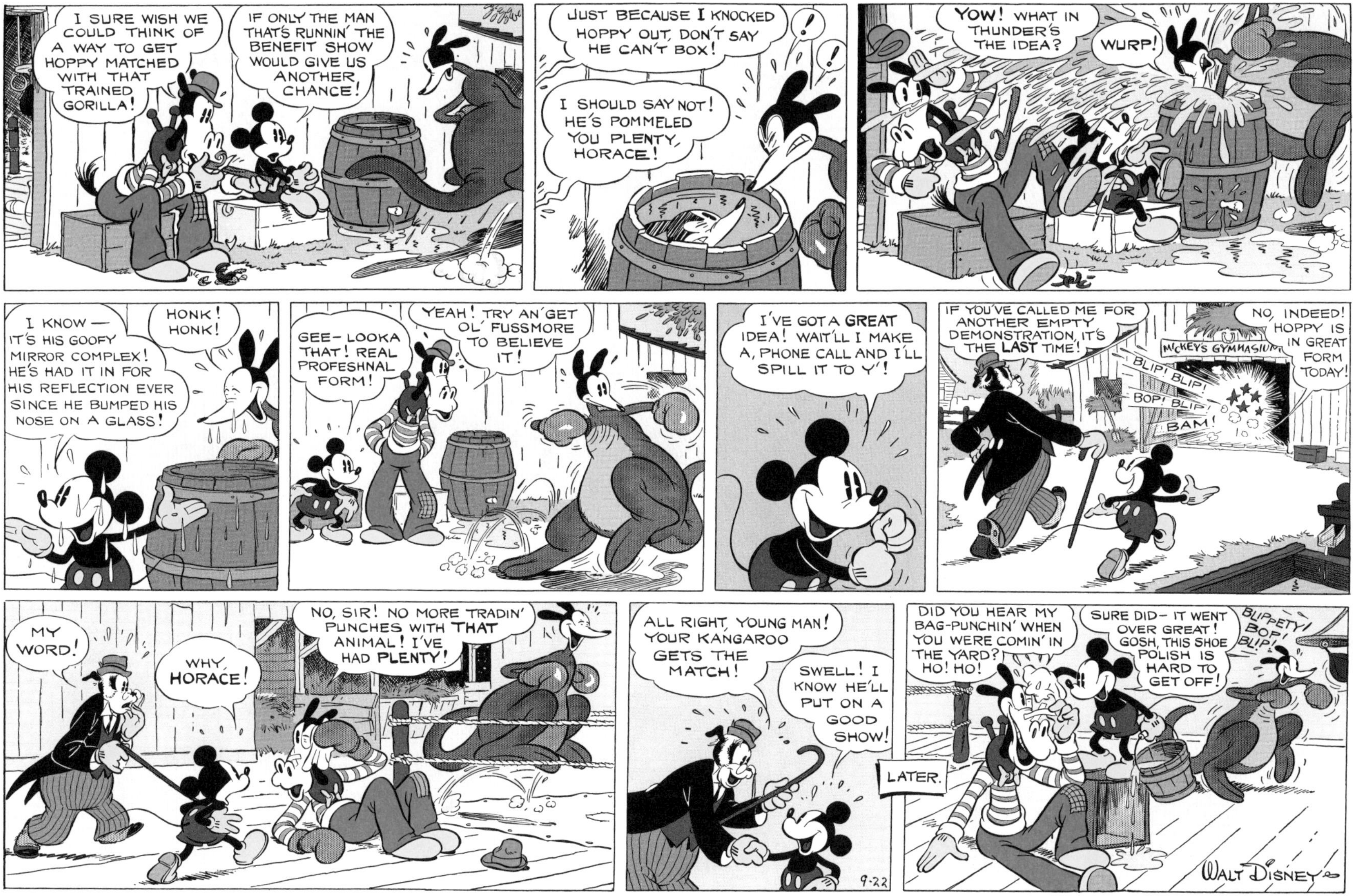
I SURE WISH WE COULD THINK OF A WAY TO GET HOPPY MATCHED WITH THAT TRAINED GORILLA!
IF ONLY THE MAN THAT'S RUNNIN' THE BENEFIT SHOW WOULD GIVE US ANOTHER CHANCE!
JUST BECAUSE I KNOCKED HOPPY OUT, DON'T SAY HE CAN'T BOX!
I SHOULD SAY NOT! HE'S POMMELED YOU PLENTY, HORACE!
YOW! WHAT IN THUNDER'S THE IDEA?
WURP!
I KNOW — IT'S HIS GOOFY MIRROR COMPLEX! HE'S HAD IT IN FOR HIS REFLECTION EVER SINCE HE BUMPED HIS NOSE ON A GLASS!
HONK! HONK!
GEE- LOOKA THAT! REAL PROFESHNAL FORM!
YEAH! TRY AN' GET OL' FUSSMORE TO BELIEVE IT!
I'VE GOT A GREAT IDEA! WAIT'LL I MAKE A PHONE CALL AND I'LL SPILL IT TO Y'!
IF YOU'VE CALLED ME FOR ANOTHER EMPTY DEMONSTRATION, IT'S THE LAST TIME!
NO, INDEED! HOPPY IS IN GREAT FORM TODAY!
MICKEY'S GYMNASIUM
BLIP! BLIP! BOP! BLIP! BAM!
MY WORD!
WHY, HORACE!
NO, SIR! NO MORE TRADIN' PUNCHES WITH THAT ANIMAL! I'VE HAD PLENTY!
ALL RIGHT, YOUNG MAN! YOUR KANGAROO GETS THE MATCH!
SWELL! I KNOW HE'LL PUT ON A GOOD SHOW!
9-22
LATER.
DID YOU HEAR MY BAG-PUNCHIN' WHEN YOU WERE COMIN' IN THE YARD? HO! HO!
SURE DID- IT WENT OVER GREAT! GOSH, THIS SHOE POLISH IS HARD TO GET OFF!
BLIPPETY! BOP! BLIP!
WALT DISNEY

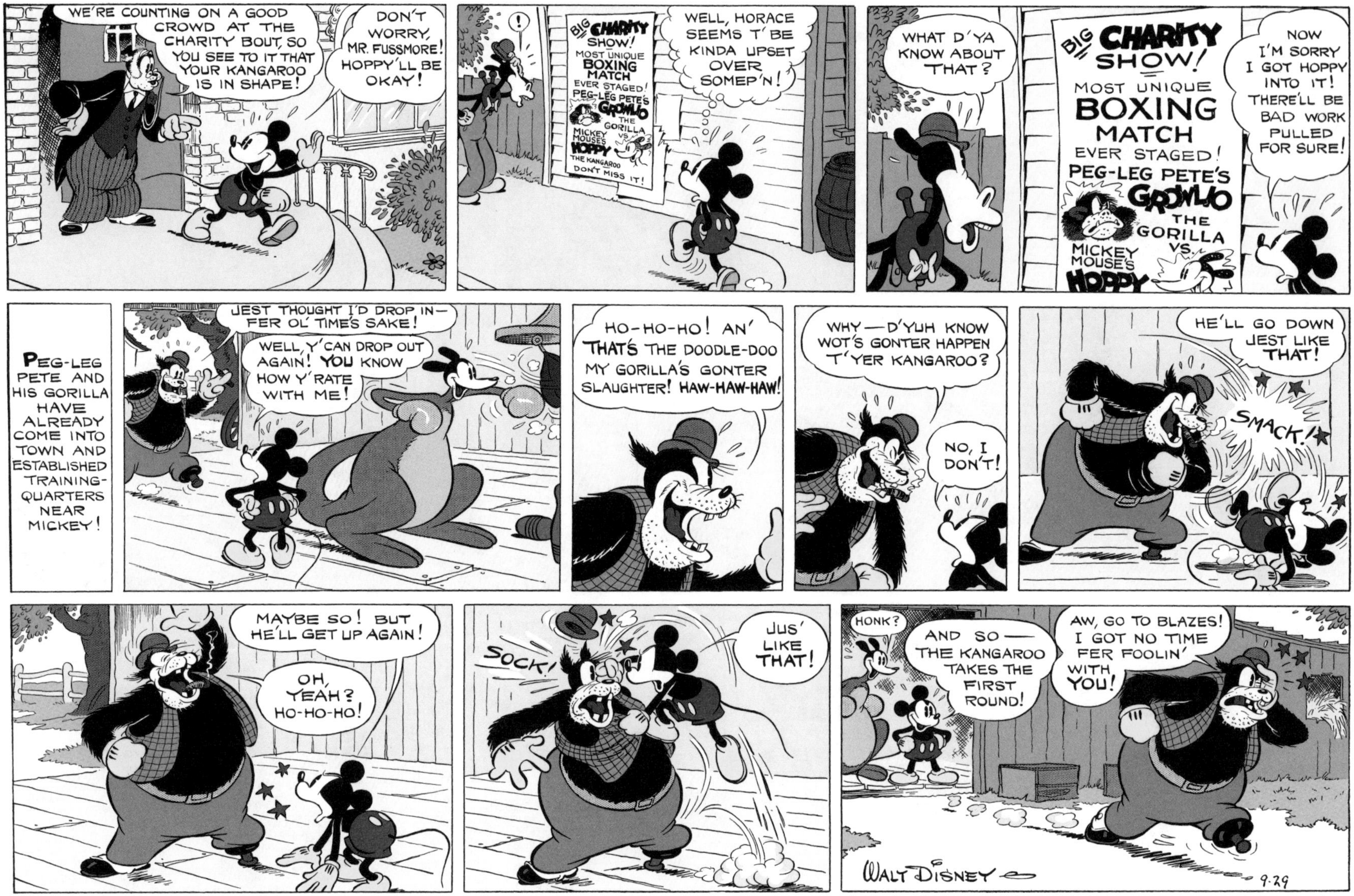
WE'RE COUNTING ON A GOOD CROWD AT THE CHARITY BOUT, SO YOU SEE TO IT THAT YOUR KANGAROO IS IN SHAPE!
DON'T WORRY, MR. FUSSMORE! HOPPY'LL BE OKAY!
!
BIG CHARITY SHOW! MOST UNIQUE BOXING MATCH EVER STAGED! PEG-LEG PETE'S GROWLIO THE GORILLA VS. MICKEY MOUSE'S HOPPY THE KANGAROO DON'T MISS IT!
WELL, HORACE SEEMS T' BE KINDA UPSET OVER SOMEP'N!
WHAT D'YA KNOW ABOUT THAT?
BIG CHARITY SHOW! MOST UNIQUE BOXING MATCH EVER STAGED! PEG-LEG PETE'S GROWLIO THE GORILLA VS. MICKEY MOUSE'S HOPPY
NOW I'M SORRY I GOT HOPPY INTO IT! THERE'LL BE BAD WORK PULLED FOR SURE!
PEG-LEG PETE AND HIS GORILLA HAVE ALREADY COME INTO TOWN AND ESTABLISHED TRAINING-QUARTERS NEAR MICKEY!
JEST THOUGHT I'D DROP IN-FER OL' TIME'S SAKE!
WELL, Y'CAN DROP OUT AGAIN! YOU KNOW HOW Y'RATE WITH ME!
HO-HO-HO! AN' THAT'S THE DOODLE-DOO MY GORILLA'S GONTER SLAUGHTER! HAW-HAW-HAW!
WHY—D'YUH KNOW WOT'S GONTER HAPPEN T'YER KANGAROO?
NO, I DON'T!
HE'LL GO DOWN JEST LIKE THAT!
SMACK!
MAYBE SO! BUT HE'LL GET UP AGAIN!
OH, YEAH? HO-HO-HO!
SOCK!
JUS' LIKE THAT!
HONK?
AND SO—THE KANGAROO TAKES THE FIRST ROUND!
AW, GO TO BLAZES! I GOT NO TIME FER FOOLIN' WITH YOU!
WALT DISNEY
9-29

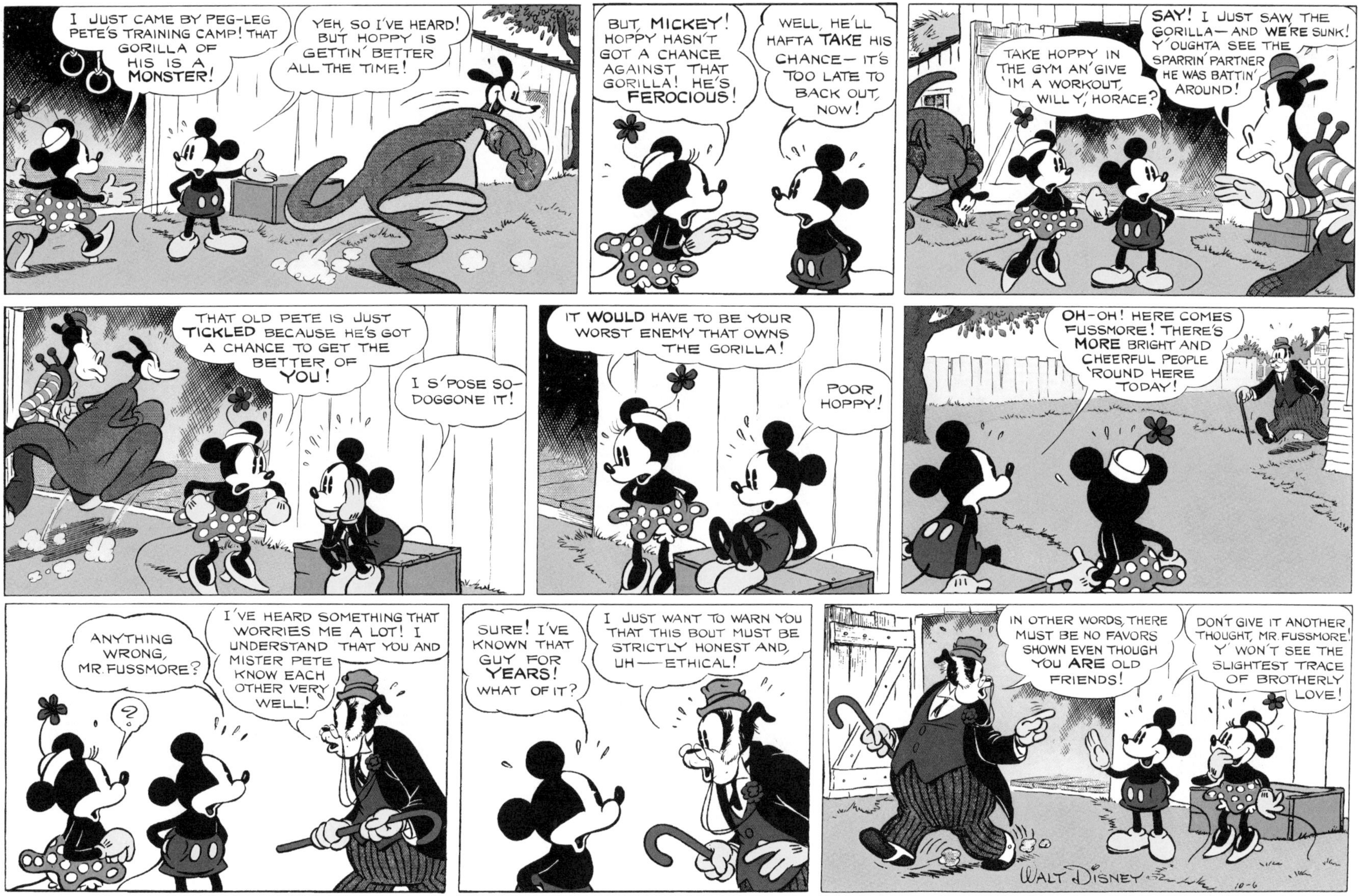

I JUST CAME BY PEG-LEG PETE'S TRAINING CAMP! THAT GORILLA OF HIS IS A MONSTER!
YEH, SO I'VE HEARD! BUT HOPPY IS GETTIN' BETTER ALL THE TIME!
BUT, MICKEY! HOPPY HASN'T GOT A CHANCE AGAINST THAT GORILLA! HE'S FEROCIOUS!
WELL, HE'LL HAFTA TAKE HIS CHANCE— IT'S TOO LATE TO BACK OUT NOW!
TAKE HOPPY IN THE GYM AN' GIVE 'IM A WORKOUT, WILLY, HORACE?
SAY! I JUST SAW THE GORILLA— AND WE'RE SUNK! Y' OUGHTA SEE THE SPARRIN' PARTNER HE WAS BATTIN' AROUND!
THAT OLD PETE IS JUST TICKLED BECAUSE HE'S GOT A CHANCE TO GET THE BETTER OF YOU!
I S'POSE SO- DOGGONE IT!
IT WOULD HAVE TO BE YOUR WORST ENEMY THAT OWNS THE GORILLA!
POOR HOPPY!
OH-OH! HERE COMES FUSSMORE! THERE'S MORE BRIGHT AND CHEERFUL PEOPLE 'ROUND HERE TODAY!
ANYTHING WRONG, MR. FUSSMORE?
?
I'VE HEARD SOMETHING THAT WORRIES ME A LOT! I UNDERSTAND THAT YOU AND MISTER PETE KNOW EACH OTHER VERY WELL!
SURE! I'VE KNOWN THAT GUY FOR YEARS! WHAT OF IT?
I JUST WANT TO WARN YOU THAT THIS BOUT MUST BE STRICTLY HONEST AND, UH—ETHICAL!
IN OTHER WORDS, THERE MUST BE NO FAVORS SHOWN EVEN THOUGH YOU ARE OLD FRIENDS!
DON'T GIVE IT ANOTHER THOUGHT, MR. FUSSMORE! Y' WON'T SEE THE SLIGHTEST TRACE OF BROTHERLY LOVE!
WALT DISNEY
10-6

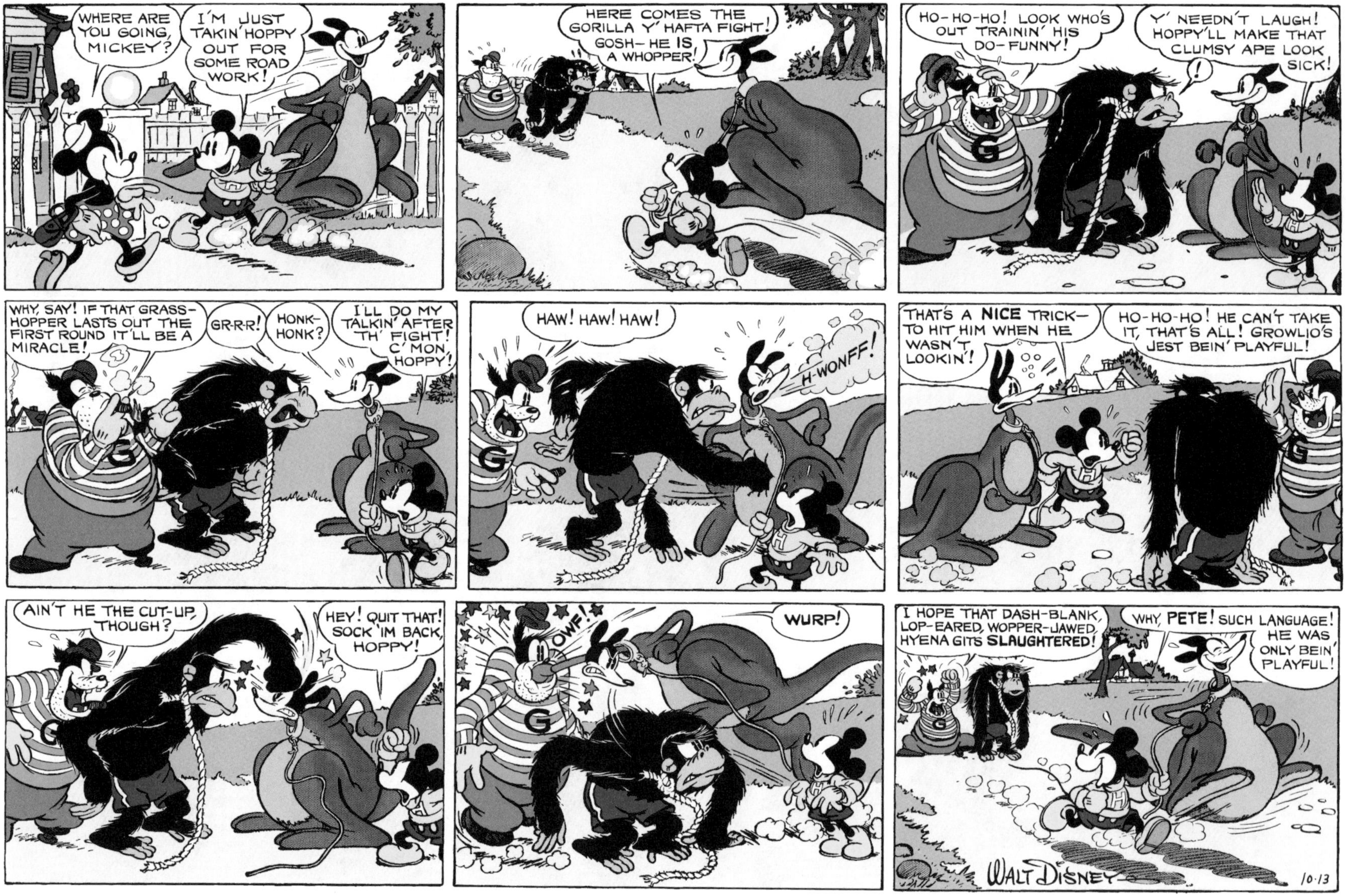
WHERE ARE YOU GOING, MICKEY?
I'M JUST TAKIN' HOPPY OUT FOR SOME ROAD WORK!
HERE COMES THE GORILLA Y' HAFTA FIGHT! GOSH– HE IS A WHOPPER!
HO-HO-HO! LOOK WHO'S OUT TRAININ' HIS DO-FUNNY!
Y' NEEDN'T LAUGH! HOPPY'LL MAKE THAT CLUMSY APE LOOK SICK!
!
WHY, SAY! IF THAT GRASS-HOPPER LASTS OUT THE FIRST ROUND IT'LL BE A MIRACLE!
GR-R-R!
HONK-HONK?
I'LL DO MY TALKIN' AFTER TH' FIGHT! C'MON, HOPPY!
HAW! HAW! HAW!
H-WONFF!
THAT'S A NICE TRICK– TO HIT HIM WHEN HE WASN'T LOOKIN'!
HO-HO-HO! HE CAN'T TAKE IT, THAT'S ALL! GROWLIO'S JEST BEIN' PLAYFUL!
AIN'T HE THE CUT-UP, THOUGH?
HEY! QUIT THAT! SOCK 'IM BACK, HOPPY!
OWF!
WURP!
I HOPE THAT DASH-BLANK, LOP-EARED, WOPPER-JAWED HYENA GITS SLAUGHTERED!
WHY, PETE! SUCH LANGUAGE! HE WAS ONLY BEIN' PLAYFUL!
WALT DISNEY
10-13

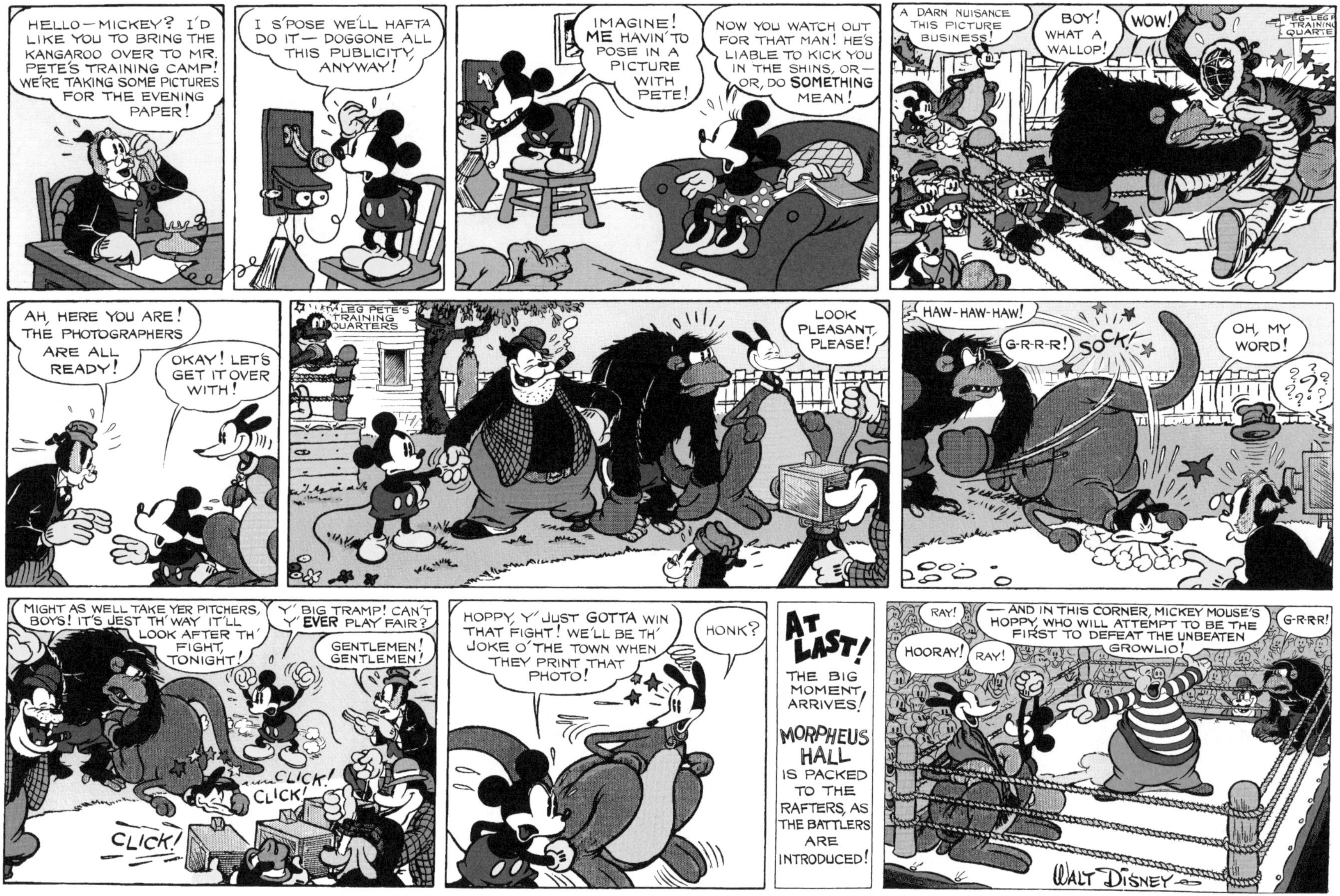

HELLO—MICKEY? I'D LIKE YOU TO BRING THE KANGAROO OVER TO MR. PETE'S TRAINING CAMP! WE'RE TAKING SOME PICTURES FOR THE EVENING PAPER!
I S'POSE WE'LL HAFTA DO IT— DOGGONE ALL THIS PUBLICITY, ANYWAY!
IMAGINE! ME HAVIN' TO POSE IN A PICTURE WITH PETE!
NOW YOU WATCH OUT FOR THAT MAN! HE'S LIABLE TO KICK YOU IN THE SHINS, OR— OR, DO SOMETHING MEAN!
A DARN NUISANCE THIS PICTURE BUSINESS!
BOY! WHAT A WALLOP!
WOW!
AH, HERE YOU ARE! THE PHOTOGRAPHERS ARE ALL READY!
OKAY! LET'S GET IT OVER WITH!
LEG PETE'S TRAINING QUARTERS
LOOK PLEASANT, PLEASE!
HAW-HAW-HAW!
G-R-R-R!
SOCK!
OH, MY WORD!
MIGHT AS WELL TAKE YER PITCHERS, BOYS! IT'S JEST TH' WAY IT'LL LOOK AFTER TH' FIGHT, TONIGHT!
Y' BIG TRAMP! CAN'T Y' EVER PLAY FAIR?
GENTLEMEN! GENTLEMEN!
CLICK! CLICK!
CLICK!
HOPPY, Y' JUST GOTTA WIN THAT FIGHT! WE'LL BE TH' JOKE O' THE TOWN WHEN THEY PRINT THAT PHOTO!
HONK?
AT LAST! THE BIG MOMENT ARRIVES!
MORPHEUS HALL IS PACKED TO THE RAFTERS, AS THE BATTLERS ARE INTRODUCED!
RAY!
—AND IN THIS CORNER, MICKEY MOUSE'S HOPPY, WHO WILL ATTEMPT TO BE THE FIRST TO DEFEAT THE UNBEATEN GROWLIO!
G-R-RR!
HOORAY!
RAY!
WALT DISNEY

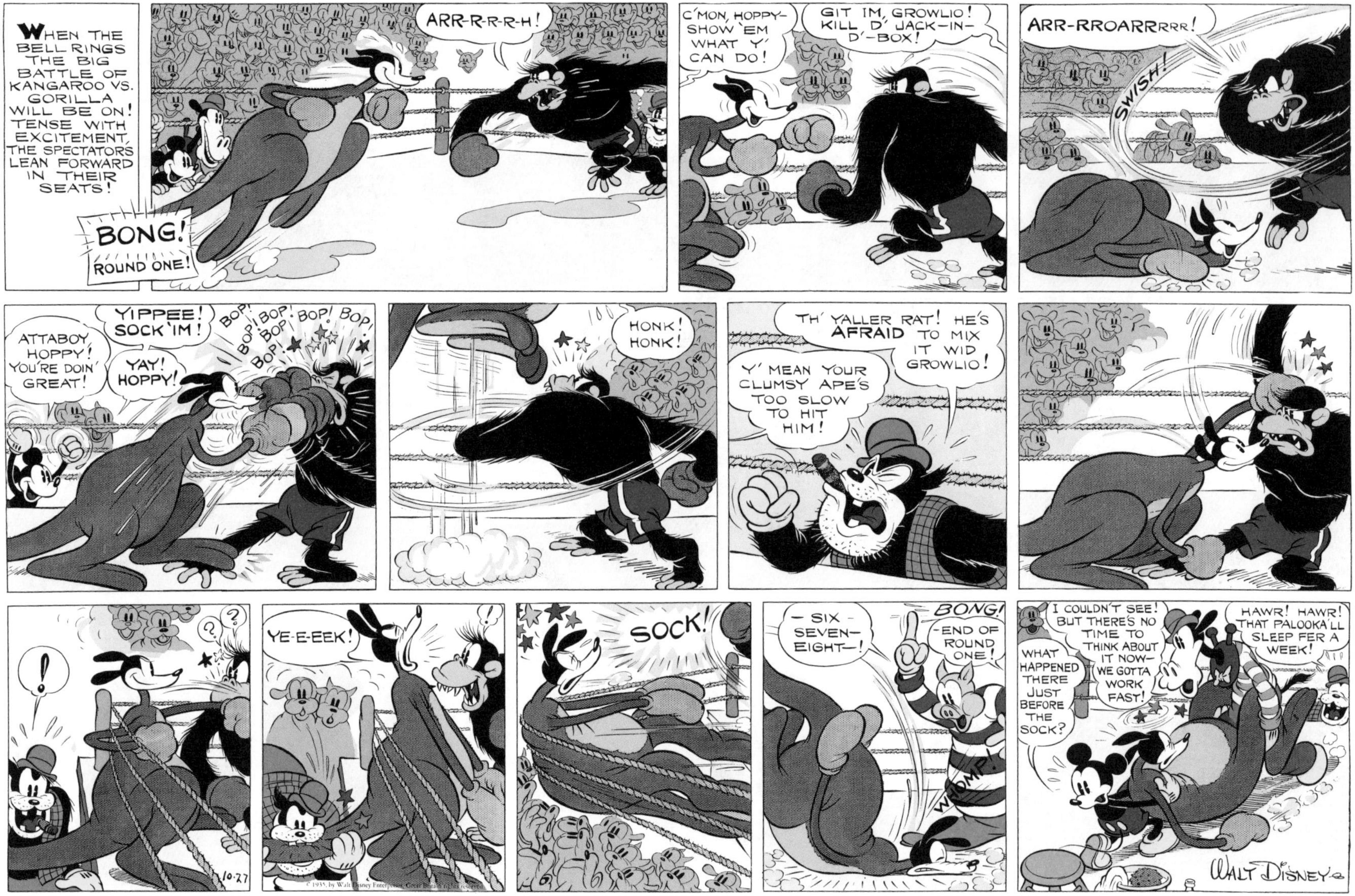
WHEN THE BELL RINGS THE BIG BATTLE OF KANGAROO VS. GORILLA WILL BE ON! TENSE WITH EXCITEMENT, THE SPECTATORS LEAN FORWARD IN THEIR SEATS!
BONG!
ROUND ONE!
ARR-R-R-R-H!
C'MON, HOPPY-SHOW 'EM WHAT Y' CAN DO!
GIT IM, GROWLIO! KILL D' JACK-IN-D'-BOX!
ARR-RROARRRRR!
SWISH!
ATTABOY, HOPPY! YOU'RE DOIN' GREAT!
YIPPEE! SOCK 'IM!
YAY! HOPPY!
BOP! BOP! BOP! BOP! BOP! BOP!
HONK! HONK!
TH' YALLER RAT! HE'S AFRAID TO MIX IT WID GROWLIO!
Y' MEAN YOUR CLUMSY APE'S TOO SLOW TO HIT HIM!
!
? ?
10-27
YE-E-EEK!
!
SOCK!
-SIX-SEVEN-EIGHT-!
BONG!
-END OF ROUND ONE!
WHOMP!
WHAT HAPPENED THERE JUST BEFORE THE SOCK?
I COULDN'T SEE! BUT THERE'S NO TIME TO THINK ABOUT IT NOW-WE GOTTA WORK FAST!
HAWR! HAWR! THAT PALOOKA'LL SLEEP FER A WEEK!
WALT DISNEY

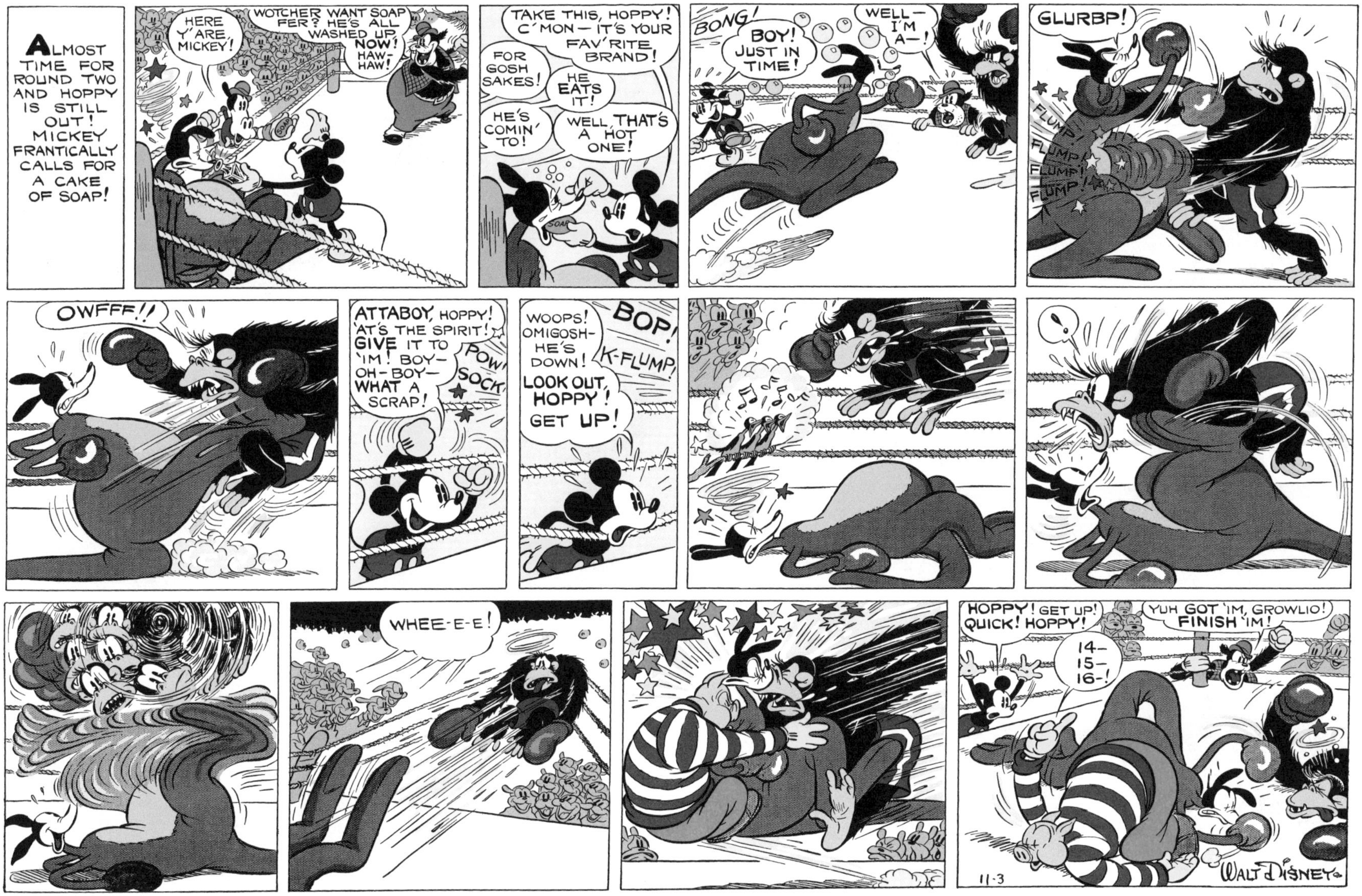
ALMOST TIME FOR ROUND TWO AND HOPPY IS STILL OUT! MICKEY FRANTICALLY CALLS FOR A CAKE OF SOAP!
HERE Y'ARE, MICKEY!
WOTCHER WANT SOAP FER? HE'S ALL WASHED UP NOW! HAW-HAW!
TAKE THIS, HOPPY! C'MON — IT'S YOUR FAV'RITE BRAND!
FOR GOSH SAKES!
HE EATS IT!
HE'S COMIN' TO!
WELL, THAT'S A HOT ONE!
BONG!
BOY! JUST IN TIME!
WELL — I'M A—!
GLURBP!
FLUMP! FLUMP! FLUMP! FLUMP!
OWFFF!!
ATTABOY, HOPPY! 'AT'S THE SPIRIT! GIVE IT TO 'IM! BOY-OH-BOY— WHAT A SCRAP!
POW! SOCK!
WOOPS! OMIGOSH— HE'S DOWN!
BOP! K-FLUMP!
LOOK OUT, HOPPY! GET UP!
!
WHEE-E-E!
HOPPY! GET UP! QUICK! HOPPY!
YUH GOT 'IM, GROWLIO! FINISH 'IM!
14— 15— 16-!
11·3
WALT DISNEY

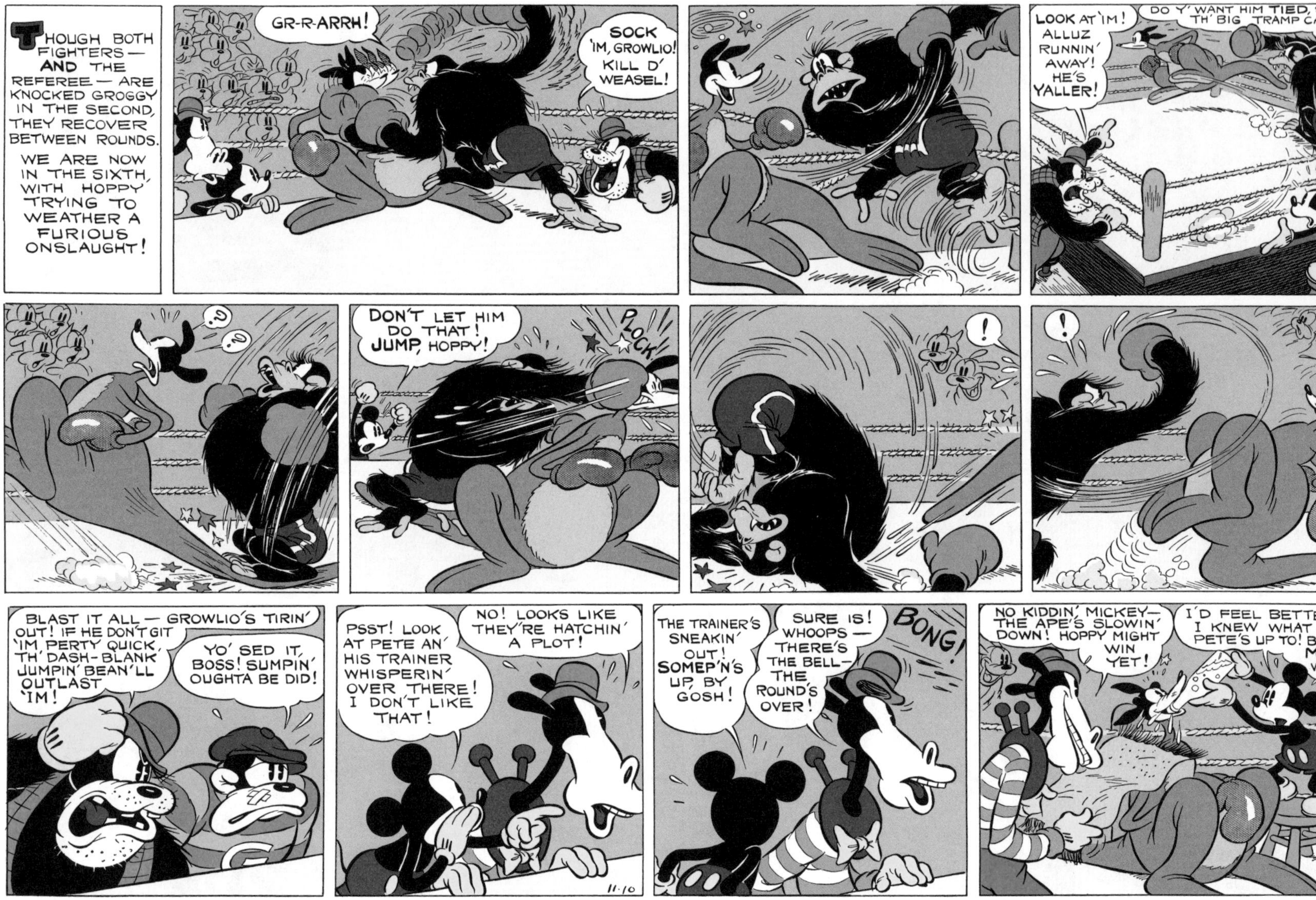
THOUGH BOTH FIGHTERS — AND THE REFEREE — ARE KNOCKED GROGGY IN THE SECOND, THEY RECOVER BETWEEN ROUNDS.
WE ARE NOW IN THE SIXTH, WITH HOPPY TRYING TO WEATHER A FURIOUS ONSLAUGHT!
GR-R-ARRH!
SOCK 'IM, GROWLIO! KILL D' WEASEL!
LOOK AT 'IM! ALLUZ RUNNIN' AWAY! HE'S YALLER!
DO Y' WANT HIM TIED, SO'S TH' BIG TRAMP CAN HIT HIM?
DON'T LET HIM DO THAT! JUMP, HOPPY!
PLOCK
!
!
BLAST IT ALL — GROWLIO'S TIRIN' OUT! IF HE DON'T GIT 'IM PERTY QUICK, TH' DASH-BLANK JUMPIN' BEAN'LL OUTLAST 'IM!
YO' SED IT, BOSS! SUMPIN' OUGHTA BE DID!
PSST! LOOK AT PETE AN' HIS TRAINER WHISPERIN' OVER THERE! I DON'T LIKE THAT!
NO! LOOKS LIKE THEY'RE HATCHIN' A PLOT!
11-10
THE TRAINER'S SNEAKIN' OUT! SOMEP'N'S UP, BY GOSH!
SURE IS! WHOOPS — THERE'S THE BELL — THE ROUND'S OVER!
BONG!
NO KIDDIN', MICKEY — THE APE'S SLOWIN' DOWN! HOPPY MIGHT WIN YET!
I'D FEEL BETTER IF I KNEW WHAT OL' PETE'S UP TO! B'LEEVE ME, I WOULD!

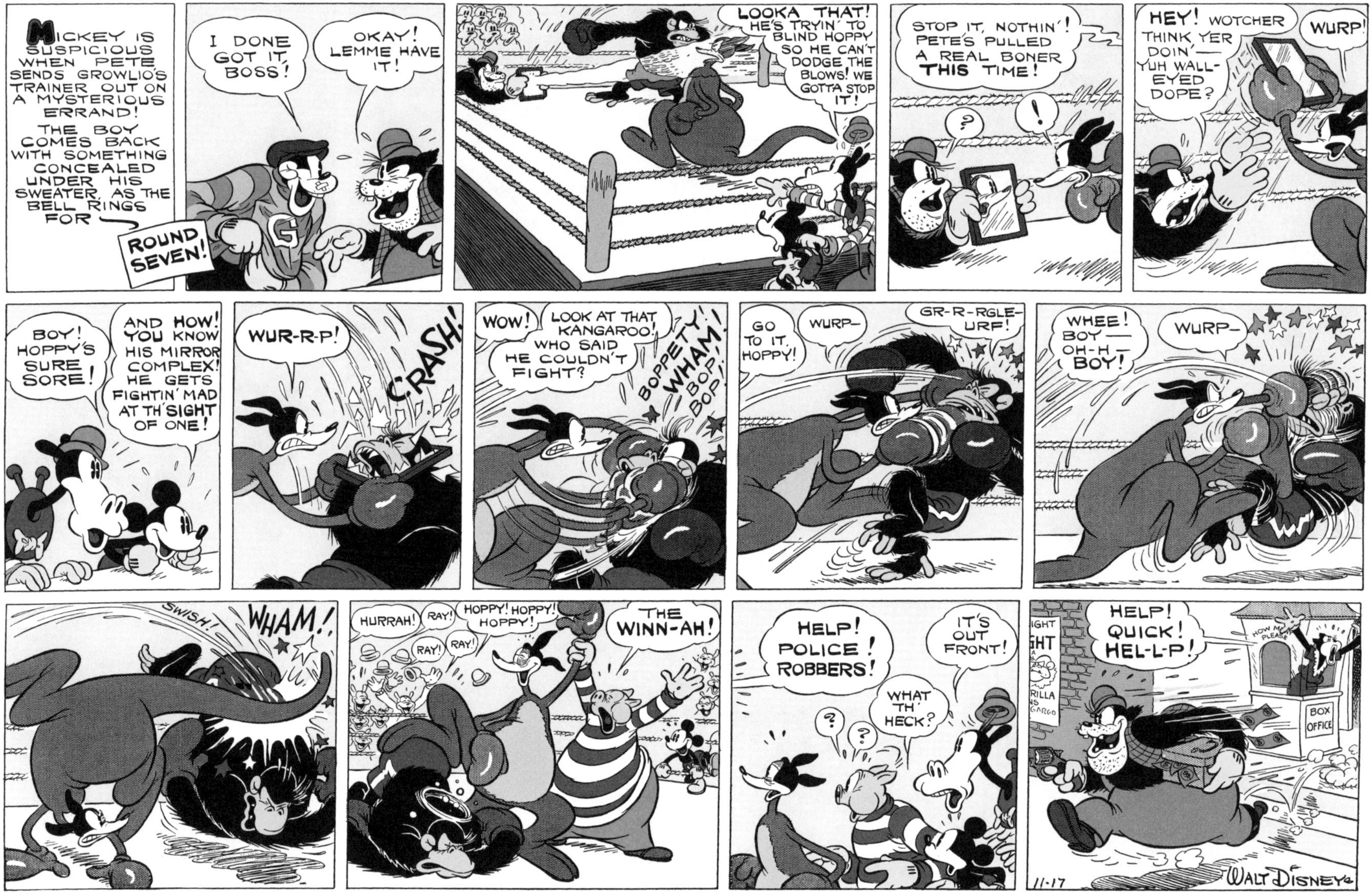
MICKEY IS SUSPICIOUS WHEN PETE SENDS GROWLIO'S TRAINER OUT ON A MYSTERIOUS ERRAND!
THE BOY COMES BACK WITH SOMETHING CONCEALED UNDER HIS SWEATER, AS THE BELL RINGS FOR
ROUND SEVEN!
I DONE GOT IT, BOSS!
OKAY! LEMME HAVE IT!
LOOKA THAT! HE'S TRYIN' TO BLIND HOPPY SO HE CAN'T DODGE THE BLOWS! WE GOTTA STOP IT!
STOP IT, NOTHIN'! PETE'S PULLED A REAL BONER THIS TIME!
?
!
HEY! WOTCHER THINK YER DOIN'— YUH WALL-EYED DOPE?
WURP!
BOY! HOPPY'S SURE SORE!
AND HOW! YOU KNOW HIS MIRROR COMPLEX! HE GETS FIGHTIN' MAD AT TH' SIGHT OF ONE!
WUR-R-P!
CRASH!
WOW!
LOOK AT THAT KANGAROO! WHO SAID HE COULDN'T FIGHT?
BOPPETY WHAM! BOP! BOP!
GO TO IT, HOPPY!
WURP—
GR-R-RGLE-URF!
WHEE! BOY— OH-H— BOY!
WURP—
SWISH!
WHAM!
HURRAH!
RAY!
RAY!
RAY!
HOPPY! HOPPY! HOPPY!
THE WINN-AH!
HELP! POLICE! ROBBERS!
IT'S OUT FRONT!
WHAT TH' HECK?
?
?
HELP! QUICK! HEL-L-P!
BOX OFFICE
11-17
WALT DISNEY

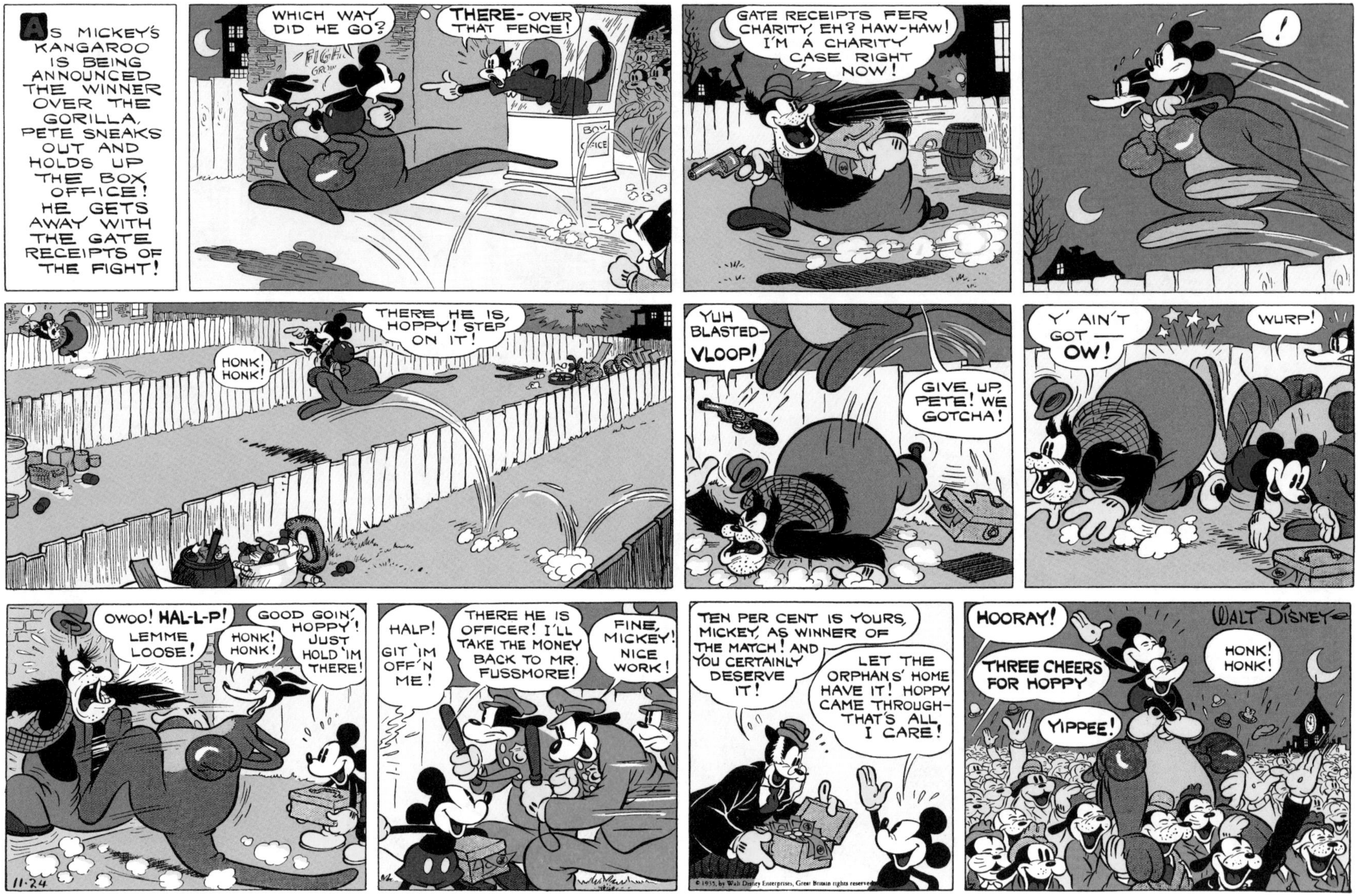

AS MICKEY'S KANGAROO IS BEING ANNOUNCED THE WINNER OVER THE GORILLA, PETE SNEAKS OUT AND HOLDS UP THE BOX OFFICE! HE GETS AWAY WITH THE GATE RECEIPTS OF THE FIGHT!
WHICH WAY DID HE GO?
THERE- OVER THAT FENCE!
BOX OFFICE
GATE RECEIPTS FER CHARITY, EH? HAW-HAW! I'M A CHARITY CASE RIGHT NOW!
!
THERE HE IS, HOPPY! STEP ON IT!
HONK! HONK!
YUH BLASTED- VLOOP!
GIVE UP, PETE! WE GOTCHA!
Y' AIN'T GOT — OW!
WURP!
OWOO! HAL-L-P! LEMME LOOSE!
HONK! HONK!
GOOD GOIN', HOPPY! JUST HOLD 'IM THERE!
HALP! GIT 'IM OFF'N ME!
THERE HE IS OFFICER! I'LL TAKE THE MONEY BACK TO MR. FUSSMORE!
FINE, MICKEY! NICE WORK!
TEN PER CENT IS YOURS, MICKEY, AS WINNER OF THE MATCH! AND YOU CERTAINLY DESERVE IT!
LET THE ORPHANS' HOME HAVE IT! HOPPY CAME THROUGH- THAT'S ALL I CARE!
HOORAY!
THREE CHEERS FOR HOPPY
YIPPEE!
HONK! HONK!
WALT DISNEY
11-24

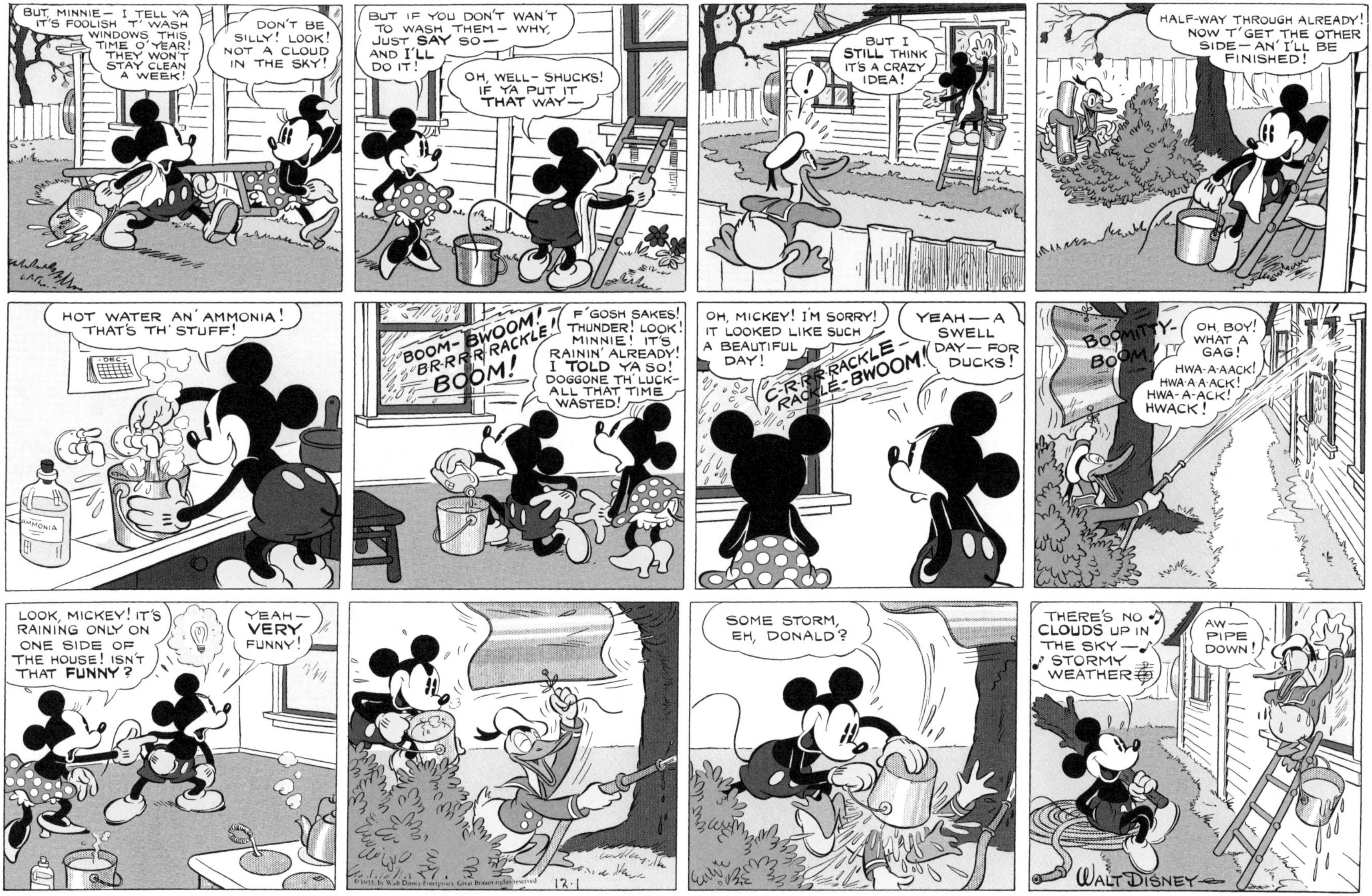
BUT, MINNIE— I TELL YA IT'S FOOLISH 'T' WASH WINDOWS THIS TIME O' YEAR! THEY WON'T STAY CLEAN A WEEK!
DON'T BE SILLY! LOOK! NOT A CLOUD IN THE SKY!
BUT IF YOU DON'T WAN'T TO WASH THEM— WHY, JUST SAY SO— AND I'LL DO IT!
OH, WELL— SHUCKS! IF YA PUT IT THAT WAY—
!
BUT I STILL THINK IT'S A CRAZY IDEA!
HALF-WAY THROUGH ALREADY! NOW T' GET THE OTHER SIDE— AN' I'LL BE FINISHED!
HOT WATER AN' AMMONIA! THAT'S TH' STUFF!
DEC
AMMONIA
BOOM- BWOOM! BR-RR-R RACKLE! BOOM!
F'GOSH SAKES! THUNDER! LOOK! MINNIE! IT'S RAININ' ALREADY! I TOLD YA SO! DOGGONE TH' LUCK— ALL THAT TIME WASTED!
OH, MICKEY! I'M SORRY! IT LOOKED LIKE SUCH A BEAUTIFUL DAY!
C-R-RR-RACKLE RACKLE-BWOOM!
YEAH — A SWELL DAY— FOR DUCKS!
BOOMITY- BOOM!
OH, BOY! WHAT A GAG! HWA-A-AACK! HWA-A-A-ACK! HWA-A-ACK! HWACK!
LOOK, MICKEY! IT'S RAINING ONLY ON ONE SIDE OF THE HOUSE! ISN'T THAT FUNNY?
YEAH— VERY FUNNY!
© 1935, by Walt Disney Enterprises. Great Britain rights reserved
12-1
SOME STORM, EH, DONALD?
THERE'S NO CLOUDS UP IN THE SKY— STORMY WEATHER
AW— PIPE DOWN!
WALT DISNEY

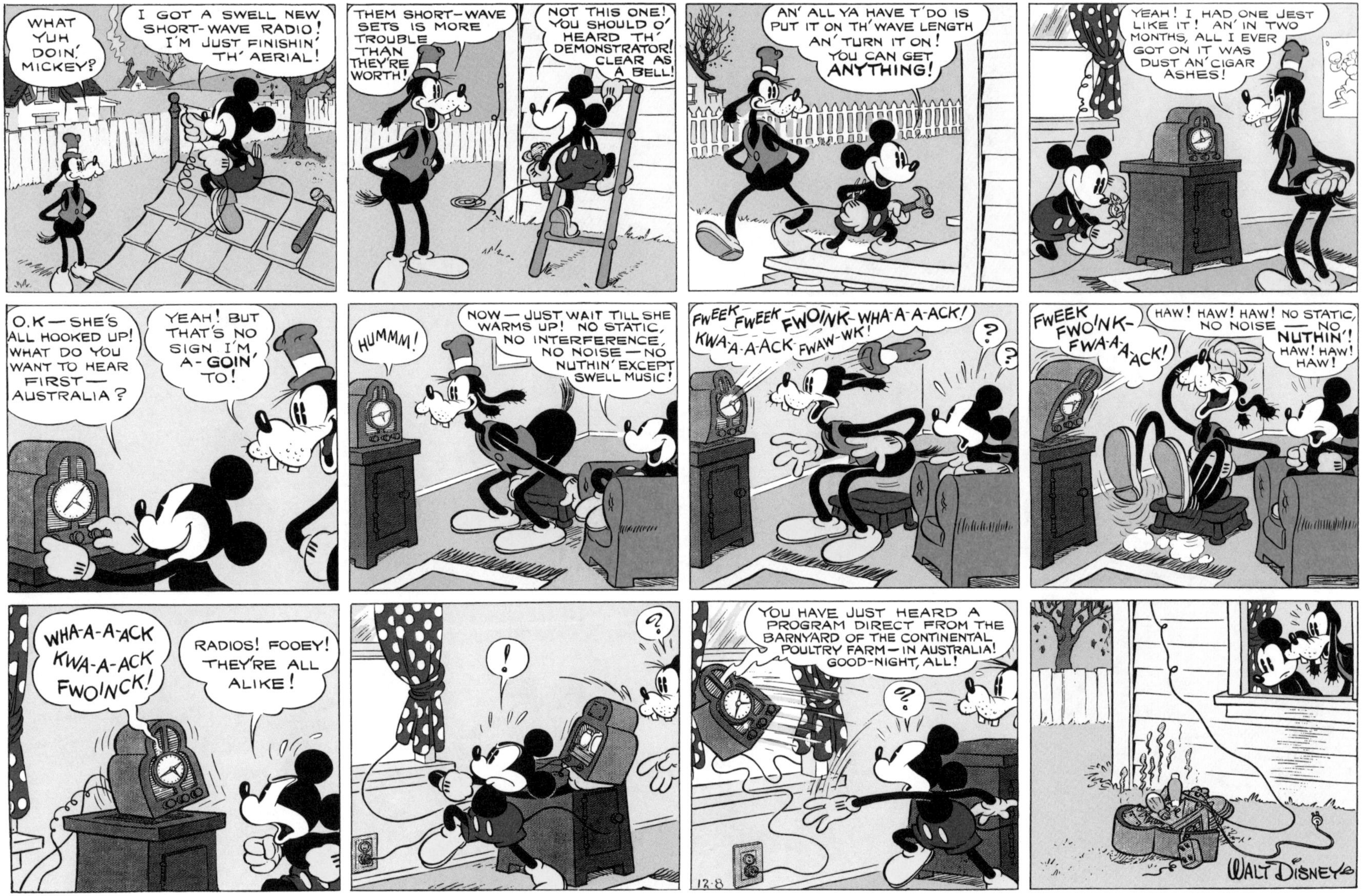
WHAT YUH DOIN' MICKEY?
I GOT A SWELL NEW SHORT-WAVE RADIO! I'M JUST FINISHIN' TH' AERIAL!
THEM SHORT-WAVE SETS IS MORE TROUBLE THAN THEY'RE WORTH!
NOT THIS ONE! YOU SHOULD O' HEARD TH' DEMONSTRATOR! CLEAR AS A BELL!
AN' ALL YA HAVE T'DO IS PUT IT ON TH' WAVE LENGTH AN' TURN IT ON! YOU CAN GET ANYTHING!
YEAH! I HAD ONE JEST LIKE IT! AN' IN TWO MONTHS, ALL I EVER GOT ON IT WAS DUST AN' CIGAR ASHES!
O.K — SHE'S ALL HOOKED UP! WHAT DO YOU WANT TO HEAR FIRST — AUSTRALIA?
YEAH! BUT THAT'S NO SIGN I'M A-GOIN' TO!
HUMMM!
NOW — JUST WAIT TILL SHE WARMS UP! NO STATIC, NO INTERFERENCE, NO NOISE — NO NUTHIN' EXCEPT SWELL MUSIC!
FWEEK FWEEK FWOINK-WHA-A-A-ACK! KWA-A-A-ACK FWAW-WK!
?
?
FWEEK FWO'NK-FWA-A-A-ACK!
HAW! HAW! HAW! NO STATIC, NO NOISE — NO NUTHIN'! HAW! HAW! HAW!
WHA-A-A-ACK KWA-A-ACK FWOINCK!
RADIOS! FOOEY! THEY'RE ALL ALIKE!
?
!
YOU HAVE JUST HEARD A PROGRAM DIRECT FROM THE BARNYARD OF THE CONTINENTAL POULTRY FARM — IN AUSTRALIA! GOOD-NIGHT, ALL!
?
12-8
WALT DISNEY

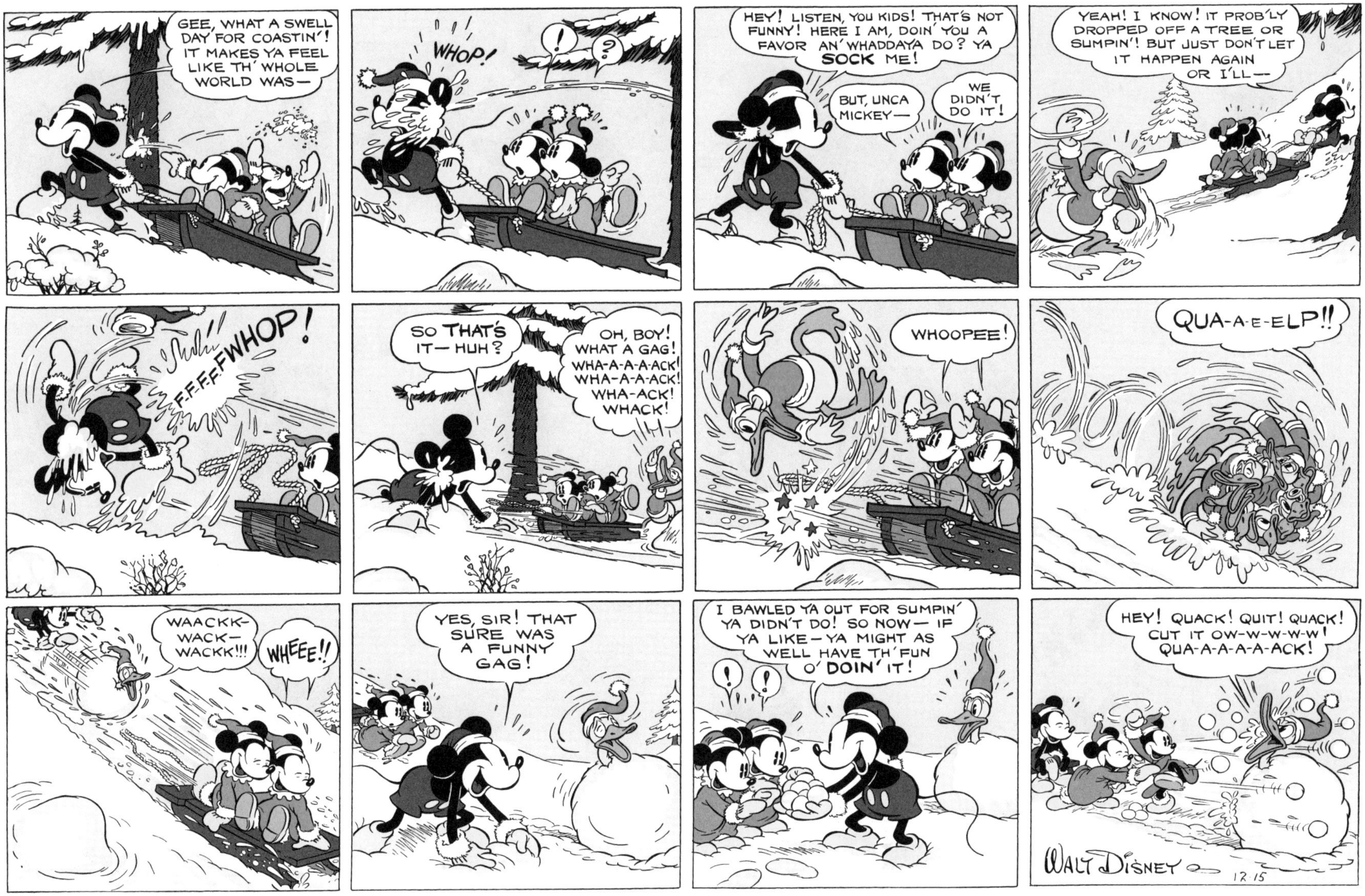
GEE, WHAT A SWELL DAY FOR COASTIN'! IT MAKES YA FEEL LIKE TH' WHOLE WORLD WAS—
WHOP!
!
?
HEY! LISTEN, YOU KIDS! THAT'S NOT FUNNY! HERE I AM, DOIN' YOU A FAVOR AN' WHADDAYA DO? YA SOCK ME!
BUT, UNCA MICKEY—
WE DIDN'T DO IT!
YEAH! I KNOW! IT PROB'LY DROPPED OFF A TREE OR SUMPIN'! BUT JUST DON'T LET IT HAPPEN AGAIN OR I'LL—
F-F-F-FWHOP!
SO THAT'S IT—HUH?
OH, BOY! WHAT A GAG! WHA-A-A-ACK! WHA-A-A-ACK! WHA-ACK! WHACK!
WHOOPEE!
QUA-A-E-ELP!!
WAACKK-WACK-WACKK!!!
WHEEE!!
YES, SIR! THAT SURE WAS A FUNNY GAG!
I BAWLED YA OUT FOR SUMPIN' YA DIDN'T DO! SO NOW—IF YA LIKE—YA MIGHT AS WELL HAVE TH' FUN O' DOIN' IT!
!
!
HEY! QUACK! QUIT! QUACK! CUT IT OW-W-W-W-W! QUA-A-A-A-ACK!
WALT DISNEY
12 15

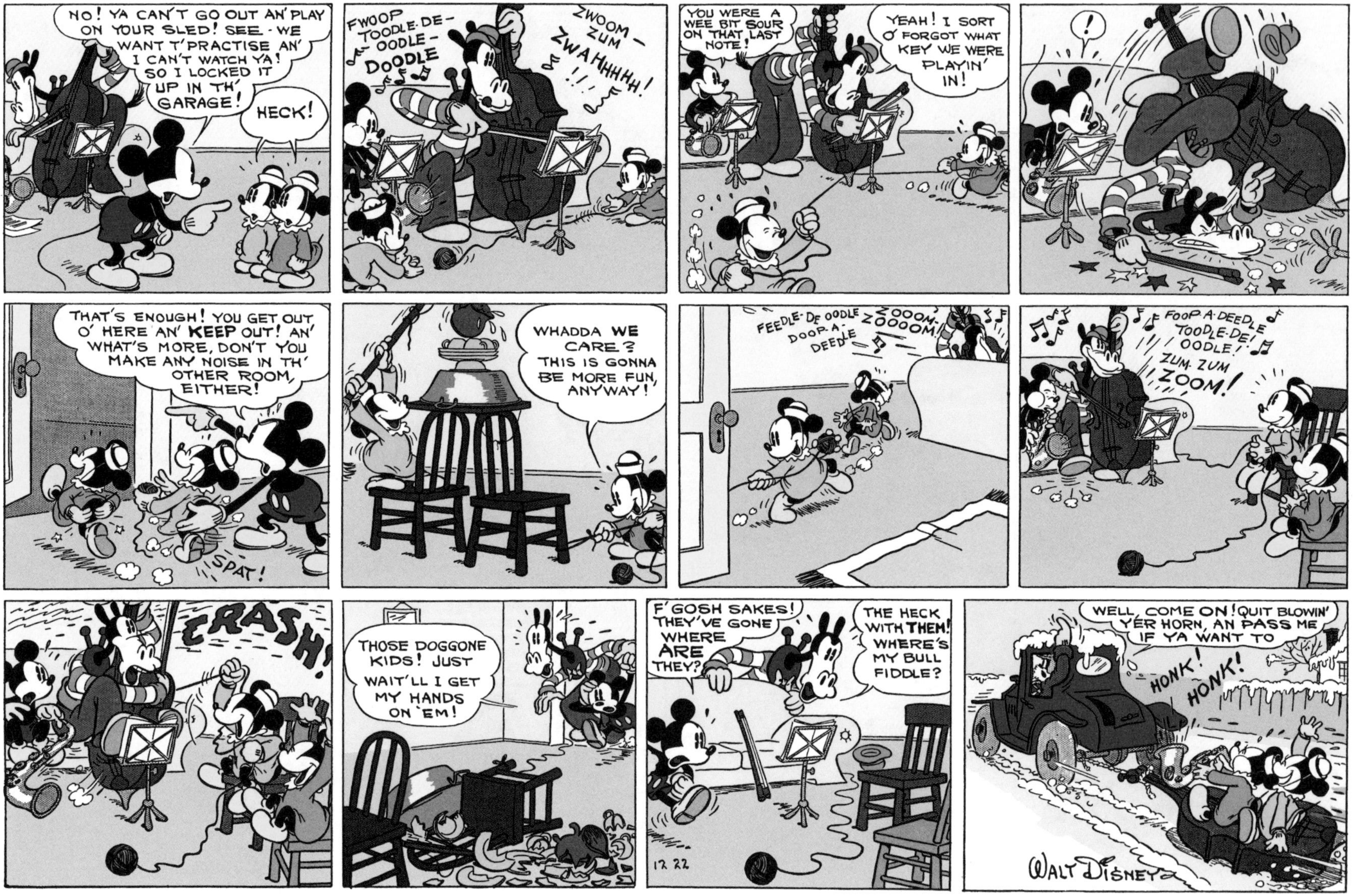
NO! YA CAN'T GO OUT AN' PLAY ON YOUR SLED! SEE - WE WANT T' PRACTISE AN' I CAN'T WATCH YA! SO I LOCKED IT UP IN TH' GARAGE!
HECK!
FWOOP TOODLE-DE-OODLE-DOODLE
ZWOOM-ZUM ZWAHHHHH!
YOU WERE A WEE BIT SOUR ON THAT LAST NOTE!
YEAH! I SORT O' FORGOT WHAT KEY WE WERE PLAYIN' IN!
!
THAT'S ENOUGH! YOU GET OUT O' HERE AN' **KEEP** OUT! AN' WHAT'S MORE, DON'T YOU MAKE ANY NOISE IN TH' OTHER ROOM, EITHER!
SPAT!
WHADDA **WE** CARE? THIS IS GONNA BE MORE FUN, ANYWAY!
FEEDLE-DE OODLE DOOP-A-DEEDLE
ZOOOM-ZOOOOM!
FOOP-A-DEEDLE TOODLE-DE! OODLE!
ZUM-ZUM ZOOM!
CRASH!
THOSE DOGGONE KIDS! JUST WAIT'LL I GET MY HANDS ON 'EM!
F'GOSH SAKES! THEY'VE GONE WHERE **ARE** THEY?
THE HECK WITH **THEM**! WHERE'S MY BULL FIDDLE?
12 22
WELL, COME **ON**! QUIT BLOWIN' YER HORN, AN **PASS** ME IF YA WANT TO
HONK!
HONK!
WALT DISNEY

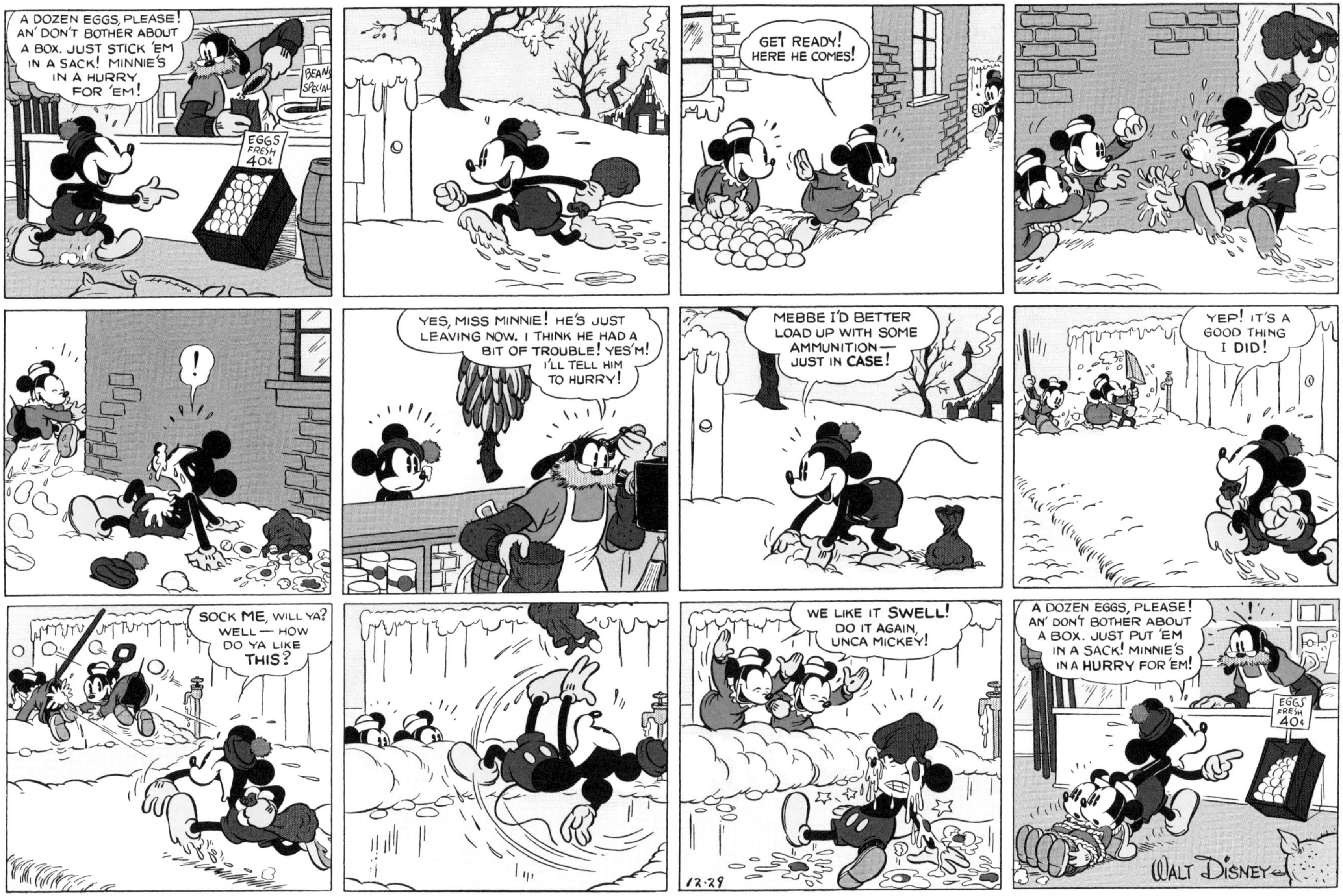
A DOZEN EGGS, PLEASE! AN' DON'T BOTHER ABOUT A BOX. JUST STICK 'EM IN A SACK! MINNIE'S IN A HURRY FOR 'EM!
EGGS FRESH 40¢
GET READY! HERE HE COMES!
!
YES, MISS MINNIE! HE'S JUST LEAVING NOW. I THINK HE HAD A BIT OF TROUBLE! YES'M! I'LL TELL HIM TO HURRY!
MEBBE I'D BETTER LOAD UP WITH SOME AMMUNITION— JUST IN CASE!
YEP! IT'S A GOOD THING I DID!
SOCK ME, WILL YA? WELL— HOW DO YA LIKE THIS?
WE LIKE IT SWELL! DO IT AGAIN, UNCA MICKEY!
12-29
A DOZEN EGGS, PLEASE! AN' DON'T BOTHER ABOUT A BOX. JUST PUT 'EM IN A SACK! MINNIE'S IN A HURRY FOR 'EM!
!
EGGS FRESH 40¢
WALT DISNEY

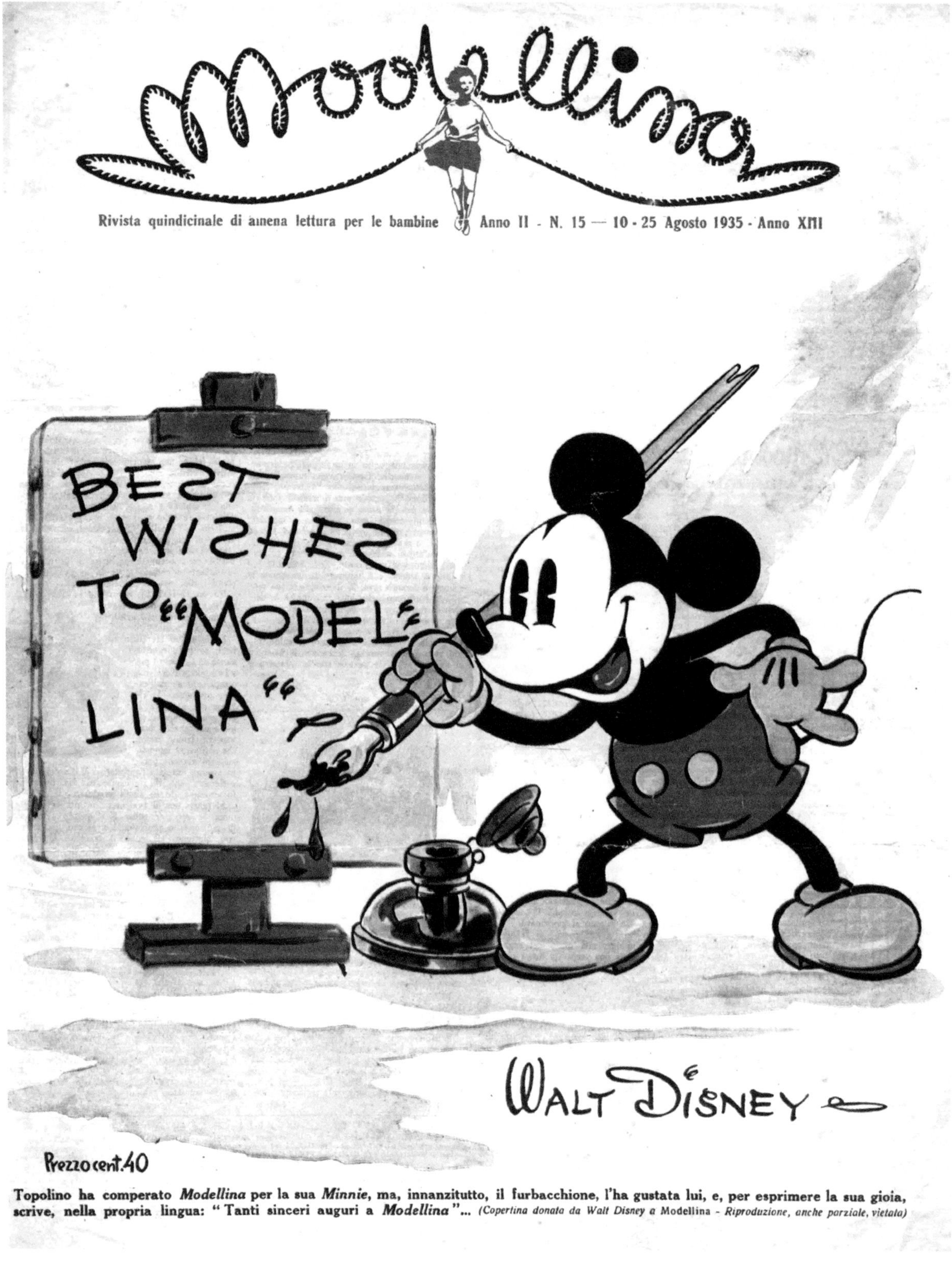
Modellina
Rivista quindicinale di amena lettura per le bambine
Anno II - N. 15 — 10 - 25 Agosto 1935 - Anno XIII
BEST WISHES TO "MODEL LINA"
WALT DISNEY
Prezzo cent. 40
Topolino ha comperato *Modellina* per la sua *Minnie*, ma, innanzitutto, il furbacchione, l'ha gustata lui, e, per esprimere la sua gioia, scrive, nella propria lingua: "Tanti sinceri auguri a *Modellina*"... *(Copertina donata da Walt Disney a* Modellina *- Riproduzione, anche parziale, vietata)*

Mickey's widespread popularity in Europe led to special publicity tie-ups, many of them handled by our domestic Comic Strip Department. The Italian children's magazine *Modellina* received this special cover in 1935; layout by Floyd Gottfredson, finished pencils and inks by Tom Wood. Image courtesy Sergio Lama.

THE GOTTFREDSON ARCHIVES

Essays and
Special Features

The Monthly

"Sundays"

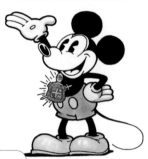

» BY DAVID GERSTEIN AND JIM KORKIS

DEMOLAY INTERNATIONAL is a Masonic youth group for boys aged 12-21, aimed at building civic awareness, leadership skills, and personal responsibility.[1] The original aims of DeMolay—named for Jacques DeMolay, 14th century Knights Templar leader—also included providing "inspiration and direction" to children left fatherless by World War I. DeMolay founder Frank S. Land earned his enduring nickname, "Dad," through his early mentoring of these troubled youths.

Land was called a "grand humanitarian" by Walt Disney, who joined DeMolay one year after the organization's 1919 founding.[2] The 19-year-old Walt became the 107th member of the original Mother Chapter of DeMolay in Kansas City, Missouri, and his fellow members remembered him as hardworking and extremely imaginative.[3]

Belief in one Supreme Being was a basic requirement for young DeMolay members. But the seriousness of religion was offset by the fun of secret passwords, handshakes, and other kid-oriented club rituals, which appealed to young boys as well as building a feeling of fraternity.

Group activities emphasized the seven cardinal virtues: love of parents, reverence for sacred things, courtesy, comradeship (friendship), fidelity (faithfulness), cleanness, and patriotism. In 1965, Walt stated that DeMolay's "precepts have been beyond value in making decisions, in facing dilemmas and crises... I am proud, indeed, still to retain my bond with DeMolay..."

TOP RIGHT: In the early 1930s, Walt Disney gave DeMolay founder Frank Land this special Mickey drawing, penciled by Les Clark. Mickey wears the 1919 DeMolay badge that Disney himself wore as a member. Image courtesy of Dale Dietzman, Past State Chapter Dad of Florida DeMolay; used with permission.

RIGHT: From Gottfredson's "Mickey Mouse and the Ransom Plot" (July 30, 1931). Since DeMolay is a boys' organization, the DeMolay remake (page 251) swaps Clarabelle and Minnie out for male bit player Percy Pig.

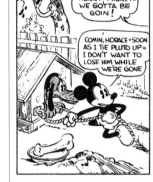

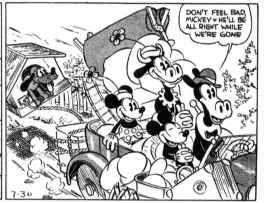

In 1931, Walt Disney was given the DeMolay Legion of Honor, an award representing outstanding leadership in civic, professional, fraternal, or spiritual endeavors. As a gesture of thanks, one year later, Walt asked studio animator Fred Spencer—also a DeMolay alumnus—to create a comics feature for the *International DeMolay Cordon* newsletter: nothing less than a companion series to the *Mickey Mouse* newspaper strip.

HURRY, MICKEY= WE GOTTA BE GOIN!
COMIN, HORACE=SOON AS I TIE PLUTO UP= I DON'T WANT TO LOSE HIM WHILE WE'RE GONE
DON'T FEEL BAD, MICKEY=HE'LL BE ALL RIGHT WHILE WE'RE GONE
7-30

The monthly "Mickey Mouse Chapter" installments, resembling slightly shortened *Mickey* Sunday episodes, began in the December 1932 *Cordon* and ran through May 1933, skipping March. The May installment promised more strips in September, but more never came. We are pleased to reprint the five published episodes here, starting on the next page.

It is unknown whether Spencer worked directly with Floyd Gottfredson's team on "Mickey Mouse Chapter," but the May segment is effectively an expanded remake of Gottfredson's July 30, 1931 daily strip. •

The authors wish to thank Didier Ghez and Paul F. Anderson for additional background research. Strips courtesy Chancellor Robert R. Livingston Masonic Library of Grand Lodge, with thanks to Director Thomas M. Savini.

1 Most information about DeMolay and Frank S. Land: DeMolay International, "What is DeMolay?" Demolay International website, http://www.demolay.org/aboutdemolay (accessed April 14, 2011).

2 All Walt Disney quotes: Paul F. Anderson, "Special DHI Guest Essay on DeMolay," Disney History Institute (blog), entry posted March 21, 2011, http://www.disneyhistoryinstitute.com/2011/03/mickey-mouse-chapter-of-demolay.html (accessed December 19, 2012).

3 "Creator Grooms Mickey Mouse for Full-Length Features on Screen." *Kansas City Star*, 6 July 1936.

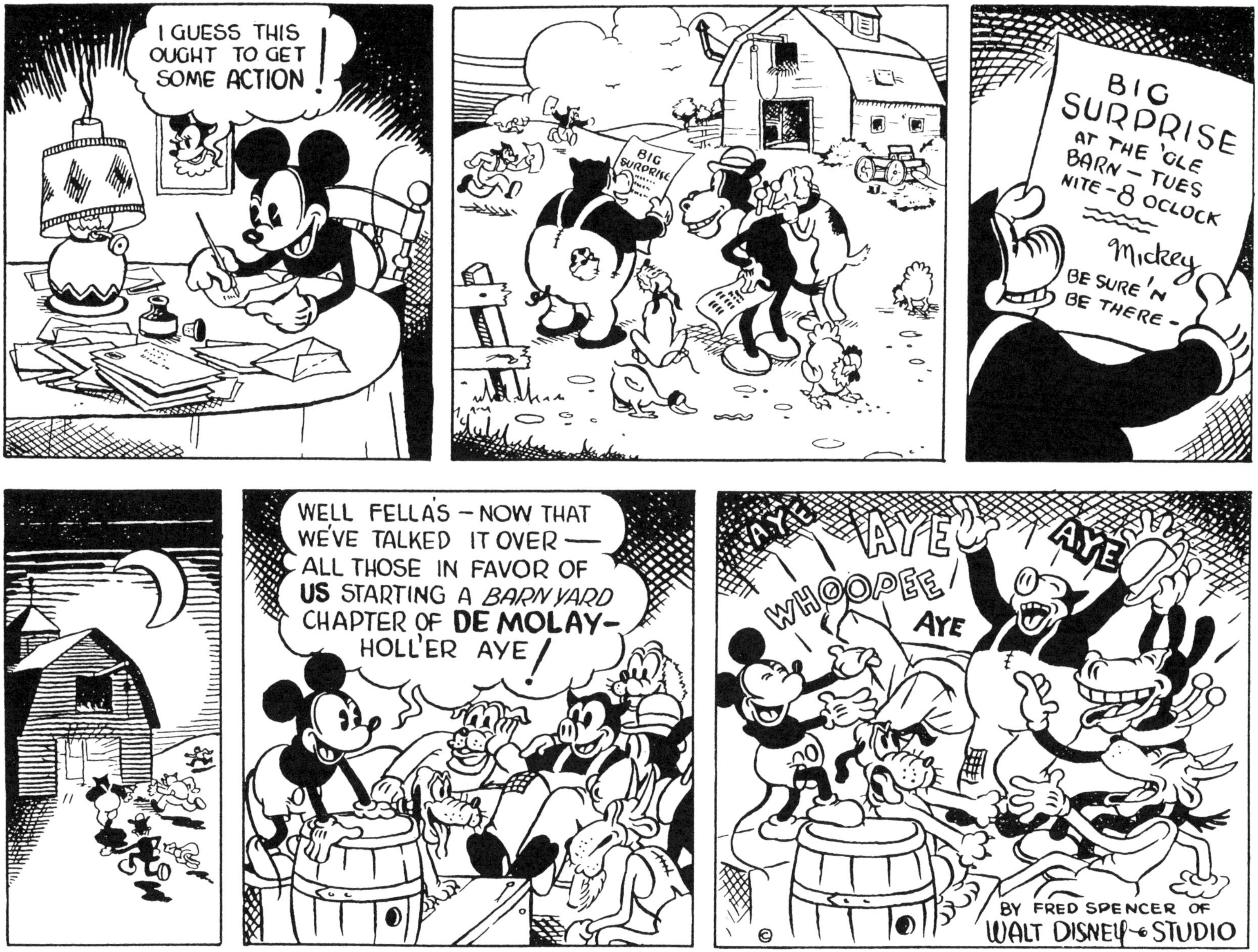
I GUESS THIS OUGHT TO GET SOME ACTION!
BIG SURPRISE
BIG SURPRISE AT THE 'OLE BARN - TUES NITE - 8 OCLOCK
Mickey
BE SURE 'N BE THERE -
WELL FELLA'S - NOW THAT WE'VE TALKED IT OVER — ALL THOSE IN FAVOR OF US STARTING A BARN YARD CHAPTER OF DE MOLAY - HOLL'ER AYE!
AYE
AYE
AYE
WHOOPEE
AYE
BY FRED SPENCER OF WALT DISNEY STUDIO

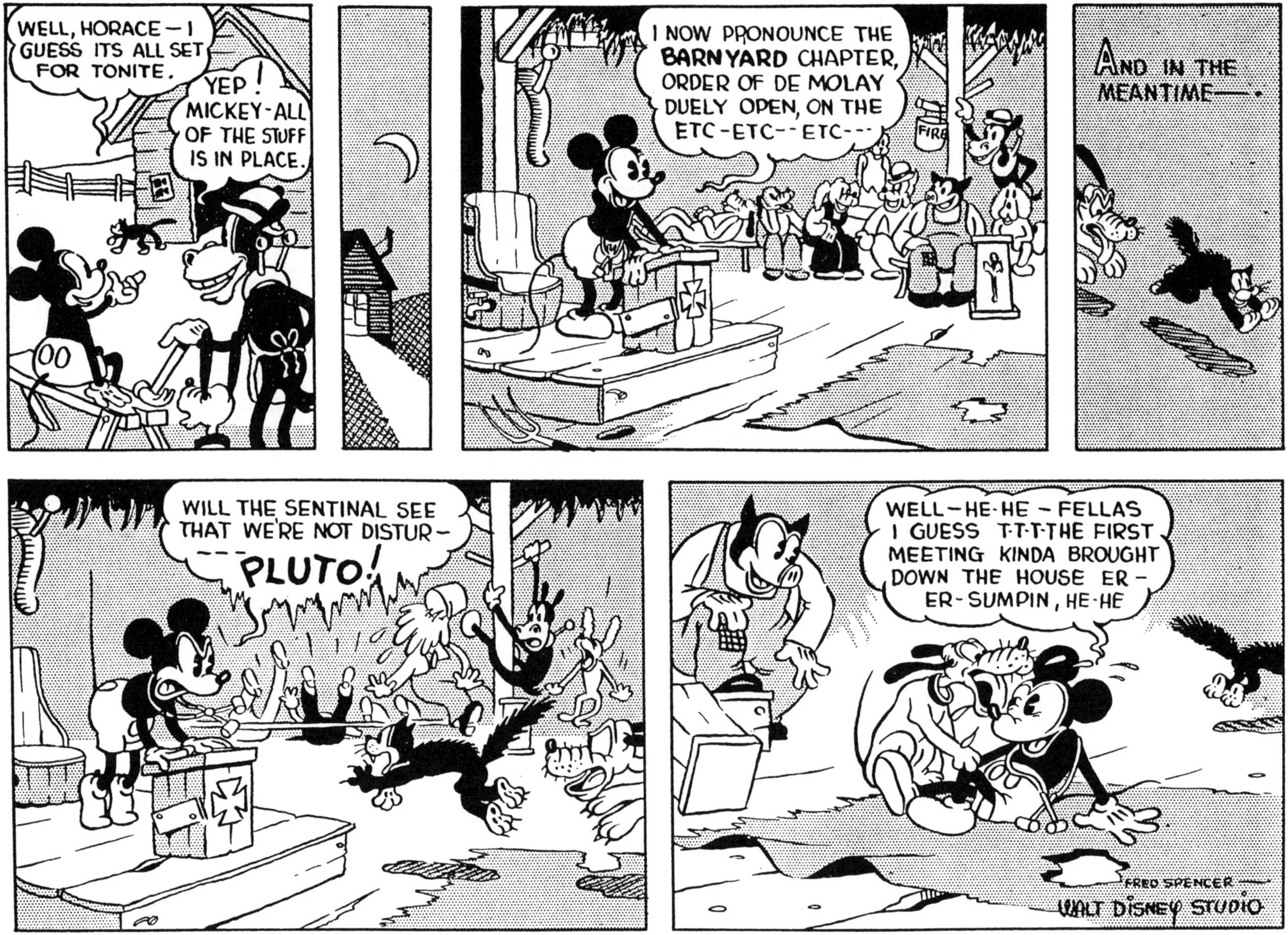
WELL, HORACE — I GUESS ITS ALL SET FOR TONITE.
YEP! MICKEY - ALL OF THE STUFF IS IN PLACE.
I NOW PRONOUNCE THE BARNYARD CHAPTER, ORDER OF DE MOLAY DUELY OPEN, ON THE ETC - ETC -- ETC ---
FIRE
AND IN THE MEANTIME —.
WILL THE SENTINAL SEE THAT WE'RE NOT DISTUR- --- PLUTO!
WELL — HE-HE — FELLAS I GUESS T-T-T-THE FIRST MEETING KINDA BROUGHT DOWN THE HOUSE ER - ER - SUMPIN, HE-HE
FRED SPENCER —
WALT DISNEY STUDIO

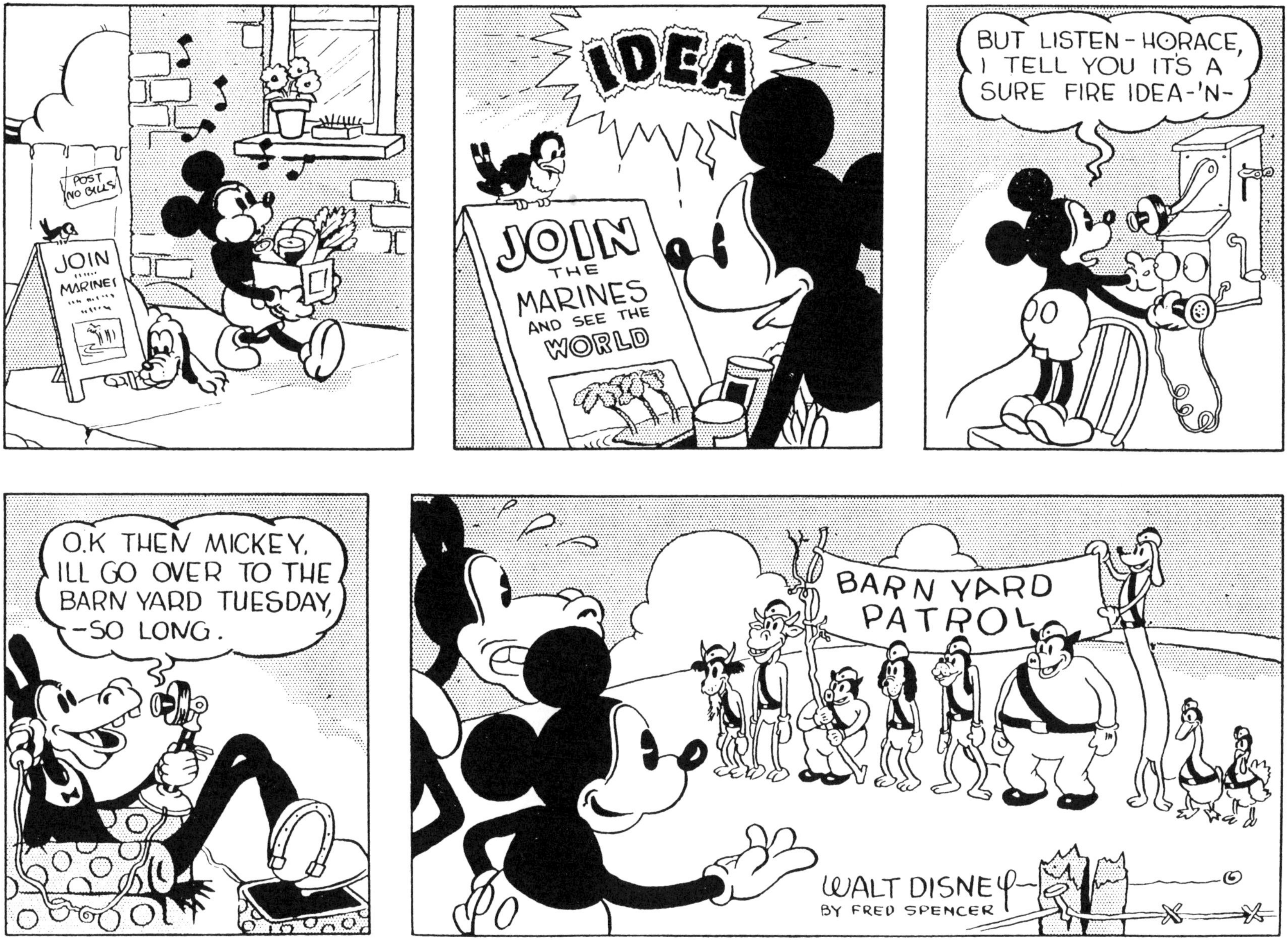
POST NO BILLS
JOIN
MARINES
IDEA
JOIN THE MARINES AND SEE THE WORLD
BUT LISTEN - HORACE, I TELL YOU IT'S A SURE FIRE IDEA-'N-
O.K THEN MICKEY. ILL GO OVER TO THE BARN YARD TUESDAY, -SO LONG.
BARN YARD PATROL
WALT DISNEY
BY FRED SPENCER

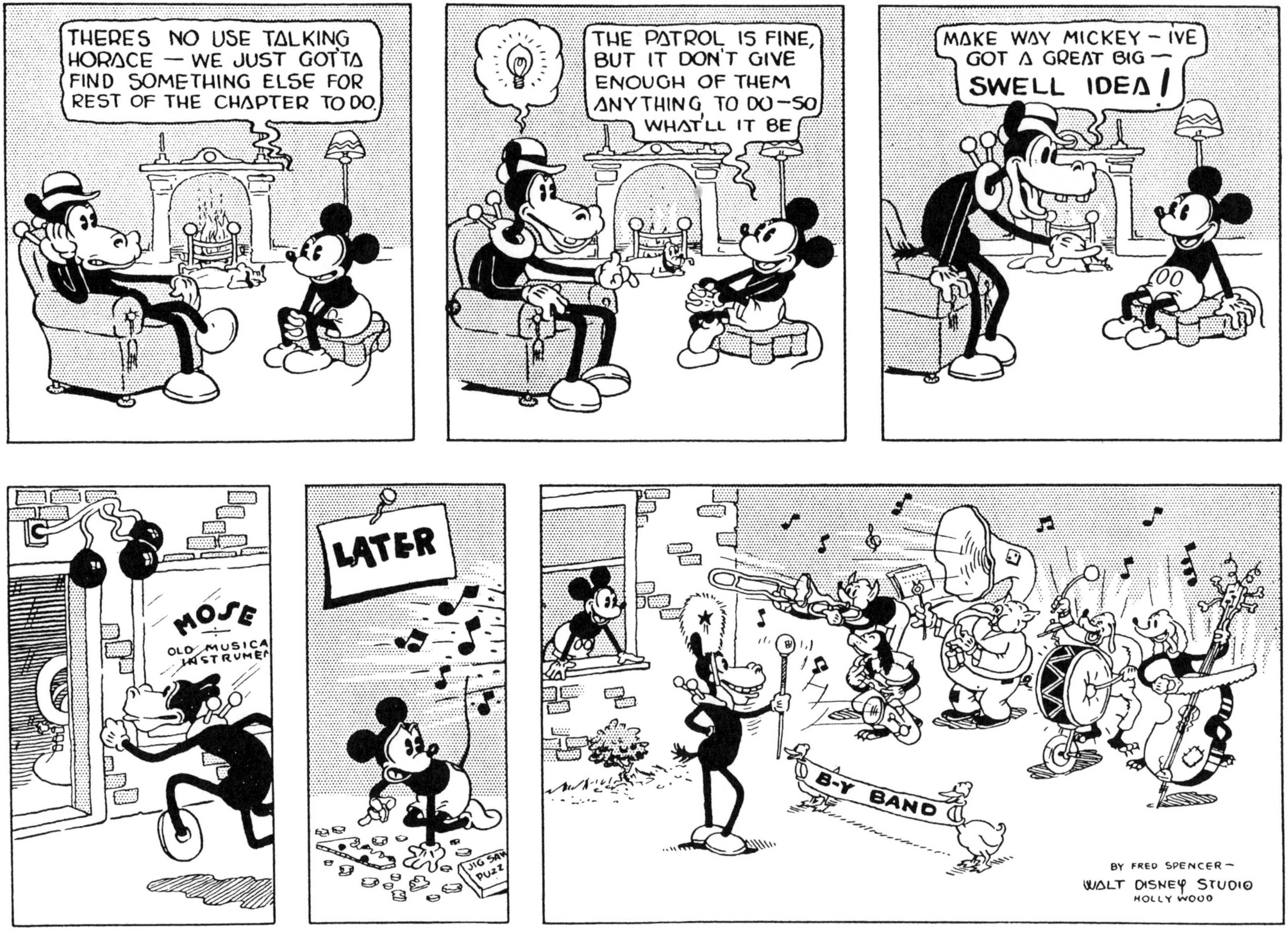
THERES NO USE TALKING HORACE — WE JUST GOT'TA FIND SOMETHING ELSE FOR REST OF THE CHAPTER TO DO.
THE PATROL IS FINE, BUT IT DON'T GIVE ENOUGH OF THEM ANYTHING TO DO—SO WHAT'LL IT BE
MAKE WAY MICKEY — IVE GOT A GREAT BIG — SWELL IDEA!
MOSE
OLD MUSICA INSTRUME
LATER
JIG SAW PUZZ
B-Y BAND
BY FRED SPENCER —
WALT DISNEY STUDIO
HOLLYWOOD

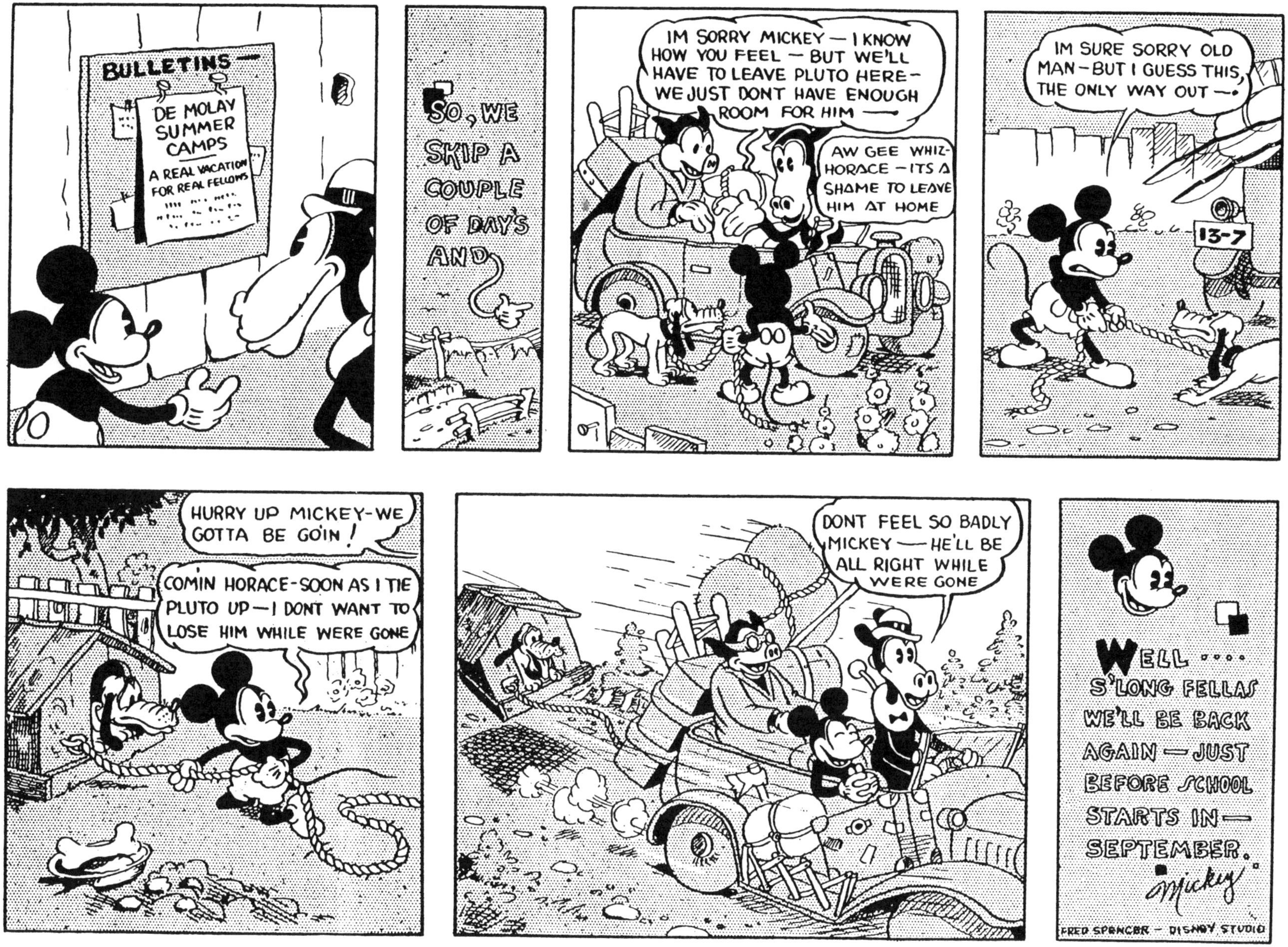

BULLETINS
DE MOLAY SUMMER CAMPS
A REAL VACATION FOR REAL FELLOWS
SO, WE SKIP A COUPLE OF DAY'S AND
IM SORRY MICKEY — I KNOW HOW YOU FEEL — BUT WE'LL HAVE TO LEAVE PLUTO HERE — WE JUST DONT HAVE ENOUGH ROOM FOR HIM —
AW GEE WHIZ — HORACE — ITS A SHAME TO LEAVE HIM AT HOME
IM SURE SORRY OLD MAN — BUT I GUESS THIS, THE ONLY WAY OUT —
13-7
HURRY UP MICKEY — WE GOTTA BE GO'IN!
COMIN HORACE — SOON AS I TIE PLUTO UP — I DONT WANT TO LOSE HIM WHILE WERE GONE
DONT FEEL SO BADLY MICKEY — HE'LL BE ALL RIGHT WHILE WERE GONE
WELL .... S'LONG FELLAS WE'LL BE BACK AGAIN — JUST BEFORE SCHOOL STARTS IN — SEPTEMBER.
Mickey
FRED SPENCER — DISNEY STUDIO

Every country that loves Mickey Mouse has had its own edition—or editions—of Floyd Gottfredson's epics. And each country's Disney comics publisher has tried to make its own version unique, usually by asking homegrown talent to create their own covers or vignettes based on the stories.

In this series we're proud to anthologize these images, both foreign and domestic, old and new—and give you a sense of how far Gottfredson's classic adventures have traveled over the years. We'll start with two covers under which "Dan the Dogcatcher" was reprinted... though the bullying Dan only dared to show his face on one. [DG]

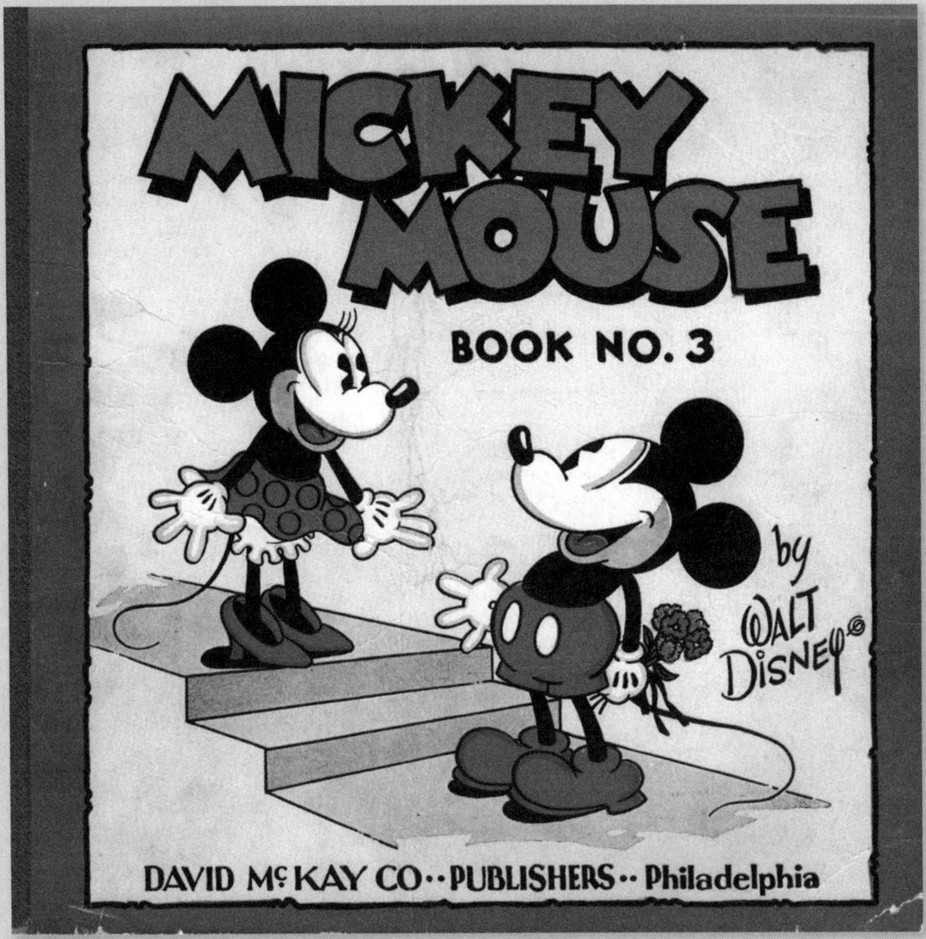
MICKEY MOUSE
BOOK NO. 3
by WALT DISNEY
DAVID McKAY CO.·PUBLISHERS·Philadelphia

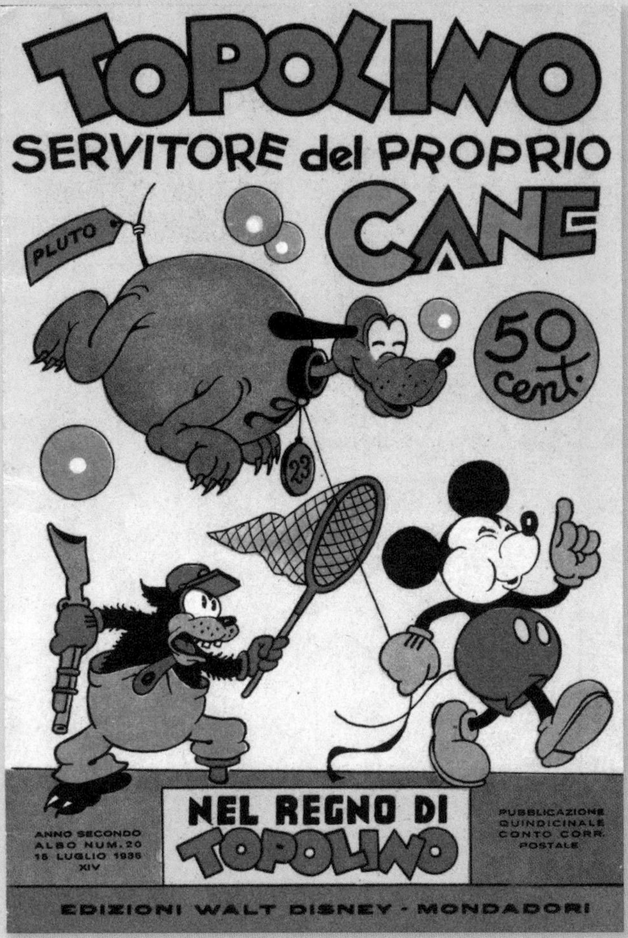
TOPOLINO
SERVITORE del PROPRIO CANE
PLUTO
50 cent.
23
NEL REGNO DI TOPOLINO
ANNO SECONDO ALBO NUM. 20 15 LUGLIO 1936 XIV
PUBBLICAZIONE QUINDICINALE CONTO CORR. POSTALE
EDIZIONI WALT DISNEY - MONDADORI

LEFT: David McKay's *Mickey Mouse Series* 3 (1933), pencils by Floyd Gottfredson. This was the first Disney comic book to consist entirely of Sunday strips—and the first to be printed entirely in color. Image courtesy Thomas Jensen.

RIGHT: Italian *Nel Regno di Topolino* 20 (1936). Art by Antonio Rubino; image courtesy Leonardo Gori.

Mickey's nephews started with a rabbit.

Well, perhaps that's a rather obvious statement. Mickey Mouse would not exist had Walt Disney not lost control of his earlier hit character, Oswald the Lucky Rabbit. So had there been no Oswald, there would be no Mickey—and thus, naturally, no Morty and Ferdie Fieldmouse.

But in fact, the pesky twins actually owe Oswald a special, separate debt apart from Mickey's own.

To understand why, we must jump back to 1927—to the cartoon *Poor Papa*, the first Oswald storyline to go into production. "Already the father of a large family,"[1] the rabbit sees red when storks bring him fifteen new Bunny Kids, with hundreds more to follow. After bathing mobs of babies in a churn and drying them on a clothesline, angry Oswald fends off further stork deliveries by taking to the roof with a shotgun.

When distributor Charles Mintz screened *Poor Papa*—its title borrowed from a 1926 pop tune about a harried husband—he got angry, too. Mintz wanted his new cartoon star to be a sympathetic youngster; Oswald was a middle-aged, unpleasant dad.[2] Mintz shelved *Papa*, then demanded Walt Disney and Ub Iwerks de-age Oswald immediately. And a younger hero, it seemed, had little need for babies: the Bunny Kids disappeared a few films later.

But perhaps they deserved a second chance. For in 1928, when *Poor Papa* was belatedly released, it got reviews as positive as any other Oswald short. This seems to have set Walt to thinking. Maybe the *Papa* plot could be remade without *Papa*'s flaws—and with a different kind of star character.

Mickey's Nightmare (1932) was the result, framing the stork invasion as a dream. While some scenes directly copied *Papa*—Minnie, like Oswald's Fanny, lying in bed with a row of kids on either side—the comedy now grew from bewilderment, not anger. Whereas Oswald had been a grown-up grump, at war with the storks and his children, Mickey is a youngster forced to play parent; comically embarrassed and endearingly sympathetic.

Walt Disney apparently loved the result—enough to bring back the dream kids as orphans in later cartoons.[3] He also asked Gottfredson to introduce two of them as nephews in the comics. In their debut story, "Mortimer" and Ferdie are the children of "Mrs. Fieldmouse," seemingly a neighbor. But the tall lady mouse is ret-conned into a de facto sister several weeks later, when Mickey begins introducing her boys as his relatives.

JOSEPH M. SCHENCK
Presents
WALT DISNEY'S
MICKEY MOUSE
'The STEAMROLLER'
UNITED ARTISTS
PICTURE

Gottfredson's early uses of Morty and Ferdie reflect *Mickey's Nightmare*; but show traces of *Poor Papa* too. The twins are mischievous to the point of anarchy, making Mickey more sympathetic by default. But should Mickey react with bossy anger—as he sometimes does—then the unsympathetic Oswald of *Papa* hops back into view. While Gottfredson never spoke of it later, his team evidently faced a balancing act: how parental could Mickey get while remaining a likeable underdog?

By 1935 a satisfying middle ground was achieved, with Mickey portrayed less as a parent, more as a big brother. We find him caught between his nephews, Minnie, and third parties in comedies of manners; he is more adult than the boys, yet still tempted to engage them on their childish level.

We're quite some ways from blasting storks off the roof. [DG]

LEFT: Morty and Ferdie's ancestors: Oswald gets even with the Bunny Kids in *Trolley Troubles* (1927). The Kids would later return as video game foes in *Disney Epic Mickey* (2010).

RIGHT: For all their comics popularity, Mickey's nephews only made a few screen appearances; *Mickey's Steamroller* (1934) was the first. Art by Tom Wood; image courtesy Walt Disney Archives.

1 Walt Disney et al. "Poor Papa: Synopsis, Gags and Situations." Studio reference document, 1928.

2 Charles Mintz, telegram to Walt Disney, April 15, 1927.

3 The cartoons run from *Giantland* (1933) to *Pluto's Party* (1952); when *Giantland* was adapted to this volume's "Rumplewatt the Giant" (1934), the orphans made their comics debut.

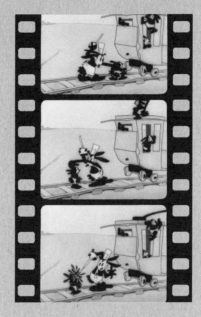

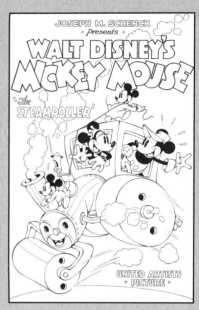

Behind the Scenes: MINNIE'S YOO-HOO

READING THE *MICKEY MOUSE* Sunday strip of October 16, 1932, the modern fan might miss the significance of the moment. As carefree Mickey paints his hencoop, he sings a silly song about barnyard noise. "Th' cows an' th' chickens, they all sound like th' dickens/When I hear my little Minnie's *yoo-hoo!*" At first, the tune seems little different from other comic songs sung in the *Mickey Mouse* Sunday, many of them written by Gottfredson himself.

But there was something different about "Minnie's Yoo-Hoo": across the United States, a million kids were singing it with Mickey.

The backstory takes us to 1929, when sound cartoons were new. Rival studios were toying with synchronized speech, an innovation Disney had yet to perfect. Early Mickey cartoons had featured more clucks than words. But Disney had resolved to change this in a big, publicity-worthy way. Let other funny animals talk; the Mouse would roar. *Sing*, that is.

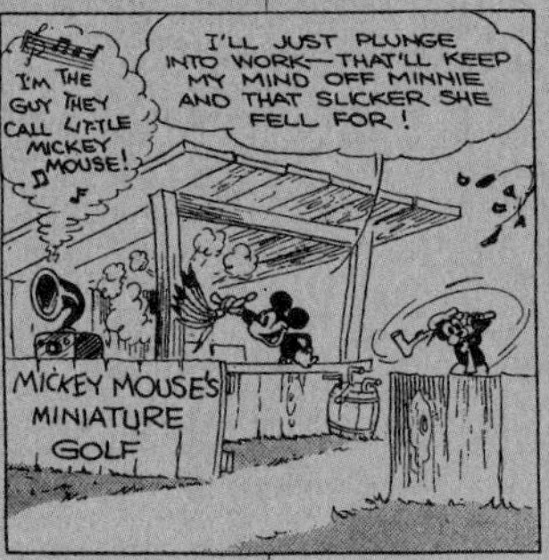
I'M THE GUY THEY CALL LITTLE MICKEY MOUSE!
I'LL JUST PLUNGE INTO WORK—THAT'LL KEEP MY MIND OFF MINNIE AND THAT SLICKER SHE FELL FOR!
MICKEY MOUSE'S MINIATURE GOLF

"The theme song [concept] seems to have passed to the studios of motion comic strips," the *Los Angeles Times* reported. "Mickey's voice will ring out clear and true for the total time space of one minute... 700 drawings will be required [to get] the song out of his system. These muscular movements of the throat and body must occur in such a fashion that they synchronize perfectly..."[1]

The resulting cartoon, *Mickey's Follies* (1929), shows that its animators had carefully analyzed the throat and body. Maybe *too* much so—or maybe it was on purpose: in singing his song, Mickey contorts into some of the funniest poses he ever struck. And the lyrics of "Minnie's Yoo-Hoo," written by Walt Disney and studio composer Carl Stalling, only helped him along.

Not surprisingly, *Mickey's Follies* was a hit; no less surprisingly, the new theme song had a long life ahead. Summer 1929 saw the launch of the Mickey Mouse Clubs: no relation to the later TV series, but rather a nationwide group of Disney-sponsored theatre clubs for kids. Boasting over a million members by 1932,[2] the Clubs featured games, contests, a "Mickey Mouse Club yell"... and a theme song. At each matinee meeting, the uniformed Song Leader led young "Mickey Mice" in singing "Minnie's Yoo-Hoo." A special sing-along film, adapted from *Mickey's Follies*, rang in theatres' rafters for years.

The music didn't stop there. Until 1933, "Yoo-Hoo" was also the theme song of Mickey's screen cartoons. Then it returned in later decades for *The Mouse Factory* TV variety show (1972) and the animated *Mickey Mouse Works* (1999). It's easy to see why Floyd Gottfredson should have picked up the song; it's amazing he didn't use it *more* often.

That said, Gottfredson faced the music often enough to engage in a playful dig at its ubiquity. In the daily strip of October 28, 1930, Mickey doesn't sing "Minnie's Yoo-Hoo" while he works; he has a radio on hand to sing it for him! At the time—in our world—a cover by bandmaster Leo Zollo was just about to come out. [DG]

1 Muriel Babcock, "Talkie Idea Strikes Animated Cartoons and Film Antics Turn Vocal." *Los Angeles Times*, 11 August 1929. By the time this article saw print, *Mickey's Follies* had already been released.

2 Cecil Munsey, *Disneyana: Walt Disney Collectibles* (New York: Hawthorn Books, Inc.), p. 102.

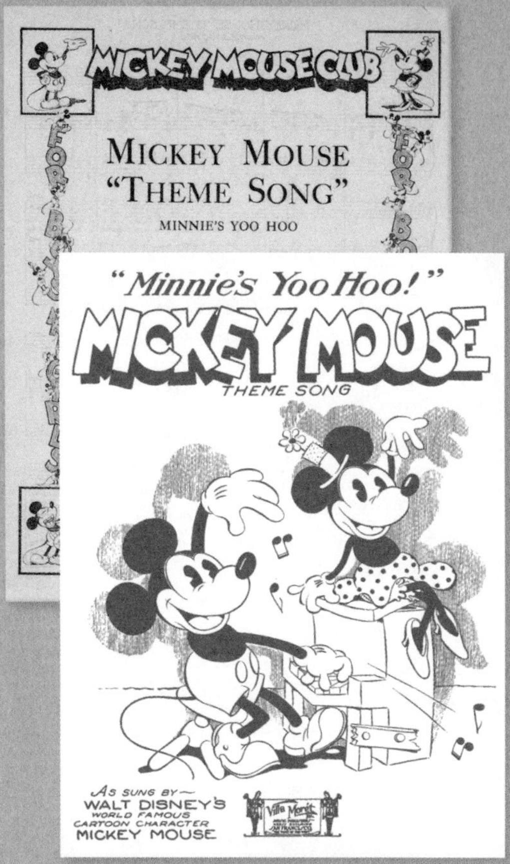
MICKEY MOUSE CLUB
MICKEY MOUSE "THEME SONG"
MINNIE'S YOO HOO
"Minnie's Yoo Hoo!"
MICKEY MOUSE
THEME SONG
AS SUNG BY— WALT DISNEY'S WORLD FAMOUS CARTOON CHARACTER MICKEY MOUSE

LEFT: From "Mr. Slicker and the Egg Robbers" (October 28, 1930). The Mickey Mouse Club campaign book stated that "The King Features Syndicate... releases a Mickey Mouse comic strip for newspapers, which is being used in some of the best newspapers in the world. Work up a cooperative proposition with them..."

ABOVE: "Minnie's Yoo-Hoo" as both Mickey Mouse Club theme song and standalone hit: sheet music, 1930. Piano-playing image penciled by Les Clark, inked by Win Smith; images courtesy Hake's Americana.

OPPOSITE: Mickey "getting the song out of his system" in *Minnie's Yoo-Hoo* (1930), the Club sing-along film. Animation repurposed from *Mickey's Follies* (1929).

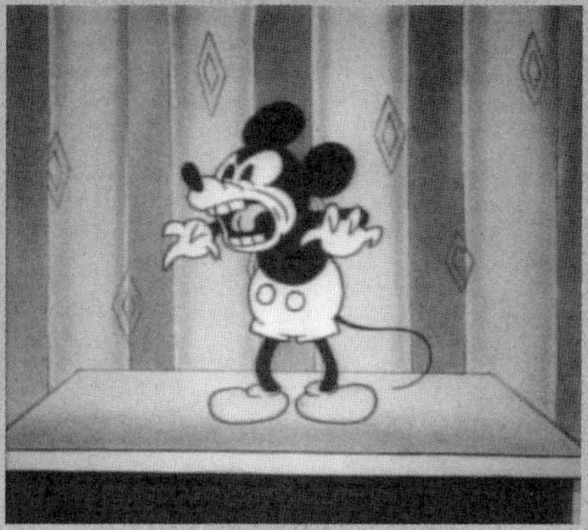

Oh! the old tom cat
With his meow meow meow

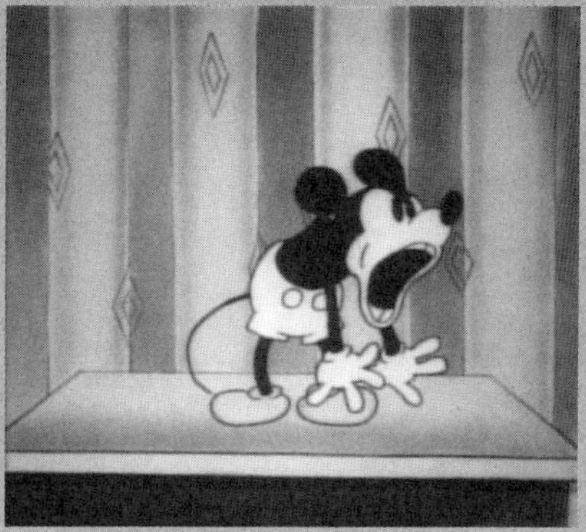

Old houn' dog
With his bow wow wow,

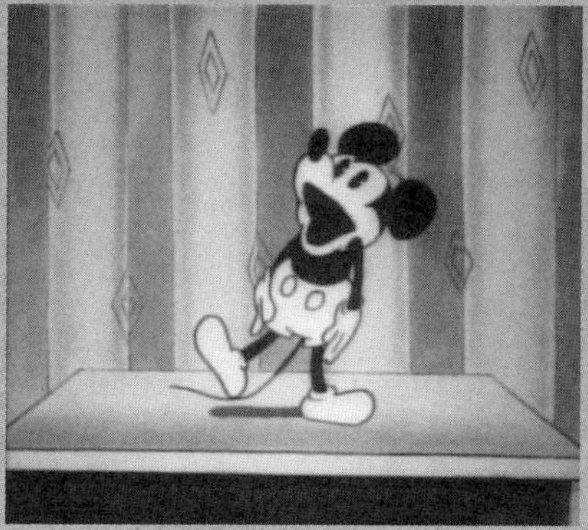

The crow's caw caw
And the mule's hee haw

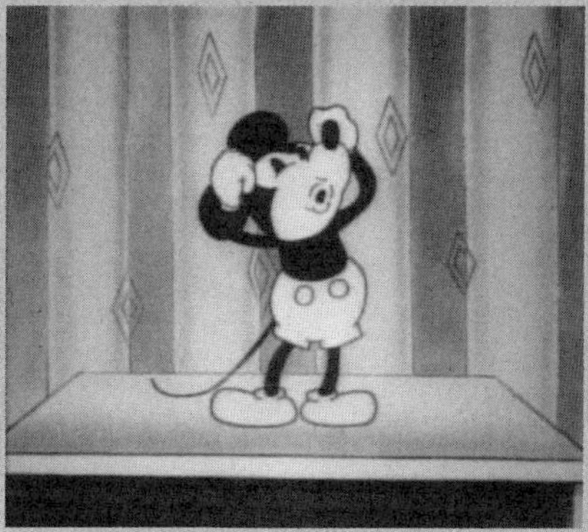

Gosh, what a racket
Like an old buzz saw

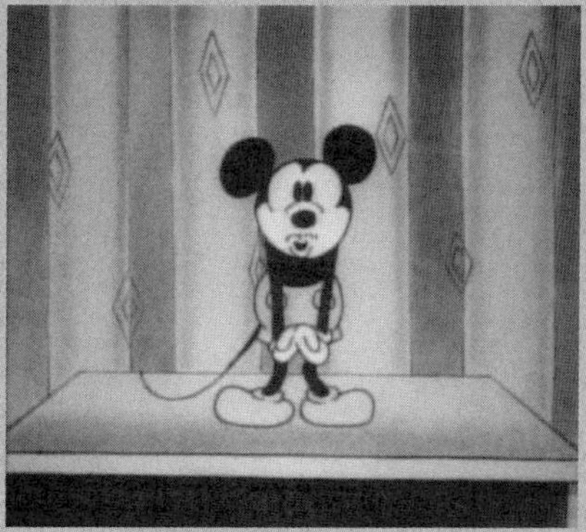

I have listened to the cuckoo
'Kuke' his cuckoo

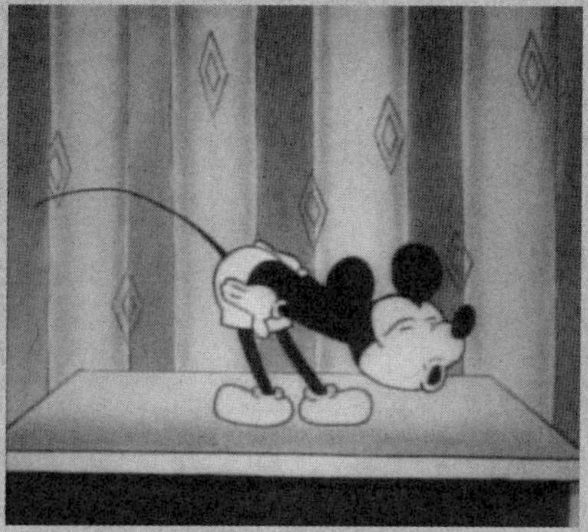

And I've heard the rooster
Cock his doodle doo-oo

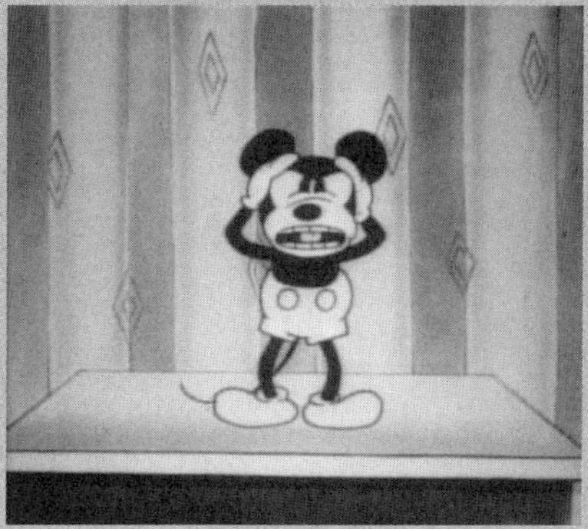

With the cows and the chickens
They all sound like the dickens

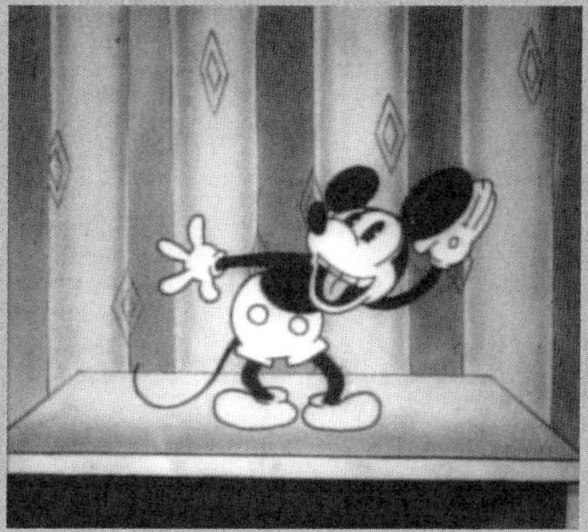

When I hear my little Minnie

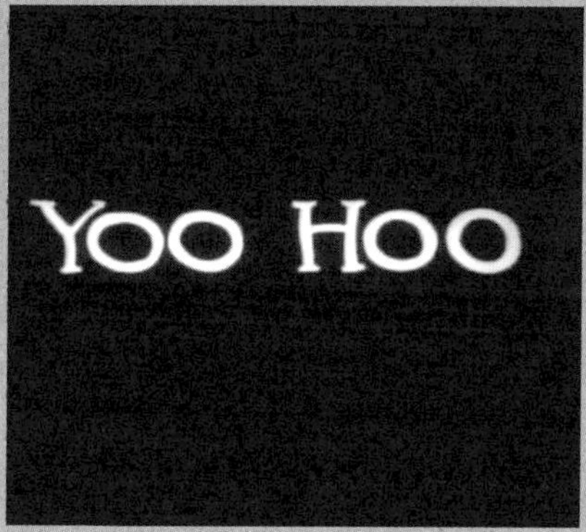
YOO HOO

Mischievous Morty and Ferdie have invaded hundreds of Disney comics covers over the years. Their debut, oddly enough, only got a front cover to itself in one country. But *what* a cover it was.

Upon landing on Italy's *Topolino* 7 (1933), the October 30, 1932 strip from "Mickey's Nephews" became the first-ever Gottfredson work to be published in Italy—displacing cruder Mickey strips drawn by local talent. While some of those cruder strips had actually been Gottfredson-inspired (see page 271), there proved to be no substitute for the real thing.

Eighty years later, there still isn't. [DG]

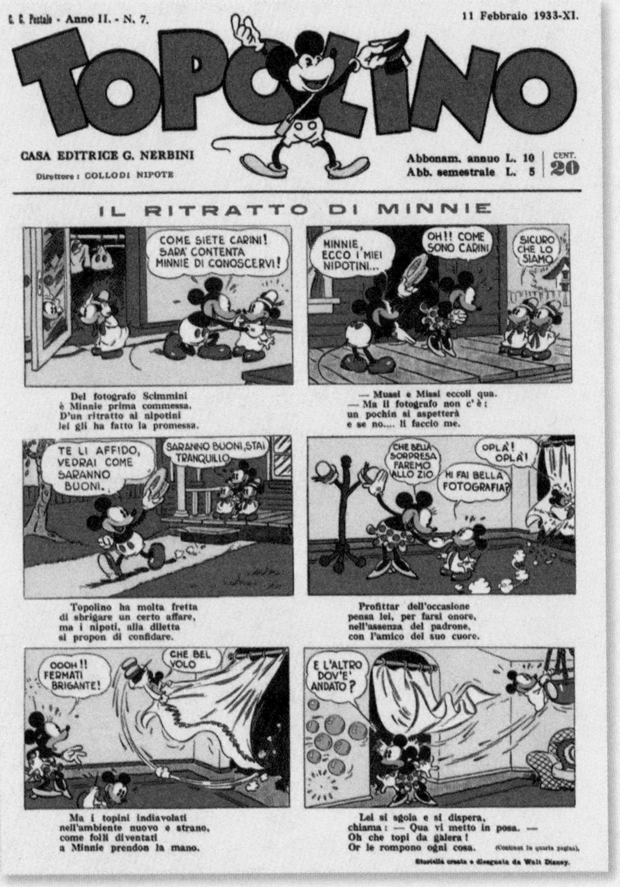
C. C. Postale - Anno II. - N. 7.
11 Febbraio 1933-XI.
TOPOLINO
CASA EDITRICE G. NERBINI
Direttore: COLLODI NIPOTE
Abbonam. annuo L. 10
Abb. semestrale L. 5
CENT. 20
IL RITRATTO DI MINNIE
COME SIETE CARINI! SARA' CONTENTA MINNIE DI CONOSCERVI!
MINNIE, ECCO I MIEI NIPOTINI...
OH!! COME SONO CARINI
SICURO CHE LO SIAMO
Del fotografo Scimmini
è Minnie prima commessa.
D'un ritratto ai nipotini
lei gli ha fatto la promessa.
— Mussi e Missi eccoli qua.
— Ma il fotografo non c'è:
un pochin si aspetterà
e se no.... li faccio me.
TE LI AFFIDO, VEDRAI COME SARANNO BUONI.
SARANNO BUONI, STAI TRANQUILLO
CHE BELLA SORPRESA FAREMO ALLO ZIO
OPLÀ! OPLÀ!
MI FAI BELLA FOTOGRAFIA?
Topolino ha molta fretta
di sbrigare un certo affare,
ma i nipoti, alla diletta
si propon di confidare.
Profittar dell'occasione
pensa lei, per farsi onore,
nell'assenza del padrone,
con l'amico del suo cuore.
OOOH!! FERMATI BRIGANTE!
CHE BEL VOLO
E L'ALTRO DOV'E' ANDATO?
Ma i topini indiavolati
nell'ambiente nuovo e strano,
come folli diventati
a Minnie prendon la mano.
Lei si sgola e si dispera,
chiama: — Qua vi metto in posa. —
Oh che topi da galera!
Or le rompono ogni cosa.
(Continua in quarta pagina).
Storiella creata e disegnata da Walt Disney.

Italian *Topolino* 7 (1933). Strip art by Floyd Gottfredson and Ted Thwaites; image courtesy David Gerstein.

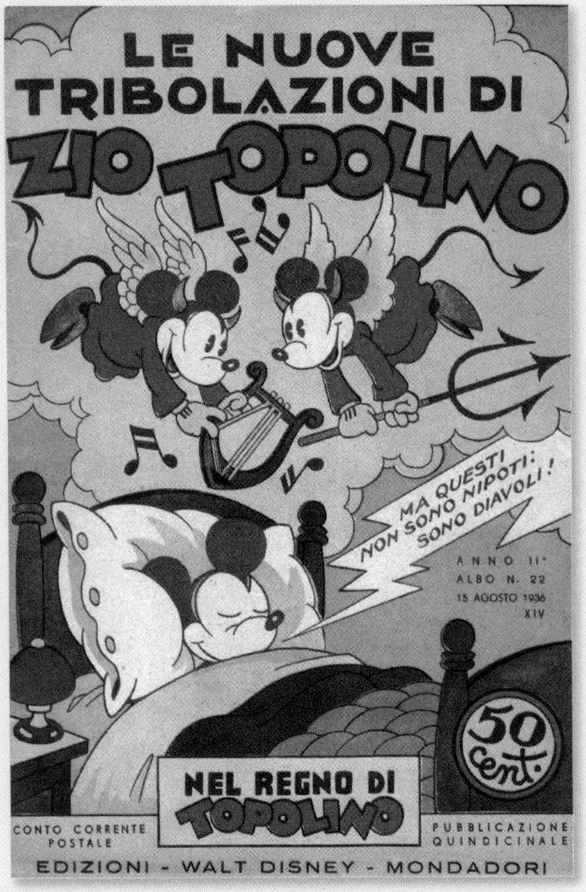
LE NUOVE TRIBOLAZIONI DI ZIO TOPOLINO
MA QUESTI NON SONO NIPOTI: SONO DIAVOLI!
ANNO II°
ALBO N. 22
15 AGOSTO 1936 XIV
50 cent.
NEL REGNO DI TOPOLINO
CONTO CORRENTE POSTALE
PUBBLICAZIONE QUINDICINALE
EDIZIONI - WALT DISNEY - MONDADORI

Italian *Nel Regno di Topolino* 22 (1936; story title translates roughly to "Unca Mickey's new agonies"!). Gottfredson art reinked by Antonio Rubino; image courtesy Leonardo Gori.

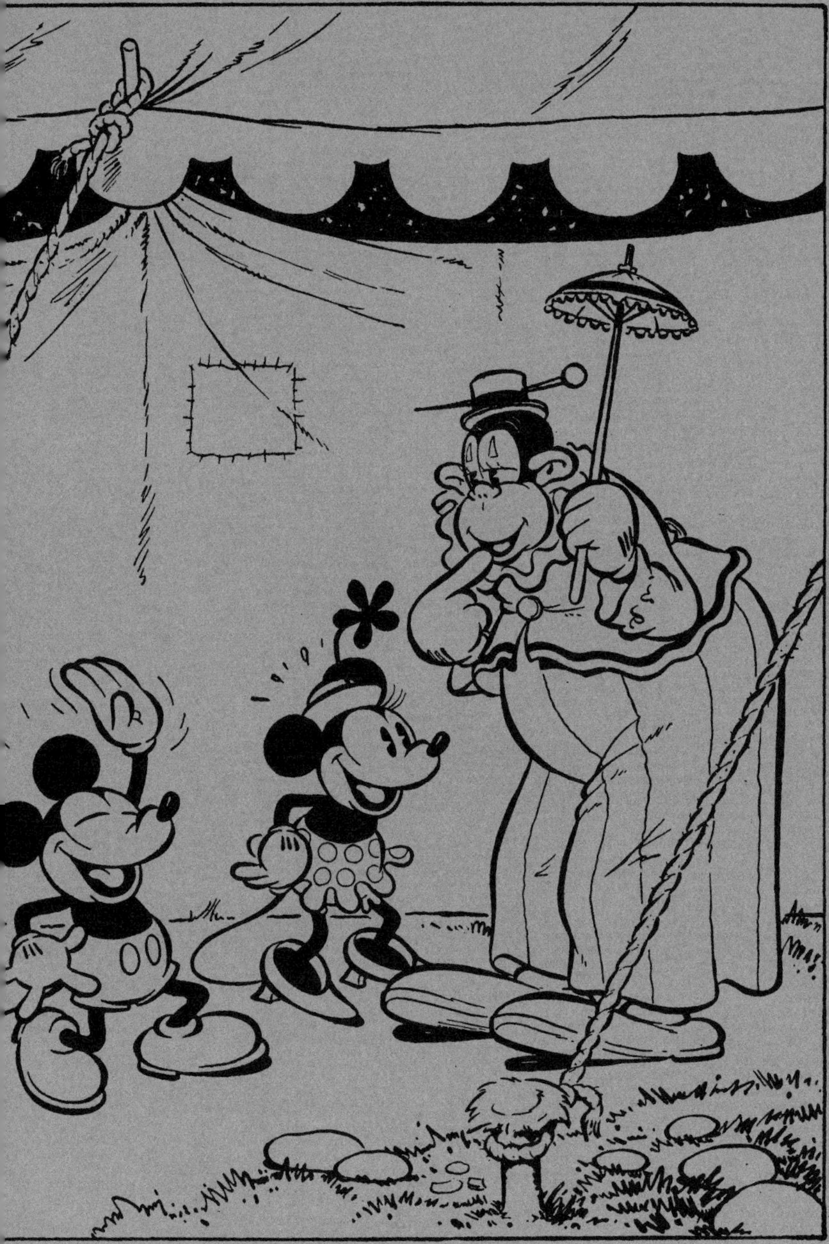

The Comics Dept. at Work: THE MOUSETON POPS

1933 found Floyd Gottfredson, Al Taliaferro, and inker Ted Thwaites moving from strength to strength. The *Mickey Mouse* daily and Sunday strips were both going strong; so was the *Silly Symphony* topper feature. And in Gottfredson's spare time—as manager of the Comic Strip Department—he supervised Tom Wood's studio publicity art. Soon afterward, Publicity would split off to become a separate branch of Disney entirely.

Before that happened, however, Gottfredson, Taliaferro, and Thwaites joined Wood for one last noncomics hurrah. The occasion was Mickey's first foray into a new kind of kids' product: pop-up books, just then recently brought to America by New York licensee Blue Ribbon Publishing. Blue Ribbon founder Harold Lentz, a pioneer in paper engineering, actually created the term "pop-up" to characterize his titles. Like "Kleenex" and "Hoover," it has since become a handy generic—applied even to other publishers' versions of the product.

Blue Ribbon's 1933 *Pop-Up Mickey Mouse* featured a cover inked by Wood. Wood seems to have drawn the *Pop-Up Minnie Mouse* cover from start to finish, along with all of the actual pop-up spreads in both books.

But only a few spreads in each book actually popped up. The rest of the art, save just one page in *Minnie*, was visibly inked by Taliaferro and Ted Thwaites—and penciled by Gottfredson and Taliaferro. Some drawings represented all-new Gottfredson pencil work; other times, Gottfredson's poses were mined from Sunday serials such as "Lair of Wolf Barker."

Reprinted on the next few pages are those vignettes that, to our eyes, show the greatest degree of Gottfredson's involvement. Read on to check out two of the strangest children's stories ever told...

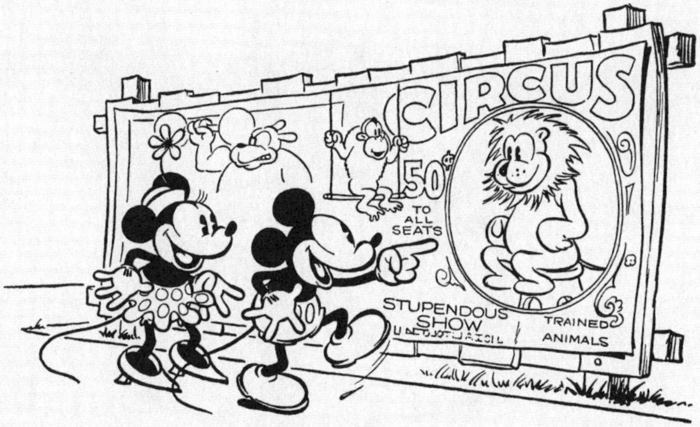
CIRCUS
50¢
TO
ALL
SEATS
STUPENDOUS
SHOW
TRAINED
ANIMALS

In *The Pop-Up Mickey Mouse*, the circus is coming to Mouseton—until the tents, animal trainers and caretakers are suddenly blown away by a huge windstorm! The circus animals are left unemployed and alone, and it's up to Mickey and Minnie to give them shelter. "The poor things would have to swim oceans, and walk thousands and thousands and thousands of miles to get back to their own countries," Minnie exclaims.

Mickey and Minnie swiftly turn their farm into a makeshift zoo. But how to fund the animals' eventual journey home? Thinking hard, our heroes utilize the critters' special talents to create giraffe butter, camel milk, and other salable taste treats. Mouseton citizens are scared to buy the odd foods—until the Mayor gives them a tasty endorsement. Soon enough money is made that a Noah-like ark can be built. Bon voyage, beasties.

"La-dies and gentlemen," he began. "Minnie and I are not going to let you go hungry and homeless for long."

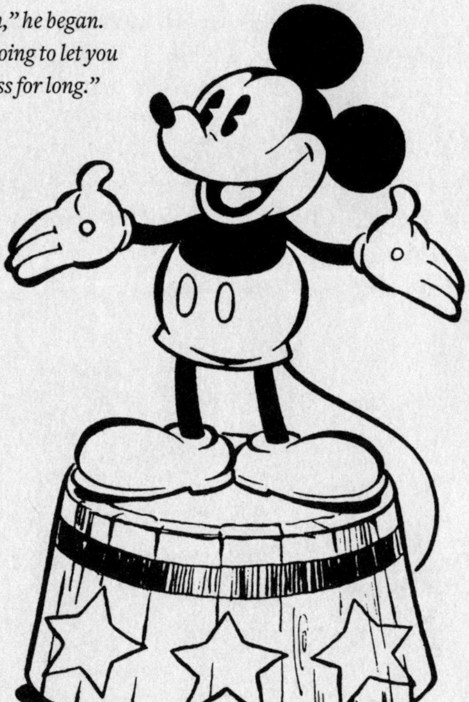

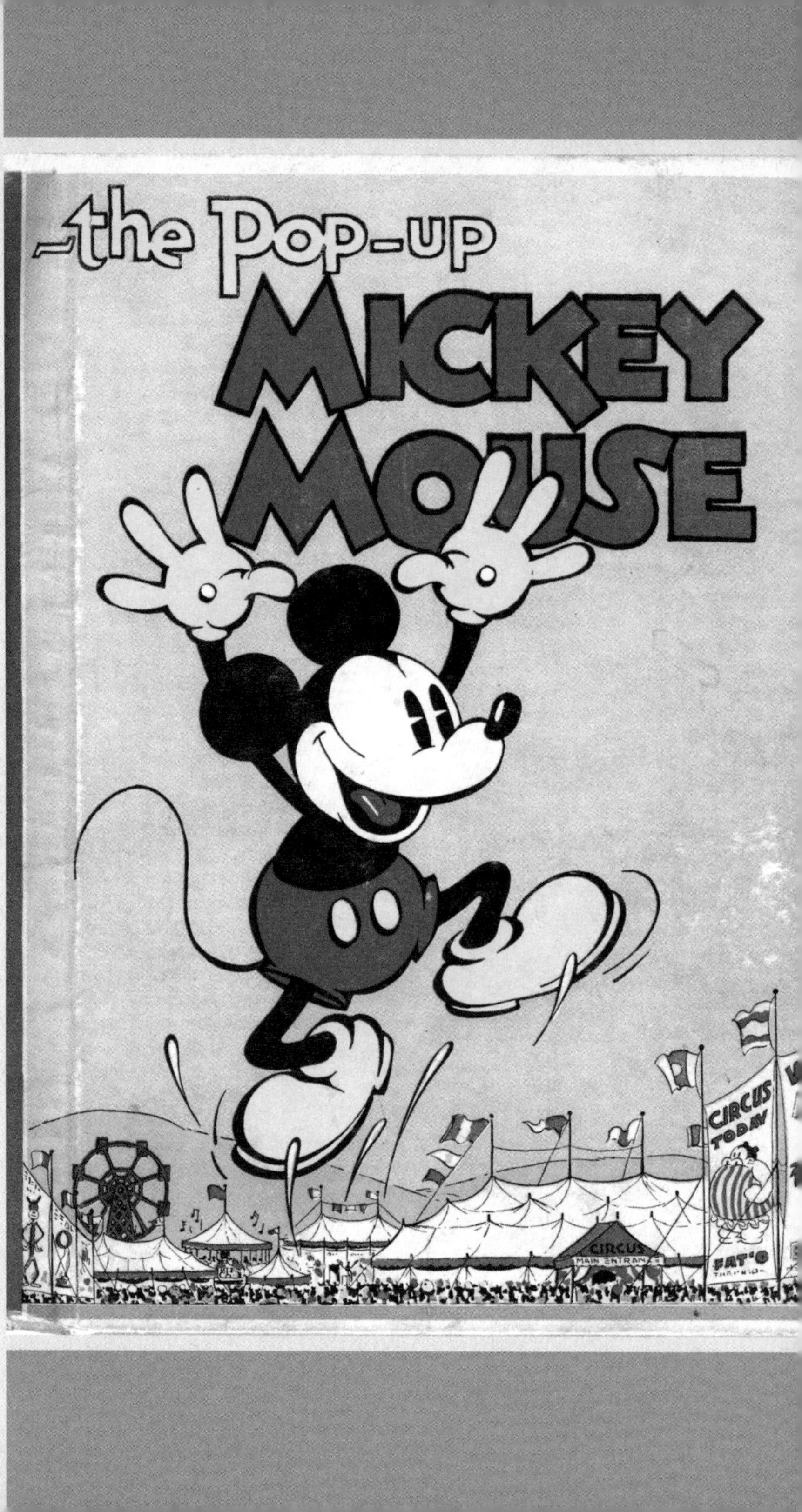
the Pop-up
MICKEY
MOUSE
CIRCUS TODAY
CIRCUS
MAIN ENTRANCE

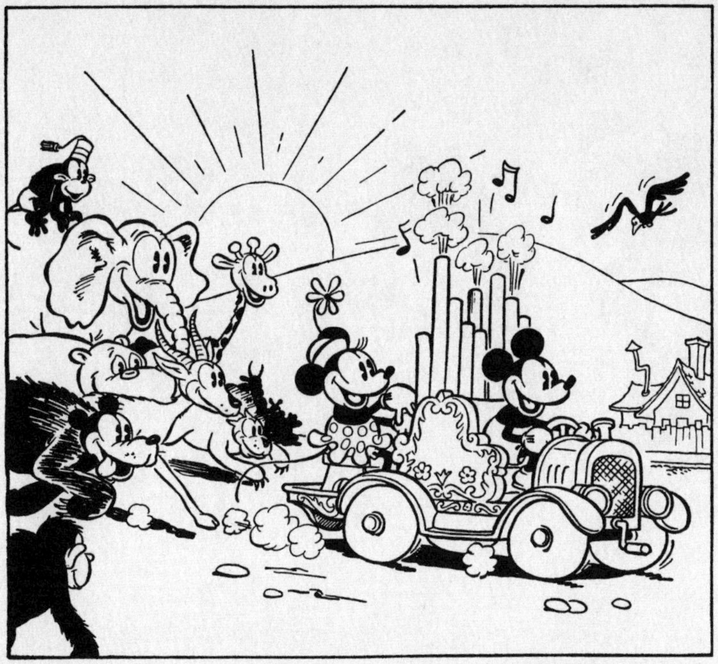

They marched in alphabetical order as follows: antelope, bear, camel, duck, elephant, fleas, giraffe, hippopotamus, ibex, jaguar, kangaroo, leopard, and lion, miscellaneous.

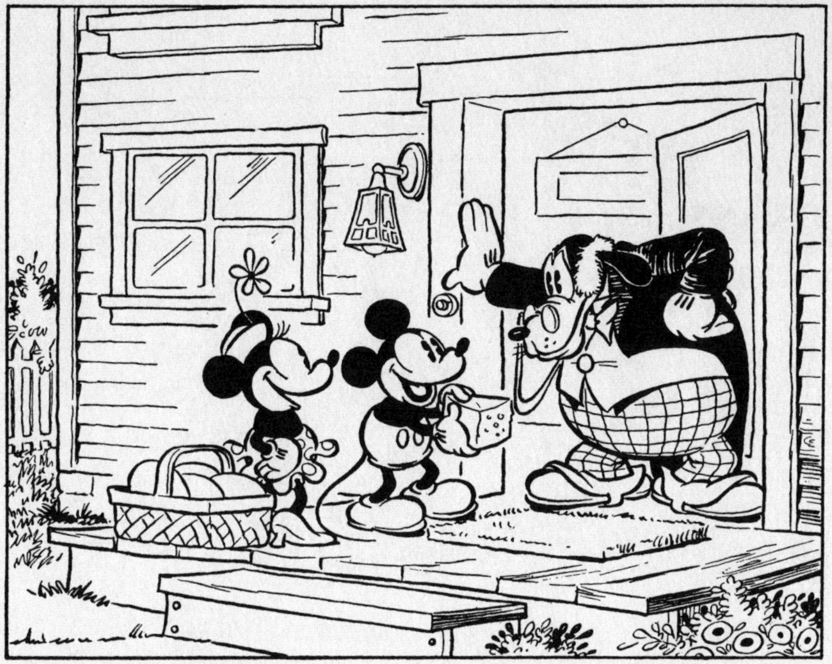

"Taste it," urged Mickey. "Elephant's cheese is very rare, and nobody ever tasted anything like it."

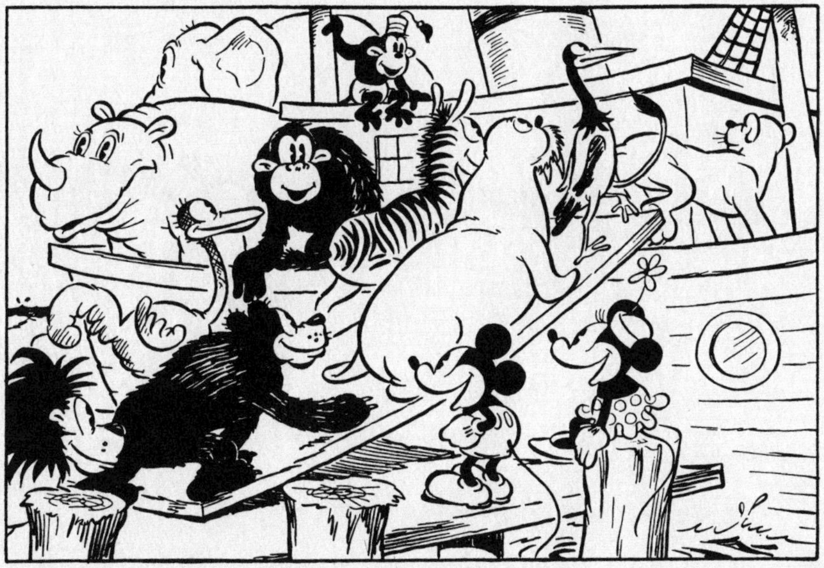

They named it "Mickey's Ark," and they all marched on board in alphabetical order.

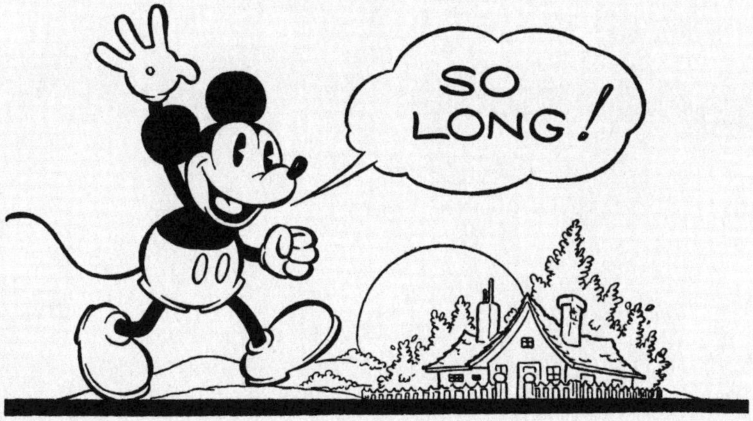
SO LONG!

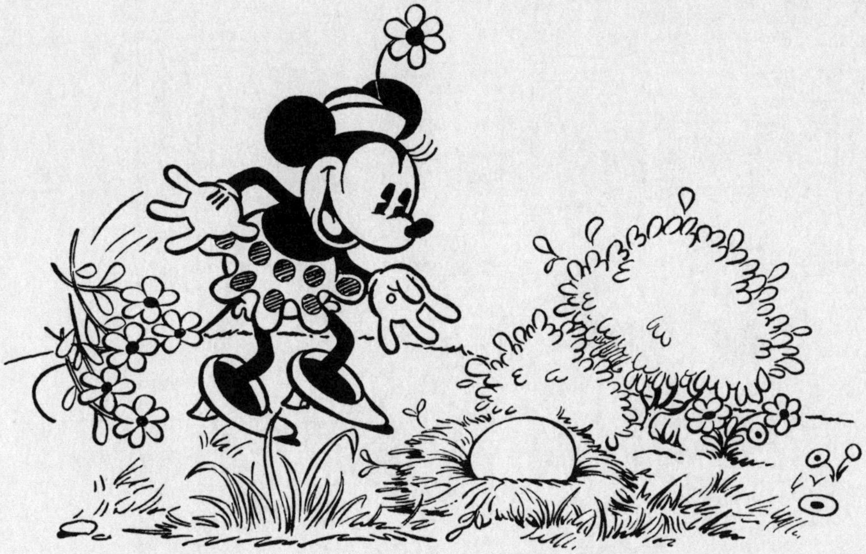

"Ohhhhh!" breathed Minnie, and her "Ohhhhh!" was very soft and round and gentle.

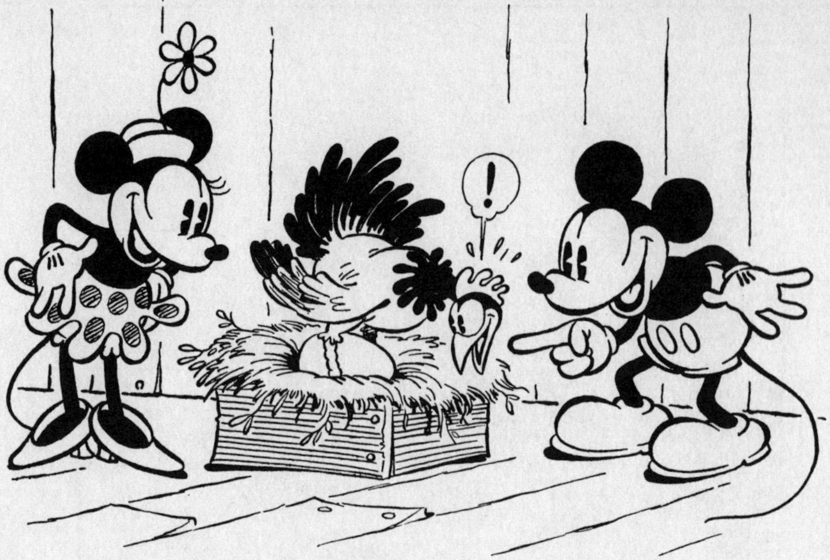

"Clara Cluck, of course," replied Minnie. "That hen can hatch anything."
"Except doorknobs," interrupted Mickey.

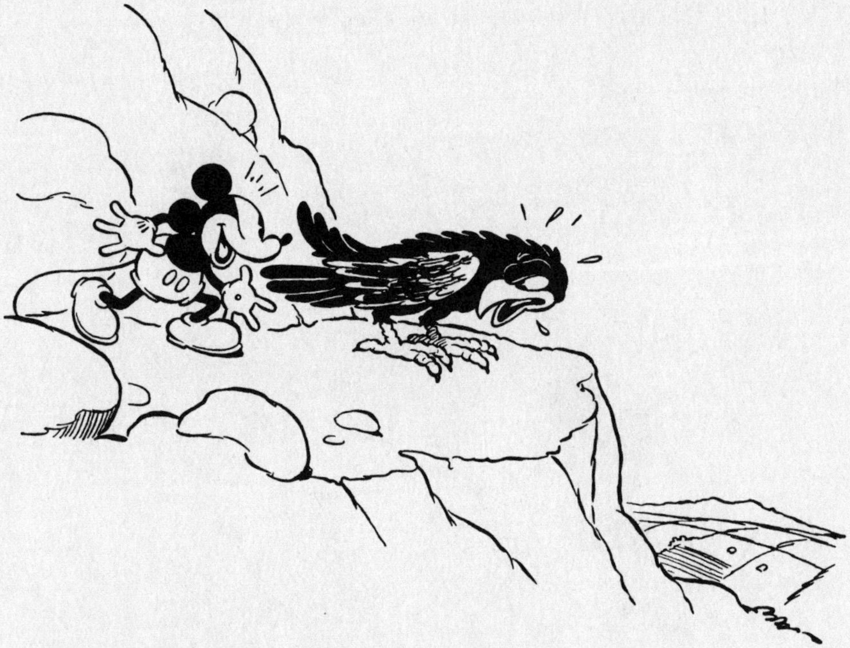

"Go home," screamed Clutch. "Go home before I kill you. I saw the brown egg first. The egg was mine. And Moby Duck is mine."

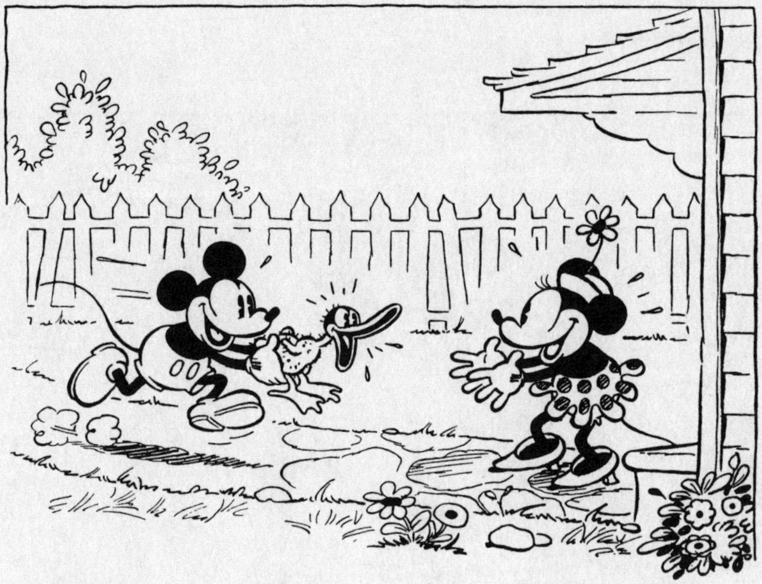

"Oh, Moby," she cried, "I thought we'd never, never see you again."

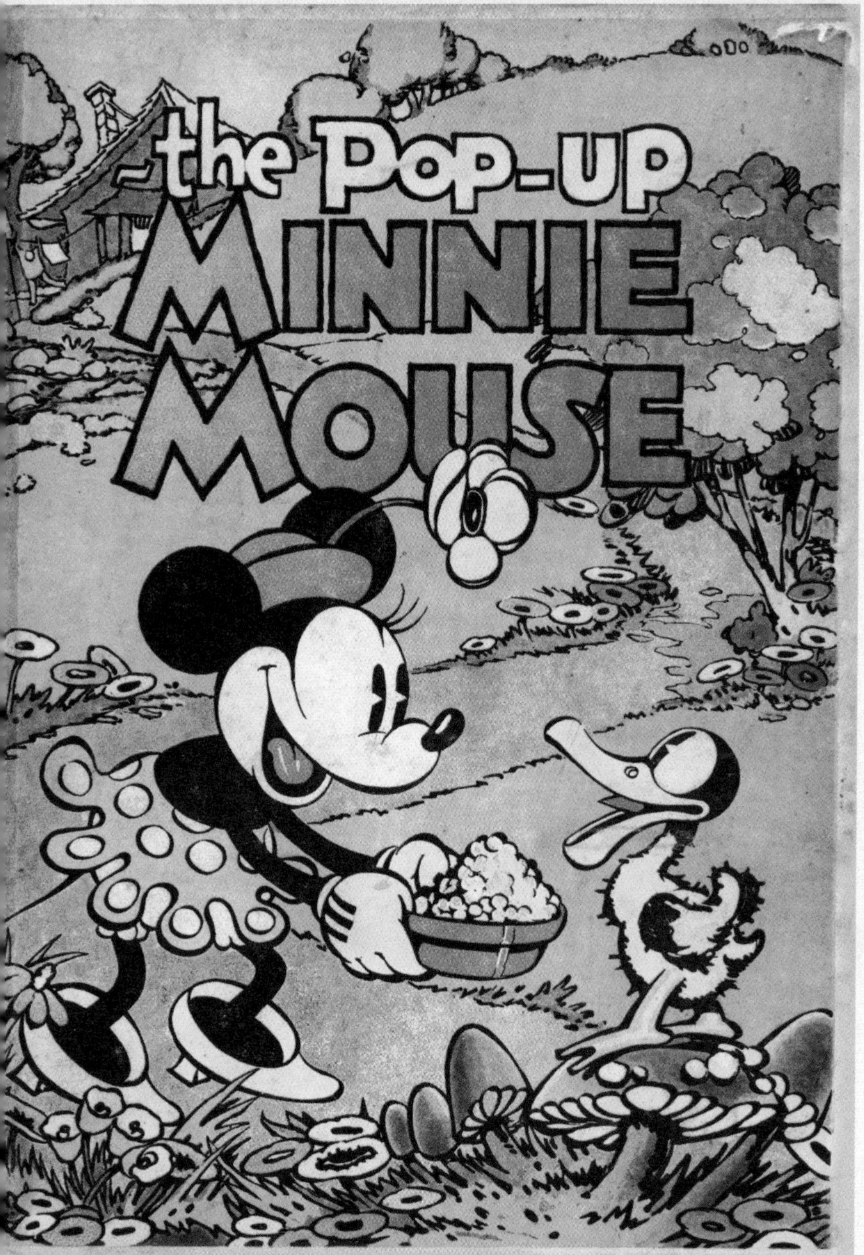
the Pop-up
MINNIE
MOUSE

Minnie's pop-up book finds our heroine and Mickey saving an orphan egg from a fearsome she-hawk named Clutch. Back home, Minnie's hen Clara Cluck (no relation to the later Disney character) hatches the egg, giving birth to a duckling named Moby Duck (no relation to... etc. etc.). But Clutch invades Minnie's farm, swearing revenge. She might have missed out on the egg—but there's nothing she'd like better than a nice duck for dinner!

When Clutch swoops down and kidnaps Moby, Mickey trails her to foreboding Bleak Mountain, where he tricks the hawk and snatches back the hatchling. But the villain still pursues them, trying to maul both Mouse and mallard! Luckily, friendly fauna rally to their rescue. Even Pluto's fleas get into the act, biting Clutch and distracting her till the hawk is hog-tied. In the end, our forest friends formally evict the bad bird. [DG]

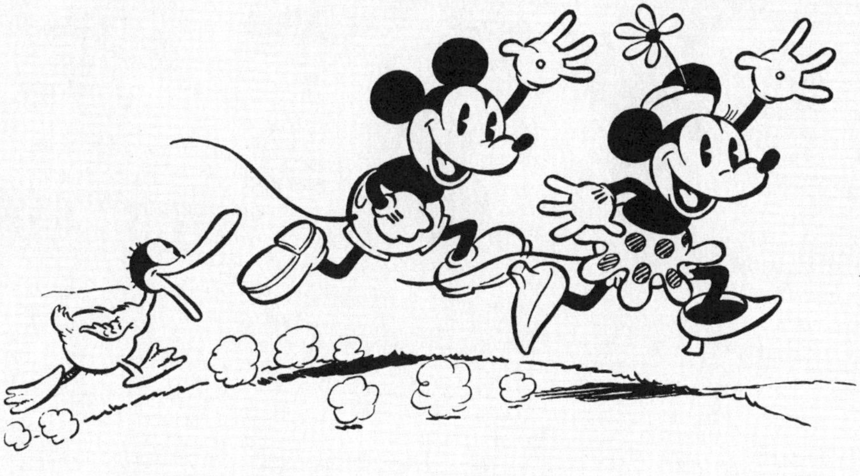

Mickey's first blockbuster color adventures, "The Lair of Wolf Barker" and "Rumplewatt the Giant," have received a lot of fan attention over the years. They've also received extra-classic cover art from the likes of Dutch master Daan Jippes—and Gottfredson's own comic strip team.

But "Rumplewatt" and "Wolf" haven't totally overshadowed their gag-strip and short story contemporaries. In Europe, even Mickey's mishap with a dentist (!) got a toothsome cover of its own. [DG]

GLADSTONE
WALT DISNEY'S
MICKEY MOUSE
3
"the LAIR of WOLF BARKER"

Spedizione in abbonam. postale
TOPOLINO
E IL BAULE MAGICO
60 CENT.
QUESTO ALBO CONTIENE 2 FIGURINE OMAGGIO TOPOLINO
ANNO III - ALBO N. 45
25 SETTEMBRE 1937-XV
Pubblicazione quindicinale
NEL REGNO DI TOPOLINO
EDIZIONI WALT DISNEY • MONDADORI • MILANO

TOPOLINO
E IL VAMPIRO DELLA PRATERIA
ALBO D'ORO N. 110
Prima ristampa - 30-5-1953
36 PAGINE - 50 LIRE

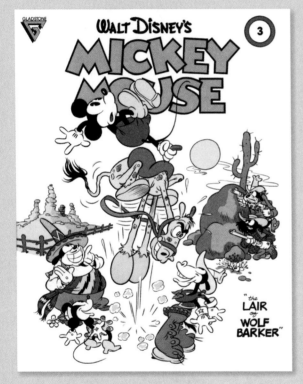

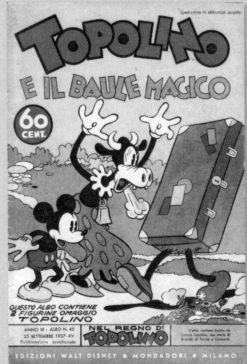

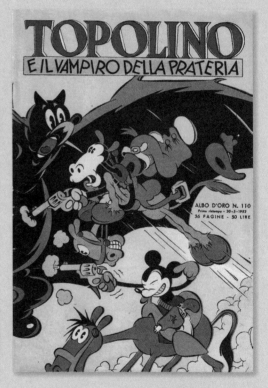

Gladstone Comic Album 3 (1987). Art by Daan Jippes; image courtesy Mike Matei.

Italian *Nel Regno Topolino* 45 (1937), illustrating "Lair of Wolf Barker." Art partly reinked from Gottfredson by Antonio and Michele Rubino; image courtesy Leonardo Gori.

Italian *Albo d'Oro* 48110 (1953), illustrating a mixed-up combination of "Lair of Wolf Barker" and Gottfredson's later "Bat Bandit of Inferno Gulch." Art by Floyd Gottfredson and Ambrogio Vergani; image courtesy The Walt Disney Company.

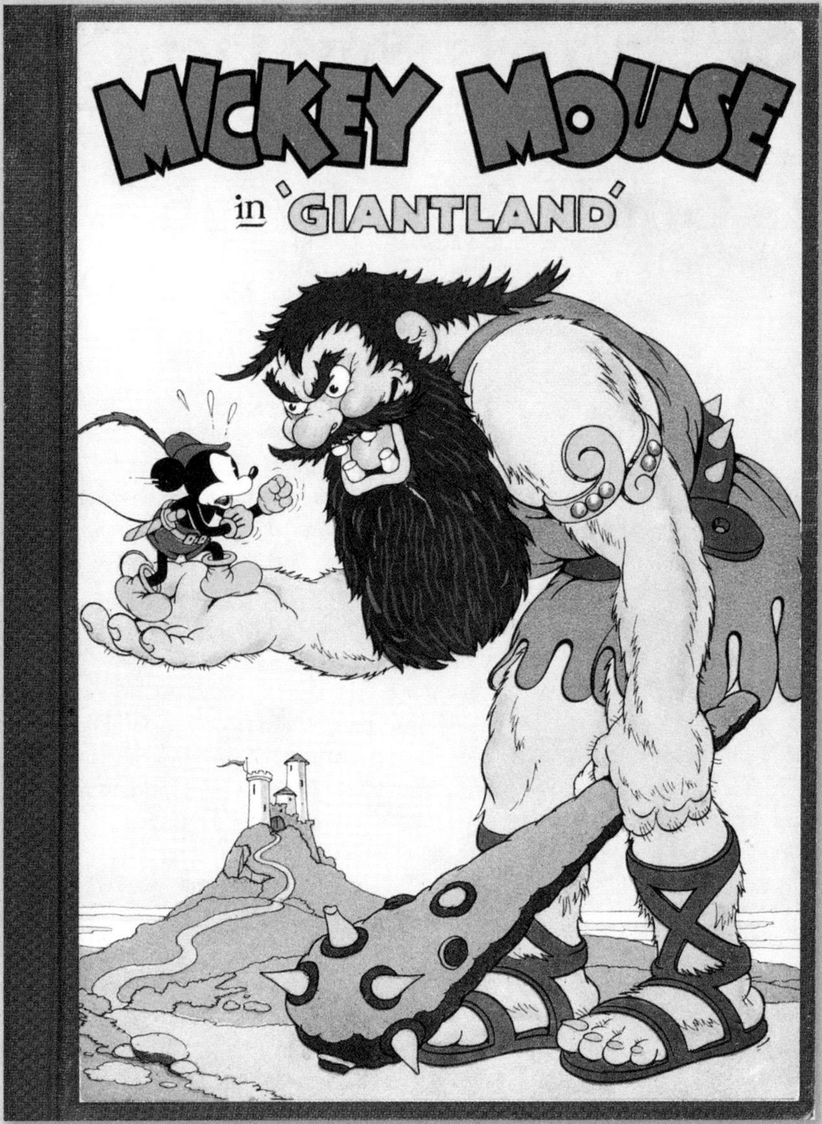
MICKEY MOUSE
in 'GIANTLAND'

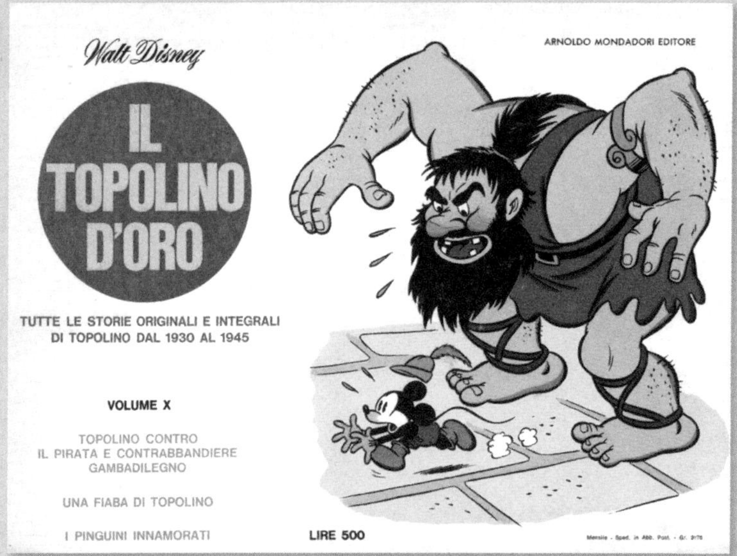
Walt Disney
ARNOLDO MONDADORI EDITORE
IL TOPOLINO D'ORO
TUTTE LE STORIE ORIGINALI E INTEGRALI
DI TOPOLINO DAL 1930 AL 1945
VOLUME X
TOPOLINO CONTRO
IL PIRATA E CONTRABBANDIERE
GAMBADILEGNO
UNA FIABA DI TOPOLINO
I PINGUINI INNAMORATI
LIRE 500

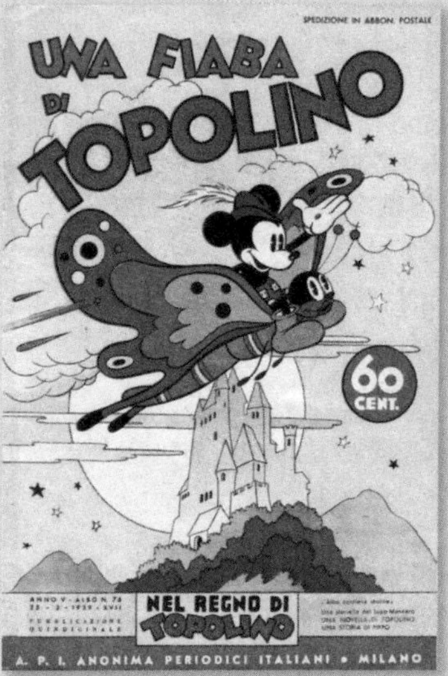
SPEDIZIONE IN ABBON. POSTALE
UNA FIABA DI TOPOLINO
60 CENT.
NEL REGNO DI TOPOLINO
A. P. I. ANONIMA PERIODICI ITALIANI • MILANO

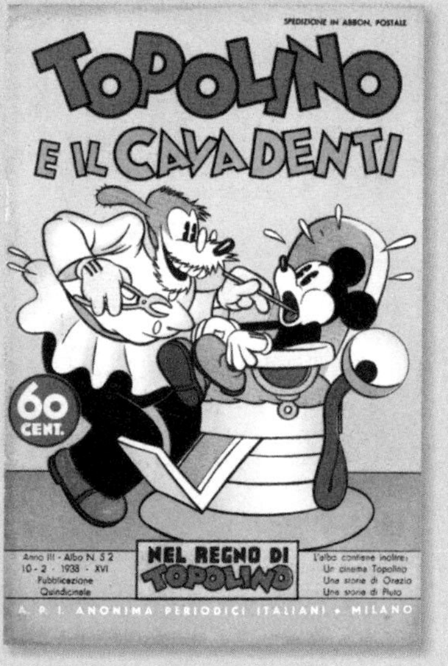
SPEDIZIONE IN ABBON. POSTALE
TOPOLINO E IL CAVADENTI
60 CENT.
Anno III - Albo N. 52
10 - 2 - 1938 - XVI
Pubblicazione
Quindicinale
NEL REGNO DI TOPOLINO
L'albo contiene inoltre:
Un cinema Topolino
Una storia di Orazio
Una storia di Pluto
A. P. I. ANONIMA PERIODICI ITALIANI • MILANO

David McKay hardback (1934), illustrating "Rumplewatt the Giant." Pencils attributed to Floyd Gottfredson, inks by Tom Wood.

Italian *Topolino d'oro* 10 (1971), illustrating "Rumplewatt the Giant." Art by Marco Rota; image courtesy Leonardo Gori.

Italian *Nel Regno Topolino* 76 (1939), illustrating "Rumplewatt the Giant." Art reinked from Gottfredson by Michele Rubino; image courtesy Leonardo Gori.

Italian *Nel Regno Topolino* 52 (1938), illustrating November 12, 1933 gag strip. Art reinked from Gottfredson by Michele Rubino; image courtesy Leonardo Gori.

Dippy Dawg Is Now Here

* * * * *Joins Mickey Mouse* * * * *

He's Got Unique Laugh

By IRENE CAVANAUGH

From the Los Angeles Illustrated Daily News, *June 3, 1932*

The Gottfredson Gang in "Their Own" Words

MICKEY AND HIS FRIENDS were box-office gold in the 1930s—thanks largely to their innovative character animation and sound. In the comics, however, Mickey had neither motion nor music. Popularity instead grew out of character complexity.

Case in point: when Dippy Dawg debuted in the funnies, he was cast as a pest full of eccentric hobbies and way-out ideas. On screen, by contrast, the future Goofy was just... goofy. He laughed; he acted yokel-like; but he would not gain depth for awhile.

How, then, to bridge the disparity between cartoons and comics? The answer lay in a masterful press campaign. Disney invited journalists to write mock-interviews with Mickey's gang, chronicling their more complex "private" lives: for instance, telling moviegoers that the offscreen Dippy was more nuanced than he looked. Then Gottfredson's strip could easily include those nuances.

1930s mock-interviews also invoked another Gottfredsonian nuance: Mickey's inability to get cultured. In the piece excerpted here, his trip to a celebrity astrologer leaves both parties seeing stars. [DG]

HARUMPH, harumph, harumph, harumph, harumph-hhh!"

If you hear a chorus of small boys disturbing the cinema capital with deep-throated and raucous laughter in this vein, do not imagine there is an epidemic of whooping cough on.

They are simply practicing the latest razz, the Dippy Dawg laugh, originated at the Walt Disney studios, which has already caught the fancy of the younger generation.

The laugh came into being with the creation of a new character in Mickey Mouse's hilarious company, which Walt Disney has christened Dippy Dawg.

But let's have Mickey Mouse himself tell us about this new aspirant for fame in sound cartoonland.

"Frequently of late we have been disturbed during our rehearsals preliminary to actual shooting by an unearthly laugh from the audience of animals that always assembles on such occasions," stated Mickey.

"Clarabelle Cow was greatly annoyed by it, and vainly tried to trace it to Horse Collar Horace, whom, as you doubtless know, came from the farm and has not yet lost all his uncouth ways, in spite of Clarabelle's efforts to reform him.

"But we soon decided Horse Collar was innocent, as I put my sweetheart, Minnie Mouse, to watch

[him under] observation on the set.[1]

"When members of the company [found the real culprit, approached] him when he was not actually [expecting it, and] dragged him into the open, he began to laugh. Such a guffaw you never heard before. It seemed to come direct from his Adam's apple. It was just such a laugh as you would expect from an ignorant country bumpkin, the village cutup, in other words.

"Mr. Disney, always on the outlook for new talent for our company, baited him into trying out his comedy on us. As proud of his accomplishments as any rube, he showed us how he could pitch peanuts into the air and catch them in his mouth.

"He was such a perfect specimen of the small town pest who thinks he is funny that Mr. Disney decided to give him a role in my company. You know the breed, the yapp that is always annoying the girls; the kind who wears a flower in his buttonhole with a tube attached to a squirt bulb in his pocket, or puts mucilage on the chairs at the country store.

"So Dippy Dawg is with us permanently. He is making his sound cartoon debut in our latest feature cartoon, titled *Mickey's Revue.*" •

1 Due to a printing error, several sentences in this article originally appeared incomplete. We have approximated the missing content as seems appropriate.

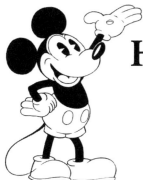

Here's My Horoscope, Folks!

* * * *

says Mickey Mouse

* * * *

Yes, Evangeline Adams does a real horoscope of Mickey, the boy wonder

MICKEY! STOP!
WHAT'S MORE, I CAN FIX THIS ONE FOR Y' SO IT'LL BE WORTH JUST AS MUCH AS THE OTHER!
Distributed by King Features Syndicate, Inc.

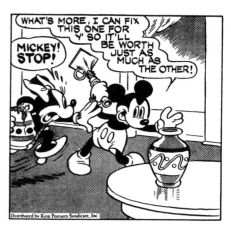

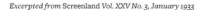

Excerpted from Screenland *Vol. XXV No. 3, January 1933*

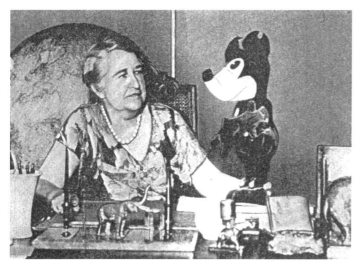

WHEN i was a youngster of two and a half or so, it was all right for me to live a gay, flibberty-gibbet sort of life, going out on all-night crumb-hunting parties, running around with kitchen-mousettes, and so on. But I reached my fourth birthday last October 1, and when a fellow gets to be four it's time he began to take life seriously.

I decided it would be a good idea to have my horoscope read, and find out just where I stood. Naturally I went to see Evangeline Adams, the famous astrologer, about it, so as to be sure of having it done right. Well, she went right to work to look up my stars; and it certainly is remarkable the way that lady can find out things about you! Talking about my popularity with the fans, Miss Adams said:

"While the fairies and Santa Claus have filled so important a part in the lives of children in the past, the trend of modern thinking is to discourage anything which does not have a physical form, and you are fortunate in being able to take the place of all the traditions of the past, as you have a very original, attractive and concrete form with which to meet the demands of the modern age."

Well, that's just about what I try to do in my work—to translate the fairy tale into modern terms, to be a sort of new "Puss in Boots" adapted to the jazz age. Take those "curiouser and curiouser" things that happened to Alice in Wonderland—wouldn't it have been even more exciting to see these fantastic things happen right before your eyes in the movies?

But I'm getting away from Miss Adams' reading. "There is everything to indicate that your influence will be felt in the far corners of the world," she continued, "and that you can be of far greater power than any of your rivals in the fable world."

All right with me! But say, wait a minute—aren't the stars going to smile on my romantic hopes? I'm engaged to Minnie Mouse, you know, and that little gal means more to me than anything else in the world. But listen to what Evangeline Adams says about that:

"Your father (meaning Walt Disney, of course) has shown great wisdom in not allowing you to become involved in anything matrimonial. For the position of Mars would bring you disaster unless you travel in single harness."

Oh, yeah? Well, we'll see about that! Career or no career, I'm going to have my Minnie some day, and if anybody tries to stop us you'll be reading about one of those airplane elopements to Yuma, Arizona. Meaning no disrespect to Miss Adams, of course; but if the stars don't encourage my romance it'll have to get along without their encouragement, that's all. •

LEFT: Evangeline Adams (1868-1932), "America's first astrological superstar," passed away shortly before her Mickey tie-in appeared. This photo was specially arranged for *Screenland*.

ABOVE: Just as Mickey lost patience with Adams' highfalutin advice, he reaches his limit with Minnie's antiques expertise in Gottfredson's "Miracle Master" (September 14, 1939).

Mickey's 1934 Sunday sagas took him deep into the Mouseton hinterlands—where North American cover artists feared to tread, but Disney's Italian talent bravely forged ahead. From mad science with Dr. Oofgay to cliff-climbing calamities, everything was covered. [DG]

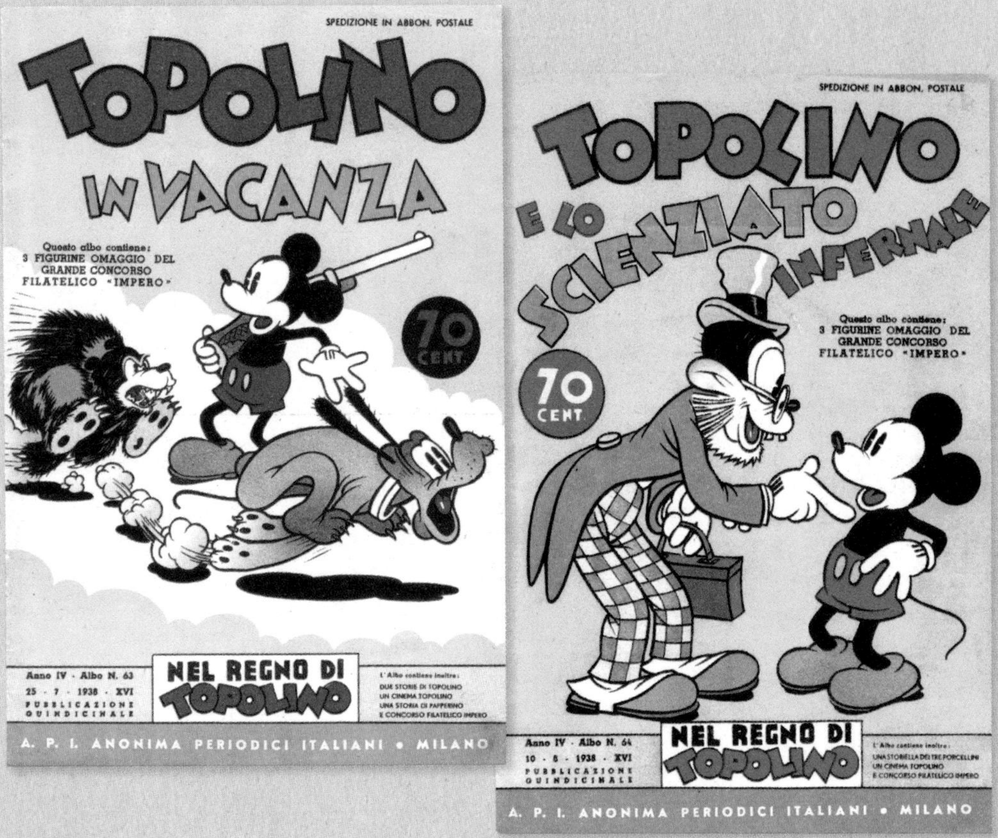
SPEDIZIONE IN ABBON. POSTALE
TOPOLINO
IN VACANZA
Questo albo contiene: 3 FIGURINE OMAGGIO DEL GRANDE CONCORSO FILATELICO «IMPERO»
70 CENT.
Anno IV - Albo N. 63
25 - 7 - 1938 - XVI
PUBBLICAZIONI QUINDICINALI
NEL REGNO DI TOPOLINO
A. P. I. ANONIMA PERIODICI ITALIANI • MILANO
SPEDIZIONE IN ABBON. POSTALE
TOPOLINO
E LO SCIENZIATO INFERNALE
70 CENT.
Questo albo contiene: 3 FIGURINE OMAGGIO DEL GRANDE CONCORSO FILATELICO «IMPERO»
Anno IV - Albo N. 64
10 - 8 - 1938 - XVI
PUBBLICAZIONI QUINDICINALI
NEL REGNO DI TOPOLINO
A. P. I. ANONIMA PERIODICI ITALIANI • MILANO

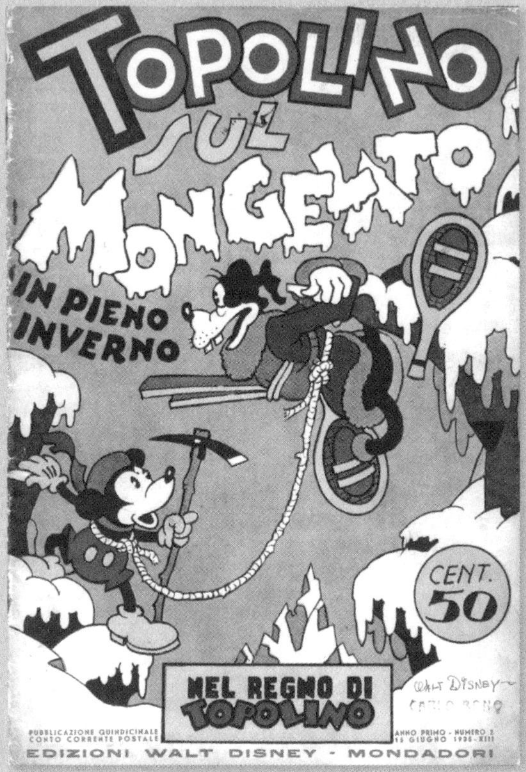
TOPOLINO
SUL MONGELATO
IN PIENO INVERNO
CENT. 50
NEL REGNO DI TOPOLINO
WALT DISNEY
PUBBLICAZIONE QUINDICINALE
CONTO CORRENTE POSTALE
EDIZIONI WALT DISNEY - MONDADORI

LEFT: Italian *Nel Regno di Topolino* 63 and 64 (1938), illustrating "Dr. Oofgay's Secret Serum." Art reinked from Gottfredson by Michele Rubino; images courtesy Leonardo Gori.

RIGHT: Italian *Nel Regno di Topolino* 2 (1935), illustrating "Foray to Mount Fishflake." Art by Antonio Rubino; image courtesy Leonardo Gori.

Behind the Scenes: INTERIOR DECORATORS

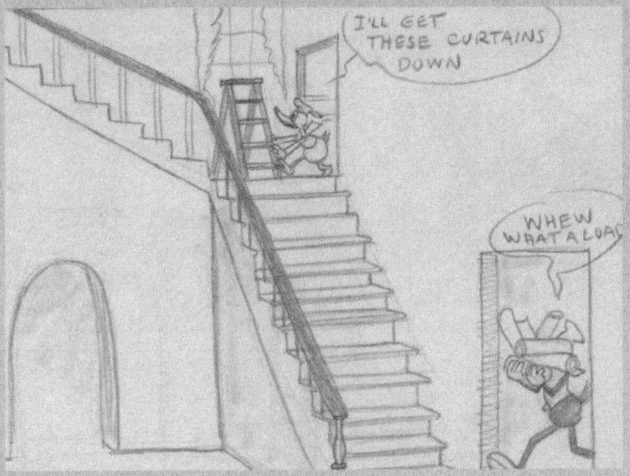

As J. B. Kaufman explains in this volume's foreword, Disney's unfinished cartoon "Spring Cleaning" inspired several *Mickey Mouse* Sunday strips. With "Interior Decorators"—a spin-off short that was also shelved—the creative process went the other way.

Here's how story man Homer Brightman planned to turn the October 21, 1934 *Mickey* strip (see page 174) into a Goofy gag for "Decorators." It's an intriguing look at the creative process—because retooling a Mickey scene for Goofy involved more than just trading one character for another.

Mickey, after all, is an intent, focused mouse. In the strip, he makes a clumsy mistake less because he's a klutz, more because he's a little *too* driven and focused on his task. Goofy, by contrast, plays the gag as the klutz to end all klutzes. Walking through a windowpane... gawrsh!

Images courtesy Walt Disney Feature Animation Research Library; special thanks to Fox Carney. [DG]

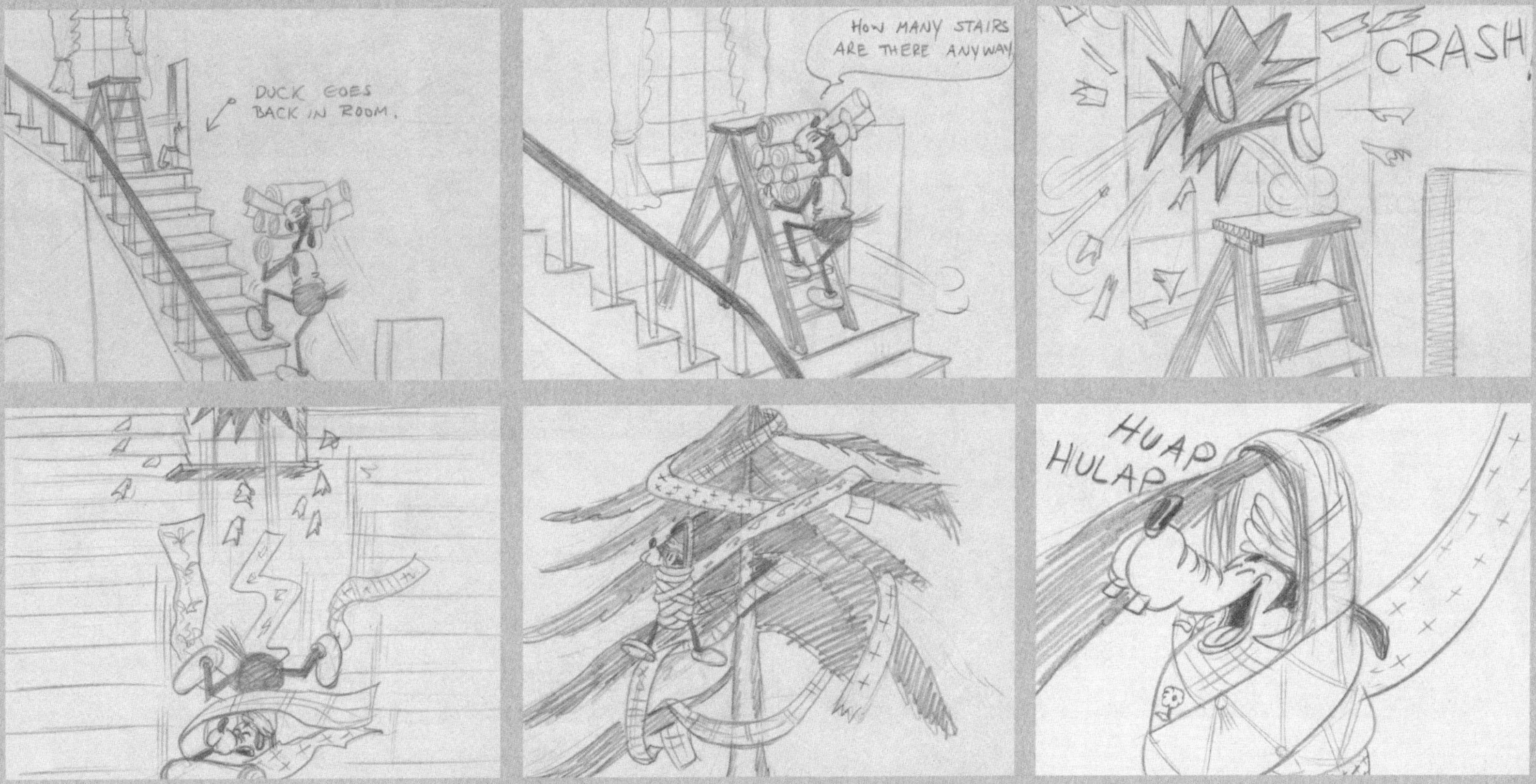

"*Wrapping Up*" THE CASE OF THE VANISHING COATS

As one of Gottfredson's few major Mickey/Donald team-ups, "Case of the Vanishing Coats" (1935) has seen many a reprint over the years. In *Donald Duck* 286 (1994), Donald's 60th birthday issue, "Coats" and other Duck-centric classics were wrapped in a new frame story by William Van Horn. It it, "Birthday Boy" Donald experiences the vintage tales as nightmares after too many ice cream sundaes! Here's how "Vanishing Coats" was interpolated—complete with a rare in-story reference to Donald's evolving beak length. [DG]

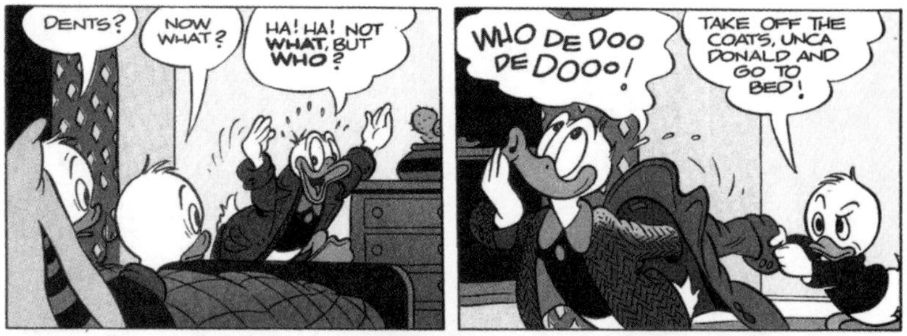
DENTS?
NOW WHAT?
HA! HA! NOT WHAT, BUT WHO?
WHO DE DOO DE DOOo!
TAKE OFF THE COATS, UNCA DONALD AND GO TO BED!

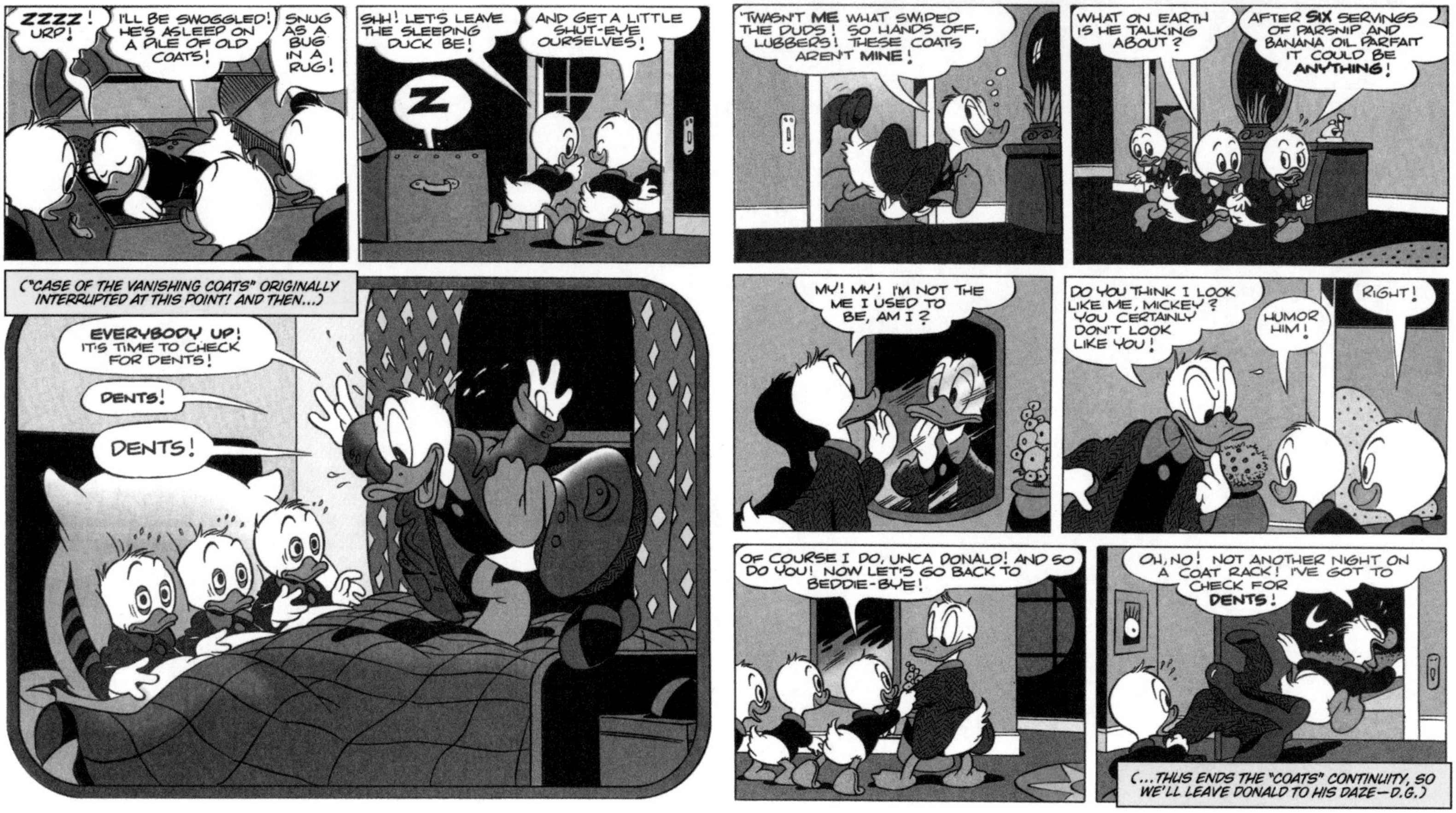
ZZZZ! URP!
I'LL BE SWOGGLED! HE'S ASLEEP ON A PILE OF OLD COATS!
SNUG AS A BUG IN A RUG!
SHH! LET'S LEAVE THE SLEEPING DUCK BE!
AND GET A LITTLE SHUT-EYE OURSELVES!
Z
("CASE OF THE VANISHING COATS" ORIGINALLY INTERRUPTED AT THIS POINT! AND THEN...)
EVERYBODY UP! IT'S TIME TO CHECK FOR DENTS!
DENTS!
DENTS!
'TWASN'T ME WHAT SWIPED THE DUDS! SO HANDS OFF, LUBBERS! THESE COATS AREN'T MINE!
WHAT ON EARTH IS HE TALKING ABOUT?
AFTER SIX SERVINGS OF PARSNIP AND BANANA OIL PARFAIT IT COULD BE ANYTHING!
MY! MY! I'M NOT THE ME I USED TO BE, AM I?
DO YOU THINK I LOOK LIKE ME, MICKEY? YOU CERTAINLY DON'T LOOK LIKE YOU!
HUMOR HIM!
RIGHT!
OF COURSE I DO, UNCA DONALD! AND SO DO YOU! NOW LET'S GO BACK TO BEDDIE-BYE!
OH, NO! NOT ANOTHER NIGHT ON A COAT RACK! I'VE GOT TO CHECK FOR DENTS!
(...THUS ENDS THE "COATS" CONTINUITY, SO WE'LL LEAVE DONALD TO HIS DAZE—D.G.)

"The Case of the Vanishing Coats" has been a comic book perennial—but very few magazines have reflected its inclusion on the cover. On a similarly odd note, another early magazine featured vintage 1935 Donald strips... but treated Morty and Ferdie as the cover stars. Maybe the mischievous nephews simply tricked Donald into standing "off-camera"? [DG]

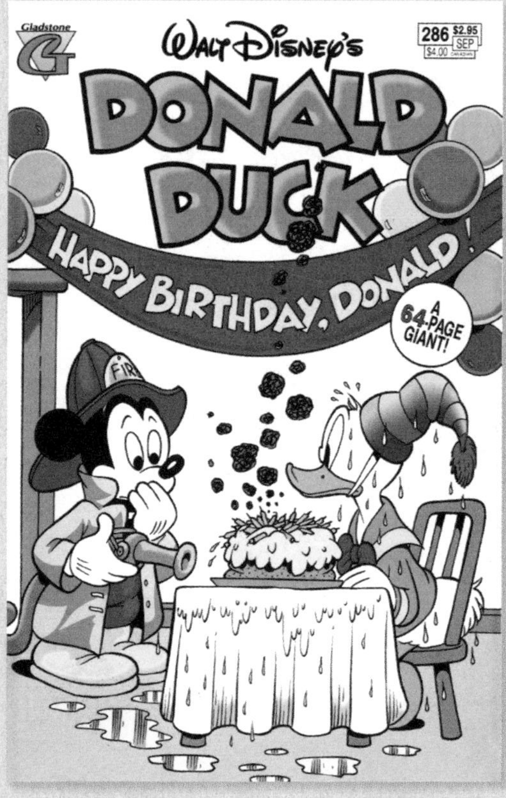
Gladstone
WALT DISNEY'S
DONALD DUCK
286 $2.95 SEP
$4.00
HAPPY BIRTHDAY, DONALD!
A 64-PAGE GIANT!

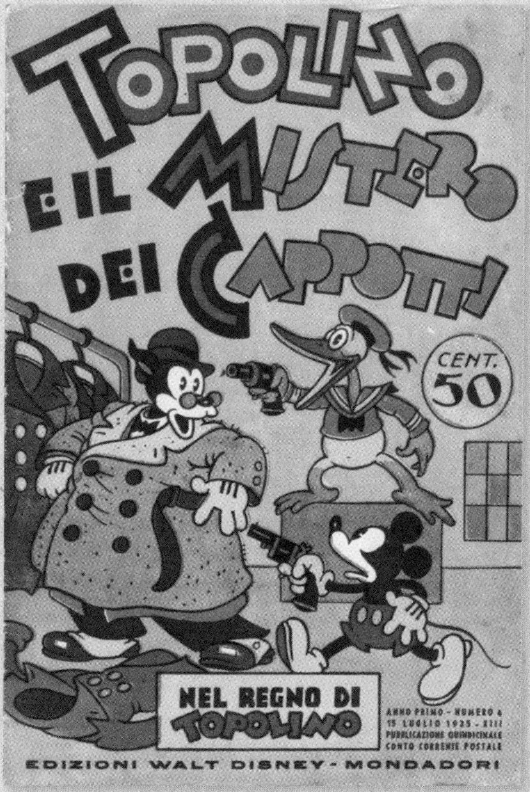
TOPOLINO
E IL MISTERO
DEI CAPPOTTI
CENT. 50
NEL REGNO DI
TOPOLINO
ANNO PRIMO - NUMERO 4
15 LUGLIO 1935 - XIII
PUBBLICAZIONE QUINDICINALE
CONTO CORRENTE POSTALE
EDIZIONI WALT DISNEY - MONDADORI

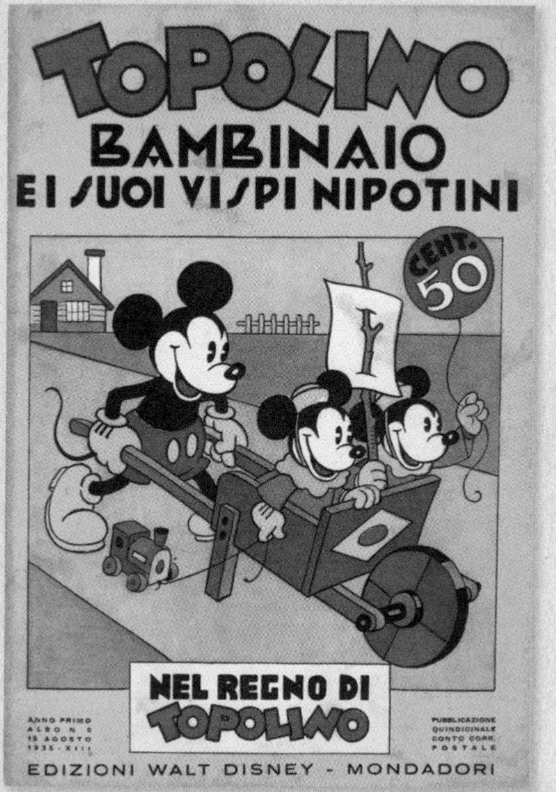
TOPOLINO
BAMBINAIO
E I SUOI VISPI NIPOTINI
CENT. 50
NEL REGNO DI
TOPOLINO
PUBBLICAZIONE
QUINDICINALE
CONTO CORR.
POSTALE
EDIZIONI WALT DISNEY - MONDADORI

LEFT: *Donald Duck* 286 (1994), illustrating "Case of the Vanishing Coats" and its modern frame story (see opposite). Art by William Van Horn; image courtesy Thomas Jensen.

MIDDLE: Italian *Nel Regno di Topolino* 4 (1935), illustrating "Case of the Vanishing Coats." Art by Antonio Rubino; image courtesy Leonardo Gori.

RIGHT: Italian *Nel Regno di Topolino* 6 (1935), illustrating the March 31, 1935 gag strip. Art by Antonio Rubino; image courtesy Leonardo Gori.

A marsupial—er, *super serial* like "Hoppy" was destined to receive a super bunch of dedicated cobbers... uh, *covers*. As local reprints piled up, fans got *bushed* trying to grab them all for a *fair dinkum*—er, a fair *price*. (Whew.)

The 'roo's most prized reprint was his first one, published in his biological country of origin: Australia! Disney's kangaroo "star" was so popular down under that he received Mickey's first story-specific comic book cover in that country.

The art shows Hoppy having such a *g'day* that he doesn't even notice the mysterious joey in his pouch—a character from the *Mickey's Kangaroo* (1935) cartoon who isn't actually in Gottfredson's comic! [DG]

MICKEY'S KANGAROO
by WALT DISNEY.
© COPYRIGHT WALT DISNEY
PRINTED & PUBLISHED BY JOHN SANDS LTD., SYDNEY

GLADSTONE
WALT DISNEY'S
GLADSTONE COMIC ALBUM SERIES
8
MICKEY MOUSE
"HOPPY THE KANGAROO"

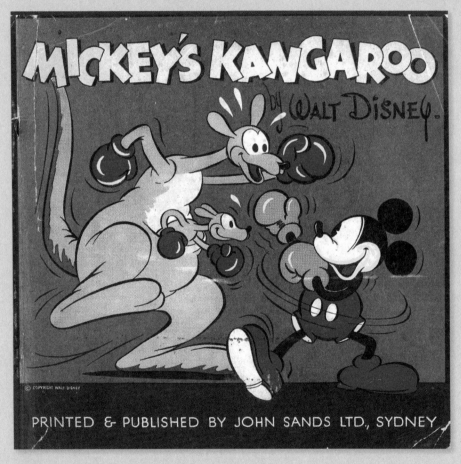

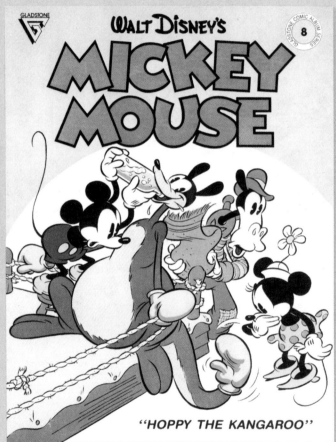

LEFT: Australian *Mickey Mouse* unnumbered issue (1935: the fourth Disney comic by publisher John Sands). Image courtesy Ricky Turner and Kosta Labropoulos.

RIGHT: *Gladstone Comic Album* 8 (1987). Art by Daan Jippes; image courtesy Thomas Jensen.

THE HEIRS OF GOTTFREDSON:
TOPOLINO

» BY SERGIO LAMA AND DAVID GERSTEIN

FLOYD GOTTFREDSON didn't create his first *Mickey Mouse* Sunday pages until 1932; yet as early as 1931, he was exerting a major, exciting influence on long-form, weekly Mickey Mouse comic strips. But how?

The answer becomes clear when we look at the strips' target market: Italy. In Italy, Disney's publishing activities bloomed faster than in the United States; in Italy, Gottfredson managed to affect local audiences *before* they had actually seen his work. For in Italy, and Italy alone, Gottfredson's "heirs"— local talents who carried on his style—actually beat him to a spot on the newsstand! This is their fascinating story.

Mickey Mouse was a film character first. Over his initial few years in Italian cinemas, Disney's big-eared star found ever-growing popularity, thanks in no small part to Sunday matinee shows for children. The same story was playing out in theatres around the world. The cartoons themselves were becoming increasingly sophisticated, and their success could be defined as global.

The same cannot be said for Mickey's comics debut. When January 1930 brought the first daily strips into print, they initially appeared in just a

small number of American newspapers. That number would increase exponentially after May, when Gottfredson began work on the series. But until then, King Features Syndicate—and its magnate CEO William Randolph Hearst—almost had to force client papers to jump on the bandwagon.

The strip had a similarly rough start in Italy. Lorenzo Gigli, an editor with the *Gazzetta del Popolo* ("People's Gazette") newspaper, published "Lost on a Desert Island" (1930), the initial pre-Gottfredson serial. It was Gigli who gave Mickey his famous Italian name of *Topolino* ("little mouse"). But Gigli dulled the serial's impact by printing the strips out of order and only once a week. After 1930, Gigli dropped *Topolino* from the *Gazzetta* entirely. Perhaps he considered the strip a flop; regardless, he never gave Gottfredson a chance to make his debut.

What next? After being dumped by the *Gazzetta*, *Mickey Mouse* might have been hard for King to resell elsewhere in Italy—Gottfredson notwithstanding. Unless, perhaps, the strip was rebooted as a totally different-looking product. But how different could it become? Quite a bit, actually...

From April 16 to August 13, 1931, the newspaper *Il Popolo di Roma* ("The People of Rome") published a weekly, long-form Mickey Mouse comic strip on its children's page. But it was not the American *Mickey*. This new product was created for *Il Popolo* by **Guglielmo Guastaveglia** (1889-1984), a well-known

Mickey sings for Minnie's sake
An aria sweet as chocolate cake.
While Minnie, poised at window, rests
And dreams of love's togetherness.

local gag cartoonist. Yet it was nevertheless authorized by Disney via King Features, as indicated by an "exclusively for Italy" notice beneath each strip.[1]

Guglielmo Guastaveglia brought decades of comics training to *Il Popolo* and Mickey. He had earlier been an editor, writer, and director for various popular humor journals; he worked a twenty-year stretch with *Travaso delle Idee* ("The Transfer of Ideas"), a comic weekly launched at the turn of the century.

Guastaveglia's first Mickey pages took an artisanal approach that reflected this past experience. Settings were typically Italian in design. Rhyming narration—another Italian tradition—usually replaced voice balloon dialogue. Gags showed Mickey outwitting a black cat reminiscent of Felix the Cat; the Otto Messmer character, while not a Disney brand, was another King-licensed property.[2]

Three weeks in, someone evidently cried foul. Either Disney or Italian King representative

RIGHT: From Guglielmo Guastaveglia's first *Topolino* strip (Italian *Il Popolo di Roma*, April 16, 1931). Image courtesy The Walt Disney Company.

NO MATTER WHAT HAPPENS, MINNIE- YOU MUST STICK CLOSE TO ME!
PLOP!
5 15

WELL, IF I CAN'T KEEP THE KNOTS IN HIS TAIL AFTER I TIE 'EM, I'LL FIX IT SO HE WON'T DARE WEAR IT IN PUBLIC!
WHITE ENAMEL

ABOVE: Guastaveglia copied a few Gottfredson scenes directly; compare strips on the following pages with these panels from May 15, 1930 (LEFT) and February 16, 1931 (RIGHT). Italy's concept of cartoon slapstick was broader: whereas Gottfredson's Mickey merely paints Kat Nipp's tail, Guasta's Mickey cuts it clean off with no harm done.

OPPOSITE AND PAGES *276-278:* early Mickey strips by Gottfredson's Italian "heirs." In chronological order: Guastaveglia strips from *Il Popolo di Roma*, May 14 and 21, June 4 and 18, July 9 and 26, 1931; Toppi strip from *Topolino* 1 (1932); Burattini strip from *Topolino* 7 (1933). Guastaveglia material courtesy Sergio Lama; Toppi courtesy The Walt Disney Company; Burattini courtesy David Gerstein. American dialogue by David Gerstein.

Guglielmo Emanuel sacked the faux Felix, then supplied Guastaveglia with Gottfredson and Win Smith photostats for future reference use.[3] Details of Guastaveglia's later Disney strips—a character pose here, a borrowed gag there—reveal that the artist carefully studied these American dailies, none yet published in Italy. Then he combined their flavor with his own.

The results seem to have been a success. *Il Popolo* gave Mickey a short run similar to the *Gazzetta*—but devoted far more space to him, suggesting greater acceptance. More importantly, in a land where no one knew "real" Gottfredson, Guastaveglia gave readers their first taste of Gottfredson's style. Guastaveglia's Mickey still cavorted though Italian backdrops, including soccer games (May 28) and a deli selling Parmesan cheese (May 21). But Mickey's peers were now Gottfredson-style dogs and pigs; his new enemy was Kat Nipp, a formidable foe from 1931 Gottfredson daily strips.[4] And their ensuing hijinks actually did Gottfredson one better. Guastaveglia began to feature escalating gags and fairly complicated setups: the kind that Gottfredson, in 1931, could not have put across in a four-panel daily strip.

In his antiquated, rhyming, Rome-centric way, Guglielmo Guastaveglia directly anticipated the Gottfredson Sunday strips to come.

Guastaveglia also anticipated later Italian events. In fall 1932, *Il Popolo*'s run had long since ended; and for the moment, there was no Disney comics presence in the country. A new publisher, Florence-based Casa Editrice Nerbini, decided to issue an entire Mickey *magazine* without Disney or King Features involvement—and without, as it happened, Gottfredson inspiration. Nerbini's *Topolino* 1 (1932) paired Mickey not with Minnie or Kat Nipp, but with a nonhumanized elephant that he mercilessly pranked. Some Guastaveglia influence was visible; Gottfredson influence was not.

The elephant-fighting Mickey, drawn by **Giove Toppi** (1888-1942), never got to evolve like Guastaveglia's. King and Disney understandably objected to the unlicensed magazine. In an effort to avoid further offense, Nerbini briefly replaced Topolino with "Topo Lino" ("Lino Mouse"), an entirely different-looking rodent.

Then a deal was struck. Nerbini became an authorized King Features partner, allowing the legitimate use of Mickey. Disney took ownership of Nerbini's earlier mouse material—even Topo Lino—and all its original Disney content going forward. Toppi and colleague **Angelo Burattini** (1891-1969) continued to draw occasional Mickey strips for Nerbini. But the "main" Disney artist in *Topolino* was now Gottfredson, who at last had a regular Italian showcase for his work—starting with many of this volume's Sunday strips.

Guglielmo Guastaveglia was Gottfredson's first Italian "heir"; Toppi and Burattini functioned more like stepping stones to later, greater successors. Yet oddly important stepping stones they were. For without their efforts, famous future heirs like Romano Scarpa might have had no Disney comics line to work for! •

1 Mark Johnson (Archivist, King Features Syndicate), conversations with David Gerstein, December 2012. Period documentation does not survive at King, but the pattern matches King's sublicensing of other comics features in Europe at the time.

2 Perhaps Guastaveglia mistook Felix for a Disney character; the somewhat Felixlike Julius the Cat was a featured player in silent era Disney cartoons. The 2005 American edition of one Guastaveglia Mickey strip interprets Guastaveglia's cat as Julius.

3 Johnson to Gerstein, *ibid.*

4 Kat Nipp, called *Maramao* by Guastaveglia, would wait five years before Italian audiences saw him in Gottfredson's hand (in *Nel Regno di Topolino* 17, 1936).

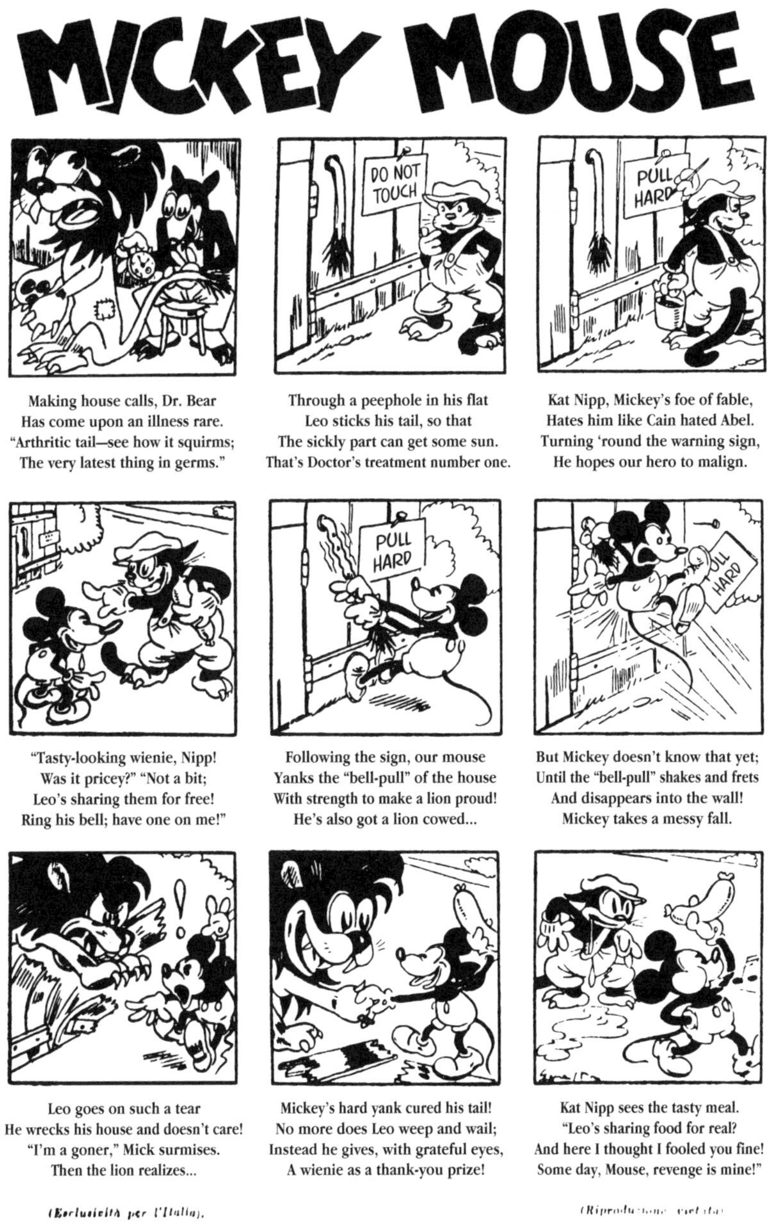
MICKEY MOUSE
Making house calls, Dr. Bear
Has come upon an illness rare.
"Arthritic tail—see how it squirms;
The very latest thing in germs."
DO NOT TOUCH
Through a peephole in his flat
Leo sticks his tail, so that
The sickly part can get some sun.
That's Doctor's treatment number one.
PULL HARD
Kat Nipp, Mickey's foe of fable,
Hates him like Cain hated Abel.
Turning 'round the warning sign,
He hopes our hero to malign.
"Tasty-looking wienie, Nipp!
Was it pricey?" "Not a bit;
Leo's sharing them for free!
Ring his bell; have one on me!"
PULL HARD
Following the sign, our mouse
Yanks the "bell-pull" of the house
With strength to make a lion proud!
He's also got a lion cowed...
HARD
But Mickey doesn't know that yet;
Until the "bell-pull" shakes and frets
And disappears into the wall!
Mickey takes a messy fall.
!
Leo goes on such a tear
He wrecks his house and doesn't care!
"I'm a goner," Mick surmises.
Then the lion realizes...
Mickey's hard yank cured his tail!
No more does Leo weep and wail;
Instead he gives, with grateful eyes,
A wienie as a thank-you prize!
Kat Nipp sees the tasty meal.
"Leo's sharing food for real?
And here I thought I fooled you fine!
Some day, Mouse, revenge is mine!"
(Esclusività per l'Italia).

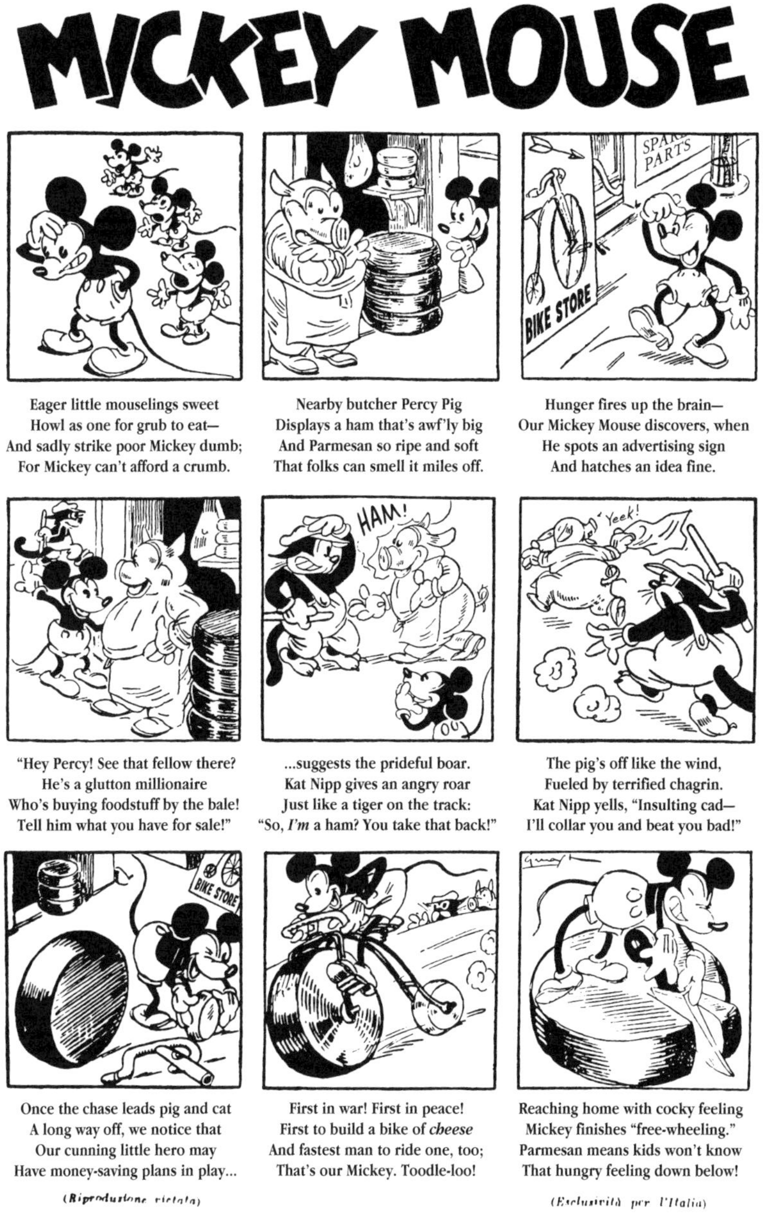
MICKEY MOUSE
Eager little mouselings sweet
Howl as one for grub to eat—
And sadly strike poor Mickey dumb;
For Mickey can't afford a crumb.
Nearby butcher Percy Pig
Displays a ham that's awf'ly big
And Parmesan so ripe and soft
That folks can smell it miles off.
PARTS
BIKE STORE
Hunger fires up the brain—
Our Mickey Mouse discovers, when
He spots an advertising sign
And hatches an idea fine.
"Hey Percy! See that fellow there?
He's a glutton millionaire
Who's buying foodstuff by the bale!
Tell him what you have for sale!"
HAM!
...suggests the prideful boar.
Kat Nipp gives an angry roar
Just like a tiger on the track:
"So, *I'm* a ham? You take that back!"
Yeek!
The pig's off like the wind,
Fueled by terrified chagrin.
Kat Nipp yells, "Insulting cad—
I'll collar you and beat you bad!"
BIKE STORE
Once the chase leads pig and cat
A long way off, we notice that
Our cunning little hero may
Have money-saving plans in play...
(Riproduzione vietata)
First in war! First in peace!
First to build a bike of *cheese*
And fastest man to ride one, too;
That's our Mickey. Toodle-loo!
Reaching home with cocky feeling
Mickey finishes "free-wheeling."
Parmesan means kids won't know
That hungry feeling down below!
(Esclusività per l'Italia)

—CONTINUED ON PAGE 276

MERRY CHRISTMAS

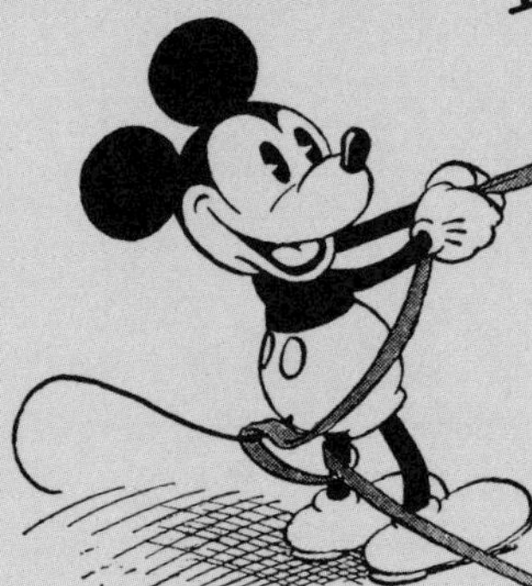

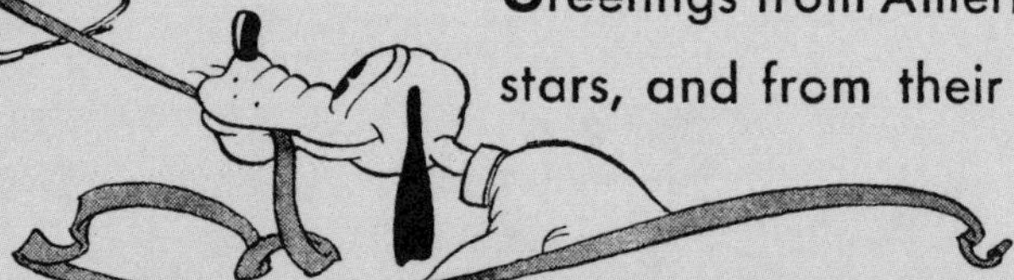

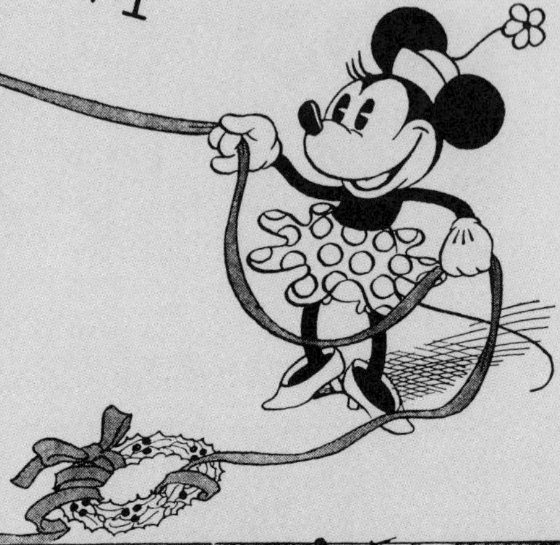

from

MICKEY AND MINNIE MOUSE

Greetings from America's most popular movie stars, and from their creator **WALT DISNEY**

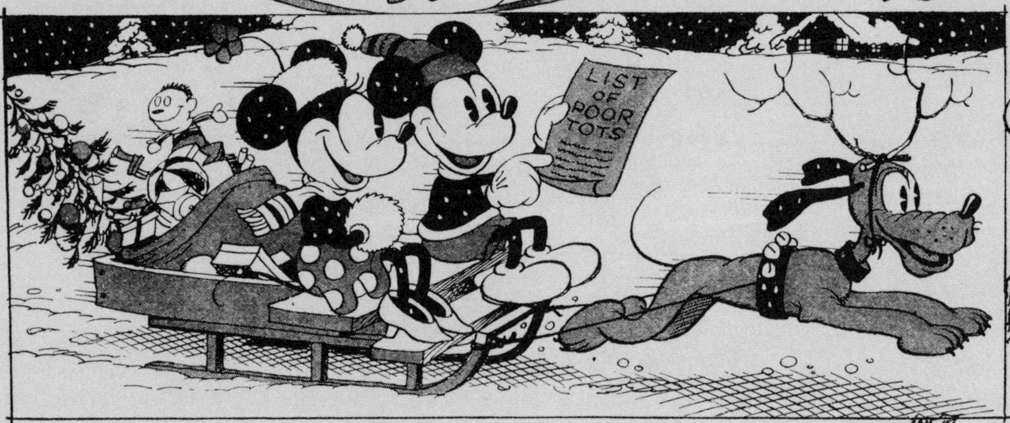
LIST OF POOR TOTS

1. "See, Minnie," said Mickey, "I've made up a list
Of children that Santa Claus probably missed!"

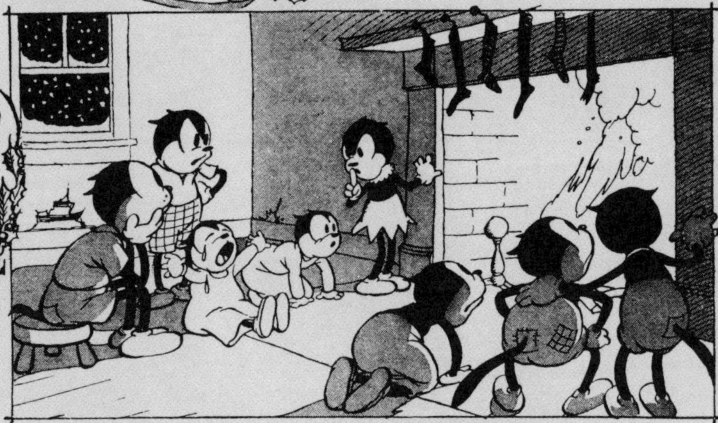

2. Tattered and starved, at the end of their rope,
These poor kids had naught in their tummies but—hope!

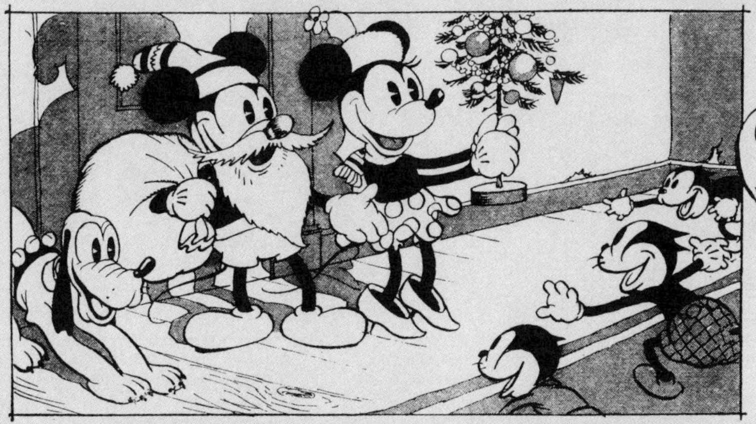

3. When suddenly, laughing and shouting, "SURPRISE!" Mickey and Minnie appeared in disguise.

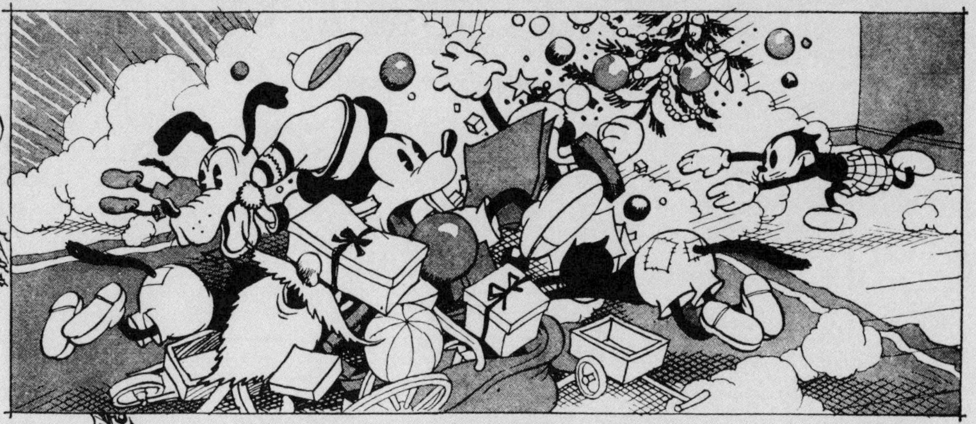

4. "Whoopee!" "It's Santa Claus!" "Look at the toys!" And they were submerged by a deluge of boys.

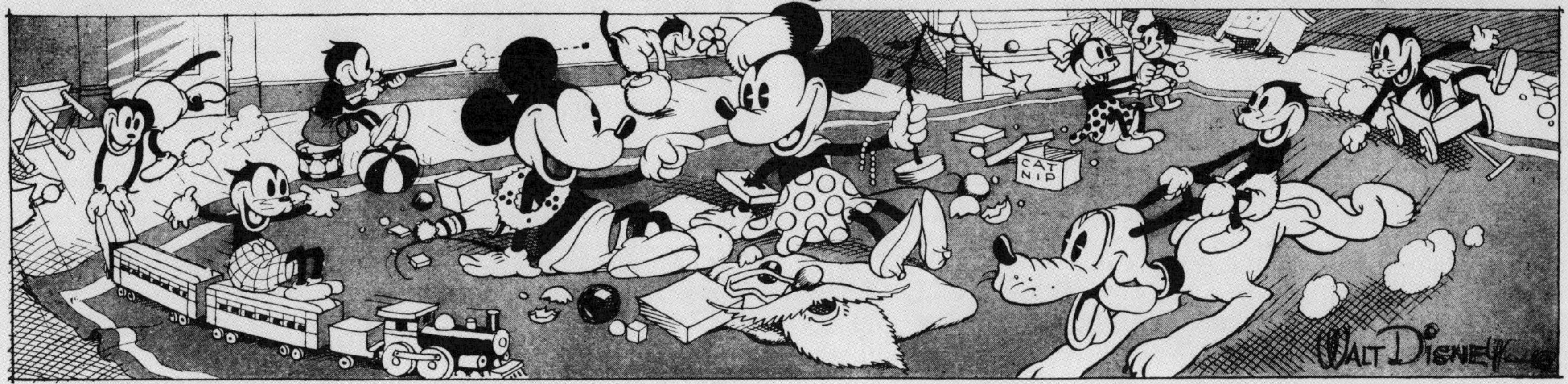
CAT NIP
WALT DISNEY

5. Said Mickey: "This proves it! I really believe That it is more blessed to give than receive."

6. "These toys will be wrecked and forgotten, I'll bet, But the pleasure WE'VE had, we will NEVER forget!"

Turnabout is fair play. American Disney staffers mimicked the Italian comics style—complete with text under the panels!—when Gottfredson's Comic Strip Department produced this special Christmas strip for *The Delineator* magazine (1932). Image courtesy David Gerstein.

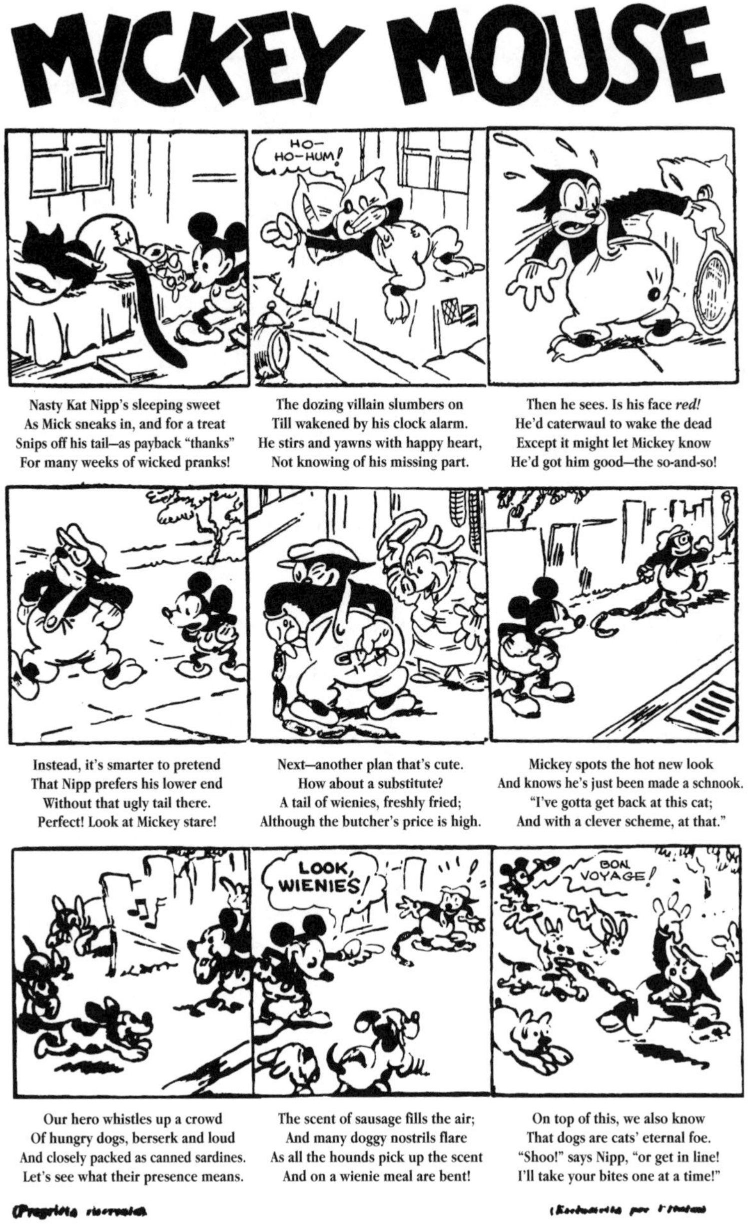
MICKEY MOUSE
HO-HO-HUM!
Nasty Kat Nipp's sleeping sweet
As Mick sneaks in, and for a treat
Snips off his tail—as payback "thanks"
For many weeks of wicked pranks!
The dozing villain slumbers on
Till wakened by his clock alarm.
He stirs and yawns with happy heart,
Not knowing of his missing part.
Then he sees. Is his face *red!*
He'd caterwaul to wake the dead
Except it might let Mickey know
He'd got him good—the so-and-so!
Instead, it's smarter to pretend
That Nipp prefers his lower end
Without that ugly tail there.
Perfect! Look at Mickey stare!
Next—another plan that's cute.
How about a substitute?
A tail of wienies, freshly fried;
Although the butcher's price is high.
Mickey spots the hot new look
And knows he's just been made a schnook.
"I've gotta get back at this cat;
And with a clever scheme, at that."
LOOK, WIENIES!
BON VOYAGE!
Our hero whistles up a crowd
Of hungry dogs, berserk and loud
And closely packed as canned sardines.
Let's see what their presence means.
The scent of sausage fills the air;
And many doggy nostrils flare
As all the hounds pick up the scent
And on a wienie meal are bent!
On top of this, we also know
That dogs are cats' eternal foe.
"Shoo!" says Nipp, "or get in line!
I'll take your bites one at a time!"

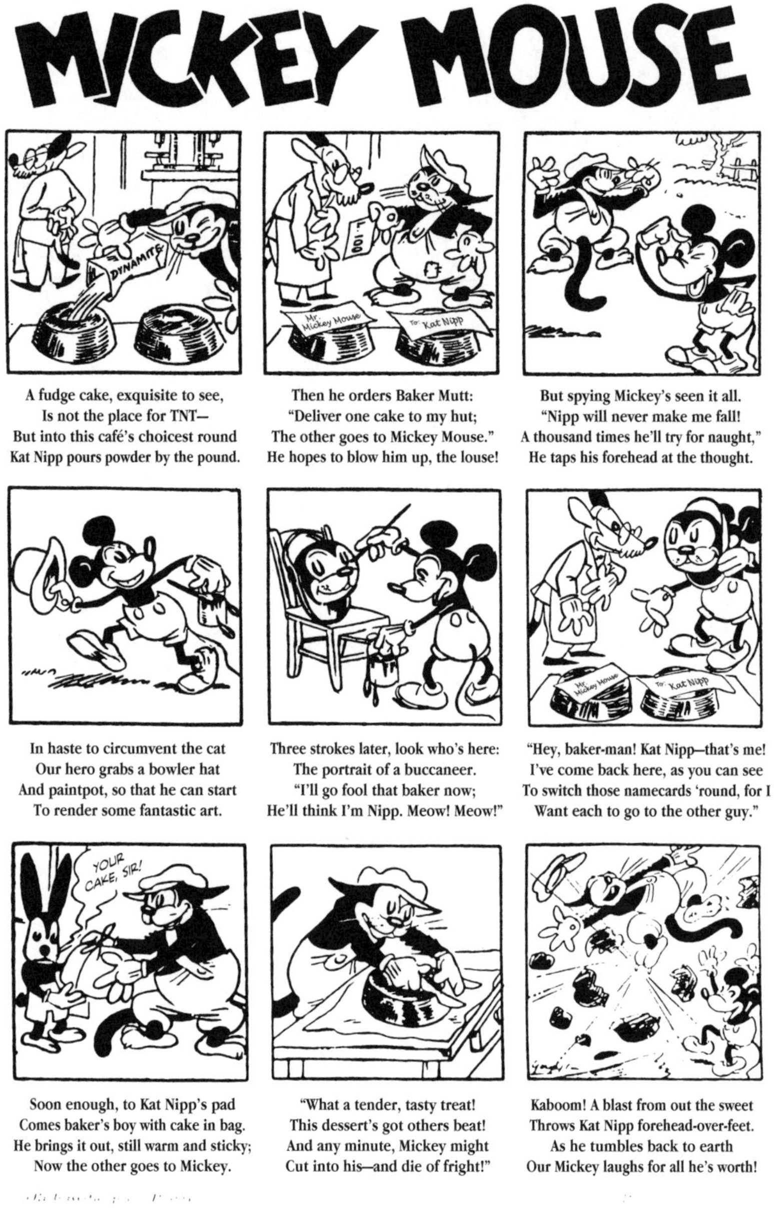
MICKEY MOUSE
DYNAMITE
Mr. Mickey Mouse
To: Kat Nipp
A fudge cake, exquisite to see,
Is not the place for TNT—
But into this café's choicest round
Kat Nipp pours powder by the pound.
Then he orders Baker Mutt:
"Deliver one cake to my hut;
The other goes to Mickey Mouse."
He hopes to blow him up, the louse!
But spying Mickey's seen it all.
"Nipp will never make me fall!
A thousand times he'll try for naught,"
He taps his forehead at the thought.
In haste to circumvent the cat
Our hero grabs a bowler hat
And paintpot, so that he can start
To render some fantastic art.
Three strokes later, look who's here:
The portrait of a buccaneer.
"I'll go fool that baker now;
He'll think I'm Nipp. Meow! Meow!"
Mr. Mickey Mouse
To: Kat Nipp
"Hey, baker-man! Kat Nipp—that's me!
I've come back here, as you can see
To switch those namecards 'round, for I
Want each to go to the other guy."
YOUR CAKE, SIR!
Soon enough, to Kat Nipp's pad
Comes baker's boy with cake in bag.
He brings it out, still warm and sticky;
Now the other goes to Mickey.
"What a tender, tasty treat!
This dessert's got others beat!
And any minute, Mickey might
Cut into his—and die of fright!"
Kaboom! A blast from out the sweet
Throws Kat Nipp forehead-over-feet.
As he tumbles back to earth
Our Mickey laughs for all he's worth!

MICKEY MOUSE

"What's your answer, Minnie girl:
Is any cyclist in the world
As safe and fast and slick as me?
Ha! Such a biker couldn't be!"

"The rocky road may dip and slope;
But on my bike you needn't mope.
Sit back and laugh—enjoy the sights.
My leather seat will hold you tight!"

. . . .
. . . .
. . . .
. . . .

"Then again, Toots, maybe we
Have had too much frivolity.
Why don't we stop and rest awhile
While you congratulate my style?"

. . . .
. . . .
. . . .
. . . .

"Sorry, Minnie; my mistake—
But one that any ace could make.
A pedal-master I remain;
Such boo-boos will not come again!"

"In fact, I'll help you to forget
That spill you took. Hang on, don't fret;
Watch my speed just knock 'em dead
As I zip past that car ahead!"

. . . .
. . . .
. . . .
. . . .

"Milord, Sir Pedal-Master? I
Would love to stay, but I must fly.
A far more modest, skilled chauffeur
Is what I'd honestly prefer."

MICKEY MOUSE

Kat Nipp's got it in his head
To kidnap Minnie Mouse;
But her beloved has a plan
To save his future spouse.

These extra shoes are needed to
Protect our hero's mate.
But pending that, the wicked cat
First has to take the bait!

"Minnie, no!" our Mickey shouts.
"Don't drown yourself, my dear!
You needn't end it all like this
Just 'cause Kat Nipp is near."

The villain thinks the girl is lost!
He dives into the drink
To rescue her—so why is Mickey
Smiling, do you think?

Nipp had yearned to capture
Minnie's kisses, you can bet;
But now, a prisoner of love,
He's captured in this net.

A wicked fate for Nipp: to hang
Immobilized like this
While Mick and Min sit down below
And share a comfy kiss!

277.

MICKEY MOUSE

Mickey takes a reckless dare,
Forgetting that it's quite unfair
To toss a rock at Jumbo's dome.
He should leave well enough alone.

Jumbo, smarting at the whack,
Bursts out of his cul-de-sac.
It looks like he'll lay Mickey low.
(And don't forget, we told him so.)

Run, run, Mickey—speedy mite!
Jumbo grabs his tail tight;
But Mickey lets the end break free
And scrambles for security.

Run, run, Mickey—find a goal!
Down the way he sees a hole
Beneath a nearby city wall.
Could it be salvation's call?

Mickey squirms in with a pop.
Elephant's too fast to stop;
Chugging like a streamline train,
He gets brickwork on the brain.

Dizzy Jumbo lies at rest
Feeling very second-best.
Mickey grins, "I may be small,
But I can save myself; that's all!"

A DEMANDING DIRECTOR

CINE
CINE

"Look sharp! Sit straight! Act resolute—
And get that grimace off your snoot!"
A bossy cameraman's demands
Bring shivers to poor Mickey's hands.

Stepping much too near the ledge,
The movie-man falls off the edge
And doesn't grab the wall in time,
So tumbles downward toward the brine.

CINE
CINE

He hits the flimsy boat, and knocks
It on its side to face the dock;
Tossing Mickey all asunder,
Toward the camera, quick as thunder.

While waiting for the puffed-up louse
To save himself, our playful mouse
Reverses roles: "Act resolute—
And get that grimace off your snoot!"

A New
WALT DISNEY
MICKEY
MOUSE
Presented by
JOSEPH M.
SCHENCK
A UNITED ARTISTS PICTURE

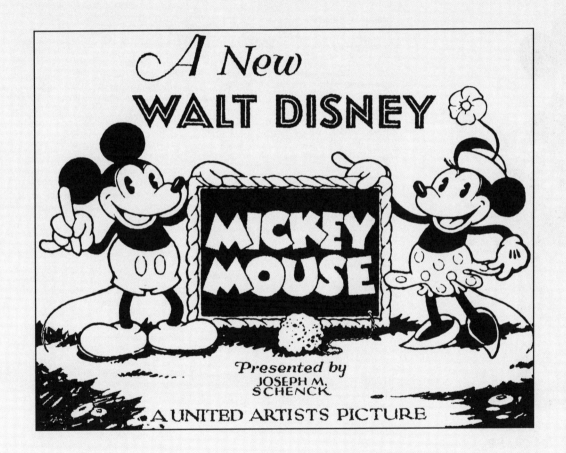

"Any time you can tell your story visually, do it. Leave [words] out if you can, or tell it in action as much as you can. Use the word to complement the drawing... your writing has to be fairly pithy... to make the point as briefly as possible... [but] once you get it down there, it's even a more perfect medium than your television or whatever, because it's there. [Readers] can go back to it if they're puzzled."

— Floyd Gottfredson to Arn Saba, 1979

LEFT: This rare 1932 lantern slide design, attributed to Gottfredson, once promoted new Mickey cartoons in cinemas. Slight distortion to the image originates with its source, a Disney exhibitors' catalog; we know no surviving examples of the slide itself. The Mickey/Minnie concept and poses are similar to, but not quite the same as, the design used for contemporary cartoons' main titles. Image courtesy Hake's Americana.

SINCERELY YOURS —
MICKEY MOUSE,
MINNIE MOUSE
AND
Walt Disney —

ABOUT THE EDITORS

DAVID GERSTEIN is an animation and comics researcher, writer, and editor working extensively with the Walt Disney Company and its licensees. Gerstein's published work includes *Mickey and the Gang: Classic Stories in Verse*; *Walt Disney Treasures – Disney Comics: 75 Years of Innovation*; and *The Katzenjammer Kids: 100 Years in Norway*. He has also worked with Disney to preserve the *Mickey Mouse* newspaper strips seen in this volume.

GARY GROTH co-founded Fantagraphics Books and *The Comics Journal* in 1976. And he is still at it.

J. B. KAUFMAN is a film historian on the staff of the Walt Disney Family Foundation. He is the author of *The Fairest One of All: The Making of Walt Disney's Snow White and the Seven Dwarfs* and *South of the Border With Disney*, and the coauthor—with Russell Merritt—of *Walt in Wonderland: The Silent Films of Walt Disney* and *Walt Disney's Silly Symphonies: A Companion to the Classic Cartoon Series*.

KEVIN HUIZENGA has published books and comics with Drawn & Quarterly, Fantagraphics and others. He also self-published mini-comics for over ten years. Many of his stories feature the character Glenn Ganges and sweatles. His most recent books are *Gloriana* and *Amazing Facts and Beyond! with Leon Beyond*. He lives in St. Louis with his wife, cat, and two snakes.

LEONARDO GORI is a comics scholar and collector specializing in Italian Disney authors and syndicated 1930s newspaper strips. With Frank Stajano and others, he has written many books on Italian "fumetti" and American comics in Italy. He has also written thrillers, which have been translated into Spanish, Portuguese, and Korean.

FRANCESCO ("Frank") STAJANO was imprinted on Disney comics at preschool age and never grew out of it: the walls of his house are covered in bookshelves and many of them hold comics. He has often written about Disney comics, particularly with Leonardo Gori. In real life he is an associate professor at the University of Cambridge in England.

JOE TORCIVIA is a comics historian renowned for decades of Disney, Warner Bros, Hanna-Barbera, and DC Comics scholarship. He has also worked as a dialogue writer for American editions of European Disney comics. He maintains

the blog "The Issue At Hand" (*tiahblog.blogspot. com*), featuring a lighthearted look at pop culture. Torcivia has also read every retelling and/or redrawing of Gottfredson's "Island in the Sky" (1936)—and lived to tell about it.

THAD KOMOROWSKI began his professional association with Disney comics as a teenager, writing character dialogue for American editions of European *Uncle Scrooge* stories. Today a historian and archivist, Komorowski maintains the blog *whataboutthad.com*, devoted to the art of animation, comics, and live-action film. He is the author of *Sick Little Monkeys: The Unauthorized Ren & Stimpy Story*.

JIM KORKIS has been an active historian of the worlds of Disney for over three decades. He has written hundreds of articles and several books on the Walt Disney Company. He worked for nearly fifteen years at Disney in a variety of capacities including performer, animation instructor, facilitator, and writer. As an approved freelance contractor, he continues to provide research and writing for Disney today.

SERGIO LAMA was born in Florence in 1936. Since childhood he has been involved in comics as an avid reader, collector and scholar. In the 1970s he became a columnist for some of the first Italian comics fanzines, including *Exploit Comics*; later, he would also write essays on early Italian magazines. With Fabio Gadducci and Leonardo Gori, he authored *Eccetto Topolino*, the seminal book on American syndicated comics in Italy during the 1930s and 1940s. Lama's research into early 20th century Italian comic artists has helped to create a serious database of their significant, previously neglected works.

LEFT: Studio fan card, 1933. Pencils by Floyd Gottfredson, inks and lettering by Ted Thwaites. Image courtesy Hake's Americana.